THE INTERNATIONAL
REFUGEE ORGANIZATION

IRO's blue insignia—the lifebelt—displayed on all its documents, publications, buildings, offices, cars, and ships, was the result of a competition organized among the refugees. The winning design, by a Hungarian now established in Canada, became the symbol of hope to thousands of his fellow men throughout the world

THE INTERNATIONAL REFUGEE ORGANIZATION:

A SPECIALIZED AGENCY OF THE UNITED NATIONS;

ITS HISTORY AND WORK
1946–1952

BY

LOUISE W. HOLBORN
CONNECTICUT COLLEGE, NEW LONDON, U.S.A.

Issued under the Auspices of the
Liquidation Board of the
International Refugee Organization

GEOFFREY CUMBERLEGE
OXFORD UNIVERSITY PRESS
LONDON NEW YORK TORONTO
1956

Oxford University Press, Amen House, London E.C. 4

GLASGOW NEW YORK TORONTO MELBOURNE WELLINGTON
BOMBAY CALCUTTA MADRAS KARACHI CAPE TOWN IBADAN

Geoffrey Cumberlege, Publisher to the University

PRINTED IN GREAT BRITAIN
AT THE UNIVERSITY PRESS, OXFORD
BY CHARLES BATEY, PRINTER TO THE UNIVERSITY

PREFACE

THIS work presents the history of an international organization—the International Refugee Organization—which performed a great humanitarian service following the Second World War from 1947 to 1952. The needs with which the IRO dealt were economic, social, and political. The means it used drew partly on the experience of the two earlier organizations—UNRRA and IGCR—which dealt with the problems of displaced persons and refugees, but went beyond them to large-scale permanent settlement. In a relatively short period of time the IRO dealt with the urgent necessities of more than $1\frac{1}{2}$ million people, and in so doing relieved not only their human sufferings but also a threatening international situation.

Two objectives have been present in writing this history: to provide a factual account of the work of the IRO for the general public, and to give enough documentary material and bibliographical references to make it a useful reference work for experts. Indication has also been given of where the specialized source material exists so that further detailed studies can be made.

The history of the IRO is based on the Organization's records, the archival files collected and sifted by the History Unit, monographs supplied to the History Unit by IRO Missions and administrative officers, and, as far as available, documentary material of the national governments concerned. Much information has also been gleaned from interviews with persons concerned with all phases of the work described in this volume.

Warm appreciation is extended to the numerous persons who have contributed to the author's knowledge and understanding of the manifold problems with which the IRO was confronted, and the way in which they were tackled. In particular the author wishes to mention Mr. George L. Warren, the US delegate to the General Council, Mr. C. J. Edmonds, the UK delegate, Ambassador Henri Ponsot, the French Conseiller, Sir Arthur Rucker, the Deputy Director General, Colonel Oliver E. Cound, the Liquidator of the IRO, and members of the Liquidation Board: M. J. Serres, Acting Chairman and Ministre Plénipotentiaire, Mr. J. C. Wardrop, UK Permanent Delegate at Geneva, Dr. Weibezahn-Massiani, Secretary of the Venezuelan delegation. Appreciation is also expressed to the British Foreign Office, the French Ministry of Foreign Affairs, the US Department of State, the Documentation Branch of the UN High Commissioner for Refugees, and the Geneva Office of ICEM. Special thanks for his collaboration are extended to M. René Ristelhueber, who prepared the French version of the history.

Gratitude for hospitality and help is expressed to the Archives Nationales in Paris, especially to the Curator Mlle Madi; to Chatham House, the Royal Institute of International Affairs in London; to the UN Library at Geneva and to the Palmer Library of Connecticut College at New London. The author would like also to express her appreciation to those who helped her prepare the manuscript for publication, in particular Miss Sylvia Brown and Miss Margaret Goldsmith.

L. H.

Quaker Hill, Connecticut, 19 October 1954

CONTENTS

APPENDIXES

CHARTS AND MAPS

LIST OF ABBREVIATIONS

ACVAFS	American Council of Voluntary Agencies for Foreign Service
AFSC	American Friends Service Committee
AJDC	American Joint Distribution Committee
AMGOT	Allied Military Government for Occupied Territories
ARC	American Red Cross
ARCS	American Red Cross Societies
ASFR	Association for Settlement of Foreign Refugees
BCAR	British Council for Aid to Refugees
BRCS	British Red Cross Society
CAD	Civil Affairs Division
CARE	Co-operative for American Remittances to Europe
CCG	Control Commission Germany (British Zone)
CCG	Control Council for Germany
CINCEUR	Commander-in-Chief, European Command (US)
CNRRA	Chinese National Relief and Rehabilitation Administration
COBSRA	Council of British Societies for Relief Abroad
CTB	Central Tracing Bureau
CTB	Combined Travel Board
CWS	Church World Service
DM	Deutschmark
ECOSOC	Economic and Social Council
EUCOM	European Command
FAO	Food and Agriculture Organization
GA	General Assembly
GC	General Council
HIAS	Hebrew Immigrant Aid Society
HICOG	High Commission for Germany
HICOM	Office of the High Commissioner for Refugees
ICAI	International Committee for Aid to Intellectuals
ICEM	Intergovernmental Committee for European Migration
ICRC	International Committee of the Red Cross
IGCR	Intergovernmental Committee for Refugees
ILO	International Labour Office
IRO	International Refugee Organization
ISS	International Social Service
ITS	International Tracing Service
JAFP	Jewish Agency for Palestine
JEIA	Joint Export Import Agency
LWF	Lutheran World Federation
MERRA	Middle East Relief and Rehabilitation Administration
MSTS	Military Sea Transportation Service

NAAFI	Navy Army and Air Force Institutes
NATO	North Atlantic Treaty Organization
NCWC	National Catholic Welfare Conference—War Relief Services
NTB	National Tracing Bureau
NY	New York
OFRRO	Office of Foreign Relief and Rehabilitation Operations
OMGUS	Office of Military Government for Germany (US)
ORT	World ORT Union (Organisation Reconstruction Travail)
PCIRO	Preparatory Commission of the International Refugee Organization
PICMME	Provisional Intergovernmental Committee for the Movement of Migrants from Europe
PX	Post Exchange
RPS	Refugee Placement Service
SAE	Swiss Aid to Europe
SCAEF	Supreme Commander of the Allied Expeditionary Forces
SHAEF	Supreme Headquarters of the Allied Expeditionary Forces
SHAPE	Supreme Headquarters Allied Powers Europe
SSAE	Service Social d'Aide aux Emigrants
TAAUN	Technical Assistance Administration of the United Nations
UK	United Kingdom of Great Britain and Northern Ireland
UN	United Nations
UNESCO	United Nations Educational Scientific and Cultural Organization
UNHCR	United Nations High Commissioner for Refugees
UNICEF	United Nations International Children's Emergency Fund
UNKRA	United Nations Korean Reconstruction Agency
UNRPR	United Nations Relief for Palestine Refugees
UNRRA	United Nations Relief and Rehabilitation Administration
UNWRA	United Nations Works and Relief Agency
US	United States of America
USAT	United States Army Transport
USDPC	United States Displaced Persons Commission
USFA	United States Forces in Austria
USMC	United States Maritime Commission
USSR	Union of Soviet Socialist Republics
WCC	World Council of Churches
WHO	World Health Organization
WRB	War Refugee Board
WRCB	War Relief Control Board
YMCA/ YWCA	World's Alliance of Young Men's Christian Associations and Young Women's Christian Associations

INTRODUCTION

THE REFUGEE PROBLEM IN THE TWENTIETH CENTURY: AN INTERNATIONAL CONCERN

'It is a judgment on our times that the age of the Atlantic Charter and of the
Universal Declaration of Human Rights should also be the Century of the
Homeless Man.'[1]

THE International Refugee Organization was the first international agency created
by the United Nations Organization. In its short period of operations from 1947 to
1952 it dealt with the most pressing refugee problem ever faced by the Western
world. In so doing it provided what its last Director General called 'the most successful example of large-scale international co-operation for humanitarian purposes
in history'.

The refugee problem is not new, but in the last half century it has expanded so
vastly in scope as to become a matter of urgent international concern. Refugees are
persons dislocated by war or persecution, in search of asylum and livelihood. Both
world wars have caused incalculable human suffering by driving people from their
homes, dispersing them over ever-widening areas. The chief causes of permanent
refugee movements, however, are intolerant nationalisms and the violence of dictatorial régimes. In the twentieth century the largest refugee movements, and those
most difficult to deal with, have been the result of political tyranny manifested in
enforced racial or political unity by National Socialist and Fascist régimes or the
political one-party system of governments adhering to Communist doctrine.

After the Second World War the devastating impact of the fighting, coupled with
the refusal of over $1\frac{1}{2}$ million people to return to areas under totalitarian régimes,
confronted the international community with a problem so far-reaching in extent
that it demanded a comprehensive international organization which could not only
give relief and aid repatriation (as the military authorities, assisted by UNRRA, had
done so magnificently) but also plan for mass resettlement, mainly in overseas
countries.

In carrying out these tasks IRO administered a network of camps, housing, feeding, and providing medical care for their inmates, and, as far as possible, providing
for their rehabilitation and retraining. It arranged legal protection as long as the
refugees were stateless. It negotiated agreements for resettlement, brought the refugees to the ports of embarkation, and, in a vast shipping operation with its own
fleet, transported them overseas.

The immediate task of IRO was to undertake a complete registration to obtain
individual and family particulars for each applicant for assistance in order to determine their basic eligibility and need for aid from the Organization. For those found
eligible a comprehensive programme was maintained offering shelter, food, clothing,

[1] Elfen Rees, 'The Refugee and the United Nations', *International Conciliation*, June 1953, No. 492,
p. 313.

health services, hospital care, employment and vocational training, education, in-dividual counselling, and child welfare services. In many respects this programme was a continuation of that initiated by other agencies which had been extending aid to refugees and displaced persons, notably, the United Nations Relief and Rehabili-tation Administration (UNRRA) and the Intergovernmental Committee for Refugees (IGCR). It differed, however, basically in that it did not merely provide supplies and a place to live, but was coupled to the resettlement programme. The care and maintenance programme was to prepare for resettlement and to make it more possible for the displaced persons to resettle. Many aspects of vocational training, the health services, and the welfare programme were developed with this definite aim in view.

Later chapters will show that this broad social welfare programme proved an in-dispensable means towards solving the refugee problem entrusted to IRO. Besides raising the physical and occupational standards of people who would otherwise have had no chance of qualifying for a new life, it enabled IRO, from the basis of a definite health and social policy, to influence successfully the attitudes of the emigration and local settlement countries.

The concept of the value and dignity of man had taken a heavy pounding over the years from the degraded social environment of the uprooted people. Ultimately, it was the human being, his faith in himself and his belief in the value of his neighbour, which had to be protected and retrieved. A response was needed to the desire, deter-mination, and willingness of the people to help themselves get back on their own feet, to become self-supporting respected members of a new society, and to take with dignity their rightful place in the ranks of working mankind.

Thus the IRO became a welfare organization on a world-wide scale devoted to solving a vast and complicated problem. Its practice required qualities of statesman-ship, combining an ability to devise constructive policies affecting many thousands of human beings, with a real and human regard for the individual tragedies and heroisms involved. It demanded a conception of care much broader than material needs—a personal interest in the individual refugee, his life, and problems.

This formidable task had to be tackled under continuous pressure of time and money and also of post-war passions and prejudices. The ever-present tension under which IRO operated accounts for some apparently harsh decisions, e.g. the limitations set on care and maintenance which, during the first two years, were found to be absorbing too high a proportion of the budget to the detriment of the resettlement programme.

In assessing the achievements of the IRO, these interrelated and to some extent conflicting aspects of its task have to be kept in mind. On the whole they were re-conciled with an astonishing degree of success, the necessity to do so generating an extremely powerful drive which is characteristic of all the IRO's activities and is apparent in the rapid build-up and progressive adaptation of most parts of its machinery.

League of Nations work for refugees, 1919–46

To see the work of IRO in perspective it is necessary to realize that the problems with which it grappled were not new nor its activities without precedent. Following the First World War, League of Nations' agencies had grappled with some of the most obvious needs of the waves of refugees caused from 1912 on by the dislocations of war, the impact of violent nationalisms, and the arbitrary action of dictatorial régimes. When German National Socialism, through its intolerance and racial legislation, created a huge exodus after 1933 and placed great numbers of individuals in an intolerable position, special intergovernmental action was organized from 1938 on under the initiative of President Roosevelt, resulting in the establishment of the Intergovernmental Committee for Refugees. This intergovernmental action, under the direction of the United States and Great Britain, was continued and broadened during the Second World War to deal with new emergencies. In the third place were the large-scale efforts on behalf of displaced persons by the military authorities once liberation of the Continent began with the second front in June 1944. These efforts were supplemented by those of relief agencies, notably UNRRA, as already mentioned, whose work, along with that of IGCR, forms the immediate background to the establishment of IRO.

Large-scale refugee movements began with the Balkan wars of 1912–14, when tens of thousands of Greeks, Bulgars, and Turks were driven from their homes. Millions more were displaced during the First World War. Many of these people, however, were repatriated after the war, and resettled as in earlier post-war periods. Civilian populations which had fled or were evacuated from the eastern fronts into Russia (estimated as 3 million by the spring of 1916) were able to return to their homes in states like Poland and the new Baltic countries. Peoples who had left the western front for Great Britain, France, and other places were able to return after the defeat of the enemy. Magyar refugees driven out of Rumania, Yugoslavia, and Czechoslovakia found refuge and final settlement in Hungary, while about 600,000 persons of German extraction, who left Poland under pressure, were settled in Germany itself.

Other refugee movements that arose during the First World War and the post-war period were more difficult to handle, however, and contributed to the political unrest and tensions in central and eastern Europe and the Near East in the inter-war period.

1. About $1\frac{1}{2}$ million Russian nationals were dispersed and left stranded mainly in north, central, and southern Europe and in the Far East in the years 1918–22 as a result of the Bolshevik revolution of November 1917, the rout of the anti-Bolshevik armies in European Russia in 1919–20, the famine of 1921, and the breakdown of White Russian resistance in Siberian Russia in 1922.[1]

2. By 1923 an estimated 320,000 Armenian refugees were scattered throughout the Near East, the Balkans, and other European countries after they had fled from persecutions and massacres in Asia Minor following the collapse of the Ottoman Empire and the nationalistic policy adopted by Turkey.

3. Under the provisions of the Treaty of Lausanne of 1923, 1,300,000 Greeks were transferred from Asia Minor to Greece, while 400,000 Turks were moved from the Balkans to Turkey.

[1] For these and the following figures see Eugene Kulischer, *The Displacement of Population in Europe*, Montreal: ILO, 1943, p. 39.

4. More than 220,000 Bulgars moved between 1913 and 1925 into the truncated territories of Bulgaria.
5. Thirty thousand Assyrian refugees, who had fought against the Turks, escaped after the Russian collapse in 1917 to the Caucasus, Greece, and Iraq, and some later to Syria.
6. The ranks of refugees from the First World War and the inter-war period for whom a full solution had not yet been found were swelled by refugees from Greater Germany, following the establishment of the National Socialist régime in 1933. Three main waves, encompassing 400,000 refugees, left Germany in consequence of this country's racial legislation, of the annexation of Austria, and the pogroms of November 1938.
7. Of the 450,000 Spanish refugees in France between 1938 and 1939, 140,000 remained in France after the end of the Civil War.

All these groups had more or less in common the fact that they did not leave their country of their own volition. They became uprooted and dispossessed by wars and their aftermath, political changes and social upheavals, massacres, persecutions, and fear. They were no longer protected by their native governments and did not or could not return to their country of origin.

There were, however, important differences in the ways in which these refugee groups could be handled. The large groups of Bulgars, Greeks, and Turks moved into countries with similar ethnic and cultural conditions. Their governments accepted moral and political responsibility for these fugitives, and so they did not become stateless persons without governmental legal protection. Their problem was basically one of economic integration and social assimilation in the receiving countries, a task which demanded not only the good will of the receiving governments, but also considerable foreign financial resources and aid.[1]

The position of the other groups, however, was far more difficult because the countries of first asylum were not able to absorb them into their economic life and/or were not willing to assimilate them into their social and cultural life. Thus the intruders, as they were looked upon in many cases, became a dangerous threat to the political and economic stability of the countries of first refuge.

How different was the fate of emigrants in earlier centuries! Small in numbers, those who left their homelands for political reasons were able to merge themselves in the great stream of emigrants who migrated for economic and social reasons, like unemployment, overcrowding, or even a yearning for adventure. The nineteenth century was still the age of uncontrolled and unrestricted 'spontaneous migration'. The 'surplus' population of the Old World could be absorbed by the New World because its economic and geographical expansion demanded man-power. In the course of a single century alone (1824–1920) 55 million people had emigrated from Europe.

In contrast, the refugees of the twentieth century found closed frontiers overseas. Today migration has become essentially a planned movement controlled by governments. The immigration policies of the earlier centuries have been replaced by

[1] For the solution of this problem cf. Sir John Hope Simpson, *The Refugee Problem*, New York, London, Toronto, 1939, pp. 11–29.

selective and restricted ones, guided not only by economic but also by the political and strategic considerations of the receiving countries. Moreover, immigration is no longer 'a purely national or even bi-national problem to be solved solely between the giving and the receiving countries', as a prominent international lawyer has pointed out.[1] 'Immigration policy is today intimately linked with wider aspects of international relations.' It has become 'super-national in character'.

Thus the refugee problem of our times is distinguished from former refugee movements by the variety of its causes, its scope, and complexity of solution. It has been the cause of grave political disturbances in the countries of temporary reception, endangering their peace and stability. It has developed a new class of people who are homeless and stateless, who live in a state of constant insecurity which wears away the essentials of human dignity. It is a human problem with serious political and legal implications. Beyond this it involves economic and social complications which surpass the administrative and economic resources of private organizations and even the political, legal, and financial capacities of individual national governments.

Since the refugee problem has 'outgrown national jurisdiction and facilities', efforts to cope with it have inevitably become international in scope and nature.

In 1920 it became clear for the first time in history that international action was the only means which could solve the refugee problem inherited from the First World War. Collaboration among the governments concerned was needed to reconcile the often conflicting interests of the countries of first refuge and those of final reception. It was imperative to provide for an international authority which would co-ordinate the various efforts already undertaken for the material relief of the refugees, develop plans for enabling them to become self-supporting, and help them to be repatriated to their country of origin or to resettle in overseas countries. Another important function that could be carried out only by an international authority was to grant political and legal protection as long as the refugees had to live in a 'no man's land' between state jurisdictions.

By the end of 1920 some governments and voluntary philanthropic agencies could no longer cope with the refugee problem which had assumed vast dimensions. They appealed to some technical organs of the League of Nations to undertake the work which they found to be beyond their scope and capability. On 20 February 1921 the President of the International Red Cross Committee (IRCC), on behalf of a large number of voluntary organizations, approached the Council stating that the League of Nations was 'the only super-national authority capable of solving a problem which is beyond the power of exclusively humanitarian organizations'.

War and post-war experience had proved the greater effectiveness of co-ordinated efforts, especially in the repatriation of the prisoners of war from Siberia which had been carried out so successfully under the direction of Dr. Fridtjof Nansen, who had acted as the High Commissioner for the League of Nations. In response to the appeal the Council agreed to put its machinery at the disposal of the governments with the understanding that it would take no responsibility for the organization or financing of relief and that its work should be considered temporary. On the request of the

[1] Wolfgang G. Friedmann, *German Immigration into Canada*, Toronto, Dec. 1951, pp. 9 and 10.

Council, Dr. Nansen assumed the office of High Commissioner for Russian Refugees on 1 September 1921. The League of Nations also availed itself of the relief services of the High Commissioner to solve some emergency problems connected with the influx of Greek and Armenian refugees from Asia Minor into Constantinople (Istanbul) in 1921, and in 1923 to improve the situation of the Bulgarians who had been turned out of western Thrace. In September 1923 the Council also transferred the protection and care of the Armenian refugees to the High Commissioner and, four years later, the Assyrian, Assyro-Chaldean, Turkish (friends of Allies) and assimilated refugees.

During his period of office from 1921 to his death early in 1930, Dr. Nansen was constantly concerned with the question of the final disposition of the refugees either by repatriation, employment in the countries of refuge, or settlement in overseas countries.

From 1921 to 1924 the preparatory work for achieving final settlements was made. Since the High Commissioner was not provided by the League of Nations with a general authority or with financial resources except for limited administrative expenses, Dr. Nansen undertook first of all to organize machinery for co-ordinating the efforts which were being made for relief and settlement by the humanitarian organizations and national governments. He kept contact through his own representatives with the refugees, and consulted with the representatives of the interested governments in intergovernmental conferences and with the representatives of the private organizations which formed an advisory committee under his chairmanship. The office of the High Commissioner thus became a clearing house for information to fit the individual efforts into a general plan and to present it to the League of Nations. During this period the work concentrated mainly on immediate relief and care in order to mitigate the tremendous stress and need of the refugees. A census was carried out and the legal status was regulated so that refugees could be dispersed from congested areas and attempt to secure employment.

From 1921 to 1929 technical aspects of the work for refugees like employment, emigration, and settlement were transferred to the International Labour Organization (ILO) as they fell within the scope of its activity. The High Commissioner retained the responsibility for legal and political questions. By the middle of 1928 the number of unemployed refugees had been reduced from about 400,000 to approximately 200,000. The majority of these unemployed were neither agricultural workers nor equipped to accept industrial contracts. Therefore at the request of the ILO, since the problem had reached another stage, the refugee administration was reconsidered in 1928. The process of assimilation and absorption of these groups in the country of residence was seen to be the main emphasis of the work and it was recognized that this would take a considerable period of time.

In view of the situation as it presented itself in 1929, Dr. Nansen believed that the work for refugees could be wound up in ten years under an organization with a definite status and possibility of planning for that period. He suggested keeping the work under the League by incorporating it in the Secretariat but this was not approved. Instead the Assembly set up the Nansen International Office for Refugees, which was to wind up the refugee work and be liquidated by 31 December 1938. The post of High Commissioner was abolished. The supreme authority in the Office was exercised by a governing body[1] of which the President was nominated by the League Assembly. The League voted grants for administrative expenses on a scale progressively diminishing to the date of final liquidation.

After the Assembly had approved the division of services for refugees, only the humanitarian work was referred to the Nansen Office, while the Secretariat of the League of Nations retained the legal and political protection of the refugees which it had exercised during the interim period 1929–30. In practice the Nansen Office undertook all phases of the work. The fact that the League kept the function of legal and political protection was of great significance, however, when the termination of refugee services was discussed in 1937. The financing of the operational work of the Nansen Office came from the sale of Nansen stamps and from surcharged postage stamps sold in France and Norway, as well as from contributions by private organizations.

Four unforeseen problems arose during the Nansen Office's period of activity, and these made it impossible for it to carry out its original plans. The first was the economic depression which drastically affected the employment of Nansen refugees. Labour permits became increasingly difficult to secure, and refugees were forced to relinquish their positions in favour of nationals. Refugees were expelled from countries for having no means of support, and at the same time were refused entry permits into other states. Moreover, the capital of charitable organizations was affected and direct relief almost ceased. The second factor was the decline of the League's moral influence owing to the setbacks which the system of collective security suffered after 1931. This inevitably reacted on the measure of protection which the League could give to the refugees. Third, there had already been a tendency noticeable in the League which operated in favour of reducing League activities on behalf of refugees. The entrance of the Union of Soviet Socialist Republics into the League strengthened this sentiment, since the Russian representatives bent their efforts to restricting the work being done for Russian refugees. The last factor was the new refugee problem which arose in Germany.

The German National Socialist Government created an acute problem, which made necessary a changed approach to the refugee problem as a whole. The German refugee problem was first brought to the attention of the Council of the League of Nations in May and July 1933 in the form of a minority petition. At the ILO conference in June, Dutch, Belgian, and French representatives pointed out that the influx of German refugees threatened to disturb the labour markets in their countries, and the conference decided that the ILO should study the means of settlement of refugees and submit resolutions to the League. The German refugee question was brought before the League Assembly by the Netherlands delegation in September 1933. Because of objections made by the German delegate to direct action by the League, a compromise was formulated and the High Commission for Refugees (Jewish and others) coming from Germany was set up as an autonomous organization, created by the League, but responsible to its own Governing Body, not to the

[1] The members of the Governing Body were to be appointed by the League, the ILO, and by private relief organizations. Refugees could become members.

League Council. The funds for the settlement of refugees as well as those for the administration of the Commission were provided by private contributors.[1]

This compromise made it even more difficult for the new High Commissioner, Mr. J. G. McDonald, an American, to solve the German refugee problem, especially since, because of the expulsion and persecution of 'non-Aryan' people and of political opponents, the number of German refugees increased continually. The administration was further complicated by the fact that in May 1935 the Council entrusted the protection of the Saar refugees to the Nansen Office. When he resigned in December 1935, Mr. McDonald pointed out that the work for refugees from Germany needed the authority of the League. In June 1935 the Norwegian Government suggested a centralized scheme under the League of Nations and an extension of assistance to all groups of refugees (Croats, Macedonians, Italians, Slovenes, Spaniards, and Portuguese). Also the voluntary organizations unanimously expressed their desire for a centralization of the work under the League. On the other hand, some governments felt that this would lead to a delicate political situation in the League because it would strain the relations between the countries of origin and those of asylum for the refugees. Also financial considerations helped to influence the decisions of the members of the League to reject these suggestions.

The Assembly of the League of Nations set up a committee of experts to examine the problem of refugees under the mandate of the Nansen Office and under the High Commissioner for Refugees Coming from Germany. However, it was not empowered to consider the extension of the Nansen Office beyond 1939, and no additional funds of the League could be made available 'without explicit permission from the Assembly'.[2]

In February 1936 Sir Neill Malcolm was appointed by the Council as High Commissioner for Refugees from Germany. His position corresponded to that of Dr. Nansen as High Commissioner for Russian and Armenian Refugees. His mandate was extended in May 1938 to include the refugees coming from Austria. It not only included the tasks of his predecessor—to negotiate and direct the international collaboration necessary to solve the economic, financial, and social problems of the refugees—but also entrusted him with their legal and political protection and the handling of their employment questions. He was a League official, obtained administrative expenses from the League to which he was responsible, and had the assistance of the Secretariat.

The work of the League of Nations for refugees was subsequently re-organized on the basis of resolutions adopted by the Assembly on 30 September 1938.[3] The Nansen International Office for Refugees and the Office of the High Commissioner

---

[1] Fifteen governments were invited to send representatives to the Governing Body, twelve accepted immediately, including all countries adjacent to Germany and in addition the UK, Italy, Sweden, the USA, and Uruguay. Yugoslavia joined later. The functions of the High Commissioner for Refugees Coming from Germany, agreed upon at the First Meeting of the Governing Body at Lausanne in Dec. 1933, were 'to stimulate the fund-raising activities of the philanthropic bodies, and to co-ordinate the efforts of the Organization in many countries for the settlement, emigration, and re-training of the refugees, and to negotiate with governments both on technical questions, such as passports, and on the admission or absorption'. League of Nations, *Official Journal*, 1933, Spec. Suppl. 127, pp. 45–60.

[2] League of Nations Doc. A.64, 1935, XII.

[3] For text see Sir John Hope Simpson, op. cit., pp. 596–8.

for Refugees Coming from Germany were replaced by a High Commissioner of the League of Nations who had his headquarters in London and who took over on 1 January 1939 the protection of all groups of refugees who had been under the two former organizations (about 600,000 persons). By Council decision of 17 January 1939 the Czechoslovak refugees coming from the Sudetenland were added to these refugees.

Sir Herbert Emerson, an Englishman, was chosen as High Commissioner for a period of five years. He was responsible for the legal protection of the refugees, the co-ordination of material assistance, and extension of aid to governments and private organizations in their endeavours for emigration and settlement. The great difficulties caused by the war crippled his activities, however, as did the virtual liquidation of the League of Nations.

At the end of 1946 the High Commissioner of the League of Nations transferred the duty of protection to the Intergovernmental Committee on Refugees (IGCR), which acted until the International Refugee Organization (IRO) took over all responsibilities for refugees on 1 July 1947.

In studying the work of the League of Nations on behalf of refugees in the period from 1919 to 1939, it is clear that the handling of the refugee problem, although it was fundamentally a humanitarian one, was constantly complicated and often hamstrung by political, economic, and social factors which demanded an international authority. Only the League of Nations, including among its members most of the countries affected and concerned with the refugee problem, could co-ordinate the efforts of governments and non-governmental organizations, negotiate with the countries of origin, and conciliate the divergent economic and social interests of different countries. It is also obvious that only an international authority could represent the moral conscience of mankind.

Certain facts about its efforts are particularly instructive. Each time the League put a new group under its guardianship the initiative came from individuals or private organizations or governments which believed in international collaboration and stood for the recognition and protection of human rights. Without the leadership of such humanitarians and statesmen as the Swiss Mr. Ador, the Norwegian Fridtjof Nansen, the British Lord Robert Cecil, Gilbert Murray, and Philip Noel-Baker, the Belgian M. Hyman, to mention only a few, the interest and imagination of the League Council and the Assembly would not have been inspired nor world public opinion stirred to action.

The very fact furthermore that the League of Nations existed made it possible to use its facilities. When the terrible disaster of the Greeks and Armenians happened in the Autumn of 1921, in Asia Minor, general and quick aid was possible only because Dr. Nansen could appeal to the Assembly of the League of Nations, then in session in Geneva. The governments were more willing to accept his plan for help immediately since their actions were in the public eye.

Immediately after the First World War repatriation of most of the Russian refugees was generally looked upon as the proper solution. Nansen and the Czechoslovak Government tried to connect repatriation schemes with their plans for the economic reconstruction of Russia as an integral part of the European economic system. It became clear, however, that the political division was too serious to be bridged. Nansen secured only the repatriation of about 6,000 Cossacks, and his efforts in 1923 to reach a general arrangement with the Soviet Union for repatriation similar to the Balkan schemes were not successful. From that time, repatriation as a general solution had to be abandoned. Attempts to repatriate Spanish refugees from France, and also German refugees, again failed due to the fact that no agreement could be secured[1] between the countries of origin and those of temporary refuge.

Thus were left only assimilation and integration in the country of refuge or, as an alternative, emigration and settlement in overseas countries. For the period before final settlement the League of Nations assumed the legal and political protection of the refugees, since these people had become stateless *de jure* or *de facto* by the negation of protection and withdrawal of citizenship rights by their countries of origin. The experience of the League's work for refugees indicated the importance of securing an adequate legal status for refugees as a basis for all other efforts which are made on their behalf. However, the League of Nations was able neither to develop large-scale migration or colonization schemes nor to influence the policies of the countries of origin. This made necessary intergovernmental action outside the League which will be described later.

It remains to sum up the achievements and limitations of the League's work for refugees. In the first place, the League accepted the responsibility only for certain groups. It provided machinery outside its own administration and only on a temporary basis. It accepted limited and specific tasks for the sole purpose of aiding these uprooted and homeless people in their transition from a refugee status to a new national status, that is to say, of dealing with the problem in such a way that it could be brought to a final settlement on the national level by the governments of final residence.

Since the refugee administration was not vested with real authority nor furnished with the necessary operational means, it served mainly as a co-ordinating and stimulating agency both for short-range or temporary functions such as care, maintenance, health, and other social welfare, and for long-range plans for final solutions like repatriation, emigration, and integration. The operational tasks were predominantly carried out by private and voluntary agencies which were served by a large group of dedicated people much experienced in relief and social welfare work.

At the same time, the amount and extent of the work accomplished through the international co-operation of governments and voluntary organizations under the guidance of the League of Nations and the use of its machinery was very considerable. Many uprooted people were saved from starvation through its efforts and helped to find a new homeland in which to settle. The work also helped to release tensions in trouble spots which otherwise might have led to more serious incidents endangering peace. It was, in effect, the first truly functional approach in peace-time to 'promote international co-operation'.

---

[1] '. . . repatriation has not provided a complete solution of any of the important post-war refugee movements, and it can be ignored as an important element in any future programme of international action aiming at a practical liquidation of the existing refugee problems. . . .' This was the final judgement of the authentic survey of the refugee problem made by Sir John Hope Simpson in 1939.

Intergovernmental organization for refugees, 1938-47

The intergovernmental efforts on behalf of refugees, which were at first supplementary to, and then virtually superseded those of the League of Nations, arose out of the tragic impasse of tens of thousands of victims of Nazi intolerance who could find no permanent asylum because of the impact of economic depression both on the countries of temporary refuge and those overseas. This situation led President Roosevelt to call a conference in July 1938, held at Evian-les-Bains in France, to consider what steps could be taken to facilitate the settlement in other countries of refugees from Germany (including Austria). This conference considered the problem of persons 'who desired to leave Germany, as well as those who had already done so',[1] thus introducing the new conception of a planned migration. 'It is essential', stated the delegates, 'that a long-range program should be envisaged, whereby assistance to involuntary emigrants, actual and potential, may be co-ordinated within the framework of existing migration laws and practises of Governments.'[2]

To undertake this comprehensive programme, the Evian conference established a permanent Intergovernmental Committee on Refugees (IGCR). The first Director, Mr. George Rublee, an American, was appointed by the Committee at its first meeting in August 1938; he was succeeded in February 1939 by Sir Herbert Emerson who combined this office with that of High Commissioner under the League of Nations. The work of the Director was threefold in character: to negotiate with Germany to improve the conditions of exodus so that they would facilitate orderly emigration; to attempt to develop opportunities for permanent settlement through negotiations with the governments of countries of refuge and settlement; and to undertake migration studies in co-operation with existing refugee services of the League of Nations and the ILO.

The efforts of the Director were mainly diplomatic in character since his tasks were more difficult to perform. The countries of temporary refuge, like France, had virtually exhausted their resources in extending hospitality, while the British felt that for economic and social reasons they could extend political asylum only within narrow limits. Overseas countries were similarly reluctant for economic, social, and political reasons to welcome large groups of immigrants, most of whom were Jewish. Above all, the negotiations with the German Government proved highly precarious, and had few, if any, conclusive results. German aggression in September 1939, in any case, brought the efforts at negotiation to an abrupt end.

A further difficulty was that during the period from 1938 to 1943 the funds of the IGCR, obtained through contributions from member governments, were used exclusively for administrative expenses. There were no operational expenditures for direct assistance to refugees at the disposal of the Committee. Thus the maintenance and assistance of refugees had to be provided by Jewish and other private organizations, by friends and relatives, or by funds granted by individual or group guarantors.

The greatest problems were presented naturally by war-time conditions. All

[1] For full text see Eric Estorick, 'The Evian Conference and the Intergovernmental Committee', *The Annals*, May 1939, Philadelphia, US, pp. 136-41. The American delegation under the chairmanship of Myron C. Taylor consisted among others of James G. McDonald and George L. Warren; the British was led by Lord Winterton who was elected permanent chairman of the IGCR.

[2] Ibid., p. 138.

Allied efforts were directed towards stemming the onslaught of the Nazi aggression. At the same time, as the German army advanced, and Nazi rule expanded over western and eastern Europe, the numbers of refugees increased vastly.

Early in 1943 the British and American governments made another attempt to expand refugee aid on an international level. Public opinion in both countries was horrified at the systematic persecution of the Jewish populations in Nazi-occupied countries. After an exchange of notes and consultations, an Anglo-American conference was held at Bermuda from 19 to 29 April 1943.[1] The two governments declared their readiness 'to investigate all possibilities for refugee havens, to give financial aid to any country caring for refugees, and to use available shipping facilities for the use of refugees'. Maintaining that they would 'aid war refugees of any race or creed wherever such measures did not interfere with war operations', they recommended a broadening of the activities of IGCR.

At an executive meeting of IGCR in August 1943, its mandate, which had previously referred only to refugees from Germany and Austria and the Sudeten area, was widened 'so as to include, as far as practicable also those persons, wherever they may be, who, as a result of events in Europe, have had to leave, or may have to leave, their countries of residence because of the danger to their lives or liberties on account of their race, religion or political beliefs'. Its functions were extended from the purely diplomatic one of co-ordinating the efforts of governments to an operational task, namely, 'to preserve, maintain and transport' persons coming within its mandate, 'so far as this may be necessary and desirable'.[2] Thus the IGCR had now responsibility for the legal protection, maintenance, and resettlement of refugees.

The Committee was enlarged to thirty-six members, and the administrative budget increased.[3] Though public opinion was disappointed that the conference had not been able to produce 'concrete results', the British and American governments did what they could, underwriting in equal shares the operational expenditures of IGCR which gradually increased from that time on.[4]

This was a departure from practices under the League, when governments expected private agencies to finance the humanitarian work for refugees. The

[1] *Report to the Governments of the US and UK from their Delegates to the Bermuda Conference*, 19–29 Apr. 1943. HM Government, Docs. 6711/6911/48, 3 May 1943. Also *New York Herald Tribune*, 30 Apr. 1943. In his statement of 23 Mar. 1943 regarding war refugees Lord Cranborne stated in the House of Lords that 'it is up to us, as to other nations, to do all in our power consistent with military security considerations . . . to provide assistance and asylum for the victims of this policy of extermination. . . . There is no doubt that it is only on an international basis that we can handle this problem.' *Parl. Deb.*, *Lords*, vol. 126, cols. 848–60.

[2] See Rules for the Constitution and Procedure of the IGCR, Article Two, in Louise W. Holborn, *War and Peace Aims of the United Nations*, Boston, 1948, vol. ii, pp. 151 f., also *New York Herald Tribune*, 30 Apr. 1943.

[3] The Soviet Union, Czechoslovakia, Egypt, Greece, Iceland, India, Luxembourg, Poland, and the Union of South Africa became additional members. IGCR, Fourth Session of the Committee held in London, 15–17 August 1944. Report submitted by the Director, Sir Herbert Emerson, London, 25 July 1944.

[4] This found its most vivid expression in the debate in the House of Commons when Miss Eleanor Rathbone, MP, the most ardent champion of the refugees, launched a severe criticism against the two governments. *Parl. Deb.*, *Commons*, 19 May 1943, vol. 389, cols. 1135–6 and col. 1201; cf. also Mary D. Stockes, *Eleanor Rathbone*, London, 1949, p. 300.

governments now stepped in with public funds, since the means of private organizations had become utterly exhausted.

Further, the Committee made every endeavour to co-ordinate its activities with those of the High Commission of the League of Nations, the ILO, and later with the War Refugee Board of the US and UNRRA. Though no Allied agency could stop the development of the Jewish tragedy, the IGCR, by its support of Jewish benevolent societies in neutral countries and assisting underground movements especially in France, Hungary, Italy, and Rumania, managed to bring some thousands to safety.[1] Others escaping across the Pyrenees were helped by Allied agencies through Spain to North Africa.

As parts of Europe were liberated from 1944 on, the Committee appointed representatives to assist in those countries; Belgium, France, Italy, Portugal, Spain, and the Middle East being the main areas of work. In addition to providing material assistance, mainly by subsidizing the relief programmes of voluntary agencies, the IGCR arranged and paid for the migration of thousands of refugees and protected the interests of persons who did not enjoy, in law or in fact, the protection of a home government. This protection was both formal and informal; it included, from 1945 onwards, the protection of Spanish Republican refugees as well as the initiative and arrangements for the conclusion, in October 1946, of an intergovernmental agreement on the issue of travel documents for refugees.

A series of administrative measures were undertaken by the British and American governments to co-ordinate and support the endeavours of the voluntary relief and welfare organizations. Already, towards the end of 1942, a number of private organizations had formed a consultative body, the Council of British Societies for Relief Abroad (COBSRA), composed of agencies 'with established international contacts and recognized experience in the field of relief of suffering, or social recovery work'. A still wider range of interested organizations were associated with COBSRA through a standing conference.[2]

After the First World War military authorities had been hesitant to use voluntary organizations in the transitional period other than British and American Red Cross societies. COBSRA, however, had 'useful consultation and negotiation' with military authorities and government officials including the Inter-Allied Committee on Post-war Requirements,[3] especially in regard to personnel. Similar arrangements were made in the US through the formation, in October 1943, of the American Council of Voluntary Agencies for Foreign Service (ACVAFS) which had sixteen organizations concerned with relief and rehabilitation work in foreign countries.

As early as 13 March 1941 the President had appointed a Committee on War Relief Agencies (later changed to War Relief Control Board). Its purpose was to control 'in the public interest charities for foreign and domestic relief, rehabilitation, reconstruction and welfare arising from war-created needs'.[4] The American

---

[1] By the Credit scheme: Report of Director to Fifth Plenary Session of IGCR.

[2] *UNRRA: Gateway to Recovery*, Washington, National Planning Association, Feb. 1944, pp. 54 and 82.   [3] Cf. p. 16.

[4] Executive Order 2905. The total collections of all agencies registered since 1939 amounted to $157,123,014, including contributions of $33 million in kind. By 1945 the War Relief Control Board (WRCB) had authorized thirty-one American voluntary agencies to help in bringing aid to displaced

Red Cross (ARC), a quasi-official organization because of its close contacts with the governmental authorities, was authorized by the President to serve as the relief agency contributing the appropriations granted by Congress through its Emergency Relief Appropriation Acts.[1]

In order to give more effect to the policy which had been suggested at the Bermuda conference and because of growing difficulties for the refugees, President Roosevelt set up the War Refugee Board[2] on 22 January 1944 and, a little later, the Office of Adviser on Refugees and Displaced Persons in the Department of State. The mission of the WRB was 'to take action for the immediate rescue from the Nazis of as many as possible of the persecuted minorities of Europe—racial, religious or political . . . ' It was to develop plans and institute 'effective measures for the rescue, transportation, maintenance and relief of the victims of enemy aggression and the establishment of havens of temporary refuge for such victims'.[3]

One of the activities of the WRB was to harbour 1,000 refugees (mainly Italians) in an emergency refugee shelter at Fort Ontario near Oswego, NY, for the duration of the war. They reached the shelter in April 1944 from Algiers.

According to an estimate about 500,000 persons from enemy occupied European countries (some 250,000 were refugees) were admitted to the US during the fiscal years ending 30 June 1934–43.

These intergovernmental efforts had served usefully to co-ordinate the work of voluntary societies, and had also introduced the significant concept of planned migration. Hampered as the IGCR was by the exigencies of war, lack of funds, and overwhelming tasks which confronted it, the organization yet helped to bridge a period of extraordinary difficulty in which the League of Nations could no longer function. Much credit is due to both the British and American governments for their unceasing concern for the refugees from Nazi persecution. From an early stage in the war, however, it was apparent that the piecemeal efforts of earlier years were

persons of different nationalities, religious and cultural backgrounds. Collectively these agencies raised and spent in 1945 about $17 million for maintenance and assistance to displaced persons.

[1] The Emergency Relief Appropriation Act of the United States Congress for the fiscal year 1941 appropriated $50 million for 'the relief of refugee men, women and children who have been driven from their homes or otherwise rendered destitute by hostilities or invasion', and in Dec. 1941 a further $35 million was appropriated for the same purpose for the fiscal year 1942 by the Third Supplemental National Defence Appropriation Act. The President, authorized by Congress, designated the Department of Agriculture, the Treasury Department, and the War Department as agencies to purchase relief supplies and the American Red Cross as an agency to receive, transport, and distribute those supplies. By Apr. 1942 the ARC had distributed supplies in twelve foreign countries (British Middle East, Greece, China, Finland, France, French Equatorial Africa, Great Britain, Iceland, Spain, Soviet Union, Yugoslavia) working together with forty-eight national relief organizations, maintaining 21,753 distribution points, and with 2,106 independent local agencies. More than 3 million foreign volunteers participated in this distribution which reached more than 15 million persons, including 65,000 alien refugees who were temporarily residing within the countries being aided. The ARC assumed not only all administrative expense incurred in connexion with the distribution of supplies purchased with government funds but maintained all personnel employed by the Red Cross in foreign service at its own expense. 77th Congress, Second Session, House Doc. No. 807: *Refugee and Foreign Relief Programs*, Washington, 1942, pp. 1–5. Also William Adams Brown Jr. and Redvers Opie, *American Foreign Assistance*, Washington, 1953, p. 82.   [2] By Executive Order 9417.

[3] A total of $563,000 of Federal funds were used for the administrative operating expenses, while $20 million were authorized for transfer by the US Treasury Department of which $16,300,000 were provided by Jewish welfare agencies, primarily AJJDC—see US War Refugee Board, *Final Summary Report of the Executive Director*, Washington, 15 Sept. 1945.

inadequate in the face of the vast suffering involved in the displacements of the war. Thus a more comprehensive approach to the refugee problem evolved along with other plans for reconstruction after the fighting ceased. This broad approach was reflected in the efforts of Allied military authorities and relief agencies once the second front began.

Inter-allied military and civilian work for displaced persons and refugees, 1943–7

The background to the more comprehensive approach to refugees and displaced persons was the magnitude of the problem, for the Second World War caused the most formidable displacements of population ever experienced. At its outbreak there had been more than a million refugees in various parts of Europe and Asia. This number was swelled almost beyond calculation by mass movements which brought vast human misery and suffering in their wake.

In Europe the principal displacements were those of Germans within Greater Germany. These were caused by various factors: the transfer of ethnic Germans into Germany, mainly from the eastern European countries; the dispersal of industry within Germany; the bombing of urban centres; and the dislocations of the German population during the rout of the Nazi armies. By early 1945 the total figure was estimated at from 21 to 30 million. In addition there were in Germany more than $8\frac{1}{2}$ million nationals of other European countries including civilians and prisoners of war. Both groups were forced to join the ranks of labourers.

Beyond these groups were about 20 million non-German displaced persons partly the result of mass expulsions from the defeated countries, partly of population transfers and exchanges agreed upon by treaties, and partly of the systematic deportation and persecution of non-German Jews. Many of the latter group were dispersed as far as India, Africa, and the Western Hemisphere. In Asia, about 20 million Chinese were uprooted, and at the end of the war there were some 12 million refugees and displaced persons in Japan, of whom 2 million were Koreans.

Already, on 14 August 1941, President Roosevelt and Prime Minister Churchill had enunciated certain common principles of policy in regard to the political reconstruction, economic rebuilding, and social rehabilitation of the war-devastated countries. The principles of the Atlantic Charter were accepted by the delegates of twenty-six countries, including the Soviet Union, on 1 January 1942, when they signed the Declaration by United Nations in which they pledged themselves 'to defend life, liberty, independence and religious freedom, and to preserve human rights and justice . . .'[1]

Both the UK and the US began early to plan for the relief of liberated areas and occupied countries.[2] In September 1941 the British Government convened an Inter-Allied conference at St. James's Palace for consultation on securing the supplies of food, raw materials, and articles of prime necessity for the post-war needs of

---

[1] The conference of the ILO, held on 5 Nov. 1941 at Philadelphia, USA, endorsed the principles of the Atlantic Charter in a resolution 'pledging the complete co-operation of the ILO in their implementation'. Louise W. Holborn, op. cit., vol. i, p. 5.

[2] Already on 21 Aug. 1940, two months after the fall of France, Prime Minister Churchill promised the enemy-occupied countries not only liberation, but that the Allied Powers would then make every effort to bring them the necessary needs for livelihood. *Parl. Deb., Commons*, vol. 55, cols. 1161–2.

countries liberated from Nazi aggression. The Allied governments (the UK and the British Dominions, the governments-in-exile, and the Free French) passed a resolution[1] concerning post-war rehabilitation and agreed to co-ordinate their individual efforts through an Inter-Allied Committee on Post-war Requirements. This Committee, under the chairmanship of Sir Frederick Leith-Ross, chief economic adviser to the British Government, also set up a bureau to make estimates of the requirements of Allied governments and authorities.

The first step towards the liberation of enemy occupied territories was the successful landing of American and British troops in French North Africa on 7–8 November 1942. Quick relief measures for released prisoners of war and refugees were necessary and a Joint Commission for Political Prisoners and Refugees in French North and West Africa was set up under the chairmanship of the British and American Consuls in Algiers.

On 21 November 1942 President Roosevelt established the Office of Foreign Relief and Rehabilitation Operations (OFRRO) as a part of the Department of State, under the direction of Herbert Lehman, later Director General of UNRRA. The purpose of the Office was to organize 'American participation in the activities of the UN in furnishing relief and other assistance to the victims of war in areas re-occupied by the forces of the United Nations'. This new agency sent some welfare experts to North Africa. They co-operated with the British Middle East Relief and Refugee Administration (MERRA) which had been established with its headquarters in Cairo, on 1 June 1942, to care for Greeks, Yugoslavs, and Albanians who had fled from their countries to North Africa.[2]

The Civil Affairs Branch of Combined British and American Military Headquarters worked together with OFRRO, MERRA, and the Joint Commission for Political Prisoners and Refugees. In fact, it became here already apparent how difficult it was to separate the spheres of responsibility of military and civil authorities, particularly in the period of active warfare. Even thereafter it remained true, for the military authorities had necessarily to have overall control for strategic reasons. Moreover, military authorities met initial relief requirements as a means of keeping order and furthering the military operations.[3] Thus they assumed responsibility for civilian affairs on a larger scale than in former wars, a result of the total and global character of the war.

Although the refugee problem of French Morocco, Algiers, and Tunis was of minor proportions, those dealing with it learned valuable lessons. These experiences were taken into account in planning the later refugee welfare policy of Supreme Headquarters Allied Expeditionary Force (SHAEF) and of UNRRA.[4]

[1] Cmd. 6315, Misc. No. 3 (1941), pp. 17–18; also Holborn, op. cit., vol. i, p. 4. The Soviet Union, however, did not participate since they 'could not accept the idea of a central bureau controlled by the UK'. The Soviet delegate proposed 'an international body built on the principle of equal representation for all governments concerned' and reserved the right of his government to put forward at a later date proposals in that connexion. This concept provided some basis subsequently for UNRRA.

[2] By May 1944 some 46,000 refugees were living in six large refugee camps. *UNRRA: Report of the Director General to the Council, 15 September to 31 December 1944*, Washington, 1945, p. 35.

[3] *UNRRA: Gateway to Recovery*, Washington, National Planning Association, Feb. 1944, p. 5 and 6.

[4] Cf. Malcolm Proudfoot, 'European Refugees of World War II', MS. Chatham House, London, 1953, ch. vi; also for the following part.

The landing of Anglo-American forces in Sicily early in July 1943 and the movement of the troops northward in Italy to Monte Cassino brought approximately 50,000 non-Italian refugees under Allied care and responsibility. They included civilian internees, ex-soldiers, and workers of all European nationalities, though predominantly Yugoslavs. In Italy, the Allied Military Government for Occupied Territories (AMGOT), which undertook all emergency relief and rehabilitation measures, was confronted with a difficult administrative task, since Italy, though initially an enemy country, became a co-belligerent under an Italian government after the Armistice. Furthermore, fighting still went on since the north was still occupied by the Germans. Lack of experienced people and an overlapping of functions and responsibilities of the various agencies working in Italy also made the work not too effective.

Conscious of these inadequacies, and of the magnitude of the tasks which were confronted, three different kinds of authorities worked on plans to deal with the broad tasks of relief and rehabilitation of the war-devastated areas, within which relief and repatriation of uprooted persons formed a significant part. In the first place were the governments of the UK, US, and governments-in-exile, each of which had an individual programme for its area of immediate responsibility, and also co-operated through the Inter-Allied Committee on Post-war Requirements of which the US had become a member after its entry into the war. Secondly, the Anglo-American military authorities had to make their plans in connexion with the invasion of western Europe. Finally there was the project for an international organization for relief and rehabilitation out of which came UNRRA.

Consultations between the Allied governments between May and October 1943 led to the decision to put relief and rehabilitation on a UN basis to provide an international approach to what was seen to be an issue intimately associated with the establishment of eventual peace. On 9 November 1943 an Agreement Creating the United Nations Relief and Rehabilitation Administration (UNRRA) was signed at the White House in Washington by representatives of forty-four United Nations. The purpose of this newly established organization was 'to plan and administer a relief programme supplementary to that of the Allied Military Forces', and to make 'preparations and arrangements . . . for the return of prisoners and exiles to their homes'.[1]

At its First Session, immediately following the signing of the Agreement, the General Council, UNRRA's policy-making organ, considered also the role which UNRRA would have to assume in regard to displaced persons. On the basis of the Report of the Sub-committee on Policies with Respect to Assistance to Displaced Persons, it agreed that the Administration should help to care for and repatriate certain categories of displaced people with the agreement of the governments concerned and the military authorities.

Two studies on the nature and scope of the dislocation of people provided basic data for defining the eligibility of displaced persons for UNRRA assistance. One of these studies, *The Statistical Statement on the Problems of Displaced Persons*,

---

[1] George Woodbridge, *UNRRA. The History of the United Nations Relief and Rehabilitation Administration*, New York, 1950, iii. 23, 31–33. Cf. also Brown and Opie, op. cit., pp. 76 f.

prepared under the auspices of the Leith-Ross Committee in London and finished in October 1943, estimated there would be about 22 million displaced persons not including 6 million Germans who had been moved from Western Germany. The other survey prepared by the ILO and published in 1943 in Montreal, Canada, dealt with the whole problem of the *Displacement of Populations in Europe*. This study estimated there would be 30 million displaced persons.

According to the classification in the latter study, the displaced persons fell into four broad categories which in practice were difficult to keep separate. The first group comprised the war refugees, i.e. the civilian victims of modern total war, the prisoners of war, and the civilian internees. The second group, the result of ideological policies or divisions, were the refugees who for political, religious, or racial reasons were stateless, in law or in fact, and thus were a responsibility of IGCR. In the third place were the labourers from both western and eastern Europe drawn into Germany by persuasion or force. Lastly were the Germans, both those who had been settled on occupied or annexed territory, and those 'called home' from the Baltic countries, eastern Poland, and from some of the Balkan states.

With the exception of prisoners of war, who would be taken care of by the military authorities, and persons of enemy or ex-enemy nationality 'intruded into' the territories of member governments, all these groups were declared eligible for UNRRA aid under the definition adopted by the General Council.[1] The latter also accepted a working scheme of ten specific duties to guide the work of the Administration.[2]

This plan was not implemented under UNRRA's jurisdiction and control, however, as the military authorities carried out the repatriation of almost all UN displaced persons. Not until later did UNRRA assume the care of displaced persons, mostly in enemy territory, 'who did not wish to return or did not wish immediately to do so'.[3]

From VE Day until the end of SHAEF in July 1945, the military authorities assumed the responsibility and control of displaced persons. Pre-invasion plans to handle this problem had been developed in 1943 and 1944 by SHAEF and also by the Civil Affairs Division of the Office of Chief of Staff in the US War Department.[4] These plans accepted that 'liberation of slave labourers and concentration camp inmates (representing all nationalities, religious and political beliefs opposing the Nazi system) and the liberation, care, maintenance, repatriation, and resettlement of UN displaced persons' were among the major objectives of the Supreme Allied Commander's mission. In consequence, he instructed the Allied armies to assume these duties as a direct military responsibility.[5] Thus plans for the disposition of displaced persons were included in the overall programme for the conquest of Germany.

How important the military control of the displaced persons problem was had

[1] Woodbridge, op. cit., vol. ii, p. 471.   [2] Ibid., p. 472.   [3] Ibid., p. 475.
[4] Statement on resettlement of displaced persons, by Mr. John H. Hilldring, Assistant Secretary of State for Occupied Areas, in the House of Representatives Sub-committee on Immigration and Naturalization, on 4 June 1947. Department of State, *Bulletin*, 15 June 1947, p. 1162. Cf. also his statement before the Committee on Foreign Relations, US Senate, International Refugee Organization, Hearing SJ Res. 77, 1 March 1947, p. 41, before US Senate, 80th Congress, First Session.
[5] *Displaced Persons in Europe and the Resettlement in the United States.* House Report 1507. 81st Congress, Second Session, 30 Jan. 1950. Washington, 1950, p. 6.

already become apparent to the British in the summer of 1940 when the German armies broke through the Allied lines. Masses of refugees endangered the military operations by congesting the roads, and not only hindered the movement of troops, but also the transport of supplies for the soldiers and civilians. It was for that reason imperative, once liberation of territories and people began, to provide orderly assembling, caring, and repatriation of the displaced person. It was basic for military success to control the refugees during combat operations, and also to assemble and register them, and provide care and maintenance until repatriation could take place.[1]

In October 1943 the Refugee and Displaced Persons Section was set up in the Civil Affairs Division of COSSA in London. It became the Displaced Persons Branch under SHAEF—G-5 Division, when, on 16 January 1944, General Eisenhower took over the command of the Allied armies as Supreme Commander of the Allied Expeditionary Force.

The Displaced Persons Branch had the task of drafting plans for the control and handling of the refugees after liberation and during the period of military operations in Europe. Working closely with British agencies the section evolved a registration and identity card system for the control, care, and repatriation of the displaced persons based on the studies of the Leith-Ross Committee and also the experience of OFRRO. Furthermore, the Refugee and Displaced Persons Section worked out a welfare guide for care and relief of refugees within the camps. This plan, known as the 'Outline Plan for Refugees and Displaced Persons' relating to the control, care, relief, and repatriation of displaced persons, became, by order of 4 June 1944—two days before the invasion of Normandy—part of the instructions to army group commanders. These instructions were supplemented by more detailed ones on 18 November 1944.[2]

The outline took into consideration the two stages of military operations: 'opposed advance' and 'the German collapse and surrender'. It was planned to transfer the displaced persons to assembly centres, mainly in foreign countries, from there to transfer them to border control stations, where nationality screening would take place, and finally to reception centres in the home countries. During the winter of 1944-5 local government agencies, in co-operation with the civil affairs officers of the Allied armies, operated assembly centres and camps for some 100,000 refugees; a very high percentage of these were Soviet Russians, Poles, and persons from other eastern European countries.

---

[1] These activities in liberated territory were dealt with as civil affairs while in ex-enemy or enemy territory they were under the military government.

[2] 'Under these instructions displaced persons uncovered by military forces are assembled in collecting points and directed back to transit points or areas where they are given food, temporary shelter, and first aid. From there they are directed to assembly centers, where they are cared for until they can be repatriated. When uncovered in areas of rapid military advance, they are directed to stand fast until arrangements can be made to collect them in assembly centres. As soon as conditions permit, UN displaced persons are returned to reception centers in their own countries, where their governments assume full responsibility for them. In liberated countries the care of displaced persons is the responsibility of the Allied governments concerned, assisted and advised by Supreme Headquarters, AEF, Missions. In enemy territory, UN displaced persons are a direct responsibility of the Allied forces, whereas enemy and ex-enemy displaced persons are made the responsibility of enemy authorities supervised by military government'. *The Axis in Defeat*, Department of State, Pub. 2423, Washington 1945; A Collection of Documents on American Policy Toward Germany and Japan, pp. 85-86.

At the end of the war there were more than 11 million displaced non-German people in Europe. Most of these were located in the occupied countries of Germany, Austria, and Italy which were partly under the control of the Western Allies and partly of the Soviet Union, and also in Poland and other parts of central and eastern Europe which were under the control of the Soviet Union. In addition, there were displaced persons in the liberated countries—Norway, Denmark, the Netherlands, Belgium, Luxembourg, France, and Greece, and in several neutral countries in Europe and also in the Middle East. The distribution was as follows:

SHAEF area of Germany, Austria, and Czechoslovakia	5,922,000
Soviet area of Germany, Austria, Czechoslovakia, Poland, &c.	4,502,000
France	215,000
Norway	111,000
Middle East and Turkey	81,000
Sweden	63,000
Switzerland	52,000
United Kingdom	38,000
Italy	34,000
Soviet Union	24,000
Denmark	21,000
Belgium	13,000
Netherlands	2,000
	11,078,000

Working arrangements with European Allied governments made available liaison officers to assist in the care, identification, control, and repatriation of their nationals. Further agreements with the governments of France, Belgium, Netherlands, and Luxembourg resulted in the establishment of reception facilities for their displaced nationals. This collaboration between SHAEF and the western European governments proved highly successful. In contrast, the difficulties in working with the Soviet Union liaison officers, who disregarded the authority of SHAEF and did not deal at an intergovernmental level with France, Belgium, Netherlands, and Luxembourg, were a forerunner of those which later complicated the work of both UNRRA and IRO.

The repatriation of uprooted people to and from France, Belgium, Luxembourg, and the Netherlands, although difficult, was relatively easy compared with the problem which confronted military authorities and later UNRRA and IRO in Germany, Austria, and Italy.

Realizing the difficult and prolonged task ahead, SHAEF proceeded along two lines in its preparations for controlling and handling the refugees. First, it treated the displaced persons problem in Germany almost entirely as a command responsibility. Where consistent with military operations, combat units were utilized to care for and control displaced persons, while displaced persons' camps and installations were under the direct control of military government detachments.

Negotiations between SHAEF and UNRRA, beginning in early 1944, led to the UNRRA-SHAEF Agreement, signed by the Director General and the Supreme Commander on 25 November 1944 in France. This Agreement sought to make easier the handing over of responsibilities to UNRRA, and to ensure 'a continuous uniformity

of policy in the military and post-military periods'.[1] For this purpose UNRRA
was to participate both in planning and operations in regard to displaced persons,
acting under the orders of the Supreme Commander and through military channels.
In accordance with this arrangement, UNRRA sent 322 teams of thirteen members
each into the field in the period from 1 January to the end of June 1945.[2]

When SHAEF was liquidated by July 1945, the responsibilities for displaced persons were transferred to the Quadripartite Control Council for Germany. Since the
Soviet Union did not ask UNRRA to work in the Soviet occupied zone of Germany,
the other three governments, the UK, France, and the US, each made its own
agreement with UNRRA. However, the British Agreement was not signed until
27 November 1945, the French on 18 February 1946, and the American on 19 February 1946. Up to these dates the SHAEF Agreement still remained in force.

These agreements divided responsibility between the military authorities and
UNRRA as follows:[3]

1. Military responsibilities:
    (a) Full responsibility for all basic supplies;
    (b) Coordination of movements, plans and the provision of transport
        facilities in connection with repatriation;
    (c) Security and maintenance of law and order.

2. UNRRA's responsibilities:
    (a) Internal administration of assembly centers housing United Nation's
        displaced persons;
    (b) Coordination and supervision of voluntary agencies working in dis-
        placed persons assembly centers;
    (c) Provision of amenity supplies (includes such items as tobacco, cigarettes,
        razor blades, candy for children, recreational equipment and educational
        supplies);
    (d) Operation of the Central Tracing Bureau;
    (e) Cooperation with military and governmental authorities in arranging
        repatriation of displaced persons including their reception in their home
        countries.

In its further sessions the General Council of UNRRA adjusted its policies to the
needs of displaced persons' operations, drawing also from the experiences of the
Administration gained in the areas of operations. At its Second Session, held at
Montreal, Canada, in September 1944 the Administration was authorized to assist:

(1) in the repatriation of intruded persons;
(2) in the care and repatriation from enemy areas of displaced persons nationals of
    member governments, if their governments agreed and subject to the control of
    the military authorities;
(3) in the care and repatriation of 'persecutees' whatever their nationality if found
    in enemy, ex-enemy, or liberated territories.[4]

---

[1] Woodbridge, op. cit., vol. iii, p. 180.
[2] It took a certain time until a smooth collaboration in the field could be worked out between SHAEF
and UNRRA. Six months after liberation SHAEF was still responsible for shipping and supplies. Ibid.,
vol. ii, p. 484.   [3] Ibid., p. 488.
[4] Ibid., p. 482.

At the Third Session, convened in London in August 1945, a request by the Administration for a clarification of the policy in regard to repatriation brought to the fore the different points of view of the western and the Slav countries concerning the question of voluntary and non-voluntary repatriation. From then on this question absorbed not only much time during the Council meetings, but became even more prominent during the deliberations in the various UN organizations which were concerned with the drafting of plans for the international organization for refugees, the IRO. In spite of objections by the Slavic countries, the General Council decided to assume responsibility for 'displaced persons otherwise eligible for care even though they are unwilling to be repatriated or returned to their homes'.[1] Thus although stress was also laid upon making 'every effort . . . to encourage repatriation' the General Council, adjusting its policy to the needs of the situation in the field of operations, widened the authority of the Administration to assist persecutees and to supervise the case of displaced persons, even without the consent of the country of origin.

By this time the existence of non-repatriable displaced persons or refugees had become quite evident. The General Council recommended

that in view of the temporary nature of the assistance that can be given by the Administration with respect to all of the remaining displaced persons in all areas in which the Administration is authorized to operate . . . its members shall seek to do all in their power to expedite the early creation of a United Nations body capable of dealing in an effective manner with the problem, such as is contemplated under the Resolution adopted by the General Assembly of the United Nations on February 12, 1946.[2]

Furthermore, at its last session in August 1946, the General Council decided

to continue its various operations with respect to displaced persons until such time, or times, as they are undertaken by the International Refugee Organisation, or by any appropriate interim commission or by any other appropriate body, provided that none of these operations shall be continued by the Administration after 30 June, 1947.[3]

Displaced persons cared for or supervised by UNRRA at peak periods

Location	Numbers	Time
Germany . . .	715,000	May 1946
Austria . . .	46,000	April 1946
Italy	26,000	July 1946
Middle East . .	37,000	May 1944
China	45,000	June 1947

Since the special responsibility of UNRRA as well as the military authorities was to organize repatriation, both looked towards IGCR to work out resettlement plans for non-repatriable displaced persons. Under a resolution adopted by the Executive Committee in November 1943, however, IGCR was not to deal with such persons without consultation with and the agreement of the country of origin. In July 1946, under the initiative of the US representative seconded by the British delegate, the

[1] Woodbridge, op. cit., vol. iii, p. 486.   [2] Ibid., p. 156.
[3] Ibid., p. 162: Res. 99.

Executive Committee authorized the future inclusion of refugees and displaced persons who would fall under the mandate of the future IRO and decided to plan a resettlement programme in order to assist the subsequent assumption of responsibility by IRO. After this decision the Soviet Union withdrew its membership. In its last six months of existence IGCR signed resettlement agreements or was in process of signing them with Belgium, Netherlands, France, Britain, Venezuela, Peru, Chile, Colombia, Ecuador, Argentine, Canada, Union of South Africa, Australia, Morocco, and Tunis.[1]

On 3 June 1947 the member governments of IGCR passed a resolution to transfer its funds and all its functions to IRO to take effect 1 July 1947. At the same time UNRRA's functions and remaining funds were also turned over to IRO.

Looking back on what had been done it was obvious that the military authorities had accomplished a remarkable task under unforeseen difficulties in the war-torn areas. From VE Day to the end of September 1945 SHAEF repatriated about 7 million displaced people from Germany, Austria, and Italy with the help of the governments of the liberated countries, UNRRA, and the voluntary agencies. From November 1945 to June 1947 UNRRA repatriated more than 1 million. Thus the displaced persons problem had been brought to manageable proportions.

Liberation and final repatriation had been the main objectives, but neither the military authorities nor UNRRA were in a position to deal with those who would not or could not go home. As Mr. Dean Acheson told the Committee on Foreign Relations of the U.S. Senate, there were

. . . hundreds of thousands who will not voluntarily return to their places of origin. This is due to the changes wrought by the war in prewar governmental boundaries and governmental systems within the areas from which they have come, to the aftermath of the memories of Nazi persecutions in those areas during the war, the destruction of their kindred and their former homes and former opportunities for livelihood, to differences in political views and fears of persecution or reprisal because of those differences.[2]

These people were a serious liability to the military powers of Germany, Austria, and Italy since they could not go home, nor could they stay where they were. What remained of Germany and also Austria was overcrowded. Moreover, most of the refugees had no desire to make these countries their permanent home, having come against their will and, in many cases, having been slave labourers.

Resettlement was the only solution for most of these people, but this required a new and comprehensive type of organization. In the first place it had to be a civilian agency. To administer the displaced persons' camps was 'essentially a task for civilians', as Mr. Robert P. Patterson, US Secretary of War told Congress. It had to be set up in such a way as to deal with the problems as a whole, not piecemeal. Three kinds of authorities divided responsibilities for displaced persons in the early post-war period: the British and American and French armies, UNRRA, and IGCR.

[1] IGCR Report of the Director, May 1947. Minutes of the Seventh Plenary Session, London, 30 May–3 June 1947, London, 1947, p. 15.
[2] Statement by Mr. Acheson, Under-Secretary of State, before the Committee on Foreign Relations, International Refugee Organization, Hearing . . . on SJ Res. 77, 1 Mar. 1947, p. 7.

Mr. Hilldring spoke of this division of responsibilities as 'a formula for pande-monium'.[1] He also pointed out that it was 'a formula for expensive administration in handling of this problem'.

What was needed was an international organization which could deal in an integrated way with the whole problem of refugees, so pressing an international problem in scope and nature. This was necessary partly because neither the existing agencies, nor the US and the UK could continue the heavy financial burden involved in maintaining hundreds of thousands of people in the displaced persons' camps. But beyond this was the human problem involved. Mr. Patterson touched on this when he said that a permanent life in camps was 'the last thing that, by and large, these uprooted workers, who have had the tough fiber to survive their hardships, would desire'.[2] Even more understandingly did Representative Vorys express this aspect of the problem when he said:

We should not forget that we are talking about 1,000,000 men and women and children, human beings, wise and simple, strong and weak, young and old, good and bad, sick and well, but all of them children of God, who are suffering deeply, in body and spirit, because they are separated, through no fault of their own, from the place that is dearest to us all—home.[3]

Under both these aspects, it was natural to turn to the UN to cope with the problem, since its purposes and principles are

to achieve international co-operation in solving international problems of an economic, social, cultural, or humanitarian character, and in promoting and encouraging respect for human rights and for fundamental freedoms for all without distinction as to race, sex, language, or religion; and to be a center for harmonizing the actions of nations in the attainment of these common ends.[4]

The establishment of IRO was a fitting response to these aspirations.

Though IRO was to carry out a task of great scope and importance which neither the military authorities nor UNRRA could handle, it is important for an evaluation of IRO's work to recapitulate the accomplishments of these agencies which first coped with the displaced persons' problem after the war, to recognize how IRO was able to build upon their efforts, and also to acknowledge the wealth of experience on which IRO was able to draw. In a very real sense IRO was the keystone of the relief, rehabilitation, and repatriation work already begun after the Second World War as, in another way, it was the culmination of earlier more piecemeal efforts on behalf of refugees which dated back to the end of the First World War.

Most significant of the achievements prior to the establishment of IRO was that the war displacement problem was reduced to manageable proportions by the repatriation of more than 10 million people by the Soviet Russian, French, British, and American armies. Moreover, most of the supplies needed for the care and maintenance of 'non-repatriables' was provided by the Americans, British, and French in their respective military zones in Germany and Austria. The British and

[1] Acheson, op. cit., pp. 36-37.
[2] Ibid., p. 28.
[3] Representative Vorys, 80th Congress, First Session, House of Representatives, Report No. 464.
[4] Charter of the United Nations, chap. 1. Purposes and Principles, Article 1, paras. 3 and 4.

American Control Commission in Italy performed a similar task in Italy after 1943, while the British army supported refugees and displaced persons in the Middle East and East Africa from 1942 to 1944. Any criticism of the defects of this work must take into account that, as has been rightly pointed out, 'much was done so well and so promptly' in spite of the fact that the soldiers were 'mightily pre-occupied and unacquainted with the problem which was dumped on them'.[1]

The main task of UNRRA in regard to displaced persons was to furnish administrative, medical, and welfare staff for assembly centres in the three western zones of Germany and Austria, and in Italy and the Middle East. In addition it provided some material supplies, particularly in Austria and Italy. It also repatriated Greeks, Yugoslavs, and Poles from the Middle East, Jewish refugees in Shanghai, and collaborated with the military authorities in the repatriation schemes in Germany and Austria, 'particularly by making food available for Polish repatriates in 1946 and 1947'.

Though its accomplishments were impressive UNRRA's efficiency was handicapped by the circumstances in which it had to develop its work. UNRRA was an instrumentality of forty-four governments, several of which were not in agreement with each other about the overall policies it should pursue. Apart from this basic political problem, UNRRA's work was also handicapped by a lack of efficient and trained people, since armies and national governments had already taken the cream of them.

Nevertheless, UNRRA's experience served IRO well. Statesmen, charged with the task of establishing the new organization to be responsible for the residual refugee problem, kept in mind the fact that success could only be secured by establishing a high standard for the performance of the international staff, by a clear agreement and understanding of the aim and purpose of the new organization, and by the determination of the governments concerned to take full responsibility not only for the administration but also the operational costs of the new organization.

The IGCR had supplemented in a very small way the care and maintenance programmes of the military authorities and UNRRA, mostly through small financial grants administered by voluntary organizations, mainly for Jewish and Spanish Republican refugees in France, Belgium, the Netherlands, Spain, and Portugal. In an even more minor degree it had been responsible for camp administration for non-repatriables in Italy in June 1947. IGCR was concerned mainly with aiding resettlement by furnishing financial and other aid toward the transportation of individuals and families from France, Belgium, the Netherlands, Spain, Portugal, Switzerland, Czechoslovakia, the Middle East, and Shanghai to countries of resettlement. It negotiated agreements with reception countries and maintained staffs in the western zones of Germany and Austria to aid in selection, and chartered ships for the passage of refugees. IGCR also carried on legal and political protection in the areas mentioned, and through two international conferences developed an agreement on identity and travel documents to supplement the 'Nansen passport'.

---

[1] Patrick Murphy Malin, 'The Refugee: A Problem for International Organization', *International Organization*, vol. i, 3, p. 448. Mr. Malin was American Director of the International Migration Service from 1942 to 1944. From 1944 until 1946 he was Vice-Director of the IGCR.

In addition to these agencies, many individual governments provided services for refugees either by developing their own resettlement schemes or giving grants-in-aid to national voluntary organizations.

In addition to the very real accomplishments of these agencies, and the experience they provided, there was the material setting which IRO inherited. The military authorities established and developed the installations and registration which formed the basis for the camp work of IRO. The military authorities and UNRRA also handed on valuable experience and equipment in regard to supply and transport, health services, &c. It was sometimes forgotten by the IRO officials how much they owed to the well-laid foundations for their work which they inherited.

Moreover, after a period of twenty-five years of international action on behalf of uprooted people, a wealth of political wisdom and practical knowledge lay at the disposal of those who planned for the new international organization and the administrators who had to tackle the practical side of the problem. They could hardly fail to be aware that the refugee problem of the twentieth century was not a temporary question but an outgrowth of modern political development; not only a humanitarian problem but a human one which demanded political and economic action as well as humanitarian aid.

But they knew that the causes of the refugee problem made it 'a thorny one for organized treatment'. Inevitably, there were sharply divergent attitudes towards the refugee problem between the countries of origin and those of first refuge and final settlement. The country of origin often looked upon the refugee as a kind of traitor. Thus any assistance given to him by outside bodies was considered an interference with its sovereign right over its own people. On the other hand, while the countries of temporary asylum or permanent settlement upheld the refugee's right to decide whether or not to return to his place of origin, their attitude towards international organization was not without reservations. Eager as they were to secure international support in shouldering the costly burdens of interim maintenance or final settlement, they were often averse to what they termed external interference in the affairs of their country.

Furthermore, an almost unlimited patience and optimism were needed by the sponsors and administrators of internationally organized transactions for the refugees. The refugees were concerned predominantly with their own tragedy. This can be well understood, since they suffered from insecurity and uncertainty and a vastly changed social position. However, many refugees expected virtual miracles from those who were dealing on their behalf, and often considered them unjust or inhuman when aid was not forthcoming according to their degree of suffering. On the other hand, the supporters of effective international aid for refugees had, from their side, to face many disappointments in their attempts to get quick and sufficient support. They had to plead with the public as well as with governments for a highly intricate and expensive undertaking. To bridge the gap between refugee plight and public aid taxed the resources and ingenuity of non-governmental, philanthropic, and other public-minded organizations.

In the long perspective of efforts for refugees from the end of the First World War to the establishment of IRO, it was clear that the rising crescendo of the problem had brought at least increasing awareness that the refugee problem was intimately connected with planned migration. The efforts of the League of Nations, useful as they had been, were piecemeal, and undertaken under the aspect of coping with one or another refugee group already stranded in an area of temporary refuge. When IGCR was empowered to consider the planned movement of Jews out of Germany as well as the problems of those already outside the country, the conception of planned migration was introduced. What the efforts of the military authorities and UNRRA added to this were operations on a scale hitherto unknown. IRO not only inherited their experience but also, in its mandate, reflected new comprehension that the international character of the refugee problem demanded unified and far-reaching efforts.

PART I

CHAPTER I

THE CREATION OF THE IRO

THE idea of creating an international refugee organization was first discussed at the second meeting of Committee II/3 on 7 May 1945 during the San Francisco conference, which drew up the Charter of the United Nations. Once again the Norwegian Government[1] took the initiative, suggesting that a specialized international organization 'be created now, or revised in a new form named the International Organization for Refugees and Stateless Persons'.[2] However, no action was taken at that time.

The Government of the United Kingdom, one of the two main contributing members of IGCR, moved the matter further by presenting its concern and its point of view at the Fifth Plenary Session of IGCR, held in Paris in November 1945. Sir George Rendel, the UK delegate, pointed out that a number of displaced persons would be left over who had not been repatriated or returned to their homes by UNRRA, as well as others who did not come within UNRRA's mandate since they had been under the auspices of the High Commissioner of the League of Nations or of IGCR. He stressed that the refugee problem was one which concerned all the UN, and that in the opinion of his government the work of dealing with the refugee problem could best be achieved through the organization of the UN. This, he said, would ensure the free and open discussion of all questions relating to refugees, some of which involved difficult political problems.[3] The matter was further pursued during the meetings of the Executive Committee and later of Committee III of the Preparatory Commission as one of many 'complex economic and social problems of the gravest urgency arising out of the war, which will demand the immediate attention of ECOSOC after its establishment'.[4]

On 13 December 1945, before Committee III (Economic and Social) of the Preparatory Commission, Mr. Myrddin Evans, the UK delegate, stressed again the urgency and importance of bringing the refugee problem under the UN because of its political and financial aspects and because of its concern to all the member nations. Since international organization in this field was at that time inadequate to deal with

[1] Cf. Introduction, p. 8.
[2] IGCR, Minutes of the Fifth Plenary Session, p. 13.
[3] Report by the Executive Committee to the Preparatory Commission of the UN, paras. 8 and 9. 12 Nov. 1945, p. 51.
[4] He stated: '. . . to have too many international agencies dealing with different aspects of economic or social policy does raise, as we all know, difficulties of a budgetary nature.' Preparatory Commission, Committee III, Seventh Meeting, 6 Dec. 1945 (PC/ES/16), Eleventh and Twelfth Meetings, 13 and 14 Dec. (PC/ES/25).

the matter which had taken on a new aspect and was beyond the scope of IGCR and UNRRA, he proposed that the ECOSOC set up a 'Commission on Refugees' rather than a semi-independent specialized agency. This Commission was to take over and develop as it deemed necessary the functions then performed by the IGCR and to 'advise the Council (ECOSOC) and, through it, the other organs of the UN on all questions relating to refugees'.[1] In support of this proposal, he pointed out that it seemed expedient to keep the number of specialized agencies to a minimum regardless of how closely they were affiliated with the UN. Only the UN itself could provide the solution to a question of such magnitude. The funds at the disposal of the UN would facilitate work on behalf of the refugees, whereas the budgets of the various specialized agencies would be dependent upon annual legislation by participating countries. Other delegations associated with this view agreed that a problem of such magnitude and with so many implications could be better dealt with by the UN than by a specialized agency. The suggestion of establishing a commission, however, was not accepted, although it was agreed that a preliminary study of the whole matter should be undertaken by ECOSOC. The Preparatory Commission suggested that 'ECOSOC on its own initiative or at the request of the General Assembly, should review at the First Part of its First Session the nature and efficacy of the international machinery which then existed and, if necessary, should promote improvements in the existing machinery or provide other effective means to deal with this problem'. At the same time it was recommended that the General Assembly should likewise consider the question, because of the political problems involved. The rapporteur of Committee III stated in the Third Plenary Meeting of the Preparatory Commission[2] (18 December) that the political aspects of the question could be 'thrashed out' at the General Assembly so that when ECOSOC took up the matter on its own agenda, it would have a 'clearer picture of those political considerations' which were involved in the handling of the matter. The question of the refugees was thus included in the provisional agenda for the First Part of the First Session of the General Assembly under item 17: 'matters of urgent importance, including the problem of refugees.'[3]

Third Committee of the UN General Assembly

Although the First Part of the First Session of the General Assembly was intended to be largely constituent, it proved to be inevitable that consideration had to be given to urgent world problems. In fact, more hours were devoted during the two parts of the First Session of the General Assembly to the refugee problem than to any other single question except those concerning security. The political as well as the technical implications of this humanitarian problem caused the debate on the refugee question to be so complicated that it cannot easily be followed in detail with all the manifold repetitions, withdrawals, amendments, or concessions made by the delegates who participated in the discussion in the various organs of the UN. Instead of presenting a chronological description, it may suffice to highlight the main argu-

---

[1] Journal No. 22, 19 Dec. 1945, p. 4.

[2] UN Preparatory Commission, Third Plenary Meeting, 18 Dec. Consideration of Report of Committee III (PC/ES/36), (PC/CD/3), (PC/ES/36/Corr. 1).

[3] UN General Assembly, *Official Records*, First Part, First Session, 1946, Plenary Meetings, p. 33.

ments and recommendations which led to the final resolution of 15 December 1946, in which the General Assembly accepted the Constitution, a provisional budget, and an agreement for the interim measures to be taken for establishing an international refugee organization.

The General Assembly, at its Sixteenth Plenary Meeting held on 19 January 1946, referred the matter to the Third Committee—dealing with social, humanitarian, and cultural questions—for consideration and report to the plenary meeting. From 28 January to 14 February 1946 there was in the Committee a vigorous debate on the question of refugees and displaced persons in general and upon the nature and scope of any new international refugee organization to be created. During this debate all the contentious issues involved became apparent. The representatives of the UK, US, France, and other countries considered that the problem was 'international in scope and character', and maintained that an effective solution could be achieved only through an international organization. At the Fourth Meeting of the Third Committee Mr. P. Noel-Baker, the UK delegate, presented a proposal concerning refugees recommending that 'there might be created under the United Nations, under the direct authority of the Assembly, an organ of the United Nations ... which would take over the responsibilities of existing bodies'.[1] Mrs. Franklin D. Roosevelt, the US delegate, in expressing agreement with Mr. Noel-Baker, emphasized that international action was needed 'in the interest of humanity and social stability', and to solve a problem which was 'a source of disturbance in the relationships of the nations'.[2] An alternative proposal presented by Ales Bebler, the Yugoslav delegate, maintained that the problem of displaced persons had ceased to be an important international question as the defeat of the Axis Powers permitted the return of all displaced persons to their home countries. No permanent international machinery was necessary, therefore, to organize assistance to such persons. Those not yet returned to their home countries should be dealt with through bilateral agreements between the countries of origin and those of refugees. Any displaced person not responding for repatriation within four months should not be entitled to any assistance at the expense of an international organization or of their state of origin, with the exception of the Spanish refugees. Furthermore, the General Assembly should recommend to members of the UN that they make arrangements to facilitate the seizure of war criminals.[3]

In the course of long drawn out discussions in the Third Committee and the following plenary meetings of the General Assembly these points were upheld and elaborated by the eastern European countries (Byelorussia, Poland, USSR, and Ukrainian SSR). These delegates emphasized that in their view all men of goodwill, since the defeat of the Axis Powers, could return to their home countries; quislings, war criminals, traitors, Fascists, and undemocratic elements who opposed governments of their countries should not receive any assistance from an international organization. The solution of the refugee problem was repatriation to be arranged as quickly as possible, preferably through bilateral arrangements between the countries concerned.

[1] Third Committee, *Summary Record*, p. 9, and Annex 1, p. 37.
[2] Ibid., Annex 5a, p. 56. [3] Ibid., p. 10, and Annex 2, p. 43.

Western countries, including Belgium, the Netherlands, Panama, South Africa, the UK, and the US, considered it necessary to put human considerations above political ones. In their view there was an important group of political dissidents who were neither Fascist nor war criminals nor traitors. They maintained that such persons should not be forced to return to their home countries because the right of asylum for political dissidents was an essential part of those basic rights embodied in the Charter of the United Nations.

The fate of Jews aiming at emigration to Palestine presented a specific problem as the representatives of a number of Arab states stated their opposition to political Zionism during the debates. Although expressing sympathy for Jewish victims of Fascism they emphasized that it should not be related to the problem of Palestine. If Jews left Europe as a matter of personal preference this could not be regarded as a refugee question.

On 1 and 4 February respectively the Netherlands and the USSR presented alternative draft resolutions.[1] Both alike proposed that the problem should be referred to ECOSOC and that refugees who did not wish to return to their countries should not be compelled to do so. But the Netherlands suggested that the resettlement of such refugees should be the responsibility of an international organization, while the Soviet delegation wanted to make such resettlement contingent upon the consent of countries of origin of refugees. The Netherlands recommended that an international body which would examine the refugee problem in all its aspects should be established under the Council. The Soviet resolution insisted that the main task of the UN was to give refugees all possible help for their early return to their home countries. The Netherlands, however, stressed that only persons liable to extradition in conformity with an international agreement because of their actions or attitude during the last war were to be refused refugee status. The Soviet resolution put forward that

(a) Quislings, traitors and war criminals, as persons dishonoured for collaboration with the enemies of the United Nations in any form, should not be regarded as refugees who are entitled to get protection of the U.N., and that quislings, traitors and war criminals who are still hiding, under the guise of refugees, should be immediately returned to their countries;

(b) Germans being transferred to Germany from other States or who fled to other States from Allied troops, do not fall under the action of this decision; their situation may be decided by Allied Forces of occupation in Germany, in agreement with the Governments of the respective countries.

In addition the Soviet delegation proposed that

No propaganda should be permitted in refugee camps against the interests of the Organisation of U.N. or her members, nor propaganda against returning to their native countries. The personnel of refugee camps should be comprised mainly of representatives of States concerned, whose citizens are the refugees.

After further discussion the representative of the US introduced a compromise resolution:[2] persons who objected to returning to their country of origin should not be compelled to do so, but every effort should be made to encourage repatriation. No action taken in accordance with this resolution, however, should interfere in any

[1] Third Committee, *Summary Record*, Annexes 3 and 4, pp. 51 and 54.
[2] UN Doc. A/45, included in the Constitution of the IRO as Annex III, see Appendix I, p. 588.

way with the surrender and punishment of war criminals, quislings, and traitors, in conformity with international arrangements and agreements. Furthermore, the General Assembly should recommend to ECOSOC the establishment of a special committee to make a thorough study of the refugee problem and to report to the Second Part of the First Session of the General Assembly.

In the hope that a majority would support the US resolution the Netherlands and the UK withdrew their proposals. But after the Third Committee referred the drafts of the USSR and US resolutions to a sub-committee (which reported back on 7 February), the Soviet delegation re-introduced its two former suggestions as amendments, and again, after their rejection in the Third Committee, at the Twenty-ninth Plenary Meeting of the General Assembly on 12 February 1946, when the report of the Third Committee was discussed. Once more, after considerable delays, the amendments were rejected and the draft resolution of the Third Committee adopted.

The fact that, following the rejection of the amendments by the General Assembly, the resolution as a whole was adopted by 42 votes, no delegate voting against it, nor formally abstaining, reflects the considerable effort made in working out the terms of the resolution to meet the divergent views revealed in the course of the discussion in the Third Committee.[1]

The resolution laid down some general principles that were to guide the deliberations of ECOSOC, to which the General Assembly transferred the matter 'for thorough examination in all its aspects'. It recognized first that the problem was 'one of immediate urgency, and international in scope and nature'; secondly, that no refugees or displaced persons against whom criminal charges had not been laid should 'be compelled to return to their country of origin', and that 'the future of such refugees or displaced persons' should 'become the concern' of an international body; and thirdly, that 'the main task concerning displaced persons' was 'to encourage and assist in every way possible their early return to their countries of origin'. Thus the General Assembly unanimously accepted the principle that the refugee question was the concern of the UN and that an international agency should care for those refugees who did not want to be repatriated, while the greatest possible efforts should be made to help the others to return soon to their respective countries.

While the discussion in the Third Committee enabled agreement to be reached on the points mentioned above, it also revealed the necessity of examining more closely the question of defining the term 'refugee' in the light of the entirely new situation created by the Second World War. It also proved necessary to examine how the general principles laid down in the resolution of 12 February 1946 could be applied so as to give refugees and displaced persons and the interested governments the maximum guarantees that their legitimate interests would be safeguarded. In the words of the rapporteur, it was desirable to strengthen and widen the compromise reached within the Committee, to secure the sympathetic collaboration of governments on the practical issues, and to compare the various viewpoints on questions of detail before taking decisions of a general character.

---

[1] Lebanon represented a special problem arising out of the situation in relation to refugees in the Middle East.

Special Committee on Refugees and Displaced Persons

Following this decision, ECOSOC, on 16 February of the same year, established a Special Committee on Refugees and Displaced Persons, which met in London from 8 April to 1 June 1946, under the chairmanship of Mr. Hector McNeil. The Committee consisted of representatives of twenty countries which were concerned in different ways with the refugee problem: there were countries of origin (the Soviet Union, Ukraine, Byelorussia, Poland, Yugoslavia, Czechoslovakia, and China); countries of temporary residence (Belgium, France, the Netherlands, and the UK); and countries of resettlement (Australia, Brazil, Canada, Colombia, the Dominican Republic, New Zealand, Peru, and the US). Representatives of the IGCR and UNRRA took part in a consultative capacity. The countries were represented by delegates, many of them experts in the field, e.g. Sir George Rendel and Mr. Hector McNeil of the UK Government had worked in the IGCR as well as in connexion with the planning of UNRRA. And their opposite number, Mr. George L. Warren of the US Government, was an experienced veteran in the field of international migration and the refugee problem; overseas countries were represented in some cases by experts on migration.

The Committee recommended the establishment of a specialized agency of a non-permanent character to deal with the problem of refugees and submitted to ECOSOC an elaborate report.[1] Apart from a lengthy preliminary section of observations by the rapporteur and a chapter of 'information on the settlement' containing statements by a number of countries of reception, the report dealt in three main chapters with 'the scope and nature of the problem' which was the work of the special sub-committee on fact finding; with a 'definition of the terms "refugees" and "displaced persons"', an outcome of laborious debates on the part of the drafting group and the drafting sub-committee on definitions; and finally, a chapter on 'Organization of and Financial Provision for an IRO', including a draft constitution, a product of another sub-committee.

In considering the refugee problem, the Special Committee tried to apply the broad general principles formulated by the General Assembly. It was faced with an onerous task. Its deliberations proved conclusively that it would be impossible to secure universal support for the new agency. But less than a year after the end of the war and only a few months after the establishment of the UN as an organization, there was manifest unwillingness to miss this opportunity of at least formal agreement. Both sides were accordingly willing to compromise in an effort to accommodate irreconcilable points of view. The report of the Special Committee, however, was by no means unanimous, and it was qualified at every turn by reservations and contradictions. It incorporated not only provisions adopted by a majority of votes but also various minority statements regarding points on which there was substantial disagreement. Considering the profound differences of opinion, it is astonishing that so much progress was achieved.

The delegates discussed at some length the type and character of the agency which

---

[1] UN, ECOSOC, *Official Records*, First Year, Second Session, Special Suppl. 1. 7 June 1946, Doc. E/REF/75.

would best serve the purposes they had in view. A 'truly representative and effective organization under the auspices of the United Nations' was needed, which should 'be given full authority to deal with all classes of displaced and uprooted persons', and 'be assured of the necessary funds' to enable it 'to cope adequately with this urgent, complex, and inevitably long-term problem'. Such an organization should have the advantage of being able to pool past experiences and to benefit by them; it should be able to arrange for the reception countries to accept refugees for resettlement efficiently and economically; and to secure the services of an impartial, international-trained secretariat.[1] Three possibilities were considered: (1) under Article 22 of the Charter the General Assembly might establish machinery coming directly under its own authority; (2) under Article 68 a commission under ECOSOC might be set up; (3) under Articles 57 and 63 a specialized agency could be created as an autonomous body linked with the UN by a negotiated agreement. The British delegation was in favour of either of the first two suggestions, mentioning the High Commission under the authority of the League as a precedent. Members of the Commonwealth, Belgium, France, and the Netherlands were also in favour of the integration of the new organization with the UN and expressed doubts concerning the efficacy of any refugee agency not under the authority of the UN.[2]

The Australian delegate, Colonel William Roy Hodgson, maintained that specialized agencies 'scattered all over the international landscape' were more costly in money and personnel and that, since they established their own constitutions, principles, and methods of work, they could not be so effectively controlled or directed as an instrument directly responsible to one of the main organs of the UN.[3] The countries holding this view felt that the mandates of the General Assembly and of ECOSOC were not confined to mere review and comment and that the new organization would have fuller support by all member nations as an integral part of the UN machinery.

Mr. George L. Warren, the US delegate, was opposed to this point of view, maintaining that the UN was a deliberative body for discussing and deciding policy issues, in other words, a kind of parliamentary body. An operational undertaking of the size and complexity needed for refugees would strain the UN budget and would also place demands on those members who were unable or unwilling to participate. He felt that it was unwise to impose an operational budget on the UN, and that those who had drawn up the Charter had considerably more faith in the ability of specialized agencies to conduct important international activities.[4] He pointed out that the specialized agency would function within the framework of agencies related to the UN, drawing its strength from it and co-operating with it in accomplishing its purposes. Provisions should be made for the fullest possible use of public interest and of the moral support and judgement of the General Assembly and ECOSOC in the conduct of the specialized agency. But he stressed that 'such a large operational task, to be done well, must be given authority to function quickly and with appropriate flexibility'.

The delegations representing the countries of origin agreed that from a political

E/REF/52, p. 2, and E/REF/39, p. 1.
[2] UN, Third Committee, *Summary Record*, p. 53, and ECOSOC, op. cit., pp. 144 and 156.
[3] General Assembly, Third Committee, *Verbation Record*, 4 Feb. 1946. E/REF/1, p. 29.
[4] 2 May 1946, E/REF/60.

point of view, an independent organization, specialized and not permanent,[1] would be in a better position to deal with the wishes of the countries directly concerned; they attached particular importance to the *temporary* character of the organization, which would thus be better safeguarded. The Soviet Union further suggested that the creation of a specialized agency would permit representation in its councils of the countries of origin in proportion to the numbers of their refugees and displaced persons.[2] British feeling, however, was that if it were decided to establish a specialized agency, its members should consist of those countries that would bear the financial burden of the resettlement work rather than the countries of origin, with which the refugees would, in fact, have no further connexion.

Attempts by the French delegation to achieve a compromise failed,[3] and the US proposal was finally accepted instead of the British one. In the end, the countries of origin were not represented in the IRO councils, since they did not join the organization, and British doubts proved unfounded. Later discussions in the UN on the work of the IRO plainly indicated the difficulties and delays that might well have resulted from operational supervision by those UN bodies whose treatment even of humanitarian matters was politically controversial. The Committee turned to its second task, that of deciding in the light of the resolution of 12 February 1946 how to define the terms 'refugee' and 'displaced person' and to lay down the conditions to be fulfilled by refugees and displaced persons to enable them to qualify for the protection and assistance of refugees, and finally to draw a line of demarcation between those who were genuine refugees whom it was the duty of the international community to support, and those who were not. As the rapporteur of the Special Committee stated, the definition of the term 'refugee' and 'displaced person' was the 'corner-stone of the whole edifice'.[4] More difficulty was experienced in attempting to arrive at a definition of these terms than in any other matter. The British delegate, Sir George Rendel, felt that the chief reason for this difficulty arose from varying conceptions of the rights of individuals and the rights of states, and that it concerned totally different conceptions of the relationship of the individual to the state. He added: 'I do not think we can hope, at this moment of history, to reconcile two philosophies which have that antithesis in such a way as to produce complete harmony and complete unanimity.'[5]

This difference of outlook was reflected in the attitudes of the major groups of powers to this issue. The emphasis of the western European countries was placed, as Mrs. Roosevelt said, on finding 'ways . . . in the interest of humanity and social stability to return . . . thousands of people who have been uprooted from their homes and their countries to a settled way of life'.[6] These people were defined as

---

[1] Byelorussian delegate, 24 Apr., Doc. E/REF/39, pp. 4–5.

[2] 27 Apr., Doc. E/REF/46, p. 2.

[3] It was proposed that a special commission of the Council should be created comprising an equal number of representatives of the governments of the countries of origin and of the countries of reception. This commission, meeting once or twice a year, would have the duty of ensuring the necessary liaison between the UN and the IRO (23 Apr. E/REF/35). Twelve delegates voted for a specialized agency and six against (Australia, Canada, Lebanon, the Netherlands, New Zealand, and the UK), the delegates of Belgium and France abstaining (E/REF/39, p. 7).

[4] M. Raymond Bousquet, delegate of France (Special Committee Report, p. 7).

[5] At the final meeting of the Special Committee (ibid., p. 155).

[6] General Assembly, Third Committee, 28 Jan. 1946, E/REF/1, p. 7.

persons 'displaced by the events of war, by the battles that may sway backwards and forwards, by the political consequences to which wars lead . . . people . . . unwilling to return to the homes where they lived before the war began'.[1] Other governments maintained that refugees and displaced persons consisted either of 'people committed in one way or another to the occupation authorities, or sections of the population who, owing to their anti-democratic activity, do not wish to return to their own country, or else people who, under the influence of the first two categories, are not returning when they could return . . .'.[2] In seeking a definition of 'refugee' two approaches were used. The first was to arrive at a broad definition on a common humanitarian basis, so that any political refugee or a displaced person would be eligible for international protection and assistance. The Committee decided, however, to define such refugees and displaced persons according to main categories. Sir Herbert Emerson, Director of IGCR, pointed out that 'experience has shown that for practical purposes it is expedient to define such persons in terms of categories, the right of individual assistance being dependent on inclusion of the person within one or other of the categories unless he is otherwise disqualified. This ensures a precision which is difficult to obtain by an omnibus mandate conceived in terms of the individual person in isolation and not as a member of a specific category.'[3]

During subsequent meetings a distinction (which was to become embodied in the General Assembly resolution of 12 February 1946) was drawn between 'genuine refugees and displaced persons', 'war criminals, quislings and traitors', and 'Germans being transferred to Germany from other States or who fled to other States from Allied troops'. Discussion turned chiefly on major questions of principle, particularly the question of whether political dissidents who did not actively assist the enemy, but were opposed to the new régimes existing in their countries, should or should not come within the IRO mandate. The Soviet and Yugoslav delegates stated that although they did not wish to deny the right of asylum, or even the right of émigrés who objected to a particular government or régime, to express their hostility to that régime, they were unable to accept a position in which a member government of the UN might contribute directly or indirectly to the maintenance or relief of its dissident nationals while those nationals held a hostile attitude to that government. The UK and US delegates supported the view that only active leaders of groups of political dissidents should be denied assistance, since indiscriminate suppression of all manifestations of political disagreement on the part of refugees would infringe the basic right of freedom of speech. Moreover, it should not be forgotten that immediately after the Allied victory over Nazi Germany about 8 million people had returned to their homes. The remainder, as the report expressed it, were the 'hard core of non-repatriable persons' who must be given an opportunity to resettle in countries willing to give them asylum.

On the question of the registration and screening of refugees and displaced persons, the Soviet and Yugoslav delegates maintained that the governments of the

[1] By Mr. P. Noel-Baker, UK delegate, ibid., p. 5.
[2] Mr. A. Bebler, delegate of Yugoslavia, ibid., p. 9.
[3] E/REF/12, p. 2.

countries of origin should participate in this operation, and that the information obtained should be communicated to them for verification. They considered that the objects of registration should be, first, to ascertain the names of those entitled to assistance from the Organization; secondly, to sift war criminals, quislings, and traitors from among the refugees and facilitate their surrender to the countries concerned; and thirdly, by eliminating such persons, to remove the harmful influence they exerted on their compatriots and thereby to facilitate repatriation. It would not be possible, in their view, for the staff of the IRO alone to assess the value of the information received from the refugees and displaced persons. Many of them would have no identity papers. It would thus be easy for Germans who previously formed part of German minorities in the countries of origin, and who spoke the language of those countries, to pass themselves off as genuine refugees. They believed that this kind of danger could be lessened considerably by co-operation between officers of the countries of origin and of the IRO in carrying out registration, and they felt that to communicate the results as and when they became known to the governments of the countries of origin would considerably limit the risk of errors in identifying the persons concerned.[1]

Representatives of the western countries, led by the UK delegate, insisted that refugees should be permitted to seek asylum, and that only 'the local authorities responsible for the administration of camps for refugees and displaced persons or for the protection of refugees and displaced persons' were qualified to carry out registration independently. They argued that the purpose of the Soviet and Yugoslav delegates seemed to be to ensure that governments of countries of origin should be permitted to review the international body's decisions, and that it was impossible to admit the legitimacy of such a right, especially in the case of political dissidents.[2]

Thus it became apparent that the western countries were determined to secure UN protection for political dissidents among the refugees, while the minority aim was to seek out the dissidents and turn them over to the countries of origin for punishment. Each government formulated its policy regarding categories of persons entitled to assistance from the new organization according to its own conception of the relationship between the individual and the state, and the positions of the different governments can be summarized as follows: the eastern European countries, led by Poland, the USSR, and Yugoslavia, supported the view that only those persons who wanted to return to their countries should be assisted by an international organization. All others were classified by them as Fascist collaborators, war criminals, quislings, or traitors, and were therefore not entitled to assistance; at the same time the delegates of these countries strongly recommended that the new organization should facilitate the apprehension and surrender of such persons to the country that claimed them. The representatives of the other countries, led by the UK and the US, maintained that many people who found themselves outside their country of nationality or former habitual residence owing to political changes which occurred as a result of the war could be justified in claiming the

---

[1] E/REF/22 and 23.

[2] 17 May, E/REF/73 and Special Committee Report; see comments of the rapporteur on chap. ii of the Report, p. 9.

status of refugee or political dissident, and that it was incumbent upon the UN to assist such people.

The result of the Special Committee's deliberations was a draft constitution for a non-permanent organization to be called the International Refugee Organization, a specialized agency to be brought into relation with the UN. The draft constitution included a detailed definition of the categories of persons who might become the concern of the Organization, the conditions which individuals within the categories would have to satisfy before they could become its concern, the disqualifications which would exclude individuals, and the circumstances in which they would cease to be its concern.

Committee on Finances

The ECOSOC, to which the report was submitted at its Second Session in New York, held in May and June 1946, confined itself to the consideration of the Draft Constitution and of the definitions. It provisionally approved the Draft Constitution, with certain amendments, for the purpose of submission to member governments of the UN for their observations, and at the same time appointed a Committee on Finances to prepare a draft budget for the first fiscal year of the new organization. This Committee met in London in July 1946 to prepare both the provisional administrative and operational budgets for the first financial year of the IRO, and the scales according to which contributions to these budgets might be allocated in an equitable way among the members of the UN having due regard 'to the exceptionally difficult financial situation of countries' which had formerly suffered under enemy occupation.[1]

The aims of former international organizations had often been thwarted by a lack of funds for their operational activities. Neither the League of Nations nor the IGCR had sufficient means to carry out efficiently even its administrative task. Both organs had to rely on help by voluntary agencies and on support by individual governments. Now, however, the discussions and the urgency of the problem made the governments willing to provide the means out of public funds for the administration as well as the operation of the new agency.

The governments which advocated international action for solving the refugee problem were willing to accept financial responsibilities. The matter had been discussed in the Third Committee of the General Assembly and in ECOSOC. Mr. Paul Martin, the Canadian delegate to ECOSOC, expressed the general opinion of the delegates when he declared: 'The demands of our responsibilities toward refugees will command the same measures of general support as in the case' of relief and repatriation. 'These decisions which we are taking will involve all of us in heavy financial responsibilities.' Every country concerned was aware that it was a costly business to maintain refugees in camps, and that it was even more costly to re-establish them in other parts of the world. 'We might as well understand from the outset that it is going to be expensive. It is going to cost money. Peace

---

[1] This Committee comprised delegates from Brazil, Canada (chair), China, France, Lebanon, the Netherlands, Poland, the UK, the US, and the USSR. Sir Herbert Emerson and Mr. Fiorella La Guardia, Director General of UNRRA, sat on the Committee in a consultative capacity. E/81/Rev. 1.

is costly—but nothing like the cost of war', the American people were told in a broadcast by Mr. George Warren, the American delegate to the General Council, who was one of the financial advisers of the IRO.[1]

However, past experience with the huge relief and rehabilitation problem of war-torn countries of which the refugee problem had been a part, had made statesmen more cautious in their planning. Mr. Martin, the Canadian delegate, stated: 'The mounting cost of international undertakings is already a cause of concern. . . . It will be necessary to demonstrate that every item in the budget is essential and that it is set at the lowest possible figure. For this reason the proposed budget of the new organization should be scrutinized with the greatest care.' This applied to the scales of contributions recommended for administrative and operational expenditures, and to the actual amounts estimated for administration, care and maintenance, repatriation and resettlement.

The UK delegation, supported by others, stressed that all member nations should fully share the financial responsibility. It recommended that 'the financial structure of the new organization should provide for the acceptance of financial obligations, administrative, operational, on as wide an international basis as possible . . .'. The Canadian delegate suggested in the Third Committee of the General Assembly that '. . . the constitution should be strengthened in such a way as to make the signature and approval of the constitution carry with it the obligation to contribute to its support. The new organisation will not be able to carry passengers . . . it would be most invidious if any state was able to be a party to the constitution with a reservation which would in effect allow it to avoid financial contribution. . . .'[2] In the end, the idea of universality in the sharing of the economic and financial burden of the refugee problem was defeated. The debates had shown that universal contractual support and financial backing for the operations of the IRO was unlikely. But the Constitution made contributions to both the operational and the administrative expenditures obligatory on membership of the Organization; and thus excluded the possibility that some governments, sitting in the Council of the Organization by virtue of a contribution to administrative expenses only, might destroy the whole work by cutting down the operational budget.

In making this provision, the Constitution reflected experience gained during the life of the League of Nations and UNRRA. In 1937 the Government of the Soviet Union had made it known before the League of Nations that it would object to a proposed credit designed to permit continuation of the League's work for refugees.

The task of the Committee was arduous because of the many speculative calculations involved, such as, for instance, the estimates of the numbers and location of refugees and displaced persons who would exist on 1 January 1947, or of those likely to be repatriated or resettled during that year. The same difficulties arose when it came to shaping the organizational units or estimating the supplies needed.

---

[1] 'Refugee Problems and the Economic Reconstruction of Devastated Areas', *Our Foreign Policy*, New York, National Broadcasting Company, 21 Sept. 1946, p. 10. For a similar utterance, see Mr. Riddell's address, delivered at the Canadian Institute of Public Affairs, Ottawa, Canada, Department of External Affairs, 24 Aug. 1946.

[2] General Assembly, Third Committee, *Summary Record*, Second Part, First Session, p. 92.

On the basis of information furnished by UNRRA and IGCR the provisional figures for the first year were finally decided at $4,800,000 for administrative expenses, $193,954,000 for operational expenditure (just under $10 million for repatriation, $12 million for resettlement of family units and individuals, and $158 million for care and maintenance), while $60 million were provided for large-scale operations: thus making a total budget of $250,875,400.[1]

The fact that the budget estimates had been expressed in dollars did not constitute a recommendation to the Committee that contributions must necessarily be paid in American currency; the possibility of payment in other currencies and in kind was also taken into consideration.

In respect of the proposed budgets, various government representatives made reservations. The main criticism came from the USSR which was in complete disagreement with the principle of obligatory contribution to the operational budget of the IRO and considered that this should be covered by voluntary contributions of the members. The UK delegate found the scales of contribution unacceptable and argued that war damage should have been taken into consideration as far as his country was concerned.

At its Third Session held at Lake Success, NY, in September, ECOSOC had before it the comments of the governments on the Draft Constitution, the report of the Committee on Finances of IRO, and a report of the Secretary General relating to the initiation of the work of the planned organization. It appointed an *ad hoc* Committee on Finances[2] to examine Article 10 of the Draft Constitution and the provisional administrative and operational budgets proposed by the previous Financial Committee. It also had to deal with the special question of assistance to overseas Chinese refugees.

During the discussions, formal statements or renewed reservations were made by a number of delegations. The USSR representatives, in voting again against the principle of compulsory contributions to the operational budget (Parts I and II) fully reserved the position of the Soviet Government regarding procedures for the raising of requisite funds for the operations of the IRO. They also voted against the inclusion in the budget of the items with respect to refugees in Spain and Shanghai, and reserved their position regarding the eligibility of refugees in those territories. The French delegation insisted on the principle of voluntary and non-obligatory contributions to Part II of the provisional operational budget. The Peruvian delegation emphasized that, because of the lack of adequate factual information regarding would-be settlers, it had been difficult for many prospective countries of reception to make necessary plans and budgetary estimates of the means and amount of their possible contributions. The US delegation stated that the amount provided in Part II for large-scale resettlement, now reduced to $5 million, should omit any specific estimate of the number of displaced persons and refugees to be settled during the first year of the Organization. In earlier discussions in the Finance Committee, the figure of $60 million had been accepted on the

---

[1] See UN Doc. E/REF/FIN/23, 22 July 1946.
[2] The Committee was composed of ten members as well as the representatives of UNRRA and the IGCR.

assumption that 100,000 refugees could be found new homes during the first financial year of the IRO. This reduction was also based on a further assumption— that the estimates of the *per capita* cost for resettlement operations were lower than those contemplated by the Committee on Finances of the IRO.

The US delegation, supported by the UK, France, Norway, China, and Peru, considered that many complex factors were involved in large-scale resettlement operations; they felt that as it was desirable for the Organization to consider each proposed resettlement project on an individual basis, it was advisable to include in the Organization's budget a sum sufficient for projects which might reasonably be anticipated without specifying the number of individuals who might be involved in such projects, or the *per capita* cost. The Committee reviewed both the provisional administrative and operational budgets in the light of the arguments brought forward by the various delegations and produced revised estimates.[1] In fact, the administrative budget for $4,800,000 was adopted, but Part I of the operational budget, other than large-scale resettlement, was reduced from $193,950,000 to $151,060,500. The reason for this reduction was that 'the estimates were excessive, not in relation to need but in relation to the political realities—that is, the likelihood of appropriations by the governments'.[2] The Latin-American representatives and the US delegation in particular were anxious to reduce the budget, knowing that the appropriations would have to be voted upon by the parliaments of their respective countries.

Taking into consideration full statements from UNRRA and IGCR concerning their respective organizational pattern, the Committee drafted a budget divided into administrative, operational, and large-scale resettlement sections. Because the time was very limited, the Committee was unable to gather full data from the governments and the occupying authorities. They relied on verbal information from government delegates, and on the experience of UNRRA and IGCR. 'In drawing up the estimates, the Committee assumed that the occupying Powers would make available to the IRO, without cost, maximum supplies and services from the German economy.'[3]

The Committee made some substantial downward adjustments in the operational budget in Section 1: personnel and establishment costs: salaries, allowances, &c., for operational personnel were reduced; it was taken into account that some camps would be closed and some camp duties, formerly performed by UNRRA staff, would now be carried out by displaced persons themselves. However, 700 additional persons were included for 'certain programmes such as supply, training and retraining, and screening of eligibles' and other new tasks.

In Section 2: care and maintenance, the estimates for supplies, welfare, and retraining were different from UNRRA's estimates. The cost per head per day for care and maintenance was reduced from 67 to 45 cents, because this could be supplemented from indigenous supplies. 'It has always been assumed that the

---

[1] UN Doc. E/REF/FIN/23 and E/203/Rev. 1 in UN *Official Records*, Summary Record, Second Part of First Session of General Assembly, 1 Nov. to 13 Dec. 1946, Annex 12, pp. 384–403.

[2] Report of a Special Sub-committee on Foreign Affairs (Fulton Report), Displaced Persons and the International Refugee Organization, 80th Congress, First Session, Washington, 1947, p. 14.

[3] UN General Assembly, *Official Records*, Summary Record, Second Part of First Session, p. 386.

greatest possible part of the burden (care and maintenance) will be borne by the German Economy.' The training and retraining estimates was put 33 per cent. higher than the UNRRA programme, for it was taken into account that this activity would be closely connected with emigration and resettlement.

Also under Section 3: 'repatriation', certain cuts were made on the assumption that IRO would not be responsible for transportation costs in certain areas.

According to the wording of Article 10, paragraph 1, of the Constitution, the IRO budget had a dual role: to estimate the Organization's expenditure and to assess the contributions from the member governments. A great deal of thought was given to the apportionment of the budget among the members. It was agreed that the administrative budget should be apportioned on the same scale as the apportionment of the UN. 'The Operational Budget, it was felt, should reflect a little more closely the interest of the different countries in the problem. Certain adjustments were also made in favour of countries which had suffered severe economic and financial damage as a result of the war.'[1]

The Economic and Social Council, at its fourteenth meeting on 30 September 1946, approved the Draft Constitution for transmission to the General Assembly and decided to submit an appropriate resolution relating to interim arrangements; the Council also adopted the revised estimates. The question of scales of contribution was referred to the General Assembly for consideration in the light of the discussions of the Assembly's Standing Committee on Contributions.

Draft Constitution of IRO

When the General Assembly met at Lake Success for the Second Part of its First Session, in October 1946, the item relating to refugees on the agenda was passed on to the Third and Fifth Committees for consideration. The Third Committee was required to deal with the Draft Constitution and interim arrangements. The Fifth Committee (Administrative and Budgetary), which met from 3 to 13 December, was required to consider and report on Article 10 and Annex 2 of the Constitution dealing with finances, the provisional budget of the Organization, and the provisional scales of contribution. Thirteen amendments to Article 10 and Annex 2 were submitted by various delegations. One amendment to Article 10 presented by the Byelorussian delegation concerning the financing of the Organization was discussed at great length. This proposal suggested that the cost of the repatriation of refugees should be charged to Germany and Japan as the plight of these refugees had been caused by the action of the German and Japanese governments. Some representatives maintained that Germany and Japan could not assume further burdens, for in calculating the cost of the care and repatriation of refugees it had already been considered that these two countries would supply foodstuffs. In spite of these warnings the Committee accepted the principle by a vote of 16 to 12, and after further debate adopted, by a vote of 28 to 6, the following wording:

and that the expense of repatriation to the extent practicable should be charged to Germany and Japan for persons displaced by those Powers from countries occupied by them.

[1] Mr. Dean Acheson, Under Secretary of State, before the Committee on Foreign Relations, 80th Congress, First Session, on SJ Res. 77 (IRO), 1 Mar. 1947, p. 5.

At the suggestion of the US delegate this wording was inserted in the preamble to the Constitution. In spite of opposition by certain countries the US proposal, that countries who did not fulfil their financial obligations should lose their right to vote, was adopted by the Committee.

Article 10 as a whole was adopted by a vote of 12 to 6 with 14 abstentions. The second proposal presented by the Byelorussian delegate suggested that all provisions for large-scale resettlement should be omitted from the provisional budget, as such resettlement was contrary to the main purpose of the IRO. The countries of resettlement should also pay for the expenses of transportation and installation since they benefited from the additional man-power they would obtain. This amendment was rejected. The Committee further worked out the scales of contribution which were included in the final draft budget.

The Third Committee agreed at its fifteenth meeting, 4 November 1946, to hold a general debate on the Draft Constitution in which a large number of the representatives could express their views, since it was the first time that the Draft Constitution was considered by the entire membership of the UN.

As in former deliberations the main differences which became apparent in the protracted meetings were between (a) the countries of origin of the majority of refugees and displaced persons, (b) the countries administering refugees and displaced persons camps in the occupational zones of Germany and Austria (US, UK, and France), and (c) countries interested in the resettlement of refugees.

The point of view of the eastern countries, represented mainly by the delegates of Yugoslavia, Poland, Byelorussia, and the USSR, stressed again that the first task of IRO was the repatriation of refugees, and, according to their opinion, if IRO carried out resettlement functions these should be strictly limited and should not include persons refusing to go home. Furthermore, more effective provision should be made ensuring that war criminals would not receive any aid from IRO. The eastern countries asserted that active propaganda was carried on in camps against repatriation by elements hostile to the USSR and to other governments of the countries of origin, and effective provisions for suppressing such propaganda should be inserted into the Constitution. The eastern countries also declared that more effective measures for the screening of war criminals and collaborators should be provided, and each country of origin should be furnished with lists of displaced nationals of that country. And last, the countries of origin demanded a larger representation on the various organs of the IRO than was provided for in the draft. Some fifty amendments to the Draft Constitution were submitted by the countries of origin with the aim of bringing the Constitution in line with their point of view.

As in previous discussions, many representatives of the western countries, notably the UK and the US, opposed the recommendations on the ground that the principle of forced repatriation had been rejected, that persons with valid reasons for refusing to go home were entitled to support by the IRO, and that resettlement was in such cases the only possible solution. The governments responsible for the camp administration denied the charges, and maintained that the right of free speech should be ensured and facilities be granted to representatives of countries of origin to present their government's point of view to all persons in the camps. They also maintained that the constitutional provisions were sufficient to ensure that war criminals would not receive any aid. The majority of the Assembly stressed that the Draft Constitution as a whole was the result of extensive discussion in ECOSOC and its Special Committee, approved by a majority. Therefore the General Assembly should pass the Constitution without major changes.

The general discussion was followed by a consideration of the Draft Constitution, article by article. A total of 65 amendments were submitted by various delegations of which 39 were rejected, 18 adopted without change, and 4 in a modified form, while another 4 were withdrawn. At its forty-sixth meeting on 9 December 1946, the Third Committee finally approved the Draft Constitution as a whole (with the exception of Annex 2) by a vote of 18 to 5, with 5 abstentions. On 15 December, nearly a year after the matter had first been brought before the UN, the Constitution of the IRO was approved by the General Assembly at its last plenary meeting by 30 votes to 5, with 18 abstentions, in recognition of the urgent and international character of the problem and the temporary status of the new organization.[1]

Mrs. E. Roosevelt, speaking for the US at the last plenary meeting of the General Assembly, on 15 December 1946, illustrated these points by saying:

> Each member government of the United Nations has a direct selfish interest in the early disposal of this problem. As long as a million persons remain with refugee status, they delay the restoration of peace and order in the world.... They represent in themselves political, economic and national conflicts which are symbolic of the work which lies before nations if peace is to be restored. While they remain a solid mass in assembly centres, they deteriorate individually, and collectively they present a sore on the body of mankind which it is not safe for us to ignore.[2]

The creation of an international refugee organization was an outstanding landmark in the history of international action on behalf of refugees and displaced persons and in the development of international organization itself. It was heralded as the 'first real effort' by a world-wide organization of fifty member nations to gain a clear picture of a problem painful in its human aspect, delicate in its technical side, and politically extremely difficult, and 'to find a solution for one of the most heart-breaking problems ... which ... has confronted the conscience of mankind'.[3] Moreover, for the first time, countries of origin participated in the discussions with those of temporary refuge and of resettlement, and presented the refugee problem in all its aspects—humanitarian, economic, political, legal, and technical—to a world-wide audience. The member nations who voted for the establishment of an international refugee organization thereby upheld the purpose and principles of the

[1] *Voting for*: Belgium, Canada, China, Cuba, Denmark, the Dominican Republic, Ecuador, France, Greece, Guatemala, Honduras, Iceland, Iran, Lebanon, Liberia, Luxembourg, Mexico, the Netherlands, New Zealand, Nicaragua, Norway, Panama, Paraguay, Peru, Philippine Republic, Union of South Africa, the UK, the US, Uruguay, and Venezuela.
Voting against: Byelorussian SSR, Poland, Ukrainian SSR, the USSR, Yugoslavia.
Abstaining: Afghanistan, Argentina, Australia, Bolivia, Brazil, Chile, Colombia, Costa Rica, Czechoslovakia, Egypt, Ethiopia, Haiti, India, Iraq, Saudi Arabia, Sweden, Syria, Turkey. San Salvador was absent.
[2] General Assembly, *Official Records*, Verbatim Record, Second Part, First Session, pp. 1421 f.
[3] M. Raymond Bousquet, ECOSOC, *Official Records*, First Year, Second Session, Special Supplement No. 1, p. 3.

UN as stated in the preamble and Article 55c: 'to re-affirm faith in fundamental human rights, in the dignity and worth of the human person' and 'universal respect for, and observance of, human rights . . . for all, without distinction as to race, sex, language or religion'. They also undertook the heavy financial commitments involved in a resettlement plan for more than a million uprooted and homeless persons. This was also the first time that a specialized agency received its mandate directly from the UN. Credit for the achievement was due not only to the representatives of the countries concerned (especially to the UK delegates who initiated the discussions), but also to delegations staffed by outstanding and experienced experts. During all the meetings the delegates were aware of the pressing urgency of the problem. First and most important was the desperate situation of the people outside and inside camps and the deterioration of their morale. It was also realized that other agencies dealing with displaced persons were coming to an end, particularly UNRRA, and that the responsibility of the Allied military authorities was not permanent. Another reason for quick action was the danger that these refugee groups presented to the reconstruction of the economic and social life of western European countries, in particular to the occupied and controlled countries such as Germany, Austria, and Italy.

Yet much patience had been needed to achieve the aim, propounded by the western countries, of establishing an international refugee organization with the approval of the UN and recommending participation by all member nations. As Mr. Penrose, adviser to the US delegation, stated: 'It was to achieve this aim and not to persuade the Russians to join the IRO that concessions had to be made, none of which, however, encroached on the liberties of the refugees and their right to choose freely between repatriation and resettlement.'[1]

---

[1] E. F. Penrose, 'Negotiating on Refugees and Displaced Persons, 1946', in R. Dennett and J. E. Johnson, *Negotiating with the Russians*, Boston, World Peace Foundation, 1951, p. 167. Mr. Penrose took part in the meetings as adviser on economics and social affairs to the US representative on ECOSOC.

CHAPTER II

THE CONSTITUTION

THE Constitution of the IRO provided for 'a non-permanent organization to be called the International Refugee Organization, a specialized agency to be brought into relationship with the United Nations',[1] to deal comprehensively with the whole problem of refugees and displaced persons. The Constitution had been prepared by ECOSOC according to Article 62, paragraph 3, of the Charter by which the Council 'may prepare draft conventions for submission to the General Assembly, with respect to matters falling within its competence'. IRO, like UNRRA, was a temporary organization. While no time limit had been set, it was originally understood that a period of no more than three years would be needed.

The length of the Organization's life had been discussed in the UN deliberations, and the prevalent opinion was that three years should be sufficient to accomplish its task. The same idea was inferred by Mr. Ernest Bevin, Foreign Secretary of the UK, and General Marshall, Secretary of State of the US, when, in late 1947, in discussions with the IRO's Executive Secretary and his deputy, they considered that their governments would be prepared to make funds available for three years. Only the French Parliament limited its ratification of the IRO Constitution to three years' membership; this, however, neither altered the right of withdrawal according to the IRO Constitution, nor altered the necessity of parliamentary appropriation for the IRO's yearly budgets. Some experts, however, among them the American delegate, Mr. George L. Warren, as well as Assistant Secretary of State, John H. Hilldring, had believed that it would be difficult to fix a definite time and had spoken of a period of three to five years.[2]

Scope of IRO

IRO differed from other specialized agencies such as FAO, UNESCO, and ICAI in that it was charged with a definite and specific operational task. It had the authority, the necessary administrative structure, and the financial resources to undertake certain obligations for specific groups of refugees and displaced persons with the aim of bringing about 'a rapid and positive solution of the problem of *bona fide* refugees and displaced persons',[3] either by repatriation or by resettlement and re-establishment.

The terms of reference of the Organization were not as comprehensive as some people had hoped they would be.

Historically the term 'refugees' had been used to refer to persons who had left their country of nationality or residence because of fear of danger to their lives or

---

[1] For full text see Appendix I, pp. 575–89.
[2] GC/SR/25 and US Congress, Senate, Committee on Foreign Relations, 80th Congress, First Session, SJ RES. 77: IRO, 1 Mar. 1947, p. 11.
[3] Preamble.

liberties, on account of their race, religion, or political beliefs; or who, if already absent from their country of nationality or residence, did not return to it because of such fear. Refugees were usually stateless, lacking in law or in fact the protection of any government. Whether stateless or not, they were considered to be refugees until they became re-established in their former country of nationality or residence, or became newly established in another country—with the right of nationality or, at least, the right of settled residence.

The term 'displaced persons' had been used to refer to persons who were obliged to leave their homes by reason of the Second World War, either for places elsewhere within their country of nationality or residence, or for places beyond its boundaries. Some of those displaced within their country of nationality or residence, and most of those displaced beyond its boundaries, had been obliged to leave their homes by deliberate action of an enemy power, either for purposes of forced labour or because of race, religion, or activities in favour of the united nations. Most of the displaced persons, even those internationally displaced, had been, and still were, possessed of nationality; but they were considered to be displaced persons if they had not yet returned to their homes, or found new homes, in their former country of nationality or residence.[1]

These general descriptions of refugees and displaced persons presented by Sir Herbert Emerson to the Special Committee applied only to those refugees and displaced persons enumerated in Annex 1 (an integral part of the Constitution). Annex 1, Part 1, consisted of a set of cumbersomely worded definitions which reflected compromise between the views of the western countries—which on the whole sought to expand the definitions—and those of the countries of origin, which tried to restrict them.

Briefly stated, the term 'refugee' was to apply to recognized pre-war refugees; exiled Spanish Republicans and other victims of the Falangist régime in Spain; victims of Nazi, Fascist, or quisling régimes; victims of racial, religious, or political persecution, and persons outside their countries of origin or former habitual residence who were unwilling or unable to avail themselves of the protection of the government of those countries. In addition, and as a special category, the term applied to unaccompanied children 16 years of age or under who were war orphans or whose parents had disappeared, and who were outside their own countries. The term 'displaced persons' applied to a person who had been obliged to leave his country as a result of the actions of Nazi and Fascist authorities. This distinction between a refugee and a displaced person was an innovation in that it extended refugee status to people who legally speaking were not stateless and whose governments wanted them to return. However, by refusing to be repatriated, these displaced persons became refugees, and in reality the initial distinction lost its meaning. Once repatriation ceased, the Organization had under its mandate only refugees.

According to the Constitution only those people who decided not to return became the concern of the Organization upon fulfilment of conditions which were laid down in Section C of Annex 1, Part 2. If a person wished to be resettled to

---

[1] UN ECOSOC (E/REF/12), 10 Apr. 1946: Special Committee on Refugees and Displaced Persons. Note by the Director of the IGCR.

a country other than that of his origin, it was necessary for him to have sound grounds for his refusal to go home. Such 'valid objections' could be made only after he had received 'adequate information'; this was deemed to consist of full knowledge of the facts regarding conditions in his country of nationality or former habitual residence. Such information was to be communicated to the persons concerned by representatives of the government of these countries who were to be given, for this purpose, every facility for visiting camps and assemblies.

Such 'valid objections' had to be well founded, arising from 'persecution, or fear, based on reasonable grounds, of persecution because of race, religion, nationality or political opinions, provided these opinions were not in conflict with the principles of the United Nations . . .'; from 'compelling family reasons arising out of previous persecution, or compelling reasons of infirmity or illness'; or from 'objections of a political nature judged by the organization to be "valid" '.

Refugees ceased to be the concern of IRO when they returned to their own country,[1] when they acquired a new nationality, when they became otherwise firmly established, when they unreasonably refused to accept the proposals of the Organization for their resettlement or repatriation, when they made no substantial effort toward earning their living if it was possible for them to do so, or when they were exploiting the assistance of the Organization.

Although the definitions of refugees and displaced persons differed from SHAEF, UNRRA, and IGCR classifications, virtually the same groups became the concern of the IRO. To them were added, however, those persons who, since the end of the war, had left countries behind the Iron Curtain and had infiltrated into Germany and Austria, creating new refugee groups. The largest groups of them were Jewish refugees from Poland, Rumania, and Hungary who entered Germany and Austria after an outbreak of active anti-Semitism in Poland in July 1946. A group of *Volksdeutsche* entered Austria after the defeat of the Axis, partly in implementation of decisions reached by the Potsdam conference and by the Allied Commission for Austria.[2]

The determination of eligibility was the criterion according to which the refugee could become the concern of the IRO. It proved to be one of the most difficult tasks and one of the heaviest responsibilities of the Organization to apply the provisions relevant to eligibility 'fairly and impartially'. Paragraph 2 of Annex 1 recommended entrusting this authority to a 'special system of semi-judicial machinery . . . with appropriate constitution, procedure, and terms of reference' to implement the principle of justice and equity, to *bona fide* refugees and displaced persons, as provided in the Constitution.[3]

Screening of war criminals and others was not the responsibility of the IRO. In a special resolution of 15 December 1946, the General Assembly again recommended to all governments concerned that they should expedite the screening of

---

[1] Annex 1, Part 1, section D. At the request of the Chinese delegation, at the time of the drafting, the clause referring to those refugees whose 'former habitual residence to which they wished to return (was) outside their country of nationality' would cover the so-called overseas Chinese. See Chapter X, Origin of the Refugees, p. 186.

[2] Ibid., p. 185.

[3] Annex 1, para. 19.

all displaced persons, refugees, prisoners of war, and persons of similar status in order to remove 'an obstacle to the free and unhampered exercise' of the right of the genuine refugees and displaced persons to opt between returning and not returning.[1] As will be seen later, the implementation of this policy greatly complicated the work of the IRO administrators.

The broad functions of the Organization were to care for, protect, and re-establish the refugees in a normal life. These tasks were enumerated in Article 2 as identification, registration, classification of the people, care and assistance (financial commitment, food, clothing, shelter, medical care, or vocational training), and legal and political protection as long as they had not yet acquired a new citizenship. The main task was the re-establishment of refugees by repatriation, resettlement, or local settlement. Repatriation meant voluntary return to the country of origin or of citizenship or to the country of last habitual residence if the refugee had the right of re-entry. By resettlement was understood the transfer to countries in which refugees had not had citizenship or residence with right of re-entry. Local settlement involved what was called 're-establishment in place', or absorption or acceptance in the country of refuge. To carry through these movements the IRO was equipped with transportation services by land, sea, and air. While it was in operation, the IRO became the largest mass transportation agency in the world.

Most of these functions were familiar because of the work of IRO's 'predecessor organizations', but it must be stressed that they were now centralized in a single organization, and that under its Constitution the IRO possessed the power necessary to perform them effectively. The IRO would 'undertake any project appropriate to the accomplishment of the purposes of this Organization' and could perform any legal act appropriate to its purposes. In particular, it was empowered to conduct negotiations and conclude agreements with governments, especially with those countries that were willing to receive refugees, and to make contracts with governments or with occupation or control authorities in regard to the care and maintenance of refugees and displaced persons in territories under their authority. The IRO was also able to promote the conclusion of bilateral arrangements for mutual assistance in the repatriation of displaced persons and to consult and co-operate with public and private organizations.

These powers, especially section 2 (e) of Article 2, were discussed in the hearings of both houses of the US Congress, when the bill for membership and participation by the US was considered.[2] It was emphasized that the powers were broad, but that they were 'tied definitely to the functions' of the Organization.

Membership and structure

Membership in IRO was open to all members of the UN. 'Any other peace-loving states' could acquire membership 'upon recommendations of the Executive Committee, and by a two-thirds majority of members of the General Council

[1] UN, *Resolutions adopted by the General Assembly, Second Part of First Session, 23 October to 15 December 1946*, p. 120: Sixty-Seventh Plenary Meeting, 15 Dec. 1946, Res. 62 (I) and Chapter XII, Eligibility for Refugee Status and Assistance, p. 207.

[2] Hearing before the Committee on Foreign Relations, US Senate, 80th Congress, First Session, on SJ Res. 77, 1 Mar. 1947, p. 13.

present and voting', subject to the arrangements made between the IRO and the UN (Article 3) mentioned below. Special provisions were made for countries which would not sign the IRO Constitution or could not deposit the document of acceptance within the six months following their signature. These could be admitted under paragraphs 3 (*a*) and (*b*) of Article 4 if they would either contribute in accordance with the relevant scale or would submit to the IRO a plan for the admission of refugees 'in such numbers, and on such settlement conditions' that it would be equivalent to a contribution on that scale. Some overseas countries participated in the resettlement work of the IRO under the latter conditions, as will be seen later.

The general structure of the Organization was similar to that of other specialized agencies. It was brought into relationship with the UN by an agreement[1] between the two organs drawn up after the establishment of the IRO and pursuant to Articles 57 and 63 of the Charter of the UN. The Constitution provided for three organs (Articles 5–6): a General Council, the ultimate policy-making body, composed of one representative of each member nation; an Executive Committee, consisting of representatives of nine countries, elected by the General Council for two-year terms; and a chief administrative officer, the Director General, appointed by the General Council upon nomination of the Executive Committee, and serving under a contract terminable upon six months' notice by either party. As chief officer he was to carry out the administrative and executive functions in accordance with the decisions of the General Council. The General Council was to be convened not less than once a year by the Executive Committee. Provision was also made for special sessions of the General Council. The Executive Committee was to perform such functions as might be necessary to give effect to the policies of the General Council.

The staff (Article 9) was appointed by the Director General under regulations established by the General Council. The 'paramount consideration in the employment of the staff' was to be the highest standards of efficiency, and integrity, and adherence to the principles laid down in the Constitution. Attention was to be given to recruiting on an appropriate geographical basis and to employing an adequate number of persons from the countries of origin of displaced persons. The third paragraph of Article 9, included upon a motion of the US delegate, was designed to ensure the full international character and loyalty of the staff, with freedom from any form of national pressure. This paragraph had the same wording as Article 100 of Chapter XV, The Secretariat, of the United Nations Charter.

Finance

The financial procedures were set forth in Article 10. The Director General was to submit, through the Executive Committee to the General Council, an annual budget covering the necessary administrative, operational and large-scale resettlement expenditures, and periodically such supplementary budgets as might be required. The Executive Committee was to transmit, for final approval, the budget to the General Council with its own comments and recommendations. The administrative

[1] *Agreement Between the UN and the IRO*, UN, Lake Success, NY, 1949.

budget was to be submitted annually to the General Assembly of the UN for survey and recommendation. The agreement of 26 July 1948 concluded between IRO and the UN did not in any way specify the kind of review;[1] and as the members of the UN were chiefly concerned with the programme of IRO and its political implications, the budgets were never subject to any searching review or criticism by the General Assembly.

The members had to contribute the administrative and operational expenses according to the scales embodied in the Constitution (Annex 2). They were different for the administrative and operational expenditures of the budget. In accordance with paragraph 1 of Article 4 of the Constitution, percentages within the scales of contribution were established for new members by the General Council; the contribution for Italy was determined in the administrative budget as 2·40 per cent. and in the operational budget as 2·27 per cent.; and that for Switzerland as 1·30 per cent. and 1·10 per cent. respectively.

The manner of payment by contributors was to be determined by negotiations between the governments concerned and the Administration. This provision allowed for a very broad interpretation, for it meant that governments could pay in services or in any currency which could be agreed upon in these negotiations. There were expenditures in individual countries, because the problems of refugees were, of course, both national and international in character. The negotiations between governments and the Administration, therefore, dealt with the share of each in this expenditure.

IRO was set up to assist with international funds certain governments which, as a result of the war, were overburdened by the presence of refugees on their territory. The international community decided that these governments should have the assistance of other governments.

IRO was to make its headquarters in Paris or Geneva according to the General Council's decision and could establish regional or other offices with the consent of the government of the country concerned.

Articles dealing with procedure, status, immunities and privileges, and interpretation were similar to those of the UN organs.[2] But the provisions for amendment and entry into force of the Constitution were framed with consideration of this special case.

Amendments to the Constitution were to be communicated to the members by the Director General at least three months in advance of their consideration by the General Council. Such amendments were to take effect when adopted by a two-thirds vote of the members of the General Council present and voting, and accepted by two-thirds of the members in accordance with their respective constitutional processes; provided that amendments involving new obligations for members should come into force for each member only upon acceptance by it. This was a very cumbersome procedure which actually served to hinder its use by the General Council.

[1] Article 15 of the Constitution.
[2] UN, Second Session of the General Assembly, *Official Records*, Nov. 1947: Convention of the Privileges and Immunities of Specialized Agencies. Annex X applies the standard clauses of the convention 'without modification' to the IRO.

Under the terms of its Constitution, the IRO was to come into existence when at least fifteen government members of the UN, whose contributions totalled not less than 75 per cent. of its first year's operational budget, adhered unconditionally to the Constitution.

The first paragraph of Article 18 took into account varied governmental procedures through which delay might occur, and facilitated the signature of governments by providing three means of adherence: (1) signature without reservation concerning approval; (2) signature subject to approval followed by acceptance; and (3) acceptance.

Effectiveness of the Constitution in practice

The Third Committee of the General Assembly, in its Draft Report,[1] acknowledged that 'the draft constitution . . . was far from perfect. It was an attempt, however, to reconcile two conflicting points of view.' At the same time the humanitarian aspect was emphasized by all members. As several delegates pointed out, the Constitution was only a framework for the work of the IRO, and the spirit in which this work was to be carried out would be far more important than the framework itself.

Under the test of experience, the Constitution proved to be a useful framework, wide and flexible enough, and did not reveal serious defects except in regard to the eligibility of certain refugee groups.[2] The Constitution arose out of compromise over the definition of the refugee. It must, however, be taken into consideration that without this compromise an international refugee organization could not possibly have been set up by the UN. It was not without significance that the IRO was a UN specialized agency, which could avail itself of the UN for discussing its work before the General Assembly and ECOSOC, and could draw on the services of the Secretariat and of other specialized agencies.

The statement of the Third Committee was, however, very true, in that the spirit in which the work was carried out was crucial to its success. From this point of view it was fortunate that the countries of origin did not join the IRO, and that the members were represented at the General Council by persons who had not only the right spirit, but also a wealth of expert knowledge and experience in that field. It can be stated, furthermore, that on the whole the Organization was served by a devoted and efficient staff working under the direction of three experienced chief executive officers. In addition, governments and non-governmental organizations concerned helped to bring the task of the IRO to completion.

[1] UN Doc. A/C.3/142, *Official Record* of the Second Part of the First Session of the General Assembly, Third Committee, *Summary Records*, 24 Oct.–12 Dec. 1946, p. 342.
[2] See Chapter XII, Eligibility for Refugee Status and Assistance, p. 210.

CHAPTER III

PLANNING AND ESTABLISHMENT OF POLICIES BY THE PREPARATORY COMMISSION AND THE GENERAL COUNCIL

Preparatory Commission of the International Refugee Organization (PCIRO)

ONCE the Constitution was voted upon by the General Assembly of the UN, the primary concern was to ensure the early and effective operation of the IRO. Before the IRO could be established and function as an effective organization, it was necessary to have the signatures and ratifications of fifteen members who could contribute seventy-five per cent. to Part I of the operational budget. On 31 December 1946 eight governments had signed the Constitution, i.e. the requisite number needed for the Agreement on Interim Measures (Article 8) to come into force.[1] Therefore, the Secretary General of the UN was able to convene the First Session of the PCIRO in Geneva on 11 February 1947—a year after the General Assembly had recognized 'that the problem of the refugees and displaced persons of all categories was one of immediate urgency and . . . international in scope and nature'.

The PCIRO was established pursuant to paragraph 9 of the Agreement on Interim Measures to be taken in Respect of the Refugees and Displaced Persons,[2] and charged with the task 'of taking all necessary and practical measures for the purpose of bringing the organization into effective operation as soon as possible' (Article 2). The PCIRO had been conceived as a planning body for the sole purpose of smoothing the way for the IRO itself and of enabling it to take over operating responsibilities once its Constitution was ratified. Originally the task of the PCIRO had been limited to planning the administrative and operational structure for the IRO, but, as will be seen later, it was 'thrust into the breach also as an operational agency'.

The PCIRO consisted of one representative of each of the governments who had signed the Constitution and the Agreement on Interim Measures. A representative of the ILO, the Director of IGCR, and a representative of the Director General of UNRRA sat with the Commission in a consultative capacity. The Secretary General of the UN was represented by the Director of the Division of Refugees and Displaced Persons (UN Secretariat) who acted as secretary of the Commission until the appointment of the Executive Secretary. He was assisted in his task by staff members of the UN. M. Henri Ponsot, who drew upon long experience in the French diplomatic service, notably as High Commissioner of Syria and as Ambassador to Turkey,

---

[1] Canada, Guatemala, and the US signed on the day following the vote; the Dominican Republic and France a day later; Honduras, the Philippine Republic, 18 Dec.; and Liberia, 31 Dec.

[2] Similar to the agreements for interim measures of other specialized agencies. For text cf. Appendix I, p. 589.

was elected chairman. Under his able and active guidance the PCIRO met seven times, six in Geneva and once in Lausanne, during a period of nineteen months.

One of the first actions of the PCIRO was the election of Mr. Arthur J. Altmeyer as Executive Secretary. He was released for several months by the US Government from his work as chairman of the US Social Security Board and as US representative to the Social Commission of ECOSOC of the UN. Mr. Altmeyer was especially qualified to marshal an administration and a staff for an agency that had a very complex structure due to the spread of its tasks all around the globe.

At the outset of its work the Commission was facing problems of special urgency, the most urgent being that of ensuring an early and effective operation of IRO. No government was bound to contribute funds before the Constitution was in force. The General Assembly of the UN, by a majority vote, had urged all concerned to take every measure possible to put IRO into operation and to provide for an orderly transfer of the functions and assets of its predecessor organizations.[1] Although the Constitution was finally adopted by a large majority of the General Assembly, signatures and ratifications came in more slowly and fewer in number than had been expected.

At the time the Constitution was drafted budgetary difficulties of governments and the slowness of legislative processes had been under-estimated. Moreover, the financial contributions required were far greater than those made to other international organizations and constituted a particularly heavy burden on countries which had suffered grievously under the impact of the war. Adherence to the Constitution was of importance to the US in view of the specially high proportion of the budget she had to provide.[2] Although the number of signatures to the Constitution had increased to fourteen by the time of the Second Part of the First Session, only five of these signatures represented final acceptance of the Constitution by member governments (the UK, New Zealand, China, Iceland, and Australia).

PCIRO thus had to begin its work under sombre auspices: no money, no certainty when and whether the IRO would come into being, and at the same time the immense task and responsibility of having to care for thousands and thousands of people with no real prospect for resettlement. It took the experience, all the patience, the courage, and hope of the people charged with the task to lay down plans and establish the policy for this new agency. When Mr. George L. Warren, the US delegate to PCIRO and the General Council, was asked in a radio interview: 'Are you hopeful that all of these obstacles . . . can be successfully overcome?', his answer was: 'Yes, we have *got* to be hopeful. With many thousands looking to us for rescue and help, we must meet the challenge.'[3] His statement reflects the spirit in which the members of the governing body and the Executive approached their task with its many intricate, human, political, economic, legal, and technical aspects.

Although the Agreement on Interim Measures had been signed by twenty-four governments at the end of the period in which PCIRO functioned, there were never more than between eight to fifteen governments represented at its meetings. But this

[1] Res. of 15 Dec. 1946.
[2] G. H. Dorr, delegate of US, GC/SR/3, p. 3.
[3] *Refugee Problems and the Economic Reconstruction of Devastated Areas*, NY, National Broadcasting Co., 1946, p. 11.

small group of delegates, well versed in the subject-matter and devoted to their highly responsible work, succeeded in carrying out the tasks at hand without any breach in continuity, readily gaining the confidence of all governments and agencies concerned, and last but not least of the refugees themselves.[1] Because of the delay in the ratification of the Constitution the PCIRO has to its credit eighty-five meetings held during the seven parts of its first and only session in the period from 11 February 1947 to 11 September 1948.

In these meetings the delegates drew up preliminary directives to the Executive Secretary to implement the constitutional functions of IRO, to promote repatriation and resettlement, to determine eligibility, and to establish agreements between IRO and the governments and occupation authorities; they also provided for funds and personnel to carry out the work.

Since the establishment of the IRO depended on the co-operation of the governments and their willingness to take responsibility, the PCIRO requested the Secretary General of the UN by cable to make an urgent appeal to all those countries which had voted for the Constitution as well as to those countries which either had abstained from voting or had voted against the adoption to sign and ratify the Constitution at the earliest possible date.[2] At the same time the Commission recommended to the governments represented at the First Part of the First Session that they instruct their diplomatic representatives jointly or separately to support the Secretary General's appeal. Furthermore, it directed the Executive Secretary to make similar representations to the countries concerned.

Transfer of responsibilities from UNRRA and IGCR

The situation was particularly precarious since UNRRA was to discontinue its care of displaced persons on 30 June 1947 and was already largely reducing its activities. Another problem loomed large: that of rendering care to large numbers of displaced persons in Italy which would be needed as soon as the Allied armies had withdrawn from that country in accordance with the Peace Treaty. Since the time was drawing close at which UNRRA and IGCR had to discontinue their activities, continuity of the work, crucial in the lives of so many refugees, was seriously endangered. In order to cope with this imminent problem, the delegates of PCIRO instructed the Executive Secretary to take all necessary steps for promoting a smooth transfer of the activities of UNRRA and IGCR to the IRO, and not later than on 30 June 1947. They advised him to obtain all information relevant for an orderly transfer, such as texts of agreements to which the two organizations were parties, and any reports, accounts, or balance-sheets showing the assets and liabilities of either of those organizations.

The Executive Secretary was further directed to consult voluntary agencies with a view to retaining the assistance which they had previously given UNRRA and

---

[1] Members of a Congressional Committee reported in Jan. 1950: 'The spirit of displaced persons . . . in 1949 differed entirely from their mental attitude . . . in 1946 and 1947. While a feeling of hopelessness prevailed in the camps three and two years ago, general atmosphere of expectation and hope for a better future was easily detectable in 1949 . . .' (US 81st Congress, Second Session, House Report No. 1507, p. 13).

[2] Res. 2, Appendix III, p. 685.

IGCR, and advised to obtain some additional assistance from them. The Commission considered this matter of great importance due both to the large sums of money distributed annually by these agencies and to the quality of field work which characterized the work of voluntary agencies.

He was also to consult appropriate governments and any occupation authorities concerned in regard to transfer of agreements or drafting of new agreements. In the light of his plans for the organization and operation of the IRO, the Executive Secretary was to prepare draft agreements to be entered into by the IRO with governments or authorities exercising control in ex-enemy countries, meaning Germany, Austria, and Italy; with the governments of countries where refugees were located such as France, the Netherlands, and others; with the governments of the countries of origin or former habitual residence to cover repatriation arrangements, primarily with the Soviet Union, Poland, Yugoslavia, and others; and, finally, with the governments of the countries in which the refugees were likely to be resettled, in particular with overseas countries such as Canada, US, Latin-American countries, and others. These draft agreements were designed to secure the operation of the IRO under the best possible conditions by not later than 30 June 1947.[1]

The delay in obtaining sufficient ratifications to bring the new organization into being had created difficulties for UNRRA itself when it prepared to wind up its operations. Since its activities relating to health and social affairs were not to outlive the year 1946, and its resources were very limited, the transfer of displaced persons operations had become rather pressing for UNRRA, especially since it recognized the existence of non-repatriable persons. As early as March 1946 the Fourth Session of the UNRRA Council recommended to its members 'to do all in their power to expedite the early creation of a UN body capable of dealing in an effective manner with the problem' of resettlement of the displaced persons.[2]

It can be said that UNRRA, like IGCR, did all in its power to co-ordinate its last transactions with the plans anticipated for IRO. It provided funds, supplies, and also the services of experienced personnel. Its executive officers gave any advice and help which would facilitate an unimpeded transfer. Sir Arthur Rucker, the Deputy Executive Secretary of PCIRO (appointed August 1947), stated later 'our initial problems could never have been solved but for the marvellous work of UNRRA in preparing camps and food for these refugees; we took over a going concern. Again I do not know how we could have tackled the resettlement problems if it had not been for the work and thought put in by the IGCR.'[3]

In August, after ECOSOC's adoption (11 June 1946) of the Draft Constitution of the IRO for submission to the member governments of the UN, the UNRRA Council resolved to prolong its operations with respect to displaced persons until 30 June 1947, and the Administration began to prepare for the transfer of its operations to the future new international organization.[4] In view of likely delays in the establishment and operation of IRO, the governments of the UK and the US also turned to

---

[1] See Chapter XX, Resettlement, pp. 343 and 349 f.
[2] Res. 92, see G. Woodbridge, op. cit., iii. 156 and i. 311–15.
[3] Sir Arthur Rucker, 'The Work of the International Refugee Organization', *International Affairs*, vol. xxv, No. 1, Jan. 1949, p. 67.
[4] Fifth Council, Geneva, Res. 99, G. Woodbridge, op. cit., iii. 161–4.

IGCR with an urgent appeal to take into consideration all possible measures of facilitating the work of the new organization during the interim period. Although the mandate of the IGCR was extensive, the Committee's operations after the war applied in practice only to Austrian and German refugees from Nazi persecution, to Spanish Republican refugees, and to a few other stateless persons. The Executive Committee of IGCR approved in July 1946 by 7 votes to 1 with one abstention the proposal of the two governments. These proposals were strongly opposed by the Soviet delegate as being outside the mandate and scope of the Committee. In disagreement with the new policy, the Soviets withdrew from the Committee, while the Polish government remained a member.

Implementing this decision IGCR extended operations to include other classes within the Committee's mandate, in particular, displaced persons who were unwilling or unable to return to their home countries. In regard to such persons the principles contained in the Draft Constitution of the IRO were applied by the IGCR, and the Committee, in consultation with the Allied military governments and UNRRA, collected such information as might be necessary in connexion with migration and settlement. Furthermore, IGCR discussed with potential countries of settlement both individual migration and group settlement and undertook some migration and settlement.

In December 1946 UNRRA again reviewed its programme for displaced persons at the Sixth Session of its Council in Washington. Although the main stress was still on repatriation, the Council agreed, with the concurrence of the representatives of the eastern bloc, that UNRRA should turn over its responsibilities to the IRO, or to any other appopriate organization not later than 30 June 1947. Further, the Administration was empowered to co-operate with IGCR and to adjust its eligibility regulations 'so that they might coincide with those developed by IRO'. By February 1947 a displaced persons headquarters had been set up in Paris by UNRRA, and the administration of all displaced persons operations in Europe and the Middle East was centralized. Plans were made to transfer personnel to PCIRO and also the funds covering their annual leave and their costs of repatriation. The Co-ordinating Committee, set up in the European regional office, helped transfer all operational activities. Various studies, especially on personnel and budget, were prepared for PCIRO's information and guidance. UNRRA turned over certain supplies and carried on with the procurement and shipping of others on a reimbursable basis until PCIRO could take over these responsibilities. On 29 June 1947 an agreement in regard to the transfer was signed between the two organizations. Funds amounting to $3,603,839 were included in this transaction. Of these the sum of $1,603,839 was the unspent balance of allocations earmarked for UNRRA displaced persons operations in Europe and the Far East, while the other sum of $2 million was granted for supplementary child feeding programmes and some additional child welfare staff.[1]

In a similar fashion Sir Herbert Emerson, the Director of IGCR, helped smooth the way for the new organization before the liquidation of his agency on 30 June 1947. Effective 1 July 1947, the IGCR headquarters in London were taken over by PCIRO; its staff records and equipment were later transferred to the PCIRO head-

[1] For details of UNRRA and IGCR fund see Chapter VI, Finances, Annex 6, p. 123.

quarters in Geneva. The Preparatory Commission also availed itself of the existing network of IGCR representatives in Belgium, Czechoslovakia, France, the Netherlands, Switzerland, Spain, Portugal, the Middle East, and the operational staff responsible for the Allied commission camps, screening experts *et al.* in Italy. The transfer of functions also included care and maintenance as well as assistance by short-term loans from Belgium, France, and the Netherlands, and programmes of training and retraining from these countries and in addition from Switzerland. PCIRO accepted also in agreement with the governments concerned the IGCR conventional system effective 1 July 1947, and took over the legal and political protection of the refugees.

With respect to finance sufficient provision had been made in the budget for the new organization to allow for the continuation of the activities of the IGCR, and also for the two organizations to reach agreement on the balance of payments to be made between them. There were credit items of the IGCR such as stores and equipment that had to be taken over by the IRO, apart from an appropriate share in the cost of conversion of the US ships chartered by the IGCR. The debit to IGCR included cost of repatriation of their staff taken over and not retained in IRO service for more than three months, and the transfer of humanitarian and reparation funds. The formal decision on the transfer to the IRO of both IGCR and UNRRA activities was made by PCIRO on 13 May 1947, formulated in Resolution 1 as follows: 'such functions, activities, assets and personnel as from 1 July 1947, of existing organizations dealing with refugees and displaced persons are considered to be essential in order to accomplish the orderly transfer to the IRO of such functions and activities.' Furthermore, PCIRO decided to take over IGCR commitments in Resolutions 12 and 13. By an agreement between Mr. A. J. Altmeyer and Sir Herbert Emerson in June 1947, acting for the two organizations, the transfer was legally settled.[1]

Another essential matter considered at the first meeting of the PCIRO was the securing of funds for the administrative as well as operational work of the IRO. The eleven nations who had signed the Constitution represented only the allocations of a total of 69·8 per cent. of the provisional budget; moreover, the representatives were not able 'on constitutional grounds' to secure advance contributions from their governments. Therefore they decided to appeal to the Secretary General of the UN to make an advance from the Working Capital Fund of the UN as had been done in the case of the Interim Commission of the World Health Organization and in accordance with the provisions of Part C of the Working Capital Fund resolution, adopted by the General Assembly on 14 December 1946. In the letter to the Secretary General the chairman of PCIRO pointed out that the question whether this work was to be completed or to be abandoned now depended on whether the necessary funds could be secured to enable the Preparatory Commission to continue its operations and the Executive Secretary to be appointed and to undertake his task forthwith.[2]

In response to this request the Secretary General agreed to place at the disposal

---

[1] Agreement between the Intergovernmental Committee on Refugees and PCIRO, Appendix II, p. 591.   [2] PREP/27, 21 Feb. 1947. Report of the First Part of the First Session, p. 25.

of the Organization a sum not exceeding US $250,000 in all, against which the UN paid the salaries and other necessary administrative expenses of the Organization on the understanding that these costs would later be reimbursed. These arrangements lasted over a period of approximately four months. In order to reduce the financial burden the Secretary General made available office accommodation in Geneva as well as members of staff of the Refugee Division of the UN Secretariat and other technical assistance. The PCIRO directed the Executive Secretary to present a budget for the planning period up to 30 June 1947. The total of the expenditures amounted to $158,000 set up in two quarters, calendar year 1947 ($21,000 and $137,000).[1] This entailed a reduction of nearly $100,000 from the initial estimate,[2] due to arrangements made by UNRRA and IGCR to pay the salaries, allowances, travel, and other costs of personnel loaned by them to the PCIRO: in addition UNRRA provided various other services.

Statistical Information

For planning purposes the PCIRO needed accurate statistical information regarding the numbers and categories of refugees and displaced persons. It instructed the Executive Secretary to make provisions for a small statistical and demographical staff which could produce all basic material for future planning. Also at its First Part of the First Session on 16 February 1947, the PCIRO had directed the Executive Secretary to consult 'appropriate Governments, any Occupation Authorities concerned, UNRRA, IGCR, and appropriate voluntary organizations or other similar bodies', in order to obtain 'as accurate statistical information as possible regarding the numbers and categories of refugees and displaced persons at present under their care', and to determine on this basis the approximate number of persons likely to come within the mandate of the IRO. This statistical information was to include classification according to political nationality of origin or place of former habitual residence, sex, age, family grouping, and trade, profession, or employment group, and should indicate their location and whether they are in camps or outside.[3]

The Executive Secretary presented to the Second Part of the First Session of PCIRO a report on the composition of the refugee and displaced persons population.[4] Though this was only a preliminary report on the groups which would be the IRO's concern, it gave the General Council and the Executive Secretary the needed statistical information for planning purposes.[5] It was essential to know the numbers and locations of refugees and displaced persons in order to prepare accurate estimates of expenses, to plan future operations, and to inform the general public. Exact information regarding nationality was required for repatriation. Data on age, sex, family status, and occupational skills were necessary for resettlement. All this information was needed also for planning and carrying out employment, training, health, and welfare programmes.

---

[1] PREP/40, Annexes 1 and 2. [2] PREP/12/Rev. 1.
[3] PREP/27, p. 29. [4] PREP/35.
[5] At the Second Part of the First Session, the importance of fully equipped statistical machinery was again stressed by various delegates, and the Executive Secretary was urged to prepare a report on the creation of a statistical bureau equipped with the necessary machinery to enable it to produce correct statistics. (PREP/53, p. 5.)

Decision to begin operations

The establishment of the IRO and its assumption of operational responsibility depended upon the status of signatories to the Constitution, which was the most important item on the agenda of the meeting of PCIRO at the Second Part of the First Session, 1–21 May 1947. Various members of the Commission had received informal indications that several governments, in addition to those fourteen who had already done so, were about to sign. Thus the Commission entered the session in a spirit of confidence, believing that the IRO would finally come into existence, although still reasonably doubtful as to whether the number of ratifications needed would be received by 30 June 1947, the date on which both UNRRA and IGCR were to terminate their activities on behalf of the refugees and displaced persons. The representatives agreed unanimously that the only step appropriate to this situation was to invoke paragraphs 3 and 6 of the Agreement on Interim Measures, so that PCIRO could, beginning 1 July 1947, assume operating responsibilities pending the formal establishment of the IRO. On the basis of this decision PCIRO asked member governments to make advance contributions for financing operations for a period of three months after 1 July. In accordance with paragraph 6 of the Agreement on Interim Measures, these contributions were to be advanced against and be deductable from the first contributions later to be made by these governments to the IRO itself.[1]

The burden of this momentous decision fell on eight governments[2] whose votes are a testimony to their genuine interest in international action and to their great moral courage. Faced with the immensely complicated task of integrating into a unified organization part of the assets, staffs, and policies of its two predecessor organizations, confronted with a projected annual budget of which less than two-thirds was firmly subscribed, PCIRO's assumption of operational responsibility in thirty different countries was a genuine 'act of faith'.

For a full implementation of this decision, agreements with governments and occupation authorities had to be concluded and necessary funds to be secured.[3] While working on plans for a sound and efficient administration, the representatives of the Commission forged ahead to lay down policies for the execution of operations. From this time onwards, PCIRO was actually engaged in work identical with that of the functioning body for which it was originally instituted to prepare—the General Council of the IRO. Its governing body's main concern was the approval of the budget and the general layout of operations. It received from the Executive Secretary, later from the Director General of IRO, annual and interim reports on financial and budgetary matters as well as on operational questions. On this basis the delegates discussed the operations and gave direction and counsel to the executive. Implementation of the policies arrived at by the governing body and laid down in separate resolutions, was left to the executive who retained freedom of performance in the framework of the Commission's overall policy.

[1] PREP/65, Part IV, Res. 1, Appendix III, p. 687.
[2] Belgium, Canada, China, France, the Netherlands, Norway, the UK, and the US. The Dominican Republic, Guatemala, Liberia, New Zealand, and the Philippine Republic were not represented.
[3] Chapter VII, Co-operation of Governments, pp. 127 f.

In view of the heavy responsibility which the executive had to bear as a result of the decision to embark upon operations before the final ratification of IRO, the PCIRO appointed an Advisory Committee which was to meet from time to time and advise the Executive Secretary in regard to his plans of organizing the IRO and appointing senior staff members. The Advisory Committee was also to recommend action to the Commission on all outstanding measures concerning the effective operation of IRO.[1] This Advisory Committee held three meetings in June, July, and September 1947.

At the time when PCIRO held the Sixth Part of its First Session in May 1948, twenty-one governments had signed the Constitution, fourteen of them either without reservation as to subsequent approval or with formal acceptance of the Constitution after signature. Thus only one more government was needed to complete the formalities of acceptance. The Commission, therefore, took preliminary steps to arrange for a meeting of the General Council on 13 September 1948. When, finally, the fifteenth member, Denmark, had ratified the Constitution, the Secretary General of UN declared the Constitution to be in force as of 20 August 1948, fourteen months after PCIRO's assumption of operational responsibility. Herewith IRO became the tenth specialized agency of UN. Once the Constitution was in force governments not members of the UN could accede to it. Only two did so, namely, Italy and Switzerland in March 1949.

General Council convened

It was during the Seventh Part of its First Session that PCIRO took action to convene the ultimate policy-making body of the IRO, the General Council, for its First Session on 13 September 1948. Each member government was represented by one delegate to the General Council. The representatives of fifteen member governments and a number of observers from interested governments and specialized agencies attended the First Session.[2]

The General Council took a number of steps essential to the establishment of the Organization, and adopted budgets for the second and third years of operation. Mr. William Hallam Tuck, who had succeeded Mr. Arthur J. Altmeyer after his resignation in July 1947 as Executive Secretary of the former PCIRO, was unanimously elected Director General of IRO, while Sir Arthur Rucker, Deputy Executive Secretary since July 1947 was appointed Deputy Director General. The General Council performed certain necessary formal acts, such as the approval of the agreement between UN and IRO, adoption of the official acts of PCIRO, and authorization of the Director General to act on behalf of the Organization.

During its existence for more than three and a half years the General Council held nine sessions, amounting to 102 meetings. The last session took place from 11 to 16 February 1952. The General Council was aided in its work by the Executive

---

[1] The Advisory Committee was composed of representatives of Belgium, Canada, China, France, the Netherlands, the UK, and the US, with the chairman of PCIRO representing France. PREP/82, Part IV, Res. 4. Cf. Appendix III, p. 689.

[2] Present were the representatives of Australia, Belgium, Canada, China, Denmark, the Dominican Republic, France, Guatemala, Luxembourg, the Netherlands, New Zealand, Norway, the UK, the US, and Venezuela. Official observers were: Brazil, the Holy See, Ireland, Switzerland, Italy, the UN ILO, and WHO. Iceland, a member government, was not represented.

Committee[1] which was convened immediately before the meetings of the Council, and met eighty-seven times in eleven sessions, once in Rome, and the other times in Geneva.

The Executive Committee performed such functions as were necessary to give effect to the policies of the General Council and to make policy decisions of an emergency nature, subject to reconsideration by the General Council. All in all, the Executive Committee passed eleven resolutions apart from submitting a number of recommendations to the Council.

The overall policies which were laid down for the operations were evolved in close collaboration between the governing body and the executive, and were inspired by their ultimate aim to enable the refugees and displaced persons to regain once more their status of free men, with a home country 'and to re-establish them in their dignity as individual human beings'.[2] This vital mission was constantly kept in mind when PCIRO and the General Council determined the policies for the various operations, i.e. for repatriation, resettlement, for care and maintenance, and legal and political protection.

Determination of policy

The Organization attempted to promote repatriation by all possible means. It always emphasized to the displaced persons the possibility of their being repatriated. The Executive Secretary suggested measures, approved by PCIRO, which aimed at effective implementation of the constitutional provisions for repatriation (set forth in the Preamble, Article 2, and Annex 1): to keep in touch with the principal countries of origin of displaced persons; to pass on information, supplied by the respective governments, regarding the conditions in their countries; and to permit repatriation missions to visit the camps, address the inmates, and distribute literature. In other words, all measures taken were to help the displaced persons to decide freely whether or not to be repatriated. On the other hand, PCIRO decided against offering cash allowances to them as a means of encouraging repatriation, and also against providing assistance once displaced persons had been repatriated. Later, it discontinued its earlier practice of providing inducements towards repatriation by such means as offering special food rations.[3]

The question of resettlement naturally hinged upon the readiness of governments to receive displaced persons in their countries for resettlement. Availability of shipping and of money from the budget for paying the cost of resettlement were other determining factors, especially in regard to the rate at which the number of persons receiving care and maintenance from IRO could be reduced in a given period of time. In view of the very limited prospects for repatriation, the Organization made every effort to promote a world-wide resettlement programme.

Since its inception the PCIRO had been 'fully aware of the urgency of the matter of getting immigration doors opened in as many countries as possible without delay',

---

[1] Article 7 of the Constitution. Cf. Appendix I, p. 578.
[2] Mr. Jean Desy, Canadian delegate (GC/SR/3).
[3] PREP/39 and Rev. 2; PREP/83 and Res. 10 (PREP/90/Rev. 1, Add. 1, p. 10), cf. Chapter XIX, Repatriation, p. 352.

and this problem was taken into consideration at almost every meeting.[1] As early as May 1947 directives had been given to the Executive Secretary to get in touch with member governments of the UN with a view towards enlisting their co-operation and generosity to allow for immigration. Again in October 1947 the Executive Secretary was authorized to consult interested organizations (e.g. UN, ILO, Economic Commission for Europe) and member governments which had voted for the resolution of 15 December 1946 about the possibility of convening an international conference on resettlement of refugees and displaced persons. At the meeting held in January 1948 the Executive Secretary reported that the suggestion made to interested governments to accept 'quotas' of refugees for reception did not appear practicable; nor did it seem appropriate at that time to pursue further the plan for holding an international conference. As an alternative solution the Secretary submitted for consideration a 'fair share' plan according to which governments would agree to accept whatever might be determined as their reasonable share in the total number of refugees and displaced persons who remained to be resettled. As a result of this discussion, the Executive Secretary continued his conversations about a 'fair share' plan with individual governments, and at the next meeting, on 12 August 1948, PCIRO adopted a resolution bearing on this matter.[2]

While the 'fair share' plan, as envisaged by the Executive Secretary, never developed, IRO concluded bilateral agreements with such individual governments as were willing to accept refugees as immigrant settlers. In fact, in many cases, these agreements and administrative arrangements fully lived up to the spirit and intention of the 'fair share' plan.

It was of great significance that under the Organization's policy an 'organized migration' scheme was developed, setting certain standards for resettlement, such as emphasis on preservation of the family unit, and therefore resettling individual refugees only when they had no dependants. An international shipping pool was established, and new techniques were developed in migration procedures through the services of the Selection Missions.[3] Progressively the selection criteria were liberalized and humanized in a broad resettlement programme, and an attempt was made to gain permission for intellectual refugees in the countries of reception to follow their intellectual pursuits; an effort was also made to secure acceptance of persons who were not economic assets to the receiving countries, and thus to effect the completion of the task of the IRO.[4]

Quite early, however, it became increasingly clear that in spite of the many efforts devoted to establishing liberal policies a certain percentage of non-repatriables could not be resettled either, partly because of insufficient opportunities for resettlement, and partly on account of impediments on the side of the refugee, such as health, age, family composition, and the like.

---

[1] ECOSOC, Seventh Session, E/816, 10 June 1948, Report on Progress ... (Hambro Report), p. 47.
[2] PCIRO, Sixth Part, Res. 82 (PREP/217/Rev. 1); cf also Ress. 56, 59, and 63.
[3] '. . . The IRO . . . did not resettle displaced persons in doubtful conditions merely to enable a reduction in its load of care and maintenance', e.g., it suspended 'the transfer of agricultural workers to certain areas of South America in the face of reports that conditions of life and work for the immigrants were not up to a proper standard' (Fulton Report, op. cit., p. 62).
[4] GC/17/Rev. 1, 21 Sept. 1948.

Vitally important as emigration had been and continued to be as a solution of the problem of refugees and the surplus population in Europe, it was no panacea, and efforts had to be made concurrently for the re-establishment of displaced persons in Europe.[1] At the Tenth Meeting of the First Session of the General Council, M. Robert Rochefort, the delegate of France, brought the matter to the attention of his colleagues and pointed out that 'whatever method may be adopted by IRO to speed up resettlement as much as possible . . . part of the problem will remain unsolved'.[2] The Director General concurred and stated that the problem of the 'residual group' —those persons whom the IRO could neither repatriate nor resettle—was becoming increasingly urgent.[3] Facing squarely the implications of this situation, the General Council at its First Session in September 1948 referred to the PCIRO resolution of 12 May 1948 and asked the Director General to formulate and submit at the Second Session a plan for the disposition of those refugees and displaced persons who, as was then apparent, would require special measures of assistance for the completion of the mandate.[4] In July 1949, at the Third Session,[5] and again in October 1949 at the Fourth Session,[6] the Director General submitted to the Council further recommendations for the completion of IRO's task. Following his suggestion, the General Council instructed[7] the Executive to broaden and intensify the counselling programme initiated in 1948, in order to find out more about the personal wishes and capabilities of the individuals concerned. This information was to serve as a basis for developing special plans, particularly for the residual group and the 'hard core'. The term 'hard core' denoted those refugees who required continuing institutional care and who had little chance of ever being selected or sponsored for resettlement unless special efforts were directed toward that end. For the solution of the 'hard core' problem, the General Council appropriated in its Eighth Session a special fund of US $11 million, later increased to US $22 million.

Soon after the beginning of its operation, PCIRO had instituted a system for determining the eligibility of all persons taken over from UNRRA, IGCR, military authorities, and voluntary societies and had established the Review Board of Eligibility. From time to time the General Council gave special attention to problems of certain groups of refugees and displaced persons and came to decisions in regard to their eligibility, e.g. Venezia Giulians, refugees in Greece, and others.[8] The *Volksdeutsche* in Austria presented a special problem. The General Council recognized that they might come under the mandate of IRO, but decided—in view of the limited

---

[1] Mr. George L. Warren, who had participated as alternate delegate for the US in the drafting of the Constitution, gave the meaning of the two forms in the Constitution as envisaged by the drafters. 'Reestablishment' as '. . . adjusted to the local community, moving from dependence on the IRO to independence' as it might be in France or even in Germany, and 'resettlement' as '. . . moving to a final destination in a country of permanent residence with employment immediately on arrival or participation in an agricultural scheme sponsored by the Government of the country of reception' (GC/SR/9, p. 6).

[2] GC/SR/5, 1 Oct. 1948.

[3] GC/SR/6, 4 Oct. 1948.

[4] Cf. Chapters XXII and XXIII, Local Settlement and Hard Core, pp. 473 and 483.

[5] GC/80.

[6] GC/166 Annual Report of Director General; GC/167, Proposals for the Operations during the Supplementary Period.

[7] Res. 39/4 and Res. 76/C, Appendix III, pp. 726 and 740.

[8] Cf. Chapter XII, Eligibility, pp. 210 f.; Appendix III, pp. 697 and 707; III, p. 721; III p. 752.

funds—not to provide assistance on their behalf. As time went on, however, the General Council urged the administration to adopt a broader interpretation of the eligibility concept established in the Constitution, so that assistance could be given to certain groups like the Balts—especially in view of the facts that had been ascertained about them.

As long as a number of refugees and displaced persons had not yet been repatriated, resettled, or re-established, IRO retained responsibility for their care and maintenance in and outside of camps. In May 1947 the PCIRO had approved principles governing standards of care, which had also been accepted by the General Council at its First Session.[1] The care and maintenance programme covered a wide range of activities far broader in scope than a mere provision for the physical needs of life: it included such services as employment, education, religious services, vocational training, and child-care programmes, and aimed in general at adapting the persons to their future life in new and unfamiliar environment.

Although the IRO had been established as a non-permanent organization, no specific time limit had been fixed for its duration, nor was there a limitation by date-line on the intake of eligible persons. The drafters of the Constitution had foreseen the probability of an increase in the number of refugees who might eventually become its concern,[2] bringing a progressively heavier burden on its funds. As a result, the Organization was unavoidably financed on a non-permanent basis, and the General Council set the time limits within which the status of refugee and the eligibility for assistance might be claimed. Rather reluctantly, besides adopting a time limit, the PCIRO had—at the beginning of its operational period—authorized a so-called 'freeze order', which limited new admission to care and maintenance only to those eligible persons who would be threatened with genuine hardship if denied the support of the Organization. Instructions were given to the Executive Secretary to interpret 'hardship case' as liberally as possible, and to cancel the freeze order as soon as the financial position of the IRO would justify such action.

The refugee problem as a whole could hardly be solved by the IRO. The presence of refugees in Europe and Asia was a disturbing factor of international concern, both economically and politically. As the IRO had been created primarily to meet an emergency situation arising out of the Second World War, it had no authority to shoulder responsibility for the so-called permanent world refugee problem that had arisen from manifold causes at various times. The delegates of the General Council felt the urgency of the international problem, but, according to their mandate, had to decide to terminate IRO's activities at a definite date.

To this end the General Council set limits to the programme by establishing a series of date-lines with the view to circumscribing the Organization's responsibilities within manageable limits. The Director General was instructed to discontinue on 31 August 1949 all registration of refugees and displaced persons except for: (a) unaccompanied children discovered after that date under the child search programme, (b) refugees leaving their countries of origin after 31 August 1949 and arriving in an area of IRO operations before 15 October 1949, and (c) refugees and displaced

---

[1] Cf. Chapter XIII, Care and Maintenance, p. 219.
[2] E/REF/65, p. 18; E/REF/75, p. 23; E/87, p. 4; A/C.3/59, p. 2.

persons in need of legal and political protection only. After 31 December 1949 all admissions to care and maintenance in assembly centres, and after 31 March 1950, admissions to care and maintenance under the cash assistance programmes, were to be discontinued. By 30 June 1950 care and maintenance for all persons other than refugees and displaced persons in process of repatriation or resettlement and those who might require permanent assistance, such as institutional care, were to be discontinued.

At the March and July meetings in 1949 of the Council the representative of the US pressed for and insisted upon closing the operations by 30 June 1950, supported in his effort by the representatives of the UK and Canada. Realizing that the job could not be finished by that time, and afraid of being stranded with a heavy burden in their territories, the delegates of the continental western European countries strongly opposed this point of view. Actually, in October 1949, it appeared that the main receiving countries, the US, Canada, Australia, and Latin America, were falling far behind receiving the number budgeted for removal to their countries. Also, the completion of the 'hard core' problem and the local establishment programme were moving more slowly than had been planned originally. Recognizing that an early close of IRO's facilities would greatly impair both the existing and the pending resettlement programme (especially USDP programme) the General Council arrived at the conclusion that a continuation 'of IRO's activities was necessary in order to carry out the basic objectives of the Organization, to the fullest possible extent within the limits of resources available'. They then extended the programme (except care and maintenance) until 30 September 1951, approving a supplementary budget of $55,165,446 for this additional period.[1] In an amendment to this decision the General Council authorized the Director General to continue the operational programme for such length of time as would be permitted by the existing realizable resources.[2] In fact, this amendment allowed the Organization to carry on its activities until 1 March 1952, when the IRO went into liquidation.

[1] GC Ress. 61 and 78, Appendix III, pp. 735 and 741.
[2] GC Ress. 84 and 87, Appendix III, pp. 741 and 742.

CHAPTER IV

ADMINISTRATION

IN tracing the life story of an organization, one can, in most cases, follow the usual pattern of three distinct periods: the preliminary period of planning, the main period of operation, and the final period of liquidation. In the history of the IRO one finds a complicating factor. Since the Preparatory Commission had to start operating before the Constitution was in force, and therefore before IRO was in existence, there is not the same clear-cut separation of these stages. Nevertheless, constitutionally speaking, one can distinguish between three different periods. From February 1947 to September 1948 the Preparatory Commission began planning the work of the IRO and then assumed operating responsibility for it. From September 1948 to February 1952 the Constitution was in force and operations continued. Finally, from 1 March 1952 to September 1953, the work of liquidation was carried out by the Liquidator, subject to control by the Board of Liquidation which assumed the powers of the General Council.

Actual operations took place in the time between 1 July 1947 and February 1952. On 1 July 1947 PCIRO became the largest operating agency of the UN both in the geographical scope of its operations and in the numbers of people employed and served. It undertook the operation of missions and field offices in twenty-five different countries on five continents. The Organization inherited four separate headquarters—those of IGCR in London, UNRRA in Paris, UNRRA Finance in London, and the PCIRO staff in Geneva—and field missions and offices of the two predecessor organizations. The consolidation of the headquarters elements in Geneva and the field missions throughout the areas of operation was an administrative task of considerable magnitude. On 30 June 1949 the IRO story was two-thirds completed. Just after the close of the preceding two-year period, the General Council met and reaffirmed the intent of the framers of the IRO Constitution: that the agency should complete its work in three years—by 30 June 1950, and liquidate itself as soon thereafter as possible. From the autumn of 1949, therefore, preparations were made which would lead to a major change in the operational emphasis to come in the middle of 1950.

In order to place a definite limit on the scope of the remaining problem, and to ensure an orderly termination of the IRO programme, an intensive counselling programme was instituted in August 1949 to encourage refugees to make plans for their establishment; registration of new applicants for the receipt of material services was, with certain exceptions, to end by 31 August 1949; admission to care in assembly centres was to cease after 31 December 1949. Administrative and operational structures were adjusted to these changes in IRO's work, although, in the main, the structure designed by PCIRO was maintained until July 1950.

From 1 July 1950 the resources of the Organization were concentrated on resettlement. As a result there was a major alteration in the structure both of headquarters and of many field missions. From January 1951 onwards, the UN High Commissioner for Refugees became responsible for the international protection of refugees, and the IRO made consequential changes in its work and structure.

What follows is a description of the methods used in the administration of the IRO for formulating and co-ordinating policy and for directing and controlling its implementation. During its first three years, the functions of the IRO were extremely varied and interdependent and extended over many geographical areas, and the control methods were correspondingly complex. Later, as the functions were simplified, their control tightened.

It was at the First and Second Parts of its First Session in May and July 1947 that the PCIRO developed plans for the administrative and operational structure of the Organization. In its decisions it was influenced by the following consideration: to use, as far as possible, the administrative pattern of its predecessor organizations while avoiding some of the weaknesses that had been inherent in the administrative scheme of UNRRA. Some delegates levelled their criticism especially against shortcomings in the exercise of administrative control. Emphasis, therefore, was put upon such organizational features as would ensure a faithful and uniform observance of the policies of the governing body.

In the Constitution, this need for governmental control was met by the requirement that the Executive Committee should convene 'normally twice a month', and by the suggestion that the Committee might, 'either as a body or through a delegation of its members, visit camps, hostels or assembly points within the control of the Organization', and might 'give instructions to the Director General in consequence of the reports of such visits'.[1] This was one article of the Constitution that was not implemented by PCIRO, but by the time the Constitution was formally in force, confidence and close collaboration between the Executive Committee and the Director General, who reported to the General Council about the consensus of opinion reached in their private sessions, brought about a control of operations in conformity with the intention of the Constitution.

Headquarters

A balance had to be struck between the various activities at the headquarters level, and operations in the field correlated with the policy adopted. A powerful headquarters in Geneva, composed of service departments, operational departments, and advisory services was therefore needed. Control of the work of the missions in the various areas would be exercised from these departments at headquarters and each Chief of Mission's operational departments would be largely guided by instructions from the corresponding departments in Geneva.

In the two meetings of PCIRO held in May and July 1947 the delegates considered different plans for the organizational structure, presenting points of view that reflected their different national traditions. Some favoured a 'horizontal' outlay, others advocated strong lines of command through a 'vertical' plan. The tentative plan in favour of 'horizontal' structure proposed by the Executive Secretary provided for

[1] Constitution, Article 7, paras. 4 and 5, Appendix I, p. 578.

four staff offices (General Counsel, Public Information, Reports and Statistics, and Conference Secretariat), and four principal departments (Repatriation and Resettlement, Care and Maintenance, Office of the Comptroller, and Administration and Supply).[1] The headquarters, under the Director General, was to govern both field operations offices, which would be concerned in dealing with the refugees, and field liaison offices which would have to deal with governments.[2] The UK delegate, favouring a 'vertical' plan, stated that it was necessary in administrations to have a clear chain of command from the top to the bottom, in which responsibilities could be clearly fixed.[3] The US delegate, on the other hand, made the distinction between staff and operations officers, and suggested that to attach staff advisers to the Director General would increase his ability to direct.[4] He also advocated making supply an operating function, rather than placing it under the heading of Administration. The Commission unanimously approved the inclusion of a Deputy Director General. The representative of the IGCR was opposed to laying down a rigid organizational structure, as he knew from experience that dealing with the continually changing refugee problem demanded flexibility.[5]

As all the functions of the headquarters offices were considered to be indispensable, a rather large headquarters was unavoidable. It was also felt to be more practical and economical to exercise co-ordination and control from headquarters than to entrust service functions to field offices scattered throughout the world.[6]

According to instructions by the Preparatory Commission the Executive Secretary, in collaboration with the Advisory Committee, worked out a pattern which PCIRO accepted in Resolution 30.[7] With minor changes this structure served as the administrative framework for the IRO during its most active period until June 1950. As of 19 October 1947 the IRO headquarters were organized according to the following plan: Three departments directed and controlled the operational functions of IRO:

1. Department of Health, Care, and Maintenance with four divisions (Health, Family and Individual Services, Employment and Vocational Training, and Voluntary Societies).
2. Department of Repatriation and Resettlement with three divisions (Repatriation, Resettlement, and Movements).
3. Department of Protection, Mandate, and Reparations.

These operational functions of IRO were supported and sustained by the Agency's 'House-Keeping' Unit, the Department of Administration and Budget with three divisions (Personnel, Management and Budget, and Administrative Services), and by a number of independent divisions and offices reporting directly to the Director General: the Office of Supply and Transport, charged with buying and procuring food, clothing, and other supplies in shipload quantities on markets throughout the world, and with the supervision of the tremendous logistical machinery necessary

---

[1] PREP/44, p. 14, 1 May 1947.   [2] PREP/SA/32, p. 9, 14 May 1947.
[3] Ibid., p. 11.   [4] Ibid., p. 14.
[5] PREP/SA/36, p. 7, 16 May 1947.   [6] PREP/SA/42, p. 3, 20 May 1947.
[7] PREP/105/Rev. 1, 22 July 1947, Appendix III, p. 696.

to move the supplies to the consumers—the refugees. The Office of Planning and Field Service and the Office of Statistics and Operational Reports provided the Director General with counsel and basic information on which policy decisions were based.[1]

The purpose of the Office of Planning and Field Service was to develop plans in co-operation with the operating departments, to co-ordinate policy directives to the field, and to bring about unification of operation throughout the IRO. This unification was to be achieved by sending field representatives into the operational areas as ambassadors of headquarters, qualified to advise chiefs of mission on policy, and to analyse the working of local offices. They were to report whether policy was being applied as developed by headquarters. The Comptroller and General Counsel provided financial and legal advice respectively, and the Office of Public Information maintained liaison with the public through all media of communications. The establishment of the International Tracing Service, and the semi-autonomous Review Board for Eligibility Appeals were authorized by Resolutions 23 and 33 of the PCIRO. In 1948 and 1949 further special staff officers were appointed to meet particular needs, so that finally twenty people were directly responsible to the Director General. The Executive Secretary, later Director General, was the chief administrative officer who carried out the administrative and executive functions of the Organization in accordance with the decisions of the General Council and the Executive Committee. For all purposes he was the Director of the Organization with whom rested—subject to the directions of the governing bodies—the final decisions on policy and operations.

The Deputy Executive Secretary, later Deputy Director General, was a chief executive officer, second-in-command, rather than a staff officer. There were three assistant executive secretaries, later assistant directors general, who served as advisers to the Executive Secretary on policy matters, and at the same time as administrative heads of their departments (Care and Maintenance, Budget and Administration, and Repatriation and Resettlement).

The Preparatory Commission had planned to bring the three assistant executive secretaries in a direct policy-making relationship with the Executive Secretary and his Deputy, and thus to form a 'cabinet'. Long and thorough staff work would have been needed for policy to be decided at this level. But with the constant evolution of the refugee problem, as the result of frequent emergency situations, many policy decisions had to be taken in regular staff meetings, at which all day-to-day business was reviewed with officers who were in direct contact with the refugees and their urgent needs and desires. Although decisions could be made 'with an ear to the ground', without losing sight of the human implications of the work, this method of determining policy by *ad hoc* meetings of the officers concerned was not conducive to the development of an effective separate Office of Planning and Field Service, which was supposed to function as the key office. As the heads of the operating departments and the chiefs of the offices reported directly to the Director General and his Deputy, the Office of Planning was frequently not apprised of all action and

[1] PREP/AC/12, 7 July 1947, p. 2, and PREP/AC/14, 19 Sept. 1947, p. 1; PREP/130, 19 Oct. 1947; PREP/161, 5 Jan. 1948, p. 81.

policy matters, and serious difficulties arose in regard to competent planning and co-ordinating.

In the autumn of 1949 preparatory steps were taken for a thorough administrative reorganization in order to streamline the Organization's structure in the interest of greater efficiency and in preparation for the closure of operations. Reorganization was begun at the end of May 1950 and completed by 1 July. At that time IRO started to divest itself of responsibility for maintaining refugees other than those in the process of being repatriated or resettled.

The new circumstances permitted changes in the method of co-ordinating action. The cabinet system was put into full effect, and a single line of authority was established between headquarters and all missions; a regular morning meeting of the Director General with the Deputy Director General and the assistant directors general was instituted in September 1949 to deal with day-to-day matters as they arose. A larger weekly meeting was held to inform senior officers of current operations and matters on which policy decisions had been taken. A necessary corollary was to organize the staff work needed if the cabinet was to reach decisions without holding too many meetings. Two assistants were appointed, between whom there was a clear division of responsibility: one was to prepare and co-ordinate the broader questions of operational policy, and the other was to marshal the points of view of the Budget Division, the Office of the Comptroller, the Division of Supply, and others concerned with financial matters. To correspond with this division of responsibility, a Committee on the Programme of the Organization and a Committee on Financial Policy were formally established at the end of October 1949 instead of the *ad hoc* meetings that had formerly dealt with these questions.

Since the Office of Planning and Field Service had never carried out its intended function of general planning of the operations of the IRO and of controlling the execution of policy in the field, it was dissolved. In its place a co-ordinating policy-making body, the Office of Liaison and Planning, was created in January 1950. The functions of this new office were clearly defined and were to include the preparation of plans and papers for the General Council and the Executive Committee, the maintenance of relations with the UN, and the preparation of the history of the Organization.

Another change, which did not involve the structure, was also significant. It became a matter of policy to marshal the support of public opinion for specific operational projects. If the Organization spoke with one voice and concentrated on a small number of major activities, the IRO's public information could make a positive contribution to the success of operations as distinct from merely creating goodwill for the Organization as a whole. Therefore all public information activities throughout the IRO were brought under the centralized direction and control of the Geneva headquarters in March and April of 1950.

In this reorganization of the administrative structure four main objectives were pursued: to tighten the internal organization of headquarters by reducing the number of officials reporting to the Director General and by grouping related activities; to centralize directions to the field, aiming at a single line of direction; to delegate as much responsibility to the field as was possible, thus relieving the burden on headquarters; and, finally, to effect a reduction in staff by achieving greater flexibility and 'less compartmentalization'.[1]

Under the new plan of administrative organization put into force at Geneva headquarters on 1 June 1950, three major departments were established; a Department of Planning and Technical Services, a Department of Operations, and a Department of Finance and Administrative Services.

The Department of Planning and Technical Services had to perform the policy-making function. It incorporated the formerly independent Offices of Liaison and Planning (now Division of Co-ordination and Liaison) and of Statistics; and the divisions of Health, of Welfare, of Voluntary Societies, and the Office of Eligibility, which had been under the aegis of the Assistant Director General for Health, Care, and Maintenance. This officer now assumed control of the new Department of Planning and Technical Services, in which the independent Office of the General Counsel was also included.

The execution of policy was entrusted to a Department of Operations, under the control of the former Assistant Director General for Repatriation and Resettlement, with four divisions: Shipping, Repatriation and Resettlement, Resettlement Placement Service, and Field Services.

In addition to the traditional operating divisions, the Department contained a new one, the Division of Field Services, which was the key to the whole reorganization in the Administration. Its task was to co-ordinate, authorize, and issue all operational and executive instructions and correspondence to the IRO's offices and missions in twenty-two countries, including Germany, Austria, and Italy. The only communications to and from the twenty-two countries[2] that would not come within its purview were matters of a technical nature concerning repatriation, resettlement, movements, or shipping. A direct chain of command was thus established between the Director General and the chiefs of missions.

The twenty-two countries were those in which the IRO provided a variety of services to refugees—legal and political protection, emigration assistance, welfare services, and so on. Apart from these offices, the IRO maintained delegations in many of the overseas resettlement countries—Australia, Canada, Brazil, Venezuela, the US, and so on. The task of these offices was limited to promoting opportunities for resettlement, organizing reception facilities for refugee immigrants, and maintaining liaison with the national authorities. There was thus a fundamental difference between a resettlement mission and the missions providing services. As missions in overseas resettlement countries were to correspond directly only with the Division of Repatriation and Resettlement, the new plan ensured that control would have a direct bearing on the job at hand.

The third major department was the Department of Finance and Administrative Services, including the services of the Office of the Comptroller, organized as the Division of Financial Accounts, the Division of Audit, and the Division of Financial Operations; the Division of Supply and Transport; and the three divisions that had

[1] Director General's Weekly Meeting, No. 14, 18 Apr. 1950.
[2] Austria, Belgium, Denmark, East Africa, Egypt, France, Germany, Greece, Hong Kong, Italy, Lebanon, Luxembourg, the Netherlands, Norway, Philippines, Portugal, Shanghai, Spain, Sweden, Switzerland, Turkey, and the UK.

previously been controlled by the Assistant Director General for Administration—those of Personnel, Translation, and Administrative Services. The Office of Budget and Administrative Management was removed from the Administrative Department and attached directly to the Director General's staff. In addition to the budget, this office was charged with the responsibility for all staff work on the allocation of funds, position control for the personnel establishment, and general management studies related to the phasing-out of the agency's activities.

Other independent units were the Review Board and the Office of Public Information; and a small number of special advisers were retained. The International Tracing Service was shortly to be closed in accordance with a decision of the General Council taken in March 1950; but for the time being its Director continued to be responsible to the Director General in Geneva, though his headquarters remained in Germany. The old Department of Protection, Mandate, and Reparations was in a special position. The protection of refugees was undoubtedly to some extent an operational responsibility; but with the end of the IRO in view, the UN had arranged the establishment of a High Commission for Refugees to be responsible for their international protection from 1 January 1951. Further, protection involved a number of general activities which were not at all operational. Therefore, the establishment of an independent Office of Protection was part of the reorganization, the General Counsel taking over responsibility for the administration of the Reparations Fund.

By subordinating Supply and Transport, the Comptroller's Office, Statistics, the General Counsel, and the Planning Office to departmental control, the Director General emphasized the great change that had come over the IRO's operations since the time, three years before, when the independent importance of these units had been stressed by the governing body. The narrowing of the Organization's activities down to resettlement also removed the necessity for the extensive co-ordination between departments, divisions, and offices that had existed in the first two years. Yet in July 1950 it was necessary to appoint a special co-ordinator for the institutional hard core programme, an operational undertaking that concerned the Health and Welfare divisions, the Offices of Statistics, of the General Counsel, and of Budget and Administrative Management.

The Director General had intended to strengthen his control over the administration by ensuring that any conflict between planning and operations should come to him for a decision. But though the administrative pattern of June 1950 confirmed the Director General's power of ultimate decision, experience soon showed that the distinction between staff and line could not be made by merely deciding whether a service was technical or not. The big operational service of resettlement was 'technical', whereas divisions like Health and Welfare in the Department of Technical Services had definite operational responsibilities. The operational role of the Health Division led to an exception being made in the chain of command in October 1950; thereafter the Director of Health would issue all technical instructions to subordinate medical officers.[1] Thus account was taken of the special position of the medical staff.

---

[1] Letter, Director General to chiefs of missions in Germany, Austria, and Italy, 28 Oct. 1950. 'It is

As a result of the administrative reorganization, the personnel of the Organization had been reduced from some 2,400 to about 1,800, and further reductions were required to conform to the plans for closing the IRO's work during 1951. A comprehensive study of personnel administration and organization throughout the Organization was made between July and October 1950. As an outcome of this survey, a substantial decentralization of personnel operations to the field was made.

With the gradual liquidation of the IRO's work, simpler co-ordination was achieved in a second reorganization on 15 February 1951, consisting merely of placing all the divisions with operational responsibilities into the Department of Operations, and putting those with administrative responsibilities into the Department of Administration. The reorganized Department of Operations included the divisions of Health and of Voluntary Societies, and the functions of Welfare, Eligibility, and Statistics, now combined in the Division of Field Services; the divisions of Shipping and of Repatriation and Resettlement remained within the Department, but the Division of Resettlement Placement was discontinued. The office of the Comptroller was made a separate department, under an Assistant Director General. The Office of the General Counsel was again made independent as an advisory office, and assumed the remaining functions of legal and political protection for refugees, in so far as such functions had not been taken over by the UN High Commissioner for Refugees. The Office of Budget and Administrative Management returned to the Department of Budget and Administration, which retained the divisions of Personnel, Supply and Transport, Translation, and Administrative Services. The Office of Liaison was again made directly subordinate to the Director General.

A number of innovations introduced in June 1950 had been reconsidered in the light of experience; for example, a return had been made to the original principle of separating Finance and Administration. Further, the operational role of the Health Division was at last taken into account in determining its place in the Organization, and it was now on a par with Repatriation and Resettlement in hierarchical importance. The excellent arrangements for communicating with the field through the Division of Field Services and the Division of Repatriation and Resettlement had been retained unchanged.

The missions

The operational units of the IRO were its field offices or missions. The general principle followed was that the geographical responsibilities of the missions should be coterminous with the political boundaries of the governing authorities to which the missions were accredited. Thus, throughout the life of the Organization, there was one mission in each of the British, French, and US occupation zones of Germany. In contrast to Germany, a single mission was responsible for all work in Austria; and in further contrast, a regional headquarters with offices in Cairo was, for eighteen months, responsible for work in the huge area in the Middle East; when this

contrary to medical ethics for a physician to accept technical medical instruction and direction from non-medical personnel. In the event of judicial enquiry into an eventual case of serious illness or even death . . . the medical officer might be put in a very embarrassing position if instructions are signed by lay persons.'

headquarters was abolished, separate missions in the area became separately responsible to Geneva, that in East Africa covering activities in several governmental areas.

Although the PCIRO gave much thought to the form and structure of the IRO's headquarters, no similar effort was made to determine the structure of the subordinate offices. Nor did headquarters attempt at first to impose any particular organization on them. At the conference of acting chiefs of field missions held in August 1947 it had been stated that 'each area should feel free to organize its headquarters, district, regional or other areas in whatever way is most appropriate. . . .'[1] In general, it was clear that the structure of missions would depend on the conditions of work in their various areas of operations. The centralization of executive authority and control in the Geneva headquarters, however, was bound to influence the administrative pattern of the Organization in the field. If authority was to flow along functional lines, as the method of work at headquarters made the normal practice, it followed that the larger field offices would have counterparts for the headquarters officials whose activities had repercussions on local work. This implied that fairly large staffs would be employed at mission or zone headquarters, and that the latter would most resemble the Geneva headquarters in areas where the IRO's responsibilities were the most extensive.

This was most notably the case in the largest field office, that in the US zone of Germany, where the IRO was responsible for all aspects of refugee work, including the administration of assembly centres. The structure of the zone headquarters was very similar to that of Geneva, the only important differences being that Finance was a division in the Department of Administration, and that an Office of Military Liaison was attached to the Chief of Operations. The special circumstances of the medical staff were responsible for the elevation on 1 January 1948 of the Division of Health to the status of a department. In February 1949, control of finance was separated from control of budget and management. This was indeed the position which always obtained in Geneva; and the order from Geneva which established the chief financial officers (entitled Deputy Comptrollers, to emphasize their responsibility to the Comptroller in Geneva) in the large missions, and which specifically instituted an Office of the Deputy Comptroller in the US zone of Germany, laid down that 'the office of the Comptroller in the Field will report directly to the Chief of Field Office'.[2]

The organizational structure of the area offices in the US zone closely followed that of their zone headquarters. At the beginning of operations there were twenty-one such areas, which were soon reduced to seven on budgetary grounds; later, an eighth area was created in Bremen when that port became a major embarkation point.

As at Geneva headquarters, the concentration of the IRO's functions in the middle of 1950 caused alterations in the structure of the IRO's larger missions. At Geneva the result was at first a three-department structure—Operations, Planning, and Administration—from which the separate identity of Planning was later removed, while the missions adopted a two-department form—Operations and Administration—since planning was essentially a function of headquarters.

---

[1] PC/FM/3, p. 17, 16 Aug. 1947 (Director General's report to conference of chiefs of missions).
[2] Provisional Order No. 39 dated 13 Dec. 1947.

In the US zone of Germany the concentration of functions also led to a physical concentration of those refugees for whose care the IRO remained responsible. This took the form of a movement to the south of the zone of that section of the assembly centre population with prospects of resettlement; the mission headquarters too, was therefore moved in the autumn of 1950 to Munich.

In the British zone of Germany the occupation authorities provided the refugees with maintenance, shelter, medical care, welfare, and employment services through their own staffs in charge of the centres, and the IRO was entitled only to see that its standards were being complied with as far as possible. Legal protection and the determination of eligibility, however, together with resettlement and repatriation (from August 1947) were handled directly by the IRO.

The first organization of the zone headquarters conformed to the dual nature of the IRO's work by making a clear distinction between executive and supervisory functions, each of which formed a separate group within the Department of Field Operations, one of the two departments into which the headquarters was divided— the other being Finance and Administration. Since this arrangement of departments according to supervisory and executive functions was unsatisfactory, a Department of Re-establishment and a Department of Care and Maintenance were set up in September 1947, corresponding to the operational departments in Geneva with very nearly the same functions on a zonal level. The Department of Finance and Administration was not affected by this reorganization, and continued to deal with Organization and Management, Budget Control, Personnel and Administrative Services, in addition to Finance, and Supply and Transport, two specialities which, at Geneva, were handled by separate offices. The change of functions in 1950 was followed, as elsewhere, by a two-department structure in the IRO's zonal headquarters—in this case a reversion to the earlier method.

As the IRO was so intimately connected with the work of the British occupation authorities, the subordinate offices of the IRO in the zone followed the organization of the British element of the Control Commission for Germany (CCG). British operations on behalf of refugees were controlled by the Prisoners of War and Displaced Populations Division (PW/DP Division), which was part of the zonal headquarters of the British element of the CCG. This division was also represented in the Regional or Land CCG establishment. Below this were the relief detachments established at each *Regierungsbezirk*[1] of which there were thirteen in the British zone of Germany. The relief detachments, in turn, controlled the displaced persons' assembly centre staff who were in daily contact with the refugees.

To conform to this arrangement, the IRO's regional teams were established according to *Länder*, so as to co-ordinate their responsibility with that of the CCG representative. The IRO's area officers in these teams then serviced the relief detachments and the staff in assembly centres. At first the IRO had three regional offices; these became, in conformity with the British line of command, four area teams in November 1949. The internal organization of the IRO's functional departments was not very different from that noted previously for other offices. The purely

---

[1] An interim governmental unit co-ordinating the functions of *Länder* governments in respect of a group of *Landkreise*.

fortuitous circumstance that the IRO's chief zonal eligibility officer was a qualified lawyer (as were many of his staff), and the difficulty at first of finding a suitable chief legal adviser for the zone headquarters resulted in a closer connexion between legal work, protection of refugees, and determination of their eligibility for the IRO's assistance than occurred in other missions with the exception of that in Paris.

In the French zone of Germany, where fewer refugees were living than in the British and US zones, a high proportion of the refugee population was working and living outside the assembly centres, so that the IRO had to adapt its organization to the requirements of individual case-work and of work among refugees in the camps. The actual camp administration, as in the British zone, was performed by the French military authorities, and a similar pattern of organization was adopted for the IRO headquarters in this zone, with minor modifications to correspond with the French military administration of the zone.

The differing methods of dealing with the refugee care and maintenance problem in the three western zones of Germany, where no national government existed in 1947 and 1948, were reflected in the methods adopted by the Occupying Powers in their respective zones of Austria, where the Austrian Government was, in contrast to Germany, in effective control of the civilian administration. This meant that the IRO in Austria had a combination of advisory and executive functions, and also that the headquarters was responsible for negotiation with the Austrian Government to arrange for the requirements of the operation in local currency, which could not be obtained by the same mandatory means that were employed in Germany.

In the original form, the Vienna headquarters consisted of four main departments: Care and Assistance (changed in October 1947 to Care and Maintenance); Repatriation and Resettlement, containing only a Division of Resettlement and a Division of Repatriation; Comptroller's Office; and the Department of Administration, under which were included the Supply and Transport Divisions. The Health Division at that time came under the Department of Care and Assistance. Attached to the office of the Chief of Operations were the Legal Adviser, the Public Relations Unit, and the Reports Unit. In the course of a number of minor reorganizations during 1947, the Department of Repatriation and Resettlement became the Department of Re-establishment, to which were added divisions dealing with refugee movements and local settlement, and a Protective Services Unit was attached to the office of the Chief of Operations. The headquarters order establishing the Office of the Comptroller in the Field was implemented shortly afterwards, on 16 January 1948, but did not imply any change in the administrative structure, since the Comptroller in Vienna had not been subordinated to the Department of Administration as had been the comptrollers in some of the other missions. The heads of the departments of Care and Maintenance and of Re-establishment and the Comptroller[1] came to be recognized as the 'senior' department heads and, with the Chief of Operations, formed the policy-making body at mission headquarters level. From December 1948 onwards the Comptroller also acted as Chief of Administration.

The IRO's field administration in Austria consisted of five area teams, one in the

---

[1] This title was adopted, instead of the usual 'Deputy Comptroller', as local Austrian officials did not like dealing with a 'Deputy'.

British zone (split up for most of the time into two sub-units), one in the French zone, two large ones in the US zone, and one covering Vienna. The team responsible for work in the French zone in October 1947 was typical of the teams operating there and in the British zone throughout; there were ten international positions: the Area Director, Deputy Director, Eligibility Officer, Child Care Officer, Medical Officer, Care and Maintenance Officer, Nurse, Resettlement and Repatriation Officer, Supply Officer, and Administrative Assistant. For each of the two teams in the US zone, the following positions were established:

1 Area Team Director	1 Area Nurse
1 Deputy Area Team Director	2 Nurses
7 Assembly Centre Administrators	1 Area Supply Officer
1 Area Eligibility, Repatriation, and Care Officer	1 Area Special Stores Officer
	1 Special Stores Officer
2 Eligibility, Repatriation, and Care Officers	2 Supply Officers
1 Child Search Officer	1 Transport Officer
1 Employment and Training Officer	2 Accommodation Officers
2 Area Medical Officers	1 Administrative Assistant
1 Medical Officer	1 Secretary
1 Voluntary Societies Liaison Officer	2 Administrative Officers

(33 officers)

With the consolidation of operations after the middle of 1950, the headquarters of the mission in Austria was itself split up. The Chief of Mission with certain of his staff officers remained in Vienna, in contact with government and occupation authorities; the remainder of the headquarters, divided into a Department of Operations and a Department of Administration, under the supervision of the Deputy Chief of Mission, moved to Salzburg.

In Italy, some peculiarities of organization resulted from the integration of the IGCR and UNRRA, which had occurred less smoothly than in the other countries, partly because in Italy both organizations had been occupied in similar tasks of care and maintenance, and partly because of misunderstandings concerning the control of future operations.

The changes in structure which elsewhere had followed the changes in the IRO's responsibilities, neither took the same form nor happened at the same time in Italy as in other missions. The major alteration, a move of the mission headquarters to Bagnoli (near Naples) from Rome, took place in May 1950, following the consolidation in the Naples area of all assembly centres for which the IRO was responsible. Some offices, for example that of Legal Advice, remained in Rome; and from May 1950 the organizational structure was unlike that of any other mission, and primarily reflected conditions in Italy. The emphasis of the work was on emigration, as elsewhere; but assembly centres were still maintained and so were arrangements for the care of refugees out of camps. In this reorganization the health services were put on a par with other operational functions, and Supply and Transport became subordinated to operations in general.

The rapidly changing nature of operations in Italy was demonstrated by the three changes in administrative structure during 1951: February, April, and September.

The first change was a grouping of some of the offices reporting to the director of operations; this grouping was continued in another change made in April 1951. At the same time the position of the Assistant to the Chief of Mission, in charge of all offices in Rome, was defined. By mid-1951 the importance of negotiations with Italian authorities concerning the 'hard core' and the future of residual refugees caused the Chief of Mission to spend more of his time in Rome than in Naples. By September 1951 the increasing concentration on the movement of refugees from Italy caused the control even of eligibility and liaison heretofore exercised by the voluntary societies to be assumed by the resettlement divisions; by then the work in the Bagnoli resettlement centre was the major part of operations.

While missions in Germany and Austria adopted along broad lines the departmental divisions in force in Geneva, the conditions in the Middle East, throughout, favoured a two-department structure; the Department of Operations and the Department of Finance and Administration—much the same pattern accepted in the early days in the British zone of Germany and to become general after June 1950. The mission's direct responsibility for camp care and maintenance was confined to one large camp in Egypt; and since the conditions of refugees were so dissimilar in each case, the Egyptian camp at El Shatt was made a sub-unit with equal status to the units in East Africa and Palestine; and the local staff, in each case, implemented the instructions of the Health, Care, and Maintenance Department at Geneva in the light of the local situation. Such guidance as was required from the intermediate echelon at the Middle East headquarters in Cairo was furnished by the Division of Re-establishment in the Department of Operations.

The far-flung operations in the Middle East were not easily controlled from a central point, and the existence of a large headquarters in Cairo, five sub-units in the main areas, and sub-sub-units in East Africa[1] and the Levant—necessary because of the distances between refugee concentrations—made for expensive administration. Because no refugees could be left in these areas, and because it was difficult to arrange their emigration while they were so far away from the normal operations of selection missions, the Organization closed the Middle East headquarters at the end of 1948, moved refugees to Europe as far as possible, and left only skeleton staffs in five regional offices which were responsible to Geneva directly, though the former Chief of Mission continued as a special representative of headquarters in that area.

Some directives arriving from Europe in the Middle East missions were entirely inappropriate in that area. Often only conditions in the larger areas of Germany and Austria appeared to have been taken into account by headquarters staff. As a result of complaints, a special Middle East Committee was established at headquarters to co-ordinate the instructions to be sent to Cairo, and began its work on 6 July 1948.

In addition to the field offices so far described, the Organization opened operational offices on 1 July 1947 in Belgium, France, the Netherlands, and Switzerland. Conditions and needs in these countries differed widely from those obtaining in Austria, Germany, and even Italy. The administrative structure was dissimilar partly because it followed the requirements of the local work, partly because it

[1] In Northern Rhodesia there was even a sub-sub-sub-unit, dependent on the office in Salisbury, Southern Rhodesia.

followed national characteristics rather than the international or Anglo-American point of view adopted elsewhere. Emigration was not a major concern in these offices, and such emigration as was arranged was that of individuals or small parties (except for a large selection of emigrants Australia-bound from Switzerland) not requiring the complicated organization of centralized control necessary in Austria, Germany, and Italy. Again, as the IRO was not directly responsible for maintaining refugees in these countries, a department of care and maintenance was not needed there; instead appropriate methods were developed locally to provide for the supervision of the work of the voluntary societies which received subsidies and disbursed the IRO's maintenance allowances. In France, the legal protection of refugees was the major task of the IRO's mission; for this reason the officer in charge of that work was one of the senior officers of the mission; and as the service of protection was that most commonly requested by refugees, the determination of their eligibility (everywhere the necessary precursor of any form of assistance) was, for a considerable time, the responsibility of a branch of the office of protection; this was later altered to be more in conformity with practice elsewhere. Local offices at a level lower than the mission headquarters were not usual in these western European countries. But the influx of Spanish refugees across the Pyrenees made it necessary for the IRO, for some time, to establish local offices for the determination of the eligibility of refugees as soon as possible after they crossed the frontier. In Belgium, the exigencies of the resettlement scheme caused local welfare offices to be established in the Belgian coal-mining areas.[1]

The lines of control

Policies and procedures requiring wide distribution at or from headquarters were issued as instructions of four types: general orders, local orders, provisional orders, and bulletins. The most important were the provisional orders, which were initiated by the functional unit concerned, co-ordinated in draft with other units at headquarters, and issued over the signature of the Executive Secretary or Director General. In the long series of provisional orders, major policies concerning, for example, resettlement, repatriation, and the standards of care and maintenance, and minor housekeeping matters, such as staff contributions to national insurance schemes, payment of UK income-tax, or participation in the Swiss Military Compensation Plan (for Swiss staff members), were all dealt with and amended.

From September 1948 onwards, after the IRO had come into formal existence, provisional orders continued to be issued, but orders laying down operational and administrative functions were regulated by an Operational Manual, local orders, and bulletins. The Manual was ultimately published in May 1950. Provisional orders, however, could not be eliminated entirely, since the mass of instructions that had to be consolidated was so large; not until 1 May 1951, ten months before the closure of operations, were all outstanding provisional orders collected in a revised edition of the *Operational Manual*.[2]

[1] For a complete list of the IRO's missions, with their dates of opening and closing, cf. Appendix IV, pp. 763.
[2] IRO *Operational Manual*, May 1951.

During 1947 the chief concern at headquarters had been to maintain the programmes for which the PCIRO had become responsible, and to develop the general policies that were distinct from those of the predecessor organizations. By the beginning of 1948 more attention could be paid to procedural methods and to the requirements of administrative control. In order to achieve long-range planning, mature policy decisions, better staff co-ordination, and 'closer cooperation with the field',[1] a special meeting was called by the Executive Secretary in May 1948, the outcome of which was to institute monthly meetings to consider future policy in the light of financial statements, and to expand the Office of Planning.

A necessary concomitant of centralized control from the Geneva headquarters was the requirement of extensive and detailed reports, returns, and statistics on every aspect of work in the field. The number of statistical reports needed increased as the Organization developed; altogether some fifty statistical forms were produced, and reporting did not cease there. Each field office had to submit a monthly narrative report on up to twenty-two functional subjects, and one of these, the narrative report on health, was itself divided into nineteen subheadings. Further reports were rendered: weekly reports of communicable diseases, nominal rolls of refugees being resettled, and similar information within the major departments.

The Administration needed detailed information on the course of operations not only for planning and budgeting, but also in order to keep the governing bodies and contributing governments posted about the progress of work. There can be no doubt that the departmental origin of the provisional orders and the other instructions tended to make them technical, detailed, and, above all and often, appropriate only to the situation in the larger operational areas of Germany, Austria, and Italy. Though the reporting procedures were feasible in the largest missions, where special personnel could be assigned to the work, and where the largest concentrations of refugees were to be found, the Chief of Mission in the Middle East echoed the feelings of all the small offices by suggesting that statistics should be rendered quarterly rather than monthly.[2]

The demands for statistics were particularly great during the interim period when the closure of the Organization was being planned. It was essential for the governing bodies and the Administration to have exact information regarding openings for establishment and the plans of each family of refugees; the intensive counselling programme and a postal census of refugees put much additional work on staff members everywhere.[3] By 5 April 1950 the monthly narrative reports which field offices had hitherto been required to submit could be dispensed with.

[1] Memorandum, Deputy Executive Secretary to Executive Secretary, 21 May 1948, repeated in minutes of meeting held on 26 May 1948.
[2] When the Middle East area was divided into five smaller offices at the end of 1948, he wrote to headquarters in the following terms: 'One thing I beg of you. Even if it is necessary for East Africa and Lebanon to be fed with the diet of heavy workers, and to produce the reports and statistics and returns which are expected from a full-blown mission, please treat the others as unweaned children, give them the lowest diet and expect from them, in paper work, no more than Kindergarten stuff. The effect on the Turkish office of a demand for complete statistics would be disastrous' (Chief of Mission, Middle East, to chairman of Middle East Committee at headquarters).
[3] The typical strain of work is illustrated by the following extract from a letter of resignation from the US zone of Germany: 'I am morally and physically extremely tired as a consequence of a long, exhausting and unequal race with statistics on the one hand and an ever increasing amount of welfare

The flow of instructions to and reports from the missions was supplemented by personal visits of field staff to Geneva, and of headquarters staff to the field. In addition to routine visits of individuals, more formal conferences were held. There were, for example, conferences in Geneva of all or most chiefs of missions in August 1947, April 1949, and December 1949; between March 1950 and July 1951 the three chiefs of missions in Germany and their senior staffs held ten meetings (in their three headquarters by turns), known as the 'Trizonal Co-ordinating Commission'; meetings in Geneva of the chief resettlement officers in Germany, Austria, and Italy were held on the average quarterly throughout the operations; and from time to time other specialists—child care officers, eligibility officers, repatriation officers, medical officers, for example—were called to Geneva for formal conferences. Similar meetings of the local area officers in the larger missions were often attended by representatives from Geneva headquarters.

The above will indicate that the IRO's staff was individually and collectively a vital part of the lines of control. The position of the chiefs of missions calls for particular mention, as it embodies two characteristics of the IRO's methods of administrative control. First, the terms of reference in the letters of appointment given to chiefs of missions were usually far-reaching; but the actual authority enjoyed by each, as a result of a functional organization of operations in the larger offices and of the functional lines of command emanating from Geneva, was essentially that of a regional co-ordinator or integrator. Secondly, the emphasis naturally placed at headquarters on work in Germany, Austria, and Italy, where the overwhelming majority of unestablished refugees lived, caused the smaller missions, and consequently the chiefs of missions, to be relatively neglected. Both missions and headquarters depended on mutual personal contact for the success of their work. The routine visits and conferences that were possible in Europe were naturally lacking in the more distant missions.

Obviously the position of chiefs of missions was not always a happy one. But criticisms should not imply condemnation, for similar difficulties exist in every undertaking that has a score of offices of different size and functions scattered throughout the world. The IRO found itself in a position similar to that of a Ministry of Foreign Affairs, obliged to maintain contact both with important embassies and with the smallest vice-consulates, obliged to implement its common mandate through large and small missions alike, and obliged to take into account vastly different conditions in different areas of work. Foreign Offices rely heavily on settled administrative routine and long tradition; but routine and tradition were denied to the IRO by the nature of its task and the circumstances of its establishment. And, to continue the analogy, the IRO, in its dealings with governments, had several alternative channels of communication open to it, and experienced similar problems of co-ordination in informing all concerned. But it is noteworthy that most complaints were made in the earlier months of work; by the time operations had been carried on for a year, the criticisms had borne fruit, and an increasingly effective routine was

problems on the other. For more than one year the field welfare officers have been harassed with continuous new programmes, with deadlines and with such urgent statistical tasks that the care work as such became a luxury. Reports, nominal rolls, surveys, etc., filled the major part of the working days. . . .' (Welfare Officer, Ansbach, US zone of Germany, 28 Mar. 1950).

established. In August 1950 an additional contact with chiefs of missions was the issue of a confidential news-letter from the Director General, entitled 'What We Are Thinking'.

By and large the Organization operated effectively. Large numbers of refugees were maintained, repatriated, resettled, and protected in an operation of unexampled complexity. Though the arrangements for co-ordination between departments, and between headquarters and the missions, might seem in some respects to have been loose and informal, the internal working of each department was good, and led to effective results. There were differences in emphasis between one department and another; the Department of Health, Care, and Maintenance was able to give its field officers more responsibility in the implementation of its programme than the Department of Repatriation and Resettlement, which had to maintain a great deal of centralized executive power from headquarters, principally because of the need for close co-ordination of processing and movements. The operation as a whole was unprecedented; its administration depended inevitably on a measure of trial and error and on a remarkable personal loyalty of the whole staff to the leaders and particularly to the Directors General. It was surely one of the outstanding achievements of the IRO that a staff which consisted of members of thirty-five and more nationalities, with contrasting backgrounds, and with different experience to guide them, should have been welded, as it was, from an early date, into an effective administrative machine.

CHAPTER V

PERSONNEL

THE IRO was basically a service organization like its two predecessor organizations, UNRRA and IGCR. Success or failure in its mission depended on the quality and efficiency of its staff. It needed people with administrative ability, many trained in law, medicine, social work, and other professions, and a vast number of clerical and secretarial assistants. In addition to professional qualifications and experience, it needed people with self-reliance, imagination, and devotion to their job.

The Constitution incorporated the same principles for the employment of staff and conditions of service as Article 101 of the UN Charter: paramount consideration was to be given to the highest standards of efficiency, competence, and integrity and, as IRO was an international organization, attention was to be paid to recruiting on an 'appropriate geographical basis'. Article 9 of the IRO Constitution specified also the employment of an adequate number of persons from the countries of origin of the displaced persons. Since the countries of origin did not join the IRO, however, the latter clause became obsolete and recruiting on a geographical basis gave preference to nationals of the member governments. Where qualified nationals of member states were not available, other qualified applicants could be appointed.

Men and women were equally eligible for all posts on the staff of the Organization. It is worth mentioning that compared with other specialized agencies a relatively high percentage of women were employed not only on the clerical and secretarial levels, but also in responsible administrative and operational jobs.

In recruiting staff, the PCIRO had to reconcile divergent points of view and possibly conflicting interests. The major problem was to combine the aim of a truly international staff with the efficiency and experience of the predominantly American and British personnel of IRO's predecessors, IGCR and UNRRA. The French delegate and chairman of the PCIRO, M. Henri Ponsot, drew the attention of the delegates to this fact and declared on behalf of his government that it would be advisable for the personnel of the new organization to be equally representative of other nationalities if they were of the same competence. Some member governments which were particularly interested in placing their nationals in key positions reminded the delegates of PCIRO of the difficulties which UNRRA had experienced in its early efforts to recruit a suitable staff, and recommended employing new applicants. The staffs of UNRRA and IGCR, however, were the only organized bodies with experience in the refugee relief field. The representatives of both organizations who were present as consultants at the PCIRO meetings stressed how shortsighted it would be to deprive the refugees and displaced persons of the assistance of the experienced personnel of these two agencies. They pointed out that PCIRO would have at its disposal those persons who had best proved their efficiency, competence, and integrity, since the termination of both organizations had been carried out on a highly selective basis which kept only the best qualified on the pay-roll.[1] Having, moreover, an extremely short time in which to effect a smooth transfer of the functions of these two agencies to the IRO, the PCIRO decided to employ large numbers of its predecessors' employees on a temporary basis, and formed an Advisory Committee to discuss the whole question of staff distribution, salaries, and regulations.[2] The PCIRO directed the Executive Director to recruit 'from the present staffs of UNRRA, IGCR, and the voluntary agencies, from candidates suggested by governments, and from other sources'. The Executive Secretary was to submit nominations for the Deputy Director General and the principal executives (either heads of departments or of major operational organizations in the field) to the Advisory Committee for its advice.[3] Approximately 1,650 employees were taken over from UNRRA, approximately 300 from the IGCR staff of 600, and about 20 new employees were engaged when the IRO succeeded to the functions of these two organs on 1 July 1947. This compares with a total staff of 5,600 at the height of the IRO's operations. Recruitment was largely on the basis of efficiency.

Because of its financial limitations, the IRO was forced to organize on a much more modest basis than had UNRRA and SHAEF. The field personnel attached to the displaced persons camps in Europe were reduced from 5,300, which UNRRA employed in August 1946, to about 1,450. This reduction was made possible in part by employing displaced persons themselves and partly by the voluntary organizations taking over an increasing share of the responsibility for the displaced persons.

Classification of staff

During the deliberations of the Advisory Committee in the summer of 1947, the main features of subsequent personnel policy were decided. The system of employees' categories, introduced by UNRRA, was continued for reasons of economy and expediency: Class I, the international staff, and Class II, the local staff, were on the IRO pay-roll, while Class III, also local staff, were paid by the local economy in the three occupied zones of Germany.[4]

The Personnel Regulations, subsequently drawn up by the Administration in the light of legal and personnel experience, and issued by the Executive Secretary, were noted with approval by the Advisory Committee.[5] These regulations came into force on 21 October 1947 and applied uniformly in all areas of operation. They underwent several revisions and amendments, which culminated in the second revision in 1951 printed in the *Operational Manual* as well as in the form of a special reprint. The provisions in the latter revision were mostly similar to those accepted by the UN and other specialized agencies. The temporary character of the IRO and the specific nature of its operations, however, made some deviations necessary. Thus international staff members were recruited and employed in accordance with the principles laid down in Article 9 of the IRO Constitution, and those of the Staff Rules, approved by PCIRO and later by the General Council.

---

[1] PREP/SA/36 and 37, 16 May 1947.
[2] PREP/90/Rev. 1: Res. 4; Appendix III, p. 689.
[3] PREP/80/Rev. 2: Resolution on Personnel Policy, 22 May 1947, ibid.
[4] Annex 28, p. 308.
[5] PREP/AC/18 and Personnel Regulations and their Implementation in *Operational Manual*.

The principle of equal pay for equal work was adopted, with a system of job classification into grades on the model of the US Civil Service that had been used in a modified form by UNRRA. A single tax-exempt salary scale was approved, the rates to allow for higher pay in the senior posts, and, to encourage North American candidates, an expatriation allowance of $800 a year was granted 'to employees assigned to posts of duty far distant from their home stations'. As a form of security, in view of the temporary nature of the Organization, a provident fund was established to be financed (as in the IGCR and UNRRA) by 5 per cent. deductions from salary and a corresponding $7\frac{1}{2}$ per cent. contribution by the IRO; plans were also made for compensation in the event of occupational injury and for mutual health insurance. Supplementary *per diem* allowances were granted to employees serving in areas where a high cost of living prevailed.

The international staff was required to work in any service of the Organization and in any area where the IRO operated. At peak strength they numbered from about 2,500 on 30 June 1948 to 2,877 on 31 December 1949.[1] This staff was assisted by the Class II or local staff, engaged for service only in the country of their recruitment; some 3,200 employees in this category were on the rolls of the IRO on 31 December 1949. In practice, 'local' was a misnomer, since qualified displaced persons were employed wherever feasible and desirable and indeed, in Germany, this class was reserved for displaced persons occupying functions of some importance in the Organization, where a status above that of the 'indigenous' worker would increase their effectiveness. Finally, in the occupied countries, thousands of workers were used in the maintenance of camps and other installations under the IRO supervision. The number of such employees in the three zones of Western Germany was at one time as high as 90,000. This man-power was loosely labelled 'indigenous labour', although usually most of the workers were refugees, whose troubles mainly stemmed from the fact that they were not indigenous. Although the ancillary services they performed were vital to the smooth functioning of the operation, they were not members of the IRO personnel in the strictest sense—that of being a charge on the IRO budget—since they were remunerated by German paymasters out of mark funds provided by the German economy. There was in addition another relatively small group of German employees doing manual labour who were also paid by Germany.

It may be noted here that in Germany the Class II staff were also paid the greater part of their wages from moneys furnished by the German economy. They were entitled, however, to receive part of their wages in the occupational currencies (an average of $15 per month); this money was provided out of the IRO budget, and was intended for the purchase of amenity supplies such as cigarettes, chocolate, certain food items, and articles of clothing from PX and NAAFI stores.

Nationalities

Considering the first two classes of personnel who provided the actual staff of the IRO, the IRO had a truly international staff representing forty-one different nationalities and speaking nearly all the languages of the world.

[1] See Annex I, p. 99.

The principles of duties and obligations of the internationally recruited staff were laid down in paragraph 3 of Article 9 of the Constitution, and exemplified in greater detail in Part 1 of the Personnel Regulations. The IRO staff, in common with the employees of the UN and other specialized agencies, were part of the international civil service, subject and responsible only to the Director General. On accepting their appointment, all members of the staff took an oath by which they swore solemnly to exercise in all loyalty, discretion, and conscience the functions entrusted to them as members of the international service of the IRO; to discharge those functions and to regulate their conduct solely with the interests of the IRO in view; not to seek or receive instructions in regard to the performance of their duties from any government or other authority external to the Organization; or to accept any other paid employment while in the service of the IRO. In their performance of duty they were not expected to give up their national sentiments or their political and religious convictions, but at all times they were to bear in mind the loyalties, reserve, and tact incumbent upon them by reason of their international status.

At one time there was a certain criticism that some IRO officials tended toward a national rather than an international view-point, leading to insufficient staff consultation and lack of co-ordination affecting the operations of the Organization.[1] On the other hand, certain IRO officials were criticized by their governments because their actions as international civil servants conflicted with national policy. These questions were brought up and discussed in the General Council, and, by administrative reorganization and some final compromise on policy, the difficulties were overcome. It must be stressed that in general 'a high degree of team work and devotion prevailed' among the staff and that on the whole the international comity in the IRO was good.

While there was a wide representation of nationalities on the staff, the distribution of numbers and grade breakdown varied greatly. In October 1948, for example, of the 39 different nationalities represented, 753 persons were British, 346 Americans, 266 French, 138 Dutch, 117 Belgians, and 64 Canadians. A certain redistribution of the available positions took place during the lifetime of the Organization through selective recruiting both for newly constituted positions and for the small number of vacancies created by resignations and other reasons. This did not, however, change the percentages decisively, e.g. the UK representation lessened from 38 to 32·4 per cent., the US from 18 to 16 per cent.[2]

The majority of the higher-salaried positions on the policy-making level (grades 10 through 15 and unclassified) were held by citizens of the US, Great Britain, France, and Canada. The national distribution differed here from that mentioned above. On 30 September 1949, when the IRO was near its peak strength, the American nationals held 36·5 per cent. of the leading positions, while Great Britain had only 25 and France 11 per cent. Australia and Canada came next, each with nearly 4 per cent. of the key positions.

Most of the British contingent comprised clerical and secretarial personnel, since most of the Organization's work was carried on in English. Secretaries from the

---

[1] US Senate, Report No. 476, 8 June 1949, pp. 27 and 32.
[2] See Annex 2, p. 100.

US and Commonwealth countries were perhaps available, but because of expatriation allowances, passage-paid leave, expensive travel costs for recruitment and repatriation, and, in general, their slight knowledge of French, they were much more costly to employ. Moreover, the clerical and secretarial positions in the IRO did not appeal to American citizens, partly because of the lower salary level, partly because of the short-term recruitments. The distribution of nationalities varied, furthermore, according to the different areas of operations. The financial staff was mainly British, reflecting the composition of the UNRRA accounting staff in London; it provided an efficient and experienced group. It would have complicated the difficult financial operations, which already involved some thirty-five different currencies, if an attempt had been made to blend the widely divergent accounting procedures of half a dozen countries. Naturally there was a preponderance of Americans in the Supply and Budget divisions because the IRO supply operations were predicated on the availability of the US army supply lines already in existence, and the budgeting work had to be performed in accordance with methods practicable for the nation that was providing close to 60 per cent. of the funds.

When the staff of the IRO was at its peak strength, in the autumn of 1949, the highest administrative positions were filled in most cases by government nominees, most of whom had previously been active in national administrations. Most of the higher French officials, for example, were civil servants on detached service from their ministries, or had held high posts of diplomatic or military responsibility. On the executive level the majority of the employees were officials taken over from UNRRA and IGCR. Persons recruited for executive posts in general possessed good qualifications in some branch of civilian life, e.g. the public information officers and personnel in the Shipping Division; the staff hired by the IRO itself usually turned out to be highly competent. Retired officers of the armed forces with the necessary administrative and supply experience were employed in high positions. The secretarial classes, in which it was always difficult to obtain employees of the necessary standard, were recruited mainly by the IRO itself.

There was never a clear ruling that functions above a certain level would be staffed by international employees, and below that level by Class II local personnel. Headquarters office in Geneva was staffed almost exclusively by international employees during the active period of operations, but in field offices and missions the classes often overlapped, with employees of different classes working side by side on analogous tasks, e.g. refugee doctors working with international medical officers, and so on. The duality also went quite a long way up or down the scale: a duplicator operator could be Class I, while key officials such as eligibility officers could be Class II. This was partly a carry-over from the UNRRA system, and partly an attempt to conform to national policies in the countries where the IRO operated. Although member governments in general desired representation on the international staff, several of them felt that to have their nationals working in their own country and receiving tax-free international salaries that were higher than the prevailing local rates created problems.[1]

Standards varied noticeably between the different groups. The favourable

[1] Agreement between the Italian Government and PCIRO, 24 Oct. 1947.

conditions enjoyed by the international staff tended to secure for the IRO the services of good people, and their efficiency as a body was increased by a deliberate policy of eliminating undistinguished workers whenever a reduction in force had to be made. In the case of the local staff, efficiency was not on a comparable level, though the salaries were quite good by regional standards. Many were displaced persons; their resettlement and repatriation effected a 'reduction in force' that was contrary to the Organization's interests, since the best staff was siphoned off first. The practical training of those who remained was often low by Western standards. Many also displayed marked bias in carrying out the IRO policies, for their primary loyalties often went to their compatriots and fellow exiles. This reasoning did not apply in the same degree to non-refugee employees, but here the temporary nature of the jobs and the absence of any special financial inducement did not attract outstanding recruits, and the wide margin between international and local remuneration did not contribute to high morale.

Since local employees were not engaged to fill policy-making appointments, no particular significance need be attached to the statistics of local staff classified according to countries of citizenship or ethnic groups. For example, in Italy 25 per cent. of the total local staff on 30 September 1949 were of Italian nationality. Many of the available displaced persons within that mission's territory were persons of Italian nationality expelled from Venezia Giulia and other territories.

Conditions of service of the international staff

Three types of appointments to the staff were provided: temporary, indefinite, and special. Five forms of contract termination were envisaged in accordance with the conditions laid down in the contract: reduction in force, security reasons, reasons of health, unsatisfactory service, and misconduct.

At the beginning the majority of employees were given contracts for one year, beginning on 21 October 1947; most of these were renewed the following year. After 1 July 1949 no further renewals of term contracts were made[1] in view of the projected termination of the Organization, and when contracts expired after this date, they were replaced by indefinite appointments in which no term of service was mentioned. All new recruitments were made on the same basis.

Salary scales, staff allowances, and benefits

The scales ranged from an annual net salary of $1,100 (grade 1) to an annual net salary of $8,000 (grade 15).[2] All grades carried five in-grade promotions. The classified scale did not cover the Director General and the Deputy Director General, whose positions were unclassified with basic salaries at $14,000 and $12,000 per year, respectively.

A special salary scale was provided for American staff working in the US office of the IRO in Washington; it was modified from time to time in relation to the rises in civil service rates. Apart from the local scales this was the only deviation from the principle of equal pay for equal work which had the objective of providing equal living conditions for equal work. Though this scale ranged higher than the regular

---

[1] Provisional Order 19.2, 14 June 1949.   [2] See Annex 3, p. 100.

scale, the US nationals stationed in Washington did not receive certain staff benefits and allowances paid to other international personnel. The justification for these higher salaries lay in the need to attract the proper type of personnel.

At the same time, the salaries paid to the international staff by the IRO were considerably lower than those paid by the UN and other specialized agencies. Compared with UNRRA salaries, the average reduction in pay for all classes from UNRRA levels was 29·44 per cent.

In addition to their regular salaries or wages the IRO staff received ten different allowances and benefits, including staff allowances, travel, and four different kinds of welfare and insurance benefit.

The expatriation allowance of $800 per annum was paid as part of the salary to those staff members whose post of duty was in an area outside their home station, either in the Western Hemisphere, Europe, the Middle East, Africa, or the Far East (including Australia and New Zealand). The *per diem* allowances for each duty station varied in accordance with fluctuations in the cost of living. The *per diem* allowance was not intended as a supplement to income nor as a living allowance at the post of duty. It was granted only to an employee because of the fact that his post of duty was not his home station and was thus subject to increased costs for living requirements.[1] These payments were made only in local currency. *Per diem* scales were not paid in the British and French zones of Germany, and were as high as $14·50 in Manila.

Per diem was originally payable only to personnel working outside the country of their home station. From 1949 'cost of living' allowances, at lower rates than the regular *per diem*, were granted for six duty stations, including Geneva, to local staff[2] to assist international staff members who were working in the country of their home station. It should be noted that in practice *per diem* allowances possessed the characteristics of a supplement to income. Thus, a request for increase in salary presented by headquarters personnel in late 1948 was met by an increase in *per diem*; a Geneva grade 3 typist, for example, normally collected $125 in salary and $108·50 in *per diem* for thirty-one days' work.[3]

An adjustment of payments had to be made for the widespread devaluation of currencies that occurred in September 1949. The Director General terminated the contracts of the employees involved on 28 February 1950. The appointments were then re-negotiated on the basis of an artificial rate of exchange to the dollar (the 'Kingsley dollar') that would produce on future payments and accruals the pre-devaluation exchange value augmented by 40 per cent. of the difference between the old and the new rates.[4]

Leave

Normal provisions were made for sick leave and annual leave, the latter accruing at the rate of two and one-sixth days for each month of service; in periods of sick and annual leave, salary and residential *per diem* continued. After each period of eighteen months' qualifying service a return ticket was provided from the employee's

[1] Provisional Order 23, 21 Oct. 1947.   [2] Provisional Order 23.7, 11 Nov. 1947.
[3] GC/60, 22 Mar. 1949.   [4] GC/125, 18 Oct. 1949 and Staff Regulation 23.

post of duty to his home station, and UNRRA settled a sum of money on the IRO to enable the new organization to give passage-paid leave to those who had accumulated some qualifying service in UNRRA. Many employees did not desire to return home every eighteen months, however, and after April 1949 'passage-paid leave' could be commuted into cash.[1]

The home station was considered the principal city or capital of the country of residence of the employee, or the country in which he had the greatest personal attachments. It was determined on recruitment, and could only be changed in highly exceptional circumstances, e.g. the case of a Czech who became virtually a displaced person when the Communist régime came to power. The home station was of importance to the staff member's financial status. It governed the value of his passage-paid leave, his repatriation rights,[2] his *per diem* and expatriation allowances, baggage and travel allowance on repatriation, the value of repatriation of his dependants, the allowance weight of furniture and household goods which he could send home at the Organization's expense, and, above all, the currency in which his terminal emoluments were to be paid.

Termination

The home stations of most of the staff were in countries with non-convertible currency contributions, and the policy was adopted at an early stage of using this money as far as possible to pay for personal services. The most important amounts were the terminal emoluments, which in conformity with Provisional Order No. 44 of 27 January 1948, had to be paid in the currencies of the home countries, a basic decision of administrative policy that remained in force until the end of the IRO activities. Only after the beginning of 1952 did it become possible for an employee to collect his terminal emoluments in the currency of his duty station, i.e. in convertible currency—a special privilege intended to recompense those who had stayed with the Organization to the end.

When PCIRO began operations no provision had been made for the transportation of baggage on repatriation or permanent change of station. From 1 January 1948 personal baggage and household goods could be moved at the Organization's expense.[3]

The IRO followed UNRRA's practice in setting up a provident fund for those employees who had no pension rights and were seconded from other organizations. The same percentage, 12·5, of the total salary was paid to the employee as part of his emoluments at the termination of his work. Employees with less than six months' service and those discharged for misconduct were refunded only the total emoluments paid from their salaries.

During the UNRRA period few employees had their dependants at their post of duty, and at the time of the transfer to PCIRO, most staff members regarded

[1] Provisional Orders 55.3 and 55.9, 8 Apr. 1949 and 25 May 1950. For further detail on leaves see *Operational Manual*, Appendix XXII, 1, 2b, p. 225.

[2] In Jan. 1950 the privilege of repatriation or cash in lieu thereof was extended to dependants residing at the staff member's post of duty. Provisional Orders 122.1 and 2, 20 Feb. 1950 and 26 Apr. 1950; *Operational Manual*, p. 225.

[3] Provisional Orders 52 and 52.5, 12 Feb. 1948 and 15 Apr. 1950.

themselves as temporary relief workers, living far from their homes and families. As conditions improved, families came to live with the staff members wherever the regulations permitted it, and homes were set up abroad. The effect of this trend was to increase the stability and improve the morale of the personnel, and in January 1949 the Administration introduced dependants' allowances.[1] Wives (and dependent husbands) resident at the staff members' post of duty were granted 75 per cent. of the *per diem* allowance, and in respect of each other dependant, resident or not, a flat allowance of $200 a year was paid.

A fair and uniform system of determining the grades and classification titles was taken over from UNRRA, and contributed to the general efficiency and well being of the IRO.[2] Control over position grading was exercised by headquarters at first through close liaison between the Personnel and Administrative Management divisions, and from October 1948 by a Classification Board which included members of these divisions.[3] The establishment and implementation of a uniform plan through-out the Organization was an impossible task since the central office did not possess sufficient information to achieve more than approximate uniformity. The same was true when full responsibility for grading passed on 1 June 1950 to the Office of Budget and Administrative Management at headquarters.[4] Consequently in November 1950 the classification of field office posts grades 3 through 10 was decentralized to the field offices themselves.[5] Headquarters retained general budgetary control and also the determination of the classification of positions of grade 11 and above.[6]

Insurance and health schemes

The IRO Staff Compensation Plan and the IRO Medical Service Plan, circulated early in 1948, became effective retroactively on 21 October 1947. They applied to the international staff, as local staff were subject to the provisions of national social insurance legislation.

The Staff Compensation Plan was a comprehensive scheme covering occupational injuries, illnesses, and death occurring in the course of duty or arising out of special local hazards to which the staff member was exposed by reason of his employment. The benefits afforded reasonable cover. The IRO bore the cost of financing the plan, requiring no contributions from the staff. The Assistant Director General for Budget and Administration administered the plan, with a right of appeal from his decisions to an Appeals Board.

The Medical Service Plan provided a form of mutual health insurance similar in scope to many national health schemes. It provided 75 per cent. reimbursement (in-creased to 80 per cent. after 1 July 1949) of all normal expenditure on medical, dental, and maternity services not arising out of occupational hazards, i.e. which were not covered by the Compensation Plan, subject to a maximum payment of $480 in the first year. Subsequent revisions[7] raised the maximum payments during the second year of participation to $720 and $1,000 in each succeeding period of

---

[1] Provisional Order 97, 16 Feb. 1949.
[2] IRO *Classification Manual*, Nov. 1950, p. 5.
[3] General Bulletin, No. 6, 27 Oct. 1948.   [4] IRO/GEN/4.
[5] IRO, op. cit., and Annex 4, p. 101.   [6] Management Instruction, No. 30, 23 Nov. 1950.
[7] Provisional Order No. 56.7, 22 June 1949.

twelve months. All international staff members were required to participate in the Medical Plan, and their dependants were also eligible to participate upon request on the condition that they were resident with the staff member outside the country of his home station. The plan was financed by contributions from the staff which were originally from 1 per cent. to 2 per cent. of salary, according to the number of dependants, but on 1 July 1948 the contribution from an individual employee without dependants was reduced to $\frac{1}{2}$ per cent. of salary, since the Medical Plan was amassing large reserves of money.[1] IRO administered the plan without charge and assumed responsibility for any deficit.

To permit the efficient operation of these plans, and to promote efficient service generally, the IRO paid particular attention to the health of its staff. Complete physical examinations, including chest X-rays, were given on recruitment and termination and, at the IRO's discretion, at any time during the period of employment. For those in apparent good health, chest X-rays were performed at intervals of about six months; refusal to have a physical examination required by the Organization constituted sufficient grounds to terminate a staff member's contract.

Locally recruited personnel

The conditions of service of locally engaged personnel were mainly determined according to local patterns. Employment conditions and legislation differed so widely in the various countries where the IRO operated that general rules for local staff could not be laid down. In Italy, for example, the law provided for the payment of a thirteenth month's salary as a Christmas bonus, whereas in Egypt it was a statutory requirement that 75 per cent. of the staff should be Moslem Egyptians. The problem was solved by authorizing each Chief of Mission to lay down staff regulations for his local staff, subject to the approval of headquarters in Geneva, and to recruit staff freely up to the limit of his budgetary ceiling.

The most usual practice was to assimilate the IRO local staff to national civil servants, and to adopt pay scales and regulations that would not be appreciably out of line with the conditions applicable to government employees. Their wages were not normally tax-exempt. They remained subject to national health insurance and workmen's compensation legislation in the country of residence. Usually there was considerable disparity between the salaries and wages of local workers and the international staff.

Germany and Austria presented a special case. Class II, the local staff category, was reserved in Germany for displaced persons, but the military determined the numbers that could be employed and the salaries that could be paid. Policy varied widely from one zone to another. The numbers employed in this class under the IRO were never large, the US zone having a peak of 695 such employees in July 1947, while at the end of 1947 the British and French zones employed only 27 and 56 respectively. This was at a time when between 40,000 and 50,000 indigenous workers were employed in the same zone. Class II personnel performed similar duties to those of the international personnel, while the indigenous class consisted for the greater part of manual and petty clerical jobs.

[1] Provisional Order No. 56.4, 6 July 1948.

Personnel management

The Personnel Division at headquarters, numbering some thirty employees at peak strength, was the central authority for the personnel operations of the IRO, and maintained control over recruitment, reassignment, terminations, and personnel policy in the field, besides the actual management of the headquarters staff. Much of the recruitment was done at headquarters. When this authority was delegated to field offices or missions, final appointment could not be made without reference to Geneva. Until 1 December 1950 headquarters also retained financial control over personnel actions in all areas of operation, certifying each action for conformity to the established personnel procedures before payment could be made, and also administered the Compensation and Medical plans. Thereafter these functions passed to the Office of Budget and Administrative Management.

In addition, each mission possessed a personnel staff to perform the routine processing of personnel actions, and carry out recruiting. Personnel officers in the field were responsible for staff welfare and day-to-day personnel management in their areas.

Although efforts were made to ensure some stability of employment, budgetary considerations and changes both in the orientation and the duration of the Organization's activities tended in the opposite direction, and there was a sizeable load of recruitment, reassignment, and termination to be performed by the Personnel Division. The initial shortage of funds forced some reduction of the staff at the start, but from June 1948 there was an intensive recruitment campaign for nearly a year, reflecting an increase of working funds and a shift of emphasis from refugee maintenance to resettlement. The staff totals remained stable for about a year from March 1949, but changes in organizational structure and replacement of personnel involved some turnover of staff beginning 31 December 1949. At the time of the transfer of static camps to the German authorities, 30 June 1950, the jobs of a large number of employees in the field were terminated. The speed-up of resettlement in the second half of 1950, however, called for some recruitment of shipping and medical personnel, while at the same time a programme of gradual reduction in force began and continued throughout the supplementary period.

There was a fairly heavy loss of staff through normal attrition, and resignations amounted to a steady average of 1·5 per cent. of total staff each month throughout the operation. Many employees had been serving abroad for several years, and were obliged, for various family and other reasons, to return home; others left the Organization to take up employment of a less temporary character. From the end of 1949 this attrition was used as a 'painless' form of reduction; especially for the female clerical staff, however, it was often necessary to find replacements.

The main need for recruiting arose from marked changes in the Organization's programme, and the emphasis put on resettlement. In the major recruitment drive that began in June 1948, it was not possible to staff more than a few of the posts by reassignment of employees from other positions, since the budgetary compression of staff at the end of 1947 had reduced staff below the minimum required for efficiency in nearly every branch. Headquarters Personnel Division was responsible for recruiting a total of some 1,500 persons in all during the existence of the Organization.

The management of an international staff in a temporary and world-wide organization raised nearly every problem known to personnel authorities. There was delay in complete integration of the staff taken over from UNRRA and that from IGCR. There were conflicts of personality and differences in working methods. In Germany the two earlier organizations had performed distinct functions, and it was difficult to combine the staffs when the IRO took over. In Italy both bodies had maintained displaced persons camps and other facilities for refugees, and their amalgamation under PCIRO with a resulting diminution of personnel caused friction.

International employment with the Organization could have considerable drawbacks, depending on the duty station, and though few employees suffered the inconveniences of the medical officer on Samar in the Philippines, who complained that he had to sleep on the floor of his office on arrival, conditions in many field locations were far from perfect. In Germany and Austria recreational facilities were scarce, and the oppressive atmosphere of an occupied country resulted in resignations and frequent applications for transfer; moreover, the occupying authorities in the US and British zones of Germany refused to allow dependants of non-American and non-British employees to reside in the zone unless they were employed. This created hardships in certain cases, although some officials managed to circumvent this rule by making arrangements with the voluntary societies to employ their wives or husbands. Even in duty stations where conditions were excellent, such as Geneva, international staff members encountered certain difficulties in obtaining accommodation at reasonable prices, and in case of illness. Personnel welfare officers were appointed at headquarters and in the larger missions to smooth out such day-to-day troubles. On the larger issues recommendations on policy were made by the Personnel Division to the Director General, and full collaboration was extended to the Joint Board and the Staff Associations.

It was inevitable that in such a large staff there should be some cases of dishonesty and irregularity in handling stores and money, though the adequate emoluments received by the Organization's international officials kept these misdemeanours few in number among the Class I staff. Where the employee's guilt was clearly proved, he was dismissed for misconduct: perhaps a score of persons were discharged for this reason. It frequently happened, however, that responsibility for cash stores passed to a succession of employees in a given period, or that an international employee had merely been guilty of insufficient supervision of indigenous or local employees. In such cases, the Organization dismissed the persons suspected for unsatisfactory performance or on other grounds. Most of the deficiencies were repaid to the Organization by the staff member held responsible, and in general the IRO did not lose much.

The disciplinary measures available to the Administration included warnings, suspension with or without compensation, and termination of services. Because of the temporary nature of the work, sanctions applicable to national civil services, such as loss of seniority, reduction in rank, and bars to promotion did not carry sufficient weight. In practice, apart from mild admonitions concerning the quality of the work, the only punishment available was to deprive the employee of his job by some means or other. The staff member had safeguards against arbitrary treatment. If it seemed that a termination was unjust, or agreed terms of appointments not observed, he could make an appeal to the Appeals Board, constituted in July 1949.[1] This Board was composed of two members representing the staff, two members representing the Director General, and a chairman appointed by the Director General in consultation with the staff..

In 1950 and 1951, as the IRO neared the end of its work, many completely satisfactory employees lost their positions. To provide some compensation for their loyalty in remaining with the Organization and thus possibly losing the opportunity of more permanent employment, the personnel regulations were liberalized in their favour as already described. Moreover, a small outplacement service was established to recommend suitable members of the IRO for further international employment with other agencies. It collected and disseminated information on available vacancies to the staff. The Director General of the IRO also made strong representations to the UN and its principal specialized agencies[2] urging them to accord priority in recruitment to former staff members of the IRO. His efforts were supplemented by personal visits by other high-ranking officers of the Organization to such bodies as the Council of Europe, FAO, and SHAPE. The results of these visits were encouraging. In fact, many employees were appointed by UNKRA and the newly established UNHCR office and the ICEM. In this way much of the continuity of the work and the experience of highly qualified international staff in operational work was assured.

Staff representation

The task of personnel management was facilitated by the close co-operation which developed between the executive officers of the Organization and the Council of Staff Associations. The Council was established in June 1949, grouping delegates of the staff associations at headquarters and in the larger missions. Its main task was to present to the Director General through the Joint Board the views of staff members on matters affecting them in their individual capacity. Before June 1949 this staff representation had been carried out by the headquarters Staff Association in the interests of both headquarters and field employees. The local associations retained their role of arranging social activities and of representing the local staffs in matters of internal administration in each office.

The staff representation which the Council afforded contributed to the modification and liberalization of the Personnel Regulations, and dealt with a number of other matters, such as the administration of the medical plan, the outplacement service, the status of personnel, &c. The Council's main function, however, was to recommend changes in the conditions of service, and many of the recommendations made were subsequently acted upon by the Director General.

The good relations between the Administration and the staff in questions of staff welfare can largely be ascribed to the influence of the Joint Board, set up in November

[1] Provisional Order No. 105, 29 June 1949. *Operational Manual*, Appendix XXII, Regulation 20, p. 173.
[2] Visiting the UN Administrative Committee on Co-ordination at Lake Success, Oct. 1949, and at Paris, Apr.–May 1950. GC/166, 23 Aug. 1950.

1948. This Board was composed of two members representing the staff associations (and later the Council of Staff Associations) and two members appointed by the Director General, under the chairmanship of the Assistant Director General for Budget and Administration. The existence of this 'buffer' board between the staff, on the one hand, and the Administration, on the other, eliminated much friction that might have arisen. It contributed to the general satisfaction of staff members with their conditions of employment and strengthened their morale.

Justification of staff policy

The IRO was essentially a 'service' organization, in which the personnel costs were bound to be heavy. Its task was a practical, material one, and its achievements can be measured statistically in terms of refugees repatriated and resettled, displaced persons housed and fed, legal problems solved, and families reunited through its tracing activities. In such an agency the criterion of success is an obvious one, and the following chapters will show that the exertions of the staff enabled a substantial measure of success to be attained.

It is possible to criticize the way in which the money was spent. The undesirable financial distinction between international and local personnel was undoubtedly an imperfection from the theoretical point of view. But the Organization was under an obligation to employ the best possible personnel for its executive staff, and, as a temporary agency, it could not expend large sums in forming a completely international staff or in equating its salaries with those of other international agencies. Even the most highly placed staff members seem, however, not to have been overpaid.

In becoming a going concern, the initial problem of the IRO was to select personnel from staffs of the UNRRA and IGCR. This entailed very real difficulties, but at the same time provided great strength to the new organization in the form of experienced personnel. In spite of the fact that the IRO was competing for qualified people in a period when they were not readily available, very few of those recruited proved unequal to the task assigned them.

The IRO's record provides substantial evidence that welfare work, whether international or domestic, demands highly trained and well-paid workers. The IRO endeavoured, throughout, to maintain a limited personnel, efficient and adequately paid. At no time did it have numbers of idle and unassigned employees, nor a heavy turnover of staff, both difficult to avoid in a temporary agency whose mission was continually evolving. The Organization wisely integrated recruits from outside sources with able governmental nominees, with the result that its leading officials were active servants of the Organization and not mere defenders of their government's interests. The unity of purpose among the top staff was reflected on every level of staffing throughout the IRO, and thus a host of men and women of many nationalities was fused into a body dedicated to the interests of the refugees.

Smooth co-ordination and efficient performance were by no means easily achieved. The temporary nature of the Organization made it difficult to develop a high standard of performance. The various offices of the Organization were widely scattered, and it offered no security of tenure to its staff. Yet its performance gradually improved and many devoted people gave life and reality to the IRO's principles.[1] In the light of the many prejudices and dissensions that might have existed between the national and racial groups represented on the IRO personnel rosters, the fact that such differences were laid aside, and never allowed to hamper the Organization's work, is in itself a major achievement in international collaboration. This did not come about by chance; it was the fruit of just treatment and understanding management by those responsible for personnel policy. The successes of the IRO in building up a homogeneous staff would not have been reached without three experts in their fields, the Directors General who successively served the IRO, each making his distinctive contribution. Mr. Altmeyer laid the basis of a sound personnel system, Mr. Hallam Tuck set the standards and objectives, while Mr. J. Donald Kingsley, building on the foundation already established by his predecessors, was able to develop a greater efficiency in operation.

ANNEX I

International personnel (1 July 1947–30 September 1953)

	1947				1 July	.	.	.	.	1,107
1 July	.	.	.	2,040	1 October	.	.	.	.	901
31 December	.	.	.	2,142	1 November	.	.	.	.	700
					31 December	.	.	.	.	677
	1948					1952				
30 June	.	.	.	2,458	31 January	.	.	.	.	262
31 December	.	.	.	2,458						
						Liquidation period				
	1949				1 March	.	.	.	.	145
30 June	.	.	.	2,877	1 April	.	.	.	.	87
31 December	.	.	.	2,877	1 May	.	.	.	.	74
					1 June	.	.	.	.	54
	1950				1 July	.	.	.	.	39
30 June	.	.	.	2,470	1 September	.	.	.	.	19
1 July	.	.	.	1,835	1 October	.	.	.	.	14
1 October	.	.	.	1,684	1 December	.	.	.	.	13
	1951					1953				
1 January	.	.	.	1,625	1 January	.	.	.	.	6
1 April	.	.	.	1,313	1 June to 30 September	.	.	4		

[1] The quality of the staff work through years of vicissitudes cannot be appraised in better terms than in those used by Kathryn Hulme in her narrative *The Wild Place*; they were 'people who were working, not with charts and statistics, but with the living material in the mill'; 'seeing the DP's individually, each a special problem, no two of which were alike'; and finally coming to an 'identification with their individual cases as complete as if their own names were listed . . . on each blocked assurance'. Kathryn Hulme belonged to one of the first of UNRRA's field teams and worked as an IRO field officer in the assembly centre of Wildflecken, Bavaria, Germany, until 1951 (Kathryn Hulme, *The Wild Place*, Boston and London, 1954, p. 223).

PERSONNEL

ANNEX 2

*IRO staff members, by nationality, as of 31 October 1949**

Nationality	Number	%	Nationality	Number	%
Albania . .	1	0·04	Netherlands . .	192	7·47
Australia . .	39	1·52	New Zealand . .	17	0·66
Belgium . .	131	5·10	Norway. . .	74	2·88
Brazil . . .	4	0·15	Peru . . .	1	0·04
Canada . .	70	2·72	Poland . . .	36	1·40
Chile . . .	1	0·04	Puerto Rico .	1	0·04
China. . .	36	1·40	Spain . . .	2	0·08
Cuba . . .	6	0·23	Sweden. . .	21	0·82
Czechoslovakia .	21	0·82	Switzerland .	98	3·81
Denmark . .	84	3·27	Syria . . .	1	0·04
Egypt. . .	4	0·15	Turkey . . .	2	0·08
Eire . . .	10	0·39	Union of S. Africa .	9	0·35
France . .	357	13·89	USSR . . .	2	0·08
Greece . .	10	0·39	United Kingdom .	855	33·25
Hungary . .	1	0·04	United States . .	422	16·41
Israel . . .	3	0·12	Yugoslavia . .	4	0·15
Italy . . .	25	0·97	Stateless . .	15	0·58
Luxembourg .	14	0·54			
Mexico . .	2	0·08	TOTAL . .	2,571	100·00

* US House of Representatives, 81st Congress, Second Session, Hearings before the Sub-committee on Appropriations for the Department of State, Apr. 1951, Part I, p. 861.

ANNEX 3

International salary scales (tax exempt)

*Effective 21 October 1947**

Grade	I. Base	Incremental steps			
		II	III	IV	V
	$	$	$	$	$
1	1,100	1,140	1,180	1,220	1,260
2	1,300	1,340	1,380	1,420	1,460
3	1,500	1,540	1,580	1,620	1,660
4	1,700	1,740	1,780	1,820	1,860
5	1,900	1,940	1,980	2,020	2,060
6	2,100	2,160	2,220	2,280	2,340
7	2,400	2,460	2,520	2,580	2,640
8	2,700	2,780	2,860	2,940	3,020
9	3,100	3,220	3,340	3,460	3,580
10	3,700	3,840	3,980	4,120	4,260
11	4,400	4,560	4,720	4,880	5,040
12	5,200	5,380	5,560	5,740	5,920
13	6,100	6,280	6,460	6,640	6,820
14	7,000	7,200	7,400	7,600	7,800
15	8,000	8,200	8,400	8,600	8,800

O *Operational Manual*, Appendix XXII, p. 224. These amounts were increased by $800 a year
e members of the staff qualifying for expatriation allowances.

ANNEX 4

Job categories*

Titles	Grade levels							
	3	4	5	6	7	8	9	10
Accommodation Officer						+	+	+
Accountant						+	+	+
Administrative Assistant				+	+			
Administrative Officer						+	+	+
Administrative Services Officer						+	+	+
Archivist						+		
Auditor						+	+	+
Budget Officer						+	+	+
Child Welfare Officer						+	+	+
Clerk	+	+	+	+	+			
Clerk-Typist	+	+						
Commodity Accountant					+	+	+	+
Communications Officer							+	+
Driver		+						
Eligibility Officer					+	+	+	+
Employment Officer						+	+	+
Employment and Training Officer						+	+	+
Escort Officer					+	+	+	
Field Supervisor								+
Food Supervisor						+		
Insurance Officer							+	
Machine Operator	+	+	+					
Management Officer						+	+	+
Medical Officer								+
Movements Officer					+	+	+	+
Nurse					+	+	+	+
Nutritionist							+	+
Occupational Therapist						+	+	
Personnel Officer					+	+	+	+
Physical Rehabilitation Officer					+	+	+	
Protective Services Officer							+	+
Public Information Officer						+	+	+
Records Officer					+			
Registrar					+		+	
Repatriation Officer							+	+
Resettlement Officer					+	+	+	+
Secretary		+	+					
Shipping Officer						+	+	+
Statistician					+	+	+	+
Supply Officer						+	+	+
Supply and Transport Officer						+	+	+
Switchboard Operator		+	+					
Translator						+		
Transport Officer						+	+	+
Travel Officer					+		+	
Voluntary Societies Officer							+	+
Welfare Officer						+	+	+

* IRO *Classification Manual*, Nov. 1950, p. 104.

CHAPTER VI

FINANCES

THE financial affairs of the IRO naturally involved many complications and difficulties. The manner in which these problems were faced and solved reflected the outstanding humanitarian spirit with which they were approached. Only a respect for humanitarian ideals, and a determination to see that justice was done as far as possible to the unfortunate refugees and displaced persons, created the measure of co-operation which was achieved in the financial dealings of the IRO and the efficiency with which these complex monetary tasks were accomplished.

Over a period of four and a half years of operation, that is from 1 July 1947 to February 1952, the impressive total of $398,596,802 was contributed by eighteen governments, with additional incomes amounting to nearly $40 million from UNRRA and IGCR funds, from gifts, from transportation, surplus selling, and Deutschmark funds from the German economy; there were also expenditures of individual national governments and of voluntary societies.[1]

IRO's expenditures during this time amounted to $428,505,335.[2] This remarkable record presents an achievement considered impossible in 1947 by many people who could not believe that, in peace-time, a sufficient number of governments would join together in an effort to solve a great humanitarian task and accomplish its aim. IRO's financial operations reveal perhaps more strikingly than its other operations the efficiency, ingenuity, and co-operation of the administrators of the programme in a very complicated undertaking which was beset with many uncertainties.

Emphasizing the fact that it was an organization essentially charged with humanitarian and charitable duties, it received most favourable treatment for its financial operations from governments, national treasuries, central banks, as well as from commercial banking institutions and other bodies. IRO obtained conversions of currencies as a favour from various governments, and this immeasurably facilitated the execution of its programme where an approach on plain legalistic grounds would have failed. It also received a waiver of commission by central and commercial banks; it was granted reduced operating charges and special interest terms on the strength of its plea for the humanitarian and charitable cause it represented. In negotiations with shipowners the emphasis on IRO's humanitarian activity ensured considerable advantages with regard to payment provisions, and this helped to augment the resources of the Organization.

Budgets

Three annual budgets were drawn up, covering the financial years of 1 July 1947 to 30 June 1950. There was an additional budget in October 1949 for the supplementary and closure period from 1 July 1950 to September 1951 when the General

---

[1] For contributions of governments see Annex 5, p. 122; for those of UNRRA and IGCR, Annex 6, p. 123; and others, Annex 10, p. 126.　　　　[2] See Annex 9, p. 125.

Council agreed to extend IRO's period of operation. When it became apparent that former savings and other sources made still more funds available, the General Council decided to carry on the approved programme as long as realizable resources would permit. At the outset, however, the financial programme caused much anxiety and presented great difficulties to the policy-making body, the PCIRO, as well as to the Executive Secretary. Only by continuous vigilance on the part of both and by their efforts to improve financial procedures and methods could such a remarkable result finally be achieved.

The Constitution of the IRO provided for a provisional budget for the first financial year of 1947–8. The budget and the scales of contributions had been drawn up with all fifty-four member nations of UN in view. By May 1947 not enough member governments had ratified the Constitution to enable the Organization to be formed by 1 July 1947, and it had also become apparent that not all member nations would join the IRO. Thus the amount of money at its disposal for expenditures for the first financial year was uncertain. The PCIRO therefore drew up a budget on the assumption that IRO would have to plan its operations on the basis of 75 per cent. of the original amount of $156,060,500. The administrative plan of expenditure was reduced from $4,800,000 to $3,600,000, and the operational plan of expenditures was reduced from $151,060,500 to $115,611,680. This budget wiped out a contingent fund which the Executive Secretary had suggested in order to provide greater flexibility in planning and operation. This, he pointed out, was much needed for world-wide operations in view of the unpredictable extent of responsibility. Furthermore, the budget provided only $24,745,760 to be used for repatriation and resettlement, operations which should actually eliminate the very problem the IRO was supposed to handle, while the main share of the budget with $75,281,927 was set aside for care and maintenance.[1]

The budget was reduced in order to avoid a deficit. That necessitated, however, the issue of a freeze order, forbidding the acceptance of new cases for care and maintenance, except hardship cases. It would have been easier if the Administration could have planned for a three-year budget, since resettlement and repatriation, although demanding a great initial outlay, would, in the long run, bring about a decrease of the expenditure for care and maintenance. The appropriations of the supporting governments were granted annually. In view of the necessity of operating according to this annual limit, the IRO had to strike a balance between giving temporary assistance to the refugees and resettling them permanently.

The two largest supporters, the US with a contribution of 45·75 per cent. and the UK with 14·75 per cent. for operations, and 39·89 per cent. and 11·48 per cent. respectively for administrative expenses, had proceeded on the assumption that the operational period would last for three years. Late in 1947, Mr. Ernest Bevin, Secretary of State for Foreign Affairs of the UK, and General George Marshall, Secretary of State of the US, indicated to the Executive Secretary of the PCIRO that he could plan for a three-year period.[2]

---

[1] PREP/159 corrected and Annex 7, p. 123.
[2] See Senate Report No. 476, 81st Congress, First Session, p. 37: Appendix A, Original three-year plan of operations.

The first year's operation showed that the cost of health, care, and maintenance had been over-estimated, while the cost of resettlement had been under-estimated. Thus, the estimates for 1948–9 and 1949–50 were revised in accordance with the actual situation. The estimates with respect to resettlement needed considerable revision owing to the fact that shipping and other transportation expenses, major factors in resettlement expenses, had been very much under-estimated: for 1948–9 an increase of about $60 million from the original estimate were provided, and similarly for 1949–50, while in the closure and supplementary period the expenditure for resettlement was approved in the amount of about $50 million.[1]

During this period the cost of care and maintenance decreased from 57 per cent. of the total expenditure in 1947–8 to 33 per cent. in 1948–9 and to about 20 per cent. and less in the final operations.

Article 10 of the Constitution had in view a dual function of the IRO budget, namely, to assess the Organization's expenditure and allocate their shares to the member governments. In practice the drafting of the budget was combined with an estimate of possible expenditure, since the actual expenditure could not yet be accurately foreseen. In the first place, not all governments of the UN had joined the IRO. Secondly, payments could be made in kind, or partially or wholly contributed by member governments through expenditures in their homeland for immigration arrangements. Such contributions had to be adjusted by negotiation with the respective governments. Moreover, a legal currency devaluation took place in some member countries during the life span of the IRO. There were also important developments and changes in the countries in which the operations were conducted. The creation first of the bi-zonal and later of the tri-zonal economy in Germany affected the basis of costs of maintenance; refugees from China had to be transferred to the Philippines without delay; resettlement opportunities unexpectedly opened or closed. Such events not only necessitated new programmes, but sometimes a shift of emphasis in policy caused a change in established programmes: in either case, alterations in the plan of expenditure resulted. A constant two-way procedure of adjustment of programmes to conditions, resources to programmes and vice versa characterized all the work of the Organization. Nevertheless, as in all living bodies, the IRO's programme had priority over budgetary technicalities; in the words of the General Council: 'Having reached certain conclusions with regard to the character of the Organization's operations . . . the Council turned to the budgetary aspect. . . .'[2]

For these reasons a division between budget and plan of expenditure was embodied in the financial regulations of the IRO,[3] which were established in accordance with Article 10 of the Constitution and became effective from the date of approval by the General Council.

In addition to the necessity of revised estimates there were other obstacles to operational planning, especially in the first year.

First there was the Organization's inability immediately to obtain exact cost

[1] See Annex 8: Planned and actual expenditures, p. 124.
[2] GC/194/Rev. 1, p. 15.
[3] PREP/44, PREP/93, and GC/53: Financial Regulations for IRO. Scope and Application, 27 Sept. 1948.

figures covering the various supplies which were being furnished to the displaced persons by the occupation authorities when they assumed operational control in the field. To meet such liability of undetermined size, substantial reserves had to be established. Only after months of careful negotiations were initial prices ultimately reduced, thus enabling the IRO to commit the same amount of reserve as the excess of the actual liability. Two other problems arose in regard to its main source of income, namely, the contributions to the IRO: (1) the collection problem, and (2) the currency problem.

The contributions were not made regularly, and this uncertainty regarding payments of the anticipated revenue complicated planning. In each of the first eight months of operation, for example, the Organization received an average of only 6 per cent. of its anticipated revenue for the year. Then, in one month, in the third quarter, it received nearly a quarter of its entire year. These fluctuations of receipts made proper operation difficult.

Economic difficulties in many countries, furthermore, caused their respective governments to make contributions in their own currencies, most of which were either soft, blocked, or both. Belgium and France paid in their own currencies, the UK and Australia in blocked sterling, China in Chinese dollars. Only the US, Canada, Iceland, Guatemala, and the Dominican Republic paid in US dollars. Thus the IRO had a shortage of dollars, and this complicated its financial problem. Contributions which were paid in blocked currencies could be used to buy only within the contributing country. The major part of the budget was needed for purchasing foodstuffs in connexion with the care and maintenance programme and for shipping in connexion with the resettlement programme. A large portion of these foodstuffs and about 70 per cent. of the shipping costs had to be paid in US dollars, since soft currencies could not be used for these expenses. The IRO budget had to take into account expenditures in fifty-one different currencies incurred by IRO offices in twenty-seven countries all over the world. It can be stated without reservation, therefore, that the degree of progress which was made in the financial field during the period of operation was truly remarkable considering not only the initial difficulties under which this part of the work was begun in July 1947, but also taking into account the continuous shift in timing and change in type and extent of operations inherent in an emergency relief programme of a temporary nature.

The following description of the financial operations involved in collecting and utilizing the IRO funds will substantiate this statement in greater detail.

CONTRIBUTIONS

Method of collection

From the inception of its operations, the IRO was faced with the problem of devising an effective system for the collection of its member governments' contributions. This task presented many problems of considerable difficulty and complexity and necessitated continued vigilance in following up pending contributions and in continuing negotiations until actual payment of funds had materialized.

The outstanding success of the IRO in collecting nearly all of its contributions, as compared with a large percentage of arrears on the part of members of other specialized agencies of the UN, had been largely due to the Organization's un-remitting efforts to keep its member governments constantly apprised of their con-tribution positions and in requesting their co-operation in expediting their payments. Actually all member governments paid their full contribution except China (with $8,210,469 unpaid of a contribution of $21,801,982) and Guatemala (with $60,024 unpaid of a contribution of $269,850) who were in arrears when the final liquidation period came.[1]

The difficulty of obtaining favourable results in this task will be appreciated when it is borne in mind that governmental payments usually involved legislative as well as administrative procedures which often required a considerable length of time and, even with the best of intentions on the part of the contributing member governments, did not always result in an actual payment. These governmental procedures were so often protracted and inconclusive that it seemed doubtful whether the vast and complicated financial operations involved in the IRO's programme could be success-fully initiated unless it was arranged that a substantial portion of its funding re-quirements could be made available to the Organization at the very beginning of its operations. The prompt payment of contributions by the US and the UK—the two largest contributors to the IRO—was one of the principal factors which made possible the early start and successful conclusion of the IRO programme.

The prompt receipt of the US contribution instalments, deposited with the IRO bank depository in New York, enabled the Organization to cover its operational and administrative disbursements in convertible exchange on a world-wide basis, keep-ing it in funds to the extent of approximately 50 per cent. of its entire budget. Augmenting this very substantial asset, the UK contribution added materially to IRO's ability to procure goods and services, particularly shipping, and served to enlarge and extend the IRO's payment range. The timely receipt of these two major assets of its annual budgets provided the IRO with some leeway in regard to the remaining sixteen governments' payments.

The method for collecting contributions was as follows. The Administration's budget proposals were submitted to member governments either through their permanent delegates to the Organizations or directly, always six weeks at least before the session in which the budget was to be debated in the General Council. The delegates to the General Council could thus always be briefed as to the attitude they should adopt when voting on the budget. The General Council's resolution which approved the budget was coupled with a directive to the Director General instructing him to submit, through official channels to the member governments, the budgets, together with the terms of the resolution. The first step, therefore, towards initiating the necessary action for the payment of contributions was the dispatch of a letter from the Director General to the Minister of Foreign Affairs of each member government stating the amount of the contribution due in accord-ance with the relative recommendation of the Council and indicating the manner of payment.

In those countries in which the IRO maintained missions or representatives,

---

[1] For details see Annex 5, p. 122.

copies of all such communications to the governments were transmitted to the Chief of the Mission or to the representative in order to keep him appraised of the status of contributions and, in appropriate cases, to enlist his aid in expediting payment by the government concerned. It was important to be familiar with the time schedules governing parliamentary appropriation actions and budgetary provisions in the various countries in order to ensure inclusion of the IRO contribution payments in the authorized disbursements of governments.

METHOD OF PAYMENT

Estimate of currencies required

In its budgetary estimates covering the programme of operations, the IRO endeavoured to arrive at the closest possible approximation of its anticipated expenditures, not only in convertible exchange but also in the currencies of its member governments which lacked automatic convertibility. This arrangement served as an invaluable guide in enabling the Organization to determine from the outset its approximate position in the non-convertible currencies of the contributing member governments, and to subtract the estimated expenditures from the anticipated contribution payments. For the purpose of this calculation the contributions of the US, Canada, the Dominican Republic, Guatemala, Switzerland, and Venezuela were included in the US dollar group, based on original provisions for their payment to the Organization's New York account; those of the UK, Australia, and New Zealand were paid to a special sterling account and were available for disbursement within the sterling area and in other countries specifically agreed upon by the UK Treasury; finally, those of Belgium, Denmark, France, Iceland, Italy, Luxembourg, Netherlands, and Norway were classified as non-convertible assets in the currencies of the respective countries, available for procurement of goods and services within their economic spheres, subject to existing regulations.

From time to time, the position of the Organization in all of these currencies was reappraised in order to adjust the purchase of goods and services to the change in currency. When the IRO found itself potentially short of a certain country's currency because expenditure in that exchange would tend to exceed the contribution of that country, it endeavoured to modify its areas of procurement. Thus the IRO found itself able to concentrate on the utilization of surplus currencies and to avoid creating or increasing a deficit in another currency in case the pricing and quality factors were propitious.

Acceptance of contributions in non-convertible currency

In marked contrast with the practice of other specialized agencies of the UN—who had requested from their member governments payments of the greater part of their contributions in US dollars—the IRO had adopted a realistic attitude and had recognized the great burden which such a stipulation would place upon those of its member governments whose currencies were not automatically convertible, and had accepted contributions to its accounts in the form of bank deposits earmarked for expenditure within the respective countries in accordance with applicable exchange regulations. In this connexion, however, it must be remembered that the IRO had a restricted number of members and had, because of the operational nature of its activities, a very much larger budget than other specialized agencies. Therefore, due to the considerable amounts involved, governments contributing dollars to other agencies were unable to contribute dollars to the IRO. The contribution of the US, for example, amounted to between 40 and 70 per cent. of their total expenditure on membership for international organizations.[1] The contribution of the US for 1947–8 was approximately 2·1 per million of its federal budget, whereas the proportion for Great Britain was about 1·8 per million and that for France a little lower.

Once bank deposits had been made in the respective local currencies the IRO endeavoured to obtain full utilization of such funds in accordance with the wishes of the governments concerned, and mindful of the interests of their economies. This meant, at first, that these non-convertible currency assets were more in the nature of a reserve fund for potential future utilization than an immediately available fund for unrestricted utilization. The problem was finally solved almost at the very end of the IRO's existence when, after consistent emphasis on utilization of non-convertible currencies in every possible way and avoidance of expenditure of convertible exchange wherever other currencies could be employed, the IRO had achieved the position of practically 100 per cent. utilization of all of its non-convertible currency contributions. This reflects the efficacy of IRO's handling of the problem of member government contributions without mandatory conversion provisions.

Computation of rates of exchange

The IRO, though carrying out vast international transfer operations in practically all world currencies, and maintaining banking accounts in many different countries, found it necessary, for all of its operating and accounting purposes, to reduce all foreign exchange values to a single unit which it identified as the 'nominal dollar'. This term implied that any receipt or expenditure in any currency of the world carried in IRO's accounts, operating statements and reports, statistical data, and all other documents was measured by a common yardstick which represented mathematically the US dollar equivalent of any amount in any other currency at the rate of exchange determined by the IRO as appropriate for that purpose.

In September 1949 rates of exchange presented many complex problems and involved further complicating factors in regard to the IRO's member governments' contributions, because of the currency devaluations of most of the member governments. The devaluation problem arose with regard to the contributions of Australia, Belgium, Canada, Denmark, France, Iceland, Italy, Luxembourg, the Netherlands, New Zealand, Norway, and the UK, and only the contributions of the Dominican Republic, Guatemala, Switzerland, the US, and Venezuela were not affected by this development.

---

[1] Report of the Committee on Expenditures in the Executive Departments, US Relations with International Organizations, US Congress, Washington, 8 June 1949, p. 1: Out of approximately $109 million spent by this government in connexion with international organizations during fiscal year 1948, approximately $71 million went to the IRO. During fiscal year 1949, of an estimated $150 million devoted to these purposes, $70 million went to the IRO.

The member governments of the countries whose currencies were devalued in relation to the dollar were faced with the problem of providing additional funds with which to cover the deficiency created by the increase in the value of the dollar in relation to their respective exchanges, which, in the case of the pound sterling and allied currencies, amounted to almost 44 per cent. The initial reaction of the governments was not altogether favourable to the idea of adjustment. It took a long time and considerable negotiations between the Administration and the governments concerned to work out a formula which proved acceptable to the governments. Finally, the old rate of exchange was applied to the contribution for the number of days during which it prevailed, figuring from the beginning of the IRO financial year 1949–50, i.e. 1 July 1949 to the date of devaluation, and the new rate of exchange from the date of devaluation to 30 June 1950.

From the very beginning of its operations it was necessary for the IRO to establish a table of foreign exchange rates for its internal use in order to provide a working and accounting basis for its receipts and disbursements in all currencies. Using the US dollar as a base, the IRO determined the value of all other currencies in terms of dollars, based on the prevailing par values of the International Monetary Fund, and issued orders governing the use of such exchange rates for its internal purposes.

In the course of the financial year 1949–50, a general agreement was concluded with the member governments regarding the formula under which the contributions of those governments whose currencies had been devalued would be computed in relation to the nominal dollar allocations. A comprehensive contribution statement was prepared by the IRO in each case, detailing the amounts of the administrative and operational allocations and the details of the conversion calculation. These computations were made on the basis of the exact par rates of the International Monetary Fund. These statements which were presented to the respective governments also included comprehensive data relating to the apportionment of credits for services and other expenditures incurred by governments for account of the IRO in assuming hard core and other responsibilities as a charge against contributions.

Utilization of the IRO funds

Constitutionally, the payment of the contributions could be made in kind, either in goods or in services. Further, according to Article 10, paragraph 2, the contribution could be paid in such currencies as might be stipulated by a decision by the General Council, having regard to the currencies in which the anticipated expenditure of the Organization might be effected. Moreover, contractually, Article 2, 2 (d) provided that the Organization could conclude agreements with member governments according to which they undertook a part, or all, of the care, maintenance and other services for refugees in territories under their authority; this system resulted in claims and counter-claims which had to be adjusted between the Organization and the contributing members. Finally, limitation on the disposition of means based on contributions existed in the form of national legislation; for instance, the US Displaced Persons Act of June 1948 provided that all IRO immigrants had to be carried in ships sailing under the US flag. These factors had to be taken into consideration by the Organization in the utilization of the funds.

In addition to the IRO's contributions from the US, deposited, as has been said, in New York, dollar accounts were also maintained in London and in Geneva, which ensured the necessary fluidity for the Organization's operational purposes. The New York dollar account was also the repository of the Government of Canada's contributions which were paid in whole or in part in US dollar exchange, as well as those of the Dominican Republic, Guatemala, and Venezuela. This account was also credited with Switzerland's contributions whenever Swiss franc credits received by the IRO were in excess of its immediate requirements in that currency and were converted to New York exchange.

The IRO drew against its dollar accounts for all disbursements which required payment in US dollars or other currencies which could be purchased only with dollars and which the IRO did not possess. Thus, at the height of its programme, the IRO transferred from its dollar account between 2 and 3 million dollars a month to the order of the Treasurer of the US in payment of the charter hire of a fleet of US Army Transports (USATS), later renamed US Navy Ships (USNS), which carried hundreds of thousands of displaced persons from German and Italian ports of embarkation to countries of resettlement overseas, and which provided an exceptionally high calibre of service at a very reasonable cost. The IRO also had under charter certain other vessels under dollar contracts, for which US dollars constituted the only payment medium. Dollars were also required for essential purchases of supplies in the US, maintenance of the IRO's US Office in Washington, as well as salary payments and other moneys owed to US nationals employed by IRO at its headquarters in Geneva and in all of its other missions and offices. A considerable segment of the IRO's programme operations in Germany constituted another direct dollar expenditure, necessitating transfers from New York to the IRO mission accounts in the US zone of Germany.

Many other expenditures of the IRO, payable in currencies other than US dollars, necessitated the purchase of such exchanges with US dollars because the IRO did not have the required exchanges and could not obtain them by conversion from its available holdings in other currencies. For example, during the first and second year of its operations the IRO was obliged to use US dollars for the purchase of most of the currencies required by its missions in non-contributing countries, covering both operational and administrative expenditures. In the case of its programme operations in one of the contributing countries, Italy, the operation was so extensive that the contribution of the Government of Italy was quite insufficient to cover the IRO's requirements, and many millions of dollars had to be used for the purchase of the Italian lire necessary to finance this operation.

The importance of the US dollar assets in the planning and execution of IRO's programme was one of the dominant features of its operations, particularly during the first three years. In any contemplated programme to be undertaken with the currency of a non-contributing country, the natural query always arose as to how the expenditure could be financed. Since, in general, the available contributions in non-dollar currencies were non-convertible, IRO's dollar assets had to be used. If therefore an uncommitted reserve of dollars still existed, the project could be undertaken. If the dollars were committed or expended, there was no provision for this new venture unless possibly a commitment for some other project could be placed in abeyance or cancelled in favour of the new plan. The constant task of all IRO officers, particularly in the Comptroller's Office and in the Budget Office at headquarters, was to watch the Organization's dollar position and to see whether any new project could be undertaken.

Non-convertible currency utilization

This emphasis on the importance of the US dollar resources of the IRO must not detract from the significance of the non-US dollar contributions of the Organization, as the latter constituted a noteworthy element in many of the IRO's world-wide operations. These currencies were usable in most cases only within the economic areas of the contributing countries. Nevertheless, they represented considerable economic values, and, though much ingenuity was required on the part of the IRO to make use of such values, the final result was a sizeable contribution in goods and services to the IRO's programme, a contribution which helped assure the successful conclusion of its operations.

The contributions of the UK were made available to the IRO by credit to a 'Special Resident Account' maintained with its bankers in London. Australia's and New Zealand's contributions were also credited to this account. It was technically identified by the IRO's bankers as the 'IRO Non-convertible Sterling Account', from which payments could be made without any special formality to cover the procurement of goods and services in the UK as well as in the Dominions (excluding Canada) and possessions, and other countries of the sterling area. A small portion of the contributions of the UK and Australia was paid in convertible sterling, i.e. London exchange which was then translated into any other currency including US dollars; this proved most helpful in the initial phase of the IRO operations. The entire contribution of New Zealand, too, for the first financial year of the IRO's operations, i.e. 1947–8, was remitted to the Organization's account in London in convertible sterling, thereby acquiring equal value with the IRO's dollar contributions. With these exceptions, however, the contribution payments of these governments consisted entirely of non-freely-convertible sterling, subject to all the limitations and controls prescribed under the pertinent regulations of the UK Treasury.

The original practice of the IRO in the utilization of its non-freely-convertible sterling credits was to budget them for procurement of goods and services within the sterling area. This meant that goods could be procured for utilization within the sterling area, and that British vessels could be employed against payment from the Organization's Special Resident Account in London. Almost from the inception of its programme, however, the IRO was accorded broad privileges in its expenditure of non-convertible sterling which normally would not have been granted. With regard to supplies, the UK Treasury agreed to accept from the IRO a so-called 'shipping list' of the commodities required by the IRO in all areas of its operations which could be procured in the sterling area and paid for from the Special Resident Account. In practice this meant that shipments to Switzerland and to Italy, which would normally have required delivery of Swiss francs and Italian lire to the British Exchange Control, were acquired from funds in the Special Resident Account in

London, and the Organization was thus spared the expenditure of an equal amount of Swiss francs and Italian lire which would have been a drain on its dollar resources.

This latitude in regard to the monetary transactions of the IRO also applied to a certain extent to shipping. Shipping revenues were very important in Great Britain's balance of payments and were a major producer of dollars and other hard currencies. The dollars accruing in the north Atlantic service from the US passenger and freight traffic were particularly important to the economy of the UK. Nevertheless, the IRO chartered space on a number of British flag vessels against payment from the Special Resident Account, thus acquiring valuable shipping accommodation without having to pay dollars. Another use of sterling assets from the Special Resident Account was the expenditure on salaries and other emoluments of UK and other sterling area nationals employed at IRO's headquarters in Geneva and in all other offices and missions.

The sum total of the IRO's drawings against its Special Resident Account in London was at all times a rather imposing figure amounting to the equivalent of many millions of dollars during each financial year. At no time, however, during the first three financial years, did this total closely approximate the total amount of sterling placed to the IRO's account by the UK, Australian, and New Zealand governments covering their contributions. Throughout this period the Organization's sterling balances remained as a partially unusable asset, since all measures of procurement of goods and services within the existing methods could not fully absorb it.

A significant step towards alleviating this problem was taken by the UK Treasury as early as November 1948, when it approved the IRO's request for the utilization of up to £1,860,992 for the charter hire of two Norwegian vessels, the *Skaugum* and the *Goya*, which were used for the resettlement of displaced persons on voyages from German and Italian ports to Australia and other overseas countries. Subsequently, this authorization was increased by a further £1 million resulting in a total authorization of £2,860,992 which covered all the succeeding voyages of those steamers. At the same time the UK Treasury authorized the use of £1,132,269 for the charter hire of the Swedish vessel *Anna Salen*, and this authorization was subsequently increased by £750,000 to a total of £1,882,269. In March 1949 the UK Treasury further authorized the use of £100,000 for payments for French shipping which was later increased by a further £60,000 and £250,000 to a total of £410,000. In February 1950 the UK Treasury also permitted the use of £92,258 for Italian shipping and later issued two additional permits, thus increasing this total to £711,738. In 1950 authorizations were also granted for various other shipping payments including a transfer to Japan, and payments covering Netherlands air and steamer bookings as well as for shipping disbursements in several other countries. These utilizations represented a very important measure of convertibility of the IRO's sterling assets, as they extended the range of utilization of the IRO's sterling funds on an almost world-wide basis excluding only the dollar area itself.

Until the latter part of 1949, the IRO's transfers covering the needs of its missions and offices in the various countries outside the sterling area were effected automatically by its US dollar account. Occasionally a transfer to Egypt or Palestine was attempted in terms of sterling out of the IRO's Special Resident Account in London. In such cases the IRO's bankers referred the request to the Bank of England which occasionally credited them against sterling, but at other times turned them down. In the latter part of 1949 the IRO's overall funding policy was reviewed, and the Organization decided to approach the UK Treasury to suggest a formula under which the IRO's funding requirements in areas which had relatively close ties with the UK economy could be serviced out of the Organization's Special Resident Account in London.

The method worked out by the IRO was to submit a request to the UK Treasury for blanket authorization for transfers to its missions and miscellaneous disbursements in Egypt, Ethiopia, Greece, Iran, Israel, Lebanon, Portugal, Spain, and Turkey. These transfers were made on the basis of estimates covering, in each case, three months in advance, whereupon the Organization's bankers in London could execute such transfers automatically under the appropriate Treasury reference. The UK Treasury agreed to this arrangement, and subsequently all of the IRO's mission fundings and miscellaneous disbursements in the countries above mentioned were operated as a charge against the IRO's sterling account in London instead of its dollar account. The sum total of these fundings and disbursements amounted to £357,273—a very sizeable portion of the IRO's total mission expenditures. In July 1950 the UK Treasury agreed to include the funding of its China Mission, a total of £311,706 for such transfers, which had previously been funded entirely out of dollars. And in May 1950 a similar method of funding the IRO's operations in Austria was agreed upon, and a total of approximately £1 million was transferred for that operation.

The most significant transfer facility given by the UK Treasury to the IRO in connexion with the mission funding requirements was that authorized in August 1950, when the UK Treasury agreed with Sir Arthur Rucker, Deputy Director General of the IRO, to permit utilization of £1 million from the IRO's Resident Account for conversion into Italian lire, in which the IRO had a sizeable deficit position and for which it had never been able to utilize any other currency except dollars. The Italian Government, because of its long position in sterling, was not at first receptive to this suggestion, and it took all the persuasive efforts of the Deputy Director General in personal negotiations in Rome to induce the Italian Government to accept the sterling and to credit the IRO account with the equivalent in lire. The effect of this transaction—equivalent to a conversion to US dollars—was a direct saving to the IRO of $3 million in US exchange.

When, at the end of 1950, the IRO reviewed its overall funding position, it found that the sterling surplus which had been expected at the end of operations was considerably decreased. A further review of the sterling situation at the end of January 1951 showed that the estimated surplus was reduced to the equivalent of approximately $900,000. In the end, the IRO finished with no sterling surplus. Co-operation between the UK Treasury and the Organization brought about this result.[1]

---

[1] 'Throughout our relationship with the United Kingdom Government we have always had their utmost cooperation in the latitude given to us for our non-convertible sterling disbursements. We have supplied on various occasions to governments out of this account in the form of Swedish, Norwegian and French sterling in very considerable amounts to cover shipping contracts and, in some cases

It is appropriate to mention here the loan amounting to £1 million granted to the UN Agency for Relief of Palestine Refugees (UNRPR), which was made in response to a request by the Secretary General of the UN received in late 1949, and the terms of which were set forth in an agreement concluded between the IRO and the UNRPR on 19 January 1950. After the granting of the loan, and following negotiations between the Director General and the UN, the repayment of the loan was postponed on several occasions, and it was eventually agreed that the final refund would be made on 1 October 1951. Since this was later than the date originally anticipated, it caused the Organization to be temporarily short of sterling resources. However, to tide over this period, an agreement was made with the UK Treasury whereby US dollars were converted to sterling on the understanding that these funds would be reconverted to dollars when the Organization's sterling position was once again more fluid. The rights of reconversion were limited to a maximum sum of £1 million.

As in the case of the contributions of the UK, Australia, and New Zealand, the contributions of Belgium, Luxembourg, France, and Italy were made available to the IRO by credits in the respective currencies to the IRO bank accounts in these countries. Since the IRO had a slight deficit in Belgian and Luxembourg francs throughout its operations, and a very substantial deficit in Italian lire from the very beginning, the utilization of these contributions presented no problem. In the case of France, the IRO originally estimated with a considerable French franc surplus. In the end, however, the IRO was short of French francs as the result of an agreement reached with the French Government providing for the care of a considerable number of residual IRO cases. This had meant a charge of several million dollars to the IRO, and brought about complete absorption of the French contribution plus additional payments to the French Government which for the most part were paid out of the Organization's sterling holdings in London.

The surplus position which the IRO showed in the contributions of Denmark, the Netherlands, and Norway during the first three years of its operations changed at the very end, when the Organization succeeded in working out present transfer arrangements with these governments under which the full amounts of the estimated surpluses in their currencies were utilized internally for the procurement of goods and services. An outstanding example of co-operation in the solving of the funding problems of the IRO was the contribution of Norway; this was absorbed entirely through the transfer of funds to other currencies, and through the admittance to Norway of 'hard core' refugees, such as the blind, aged people, and TB patients.

In the IRO's negotiations with the Icelandic Government with regard to its contributions it was agreed that Iceland would make its contribution available in kind. Except for a small amount which was paid to the IRO in US dollars in the early days of the IRO, the contribution was made available by the delivery of cod liver oil which the IRO succeeded in transferring to another international agency against payment in US dollars. This operation resulted in an exchange loss due to a conversion basis used by the Icelandic Government which differed from that originally adopted by the

procurements, and we also obtained very liberal availments of various non-dollar currencies required for funding out missions. We are deeply indebted to them for their kind consideration of our problems and for their favours in granting necessary exchange conversions to the limit of their ability.' Report, Director of Financial Operations, Comptroller's Office to Director General, 24 Feb. 1950.

IRO. There was also an additional loss due to the difference between the value of the cod liver oil as determined by the Icelandic Government and the price realized by the IRO.

The only contributions not collected and used by the IRO during its lifetime were an insignificant part of the Guatemalan contribution and a large part of the contribution of China.[1] The percentage of the collection of contributions was creditably high; the IRO lost only 2 per cent. of its contributions by unavoidable default of its members. This excellent record was due, first, to the goodwill of the member governments, and secondly, to the fact that the IRO was an operational organization and not purely an administrative one: it had a diversity of use for all available funds. The US, through the Marshall Plan or by other means, and the European Payments Union, have helped to reconstruct and to rehabilitate the war-shattered economy of Europe, thus making it possible for IRO's members themselves to participate extensively in the financial contributions of IRO, or to help solve the difficult problem involved in the use and convertibility of IRO's funds.

Financial control and reporting

To administer the funds of IRO a financial administration was set up to supervise expenditure in thirty-eight different currencies by twenty-five principal offices and numerous sub-offices throughout Europe, the Western Hemisphere, China, the Middle East, and African territories. Auditing and accounting procedures were adopted to ensure prompt production of financial data, expedite operational planning, and render it flexible to meet the varying needs of a changing programme.

Advice in regard to allotments was given to headquarters in Geneva by field officers who made quarterly estimates of expenditures. Their requirements were reviewed, and if approved, allotments subsequently made. No subsequent commitments were undertaken unless they were cleared with the Comptroller's Department after due regard to the financial position of the Organization as a whole. Monthly expenditure reports received from the field were consolidated by headquarters which issued quarterly statements. Auditing was performed by an international firm of accountants and usually completed and presented two months after the end of the fiscal year.

The large sums at the disposal of the Organization required more than auditorial control. Control was in fact established not only by the overriding powers of the Executive Committee and the General Council, the meetings of which were attended by financial experts from several governments, but also by the regular scrutiny of the parliaments of the contributing countries. Every yearly appropriation gave rise to a discussion of the IRO programme which offered an opportunity for making its work known to the law-makers and the general public. The US Congress made intensive inquiries through several Congressional committees and was supplied, through the

[1] The status of the Chinese Government's contributions to the IRO was well reflected in the following footnote which appeared in the IRO's contribution statements for the financial year 1949–50 and for the supplementary period after 30 June 1950: 'The Chinese Government has made no contribution to the IRO since 1948–49, when they were credited with $1,316,532 in cash and services, equivalent to approximately $32\frac{1}{2}$ per cent. of their contribution for that year. Although the contribution of China has been included in this statement, it has not been taken into the resources available to the Organization for expenditure subsequent to 1948–49.'

Department of State, with special budgetary analyses. Inside the governments of other member countries this control was further strengthened by the appointment of special staff units, or committees, which dealt, in close co-operation with the respective treasuries,[1] with the affairs of international organizations. Budgetary control was thus exercised by the national legislators, and this was an advantage to the Organization. The British delegate had remarked in the UN Special Committee on Refugees and Displaced Persons that national legislators would be more disposed to allocate funds when they could be more definitely assured that the utilization of funds would be strictly supervised.[2] The delegates of the governments to the General Council were very much interested in the improvement of the presentation of finances and in good financial management in view of the fact that they had to convince their legislators about the need and justifiable use of the money before appropriations were made. Basic policy and decisions of the General Council depended on a timely and concise presentation of the financial resources. In April 1949 the US delegate expressed the wish that the financial statements be presented in a clearer and more comprehensive manner. The Executive Committee and the financial experts of the General Council were aiming at a simplified and clearer method of financial reporting which would enable 'the average delegate to see at a glance the actual financial position of the Organization on any specified date'.[3] The Executive Committee appointed a sub-committee consisting of representatives of Australia, France, the UK, and the US to discuss with representatives of the Director General and of the external auditors the possibility of making changes in the financial reports which would ensure quarterly an up-to-date picture of the exact financial position of IRO. The main concern of the sub-committee was that funds committed for goods or services were not shown in the accounts until payment was made or until the goods or services had actually been received. To meet the needs of the delegates of the General Council in representing the financial situation to their parliaments, the sub-committee suggested that a new form of statement of 'resources and application thereof' should be drawn up showing clearly the resources of the Organization and the obligations to be met, and the expenditures projected for the remaining period of the financial year. This statement, in addition to the annual balance-sheet, which covered only funds already spent, would show the actual financial position of the Organization at a glance. Furthermore, while recognizing that the terms of reference of the external auditors required an audited statement of assets and liabilities only once a year, the sub-committee was anxious that member governments should have a full picture of the financial position of the Organization as frequently as possible. Accordingly it was decided that the Director General should submit to member governments, at an early date, an unaudited financial statement covering the period 1 July to 31 December 1949 and thereafter a quarterly report including all essential figures except currency charts. It was also suggested that the Director General should maintain a continuing review of all contracts for supplies and other commitments of the Organization, so that prompt cancellation or other appropriate

[1] Report of the Joint Enquiry of the International Institute of Administrative Sciences and UNESCO, Brussels, 1951.
[2] UN, Committee on Finances of the IRO, *Summary Records*, 25 May 1946.
[3] GC/163/Rev. 1, Report on the Fifth Session of the General Council, p. 15.

action might be taken to avoid an accumulation of supplies and services. These proposals were unanimously adopted by the General Council at its Fifth Session.[1]

At its Sixth Session, held in October 1950, the General Council noted its satisfaction that a complete, readable, and satisfactory financial report had been achieved by the Administration and external auditors, and that substantial progress had been made in controlling and reducing the inventory of supplies and in disposing of items considered surplus to operations.

Mandatory budget for the care and maintenance of displaced persons

The budgeted expenditures from the contributions of member governments were not the only resources of IRO. In addition, the countries of resettlement bore the expense of the reception of refugees by the local governments or communities; and every country in which refugees and displaced persons were living when the Second World War came to an end contributed directly to their survival by providing goods, services, or money.

The question of Germany's participation in the problem had been raised when the Constitution of IRO was being drafted. There were two contending points of view. On the one hand, it was considered that as Nazi Germany had been the promoter of the war and of the deportation of displaced persons, the German people had a political and moral obligation to contribute to the limit of its ability to their re-establishment and to bear the cost of their upkeep. On the other hand, it was argued that such a decision embodied in the Constitution of IRO would be tantamount to imposing reparations on Germany, and this was a matter for the decision of the final peace treaty rather than a matter exclusively relating to refugees. The latter opinion prevailed, and, in signing the Constitution, governments only recognized that Germany and Japan should bear certain expenses of repatriation.

German opinion also was divided.[2] But when Germany, through its Federal and *Laender* governments, came to decide the financial burden to be borne, responsibility was accepted; sums for the financial support of the refugees were voted and liberal legal arrangements were made for those refugees who remained in Germany.

The legal framework for the support of the refugees from German funds was Law No. 2, promulgated by the Allied Control Council for Germany in 1945. It provided that the German authorities and the German people had to ensure the care and maintenance of persons who were not German citizens and to safeguard their property. The agreements, concluded two years later, between IRO and the occupation authorities, determined the scope and cost of all support—financial and logistic—carried by the German economy.[3]

The Deutschmark funds were drawn from the German economy through the 'Mandatory Budget for the Care and Maintenance of Displaced Persons'. 'The DM budget was a EUCOM responsibility, along with all other Army budgets', and 'the

[1] Res. No. 65; cf. GC/163/Rev. 1, op. cit., pp. 14–16. For Report of the Sub-committee on Methods of Accounting, GC/157, 21 Mar. 1950.
[2] Institut für Besatzungsfragen, *Sechs Jahre Besatzungslasten*, Tübingen, 1951, p. 197; and *Das DP Problem*, Tübingen, 1950, pp. 2 and 3. Cf. US, 80th Congress, First Session, Hearings before Special Sub-committee on HJ Res. 207, 15 May 1947, p. 27.
[3] See Chapter VII, Co-operation of Governments, pp. 128 f., and Appendix II (b).

final responsibility was in the hands of the military post budget and fiscal officers'.[1] The full story of the utilization of means derived from the German economy for the support of the refugee programme can only be given on the basis of the records of the governments of the three Western Powers which are not yet available.[2]

Reparations

Article 8, Part I, of the Final Act of the Paris Conference on Reparation, signed in January 1946 by eighteen Allied governments whose reparation claims were to be met, in part, from appropriate German external assets, allocated three sources of assets for rehabilitation and resettlement of limited categories of non-repatriable victims of German action—persons who stood in dire need of aid to promote their rehabilitation but were ' . . . unable to claim the assistance of any Government receiving reparation from Germany'.[3] These assets were: (1) $25 million from German assets in neutral countries;[4] (2) 'non-monetary gold' uncovered by Allied forces in Germany[5] (i.e. unidentifiable looted jewelry, silverplate, rugs, &c.); and (3) 'heirless assets'[6]—assets in neutral countries of Nazi victims who died and left no heirs.

The Paris Conference established the broad programme and directed five governments (US, UK, France, Czechoslovakia, Yugoslavia) to work out a specific plan, in consultation with the Intergovernmental Committee on Refugees, to accomplish the objectives. Thereafter, the designated governments adopted a plan embodied in the Five-Power Agreement of 14 June 1946[7] and in the Letter of Instruction[8] to the Director of the IGCR, Sir Herbert Emerson. This Agreement (1) allocated 90 per cent. of the $25 million and of the proceeds of liquidation of 'non-monetary gold', together with 95 per cent. of 'heirless assets', for assistance to Jewish victims, in recognition of the overwhelming preponderance of Jews among the victims who were unable to claim assistance of any government receiving reparation from Germany;[9] and 10 per cent. (with 5 per cent. of 'heirless assets') for assistance to non-Jewish German and Austrian victims; (2) placed primary responsibility for rehabilitation and resettlement assistance upon operating voluntary agencies; (3) designated the AJDC and the JAFP to receive funds to assist Jewish victims and empowered the Director of IGCR and his successors to select appropriate voluntary agencies to administer funds for assistance to non-Jewish eligibles; (4) placed

---

[1] Minutes of Joint Meeting of IRO the US European Command, and the German bizonal authorities, 17 Jan. 1950.

[2] In the US zone of Germany the IRO spent approximately $153 million from 1 July 1947 to the end of Mar. 1952, including the transportation costs from Germany of those refugees who had been in the US zone and had left to be resettled. During the same period IRO administered DM funds from the German economy exceeding 572 million DM (equivalent to approximately $136,500,000). Besides, before the 1948 currency reform, IRO apportioned additional sums in Reichsmarks; it is estimated that the DM equivalent of these Reichsmarks would be about 200 million DM ($47,600,000). (Cf. Report to the US HICOG on the IRO, US Zone of Germany, 22 Oct. 1951, p. 18, and Annex I, p. 3.)   [3] Preamble to Article 8, Part I, Final Act of Paris Conference on Reparation.

[4] Final Act of Paris Conference on Reparation, Part I, Art. 8.

[5] Ibid., Article 8 (A).   [6] Ibid., Article 8 (C).

[7] Agreement on a Plan for Allocation of a Reparation Share to Non-Repatriable Victims of German Action, generally referred to as the Five-Power Agreement.

[8] Letter of Instruction Transmitted by the Government of France on Behalf of the Signatories to the Five-Power Agreement, dated Paris, 21 June 1946, incorporated by reference in the basic Agreement. It is considered an integral part of the Agreement.

[9] Paragraph A, Five-Power Agreement.

responsibility upon the Director of IGCR and his successors to approve specific projects of the voluntary agencies prior to payment of funds; and (5) imposed general supervisory responsibilities of the programme upon the Director of IGCR and provided for transfer of the responsibilities to the Director General of IRO.[1]

The first payment of 50 million Swedish kronor ($12½ million) was received by the Executive Secretary of PCIRO in July 1947.[2] One year later 20 million Swiss francs were collected from Switzerland,[3] making a total of $17,151,163 received and disbursed by the Directors General of IRO, from the first source of assets, during IRO's lifetime. To implement approved projects, the funds were paid in the agreed proportions to the designated Jewish agencies and to other voluntary agencies selected by the Directors General of IRO, including the NCWC, CWS, ISS, and others.

Specialized IRO staff collected and assorted 'non-monetary gold' found mainly in the US occupation zones.[4] Over $3 million was realized from proceeds of liquidation[5] through the efforts of a group of New York businessmen, headed by Colonel Ray C. Kramer, who volunteered their services in a 'Merchandizing Advisory Committee' and who assisted IRO personnel in best disposing of the property.[6]

The third source of funds—'heirless assets' in neutral countries—did not materialize. None of the neutrals made such funds available.[7]

This programme of special assistance to victims of German action in limited categories was not part of IRO's general programme. It was not subject to direction by the IRO General Council but was administered by the Directors General of IRO as a trust, under specific terms and for limited purposes. The funds accruing to this programme, therefore, were not part of IRO's general budget and did not affect the contributions of member countries to IRO.[8]

Over $7½ million was still due to be paid to the $25 million fund from German assets in neutral countries when IRO liquidated. Fully appreciating the technical aspects and difficulties of the programme, and anxious to implement it in full, Mr. J. Donald Kingsley agreed to continue as its Liquidating Trustee, thereby assuring continuity of a programme which has contributed materially to the rehabilitation of thousands of persecutees. A separate and complete report of all phases of this programme will be published by Mr. Kingsley and his Deputy Trustee and Counsel, Mr. Abba P. Schwartz, when the balance of the $25 million allocation is received and the Trustee's final report is submitted to the Government of France, representative of the Five Powers, to whom Mr. Kingsley remains responsible.

[1] Administration of the programme passed to the Executive Secretary of PCIRO on 1 July 1947 and subsequently to the Director General of IRO.
[2] PCIRO Res. PREP/111; PCIRO press release No. 255, 23 July 1947.
[3] Interim Progress Report of Director General, IRO, for Period 1 July 1947–30 Sep., 1948, pp. 8–9; Rapport du Conseil Fédéral à l'Assemblée Fédérale sur l'execution de l'accord conclu à Washington le 25 mai 1946 (du 13 avril 1949), pp. 10–11; IRO press release No. 334, 24 July 1948.
[4] See PCIRO Res. PREP/134, Oct. 1947; see also Joint Chiefs of Staff Directive addressed to Commanding Generals, United States Forces, Austria, Nov. 1946, reprinted in Interim Progress Report of Director General, IRO, for period 1 July 1947–30 Sept. 1948.
[5] Interim Report, op. cit., supra, note 11, at 9 et seq.
[6] Annual Progress Report, Director General, IRO 64 (1 July 1949–30 June 1950).
[7] See Interim Report, op. cit., supra, note 11, at 15; Report of the Executive Secretary (PCIRO) on the status of the Organization and its Activities during the First Three Months, Doc. PREP/130, Oct. 1947; PCIRO Res. PREP/112, July 1947.
[8] See PCIRO Memorandum, PREP/6, 13 Feb. 1947.

It seems appropriate at this juncture to review the background of the IRO's endeavours on behalf of displaced persons in Germany, for some people tend to overlook the essential basis of this programme. The Director General outlined this policy on 28 September 1950 to the Allied High Commission at a discussion of the problems relating to the continued operation of IRO in Germany after the Organization had transferred the responsibility for the care and maintenance of the refugees to the German authorities.

'The problem of displaced persons [he pointed out] was created by the Germans. The German people are morally and materially responsible . . . the humanitarian challenge so created has met with the collective response of seventeen Western nations —and China—who have contributed more than $500,000,000 to the solution of this grave problem through the IRO. At no time did they propose to bear this heavy burden without an equitable measure of support from the German economy. . . . The pooled resources of the Allied governments plus those justly contributed by Germany have enabled IRO to accomplish the unprecedented task . . . of re-establishing outside Germany 600,000 displaced persons who otherwise would inevitably have remained a permanent charge on the German economy, and a continued burden of heavy proportions on German housing. In the remaining period of IRO activities—and with the substantial financial support of the Western Governments—IRO hopes to remove 175,000 more persons from Germany, thus making a significant contribution to the solution of the onerous problems confronting the German Federal and *Laender* Governments. I have stressed this, because it might appear to those who must deal with the Germans on the mandatory budget that IRO represents a charge or burden on the German economy. Viewed in its true perspective, however, IRO is an instrument through which the Western Powers have, in fact, made an incalculable contribution toward the solution of the German problem of over-population. It can, with continued support, achieve more. . . .'

This point of view, expressed by the Director General of the IRO, should be borne in mind when considering further aspects of IRO's activities in Germany. While the Germans paid for the care and maintenance of the displaced persons in Germany, in 1948, IRO's blocked DM accounts were established. An employed displaced person was required to make reimbursement for the cost of his care. The British zone first introduced this practice by an order of 10 May 1948. The weekly contributions varied from 3 to 7 DM for each member of a family. In the US zone a similar regulation was enforced on 10 August 1948, providing that employed displaced persons should contribute 70 DM a month. Fifty DM a month of this contribution were refunded to the German economy, and 20 DM were retained by the IRO in a so-called Blocked DM Account. The regulation of 1 October 1948 in the French zone stipulated that payments would range from 25 to 70 DM monthly for displaced persons with free lodging, and between 15 and 50 DM for those who paid for their lodgings. The amounts kept were paid into an account of the DP Service and were used for the care and maintenance of displaced persons.

In order fully to understand the fiscal aspects of the German mandatory budget it should be borne in mind that employed refugees paid taxes to the German Treasury; that the mandatory budget, whatever its size, saved the German Treasury expense on social assistance, health schemes, education, community activities, welfare, and similar services; and that the payments for maintenance made by employed refugees during

IRO's time in the US zone probably amounted to over 35 million DM, and in the British zone to over 30 million DM. From the point of view of Germany's national economy it should be emphasized that little of the money spent by the German Treasury was exported by IRO or the emigrating refugees. This fact is indicated by an example showing the apportioning of the German expenditure in Württemberg-Hohenzollern, where 25 per cent. were allocated for wages, 41 per cent. for lodging, and 34 per cent. for food.[1] The severe customs check on the export of any goods forestalled the buying of goods with savings from wages; moreover, the German currency was legally non-transferable.

There is conclusive evidence that throughout IRO's life, and especially after the year 1949, a fair amount of the funds listed as expenditures for lodging was devoted to fundamental improvements in the housing of refugees, a development from which the German economy benefited permanently. The housing programme was substantially helped by imports of materials not available in the German economy and paid for from the mandatory budget. In the financial year 1949–50, for example, imports of this kind cost the IRO budget $1,143,000.

For Germany the major credit item was, however, the so-called Food Credit. IRO imported and turned over to the German authorities dollar-procured foodstuffs to replace food supplied from indigenous production over and above the average amounts provided by the German economy for the German population. The latter amounts were furnished free from the German economy under the terms of the Byrnes–Bevin Agreement; the supplementary amounts were to bring the refugees' diet up to the level considered desirable by the IRO. Purchases had to be made by the IRO in advance when German production could only be estimated. As a result of inevitable miscalculations of German production the IRO actually imported and turned over to the German economy more food than this economy produced for IRO's refugees by way of supplements to the free supplies. This excess resulted in the Food Credit which at one time in IRO's estimate exceeded $7 million. After discussions with the Allied High Commission for Germany and the German Federal Government, 12 million DM were credited to the IRO in liquidation. This sum could not be transferred abroad; it served to support the refugees remaining in Germany.

A similar use was made of the Blocked DM Account in the US zone which amounted at its peak to over 14 million DM. Part of this sum was spent by IRO to meet those expenses in Germany which could not be covered by the normal DM budget, such as fees for documentation, translations, the transportation of luggage in connexion with resettlement, equipment for vocational and rehabilitation programmes, and unusual administrative expenses. The principal use of the Blocked DM Account, however (more than 12 million DM), was for the construction and furnishing of institutions for the 'hard core'. These funds were also used to establish the DP Fund in the Expellee Bank and for grants to voluntary societies.[2]

For all the countries sharing the responsibilities for the financial direction of IRO

[1] *Sechs Jahre Besatzungslasten*, op. cit., p. 209.
[2] See Chapter XXII, Local Settlement, p. 477, and Report to the US HICOG on the IRO, op. cit., p. 19, and Annex IX: IRO Blocked DM Account as of 31 Aug. 1951.

and for the general financing of the refugee problem, the IRO budget was a clearing house providing for the equalization of burdens. Germany and Austria benefited politically and economically by the removal of the majority of refugees from their territories. In other European countries, which had contributed heavily to the IRO's budget, the financial burden involved in the care of refugees was somewhat lightened by the IRO's expenditures within their territories or for the purchase of their services. The overseas countries, by permitting immigration, contributed to the solution of a problem international in scope and in nature.

ANNEX 5

Statement of contributions made by member governments

Member governments	*Accumulated totals* *1 July 1947 to 7 Feb. 1952* *Contributions due and received*
	$
Australia	9,194,156
Belgium	5,262,255
Canada .	18,164,674
China .	13,591,513
Denmark	2,491,948
Dominican Republic	209,826
France .	21,652,462
Guatemala	209,826
Iceland .	75,272
Italy .	8,290,709
Luxembourg .	147,002
Netherlands .	4,766,750
New Zealand .	2,299,784
Norway.	2,299,784
Switzerland .	4,033,698
United Kingdom	76,218,086
United States.	237,116,355
Venezuela	843,195
TOTAL CONTRIBUTIONS DUE	406,867,295
Less total contributions unpaid .	8,270,493*
TOTAL CONTRIBUTIONS RECEIVED	$398,596,802

* Total China contribution unpaid   8,210,469
     Total Guatemala contribution unpaid   60,024

                    $8,270,493

ANNEX 6

Contributions from UNRRA and IGCR to the IRO

		$	$
UNRRA			

1. Contributions in cash:

    (*a*) For displaced persons operations in the Far East and Western Hemisphere.   1,000,000

    (*b*) Balance to complete the above grant .   .   .   603,839

    (*c*) Grant for supplementary feeding of children and employment of additional welfare staff   2,000,000

                                            3,603,839

    Claims raised against IRO.   1,367,646

                                            2,236,193

2. Transfer of supplies and equipment for displaced persons on a non-reimbursable basis:

    (*a*) Services: salaries and expenses of personnel made available without charge   4,587

    (*b*) Supplies and equipment transferred at appraised values based upon actual or estimated cost★   12,899,761

                                            12,904,348

        TOTAL $15,140,541

IGCR

1. Residual IGCR assets; free gifts from IGCR member governments.   37,657

2. Portion of IGCR residual assets; free gifts from IGCR member governments   1,486

3. IGCR surplus funds   39,006

4. Inventory values on the USATS (approx.) .   .   .   321,000

5. Operating reserve on the USATS   118,177

        TOTAL $517,326

★ Transfer of supplies and equipment on a non-reimbursable basis valued by UNRRA at $12,904,348, applied on the balance-sheets of IRO financial statements as equipment on hand at a nominal value of $1.

ANNEX 7

Expenditure on care and maintenance and ratio of total expenditure
(US dollars)

	Period			Supplementary period
	1947–8	*1948–9*	*1949–50*	
Expenditure	$42,476,834	$43,227,193	$25,581,481	$17,388,210★
Per cent. of total expenditure in the period	57%	33%	21·5%	16·3%

★ Expenditure on 'hard core' settlement is excluded.

ANNEX 8

Planned and Actual Expenditures (US dollars)

Item	1947-8 — Approved plan of expenditure PREP/159 corrected	1947-8 — Actual expenditure GC/9	1948-9 — Approved plan of expenditure GC/63 Rev. I	1948-9 — Actual expenditure GC/105	1949-50 — Approved plan of expenditure GC/138	1949-50 — Actual expenditure GC/169	1950-2 — Approved plan of expenditure G/265	1950-2 — Actual expenditure IRO/FIN/107
Administrative Budget	3,476,540	3,475,306	4,797,800	4,299,985	4,500,000	4,489,730	5,444,179	5,437,803
General Council	100,000	98,666	159,000	60,640	100,000	...	...	...
Headquarters	1,457,780	1,457,780	3,356,062	3,186,374	2,768,831	...	...	...
Other offices	1,918,860	1,918,860	1,221,422	1,052,971	803,010	...	...	...
Reserve			70,316		828,159	...	...	...
OPERATIONAL BUDGET—PART I								
Personnel and establishment	11,823,613	11,370,714	13,700,699	13,482,953	15,173,075	15,468,431	12,887,656	12,877,268
Purchase and maintenance of vehicles	3,760,380	2,976,806	4,639,463	3,882,608	2,685,175	1,645,615	1,025,000	1,010,255
Health, care and maintenance	75,281,927	42,476,834	50,417,748	43,227,193	41,982,465	28,146,399	33,924,542	33,575,709
1. Direct care	56,177,177	28,245,311	33,632,246	27,861,093	16,317,819	11,352,650	11,203,659	11,010,375
2. Medical care	966,347	217,078	1,525,600	1,236,793	1,959,000	1,417,125	1,242,462	1,110,260
3. Vocational training	750,000	197,235	1,500,000	1,297,854	600,000	506,475	55,153	55,156
4. Employment programme								
5. Rehabilitation training								
6. Cash assistance	3,094,947	2,581,818	850,000	4,052,610	700,000	402,525	113,816	112,973
7. Per capita costs	14,293,456	10,952,392	4,146,567	8,398,102	5,035,599	4,794,408		
8. Community organization and welfare			8,113,335	380,741	6,770,047	6,631,883	1,063,095	1,063,049
9. Voluntary societies special projects			650,000		400,000	289,895		
10. Inter-camp movements					100,000	52,678		
11. Care of residual cases					100,000	41,507	16,536,332	16,513,911
12. Special projects					10,000,000	2,564,918		
13. Reimbursement to governments						92,395	3,710,025	3,710,025
Repatriation	3,850,930	1,483,057	997,195	668,332	646,728	233,666	86,945	82,945
Resettlement	20,749,830	13,844,765	79,465,750	65,012,461	77,005,243	67,743,120	48,287,118	48,283,652
1. Transportation†			57,057,000	43,692,456	67,523,013	61,270,072	44,725,986	44,851,529*
2. Other mass resettlement costs			1,388,750	1,990,860	2,346,305	2,049,980	2,639,772	2,511,753
3. Individual resettlement costs			10,020,000	8,935,069	5,718,000	3,597,427		
4. Migration to Israel			9,000,000	9,000,000	1,417,925	553,640	696,360	696,360
5. Shanghai emergency move								
6. Refugee service committee			2,000,000	1,394,076		280,000	225,000	224,010
7. Special projects								
Local re-establishment loans	145,000	48,358	150,000	133,741	150,000	97,513		
Contingency reserve			858,403	1,460,203	3,089,895	1,578,423		
1. Programme reserves			858,403	766,332	1,324,851	79,508		
2. Losses on exchange				693,871	1,765,044	1,498,915	35,000	(7,510)
TOTAL OPERATIONAL—PART I	115,611,680	72,200,534	150,229,258	127,867,491	140,732,581	114,912,167	96,246,261	95,822,319
Total Admin. and Op. Part I	119,088,320	75,675,840	155,027,058	132,167,476	145,232,581	119,401,897	101,690,440	101,260,122
Large-scale resettlement, Op. Part II			48,712		199,537			
GRAND TOTAL	$119,088,320	$75,675,840	$155,075,770	$132,167,476	$145,432,118	$119,401,897	$101,690,440	$101,260,122

* This amount is made up as follows: (a) Costs of ships sublet ... 1,806,573   (b) Transportation costs of IRO refugees ... 43,044,956   = 44,851,529

† Including cost of transporting refugees from E. Africa and the Middle East to Italian and other European ports and forwarding immigrants from S. American ports ...

ANNEX 9

Major items of IRO's expenditure (US dollars)

	Period 1947–8 GC/9	Period 1948–9 GC/105	Period 1949–50 GC/138	Period 1950–2 (28·2) FIN/107	Total of section and grand total
	$	$	$	$	$
Administrative Expenses	3,475,306	4,299,985	4,489,730	5,437,803	17,702,824
Operational Expenses:					
1. Personnel and establishment	11,370,714	13,482,953	15,468,431	12,877,268	53,199,366
2. Purchase and maintenance of vehicles	2,976,806	3,882,608	1,645,615	1,010,255	9,515,284
3. Health, care, and maintenance	42,476,834	43,227,193	28,146,399	33,575,709	147,426,135
4. Repatriation	1,483,057	668,332	233,666	82,945	2,468,000
5. Resettlement	13,844,765	65,012,461	67,742,120	48,283,652	194,882,998
6. Re-establishment loans	48,358	133,741	97,513	..	279,612
7. Losses on exchange (gain on exchange of currencies)*	..	693,871	1,498,915	(7,510)*	2,185,276
8. Programme reserves	..	766,332	79,508	..	845,840
Operational totals	72,200,534	127,867,491	114,912,167	95,822,319	410,802,511
TOTAL OF PERIODS AND GRAND TOTAL	$75,675,840	$132,167,476	$119,401,897	$101,260,122	$428,505,335

ANNEX 10

Analysis of miscellaneous income (US dollars)

	1947–8	1948–9	1949–50	1950–2	Total
	$	$	$	$	
I. Funds reported as miscellaneous income derived from expenditures made from contributions:					
1. Reimbursements on resettlement:					
Australian reimbursement .	358,930	1,608,952	1,763,610	296,314	
Close relatives . . .	1,107,511	1,960,357	475,228	270,016	
Other sponsors* . .	30,945	175,342	128,418	168,872	
Refunds and sublet shipping .	..	..	5,309,844	3,598,551	
Refunds of New Zealand Government . . .	..	..	..	90,832	
					17,343,722
2. Reduction of liabilities, &c.:					
From UNRRA for services rendered	31,212	..	..	..	
Polish family centre revenue .	..	131,003	..	..	
Collection of messing charges and surplus† . . .	..	12,214	62,335	402,711	
Settlement of liabilities . .	..	2,714,505	1,890,378	1,539,705	
Miscellaneous . . .	..	8,243	104,594	..	
					6,896,900
3. Sale of IRO property, PX and amenity supplies and clothing:	147,665	..	..	..	
Stamps of eligibility Certificates	20,108	12,896	3,671	..	
Motor and transport supplies	61,805	269,612	636,137	3,489,012	
Other surplus items . .	..	58,580	65,820	..	
Credits for supplies removed from de-commissioned US navy ships . . .	..	..	..	1,488,098	
					6,253,404
4. Refund on loans . . .	79,567	48,265	41,302	5,741	174,875
5. DM blocked account‡ . .	..	..	..	2,825,365	2,825,365
					33,494,266
II. Funds derived from sources other than government contributions:					
1. UNRRA and IGCR funds:§					
Grants under UNRRA agreement	1,500,000	..	..	..	
Adjustment under UNRRA agreement . . .	103,839	632,354	..	..	
Residual IGCR assets . .	37,657	1,486	..	..	
IGCR surplus funds . .	..	39,006	..	..	
					2,314,342
2. Donations and gifts:					
Gifts for care and maintenance	1,523	..	..	..	
Donations	8,091	11,816	14,047	266,416	
					301,893
3. Proceeds of investment of funds including bank interest . .	70,627	197,442	268,677	746,378	1,283,124
					3,899,359
III. Funds derived from donations and gifts by governments:					
1. Swiss gift	61,772‖	2,431‖	..	..	
2. Belgian gift	..	50,000‖	..	..	
3. Brazilian gift . . .	..	85,333‖	..	..	
4. Brazilian donation . .	..	655,277	..	..	
5. Belgian students fund . .	..	..	100,000	..	
					954,813
GRAND TOTAL . . .	$3,621,252	$8,675,114	$10,864,061	$15,188,011	$38,348,438

* Including *ex gratia* contribution of Swiss Government to emigration from that country.
† Revolving fund for staff supplies.
‡ Contribution paid by refugees in employment towards their care and maintenance.
§ Details of contributions from UNRRA and IGCR, including both cash and transfers of supplies and equipment are given in Annex 6, p. 123.
‖ These amounts, totalling $199,536, have been transferred to Operational Budget—Part II, large-scale resettlement.

CHAPTER VII

CO-OPERATION OF GOVERNMENTS

THE problem of refugees has been of international and national concern. What share of responsibility should be assumed by the international organization, and what share by the national governments with refugees on their territories, was, therefore, a matter for negotiation between the governments and the IRO. The IRO was established to assist, with international funds, intergovernmental facilities, and staff, those governments which, as a result of the war, were overburdened by the presence of refugees and displaced persons on their territory.

The intention behind the creation of the IRO was not solely to relieve the national governments of their responsibilities, but to cope with a situation which had out-grown national jurisdiction and facilities, and to solve this problem in such a way as to leave it manageable at the national level. The success of IRO, therefore, depended not only on the support given by the member governments through the policy-making bodies, the General Council and the Executive, and their financial con-tributions to the IRO; it was equally important that the delegates to the General Council and the Administration should establish co-operation and understanding with the parliaments and the executive branches of those countries which had refugees on their territory; it was also essential to conclude agreements and secure help from those governments who were not members of the Organization, but might be concerned with the problem because they were countries of origin, or of first refuge or permanent residence.

It can be said at the outset that the very close and fruitful co-operation which developed between the IRO and the member governments, on the one hand, and between the IRO and the governments of the countries of first refuge and permanent resettlement, on the other, contributed decisively to the positive results achieved by IRO in its four and a half years of operation. While the contribution of the former was a question of policy and administration of the IRO (discussed in the preceding chapters), the latter was a question of agreements between the government of each respective country and the IRO, based on the policy of the governments concerned. The President of the US, in his Message to Congress in 1947, specially referred to Article 15 of the IRO Constitution, and stated that, as the Organization would not have governmental powers, it 'could in no way alter the statutes of any of its members. . . . It will be solely a service organization to aid in the solution of a common prob-lem.' At each stage of its operations IRO had to act through the governments concerned, and the scope of its authority as well as the adequacy of its instruments were conditioned by the voluntary grants made by these governments.

Article 2 of the Constitution had invested the IRO with the power 'to conduct negotiations and to conclude agreements with governments' for the purpose of carrying out its functions, such as temporary care and maintenance, repatriation, resettlement and re-establishment *sur place* as well as giving legal and political protection. Article 15 of the Constitution, in particular, stipulated that the relationship of IRO with the governments or administrations of countries in which displaced persons or refugees were located, and the conditions under which it would operate in such countries, had to be determined by agreements to be negotiated by IRO with those governments in accordance with the terms of the Constitution.

The PCIRO, at its First Part of its First Session, authorized the Executive Secretary to negotiate on the basis of these constitutional provisions with the governmental authorities of the areas where the IRO had to conduct its operations, and with the countries of resettlement. The hope of the Administration to come to some formal arrangement for repatriation did not materialize (these efforts will be dealt with in the operational chapter on repatriation).

Occupied countries

The majority of the refugees and displaced persons—80–85 per cent., who came under the mandate of the IRO on 1 July 1947—were living in the three defeated countries of central Europe. As the operations of UNRRA and IGCR had come to an end, new agreements with the Occupation Authorities in the three zones of Western Germany, with the control Powers in Austria, and with the Italian Government were most urgently needed. The ultimate authority in regard to law, order, security, and economic control in each of the occupied zones, as in other territories of first residence, rested with the military government of the Occupying Power or with the sovereign governments. The primary responsibility for the care of displaced persons was vested in the IRO, but the range of its authority was not uniform from country to country nor from zone to zone in occupied countries, and its role had to be worked out in specific agreements with the governmental authorities concerned.

Germany was jointly occupied by the armies of France, Great Britain, Soviet Russia, and the US. After SHAEF's dissolution in July 1945, Germany was governed by the military governments. The commanding generals of the four zones exercised supreme control both in the military field and as the Governor members of the Allied Control Council, with its seat in Berlin, also divided into four zones. Austria, on the other hand, the first victim of Nazi aggression, being a liberated country, had a freely elected national sovereign government though limited by the presence of the Allied Commission for Austria. It was divided into four zones of occupation, and all major governmental decisions were subject to the Quadripartite Allied Commission's approval or veto.

The agreements for the US zones of Germany and Austria were concluded after long negotiations. On 28 July 1948 the so-called IRO/CINCEUR Agreement concerning the US zone of Germany was concluded between the IRO and the Commander-in-Chief of the European Command.[1] It was prolonged by an exchange of letters between the US HICOG, and the IRO Chief of Mission in August 1949. On 12 September 1947 an interim agreement for a period of three months concerning Austria was signed between PCIRO and the US Forces in Austria (USFA); this

---

[1] For text see Appendix II (*b*), p. 661; cf. also Lucius Clay, *Decision in Germany*, New York, 1950, p. 233.

was extended by an exchange of letters between the Commanding General and the Executive Secretary of the PCIRO, until a final agreement was signed between the US High Commissioner for Austria and the IRO Chief of Mission on 11 August 1948.[1]

The agreements concerning the US zones in Germany and Austria were essentially similar. Provision was made for a close liaison between the Organization and the occupation authorities at all levels to ensure smooth functioning of the programme and the effective performance of their mutual responsibilities. The IRO's principal responsibilities were: care and maintenance of refugees and the operation of assembly centres; co-ordination and supervision of voluntary societies; determination of the eligibility of applicants for assistance by the IRO; arrangements for repatriation movements and plans for resettlement; co-operation with military government authorities in plans for employment of employable refugees.

The principal responsibilities of the occupation authorities were: the maintenance of law, order, security, and public health; provision of living accommodation, usually in assembly centres; provision of rail transport for refugee movements in the US zones; provision of food, fuel, clothing, medical supplies, and household equipment from the local economy to the extent available. When imported supplies were required to bring living conditions up to the standard determined by the Organization, the costs were borne by the Organization. In Austria the occupation authorities were to take appropriate measures under the control agreement of 28 June 1946 to assure the provision of similar accommodation and supplies by the Austrian Government to the extent available. As a result of greater stringency of the economy in Austria, the diet in that country was lower than that provided in Germany. To the extent available from the local economy, working and living accommodation were to be provided by the Austrian Government.

In addition the occupation authorities had to provide logistical support. The agreements also provided for the legal status of IRO staff and of displaced persons in the zone, as well as for the legal care and protection of displaced persons by the Organization within the framework of military-government law.

The original agreement with the British Element of the Control Commission for Germany, providing for the IRO's assumption of certain operating responsibilities hitherto performed by the British authorities, was signed on 28 June 1947; it remained the basis for operations in the British zone of Germany until a redefinition of responsibilities concerning the displaced persons operation in the British zone of Germany became effective on 1 January 1951.[2] Agreement between the British Element of the Allied Commission for Austria (responsible for the administration of the British zone of Austria) and IRO was not signed until 7 November 1947.[3] Agreements covering IRO operations in the French zones of Germany and Austria were signed on 6 September 1947.[4]

In the British and French zones, the actual operation of assembly centres and the direct care and maintenance of refugees were to be performed, not by IRO as in the

---

[1] PC/LEG/29.　　　　　　　　　　[2] For text see Appendix II (b), p. 653.
[3] PC/LEG/5.
[4] For text see Appendix II (b), pp. 603 and 605, and PC/LEG/2.

American zone, but by the occupation authorities under the supervision of IRO in accordance with the policies laid down in the IRO Constitution. The costs of such operations were to be borne by the Organization which maintained staff in the zones to supervise and check on the implementation of refugee programmes by the occupation authorities.

The British Government did not recognize the primary responsibility of IRO in the operation of displaced persons' camps in their zone, as was done by the US authorities in the US zone. This British attitude was based chiefly on the point of view that, as the displaced persons problem was of such great political and economic importance, operational responsibility should remain primarily with the Government rather than be transferred to an outside organization. British authorities had reached this particular conclusion as a result of the difficulties and anomalies they had experienced in connexion with a division of responsibility with UNRRA. They did not anticipate differences with IRO, but believed that an arrangement under which they would act as the operating agents for IRO would be more satisfactory.

From the point of view of the IRO's central administration, the method used in the US zones was more convenient; for the programme of migration for settlement required a degree of uniformity that was perhaps more easily and quickly achieved by giving directives than by initiating negotiations. In Austria, on the other hand, there was the additional burden on the occupation authorities to consult with the Austrian Government and to ensure that the IRO's policies did not conflict with the Government.

Standards were not always the same, and certain welfare programmes differed from zone to zone; the voluntary societies were used differently, and logistical support for them varied. At the same time the situations confronting the authorities in each of the three zones raised problems not shared by the other zones. The US zone was the only one linked with the Eastern world by its common frontiers with Austria and Czechoslovakia. Both the British and US zones bordered in the east on the Soviet occupational zone which had become the Eastern German Republic, while the small French zone in the west was separated from the east by the US zone which was the first place of arrival for fugitives from Soviet-controlled countries. Food conditions were better in the US zone, since it included the rural and agricultural regions left to Western Germany, after the loss of its large agricultural territory in the east to Poland and Soviet-dominated Eastern Germany, while the British zone included many destroyed cities and devastated industrial districts.

The division into separate occupation zones was greatly complicated by the huge exodus of Germans from the territories occupied by Poland, Czechoslovakia, Hungary, and Yugoslavia, in addition to those Germans who had already entered the West during the final retreat and rout of the German armies. The Control Council's plan of November 1945 provided for compulsory evacuation of $6\frac{1}{2}$ million people, bringing the figure up to 10–12 million. The Allied policy assumed that these refugees were the responsibility of the German people. The larger number of refugees, although not the responsibility of IRO, aggravated the Organization's housing, supply, and employment problems in regard to the displaced non-German refugees in camps.

The policy and work of the three governments, British, French, and US, and of the IRO, for the refugees must be regarded from the point of view of this background if the problems and difficulties with which the authorities were confronted, and the ways and means by which they approached them, are to be clearly understood. The refugees presented not only political complications, but also an economic burden for both the occupation authorities and the emergent governments of Germany and of Austria.

Politically, the existence of large groups of persons unable or unwilling to return to their own countries, of which they were critical and in some cases even hostile, was disturbing; the more so since some of these countries had common borders with Germany and Austria. The security aspect was increasingly important as the cleavage between the Western and Eastern blocs developed. Incidents occurred, sometimes affecting the local population and sometimes the refugees; in addition, there was the need to check infiltration of agents and spies in the guise of refugees. The British authorities in Austria, for instance, had to cope with a precarious situation created by the presence of Yugoslav displaced persons, since their zone bordered on Yugoslavia. The Yugoslav Government pressed for a joint effort to reach final settlement of the question of Yugoslav displaced persons and collaborators under British control. On 8 September 1947 an agreement was signed at Bled (Yugoslavia) between Marshal Tito and the British Commander-in-Chief in Austria, according to which a special refugee commission was to perform screening functions in the British zone of Austria, similar to those it had already carried out in Italy. This caused a delay of IRO's registration of refugees, although the commission's findings were later made available to the IRO, when the denunciation of the Bled Agreement brought with it the winding up of the Commission in Austria.

At the end of the war the Occupying Powers had adopted the policy of granting the displaced persons in both countries special privileges such as priority of care and protection against interference or ill-treatment by the indigenous population or authorities. In Germany, the original policy of the Supreme Commander of the Allied Expeditionary Force had been to relieve want among the UN refugees and to use all available resources for their protection against interference or ill-treatment by the German authorities or population. The German authorities had been expressly required to provide the means, as directed, for their care, shelter, maintenance, and medical attention as a matter of priority over the needs of the German population. Some refugees were not to be billeted on the German civilian population, although German billets would, when necessary, be requisitioned to provide accommodation for them.[1] Thus refugees were accorded a standard of living higher than that which they had known in prison, and received special legal protection by the Occupying Powers.

The evolution of Allied policy gradually brought refugees in most respects under the authority of the Austrian and German governments, subject to the general protection of their interests by the occupation authorities and the IRO.

During the first stage of this development, refugee nationals of any of the UN countries—generally known as displaced persons—were cut off from the German

[1] SHAEF, Administrative Memorandum No. 39, Rev. 16 Apr. 1945.

population both economically and legally; there was no need for contact unless an individual chose not to live in an assembly centre. After the monetary reform in 1948, which will be discussed later in this chapter, when German currency became of some value, there was reason for and possibility of economic contact; as a result of the monetary reform, however, when harder economic conditions prevailed for people not living in assembly centres, many applications for admission to them were received. At the same time, contact with German legal authorities became desirable in order to improve refugees' chances of migration by regularizing their personal status. Later the IRO deliberately brought refugees within the competence of German courts just as the practice of the British authorities in Austria, from 1948 on, had been to bring nearly all cases involving refugees before Austrian courts. This was part of the effort to establish normal contact between the local communities and the camps. Contact with German administrative authorities became necessary for refugees living in assembly centres after the middle of 1950 when those authorities assumed responsibility for the upkeep of such centres and all activities in them.

This was a normal process of development whereby an emergent national state assumed control of the population within its borders, so that gradually the foreigners were less sharply divided from the local population. However, in view of post-war antipathies, this development was not without difficulties. The Jews particularly, and all persons deported for forced labour during the war, felt a justifiable resentment against their former oppressors; this naturally created all manner of political and psychological complications on both sides.

The situation was handled somewhat differently by the three Western Occupying Powers. They agreed in general to help as many refugees as possible to leave Austria and Germany. While the refugees remained, they were to be assisted in so far as funds were available for their maintenance, and they were to be prepared for their departure. The British authorities early recognized that refugees were 'part and parcel of the occupation population', and that they should, therefore, have the same treatment as the indigenous population, i.e. the refugees received the same food rations as the Germans. The refugees were also asked to make a contribution in the form of work in return for what they received. The British authorities maintained that the integration of the refugees in the British zones was easier later, because this policy had built up goodwill between the indigenous population and the refugees which helped to stimulate the assimilation of those refugees who had to be integrated in the German economy when IRO's activities ceased.

The French authorities emphasized the desirability of work for refugees to keep them fit for migration. They did not favour assembly centres, and many refugees in the French zones did not live in them. The US authorities, from the beginning, kept the refugees in their own community, emphasizing the necessity for total evacuation.

In Austria, partly because of the position of the Austrian Government and partly because a higher proportion of refugees lived privately or worked outside their assembly centres, the situation did not follow the German pattern; throughout the period of IRO's work, refugees were more closely in contact with Austrian life and civil administration. Most applicants for admission to centres were persons who, falling out of seasonal employment, were threatened with eviction from their lodgings; normal residence permits were always required.

As conditions developed, the IRO's working relations with various governments, too, changed, and were no more static than were the masses of refugees. IRO's case-load was augmented as persons living outside assembly centres came within the Organization's mandate, and, in addition, new refugees, potentially within the mandate, were arriving in both countries from eastern and south-eastern Europe. Whether the exit of this latter group was controlled or clandestine, their entry into Austria and Germany was certainly illegal. For both economic and political reasons, control of entry remained officially the responsibility of the occupation authorities throughout the IRO's operation, although the local governments performed increasingly important functions. Frontier controls as well as the control of movements between zones, introduced soon after the war, were an attempt to prevent infiltration. A great deal of clandestine movement, both inter-zonal and international, however, was directed towards the US zones of Austria and Germany; the latter especially was considered the ideal stepping stone to final re-establishment. The only means of reducing the international financial commitment was by limiting admittance to assembly centres. But in view of the human needs resulting from an influx of refugees, changes in occupation policies were inevitable and commitments were assumed by the IRO—as before by UNRRA—which had not been envisaged when their agreements with the occupation authorities were concluded.

For example, a large number of Jews from Poland entered Germany in 1946. Their movement had been precipitated by the outbreak of active anti-semitism in Poland. They were admitted to UNRRA centres in spite of an earlier and contrary order by the military authorities which was based on the belief that transfers under the Potsdam Agreement would put an end to population moves.

When this influx of Jews from Poland had somewhat abated, the US Occupation Authorities in Germany issued instructions that, as from 21 April 1947, admission to US displaced persons assembly centres, as well as any other form of gratuitous assistance from the US army, would be denied to all persons who entered the US zone of Germany or the US sector of Berlin on or after that date. Exceptions were permissible only by special authority, e.g. in case of illness or injury causing extreme hardship; when heads of families could not secure adequate employment; or when applicants for admission had been accepted by representatives of the governments concerned for repatriation or resettlement. These instructions were incorporated, as an annex, in the agreement between the IRO and the US Occupation Authorities. But just as the earlier rule had to be amended because of the needs of Jewish refugees, this later one, too, had to be changed to meet the needs of the Czech refugees who left their country in 1948 after the Communist revolution.

The US Government, therefore, requested the IRO to examine the situation of Czech refugees in co-operation with the military authorities, and to consider Czech refugees in the US and British zones of occupation in Germany as eligible for assistance on the same basis as displaced persons already in camp. Furthermore, Czech voluntary societies in the US were requested to organize the most far-reaching assistance possible as soon as this could be done.

Although the influx of Czech refugees across the borders and the necessity to care for them brought about a change of policy on the part of the occupation authorities, admittance into camps was not the only solution envisaged; it was also arranged to split the commitment and to remove Czech refugees into other countries. It was felt that antipathy between Czechs and Germans was generally so strong that any large-scale absorption of Czechs into the German economy appeared neither likely nor desirable. Their stay in Germany was therefore looked upon as transitory, and several thousand Czech refugees from the US zone of Germany were transferred to Italy. This move was counter-balanced by the movement of certain refugees from Italy to Germany at the time of the first Italian post-war elections in April 1948.

Following the arrangements for the control of the reception of refugees in Germany, economic arrangements for their maintenance were made. During the year before the assumption of responsibility by IRO, economic and political developments had gradually caused occupation restrictions to be lifted, and an improvement of the general living standard of Germans and Austrians had occurred. Foremost amongst the measures taken was the conclusion, on 2 December 1946, of the agreement between the US Secretary of State and the British Foreign Secretary, known as the 'Byrnes–Bevin Agreement', on the 'Economic Fusion of the United Kingdom and United States zones in Germany'. Its aim was the achievement, before the end of 1949, of a self-sustaining economy in the two zones. It provided for the joint management and financing of the British and US zones of Germany, and the sharing of financial responsibility by Britain and the US. The first charge against German exports was to be the maintenance of the German economy, rather than payment of occupation expenses, which included the costs of maintaining the IRO's refugees. The agreement provided *inter alia* that subject to any international arrangements which might subsequently be made, the maintenance from the German economy of refugees in both occupation zones should not exceed the maintenance of German citizens from that economy, and that supplementary rations and other benefits which might be provided for displaced persons in excess of those available from German production for German citizens would have to be imported into Germany without cost to its economy.[1] Before the 'Byrnes–Bevin Agreement', such supplementary supplies had been financed by each occupying Power for its own zone; after the agreement, such supplies for the British and US zones were jointly financed under the bi-zonal arrangements, and after the IRO's work began, they were financed from the IRO's budget.

The object of the 'Byrnes–Bevin Agreement' was to reduce the support previously needed from Britain and the US to prevent the collapse of the German economy; Germany was to become self-supporting and its economy viable. A necessary corollary was therefore a stable currency in which the German people would have confidence. The inevitable war-time inflation and the disintegration of the German State had led to a distorted economy in which it was profitless to buy, to sell, or even to work for money. The counter action was a reform of the currency in August 1948; the old Reichsmark became valueless and all currency holdings and bank

---

[1] *Germany, 1947–1949; the Story in Documents*: Dept. of State Pub. 3556 (European and British Commonwealth Series 9), Mar. 1950, p. 452, par. 11.

balances were converted into the new Deutschmark at a rate of 10 Reichsmarks for 1 Deutschmark. To refugees, whose amenity supplies, freely given by UNRRA and the IRO, had been used for barter, the conversion meant a contact with more real economic values and a concomitant hardship for those not living in assembly centres. Goods came into the German shops; people were anxious to work to earn money to buy them, and refugees obtained employment less easily. For the Organization the conversion also brought reality in the expenditures debited to the mandatory budgets.

An agreement between the three Occupying Powers on an Occupation Statute for Germany came into force on 21 September 1949, simultaneously with the Charter of the Allied High Commission for Germany.[1] At the same time, with the establishment of the West German Federal Republic, the penultimate step was reached in restoring independence to the western part of the former Reich.

The Occupation Statute expressed the desire and intent of the governments of France, the UK, and the US that, during the period in which it was necessary to continue the occupation, the German people should enjoy self-government to the maximum degree consistent with such an occupation. The Federal State and the participating *Laender* should, therefore, subject to the limitations of the Statute, have full legislative, executive, and judicial powers in accordance with a basic law and their respective constitutions.

In order to ensure the accomplishment of the basic purposes of the occupation, the Allied Powers reserved certain spheres of activities for themselves; among these were foreign affairs and the question of displaced persons and refugees. The German Federal Government and the governments of the *Laender*, under the Occupation Statute, had the power, however, after due notification to the occupation authorities, to act and legislate in the fields reserved to these authorities, except as the occupation authorities otherwise specifically directed, or as such legislation or action would have been inconsistent with decisions or actions taken by the occupation authorities themselves.

While, therefore, the question of displaced persons and refugees remained nominally the responsibility of the occupying Powers, the indigenous authorities were also competent in the matter, and the later stages of the IRO's operations were increasingly dependent upon a close co-operation with the Germans.

In Germany, the Occupation Statute and the resultant readjustment of responsibilities were by-products of the setting up of a German Government; in Austria, as has been said, a government had already been in existence since 1945. Though nominally independent, it could not assume complete sovereignty until a State Treaty had been signed and occupation troops withdrawn.

The Austrian economy was controlled by the Austrian Government with such advice or directions as might be given by the Allied Council or by the administration of economic aid through the Marshall Plan, and by the Soviet authorities in their zone of occupation. There was, therefore, no exact similarity between the economic development of Austria and that of Germany. Although, as a continuation of the occupation régime, the IRO was at first supported by payments for certain purposes

[1] Ibid., pp. 88–96.

made locally in Austrian schillings on occupation account, such disbursements were supervised by the Austrian authorities; they were the subject of lengthy negotiations between the IRO and the Austrian Government in which the IRO tried to insist that the Government should pay for the maintenance of refugees in assembly centres. Later, the Organization had to pay in foreign currency for such schillings as it needed, and, from the financial point of view, its operations were similar to those in any other independent country.

Prolonged negotiations for a State Treaty had taken place through the years. In 1949, during the discussions in London between the Deputies of the Foreign Ministers, IRO was represented for consultation on behalf of those refugees who would remain in Austria after IRO ceased to exist or a State Treaty was completed, whichever was the earlier. The draft clause on refugees was one of those on which agreement could not be reached between the four Powers; the Western powers, desiring assurances that there would be no forcible repatriation, were in favour of the continued residence in Austria, with appropriate social rights, of refugees who wished or were forced to stay there. In view of this disagreement, the IRO discussed with the three Western governments and the Austrian Government what might alternatively be done. The latter based their point of view on a declaration of April 1948 according to which the Austrian Government would apply to refugees the terms of the resolution adopted by the General Assembly of the UN on 12 February 1946—that is to say, that there would be no forcible repatriation of bona fide refugees.[1] In the end, though no formal agreement was reached and though, at the time of IRO's closure, completion of a State Treaty seemed as remote as when the Organization began its operations, suitable arrangements were finally made, thanks to the understanding attitude of the Austrian Government, for the issue of residence and work permits to refugees remaining in Austria.

But the basic reason for a relatively satisfactory conclusion of this affair was the emigration of over 80 per cent. of the refugees registered with IRO in Austria who did not wish to be repatriated and who, had they stayed in the country, would have become a burden to themselves and an embarrassment to the Government. This successful migration had not been uniform: in the first year of work, the IRO administration in Austria frequently complained of a lack of attention to their needs as regards migration quotas and availability of ships; yet by 1950 it was the policy of the US Government to give priority to movement from Austria.

Italy

In addition to the agreements between IRO and the three Western occupying Powers in Germany and Austria operation agreements were also entered into with the governments of a number of sovereign countries in which the Organization operated. Formal agreements were concluded with the governments of Italy and France. With other countries the arrangements were less formal. These agreements and arrangements differed according to the Organization's programme in the respective countries, but they were all in accordance with the principles of the Constitution and with the specific local requirements.

[1] Cf. Chapter XVII, Legal and Political Protection, p. 315.

Italy, a co-belligerent with the UN since 13 September 1943, was restored to sovereignty on 15 September 1947, two and a half months after the creation of IRO. While the country was still under Allied occupation, arrangements for the assistance of refugees had been made by UNRRA, the IGCR, and the Allied Commission. PCIRO concluded an agreement on the international assistance programme for displaced persons in Italy at Rome on 24 October 1947.[1] This Agreement authorized IRO to conduct activities in Italian territory in connexion with the care, repatriation, and resettlement of refugees, and provided for the co-operation of the Italian Government toward these ends. A joint committee, consisting of delegates of the Government and of representatives of the IRO, was set up to implement the Agreement, and to discuss both policy and day-to-day practical problems. This successful committee arrangement was not made in any other country except Brazil.[2]

Under the terms of the Agreement the IRO was 'responsible for carrying out, to the limit of its available resources', the operation and administration of camps, the determination of eligibility of refugees for its assistance, for providing facilities for repatriation and resettlement, and for protection of the refugees' legitimate interests. The Italian Government granted the Organization free use of such property as was needed by IRO. The Government also allowed tax and customs exemptions on supplies imported by IRO, and transportation priorities for the movement of refugees. The entire burden of subsistence, however, fell upon the Organization, and special financial provisions facilitated the early period of operation.

Although the actual number of refugees who came under the mandate of the IRO was much smaller in Italy than in Western Germany, they were, nevertheless, a burden, and hampered the full recovery of the country because of permanent unemployment due to over-population. This situation resulted in a strong pressure towards emigration, especially as the Italian Government was greatly embarrassed by a phenomenon peculiar to Italy: the presence of a very great number (about 150,000 in the autumn of 1946) of refugees, who, unrecognized by any Allied authority, lived out of camp. The immigration of Italian refugees from the African colonies, the Dodecanese, and Venezia Giulia transferred under the Peace Treaty, was a related and complicating factor. The presence in Italy of these miscellaneous groups of refugees was a matter of grave concern especially to the British and US governments in view of the impending withdrawal of their troops from Italy, and of their wish to relieve the Italian Government of unnecessary financial and political burdens.

On 14 November 1950 a further agreement between IRO and the Italian Government, supplementing the basic agreement of 1947, was concluded. The two main objects were the resettlement of a further 20,000 refugees from Italy before operations closed, and the assumption of government responsibility for the well-being of the residual group.[3]

[1] PC/LEG/4, 28 Oct. 1947: Agreement between the Italian Government and the PCIRO, signed 24 Oct. 1947.
[2] In the Agreement of 15 May 1947 between the IGCR and the Italian Government such a Joint Committee had been provided for for the first time.
[3] Cf. Chapter XXII ,Local Settlement, p. 478.

Trieste

Work in Trieste was administered as part of IRO's Italian operation. Neverthe-less, working conditions encountered there were by no means identical with those in Italy, although there was the connecting link of refugees who had crossed the Yugo-slav border into the Free Territory of Trieste and from there had entered Italy.

At the time of the IRO's operations, conditions in Trieste resembled those in an occupied rather than in a liberated or sovereign country. The Yugoslav Partisan Provisional Government had, as early as 1943, declared that Venezia Giulia and Trieste had been annexed to Yugoslavia. In April 1945 the Yugoslav army, after heavy fighting against the Germans, forced its way into Trieste where it met Commonwealth forces advancing from the Po.

In June 1945 a provisional agreement divided Venezia Giulia between the Anglo-American and the Yugoslav armies; the Peace-Treaty with Italy of 10 February 1947 which came into force later that year, created the Free Territory of Trieste and laid down the frontier between Italy and Yugoslavia. The greater part of Venezia Giulia went to Yugoslavia, but the ship-building centre of Monfalcone and the railway through Gorizia, including the latter town, went to Italy. The territory of Trieste was divided into two regions: Zone A, the northern part with the city Trieste, and Zone B, the southern area. Pending the appointment of a Governor by the UN Security Council the Free Territory was administered by an Allied military government; the northern zone by joint British–US forces, and the southern zone by the Yugoslav army. Repeated attempts to elect a governor of the Free Territory failed. Meanwhile, the Yugoslav authorities treated their zone as if it were incor-porated in Yugoslavia as an integral part of the country, while the Anglo-American occupation of the other zone continued.

The IRO was directly concerned only with affairs in the Anglo-American zone, where the situation was very similar to that experienced by IRO in Austria. In Trieste, as in Austria, a relatively large number of refugees in a small territory created many political and economic difficulties. In close co-operation the military government and the IRO aimed to remove as many refugees as possible.

Greece

Fundamentally, the attitude of the Greek Government towards foreign refugees was the same as the Italian—there was no room for them, especially as the post-war dislocation of essential Greek cash-crops, tobacco, fruit, and the like, had caused Greece, economically speaking, to be overpopulated. The civil war, following the Second World War, was the immediate cause of the existence in Greece of purely Greek refugees, who had been displaced by the fighting. They numbered 50,000 in the spring of 1947 and 700,000 by September 1949, one-tenth of the population, and represented a heavy burden for the Greek Government. This problem of internally displaced Greeks, however, was not within the mandate of the IRO, but other ethnic Greeks, such as the refugees from Rumania, became the concern of the IRO. Another group were the Northern Epirots, refugees from southern Albania, who had been entering Greece illegally since the end of the war. The Greek Government requested the IRO's assistance in the resettlement of this group. After a careful survey of conditions leading to the exodus of this group and their status in Greece, a considerable number were found to be within the mandate of the Organization. Some of them were, in fact, in a group scheduled to embark for Italy, when, in August 1949, the Greek Government had reconsidered the position and informed the IRO that, in view of a possible peace treaty with Albania, it had decided not to press for their departure from Greece, and therefore wished to relieve IRO of the responsibility for these people. IRO accordingly considered them outside its mandate.

In addition, there were smaller numbers of political dissidents, not of Greek stock, from Bulgaria and Yugoslavia, and there were many pre-war Armenian refugees near and in Athens, but the Organization assisted only a few individuals among them, and most of them remained a burden on the Greek Government.

Initial contact between the Chief of the IRO Mission in Italy and the Greek Government was established in June 1948, so that procedure for registration of post-war refugees could be discussed and a policy for operations in Greece could be formulated. The Greek Government in August 1948 formally requested IRO to begin operations. An IRO representative, working under the Rome Office, was therefore appointed, and an assembly centre at Lavriou, which finally came under direct IRO administration in July 1949, was set up. This was the only assembly centre administered by the IRO in Greece, and the number of refugees there never exceeded 400.

During these initial discussions the civil war in Greece had continued, and martial law was extended throughout Greece by 29 October 1948. Several problems required immediate attention, such as, above all, the removal of refugees from Greece to Italy for presentation to selection missions of immigration countries. This selection was not possible in Greece owing to civil war conditions, whereas in Italy such selection missions were already operating.

Thus, as early as October 1948, 620 refugees were moved to Italy. A further 630, including 480 Moslems, were moved there in March 1949, and a third group of over 150 Bulgarians, followed later; over 100 of this group were accepted by the French Government as agricultural workers. These transfers involved the risk that persons not accepted would either have to be returned to Greece or further increase Italy's unemployment problem by staying there pending future resettlement possibilities; some of these Greek refugees, therefore, were not looked upon favourably by the Italian authorities.

By the autumn of 1949 it was possible to establish an independent Greek mission which was opened in November 1949. Thereafter resettlement missions came to Greece and arranged for direct selection with a view to movements from that country. The first full-scale move of persons actually selected in Greece was that of 599 persons to Australia in February 1950, the first Australian selection team having arrived in Greece in December 1949; an additional 4,000 were removed in 1950 and 1951. The successful operation of this plan, which also made it possible to combine movements of refugees from Greece with the move of certain refugees from Turkey, is greatly to the credit of the Australian, New Zealand, and Brazilian governments.

France

'Of all the countries in Europe France is probably the one that', in the twentieth century, 'has welcomed the greatest number of foreign refugees on her soil.' To France, perhaps more than to any other country, the problem of refugees has been one of long standing. In offering asylum to refugees, France 'has been following that traditional hospitality which has been peculiarly her own from time immemorial and which she has extended to the victims of all political regimes in turn', receiving sympathetically Stuart kings, Polish insurgents, Russian Bolsheviks or royalist emigrés, uprooted Armenians, refugees from the Hitler régime, and Spanish Republicans.

France was popular as a country of refuge partly because of its geographical proximity to Germany, Italy, and Spain, countries of origin of many refugees before the war; partly on account of its tolerance based on the 'Déclaration des Droits de l'Homme et du Citoyen' which established everyone's equality before the law. On the other hand, refugees were welcomed because demographic and economic conditions were in their favour. Industry and agriculture in France both needed workers because of the depopulation of the country as a result of wars and the declining birth-rate.[1]

France, therefore, was not only a country of first asylum, but also one of permanent settlement. When IRO began its work there were about 2 million aliens in France of whom 350,000 to 400,000 were refugees. Therefore, the task of IRO in France was entirely different from that in the occupied countries and in Italy, Trieste, and Greece. While in the latter countries IRO gave assistance to the military authorities and respective governments by moving out as many refugees as possible, in France its main object was to give legal protection and cash assistance to refugees until they could finally be absorbed in the local economy and integrated into the political community or be resettled in other countries.

The major categories of those to whom asylum was offered in France before 1939 were Russians and Ukrainians, Armenians, Saarlanders, Italians, refugees from Germany, Austria, and Czechoslovakia, and Spanish Republicans. Those admitted after the war, whether arriving at the frontier as refugees or selected as immigrants in Germany and Austria, were a cross-section of the nationalities dealt with by IRO during its activities.

In France, a distinction is made between 'statutory' and 'non-statutory' refugees: The statutory refugees belong to one of the categories defined before the war as those who enjoy a legal status in their country of residence; the non-statutory refugees are the displaced persons who, as a result of the upheavals of the war, are in search of a place of refuge.[2]

The f— . . . he Russians, Armenians, and other refugees to whom the inter-
. . . s and agreements relating to Nansen passports and quasi-
. . . ply. Similarly, refugees coming from Germany and Austria

glementation des Etrangers en France, editions Berger-Levrault, Paris, 1950,

's speech (Mme Lefaucheux) at the Sixth Meeting of the Third Committee
mbly, on 1 Feb. 1946 (UN, *The Question of Refugees*, op. cit., pp. 24 f.).

are entitled to benefits accruing from other international conventions, as are Spanish refugees on whose behalf, at the request of the French Government on 21 May 1945, the IGCR assumed the functions of legal and political protection with corresponding responsibility to give assistance.

The latter ('non-statutory'), broadly speaking, are all refugees other than those enumerated above. Though they are not covered by the terms of the various conventions applicable to statutory refugees, the French Government, at the request of the IGCR and the IRO, gradually extended protection to most of them. Thus, by the application of the agreements made between the Government and the IRO, all refugees coming within the mandate of the Organization had substantially the same rights in France; and after the closure of the IRO there was little practical difference between the position of the statutory and the non-statutory refugees.

On 13 January 1948 three agreements were concluded between IRO and the French Government to define the functions of the IRO in France and to establish a formal basis for mutual co-operation.

The first covered the status of the Organization and its representatives in France, and arrangements for the privileges, immunities, and facilities necessary to enable it to carry on its work on French territory. The second concerned the protection of refugees and displaced persons coming within the mandate of the IRO and the quasi-consular functions of the IRO representatives in France. (Details will be dealt with in the chapter on legal and political protection.)[1]

The third agreement[2] concerned the establishment and the activity of the IRO office in France. It stressed the common aim of the French Government and of the IRO in implementing the principles embodied in the Constitution of IRO, and determined the best methods to be employed by the French Government and the IRO to give each other the greatest possible assistance in the solution of all questions regarding those refugees in France who were the concern of IRO. It specified that IRO was responsible for the protection of all refugees and displaced persons coming under its mandate who were already in France or might come to reside in France during the period of validity of the agreement; that, at the request of the Government, IRO would undertake to maintain, for the so-called 'statutory' refugees, the advantages granted to them under international agreements and conventions, and the laws in force in France in respect of them; and that the IRO would maintain general administrative and financial supervision of the refugee national offices, and would keep the Government informed about the activities of these offices as well as, with the approval of the Government, appointing their directors. A fourth agreement signed on the same date concerned the immigration of refugees into France and Algeria; later agreements referred to Morocco and French Guiana.[3]

Belgium, Luxembourg, and the Netherlands

In these countries the situation was in some respects similar to that in France, since, because of their geographical position and liberal tradition, they were countries

---

[1] Cf. Chapter XVII, Legal and Political Protection, pp. 317–18.
[2] Cf. Appendix II (b), p. 619.
[3] IRO/LEG/GOV/14, 21 Apr. 1949, and Corr. 1 and 2; IRO/LEG/GOV/28, 21 Feb. 1950.

of first refuge. They had a considerable population of pre-war refugees to which was added a number of war-time displaced persons. At the same time they were able to use additional man-power and took the initiative, especially Belgium, in admitting refugees from Germany and Austria for work in the mines or on the land. These countries were also continuously troubled by refugees entering or attempting to enter their countries illegally. Refugees in these countries were not, as a matter of principle, separated from the indigenous population, and when in need they were assisted by the normal social services, with such co-operation as voluntary societies, supported by the IRO and disbursing IRO's funds, were in a position to give.

Therefore, IRO's work in these three countries was similar to that in France, centring on legal protection, care and maintenance, and local settlement. However, when the Netherlands in the course of a few years became over-populated, the IRO in this country concentrated on giving assistance in resettlement.[1]

Switzerland

Switzerland, the traditional country of freedom and humanitarianism, and long the seat of private and public international institutions, invited the IRO to have its headquarters in Geneva. A special agreement, concluded between the Swiss Government and IRO on 15 September 1948, legalized the status of IRO, giving the Organization the same privileges and immunities as those enjoyed by other international bodies.

Switzerland had refugees of all categories: Nansen refugees, pre-war Jewish refugees, persons liberated from concentration camps in Germany during the war, and post-war political fugitives from eastern Europe.

It was never determined how many refugees within the mandate of IRO were living in Switzerland at any given time. At the end of the war the estimated number was about 115,000 refugees. As a rule refugees registered with IRO only when they needed some form of assistance, which was often only in connexion with their emigration. Financial assistance for care and maintenance did not come within the scope of this office, since these aspects of refugee work were adequately handled by the Swiss governmental authorities and voluntary societies.

Over-population and the economic balance of the country led the Swiss authorities to limit permanent residence permits—the so-called 'asile durable' or 'Dauerasyl'— to about 1,500 compassionate cases. In theory the remaining refugees in Switzerland live there on a temporary or semi-permanent basis, but in fact residence and work permits are accorded as long as economic conditions allow; in many cases this temporary status has lasted almost ten years—and therefore, in 1950, the Swiss authorities decided that refugees who had come to Switzerland before and during the war should no longer be obliged to make preparations for further migration, but should be allowed to establish themselves in the country.

Denmark

In another country on the borders of Germany, Denmark, the work of the Organization was characterized by the fact that the majority of refugees dealt with

---

[1] Cf. for Belgium, Chapter XX Resettlement :p. 377, and for the Netherlands, Chapter XXIII, Hard Core, p. 489.

by the Danish Government after the war were Germans, rather than UN nationals. On the day of liberation there were some 250,000 persons evacuated from Germany, mostly Germans, in Denmark, and it took four years to complete their repatriation to Germany. The Danish authorities housed and maintained these refugees in some 1,100 camps and other quarters, including some 200 schools. This was a heavy burden on the country since the number of refugees amounted to 4 per cent. of the Danish population.

The non-German displaced persons, mostly of east European origin, who lived in these camps, totalled approximately 31,000. These people, at their request, were separated from the Germans in camps by the Danish authorities, and were accorded special privileges. Repatriation of UN nationals began immediately after Germany's surrender and lasted until 1947. At the same time steps were taken to make provision for those refugees who did not wish to be repatriated, either by resettlement or absorption. The relation between the Danish Government and the IRO was for- malized in an agreement concluded 19 November 1948. Under Article V the Government continued the direct operation of refugee camps and the direct admini- stration of care and maintenance of refugees in and outside camps under the general supervision of IRO. The Organization undertook financial responsibility for the cost of care and maintenance. Under the Protocol of 1 August 1949 responsibilities formerly carried by the Government were assumed by IRO from that date until June 1950.[1]

The Middle East, East Africa, and Far East

Outside Europe refugees and war evacuees had been dispersed in countries as far apart as the Middle East, East Africa, and the Far East. When IRO took over, in July 1947, there were about 27,000 people scattered in the enormous area known as the Middle East theatre of operations which had its headquarters in Cairo. IRO's Mission in Cairo controlled the Organization's activities not only in Egypt, Lebanon, Syria, Palestine, and Turkey, but as far as Kenya, Nyasaland, the Rhodesias, Tanganyika, Uganda, and India.

The conditions and problems in this area bear little relationship to those in Europe. Apart from Palestine none of these countries were countries of refuge in the real sense or suited for permanent settlement, some for climatic, some for political or economic reasons. The refugees had been accepted on the understanding that their stay was temporary and that they would repatriate after the war.

During the war, members of the Polish, Yugoslav, or Greek armed forces, civilian refugees from countries bordering on the Mediterranean, and dependants of refugees, mainly Polish, had been admitted into the Middle East, East Africa, and India as a British responsibility, the British Government giving its undertaking to the sovereign or colonial governments that the persons concerned would not become a public charge and would ultimately be removed. Most of these were originally assisted by the Middle East Relief and Rehabilitation Administration and later by UNRRA. IRO continued UNRRA's activities under an agreement concluded with the Government of the UK covering the Organization's activities in the Middle

---

[1] For text see Appendix II (*b*), p. 601.

East (India, the Lebanon, Palestine, and East Africa). The administrative respon-sibility was entirely British, and the IRO took over the arrangement already in existence whereby the Organization paid the British Government a *per capita* charge to cover all costs.

The distinct groups with which the IRO was concerned in the Far East were European Jews, pre-war Russian emigrés, especially in Shanghai, and overseas Chinese. Evacuation of the Europeans became essential for political reasons, and for their removal and final resettlement IRO had to rely in particular on the co-operation of the governments of the Philippines, Israel, the UK, and the US.[1]

Co-operation for resettlement

This chapter has dealt with the co-operation between IRO and governments or military authorities in countries of first refuge, which, to a certain extent, became also countries of resettlement, especially for refugees and displaced persons from German and Austrian camps and for the residual group. For the latter, agreements and arrangements were made by IRO at the closure of its programme for care and maintenance after June 1950.[2]

A final winding up of the whole programme depended, however, to a decisive degree on large countries most suitable for permanent resettlement, such as overseas countries. Prolonged negotiations between their respective governments and IRO preceded resettlement agreements, and varied according to the individual circum-stances in each country. Normally a resettlement agreement provided for recognition of the status and functions of the Organization and of its right to determine the eligibility of refugees and displaced persons under the Constitution; the selection of refugees by the government of the country of reception; the acceptance of close relatives; the establishment of civil rights for refugees, and recognition of the Organization's functions in connexion with legal and political protection.[3] When the co-operation between IRO and governments had successfully implemented the resettlement agreements, all responsibilities could finally be transferred to govern-ments and voluntary agencies.

[1] Cf. Chapter XX, Resettlement, p. 421.
[2] These agreements are dealt with in Chapter XX, Resettlement, under the respective countries.
[3] Cf. Chapters XXII, Local Settlement, and XXIII, Hard Core.

CHAPTER VIII

PARTICIPATION OF VOLUNTARY SOCIETIES

THE solution of far-reaching social problems always requires official action either on the national or international level. Yet private efforts, inspired by humanitarian impulses, are indispensable to public services which, by their very nature, are impersonal, and are supplemented by the services of voluntary agencies geared to the needs of the individuals concerned.

The term 'voluntary agencies' includes those private relief and welfare organizations, non-governmental agencies (the term employed by the UN), and other groups engaged in refugee work which are primarily financed by voluntary contributions from the general public.[1] The primary purpose common to all philanthropic societies is service to mankind, yet they originate in response to different needs and do not conform to one pattern. Some organizations permanently engage in humanitarian work, others render service to members of their own faith only, and still others function temporarily during emergencies, such as post-war conditions, and respond to the emotional impetus of men of goodwill.

Rarely, if ever, has a closer and more effective partnership between statutory and voluntary agencies been achieved than the co-operation of IRO and its associated voluntary agencies. Their collaboration with the Organization resulted in a combined operation which mobilized and considerably increased the organizational resources. The work of the voluntary agencies has been complementary and supplementary to that of IRO in many respects. With their help, the IRO was able more adequately to discharge its functions, especially its care and maintenance of refugees, the implementation of its resettlement programme, its welfare services, and its legal aid. The help of the voluntary societies also contributed, though in a lesser degree, to the IRO's work in connexion with repatriating refugees. In areas where the IRO did not maintain missions or have representatives, voluntary societies acted on its behalf; in other cases they assumed responsibility for some particular phase of IRO's programme. To name but a few of the outstanding examples: they assisted in the administration of the care and maintenance of refugees in France; they arranged sponsorships for refugees bound for the US; they offered programmes of orientation to refugees prior to their resettlement. In all these cases their contribution was invaluable by virtue of their interest in individual refugees and of the continuous care they extended to them. Thus, the refugees were given a new feeling of personal assurance and identification, and, as a result, they adjusted more readily to their new homes, and became more firmly re-established than would have been possible under public guardianship. Special

---

[1] Julius A. Elias, 'Relations Between Voluntary Agencies and International Organizations', *Journal of International Affairs*, vii. 1, 1953, p. 30.

L

arrangements made by voluntary agencies also enabled IRO to ensure the welfare of many institutional and other hardship cases at the time of the Organization's closure.[1]

Principal types of voluntary societies

The main group of voluntary societies organized to give aid to refugees had a denominational origin, and about 90 per cent. of all cash, goods, and personnel placed at the disposal of refugees was furnished by them.[2] Among the Catholic organizations the most significant were the War Relief Services of the NCWC organized for relief operations abroad; others were the Catholic Immigrant Aid Society of Canada; Caritas Internationalis, an organization linking several national associations, and representing them in dealings with intergovernmental bodies; Pax Romana, an international movement of Roman Catholic students and intellectuals.

The Protestant and Orthodox federations included the Refugee Commission of the World Council of Churches which had representatives of the Protestant and Orthodox churches of fifteen countries; the refugee assistance branch of the Lutheran World Federation; the Church World Service, which represented the majority of Protestant and Orthodox churches in the US; and the Mennonite Central Committee which had its headquarters in the US. These societies tended to concentrate on helping refugees belonging to their own denominations. There were other societies of Protestant affiliation, such as the American Friends Service Committee and the Unitarian Service Committee, which helped many other categories of refugees; the World's YMCA and YWCA Emergency Services.

The most powerful groups were the Jewish societies, based on ethnic or religious qualifications, comprising among others the AJDC, set up in 1914 to assist the Jewish victims of the First World War, and later taking the lead among the voluntary societies in the extent and the diversity of services rendered to refugees; the JAFP, founded in 1921 to promote Jewish emigration to Palestine, and destined to play an official role in the State of Israel's immigration affairs; HIAS, organized in 1884 to assist immigrant Jews in the US, whose sixty emigration offices were spread over twenty-five countries; the Jewish Committee for Relief Abroad, the organ of the Jewish community in Britain for foreign relief; the World ORT Union, created in 1880 to develop agricultural and industrial work among Jews, which had established schools and vocational training centres in many countries; Vaad Hatzala, founded by the Rabbinical Union of the US and Canada to give assistance to the spiritual leaders of orthodox Jewry.

The non-denominational societies included *inter alia* the international and national organizations of the Red Cross, various sections of the Scout Movement (Boy Scouts' International Bureau, Guide International Service, World Association of Girl Guides and Girl Scouts); the ISS, which specialized in individual case-work and was noted for the high professional standing of its welfare workers; the World Student Relief, set up under the auspices of four international student

---

[1] See letter of 31 July 1951 to the voluntary agencies of Myer Cohen as Acting Director General. Details of the work and various functions will be found in the chapters on operation in Part III.

[2] J. A. Elias, op. cit., p. 30.

organizations collaborating with national committees established in eight countries;[1] the International Rescue and Relief Committee (later the International Rescue Committee), founded in the US in 1933 to succour the victims of Nazism and Fascism; and the US Committee for the Care of European Children, which facilitated immigration into the US of orphans or homeless children.

Other important associations were the 'helping hand' societies created in the US and in Canada by former emigrants belonging to different national groups: the American Committee for Resettlement of Polish Displaced Persons, the American Fund for Czech Refugees, the American National Committee to Aid Homeless Armenians, the American Polish War Relief, the Tolstoy Foundation, the United Lithuanian Relief Fund of America, the United Ukrainian American Relief Committee, and the Ukrainian Canadian Relief Fund.[2]

In addition to the big associations organized for work on an international level, a large number of private organizations whose normal activities were mainly on a national scale collaborated with the IRO, particularly in western European countries.

Moral and material resources of the voluntary societies

The private charitable organizations were able to contribute material and spiritual assistance to the international refugee work: they had funds at their disposal and could offer the services of their specialized and often highly trained staff; they had experience acquired in earlier relief operations and a thorough knowledge of the complexities of public assistance and aliens legislation; they were familiar with local conditions in the communities where refugees were to be placed and enjoyed the moral support of people in a position to offer homes to refugees; and last, but not least, they had the confidence of their refugee clientele and could appeal to old beliefs and traditions they shared with them, thus facilitating their adjustment to a new life.

Immediately after the war, a society's contribution of supplies for material relief was often its most important work. Later, however, the displaced population needed the whole range of social services required by any community, or even a wider range because of the exiles' situation. The largest agencies covered many specialized programmes departmentalized within the agencies themselves. In other cases, the agency itself performed specialized functions, such as providing legal aid or migration services only, while others limited their services to programmes for children or youth and the like.

The financial resources of the agencies were often quite limited, but varied from one to another, and from country to country. The funds of many agencies in Europe were exhausted as a result of the extensive calls upon them during the war for helping their own people. The British Government encouraged the work of the voluntary agencies abroad by granting them 50 per cent. of their expenditures. This was also of advantage to the Government, since expenses for voluntary workers were lower than those for government civil servants.

[1] The functions of the World Student Relief were later taken over by a new organization, the World University Service, with headquarters in Geneva.

[2] For a detailed description of the work of American societies abroad see Fulton Report, op. cit., pp. 49 ff.

The philanthropic organizations on the north Atlantic continent were often heavily endowed, thanks to the tradition in these countries of reliance on self-help and mutual aid rather than on organized government assistance. Legislation by the governments of the US and Canada supported this tradition by enabling citizens to deduct from their taxes a part of the contributions to recognized charities which, as a result, had very considerable funds at their disposal. The work of these organizations abroad had the further advantage of facilities granted by the Government, subject to the approval by a special body of the societies' programmes. This special body was the Advisory Committee on Voluntary Foreign Aid, set up within the framework of the State Department to co-ordinate governmental action with that of the private relief societies.

The voluntary societies' financial contribution to the work of relief stemmed either from their own funds or from funds collected from the public or from certain foundations. It has not been possible to estimate the total amount of this contribution, as the societies did not submit their own accounts to the IRO, nor did they always separate their expenditures for refugees eligible under the IRO's mandate from expenditures on behalf of others. A small number of societies, however, did publish some figures, which relate to agencies with varying resources and fields of activity and cannot therefore be compared among themselves.

One British voluntary society, the Guide International Service, which aided refugees only in the British zone of Germany, spent £103,214 from 1947 to 1950 for the benefit of persons within the IRO's mandate, excluding the grants made by the Organization.

A society specializing in assisting children's emigration to the US, the US Committee for the Care of European Children, spent $991,018 from July 1947 until the end of 1951 for the benefit of children under the IRO's protection.

The International Rescue Committee collected more than $800,000 to carry out only one of the items on its programme, the re-establishment of refugee intellectuals in the US and Canada.

The contributions of the largest societies to refugee relief amounted to millions of dollars. HIAS, which employed 600 persons in Europe and maintained emigration offices in twenty-five countries, estimates that, during the life-span of IRO, it spent more than $10 million on the transportation, accommodation, and sundry emigration costs of Jewish refugees. AJDC estimates that during the same period it spent about $27 million (of which over $22 million was required for transportation costs) on the emigration of 192,000 Jewish refugees, of whom 111,000 went to Israel, 53,000 to the US, and 28,000 to other countries.

The Lutheran World Federation, working for various categories of refugees of whom the great majority were within the IRO's mandate, spent $532,445 on its programme of material and spiritual assistance and $712,203 on its re-establishment service in the years 1948–52. It further advanced $504,838 to emigrants in the form of loans for travel expenses, and distributed relief supplies in kind collected by the Lutheran World Relief valued at more than $1 million.[1]

---

[1] These amounts do not include the grants, totalling more than $1 million made by the IRO to the Lutheran World Federation to carry out various projects in favour of the refugees.

Apart from administrative expenses and the expenditures for various services, the relief distribution programmes, both in cash and in kind (foodstuffs, clothing, medicines, cigarettes, books, &c.), undertaken by the voluntary societies, cost tremendous sums. The Ukrainian Canadian Relief Fund distributed supplies in Germany from 1947 to 1951 valued at $165,198. In Germany, Austria, Italy, and France the value of the relief issues made by the United Lithuanian Relief Fund of America from 1947 to 1950 exceeded $1,300,000, that of the American Polish War Relief distributions in the same countries from 1948 to October 1951 amounted to more than $550,000. From the end of the war to 31 December 1951 the NCWC handed out to refugees and the civilian population in Germany relief supplies representing more than $26 million, a large part of which went to the refugees under the protection of the IRO. The supplies shipped by the AJDC from 1946 to 1951 to Germany, Austria, Italy, Shanghai, and Cyprus attained a total weight of 100,664,368 lb. Similar supplies going to Belgium, France, the Netherlands, and Greece between 1946 and 1950 weighed 15,541,374 lb. The total cost of the AJDC's relief programmes in the former group of countries during the period of the IRO's operations (1 July 1947 to 31 December 1951) on behalf of refugees within the IRO's mandate was about $48 million; its programmes during the same period for similar refugees in Belgium, France, the Netherlands, Portugal, Spain, Sweden, and Switzerland was about $7 million; these figures include the emigration expenses mentioned above.[1]

Currency restrictions frustrated many societies in other countries. Various societies were able to raise money at home but none could meet the dollar requirements of the principal areas where there were refugees.

Among the agencies working on a national scale in western European countries there were many whose own resources were insignificant, and whose activities could only be carried on by virtue of the funds contributed by the IGCR and later by the IRO.

The IRO's policy in regard to voluntary societies

When PCIRO, in the spring of 1947, prepared to take over UNRRA's commitments in the field of refugee assistance, more than sixty societies, including ten international organizations and national philanthropic agencies from twelve different countries, were participating in the programme of relief distribution and the various services for refugees. The policy of IRO required that voluntary societies operating under its auspices were to avoid political activity of any kind.

In their consultative capacity the societies had been instrumental in the creation of IRO itself. In 1946 a sub-committee of the Special Committee on Refugees and Displaced Persons examined the various statements submitted by private organizations and reported back on this subject to the plenary committee.[2] Recognizing the

---

[1] According to a paper presented to the Ford Foundation in Mar. 1952 by WCC, NCWC, AJDC, and LWF, these four organizations have distributed between them, since the end of the war, relief supplies and grants to refugees and the populations of various countries that represent a value of more than $240 million.

[2] UN, ECOSOC, Official Records, First Year, Second Session, Annex 12: Report of the Special Committee . . ., p. 8.

important contributions of voluntary societies in services and material aid to refugees, the PCIRO decided, as early as February 1947, to consult the societies in connexion with securing the continuance of their assistance and in order to ascertain whether additional assistance could be obtained. In May 1947 the PCIRO authorized the Executive Secretary to negotiate new agreements with them or to extend the validity of agreements existing between the voluntary societies and IGCR or UNRRA.[1] The existing agreements were prolonged for a period of three months during which the IRO defined its policy concerning official relations with voluntary societies.[2]

The policy laid down by the IRO provided for the participation of qualified societies in the IRO's operations; it was stipulated that the objectives of these agencies were in harmony with the Constitution and policy of IRO. The societies were to make available the services of their qualified staff selected in accordance with field requirements of the agencies, and to submit reports on operations and accounts in view of the advancement of funds. The IRO in turn granted recognition, status, and facilities for approved operations, and accorded the same status and facilities to the field personnel of the agencies as the Organization provided for its own personnel.

The application of this policy led to the establishment of various forms of co-operation with the voluntary societies. General agreements were concluded with agencies providing a variety of services in the operational zones of Germany, Austria, and Italy where foreign voluntary societies could function only if an agreement had been concluded with the IRO. The Organization assumed responsibility to the occupation authorities or, in the case of Italy, to the Government, for the orientation and co-ordination of the societies' work. Through the IRO, recognized societies could obtain from the competent authorities in the occupied zones the permits and material facilities covering billeting, subsistence, staff movements, use and maintenance of vehicles, and the entry and distribution of relief supplies in kind. The general agreements, applicable to one or several operational zones, constituted the basis of collaboration in the field between the IRO and the voluntary societies; they were permissive rather than mandatory, defining, on the one hand, the scope of the programme of the agency concerned, and, on the other hand, the conditions of service and the status and facilities to be accorded. During the course of IRO operations, agreements of this nature were concluded with many voluntary societies.[3]

Apart from general agreements, special agreements were entered into between the IRO and the voluntary societies for the purpose of carrying out particular operations or projects limited to a special area or a given category of refugees. The general agreements usually covered programmes in areas where normal civilian facilities did not exist, i.e. the occupied areas; for work to be done outside the functional scope or the geographical area of a general agreement, a special agreement was made defining a specific service to be rendered in one of the IRO's basic

[1] PCIRO Res. 20, 20 May 1947, cf. Appendix III, p. 693.
[2] General Bulletin, No. 5, 18 Sept. 1947, PCIRO Policy in Respect to Formal Relations or Agreements with Voluntary Agencies. *Operational Manual*, pp. 12 and 125.
[3] Cf. Appendix II (d), p. 679.

programmes. The agency would be responsible for the partial or total management of such a programme, while financial aid was to be given by IRO. Sometimes a special agreement covered a supplementary programme for which a grant would be made beyond the normal logistical support given to the agency. Notable agreements were those made in connexion with the transportation of refugees by the AJDC and the JAFP. Other important ones concerned vocational training, orientation and language training, distribution of maintenance grants, and management of special institutions such as homes for the aged, hospitals, and summer camps.

A number of voluntary societies, without concluding written agreements with the IRO, contributed to the work of aiding the refugees, either by supporting the work of organizations having authority to operate in the zones, or by working on a national scale in co-operation with the IRO's missions.

In general, only agencies operating in Austria, Germany, and Italy under general or special agreements with the IRO received administrative support from the Organization. In the other countries, notably in France, where the societies played an important role as the agents of the IRO, they received no subsidies and no facilities from the Organization. The sums made available to them by the Organization were intended solely to be paid out to the refugees or to finance special undertakings (establishing old-age homes, equipping sanatoria, and so on) for their benefit. The funds of many of these societies were very limited, and they were able to give more assistance to the refugees as a result of the IRO's resources entrusted to them.

Co-ordination of the activities of the societies and those of the IRO

To effect the necessary co-ordination between its own services and those of the voluntary agencies, particularly in Austria, Germany, and Italy, the IRO established a special administrative unit at headquarters, the Division of Voluntary Societies. The officers of this Division were in close touch with headquarters or missions of the voluntary agencies, worked with them in a mutually advisory capacity, and exchanged views regarding the many subjects requiring consideration and action. This added to the effectiveness and scope of the IRO's total programme. Each of the IRO's major missions had a similar administrative unit for the exchange of information and for the achievement of a greater degree of co-ordination.

The IRO also held frequent conferences or periodical meetings to enable representatives of the IRO and the voluntary societies working in the same zone to discuss problems of common interest. In January 1949 the IRO called a combined conference in Geneva of representatives of IRO and associated voluntary organizations. Some 104 representatives of IRO headquarters and field operations from 15 field areas, and 100 representatives of 49 voluntary societies from 13 countries or field areas reviewed the progress in operations at the half-way mark in IRO's three-year mandate and considered plans for the remaining period of work.[1]

The voluntary societies themselves set up committees or councils in several areas,

---

[1] GC/60, Annex: Conference of IRO and Voluntary Organizations, Geneva, 18–21 Jan. 1949, Summary Report, p. 17.

which enabled them to exchange their views or in some cases to make collective representations to governmental authorities or the IRO. Among the more important of these bodies were the Standing Conference of the Voluntary Societies, meeting in Geneva; the American Council of Voluntary Agencies for Foreign Service in the US; the different councils or committees created in most of the zones of operations; and, finally, the groups of national societies operating principally in their own countries, such as the Liaison Committee of Societies working for the refugees in France, or the Swiss Central Office for Refugee Aid in Switzerland.

Figures or diagrams cannot give an exact idea of the extent of the voluntary societies' participation in the overall efforts and achievements of the refugee assistance programme. The operations of IRO and the services of the societies were complementary and mutually necessary. In raising the health standards of the refugees, broadening their education, and increasing their occupational skills, assisting to reunite scattered families, and helping to solve thousands of individual problems, the voluntary societies performed an indispensable function which the IRO could hardly have assumed, since the greater part of its funds were needed to meet the costs of shelter and subsistence for refugees and to finance mass resettlement operations.

Austria, Germany, and Italy

In the IRO's main areas of operations in Austria, Germany, and to a certain degree in Italy, workers from some thirty-five voluntary societies worked in close collaboration with the IRO's own staff in carrying out the joint programme.

By December 1947 the number of personnel of the voluntary agencies receiving official status (not including the so-called 'indigenous' staff), amounted to a total of 1,256, more than half of whom belonged to the five Jewish organizations, AJDC (338), JAFP (147), JCRA (55), World ORT Union (100), and HIAS (45). Other major groups were the British Red Cross and COBSRA (200), Church World Service (53), NCWC (54), Polish Red Cross (53), World's YMCA/YWCA (123).

The principal services rendered by the voluntary societies were as follows:

Counselling and specialized services to the individual family;
assistance to refugees living outside camps;
training programmes for self-management, leadership, welfare and nursing aides, recreation leaders, teachers, and vocational instructors;
vocational training;
religious, recreational, educational, cultural, and community activities;
legal aid, visiting, and re-establishment of prisoners, assistance to the disabled, and surveys of the problem of the disabled to ascertain numbers, types of disability, need for corrective treatment, retraining or residual care;
individual emigration assistance, linking up with relatives or other sources of help, exploiting opportunities for selected individuals or groups by finding the people to fit the particular opportunities;
operation of special institutions (children's homes and summer camps, convalescent homes, special hospitals, clinics);
general tracing and inquiry services; aids to repatriation through links with home countries;

assistance given by personnel with national and language backgrounds in child
  search, identification, and repatriation of children;
  supplies for supplementary relief and amenities.

In Austria and Germany the IRO adopted the various methods of work previously followed by UNRRA in the different areas; it dealt almost exclusively with
foreign, or international, societies. As has been seen previously,[1] the IRO's own
position was not the same in each area or country; the tasks for which it was
directly responsible, the facilities it received, and consequently could make available
to others, differed from country to country and from zone to zone. These varying
circumstances, some inherited and some new, brought about inconsistencies and
inequalities as regards both policies towards the societies and the support given to
them. The IRO tried as far as possible to remove these inconsistencies, but it was
impossible to achieve uniformity.

In Italy, societies required the IRO's sponsorship to a more limited extent. The
previous method of work continued under the IRO in its two main aspects: firstly,
certain agencies lent personnel to the Organization in support of the IRO's own
staff; and secondly, certain voluntary agencies, notably the Jewish agencies, carrying
out relief programmes were granted various facilities by the IRO.

RELATIONS WITH VOLUNTARY SOCIETIES IN OTHER COUNTRIES

In western European, Scandinavian, and overseas countries the relations between
the IRO and the voluntary societies differed according to national circumstances.
In general the IRO employed the services of local societies to distribute material
relief to refugees, and to make available to them certain welfare services on behalf
of the Organization. In certain countries, Great Britain and Norway in particular,
the societies also took an active share in immigration operations.

Belgium

From the very beginning of its activities in Belgium the IRO maintained close
contacts with various national benevolent associations, with the Belgian branches
of a few private international agencies, and some mutual aid groups created by
refugees who had a common national, ethnic, or religious bond.[2] The Belgian
Refugee Committee, formed in 1950, embraced various benevolent and trade union
organizations such as the Caritas Catholica International Relief, the Socialist Mutual
Aid Movement, and the YMCA, and was entrusted with the relief functions
formerly performed by the IRO. The Belgian Refugee Committee, among other
notable contributions, kept open for several months the regional welfare offices
established by the Organization in the mining districts where the refugee population
was especially dense. In addition, the Belgian societies were most generous in their
care of aged, sick, and infirm refugees.[3]

The Netherlands

In the neighbouring country, the Netherlands, the IRO was mainly assisted by
religious agencies representing various denominations.[4] Special contributions were

[1] Cf. Chapter VII, Co-operation of Governments. [2] Cf. Appendix II (d), pp. 679 f.
[3] Cf. Chapter XXIII, Hard Core, p. 455. [4] Cf. p. 455.

made by ethnic organizations such as the Polish Catholic Association and the Hungarian Club who assisted their co-nationalists, and by international organizations sponsored by Dutch groups, such as the World Student Relief and the International Student Service who worked in co-operation with Dutch university circles to assist refugee students, mostly Czechs who had fled from the American zone of Germany.

France

France was by far the most important operational area among the non-occupied countries because of the very large number of people who had sought refuge there as a result of French social security legislation, which was particularly liberal towards foreigners. The fact that the IRO was able to take the maximum advantage of the resources open to it under French legislation was due to the help of the voluntary societies who made available their knowledge of national problems and resources, their trained staffs, and a system of relief services covering the whole country.

The aid the Organization gave to the refugees took on diverse forms, but was always given through the medium of voluntary associations specializing in some particular branch of activity or in assistance to some particular group of refugees.[1]

In effecting its assistance programme, the IRO's mission in France met with invaluable support from a French agency, the Service Social d'aide aux Emigrants (SSAE), the French branch of the International Social Service. Founded in 1921 and granted a public charter in 1932, the SSAE, in common with the ISS, based its activities on individual case-work. It had acquired vast experience of refugee aid, for it had assisted the Russian and Armenian refugees arriving in successive waves at Marseilles from 1921 onwards; persons driven from Germany and Austria after 1933; refugees from the Spanish civil war in 1937; and later Polish refugees; and refugees from the Saar and those of the post-war period. The SSAE had not only collaborated with the Nansen Office and the IGCR but also, over a long period, with the French authorities, who had charged the SSAE with specific tasks, such as paying out certain funds to Spanish Republican refugees, and had, in 1948, entrusted to SSAE welfare workers the thirty-one departmental offices of the Social Service for Foreign Labour (Service social de la main-d'œuvre étrangère) set up by ministerial decree in 1939. On behalf of the IGCR the SSAE made relief payments amounting to 1,269,607 French francs to stateless persons, 9,693,645 French francs to Spaniards, and had investigated 3,107 individual cases covering 9,320 refugees.

Due to its record of service, the SSAE was an ideal associate for the IRO both in the task of assistance and in that of co-ordinating the work of the other voluntary societies. In agreeing to work with the Organization the SSAE concerned itself with individual case-work, leaving relief distribution to other bodies. An agreement signed in 1948 made the SSAE the 'technical adviser to IRO for all individual assistance work in France'. In this capacity the SSAE made a survey for the IRO of all assistance cases in France. This necessitated the review of 10,000 case files.

[1] For list of societies see pp. 162 f.

Thus the number of refugees requiring hospitalization was exactly determined so that appropriate measures could be taken.

Co-ordination of work between the IRO and its several agents was achieved by means of weekly meetings. The IRO representatives supervised the standardization of the criteria for assistance and the grants made by the voluntary societies. Similar meetings were held fortnightly at the Ministry of Labour, in which a Bureau for the Orientation and Employment of Foreign Refugees (BOPRE) had been established in September 1948.

When in February 1950 an agreement was signed between the IRO and the French Government, whereby the latter took over responsibility for assistance to refugees in France, the SSAE was chosen by the Government to perform this task. As the result of this agreement, the SSAE received 11,492 case-files from the IRO's mission on 30 June 1950; they concerned 31,049 individuals who had received either a loan, a scholarship, donations from the reparations fund, or monthly financial assistance; and SSAE thereafter became responsible, under the supervision of an interministerial commission, for an assistance programme that aimed at making the refugees self-supporting or relieving sick and aged persons awaiting hospitalization.

United Kingdom

In keeping with the British democratic tradition, and motivated by a keen sense of responsibility for the common welfare, individuals in local communities have always worked through voluntary societies. When faced with the challenge of the refugee problem British societies were ready to continue in the old spirit. In order to co-ordinate their efforts during the war for work abroad, the British societies, as early as 1942, constituted the Council of British Societies for Relief Abroad (COBSRA). Eleven societies organized 'field teams' for foreign service, while some thirty other societies shared the work in the common cause by collecting gifts and funds, or by lending staff to the organizations forming the field teams. Under the auspices of the British armed forces, the field teams went to Egypt and Palestine in 1942, Italy in November 1943, north-west Europe in 1944, and Greece in 1945. In April 1945 these teams consisted of 907 persons: 115 in Italy, 300 in Greece, 37 in Yugoslavia, and 455 in north-west Europe.

A team that had landed in Normandy in 1944 and had continued to be increased in number throughout the operations in Belgium and Holland established itself in the British zone when Germany was occupied. It divided its relief work between the German population and the displaced persons. COBSRA concluded a general agreement with the IRO regarding work on behalf of displaced persons. After the termination of the work in Germany, in June 1950, the Council was dissolved on 30 September of the same year.

When the British Government decided to admit 2,000 refugees in the 'hard core' category from Germany and Austria, providing that maintenance and accommodation could be guaranteed for them by individual sponsors of charitable foundations (the '2,000 Scheme'), twenty-three voluntary organizations, concerned with the welfare of refugees, called in conference by the National Council of Social Service in June 1950, formed a new body, the British Council for Aid to Refugees (BCAR).[1] The Council was the first of the national refugee service committees to be set up in response to an appeal made by Mr. J. D. Kingsley that existing agencies engaged in refugee work should unite to guarantee a continuity of voluntary effort.

The BCAR, which had assumed the task of assisting refugees who had arrived in Great Britain after 31 December 1946, and of facilitating immigration for refugees requiring hospitalization or special care, took a leading part, in co-operation with the Home Office and subsidized by IRO, in carrying out the '2,000 Scheme', under which nearly 1,300 refugees immigrated between June 1950 and May 1952. It also assumed certain of the commitments of the IRO's mission in Great Britain, e.g. the reception of immigrants, after the mission was closed on 30 June 1951.

Norway

In Norway the Norwegian Refugee Committee formed by eight voluntary societies, the General Confederation of Trade Unions and the Employers Confederation, took over the task of facilitating the immigration of refugees. The Committee established municipal refugee committees all over the country. Their mission was to find in each locality housing or reception possibilities for refugees, and to aid them in adapting themselves to their new surroundings. The Norwegian Refugee Committee also sent material relief to refugees in central Europe, and financed the establishment of children's homes, vocational training centres, old people's homes, TB hospitals, and welfare centres in Germany and Austria.

Switzerland

In Switzerland voluntary organizations played a significant and early part in aiding refugees. As early as 1936 several organizations established the Office Central Suisse d'Aide aux Réfugiés (Swiss Central Office for Aid to Refugees) which was to be the liaison between the relief organizations and the authorities. Some of the organizations gave far-reaching assistance to refugees, while others devoted their efforts, in co-operation with the IRO, to arranging the emigration of those refugees who could neither be repatriated nor remain in Switzerland. These organizations included, among others, the Swiss branch of Caritas, the Œuvre Suisse d'Entre'-Aide ouvrière, the Swiss section of the ISS, and the Swiss Union of Jewish Refugee Aid Committees. IRO also co-operated with Swiss Aid to Europe which was primarily concerned with helping refugees abroad. It was Swiss Aid also to whom the Federal authorities entrusted the task of accepting 250 aged, infirm, or sick refugees within the IRO's mandate.[2]

Spain and Portugal

The IRO did not maintain missions in the Iberian Peninsula, but work there was carried out on its behalf by American voluntary societies. During the war, five societies had joined together to open an office in Madrid known as the Repre-

---

[1] Cf. list, pp. 164 f.
[2] Cf. Chapter XXIII, Hard Core, pp. 455 f.

sentation in Spain of American Relief Agencies; they were the AFSC, the AJDC, the Brethren Service Committee, the War Relief Service of the NCWC, and the USC. Their activities were chiefly concerned with victims of the Nazis escaping over the Pyrenees, and with those refugees who had not managed to move on from Spain and Portugal. There were also a small number of political dissidents and, in Portugal, of Spanish Republicans. The three centres of work were Madrid, where AJDC took an increasing share in the responsibility and ultimately became entirely responsible for the work; Barcelona, where the AJDC functioned solely on the IRO's behalf; and Lisbon, where the AJDC, the NCWC (until 1949), and the USC maintained separate offices all of which dealt separately with the IRO on behalf of their different case-loads.

The Far East

In Shanghai the AJDC also played an essential part in refugee assistance and emigration operations. Besides, it helped to create a Council of the Jewish Community, which was given funds by the IRO under an agreement concluded in November 1950 for assisting those refugees who had not yet been able to emigrate. Another agreement was signed between the IRO and the World Council of Churches in December 1951 on the basis of which this organization was to take over responsibility—after the cessation of the IRO'S activity—for the remnants of the group of refugees who had been given temporary asylum in the Philippines.

After the close of the Organization, various 'Refugee Service Committees' in several countries continued assistance to refugees at the IRO's suggestion, and dealt with refugees who had been resettled by the IRO as well as with the residual groups.[1]

RESETTLEMENT COUNTRIES

The role of non-governmental agencies overseas was of equal importance. Without their contribution the purpose of the IRO could not have been achieved. While the problems relating to an organized administration of mass movements can be solved only by public agencies, that is to say, either by national governments or intergovernmental organizations with legislative and executive authority, the application of special measures to individual groups is more successfully handled by voluntary agencies. As a rule, they have a better understanding of individuals and of their experiences and difficulties. This is due to a 'bond of affinity and sympathy' which develops so frequently between the organizations and the people they are helping as a result of the agencies' knowledge of a special field—religious, professional, trade union, or ethnic.[2] Formerly, when voluntary organizations were often the only source of aid to migrants, they had experience in organizing reception and welfare services which facilitated resettlement. Because of their freedom of action voluntary organizations can adjust their work to the migrants' needs and can follow their humanitarian aims more freely without restrictions imposed by political or economic considerations.

[1] Cf. Chapter XXVI, Final Transfer, p. 562.
[2] Suzanne Ferrière, 'Role of Non-Governmental Organizations in the Assistance of Migrants', *International Labour Review*, lxiv. 5–6, Nov.–Dec. 1951.

The United States

In view of this traditional assistance to migrants, it is not surprising that the voluntary agencies immediately grasped the opportunity to help the recent wave of refugees who, as political emigrants, were much more dependent on assistance than were emigrants who had left their home countries voluntarily. The organizations which have specialized in aiding refugees are only one group among the many large American voluntary relief organizations to which private citizens have contributed funds or voluntary service. These relief organizations serve by giving general or emergency relief to their country as well as by providing aid on an international level in times of war and post-war emergencies. New methods have been evolved by the collaboration between the US Government and these societies so that their resources can be most effectively used and the private citizen is given a guarantee that his contribution will not be misused or wasted.

Mention has already been made of the Advisory Committee on Voluntary Foreign Aid which was established on 14 May 1946 within the US Department of State by a Directive of the President of the US. The purpose of this Committee was to 'coordinate the governmental and private programmes in the field of foreign relief, to work with interested agencies and groups', and to 'guide the public and agencies seeking the support of the public in the appropriate and productive use of voluntary contributions for foreign aid'.[1] Subsequently the responsibility of the Advisory Committee was extended, and it then became the duty of the Committee to approve and register those American voluntary agencies which were entitled to specified privileges in connexion with the shipping of relief goods[2] or which assumed responsibilities under the DP Act of 1948, as amended on 16 June 1950. The Advisory Committee assumed certain responsibilities previously held by the President's War Relief Control Board with which UNRRA and IGCR had co-operated closely.

During the period of the PWRCB's activities it had been necessary for an American agency wishing to engage in overseas programmes of aid to refugees and displaced persons to secure the approval of the PWRCB before making a working field agreement with UNRRA or IGCR. When PCIRO succeeded UNRRA and the IGCR on 1 July 1947, the existing agreements with the voluntary agencies were maintained until such time as they could be revised. Similarly the basis of approval of agencies by the PWRCB was continued by the Advisory Committee on Voluntary Foreign Aid.

The IRO concluded agreements only with a voluntary society which 'had obtained a satisfactory clearance from the appropriate government authorities of its own country'[3] and, as a result of this consistent policy, the IRO agreed to request all American agencies to register with the ACVFA and secure its approval before agreements could be made with IRO. The IRO, however, continued its policy of negotiating directly with the voluntary agencies.

The Displaced Persons Admissions Act of 1948 made necessary the approval

---

[1] Advisory Committee on Voluntary Aid, Circular No. 7, 10 Feb. 1947.
[2] Under the Economic Co-operation Act of 1948, the Foreign Aid Appropriation Act of 1949 (especially with reference to 'Government and Relief in Occupied Areas'), the Act of 31 May 1947 (Section 2 (*f*), 'Relief Assistance to War Devastated Countries'), and the Export Control Law.
[3] PCIRO General Bulletin, No. 5, op. cit.

of certain voluntary agencies by the US Displaced Persons Commission for the resettlement programme in the US. An agreement was concluded between the US IRO office, the ACVFA, and the DPC, whereby the DPC, before 'recognizing' an American voluntary agency for resettlement services, required from the agency written evidence that it was registered with the ACVFA and had a field operations agreement with IRO.[1]

By 15 January 1948 a total of sixty-nine American agencies had registered with the Advisory Committee. With the liquidation of many war relief programmes after the war this list was reduced by 1 September 1949 to forty-three registered agencies and seven agencies whose overseas programmes were approved as affiliates of a registered agency.

The American Council of Voluntary Agencies for Foreign Service, established in the winter of 1943–4 by a group of American voluntary agencies, organized for programmes of war relief and assistance to refugees, served as a centre for the co-ordination of the relief activities of its sixty member agencies and as a liaison with governmental and intergovernmental organizations. The IRO, since its inception and, before that, UNRRA and IGCR, had co-operated very closely with the Council.

The US IRO office often influenced plans and programmes being developed by the agencies, either to assist the IRO directly or to carry out the US Resettlement Programme under the DPC. This brought about a close working relationship between the IRO and the American Council Office, and was of the utmost importance, both to the IRO's overseas programme and to the agencies.

Some seventeen American voluntary agencies actively participated in a great variety of programmes of assistance to the displaced persons living in and outside the IRO camps in Germany, Austria, and Italy and also, as has been mentioned, in a lesser degree, to certain groups of refugees resident in Belgium, Holland, France, Spain, Portugal, the Middle East, and China.

In connexion with the immigration programme into the US, the voluntary agencies provided assurances for the admission of approximately 85 per cent. of the displaced persons who immigrated under this law. The responsibilities of the voluntary agencies included obtaining assurances, helping to document the displaced person overseas, sponsoring him through the processing of the US government agencies, arranging for his reception at the port of disembarkation in the US and for his transportation to his final destination, and general supervision of his long-term sponsorship in the US.[2]

Both the IRO and the voluntary agencies markedly contributed to the success of the DP Act by counteracting its shortcomings: the IRO and the agencies made persistent efforts to cope with the involved details of the Act, and they used their imagination to the utmost in their endeavours to match, with individual displaced persons, assurances obtained for unnamed individuals, by agencies, denominational in 90 per cent. of the cases.[3]

---

[1] Cf. list, Annex 11, p. 162.
[2] Cf. Chapter XX, Resettlement, p. 414.
[3] Cf. Kathryn Hulme, op. cit., pp. 190 ff.

Israel

The Jewish societies on a large scale supported the emigration movement of refugees to the State of Israel. This movement was never interrupted, not even when for eight months the IRO suspended its assistance to refugees for Palestine. The Jewish agencies, by handling migration movements to Israel throughout the existence of the IRO, relieved the Organization of a very heavy task, thus freeing a large part of its administrative resources for other operations.[1]

Special services

Some of the societies associated with the IRO, to complete the work begun in the refugee centres of Europe, dealt with special projects or certain services in overseas countries. Examples in Australia were the representative bodies of the Protestant and Lutheran Churches. In Canada the Canadian Council of Churches, the Canadian Lutheran World Relief, and the Canadian National Institute for the Blind helped with the resettlement of handicapped groups; the Canadian Jewish Congress and the Catholic Immigrant Aid Society carried out projects for the resettlement of unaccompanied children. In Chile the YWCA gave assistance to the settlement of refugees. In the US the American Committee for the Resettlement of Professionals, the American Committee for the Welfare of Cripples, the American Foundation for the Blind, the National Lutheran Council, and the United Service for New Americans made their contribution in the settlement of refugees belonging to the groups which were difficult to resettle. An arrangement was made with the National Travellers Aid Society for the reception and forwarding of immigrants not assisted by other societies.

In 1950 and 1951, when the IRO approached its end, the voluntary societies gave particular help in placing the infirm, the chronically sick, and aged persons in appropriate institutions.[2]

Conclusion

The refugee relief operations under the auspices of IRO from 1947 to 1952 were characterized by the unprecedented extent and scope of the collaboration between an international body and the voluntary societies. The IRO, in common with IGCR, enlisted the local societies which became its distributing agents, for instance, in France and Belgium. Like UNRRA, it turned to foreign organizations for its operations in Austria, Germany, and Italy. It also followed the example of its predecessors in that it asked the agencies to supply services that were complementary to its own, but, in contrast to them, the IRO often delegated to the societies various basic services which, according to the IRO Constitution, were its own primary tasks and not those of private charities. Among such basic services often delegated to the societies were the care and maintenance of refugees, and the series of operations required for repatriation or resettlement.

The independence of the voluntary societies with respect to political problems gave them freedom of action in cases where the IRO was limited by its mandate.

[1] Cf. Chapter XX, Resettlement, p. 415.
[2] Cf. Chapter XXIII, Hard Core, p. 483.

In certain cases where refugees were excluded from the Organization's mandate (e.g. certain Russians who had served in the Rogozhin or Vlassov Corps), assistance was given them by voluntary societies, e.g. the Tolstoy Foundation, until such time as the IRO could take them under its protection. On occasions when the Organization had to postpone its assistance to refugees because of the uncertainty of its future financial resources and of final estimates of the number of refugees to be provided for, the voluntary agencies frequently filled the gap by helping refugees who otherwise would have been temporarily stranded.

When the IRO was disbanded the voluntary societies took over the management of a large number of institutions affording shelter to 'hard core' refugees, and apart from continuing their respective traditional activities they participated either independently or through their membership in refugee service committees which assisted refugees wherever they had been resettled.[1]

The advantages derived from the collaboration between the IRO and the voluntary societies did not benefit only the IRO. The societies, too, enjoyed advantages as the IRO bestowed upon them its own international status. In Austria, Germany, and Italy the voluntary societies obtained from the IRO or through its good offices facilities indispensable to their activities. The IRO estimated that it contributed some $3,800,000 from its funds, together with nearly $8 million from the Deutschmark mandatory budgets, to meet the societies' administrative expenses.

Apart from subsidies granted to the voluntary societies for their administrative expenses, the IRO entrusted to them considerable sums of money with which to implement certain special projects, or to give cash assistance to refugees, or to reimburse them for basic services rendered on behalf of the IRO. These sums did not represent subsidies to the voluntary societies, but financial contributions which enabled the societies to attain objectives that were as much theirs as the IRO's. The IRO spent, through the medium of voluntary societies for their administrative expenses and for the completion of certain tasks, a total estimated to exceed $40 million.

If left to their own devices the societies would in many cases have been unable to expand their activity beyond the limits of emergency aid. Only agreements between member governments of the IRO made possible the launching and the financing of the great operations that led to the resettlement of more than a million refugees, and only by becoming the agents or associates of the IRO could the societies arrive at a permanent solution of the problems of the refugees whom they had served with such devotion and so great a feeling of responsibility.

The societies themselves in turn played a great part in paving the way for the operations of the IRO. Before public action was taken they demonstrated by their work the benefits to be derived from an international organization, and were thus instrumental in creating a public opinion favourable to giving its full support to international co-operation.

[1] Cf. Chapter XXVI, Final Transfer, p. 562.

ANNEX 11

VOLUNTARY SOCIETIES ASSISTING IN IRO FIELD OPERATIONS

Germany, Austria, and Italy

American Committee for the Resettlement of Polish Displaced Persons
American Friends Service Committee (AFSC)
American Fund for Czechoslovak Refugees
American Joint Distribution Committee (AJDC)
American National Committee for Aid to Homeless Armenians
American Polish War Relief
Baptist World Alliance
Boy Scouts International Bureau
British Red Cross
Catholic Immigrant Aid Society
Church World Service
Council of British Societies for Relief Abroad
Hebrew Immigrant Aid Society (HIAS)
International Committee for Rehabilitation and Immigration
International Rescue Committee (IRC)
International Social Service (ISS)
Italian Red Cross
Jewish Agency for Palestine (JAFP)
Jewish Colonization Association
Jewish Committee for Relief Abroad
Lutheran World Federation
Mennonite Central Committee
National Catholic Welfare Conference—War Relief Services (NCWC)
Polish Red Cross
Tolstoy Foundation
Unitarian Service Committee (USC)
United States Committee for the Care of European Children
United Lithuanian Relief Fund of America
United Ukrainian American Relief Committee
Ukrainian Canadian Relief Fund
World Association of Girl Guides and Girl Scouts
World Council of Churches
World ORT Union
World's YMCA
World's YWCA
World Student Relief

France

Accueil Catholique Français
American Joint Distribution Committee (AJDC)
American Polish War Relief
Aumônerie protestante
Caisse israélite de prêts
CARE (Committee of American Relief for Europe)

Centre de formation professionnelle
Centre de reclassement professionnel (CRP)
Centre d'orientation sociale des étrangers (COSE)
Comité intercontinental de reclassement et d'immigration
Comité international pour le placement des intellectuels réfugiés (CIPIR)
Comité inter-mouvements auprès des évacués (CIMADE)
Comité juif d'action sociale et de reconstruction (COJASOR)
Comité luthérien et réformé d'aide aux travailleurs étrangers
Entr'aide française
Entr'aide universitaire française
Fédération des sociétés juives de France (FSJF)
French Red Cross (CRF)
Hebrew Immigrant Aid Society (HIAS)
International Rescue and Relief Committee (IRRC)
National Catholic Welfare Conference—War Relief Services (NCWC)
Œuvre de protection des enfants juifs (OPEJ)
Œuvre de secours aux enfants (OSE)
ORT Français (Organization for Rehabilitation through Training)
Russian Children's Welfare Society
Secours Catholique
Self Help, Inc.
Service d'aide aux émigrants (SSAE)
Service social des jeunes (SSJ)
Société de St. Vincent de Paul
Société de Secours aux Polonais (Relief Society for Poles)
Quaker Service (AFSC)
Union des étudiants juifs de France (UEJF)
Unitarian Service Committee (USC)
YMCA
YWCA

Belgium

Aide aux israélites victimes de la guerre
American Joint Distribution Committee
Belgian Red Cross
Caritas Catholica
Catholic International Union for Social Service
Comité belge d'aide aux étudiants ex-prisonniers de guerre et autres Yougoslaves
Comité belge d'assistance aux universitaires slaves orientaux—COBAUSO
Comité d'aide aux israélites victimes des lois raciales
Comité d'aide mutuelle des étudiants polonais en Belgique
Comité central israélite
Comité des réfugiés est-européens
Comité international pour le placement des intellectuels réfugiés
Fédération belge des femmes universitaires
Hebrew Immigrant Aid Society (HIAS)
International Rescue Committee (IRC)
Œuvre Notre-Dame de Sion
ORT Belge
Relief Society for Poles
Ukrainian Relief Committee
Union des Invalides de guerre russes

United Lithuanian Relief Fund of America
World Jewish Congress
World Student Relief
YMCA

Netherlands
Catholic Committee for Refugees
International Quaker Bureau
Jewish Coordination Committee
ORT Hollande
Vereinigung Deutscher Staatenloser Antifaschisten

Portugal
American Joint Distribution Committee (AJDC)
National Catholic Welfare Conference (NCWC)
Unitarian Service Committee (USC)

Spain
American Joint Distribution Committee (Barcelona) (AJDC)
Representation in Spain of American Relief Organizations (Madrid)

Council of British Societies for Relief Abroad (COBSRA)
Boy Scouts Association
British Red Cross Society and Order of St. John of Jerusalem
Catholic Committee for Relief Abroad
Friends Ambulance Unit
Friends Relief Service
Guide International Service
International Voluntary Service for Peace
Jewish Committee for Relief Abroad
Salvation Army
Save the Children Fund
YWCA

Members of the British Council for Aid to Refugees (BCAR)
British Federation of University Women Ltd.
British ORT
Catholic Women's League
Central British Fund for Jewish Relief and Rehabilitation
Family Welfare Association
Guide International Service
Inter-Church Aid and Refugee Service
International Friendship League
National Association for Mental Health
National Council for the Unmarried Mother and her Child
National Council of Social Service
National Council of Women of Great Britain
National Council of YMCAs
National Institute for the Blind
National Union of Townswomen's Guilds
Refugee Housing Society Ltd.

Rotary International in Great Britain and Ireland
Salvation Army
Scottish Council for Aid to Refugees
Society of Friends
Toc H
World University Service
YMCA of Great Britain

Canada

Canadian Citizenship Council
Canadian Council of Churches
Canadian Jewish Congress
Canadian Lutheran World Relief
Canadian National Institute for the Blind
Canadian Red Cross
Canadian Welfare Council
Catholic Immigration Aid
International Student Service
Jewish Immigration Aid Society
Travellers' Aid
Ukrainian Canadian Committee

Voluntary Societies Accredited to the US DP Commission

American Committee for the Resettlement of Polish Displaced Persons
American Federation of International Institutes
American Friends Service Committee (AFSC)
American National Committee to Aid Homeless Armenians
Church World Service (CWS)
Hebrew Sheltering and Immigrant Aid Society (HIAS)
International Rescue and Relief Committee (IRRC)
Mennonite Central Committee
National Lutheran Council (NLC)
Order of AHEPA
Serbian National Defence Council—Division of Displaced Persons
Travellers Aid Society
Tolstoy Foundation
Unitarian Service Committee (USC)
United Friends of Needy and Displaced Peoples of Yugoslavia
United Service for New Americans, Inc.
United States Committee for the Care of European Children
United Ukrainian American Relief Committee
War Relief Services—National Catholic Welfare Conference (NCWC)

ANNEX 12

Estimate of grants and payments to voluntary societies from IRO funds and from facilities made available to them from other sources, through IRO (occupational budget in Germany)

Period	Logistical support	DM budget	Special projects	Reimbursement for basic IRO programmes	Hard core	Refugee service committees	Grand total
	$	$	$	$	$	$	$
1947–8	1,000,000	1,720,635	..	972,500	..	..	3,693,135
1948–9	1,021,509	1,720,635	184,062	14,058,662	..	..	16,984,868
1949–50 . . .	794,755	1,892,857	420,637	4,740,299	..	280,000	8,128,548
July 1950–Dec. 1951 .	652,119	2,619,047	2,511,271	1,942,396	4,991,092	100,000	12,815,925
TOTAL . . .	$3,468,383	$7,953,174	$3,115,970	$21,713,857	$4,991,092	$380,000	$41,622,476

Notes: The figures for the eighteen months' period July 1950–Dec. 1951 include certain items for which actual payment was delayed until after the closure of operations on 31 Jan. 1952.*

The estimates in column 3 were not a charge on IRO funds. This assistance came from the occupational budget in Germany.

* Delayed allotments from blocked DM account, final payments on some projects or reimbursements, some logistical support beyond December.

CHAPTER IX

RELATIONS WITH THE UN AND SPECIALIZED AGENCIES

THE IRO became a full-fledged specialized agency in August 1948. On 18 November 1948 the UN General Assembly approved a draft Agreement between the UN and the IRO. A protocol concerning the entry into force of the Agreement was signed on 7 February 1949 by the UN Secretary General and the Director General of the IRO. Article 13 of the Constitution of the IRO, stipulating that the privileges and immunities of the Organization should be defined, was fulfilled by bringing into force for the IRO the UN Convention on the Privileges and Immunities of the Specialized Agencies.[1]

As a whole relations between IRO and the UN were of mutual advantage, though not without friction because of the complex situation prevailing among member governments of the UN. The cleavage between East and West cast a marked shadow on an otherwise beneficial liaison between the two organizations.

Article V of the above-mentioned Agreement laid down that the IRO was to submit annual reports about its work to the UN. Both the ECOSOC and the General Assembly carefully considered the matters presented, but the discussions before these two UN organs developed into a bitter contest between the Eastern and the Western Powers. The former consistently voted against the work of the IRO, while the latter invariably supported it. The Asiatic group, remaining aloof from these two camps, tended towards an intermediary position, and, in the later period of IRO, Yugoslavia abstained from voting.

Each year the representatives of the Soviet bloc reiterated their point of view that IRO's function was mainly and foremost repatriation, regardless of the specific wishes of individuals. In acrimonious terms they brought forward allegations regarding IRO's failure to carry out the function they expected of the Organization.

Yet with the sanction of the majority of the member governments of the UN, the IRO carried out the tasks that had been envisaged and decided upon by its own member governments. The IRO received moral, practical, and material support from the UN. The General Assembly was a world forum to which the facts and problems concerning its work could be presented. The Second Session of the General Assembly in November 1947[2] requested the Secretary General to submit, in collaboration with the Director General of IRO, a report on the progress and prospect of repatriation, resettlement, and immigration of the refugees and displaced persons for consideration by ECOSOC. The so-called Hambro Report,[3] prepared

[1] GC, Res. 31, Appendix III, p. 723.
[2] General Assembly, Res. 136 (II) and ECOSOC, Res. 122 (VI) A.
[3] The Secretary General of UN entrusted the preparation of the report to a mission composed of Dr. C. J. Hambro of Norway and Mr. Pierce Williams of the US, 'two independent persons of international standing'. Both made an elaborate field study by visiting camps in Italy, Austria, and Germany,

on the basis of careful studies on the spot, pointed out that prospects of voluntary repatriation were becoming increasingly poor, and that resettlement was the practical solution of the problem. The Hambro Report recommended, therefore, that countries should generously increase possibilities for immigration and should observe the family unit principle which was one of IRO's chief immigration policies.

At the request of the ECOSOC[1] an IRO report on the resettlement of non-repatriable refugees and displaced persons was submitted at the Eighth Session, held in March 1949. After lengthy discussions the Council passed a resolution in which an appeal was made to resettlement countries to broaden their definition of a family unit and also to admit a greater proportion of intellectual refugees.

The Secretariat of the UN consistently extended active help to the Organization, especially in its preparatory period when the PCIRO was provided by the Secretariat with a loan and with administrative facilities.[2]

The relationship between the two organizations was, on the other hand, also favourable to the UN. In its deliberations regarding the status of refugees and stateless persons the UN consulted the IRO, drawing on the knowledge and experience gained by the Organization.[3] In regard to operational activities, too, the UN appealed to the IRO for assistance, for example, when the emergency situations arose in Palestine and Korea. In this connexion the UN availed itself of the outstanding services of Mr. J. Donald Kingsley, the Director General, by appointing him UN Agent General for Korea, and of other leading and experienced IRO officials such as Sir Arthur Rucker, the Deputy Director General, who accepted the position as Chief of the European Regional Office of UNKRA.[4]

However, when in August, at the suggestion of the Security Council, the Secretary General of the UN asked the IRO to accept responsibility for the Arab group, the Director General informed him that, due to constitutional and financial limitations, the IRO could not undertake a programme of assistance for this group. But the Organization gave technical advice as well as stocks and equipment valued at more than $800,000 to the United Nations Relief and Works Agency for Palestine Refugees (UNWRA). At the beginning of 1949 it also made an interest-free loan of $2,800,000 which was repaid on 5 October 1951.[5]

In response to a request from ECOSOC of August 1950 to all specialized agencies to give whatever help they could afford to assist the civilian population, the General Council, at its Fifth Session,[6] approved an offer by the Director General to the Unified Command of the UN in Korea which made available medical and other supplies and the loan of welfare officers and other trained personnel. Up to 31 December 1950 the IRO had sent to Korea surplus medical supplies, clothing, sewing machines, &c., valued at more than $300,000.

interviewing refugees, field and headquarter officers, and representatives of the occupation authorities (E/816, 10 June 1948).   [1] ECOSOC, Res. 157 (VII).   [2] Cf. Chapter III, p. 59.

[3] Cf. Chapter XVII, Legal and Political Protection, p. 325.

[4] Mr. Kingsley accepted this position with the approval of the General Council of the IRO, while he continued to serve as General Director of the IRO (GC, Res. 81, GC/224/Rev. 1, p. 17); see also GC/256, p. 31: 169 staff members had been appointed by UN, other specialized agencies, and other international bodies by Jan. 1952.

[5] Executive Committee, Ress. 2 and 9, Appendix III, pp. 750 and 753.

[6] GC, Res. 69, Appendix III, p. 738

The Organization also participated fully in the activities of the Administrative Committee on Co-ordination and its Preparatory Committee which were established by ECOSOC to co-ordinate the activities of the specialized agencies. Naturally IRO, as a specialized agency, also associated itself with the work of the other functional organizations, especially ILO, WHO, UNESCO, &c.

Continuous liaison was established between the Secretariats of IRO and WHO on a number of matters, including the dietary scales laid down for displaced persons, and resettlement of refugee doctors, dentists, and nurses, the treatment of venereal diseases, and the classification of the tuberculous patients. Experts from WHO attended meetings of the IRO Health Division as advisers. Continuous contact was maintained with the ILO which gave valuable assistance in the field of vocational training and employment, while an exchange benefiting both agencies took place in the field of migration.

In order to further the refugees' cause close contact and co-operation was also maintained with the UN High Commissioner for Refugees, as well as with the Intergovernmental Committee for European Migration (ICEM), newly established at the end of 1951, and with other international bodies such as the Council of Europe and the Interparliamentary Union.

PART II

CHAPTER X

ORIGIN OF THE REFUGEES AND DISPLACED PERSONS

WHEN the IRO was established there were still, according to some estimates, about 10 to 12 million refugees in Europe, and many more in the Far East and the Middle East. However, only about 2 million refugees came under the mandate of the IRO; the smaller group, pre-war refugees who had remained in the countries of refuge, and had been cared for by former international agencies, the League of Nations, IGCR, and UNRRA; the larger group, displaced persons who, as a result of the Second World War, had left their countries of origin or residence 'forcibly, or under compulsion, threat, or duress of the Nazi, Fascist or similar regimes, as forced labour, or for racial, religious or political reasons',[1] and had not yet returned to their homeland. The UN had promised these people liberation and a new life according to the principles of the UN; they had particularly been assured that they would have freedom of thought and of movement. The governments who joined the IRO felt an obligation to these people. They came from the UN countries and had been up-rooted; they had suffered during the war and its aftermath, and had no hope of building up a new life in those countries in which they found themselves. Their presence, particularly in Germany, Austria, and Italy, endangered the valiant efforts of the western countries to achieve political stability, economic recovery, and social peace in former ex-enemy countries.

Pre-war refugees

Thus certain pre-war refugees, persons deported and uprooted during the war, and certain groups of post-war refugees, became beneficiaries of the IRO. The pre-war refugees included the so-called 'Nansen' refugees, the Spanish Republicans, and certain German and Austrian refugees of whom the majority were of Jewish descent, who had been driven into exile by Hitler, and the Italians who had fled the Fascist régime in Italy. The second group were liberated foreign labourers who had been forcibly deported into greater Germany during the war, people persecuted for racial reasons or for their religious or political opinions who refused to return to their homes, and a limited number of Soviet prisoners of war. The third category of post-war refugees, or so-called neo-refugees, was comprised of those persons who preferred liberty at any price to living in a country under a Communist régime.

[1] IRO, *Manual for Eligibility Officers*, n.d., p. 20.

Those refugees who had been looked after by successive international agencies were of diverse origin: they came from many regions, and had been forced into exile for a variety of reasons, they were united only by a common misfortune, the loss of their homes.

The 'Nansen' refugees were the White Russians, the Armenians, the Assyrians, Turks, and the Saarlanders, as defined in the arrangements of 12 May 1926, 30 June 1928, and 30 June 1935.[1] By 1937 about 450,000 White Russians, or one-half of the 1922 number, still retained refugee status. Of these, 111,000 lived in Poland and the Baltic countries; 56,400 in the Balkan countries; 50,500 in central Europe; 110,000 in France; 7,000 in other western European countries; and 94,000 in the Far East.[2] Many of them were older people and did not survive the hardships to which they were exposed during the Second World War. Others had sought naturalization. Their number, therefore, declined decisively from 1938 to 1946.

The Second World War created a problem of loyalties for some groups of the anti-Communist Russians. On 22 October 1941 Hitler issued an order providing for the formation of the so-called Cossack units to be attached to the German army. These units were recruited from among Russian émigrés who had settled in Germany after the 1917 revolution, prisoners of war, and dissatisfied Russians and Ukrainians who came from parts of the Soviet Union conquered by Germany. Many who joined were volunteers and therefore considered collaborationists, not eligible for IRO assistance.

In German-occupied Yugoslavia, White Russians joined the 'Autonomous Russian Corps' on 12 September 1941. By the end of 1942 the Germans assumed control of the group. At Klagenfurt on 12 May 1945 this group, now called the Rogozhin Group (after their last commander Rogozhin), about 10,000 strong, surrendered to the British.[3]

When the Russian armies swept across Poland, the Baltic countries, eastern Germany, and the Balkans, many White Russian refugees fled into western Europe. About 20,000 of them were living in camps at the beginning of 1946. By the end of the war the 8,000 Russian refugees who had been living in Yugoslavia since 1920, who had Nansen certificates or were Yugoslav citizens, were compelled by the Government of the Soviet Union to adopt Soviet citizenship although they were not allowed to return to the Soviet Union. After the dispute between the Soviet Union and Yugoslavia, the latter, in 1949, carried out a mass expulsion. About 3,000 of these refugees moved illegally into Trieste, others went to Austria, Italy, and other countries. The existence of those Russian émigrés who lived in Manchuria and China also became more precarious, owing to the advance of Communist China. Organizing their evacuation was one of the most difficult tasks the IRO had to face.

After the Russians, the Armenians were among the first protégés of the League of Nations and beneficiaries under the Nansen Statue. Many Armenians had left their homes under the Ottoman Empire. By the end of the First World War, after the final collapse of this Empire, large groups fled to the Erivan region where they tried

---

[1] See Introduction, pp. 3 ff.

[2] Sir John Hope Simpson, *The Refugee Problem*, London and New York, 1939, p. 561.

[3] *Manual for Eligibility Officers*, pp. 87–88, also Jacques Vernant, *The Refugees in the Post-War World*, London, Allen & Unwin, 1953, pp. 54 and 222–4, also for the following.

to create an independent republic. The Erivan Republic, however, became one of the Soviet Socialist Republics. After 1921, when the Soviet Union had reached the Caucasus, many Armenians, because of their political objections to the Soviet Government, were once more dispersed. A great number established themselves in France, Great Britain, Greece, and the US.

These Armenians had an ancient cultural background. They were intelligent and had a remarkable business sense. Unlike the White Russians, they were not opposed to naturalization, and took a successful part in the economic life of their countries of refuge. This was particularly noticeable in Egypt and in the former French mandated territories of Syria and Lebanon. Their natural gifts and capacity for hard work enabled some of them to become wealthy in the US, Latin America, England, France, and Egypt. They were generous in helping refugees of the Second World War to emigrate to the US and other overseas countries. Those Armenians who had left Russia and Turkey before 1 September 1939, and had not acquired another nationality, enjoyed Nansen status. Before the war their numbers were estimated as follows: in France there were 63,000; in Greece 25,000; in Bulgaria 14,500; in Rumania 6,000; in Cyprus 2,700; and in other countries 3,800.[1] These numbers decreased during the Second World War owing to deaths from natural causes and to naturalization. At the end of the war there remained about 35,000 Armenians in France who came under the IRO mandate, and about 4,100 were among the displaced persons in western Europe. After 1945, 500 additional persons came from eastern European countries.

Another group of Nansen refugees, the Saarlanders, were persons who left their homeland after the plebiscite of 13 January 1935, and were not in possession of national passports.[2] They received Nansen certificates after the plebiscite if they could prove that they were domiciled in the Saar on 30 October 1934. The great majority of these refugees settled in France (about 3,500 persons), while others emigrated to overseas countries. After the war the Saar became an autonomous territory and these refugees had to produce 'valid objections' against repatriation in order to remain under the IRO mandate.[3]

Some 400,000 Spanish refugees came to France between 1937 and 1939 as a result of the Spanish civil war which began in September 1936 and the final collapse of the Republican Government in February 1939. France, the nearest country and the one most willing to accept people who were victims of their democratic convictions, received 200,000 soldiers, who were followed in turn by 170,000 women and children, and 10,000 wounded. The French authorities interned the soldiers in camps in the south-east and south-west of France and in North Africa, institutionalized the disabled and wounded persons, and organized other shelters for the civilians where they were at least housed and fed—a task which the number of refugees, their absolute penury, and, in many cases, their poor physical condition, rendered very difficult. In June 1939 the French Government paid 7 million francs a day for maintenance of these refugees. Aid was also given by various private French and

---

[1] Simpson, op. cit., p. 558.
[2] Arrangement of 30 July 1935; see Chapter XVII, Legal and Political Protection, p. 328.
[3] *Manual for Eligibility Officers*, p. 42.

international organizations.[1] In 1938 an international committee was set up to assist the Spanish refugees, primarily to aid the children by means of contributions from different governments and with the help of various charitable organizations such as the American Friends Service Committee. On 14 June 1945 IGCR assumed responsibility for them, and between 1945 and 1947 it helped several thousands to emigrate to Latin America, especially Mexico. Some of the soldiers joined the French army during the Second World War. About 12,000 of them became prisoners of war and were deported for forced labour to Germany, and it was estimated that altogether 10,000 died in the war or in captivity.[2]

As in the case of the Russians and the Armenians, the task of the IRO was mainly that of giving the Spanish refugees legal and political protection and of aiding them to resettle. While many of them returned to Spain after the war, new groups, an estimated 22,000, entered France during the period 1946–53, among them some who came for economic reasons. The French Government therefore granted asylum only to those who could give convincing proof of their status as political refugees.

Victims of anti-semitism

To these different groups of pre-war refugees must be added the victims of the Nazi and Fascist régimes; the refugees from Germany, Austria, and the Sudetenland, protected by the Convention of 10 February 1938, the Additional Protocol of 14 September 1939, and the resolution of the 104th Session of the Council of the League of Nations of 19 January 1939.[3]

The majority of these were Jewish and their plight was due to active anti-semitism in central and eastern Europe, culminating in the anti-semitic legislation promulgated by Hitler from April 1933 onward. Economic and professional discrimination was legalized, citizenship under certain conditions was withdrawn, and other provisions made people of Jewish descent outcasts in their own country. In 1935 these regulations were extended to the Saar, in 1938 to Austria, and in 1939 to the Czechoslovakian Protectorate.

During the war, from 1939 to 1945, anti-semitism spread to the areas conquered by the German army and to those governed by the Axis satellites. Jews were subjected to deportations, transfers, purges, and concentration. In certain territories they were forced to live in ghettoes or concentration camps and many of them were conscripted for forced labour.

The great number of such transfers of Jewish people reflected the terrible uprooting and suffering to which this group was subjected. It was estimated that from 1939 to 1940 over 300,000 Jews from western Poland (i.e. one-half of the Jewish population in that territory) were deported to the *Gouvernement General*, a part of German-occupied Poland. At the same time an additional 125,000 fled from that area to eastern Europe including Rumania, Hungary, and the Baltic states. In 1942 mass

[1] See Simpson, *Refugees, a Review of the Situation since 1938*, London, Oxford University Press, 1939, pp. 54–63, and Appendix 2, p. 114.
[2] For other details see Vernant, op. cit., pp. 58 and 279.
[3] See *Manual*, p. 43, and Chapter XVII, Legal and Political Protection. Also a number of Italian political refugees and Jews from Italy who mostly went to the US and Latin America, see Vernant, op. cit., p. 60.

deportations to eastern Europe were carried out from France and the Low Countries, while in the opposite direction Jews from Albania and south-western Germany were shipped to the French border and left there to their fate.

Jews in the Bohemian Moravian Protectorate were sent to the concentration camp at Theresienstadt, and those in Rumania were assembled in large ghettoes in that area. In Hungary they were excluded from employment and deprived of their property and thus, without means of livelihood, brought to starvation level.

The farther east the German armies moved, the more Jewish people fled to Soviet-occupied territory. After September 1939 approximately 200,000 Jews from eastern Poland and, in 1941, large numbers from Rumania left for Russia.

It was estimated that during the war more than 1 million Jews either outside or within their own country were transported by the German authorities, while over 2 million became evacuees, fugitives, and emigrants. After the war the majority of evacuees who sought refuge in Soviet-occupied territory were repatriated to eastern European countries. In common with those who had stayed in central and western Europe, they joined in the large-scale movements southwards through Austria and Italy toward Palestine, or resettled individually in the west.[1] The total number of Jewish refugees in Europe and the Far East was estimated to be 450,000 in July 1947.[2]

POPULATIONS UPROOTED BY THE WAR

It is clear from this survey of the refugees of Jewish origin that some groups among them were included in the category of pre-war refugees, while the majority belonged to those refugees and displaced persons of the war and post-war period who became the concern of the IRO. The majority of non-Jewish, as of Jewish, refugees and displaced persons came from eastern European countries, predominantly from Poland, the Baltic countries, the Ukraine, Czechoslovakia, Hungary, Rumania, and Yugoslavia. Most of these countries had experienced great political, economic, and territorial changes since the end of the First World War. The war had changed not only their relationships to each other, but also their connexion with the two neighbouring Great Powers, Germany on the west and Russia on the east, upon whom they were dependent in one way or another for their political existence.

During the Second World War, Germany and Soviet Russia were competing, first as Allies and later as enemies, to dominate these territories or to incorporate them into their realms. To a greater or lesser degree, all of these countries became battlefields over which the German and Soviet armies moved back and forth. Many people of these countries were forced into the dilemma of supporting either Soviet Russia or Germany, often choosing the latter as the lesser evil, not because they believed in the Nazi ideology, but because they were hostile to Communism. Later it was one of the intricate problems faced by the eligibility officers of the IRO to determine who, among the survivors applying for the IRO assistance, had voluntarily assisted the enemy forces during the war.

[1] *Manual*, pp. 100–3.
[2] See Vernant, op. cit., pp. 60 and 63.

Poles

During the post-war period the Poles were the most numerous refugees. No country has experienced an unhappier fate than Poland. Squeezed between two enemies, the Poles suffered violence at the hands of both Germans and Russians, and even from both at once. This was the case in September 1939, when the Nazi attack in the west, followed by their rapid advance, brought about an invasion in the east by Soviet troops. During the period of this double pressure about 100,000 Poles succeeded in crossing the Hungarian and Rumanian frontiers, and most of them reached France and the Middle East. A government-in-exile was constituted at Angers in France, while with the help of numerous compatriots established in France, the military refugees were formed into units in order to continue the fight against Germany. After the military collapse in France, the Second Polish Division and a French Army Corps reached Switzerland and were interned there. Another group of 24,000 were transported to the UK, joining 3,800 air and naval personnel. Another 5,000 crossed from Syria into Palestine. After the retreat from Dunkirk in 1940, the Polish Government-in-exile, as well as numerous Polish civil servants, left for London where they remained for the duration of the war.

In the meantime mass deportations had been taking place from Poland. Three million inhabitants were sent to Germany, and over a million to various parts of Soviet Russia, even as far as Siberia. Within the frontiers of Poland arrests, internments in concentration camps, forced labour, and attempts to exterminate the Jewish population continued.

After Germany attacked Russia in June 1941, the Soviet Government came into the war on the side of the Allies, and consequently on that of Poland. A Polish army was formed in Soviet territory consisting of former deportees who were returning to their country on the heels of the retreating German armies. Under an agreement concluded by the Polish Marshal Sikorski and Stalin, approximately 112,000 persons (72,000 military personnel and 40,000 civilians) were released from Russia, and went to Iran in 1942 where they formed the so-called 'Anders Army', joining part of the Second Corps which had gone to the Near East, and later fighting in Italy and participating in the Normandy landings. The civilians were received in various countries of temporary asylum, and were dispersed in a way probably never before seen in history. Four thousand were sent to India whence half left for Mexico; 7,000 were divided between Lebanon, Palestine, and Egypt; no less than 16,000 were taken over by the British Government in East Africa, mostly in Kenya, while 3,000 went to Rhodesia.

At the end of hostilities, a Polish unit of about 170,000 was re-formed in Great Britain where the Government gave them generous facilities for integration into the economic life of the country and even for naturalization. However, nearly 50,000 preferred to be repatriated, while others were in time joined by their families, making a total of some 150,000 among whom the young male element predominated.

To these movements were added other large groups of refugees. Beginning with the invasion in September 1939 and continuing throughout the war, the movement increased in the early post-war period when the Polish Government of Unity, established under the Allied agreement at Yalta, was thwarted in its efforts to hold free elections with a secret ballot and M. Mikolajczyk, one of the two Vice-Premiers and former Premier of the Government-in-exile, had to flee from his country. Many of his compatriots, also disheartened, followed his example.

Balts

The coming and going of the Soviet and Nazi armies had caused a great deal of misery in the Baltic states of Lithuania, Latvia, and Estonia, which had received their independence as a result of the First World War. Annexed by the Soviet Union in June 1940, occupied the following year by the German armies at that time victorious in the east, these countries were again conquered by the advancing Soviet armies in August 1944, and re-incorporated into the USSR.[1]

From 1939 to 1946 Baltic people moved away from their homelands in three main waves. The first group were the ethnic Germans who were repatriated to Germany as a result of agreements of 1939 concluded under the 'Back to the Reich' policy between each of the Baltic states and the Nazi Government.[2] A further move took place at the beginning of 1941 following arrangements between Germany and the Soviet Union. Finally, in 1944, there was another large migration to Germany and to the Scandinavian countries by Balts escaping before their countries were re-occupied by the Red armies.[3]

The figures vary greatly, but it is generally estimated that more than 250,000–300,000 Balts lived in the north-western adjacent countries, particularly in Germany. Some of these refugees came to Germany as *bona fide* refugees, others as *Umsiedler* (resettlers), and still others because of their activities in those countries during the German occupation.[4] During the latter period compulsory military service had been introduced by the German authorities. Others volunteered in partisan units, or worked forcibly or voluntarily in labour units.

The situation of the Lithuanians in Memel should be especially noted. Their territory had been annexed by Germany as early as March 1939, and the distinction between those of German origin and those of Lithuanian race was often difficult for the IRO to determine, since it was not considered that a nationality which had been forcibly imposed should be taken as the only criterion.

Generally speaking, the Baltic elements were among the best disciplined and the most hard working of the refugees. There were also a considerable number of intellectuals among them. Although nationals of each of these small nations wished to emphasize their own nationality and culture, they all managed to ignore their differences and to unite in their common misfortune. A Baltic university was established near Hamburg and an Arts Institute near Fribourg, achievements which illustrate the

---

[1] The Western Powers never recognized *de jure* or *de facto* the absorption of the Baltic countries into the Soviet Union, but the Soviet Union maintained that by the 'elections' carried out in all those countries, each of these former independent republics had elected to become a Soviet Socialist Republic within the USSR.

[2] From Estonia approximately 12,000 persons of German ethnic origin were registered; from Latvia about 51,000 persons left for Germany and 40,000 from Lithuania.

[3] J. A. Swettenham, *The Tragedy of the Baltic States*, London, Hollis & Carter, 1952, p. 192.

[4] *Manual*, pp. 53–57.

understanding that united them. They published newspapers and books in their national languages, organized theatrical performances and scientific and literary studies, and they were outstandingly gifted in music, dancing, and painting.

As will be seen, they were much in demand by the countries of reception, some of which gave distinct preference to the Balts on learning of their reputation for hard work and their high cultural level.

Ukrainians

The Ukrainians were more or less an ethnic group with a strong national feeling, though they came from various countries. After the Bolshevik Revolution of November 1917 and the break-up of the Hapsburg Empire in 1918, the Ukrainian national movement achieved its independence. The two Republics, the Eastern and Western Ukraine, created in successive years, united on 22 January 1919. The Eastern Ukraine, however, ultimately became incorporated in the Soviet Union, although it was granted a certain autonomy, while the Western Ukraine, also guaranteed a degree of local autonomy, was partitioned between Poland, Rumania (receiving the Bukovina and Bessarabia), and Czechoslovakia (incorporating the Carpatho-Ukraine). Thus, until 1938 the Ukraine was divided between four states. From 1938 to 1945 the Germans and their satellites partitioned this area, only to leave it finally to the Soviets, who incorporated the entire Ukraine in the Soviet Union.

This historical background explains some of the problems which arose in connexion with the various groups of refugees. Often their nationality was a source of controversy. Some were legally Soviet citizens, others were Polish citizens, and many of the former tried to join the latter because they feared forced repatriation. Despite all this, the Ukrainians managed to remain a nationally coherent group because they always emphasized that they belonged to a common race, with a common language, culture, and religion. Whether they were of Galician, Ruthenian, or Bessarabian origin, they clung together in the camps and kept separate from the Poles and the Russians, showing a strong spirit of nationalism.

Those who left their country after the First World War were given Nansen status. Most of them, however, did not leave until the Second World War. While the Germans were still victorious in Russia, they were alternately cruel and persuasive. Some Ukrainians underwent mass arrests and were sent to Germany for forced labour, or they went to swell the ranks of the Soviet prisoners of Ukrainian origin. Others were victims of propaganda which asserted that their country would be resurrected, and pressure was brought to bear on them, on this patriotic pretext, to enroll them in the German army. As a result of this propaganda, a Ukrainian-Galician Waffen SS division was formed allegedly as the nucleus of a national army.

As the Nazis retreated before the Russian armies some Ukrainians, including women and children, were evacuated. Later this gave way to disorderly flight. A large number left the Soviet zone and entered Western Germany, while others, generally members of anti-Communist organizations or military insurgents, succeeded in arriving later.

It is estimated that at the end of the war 2 million people of Ukrainian origin lived in the western zones of occupied Germany and Austria. The majority were repatriated. In November 1946, 201,000 remained in central Europe; these were divided as follows: 178,000 in Western Germany (104,000 in the American zone, 55,000 in the British zone, 19,000 in the French zone); about 23,000 in Austria; and several thousand in Prague, mostly refugees of long standing with Nansen papers. About 71 per cent. of them came from southern Poland and Volhynia, and about 30 per cent. from the eastern Ukraine in Soviet territory. Approximately 54 per cent. were Greek Catholics; 43 per cent. Orthodox; and the rest of other denominations.[1]

The advance of the German armies from 1942 until their final defeat in January 1943 at Stalingrad was the occasion for the deportation to Germany of numbers of Soviet citizens as forced labourers. From these groups and from the ranks of the prisoners of war the Germans also formed the Cossack Regiment, which the White Russians joined, and the Vlassov army. Vlassov, a former General in the Soviet army, who had been taken prisoner at the beginning of 1942 and had denounced Communism, called this the Liberation army organized to fight against their compatriots side by side with the German forces.

At the Yalta conference an agreement was signed on 11 February 1945 (and made public on 8 March 1946) between the US and the Soviet Union 'relating to the prisoners of war and the civilians liberated under Soviet Command and Forces operating under the US command' which provided for the immediate repatriation of civilians and prisoners of war of both nationalities after their liberation.[2] Similar agreements were concluded by the UK with the Soviet Union on the same day and at the same place, and by the French on 29 June 1945. These agreements had no provision for forcible repatriation. The military authorities in the western zones of Germany insisted on repatriation as far as possible. It was reported by the chief of the Soviet Repatriation Mission that 5 million Soviet prisoners of war and civilians returned to their homelands. Some, however, were more hesitant, since the fact that they had been in enemy hands or had worked in war factories might make them suspects at home. Others dreaded repatriation for political reasons. Their attitude presented a difficult problem for the Western authorities, who wanted to carry out the provisions of their agreements with their former ally and yet wished to safeguard the individuals' free choice in accordance with the principles of individual liberty laid down in the United Nations Charter. When they realized that Soviet citizens, terrified at the idea of repatriation, opposed it with all their might—some even committed suicide—the military authorities no longer persisted in carrying out the letter of the agreement which, from the beginning, had not been fulfilled by the Soviet authorities. This explains why there were many thousands of Soviet citizens who did not go home, of whom, however, only some 10,000 received IRO assistance at the beginning of its operations.

[1] Vernant, op. cit., p. 87.
[2] For text see *World War II, International Agreements and Understandings* . . ., Washington, 1953, pp. 46–49, see also John R. Deane, 'Negotiating on Military Assistance, 1943–45', in Der op. cit., p. 14, General Deane signed this agreement for the US, later negotiated General Staff about the implementation of this agreement in regard to the America most of them in German camps or western Poland. 'The Agreement was a good on Russians were concerned, it turned out to be just another piece of paper. . . . Our Yal not carried out by the Soviet Russians.' Ibid., pp. 14–15.

Yugoslavs

Yugoslavia also suffered badly during the war. Divided racially into southern Slavs, Croats, Slovenes, and Serbs, the country was also divided by internal as well as external political allegiances. When, under pressure from the victorious Germans, the Prince Regent joined the Tripartite Pact, public reaction was spontaneous in denouncing this act. But the Nazis exacted full payment. In spite of attempts to resist after the severe bombing of Belgrade, Yugoslavia, in April 1941, had to capitulate to the Germans and was occupied by them. A quisling government was formed in Serbia under General Nedic. Serbia was partially dismembered, parts of it coming under the newly formed independent state of Croatia, and under Hungary, Bulgaria, and Albania. Slovenia was dismembered by the Axis Powers, the northern part being annexed by Germany and the southern occupied by Italy. After the collapse of the Italian Fascist Government, Germany took Italy's place. About 130,000 prisoners of war were taken to Germany. Of these, about 30,000 were soon liberated owing to their supposed pro-German sentiments. At the end of hostilities many prisoners returned to their country, but many also, in particular the officers, refused, either because they were in opposition to the régime, or because they were royalists.

As in the other countries she occupied, Germany exploited to the full potential labour for her industrial and agricultural needs. Bosnia, Herzegovina, and Croatia provided a great number of workers. The inhabitants of the annexed Slovene territory were mobilized. In Croatia, which had long been jealous of Serb predominance, the Germans cleverly exploited these sentiments and succeeded in raising several divisions that willingly fought side by side with them.

During this period in Serbia, which had been reduced to its 1914 territories, tension reached the pitch of civil war. The Serbian Volunteer Corps and the Serbian State Guards supported the Government, which was accused of siding with the conqueror and of putting down insurgent movements. The insurgents belonged either to the *Chetnik* movement, 'The Royal Yugoslav Army in the Woods', mostly former members of the regular army, who, under the leadership of General Mihailovic, had resisted the Germans and put their faith in the Western Powers—or to the other resistance forces under Tito, who had rallied the Communists after the Soviet Union joined the Allies in June 1941. After a brief truce, the two groups quarrelled. Soviet successes had done much to enhance the prestige of Tito, while Mihailovic was playing a waiting game. Finally the latter, whose group was repudiated by the British and Americans in February 1944, was captured by Tito's partisans, whose importance and efficacy had been steadily increasing. *Chetnik* units, joined by the Volunteer Corps and the State Guards, withdrew to Italy where they surrendered to the Allied forces; 10,000 were interned in a camp near Naples. There was much confusion between these troops and the Croat units who had voluntarily fought with the Nazis. Even though most of the *Chetniks* had placed themselves at the disposal of the Allies, they were for a long time the object of suspicion.

The origins and antecedents of the Yugoslav refugees, therefore, were complex.

Ethnically they were composed of Serbs (mostly anti-Communist, often royalist, and sometimes germanophile), of Croat prisoners of war and deportees (many of whom had also been drawn into the Nazi forces or had been volunteers in the *Ustashi* units and other groups comparable to the SS), and lastly of Slovenes (either mobilized, or deported, as was the case of the 150,000 who had been forced to go to Serbia and were replaced by German settlers). Hostile to the Serbs, to the Croats, and to Communism, most of the Slovene refugees refused to return to their homes. Joined by numerous compatriots fleeing from the partisan troops, whole groups transported themselves to Italy with priests and civil servants at their head.

During the deliberations in the Third Committee of the US General Assembly in February 1946, and in the Special Committee on Refugees and Displaced Persons, the Yugoslav delegate maintained that most of the displaced persons coming from Yugoslavia who refused to return after the war were people who had 'in one way or another collaborated with the aggressor, that they were traitors to their country, and thereby traitors to the cause of the United Nations'.[1]

In 1945–6 the Yugoslav Government promulgated legislation which denationalized former members of the army who refused to return, members of those organizations that were accused of having served the occupying powers such as the *Chetniks*, the *Ustashi*, the *Domobranci* and others, and those who had left Yugoslavia with the Germans or later. The people concerned were given two months in which they could return without loss of their nationality.[2] But in spite of the fact that many displaced persons did not avail themselves of this opportunity, the Yugoslav Government did not implement the provision. On the contrary, it appealed to them in various ways to return. In December 1951 the Minister of the Interior declared in the National Assembly that the Yugoslav Government would continue 'to do everything within its power to facilitate the return of the emigrés' and that the refugees would 'have absolutely nothing to fear for having failed to return sooner'.[3]

Thus the Yugoslav refugees of the Second World War originated from four groups. The first was comprised of former prisoners of war of the Germans who were liberated by the Allies. The second were the forcibly deported labourers of whom the largest part was repatriated. The third were those who fled to Austria and Italy after the collapse of the German armies and the fourth those who escaped in 1944, consisting mainly of the Croatian *Domobranci* and a few *Chetniks*.[4]

Czechs

Czechoslovakia, which valiantly tried to save its independence under a genuinely democratic government, was caught between the German and Soviet struggle for domination of this economically rich territory. The crisis, beginning with the founding of the nationalist Sudeten Party in May 1935, ended with the Munich Pact of

[1] E/REF 1, p. 9, and E/REF/75, p. 163. In 1947 the British Government entrusted to the Maclean Screening Commission 'the task of sorting out those Yugoslavs surrendered enemy personnel who were found in Italy' and Austria at the end of the Second World War, and to determine which of them would fall within the mandate of the IRO. See *Manual*, p. 88.
[2] Law of 23 Aug. 1945, amended by Law of 23 Oct. 1946.
[3] Vernant, op. cit., p. 89.
[4] See *Manual*, pp. 83–84.

September 1938 when the Sudetenland fell into Hitler's orbit and the Benes government fled, forming a government-in-exile in London. In October 1938 some $2\frac{1}{2}$ million subjects, including about 100,000 Czechs, automatically became German subjects. As has been described, many left their country and became refugees.[1] In March 1939, after instigating an uprising in Slovakia, the Nazi Government declared the Czech territory a 'protectorate of Bohemia and Moravia' and Slovakia an 'independent state under German tutelage'. Most of Ruthenia was given to Hungary, and Poland took Silesian Teschen with some additional districts. In all these territories resistance movements were active. Other groups, however, tried to flee, or collaborated with the new régimes.

One of the events that had a profound repercussion on the whole of eastern Europe, and which caused a mass exodus, was the Communist *coup d'état* in Czechoslovakia in February 1948, followed by the death of Jan Masaryck. Immediately afterwards about 5,000 persons took refuge in the US zone of Germany, and a number impossible to determine (perhaps about 10,000) because of the relative facility for clandestine entry, into Austria. Half of them were put into camps. Following the elections in May, the flood of refugees increased in spite of the efforts made to prevent them from entering. Finally, about 50,000 Czechs succeeded in crossing the frontiers and reached France, Italy, Switzerland, Great Britain, and elsewhere overseas. There were many Jews among them and members of the professional classes. Not all the Czech refugees came under IRO, and, unlike the nationals of other countries, the majority were not in the operational zone when the Organization began to operate, but arrived subsequently.

Hungarians

Hungary, Rumania, and Bulgaria, who joined the Axis, followed the German policy of persecuting the Jews, and drafted many people into their fighting and labour forces.

Following the example of Germany, Hungary was at war with Russia in June 1941 (with US and Great Britain in December of the same year), but this war was so unpopular that, after one defeat at the front, the Hungarian forces, except an army of occupation, were withdrawn from the front.

When things began to go against the Reich, support from Budapest became more and more uncertain. At the beginning of 1944 the Germans imposed a pro-Nazi government whose first act was to deport the Jews, who were very numerous and often very influential in Hungary. An attempt to conclude an armistice with the Allies was circumvented, and the Germans exercised complete control. Before the rapid Soviet advance, they forcibly evacuated numerous civil servants, as well as engineers and factory workers, with their families. About $1\frac{1}{2}$ million Hungarians thus left their country, about 500,000 of whom reached Germany and, in particular, Bavaria.

At the end of the war the Allies undertook to repatriate them with the help of the Hungarian Red Cross. But about 10,000 refused to return to their country since it

[1] Introduction, p. 9.

was occupied by the Soviet army, and several thousands more were prevented from going back by the Soviet authorities' refusal to continue supplying any means of transport. Finally, as Communist tendencies began to increase in Budapest, the Hungarian refugees gave up the idea of returning. Others succeeded in escaping, usually the younger ones who wished to evade military service, or small tradespeople who were not able to weather the economic conditions. According to an estimate nearly 100,000 were Hungarians, of whom about a half were Jews.[1]

Rumanians

In common with Hungary, Rumania declared war on the Soviet Union in June 1941, hoping to regain the territories ceded in 1940. After initial successes the Rumanian troops were defeated. On 23 August 1944 Rumania surrendered to the Allies and joined their side in the war against Germany and Hungary. In March 1945 a puppet government imposed by Russia was formed, which was succeeded by the People's Democratic Republic by December 1948.

Several groups of refugees and displaced persons owed their fate to the political changes which occurred in Rumania from 1938 to 1948: those formerly transferred and displaced persons who refused to return; political refugees fleeing from their country after the establishment of a Communist government; and several thousand Rumanians of Greek origin who took refuge in Greece in 1947. The first group resulted mainly from the transfers of population agreed upon by Germany and the Soviet Union, and by Germany and Rumania. Before the war 28·1 per cent. of the total population in Rumania was comprised of minority groups. The largest groups were 7·9 per cent. Hungarians, 5·7 per cent. Jews, and 4·1 per cent. Germans.

After the incorporation of Bessarabia and northern Bukovina into the Soviet Union, under a German-Soviet agreement concluded in September 1940, 137,000 ethnic Germans were transferred to Germany. A transfer of about 76,700 ethnic Germans from northern Dobruja and southern Bukovina took place under a similar agreement made a month later between Germany and Rumania. There were minor transfers between Hungary and Rumania and, as mentioned above,[2] the transplanting of the Jewish minority into ghettoes. The ethnic Germans were not refugees in the real sense of the word, but with them came some people from Bukovina and Bessarabia; later labourers, army officers, and students accompanied the retreating German army. The numbers were not as high, however, as in the case of Hungary. Several thousand belonging to another German group left their country after March 1945, and later, when the Communist element took over the government, they crossed into Hungary. People leaving after 1947 sought asylum in Yugoslavia where, however, the turn of events made their situation very precarious.

A group of about 7,500 Rumanians of Greek origin left for Greece after 1947 when the Rumanian Government took action against middle class people, especially those of foreign descent.

---

[1] Vernant, op. cit., p. 72. James Parkes, 'The Treatment of the Jews', in *Hitler's Europe*, Survey of International Affairs, 1939–46, ed. by Arnold and Veronica M. Toynbee, pp. 153–64; and Elizabeth Wiskemann, 'Hungary, Rumania and Bulgaria', 1941–4, ibid., pp. 604–31.

[2] See p. 174.

Bulgarians

Bulgaria, aiming at the establishment of a homogeneous Greater Bulgaria, joined the Axis and declared war, if but a 'hypothetical' one, on the UK and the US in December 1941.[1] The government carried out deportations and persecutions against minorities in the territories ceded from Greece and Yugoslavia. In August 1944 Bulgaria withdrew from the war and after Soviet Russia, in October 1944, had declared war on Bulgaria she declared war on Germany, and requested an armistice with Soviet Russia. Several thousand refugees left for western Europe after the establishment of a Soviet-influenced government.

Mennonites

Two other groups of refugees who became the concern of the IRO have to be added: the Mennonites, who came from Soviet Russia, and the Venezia Giulians, who came from the region on the Italo–Yugoslav frontier. The Mennonites belonged to the Mennonite Church, founded in Zürich, Switzerland, in 1525. One of their principles is non-resistance and conscientious objection to the use of armed force. They have been persecuted for centuries and in various countries because of their heretical religious belief. They had been persecuted in Switzerland, and persecutions continued in Holland and in Flanders during the Spanish Inquisition. In the middle of the sixteenth century they found refuge in Prussia. A century later, chiefly to escape conscription in the Prussian army, the Mennonites moved to southern Russia. They increased in Russia to approximately 45,000 people, retaining German customs and language, and their own religion.

When, however, in the nineteenth century, the Tsar tried to russify this group and deprived them of their privileges, one-third of them emigrated to the American continent. A second and larger exodus occurred in 1929–30, when about 25,000 Mennonite refugees went to Canada, Brazil, and Paraguay, and a third from 1941 to 1945, when about 35,000 went to Germany. Some of these people were sent by the German authorities to Rumania, Czechoslovakia, and Poland (Warthegau), while others left Russia with the retreating armies. It is estimated that about 25,000 returned to the Soviet Union, while most of the others went overseas.

As a result of their wanderings during a period of more than 300 years from western Europe to central Europe, to Russia and back to central Europe, there were, at the end of the war, four different categories of Mennonites in Germany, Austria, and Italy. Two groups, the so-called *Danzig Mennonites* and the *East* and *West Prussian Mennonites*, came to Germany during the war either voluntarily or because of their expulsion by the Poles as a German minority group. Approximately 2,500 of the first group came to Western Germany, predominantly to Schleswig-Holstein in the British occupied zone, and about 5,000 of the second group. There were about 25,000 *German Mennonites* who were established residents of Western Germany, and finally the *Polish* and *Russian Mennonites*, about 11,500 of whom were eligible for IRO assistance.[2]

---

[1] Cf. Elizabeth Wiskemann, op. cit., p. 605.
[2] See Chapter XII, Eligibility, p. 210.

Venezia Giulians

As a result of the cessation of part of the Venezia Giulian territory to Yugoslavia under the terms of the Italian Peace Treaty, which came into force in September 1947, many persons left the ceded territory and entered Italy. Some of them spoke Slovene as their customary language, and others spoke Italian. Although all persons in the ceded territory were granted Yugoslav citizenship by the terms of the Peace Treaty, those who had been domiciled in the ceded territory on 10 June 1940 and whose customary language was Italian had the right to opt for Italian citizenship during the twelve months ending on 15 September 1948. After that date, refugees from Venezia Giulia located in Italy whose customary language was Italian were either Italian citizens who had retained their Italian citizenship by option under the terms of the Peace Treaty, or persons who had not opted to retain their Italian citizenship and were legally still Yugoslav citizens. It was at this time that the IRO, at the request of the Italian Government, became actively concerned with the possibility of assisting the Italian-speaking Venezia Giulian refugees.

By agreement between the Italian and Yugoslav governments, a procedure had been established for persons desiring to retain Italian citizenship. Application had at first to be made to the Yugoslav authorities, who might accept or reject it. Options accepted by the Yugoslavs were then passed on to the Italian authorities, who likewise had the power to accept or reject them. The procedure was substantially similar whether the applicant was in Yugoslavia or in Italy at the time of application.

The Italian Government had officially requested the IRO to care for all Venezia Giulians who had not opted for Italian citizenship within the period ending 15 September 1948, since they were deemed to have acquired Yugoslav citizenship. In 1950 the IRO finally decided to care for about 24,000 people with an 'indeterminate citizenship'.

Volksdeutsche

The Organization was not required under its Constitution to handle the difficulties created by the influx into Western Germany and Austria of German refugees and displaced people, the so-called *Volksdeutsche*. This expression was coined by the Nazi Party to designate all persons outside Germany and Austria who qualified as members of the German race. It differed from the term 'German minorities' only in that it included Austrians as well as Germans.[1]

The mass exodus and mass expulsion of ethnic Germans who came mainly from Poland, Czechoslovakia, Hungary, and Rumania, can only be understood as a result of the terrible tensions which the policies had created in those countries whose political and military plight has been outlined above. It has been stated in another context that Hitler's *Zurück ins Reich* (back to the homeland) policy had caused more than half a million to be brought to Germany, and in addition nearly 400,000 people were transferred from the Balkans and other eastern areas when the Germans retreated to the west. This stream was endlessly swelled by people coming from liberated Poland, Czechoslovakia, and Hungary, and from the occupied territories

[1] *Manual*, p. 51.

of East Prussia, Pomerania, and Silesia. In June 1945 the Czech Government had announced officially its intention to expel Germans from its territory, as had Poland, although unofficially. Stalin confirmed this large-scale spontaneous exodus of Germans from the former German-occupied eastern European areas into Germany as early as at the Yalta conference, in February 1945, by saying: 'Where our troops come in, the Germans run away.' He maintained that nothing could stop this move-ment 'because of deep-rooted and bitter feelings of the people against the Germans'. He emphasized that not only the Big Three but also the Polish and Czech govern-ments themselves were powerless to prevent the exodus.[1]

Against this 'background of accomplished fact of large scale expulsions, coupled with Soviet unwillingness to do anything about them', the Big Three agreed on Article XIII of the Potsdam Agreement in order 'to make more orderly and humane the inevitable expulsion of those Germans remaining in Poland, Czechoslovakia, and Hungary', and 'to open occupied Germany to those who were faced with deporta-tion to remote sub-Arctic territories of Soviet Russia, an equivalent to annihilation'.[2]

The Control Council for Germany was entrusted with the development of a plan for 'humane and orderly reception' and for equitable distribution of these people within Germany. The so-called Berlin plan was put into effect in November 1945. It is estimated that about 15 million *Volksdeutsche* were uprooted during the period 1938–46, although only 12 million entered the occupied zones of Germany. Of these, 6,650,000 transfers were spaced out between December 1945 and July 1946 under the Berlin plan. The request contained in Article XIII of the Potsdam Agreement to Czechoslovakia, Poland, and Hungary, for a suspension of further expulsions until adequate preparations could be made, was not heeded; nor was attention paid to the later monthly allocation quota with a fixed total, as forwarded to these countries by the Control Council officials. It was the joint policy of the Allied Control Council that the expelled persons, after arrival in Germany, were considered as Germans and subject to the same rights, privileges, restrictions, and responsibilities as the indigenous population. Their needs were to be cared for by the agencies responsible for similar needs on the part of the native population. The military government directed that adequate reception and distribution facilities should be provided. It was in this task that, in time of emergency, the IRO camps gave help by harbouring fresh arrivals for one or two nights until other provisions could be made.

Refugee groups in China

Mention must be made of a group of refugees—those who lived outside Europe—which became the concern of the IRO. In the Shanghai region there was a group of 16,000 Europeans whose situation was pitiable. They were White Russians who had been in China for over thirty years, chiefly in Manchuria, where they had a very difficult existence, and German Jews or Jews from neighbouring countries whom panic had pushed to the shores of the Yellow Sea after an extraordinary odyssey across all Europe and Asia.

The IRO was interested in these as well as in the overseas Chinese refugees who,

[1] House Report No. 1841, 81st Congress, Second Session, pp. 6–9.
[2] Ibid., p. 6.

curiously enough, enjoyed refugee status in their own country. They were members of the numerous and flourishing business communities which had prospered round the Indian Ocean and even in the Pacific, in French Indo-China, Thailand, Burma, Singapore, Malaya, Indonesia, and the Philippines. Established a long time ago in these regions, they had been forced to flee as hostilities developed and to seek shelter in China itself, where they awaited the opportunity to regain their homes. Many of the wealthy among them returned of their own accord and by their own means. But about 12,000 could not do so, and had been taken over by UNRRA and then by the IRO which endeavoured to evacuate them in the same way as their European companions.

Having in mind the national, ethnic, and religious origin of the European and Asiatic refugees and displaced persons and the variety of political and military causes that led to their uprooting and far-flung dispersal, one can easily visualize the difficult task authorities took upon themselves when they cared for, protected, and re-established a normal life for the fugitives—a task that demanded firmness and determination, on the one hand, and great human understanding, patience, and imagination, on the other.

CHAPTER XI

THE COMMUNITY IN EXILE

STATISTICAL lag and discrepancies in classification from area to area made it difficult in the period from 1945 to early 1948 to arrive at reliable figures as to the recorded number of refugees and displaced persons. Such figures as are available can only give some idea of the general dimension of the task.

In order to plan for the work of the IRO, the UN Special Committee on Refugees and Displaced Persons tried to collect statistics as accurate as possible through its Fact-Finding Sub-Committee. The available statistics varied according to their sources, because of the dislocation in Europe, the intricate political situation in eastern and central Europe, and the loss of many identity documents, as well as the fluctuation of refugee groups.

The Allied military authorities estimated that by 31 December 1946 a total number of 1,037,404 displaced persons were living in and out of camps in Germany, Austria, and Italy.[1] These figures included only the displaced persons who were left over after the repatriation movements had been carried out under the military authorities and UNRRA in collaboration with the respective governments.

The Special Committee included in its report to the ECOSOC figures, dated 31 March 1946, on refugees and displaced persons in Europe, the Middle East, and Africa, except the Far East.[2] This estimate amounted to 1,675,000 refugees (the terms refugees and displaced persons were used in a wider sense than those used in the IRO Constitution) including persons assisted in one way or another by UNRRA, by the League of Nations High Commissioner for Refugees, by IGCR, or by the UN governments; in fact, those groups who became more or less the concern of the IRO. In addition to these, IRO had to deal with a fifth group, the so-called neo-refugees, who were flowing into western from eastern Europe during the period of operations of the IRO.

Number of refugees

Thus when the PCIRO took over the operations on 1 July 1947, the numbers of refugees within the terms of reference stipulated by the Constitution was estimated as being somewhere between 1 and 1½ million,[3] and in fact during the entire period of operations of four and a half years (1 July 1947–31 December 1951) a total of 1,619,008 refugees and displaced persons were registered and assisted by the IRO.[4]

The refugees and displaced persons under the IRO mandate were dispersed over a wide geographical area. The majority lived in the three western zones of Germany

---

[1] Annex 13, p. 197.
[2] Annex 14, p. 198.
[3] Annex 17, pp. 200–1.
[4] This estimate of PCIRO as of 31 Mar. 1948 included some 47,000 Jewish refugees, most of them in the US zone of Germany. (UN, ECOSOC, *Report on the Progress . . .*, op. cit.,'p. 9.)

(604,556); in Austria (33,049); and in Italy (29,170). Of the rest 117,370 were in Belgium (1,800); France (6,300); the Netherlands, Portugal, Spain, and a very few in Czechoslovakia.[1] In addition there were 27,600 in the Middle East as well as 16,090 in East Africa and 4,250 in India. A group of 9,300 Europeans—mostly of Jewish or White Russian origin—in Shanghai were waiting for an opportunity to leave China.

There were three groups of beneficiaries divided into categories according to the type of assistance they needed from the IRO. On 1 July 1947, 712,675 refugees and displaced persons received care and maintenance, in other words, their full livelihood. Of these, 626,000 had been taken over from UNRRA camps; 60,550 from military camps; 9,000 from IGCR; and 9,300 from AJDC.

366,000 refugees, receiving only aid in resettlement and legal assistance, lived out-of-camp in the following countries:

193,000 in three zones of Western Germany
55,000 in Austria
50,000 in Italy
50,000 in France
5,000 in Belgium
5,000 in the Netherlands
1,000 in the Middle East
7,000 in China

Lastly, there were those who were *de facto* or *de jure* stateless persons and who received only legal assistance, the so-called Nansen refugees.

The figures naturally fluctuated during the period of IRO operations. New applications were continually received from refugees already in the operational zone, who had not previously made themselves known, and from the neo-refugees who had succeeded in escaping from behind the Iron Curtain. On the other hand, the departure of the repatriates, and above all, of the emigrants, progressively decreased the number of the IRO's protégés.

The main groups receiving care and maintenance from the PCIRO on 31 August 1947 were chiefly of eastern European origin; according to their citizenship or last habitual residence, there were 278,293 Poles, 98,256 Ukrainians, 29,336 Yugoslavs, 22,192 Estonians, 77,550 Latvians, 47,884 Lithuanians, 7,559 Czechs, 9,026 Hungarians, 8,460 Rumanians, and 1,143 Turks. There were an additional 20,000 without, or with an undetermined, citizenship.[2] Of these, about 154,334 people of Jewish origin who came from thirty-five different countries of habitual residence, received care and maintenance from the IRO in Germany, Austria, and Italy.[3]

A statistical survey of 31 December 1948 regarding the religious affiliation of refugees and displaced persons showed that more than three-quarters of 523,259 refugees in IRO camps and assembly centres were: Roman Catholics (204,636), Jewish (92,944), and Protestants (87,648); while 78,616 were Greek Orthodox and 44,649 Greek Catholics.[4]

[1] Fulton Report, pp. 4–9 and Annex 17: Summary of IRO Statistics, p. 8.
[2] Table in Fulton Report, p. 5.
[3] Annex 15, p. 199.　　　　[4] Annex 16, p. 200.

Demographic character

The refugee population reflected the abnormal conditions which had brought it into being. Its demographic characteristics were unlike those of other populations. Most striking was the large proportion of young people compared with old people. The first detailed statistics compiled in 1948 in Germany, Austria, and Italy showed the following features in regard to age, sex, professions, and skills. 22·4 per cent. were under 14 years of age; 77·2 per cent. between 14 and 65; and 0·4 per cent. were above 65 years of age. The corresponding figures for the German population were: 24·3 per cent. under 14; 66·9 per cent. from 14 to 65; and 8·8 per cent. above 65 years of age. Among the children under 14 an especially large group was under 4 years of age, indicating a high birth-rate (31·9 per 1,000) and a low death rate (5·9 per 1,000), compared with the birth-rate in 1934 in Germany, 7·1 per 1,000, in England 3·3 per 1,000. One of the reasons for the extraordinarily high birth-rate was the proportion of women of 18–44 to the total female population, which was much more favourable than among a normal population. Another factor was the unusual numerical relation between the sexes, with the great predominance of males.

Among the displaced persons there were only 37·2 per cent. females compared with 55·5 per cent. in the population of Germany, and a much smaller proportion were unmarried. Thus it was a population at the height of fertility and potential strength, though mainly destitute and physically impaired by ill-treatment, hard labour, and bad living conditions.

A high percentage of the refugees of both sexes were employable and had many and diversified skills, as will be described in detail later.[1]

It might be mentioned here that the first classification of occupational skills, taken in March 1948 among 55 per cent. of the people receiving care and maintenance, showed a high population of skilled labour (38·6 per cent.) and fewer (22·3 per cent.) agricultural workers. This was partly due to the fact that the professional classes (specialists, managers, &c.) did not register themselves as such, but as skilled labourers, because they tried thus to circumvent the barriers raised by reception countries against members of the professions. In spite of this fact the proportion of the professions was still very high, i.e. 12·5 per cent. These figures indicate that a markedly large group of the intelligentsia formed part of the refugee movements of the war and post-war periods. The total number of intellectuals and their families was given as 40,000 persons.

Human problems

'Statistics tend to conceal the realities of human tragedy behind a curtain of useful administrative data.'[2] There is the danger of forgetting the personal disasters—the misery of families torn apart, the uprooting of people from their homes, and the difficulties of living in strange and not always congenial communities, the frequent and pernicious condition of lethargy, so often an aftermath of the shock of sudden

---

[1] Chapter XVI, Adaptation to a New Life, p. 277.

[2] From her sympathetic understanding the writer, K. Hulme, gave a vivid and convincing description of the camp life. Cf. Kathryn Hulme, op. cit.

catastrophe. This should be kept in mind when it is considered how and where the displaced persons lived in their temporary abodes in the countries of first asylum while awaiting a permanent settlement, and how the governments of first asylum, in co-operation with the IRO and the voluntary societies, tried to ameliorate their plight.

The fate which refugees had experienced made them feel physically and morally uprooted. They were isolated in a strange world, separated from their own culture by all the things around them: by language, by customs, by an unfamiliar approach to things, and, worst of all perhaps, by the lack of solutions to their own problems. They had lost their standing in a closely integrated society, and were living in an inhuman condition of insecurity.

They were weakened physically by poverty and privations, and morally by their abnormal life, forced into long periods of inactivity in unstable conditions in camps. The monotony of a purposeless existence under conditions of overcrowding and total lack of privacy had sapped their initiative. Many resigned themselves and became apathetic, worn out by long waiting and idleness, for which they were not always responsible. Many, too, were embittered, full of hate and desire for revenge against the people in whose territory they had found refuge. In addition, they were often at odds with each other, because of different political opinion and social and economic backgrounds.

Communal life

However, the fact of not belonging to the society in which they lived developed a community spirit among them which was naturally encouraged by living in corporate groups. In the Middle East during the war, and in Germany, Austria, and Italy immediately after the war, the military and other authorities had tried to make orderly arrangements for refugees by urging them to live in assembly centres; these, for temporary shelter in the occupied areas, were barracks, churches, schools, youth hostels, and even forced labour camps. They provided primitive family homes and communal living arrangements, as well as food, welfare, and medical services. As the period of waiting for re-establishment became longer, so the assembly centres developed; by the time the IRO started work they had emerged as complete communities, each with its own police force, public health unit, central registration or vital statistics bureau, dispensary, schools, churches, recreational facilities, communal feeding arrangements, and libraries; and in some cases attempts were made to establish small parks within the limited area of the centre.

Wherever possible, it was arranged for each assembly centre to be inhabited by a homogeneous national group. But there were exceptions. Frequently refugees from Estonia, Latvia, and Lithuania were assigned together to a given centre which was then designated as a Baltic centre. This, however, destroyed neither the principle of assembly-centre organization nor the concept of community, because there was a common political allegiance to certain ideals and experience which created a basic unity among these people. Another similar exception was the establishment of Jewish centres in which previous national affiliations were completely disregarded and the characteristic spirit was purely Jewish. There were rarely more than a few non-Jews in Jewish centres, but in other centres with any predominant national character, there were nearly always groups of refugees of other nationalities.

The community spirit among refugees was greatly assisted by national pride; Jews and non-Jews, however, showed a different kind of national pride. The Jewish population, motivated by the will to establish a state of their own, looked forward to it with an enthusiasm which completely effaced any sense of previous national ties. The non-Jewish population meticulously followed each national holiday and paid respect to their honoured national citizens. The hope of returning to their countries as they knew them before the war was constantly present. The Jewish population directed their energies towards the future; it was a hope within the realm of possibility. The non-Jewish group looked back to what had been.

The deep sense of national or communal pride was evident in every centre. There were streets named after familiar surroundings in their home countries; and many assembly centres were called by the name of a national hero. The art and literature of particular national groups were preserved by those of them who possessed the technical skill to produce replicas of past glory. The production and exhibition of national handicrafts always provided an opportunity to display to the public the aspects of national culture which had a universal significance.

Jewish cultural activities were highly developed and centrally encouraged. There were, for example, more than twenty newspapers and periodicals published by the Central Committee of the Jewish Displaced Persons in Austria, Germany, and Italy. In the US zone of Germany the Central Committee in 1947 was responsible for 62 kindergartens, 62 elementary schools, and 4 high schools; they provided for the education of 14,000 children, and of the 600 teachers in these schools some came specially from Palestine. Jewish artists and musicians, too, were brought from Palestine to the UK and the US zones by the AJDC and the JAFP, to lecture and perform in the institutes of adult education which existed in all centres.

To an Estonian, the relatively high standard of living prevailing in pre-war Estonia was a matter of pride; and a Latvian viewed Riga as the little Paris of eastern Europe. The pre-war White Russian and Armenian refugee groups were notably loyal to their national origins, despite their wanderings since the First World War. Within the framework of their communities the refugees were able to preserve their customs and usual patterns of life; and their basic institutions, such as churches and schools, were established along traditional lines. The sense of community and pride in it were doubtless another reason why—despite the propaganda efforts to picture the refugees as undisciplined—refugees were, in fact, more law-abiding than the populations among whom they were forced to live.

Community spirit was further encouraged by the arrangements for the administration of centres by the refugees themselves. As early as 1945 it had been contemplated that the refugee population should be charged with the performance of certain functions essential to the administration of the centres, such as registration, billeting, welfare, supply, health and sanitation, education, recreation and employment. It became the policy of both the Allied military authorities and of UNRRA that the refugee populations should resume these responsibilities. The first step was the formation of an advisory council of refugees in each centre; such councils later became elected centre committees responsible to the international staff for the conduct of the centres. When the IRO became responsible for assembly centres in Italy and in the US zones of Germany and Austria, it continued the policy of self-administration previously established. In the US zone of Germany, this policy was laid down in an administrative order of 12 August 1948; the general policy already accepted was published for the IRO as a whole in an order from headquarters dated 15 June 1949. In the British zones of Germany and Austria, British officers were in charge of individual assembly centres. Where the IRO was responsible, the international staff supervised a number of centres together.

Naturally, the scope and pattern of self-administration varied according to the personality of the IRO's field administration. Elections for the centre committees were a serious business, for leaders had to be chosen who could adequately represent the population before the Allied and international authorities. Such elections in themselves helped to maintain the self-respect and pride of the individual, for they gave him the chance of giving form to his concept of how the community should function. Although far from their countries of origin, past political and class relationships played an important part in the selection of persons as members of the committees. Former public servants, professors, leading business men, and jurists were frequently chosen as members of the representative bodies elected by the displaced population. This became significant when, in the latter years of the IRO operations, many leaders left because of their resettlement, so that certain functions of centre life had to be taken over by members of the IRO staff. Difficulties with language were not unknown. The population of a centre often considered it wiser to appoint to the committee persons who could speak English or the language of the country in which the centre was located, rather than persons who might, on other grounds, be more suitable. Thus it happened from time to time that the elected committee was in fact instructed on its policies by an informal group of 'elder statesmen'.

The assembly centre community greatly strengthened group relationships. Refugees daily discussed all problems with each other, especially the important matters which might affect their temporary status as exiles. In the semi-isolated life of the centres the refugees tended to live among themselves almost entirely; there were few moderating contacts with the local population and the outside world. Life in the centres was either completely apathetic or exceedingly tense; the community was on the defensive, either not caring about anything or sensitive about everything.

This situation markedly affected the personality of the refugee. He was deferential to the authorities, yet showed particular sensitivity with respect to his status. His sense of not belonging was the common lot of the stateless. The complete uncertainty as to the future and the memories of the past inevitably increased his feeling of insecurity. Since his whole life hinged on resettlement opportunities, he was bitterly envious of refugees more fortunate than himself in this respect; and since his day-to-day existence was based on fair shares, he would protest against the slightest inequality in treatment.

Where the material conditions were suitable, the bonds of comradeship—the common language and other cultural elements—could become strong, and the communal solidarity of the centres and loyalty to the refugee community were further strengthened by the IRO and the voluntary societies. This fellowship in adversity sustained the refugee, and enabled him to withstand disintegrating effects of exile.[1]

Though the assembly centre community was at first separate from the wider community of the country in which it was placed, i.e. Germany and Austria, the two communities gradually came closer together, and the relationship between the specially protected exile and the local population began to assume a more normal pattern.

Nevertheless, in the assembly centre countries, economic conditions prevented complete assimilation. The widespread unemployment in Italy in general prevented refugees from working in the free market; by agreement with the Italian Government refugees under the IRO mandate receiving care and maintenance could not compete for work in the local economy. In Germany there was a deep resistance on the part of refugees to working for German firms. The breakdown of this attitude was slow, and even after the currency reform in August 1948 there was no noticeable increase in the employment of refugees in private enterprise until the middle of 1949. Although it was the policy in Austria to subject refugees to the local compulsory labour law, jobs, except in unskilled labour and farm work, did not, in practice, exist. In the Middle East, individuals sometimes found work outside the centres. In Samar the refugees were so isolated that it was impossible for any individual to work in private employment.

The spirit of the community of exiles was so strong that there existed a common desire to hold the community together by group migration. But under the criteria established by the immigration countries, the young and the technically trained departed first, and with their departure the communities in the assembly centres began to deteriorate. Despite the efforts of the IRO to encourage resettlement by families there was evidence that families were breaking up to enable individual members to emigrate. Those who had made the decision to settle overseas began to prepare themselves for a new life and for assimilation in their future countries. They were supported in these efforts by the governments of the reception countries as well as by the IRO. Gradually the governments realized that the newcomers would be assimilated more quickly if they would settle with their families. With the efforts of the Organization and the co-operation of voluntary agencies in the reception countries the refugees submerged soon into the melting pot, and though they still clung to their personal background, the next generation started a new life as members of the country of their adoption.

Refugees outside the assembly centres

The special arrangements made by the Allied Powers to provide assembly centres for the displaced populations did not prove attractive to all persons con-

[1] The Latvian Professor P. Jurevics' statement expresses very poignantly the difficulty arising from the separation of the refugees from their own culture: 'In so far as we save our cultural inheritance and develop it further we can hope to preserve our full human dignity and not slide into barbarism. . . . Let us not forget that among the cultural values safeguarded by the national community are also the moral values. If a person has torn himself away from his old community, and at the same time has not been able to become a member of another, then that type of man is created who initiates all catastrophes

cerned. There was a strong suspicion that refugees and displaced persons might be forced to return to their countries of origin. It was thought that there would be endless 'registration' and 'screening', as well as constant 'propaganda' in respect of repatriation. And finally there was a tendency to cling to existing arrangements. For when refugees were moving westwards in Europe at the end of the war, many sought refuge wherever they could find it. In some instances it may have been a small hotel; in other cases a farm or a private house. This was possible whenever the persons concerned had managed to take valuables with them. Moreover, forced labourers, who had been assigned employment with farmers, in many cases remained on the farm where food and lodgings were assured. Some might have been eligible for care by UNRRA had they applied to go into a camp; but there were very many more who, though they had not been considered eligible by UNRRA, became the concern of the IRO by virtue of the broader definitions under which it operated. It was estimated that in addition to the 712,000 in centres, there were approximately 500,000 refugees within its mandate living privately in Germany, Austria, Italy, and China, most of them in Germany.

In the French zone of Germany, out of a population of approximately 44,000 which became the concern of the Organization on 1 July 1947, nearly one-half was dispersed, living privately throughout the occupied area. From the early days the French authorities had encouraged refugees to accept local employment, and every effort was made to secure private housing for them. At the same time, the refugees were entitled to draw their rations from the French occupation authorities. This system was adopted because the military administration was sensitive to the disadvantages inherent in the development of isolated assembly centres.

In other zones of Germany the proportion of refugees living outside assembly centres was lower, although in one locality of the US zone there were nearly 1,200 persons living in the immediate neighbourhood of an assembly centre which itself housed about 5,000 persons. In this instance special arrangements had been made to enable these refugees to draw their food rations from the centre; to this extent, they were considered a part of the total population of the centre community.

In Austria, very many refugees lived privately; in Styria, particularly, conditions were not good, but refugees occupied the same type of housing and lived under the same conditions as Austrians in similar employment. Where work had been obtained with local farmers, they were usually given a room in the employer's house.

The persons living on the local economy of the countries of operation were known as 'out-of-camp refugees', as 'persons living on the local economy', or as 'free living DPs'. These terms distinguished them from the refugees who remained in assembly centres receiving care and subsistence at the expense of the Organization. The existence of out-of-camp refugees was a precarious one at best; and as the immediate effects of war receded into the past, they found it more difficult to live outside the established assembly centre communities. Although often enjoying a better standard of housing than the centre residents, the out-of-camp refugees found themselves isolated from their national groups. Whenever possible, they joined their comrades

—the completely isolated human being.' H. E. Holt, *Australia and the Migrant*, London and Sydney, 1953, p. 15.

in centres to celebrate a national holiday or to participate in the political life of the centre community.

Before the establishment of the IRO, and even during its first year, the out-of-camp refugees were looked upon with considerable suspicion in the occupied countries. Very often they were charged with being collaborators, *Volksdeutsche*, or persons who had come to Austria or Germany because they were pro-German. Doubt concerning this group was sometimes expressed by the IRO's international staff, who felt that the Organization should be protected from exploitation. In the latter period of the IRO's work, however, this group provided a large number of acceptable resettlement candidates; indeed, for the whole period of work, approximately 40 per cent. of the persons resettled came from the out-of-camp population.

ANNEX 13

*Displaced persons in Germany, Austria, and Italy, 31 December 1946**

I. *Total number*

      850,774 in Germany
      147,864 in Austria
      38,766 in Italy
    1,037,404 in and out of camp.

II. *Displaced persons in and out of camp*

About 8 out of every 10 displaced persons lived in camps (300 alone in the US zone).

In camps	Germany		Out of camps	Total
US zone	375,931	59%	142,419	518,350
UK zone	271,088	35%	15,675	286,763
French zone	35,494	6%	10,167	45,661
	Austria			
US zone	44,933		24,867	69,800
UK zone	21,930		40,531	62,461
French zone	6,593		9,010	15,603

Italy

Not allocated by zones 38,766 (13,591 in army camps including 3,000 estimated Royal Yugoslavs employed by British army; 25,175 in UNRRA camps exclusively UNRRA responsibility).

III. *Nationalities in camps of all three countries*

Yugoslav	39,494
Polish	278,868
Baltic	180,838
Jewish	193,332
Western European	2,400
USSR	13,800
Other—including stateless	86,003
	794,735

IV. *Ages*

    21% of the total children up to 18
    66% between the ages of 18 and 44
    13% above the age of 44.

V. *Occupations*

About 40 per cent. were employable; of this number about 80 per cent. were working in regular jobs, either in camps or otherwise in professional, administrative, technical, and manual jobs.

* According to the statistics of the Department of State, presented by Assistant Secretary of State, John H. Hilldring, at hearings before the Committee on Foreign Relations US Senate, 80th Congress, First Session, op. cit., 1 Mar. 1947, pp. 30–36.

ANNEX 14

UN Data on refugees and displaced persons (the Far East excepted)*

1. The number of displaced persons receiving UNRRA assistance in Europe and in the Middle East on 31 March 1946 was, as nearly as can be ascertained, 850,000.

2. The number of persons in Europe and in the Middle East being the concern of the League of Nations High Commissioner for Refugees (Nansen refugees), and not included in the total shown in paragraph 1 above was on 31 March 1946, as nearly as could be ascertained or estimated, as follows:

(a)	Russian refugees	150,000
(b)	Armenian refugees	100,000
(c)	Assyrian refugees	1,000
(d)	Saar refugees	5,000

3. The number of persons receiving assistance from or being the concern of the Inter-Governmental Committee in Europe, North Africa, and the Middle East, and not included in the totals shown in paragraphs 1 and 2 above, was on 31 March 1946, as nearly as could be ascertained or estimated, as follows:

Refugees coming from Germany, Austria, and the Sudetenland	110,000
Spanish Republican refugees	212,000

4. The number of refugees and displaced persons in Europe, the Middle East, and Africa receiving assistance from or being the concern of UN governments, and not already included under paragraphs 1, 2, and 3 above, was on 31 March 1946, as nearly as could be ascertained or estimated, 250,000.

5. The total number of refugees and displaced persons in Europe, the Middle East, and Africa receiving assistance from or being the concern of UNRRA, the League of Nations High Commissioner for Refugees, the Inter-Governmental Committee and UN governments, was on 31 March 1946, as nearly as could be ascertained or estimated, 1,675,000.

* UN Doc. E/REF/75, op. cit., p. 42.

ANNEX 15

Jews receiving IRO care and maintenance in Austria, Germany, and Italy,
*31 July 1947**

Country of last habitual residence	Austria	Germany		US zone	Italy	Total
		British zone	French zone			
Albania	1	..	..	1	..	2
Argentina	..	..	..	..	1	1
Austria	..	20	8	323	196	547
Belgium and Luxembourg	1	..	..	8	5	14
Bolivia	..	..	1	..	..	1
Brazil	1	..	..	2	..	3
Bulgaria	..	..	..	4	9	13
Czechoslovakia	221	112	4	5,822	846	7,005
Denmark	..	..	1	1	..	2
Egypt	..	..	..	1	..	1
Estonia	1	..	3	3	1	8
France	..	..	..	28	3	31
Germany	3	95	1,149	3,969	110	5,326
Greece	10	2	..	135	68	215
Hungary	295	1,132	11	5,383	1,213	8,034
Iran	..	..	2	..	..	2
Italy	7	1	1	19	..	28
Latvia	6	38	2	203	33	282
Lithuania	24	38	6	1,542	204	1,814
Mexico	..	2	..	..	..	2
Netherlands	..	..	..	10	..	10
Palestine	19	5	..	41	13	78
Paraguay	..	..	10	..	..	10
Poland	4,466	7,870	608	96,780	11,262	120,986
Rumania	386	1,451	4	3,232	2,513	7,586
Spain	2	..	..	6	22	30
Switzerland	..	..	..	4	3	7
Turkey	..	..	..	9	19	28
UK	..	..	1	2	..	3
US	..	..	1	8	2	11
USSR	5	7	1	1,285	118	1,416
Yugoslavia	23	6	..	177	279	485
Stateless	..	8	8	23	32	71
Other	..	21	64	102	95	282
TOTAL	5,471	10,808	1,884	119,124	17,047	154,333

* Fulton Report, p. 8.

ANNEX 16

Total number of displaced persons and refugees under IRO care and maintenance as of
31 December 1948 (classified by religion)*

Religion

Roman Catholic	204,636
Jewish	92,944
Protestant	87,648
Greek Orthodox	71,616
Greek Catholic	44,649
None	1,804
Others	5,040
Unknown	8,522
TOTAL	523,859

* Statistics prepared and furnished by the IRO. They include only those who are in IRO camps and assembly centres.

ANNEX 17

Summary of IRO statistics

	Total	Austria	Belgium	Denmark	Far East / Shanghai / Europeans	Far East / Shanghai / Overseas Chinese	Philippines	France
TOTAL REFUGEES WHO HAVE BEEN REGISTERED AND ASSISTED BY IRO	1,619,008	188,498	20,074	3,105	23,585	11,122	5,537	224,890
Refugees resettled, repatriated, or whose cases have been otherwise closed	1,208,586	165,328	8,797	2,547	18,668	11,122	5,407	32,180
1. Resettled in new countries*	1,038,750	145,233	8,672	2,034	13,957	..	5,308	31,434
2. Repatriated to their country of origin or former domicile	72,834	4,667	125	32	1,809	11,122	21	746
3. Deaths, disappearances, &c.	97,002	15,428	..	481	2,902	..	78	..
Other refugees who had not been resettled or repatriated	410,422	23,170	11,277	558	4,917	..	130	192,710
4. Who wished to be resettled*	127,080	15,450	2,004	196	2,755	..	75	11,600
i. Considered by IRO to have prospects for resettlement which had not been effected	35,386	4,450	977	91	1,483	..	75	3,000
ii. Considered by IRO to be without prospects or possibilities	91,694	11,000	1,027	105	1,272	..	..	8,600
5. Institutional hard core and their dependants	523	13	..	..	353	..	54	..
i. Awaiting final movement or placement	157	13	..	..	20	..	25	..
ii. For whose establishment no satisfactory plans were possible	366	..	..	..	333	..	29	..
6. Desiring repatriation which could not be effected	144	15	..	..	26	..	..	..
7. Others for legal and political protection only	282,675	7,692	9,273	362	1,783	..	1	181,110

* Arrangements made to resettle a further 7,000 during January.

ANNEX 17

July 1947–31 December 1951

Germany			Greece	Italy	Luxembourg	Middle East				Netherlands	Portugal	Spain	Sweden	All other areas
British zone	French zone	US zone				East Africa	Lebanon	Syria	Turkey					
326,738	61,426	585,589	9,198	106,806	1,060	15,774	6,403	188	1,117	4,749	610	795	4,031	17,713
274,911	50,156	508,675	4,972	80,865	384	15,774	6,256	114	530	1,772	485	389	1,541	17,713
224,261	38,087	457,188	3,137	70,535	200	14,044	5,857	71	405	1,691	348	319	1,539	14,430
23,168	2,793	20,974	4	3,085	2	1,311	354	1	41	81	21	69	2	2,406
27,482	9,276	30,513	1,831	7,245	182	419	45	42	84	..	116	1	..	877
51,827	11,270	76,914	4,226	25,941	676	..	147	74	587	2,977	125	406	2,490	..
28,577	5,157	34,800	2,611	22,146	48	..	29	50	122	..	16	76	1,368	..
3,661	557	15,800	907	4,000	37	..	29	50	122	..	..	76	71	..
24,916	4,600	19,000	1,704	18,146	11	..	..	..	..	..	16	..	1,297	..
13	17	..	20	40	..	..	5	..	..	..	..	8	..	..
13	17	..	20	40	..	..	5	..	..	..	..	4	..	..
..	..	..	..	..	..	..	..	..	..	..	..	4†	..	..
3	..	65	..	25	..	..	..	2	..	..	..	8	..	..
23,234	6,096	42,049	1,595	3,730	628	..	113	22	465	2,977	109	314	1,122	..

† Possible that satisfactory establishment wil lbe realized for these four in the near future.

ANNEX 17a

Summary of IRO statistics, 1 July 1947–31 December 1951

	1 July 1947	31 Dec. 1947	30 June 1948	31 Dec. 1948	30 June 1949	31 Dec. 1949	30 June 1950	31 Dec. 1950	30 June 1951	31 Dec. 1951
TOTAL REFUGEES REGISTERED	712,675	850,000	1,000,000	1,138,000	1,300,000	1,420,096	1,490,452	1,532,560	1,577,873	1,619,008
Refugees resettled, repatriated, or whose cases were otherwise closed	..	173,463	295,831	417,675	615,818	840,793	955,559	1,061,295	1,125,795	1,208,586
Refugees not resettled or repatriated (total)	712,675*	676,537*	704,169	720,325	684,182	579,303	534,893	471,265	452,078	410,422
Austria	33,049	47,664	63,428	73,671	62,826	50,139	42,394	33,137	28,971	23,170
British zone	12,561	10,913	16,409	21,840	20,555	16,744	12,953	NR	NR	NR
French zone	5,558	5,361	11,485	10,807	8,495	6,483	4,609	NR	NR	NR
US zone	14,930	31,390	33,160	37,439	28,693	21,455	18,490	NR	NR	NR
Vienna area	..	..	2,374	3,585	5,083	5,358	6,282	NR	NR	NR
Belgium	1,800	1,509	3,532	4,966	9,660	12,404	12,183	12,227	12,116	11,277
Czechoslovakia	20	8	294	248	380	386	..	..	..	..
Denmark	..	..	..	2,870	2,647	1,845	1,560	927	768	558
Far East	9,300	5,944	8,169	10,443	10,700	9,447	8,823	7,538	5,865	5,047
Shanghai	9,300	5,944	8,169	10,443	5,659	6,165	5,812	5,409	5,505	4,917
Philippines	..	..	..	..	5,041	3,282	3,011	2,129	360	130
France	6,300	6,421	16,646	39,598	80,600	122,049	148,884	165,907	182,010	192,770
Metropolitan France	6,300	6,421	16,457	39,405	80,405	121,687	148,624	NR	NR	NR
French North Africa	..	..	189	193	195	362	260	NR	NR	NR
Germany	604,556	562,283	570,264	555,268	481,072	342,503	277,136	211,160	178,196	140,011
British zone	223,747	195,094	206,792	184,401	163,266	125,586	100,610	78,338	64,816	51,827
French zone	44,109	44,105	40,855	37,602	31,508	24,363	19,456	15,876	13,453	11,270
US zone	336,700	323,084	322,617	333,265	286,298	192,554	157,070	116,946	99,927	76,914
Greece	..	..	..	524	2,575	3,750	1,206	1,188	3,797	4,226
Italy	29,170	29,495	28,541	21,808	22,890	24,757	30,028	30,384	31,880	25,941
Luxembourg	..	..	..	452	728	812	842	857	715	676
Middle East	27,600	22,302	10,890	6,279	6,010	4,830	3,424	1,008	925	808
East Africa	16,990	15,261	7,288	4,260	3,779	3,022	1,672	..	..	..
Egypt	700	675	1,104	112	116	149	..	..	..	..
India	4,250	1,831	526	2	..	..	..	..	..	..
Israel	2,750	1,700	1,921	1,592	1,710	1,085	945	150	156	147
Lebanon	3,810	2,835	..†	..†	..†	136	122	113	104	74
Syria	..†	..†	51	313	405	438	685	745	665	587
Turkey	..	..	..	..	..	..	..	..	..	..
Netherlands	170	177	1,693	2,196	2,215	3,182	3,015	3,081	3,037	2,977
Norway	..	..	..	..	..	235	378	361	345	..
Portugal	230	324	281	252	199	209	61	35	126	125
Spain	480	410	431	450	380	310	193	228	440	406
Sweden‡	..	..	..	..	..	1,145	3,466	3,227	2,887	2,490
Switzerland	..	..	..	1,300§	1,300§	1,300§	1,300§	..	..	..

Note: Refugees departed for resettlement but receiving IRO care and maintenance in embarkation centres are excluded from the case-load from 1 July 1948.

* Refugees receiving IRO care and maintenance only. Statistics on refugees not receiving IRO care and maintenance are not available prior to 30 June 1948.

† During this period refugees in Syria were included in Lebanon and Egypt figures, exact details of which were unobtainable.

‡ Under the auspices of the IRO Office in Denmark.

§ Static figure for which IRO assumed financial responsibility under agreement with the Swiss Government.

PART III

CHAPTER XII

ELIGIBILITY FOR REFUGEE STATUS
AND ASSISTANCE

T H E IRO had been established 'to bring about a rapid and positive solution of the problem of *bona fide* refugees and displaced persons'. The eligibility of refugees and displaced persons for the assistance[1] of the Organization had to be determined by the basic criteria set forth in Annex I to the Constitution.

In its definition of persons to be assisted by IRO, the Constitution broke new ground. Before the war, membership of a particular group of refugees qualified a person for such international assistance as might be available, e.g. under the Intergovernmental Arrangement of 12 May 1926 Russian refugees included 'Any person of Russian origin who does not enjoy . . . the protection of the Government of the Union of Socialist Soviet Republic and who has not acquired another nationality.' The reason for this, at least in part, was that the available assistance did not usually consist in valuable material benefits, but mainly in the establishment of a satisfactory legal status for the refugees concerned, and the international agency did not concern itself with the situation of large numbers of individuals as such; individuals assisted were either hard cases or test cases.

By contrast, the IRO was designed to feed, clothe, counsel, legally assist, educate, and transport the refugees who came under its mandate. These were services provided by the Organization to individuals; and eligibility to receive them would require quite as much investigation as would the eligibility of the recipients of any social benefits. Thus the Constitution of the IRO included detailed provisions governing not only the categories of persons to be regarded for its purposes as refugees and displaced persons, but also the conditions under which they would qualify for assistance or be excluded from it. These provisions also took into account certain political aspects. The governments who had been opposed to the establishment of the IRO claimed that if any refugees at all were to be given assistance apart from help needed for their repatriation, then all those whose activities had been suspicious during the war should be excluded from international assistance. The question was to be investigated by semi-judicial machinery. Therefore the determination of eligibility—the determination whether or not they were within the mandate of the Organization—

---

[1] Assistance included any combination of the IRO care and maintenance, services for repatriation or resettlement, and any other services rendered to refugees on an individual basis by IRO.

was an essential part of the IRO's task, and was beset by human and political complications. It was the initial contact of the refugee with the Organization. Persons who had been accepted within the mandate of the Organization were given counselling on the results of which they were registered and classified for services. Admissibility to services was different from constitutional eligibility, as will be described later.[1]

Registration procedure

The function of 'identification, registration, and classification' served a dual purpose: to segregate the persons who might receive assistance from the Organization from those who were not entitled to receive it; and to provide the General Council and the Executive Committee with reliable data as a basis for planning the expenditure and operations of the IRO.

For this purpose the administration introduced a comprehensive single reporting system. It required the development of a common terminology and of definitions, and full co-operation between the IRO and the military authorities, in order to avoid overlapping. For the compilation of accurate statistics, detailed records of numbers, nationality, age, sex, family status, occupation, and repatriation or resettlement desires were collected at the field level and passed on to headquarters for collation. The administration tried to improve the technique of reporting during the course of the work and overcame some of its initial difficulties.[2]

In order to determine whether a person fulfilled the conditions set forth in the Constitution for being within the mandate of the IRO, he was registered and interviewed. This procedure had to establish two points: one, basic eligibility, to find out whether the applicant was or was not fundamentally a displaced person or a true refugee who had been bereft in law or in fact of national protection and also whether he fell within the mandate of the Organization according to its Constitution; two, to determine in cases where a person's eligibility had been proved, what services, if any, should be provided for him. The status of an IRO refugee made a person eligible for legal and political protection, but it implied only the possibility of material assistance, not an obligation on the Organization's part to render any particular service.[3] 'Admission policy notably to care and maintenance or to settlement movements financed by the Organization had to be determined in the light of administrative and budgetary considerations.'[4]

The administration of the IRO's eligibility programme was the responsibility of one office at Geneva headquarters, which issued policy directives within the general rules laid down by the Director General. But the complexity of the subject, as well as its semi-judicial nature (the law being one of civilization's highly developed means of ensuring consistency), caused the Review Board for Eligibility Appeals,

---

[1] p. 211.

[2] See Senate Report No. 456, 81st Congress, First Session, op. cit., pp. 30–32. IRO *Operational Manual*, Revised May 1950, Appendix VI, pp. 6 and 59–68.

[3] Ibid., p. 4.

[4] PREP/165. Report of the Executive Secretary on Eligibility and Semi-Judicial Machinery, 15 Jan. 1948, p. 2.

which is described later in this chapter, and the Chief Legal Adviser's Office (and its successors) to take part in the determination of policy.

Each of the field offices in Germany, Austria, and Italy had a similar office which was under the control of a Chief Eligibility Office. Below that level there were area offices or control centres which received applications from refugees and which were located where they would afford refugees within the area as much opportunity as possible of applying for IRO assistance. Problems encountered by subordinates were forwarded to the Chief Eligibility Officer of the mission, who judged the case in the light of the instructions issued from Geneva headquarters, or, if there were any doubts, submitted the case to headquarters. Meetings between the Chief Eligibility Officer of a mission and his area officers were held monthly in most of the larger areas; copies of minutes of such local meetings were forwarded to Geneva headquarters for perusal, study, and such action as was appropriate. Moreover, the Chief Eligibility Officer of any mission made tours of inspection in order to ensure that correct procedures were applied by those offices. The administrative procedures and personnel establishments varied in detail from mission to mission according to circumstances, local conditions, adequacy of staff, and the attitude of occupation authorities or governments. But officials from Geneva did their best to ensure uniformity in principle.

A person who applied for assistance was normally first registered on the specially provided form,[1] either in the assembly centre or in the local IRO office. The first registration of all assembly-centre inhabitants was completed by March 1948; but the influx of new refugees, as well as the applications of those who had been residing among the indigenous population, prevented the Organization from ever completing the registration of all persons who might be the concern of the Organization.

In some areas, eligibility officers interviewed all applicants for assistance either in the assembly centres or in the area office; in other areas, such as Austria and Italy, the interview was carried out by specially trained interviewers from among the refugee population or locally recruited staff of the mission. In all cases, interviews were conducted as discreetly as possible. The decision as to eligibility was always made by an IRO eligibility officer, usually after a private interview with the applicant, though sometimes simply on the basis of information recorded on the application form by the preliminary interviewer.

To be fair to all required consistency. Therefore the Administration laid down rules concerning both substance and procedure.

The determination of basic eligibility proceeded in three stages. The first ascertained whether the applicant belonged to any one of the main categories of refugee or displaced persons envisaged in Sections A and B of Part I of Annex I of the Constitution or to a new category which had been established by the General Council.[2]

The second step was to examine whether or not the applicant was disqualified from becoming the concern of the Organization under Part II of Annex I.

After having successfully passed these two stages, the applicant was considered

---

[1] The CM/1 Form. IRO *Operational Manual*, Revised, May 1950, p. 47.
[2] See Chapter II, Constitution, p. 45 and III, Preparatory Commission: General Council, p. 60.

a 'genuine refugee or displaced person'. He had, however, to pass a third stage; he had to express—'definitely' in 'complete freedom', and after receiving 'adequate information'—'valid objections' to returning to his country of nationality or former habitual residence according to Part I, Section C (*a*) of the Definitions. At this stage he was recognized as a political dissident, a person who was unwilling to return to his country although his country of origin was willing to receive him. He thus acquired the status of a political refugee.

The general principle in this process of eligibility was that the person applying for the recognition of a right had to prove to the satisfaction of the authority granting it that he was entitled to it. He had to supply information and to support it by documentary evidence.

Establishing eligibility

Registering the individual constituted a record of his application for assistance. Though the registration procedure varied in each sector according to local conditions, the guiding principles of registration and interview were the same. It was stated in the Constitution that the identity of the applicant had to be established, and that it had to be established furthermore how and why he had been displaced or had fled from his country of origin. Normally the accuracy of such information was checked through documents which the applicant produced at the time of registration; but it was the interview between the IRO eligibility officer and the applicant which served to elucidate the evidence at hand and thereby decide whether the applicant was in fact a *bona fide* refugee or displaced person. The documents, when they existed, might consist of a passport, or identity card, a German labour card issued to forced workers, a demobilization certificate, official letters, and so on. However, when the candidate had no papers, he was not automatically eliminated; IRO gave him the benefit of the doubt if his story sounded plausible.

On the other hand, the expected advantage of documentary evidence in itself induced many otherwise *bona fide* refugees to produce false documents and to give false testimonies. For example, many Soviet citizens, fearing forcible repatriation at the end of the war, supplied themselves with sets of identity papers as Polish or other Slavic nationals. Obviously, the initial registration was made on the basis of these documents, and in many cases the decision on eligibility was in the applicant's favour. In other cases, however, discrepancies in personal histories eventually led to disclosure of the true facts, and then the applicant was re-interviewed. When, on the basis of the true facts, an applicant would be recognized as being within the mandate, the previous false statements were disregarded.

The checking of conditions was particularly difficult if the candidate had voluntarily helped the enemy in operations against the UN countries, or if he was of German ethnic origin, a *Volksdeutscher*;[1] or if he had acquired German citizenship during the war, in which case he was outside the mandate because he was within his country of nationality, presumably with the rights inherent in citizenship. An exception was made if the citizenship was acquired under duress.

If there was no apparent reason to exclude a candidate from the mandate it was

---

[1] See Chapter X, Origin of Refugees and Displaced Persons, p. 185; and below, p. 211.

not his duty to furnish proof of his right to be included. On the other hand, a candidate could be turned down because he could not furnish proof in order to correct an unfavourable impression. Sometimes it was impossible to check one way or the other. IRO made it a rule to make individual decisions only, and, except for the *Volksdeutsche*, not to eliminate a candidate merely because he belonged to a certain group, even if the fact of belonging could be held against him.

The information used by the Administration in determining the eligibility of any applicant was obtained from official government sources, private agencies, and, above all, from interviews with the refugees themselves. Although war-time events were publicly known, the history of an individual developed its criteria empirically as the interviews of individual members of the various refugee groups were made and reported to Geneva headquarters. As the information was received from the field missions, it was consolidated by the various offices concerned in Geneva headquarters and re-issued in the form of policy directives by the Director General.[1] Three editions of the criteria were issued: The first as a relatively short interpretative guide in January 1948; the second, considerably expanded, in manuscript in January 1949, and the third as the printed *Manual for Eligibility Officers*, published in May 1950. This Manual provided the officers with valuable historical data about the origin of the various categories of refugees and displaced persons, with a carefully drawn up commentary to the definition of the Constitution, Annex I and II, and examples of actual cases which were to serve as guides, but not as precedents, since each case was decided on its individual merits.

Among the underlying principles of interpretation some deserve special mention. Every effort was made to strike a balance between strict adherence to the constitutional provisions, as interpreted by their legislative history, and considerations of humanity. The applicant was given the benefit of the doubt. In pursuance of the social policy of keeping together the family unit, a positive basic eligibility determination of the head of the family implied the eligibility of the wife, children, and other dependants unless there was a formal disqualification of an individual member of a family under Part II of Annex I of the Constitution.

War criminals

In regard to war criminals, quislings, and traitors the Directives followed the Resolution of the General Assembly of the UN of 12 February 1946, whereby nothing should be done to 'interfere in any way with the surrender and punishment of war criminals, quislings and traitors'. Screening, arresting, and surrendering them was entirely the responsibility of the governments and occupational authorities. IRO was not charged with actively carrying out a task which had proved too much for UNRRA, but had to assist only by informing the authorities of the presence of such persons, unless expressly ordered otherwise.[2] But the previous history of the screening operations affected IRO's eligibility procedure, and in some areas the operations were preparatory to it.

For example, in Italy, in 1946, in view of the impending peace treaty with the

[1] The first Eligibility Directive was issued 25 June 1947.
[2] *Manual*, op. cit., p. 33.

Italian Government, the various military authorities screened some 20,000 Ukrainians and Yugoslavs in order, first, to isolate war criminals, quislings, or any other wanted persons who were liable for subsequent surrender to the country of origin; second, to establish which persons were likely to be acceptable to the IRO; third, to isolate those elements capable of organizing opposition to the policy of the Allied governments; and fourth, to persuade as many dissidents as possible to return to their countries of origin.

By January 1947 a British official screening team was dealing with the Ukrainians and Yugoslavs, and a team of the IGCR was determining the eligibility of persons who would come under its control in assembly centres. Both teams used criteria based on the IRO Constitution, though these were somewhat different from those afterwards developed by the IRO itself in the missions and at headquarters; and both endeavoured to determine which refugees were likely to be within the IRO's mandate and which would require other arrangements. The British team was the Special Refugee Commission, headed by Brigadier Fitzroy Maclean, formerly head of the war-time British military mission to the Yugoslav partisan headquarters.[1]

The Review Board

Eligibility was determined administratively by eligibility officers in the field under directives of the Director General. An applicant excluded could appeal against their decision. 'To ensure the impartial and equitable application of its principles and definitions', the Constitution of the IRO provided, in paragraph 2 of the General Principles under Annex I, for a special system of semi-judicial machinery, with appropriate constitution,[2] procedure, and terms of reference.

The Review Board for Eligibility Appeals was formally established on 29 November 1947, and began work at the beginning of 1948. The Board had two functions: (1) to serve as an appeal tribunal for final review of a decision made by the field staff as to whether a person was within the mandate, and (2) to advise the Director General on questions of eligibility which he submitted to it.

The Board consisted of a chairman, Mr. de Baer, former Justice of Appeal in Brussels and Professor of Law at the University, who presided during the war over the Belgian Military and Maritime Courts of Appeal in Great Britain, and 28 persons (3 members, 4 deputy members, 1 recorder, 1 case reviewer, 8 assistants, and 11 clerks), some with long legal and judicial experience, others with a broad knowledge of refugees and conditions in central Europe, and all speaking several languages. By May 1948 the Board was sufficiently organized to deal with most appeals by sending its members on circuit to field missions where appellants were given the opportunity of being heard personally. These circuits (the maximum number was 32) were systematically planned to cover most areas of the IRO operations in central Europe, mainly Germany, Austria, and Italy, but shortage of staff and the progressive increase in the number of appeals made it impossible to visit regularly the outlying missions such as those in the Middle East and the Far

---

[1] *Manual*, op. cit., p. 88. For further material see Chapter XIX, Repatriation, p. 343.
[2] Constitution of Review Board for Eligibility Appeals, GC/65, 26 Mar. 1949, p. 5, cf. Annex 18 pp. 213 ff.

East. Appeals originating in those areas were decided at headquarters by review of the case files.

The decisions of the Board were based on the same criteria as those used by the eligibility officer in the first instance; these were the Constitution and its interpretation by the administration and the General Council as embodied in the policy directives of the Director General. The evidence was also similar to that presented to the eligibility officer: registration form, personal documents, sworn statements and testimonials, information obtained by the Board from intelligence sources, and, finally, the interview itself. In the same way, the Board was faced with the problems of burden of proof, false pretences, and conflicting statements.

In its judicial capacity the Board enjoyed the same independence of judgement as members of Courts of Justice, and consequently, in dealing with appeals, the Board sought to determine the validity of the initial decision in the light of the Constitution. It could thus either confirm or reverse the original decision of the eligibility officer. It was mainly to give justice to individuals whose eligibility had been mistakenly determined that the Review Board was originally established. As the field staff gained greater proficiency in the determination of eligibility, however, the role of the Board was essentially one of ensuring that the negative decisions were constitutionally justified. This was reflected in the fact that during the periods of operation when appeals had accumulated faster than the Board could deal with them the establishment of Zonal Review Commissions, composed of the senior eligibility officers in each mission, was authorized. These commissions had authority to review appeals in the same way as the Review Board, but they were restricted in their decisions to those cases in which the original determination of 'not within the mandate' could be reversed. All others were referred to the Board. This was essential in the interests of justice, for if the field staff had been empowered to confirm such decisions, the same authority which had rejected an applicant would also have been empowered to reject his appeal, thereby depriving him of an impartial judgement on appeal.

Although all decisions made by the Board on individual cases were final, the Board was not prevented from reversing its own decision against the appellant if new facts, supported by authentic documents, were adduced. If, for example, the Board declared a person not within the mandate because of a lack of valid objections to repatriation, the case could be re-opened if the appellant later expressed objections which could be considered as substantially valid.

From its inception until 31 December 1951, the Board delivered 36,742 decisions involving approximately 80,000 persons, and granted 21,906 personal hearings. It served as a valuable safety-valve for the individual refugee, giving him in most cases a personal hearing and a statement of the reasons for the acceptance or dismissal of his appeal.

Surveying the work, the acting chairman of the Board emphasized that an

evolution had taken place over a five-year period in the implementation of IRO policy with regard to the problem. From being a body established to apply the Constitution of the IRO, the Review Board had developed into an organ having the character of an investigator, psychologist, and judge. As a result, an unexpected amount of information on events during the war had been collected, and the Review Board's jurisprudence had undergone some changes, more especially in the interpretation of criteria. Thirty-seven thousand decisions had been taken during the lifetime of the Organization by the Review Board, but its influence had extended far beyond the number of cases actually decided and had promoted justice and equity in all areas.[1]

Revisions of policy

It is evident how difficult a task it was to select genuine refugees and displaced persons among the huge mass of uprooted humanity. Several policy changes developed in the course of the period which affected the eligibility programme and the work of the Review Board. A more liberal interpretation of 'valid objections' and the granting of the benefit of the doubt was practised with a degree of understanding acquired by experience. The interpretation of the exclusion clause (paragraph 2 (*b*) of Part II of the Constitution), concerning voluntary assistance to the enemy forces, was modified. Whereas previously the criterion had been solely the action of the individual rather than his moral intentions; it was decided that a more lenient approach was necessary in view of the increased knowledge of the background and motives of various national groups.

The jurisprudence of the Review Board evolved in line with the Organization's policy of greater leniency in deciding eligibility. As more was learnt of the past experience of various groups of refugees the Organization had been able to apply the criteria with greater equity and understanding. Moreover, although the Constitution was not altered, it became apparent, from statements made during the sessions of the General Council, that member governments were developing a wider conception of a *bona fide* refugee than that which had prevailed at the beginning. The Board therefore endeavoured to apply leniency to the widest extent possible.

The question of eligibility was peculiarly complicated and difficult, and could only be rightly handled if sound legal thinking was tempered with generosity and wisdom. The criteria of eligibility imposed on the IRO by its Constitution limited its freedom in meeting demands for help. These limitations were in line with the general idea at that time as to who should be considered as a deserving refugee or displaced person.

While the determination of eligibility was scrupulously carried out by specialized personnel on the basis of the principles and definitions laid down in the Constitution, in course of time a marked evolution took place in the attitude of the international community. As a result of the changes in the political scene after 1948 and greater knowledge of the facts, the IRO endeavoured 'to liberalize the interpretation of its own definitions, in order to fall into line with the wider conception of a refugee', and thus be able to assist a greater proportion of all refugees who were in need of assistance.[2]

The groups which benefited particularly from the more liberal assessment of eligibility were the Balts, the Mennonites, some military organizations like the Rogozhin Group,[3] the Vlassov army and others, and the Venezia Giulians.

[1] GC/SR/95.
[2] See Mr. Donald Kingsley's letter of 25 Feb. 1952 which he wrote to the member governments at the request of the General Council after its Ninth Session, when the matter had been thoroughly surveyed.   [3] Executive Committee, Res. 10, 12 Oct. 1950.

In the early days of the IRO the delegates of France, Belgium, and the Netherlands took a great interest in the Balts and, after constant preoccupation with the problem, the Administration accepted the judgement of the General Council[1] and considered certain groups of Baltic origin within its mandate. When the IRO Constitution was written in 1946, collaborators with the enemy were excluded from assistance by the new organization. However, as difficulties with the Soviet Government increased and the cold war developed, during the life-span of the IRO, there was growing appreciation in the General Council of the fact that many persons might technically have collaborated with the Germans and yet were in refugee status.

The issue regarding the Venezia Giulians, who were Italian-speaking and came from parts of pre-war Italy ceded to Yugoslavia under the Peace Treaty of 1947, was whether or not they had successfully exercised the right of option given them by the Treaty. After lengthy discussions in November 1950, an agreement was concluded between the IRO and the Italian Government whereby the IRO undertook to re-settle 20,000 refugees from Italy during the remaining period of operations. In this way the emigration of considerable numbers of these unfortunate people was assured.

Under the Constitution, persons of German ethnic origin, whether German nationals or members of German minorities in other countries (Part II, paragraph 4), were not the concern of the IRO. There were, however, a group of about 200,000 *Volksdeutsche* in Austria. These were members of German-speaking minorities, mostly of German ethnic origin, who had settled in the past in various countries of eastern and southern Europe over a period of centuries and had their origin in different and widely separated geographical areas. After the defeat of the Axis, partly in implementation of decisions reached by the Potsdam conference and by the Allied Commission for Austria, the countries of eastern and southern Europe expelled these minorities and started them on their way to Germany and Austria, areas in which they had no economic roots. The question was whether these groups should be considered ethnically, that is to say, as belonging to the peoples who were former enemies of the UN and therefore ineligible for the IRO service, or as expelled minorities who were victims of political and racial discrimination in the eastern and southern European countries.

In the summer of 1947 the PCIRO passed a resolution recognizing the eligibility of these *Volksdeutsche* and extending to them legal protection and resettlement opportunities, although leaving the responsibility for their care and maintenance to the indigenous population in Austria. Though the Organization did not have sufficient funds available to implement this resolution, the *Volksdeutsche*, however, were considered for migration under other schemes developed later to relieve the population pressures by emigration from certain central European areas.[2]

Admission to services

Reference has already been made to the provisions whereby admissibility to services was not a constitutional right, but depended on the policies determined by

___

[1] Resolution of the Executive Committee EC/27 and EC/SR/25, pp. 3–5, 30 Mar. 1949.
[2] Chapter XXII, Local Settlement, p. 478.

the General Council and the Administration. The degree of hardship in the individual case, the availability and extent of the IRO resources, the application of sanctions, and other criteria were the guides for granting services to basically eligible refugees.

An important restriction of material help was one of the first decisions of the Administration when on 1 July 1947 it had assumed operational responsibility for the care and maintenance of refugees and displaced persons. As one of the first measures of economy in July 1947, necessitated by its limited initial budget, the PCIRO restricted the care and maintenance programme to persons already located in assembly centres, and no new admissions were authorized. The chiefs of mission were given authority to declare other persons eligible for care only where refusal to admit an applicant to an assembly centre would result in severe material hardship.

During the first year of operations the main assistance granted to refugees was largely in the form of care and maintenance or cash relief subsidies. However, more applications were received for this service than had initially been expected, because large numbers of people were crossing the frontiers into Germany from Poland and Czechoslovakia, and from Hungary and Rumania into Austria. Under the restriction only hardship cases could be granted care and maintenance.

The problem of persons who preferred to remain idle in assembly centres raised the question how far the constitutional provisions regarding cessation of the Organization's concern for a refugee should be applied. In the British zones of Germany and Austria, where the maintenance of refugees in assembly centres was the responsibility of the occupation authorities, all refugees capable of working were encouraged to do so and were required to make a token contribution to their upkeep; this was done in order to maintain discipline as well as to develop a sense of social responsibility. The occupation authorities were strict in carrying out this programme, and the IRO missions formulated the policy whereby persons who refused to work or absented themselves from work without just cause[1] would be refused care and maintenance without forfeiting their fundamental status. The co-operation of the British authorities permitted these measures to work, but there was little need to enforce them on a large scale, for invariably, when a complaint reached the eligibility officers in the field, a warning to malingerers sufficed to bring them to order. In other areas, such as the US zones of Germany and Austria, the control of the camps by the IRO made it possible to deal with the matter in a similar manner, directly by the IRO's local welfare officers.

Services were restricted also by a number of decisions of the governing bodies, fixing dates after which certain services would not be provided by the Organization, or registration with the Organization would be only a determinant of status.[2]

IRO's eligibility procedure was bitterly resented at the time by some of the excluded persons and groups, and the working of this complex machinery gave rise to a great deal of criticism. While it is true that mistakes were made at the beginning and suffering was caused thereby, the policy must be judged in its context. It is already becoming difficult to recall the violence of the post-war partialities and enmities, the confusion and political tension in which the Constitution was laid down. The

---

[1] Chapter XVI, Adaptation to a New Life, p. 278.
[2] Chapter III, p. 66.

important fact is, however, that in applying it there was a steady pressure at all levels towards humanity and realism, which far outweighed the tendency of some minds to take refuge in strictly legalistic interpretations.[1]

ANNEX 18

Constitution[2] of Review Board for Eligibility Appeals

1. In accordance with the 'Constitution of the International Refugee Organization' which in paragraph 2 of the General Principles of Annex I provides for the creation of a special system of semi-judicial machinery, there has been established a Review Board (Conseil des Recours de l'OIR) for Eligibility Appeals. It will be referred to in this document as 'The Board'.

A. TERMS OF REFERENCE

2. The Board has two functions:

(a) to serve as an Appeal Tribunal for the purpose of finally reviewing, in appropriate cases, the determination made by the field staff of whether a person is within the mandate;

(b) to advise the Director General upon any eligibility matter which he may refer to the Board.

3. The Board is an autonomous body. In respect of its judicial activity the Members have the same independence of judgement as members of Courts of Justice.

4. The purpose of the Board in the judicial field is to ensure the impartial application to individual cases of:

(i) the principles and definitions contained in Annex I of the Constitution;

(ii) the decisions of the General Council;

(iii) the general eligibility rulings and instructions issued by the Director General in implementation either of the definitions or the decisions of the General Council.

B. CONSTITUTION

5. *Seat.* The seat of the Board is at the Headquarters of the Organization. The Board may delegate individual Members, as directed by the Chairman, to sit in any area of operation of the Organization, or to travel from place to place according as best calculated to ensure the expeditious hearing of applications for review.

6. *Language.* The working languages of the Board are English and French. Proceedings may make use of another language when this is in the interest of justice.

7. *Composition.* The Board shall consist of persons appointed by the Director General subject to the approval of the Executive Committee. It shall consist of one Chairman, and a number of associate Members. Provisionally the number of associate members shall be three. Should the need arise, this number may be increased by a decision of the Director General. Deputy members may be appointed for a period of time.

8. The Chairman shall be chosen from among experienced jurists who have held high judicial office in their own countries and who are conversant with the English and French languages. He shall be charged with the administration of the Board as specified hereafter. The Members shall be chosen among persons who have, in the opinion

[1] GC/25H, 22 Jan. 1952. [2] IRO, GC/65, 26 March 1949.

of the Director General, the necessary qualifications to fill these posts, with due respect to the requirements laid down in Article 9 of the IRO Constitution and in accordance with the recruitment of members on an appropriate geographical basis.

9. *Quorum.* The normal quorum of the Board shall be three except in cases of extreme urgency where a quorum of two, concurring, shall suffice. This provision does not apply when one Member has been delegated to represent the Board, in accordance with provisions of Clause 14.

C. PROCEDURE

10. Appeal to the Board may be taken:
(a) by any refugee or displaced person in the form of a petition for review;
(b) by the Director General or as directed by him.
The Board is enjoined with the reviewing of the petition once it has been filed.

11. *Petitions.* Any petition for review shall specify:
(a) the name of the individual refugee or displaced person concerned;
(b) the specific grounds for challenging the administrative determination including specific statements of any facts (such as dates and places) which it is alleged relate to the application of the mandate to the individual concerned;
(c) any facts which it is alleged have not been properly taken into consideration.

12. A petition to the Board should normally not be an appeal on the facts, but on the application of the definitions of the scope of the mandate to the facts as found by the Field staff. In exceptional cases, however, where substantial grounds for re-examining the facts are alleged, the appeal may be based on the facts.

13. A petition for review may be delivered by the party appealing to any Eligibility Officer of the Organization, who shall give a receipt for it and forward it to Headquarters, unless other arrangements have been made with the Review Board.

All Officials of the Organization are authorized to use the official mail for this purpose.

14. Petitions for review shall be made not later than 31 days after the refugee or displaced person has been informed of the decision by which he was declared not within the mandate. The Board shall use its discretion in accepting petitions made after the 31-days period.

15. All petitions for review must be submitted to the Board, and it is for the Board to decide whether or not they will be accepted as appeals.

16. The submission of a petition for review *ipso facto* suspends the effect of the decision against which the petition is made. No action shall be taken until the Review Board has decided on the case.

Functioning of the Board

17. The Board shall function in the following manner.

The cases shall normally be reviewed in the area of the Field Officer. To this effect, the Chairman may delegate in each area a member who will sit on circuits and decide upon all cases in which he is satisfied that application of principle is clear. That member shall function in the name of the Board and his decisions shall be deemed to have been taken by the Board itself. He may solicit advice from the local legal or eligibility officer or both. However, it will be his duty to refer to the Board sitting at Headquarters, Geneva, any case in which he has a doubt as to the proper decision which should be taken. In such cases and in any other cases or group of cases which the Chairman may determine, the Board shall examine the petition and take the appropriate decision.

18. In any case in which the Board or its representative regards the grounds set forth in the application for review as indefinite, or frivolous, it may require the applicant to specify proper grounds for his application before the review will be granted. The same applies when the case is governed by a previous decision in respect of which no valid reasons are brought which would justify its reversal. In such cases the petition may be rejected or the case summarily dismissed.

19. The Board or its representative is empowered to refer the case back to the administrative staff for further investigation if it is of the opinion that certain facts have not been properly investigated.

20. Although the petitioner has the right to be heard in person if he so requests in his petition for review, the presence before the Board, or its delegate, of the party petitioning for review is not required. However, any party petitioning for review shall be entitled to submit to the Board any memorandum stating his case, and any documentary evidence. If necessary, the Organization may provide an officer to watch his interests.

21. Whenever possible and expedient, the practice shall be to take a decision upon the documents produced. However, when the Board is of the opinion that, in order to make a proper review, it should itself examine the facts, the Board or its representative may itself conduct a hearing, call for information and documents or any particular witness or witnesses if it thinks fit, and examine such facts as may be presented to it. Expert advice may be solicited as necessary.

22. The decisions of the Board shall be taken by a majority of the Members sitting in the case and the decision shall be deemed to be the opinion of the Board as a whole. When voting, all Members who have sat in a case will have an equal right to express their opinion and to cast their vote. Every decision of the Board shall state the reasons therefore. Dissenting opinion may be placed on record.

23. The decision of the Board or of its representatives on any petition for review shall be final. However, the Board is not precluded from rectifying errors, or from reconsidering cases in which additional information has been received.

24. A Recorder shall be appointed to the Board. He will keep the appropriate registers, records, archives, and originals of the decisions, as directed by the Chairman, and will see that the competent services of IRO and the parties concerned are informed of the decisions of the Board or its representatives.

25. The Board may when necessary issue rules to govern its own procedure. It will have power to require the Eligibility Officers at all levels, through appropriate channels to observe certain rules of procedure relating to application for review, as it may determine.

26. In the absence of a sufficient number of Members to form a quorum the Chairman of the Board or the Member present at Headquarters Geneva shall himself be empowered to take decisions and review cases which are urgent or whose accumulation would add to the administrative difficulties in the Zones.

ANNEX 19

Applications for IRO assistance

Dates of application and determination within the IRO mandate

IRO area	Total	Refugees who applied on 31 Aug. 1949	Refugees determined to be within the mandate of IRO, 1 July 1947–31 Dec. 1951						
			Total	Refugees who applied after 31 Aug. 1949					
				Refugees who left country of origin after 31 Aug. 1949 and arrived in IRO area before 15 Oct. 1949		Other refugees who arrived in IRO area before 1 Oct. 1950		Refugees who arrived in IRO area on or after 1 Oct. 1950	
				For legal and political protection	For other services	For legal and political protection	For other services	For legal and political protection	For other services
TOTAL	1,337,749	1,173,888	163,861	306	3,961	97,883	43,600	5,779	12,332
Argentina	2	2	..	..	..	..	..	..	..
Austria	148,804	136,530	12,274	95	598	1,884	7,460	409	1,828
Belgium	18,865	14,481	4,384	1	102	1,578	2,558	103	42
Brazil	97	37	60	..	..	60	..	..	..
Czechoslovakia	2,870	2,870	..	..	..	..	..	..	..
Denmark	2,880	2,803	77	..	3	26	28	..	20
Far East Shanghai	26,436	24,543	1,893	..	..	1,840	52	1	..
France	213,835	118,921	94,914	..	282	86,242	4,642	3,748	..
Germany British zone	809,409	788,409	21,000	85	2,197	3,361	12,466	844	2,047
French zone	236,523	232,074	4,449	14	104	1,229	2,523	440	139
US zone	54,478	52,462	2,016	56	197	344	1,099	145	175
US zone	518,408	503,873	14,535	15	1,896	1,788	8,844	259	1,733
Greece	10,519	5,187	5,332	48	55	88	2,827	186	2,128
Italy	86,055	64,473	21,582	75	647	866	13,283	465	6,246
Luxembourg	988	773	215	..	5	182	14	13	1
Middle East	7,522	6,708	814	..	51	491	248	4	20
East Africa	5,504	5,503	1	..	..	1	..	..	..
Egypt	212	83	129	..	..	129	..	..	..
Lebanon	215	172	43	..	..	24	13	..	..
Syria	190	182	8	..	..	2	6	2	4
Turkey	1,401	768	633	..	51	335	229	2	16
Netherlands	3,784	2,945	839	..	..	824	15	..	..
Norway	573	396	177	..	..	173	1	3	..
Peru/Bolivia	105	105	..	..	..	..	..	..	..
Portugal	291	251	40	..	..	38	..	..	..
Spain	340	299	41	2	21	17	..	..	..
Sweden*	4,029	3,810	219	..	..	213	6	3	..
UK	268	268	..	..	..	..	..	..	..
US	77	77	..	..	..	..	..	..	..

* Applications received by the IRO Office in Denmark

ANNEX 19a

Applications for IRO assistance

IRO area and month

IRO area	Refugees determined to be within the mandate of IRO, 1 July 1947–31 Dec. 1951			
	Total 1 July 1947–31 Dec. 1951	Total 1 July 1947–30 June 1949	Total 1 July 1949–30 June 1950	Total 1 July 1950–30 June 1951
TOTAL	1,337,749	1,008,839	221,995	79,404
Argentina	2	..	2	..
Austria	148,804	111,548	24,258	9,080
Belgium	18,865	9,660	5,733	1,766
Brazil	97	27	62	8
Czechoslovakia . . .	2,870	1,468	1,402	..
Denmark	2,880	2,130	701	36
Far East Shanghai	26,436	21,047	3,929	1,105
France	213,835	87,328	69,020	41,351
Germany	809,409	716,991	77,383	9,162
British zone . . .	236,523	209,030	23,913	2,318
French zone . . .	54,478	50,963	2,322	673
US zone	518,408	456,998	51,148	6,171
Greece	10,519	3,825	1,285	3,528
Italy	86,055	45,213	20,902	12,471
Luxembourg	988	696	222	70
Middle East	7,522	6,386	858	241
East Africa . . .	5,504	5,499	5	..
Egypt	212	71	141	..
Lebanon	215 ⎱	281	104	15
Syria	190 ⎰			5
Turkey	1,401	535	608	221
Netherlands	3,784	1,715	1,842	227
Norway	573	..	395	62
Peru/Bolivia	105	98	7	..
Portugal	291	235	56	..
Spain	340	224	100	13
Sweden*	4,029	..	3,741	284
UK	268	177	91	..
US	77	71	6	..

* Applications received by the IRO office in Denmark.

CHAPTER XIII

CARE AND MAINTENANCE

IN the principal areas of operation the refugees and displaced persons lived in camps or assembly centres which were taken over from UNRRA in the three western zones of Germany, in Austria, Italy, Middle East, India, Lebanon, and Palestine, and from the military authorities in Germany and Italy, and from the AJDC in Shanghai.[1]

In other areas, mainly the countries of western Europe, the refugees lived out-of-camp within the economy of the country of refuge and received cash assistance. An assembly centre was a camp or a group of camps, a community of detached dwellings, or any other agglomeration or individual housing arrangements for which the IRO took responsibility, e.g. by finance, physical maintenance, supervision, or assignment of space (billeting). In addition to the living centres (the so-called static centres) a number of transit centres were established in which the refugees could be assembled for the purpose of selection, movement, and embarkation.[2] There were repatriation centres in which refugees were collected for return to their country of origin; resettlement processing centres for those collected for presentation to selection teams. From there they went through the staging centre, to which fully processed emigrants were passed ready for movement to final destination through an embarkation centre, whence they were called forward for shipment on a special vessel or aeroplane.

In addition there existed specialized centres such as the medical centres (hospital, sanatorium, convalescent home, children's nutritional centre); rehabilitation and vocational training centres; children's and youths' centres and homes for aged refugees. The majority of refugees received full care and maintenance and shelter, though in the most varied types of accommodation.

In Germany and Austria, and to some extent in Italy, the people lived in six characteristic types of shelter: (1) *Kaserne* (formerly used by the German army, or by the Nazi Stormtroopers), usually a several-storied brick or concrete building with paved courtyards; (2) temporary wooden barracks; (3) German tenement houses which had been requisitioned; (4) sections of villages from which Germans had been moved; (5) former slave-labour and even concentration camps; and (6) public buildings such as school-houses and sanatoria, which had been taken over. Certain of these installations provided very adequate standards of housing, others were hardly fit for human habitation. Some lacked the basic facilities such as heating, cooking, washing, and sanitary accommodations. The rooms within the barracks were often only partitioned off with blankets swung across ropes. The greatest problem nearly everywhere was the overcrowding which prevented normal

---

[1] See Annexes 20–22, pp. 236–8.
[2] See Chart, IRO Pipeline.

family living arrangements. The Organization made great efforts to provide the refugees with adequate housing, but it was practically impossible at times to implement the approved standards. As early as May 1947 the PCIRO had approved principles governing standards of living and care which were later approved by the General Council at its First Session.[1]

Living Standards

Housing was to meet minimum standards of health and decency; living quarters were, if possible, to be reasonably heated, have sufficient light, and adequate sanitary facilities, and adequate sleeping accommodation with due respect for differences in age and sex.

The diet was to be no lower than that of the local population. When the diet of the general population did not provide a minimum emergency standard of health, the Preparatory Commission, taking into account the climatic and other conditions, was to augment the diet of refugees to the minimum emergency standards approved by medical and nutritional authorities. Particular consideration would be given to special groups such as children, nursing mothers, sick persons, and workers.

Clothing was to be provided as needed to meet climatic conditions, and was to be of a standard to meet the needs of the individual.

In co-operation with the governments or occupying authorities, the Preparatory Commission was to maintain and safeguard health, including health during repatriation or resettlement movements.

In co-operation with governments or occupation authorities useful employment was to be ensured to as many displaced persons as possible within their skills, and vocational training and refresher courses were to be provided as far as possible to enable persons to learn new skills, or to become adept again in previous skills. Such training was to be related to the individual's prospective repatriation or resettlement.

Educational opportunities for children and youth were to be provided whenever possible. The development of community activities of the kind to which the particular groups were accustomed were to be encouraged, and space and equipment for such activities provided. All groups were to be given facilities for conducting their own religious services—the IRO was to ensure that persons not living in groups should have access to religious services.

Once these standards had been established in general terms, they had to be translated into specific items of food, clothing, &c., and applied to the daily life of the refugees. The former task became the responsibility of various organizing units at headquarters;[2] the latter depended, in areas of Austria and Germany under British and French control, on agreements with the appropriate authorities;[3] where the Organization administered the centres itself, as in the zone of Austria and Germany and in Italy, it applied its own standards subject to the availability of supplies.[4]

[1] PREP Res. No. 19, Appendix III, p. 692.
[2] Chapter IV, Administration, p. 65.
[3] See Chapter VII, Co-operation of Governments, pp. 128 ff.
[4] See Chapter XXV, Supporting Services, p. 528.

The basic agreements with the governing authorities of the British and French zones have already been described.[1] As far as care and maintenance were concerned, such agreements assured the Organization that adequate standards would prevail for housing, its maintenance and repair, feeding, clothing, fuel, medical supplies, household materials and equipment, kitchen utensils, and amenity supplies. The material standards of care were to conform as far as possible to those approved by the Preparatory Commission, and to this end consultations were to be held with the appropriate authorities.[2]

In the Middle East the UK Government continued the arrangements made with UNRRA whereby the local British representatives were responsible for the care and maintenance of the refugees in exchange for a monthly payment for each refugee. The rates of payment varied in different areas.[3]

The Far East programme established by UNRRA and the Chinese National Relief and Reconstruction Agency (CNRRA), provided for the relief of European refugees in matters of housing and food. Local medical facilities were also placed at the disposal of the international agency. When the PCIRO took over this programme, appropriate steps were taken to establish formal arrangements with the Nationalist Government in respect of its operation.

In 1947 agreement was reached between the IRO and the Chinese Ministry of Health regarding the provision of free health services in connexion with the overseas Chinese repatriation programme. A draft basic agreement between the Nationalist Government and the IRO was approved and was awaiting signatures in January 1949. In this document the IRO assumed responsibility for the care and maintenance of non-Chinese refugees, and also agreed to establish and administer such assembly centres as were considered necessary to carry out its basic intentions. The Chinese Government was to provide all necessary housing, including medical installations, and was to relieve the Organization of any liability in connexion with demands arising from the use of such property. Owing to political changes in the country this agreement was never signed, but its principles were accepted as a basis for operation as long as the National Government remained in power.

Administration

The administration of the installations was either delegated to the occupation authorities or local governments or retained by the IRO. In the US area of control in Austria and Germany, and also in Italy, the Philippines, Shanghai, and Egypt, the administration of the centres was the responsibility of the Organization. In respect of certain functions, such as security in the occupied areas, the military or local units of governments were joint partners in the particular function. The administrative arrangements made to control the installations under the direct supervision of the Organization varied according to the type of agreement that had been reached with the governing authority.

[1] See Chapter VII, p. 129, and Appendix II (b).
[2] This was particularly specified in the agreement with the French Government, dated 6 Sept. 1947.
[3] Letter from Executive Secretary, PCIRO, to the Under Secretary of State, Foreign Office, London, 3 June 1947.

In Austria the US zone was divided into two areas with headquarters located in Salzburg and Linz. In each of these areas a team of specialists under the direction of a senior officer supervised the many activities and programmes in the several assembly centres. In each centre, there was an international staff usually consisting of a centre administrator with welfare supply officers. These officers were assisted by local staff who, in most cases, were made chiefs of particular sections and were designated as local employees. They were recruited from the duly elected centre committee, and in this respect served a dual purpose. In the British and French zones of Austria, similar area staffs were appointed, but the IRO had no staff in assembly centres which were administered by the British and French elements of the Allied Commission for Austria.

The programme in Italy was different from that in Germany and Austria, in that the Government of that country joined with the Organization as a partner. Although assembly centres were operated by the IRO, Italian police had jurisdiction in matters involving breaches of law wherever the centres were located.[1] A special division was established to control the administration of assembly centres; this, in turn, was supervised by a senior officer responsible for all care and maintenance activities. Three international officers were assigned to each centre: a centre director, a welfare officer, and a supply officer. This staff was supplemented by a staff of refugees and Italians. Every effort was made to employ Italians in the operation, especially where the position required frequent contact with local administrative authorities.

For Jewish refugees in Italy, a special community programme was adopted, and the people, both old and young, who intended to emigrate to Palestine received agricultural and cultural training in accordance with the principle of the collective settlement in Palestine. These Jewish communities in Italy were designated as 'Hachsharoth' or communities for 'preparation'. This programme was under the joint sponsorship of the AJDC and the JAFP, assisted by the World ORT Union, the IRO giving financial assistance as part of its care and maintenance programme.

In Germany the administrative control of assembly centres was more complicated. Of the 776 for which the IRO became financially responsible, 732 were located in Germany, housing approximately 89 per cent. of the refugee population for whose maintenance the IRO was responsible.[2] The administration of this large number of assembly centres was a serious task.

In the British zone of Germany the operation of all centres was the responsibility of the occupation authorities. In so far as it was consistent with their general policies, the British authorities followed the policies established by the IRO; and the IRO's specialist staffs made periodical inspections of accommodation, welfare and community services, the issue and preparation of food, employment, distribution of relief items and amenity supplies, and any other activities incident to the care of the refugees.

The French zone operated on the same principle as that adopted in the British zone. The zone was divided into three areas, in addition to the zone headquarters.

[1] Agreement between the Italian Government and the PCIRO, Oct. 1947, Articles II, III, and VII.
[2] See Annexes 20 and 21, pp. 236–7.

222 CARE AND MAINTENANCE

In the US zone the control of assembly centre administration was the direct responsibility of the IRO. In the early days the operations of IRO were conducted through seven area offices in the zone proper, in addition to the embarkation area in Land Bremen and the Berlin Office. Reductions in the population of refugees and displaced persons and consolidation into the southern part of the zone brought about a gradual reduction of this administrative structure to field offices corresponding to the three *Länder* of the US zone (Württemberg, Hesse, and Bavaria) and Bremen and Berlin. Within each area, sub-administrative units were developed to control groups of assembly centres according to the number of separate centres and the size of the population. The areas were, in a certain sense, operationally autonomous and were required to work closely with the military government. The actual supervision of the standards of care was the joint responsibility of the staff at area headquarters and the sub-area offices. Within the centres, staffs of displaced persons and refugees assumed day-to-day responsibilities for all welfare and relief services.

One important result of the IRO's direct responsibility for the administration of assembly centres in the US zone of Germany was the application of the principle of self-administration. Under the administration of SHAEF,[1] refugees had played a large part in handling their own community affairs. The policy was affirmed by the IRO on 15 June 1948 in Provisional Order No. 74 on 'Community self-administration and relationship with national groups of displaced persons'. This order was to encourage the participation of displaced persons and refugees in the administration of camps and assembly centres and to co-ordinate the various existing systems. By accepting the policy of self-administration in centres, Geneva headquarters opened the way to dealing officially with national committees: 'It is the policy of PCIRO to give full consideration to proposals put forward by National Groups of displaced persons, and to establish, at field level, operating relationships.'

All missions reviewed this question carefully, but the US area control was the only one in which it was fully implemented. On 12 August 1948 an administrative order was issued setting forth the policy and procedure of self-administration to be established in the zone for the administration of assembly centres. The operative sections read as follows:

VI. *Policy*

C. The responsibility for supervision of camp operations had been placed upon the Organization, both by the IRO Constitution and through agreements with the governing authorities in each area of operation. Although it is within the authority of PCIRO to delegate authority for assembly centre administration to displaced persons, the ultimate operational responsibility remains with PCIRO. The administration cannot relieve itself of its responsibility to the Preparatory Commission and the General Council with respect to the welfare of displaced persons and refugees and with respect to the control of property and funds. Therefore, in connexion with all programmes of camp administration PCIRO must continue to exercise the right of supervision and overall control.

[1] The SHAEF *Manual*, issued in May 1945, stated that displaced persons were to be used as extensively as possible for assembly-centre administration.

VII. *Procedures*

A. Elections will normally be held in all assembly centres at annual intervals and on such other occasions as are authorized by area directors for the purpose of electing a camp committee.

B. The elected camp committee will nominate a camp administrator who will assume his office and functions when approved and appointed in writing by the area director. Pending elections, subsequent nominations and approval by the area director, the area director may appoint a camp administrator.

C. The camp administrator will serve as the senior member of the displaced persons administrative staff.

1. The displaced persons administrative staff is the executive instrument of PCIRO in the assembly centre. It consists of:

a. A camp administrator

b. His deputy or deputies (maximum 2)

c. The staff (varying in size depending on circumstances): Reports and statistics—health—repatriation—resettlement—supply and transport—employment—welfare—child care officers—food supervision—police chief—legal counsellor and commodity accountant.

The importance of continuity in the technical tasks of the displaced persons administrative staff is apparent.[1]

In Italy every effort was made to establish a similar programme but circumstances prevented its development. The Austria mission decided against the full implementation of the policy, but refugees were employed in centres and committees were formed.

Self-government

One of the essential points in the success of self-administration was to devise a method whereby the refugee could participate in the management of the assembly centre, free of any influence on the part of the official agencies responsible for the programme. Originally the occupation authorities had encouraged the formation and use of centre advisory councils,[2] and as a result of this policy, the centre committee had become an integral part of the assembly centre administration. When the IRO's work started, centre committees were in existence in all assembly centres. Their essential task was to review the programme of international aid as it affected the lives of the particular refugees whom they represented. Since they were bodies elected through popular balloting, they were also concerned with the future plans being made for the particular national groups involved.

One of the most important communal organizations was that of the displaced Jewish population. In Germany, Austria, and Italy local committees were established in centres and in all localities where the refugees were living privately in cities and towns. In 1946–7 all these committees were united in centralized organizations, on a zone level in Germany and Austria, and on a national level in Italy. These centralized bodies were headed by democratically elected central committees.

[1] A special centre was established in Bad Wiessee, a small resort in Lower Bavaria, US zone of Germany in 1946, to train refugees for positions in assembly-centre administration. This programme was designed to aid in the gradual withdrawal of international staffs from direct administrative work in the refugee communities. By the spring of 1947 this had been largely accomplished.

[2] SHAEF Civil Affairs Division, *Guide to Assembly Centre Administration*, issued by the Displaced Persons, Refugees and Welfare Branch, revised Sept. 1944, p. 10, section 106.

These local and central committees constituted a self-government of displaced Jews and formed governing bodies of a peculiar society of people in transit, aspiring to create a substitute for a normal life which would help them to bear the hardship of a displaced person's existence.[1]

The central committee in Italy served as co-ordinating and liaison agency for the regional and local centre committees. The regional committees dealt with all matters concerning the Hachsharoth communities, and also co-ordinated the work of local committees in the northern and southern parts of the country. Serious problems involving registration, ration issue, relations with the Italian governmental authorities, the arrival of new refugees, and movements were discussed by the IRO administration with the central committee. The latter transmitted information received and decisions reached to the regional and local committees for necessary implementation when required.

Local centre committees constantly came before the population as leaders, and served to develop the principle of self-government. In the Adriatica centre in Milan monthly meetings were arranged so that the centre population could hear the report of the centre committee. These meetings had a moral effect on the population, since they received news that concerned individuals as well as the welfare of the camp. Statistics informed them how many people had been given clothing during the month, how much wood was distributed, how many individual welfare cases were handled, how much food was consumed, and the tonnage of supplies received. Future projects were discussed. All this tended to build up the morale of the camp.[2]

In Germany not only was the Jewish refugee population well organized, but the Baltic, Ukrainian, and Polish national committees, too, were very active. With the agreement of the occupying authorities the US zone headquarters established a working relationship with the following nine national committees and a liaison officer of these committees was appointed to the IRO staff:

Esthonian Central Committee
Latvian Central Committee
Lithuanian Central Committee
Polish Union
Hungarian Office
Ukrainian Central Relief Committee
Central Representation of the Russian Emigration
National Alliance of Czechoslovakian Democratic Refugees in Germany
White Ruthenian (Bielo-Russian) National Committee (Central) Representation of
　　White Ruthenian Emigration in Germany)

Late in 1951 the national committees, in co-operation with similar representatives in the British and French zones, formed a Central Council of National Committees of Alien Refugees in Germany in an effort to develop group representation for the remaining refugees in Germany.

The press, supported by IRO, through grants of newsprint and travel facilities

---

[1] Report of Activities on behalf of the Jewish Displaced Persons and Refugees by AJDC and JAFP, July 1952.
[2] Report of the assembly-centre administrator for Dec. 1947.

for reporters, contributed to the good relations between the refugees and the IRO authorities. At the same time the press served as a useful medium for information to the refugees. In monthly news conferences with headquarter officials, the representatives of the refugee press obtained first-hand information and answers to questions. IRO supported eighty-two refugee publications representing fourteen different languages.

The administrative structure of assembly centres was essentially like the administration of any modern town. These camps—some of them housing over 10,000 people—were complete communities in themselves with all the problems of normal community life, complicated by their situation in the midst of the generally hostile population. Provision had to be made to meet such problems, and the refugees proved to be versatile and reliable in the camp administration. They had their own police and fire department, their schools and churches, and entertainment; they handled their food supply, clothing distribution, medical care, and public health. 'Crowded camp life was a necessary evil, but the refugees themselves did much to offset its demoralizing influence.'

The centre committee, whose members were elected by the refugees and who were themselves not permitted to undertake any paid employment in the camp, functioned in a manner similar to that of a town council. All administrative positions within the centres were assigned to refugees who were appointed by the IRO on the recommendation of the duly elected centre committees.

Organization of camp services

The IRO retained the general responsibility for the welfare of the refugee community, and the camp administrator was responsible for the implementation of its policies. The camp administrator knew that his appointment was due to the recommendation of the centre committee, and, acting in accordance with public opinion, he conformed to its wishes in so far as they did not conflict with the IRO's policy. Thus the administrator was comparable to a city manager, mayor, or town clerk, and the staff officers operating under his direction supervised the important functions necessary to the smooth operation of the centre.

The registration office, or bureau of vital statistics, contained all basic records on the refugee population. The main tasks of this office were the preparation of official reports on the age and sex distribution of the population, absentees, transfers, and admissions; lists of final departures were also kept.

The function of the medical office, or the bureau of public health and medical care, was to supervise the medical inspection, examination, and treatment of individuals in the centre, and to operate an infirmary and the necessary clinics to meet emergencies. Closely related to this was the routine of sanitary inspection of communal facilities such as latrines, baths, showers, garbage collection, and similar essential services.

The department of re-establishment of the office of repatriation and resettlement was mainly concerned with the preliminary documentation required as a first step in sending a person home or to a new country.

Supply, transport, and engineering work was consolidated into one office, whose main responsibility was to ensure that food supplies were properly stored and issued only against authorizations from the food distribution office. Centre maintenance was also one of its functions, and all vehicles assigned to the centre were controlled by the supply officer.

The food supervisor was the counterpart of the area nutritionist and authorized the issue of rations according to approved scales established by the Organization. Planning the daily menu and supervising the preparation of the food in central messing units took up a considerable part of the time of the employee assigned to this position.

The employment office maintained an up-to-date record of all employable refugees. Theoretically, contacts were to be maintained with indigenous labour offices with a view to securing as many positions as possible for the refugees. In occupied countries, liaison was maintained with local military unit commanders or civilian personnel offices in order to stimulate the employment of centre residents. Labour required for the centre administration was recruited through this office, whether it was for paid employment or voluntary work.

The welfare office rendered many services, as there were always individuals in any group who had problems which were difficult for them to resolve unaided. The prevailing concept of social service, in the minds of refugees, required that centre welfare officers should above all else be able to listen sympathetically to any problem; personal counselling meant more than securing information regarding a refugee's future plans. But in addition, this office arranged special care for the aged, the infirm and physically handicapped, and the unaccompanied children; saw to registration and the personal documents of refugees, and was responsible for education, leisure time, and recreational activities.

The public safety programme was largely concerned with internal problems of law and order. Rules and regulations were issued by the Organization, and in liberated and occupied countries the occupation authorities and the local government were also involved, as military government regulations and local laws were applicable to the refugees. The centre public safety force, consisting of the police and fire brigade, were established to maintain law and order within the centre and to develop a fire defence system in accordance with instructions issued by the army or the local government, or both. For detention purposes special arrangements were made in each centre, although on occasions local facilities of the military or the local government had to be used.

The essential task of the centre legal counsellor was to assist the centre residents on all legal matters. One of his very important functions was the preparing of documents in support of resettlement applications. Closely related to this were the services in respect of divorces, adoptions, and similar legal problems which might have prevented refugees' migration and settlement.

Briefly, the above indicates the functions of the various staff offices in the assembly centre. The centre administrator bore a heavy responsibility in co-ordinating the work of a staff which dealt with every aspect of communal life. Self-administration in a broad sense existed, but the system was technically a joint relationship between the Organization and the refugee. This assured the IRO that its standards of care and administration would be maintained, and at the same time made the refugees responsible for all activities in the centre.

This system of self-administration was developed almost exclusively in the US zone of Germany. In this area were located more than half the centres for which the IRO was administratively responsible, housing more than half the refugees living in assembly centres. In practice, the internal administration of centres was similar elsewhere, whether the responsibility lay with the IRO or not. The centre administrator, however, instead of being a refugee, was an official of the IRO, or of the responsible authority; similarly the chief welfare officer and the supply officer came from outside. But it was usual for the greater part of the staff necessary for administering these complex communities to be recruited from among the refugees.

Out-of-camp refugees

Not all refugees receiving care and maintenance lived in assembly centres; the major groups living outside centres were in the Middle East and in western Europe.

In the Lebanon and Palestine, assembly centres as such did not exist, and the relief operations for the refugees were administered by the 'Polish Refugee Office' under the supervision of the British Consul General in the particular areas concerned. This system had been in operation since 1943, and was later continued by UNRRA and the IRO.

Its costs were a source of considerable concern throughout the whole period of the IRO's operations; but by reducing the *per capita* grant to persons receiving assistance who were also obtaining a pension from the British Government, the IRO was able to set up a budget which allowed for 1·3 per cent. of the total grant to be assigned to administrative costs and approximately 13 per cent. for medical, welfare, cultural, and material expenses such as transport, supply, storage, and equipment. Apart from this, a reserve fund was created to take care of emergency cases which arose among the refugees. Most of these accumulated reserves were later returned to the remaining refugees to increase their relief allowances.

A cash assistance programme was provided also in Belgium, and similarly administered through agents who, in this case, were the voluntary societies. Nearly all refugees assisted were living privately, but there were a few aged people and some unaccompanied children residing in special homes. While the case investigations by voluntary societies were accepted as a basis for issuing cash grants, the IRO's office in Belgium employed a staff of case workers who made subsequent visits to the homes of the clients to ensure that the resources of the Organization were not being exploited. Responsibility for the assistance of 1,800 persons was taken over by the IRO on 1 July 1947, and the number remained more or less constant (2,111 at the end of 1949 and 1,424 on 30 June 1950) until the Belgian Government assumed responsibility.

The assistance programme established in France emerged from the work the IGCR had undertaken in May 1945. At that time there were three principal groups receiving material aid—German and Austrian refugees; a few stateless persons other than Nansen refugees; and the Spanish refugees. The programme for the

Austrians and Germans included cash assistance to individuals and grants to institutions caring for the aged, infirm, and children, short-term rehabilitation loans, and vocational training. This programme was administered through recognized voluntary societies which were experienced in the field of social welfare. The Spanish refugees received primarily individual cash assistance, although vocational training programmes were established to help re-train some of the youths.

The IRO's cash assistance in France did not differ in principle from that in other countries. In effect, the existing programme was continued and developed. The IRO supported programmes of vocational training, cash assistance, support for institutions, and grants to individuals for varying purposes.

Certain details of these services were of significance. Assistance was granted on a monthly basis to persons unfit for work, the amount varying in accordance with the degree of incapacity and with their domestic responsibilities. Assistance was granted to unaccompanied children, and to a large number of persons were given CARE packages as well as cash relief. Grants were made to students who were sufficiently advanced in their education to warrant aid, and loans were made to assist refugees in establishing small businesses. None of this work was done by the Organization direct; it was all done by voluntary societies, acting as agents of the IRO. As a result of an agreement with the SSAE (Service social d'aide aux émigrants), the Paris office of the Organization was able to secure the services of expert social workers to assume responsibility for case-work required in connexion with the cash assistance programme. These professional workers investigated all cases making application for relief, and through their efforts many individuals were assisted in obtaining the type of aid best suited to their individual needs. The use of this organization had many advantages because, on account of its wide establishment in the country and its international affiliation, it was able to take direct action in other countries in respect of social inquiries, tracing missing persons, re-uniting families, obtaining original documents, and other similar activities. In addition to the SSAE some twenty-six other welfare organizations, both French and international, denominational and non-denominational, co-operated with the Organization in its work in France. Some indication of the magnitude of the cash assistance programme in France is indicated below:

Cash assistance in France for the financial years 1948–9 and 1949–50

Types of expenditure	Financial year 1948–9	Financial year 1949–50
	$	$
Cash assistance	1,949,330	2,025,392
Vocational training	138,583	72,876
Loans	130,202	..

On 1 July 1947 responsibility for the material support of 6,300 refugees was assumed by the Organization; at the end of 1949 over 26,000 refugees were being maintained at the IRO's expense.

Most refugees in the Netherlands were eligible to benefit under the generous social security arrangements of that country. The IRO's care and assistance activities were confined to payments to supplement public assistance benefits, medical assistance, and emergency relief to the small numbers not qualified to benefit under social security schemes; these activities covered 170 persons on 1 July 1947 and 159 at the end of 1949. This emergency relief was administered directly by three voluntary societies, who reported in detail to the IRO each month.

In Spain and Portugal the programme of assistance established by the IGCR in December 1945, whereby monthly payments equivalent to $48 and $40 respectively for each eligible refugee (with small supplements for medical expenses) were paid on behalf of IGCR by the voluntary societies, was retained by the IRO. Seven hundred and ten persons were assisted in these two countries at the beginning of operations; the number had been reduced to 460 by the end of 1949.

Nutrition

The question of adequate food was very important particularly in view of the abnormal environment in which the refugees lived. When the PCIRO assumed responsibility for refugees in July 1947, the dietary standards for displaced persons in Germany and Austria were inadequate in quantity (normal consumer 1,500 to 1,900 calories in Germany, 1,500 in Austria), unbalanced, with excessive carbohydrate as compared with fats and protein, and of generally poor quality. Ration scales were in practice inferior to the consumption levels of local nationals in many instances. Quantities of items allocated to refugees were shown in the scales in gross, no allowance being made for wastage in distribution or bone content in the case of meat. While the Germans, for instance, were entitled to exchange their sugar ration for dried fruit, the refugee had no choice of items. The German national received limited quantities of eggs and fresh fruit: in the refugee community, eggs were supplied only to hospitals. Unemployed refugees, such as elderly people, had no money to supplement their meagre ration by the purchase of unrationed foods. Few of the refugees were able to resort to the various expedients practised by the local population to supplement the rations.

The unsupplemented official ration level for refugees would have been seriously detrimental to their health. Fortunately the voluntary societies helped considerably by contributing extra supplies during the most critical period. They gave generously, especially to the children, in hospitals and schools. During the first half of 1948, school feeding was maintained almost entirely by the voluntary societies. In addition, under a scheme financed by a grant of $2 million from UNRRA, children from 3 to 17 years of age received a supplement between-meals-ration of 350 calories in schools, children's centres, summer camps, and youth clubs. Even so, large numbers of under-weight children were reported from all areas, though weight in itself was not always conclusive. But such evidence as was available, both clinical and otherwise, substantiated the fact that the health of refugees, especially children, was being undermined by inadequate nutrition.

In May 1947 the PCIRO had laid down in its Resolution No. 19, that

the diet provided to displaced persons and refugees should not be lower than that of the local population. To the extent that the diet of the general population does not provide a minimum emergency standard of health, the Preparatory Commission should, taking into account climatic and other conditions, augment the diet of eligible displaced persons and refugees to the minimum emergency standards approved by medical and nutritional authorities.[1]

Accordingly, the health service strove to attain a satisfactory dietary level, based on the temporary maintenance standard of an intake of 1,900 calories daily, set by the National Research Council of the US. Since calorific levels were set by agreement with the occupation authorities of the zones in which the IRO camps were located, this standard did not immediately become effective in all zones.[2] As calorific content was only one measure of a satisfactory diet, the Organization issued a provisional order in 1947 which outlined the desired amounts of qualitative diet elements such as fats, proteins, &c., for the temporary maintenance standard.

By the end of the year 1948, revised dietary scales, based on a weighted average of 2,230 calories per person per day, were instituted for the indigenous population in the new officially amalgamated three occupied western zones of Germany. The new scales became effective in the US and British zones on 1 October 1948 and in the French zone on 1 January 1949.[3]

The new scale in the US zone, though lower in calories for some categories than the scale previously obtaining, was better balanced, providing essentials hitherto lacking, such as eggs for children and for pregnant and lactating mothers, and whole milk for children up to 2 years. In the British zone the new levels provided a considerable increase in diets for children and young people of from 6 to 20 years of age, and for the normal consumer, as well as raising the fat and protein content.

In Austria the Federal Government's standards providing for 2,213 calories per person, which came into force on 6 December 1948, were adopted as the basis of refugee ration scales. These standards made no provision for fresh vegetables and fruits, as these were on free sale, nor did they set a fixed scale of rations for hospitals. In formulating the scales for refugees, the Organization had to supplement official nutritional levels for children of 0–3 years, pregnant and lactating mothers, and hospital categories, the calorific values of general hospital diets being 2,860, and TB hospitals 3,640.[4] From February 1950 all rations for refugees were increased in an attempt to match the great improvement in the food situation in the local economies. The normal consumer category was augmented from 2,000 to 2,230 with an increase in eggs, meat, vegetables, and fruit. Nevertheless, the refugee level of feeding never did equal the improved local position. The sick, the elderly, the young mothers, and the unemployed did not possess the means to purchase supplementary rations.

The new scales did not provide for adequate transit rations. At this period resettlement operations were in full swing. After selection, refugees were transferred to staging centres. Often they had to make long overland train journeys to Italian ports, and subsequently to Bremerhaven in Germany. Many of these refugees had

---

[1] PREP/90/Rev.1/Add.1.
[2] Chapter VII, Co-operation of Governments, p. 134.
[3] GC/60, Report of the Director General, Sept. 1948, p. 11.
[4] For food standards and dietary categories in all three countries and in Samar see IRO *Operational Manual*, revised 1 May 1951, Appendix XIII.

formerly been employed by the IRO or the occupation authorities and had drawn higher rations than in these camps. After much discussion, the nutritional levels prevailing in transit centres were raised to the scale obtaining for the 10–20 years group. Communal feeding arrangements were largely employed in transit installations.

The multiplicity of ration scales in use meant increased supervisory and administrative difficulties. Without this system, however, it would have been impossible to secure adequate nutrition for vulnerable categories under the existing abnormal circumstances.

Clothing

Clothes were provided by the IRO as needed, having regard to climatic conditions and to occupation, physical conditions, age, and sex. Policy on distribution was somewhat complicated. It was to be governed by a 'basic allowance' and a yearly 'replacement allowance'. Preferential treatment was to be given to workers; and individuals engaged in particular types of employment, such as work in hospitals, heavy duty in the centres, police work, truck driving, and similar occupations were to be given special types of clothing according to their occupation. Personal and household allowances were to be made available periodically, depending upon the item and the age and sex of the individual. In the several assembly centre countries distribution of supplies, in accordance with the above principles, was developed in different ways.

The high incidence of employment in Austria made free distribution unnecessary. Economic conditions in the country as a whole were extremely bad, but refugees had from 1946 onwards received the same rations as the indigenous population, and had also been required to work, many refugees living in centres having proper employment outside, and others being employed in centre administration.

Each centre resident was issued a basic number of units—a restricted type of currency. The number of units received could be used to purchase up to the authorized basic allowance of clothing and amenity supplies. Where individuals were gainfully employed, they were permitted to purchase additional units over and above the basic issue, and persons employed by the IRO on approved projects were also given additional units; this procedure took care of the priority for workers.

To implement this plan, assembly centre service stores were established in each installation, proper staff employed, and a pricing system on a commercial basis created.

This system proved to be attractive and, as it was a form of business, allowed the refugees to receive assistance from the Organization without impairing their dignity. Not only was this method better for the refugees, it also enabled the IRO to know what items were in demand and to control supply—by requisition or purchase—accordingly.

In the British zone of Germany the issue of clothing and amenity supplies was the responsibility of the PW/DP Division of the Control Commission. In each assembly centre a clothing card was made out for each refugee and placed in a card index in the centre office. As the refugee received items of clothing he was required to sign an issue voucher which was filed and listed in a ledger. Subsequently, the item received by the refugee was entered on his clothing card, which would at all times show whether the basic and replacement allowance had been received.

Wherever possible, clothing was issued on an exchange basis; thus if a man wanted a shirt, he was required to produce one that was worn out. Refugees leaving assembly centres to live privately were given a complete set of serviceable clothing and footwear.

In the US zone of Germany, a system comparable with the one in the British zone prevailed. The centre administration, in co-operation with the refugee committee, distributed clothing and amenity supplies in accordance with instructions prepared by the IRO field welfare officers, assigned to sub-areas, who made periodical checks of the clothing cards to ensure that equity and justice prevailed.

In Italy the distribution of clothing was the direct responsibility of the IRO's welfare officers. In most centres the assistance of the refugee committee was sought.

Welfare Services

The IRO's conception of care and maintenance included the promotion of welfare and cultural activities, which were particularly important in the refugee communities because the physical conditions of life were inevitably hard. IRO modified some of the previous practices under UNRRA, but its own welfare policy was by no means uniform, owing to the varying circumstances in the different areas of control. The voluntary societies undertook a large part of the welfare work in the assembly centres. In the British zones of occupation voluntary society personnel replaced the former UNRRA staff. In Austria the IRO itself abolished the post of welfare officer altogether and appointed field care and maintenance officers, who were, however, largely supervisory personnel.

Certain programmes emerged which gave definite responsibilities to international welfare staff, and which included the counselling and registration of refugees and the establishment of standards of relief distribution, reuniting families, and dealing with the care of special categories such as children, the aged, the physically handicapped, and unmarried mothers. The international staff rendered services supplementary to vocational training and rehabilitation, and established special services in hospitals and other institutions operated by the IRO.

Education

Education, inside and outside assembly centres, depended a great deal on the interest of the intellectuals among the various national groups. Basic education, established in every centre under UNRRA control, was continued by the Organization.

The facilities made available for primary and secondary schools varied from one centre to another. In every centre of reasonable size there were kindergartens and elementary and high schools. Since the refugee population was not stabilized, and since the programme of the Organization was directed towards resettlement, repatriation, or local settlement, it was impracticable to retain fixed school organization for refugees.

The administration of the refugee school system was mainly the responsibility of the national educational committees in the centres. There were notable differences in the various missions. In Italy basic education was one of IRO's responsibilities, but was organized by voluntary societies and the refugees themselves. The welfare officer was directly concerned with matters of curricula, attendance, and school organization in the centres. In the British zone of Germany, where education was a responsibility of the Control Commission, the pattern of educational administration for refugees followed closely that of the local authorities. Regional educational boards, composed of refugees of the various nationalities, were established: the Control Commission and the IRO had permanent representatives on these boards. A system of inspection was set up to ensure that all refugee children attended school. In the US zone of Germany the national committees established educational boards which assumed responsibility for setting standards of training, for selecting teachers, and preparing examinations. In Austria the responsibility for schools in centres was considered to be a public one, shared by the IRO, voluntary societies, centre committees, teachers, and parents. In this mission the Austrian school law was adhered to as much as possible.

Specialized agencies also helped with the education of refugee children and youth. The United Nations Educational, Scientific, and Cultural Organization (UNESCO) indicated its interest by passing a resolution appealing for aid towards education in 'devastated countries'. The education of Spanish refugee children and students in exile was to become a special concern of this organization.

Educational supplies in all areas were difficult to obtain, despite the efforts of voluntary societies and the refugees themselves to meet the demand. UNESCO was successful in stimulating material aid from the Canadian Council for Reconstruction. This organization shipped some fifty boxes of classroom supplies for the educational programme for refugees. The shortage of supplies throughout the operation was reflected in the first appropriation made by the organization for education which was limited to the purchase of necessary classroom materials.

The Organization's efforts in the field of refugee education could not achieve complete success, for stability is essential for education. The refugee schools were, however, maintained to the end, and the children advanced as far as was possible in the circumstances.

Although the Organization clearly recognized its responsibility for basic education, higher education was a subject of considerable discussion. The Organization demanded assurances from refugees that its assistance to students in universities and technical colleges would represent an integral part of their plans for re-establishment, and that the studies had to be completed by October 1949; in certain cases by June 1950. Though many complaints arose over this policy, the very nature of the programme precluded the acceptance of commitments for university education that would have been extended beyond the lifetime of the Organization. It was the policy of the Organization to guide many of the students into a trade rather than encourage them to continue academic studies which would last several years, by which time they might have lost their opportunity to resettle under the IRO's auspices. There was a risk that students who were beginning their university education would not prepare for emigration, and it seemed right to persuade them to concentrate on their emigration plans, especially as many resettlement countries had very little interest in people with a purely academic training from another country and with no practical experience. For this reason, the Organization offered students the alternative of taking a course of vocational training or participating in one of the schemes for resettlement as students, such as those offered by the US or by the Netherlands. Among those whose studies were supported by the Oganization, preference was given to students of technical sciences, as their resettlement chances were better.

The training of illiterates proved to be most difficult. In the US zone of Germany more than 2,300 illiterates were found. Of this number only 206 were receiving instruction. An agreement was concluded with the World's YMCA/YWCA whereby that association undertook the responsibility for training this group, the IRO providing necessary supplies and equipment. This programme enabled many persons in this special group to meet the immigration requirements of receiving countries.[1]

Great emphasis was placed on the care and education of unaccompanied youths from 16 to 21 years of age (later amended to 17 to 21 years of age), who were unattached or in need of special guidance. It was difficult to give sufficient attention to the needs of young people in assembly centres; owing to the scarcity of facilities, adolescents tended to seek their recreation among the less desirable elements of the German community. An attempt was made to improve the situation by means of recreational programmes, including organized basket-ball, football, indoor gymnastics, table tennis, chess, checkers or draughts, and cinema shows; art classes were established and other pastimes and hobbies encouraged with the co-operation of the voluntary societies. But all this was felt to be insufficient to meet the needs of the young people in the IRO's charge. Special youth centres were therefore established whose aim was to give young people a basis for good physical and moral health, civic training and vocational guidance following individual tastes, skills, and aptitudes, so that they should not remain at the lowest social level—that of unskilled labourers—in the country of their re-establishment. Community responsibility was encouraged in these centres by letting the boys and girls participate in the running of the home and in providing a normal atmosphere as far as possible. It was not easy to develop community spirit among young people with very varied backgrounds. The youth centres gave young people a six-month training after which the Organization made recommendations for their future. Although the stay in the centre was too short to give them full courses of vocational training, many had improved opportunities to emigrate after they had completed their training.

The first unaccompanied youth centre was established in August 1948 at Verden in the British zone of Germany. The centre was run in conjunction with the technical trade school and was under the control of the Unitarian Service Committee. Another youth centre was founded in the US zone of Austria at St. Gilgen. There, after many difficulties, a suitable location was found, and a joint programme was undertaken with the World's YMCA/YWCA. Approximately 200 youths were listed, 40 were admitted to the youth centre, and after more than 160 had been

---

[1] See Chapter XVI, Adaptation to a New Life, p. 299.

interviewed and documented, a further 200 were declared eligible.[1] As it was not possible for the IRO to establish a youth centre in Italy, recreational facilities were made available in Bagnoli; and, during the summer months, in a large sea-side camp near Naples.

In regard to religion, the assistance of the voluntary societies was of immeasurable importance. Apart from material aid to their co-religionists, staff from the voluntary societies was made available to consult with the refugee clergy and to arrange special conferences to further the work of the various faiths concerned. The work of the Vatican mission in Germany was of particular help, as it was composed of a number of Catholic clergy of national origins corresponding to the principal nationalities among the refugees; the Pontifical Assistance Commission in Italy was similarly organized. The post-war reconstruction of Jewish life in Europe implied support of religious activities; this was the concern of the Jewish voluntary societies. The Lutheran World Federation and the World Council of Churches also retained special representatives on their operational staffs to deal with the religious needs of refugees. The former agency arranged for young theological students to come to Germany and other countries for the express purpose of promoting the spiritual welfare of the refugee population.

Recreation

Recreation and cultural activities were considered essential to the smooth functioning of assembly centre communities. The IRO inherited a well-established programme. Each centre had its recreation specialist, and supervisory staff from voluntary societies continued to direct the programme.

In the British zone of Germany leisure and cultural activities were entirely supervised by the voluntary societies. Training institutes, study centres, summer camping programmes, athletic contests, scouting, and the supply of equipment to support these services were all controlled by them. In Italy, by contrast, community activities were directly supervised by the IRO. International welfare officers responsible for one large centre each, or supervising several smaller centres, were concerned with sports, cinemas, nurseries, and special holiday celebrations, in addition to the normal social services such as counselling, relief distribution, education, and liaison with voluntary societies. The importance of cultural and recreational activities in the mission led to the appointment of a field supervisor, who co-ordinated this programme in co-operation with welfare workers and their centre staffs. Austria provided an example of the ingenuity and interest of refugees in maintaining their own community service programmes, supplementary aid being given by voluntary societies.

Although the Administration made no policy statement about community services in centres, the programme established by UNRRA was continued and improved largely through the able assistance of voluntary societies. For example, the summer camp programme for boys and girls inaugurated by the World's YMCA/YWCA in 1947 was an annual event until 1950.[2]

---

[1] The capacity was originally forty boys and was increased to sixty boys. This centre was later moved to Hellbrunn, and closed on 22 Sept. 1951.

[2] The YMCA/YWCA reported on 26 Aug. 1947 that: 'Before the end of the season, it is expected

The success of such programmes required continuous preparation in the centres throughout the autumn and winter. Leadership courses were necessary to train personnel, and the stimulus provided by the summer camps had to be translated into better community programmes in the assembly centres.

ANNEX 20

Total number of assembly centres (1 July 1947)

Area of operation	Assembly centres in operation 1 July 1947	Assembly centres under UNRRA control 30 June 1947	Assembly centres taken over by PCIRO on 1 July 1947
TOTAL . . .	*1,008*	*762*	*776*
Austria	*46*	*21*	*21*
British zone . .	5	5	5*
French zone . .	2	2	2
US zone . . .	39†	14	14
Germany . . .	*939*	*732*	*732*
British zone . .	472‡	272	272*
French zone . .	51§	44	44
US zone . . .	416	416	416
Italy	22‖	*8*	*22*
Egypt	1¶	*1*	*1*

(Information from UNRRA final statistical report to PCIRO on the displaced persons operations, 30 June 1947, with additional information from Monthly Statistical Reports, Austria—June 1947–July 1949.)

* These centres were operated by the occupation authorities subject to reimbursement of costs by the IRO.

† Includes twenty-two assembly centres in the US zone operated by the Austrian civilian authorities and three centres operated by the AJDC.

‡ Includes 200 centres in the British zone of Germany operated by the military authorities and voluntary societies.

§ Seven centres were under military control in the French zone.

‖ Includes fourteen centres operated by the IGCR.

¶ This was the centre at El Shatt. Poles residing in East Africa and India, the Lebanon, and Palestine are not shown.

that 41,000 DP boys and girls will have passed two weeks each in summer camps. This is practically the entire DP population between the ages of 10–17. The distribution of campers is as follows: US zone 24,000, British zone, 11,000, French zone 6,000. Thanks to the number of experienced camp directors available in different zones and as a result of the 1947 camping experience, the DP camps for 1947 were very well organized.... In the DP camps, we have had the full co-operation of UNRRA and IRO as well as of many volunteer agencies.'

ANNEX 21

Types of assistance programmes and number and location of refugees receiving assistance on 1 July 1947*

Area of operation	Number of refugees and type of assistance programme in operation as of 1 July 1947	
	Assemby centre care	Cash assistance
TOTAL	681,290	31,385
Austria.	32,719	..
British zone	12,231	330
French zone	5,558	..
US zone	14,930	..
Germany	604,556	..
British zone	223,747	..
French zone	44,109	..
US zone	336,700	..
Italy	22,170	7,000
France	..	6,300
Belgium	..	1,800
Netherlands	..	170
Portugal	..	230
Spain	..	480
Czechoslovakia	..	20
Middle East	21,040	..
East Africa	16,090	..
Egypt	700	..
India	4,250	..
Palestine	..	2,750
Lebanon	..	3,810
Far East Shanghai	805	8,495

* Compiled from the official IRO Statistical Report for December 1951 and Statistical Report from the IRO's field office in each major area of operation.

ANNEX 22

Care and maintenance

Location of refugees

IRO area	Refugees who were receiving IRO care and maintenance, 1 July 1947–31 Dec. 1951									
	1 July 1947	31 Dec. 1947	30 June 1948	31 Dec. 1948	30 June 1949	31 Dec. 1949	30 June 1949	31 Dec. 1950	30 June 1951	31 Dec. 1951
TOTAL	712,675	676,537	601,937	525,249	419,991	318,323	248,441	80,903	51,150	25,539
Austria . .	33,049	47,664	42,170	35,298	28,254	20,950	16,890	2,221	2,001	1,389
British zone .	12,561	10,913	9,740	8,831	7,091	6,053	3,989	..	7	NR
French zone.	5,558	5,361	6,557	4,785	3,666	2,723	1,999	..	..	NR
US zone .	14,930	31,390	25,873	21,682	17,497	12,174	10,902	2,221	1,994	NR
Belgium . .	1,800	1,509	1,397	1,388	1,460	2,111	1,424	..	..	..
Czechoslovakia	20	8	16	13	21	27	..	..	..	..
Denmark .	..	..	..	2,870	2,647	1,825	1,533	766	230	..
Far East . .	9,300	5,944	6,782	8,399	8,461	6,644	6,241	4,644	2,753	2,244
Shanghai .	9,300	5,944	6,782	8,399	3,420	3,362	3,230	2,515	2,393	2,114
Philippines .	..	..	..	..	5,041	3,282	3,011	2,129	360	130
France . .	6,300	6,421	9,877	14,452	22,461	26,199	24,693	..	..	..
Metropolitan France .	6,300	6,421	9,688	14,259	22,266	25,837	24,433	..	..	..
French North Africa .	..	..	189	193	195	362	260	..	..	..
Germany .	604,556	562,283	506,452	438,466	325,275	231,666	176,912	60,062	39,664	19,325
British zone .	223,747	195,094	174,214	151,200	123,573	92,235	76,357	8,854	9,064	3,790
French zone.	44,109	44,105	39,358	34,961	20,384	13,709	6,646	2,764	1,774	117
US zone .	336,700	323,084	292,880	252,305	181,318	125,722	93,909	48,444	28,826	15,418
Greece . .	..	..	..	..	101	327	381	267	172	..
Italy . .	29,170	29,495	24,541	16,296	23,558	22,218	15,884	12,549	6,085	2,575
Luxembourg .	..	..	..	51	164	181	144	..	..	..
Middle East .	27,600	22,302	9,785	5,877	5,592	4,256	2,799	268	157	2
East Africa .	16,090	15,261	7,211	4,205	3,741	2,990	1,652	..	..	..
Egypt . .	700	675	629	12	16	8	..	..	..	..
India . .	4,250	1,831	..	..	..	..	..	..	..	..
Israel . .	2,750	1,700	8	2	..	..	..	..	..	..
Lebanon .	3,810	2,835	1,913	1,575	1,673	1,014	870	38	27	2
Syria . .	..	..	..	..	..	110	99	82	73	..
Turkey .	..	..	24	83	162	134	178	148	57	..
Netherlands .	170	177	222	176	154	159	77	..	..	..
Portugal . .	230	324	276	247	199	194	34	26	9	..
Spain . .	480	410	419	416	344	266	129	100	79	4
Switzerland .	..	..	..	1,300	1,300	1,300	1,300	..	..	..

Note: Includes refugees receiving care and maintenance while in embarkation centres awaiting final movement to country of resettlement.

CHAPTER XIV

MEDICAL CARE

WHEN the IRO began to put into execution a medical programme for refugees, the immediate exigencies of medical assistance and public health in Germany, Austria, and Italy had been successfully met by UNRRA and the military authorities. The work described in this chapter was done exclusively in Germany, Austria, and Italy. The medical care of refugees for whom the IRO was in any way responsible in other countries was the concern of the various governments—either the refugees were, as in France, treated as ordinary citizens or, as in East Africa, special arrangements were made for them locally.

The programme inherited from UNRRA was comprehensive. Housing and sanitation standards were established. Nutrition and health policy were closely coordinated, and special diets were available for certain medical categories. Medical, nursing, and dental services were established in assembly centres, staffed by qualified refugees. Elaborate measures for the control of infectious diseases in a more or less static population had been put into practice, including notification, quarantine, and hospitalization. Special clinics existed for maternal, infant, and child welfare services for cases of tuberculosis and of venereal diseases.

A hospital survey carried out in October 1947 in the major theatres of operation showed the following position.[1] In the British zone of Germany three types of hospital accommodation were in use: (a) German civil hospitals with beds reserved for refugees, payment being made on a *per capita* basis; (b) German hospitals used regularly by a few refugees without any special allocation of beds; and (c) requisitioned hospitals, used solely for refugees, and charged to occupation costs. The hospitalization rate was rather high, 2·8 per cent., but beds were always available.

In the US zone of Germany the greater part of hospital care was provided in hospitals directly taken over from UNRRA by the PCIRO. Beds were available for 3·1 per cent. of the refugee population while the demand was only 2·25 per cent. In Austria general beds available in hospitals taken over by UNRRA were equivalent to to 1·2 per cent. of the in-camp population with 0·7 per cent. for tubercular cases. In Italy, with its high hospital costs, available beds were scarce and only cases requiring specialized treatment were referred to Italian hospitals. One hospital at Trani was taken over and maintained by the IRO.

IRO thus had at its disposals a hospital network sufficient for basic care. The refugees, however, were not a normal population in regard to health. Mass checks revealed the inroads of hidden illnesses, especially for the liberated inmates of concentration camps, tuberculosis, heart ailments, and the many secondary effects of malnutrition and hardship. Most refugees were undernourished and most of them needed dental treatment. In 1948 a check of more than 100,000 refugees carried out in Germany,

[1] PREP/161. Report of the Executive Secretary on Operations, Jan. 1948, pp. 16–21.

Austria, and Italy revealed that half of them had defects of health. The Organization could not be the permanent custodian of the sick or other groups for whom difficulty in re-establishment might be envisaged. It had to find a solution to their problems. The medical programme, as it was being developed, played an important part. All public health services needed by a large community, such as general supervision and nursing, clinics and sanatoria, surgical operations, maternity services, dental treatment, &c., were made available to the refugees by the IRO. Immunization was carried out as a routine measure against smallpox, typhoid, diphtheria, and against epidemics of typhus, cholera, and yellow fever when necessary. In addition the IRO concentrated more specifically on the very important problems of nutrition, control of tuberculosis and venereal diseases, repatriation of the sick, medical processing of refugees for resettlement, the resettlement of displaced medical personnel, and the vocational training and rehabilitation of the disabled.

The strict medical criteria employed by missions engaged in the selection of emigrants rendered maintenance of a high standard of health essential in refugee communities. As well as detection and treatment of incipient disease, the importance of the symptomless hernia, varicosities, orthopaedic troubles, and dental defects as handicaps to resettlement had to be stressed.

As the refugees were often moved about, it was essential to control infectious diseases. It was important to prevent the spread of serious and crippling diseases such as poliomyelitis, diphtheria, typhoid, &c., among the communities, and refugees in transit had to be subject to strict care with regard to relatively minor diseases such as measles or whooping cough. If the adults were examined and vaccinated before leaving there was little danger, but in the case of the children, the risks were far greater. An outbreak of illness during a journey often meant a loss of time and money and the dislocation of transport. Therefore the regular functioning of transport was in a large measure dependent on the efficiency of the health service.

Refugees impatient to leave Europe very often took advantage of the post-war disorganization by trying to utilize false papers. The IRO had to take all possible precautions to make sure that the papers presented to the selection missions were genuine. This necessitated an identity check in conjunction with the medical services.

Protection of health during the journey involved not only the control of infectious diseases but also provision of adequate food, sanitation, and standards of accommodation on ships and trains, study of the special needs of 'vulnerable' categories such as aged people, pregnant women, infants, and children; transmission of essential medical data on groups in transit; provision of medical escorts where indicated; and performance of pre-movement medical checks. All these were indispensable in ensuring the expeditious and safe movement of refugees to their destinations. And the movement of sick or physically handicapped persons was, of course, a major concern of the health services.

Most of the refugees rejected by the selection missions were disqualified on grounds of health. The medical service therefore had to try in every way possible to improve their physical condition. The refugees, for whom resettlement was the door to a new world and a new life, fully realized the importance of a clean bill of health. The high standard insisted upon by the selection missions was the best health propaganda, and resulted in greater co-operation by the refugees in the IRO's health measures.

Such a vast network of operations necessitated a close collaboration of many tangential units and personages both within the Organization and without. The IRO's health services impinged on all aspects of its work and maintained close touch with other international organizations, with the medical services of the occupational authorities and governments, and with related divisions of the IRO.

A detailed account covering all areas of operations cannot be given here. The most comprehensive and efficient medical programme was developed in the US zone of Germany because of the executive position of the Organization in this theatre together with effective local resources. This area sheltered the greatest refugee concentration to be found under the Organization's mandate. Therefore, programmes in this zone have been taken as the prototype of medical efforts on behalf of refugees. Differences in the other zones will be mentioned as they arise.

Medical equipment in centres

The elaborate system of medical care in assembly centres inherited from UNRRA was adapted to resettlement requirements. Great emphasis was laid, for instance, on prophylactic treatment of conditions like hernia and varicosities and on essential dental care. In fact the refugees received more medical care than people living in a normal community. For circumstances in refugee camps were not ordinary: the Organization dealt with a population living under minimal accommodation standards and on restricted rations within war ravaged economies where facilities for health-care had been gravely impaired.

Medical care in centres conformed to the following general pattern throughout the operation.

I. The full medical services comprised:

(*a*) The medical inspection room for medical and surgical examinations.

(*b*) The sick-bay, an infirmary of varying size with male, female, and children's facilities, and an observation section for suspected contagious diseases. Minor illnesses and infectious cases were treated there. Obstetrical and surgical cases were hospitalized; the camps were too overcrowded to permit treatment in the living quarters. The sick-bays were very useful in reducing the need to send cases to already overcrowded hospitals.

(*c*) Pharmacy and medical stores containing general orthopaedic, optical, and dental supplies.

(*d*) Crèches: though these were very useful in taking temporary care of infants and children whose parents were unable to look after them, they did not exist in all camps.

(*e*) Clinics providing communal prophylactic measures for mothers, infants, and children, and dental care, &c. These clinics instructed the refugees in the adverse effects of a prolonged sub-standard environment. The principles of infant and child care were expounded, and the T.B. and V.D. units carried on propaganda against these social scourges.

(*f*) Immunization centres: for smallpox, the typhoid group of fevers, and diphtheria.

(*g*) Nursing and home visiting programme; health education.

(*h*) Ambulance services.

(*i*) Hospital care for the camp population (general, infectious diseases, T.B., mental, chronic sick).

II. Services connected with food and nutrition, including dietary kitchens for infants and for tubercular cases, communal kitchens, dining rooms, and food stores.

III. Environment sanitation including supervision of water supplies, garbage and waste disposal, supervision of accommodation standards, and of latrine and washing facilities.

Thanks to the ample preventive measures taken by the IRO, the refugee population was practically immune from the two widespread epidemics of typhoid and poliomyelitis in the British zone of Germany in 1947.

It was, however, difficult to control communicable diseases, especially those of childhood, because the refugees often concealed actual cases. They did not consider for instance that measles was a serious disease, and they opposed the vaccination and quarantine precautions. They resorted to all sorts of expedients to evade detection; a sick child would be hidden during a medical inspection or a healthy child substituted. The chief motive was fear of rejection by the selection missions. House-to-house inspections by nursing staffs was the counter-measure adopted to deal with deliberate evasion of communicable diseases control. This proved to be one of the most important single factors in achieving a successful control programme, and resulted in the saving of many infant lives. Carrying out the inspection was far from easy. Police assistance was frequently necessary to secure entry into living quarters.

Medical personnel

In its health programme, as in other aspects of the care and maintenance programme, the IRO relied greatly upon the services of the refugees and displaced persons themselves. In the first year of operation more than 2,500 refugee physicians and 2,000 refugee nurses collaborated with a small staff of IRO medical personnel.[1]

Notwithstanding the generally good work of refugee doctors and nurses, their need of education in the environmental hygiene and medical administrative practices was often apparent. Lack of many important medical supplies was frequently found to have been due to inaccurate indenting. Public health courses were instituted for local and refugee nurses scheduled for supervisory positions. These courses later assumed a vital aspect in helping to fill the gap created by the exodus of large numbers of refugee nurses on resettlement.[2] Physicians also were briefed in the principles of reporting and indenting, and in the far-reaching effects on populations of sub-standard environment. In spite of this it eventually became necessary in the interests of efficiency to reintroduce international staff anew at certain levels of

[1] GC/7, Report to the General Council by the Executive Secretary of PCIRO, 1 July 1947–30 June 1948, p. 11.
[2] See Chapter XVI, Adaption to a New Life, p. 285.

operation: for instance, in the British zone of Germany international staff replaced local staff in resettlement centres, partly because of the high rate of resettlement among refugee doctors and partly because of the importance of the British zone as a staging area for refugees coming from other zones.

Supplementing the IRO's international and indigenous staffs in the field of international action were medical and nursing staffs working on behalf of certain international voluntary societies primarily concerned with their own special groups. Their provision of international medical and nursing staffs in certain institutions, sanatoria, and rehabilitation centres proved invaluable. The voluntary societies, in addition to providing staff, assisted with foodstuffs and medical supplies.

The largest of these supplementary health services was that organized by the AJDC and JAFP.[1] The former's staff included public health and tuberculosis specialists, dentists, nurses, medical and psychiatric social workers, and sanitary engineers as well as a consultant psychiatrist and a chest surgeon. At the peak of its operations in 1948 the AJDC employed fifty-three foreign service medical workers, mainly in Germany, Austria, and Italy. In 1947 and 1948 more than 1,000 medical personnel served approximately 300 institutions, nearly all under the supervision of the IRO; about 700 in Germany, 100 in Austria, 70 in Italy, and over 80 in Shanghai. This total included more than 350 physicians and more than 550 nurses. As a rule the AJDC compensated any refugee doctor with one year's service, giving him a $500 scholarship for medical studies in his country of final settlement. By the end of 1951 ninety-five persons had been helped in their final establishment through this scheme.

Hospital facilities

In planning the institutional care of the sick, the policy of the IRO differed somewhat from that of UNRRA, whose primary concern had been the basic care of the refugees. The IRO's principal aim was to group the sick and establish installations with a view to possible opportunities for resettlement. Cases of chronic illness naturally had restricted opportunities. Whether these were finally repatriated, resettled, or integrated within the local economy, the first need was to classify them into categories and to place them in the minimum number of institutions.

The IRO put them in its own hospitals as far as possible, then into hospitals run by the occupation authorities or in local hospitals where beds were reserved for them, and as a last resort in ordinary civilian hospitals. By October 1947 the Organization had thirty-seven hospitals with 6,933 beds for general cases, and ten sanatoria with 2,921 beds for tuberculosis in the US zone of Germany. This was far above the accepted standard of 4·6 general beds per 1,000 of the population. Small and uneconomic installations were turned over to the local authorities, which simplified the administrative problems and helped to maintain larger and better facilities for long-term cases.

It might be asked why the Organization found it necessary to maintain a refugee hospital structure superimposed on existing facilities located in the various local

---

[1] The services of the JAFP established in Germany in 1946 were principally to screen the health of candidates for immigration to Israel.

economies. The inadequacy of local civilian institutional arrangements for medical care, even for local populations, and the overcrowded conditions and poor technique in many, were compelling factors initially for preserving separate institutional facilities for refugees. With the passage of time the objections to the use of local institutions diminished, but even at the end of operations they were still apparent in modified form. By having its own medical institutions the IRO was able to orientate medical policy in accordance with the special requirements of the programme. Resettlement activities required the hospitals to investigate the significance in many cases of findings observed during clinical examinations in centres. These investigations, in the large numbers required, would have placed an impossible burden on civilian hospitals, with resulting delays. Again, adequate isolation facilities were most important in checking epidemics of communicable diseases. As a general rule, local hospitals refused to accept uncomplicated cases of measles or whooping cough. Lastly, the substandard environment in refugee camps made it necessary to send chronic sick and disabled cases to hospitals, who in a more normal community would have been looked after at home. By placing these patients in selected institutions the IRO was able to look after them in conjunction with the local authorities who became responsible for them after the closing of the IRO operations. They were part of the so-called residual cases.

Two major obstacles confronted the IRO in carrying out this concentration policy: opposition by refugees themselves and the decentralized system of German institutional care. Under this system, each *Land* was required to assume financial responsibility for the upkeep of persons, including refugees, located within its administrative boundaries. Centralization would thus mean that the entire financial burden would fall on the area selected for concentration. Sometimes this ruling was relaxed, mostly when the incentives were sufficiently compelling. But in general the regulations were rigidly upheld.

In admission procedures for homes for the aged and children's institutions the health services supported the wider welfare programme. Further tasks included supervision of their nutritional and sanitary aspects, provision of medical care where required, and the exercise of preventive medicine in children's installations.

Medical supplies

Obviously the fulfilment of the health programme depended to a great extent on the availability of supplies. Medical supplies were procured through three channels: army or occupation authorities, indigenous sources, and the IRO itself. The relative importance of these pipe-lines varied with the locality. Large quantities of UNRRA supplies had been made available to the IRO and proved of the greatest assistance during the early months of operation. With their gradual depletion and the IRO's increasing needs, more and more supplies had to be purchased. In the early part of 1948 the position in the field was most difficult, particularly in regard to equipment and supplies needed for the resettlement scheme.

Former army or occupation stocks, although sufficient for normal medical needs, were often composed of materials of somewhat antiquated origin which were no longer used in modern therapeutic treatment. At that time German production was negligible, though it increased considerably later. Thus at this stage the IRO's problem was to procure antibiotics and radiological and laboratory equipment for the resettlement centres. The orders were channelled through various services, which complicated matters as did the necessity to make certain purchases in soft currency. However, these initial difficulties were overcome. With the advent in 1949 of the special programmes of rehabilitation and occupational therapy, the cycle of inadequacy with ensuing frustration was repeated.

Sanitation and accommodation standards

The lodging provided for refugees varied considerably, and strict supervision was essential in order to ensure the minimum standards of environmental hygiene. From this point of view the living conditions of refugees in some places, and the manner in which many movements of population were effected, were substandard.

The allocation of living space for refugees was dependent almost entirely in Germany and Austria upon the policies of the occupation authorities. Standards of accommodation in such war-torn economies were understandably minima. In the emergency period following the war, a standard of 30–36 sq. ft. of floor space for each person was ordained by the military authorities, representing an absolute minimum. In 1947 and subsequently efforts were made to raise the standard to at least 50 sq. ft. per person. Eventually a scale of 46 sq. ft. of billet space exclusive of hallways, entrance, storage, or other non-living space was approved by the occupation authorities as the best they could do in view of the parallel German shortage of accommodation.

Redistribution of people was frequently effected in extremely adverse circumstances; the capacity of installations was assessed on an arbitrary basis in many cases. The results of such ill-advised action were to be seen in raised morbidity rates for respiratory infections, especially measles, augmented hospitalization costs, and an appreciable incidence of parasitic diseases.

Other difficulties arose from the refugees' attitude. In general they appreciated the efforts made on their behalf, but some of the more ignorant or prejudiced were unwilling to participate in the health programmes. Ordinances about immunization or sanitation were especially unpopular, and very often had unexpected results. It was forbidden to keep livestock in the camps, but on one occasion some refugees had managed to keep some pigs in one of the modern billeting quarters. A search was made without success, and it was learnt afterwards that the pigs had been shut in a lift which had been kept in motion between floors in order to evade the search team.

The dangers of overcrowding were mitigated by a generous application of DDT and by other precautions, but unfortunately such essentials as soap, cleansing materials, and disinfectants were frequently in short supply. The bad living conditions caused infant mortality to be higher than it probably would otherwise have been. For example, in 1948 the infant mortality rate in the British zone of Germany was 72 per 1,000, whereas that for the US zone was 52; equivalent ill-chance reversed the positions in 1950, when the rate for the British zone had fallen to 67·9 and that for the US zone had risen to 69·6.

Tuberculosis

Pulmonary tuberculosis constituted the greatest challenge numerically that confronted the health services and it was the most difficult disease to combat. Because of the public health objection to admitting new potential sources of infection, immigration criteria in all countries were extremely strict about tuberculosis. Allied to this was the almost universal shortage of adequate institutional facilities for treatment. The economic burden likely to be placed on social services by the admission of tuberculosis cases was another factor making the placement of patients extremely difficult.

Different concepts of what constituted clinical tuberculosis added to the complexity of the task. Radiological criteria for the diagnosis of active disease differed according to the school of thought in which the physician had been educated. Selection missions were more concerned with the prognosis of the case than with the existing clinical state. Their medical officers were admittedly frequently faced with the onerous task of endeavouring to estimate the possible effects of transporting a currently arrested case to a new way of life in an untried climate.

These considerations lent a peculiar urgency to the efforts to control tuberculosis. Compulsory notification was enforced and registers were kept in all areas of cases detected by modern methods, including miniature radiography and tuberculin testing. Notification criteria were standardized and applied by a few selected refugee officers with special experience in tuberculosis, operating under the direction of a zone consultant. Precautionary measures were carried out in an extensive network of diagnostic and therapeutic clinics.

The dispensary was the essential nerve-cell in the system of control, referring patients to hospital or following up sanatorium cases discharged as tentatively arrested. All established cases were duly registered, and a registry card completed showing essential personal data, medical history, results of investigations, treatment recommended, and subsequent progress noted. It is important to note that only TB dispensaries and hospitals possessed the power to register a diagnosis of tuberculosis. The number of dispensaries were kept to a minimum. By such means standard notification and classification should have been possible; in practice, however, it was not fully achieved. Refugee staffs were by no means always of the required calibre, and as the programme progressed personnel changes were too frequent. Nor was it easy to maintain accurate statistics in a fluctuating population.

Dispensaries were operated under the control of the zonal TB consultants mentioned above, through the medium of a number of regional control officers. As numbers declined, such units were merged in the local system of tuberculosis control. The dispensaries played an important part later in promoting the resettlement prospects of many of their patients. Under the United States Displaced Persons Act, persons with a previous diagnosis of pulmonary tuberculosis were eligible for immigration, provided documentary evidence could be presented that the condition had been arrested for one year. The records of serial checks and investigations available in the archives of the dispensaries were of the greatest possible assistance in establishing the existence of the above criterion in a given case. This is an interesting example of a public health measure helping to solve the refugee problem.

Diagnosis was carried out by means of tuberculin tests for children, fluoroscopy and radiography, estimation of blood sedimentation rates, full clinical examination, weight records, and bacteriological examination of sputa or laryngeal swabs.

Mass radiography was an essential adjunct in case finding. The use of 35 mm. X-ray sets for this purpose, however, required a high degree of professional and technical skill, with carefully established follow-up procedures. The margin of error in the miniature film is considerably lessened by the use of a subsequent large film, taken in all cases where appearances in a small film are ambiguous. This was done in all the IRO's surveys. The significance of potentially abnormal lung shadows and calcifications was further evaluated by tuberculin tests and by bacteriological examination of sputa or gastric washings, positive findings being necessary in both investigations before a suspect became a positive case of tuberculosis. Abnormal findings demonstrably non-tuberculous in origin were referred to the out-patient department of general hospitals for further diagnosis.

BCG vaccination was made available to all refugees, particularly children (6 months–20 years) and workers in exposed occupations, such as doctors and nurses who were tuberculin negative and showed no evidence of infection on X-ray. Owing to an unfortunate error which had taken place in a Lübeck laboratory in 1930, many refugee and German doctors were violently opposed to the use of BCG.

The system of tuberculin tests which needed repeated checking was very unpopular. In any case with such a mobile population it was very difficult to see that the isolation periods before and after the vaccination were observed.

In spite of these drawbacks, vaccination helped to decrease the danger of infection among a community living in overcrowded and unfavourable conditions. Statistics showed that there were more positive reactors to the tuberculin test among the camp population than among the refugees living outside. The Danish and Swedish Red Cross were largely instrumental in carrying out the tuberculin tests and vaccination programmes.

Isolation measures in the case of pulmonary TB helped to control the disease, but the implementation of disciplinary measures in the sanatoria sometimes caused difficulties and aroused protestations. For instance, certain refugees were very incensed at not being allowed to keep their personal belongings in their rooms. In several cases attacks were launched against the IRO personnel when the IRO wished to group the patients, and all change was opposed. Complaints were addressed to the President of the US, the Vatican, the Red Cross, &c., by refugees who did not wish to be moved from their residences.

Compulsory boiling of milk probably helped to keep down the rate of non-pulmonary TB as well as other milk-borne infections.

Modern therapeutic treatment by means of antibiotics, including streptomycin and para-aminosalicylic acid, alone or in combination, were made available. Usually these remedies were only applied in acute cases. This treatment resulted in numerous cases being accepted by the selection missions.

Certain patients accused the IRO of failing to give them proper antibiotic treatment.

In 1948 the IRO produced streptomycin for the operational zones, but this was a very costly product and had to be strictly controlled. Expert advice was needed before the drug was used, therefore its use was restricted to a small number of establishments where there were adequate facilities. Permission had to be obtained from a committee or from specialists before the drug could be given. At first streptomycin treatment was reserved for cases of TB meningitis and miliary TB. Later it was used in bronchopneumonic forms and TB of the bones and joints before and after operations, and complications such as laryngitis and enteritis.

The following shows the quantities of streptomycin issued in the different operational zones in December 1948:

		gm.
US zone, Germany	. . . . .	37,500
British zone, Germany	. . . .	25,000
French zone, Germany	. . .	7,500
Austria	. . . .	7,500
Italy	. . . .	7,500

In addition to streptomycin, other anti-tuberculous drugs, such as PAS and the German compounds TB 693 and 698 were available. Ample supplies of streptomycin were thus freely available for all types of cases likely to benefit from its use. The refugee community, however, in common with many members of the public in other lands, regarded streptomycin as a panacea for all types of tuberculosis. In particular, the fallacy was widespread that a series of injections with this drug served to prevent pathological signs appearing on an X-ray plate, thus enabling the refugee to present an unblemished radiological picture.

Many refugees harboured the misconception that the Organization either would not or could not supply the antibiotic which would have cured them, and tried to obtain the drugs by various other means. Very often they were in possession of a considerable quantity which was used indiscriminately, sometimes with dire results.

Occupational therapy was part of the treatment applied in the sanatoria. Apart from benefiting morale and discipline, occupational therapy tested the stability of the TB process under controlled working conditions. In addition it assisted the choice of cases for rehabilitation by indicating in the sanatoria those most likely to benefit by the more advanced courses in rehabilitation centres on the basis of aptitudes shown and stability of the disease process.

For cases achieving the quiescent stage and manifesting promising trade aptitudes, rehabilitation units were established where the patient could perfect his skill under controlled medical surroundings. It was hoped that patients leaving such centres would later have an opportunity of resettlement or at least of successful placement in their trades in the local economy.

The tuberculosis statistics, more than any others, should be treated with reserve as it was difficult to carry out accurately the instructions concerning notification of this disease. In the beginning the extra rations issued to tubercular cases incited declarations. Sometimes the numerous moves entailed the same person appearing on several registers. Many children especially were registered as tertiary, while in reality the infection was only primary, generally fleeting, or already healed but showing under radiological examination. It was not always easy to register cures, transfers, and departures. Altogether, the mortality rate is probably the most accurate criterion of the extent of this disease.

The results of a survey made in the British zone of Germany before notification methods were standardized confirms these observations.[1] On 31 March 1948 the reports showed 7,094 cases of tuberculosis: 2,319 in hospital and 4,775 others in the camps. In a population averaging 200,000 persons this is an incredibly high figure, representing 3·5 per cent. or 35 times the mortality rate for the period 1 July 1947 to 31 March 1948 (0·1 per cent.).

It is interesting to note the TB mortality rate among the different nationalities. In a study of Mantoux reactions among Latvians, Poles, and Estonians, the Latvians showed the lowest positive Mantoux rate, especially the children and adolescents. This can perhaps be put down to the fact that they had previously enjoyed a relatively high standard of living and suddenly found themselves living under conditions much changed for the worse. Thanks to the measures taken by UNRRA most of the cases had been detected and treated. The new TB percentage compared favourably with that of the civilian population (in 1948, 1·1 per 1,000 instead of 2·3 among the German population in the American zone). This improvement was largely due to the large number of beds available to the refugees in the sanatoria. Normally the number of beds is in relation to the prevailing death rate. In 1947 in the British zone of Germany the proportion of TB beds in relation to the mortality rate was 2·2 to 1 for the local population and 10 to 1 for the refugees. It is probably fair to say that no population had a more effective tuberculosis control programme than the displaced persons.

Venereal diseases

The control of venereal diseases presented a serious problem in a mixed population of different social levels living in crowded conditions. Notification and compulsory registration were of doubtful value in an operation where local population and administrative personnel were in a continuous state of flux. Further, as in most communities, those who had contracted a venereal disease endeavoured to hide the fact and often consulted outside physicians. As the tempo of resettlement mounted, the severity of the selection missions with regard to these diseases made the refugee more than ever anxious to conceal his illness from camp medical staffs. One of the missions went so far as to exclude any refugee who had suffered from this disease.

Every effort was made to secure cross-notifications from local civilian practitioners patronized by infected refugees, but without much success. The IRO itself punctiliously observed notification requirements of local authorities, and its assistance was frequently sought in the application of control measures.

For those reasons, statistics of these diseases must be interpreted with reserve. The rate was probably higher than given in official figures. In order to appreciate efficacy it must be noted that many out-of-camp refugees only presented themselves for medical examination during the last stage of operations and had had no preventive treatment. Only refugees receiving care and maintenance were fully under IRO's

[1] PREP/179, Special Report of the Executive Secretary on Health Programme, 27 Jan. 1948, p. 18.

medical jurisdiction. According to extensive field experience in different theatres of operation, the venereal diseases were not as high as the social conditions under which the refugee lived would lead one to expect. Venereal disease rates among local civilians in broadly similar circumstances were, in many instances, higher, especially in Germany. Sex distribution of venereal diseases in refugee camps suggested that a large proportion of the infection was exogenous, derived from the local population. Among the factors responsible for the relatively low rate of venereal diseases was the strict health control. Even if the refugee managed to conceal his condition from camp authorities, he was subsequently bound to be found out later in the resettlement centres. Serological surveys carried out in certain areas and the examination of pregnant women was a form of control only a few were able to circumvent. Further, the introduction of modern antibiotic therapy in 1949 helped considerably to control the spread of infection. Penicillin treatment was employed in schedules approved by the WHO. The drug was freely available to refugees, while restricted in the early days in the case of civilians.

The rapidity with which the antibiotic treatment rendered the case non-infectious, and the convenience of this form of therapy from the patient's standpoint, undoubtedly ensured a high completion rate in treatment which was especially advantageous in the control of disease in a population subject to considerable movement. The IRO was also able to procure procaine penicillin in oil with 2 per cent. aluminium monostereate as soon as this product became available. Treatment was only permissible in hospitals and sick-bays recognized as suitable for the purpose. Details of treatments were entered on a special treatment card, of which the patient received a copy in order to ensure continuation of treatment and standardized therapy.

After a standard course of therapy the patient was kept under surveillance for a period of nine months. This was less than the prescribed year, but the exigencies of the resettlement programme demanded that the treated case be available for representation to selection missions as soon as possible after therapy. Negative blood tests taken at three-monthly intervals, together with a negative spinal fluid examination at the end of the ninth month, were considered sufficient proof of cure for syphilis. Gonorrhoea patients were under surveillance for a period of three months, during which control examinations were performed at monthly intervals with a final blood test at three months. Negative results for all tests were regarded as evidence of cure.

Health propaganda and nationality background played a part in the epidemiological picture. The incidence of disease in Yugoslav and Polish nationals was substantially higher than in Baltic communities. This was well exemplified in a series of Baltic, Yugoslav, and Polish centres near Osnabrück in the British zone of Germany. Camps with high employment rates had in general a low incidence of venereal disease. Probably, however, the realization of the importance of a clean bill of health for resettlement purposes was the most compelling 'propaganda' factor in the maintenance of low venereal disease rates. Lectures, films, and the distribution of literature depicting the mode of contraction of infection, and its dire results if untreated, held a prominent place in the drive against venereal disease. The compulsory examination and treatment of cases and contacts enforced by law in many areas of operation was undoubtedly of assistance in the fight against disease, but its role in the refugee programme is difficult to evaluate.

Mental illness

Of the medical categories under the IRO's care, the mental cases needed the most careful and conscientious consideration. The fact that they were of many different nationalities speaking diverse languages made the treatment all the more complicated. The patients felt very isolated in spite of what was done for them. Repatriation where possible provided the only solution for these unfortunates.

Standards of care in German institutions, though varying considerably, were not up to American or British standards. Overcrowding was common, and segregation of patients according to the severity of their case was not effectively carried out. Facilities for treatment were average, including insulin and electro-convulsive therapy, but selection of patients for shock treatment was sometimes faulty and surgery was seldom practised. In most hospitals some form of 'work-therapy' could be found, but the results were negligible, activities seemingly designed to assist the institution rather than the patients.

The IRO introduced a programme of occupational therapy into the mental institutions in Germany and Italy which was very successful. In one institution especially, a group previously noisy and troublesome, requiring continuous sedation, became amazingly tractable and docile after a period of occupational therapy. The hospital management, previously antagonistic to the project, became enthusiastic converts to this new method.

The general lack of suitable institutions and modern facilities gravely prejudiced plans for the care of mental patients. Even though many mental cases were repatriated to Poland in the early days of the IRO's operation, it was apparent that the majority would have to be looked after in local institutions. In the British zone of Austria alone, more than 100 mental cases were left in local mental homes at the termination of the IRO.

In order to safeguard the rights of the insane, it was essential to group them in institutions where the standards of care could be easily supervised. Regrettably this proved impossible in the desired degree, largely because of the decentralized system of local care previously referred to.

Medical aspects of repatriation and resettlement

The medical programme was basic to the final settlement of the refugees and displaced persons. The health services played an important part in repatriation as in other phases of movement. Their job was to prevent possible transmission of infectious diseases to other countries by large-scale movements, and to ensure that the health of prospective travellers was adequate to sustain the journey. Pre-movement physical examinations and immunization checks were part of a well-tried routine that during a number of years had enabled such movements to be carried out with little or no health hazard.

In the movement of chronic sick the health services made a great contribution to the programme. For the majority of such cases, repatriation represented the most concrete solution, but possibilities were limited beyond the control of the IRO. At that time the journey across Europe for chronic sick was very complicated and necessitated careful organizing. At first the IRO had to come to an agreement with the governments concerned as to which categories would qualify for repatriation. The choice and numbers largely depended on the availability of institutional places in the countries of reception. Poland, for instance, which lacked hospital accommodation and medical personnel, could initially receive only a limited number of the chronic sick. Cases of advanced tuberculosis were acceptable only if their relatives in Poland undertook to look after them at home.

Tubercular and mental cases, the less serious medical cases, women over seven months pregnant, unaccompanied children, aged and infirm persons, and young children under 1 year were eligible for travelling by ambulance train. The ambulance trains were staffed, equipped, and operated by the Polish Red Cross on behalf of the Government. The IRO gave help if needed. The health services were responsible for selecting the cases, seeing to their medical documentation, and supervising the preparations for the departure of trains. During the first six months of operations 2,151 sick refugees and their relatives were repatriated from all zones by ambulance trains or coaches. In addition to these serious cases, refugees with minor illnesses travelled with their relatives on all repatriation trains.

In February 1948 a remarkable achievement was the transfer of 219 Polish mental cases from the British zone of Germany to Poland. Investigation of the patients scheduled for travel was accomplished in conjunction with a Polish-speaking officer of the repatriation section. In many instances it was difficult to determine the individual nationality as documentary evidence was insufficient. Sometimes a clue appeared during a flood of incoherency thanks to a chance allusion to people, places, or events in Poland. The eagerness with which patients responded to spoken Polish seemed indicative of how rigorous their isolation had been in the past, at the same time providing a hopeful augury for their future.

Under the IRO mandate, the refugees could not be repatriated unless they consented. Mental patients thus presented an unusual problem. From a legal point of view they were incapable of taking a decision and the question of legal guardianship was involved. Repatriation could be effected, when the country of nationality was prepared to accept the patients and guarantee to look after them adequately, on condition that there was no opposition on the part of the legal guardian. If information was insufficient a search was made for close relatives over 21 years of age. Where such relatives existed, the decision as to repatriation of the patient, or otherwise, was regarded as their prerogative.[1] The mental status of each patient was carefully reassessed by two outside physicians working in conjunction with an international medical officer.

All medical documents relevant to the patients, indicating information concerning the history, diagnosis, treatment, and prognosis were meticulously completed and subsequently transferred to the Polish authorities. Meanwhile, negotiations between the Polish Government and the IRO to establish the procedure for transfer

[1] For the not dissimilar problem of unaccompanied children see Chapter XXIV, p. 497.

were taking place. Shortage of hospital beds and facilities was the major obstacle. The total hospital bed accommodation in Poland in 1947 was 4·2 per 1,000 of population; mental hospital beds totalled only 11,771 as of 31 December 1947; this was 5,009 fewer than ten years before.

As the total number of cases proposed for transfer was 240 patients, the only way was for the Polish authorities to evacuate some 200 German mental cases hospitalized in Poland at that time. In Germany, too, hospital space was very inadequate. No holding space could be provided for the incoming German patients should circumstances require the simultaneous accommodation in the British zone of both incoming and outgoing groups. Therefore the complicated procedure of a coach-by-coach exchange of patients had to be adopted, the coach from which German patients had been removed being disinfected before the entrainment of the refugee group. A further difficulty was to provide the escort staff at the British end for the return journey, since the refugee medical personnel were reluctant to undertake a journey through the Soviet zone. Therefore the staff caring for the German patients in Poland accompanied them to Germany where the exchange with the incoming group of Polish patients took place. In this way some 238 German patients were exchanged for 219 mental cases on 19 February 1948. It was noted that the Germans were in better physical condition and better clothed than the Polish refugees. The Soviet medical authorities concurred in the Organization's recommendation that a prolonged inspection in the Soviet zone would not be in the interests of the patients, and allowed the ambulance train to be cleared on the basis of authenticated nominal rolls with a minimum of inspection.

The vast resettlement programme which was developed in 1947 required substantial re-orientation of medical services.[1] The resettlement medical examination was carried out in three phases. The first took place in the assembly centre, the second and third in the resettlement processing centre. The second was performed by the Medical Board which was established in each resettlement processing centre and consisted of an IRO medical officer as the president and two or more refugee medical officers as the members of the Board. After the President and a member of the Board had signed Part IV of the IRO Resettlement Medical Examination form,[2] the Selection Mission Officer took over. His decision was final. He had the right of access to each stage of the physical and special examination at the resettlement processing centre. Centralization of processing arrangements in special resettlement processing centres was particularly essential for the large number of persons to be dealt with. This method enabled costs to be kept low, and experienced staff were able to deal with large numbers of people in the shortest time. The average resettlement medical unit handled about 200 persons daily, including radiology and serology. Uniform documentation was possible and pre-movement examination of documented persons proceeding from resettlement centres to staging or embarkation points could be undertaken so as to avoid any damaging incidence of quarantinable disease in the latter centres. Further, adequate control of immunization schedules, so vital in mass

---

[1] See Annex 23, Medical Services in Resettlement Centres, p. 260.

[2] See Annex 24, Part IV, p. 263: the so-called FFI examination. First it meant free from infection, later changed to Medical Examination for Fitness to Travel. (See IRO/HCM/MED/99: Medical Conference at Headquarters, Nov. 1949, p. 4.)

movement, took place at a single checkpoint before the decisive stage of embarkation was actually reached.

The security aspect of documentation also necessitated the central control of all aspects of processing. Very often refugees turned down for TB practised all sorts of tricks to conceal their condition. Substitution of X-ray films and even of persons was difficult to detect, to say nothing of forged signatures and stamps, false papers, and attempts at bribery. The only method at circumventing these manœuvres was to confine acceptance of resettlement medical reports to those coming from the special centres where all aspects of examinations were performed under strictly controlled conditions. The concentration of the welfare services, the preparation of documents, and the orientation and selection in the same centre enabled the refugee to pass through conveniently. Living accommodation was the weak point of the resettlement centres. Sometimes they had to house the refugees for a considerable period, and their conditions compared unfavourably with those in the camps. This, with the inevitable aggregation of susceptible groups, produced conditions highly conducive to the occurrence of local epidemics, especially of childhood diseases.

In accordance with specific requirements of each receiving country, the refugee was provided with the documents necessary for presentation to the selection mission. In most cases the basic documents were uniform: 'IRO Resettlement Registration Form' containing all relevant data on the refugee, and a preliminary medical report established by the resident doctor. In the early stages, requirements for medical documentation varied considerably between different missions, but PCIRO, in co-operation with the mission doctors, soon established a uniform 'IRO Medical Examination Form' which was accepted by all receiving countries.[1]

In theory the medical examination form appeared well adapted to the needs of the operation. In practice it proved to be vulnerable at many points. The medical history section was signed only by the candidate. Many camp physicians interpreted this as exonerating them from any responsibility for the accuracy of statements made. In point of fact the only advantage in history-taking at assembly-centre level lay in the fact that statements of individuals could be checked against camp records and their authenticity certified by the examining physician. In the case of childhood diseases, an accurate history supported by camp registers would in certain cases (particularly measles) have saved the Organization considerable financial sums in respect of immunization procedures and immensely eased operational procedures. The assembly centre medical examination never fully accomplished its purpose of screening out obvious cases of physical unfitness and so of obviating superfluous examinations and unnecessary journeys to resettlement centres.

The explanation of much of this laxity in pre-selection at assembly centres lay in the desire of refugee physicians to assist their fellows where possible, and also in the vulnerability of camp medical staffs to the influence of refugee groups when decisions to effect rejections at camp level were to be taken. The report of the examination by the IRO's Medical Board in the resettlement centre was therefore the important part of the form. This examination was designed to determine the fitness of candidates to appear before the selection missions.

[1] IRO *Migration from Europe* (GC/199/Rev. 1), p. 48, and Annex 24, pp. 261 f.

For reasons of economy and speed, miniature radiography was introduced, checked by large films in cases of doubt. These operations necessitated specialized personnel who understood the operating and interpretating of 35 mm. radiographs. But persons of the required technical standing were difficult to acquire. Thirty-five millimetre radiography was therefore carried out under considerable disadvantages. Elementary errors in developing and storage of films were common. Faulty positioning and erroneous exposure techniques were equally frequent, not unassociated, however, with the excessive speed of operation often required to meet the exigencies of the programme. The poor quality of films supplied in some instances served to accentuate errors in processing. The appointment of a consultant radiographer was a major factor in raising effectively the standard of dark-room techniques. Endeavours were also made to reduce the complexities of film processing by the mandatory use of one reputable make of film only, in all centres. This was, however, impaired to a considerable extent by the stock-piling of X-ray films in many countries consequent on the outbreak of war in Korea, resulting in shortages of most reputable makes of film.

The greatest possible precautions were taken to prevent bribery or impersonation. Attempts were usually made in relation to radiography and serology. When reaction was doubtful another check was made, so that even if a refugee managed to clear the selection mission he was often detected when further checks were made.

When an individual was rejected, all medical information was sent to his camp doctor by the resettlement centre. The person concerned was helped and advised by welfare workers who helped to safeguard his rights and interests. Even if an individual was rejected by one selection mission he might be accepted by another. There were also the 'deferred', in other words those persons about whom the selection missions had not made a final decision and who would undergo a further check. It was in the interest of the refugee that this waiting period should be spent under the best conditions possible in order to further his chances of acceptance—this was especially the case with pulmonary diseases which were the most frequent reasons for deferment.

In 1948 resettlement possibilities, so far restricted to single workers, were extended to include married workers and their dependants. This meant the concentration of a large number of children in the resettlement centres, further complicating the work. Efforts to control infectious diseases such as immunization and quarantine proved exceptionally unpopular.

Medical care in transit

Once the departure formalities were finished and the candidates accepted, the medical services took all necessary precautions to safeguard the health of the refugees waiting to leave in staging and embarkation centres and during transit. A health ordinance was drafted establishing standards of care, nutrition, accommodation, and medical supervision of transit groups, and dispatched to field staffs for guidance.[1]

Observance of international sanitary conventions was mandatory. Medical escorts were established on scales varying with the number and type of refugees proposed

[1] Provisional Order Nos. 27 and 27.1. Health Standards on Refugee Movements, 12 Nov. 1947 and 7 Oct. 1949.

for transit. Accommodation standards for the refugees on their journey by rail and boat were applied, and adequate feeding facilities were ensured. Arrangements were made for the care of accidents or illness, quarantine, and the hospitalization of infectious cases. It was not always easy to observe these standards. Sometimes there were cancellations or refugees were called suddenly for departure or to occupy places which had become vacant on the trains or boats. Much of this could not be foreseen in advance.

The medical services did not always have sufficient personnel or adequate means of preparing the necessary documents in the short time allowed by the sudden and increasing development of resettlement operations. Sometimes the lack of adequate warning before a departure meant the speeding up of emergency transport. Each transit refugee had to be in possession of a medical certificate and an international inoculation certificate recording immunization against smallpox, measles (depending on local regulations), diphtheria, and typhus. Pregnant women were given a prenatal certificate. Leaflets were issued about the feeding of small babies during the journey. All the transit centres had special kitchens for child feeding.

Special attention was paid to feeding arrangements on the long overland train journeys to embarkation centres. The seventy-two hours' trip from the British zone of Germany to Naples was particularly hazardous for the health of the young, unless special measures were taken to ensure proper food. Arrangements varied from food parcels and army packed units in the beginning to the adaptation of baggage coaches for use as kitchen cars to be attached to refugee trains. A proposal for the establishment of food halts in the US zone of Germany proved abortive; but a very successful halt was operated for a period at Trento, in Italy. Endeavours to secure the services of commercial caterers on trains to Bremen were unsuccessful.

Children arriving in Italy parched and exhausted were markedly predisposed to infection. To ensure continuity in feeding, the issue of fresh milk was replaced by unsweetened evaporated full milk for the age 0–3 years. This was most important in preventing the dehydration likely to result from infant digestive disturbances, occasioned by qualitative changes in diet *en route*. This principle in infant feeding extended from the static assembly centres, through staging centres, and to trains and ships.

In spite of efforts to speed up the departure of pregnant women, many of them were too far advanced to travel by sea, and the Organization sent them by air: this privilege was extended to aged people. People in categories not entitled to air transport often tried their best to obtain passages and this had to be strictly controlled. Children up to 10 years of age were put under observation in a medical centre at least ten days before the scheduled departure. Then they underwent a thorough examination during their stay. This examination was repeated four days before departure, and only eight hours before they were due to leave the final decision was taken by means of a last check.

The control of communicable diseases among children

Preventive medical care in the assembly centres had been very successful in preventing epidemics such as typhoid, diphtheria, typhus, cholera, scarlet and yellow fevers. A serious health problem, however, which affected many phases of the operation was the communicable children's diseases, in particular, measles and whooping cough. Children comprised a large proportion of the refugee population. The birthrate of the refugees was far higher than that of a normal population, which had a lower proportion of the younger age groups.[1] At the beginning of 1949 the IRO had in its care a population of some 450,000 persons, including 80,000 to 100,000 children under 10 years of age.

Measles in an epidemic form in all areas of operation was a severe handicap to movements of refugees overseas in the spring of 1949. The main focus of infection was in the US zone of Germany, and despite quarantine measures in camps there was a high incidence. The long tiring journey from Germany and Austria to the embarkation camps in the Naples area for transportation to Australia presented many hazards which were particularly intensified in the case of children of 6 months to 3 years of age. There was a high rate of sickness, with a consequent rise in the mortality rate, among young children in the camps, on ships, and after arrival in Australia. The first epidemic wave in transit camps started in March 1949, after the arrival of 1,700 people, including some children in the incubation stage of measles and whooping cough. Seventy-three cases were reported in that month in the staging camps in Italy (Bagnoli, Capua, and others) and 81 in April, and during May, June, and July about 50 cases per month. During the latter months, epidemics were reported from ships. Between April 1949 to April 1950 there were 900 cases in transit camps and 1,400 on ships.

This situation was a matter of extreme concern to the Administration and everybody working in the resettlement pipe-line. Thorough investigations were carried out in the most comprehensive way, and finally measures were taken which virtually eliminated the incidence of measles.[2]

Initially, the blame was attributed to the bad conditions in Italy. It is a fact that the accommodation in the camps in Italy were very unsatisfactory at that time. In order to shorten the sea voyage from Germany and Austria to Austrialia, it had been decided in 1948 to convert several large buildings around Naples as transit centres. Three months was the estimated time for converting four buildings suitable for lodging 10,000 persons. Actually the installation took longer and cost more, and mass movements from Germany were under way before the buildings were completed. The IRO was obliged to house some of the emigrants in tents and others in inadequate camps. While these deplorable conditions lowered the resistance of the children further, the intensive survey revealed that the problem had developed as an accumulation of various factors detrimental to the health of the children on the strenuous and long journey from the assembly centres in Germany and Austria to the resettlement centres and staging and embarkation centres and during a long sea voyage.

In general, of course, the incidence of infectious diseases in mass movements has

[1] See Annex 25, Comparative Statistics, No. 1, p. 264.
[2] R. L. Coigny, the Director of the Health Division at Headquarters, in collaboration with P. Straus and the assistance of the entire staff of the Health Division carried out a study about the epidemics and their final prevention. (R. L. Coigny and P. Straus, 'Role de la gamma globuline dans la prévention de la rougeole résultats d'une étude epidémologique',¹ in *La Presse médicale*, 59e Année, No. 31, 9 mai 1951, pp. 634–9.)

always been a problem for which no really satisfactory methods of control existed. There was always the possibility that a person might be incubating a common infectious disease before departure. This unavoidable risk was increased by the special circumstances under which the medical control had to be carried out. The last check for detecting contagious diseases took place, as has been described, before leaving the resettlement centre on a three-days' railway journey. At this stage the displaced persons used all sorts of tricks to ensure getting on the appointed train, e.g. hiding or substituting children. In the course of the journey, young children were moved across Europe through the hot and dusty Naples area, put on ships under crowded conditions, and passed through the Red Sea—one of the hottest places in the world— at the hottest time of the year.

Thus the closest attention to detail to safeguard the health of the lower aged groups had to be observed throughout all the stages. The procedures of thorough immunization and 'fit to travel' inspections were tightened.[1] The hospitals at Bagnoli and Naples were reconstructed, and food and feeding facilities were improved.

Concurrently with these measures, steps were taken to remedy certain defects in the IRO chartered vessels. Provision was made for a paediatrician to be engaged on each of the chartered commercial vessels and for an increase in the staff of international nurses. Extensive reconstruction of two ships were undertaken, and alterations and modifications were carried out to improve accommodation and feeding arrangements on other vessels. Rigid limits on the number of children up to the age of 3 years were imposed on all ships. Family groups were no longer split up, whether in centres, on trains, or on ships. Experience had proved that the concentration of women and children without husbands created far greater danger of infection than when the family was kept together.

As a result of these comprehensive measures, the situation showed improvement, but the incidence of measles remained at a high level until in December 1949 obligatory injections of gamma globulin to the children between the ages of 6 months and 6 years, who were in the process of moving, were given. This immunization was repeated every three weeks if necessary and no embarkation was authorized unless the child's first immunization had taken place within a minimum of sixteen days before the date of departure. The results obtained by this first mass immunization with gamma globulin were highly satisfactory and the incidence of morbidity and mortality declined rapidly. Apart from the fact that the children's health was effectively protected, the high cost of this measure was justified also in that quarantine measures for measles became unnecessary, which had caused financial loss by interrupting the time schedule of ships.[2] And further, it guaranteed to Australia that it did not have to impose restrictive conditions which would limit the resettlement of family units.[3]

---

[1] IRO/HCM/MED 100, Recommendations and Decisions of the Chief Medical Officers, Chief Nurses, and Chief Nutritionists, Geneva, Nov. 1949.

[2] On 30 Mar. 1949 the departure of a vessel to Brazil had to be delayed due to the outbreak of measles, whooping cough, and chicken pox among the passengers.

[3] Australia was one of the overseas countries which had most generously responded to the IRO policy of resettlement of family units. With the arrival of many serious cases, several times, the vessels had to be diverted to Freemantle in Western Australia to take off hospital cases before embarking the rest of the passengers at Melbourne. This put a heavy strain on the hospitals at ports of disembarkation

The closing of the embarkation centres at Naples in April 1950, and the trans-ference of all major embarkations to Bremerhaven, materially lessened the strain on the health of the refugees by reducing the overland train journeys.

In February and March 1950, at the request of the IRO, a team of five specialists seconded by the WHO travelled through the British and US zones of Germany, Austria, and Italy surveying the health services, especially in connexion with move-ments of children. The report of these specialists expressed general approval of the steps taken by the Administration to safeguard the health of vulnerable groups and also provided 'most helpful technical advice'.[1]

It is hard to apportion responsibility for the difficulties which occurred in con-nexion with movements, particularly of children, and to answer the question whether they could have been avoided by greater vigilance of the persons in charge and greater foresight of the Administration at headquarters. It is possible that continual pressure of time and shortage of money, and the temporary emergency character of the work, might have led the field missions, as well as headquarters, to take risks for the sake of administrative convenience and economic stringency. On the other hand, the problem was exceedingly complex and no experience in similar mass movements of children was available which could have guided medical and administrative officers. It is worth stressing that the experience which the IRO built up in controlling com-municable diseases in mass movements, especially of children, has produced valuable results. That these results had to be achieved by trial and error was deplorable, but, for example, the outbreak of an epidemic of measles in Bremen in January 1951 proved that even the use of gamma globulin was a complex procedure, and safe control measures could only be worked out after a critical review and further experience. It is probably true that some of the hardship and suffering of the refugees could have been avoided. However, every measure was taken to remedy the short-comings of an emergency situation as quickly, as generously, and as basically as possible, and in so doing close co-operation developed between administrators and specialists as well as the representatives of the governments concerned.

Summary

In general, remarkable results were obtained by the public health programme. Serious epidemics were avoided, and the state of health of the displaced persons as a whole was maintained at a level seldom before achieved in similar circumstances. This was mainly due to the experience gained during the First World War, to the advance of medical science, and also to the availability of a fairly large medical personnel.

UNRRA had already laid the groundwork in the medical field with its mobile teams of doctors and nurses and the medical supplies and facilities at its disposal. But only a comprehensive public health programme such as the IRO developed over a period of time, and continuously adjusted and improved on the basis of experience,

or at immigration reception and training centres, and was a cause of criticism reflecting generally on the resettlement scheme. (See cable from Ministry of External Affairs, Canberra, 26 Oct. 1949.)

[1] GC/166, op. cit., p. 42.

could have secured such a good standard of health as the low death- and high birth-rates among the refugee population indicated.[1]

It is difficult, however, to assess the work done by the IRO medical services in terms of statistics. In Annex 25 will be found certain comparative statistics showing that in 1948 the birth-rate was almost double among the refugee population (31·9 per 1,000) that of Germany and Austria (16·6) and greater than that of Italy (22·0). The general mortality rate (5·9 per 1,000) was far lower than that of other European countries which varied from 10·3 to 12·1 per 1,000. Infant mortality was higher (66 per 1,000) than in the UK (34), but lower than in Germany (68) and Italy (72).

In spite of unfavourable circumstances the IRO kept a population equivalent to that of a small European state in reasonable health. Though the methods applied were not always popular with the refugees, they were justified by results. Hundreds of thousands of persons were transported overseas and their health maintained, and the Organization did everything possible to make adequate future provision for those who were unable to emigrate.[2]

ANNEX 23

Medical services in resettlement centres

Extract from Memorandum dated 7 December 1951, from Chief Medical Officer, United States zone, Germany, to Division of Field Operations, United States zone, Germany, describing the medical establishment in the resettlement centre in Munich when preparations were being made to transfer it to the German authorities.

Medical services fall into two categories:
  A. Those essentially concerned with processing and movements, and
  B. Services required to maintain day-to-day medical care.

A. *Services for Processing and Movements*:
  (i) The Medical Processing Unit, consisting of administrative section, documentation and registration section, with related security checks, medical examination rooms plus annexes, immunization, X-ray and laboratory units, counselling section, supply stores for essential equipment, and record archives.
  (ii) The complement of the IRO Medical Unit indicated above, is of course the medical unit attached to the various missions.
  (iii) Facilities for confirmatory and special investigations required to verify findings above units. (These by agreement will continue to be provided by Altersheim Hospital until March 1952.)
  (iv) Hospital facilities for observation cases (Altersheim).
  (v) Transport required to service above-mentioned unit.
  (vi) Quarters for staff assigned processing and movement units.

[1] Annex 25. After the transfer of responsibility for some of the refugee population to local authorities in the countries of residence the vital statistics as a whole were no longer available. GC/227/Rev. 1, Annual Report of the Director-General for the Period 1 July to 30 June 1951, p. 37.
[2] See Chapter XXIII, The Hard Core.

Movements unit:

This is essentially built around the following:

(i) Facilities for performance of medical examinations required in connexion with movements. This includes pre-movement examinations (fitness to travel, determination of pregnancy status) and also medical inspection of groups entering the centre.

(ii) Escort staffs required for movement.

(iii) Special billeting for vulnerable categories awaiting movement, including aged, unaccompanied children, physically handicapped cases.

Special care and maintenance functions having a vital bearing on processing and movements:

(a) Nursery for the care of temporarily unaccompanied children.

(b) Quarantine blocks, for observation of contacts of infectious diseases.

(c) Home visiting service for the detection of hidden cases of infectious diseases.

(d) Hospital facilities for minor infectious diseases. (By agreement to be provided by Heckscher Clinic.)

(e) Other aspects of infectious diseases control, i.e. immunization notification.

B. *Day to Day Medical Care*

(i) Dispensary for treatment minor cases.

(ii) Infirmary for treatment minor cases.

(iii) Clinics, including infant and children's ante and post natal, T.B., V.D., dental clinics and laboratory.

(iv) Hospital facilities for treatment, including general, T.B., mental, &c.

(v) Nursing services, including supervision of formula kitchen.

(vi) Messing and nutrition including special diets.

(vii) Environment sanitation (water and food store hygiene, latrines, ablutions, garbage disposal, &c.).

(viii) General medical supplies, including orthopaedic, optical, and dental.

(ix) Ambulance services.

(x) Reports on community health, including infectious diseases, births, deaths, other statistics.

(xi) Accommodation in accordance with existing standards.

ANNEX 24

IRO resettlement medical examination form[1]

Part I. Identification form to be completed by Assembly Centre doctor.

1. Name................................2. Camp....................3. Location...................
4. Age.............................5. Sex..................6. Colour of hair.............
7. Colour of eyes ....8. Height.............9. Weight.................
10. Scars or other means of identification...
11. DP Number....................12. Claimed nationality..........................

[1] IRO *Operational Manual*, revised, p. 118.

I certify that I have seen

Mr.

Mrs. ....and

Miss

examined his/her DP I. Card, his/her photograph
and his/her appearance, and am satisfied the
particulars given are correct and that he/she has
signed in my presence.

Date ....

_____

Photo of Candidate
to be attached
here and stamped

Stamp of
Assembly
——————Centre.

Signature of Medical Officer   Signature of Candidate

_____

Part II. To be completed by Assembly Centre doctor and signed by the Candidate.

1. Family medical history ....
   No. of children: (a) Alive ....(b) Dead ....(c) Cause of death ....
2. Have any of your family suffered from (a) Tuberculosis, (b) Mental illness,
   (c) Epilepsy? If 'yes' give details ....
3. Personal medical history: Have you suffered from any of the following illnesses?
   (a) Tuberculosis, (b) Mental illness, (c) Epilepsy, (d) Venereal disease, (e) Kidney
   disease, (f) Nervous breakdown. If 'Yes' give details: ....
4. Previous illnesses, injuries and operations of candidate, indicating whether he has
   or requires prosthesis for amputation: ....

   I certify that the above statements made by me in answer to the foregoing questions
   are true and complete to the best of my belief.

   Date ....Signature of Candidate ....

PHYSICAL EXAMINATION

Part III. To be completed by Assembly Centre doctor.

1. General build ....
2. Visual acuity (a) without glasses ......R........................ L........................
           (b) with glasses ....
3. Hearing ....R........................ L........................
4. Trachoma ....Yes........................ No........................
5. Teeth and gums ....
6. Abdomen ....
7. Hernia ....
8. Operation scars ....
9. Central Nervous System:
   (1) Mental status ....
   (2) Reflexes (note response) ....
       Pupils: (a) to light ....
           (b) on accommodation ....
           (c) Knee jerks ....
           (d) plantar ....
   (3) Remarks ....
10. Respiratory system ....
11. Cardiovascular system: ....
        (a) Pulse rate ....

(b) Rhythm and regularity...

(c) B.P...

(d) Ausculation...

12. Genito-Urinary...

13. Urine.....................Sugar....................Albumen..........................

14. Gynaecological (where necessary)..

15. Locomotor Function (Note disabilities).......................................

16. Date of last immunizations:...

    (a) Smallpox..

    (b) Typhoid and Paratyphoid...

    (c) Epidemic Typhus...

    (d) Diphtheria...

    (e) Others...

17. Further notes...

I hereby certify that I have examined.........................on........................
and that the above findings are true to the best of my belief and knowledge.
I consider he/she is fit to proceed to a Resettlement Centre for medical examination.

Date........................Signature...
                              Assembly Centre Medical Officer.

Part IV. To be completed by Medical Board in Resettlement Collecting Centre.

R	L
R	L
R	L
Yes	No

Sugar... Albumen..

The above person has been examined by me and is considered fit/unfit to appear
before a Selection Mission.

Date.. Signature...
                                 Examining Physician.

                                 Signature...
                                 President DP Medical Board.

                                 ....Resettlement Centre.

Part V. Special examinations:

    (a) X-ray of chest   Date Stamp....................................

        Heart...

        Lungs...

    (b) Blood test....................................... Date Stamp....................................

    (c) 'Others... Date Stamp....................................

Part VI. For Selection Team Medical Officer only.

I have examined...
and certify: (1) he/she is fit for emigration to..
            (2) he/she is unfit by reason of...

Date................................ Signature...

                       Mission..

MEDICAL CARE

ANNEX 25

Comparative statistics

1. Birth-rates per 1,000 population
   German Federal Republic
   1946 = 16·0   1947 = 16·6   1948 = 16·6   1949 = 16·8
   Austria
   1946 = 15·9   1947 = 18·6   1948 = 16·6   1949 = 16·3
   United Kingdom
   1946 = 19·2   1947 = 20·5   1948 = 17·8   1949 = 16·7
   Italy
   1946 = 23·0   1947 = 22·3   1948 = 22·0   1949 = 20·4
   Refugees (Germany, Austria, and Italy) 1948 = 31·9

2. Infant mortality rates (WHO epidemiological reports 1952)
   German Federal Republic
   1946 = 90   1947 = 84   1948 = 68   1949 = 58
   + Average 1936–8 = 63 all Germans

   Austria
   1946 = 81   1947 = 78   1948 = 76   1949 = 75
   + Average 1936–8 = 88

   United Kingdom
   1946 = 43   1947 = 41   1948 = 34   1949 = 22
   + Average 1936–8 = 56

   Italy
   1946 = 87   1947 = 84   1948 = 72   1949 = 74
   Average 1936–8 = 105

   Refugees (Germany, Austria, and Italy) 1947 = 59·8   1948 = 66

3. General mortality per 1,000 population
   German Federal Republic
   1946 = 12·0   1947 = 11·6   1948 = 10·3   1949 = 10·2
   Austria
   1946 = 13·4   1947 = 13·0   1948 = 12·1   1949 = 12·9
   United Kingdom
   1946 = 11·5   1947 = 12·0   1948 = 10·8   1949 = 11·7
   Italy
   1946 = 12·1   1947 = 11·5   1948 = 10·6   1949 = 10·5
   Refugees (Germany, Austria, and Italy) 1947 = 4·87   1948 = 5·9

CHAPTER XV

COUNSELLING

THE care and maintenance programme of the IRO was primarily directed toward the material relief and physical and vocational rehabilitation of refugees and displaced persons through the provision of food, clothing, shelter, medical aid, employment, and education; the process by means of which a person's need for these services was determined was known as counselling.

The services for the most part corresponded to the immediate social needs of the population for which they were destined. But problems not directly deriving from those needs were frequently presented to the Organization by persons whose difficulties were more psychological than material and arose mainly from anxiety about the future.

The Personal Counselling Service had been prescribed, immediately after the war, by the military authorities and carried out by UNRRA's welfare staff in the assembly centres.[1]

Before the demise of UNRRA, PCIRO headquarters had drawn up instructions about the registration and interviewing of refugees and displaced persons. Immediately upon beginning operations in July 1947 these instructions were issued to all field offices. Registration consisted of completing an application for assistance form, one of the main purposes of which was to record the personal history of the individual or family unit.

The interview was primarily for the purpose of determining the eligibility of the registrant individual or family group. But having done so, the interviewer was normally responsible for discussing the future plans of the persons interviewed, and explaining to them the IRO programme, its limitations, the services which were available to refugees and displaced persons, and the procedure to be followed in using such services. This explanation was deemed necessary since the persons interviewed had been subjected by previous organizations to numerous registrations, screenings, and interviews in the past, so that their relationship to the new Organization required restatement.

It was conceived that the eligibility interviewers, normally the first persons of the Organization with whom a refugee or displaced person came into contact, would be responsible for following through any information disclosed during the interview which would assist in solving the family's problem. For example, if there was an evident need for medical services, reference was made to the Health Division; if the refugee or displaced person requested a particular type of re-establishment, he was referred to the appropriate IRO official; and if there was a question of reuniting the applicant with relatives in other areas of the IRO operations, correspondence was initiated to attempt this. This follow-up of the eligibility interview was the beginning

---

[1] SHAEF, *Guide to the Care of Displaced Persons in Germany*, May 1945.

of the Organization's programme of social service counselling. It introduced the refugees to the IRO services and showed them ways in which their problems could be solved.

The early experience of combining the eligibility procedure with counsel service proved to be unsatisfactory. Trained and experienced welfare officers were needed for the latter. This led in June 1948 to the separation of the two functions.

The counselling programme was directed mainly toward those cases which required specialized assistance to prepare them for re-establishment. Although the service was available to all persons who desired to make use of it, it was primarily established for families and individuals whose immediate re-establishment appeared impossible or uncertain. In analysing cases, the officers who performed the counselling service normally met three types of personal situations: those which required social welfare or case-work service; those which required reference to other PCIRO departments or to a voluntary society for specialized service before re-establishment plans could be made; and those for which no immediate solution could be found. In order to deal with these situations it was essential that the welfare officers follow up cases referred to other departments or voluntary societies. The counselling of an individual case represented a continuous process which would only be completed when the individual or family group had been successfully re-established.

When provision had finally been made for the recruitment of the necessary staff to carry out the counselling programme, the field missions were, by the end of 1948, able to apply systematically the methods of social case-work to the refugee problem. The objective at this stage was to elucidate the general impediments to re-establishment as well as the extent of the group of persons for whose problems no solution could be found in terms of resettlement—the so-called 'hard-core'.

The difficulties were both administrative and operational. Because emphasis in the counselling procedure was directed towards obtaining a statistical analysis of the refugees for whom special measures would have to be taken, the field officers responsible for implementing the programme were over-burdened with administrative details. The solution in many cases was impeded through delay in contacting other field operational officers whilst following up cases. On the other hand, counselling officers had no official authority to recommend action in respect of re-establishment; the work of the counselling officer was to diagnose the particular difficulties of each refugee and the decision as to action was the responsibility of the re-establishment officer. The operational difficulty within the programme itself concerned the unification of social case-work techniques among the varied international field staff. In the British zone of Germany, for instance, eight different nationalities were represented on the counselling staff.

The first half of 1949 was spent in organizing and co-ordinating the counselling programme and in overcoming operational difficulties as they arose. Analysing the case-load was the first step in determining the extent of the residual group. However, before an individual or family could be definitely considered as part of the residual group, every effort had to be made to overcome personal difficulties and to explore all possibilities of re-establishment.

By this time the Organization had established sufficient vocational and rehabilitation services to enable counselling officers to make effective reference to them. Consultations with legal advisers in the zones enabled the counselling officer to recognize problems involving legal action. Resettlement criteria, however, were neither fixed nor constant, so that up-to-date information on resettlement could be given to the person interviewed only by the resettlement officer. As the Organization had no control over the government selection standards for resettlement, counselling and resettlement officers could never with certainty assure the person interviewed that he would be resettled to any given country. It was therefore impossible to estimate the number of persons who would definitely form the 'hard core', and a change in resettlement criteria could alter the figure at any time. The experience of the Austrian mission demonstrated the difficulty of arriving at a firm classification of each case.

As a means of unifying the counselling techniques the Administration arranged for counselling officers in Germany, Austria, and Italy to attend a two-weeks' training course in social service case-work given by the International Social Service in Paris between April and June 1949; in addition the field staff held frequent conferences to pool up-to-date information and to improve the technique of the counselling staff in establishing personal contact between the interviewer and the refugee, which was essential to successful counselling.

That the case-work approach was having a positive effect on the re-establishment programme of the Organization was shown by the expansion of the other social services such as language courses for illiterates, vocational training, and rehabilitation programmes. In some cases, such as those of unmarried mothers, the Organization, as a result of the counselling surveys made in the early part of 1949, was able to promote resettlement schemes with various countries, notably Australia, to receive the socially unfortunate groups.

In July 1949 the Administration, on the advice of the General Council,[1] introduced an intensified counselling programme with the object of getting each and every refugee to make some plan for his future. All refugees receiving assistance from the IRO were interviewed for the purpose of encouraging early re-establishment. Through classification of nearly all refugees still receiving IRO assistance which was completed in the summer of 1950, the dimensions of the remaining problem became known to the Organization. At the same time many refugees were helped to make up their minds about the best solution for their individual problems under existing conditions.[2]

All refugees and members of their families were classified in one of six categories: those desiring repatriation; those deemed acceptable for resettlement; those who wanted local settlement and would be acceptable for such settlement without continuing assistance; those eligible only for legal and political protection; the residual cases (not requiring institutional care or classified as hard core cases); and finally those to whom services would be denied because of refusal to accept proposals.

In order to contact all persons registered and within the mandate of the Organization, field officers were instructed to send postcards to all persons not receiving care

---

[1] General Council Res. 39, dated 7 July 1949; cf. Appendix III, p. 725.
[2] GC/166, Aug. 1950.

and maintenance. These cards, printed in the language of the country of residence, required the refugee to express his wish concerning re-establishment and to indicate what action he had personally undertaken to effect it. Persons living in assembly centres, or otherwise receiving care and maintenance, were interrogated in the camps. The justification of the new policy, which was thought to reflect the wishes of the member governments, was that the assistance the Organization could provide was limited by both time and funds, and it was therefore necessary for refugees to decide which course of action they would take within the limited alternative of repatriation, resettlement, or local settlement. Those who were unwilling to be repatriated and unable or unwilling to be resettled must realize that they would have to remain in the country of their present residence. It was recognized that the individual refugee was entitled to a certain freedom of choice among the possible alternatives. The Organization was responsible for assisting the refugee in making his choice: if he chose resettlement he must accept the opportunities for resettlement open to him. As he had applied for and accepted assistance from the Organization with full knowledge of the conditions attached, he was bound to respect these conditions. The refugee and the Organization together were to decide and put into execution a plan for his future life; or else the assistance of the Organization would be withdrawn from him and he would be left to make his own plans, thus relieving the Organization of responsibility.

The short period in which the entire assembly centre population in Germany, Austria, and Italy had to be interviewed necessitated long hours of work on the part of the welfare officers and limited the time for considering each case. The interviewing procedure for encouraging re-establishment was carried out by what was known as a counselling team, and consisted in interviewing family units and each refugee 17 years of age or over with the aim of persuading them to accept the possibilities for re-establishment which were available at the time. The team was composed of a welfare or counselling officer, a repatriation officer, and a resettlement officer: an eligibility officer was available to each team of interviewers to deal with any question of eligibility that arose.

The repatriation interviewer sought to encourage the refugee or displaced person to return home if this seemed at all feasible. If repatriation was accepted, all necessary steps for immediate repatriation were undertaken. When objections to repatriation did not appear to be valid the refugee was referred to the eligibility officer. If it was considered that valid objections to repatriation did exist, the individual was then seen by the resettlement officer.

If a refugee had any preference in resettlement which appeared to be practicable, he was immediately referred to the appropriate selection mission. If in the opinion of the resettlement officer the choice was impracticable within current opportunities at the time of the interview, the officer himself proposed one or more other resettlement opportunities for which he believed the person to be qualified. On accepting an alternative proposal the individual was immediately referred to the selection mission.

A refugee or displaced person was deferred from having to register for immediate resettlement scheme only if, in the opinion of the resettlement officer, he had a good prospect of resettlement in the reasonable future through nomination or individual emigration: if, for instance, a refugee was being assisted by a voluntary society which was prepared to confirm the probable receipt of an assurance for the US, he was deferred. Similar concessions were made if the individual could show that he was awaiting receipt of a visa arranged by a close relative in the country of reception.

When local settlement was desired by the refugee, representations were made to the appropriate local authority for obtaining accommodation, ration cards, and other documents necessary for civil purposes.

Persons who, because of age or infirmity or for any other reason, were unlikely to be accepted as immigrants (i.e. the 'residual group' or the 'hard core') became the responsibility of the Welfare Division or a voluntary society for such services as were required.[1]

There were instances where, with no apparent physical handicaps or social difficulties, the person interviewed was reluctant to make an immediate choice between repatriation, resettlement, or local settlement, or else refused all current opportunities for resettlement. Such cases were frequently those of young men who were working in guard units and labour companies employed by the Allied military forces, or by private firms, and hoped eventually to be given long-term contracts with their employers. The counselling officer in the first instance advised the persons that such an attitude was unsound, and where it was clear that no attempt had been made toward re-establishment, the individual was given a time limit to apply for inclusion on a resettlement scheme; failure to do so was followed by withdrawal of care and maintenance services, on the proposal of the counselling officer.

Some persons remained adamant in their desire to go to one specific country for which no resettlement scheme was operating at the time, or else to emigrate to the US without being in possession of the necessary guarantee. Usually, the persons claimed to have registered with a voluntary society, in which case the society was contacted, and if it considered that there was little or no hope of the refugee obtaining a guarantee, the counselling officer urged him to try elsewhere. If the refugee did not accept the suggestion of the interviewer, he was subject to withdrawal of care and maintenance.

In many cases circumstances, such as having an aged relative or a minor physical disability, prevented a whole family from emigrating. The counselling officer was able in such cases to make proposals for the aged relative to be placed in an old persons' home or for the handicapped member to be given a course of rehabilitation, thereby enabling the whole family to become candidates for immigration. Once these difficulties were overcome, the welfare or counselling officer was in a position to refer the case to the resettlement officer for further action. Such cases were usually exempted from the requirement to register an immediate choice for re-establishment during the intensive counselling survey.

Although the majority of persons were in a position to decide, in the light of existing possiblities, what course of action they wished to take, some family groups presented a complex of factors which did not lead themselves to a rapid solution through the intensive counselling programme. The pressure of the interviews,

---

[1] Chapter XXIII, Hard Core.

created by the necessity for reaching an immediate decision on each case, sometimes produced bewilderment among the refugees.

The area in which the intensive counselling programme was perhaps most difficult to implement was Italy; this was because of the extremely large number of persons receiving out-of-camp assistance and consequently were not easily contacted. A serious shortage of staff prevented adequate co-ordination between the counselling and resettlement staff. Five reasons were given for failure to complete the programme in Italy: first, the entire family was not interviewed, but only the head of the family; second, the interview was generally conducted through the resettlement officer and emphasis was on recruitment for resettlement schemes, relegating counselling aspects to the background, so that if the person interviewed presented his problems and doubts concerning emigration he received very little advice and nothing was done to follow up the case; third, since counselling of new applicants in the centres was done by the persons in charge of the registration and eligibility interview, counselling resembled statistical counting; fourth, a large number of long-standing cases were never dealt with; fifth, the programme was too unwieldy for proper co-ordination and supervision because of the long distances involved, the unequal experience of the interviewers, and the general differences in approach of the three co-operating units—welfare, re-establishment, and eligibility—which were never completely reconciled. The underlying cause of failure was that the field staff were in most cases unable to adapt their machinery to emergency requirements.

The intensive counselling programme was restricted to those persons in Germany, Austria, and Italy who according to their records had not yet taken steps to be re-established; when the time limit imposed by the General Council in July 1949 was reached,[1] preliminary estimates of the results showed that the number of persons who would eventually be forced, because of limited resettlement opportunities, to remain in those countries would be higher than the member governments of IRO wished.[2] In the US zone of Germany, for example, the final results of the programme showed about 23,000 persons classified as institutional and non-institutional 'hard core', and it was estimated that an additional 30,000 persons, composed of those rejected after being presented to a selection mission and those who for other reasons were not included in the counselling programme, would be likely to form a residual group. This residual group was not a homogeneous one, which could be defined as having certain characteristics that made repatriation or resettlement hopeless, and the Organization was morally obliged to make every attempt to re-establish all persons eligible for its services. Once the relatively firm group desiring re-establishment had been determined, the Organization proceeded to classify all refugees in all areas of operation under the above stated categories.[3]

The main purposes of this continuous process of classification were to ensure that this residual group would finally be limited as far as possible to the persons requiring further institutional care after the demise of the IRO; to ensure that each case would systematically receive all necessary attention from every operating

[1] General Council Res. No. 39, dated 7 July 1949. Cf. Appendix III, p. 725.
[2] Summary Records of Meetings of the General Council, Doc. GC/SR/56, 22 Oct. 1949.
[3] p. 267.

division of the Organization; and to ensure a uniform reporting system in all areas of the IRO's operation. The division of responsibility between the social service departments of the Organization and those concerned with re-establishment was clearly defined through this classification system in that a case falling into a specific category was subject to action by one department only, and if an individual was reclassified into another category, his case could easily be referred to the department responsible for cases in the new category. The point was eventually reached where the Organization, aware of the wishes of each individual and family group in relation to the opportunities for re-establishment which the Organization was able to offer, could proceed with systematic case-work in expediting a solution.

After the middle of 1950 counselling as social case-work became largely the responsibility of the voluntary societies both international and local, and the IRO's counselling was more closely connected with resettlement proper. Thus counselling officers were assigned to resettlement processing centres mainly to help persons who had been rejected or deferred from a resettlement scheme to which they had been presented.

CHAPTER XVI

ADAPTATION TO A NEW LIFE

REFUGEES generally welcomed at first the relative security of the assembly centre care provided by the Organization. Even in later days some persons tended to cling to the sheltered camp life they had come to know so well. Yet in all there were few persons who did not continually pray and strive for the day when the seemingly interminable waiting would end and once again they could lead normal independent lives—become self-supporting at last through their own work and efforts.

For most able-bodied men the worst part of this waiting was the enforced idleness, the lack of opportunity to pursue their crafts or professions, or to practise and maintain former skills; young people particularly were eager to acquire new skills for chosen work they hoped some day to do in the outside world. These and other refugees who expected to begin life anew in unfamiliar countries were anxious to prepare themselves so far as possible for the new pattern of living to be encountered.

One of the objectives of the IRO was, as stated in the Preamble to its Constitution, to put the refugees and displaced persons 'to useful employment in order to avoid the evil and anti-social consequences of continued idleness' until their repatriation or resettlement was effectively completed.

At an early stage the PCIRO and the Executive Secretary recognized that a programme of employment and vocational training was an essential part of the work of the Organization closely related both to the care of displaced persons and to their re-establishment. The object was to ensure that as many persons as possible should be employed up to the time of their final settlement. Most resettlement countries placed considerable emphasis on occupational skills in selecting refugees for resettlement, and experience proved that the best way to ensure the retention and development of an occupational skill was to provide employment opportunities.

Thus the Administration developed an employment and vocational programme promoting useful employment in the IRO administrative and maintenance functions and with occupation authorities and private employers; and providing for determination, registration, and classification of skills and maintenance of occupational registration; verification of skills by trade testing; occupational pre-selection of candidates for resettlement missions; the selection of workers for employment in occupied zones; providing occupational data in the preparation of dossiers for specialists; establishment and effective operation of work units, or production units, for the manufacturing of goods to be supplied to refugees by the Organization.

A. EMPLOYMENT

By the time the new organization had completed its first six months of operation, approximately one-half of the total refugee population was actively employed or receiving vocational training. This proportion was considered extremely high in view of the fact that many refugees were under 16 years of age, or women with young children, or elderly, or physically handicapped, or remote from employment opportunities. It had been found, however, that the extensive activities taken over from UNRRA did not constitute a programme directed specifically toward the objectives of the IRO. The employment of refugees varied considerably from area to area and there was no co-ordinated programme of vocational training to meet the needs of refugees as a whole. At the time it was suggested that short courses in languages and in general orientation regarding the country of reception might also be established.

On 1 January 1948 a Division of Employment and Vocational Training was established at Geneva headquarters. A conference of the PCIRO employment officers from Germany, Austria, and Italy, and vocational training officers of voluntary agencies from these areas, was held in Geneva a week later. Considerable attention was given to a system of occupational registration and classification which was then being developed by a representative of the Employment Service of the US Department of Labor who was loaned to the Organization to make the first survey of the occupational skills of the employable refugees and displaced persons.[1] Plans were made for future employment and vocational training work, with many suggestions contributed by representatives of the four most active voluntary societies in this field, one of which recommended that the Organization should undertake vocational training and rehabilitation of disabled refugees. Most significant was the agreement reached as to the vital need for the Organization to formulate an employment policy for refugees which would define the extent to which refugee employment was or was not compulsory, what sanctions, if any, should be imposed for refusal to accept employment, and what sort of work incentives might be offered.

The role of headquarters in this programme at all times was mainly co-ordination. Throughout the entire operation there were never more than two senior staff members at Geneva in this division, and their efforts were concentrated largely on broad planning, personnel and finance, general direction of the programmes and supervision through field reporting, and inspection tours of the principal areas of operation. $750,000 had been budgeted for these programmes to cover expenses in the first half of 1948, but less than $200,000 were spent. For the following financial year, however, a budget of $1½ million was established and an additional $850,000 for rehabilitation; though there were no expenditures in the latter category during the year, costs of vocational training totalled almost $1,300,000.

Several general objectives for the programme of employment and vocational training developed as the result of study and planning which preceded and followed the first meeting of field representatives in Geneva. It was necessary to continue the registration and classification of refugees' occupations according to improved methods; in particular, trade testing should be accelerated. Obstacles to the employment of refugees had to be overcome. Vocational training had to be made more uniform and eventually extended to the training of disabled refugees. Above all,

[1] Later a uniform list of occupation titles or job classifications was released for regular surveys in the field. These definitions, which had been based largely on the classification system of the US Employment Service, were developed with the co-operation and assistance of the ILO into a dictionary of some 400 job descriptions.

activities should be directed toward resettlement of specialists and of employable refugees generally. Occupational data were important for the immediate recruitment and employment of refugees and as a basis for planning on the part of countries interested in recruiting refugees for resettlement.[1]

Occupational classification

In the light of proposed legislation providing for large-scale immigration of refugees to the US, the first objective of the Organization was to bring up to date the occupational information compiled by UNRRA in 1946. UNRRA had developed a classification system generally based on those of the US army and the US Employment Service; but the German system had been used in the British zone of Germany and, since UNRRA had been forced to use untrained personnel in making its registration, the results were not entirely accurate or uniform.

The IRO proceeded with the classification of occupational skills of refugees between 16 and 65 years of age receiving care and maintenance on the basis of a system derived from the US Employment Service Dictionary of Occupational Titles in co-operation with the ILO. The first partial survey at the end of 1947 made it clear that the 330,000 refugees registered represented a rich source of labour in a world in which nearly all countries were confronted with severe labour shortages. Most refugee men were skilled workers, there were almost as many agricultural workers, and the next largest group consisted of professional workers. Women refugees were found to have a wide variety of skills, with the largest group in service occupations, although there were almost as many in professional and clerical categories and in agricultural work.[2]

The second more comprehensive survey of 31 March 1948 achieved greater uniformity as to classification and age groups. Of a total of 630,000 refugees, more than 340,000 could be classified occupationally; men accounted for two-thirds of this total and about one-third of them fell in the skilled category, one-quarter agricultural, and about one-eighth professional or managerial; among employable women surveyed, 19 per cent. were classified as skilled workers, and service occupations accounted for almost 14 per cent. of the total. Among the men, occupations most frequently encountered were those of tailor, shoemaker, saddler, locksmith, carpenter, and mechanic; important group for women workers were seamstresses, domestic workers, teachers, nurses, and agricultural workers.[3]

By January 1950 the number of classified workers in Austria, Germany, and Italy had decreased to 132,000 largely by resettlement. The proportions in the major occupational groups remained roughly the same. For example, between March 1949 and January 1950 the number of tailors declined from 4,370 to 1,776; of electricians from 2,888 to 1,443; and of teachers from 2,528 to 1,124.[4]

[1] PREP/177, 12 Jan. 1948: Report on Occupational Skills of Refugees in PCIRO Assembly Centres in Europe, 39 pp.

[2] PREP/178, 27 Jan. 1948: Report of the Executive Secretary on Employment and Vocational Training.

[3] First Annual Report of the IRO to the Ninth Session of ECOSOC of the United Nations, 31 Mar. 1949. E/1334, 17 May 1949, pp. 28–31. See also Table: Major Occupational Groups, Annex 26, p. 305.

[4] For a condensed summary of the surveys of 1948 and 1950 see Annex 27, p. 306.

While regular half-yearly statistical reporting on occupational skills was required from field officers in Germany, Austria, and Italy only, voluntary reporting by other offices was welcomed and special reporting was required for certain purposes. At the end of 1949 a special registration was completed of refugees in France which covered almost 2,700 refugees of whom about 70 per cent. were Spanish. Compared to a survey in Austria, Germany, and Italy made at about the same date, the registration in France showed almost twice the relative number of skilled and semi-skilled workers, but only one-fifth as many agricultural workers; the proportion of professional workers and unskilled workers was about the same in both surveys.

Realizing that registration and classification might be somewhat unreliable if based on information obtained from labour cards or interviews, the Organization developed an extensive programme for testing refugees in the skills they claimed. By 15 December 1947 about one-third of the employable population in the US zone of Germany had been given trade tests; each person was classified as master craftsman, first-class worker, second-class worker, apprentice, or helper. This qualitative analysis of skills claimed by the displaced persons indicated that they possessed a relatively high level of skills; for example, of 629 machinists tested, 101 were rated as master craftsmen, 208 as first-class, 233 as second-class workers, 86 as apprentices, and 1 as helper.[1]

Another important and related survey made during 1948 revealed that the displaced persons 'offered youth as well as skills to the world'. Eighty-three per cent. of those in camps were under 45 years of age. Among men, 26 per cent. were under 18 years of age, 51 per cent. between 18 and 45, and only 17 per cent. over 45. Among women, 29 per cent. were under 18, 55 per cent. between 18 and 45, and 16 per cent. over 45.

Trade testing was at first done largely by special commissions composed of refugees who were outstanding craftsmen in their own occupations. The standards used for the tests were largely those of the German occupational bureaux, *Berufs-kammern*. The commissions worked in co-operation with the military government, the German government, and German trade unions, and use was made of the Organization's vocational training schools, German factories, and other facilities. In time it became more difficult to find qualified refugees for the testing commissions, and increasing use was made of the *Handwerkskammer*, the official German testing agency.

Skills outside the specialist categories were tested by practical work tests, oral trade questions, review of documents, written examinations, or by other means available to the testing commissions. The testing of intellectual and professional workers consisted chiefly of examining and certifying the authenticity of diplomas, documents, and other papers presented as proof of professional qualifications. Such qualifications varied considerably according to the standards of the country of origin. Arrangements were made for German universities and professional institutes to help in the testing of professional workers. Medical and nursing personnel were tested by special professional screening boards. Apart from such medical workers,

---

[1] First Annual Report of the IRO to the Ninth Session of ECOSOC, op. cit., p. 29.

who received a special certificate, all other refugees were awarded a trade testing certificate which indicated their degree of proficiency.

As time went on, the classification programme played an increasingly important part in testing graduates of the vocational training courses and, particularly, in the selection of refugees for resettlement. Special testing also was completed for local settlement purposes, and in the US zone of Germany in June 1949 arrangements were made to re-test through the German *Handwerkskammer* all persons registered as having limited opportunities of migration, inasmuch as German firms would not accept the IRO's official testing certificates.

In the US zone of Germany, where trade testing was organized earlier and more comprehensively than in the other zones, all testing had been completed by 30 June 1948, and a few months later the results of tests were available for a total of 185,000 refugees, including 13,500 in labour service companies, 15,500 employed by military authorities, and 11,000 refugees living out of camp. At that time, 10,000 DM were being spent monthly for testing in German factories.

In the British zone of Germany the programme was slow in starting because of difficulties in obtaining staff and necessary funds, and it was not until towards the middle of 1949 that trade testing gathered momentum. The basic routine testing of refugees in that zone was then largely completed in the following six months, but the lack of Deutschmarks for testing fees and facilities continued. These difficulties were overcome to some extent by arranging for much of the trade testing to be done by staff of the World ORT Union after that organization had done some emergency testing in the first year for the resettlement of workers in Venezuela.

In the French zone of Germany, only 1,700 refugees had been tested by the end of 1948. By the middle of 1949 limited funds became available for trade testing by the *Handwerkskammer*, and the work was completed about six months later.

In Austria, trade testing began in the middle of 1948, and was carried out by the Austrian Chamber of Commerce with satisfactory results. In the middle of 1949 lack of funds put an end to testing except for refugees being selected for resettlement schemes, and all refugees, except hardship cases, paid for their tests. Trade testing in Italy was not substantial until the middle of 1949 and was not completed for a further six months.

In addition to routine trade testing to verify claimed skills, special tests were conducted at the request of selection missions to evaluate proficiency in specific operations or skills required, and at times missions supplied their own technical experts to direct the testing. But as the selection missions came to appreciate the validity of the IRO testing, the certificates of the Organization were accepted as proofs of skill, and special testing was not demanded except in unusual situations.

The use of occupational and testing records for assistance in administering the resettlement programme was greatest in the US zone of Germany. From consolidated records at zone headquarters it was possible to tell at any time exactly where to locate refugees with the specific skills desired. Selectors could then visit the areas and make a pre-selection of refugees by a study of the occupational record files maintained there. Later, the most likely candidates screened in this way could be presented for personal interview and then, if advisable, trade tests could be arranged for all or certain of these pre-selected candidates. While methods of pre-selection varied in detail according to zones and to various selection missions, the use of occupational records for selection generally followed the same general pattern; the records were also used to fill anonymous assurances under the US Displaced Persons Act.

In June 1948 more than half of the 598,000 persons receiving care and maintenance were classified as employable.[1] Six months later, approximately 110,000 of these were employed full time. While most of them worked in the administration and maintenance of assembly centres, some 6,000 were engaged in work projects devoted primarily to producing clothing and other things for the refugees themselves, and another 7,000 persons were engaged in some form of self-employment.[2] But many refugees could not find work, and many difficulties were encountered in carrying out the policy of assisting refugees to regain their status as useful working members of the community and to salvage the skills and habits impaired through disuse.

Obstacles to employment

The greatest obstacle was the unfavourable employment situation which prevailed in Germany, Austria, and Italy. During the first year when the currency in occupied areas was of low value there was little or no incentive to work; after the German currency conversion opportunities for refugee employment decreased as there was greater incentive for German nationals to work and German employers preferred to employ them. At the same time, there was widespread unemployment in Italy and to a somewhat lesser degree in Austria, with the result that the Italian Government looked with disfavour on the employment of refugees, and the Austrian Government required that preference should be given to Austrians. During the second year there was considerable unemployment in all three countries, and economic difficulties caused increased unwillingness on the part of governments and authorities to pay for the employment of refugees; therefore assembly-centre payrolls were reduced.[3] As a result, less than one-third of the employable refugees were employed, and the proportion decreased further in the following year as permitted maxima for assembly-centre employment were reduced and the number of installations diminished.[4] Another obstacle to employment was found in the attitude of certain refugees. Apart from the early disinclination to work for virtually worthless money, displaced persons who had suffered under German rule were reluctant to work under German and Austrian employers. Consequently, employment in the beginning was primarily with the specially established labour service companies of the occupation forces and in assembly centres; and relatively few refugees were absorbed economically in the countries of refuge.[5] Some refugees

[1] Report of the Executive Secretary of PCIRO to the General Council of IRO for the period 1 July 1947–30 June 1948, p. 16.
[2] GC/60, Report of the Director General on the activities of the Organization from 1 July 1948–22 Mar. 1949.
[3] GC/100, Report of the Director General to the General Council of the IRO, 1 July 1948–30 June 1949.
[4] GC/140, Semi-Annual Report of the Director General, 1 July 1949 to 31 Dec. 1949.
[5] Report of the Executive Secretary, op. cit., p. 20.

developed an apathy towards employment as the result of protracted camp life, and others were afraid that employment would interfere with their repatriation or resettlement; conversely, some who had found satisfactory employment sought to delay their ultimate re-establishment.

In most other countries of temporary refuge, e.g. in the Middle East and the Far East, work opportunities for refugees were limited, and difficulties were encountered in placing even relatively few refugees in jobs. In western European and in other countries which offered better prospects for permanent residence, the opportunities for employment and local establishment were much greater; e.g. in France the Ministry of Labour made very effective efforts towards the employment of refugees, even to the extent of establishing a special employment office for psychotechnical testing and placement of intellectuals. Indeed, France and the other countries of western Europe, which already had considerable refugee population, were, by 1947, encouraging the further immigration of refugee workers.

Although there were other obstacles to employment besides those mentioned—including the remoteness of some assembly centres from employment centres and lack of suitable clothing, especially shoes—it was the unanimous opinion of employment officers in the field that the Organization should announce a policy of compulsory employment in appropriate projects, and that additional rations, cigarettes, and other amenities should be used as employment incentives.

Sanctions and incentives

The order on employment policy, released some six months after its first discussion, provided that repeated refusal to accept available and suitable work would result in the denial of amenities or, in serious cases, of all care and maintenance. The order further provided that a refugee would have the right of appeal to the Chief of Office when an area team director had decided that care and maintenance should be rescinded. This order set forth officially the objectives and methods of the employment programme, namely, that in order to avoid idleness the Organization would assist able refugees to earn their own living and maintain and develop professional and trade skills by employment, thereby increasing opportunities for successful re-establishment.

Employable refugees who had reached the age of 16 or who had not passed the age of 65 in the case of men and 55 in the case of women were defined as fit persons except for women caring for young children, for the sick, or for aged relatives. A minimum working week of forty hours was necessary to constitute employment, and various criteria were outlined to determine the suitability of employment. Under the order, refugees were to be given priority of employment over all other persons, any attempt to discriminate in employing refugees should be combated, and the primary aim would be to place refugees in employment which did not depend on local employers. The order applied only in Austria, Germany, and Italy.

There was some reluctance on the part of the field offices in issuing and carrying out the order. In the US zone of Germany, for example, there was fear of adverse publicity, and the feeling that the refugees would construe the order as an added harassment. This zone added a clause requiring eight hours per week in camp maintenance, and other areas made similar amendments in this respect. Other modifications followed, such as the decision in the French zone of Germany that a refugee must work a minimum of forty-eight hours per week to be counted as a worker.

After the currency reform in Germany, non-financial incentives to work ceased to have the same importance as previously: it was no longer necessary to give workers better billeting, additional clothing, and amenity supplies. When most refugees were employed in assembly centres for wages which had real value, attention turned from incentives to requiring employed refugees to contribute from their earnings toward their care.

In August 1948 the military government in the US zone of Germany ordered that a monthly sum of 70 DM should be taken from the pay of refugees paid from the mandatory budget (the so-called *Bürgermeister's* pay-roll); and that of this partial payment for food and rent, 20 DM would be deposited in a blocked account in favour of the IRO.[1] The reasons for this order were that employed displaced persons should, in the interests of rehabilitation, contribute in the normal way towards the cost of their upkeep; that the disparity between the net savings of refugees and comparable German employees should be diminished; and that the total amount of money in free circulation following currency conversion should be reduced.

Wage deduction schemes had been initiated earlier in the British zone of Germany and in Austria, and a system of salary deductions came into force at the end of October 1948 in the French zone of Germany. In Italy deductions were made at source and were reflected in the slightly lower wages paid to refugees. While the objective of wage deductions was the same in all areas, methods varied greatly: some deductions were made as fixed amounts, others on a sliding scale for workers and dependants, or for workers only. The results also were dissimilar, single and family workers fared differently in different areas and the advantage generally was to the single worker as against the family man. Wage deductions, combined with other deductions for social insurance and other taxes generally, left a 'take-home' wage which offered limited incentives for obtaining employment. The earliest plans proved to be unsatisfactory in some instances and were subsequently amended.

Opportunities of employment

The administrative functions of the Organization provided most employment for refugees. In Germany the wages of refugees thus employed were paid in German marks from the mandatory budget in accordance with terms negotiated with the military authorities. At the start of operations, a maximum of 10 per cent. of the refugee population could be employed in the US zone of Germany in the operations of the Organization, but this limitation was lifted later and employment limits were based on actual needs and funds available. This employment involved nearly 50,000 workers at a time when the camp population in the zone was approximately 300,000. Germans were employed only when refugees were not available, but the limit of 4,000 originally established by the US authorities for the employment of Germans

[1] Chapter VI, Finances, p. 118.

was not enforced later when it became increasingly difficult to replace refugees who left for resettlement.

In other zones of Germany the military authorities were responsible for the employment of refugees in the operation of assembly centres under similar quantitative limitations; relatively few positions paid from the mandatory budget were allocated to the Organization, and then for special jobs only. In Austria and Italy refugee labour was paid for by the Organization which established its own limits.

In all main areas employment of refugees by the Organization declined as installations were amalgamated and closed and the refugee population decreased. In June 1949 more than 45,000 refugees were employed by the Organization in administrative functions, but a year later this figure had fallen to only some 18,000. Simultaneously there was an increase in the employment of refugees not living in centres, and of Germans. In the US zone of Germany in the first six months of 1949 employment of refugees living outside camp increased by 16 per cent. and employment of Germans by 25 per cent. At the end of 1951 non-refugee employees accounted for 45 per cent. of the IRO's non-international staff, as compared to 34 per cent. a year earlier.[1]

Refugees were employed also by the military authorities, primarily in Germany. In July 1947 there were, in the US zone of Germany alone, almost 45,000 refugee men employed with the US army in labour service companies; they worked in building and construction, vehicle maintenance and trucking, as well as in quartermasters' and guards' activities. At this time, a change of policy led to considerable demobilization of these forces, many of the workers being replaced by German nationals, and six months later the total had declined to some 14,000, reaching around 3,400 by June 1949.[2] In the British zone of Germany similar employment was provided in a civilian mixed labour organization and a civilian mixed watchmen's service, and the occupation forces also employed refugees in smaller numbers in the French zone of Germany and in Austria. As late as January 1949 almost 15,000 refugees were thus employed, but a year later the total had fallen below 6,000 and declined further to slightly more than 3,000 by the end of the third year of operations.[3]

Comparatively little work was offered by employers other than the Organization or the military authorities. After the currency reform in Germany, most of the more desirable jobs were given to German nationals despite vigorous efforts to prevent discrimination on the part of employers. As a means achieving the highest possible employment of refugees, employable persons were required to register for employment in Austria and Germany with the national employment offices through which the Organization attempted, without notable success, to develop job opportunities, particularly in the later days for persons not expected to resettle. In the US zone of Germany a pilot project was instituted at Hanau for this last objective. In the British zone of Germany efforts were made to house refugees near work opportunities, and a special employment camp was the first to be turned over to the Germans. But a high level of employment by German firms was never attained. In January 1949 some 17,000 refugees were employed by local employers in Germany

---

[1] See Annex 28, p. 308. [2] See Annex 30, p. 310. [3] Ibid.

and another 3,000 in Austria and Italy together; but eighteen months later, as the third year of operations ended, these workers numbered only some 2,300 in Germany and approximately 1,000 in Austria.[1]

Self-employment of refugees was encouraged, particularly in the earlier days. Such employment within assembly centres made it possible for many craftsmen to maintain their skills and provided needed services for all refugees under arrangements which generally ensured that benefits did not only accrue to the self-employed person but were distributed as widely as possible. Self-employment outside assembly centres was arranged only with great difficulty, but there were many instances where a single person or a group managed to establish successful ventures outside of camp. The number of self-employed refugees in all areas was more than 5,400 in January 1949, but by June 1950 the total had declined to little more than 800.

For workers whose skills did not lend themselves to self-employment, employment was available in the work projects supported wholly, or partly, by the Organization in co-operation with voluntary societies. The formation of these work projects stemmed from a suggestion made in October 1946 to UNRRA by the military authorities in the US zone of Germany. At that time the military authorities indicated willingness to turn over material for refugees to use in making some of their own clothing, and UNRRA encouraged the idea as a means of providing needed employment and contributing to the care programme. But the army was unable to arrange to carry this out with German firms, and UNRRA finally enlisted the aid of certain voluntary societies to set up the project in its own assembly centres.

When the IRO began operations there were seventeen clothing projects employing more than 2,500 refugees, and it had been demonstrated that refugees could produce for their own needs. A few months earlier, Jewish voluntary societies interested in employment had organized an employment board, Jewish Agency for Palestine (JAFP).

World ORT Union (Organization for Rehabilitation through Training) and the AJDC, by January 1948, was employing 1,300 refugees in AJDC work projects in the zone and taking responsibility for some 1,100 Jewish workers in the IRO work projects there. At about the same time there were almost 4,600 workers in AJDC work projects in Austria.

By the end of the first year, however, this programme had come to a complete halt in the US zone of Germany after having attained an employment total of more than 3,200 workers in seventy-two different locations. The main reason for this collapse had been the lack of orders received from the supply section, which had been able to obtain surplus military clothing at a low cost not to be matched by manufacturing. But in the following months the programme was reinstated on a more efficient and orderly basis so that commitments for $1\frac{1}{2}$ million clothing items could be made to the zone supply division; and before the end of the second year more refugees were employed in work projects and more items were produced than ever before. The work projects programme in this zone at times attained the limit of 4,000 workers which had been approved by the occupation authorities.

[1] See Chapter V, Personnel, p. 90.

At the beginning of 1949 some 4,000 refugees were employed in work projects in Austria, the US zone of Germany, and in Italy, but this total had dropped to less than 1,500 one year later, and the programme was virtually finished at the end of the third year of operations when only 380 workers were employed in Austria and 160 in the US zone of Germany.

B. VOCATIONAL TRAINING

Vocational training had been developed by the IRO's predecessor agencies. UNRRA had established workshops in assembly centres as well as residential vocational training centres. IGCR had sponsored vocational training undertaken by private agencies in Belgium, the Netherlands, France, and Switzerland. The voluntary societies which were making substantial contributions in this field were ORT, AJDC, JAFP, World's YMCA/YWCA, CWS, and others. They supplied the technical specialists to develop and supervise the vocational programme, and selected, trained, and employed as instructors many hundreds of refugees with basic qualifications in the vocational skills required, and also provided valuable supplies and equipment, motor transport, and other facilities necessary to support these programmes.[1]

In addition several governments had their own schemes. That in Switzerland was important, particularly during the war, when several hundred thousand refugees were given asylum. Courses of professional training covering a score of professions were organized at government expense in special centres; they were begun in 1942 and reached their peak in 1944. Further, several hundred refugees took either complete apprenticeship courses or refresher courses in Swiss factories and workshops. Several thousand refugees were thus enabled by the support of the Swiss authorities and voluntary societies better to fit themselves for repatriation or further migration after the war.

The training programmes of the voluntary societies were many and varied, ranging from courses in sewing, machine-shop practice, and carpentry to more exceptional training opportunities in such skills, for example, as typewriter repair, watchmaking, radio-mechanics, and well-drilling.

A substantial number of refugees not under care and maintenance were receiving vocational training through voluntary agencies when the PCIRO began to develop these operations. In the US zone alone ORT was training over 6,000 refugees and some 600 refugee instructors and other personnel were employed for this purpose; in all, this voluntary society was providing training for approximately 9,000 students in Austria, Germany, and Italy in a wide range of skills. AJDC was operating workshops and co-operating closely with the ORT, while other vocational training was being given by the JAFP in agriculture, by the CWS, the YMCA/YWCA (particularly in the French zone of Germany), and the Polish Red Cross.

The Organization was determined to continue to support the voluntary societies in their work on vocational training. Despite the excellence of much of this work, however, there was considerable variation between areas. Many of the vocational

---

[1] PREP/148, 30 Oct. 1947. Vocational Training of Refugees receiving PCIRO Care and Maintenance.

training projects of the voluntary societies and the Organization functioned more or less independently, and there was great need to co-ordinate the various programmes.[1]

The first twelve months of operation from July 1947 to June 1948 was largely devoted to developing plans and standards for the future and to the consolidation of the large number of scattered projects inherited from the predecessor organizations.

Training centres

In the British and US zones of Germany early efforts were made to standardize and consolidate these activities. A concentrated drive was made to group all scattered activities into a few central vocational training centres. The object of this plan was to eliminate duplication of projects and to pool centrally qualified instructors, equipment, and supplies which were all scarce. Further, it had been demonstrated that the residential type of training centre permitted more effective supervision, and more concentrated instruction became possible when trainees were removed from the distractions of assembly-centre life.

In May 1947 the PCIRO had adopted a resolution defining the policy of the Organization on basic education and instructing the Executive Secretary to make arrangements for the vocational training of youth.[2] Vocational guidance and training should be directed towards the development of skills and should be provided for young people and adults who had no skills, and for adults who needed a new skill or the refreshing of their acquired skill to further their re-establishment. The emphasis of vocational training was laid on the preparation of refugees for resettlement and repatriation; thus the selection of courses and of trainees became geared directly to resettlement needs. Courses were intensive in nature and generally of short duration: usually they did not exceed six months in teaching new skills, and three months for refresher and re-training purposes. Wherever possible, residential centres were established, but apprentice training outside centres was also encouraged. Certificates of accomplishment were given to trainees, and vocational training was entered on appropriate records used when registering skills. By 1 September 1947, 31,941 refugees under PCIRO care and maintenance in Germany, Austria, and Italy were registered in vocational training courses.

Among the difficulties facing the IRO in arranging vocational training was the lack of qualified staff. Until late in the programme, international staff could not be found, and suitable refugees, always scarce, became even rarer as resettlement progressed. While the consolidation of projects had served to use more effectively the abilities of the best teachers, these were the persons most likely to be selected for resettlement because of their exceptional skills. As the most proficient instructors were lost in this way, it became increasingly difficult to find suitable replacements, but experience made it possible for less skilled instructors to follow out satisfactorily the work of their predecessors.

As the programme developed, still another recruitment problem presented itself —that of obtaining sufficient trainees to maintain centres at capacity. At first, many

[1] PREP/177, 27 Jan. 1948, p. 4.
[2] PREP/90/Rev. 1/Add. 1, p. 16. Res. No. 19.

trainees were reluctant to enter the residential type of centre either because they did not wish to be separated from families and friends in the assembly centres, or because they had jobs or other sources of income which they did not wish to abandon. Others were afraid that they would be isolated in the centres from resettlement opportunities; and, finally, there were refugees, usually of low intellectual level who had become accustomed to idleness and were apathetic or antagonistic to the discipline and hard work required.

Resistance to enrolment was first overcome by recruiting campaigns, but a large proportion of the recruits came forward as a consequence of favourable results witnessed and recounted by trainees. For there was ample evidence that vocational training not only produced skills which made it possible for graduates to earn a livelihood, but also placed them in a preferred position for resettlement selection. As centres became established, a wide range of courses, including almost every practical skill, became available to trainees who generally could undertake training of their own choice.

At the beginning, vocational guidance consisted mostly of practical tests and interviews between the trainees and instructors within the centre. Later, however, trainees were interviewed by qualified persons before they were directed to vocational training centres, and in certain areas effective use was made of aptitude testing.

Great difficulties were experienced throughout the vocational training programme in obtaining equipment and supplies at the time when they were needed. Most of the supplies obtained from the military authorities were usable and basic needs for heavy machinery and equipment were largely met. In general, however, the programme was plagued throughout by the lack of vitally needed small parts and specific items which, insignificant in themselves, often disrupted training schedules.

Training courses

The selection and development of the training courses were important in the earlier period. From the beginning the Organization placed great emphasis on training courses of short duration. In general, it was not possible to provide training for a period long enough to develop highly skilled workers: limitation of funds, and the vast numbers of refugees to be trained, dictated a pattern of rapid refresher training to enhance the resettlement prospects of skilled workers, and somewhat longer courses to provide unskilled workers with a start in their chosen occupations.

In the US zone of Germany the system of training was brought into conformity with the international normalization system which existed in Europe. Known as the 'IN' system in Germany, this method minimized the need for highly skilled teachers by making it possible to substitute skilled technicians; it also permitted great flexibility in meeting the particular needs of individual students. In this zone, in particular, stress was laid on the accelerated or rapid training methods of well-known international systems in use both before and during the war; with few exceptions courses were designed for a period of ninety days. In order to standardize training, the zone developed comprehensive outlines for almost thirty basic courses, including schedules of training equipment and materials needed and methods of instruction.

Similar emphasis on short-term training was observed in other areas and a general uniformity in the development of courses and training methods gradually came about, largely through informal exchange of information among vocational training staff in the field missions. In all zones vocational training offices maintained constant contact with resettlement staff and with government selection missions in order to obtain information as to the type of skills most in demand in the countries of resettlement.

At the start, there was considerable controversy with the voluntary societies, particularly the ORT, over the Organization's policy of short-term training. Generally the objective of ORT was to develop finished craftsmen in courses often of six to nine months' duration, and sometimes longer.[1] As time went on, however, there proved to be room for both types of courses. While the Organization continued to concentrate on short courses, trainees were permitted to progress beyond the elementary training as facilities and funds allowed. The voluntary societies were also able to provide more extended training when justified. But the basic IRO policy of giving as many refugees as possible a start towards learning a skill was maintained at all times.

At the beginning, a variety of courses were given, at one time or another in approximately 100 different subjects. As the centres were consolidated, however, the bulk of the training was accomplished in some thirty basic courses in industrial, agricultural, commercial, and service trades. For men, popular courses were in the construction trades, mechanical work, and farming. For women, emphasis was placed on domestic service, nursing, garment and textile work, and typing.

The PCIRO also developed its training programme for medical, nursing, and related personnel both for resettlement preparation and for ensuring the maintenance of essential health and medical services in camp operations. A continuous programme was maintained to refresh the skills of trained medical personnel and to provide new medical and nursing aids. Following the UNRRA experience in Germany and Austria since 1945, medical personnel was given, in hospitals by international staff, four to six weeks' refresher courses in new methods of treatment, application of new drugs, current public health practice, and the latest principles of medical nursing and dental practice.

Shortly after the IRO began operations, arrangements were made with voluntary societies regarding post-graduate courses for medical specialists; and at the start of the second year the first of such courses was held, arranged by the Organization and the Unitarian Service Committee of New York, with financial assistance from the AJDC and the World Council of Churches. A total of seventy-one refugee doctors from the three zones of Germany and the US zone of Austria attended training courses given by a teaching staff of five prominent medical professors from the US; a second course immediately followed for an additional seventy-five refugee medical specialists. The chairman of the teaching mission expressed the opinion that the refugee doctors were men of the highest calibre who would be of great value to any country.

The excellent results obtained through these conferences stimulated the Organiza-

---

[1] Report of the Executive Secretary 1947/1948, op. cit.

tion to undertake similar two-week refresher courses in various subjects through its own facilities, and to arrange for a subsequent refresher course by visiting specialists. This second session was successfully conducted the following year, and while the arrangements were again undertaken by the Unitarian Service Committee, the Organization met all expenses. For these courses quantities of technical medical books were obtained and distributed to the refugee specialists, and on various other occasions the Organization was able to make available medical textbooks which had been obtained as the result of an appeal for donations, as unsolicited gifts, or by purchase.

The Organization also established seven weeks' courses for nursing aides. In the early period from January to 1 October 1947, a total of 2,360 young women in Germany, Austria, Italy, and the Middle East received training as hospital ward aides and nursery nurses. The medical and nursing manuals prepared by the Health Division of UNRRA were revised by the PCIRO with new chapters relating to resettlement.

During its first year of operation the IRO consolidated the efforts of the past. By the end of the first six months 9,000 refugees were in the centres of the IRO, 6,500 in ORT classes, and 500 under the CWS, with another 240 receiving training under other arrangements, bringing the total to more than 16,000. By the end of the year the vocational training of the IRO in the US zone of Germany had been concentrated in seven residential training centres with some eight subsidiary centres for special courses, primarily for farm workers and nurses. At the same time, the World ORT Union had thirty-nine centres teaching 114 courses. In the British zone sixteen training centres were established; in addition ORT was conducting training in eight different installations. Here, as in the US zone, the programme deteriorated due to lack of supplies, accommodation, instructors, and proper supervision and control at the end of the year; but after close investigation of all vocational training activities, a joint CCG/IRO instruction was released outlining a formal organized programme in large central schools. In the French zone of Germany there was a limited programme in one technical and one agricultural centre, apart from scattered and unorganized small groups of trainees.

In Austria, where ORT had conducted vocational training since January 1947, the first centre of the Organization was established in March 1948, and the first course commenced some three months later. In Italy all vocational training was conducted by ORT, mostly in its own schools; in December 1948 only 300 trainees out of a total of 1,600 were in schools maintained by the IRO. The ORT programme had expanded rapidly in the early months and outran the provisions for financial support by the Organization. But near the close of the year the original working plan was replaced by a formal agreement outlining conditions under which ORT would do all vocational training in Italy for both Jews and non-Jews, under close supervision by the Organization. At that time there were more than 70 *Hachsharoth*, and ORT conducted and provided most of the supplies for these centres training in a wide variety of skills; in one, instruction was given in fishing trades and seamanship by using a fishing boat made entirely by trainees.

In France more than 700 trainees and in Belgium a smaller number received support from the Organization in vocational training and apprenticeship courses provided through ORT and other voluntary societies. In the Middle East courses in welding, carpentry, bricklaying, and cement work were started in El Shatt camp in the early months of the first year. No vocational training was established in the Far East.

During the second year's work, from July 1948 to June 1949, great strides were made in standardizing and improving the programme of the Organization, and the quality of the training improved at the same time as the number of trainees was diminishing through resettlement. The Organization budgeted $600,000 for vocational training during this financial year. As France alone had requested the allotment of $120,000, the total was considered to be small. This proved to be the case as further consolidation of schools throughout the year raised costs and, as the previous insistence on three months' courses was relaxed somewhat, an increasing number of persons without skills were given longer periods of training to improve their resettlement chances.

In October 1948 a vocational training expert from the US Department of Labor made an inspection tour of centres in the US zone of Germany with the IRO's chief of employment and vocational training. This authority, whose services had been made available by the ILO where he was engaged as a consultant, was favourably impressed with the progress made in the centres, but listed the lack of supplies and equipment as a serious obstacle to future achievements. By June 1949, however, some of the most serious supply problems in the zone had been overcome.

In the British zone of Germany training centres were generally over-subscribed, one reason being that university courses were no longer open to refugee students, and large numbers of them entered vocational training schools. The difficulty of obtaining instructors to replace those who resettled was acute in this zone. In the French zone of Germany a joint programme with the refugee division of the French military government was being formulated in July 1948, but very little was accomplished until activities were completely reorganized nearly twelve months later: earlier progress had been blocked by difficulties in obtaining needed German currency funds. A normal programme of four months' courses, with a forty-hour working week, was established in the following year.

In Austria the programme also suffered from difficulties in obtaining Austrian schillings, but active programmes were carried out both by the Organization and by ORT. By mid-year ORT had 949 students enrolled against 523 by the IRO. While the ORT programme increased steadily at that time, it decreased later until some 300 refugees were enrolled in ORT courses at the end of the year. For the last six months the Organization had paid ORT a grant equivalent to the costs of its programme which otherwise would have been paid by the Organization in its own classes, and this support was continued. In this period supplementary food rations for vocational training students, which had been established generally in other areas, were obtained for Austria.

In Italy the ORT/IRO programme continued satisfactorily and, despite consolidations, enrolment did not suffer. Training in this area was relatively expensive, however, and a budget of $103,000 had been requested for the year.

Vocational training activities in other western European countries were limited, but the programme in France was based on an increase of over 50 per cent. in the number of trainees, and the vocational training budget was almost four times as great as in the previous year.

Evolution of the programme

By June 1949 nearly 10,000 refugees were attending vocational training courses in Austria, Germany, and Italy,[1] but the total enrolments had decreased by almost 2,000 students in the last six months. As the year ended, almost one-third of the trainees were following courses operated by voluntary societies, but the proportion of the total who were in the IRO's schools had increased steadily as the other courses, particularly those established by ORT, were curtailed or closed.[2]

In the third year, which ended in June 1950, the numbers attending vocational training courses decreased from almost 10,000 to some 4,000, and the schools were consolidated further.[3] This was due mainly to the reduction in the refugee population, although vocational training continued to be recognized both by refugees and by the Organization as an important aid to resettlement.

During this period, however, plans were accelerated for the winding up of the programme. Preparatory action included the disposal of surplus supplies and equipment as vocational training activities were consolidated into a few large centres, and preliminary negotiations with local governments for the possible transfer to them of responsibility for the schools so that vocational training might continue to be available to refugees after the demise of the IRO. The closure period for the programme occurred just at the time when major problems had largely been overcome and a high level of efficiency had been achieved—particularly in the French zone of Germany and in Austria, where the programme had developed more slowly. By June 1950 total enrolment in vocational training courses in Austria, Germany, and Italy had declined to some 3,900 from a maximum of about 16,000, but a limited programme was continued for an additional nine months until the final closure of the programme on 30 March 1951.

Vocational training developed gradually from an unorganized and largely unsupported activity in large numbers of scattered projects into an effective system of large consolidated centres under close supervision and control. The method of accelerated group training on a full-time basis in residential schools produced results even more satisfactory than had been expected in the development of skills. The excessive variety of courses which had existed at first was gradually reduced by eliminating subjects unrelated to resettlement, and the courses remaining were standardized to a high degree. The consolidation of training centres eased the problems of suitable accommodation, supply, and personnel; after the end of 1947 international staff concerned primarily with vocational training did not exceed twenty-five persons in all areas, and the programme was carried out chiefly by non-international staff, whose numbers were progressively reduced.

Apart from the cost of supplies and equipment, much of which was recovered

[1] Annex 30, p. 310.   [2] GC/100, op. cit.
[3] GC/166, Annual Report of the Director General to General Council, p. 44.

ultimately through disposal, the programme was relatively inexpensive. Many courses were virtually self-supporting through essential repair work and the manufacture of furniture and other things needed in assembly centres; proceeds from the sale of goods manufactured in vocational training classes either reverted to the Organization or provided needed funds for welfare purposes. As the result of strict safety measures including special instruction, safety guards on machinery, posters illustrating dangers, and protective clothing, an exceptionally low accident rate prevailed.

All students in vocational training centres were required to attend language classes as part of their curriculum. This connected with the IRO's wider policy of language instruction, and helped to overcome the problem of instructing classes where students understood different languages; as another step toward overcoming this language barrier, the Organization developed vocational language guides for eleven basic trades, listing some fifty technical terms for each trade in English, German, Polish, Spanish, and Russian.

C. REHABILITATION

From the outset refugees with physical handicaps were encouraged to attend vocational training classes if they were able to benefit from them. At all times, medical services for refugees with physical disabilities were available, but in the early days of the IRO, although certain voluntary societies attempted rehabilitation services on a small scale, no formal programme was organized to bring together special medical and occupational rehabilitation services for the numerous physically handicapped refugees. When the basic vocational training policy of the Organization was being determined in March 1948, the Health and Vocational Training Divisions were working on an extensive programme of medical and occupational rehabilitation.

With the progress of resettlement the Organization was faced with an increasing number of refugees considered ineligible for resettlement on the grounds of physical disability, or lack of vocational skill because of physical disability. It was also clear that rehabilitation would be a highly specialized task meriting the special efforts of staff trained in this field.

On the advice of two experts in this field, seconded to the IRO by the British Ministry of Health, a survey was made in Austria, Germany, and Italy in the late summer of 1948 to obtain estimates of the numbers of handicapped refugees, the nature of their disabilities, and the medical and training facilities and staff which might be available for rehabilitation and training centres. Medical rehabilitation boards, composed of medical and vocational training staff, were appointed to examine each disabled refugee in order to determine and report upon the precise nature of the disability and its relation to employability and to treatment.

Aim of the programme

The results of the survey indicated the scope and importance of this programme. In all, a total of almost 26,000 refugees were physically handicapped; almost half of them were victims of pulmonary tuberculosis. These handicapped refugees had more than 29,000 dependants among the refugees, producing a total of more than

55,000 persons directly affected by physical handicaps. Almost 60 per cent. of the disabled and almost 70 per cent. of the dependants were in the US zone of Germany. Of the total of disabled persons and dependants, 64 per cent. were in the US zone of Germany, 22 per cent. in the British zone of Germany, 12 per cent. in the French zone of Germany and in Austria, and 2 per cent. in Italy. It was estimated that between 7,000 and 8,000 of those classified as disabled could benefit from medical treatment and vocational training.[1]

The IRO rehabilitation programme, which officially came into being in the first days of February 1949 and lasted to September 1951, covered all categories of the disabled and had one goal, the re-establishment of the ability to be self-supporting. The process of rehabilitation included physical and psychological reconditioning, development of basic skills, and specific trade training. Residual ability was utilized to the fullest extent and this, coupled with determination and efficient training, produced numbers of skilled workers.[2]

The rehabilitation programme envisaged a maximum cost of $1,250,000 for its first year of operation. It was estimated that more than $800,000 would be required for equipping ten centres, one for tuberculous and one for the non-tuberculous in the area of each mission, and one special centre for the blind. The policy was that a disabled refugee should be included in the programme if he had good prospects of becoming employable. A disability was defined as 'an injury or condition which causes a substantial handicap to obtaining or keeping employment of a kind suited to the person's age, experience and qualifications'. It was expected that the programme would have an important effect in reducing the potential 'hard core', and in the long run might well pay for itself. Responsibility for the programme was to be shared co-operatively by the Divisions of Health, Welfare, Voluntary Societies, and Employment and Vocational Training, the last having primary responsibility for its implementation. After about a year primary responsibility was transferred to the Division of Health.

Rehabilitation centres

As with vocational training, rehabilitation became fully effective only when carried out in residential centres specially selected and equipped for this work.[3] It was important for health and psychological reasons that conditions in the centres should be good. With few exceptions, this was achieved, in spite of war-damaged buildings and other difficulties.

By November 1949 twenty centres were in use in Germany, Austria, and Italy; in addition, related occupational therapy and physiotherapy were carried out in hospitals and sanatoria. More than 130 separate courses were reported in some forty different subjects. Activities were generally most advanced in the US zone of Germany. In the British zone of Germany the programme was retarded by staff shortages, and in the French zone of Germany rehabilitation was confined to a single centre at Lindich. In Austria there was difficulty in obtaining local currency; and in Italy improvement was expected with the recruitment of needed staff.

[1] GC/60, op. cit., p. 28.   [2] IRO, *What is our Future*, Jan. 1951, p. 6.
[3] See Annex 30, p. 310.

Three months later, after the closure of peripheral activities, there were sixteen centres in operation with a total capacity of some 2,700, and more than 1,800 refugees enrolled.[1] By June 1950 twelve centres were being operated, serving about 2,000 refugees, and occupational therapy had been extended and improved in closer relationship with the courses in rehabilitation centres.[2] Attention was also being given to the problem of finding employment for refugees who had completed their training. The closure of the programme was accelerated during the year; by July 1951 rehabilitation activities had been consolidated into three centres, and by September 1951 the IRO's rehabilitation programme was closed.

Courses were designed for three groups of disabled people, the tubercular cases, the non-tubercular, and the blind in separate centres, each staffed by a medical consultant trained in medical rehabilitation, a nurse, a physiotherapist, a welfare officer, and a director of vocational training. In the US zone of Germany, where the rehabilitation programme was to be most extensive, a total of some twenty international personnel was approved for the programme; as in other programmes, rehabilitation work there and in other areas would be carried out largely by refugees and other local staff. While staff at headquarters was not increased for the programme, the two rehabilitation experts from the UK were retained as part-time medical consultants.

Initial difficulties were experienced in recruiting qualified international staff: at the end of six months the total recruited was only thirty-six out of sixty-three authorized positions. For most newly recruited personnel, as well as other key staff associated with the programme, training visits were arranged to established rehabilitation institutions in the UK. Visits were also made to a rehabilitation centre operated in the French zone of Germany for disabled French servicemen, and throughout the programme staff members were urged to exchange information and experience through visists to the IRO's rehabilitation centres outside of their areas.

Equipment was obtained mainly by the local centres, but a member of headquarters supply staff was responsible for speeding up supplies. The cost of equipping rehabilitation centres proved far lower than estimated because many of the materials were obtained from the vocational training programme, which was decreasing as the rehabilitation programme increased. Many needed supplies were also in warehouses. Total costs were reduced substantially by purchasing in the US zone of Germany against payment from the Blocked DM Account, but the lack of local currencies caused difficulties in other zones, as did the prescribed policy of requiring bids from at least three possible suppliers.

At the start, until the benefits of rehabilitation became clear, the refugees were generally reluctant to enter training centres. Many had lived with their disabilities for years and were uninterested in improving their condition. Others hesitated to leave whatever employment they might have obtained, and some even accepted work against medical advice rather than enter a rehabilitation centre. Others disliked the isolation of the centres, or were unwilling to leave their families. To counteract resistance to entering rehabilitation centres and to obtain sufficient applicants to

[1] See Annex 26, p. 305.
[2] GC/166, op. cit., p. 40.

keep the centres running at capacity, recruiting campaigns were conducted in the zones. A number of documentary and training films were obtained—mostly from Canada, the UK, and the US—which were shown to general refugee audiences, rehabilitation trainees, and staff concerned with the rehabilitation programme. Another measure was to transfer family members to camps readily accessible to the centres, but the difficulties of obtaining suitable accommodation defeated this; later it was found possible to admit limited numbers of families to the rehabilitation centres. Despite all efforts, few of the centres operated at capacity at any time.

In the British and French zones of Germany the occupation authorities were themselves responsible for the care of refugees in the rehabilitation centres, as they were for refugees in all other centres, but they did not control the technical phases of the rehabilitation programme. In centres jointly operated by the Organization and voluntary societies, all activities were required to meet the standards of the IRO which provided general direction, supervision, and control.

When the disability of a refugee had been identified by the tuberculosis or the rehabilitation board, which would indicate the treatment needed and the urgency of the case, the refugee would be counselled by welfare officers who would arrange for him to leave the assembly centre and enter the appropriate rehabilitation centre. The medical, vocational training, and welfare officers in the centre would then consider the case individually and jointly, and determine what treatment was required.

The aim was to provide vocational guidance for trainees before they reached the rehabilitation centre, so that occupational therapy could be adapted to their ultimate vocational training objectives. This responsibility was also regarded as continuous, inasmuch as either the health or the aptitude of a refugee might make it necessary at any time for him to change from one course of instruction to another. Group training was given to the greatest extent possible in vocational courses, but individual instruction was provided as required, particularly with respect to specific disabilities.

The responsibilities of the international staff of the rehabilitation centres were defined by their technical qualifications, but the emphasis at all times was on team-work; and operations were carried forward as much as possible by panel or team decision. The centre director, usually the senior staff member, was responsible for all aspects of administration and operation, including relations with voluntary societies and authorities involved. The medical officer was responsible for medical supervision of centre activities and particularly for the medical aspects of physical and mental rehabilitation. The public health nurse was responsible for supervision of clinical nursing care in addition to the more usual duties of public health nursing and health teaching, which included the instruction of trainees' families. The vocational training officer had the duties of establishing suitable training courses and assuring that vocational guidance was effective, and that medical and training aspects were closely co-ordinated at all times; he was also responsible for co-ordinating vocational training within the centre and outside occupational therapy. The welfare officer was responsible for all welfare activities within the centre; in addition to providing counselling services, this officer undertook to obtain needed assistance from voluntary societies, maintained case records, and sought to ensure that resettlement, employment, or any necessary additional training would be made available to trainees after they had left the centres.

It became evident that welfare problems were among the most important. Most of the centres were isolated and remote from cities. Many of the trainees were separated from close family members, and their health severely restricted their recreational activities; and many of them were eager to work for longer periods than their disability allowed. But generally morale was well maintained, thanks not only to the efforts of the staff of the centres but also to those of the voluntary societies, particularly the YMCA/YWCA, which provided extensive welfare and recreational services in several centres.

TB cases

Rehabilitation services were available for tubercular refugees for whom physical and mental rehabilitation as well as vocational training was needed in order to prepare them for employment in a suitable occupation. Among these were unskilled persons and others barred by the disease from employment in trades in which they were skilled. Persons had priority whose disease had been arrested for the longest period, and who were physically able to undertake the most hours of vocational training daily with their required medical treatment. As a minimum, persons were admitted whose condition was classified as quiescent and who had reached a minimum of three hours daily of work tolerance.

Upon admittance to the centre, the tubercular trainee was examined by the medical officer who decided the number of hours he might work at the start. From then on, his physical condition was scrutinized periodically. As his health improved he was permitted to work more hours daily until he was able to work a full day. Under this routine, it was estimated that TB trainees could accomplish in from six to nine months the same training as might be concluded by a fit person in three months.

Early in the programme the need was recognized for more and better occupational therapy. To aid development, experts from the Liverpool School of Occupational Therapy in the UK were called in as consultants. Subsequently this school supplied a number of qualified occupational therapists to develop the work in the IRO's hospitals in the US zone of Germany. A satisfactory programme was developed by the fully qualified occupational therapists when special equipment and adequate space had been found, when the new staff had become used to the unfamiliar conditions of work, and when smooth co-operation was effected with voluntary societies active in the programme. Occupational therapy services were concentrated chiefly in TB hospitals and sanatoria and, so far as possible, began as soon as the patient's health permitted. Although these services were of value also to patients unable to participate in the rehabilitation programme, they were particularly valuable as vocational guidance and pre-vocational training for courses to be pursued later in the rehabilitation centres. For this reason the trades taught in the occupational therapy classes included the main courses to be found in the tubercular rehabilitation centres: tailoring, dressmaking, leather work, watch repair and assembling radio, bookbinding, shoemaking, technical drawing, electrical work, and so on. To a large degree the formalized programme of occupational therapy achieved what was hoped for in assisting in the recovery of patients and equipping them to take full advantage of medical rehabilitation and vocational training.

The physically disabled

Originally the centres for non-tubercular disabled persons were concerned with reconditioning and physical therapy, with stress on the procurement of proper prostheses as required by occupational demands, and instruction and assistance in using them. Emphasis was placed on preparing non-TB trainees to take employment or to enter regular vocational training centres in the shortest possible time. As the regular vocational training programme was reduced, the rehabilitation services were continued as long as possible. Sufficient vocational training equipment and supplies for complete courses were brought into the rehabilitation centres. Except in unusual circumstances a stay of not more than six to nine weeks was adequate in non-TB rehabilitation centres. Admissions to the centres were almost exclusively cases of amputation, primarily because of the large numbers existing, but also because the services would have suffered by having to cover widely different types of disablement.

Great difficulties were encountered in obtaining suitable artificial limbs or prostheses. For the first year of the programme, needed prostheses were obtained mostly from local sources, but results proved most unsatisfactory. More than half were inadequate or were in need of repair or alteration. A large number of patients did not wear their prostheses because they did not fit properly; the medical officers of the IRO generally were not trained in this highly specialized field of limb fitting, and the task had been left to the manufacturers or suppliers of the prostheses. The Ministry of Pensions in London made an expert available to visit the rehabilitation centres. On the basis of his very helpful recommendations, an active prostheses programme was inaugurated. The full co-operation of the Ministry also made it possible for the Organization to send selected refugee medical officers to the UK for an intensive three weeks' course in limb fitting.

One of the early steps was to concentrate amputation cases in a few centres, the largest of which was at Neuburg in the US zone of Germany. At this centre a vocational training officer developed an ingenious prosthesis which combined the best features of known commercial products. Generally referred to as 'the Neuburg arm', this device was produced in sufficient quantities within the centre, largely by the trainees working in the regular vocational training shops. Later in the programme it was possible to transfer to this centre disabled cases from the other two zones of Germany. It was difficult to obtain proper prostheses in Austria and Italy, and many were manufactured in Germany from plaster casts.

An expert, made available by an outstanding manufacturer of artificial limbs in the UK, completed a tour of all centres to advise on requirements for special prostheses, which in certain cases were procured in the UK.

In addition to the special classes and facilities established for trainees in the use of prostheses, gymnasium and physical conditioning were a most important part of the training in the centres. Again, a qualified expert from the UK was retained as consultant and later employed to develop these activities under qualified remedial gymnasts; and an extensive programme of physiotherapy was also carried out by qualified personnel. Sports were an important part of these programmes and led to the development of basket ball and table tennis teams which were victorious over non-handicapped opponents. The morale and recovery of trainees was considerably aided by these activities.

The blind

Rehabilitation services for the blind constituted a more limited programme than was carried out for persons with other disabilities. In January 1949 it had been determined that among the refugees only 212 were totally blind and 427 partially blind; moreover, many of these, for senility or other reasons, could not be expected to benefit from rehabilitation. Services for the blind were consolidated in the British zone of Germany at Neustadt and in the US zone of Germany at Weyarn and later at Neuburg.

Inasmuch as relatively few of the blind trainees could be expected to find later employment except in sheltered conditions, training was given in the traditional handicrafts of pottery making, carpet weaving, broom and brush making, and basket work. Illiterate trainees were taught to read and write Braille. Some of the better educated trainees were given instructions in Braille typing, steno-typing, and shorthand. Others received instruction in type setting. A few trainees with previous experience as masseurs were aided in finding local employment, and in the British Red Cross, with assistance from German welfare authorities, conducted courses in elementary manual massage, for a number of trainees. So far as possible, blind instructors were utilized and certain of these were able to achieve excellent results, not only in classroom instruction but also in aiding the trainees to achieve a degree of physical and psychological independence. For all trainees, emphasis was placed on physical training, gymnastics, dancing, and training in walking under various conditions. Special classes were conducted in the use and care of a number of 'seeing eye' dogs which had been trained by the Bavarian Red Cross and supplied to selected trainees.

Resettlement opportunities

Aware that much or all of the benefits of rehabilitation would be lost if trainees were unable to progress further toward self-sufficiency, the programme early emphasized the need for developing opportunities of resettlement, local employment, or continued vocational training. But because of general unemployment, insurmountable trade union requirements and other factors, opportunities were limited for obtaining suitable employment where the suitable working conditions existed. So far as possible, trainees released from the centres were given priority in employment available with the Organization. But migration remained the major objective.

It was urged that disabled refugees should be brought to the notice of selection missions, and that requests for handicapped workers should be filled with persons rehabilitated by the Organization or in rehabilitation centres. The Resettlement Placement Service instructed all missions to register all disabled persons, and full dossiers were prepared for refugees with physical handicaps so that they might be adequately brought to the attention of potential employers. Publicity was also given to voluntary societies, and appeals made to give special consideration to displaced persons were particularly successful.

The US Committee for the Resettlement of the Physically Disabled, composed of prominent persons in the field of rehabilitation, in governmental and in charitable and private organizations, helped substantially to pave the way for the resettlement of disabled persons in the US. Agreements were concluded by the IRO with four of the major voluntary societies there—the National Catholic Welfare Conference, National Lutheran Council, United Service for New Americans, and Church World Service—and monetary grants made to expedite the resettlement of disabled refugees to the care of rehabilitation services in the US, in co-ordination with the International Society for the Welfare of Cripples in New York.

In the final days of the programme, when resettlement possibilities had been virtually exhausted, rehabilitation cases were referred direct to voluntary societies responsible for the residual group programmes. When the rehabilitation centres in the British zone of Germany were finally closed, a total of 330 persons were referred to the voluntary societies. Some 160 were received by one society which was interested in assisting them to set up a co-operative project; some thirty others were given work opportunities in newly built settlements where they were under the supervision of resident voluntary society welfare workers. Other cases were transferred to institutions where they received regular visits from representatives of voluntary societies who submitted monthly reports to the IRO.[1]

As with so many of its activities, the efforts of the IRO to rehabilitate refugees with physical disabilities was a combined operation with the voluntary societies. The World ORT Union was able to extend its activities to rehabilitation work. In Austria and the US zone of Germany this organization provided vocational training in rehabilitation centres established for Jewish trainees; in Italy ORT conducted vocational training for both Jewish and non-Jewish trainees. In addition to regular vocational training courses, ORT also conducted occupational therapy activities in TB hospitals in both Italy and Germany.

In another project, financially supported by the IRO, ORT provided vocational training to tubercular refugees in several localities in Switzerland; in this activity, supported by the Swiss authorities, the IRO also provided financial support for medical and other expenses incurred by OSE, a co-operating society.[2] Here, as in other areas, rehabilitation efforts on behalf of Jewish refugees received substantial financial support from the AJDC. In all agreements with ORT, the IRO had general direction of the programme according to its own standards. Other voluntary societies assisted in providing needed recreational and welfare services in the centres, particularly the World's YMCA/YWCA which provided even more extensive co-operation in the non-Jewish rehabilitation centre in Austria.

Apart from the programme carried out in Austria, Germany, and Italy, substantial rehabilitation projects were supported by the Organization in France. There, rehabilitation services were provided to refugees through cash grants to

---

[1] Chapter XXIII, Hard Core.
[2] Œuvres de Secours aux Enfants et de Protection de la Santé de la Population Juive.

various French voluntary societies which developed and carried on projects under agreement with the Organization. For the nine months' period after 1 July 1950, plans were made for rehabilitation services to 580 refugees, together with 150 family members, at a cost of slightly less than 100 million French francs.

In July 1950 the ECOSOC of the UN requested the Secretary General 'to plan jointly with the specialized agencies and in consultation with the interested non-governmental organizations a well co-ordinated international programme for the rehabilitation of physically handicapped persons'.[1] This action followed a meeting of specialized agencies which the UN had convened some four months earlier in Geneva to consider the rehabilitation of the physically handicapped. Participating in this meeting the IRO presented a statement describing in detail the activities of the Organization in the field of rehabilitation[2] and pointing out that its programme probably could not extend beyond March 1951.

A UN *ad hoc* technical working group on the rehabilitation of the disabled met in Geneva in December 1950, and at that time the Organization suggested that the UN or the specialized agencies might consider assuming responsibility for the technical direction of one or more of the IRO's rehabilitation centres to be operated as a demonstration or pilot centre. Alternatively the IRO suggested that it might furnish vocational training and medical equipment for a centre sponsored by the UN, to be located in some other country if considered necessary, also that it was prepared to make a contribution towards the initial administrative costs of such a centre;[3] this offer was later accepted. At the time of the meeting the Organization was the sole UN specialized agency with a programme of rehabilitation work in operation, while the other specialized agencies were limited to supplying technical advice in their special fields as requested by governments.

D. ORIENTATION

While the programme of vocational training and rehabilitation served only a small part of the total refugee population, the majority of the displaced persons needed information about their new homelands. Most of these people who had left their native countries for the first time were ignorant of conditions outside their own limited sphere of life and had not even heard the names of those countries which were offering them new homes. From the beginning the IRO was aware of the need of careful preparation for life in the reception countries. It developed a broad and intensified orientation programme with the assistance of voluntary societies and in co-operation with the governments of the receiving countries.

Language and literacy training was an integral part of these activities. Knowledge of the language of the new country was naturally highly important in the adaptation of the refugees. In fact for many, one of the greatest deterrents to resettlement was frequently that their linguistic knowledge was limited to Slavic languages, their

---

[1] Eleventh Session, Res. No. 309 E (XI).
[2] Statement of the IRO to the Meeting of Experts of the UN and the Specialized Agencies on Social Rehabilitation of the Disabled, Geneva, 27 Feb.–3 Mar. 1950.
[3] Statement submitted by the IRO to the First Session of the United Nations *ad hoc* Technical Working Group on Rehabilitation of the Disabled, 19 Dec. 1950.

mother tongue, and in addition perhaps to a little German or Italian which had become their common language for everyday use.

Language teaching

Thus at the beginning of 1948 the PCIRO considered the establishment of courses in language training and orientation in Germany, Austria, and Italy under qualified supervision.[1] As a result the Administration's first comprehensive order on language training was issued at the beginning of March 1948. In the following month the mission in the US zone of Germany was planning to provide language teaching in all schools and assembly centres, was recruiting staff to supervise it, and had arranged for 95,000 copies of a standard textbook to be printed. The same textbook was printed in large quantities in the British zone of Germany. Progress was hampered by the lack of qualified instructors and by the lack of a method of instruction that could be universally applied; but language training extended continually, and by the end of 1948 more than 29,000 persons were receiving more than two hours' instruction weekly. Six months later the total had risen to 38,000.[2] The majority of trainees were learning English, but many were studying French, Hebrew, Portuguese, and Spanish. As regards the training of teachers the IRO supported a special school established by the CWS in the US zone of Germany, schools were opened for teachers in English and Spanish in the British zone of Germany, and in Austria the *Berlitz* method was used.

Uniformity of method and improved training of teachers resulted from the introduction, in the spring of 1949, of the method of instruction by gramophone disks and related texts. This made a wide range of languages available, and the materials were easy to transport and could be used with large or small groups. Perhaps most important, the method did not require qualified teachers, but could be used effectively by the students themselves, usually under the direction of a fellow student with some instruction and practise in the use of the equipment. Students had the great advantage of hearing correct accents, and they responded to the recreational appeal of the method to the extent that enrolment in language training courses increased considerably and rapidly after the introduction of the system, despite the fact that the refugee population was diminishing.

Representatives of the equipment manufacturer, the Linguaphone Institute, visited all areas to demonstrate the method, assisting in the recruitment and preliminary training of group leaders, and providing expert consultation on the future development of the programme. These visits were continued throughout the programme. More than 1,000 separate sets of disks were purchased, and somewhat less than the 60,000 related texts which would have been required to equip fully each set in classes for twenty students. For these original sets it was later necessary to procure more than 30,000 additional replacement disks as the originals became worn, and additional textbooks and gramophone needles were needed.

The new method allowed language training to be accelerated in the British zone of Germany where the World's YMCA/YWCA was particularly helpful, and did much to develop the smaller programmes in Italy and in the French zone of Ger-

[1] PREP/177, Jan. 1948.   [2] GC/60 and GC/100.

many. Despite a high rate of movement for resettlement and for camp consolidations, the new method permitted the language training programme to attain its highest development during the twelve months from July 1949. There was a peak enrolment of more than 48,000 students which decreased to about 42,000 by June 1950 and enrolment increased from about 10 per cent. of the total population in assembly centres to approximately 25 per cent.[1] Of the 42,000 refugees enrolled, 28,000 were in the US zone of Germany, 12,000 in the British zone, and 600 in the French zone, 1,500 in Austria, and 800 in Italy.

The teaching of illiterates was another concern of World's YMCA/YWCA. In the British zone of Germany it conducted literacy courses for seventy-five different groups; in the US zone of Germany some 150 teachers were trained, and their activities were put in the charge of a recognized specialist. In Austria the IRO established, near Linz, a special assembly centre for illiterates, and it was found that excellent results could be obtained by three months' intensive work.

Orientation courses

The employment programme, vocational training, rehabilitation, and language courses were part of the general preparation of the refugees for a new life wherever they would settle. This preparation was called orientation. The IRO developed a broad orientation programme in co-operation with the governments and the collaboration of the voluntary societies. A general orientation was given to the refugees during the pre-selection period (before they had been selected for re-establishment in a specific location) to prepare them for a normal community life in new countries. Specific orientation was given to those who had been selected, preparing them for a life in a particular country of destination.

Carrying out the orientation programmes was mainly the responsibility of the governments of the receiving countries and of the voluntary societies. The IRO co-ordinated their orientation efforts within the areas of the IRO operation to ensure the best application of materials, personnel, funds, and to avoid duplications and omissions. This co-ordinating work was delegated to the Department of Health, Care, and Maintenance.

Orientation during the pre-selection period was chiefly concerned with adult education through language courses, vocational training, medical rehabilitation training, films, libraries, community activities, lectures, newspapers, periodicals, and radio programmes all designed to assist in re-orientating the refugees. The orientation during the post-selection period, which was given primarily at staging centres and on board ship and embarkation centres, laid emphasis on language training for the new country, information about the form of government, climate, housing, currency, cost of living, transportation, job seeking, educational facilities, trade unions, churches, and the history and physical geography of the reception country.

While expenses of specific programmes were normally paid by governments and voluntary societies, the IRO allocated a nominal sum from which allotment was

[1] GC/166, op. cit.

made for supplies and equipment necessary for the orientation programme and not made available by governments or voluntary agencies.

At the request of the IRO the World's YMCA/YWCA undertook the management and operation under the IRO direction of the language and literacy training programmes, and of the orientation programme in the three zones of Germany and Austria. In the spring of 1948 it initiated the orientation activities in the staging centre at Diepholz in the British zone of Germany, followed a little later by extensive programmes in the resettlement centres in the US zone and in Austria, and much later in Italy.

By the middle of 1950 an agreement was concluded between the IRO and the World's YMCA/YWCA whereby the IRO made a financial grant to the society, which undertook the management and operation of all orientation, language and literacy training in Germany, and orientation in Austria. In Austria the society took over from the IRO the management of language and literacy teaching on 1 April 1951.

During 1949 and 1950 the services of orientation and information for refugees were expanded in all areas to meet the great increase of resettlement opportunities offered and accepted.

Orientation work, an integral part of the resettlement programme, was directed chiefly to refugees going to Australia, Canada, the US, and South American countries.[1]

Orientation for Israel was actively carried out by Jewish voluntary societies, and the activities of the IRO were confined to facilitating language-training in Hebrew.

Without adequate information and orientation no selection schemes of these countries could be fully successful. Information was given about the conditions under which refugees would be accepted, about housing and education in the countries of reception, the possibilities of changing employment, and of being able to nominate dependants or friends after they had settled down; about price levels of consumer goods as compared with their earnings and other information supplied by the respective governments. The history and customs of the country and its political structure and practices were explained to the prospective settlers. Literature, visual aids like films, posters, travel folders, and maps were provided by Australia, the US, to a lesser degree by New Zealand, Canada, Brazil, and Venezuela. Similar material was obtained through the UN and the American Red Cross, and voluntary societies. Lectures were given by the personnel of voluntary societies and by members of selection missions and officials of the Organization and followed up by discussion groups and exhibits.

As with language teaching, orientation did not end with embarkation. Extensive orientation activities were carried out on board ship, and on several occasions on long rail journeys; it was continued in the reception countries.[2]

The means developed in Austria for the orientation of refugees towards resettlement were interesting in that they depended more than elsewhere on the IRO's

---

[1] GC/100, op. cit., p. 26.

[2] H. B. M. Murphy, 'The Assimilation of Refugee Immigrants in Australia', *Population Studies*, vol. 3, Mar. 1952, p. 188.

own staff which administered the programme as a combined operation involving several units. In 1947 initial efforts were made locally to provide refugees with the information they were requesting about conditions in their prospective countries of resettlement. The offices in the British and French zones of Austria published mimeographed and, later, printed news bulletins. These contained current news about the IRO, information about resettlement countries, and extracts of letters received from displaced persons who had already been resettled. Information centres were opened and stocked with booklets and posters as part of a general campaign for registration, counselling, and resettlement. These centres, which were not only in assembly centres, were important because about half of the refugees within the IRO's mandate in Austria did not live in assembly centres.

Voluntary societies, especially the World's YMCA/YWCA, showed considerable interest in this undertaking and in the orientation of refugees already selected by resettlement missions. Each assembly centre in Austria was provided with an attractive World's YMCA/YWCA information board and World's YMCA/YWCA workers in camps and transit centres gave lectures and distributed material. In July 1949 a special Resettlement Information Service was created at the IRO's mission headquarters in Vienna to co-ordinate production and distribution of such information material throughout Austria. Its task was to centralize and increase the local supply of information, to obtain additional material from outside sources, and to ensure an adequate distribution throughout Austria.

This service supplemented general publicity by means of a *Nachrichtenblatt* and by widely distributed leaflets, maps, and posters. Special broadcasts were arranged by the IRO; the local press and radio co-operated whole-heartedly. Of the outside sources, the Australian Information Attaché, the Canadian Mission, and the various consulates, as well as the Geneva headquarters, assisted the Resettlement Information Service to obtain material on practically every subject which was likely to interest refugees about to be resettled. In each area one resettlement officer was entrusted with information functions. His task was primarily to ensure distribution of the *Nachrichtenblatt* and other communications to refugees in his area. All means were employed: distribution through national groups, voluntary societies, counselling teams of the IRO, Austrian services, and normal postal facilities. Up to the end of operations, letters sent off by refugees already resettled to officials of the IRO or to refugee friends still in Austria were published and proved to be one of the best means of winning the confidence of those who still hesitated to emigrate.

While most resettlement countries were interested in orientation, supplying informative material, and arranging for members of selection teams and other nationals to give lectures to refugees, the most generous in terms of funds and staff were Australia and the US.

Australian scheme

Australia was the only country which, from the beginning, conducted its own orientation work. An Australian educationalist was sent to Italy, where there was a staging centre for all migrants going to Australia, to organize and develop orientation services for refugees. The policy adopted by Australia that the work contract would be reduced substantially from the usual two years' period for certain refugees who had a good knowledge of the English language and who were able to fit rapidly into their new way of life gave impetus to the programme. Australia also accepted for resettlement refugees willing to serve as language instructors for three months and during the sea trip to Australia, under the arrangement that their work contract would be reduced by a period of three months. To implement this arrangement and to assist Australia in obtaining the necessary teachers, the Organization arranged for the payment of as many as thirty teachers at a time on a three months' rotation system. The Australian programme, which was begun in staging centres, was noteworthy in that it was continued on board ship and later in the reception camps in Australia.[1] Activities were well established by the middle of 1949 and were extended and improved when the whole programme was transferred with the Australian embarkation point to the Bremen area a year later. At the height of the programme, several Australian education officers were working in Germany and others were serving on board ship. More than 90 per cent. of all refugees going to Australia were enrolled for this exceptionally successful programme and at times there were as many as 5,000 students in some 175 classes.

United States scheme

The US Displaced Persons Commission which began its formal operations by 27 August 1948 and completed its regular programme activities by 30 June 1952 included orientation as an important part of its resettlement operations. Orientation for the US had started early in scattered activities, conducted mainly by: the American Friends Service Committee, the American Red Cross, and the World's YMCA/YWCA. But only the first society directed its efforts entirely to the orientation of settlers destined for the US. The voluntary agencies, both in Europe and in the US (the American Council of Voluntary Agencies for Foreign Service) requested the Commission to establish an education service on behalf of displaced persons, because 'it was generally recognized by all who participated in the programme that orientation programmes promoted by specialized agencies, whether sectarian or international, had not developed a programme suitable to the total national needs of the United States'.[2]

Though it began early in 1949, the orientation programme under the Commission's leadership did not fully develop until 1950. The Commission was then required to:

Disseminate among persons selected by the Commission through orientation courses, lectures, films, and other appropriate means, facts and data concerning the history, customs, traditions, and geography of the United States, better to enable such persons to understand the obligations they assume under the Act and to become adjusted to life in the United States, and seek the co-operation of public and private agencies to achieve this object.[3]

Under a director of orientation with headquarters in Frankfurt, supported by

[1] Murphy, op. cit.; Wolfgang G. Friedmann, *German Immigration into Canada*, Toronto, 1952, p. 36; V. C. Phelan, 'Organization of Migration into Canada', *International Labour Review*, lxv, 3 Mar. 1952.
[2] *The DP Story*. The Final Report of the US Displaced Persons Commission, Washington, 1952, p. 201.   [3] Ibid., p. 202.

a staff officer in each of the ten primary resettlement centres, the Commission set up an orientation programme throughout Germany, Austria, and Italy. Each of the ten orientation units operated in co-operation with a central steering committee composed of representatives from World's YMCA/YWCA, ARC, IRO, HICOG, and the American Voluntary Agencies.

The Commission emphasized in its report that while this project suffered from delay and limited scope, a full and vigorously operated orientation programme would benefit not only the new-comer personally but also the community to which he was coming and the country as a whole.[1]

Resettlement of specialists

Experience showed that the resettlement of highly qualified specialists could not be successfully carried out through the ordinary channels but required an individual approach. A Resettlement Placement Service was organized in October 1949 to assist business enterprises and interested persons all over the world by putting them in contact with the 'refugee specialists'. These included 15,000 highly trained men and women, qualified practitioners of all the arts, sciences, and professions. Under the new programme six special representatives were appointed to cover wide areas of the world and approach governments and public and private organizations, on the basis of special individual dossiers, in order to find individual opportunities for resettlement. The UN specialized agencies, particularly UNESCO, WHO, and ILO, were of great assistance in this programme. Publicity was given to the problem of specialists in an effort to arouse public interest. For that purpose *The Forgotten Élite, the Story of Refugee Specialists* was published in January 1950, presenting some case-histories of individual specialists and calling upon individuals in overseas countries to sponsor this work, 'While the process of finding a particular job for each refugee belonging to the "difficult" groups is slow, the response from many countries was encouraging and the effort proved to be worthwhile'.[2]

Among the professional trained refugees were also a large number of qualified and para-medical personnel for which a special screening and identification procedure was established. By September 1948 screening boards had established qualifications in regard to 2,560 physicians working in camps, hospitals, and administrative appointments. Included in the group were 40 persons of professional status, 15 of associate professional status, and 26 with the former standing of lecturers in universities. Several, before the war, had held fellowship appointments for study abroad, and were thus internationally known. Age groupings were:

20–25 years	.	.	.	.	29
26–35 ,,	.	.	.	.	692
36–45 ,,	.	.	.	.	840
46–55 ,,	.	.	.	.	696
56–65 ,,	.	.	.	.	253
Over 65 years	.	.	.		50
TOTAL	.	.	.	.	2,560

[1] Ibid., p. 205.
[2] E/1675, 2 May 1950, Second Report of the IRO to ECOSOC, Eleventh Session, p. 25. See Annex 31, p. 310.

To evaluate the findings of these special boards, attention must be drawn to the procedure of these bodies. The presidents of the boards of the British and the US zones both were former professors of medicine, respectively of the Baltic University at Riga and the Hungarian University at Sneged. University rules and curricula in all European countries were carefully studied for the determination of qualifications. The applicant was required to attend in person the screening by the board, presenting proof of identity and of qualifications and production of diploma in original or photostats. Reference to former medical registers and affidavits by former teachers or fellow graduates of known integrity were used. When the authentic original diploma did not exist, candidates were subject to examination, including clinical examination for specialists, by the entire board. When qualifications were verified, a certificate of professional status was issued. These registered refugee physicians were possessed of all the qualifications and experience required by any country.[1] However, little disposition was shown to open national doors to refugee physicians. The various national laws governing registration and right to practise in a community restrict such privileges to graduates of recognized schools. It was the IRO's earnest hope, however, that to alleviate the distress immediately following the war, and to ensure the efficient use of available medical personnel, some relaxation of conditions governing medical practice by foreign physicians might have proved possible. A memorandum outlining the problem was presented by the IRO to the Fourth Meeting of the Interim Commission of the WHO in September 1947. A resolution was subsequently adopted requesting governments to consider this question and to indicate the conditions under which foreign doctors and dentists could be admitted to practise. The response was disappointing. Although a few opportunities were offered for resettlement in professional practice (a Pakistani scheme for army medical officers; US requirements for the Pacific Islands; Norway's offer to absorb dentists) the majority of physicians emigrated under labour schemes or by nomination to the US. There, requirements for registration varied in different states: the qualification might be full citizenship, the taking out of first papers, performance of an internship, undergoing 'further training', or an examination after a period of one year. In spite of language difficulties, many refugees were highly successful, and today occupy an honourable place in the US medical world.

For doctors remaining in Germany, the text of the German Federal law governing the rights of displaced persons grants permission to practise medicine on the same terms as Germans, provided the candidate is a graduate of a German university or of a foreign medical school recognized as possessing equivalent status. As recognition of foreign schools is accorded in each *Land* separately, by the local medical authorities, claims are in effect decided individually.

[1] IRO Displaced Persons Professional Medical Register, compiled by Health Division Headquarters, Geneva, 421 pp.

ANNEX 26

Occupational skills of refugees in Austria, Germany, and Italy

Major occupational groups, March 1948

Major occupational group	Total	Totals		Polish		Baltic countries		Ukrainian		Other non-Jewish		Jewish	
		Men	Women	Men	Women	Men	Women	Men	Women	Men	Women	Men	Women
TOTAL . . .	340,478	226,690	113,788	55,440	25,581	49,363	32,484	33,613	15,112	32,888	11,654	55,386	28,957
Professional and managerial	43,547	28,970	14,577	3,537	1,812	11,273	6,680	4,289	1,965	5,111	1,835	4,760	2,285
Professional . .	30,437	19,970	10,640	2,337	1,128	8,087	5,053	3,316	1,499	3,473	1,426	2,584	1,534
Semi-professional .	7,126	4,137	2,989	488	571	1,295	1,190	591	376	949	317	814	535
Managerial and official	5,984	5,036	948	712	113	1,891	437	382	90	689	92	1,362	216
Clerical and sales . .	20,953	11,289	9,664	1,850	1,453	3,650	4,330	1,030	626	1,752	943	3,007	2,312
Service . . .	26,449	6,313	20,136	1,332	4,823	1,221	8,256	620	2,536	1,362	2,041	1,778	2,480
Domestic service .	14,339	250	14,089	39	3,297	86	6,387	30	1,768	51	1,252	44	1,385
Personal service .	10,781	4,804	5,977	1,018	1,522	770	1,854	566	768	945	787	1,505	1,046
Protective service .	1,329	1,259	70	275	4	365	15	24	..	366	2	229	49
Agricultural, fishery, forestry, and kindred occupations .	75,964	57,351	18,613	21,072	8,567	11,414	3,165	11,797	4,468	9,661	1,656	3,407	757
Skilled . . .	98,192	76,609	21,583	16,836	3,712	13,229	5,071	10,462	2,600	9,669	2,040	26,413	8,160
Manufacturing . .	64,911	43,881	21,030	8,318	3,514	6,485	4,964	5,802	2,549	4,889	1,964	18,387	8,039
Non-manufacturing .	33,281	32,728	553	8,518	198	6,744	107	4,660	51	4,780	76	8,026	121
Semi-skilled . .	18,750	15,668	3,082	3,724	409	3,771	682	2,364	181	1,967	161	3,842	1,649
Apprentices . .	4,997	3,771	1,226	335	74	549	174	278	85	353	122	2,256	771
Helpers . . .	2,722	1,824	898	671	380	277	105	341	154	268	52	267	207
Labourers . . .	10,647	6,816	3,831	1,400	390	600	535	450	213	881	316	3,485	2,377
No previous work experience .	38,257	18,079	20,178	4,683	3,961	3,379	3,486	1,982	2,284	1,864	2,488	6,171	7,959

ANNEX 27

Occupational skills of refugees

An investigation carried out in March 1948 to assess the occupational skills of refugees was completed among 597,000 persons receiving assistance in Germany, Austria, and Italy—at that time the total number of refugees receiving assistance amounted to 630,000. In this computation no refugee falling in one of the following categories was included: persons under 16 or over 65 years; those who were either in transit camps or hospitalized; mothers with children under 12. After these conclusions 340,478 were classified. The major occupational groups were as follows:

	Men	Percentage	Women	Percentage
TOTAL.	226,690	100·0	113,788	100·0
Professional and managerial .	28,970	12·8	14,577	12·8
Clerical and sales . . .	11,289	5·0	9,664	8·5
Service	6,313	2·8	20,136	17·7
Agriculture	57,351	25·3	18,613	16·3
Skilled	76,609	33·8	21,583	19·0
Semi-skilled	19,439	8·5	4,308	3·8
Others	26,719	11·8	24,907	21·9

Men refugees represented two-thirds of this great potential labour force, and exceeded the number of women in all broad classifications except service (domestic and personal).

A more even distribution of skills among women was noted in the survey. While men were concentrated chiefly in the skilled and agriculture occupations, women workers were more uniformly distributed among skilled, agricultural, professional, and service occupations.

The 'other' group, which comprised helpers, labourers, and those persons without previous work experience, was proportionately larger for women than for men because 18 per cent. of the women classified were previously inexperienced, compared with only 8 per cent. of the men.

1. Of the total of 340,478 refugees classified, 43,547 had occupations in professional or managerial grades. Teachers represented the largest single group among the professionals—3,079 men and 2,880 women. Other professions in which many men refugees were found included:

Accountants	1,950
Agronomists	1,423
Lawyers	1,283
Physicians and Surgeons . .	1,150
Clergymen	1,119
Civil engineers . . .	1,089
Foresters	1,021
Musicians	938

There were, in addition, 3,116 business managers and executives and 602 office managers. Photographers, surveyors, and draughtsmen were heavily represented among the semi-professional group.

One-third of all the refugees classed as professional were women, and the majority of these were teachers or nurses. There were in all 2,566 nurses, half of them of Baltic origin. Other professions in which many women refugees were experienced include: accountant child-care worker, dentist, pharmacist, and physician.

2. One-third of all male refugees and almost one-fifth of the women refugees who were classified were skilled workers. There were 7,057 men and 12,502 women in the category of tailor or seamstress alone. There were in all 11,278 men and 18,359 women classified in the clothing and textile industries.

Among other skilled categories in which there were significant numbers of men refugees were:

Shoemaker, shoe repairman	7,607
Carpenter	5,664
Auto and truck mechanic, repairman . .	5,315
Electrician.	3,500
Butcher	2,969
Baker	2,523
Painter	1,862
Bricklayer	1,830

Skilled construction workers included, besides the specialized classifications shown above, plumbers, steamfitters, stonemasons, and plasterers.

3. Among the refugees were over 70,000 farmers and farmhands (men and women). Farming was, by far, the most important single occupation of male refugees and the third most important for women.

There were significant numbers of farmers in every major national or ethnic group, although Poles were most heavily represented in the total. Of the 75,964 refugees classified in agriculture, fishery, forestry, or kindred occupations, 39 per cent. were Polish, 21 per cent. Ukrainian, 19 per cent. from the Baltic countries, 15 per cent. other non-Jewish, and 6 per cent. Jewish.

In addition to the three leading occupational groups (professional, agricultural, and skilled), there were considerable numbers of refugees in clerical, service, semi-skilled, and unskilled classifications. Of these latter, service categories included the largest number, as there were 14,089 women in domestic service alone. Domestic and personal service together accounted for about 18 per cent. of all employable women refugees. In contrast, only 3 per cent. of the men refugees were in service classifications.

Included in clerical and sales classifications were clerks, book-keepers, and salesmen, comprising only 6 per cent. of all who were classified.

The semi-skilled and apprentices who represented about 7 per cent. of the total employables were principally truck drivers. Helpers and other labourers accounted for another 4 per cent. The remaining 11 per cent. comprised 18,079 men and 20,178 women who had had no previous work experience. These were not necessarily unemployable, but persons who by reason of age or background had not until then been employed.

The classification of occupations according to the country of citizenship, last habitual residence, or ethnic group of the refugees revealed marked differences in the kinds of skills possessed by refugees of different origins. Jewish refugees were predominantly skilled workers. The exceptionally high proportion (48 per cent.) of Jewish men in this category was supported by an unusually large proportion (28 per cent.) of women workers as well. Relatively few Jewish refugees, on the other hand, were agricultural workers (6 per cent.) or professional and managerial.

The largest numbers of professionals were of Baltic origin. More than one-fifth of all refugees from Baltic countries who were classified were in the category professional and managerial. The number of clerical workers was also higher among these refugees than other groups. There were correspondingly fewer farmers and skilled workers. Among women from Baltic countries, the largest numbers were in domestic and personal service.

Polish and Ukrainian refugees indicated a fairly similar occupational distribution.

Approximately two-thirds of the men were in skilled or agricultural occupations. Relatively more of the refugees of Ukrainian origin were professionals; the proportion of Polish men and women in professional classification was the lowest of any group.

In January 1950 another investigation was carried out on the same basis covering 132,210 classified workers who with their families constituted a group of about 245,000 refugees in IRO camps or receiving the IRO cash assistance outside camps in Austria, Germany, and Italy who were available for resettlement. An additional number of nearly 100,000 supporting themselves outside camps were also seeking new homes.

The 132,210 classified refugees were about 59 per cent. of the number receiving the IRO care and maintenance on the date of the study. Of the 41 per cent. not classified, 14 per cent. were in transit or embarkation centres, 4 per cent. hospitalized, and 31 per cent. either not within the defined age limits or mothers with children under 12 years of age.

These 345,000 refugees, counting workers and family members, included about 86,000 refugees in agricultural families, 90,000 in families of workers skilled in industry, and about 38,000 in families of professional and managerial workers.

ANNEX 28

Refugees and indigenous staff employed by IRO at specific dates

	31 Dec. 1950		31 Dec. 1951		29 Feb. 1952	
	Refugee	*Indigenous*	*Refugee*	*Indigenous*	*Refugee*	*Indigenous*
TOTAL . .	*13,785*	*7,196*	*5,508*	*4,554*	600	..
Austria* . .	482	..	..	..	..	..
Denmark* . .	60	..	..	..	..	..
Germany:†. .	*10,546*	7,196	4,263	4,554	..	..
British zone .	307	1,330	272	1,423	..	..
French zone .	157	234	79	172	..	..
US zone . .	9,881	4,843	3,912	2,959	..	..
ITS . .	201	789	..	..	..	..
Greece* . .	25	..	25	..	..	..
Italy* . . .	2,322	..	1,190	..	600	..
Philippines* .	350	..	30	..	..	..

* Refugee labour paid by the IRO.
† Refugee labour not paid by the IRO (paid from Deutschmark budgets).

ANNEX 29

Employment and vocational training of refugees in Austria, Germany, and Italy

	Number of refugees employed					Numbers in vocational training	Total employed and in vocational training	Percentage of care and maintenance population employed and in vocational training	Numbers receiving language training
	By IRO administrative functions	Work projects	By occupying authority	By other employers	Self-employed				
January 1949	53,710	3,987	14,737	20,389	5,428	11,417	109,668	23·0	31,293
Austria	3,486	384	690	3,288	317	1,232	9,397	28·7	2,331
Germany: British zone	13,450	..	7,321	7,890	434	3,660	32,755	22·2	10,622
French zone	267	..	2,421	6,255	1,189	489	10,621	30·9	983
US zone	34,064	3,412	4,305	2,823	3,379	5,304	53,287	21·7	16,436
Italy	2,443	191	..	133	109	732	3,608	22·4	921
June 1949	45,375	2,778	9,906	12,801	3,161	9,661	83,682	22·2	38,483
Austria	2,405	653	1,985	1,793	259	1,030	8,125	28·7	3,009
Germany: British zone	9,831	..	4,040	4,028	327	3,175	21,401	17·3	14,438
French zone	2,044	..	506	4,531	652	302	8,035	39·4	723
US zone	27,506	1,880	3,375	2,356	1,849	4,427	41,393	22·8	19,218
Italy	3,589	245	..	93	74	727	4,728	20·0	1,095
January 1950	30,692	1,486	5,732	6,671	1,752	6,590	52,923	20·1	45,019
Austria	2,042	400	1,660	1,409	265	1,214	6,990	34·0	2,922
Germany: British zone	5,898	..	2,128	2,165	204	1,827	12,222	14·0	17,600
French zone	1,060	..	142	1,327	207	602	3,338	25·0	899
US zone	18,397	1,024	1,802	1,751	1,037	1,998	26,009	21·8	22,551
Italy	3,295	62	..	19	39	949	4,364	18·3	1,047
June 1950	18,100	540	3,293	4,196	828	3,937	30,894	14·7	42,635
Austria	1,505	380	989	1,329	205	842	5,250	31·0	1,412
Germany: British zone	3,223	..	1,239	1,347	149	175	6,133	0·8	12,029
French zone	641	..	10	306	28	470	1,455	21·8	573
US zone	10,343	160	1,055	1,159	427	2,267	15,411	16·4	27,800
Italy	2,388	..	..	55	19	183	2,645	16·6	821

ANNEX 30

IRO rehabilitation centres

Location	Trainees	Enrolment 31 Jan. 1950	Training capacity
TOTAL		1,840	2,695
Italy		352	378
Pagani*	TB and non-TB	232	235
Grottaferrata†	TB	120	143
Austria		161	400
Ried‡	TB and non-TB	27	200
Ebelsberg†	TB and non-TB	134	200
Germany			
French zone		113	192
Lindich	TB and non-TB	113	192
British zone		439	600
Eversburg	Non-TB	300	400
Warta	TB	139	200
US zone		655	1,005
Neuberg	Non-TB	140	150
Weyarn	Blind	43	80
Aschau†	Non-TB	39	150
Luttensee	TB	148	250
Lauf	TB	40	80
Wartemburg	TB	83	95
Bayrisch-Gmain† . . .	TB	105	120
Esslingen†	TB	57	80
Switzerland		120	120
Montana§	TB	120	120

* Operated in co-operation with ORT.   † Operated in co-operation with AJDC.
‡ Operated in co-operation with World's YMCA/YWCA.
§ Operated in co-operation with OSE and ORT.

ANNEX 31

Resettlement of specialists by countries of destination

Statistical Report, 6 October 1950

	Employment and sponsorship offers received by RPS Geneva	No. of candidates accepted: family heads	Family members
	Summary		
Australia	3	..	..
Canada	54	86	171
New Zealand . . .	81	3	12
Europe	810	409	704
Africa	208	145	263
Asia	216	54	127
Latin America . . .	457	185	362
US	90	122	261
Trust Territories . . .	21	27	66
GRAND TOTAL . . .	1,940	1,031	1,966

CHAPTER XVII

LEGAL AND POLITICAL PROTECTION[1]

The disabilities of refugees

THE refugee is a stateless person, either *de facto* or *de jure*: *de facto* when he has retained his nationality but is not granted protection and assistance by his country of nationality, or, as a displaced person, is not willing to avail himself of the protection of the government of his country of origin; *de jure* when his country of origin has deprived him of his nationality.[2] The refugee, in either case, is thus a person who does not enjoy the protection of a government, a person who has no consul or diplomatic mission to whom to turn, and who does not benefit from reciprocal agreements between countries maintaining friendly relations which protect the nationals of one country living on the territory of another. A refugee is therefore most often confronted with serious legal disabilities at the very time when he is destitute and homeless. In short, he finds himself in a legal and political vacuum.

IRO's function as defined in the Constitution

The IRO, by virtue of Article 2 of its Constitution, was to give all refugees within its mandate legal and political protection. This protection was guaranteed by Article 4 which stipulated the general support the member governments were to give the work of the Organization. Moreover, according to Article 13, the Organization was to enjoy, in the territory of each of its members, such legal capacity as was necessary for the exercise of its functions and the fulfilment of its objectives. IRO had a position somewhat similar to a diplomatic representation and could exercise its rights to initiate protective measures as far as they were laid down in the Constitution.[3]

When, in May 1947, PCIRO made preparations to take over the functions of IGCR, its immediate policy was determined as follows:[4] (1) to ensure the smooth transfer of the protective services for Nansen refugees, refugees coming from Germany and Austria, and Spanish Republican refugees in France, then entrusted to IGCR; (2) to secure the extension of protective services to refugees and displaced persons in Austria and Germany, for whom local arrangements had been made by the occupation authorities; (3) to arrange for necessary consultations and surveys in order to facilitate the early assumption of its protective functions regarding

---

[1] Gustav Kullman, Legal Adviser IRO, 'Problems and Prospects in Legal and Political Protection' in GC/60, Annex, op. cit., p. 12. Paul Weis, Legal Adviser, Office of the UNHCR, 'The International Protection of Refugees', *American Journal of International Law*, vol. 48, no. 2, Apr. 1954, pp. 193–221.

[2] UN Dep. of Social Affairs, *A Study of Statelessness* (UN Publications, 1949, XIV, 2), p. 9; cf. Constitution of the IRO, Annex I, First Part, Section A.2: The term 'refugee ... applies to a person ... who ... is unable or unwilling to avail himself of the protection of the Government of his country of nationality or former nationality'.

[3] Cf. UN Convention on the Privileges and Immunities of the Specialized Agencies.

[4] PREP, Res. 18, May 1947, cf. Appendix III, p. 692, and PREP/90/Rev. 1, 22 May 1947, p. 16.

the categories of refugees other than those benefiting from the protection of the IGCR, and those staying in Germany, Austria, and Italy.

At the same time some members of the PCIRO stressed the desirability of changing the phrase in the Constitution 'legal and political protection' into some other phrase such as 'legal and other protection'. In the opinion of these members the former term seemed to imply a political activity.[1] The Commission directed the Executive Committee to submit to the First Session of the General Council proposals for the modification of the phrase, with a view to facilitating a possible amendment, according to the procedure laid down in Article 16, of Article 2, 1 of the Constitution relating to protection. In his statement[2] the Executive Secretary, however, proposed that the term 'legal and political protection' should be retained, because 'this expression does not cover two different kinds of protection . . .'. Referring to the Report by the Secretary General of the League of Nations on the future organization of refugee work,[3] he emphasized that legal and political protection had been regarded as one indivisible function.

It is one single form of protection, which is both legal and political in character. It is legal in so far as its object is to safeguard the rights and legitimate interests of refugees, and in particular to provide for, observe and regulate the application of existing agreements on the legal status of refugees; to provide, if necessary, for their revision; to supervise their day-to-day application in particular cases; to provide, if necessary, for the conclusion of new agreements; and to exercise quasi-consular functions . . . this (legal) protection is at the same time of a political nature, in that it implies relations with the Government.

On the basis of the proposal made by the Executive Secretary, the PCIRO decided not to amend the Constitution 'for a mere question of terminology, since in such cases a sound interpretation of the Constitution' was 'sufficient to ensure that its basic principles were respected, in accordance with the directives to be drawn up by the General Council'.[4]

However, in 1950, when this function of the IRO was transferred to the UNHCR, the term 'international protection' replaced the term 'legal and political protection' in the Statute of the Office of the UNHCR.[5]

Legal and political protection under IRO

The protective measures carried out by IRO aimed at preventing discrimination against refugees and at ensuring that refugees were granted economic and social rights and freedom of movement within and outside their country of residence.[6] Accordingly, two kinds of measures were adopted to guarantee a legal status which would place refugees above the normal status of stateless persons and at least mitigate the disabilities which the condition of statelessness involved; and to

---

[1] PREP, Res. 18, 21 May 1947.

[2] PREP/226, May 1948.

[3] League of Nations, A.28, 1930, XIII, p. 5: '. . . this function of the League of Nations is to a great extent political, in that it implies relations maintained in its name with Governments and their competent departments for the purpose of applying international agreements initiated by the League. . . .'

[4] PREP, Res. 89 (PREP/240, p. 9).

[5] UN, General Assembly 428 (V), 14 Dec. 1950, and Annex (chap. ii, Article 8).

[6] IRO *Operational Manual*, p. 6.

guarantee international and national recognition of human rights as far as they affected refugees, particularly the right of asylum, the right of the individual to have a nationality, and the right of immigration.

Of paramount concern to the IRO, in providing refugees with a status recognized by the authorities of the countries giving them asylum, was the determination of eligibility which has been described elsewhere.[1] This constituted the first and essential element of legal protection as required by the IRO Constitution.

The process of determination of eligibility, i.e. of establishing the identity of a person as a refugee and of deciding whether or not he came within the mandate of the IRO, had a dual effect: it conferred upon the refugee the status of a person who was the concern of the IRO (a 'United Nations protected person'), and it imposed upon the Organization the obligation to extend to him such legal and political protection as it was in a position to give. While other functions of the Organization, such as care and maintenance, repatriation and resettlement, as has been pointed out earlier, were carried out at the discretion of the Organization and depended upon the determination of admissibility to services, legal and political protection had to be granted automatically to every person eligible under the Constitution of the IRO.

By and large the legal and political protection granted by IRO was a fundamental function in that, by safeguarding the most essential rights of human beings and by facilitating material, cultural, and moral assimilation, it ultimately led to the acquisition by the refugee of a new nationality.

The so-called eligibility certification of the identity of a refugee and his status, verifying the fact that he was a refugee under the protection of the IRO, became increasingly important under the conditions prevailing during the life of the Organization.

For example, in Italy refugees entering the country illegally were put into 'collecting centres', but were released and their status in Italy regularized upon individual certification by the Organization. In France and Luxembourg a similar certificate of eligibility was required before a residence or work permit could be obtained. In Germany such a certification was necessary if the refugee was to enjoy the rights and benefits accorded to non-German refugees under the Federal Law concerning the Status of Homeless Aliens and under the Law No. 23 of the Allied High Commission. In other countries where fewer persons had sought refuge, e.g. in Turkey, residence was permitted after the IRO representative in the country had certified that they came within the mandate of the Organization; and in a number of countries the eligibility certificate was a prerequisite for the issue of a travel document under the Convention of October 1946.

Admission and the grant of asylum

The first problem, both in time and importance, facing an organization protecting the interests of refugees, is to ensure that governments are willing to give them asylum. On the one hand, it is the sovereign right of every state to decide whether or not a foreigner shall be admitted to its territory; on the other hand, in accordance

---

[1] Cf. Chapter XII, Eligibility, p. 203.

with an old tradition, asylum should be granted to persons who have valid reasons for seeking it.

The right of asylum was vehemently discussed at length during the deliberations of the Third Committee of the First Session of the General Assembly in 1946. The Belgian delegate, representing the point of view of most of the non-Soviet bloc powers, stated that 'the right of sanctuary represents a slow and lengthy conquest in human progress. It took centuries to obtain and safeguard this right, and even now it only exists to a more or less relative degree. . . .' 'The right of sanctuary is an integral part of what is known today as "human rights"', which, according to its Charter, the UN was to 'promote universal respect for and observance of'.[1] There is a modern tendency to provide a legal basis to the right of asylum, which is specifically mentioned in the constitutions of a number of states as well as in the UN Universal Declaration of Human Rights.[2] 'It applies equally to persons whose residence in the territory has been authorized, and to illegal entrants.'[3]

The right of asylum covers at least temporary admission, and safeguards the refugee against forcible repatriation. The primary concern of any refugee is not to be forcibly repatriated to the country from which he has fled, or, as regards the displaced person, to the country to which he does not want to return. Security against forcible repatriation is the most fundamental principle of any status for refugees. The UN reaffirmed this right of asylum by accepting the principle of voluntary repatriation in the resolution of 12 February 1946: 'no refugees or displaced persons . . . shall be compelled to return to their country of origin.'

The majority of refugees who came under the mandate of IRO found temporary asylum in Austria, Germany, and Italy, and more or less permanent asylum elsewhere, especially in France[4] before the Organization began its work.

A different situation involving the admission and grant of asylum to refugees faced the Organization in connexion with persons who became refugees during its operation and persons illegally entering countries in which it was at work. Refugees were frequently compelled illegally to leave their country of origin, and illegally to enter their country of asylum. This illegal entry could have penal consequences, and the state could refuse entry or expel the person concerned. This situation naturally affected mainly the countries of continental Europe adjacent to the countries of origin.

The matter was particularly complex in Germany because of the various competences of the occupation authorities, the German authorities, and the IRO. The admission of non-German political refugees to the western zones of Germany came within the competence of the military occupation authorities.[5] After the war, many refugees left Poland, Yugoslavia, Hungary, and Rumania and went to Germany. About 60 per cent. of them were Jews. All of them were given asylum

---

[1] UN Doc. E/Ref. 1, op. cit., p. 18.
[2] UN Charter, Article 55, paragraph (c). Universal Declaration of Human Rights, Article 14: 'everyone has the right to seek and to enjoy in other countries asylum from persecution.'
[3] P. Weis, op. cit., p. 198.
[4] Cf. Chapter VII, Co-operation of Governments, pp. 140 f.
[5] Ibid., pp. 128 f.

in Germany, most of them in the US zone, and were protected by the military authorities and by UNRRA. Similarly, in 1948, after the *coup d'état* in Czechoslovakia and the trial of Cardinal Mindszenty, Czech and Hungarian refugees sought and found asylum in Western Germany.

After the establishment of the Occupation Statute in Western Germany and the creation of the Bonn Federal Government, the latter was empowered, on 2 December 1949, by the Allied High Commission for Germany to assume certain responsibilities connected with the admission of German and non-German refugees into the territory of the Federal Republic. Although the tendency of the occupation authorities was to widen the competence of the Bonn Federal Government with regard to the admission of non-German refugees, the final decision on admission or expulsion remained with the occupation authorities.[1]

The Allied High Commission ensured the IRO's right to have access to new political refugees, and the Organization's officers in the western zones of Germany protected them, visiting the German refugee camps and prisons and obtaining their discharge, and getting for them German identity documents, labour and ration cards.

The Austrian Government had stated repeatedly that it was resolved to grant asylum to refugees fleeing from persecution. In a letter, dated 29 April 1948, Chancellor Figl declared: 'Austria will apply to refugees and displaced persons living on its territory the principles adopted on 12 February 1946 by the GA of the UN concerning the treatment of refugees and displaced persons.'[2]

Refugees entered Italy by way of the north-east frontier or across the Adriatic. They were apprehended by the Italian police and taken to collecting centres administered by the Italian authorities to await the IRO's decisions. A favourable decision resulted in release for resettlement, for transfer to an IRO camp, or for private residence if a refugee was able to support himself, since, in principle, asylum was granted by the Italian Constitution. In 1949 the IRO established a large interviewing team in Venezia Giulia on the north-east frontier, and many refugees were sent direct to IRO camps.[3]

France was faced with a particularly complicated problem in respect of her Spanish frontier which was crossed both by persons claiming to be refugees and by others making no such claim who were only looking for work. It was a problem to distinguish the one type of entrant from the other; early in 1948 they numbered about 1,000 a month. When IRO began operations, Spaniards were first interviewed by the local French authorities who made decisions regarding their admission to the country and sent their papers to IRO in Paris. There a further decision, taken in co-operation with the Office for Spanish Refugees, was made on the relevance of each individual to the IRO's mandate. The IRO was financially responsible for the temporary maintenance of an illegal entrant until it was shown that he was not the concern of the Organization. Later, the IRO established special offices near the frontier for interviewing entrants and, in conjunction with the local authorities and officials of the French National Office of Immigration, determined on the spot

[1] Occupation Statute, paragraph 2.   [2] Cf. Chapter VII, p. 136.
[3] Ibid., p. 138.

whether or not they should be considered as refugees. In the autumn of 1950 the IRO offices were replaced by offices of the French administration.

In Luxembourg holders of certificates of eligibility issued by the IRO's mission in that country were usually admitted. The holders' requests for identity cards were examined by the Luxembourg authorities, as were such requests by all foreigners, and were granted or refused as was appropriate. Throughout the IRO's period of work, admissions to Luxembourg were liberal, especially for persons willing to work in under-manned industries.

Political refugees did not encounter difficulties in finding asylum in the Scandinavian countries. In Denmark the police submitted to the Ministry of Justice cases of persons who gave plausible reasons for being political refugees, and admission was not refused if the person concerned had reason to fear persecution. The opinion of the IRO mission in Copenhagen was considered in each case.

Residence

There was naturally a difference between a country of first asylum and a country of definite admission. The countries adjacent to those from which refugees had fled were frequently under great pressure from refugees who wished to enter. Yet as these countries wanted to avoid the political complications with a neighbour which might result from the presence of the refugees, many of them granted only temporary residence permits and encouraged emigration. The IRO made an effort to ensure that refugees should be able legally to remain in their countries of first asylum, even if only temporarily.

The question of residence for refugees was also determined by the conditions of occupation in Western Germany after the war. According to German law, legal residence in Germany required a German identity card (*Kennkarte*), and permission to reside in a specific town or village required a special residence permit (*Zuzugsgenehmigung*) issued by the local authority. Refugees living privately had to comply with German regulations, while those living in German refugee camps, though holding IRO identity cards, needed no residence permits. Before the end of June 1950, when responsibility for assembly centres in the British and US zones was transferred from the Control Commission for Germany and IRO respectively to the German authorities, the camp population was virtually given extraterritorial status, for the inhabitants of the camps were not registered with the German authorities and had no German identity cards. They were, therefore, not considered as being legal residents in a German land.

Sometimes refugees secured work and accommodation for themselves and left the camps. Before the transfer of assembly centres to the German authorities, refugees electing to live privately were given certificates issued by IRO offices requesting the German authorities to grant to the applicant a permit to reside in a certain town or village. IRO officials were often obliged to intervene with German authorities who refused to accept refugees in their towns or villages. From the spring of 1949 onwards some German authorities began to stamp the identity cards of new refugees with a statement that the holder would not be entitled to a residence permit. This resulted in hardship, particularly for some Czech refugees who had previously married girls coming from the German-speaking minority in Czecho-slovakia. In accordance with the Potsdam Agreement, the wives were expelled with the whole minority group in 1945 and 1946, and resided lawfully in Germany; but the husbands, coming over in 1949, were prevented from joining their wives legally even when accommodation was available. IRO officials interceded, very often successfully in individual cases, but no general solution was possible before the passage of the Federal German Law on Homeless Foreigners in 1950 (effective in April 1951).

Conditions in the French zone of Germany were somewhat different: there the majority of refugees had lived privately from the beginning. Temporary residence permits were issued direct by the French military authorities, which in principle contacted the IRO in every case.

With the increase of the power and competence of the German authorities in Western Germany, pre-war German regulations were increasingly applied, and in 1951 the German police authorities began issuing an aliens' registration certificate to non-German refugees in addition to the normal identity card. This certificate was valid for one year and was renewable. The increase in German responsibility was paralleled by a liberalization of the law to meet the needs of those refugees who wished or who had no alternative but to remain in Germany. Negotiations between the Allied High Commission, the German Federal Government, and the IRO resulted in the approval on 25 April 1951 of the Federal Law on Homeless Foreigners. This law included a provision concerning the unconditional right of residence of non-German refugees within the mandate of the IRO who were in Germany on 30 June 1950. The implementation of this liberal measure raised issues of jurisdiction common in all federal states.

In Austria the issue of residence permits to refugees was normal throughout IRO's period of work; but it was only in the last year of operations that the Organi-zation's interventions resulted in the issue of permits to those refugees who had to remain in the country. These permits, the most liberal given to any foreigners, entitled the holder to an indefinite period of residence, subject to the possibility of cancellation of the permit.

Italy, on the other hand, owing to the over-population of the country and the high degree of unemployment, was not in a position to give refugees a right to permanent residence. As the majority of refugees were in the country illegally and liable to internment, it was IRO's task to bring them within the law. By December 1948 it had been possible to establish a procedure whereby IRO issued identity cards to all refugees within its mandate; these cards, when stamped by the Italian authorities, were considered equivalent to residence permits. Such permits, valid for four months, were renewable, whereas residence permits for normal aliens were valid for three months.

France is a country which, despite a considerable alien population, has not usually taken exceptional measures in connexion with the large-scale admission of immigrants. In France there is a precise procedure according to which foreigners wishing to stay more than three months are required to present, in support of their application for a residence permit, certain documents attesting their identity and nationality; normally a passport suffices. A refugee who had been legally admitted to the country, therefore, obtained from the IRO, acting in its quasi-consular capacity, a certificate stating his identity and nationality and indicating to which category of refugees he belonged. He was issued a 'temporary residence permit' for one year's stay and afterwards a renewable 'ordinary residence permit' for three years. Finally, an alien who had resided in France for an uninterrupted period of three years could obtain the 'privileged residence card' which was valid for ten years.

In Belgium the refugees were registered as regular residents. Those who were mine workers, recruited by the Belgian Government on the basis of special agreements, and their families, were listed in the ordinary register of the population. Difficulties arose after the expiry of the contract for mine work if a refugee was unwilling to continue working in the mines and sought other employment: after negotiations the Government agreed to give such persons a regular residence permit after they had done mine work for two years.

Bilateral agreements with governments

Once refugees were admitted to a country and had obtained residence permits, they had other urgent needs which were subject to legal provisions and called for conventional agreements between IRO and individual governments.

The IRO Constitution stipulated that member governments would not only pay their contributions but would also give the Organization general support (Article 4, paragraph 9). This enabled the IRO to entrust to their representatives accredited to these governments the task of legal protection, and to ask for formal recognition of their right to exercise this function (Article 13). The IRO succeeded in inserting in most of its agreements with governments (with occupation authorities, countries of western Europe, Italy, and some reception countries in the Western hemisphere) two provisions: the first provided recognition that IRO, by virtue of an international mandate, was entrusted with the function of protection. This meant that IRO's properly accredited representatives could make representations regarding any matters which, in their opinion, required the consideration of the governments concerned. The second provision dealt with the non-discriminatory treatment of refugees, their access to the labour market, and to the national system of social benefits. This provision, in other words, provided for treatment similar to that granted to nationals of most-favoured nations. Thus the aim of these bilateral agreements between IRO and individual governments was to ensure a status similar to that provided by the multilateral conventions already mentioned. In this way IRO provided, in some countries of asylum at least, a temporary substitute for a full-fledged conventional régime.

In practice the exercise of IRO's protective functions involved two entirely different aspects of protection. The first, primarily a headquarters activity, aimed at bringing about special agreements, or inserting in more general diplomatic instruments, clauses which would provide for an improved status of refugees not so far covered by special arrangements. The second of IRO's protective functions was primarily the task of IRO's chiefs of missions and included the exercise of the so-called quasi-consular functions.

The problems involved in the task of protection differed greatly from country to country, first according to their geographical position as adjacent or non-adjacent countries; secondly, to their tradition in regard to the treatment of aliens; and, lastly, according to their status as sovereign states or as occupied zones. In some countries IRO's chief efforts were directed towards procuring a legal status for its charges; in others with obtaining for them civil rights such as the right to work; in still others IRO was concerned with getting travel documents to clear the ground for emigration.

Personal status and conflict of laws

In the Anglo-Saxon countries the principle of domicile governs the legal status of an individual,[1] while in the chief countries of first asylum in western Europe the legal status of a person was closely connected with his nationality. The technical problems involved in legal and political protection in the so-called common law countries, which apply the law of domicile, was primarily to discover the exact legal provisions applicable, and these problems were less urgent than those encountered in the countries applying the law of nationality. In the latter countries with a large number of refugees to whom opportunities for naturalization were not always available, the establishment of a satisfactory status was imperative, and this need gave an impetus towards the development of routine international protection.[2]

While the principles adopted in France, Germany, and Austria—the countries with great numbers of refugees—were similar, the methods of meeting the problem of personal status of refugees differed decisively from one to the other, and the activities of IRO varied accordingly.

In France, when IRO began its work,[3] the Government had the benefit of a long experience and an old-established tradition. The conception of granting special legal status to stateless refugees by means of multilateral international conventions had originated in France. From 1922 to 1946 the French Government had signed and ratified international agreements and conventions concerning refugees.[4] The various agreements[5] which France concluded with the IRO and the conventions mentioned above provided the foundation for IRO's extensive activities in the field of legal and political protection of refugees in France. This was particularly effective because of the close and friendly liaison between the various French departments concerned and the IRO mission.

The protective services concerned (1) statutory refugees, the Russians, Armenians, Germans, Austrians, Saarlanders, and Spaniards. These refugees were entitled to the quasi-consular services which the High Commissioner's representative was

---

[1] In the UK the refugee is considered as an alien.

[2] In countries of immigration the fact that refugees were usually treated like other immigrants and were able to benefit from the possibility of early naturalization made it generally unnecessary to attempt to create a separate status for refugee immigrants.

[3] Cf. Chapter VII, p. 130.

[4] Cf. Annex 32, p. 328

[5] Cf. Appendix II (b), pp. 603–30.

authorized to render to Nansen refugees, and were listed in Article 1 of the Arrangement and in the Agreement, both of 30 June 1928. These services had also been made available to Spanish refugees by a decree of 3 July 1945. By a decree of 15 March 1945 the benefits of the Convention of 28 October 1933 had been extended to these Spanish refugees. (2) Non-statutory refugees within the IRO mandate who received protection in accordance with the terms of the Agreement between France and IRO of 13 January 1948.

France is one of the countries whose administrative practice presupposes the existence of consulates; and when refugees could not or would not avail themselves of the protection of such consulates, their position was safeguarded by the official establishment of special national offices—Russian, Armenian, Spanish Republican, as well as a Jewish committee—which were authorized to issue identity and other documents. These documents helped holders not only to regularize their sojourn in France but also to find employment.

The Russian, Armenian, and Spanish refugee offices continued to function under the Agreement mentioned above. They drafted the documents needed by the refugees which were then made legal by the representative of the IRO. The documents acquired the same weight in probative evidence as those issued by the countries of origin. Documents for non-statutory refugees and displaced persons were drawn up, visaed, and authenticated by the representative of the IRO, and had the same value as similar documents issued by foreign consuls to their nationals living in France.

Thus the IRO office provided documents to take the place of those normally issued by the authorities of the country of origin, and which the refugees were no longer able to obtain (evidence of nationality, registry office documents, academic diplomas, certifying refugees' signatures, copies and translations of documents in their language, &c.).

In a letter of 4 July 1950 the French Government denounced, as far as they related to protection, the two agreements of 13 January 1948 (PC/LEG 11 and 12) in order to transfer the protective measure to a newly created French authority which was to be established as the French Office for the Protection of Refugees and Stateless Persons.[1] When, on 22 April 1954, the Convention of 28 July 1951 came into force, the personal status of a refugee who qualified under the Convention signed by France was to be governed in accordance with Article XII 'by the law of the country of his domicile or, if he has no domicile, by the law of the country of his residence'.

The consequences of the law of nationality were particularly difficult in Germany. A great many persons who *de jure* were still nationals of their country of origin were without contact with the authorities of their former country, partly because the latter were unwilling to give assistance by issuing them with the necessary certificates, and partly because the refugees themselves were unwilling to approach these authorities both for political reasons and because they were afraid that any national protection would deprive them of the status of refugees within the mandate of the IRO.

[1] Cf. Chapter XXII, Local Settlement, p. 474.

In Germany there was no established procedure for dealing with these refugees who theoretically possessed their old nationality, but in the solving of this problem the ingenuity of individual legal officers was exercised to the full.

The Organization submitted to the Allied High Commission, competent to legislate on matters concerning refugees, a request that a law should be passed making it possible for the law of the country of residence to be applied to refugees, and giving the German courts competence in the matters concerned. Consequently the Allied High Commission, on 17 March 1950, promulgated Law No. 23 concerning the Legal Position of Displaced Persons and Refugees.

Under Part I of this law the status of a refugee or displaced person was determined with reference to the law of the state of residence, replacing the provisions of the Introductory Law to the German Civil Code regarding the application of natural law to aliens (Article 1). In civil cases the provision of the Civil Code became applicable to refugees and displaced persons and they were regarded as though they were German nationals (Article 3). Furthermore, certification of nubility was no longer demanded (Article 4).

Under Part II of the law, marriages between displaced persons or refugees concluded in Germany between 8 May 1945 and 1 August 1948 before a minister of a church to which they belonged, but not registered with the German authorities, could be validated. Either party to such a marriage or, if they were both dead, any surviving child of the union, was entitled to apply for validation by producing at the Chief Registry Office (*Hauptstandesamt*) in Hamburg a certificate issued by the minister who performed the ceremony.

The difficulties overcome in Germany by Law No. 23 continued in Austria, where the status of refugees was still governed by the law of the country of origin. The Austrian courts could not assume jurisdiction to act in civil law cases involving refugees when their decisions were not recognized by the country of nationality, or when refugees were unable to comply with the requirements of the law of their country of nationality. As the Soviet authorities refused to issue to Russian refugees certificates of nubility the Austrian authorities were unable to marry them. Following intervention by IRO and on the basis of certificates issued to individual refugees by the Organization, the Austrian authorities adopted a liberal attitude and considered refugees, if possible, as persons of undetermined nationality, and subjected them to Austrian law. On the intervention of IRO an order, issued by the Minister of Justice, notified the courts that refugees from Czechoslovakia, Hungary, Poland, and Yugoslavia were usually unable to produce certificates of nubility from the countries of origin and might therefore be exempted from the requirement.

Restitution and indemnification

IRO represented the interests of refugees regarding the restitution of property which they had lost during the war and regarding the indemnification for losses suffered by them. IRO watched the development of the various restitution and indemnification laws in the western zones of Germany and in Austria, and suggested to the occupation authorities various measures which would aid refugees in filing their claims. Certificates issued by the IRO and the International Tracing Service greatly assisted refugees by providing evidence in support of their claims.

The law on indemnification in the US zone, usually known as the General Claims Law, provided, on the other hand, for indemnification for damages to life, limb, health, and liberty, damages to possessions and property, and damages to economic advancement. IRO participated in the drafting of this law. After it had been passed IRO's main task was to accelerate procedures so that the resettlement plans of the refugees concerned would not be delayed. Sometimes refugees refused to leave Germany before having received compensation. All overseas missions of the IRO were informed about the legislation and the procedures for its implementation in Germany. The missions passed on the necessary information to refugees in their areas, providing them with application forms as prescribed by the legislation, and assisted the refugees in completing them and sending them to Germany.

Another service of the IRO was developed when, in occupied Germany, the conditions of life in assembly centres made it difficult for the refugees to acquire any considerable possessions. Sometimes household goods were confiscated by the German authorities when the refugees were emigrating, and it was suspected that the goods had not been lawfully acquired. But many refugees left the ports with miscellaneous property which had been legally acquired. Individual cases of this kind required intervention by IRO officials, and in the end, at the instance of the IRO, restrictions concerning possessions were removed, with some exceptions.

Travel document

Aid given to refugees to overcome the disadvantages of statelessness in the country of residence was only part of the work of the IRO. Efforts to ensure their freedom of movement within and outside their country of residence was equally important.

Since, as has been pointed out, most persons within the mandate of the IRO did not enjoy the protection of any government, they were not able to obtain a national passport. Therefore it was imperative to provide them with an internationally recognized travel document on which entry or exit visas could be affixed, in lieu of a national passport, which would be recognized by countries of transit and final settlement. The international agreement for the protection of refugees of 1922 provided for a novel kind of document known as the 'Nansen passport', which served as a travel document. It was adopted by fifty-three governments and removed a serious handicap which had hampered the resettlement of Russian refugees. Subsequent agreements extended the benefit of the Nansen passport to other categories of refugees. However, after the Second World War when the IGCR made arrangements for resettling post-war refugees and displaced persons, some new form of travel document had to be devised, since the existing agreements and conventions applied only to certain specific categories of refugees and did not cover all groups coming within the mandate of the IGCR. At a conference held in London on 15 October 1946, prepared and convened by the IGCR, an Agreement was adopted relating to the issue of a travel document to refugees. This Agreement came into force on 13 January 1947. It applied to refugees who were the concern of the IGCR, but Article 20 provided the transfer of all provisions relating to the IGCR to its successor organization, the IRO.

The so-called 'London travel document' is similar to the Nansen passport with one notable addition, the so-called 'return clause' under which holders of the document can re-enter any country in which the document has been valid for entry on the same terms as can the holder of a visaed passport. At the same time when this clause was inserted in the London travel document, a similar provision was made for Nansen passports with which the older categories of refugees continued to travel. Difficulties and confusion arose in connexion with the Nansen passports since it was doubtful whether the many persons who claimed such a paper were eligible to be given it. The suggestion was made in the Special Report on Progress and Prospects . . .[1], prepared by the Secretary General of the UN in collaboration with the Executive Secretary of PCIRO, 'to revise or denounce the Geneva Convention of 28 October 1933, giving a number of governments the privilege of issuing Nansen passports'. It was pointed out that some countries refused to grant citizenship to individuals born in the country of 'stateless' parents, which resulted in the issuing of Nansen passports to persons who were second- or third-generation refugees. This situation constituted a peculiar problem for the PCIRO officers in connexion with their resettlement efforts.

According to Article I of the London Agreement a person wishing to obtain a travel document had to fulfil four conditions: (1) to be the concern of IRO; (2) to be stateless in law or in fact; (3) to be residing lawfully in the territory of a contracting government; and (4) not to be subject to provisions of other agreements providing for a Nansen passport.

The agreement was signed by twenty-three and ratified by twenty-one countries. In addition twelve governments formally recognized travel documents issued under this agreement, and the majority of other countries recognized it *de facto*. The fact that the IRO travel document had achieved such wide recognition in a relatively short time gives some indication of the practical value it achieved. The return clause (Article 15) made it easier for holders of this document to secure emigration visas than it was for refugees whose documents contained no return authorization.

Although in granting the IRO travel document the countries of asylum accepted the risk that a few refugees might return, in practice it represented an advantage since the 'automatic return visa' facilitated the movement from their territory of many refugees who, without it, might not have left or been able to emigrate. The document was also widely used by refugees undertaking temporary journeys outside their country of residence, serving increasingly as a 'normal' travel document in lieu of a passport. The psychological importance to the refugee of having a document similar in appearance to that of a national passport was an added advantage.

It becomes the task of an intergovernmental body to see that the documents specified by an international agreement are, in fact, issued and are recognized by other governments. During the life of the Organization seven governments (Brazil, Denmark, Germany, Italy, Liberia, Norway, and South Africa) signed the Agreement of October 1946, and consequently issued documents under its terms; a

---

[1] UN, ECOSOC, Report on Progress . . ., op. cit., p. 15.

number of other governments agreed to recognize the document. In most countries documents issued under this Agreement were issued by the government concerned without consultation with the IRO, e.g. by the UK. In so far as the document was specifically restricted to refugees within the mandate of the IRO, some governments, e.g. the Swiss Government, consulted the local IRO office regarding the eligibility of applicants; other governments issued the document only to holders of the IRO's eligibility certificate. In Italy co-operation between the Government and the IRO went much further, and the Organization prepared the documents for refugees and transmitted them to the appropriate department of the Italian Government for validation before issue.

The Nansen passport and the London travel document were not the only travel documents available to refugees. Some governments made available a standard travel document to aliens resident in their territory who were unable to obtain a national passport; such documents were available to refugees if necessary, and some governments, e.g. the Government of France, issued only such documents and the Nansen passport; the French authorities issued these documents to a refugee only on presentation of a certificate from the IRO. At the time when, in Germany, travel was controlled by the Allied Combined Travel Board, refugees were issued with individual temporary travel documents by that Board in cases where travel was not organized on the basis of nominal rolls carrying block exit permits and group visas. Similarly, refugees living in the French and US zones of Austria, with the approval of the occupation authorities, received special certificates of identity. Documents were issued in some countries by the delegates of the International Committee of the Red Cross which were particularly useful immediately after the war and during the IRO's work in Italy before other arrangements had been made.

Certification of records

A problem of great day-to-day importance to the officers of the IRO was the issue, validation, and translation of the various documents required by refugees to support their applications for resettlement in new countries. When refugees had lost their original documents, duly certified notarial copies were required. When the original documents were in languages not understood by immigration authorities, certified translations were demanded. This applied, for example, to birth and marriage certificates and other documents concerning civil status. For other purposes refugees needed the originals or copies of school certificates, diplomas testifying to their academic degrees, and certificates attesting to their professional skill. At the end of 1949 this work constituted about half the activities of legal officers of the IRO in the US zone of Germany, since each prospective immigrant had to have an average of ten to fifteen translated and authenticated documents when he appeared before the selection mission (or visa-issuing authority) of most countries of immigration.

In addition to providing adequately documented records the IRO officers had to see that these records were not defaced in order to conceal criminal sentences passed on refugees for minor offences. Conditions of life in Austria and Germany immediately after the war were not conducive to law-abiding behaviour. Even minor offences sometimes barred a refugee from acceptance by many countries, and it was not possible totally to erase any mention of a conviction from the documents presented by refugees in support of their applications. In certain cases and under certain circumstances, however, convictions could be expunged or pardoned in Austrian and German law, and when this occurred the IRO attached a certificate to the refugee's documents to the effect that such legal action had taken place and giving all relevant information.

When a refugee had entered his country of final resettlement he could be expelled or deported. Between the two world wars such action was not unusual, particularly during periods of economic depression. While the IRO was functioning, expulsion and deportation were very rare. In practice nearly all governments restricted expulsion to cases where security and public order were involved. Similarly, deportation of refugees admitted by arrangement with the IRO was restricted to cases of mental disorder, to those involving public order and security, and those concerning an unreasonable refusal to work or an unreasonable breach of work contract. The IRO was usually approached by the governments concerned, so that the re-entry of the refugee into the country from which he had come (Austria, Germany, or Italy usually) could be arranged. In some instances unjustifiable deportation orders were cancelled on the intervention of IRO.

Refugees liable to extradition were excluded from the IRO's mandate,[1] because extradition proceedings were based on the terms of treaties, the interpretation and application of which were entirely decided upon by the contracting parties. The Organization therefore tried to ensure that such persons should receive fair treatment in the courts.[2]

The IRO ameliorated the consequences of the uncertain and anomalous position of persons who were stateless in fact and in law. In performing its function of giving legal and political protection it helped towards the final solution of the refugee problem, namely, the establishment and naturalization of refugees in a new country. Beyond its contribution to the work for refugees in individual countries, IRO was instrumental in helping develop international conventions and agreements covering subjects of concern to refugees.

International conventions

IRO took part in the activities of the UN, specialized agencies, and other international bodies dealing with matters affecting the status of refugees. At international conferences concerned with the stabilization of the refugees' legal position in international law it represented the interests of refugees. At the same time the Organization was called upon for counsel by the UN and other international bodies, and asked for suggestions regarding the elaboration of general international

[1] Constitution, Annex I, Part II, paragraph 3.
[2] An example is a procedure adopted by the Italian Government for the implementation of Article 45 in the Peace Treaty with Italy relating to the extradition of war criminals, traitors, and collaborators who were citizens of the UN. Article 45 was implemented by the Decree Law of the President of the Italian Republic dated 26 Feb. 1948, No. 363. Cf. the verdict of the Rome Court of Appeal on 5 Oct. 1949 in the case of twenty-five alleged war criminals interned in Lipari.

instruments such as the Universal Declaration of Human Rights and the Draft Covenant on Human Rights.

The Director General submitted a memorandum to the Second Session of the Human Rights Commission. This memorandum dealt with the following matters vital to persons coming within the mandate of the IRO: equality before the law; prevention of discrimination; problems of nationality and statelessness; questions relating to emigration, expulsion, and right of asylum. As has been mentioned, the Universal Declaration of Human Rights, adopted by the General Assembly of the UN in December 1948, lays down three basic rights (Articles 13–15) essential to refugees.

Furthermore, the Secretary General of the UN, instructed by the Sixth Session of ECOSOC in March 1948, consulted the Director General of IRO at the various stages of his work while he was preparing a study on the protection of stateless persons.[1]

IRO initiated the co-ordination on an international level of the procedure for the declaration of death of missing persons.[2] The disappearance, due to the upheavals of war or of persecutions, of hundreds of thousands of persons whose death could not be conclusively established caused legal difficulties for their families, who were thus prevented from settling questions fundamental to their family and economic life, e.g. questions of re-marriage or inheritance. Since refugees and displaced persons were among those chiefly affected, IRO in 1948 proposed to the ECOSOC that an International Convention on the Declaration of Death of Missing Persons should be drawn up. During its Seventh Session the ECOSOC adopted a resolution requesting the Secretary General to prepare a draft convention,[3] in collaboration with the IRO and other competent organizations.

On 3 December 1949 the General Assembly of the UN decided to convene an international conference of government representatives with a view to concluding a multilateral convention on the subject of a declaration of death of missing persons. This intergovernmental conference met at Lake Success, New York, from 15 March to 6 April 1950, with thirty-one governments represented, and established the Convention on Declaration of Death of Missing Persons,[4] which was open to accession by states. The Convention contained regulations on declaration of death of persons who had disappeared in Europe, Asia, or Africa during the years 1939–45 as a result of the war or of racial, religious, political, or national persecution (Article 1). It provided also that an International Bureau for Declarations of Death (Article 8) was to be established within the framework of the UN on October 1952. This Bureau published the applications and decisions of the competent courts in order to eliminate possible parallel proceedings and contradictory decisions.

IRO participated in the diplomatic conference of the International Red Cross which was concerned with the protection of victims of war. This conference was held in Geneva in 1949. The Director General submitted two memoranda: the first recommended that the IRO or the agency which might replace it, in their capacity

---

[1] UN, *A Study of Statelessness*, op. cit., pp. 3–4.
[2] PREP, Res. 75, May 1948, see Appendix III, p. 710, and PREP/203.
[3] GC/60.
[4] UN Publications 1950. V. 1, A/Conf. 1/9. The Convention came into force on 24 Jan. 1952.

as humanitarian organizations, should be authorized to act as a substitute in the absence of a protecting power in time of war. The second memorandum, dealing with the question of forcible repatriation, internment, and assigned residence, stressed in particular that refugees should not be considered enemy aliens by reason of their origin, and that internment and/or assigned residence should be applied only after each individual case had been examined. The Geneva Convention of 12 August 1949 Relative to the Protection of Civilian Persons in Time of War contained provisions in Articles 11, 44, and 45, paragraph 4, covering the suggestions of IRO.[1]

As a result of IRO's efforts, provisions were incorporated in the instruments dealing with migration for employment drafted at the International Labour Conference in 1949 to secure protection of refugees and to ensure that an international body could represent their interests.[2]

The most important contribution of the IRO concerning international agreements, however, was its initiative and active collaboration in the preparation by the UN of a new and comprehensive international convention which was to replace the existing conventions concerning the status of refugees, and was to extend the legal rights of all refugees eligible for international protection.

The Convention Relating to the Status of Refugees of 28 July 1951, adopted by the UN Conference of Plenipotentiaries at Geneva, contained a more comprehensive definition of refugees than any previously achieved,[3] but did not follow the suggestion of France and the UK to apply a single convention to all stateless persons whether or not they were already covered by existing conventions. The term 'refugee', according to Article 1, applied to: refugees eligible under the Arrangements of 12 May 1926 and 30 June 1928, or under the Conventions of 28 October 1933 and 10 February 1938, the Protocol of 14 September 1939, or the Constitution of the IRO.

Article 1 stated explicitly that 'decisions of non-eligibility taken by the IRO ... shall not prevent the status of refugee being accorded to persons who', because of events occurring before 1 January 1951, have a 'well-founded fear of being persecuted for reasons of race, religion, nationality, membership of a particular social group, or political opinion', are outside their country of nationality, and cannot 'or owing to such fear' are unwilling to avail 'themselves of the protection of that country'. This provision was included in response to the suggestion of the IRO that 'in the light of the then present situation Part II, para. 6 of the IRO Constitution should no longer be applicable to the services of protection and that para. 2 (b) of Part II should be interpreted as taking into account the real reasons which had inspired the persons concerned rather than indications of a purely formal nature'.[4]

---

[1] Cf. P. Weiss, op. cit., pp. 204 and 218; and Gutteridge, 'The Geneva Conventions of 1949', *British Yearbook of International Law*, xxvl, 1949, p. 294.

[2] GC/60, p. 73. The Model Agreement Concerning Temporary and Permanent Migration for Employment and the Convention Concerning Migration for Employment (ILO, Recommendation No. 86, Article 25; and ILO, Convention 97, Article 8).

[3] Cf. Annex 32, p. 328.

[4] GC Res./62, Appendix III, p. 735.

The Convention furthermore established a number of basic rights for refugees which gave assurances that they should be treated at least as well as aliens in the countries to which they came. These basic rights also included 'freedom of religion, access to courts, participation in non-political voluntary organizations and trade unions, housing, acquisition or lease of property, commercial activities and freedom of movement, no expulsion except for reasons of national security or public order and then only with proper legal proceedings'. This Convention[1] came into force on 22 April 1954 and concluded the protracted efforts to improve the status of refugees begun under the League of Nations in 1921 and furthered by the various international agencies, foremost among them the IRO.

ANNEX 32

International conventions, agreements, and arrangements concerning refugees

1. Arrangement of 5 July 1922, with Regard to the Issue of Certificates of Identity (Known as Nansen Passport) to Russian Refugees. (*League of Nations Treaty Series*, vol. xiii, No. 355.)
2. Plan of 31 May 1924, Relating to the Issue of a Certificate of Identity to Armenian Refugees.
3. Arrangement of 12 May 1926, Relating to the Issue of Identity Certificates to Russian and Armenian Refugees. (Ibid., vol. lxxxix, No. 2004.)
4. Arrangement of 30 June 1928, Relating to the Legal Status of Russian and Armenian Refugees. (Ibid., No. 2005.)
5. Arrangement of 30 June 1928, Concerning the Extension to Other Categories of Refugees of Certain Measures Taken in Favour of Russian and Armenian Refugees. (Turkish, Assyrian, Assyro-Chaldean, and assimilated refugees.) (Ibid., No. 2006.)
6. Agreement of 30 June 1928, Concerning the Functions of the Representatives of the High Commissioner for Refugees of the League of Nations.
7. Convention of 28 October 1933, Relating to the International Status of Refugees. (Ibid., vol. clix, No. 3663.)
8. Plan of 30 July 1935, for the Issue of a Certificate of Identity to Refugees from the Saar.
9. Provisional Arrangement of 4 July 1936, Concerning the Status of Refugees Coming from Germany. (Ibid., vol. cxxi, No. 3952.)
10. Convention of 10 February 1938, Regarding the Status of Refugees Coming from Germany. (Ibid., vol. cxcii, No. 4461.)
11. Additional Protocol of 14 September 1939, to the Provisional Arrangement and to the Convention, Signed at Geneva on 4 July 1936 and 10 February 1938, respectively, Concerning the Status of Refugees Coming from Germany. (Extended to refugees from Austria.) (Ibid., vol. cxcviii, No. 4634.)
12. Agreement of 15 October 1946, on Travel Document (Known as the London Travel Document). (*UN Treaty Series*, vol. xi, No. 150.)
13. Convention of 28 July 1951, Relating to the Status of Refugees. UN Doc. A/CONF, 2/108, Aug. 1951. (UN Publications, 1951, IV. 4.)

[1] For text of the Convention see James M. Read, *Magna Carta for Refugees* (UN Publ. 1953, I. 33) rev. ed. 1953; and UN Conference of Plenipotentiaries on the Status of Refugees and Stateless Persons, *Final Act*, Geneva, 1951 (UN Publications, 1951, IV. 4).

CHAPTER XVIII

INTERNATIONAL TRACING SERVICE[1]

THE displacement of millions of people during the Second World War resulted in the separation of families whose members completely lost touch with each other. Inmates of concentration camps and prisons particularly had no contact with the outside world and their relatives often did not know where they were held or even whether they were alive. The main victims were the political opponents of the Nazi régime, the Jews, and the foreign labourers in Nazi conquered territories. Those who survived the war had to be found and the dead and missing traced.

For many refugees food, shelter, clothes, and work were not enough; they needed news of their lost relatives and the possibility of reunion with them. They also needed proofs regarding their civil status (widowhood, succession, and so on), and evidence in matters of restitution and indemnification in order to support their claims.

In the latter part of 1943 the Committee on Displaced Populations of the Allied Post-war Requirements Bureau[2] in London considered the establishment of suitable machinery for tracing missing persons. Tentative plans were made for setting up National Tracing Bureaux (NTB) in various European countries and for developing a Central Tracing Service along the lines of the International Committee of the Red Cross (ICRC) Prisoner-of-War Card Index.

Communications from and about UN military and civilian persons in liberated and occupied areas were within the competence of the military authorities. SHAEF, therefore, developed a tracing system during 1944 in connexion with registering the displaced persons on DP2 cards. In May 1945 it established a tracing and locating unit for collecting nominal rolls of concentration camps inmates for the National Tracing Bureaux (NTB) which the individual governments had set up for tracing their missing nationals, and also to maintain, by means of the DP2 cards, a central register of non-repatriable refugees and displaced persons. UNRRA provided the staff for this SHAEF unit which in June 1945 moved with SHAEF headquarters from Versailles to Frankfurt. In July 1945, when SHAEF was dissolved, the Combined Displaced Persons Executive (CDPX) set up a central records office and a Central Tracing Bureau (CTB) which provided the foundation for the plan accepted by the Co-ordinating Committee of the Allied Control Council for Germany on 17 September 1945 and approved by the Council of Foreign Ministers at Moscow in April 1947. Under this plan UNRRA took over the responsibility for this work in November. The agreed objectives were to search for missing military and civilian persons of UN nationalities and to establish the fate of those who could not be found; to locate, collect, and preserve all available records regarding refugees and

---

[1] GC/198. *The ITS, Brief Review of its History and Activities*, 16 March 1951, submitted by the Director General to the General Council. Report on ITS written by the Director of ITS, Mr. Thudichum, 146 pp., with appendixes.

[2] Introduction, p. 16.

displaced persons in Germany, and to serve as a link to bring interested persons into communication with each other. UNRRA traced, through its CTB and zonal bureaux, those individuals who came under its mandate, and searched only in Germany and Austria; tracing outside these two countries was the responsibility of national tracing bureaux. The headquarters of the CTB was established at Arolsen in the US zone of Germany together with the UNRRA headquarters.

In February 1947, with the end of UNRRA in sight, responsibility for individual search and for child tracing was transferred to the zonal offices while a central records office and control of mass tracing by means of cinema slides, radio, posters, and so forth remained with the central office. This arrangement was continued till the end of UNRRA's work on 30 June 1947.

The SHAEF tracing unit and the CTB operated only in Germany. The needs in Austria were similar. Here the Foreign Relations Branch of the British Red Cross established in June 1945, with the co-operation of the British occupation authorities, a Central Tracing Bureau at Klagenfurt in the British zone. This Bureau also dealt with all tracing inquiries from the French, Soviet, and the US zones. The Bureau later moved to Vienna where it reached a high state of efficiency as a quadripartite agency operated by the British Red Cross. In late 1946 the British Red Cross had to curtail their overseas commitments on economy grounds, and responsibility for the Bureau was handed over by the British authorities to UNRRA. In July 1947 arrangements were made by the British authorities in Vienna, with the agreement of UNRRA, for the Tracing Bureau to be handed over to and operated by the Austrian Red Cross as a National Tracing Bureau. At that time a certain limited number of records were sent from Vienna to Arolsen.

During the first meeting of the PCIRO in February 1947 the Executive Secretary was requested to study 'the special problem raised by the continuation of the activities of the CTB after 30 June 1947', and to make suggestions at the following meeting.

In his report[1] the Executive Secretary stated that according to an estimate approximately 3 million persons were missing. The majority of them were dead, but in most cases there was no official confirmation of this fact. He pointed out that two problems connected with tracing had a bearing on the moral, social, and material considerations of the refugees. The first was the tracing and determination of the civil status of children, with the aim of returning them to their families. The second, which had a wider scope, was the reuniting of families. He stressed that the success of the repatriation and resettlement schemes depended to some extent on the re-uniting of families, since many displaced persons were loath to take any decision without knowing what was happening to their families.

Alternative schemes

Two schemes, differing in principle and in scope, were submitted for the consideration of the PCIRO: the one arranging for the greatest possible centralization by setting up a Central Indexing Service and entrusting the work to the ITS; the

---

[1] PREP/37, 26 Apr. 1947.

other a decentralized system providing for the continuation on a European scale of the activities organized by the CTB in Germany. The second scheme, which had been modelled on the proposals of the National Tracing Bureaux conference held in Brussels in September 1946 and had been supported by the conference held in Prague in March 1947, was suggested by the Executive Secretary as the more economical and expedient plan. The PCIRO became 'convinced of the supreme importance of the tracing of missing persons', and resolved to ensure the continuation of tracing through an International Tracing Bureau.[1] Thus, the UNRRA CTB was taken over by PCIRO on 1 July 1947. Its activities were to be centred on three main functions: tracing on an international scale, collective search, and the formation of a library and catalogue, while NTBs dealt with the individual tracing of their respective nationals and the CTB was responsible for co-ordinating their work.

The PCIRO was very fortunate in that the ICRC, helping the Executive Secretary in implementing the decision, seconded their senior tracing expert, Mr. Maurice Thudichum, to the new organization. The Executive Secretary was directed to convert 'the present CTB, its staff, facilities and functions' into an International Tracing Service (ITS) and 'to extend the mandate of the ITS to include as far as possible the tracing of all non-German nationals, and of such German nationals as would be eligible under the Constitution of the IRO, who have disappeared by reason of the War'.[2]

For systematic tracing, integration and co-ordination of all efforts were essential. All interested governments, therefore, whether or not members of the PCIRO, as well as voluntary societies engaged in tracing activities, were invited to relate their work to that of the ITS and arrangements were made for the exchange of basic tracing information.

It was made known to interested countries that since the IRO was a temporary organization, the ITS could continue to function for a maximum of two or three years. It would, during that period, organize its work with a view to turning over to some long-term body such tracing functions as remained incomplete at the conclusion of its own activities.

On 1 January 1948 the ITS came into being, its headquarters remaining at Arolsen. Two major jobs had to be done: co-ordinating the international tracing activities and reorganizing and realigning the former CTB and zonal bureaux. Contacts were made with all the countries primarily interested in tracing. Liaison officers from France, Belgium, Luxembourg, the Netherlands, and Italy, who had previously been attached to the CTB, were transferred to the ITS headquarters and support was given to them mainly as regards certain supplies and transport.

The ITS, responsible for general policy, supervised the activities of the zonal branches at Esslingen in the US zone (established in April 1947) and at Göttingen in the British zone (set up in March 1948) and maintained close relations with the Searching Service of the military government of the French zone at Rastatt. The original CTB Liaison Office in the US sector of Berlin was absorbed by ITS and

---

[1] PREP/55, Res. No. 23, adopted 21 May 1947 (PREP/126/Rev. 1, p. 20, and 131/Rev. 1, 6 Nov. 1947).
[2] PREP/146/Rev. 1. Resolution on the Establishment of an ITS, 31 Oct. 1947.

continued as a collecting and distributing office for the three western zones and maintained liaison with the Soviet sector and Soviet zone.[1]

The first year of ITS, 1948, was a period of reorganization, consolidation, and co-ordination, entailing considerable re-equipment in terms of personnel and materials; 1949 was the peak year of effective work. Search plans were in full swing and the processing of documents was accelerated. Full co-operation existed between the ITS and the NTB and tracing agencies; assistance was also given by the occupying authorities and German officials. During this year the Child Search Programme was launched by the ITS. Its mandate was to find and identify the maximum number of displaced persons' children in the minimum amount of time, as well as to locate the relatives of these children. The method adopted to achieve this task in Germany was known as the Limited Registration Plan.[2]

Although it was necessary to begin as early as 1949 planning for the eventual transfer of the ITS to some other body, the volume of work in progress remained undiminished until the spring of 1950, and even during the unavoidable curtailment of personnel and of means the most important activities continued until its transfer to the Allied High Commission of Germany on 1 April 1951. Apart from and in addition to the considerable results of the UNRRA CTB and those agencies working with it, the achievements of ITS during its three and a quarter years' existence were most impressive.[3]

Documentary sources

The main sources from which documents were gathered were the German civil administration, the national and international records of war crimes and criminals, and the IRO itself.

By the end of 1947 a vast accumulation of material had already been collected by the CTB and zonal tracing bureaux and was in course of processing. Most of this material had been assembled as a result of the military directives issued in 1946, which required the Germans to report and return records concerning UN nationals, though it was found that such reporting was often extremely inaccurate and incomplete. Therefore, a general coverage documents search plan was carried out by the ITS zonal divisions operating through teams, numbering from ten to twenty persons, which were attached to the various IRO area installations. In the British zone the plan was to check the material already received against records held by the Germans, as well as to obtain information hitherto unknown. A comprehensive re-combing and physical re-checking on a geographical basis of hospitals, factories, prisons, registry offices, cemeteries, &c., was undertaken. Material found was requisitioned or, where this was not possible, copied on the spot by mobile photostat teams. Some 1,570 hospitals and 248 prisons had to be visited. In the US zone, apart from a physical re-checking of graves, approximately 168,000 returns from hospitals, factories, prisons, &c., were checked.[4]

---

[1] For the organizational structure of headquarters see Annex 33, p. 337.
[2] See Chapter XXIV, Unaccompanied Children, p. 503.
[3] See Annex 34, p. 338.
[4] GC/198, 16 Mar. 1951, p. 9.

Valuable and unexpected finds were made even up to the end of 1949. For example, new sources included the Gestapo and criminal police records in Wuerzburg, a card index found in Kassel containing 11 million names of workers, Gestapo records found in the basement of the Polizei-Praesidium in Karlsruhe, and 3,215 urns containing the ashes of inmates of Dachau concentration camp kept in the cellars of the Perlacher Forest Cemetery near Munich, which had never been reported. Nor were normal graves neglected, the ITS linking its work with the foreign missions responsible for the exhumation and repatriation of bodies.

The second main source of information on displaced persons, refugees, and victims of the Nazi régime were the records held by the occupying authorities (documents centres, war crimes, &c.) who held title to these records by virtue of capture. Such records comprised concentration camp documents, transport lists, interrogations of Nazi personnel, &c. Permission had to be obtained by the ITS to procure the loan of this material. Unfortunately, most of it could be released to the ITS only after the end of the war crimes trials, thus retarding the work of the ITS by two to three years.

The third source of information was from the IRO, i.e. registration cards of persons eligible under the IRO mandate, together with nominal rolls giving disposal plans (repatriation, resettlement, &c.).

Once assembled, all record material had to be sorted into appropriate categories; collated (i.e. all information concerning the same person brought together, irrespective of the source); copied where necessary; distributed to outside agencies; and carded for inclusion into the master card index to form a permanent reference against which to answer incoming inquiries.

Meanwhile, the ITS headquarters, where all this information was finally integrated, was collecting, exchanging, and centralizing information of vital importance from NTB and tracing agencies in many other countries. It frequently happened, for example, that the missing data essential to complete records of a particular concentration camp were found partly in one country, partly in another.

Through these activities 100 tons of documents were collected, involving 20,110,875 names of Allied nationals. The distribution of records to NTB and other tracing agencies had involved more than 1 million pages of documents and nearly 1 million persons. The checking of individual graves of Allied nationals yielded information on 155,093 persons. On the basis of records in possession of the ITS, 721 notifications of death were issued and 13,774 certificates of incarceration, particulars needed by persons claiming indemnification. It might be stressed that by the distribution of this material hundreds of thousands of inquiries were stopped at the source. These records enabled countries concerned to establish the place of residence and the civil status of their nationals and to reconstruct vital statistics and, by the location of graves, helped the repatriation work of the various graves commissions.[1]

The ITS also published a two-volume catalogue (821 pp.) and a 152-page supplement of concentration camps and commandos operated by the Nazis in Germany, Austria, and occupied territories. This catalogue was especially useful to Allied

---

[1] These figures are given in GC/198, p. 10. For more detailed figures see Annex 34, p. 338.

governments in determining the categories of their nationals who were imprisoned and claimed compensation.

Further, the ITS constituted the main source of providing documentary evidence on the basis of which the German Civil Registration Office (*Sonderstandesamt*), established at the ITS headquarters in 1949, issued certificates of death for persons who died in German concentration camps, as well as the registration of births which occurred in camps and *Lebensborn* homes. Altogether, 1,990 death certificates had been issued.

These research activities had built up the most important source of information pertaining to UN nationals who were in Germany and German occupied countries between 1939 and 1945. It became, for the Germans as well, the most authoritative and authentic source against which the justice of claims made by former concentration camp inmates and prisoners for indemnification could be certified.

Central index

The core of the ITS was the master card index. This was arranged in an alpha-betical/phonetic system, which was adopted in 1949 and based on the phonetic principles developed by the ICRC. By this means all variations of the spelling of one particular name were brought together. There were, for instance, 77 different spellings for the name Kusnezow. As a result of the introduction of this system 20,000 cases were solved. This index contains individual information extracted from the documents already mentioned; a register of most of the refugees and displaced persons from UNRRA days up to the present; and notes of all incoming inquiries.

At the beginning of 1948 this index contained 1,876,499 cards; by the end of 1950 it contained 10,538,358, and 28,000 new cards were inserted daily. It was against this master index that all incoming inquiries were checked until the cessation of individual tracing in March 1950. During this period the ITS was in contact with more than 100 NTB and tracing agencies in thirty-five countries. This correspon-dence was conducted in six languages. Altogether nearly 220,303 individual tracing requests emanating from approximately 100 countries were handled from 1 January 1948 to 1 January 1951. The fate of more than 26,797 missing persons was positively established, and tentatively of a further 18,997. Those cases on which no information had been received were not closed. They remained open in the master index until such time as some information was forthcoming.

In addition the records from certain tracing agencies which had ceased activities (Central Location Index, AJDC, &c.) were integrated into the files of the ITS. These amounted to approximately 200,000, and resulted in many locations and pre-vented a considerable amount of duplication in tracing work.

For 'desperate' cases, where all other tracing action had failed to produce positive results, the last resort was mass tracing, which consisted of publicizing by means of newspapers, radio, cinema slides, and search lists the names and data concerning missing persons. From 1948 until its cessation in March 1950, this branch publicized 560,000 names through the media of 154 different language newspapers in Germany and other countries; radio stations in Germany and elsewhere; cinema slides; and the distribution of approximately 1,000 weekly search lists sent out to the IRO camps, agencies in Germany, Austria, Italy, and to NTB and other tracing agencies elsewhere. A total of 7,000 positive locations resulted from these methods of inquiry until their termination in March 1950.

The ITS was staffed in the main by displaced persons and Germans, as the following figures show:

Total personnel of the ITS on			1.1.48	267	(36 international)
,,	,,	,,	1.1.49	1,136	(108 ,,)
,,	,,	,,	1.1.50	1,789	(141 ,,)
,,	,,	,,	1.1.51	1,037	(29 ,,)

A high proportion also of the cost of administration was carried by Germany:

	CTB		ITS	
	1947	*1948*	*1949*	*1950*
1. Cost in dollars	270,000	627,809	786,261	440,000
2. Cost in Deutschmarks	..	1,210,880	2,349,472	2,500,000

Termination

It was evident before the end of 1949 that the work of the ITS would not finish simultaneously with the closure of the IRO's other work in June 1950. Money for the continuation of the ITS at IRO's expense during the supplementary period was not available. The western European countries, however, in particular, were very anxious that valuable information concerning their nationals, and needed for indemnification, for succession, for remarriage, and so on, should not be lost to them.

The General Council was unwilling to vote more money, and directed the Director General of the IRO to re-examine the budget in detail and to make savings by simplifying operations so that most field tracing and search might be completed by 30 June 1950; he was further to negotiate with interested governments and with occupation authorities for the transfer by 30 June 1950 of the remaining tracing functions of the ITS to governments or to another international or intergovernmental body.[1]

During the first quarter of 1950 every effort was made within the ITS to implement the first part of these instructions. Both general and individual tracing were closed down, and thereafter incoming inquiries were answered only by reference to records already held by the ITS.

In the meantime the Director General tried to secure that the ICRC would take over responsibility for the ITS, or at least the custody of the archives and certain essential functions. The ICRC was, however, unwilling to assume this responsibility. After the failure of this attempt the Organization was able to economize in the running of the ITS, and even found it possible to extend its life, somewhat reduced in scope, beyond 30 June.

In March 1950, at its Fifth Session, the General Council instructed the Director General to make provision in the Plan of Expenditure for the Supplementary Period of the IRO of the necessary funds for the maintenance at Arolsen after 1 July 1950

[1] GC/135, 5 Nov. 1949.

of a reduced IRO supervisory staff, provided that such provision did not exceed the amount of the savings which could be made in the sum allocated for the ITS, including child search, in the plan of expenditure for 1949–50. The Director General was also requested to negotiate with the Allied High Commission in Germany the transfer of the operations of the ITS before 31 March 1951.

In all sections of the ITS the number of staff was curtailed, meanwhile concentrating on the major work of processing material for the National Tracing Bureaux. The Berlin Liaison Office was closed. The US zone division closed down in September and the British zone division in December, leaving only field representatives with a very reduced staff to complete the work of locating and checking graves. Records from these field offices were transferred to the ITS headquarters at Arolsen.

In September 1950 the Allied High Commission agreed in principle to assume responsibility as from 1 January 1951. Although the collection of documents had in the main been completed, there still remained a considerable amount of work to be done. Therefore the High Commission proposed to take over operational responsibility as from 1 April 1951 in return for certain advantages granted on the part of the Organization. The IRO seconded eight members of its key personnel, the costs of whose services were borne by the IRO, to be attached to the ITS for a period of six months, and transferred certain office supplies, equipment, and vehicles to the Allied High Commission.

Summing-up

Although ITS was placed under IRO jurisdiction, it kept its own standards within IRO administration and IRO policy. The scope of ITS was in fact larger than that of IRO, since it was not concerned with refugees only but with many other categories of people. As can be seen from this survey, the task of ITS went beyond the main functions of the IRO and its eighteen government members. IRO did a valuable service to other governments and voluntary agencies when it made the decision to be the successor to CTB and to develop an international tracing system. In fact today the US Government, contrary to its expressed policy in 1950, avails itself of the ITS card index and other documentation material for securing information on refugees who apply for admittance under the Refugee Relief Act of 1953.

The ITS was never fully integrated into the administrative structure or with the other operations of the Organization, but it was no less valuable to the displaced persons. Tracing the missing was a work of great humanitarian significance. The importance of feeding and clothing refugees and establishing them permanently was evident. What was not so evident and yet perhaps of equal importance was the effect on the morale of these unhappy people of successfully tracing and reuniting lost relatives.

ANNEX 33

International Tracing Service Headquarters

LIAISON MISSIONS	HEADQUARTERS		BERLIN OFFICE
	ZONE DIVISIONS	ZONE DIVISIONS	
	Tracing	Child search	

TRACING BRANCH	MASS TRACING BRANCH	RECORDS BRANCH	INDEX BRANCH	ADMINISTRATION
Sections	*Sections*	*Sections*		*Sections*
Registration	Radio	Documents Intelligence	Master index[1]	Supply
Reports	Press	Certificates	DP2 index[2]	Transport
Case review	Search list	Documents intake and library		Personnel
Files		Records checking		Travel and accommodation
Correspondence		Concentration camps Processing Typing pool Photostat		Finance

[1] Made out of typed cards with names of persons sought for, of inquirer, and persons on whom information was found in documents.
[2] Cards on displaced persons under UNRRA, later IRO care.

ANNEX 34

Central Tracing Bureau and International Tracing Service

Statistical survey of activities 1945–50

	CTB			ITS		
	1945	*1946*	*1947*	*1948*	*1949*	*1950*
I. ADULT TRACING						
(1) Inquiries received	52,258	296,437	354,689	402,810	454,390	535,346
(2) Replies sent	1,550	49,139	96,196	134,776	164,850	228,832
(3) Reports sent out	..	..	..	10,066	40,140	105,470
(a) of those, positive findings were	..	..	..	5,014	18,094	26,797
(b) negative	..	..	..	3,306	15,685	59,686
(c) interim	..	..	..	1,746	6,441	18,997
(d) of all positive:						
(i) found alive	..	..	..	3,008	10,807	15,426
(ii) found dead	..	..	..	2,006	7,207	11,371
(4) Closed cases	..	..	..	12,312	89,948	223,283
(5) Registered cases	..	..	..	44,850	128,269	220,303
II. CHILD SEARCH AND TRACING			Since 1945:			
(1) Inquiries received	..	..	..	17,087	22,314	22,613
(2) Inquiries solved	..	..	..	1,745	3,369	4,798
(3) Unaccompanied children located	..	..	..	18,817	21,768	22,985
(4) Cases solved by locating relatives	..	..	..	5,036	5,583	6,002
III. INDEX						
(1) Number of cards in index (Master and DP2)*	20,250	651,173	1,876,499	3,381,747	6,040,117	10,538,358
(2) Number of cases†	..	..	..	..	3,735,908	5,793,393
of these cases:						
information only	..	..	..	..	3,439,174 (92·07%)	5,461,103 (94·26%)
inquiries only	..	..	..	..	230,808 (6·17%)	208,993 (3·61%)
meetings	..	..	..	..	65,926 (1·76%)	123,297 (2·13%)
(3) Inquiries checked	..	..	..	42,363	111,203	183,585
IV. RECORDS						
(1) Documents received (names contained therein)	..	1,897,870	5,549,647	6,783,647	8,672,098	12,410,145‡
(2) Documents distributed§ (names contained therein):						
by headquarters	..	1,228,199	12,076,596	15,309,713	18,284,119	20,583,180
by US zone	..	8,034,359		..	..	..
(3) Cards typed in pool	..	No record	448,126	1,467,914	2,289,508	3,247,432
(4) Certificate of incarceration requests	..	..	..	810	6,497	14,023
Certificates issued	..	..	..	722	4,279	12,948
Negative replies	..	..	..	88	3,028	8,382
(5) Death certificate requests	..	..	..	233	1,383	6,352
Death certificates issued	..	..	..	..	224	1,578
ITS notifications of death issued	..	..	..	163	571	688
Negative replies	..	..	..	70	588	3,933
(6) Photostat copies made of records	..	No record	42,876	59,447	132,287	755,275 +600,000‖

* Master index: made out of cards typed with names of persons sought for, of inquirer, and persons on whom information was found in documents. DP2 index: cards on displaced persons under UNRRA and IRO care.

† Persons known in index through information or inquiry cards, or both.

‡ Documents were also received from 147,559 sources (German civil administration) in the US zone, containing uncounted names. In addition, approximately 1,370,000 individual records and 721,000 lists and registers with uncounted names were received from the US army after the war criminals trials. No figures are available for the British zone for the years 1945–7 when the British zone search bureau was not controlled by UNRRA or ITS. The increase in 1950 is partly due to the re-check of the 1946 returns submitted by the Germans.

§ In 1946–7 the CTB made general distribution, but from 1948 onwards ITS distributed only to the five western European National Tracing Bureaux, hence the fall off of the figures.

‖ Done by outside contract.

CHAPTER XIX

REPATRIATION

THE Constitution of the IRO provided for three permanent solutions: repatriation, emigration and resettlement in other countries, and local settlement or integration in the country of first refuge. Repatriation, that is, return of refugees and displaced persons to their countries of origin or previous permanent residence, was repeatedly stated in the Constitution as a primary means of reducing the refugee problem. In the preamble, as well as in Article II, paragraph 1 (*a*), and in Annex I, paragraph 1 (*b*), emphasis was put upon encouraging and assisting 'in every way possible their [the displaced persons] early return to their countries of origin'. It is well to remember that about 12 million displaced persons returned voluntarily to their countries under the displaced persons operations planned by SHAEF and carried out by the Allied military authorities and UNRRA and IGCR after their liberation throughout 1945 and 1946.[1]

Those officials responsible for the planning of these repatriation operations assumed 'that once the fighting was over and transportation became available, practically all of the displaced persons would be eager to return to their former homes to participate in the painful reconstruction of their countries'.[2] But in mid-summer of 1946 it was already apparent that by July 1947, when UNRRA and IGCR would end their operations, there would be left a large group of unrepatriables, composed chiefly of natives of Estonia, Latvia, and Lithuania, Poland, Yugoslavia, Czechoslovakia, Hungary, and the Polish and Soviet Ukraines, including a large group of Jewish people as well as the Jewish population of Germany and Austria.

With the political and social upheavals and the re-making of national maps which had taken place in their former homelands, many of those felt that they no longer had a country. Many were reluctant to return to an area whose boundaries had been changed, and where their nationality would therefore be different from that held before their deportation to central Europe. Many of them were 'in fundamental disagreement with the type of new government in power and the new economic pattern'. Those who had been politically active feared persecution or victimization; the persons with strong religious convictions deplored the supposed lack of religious freedom or the toleration of atheism under Communist rule. The peasants and farmers suspected the Communist intention to nationalize land and institute collective farms; and the small business man had doubts as to his rights and his status in a form of government that advocated the suppression of private enterprise and the national ownership of the means of production.

For the surviving Jews in the countries that had been occupied or dominated

---

[1] See Introduction, p. 18.

[2] Mr. Hilldring, Assistant Secretary of State, at hearings before the Sub-committee on Immigration and Naturalization . . ., op. cit., p. 126.

by the Nazis, repatriation did not appear to many to be a solution of their difficulties. Tens of thousands of Jews had returned to their former dwelling-places immediately after the war in search of their families and their belongings, only to reappear after a short time in the occupied countries embittered and disappointed. They found only the graveyards of their families; their belongings had often been appropriated by their former neighbours; and they realized that the pogroms and persecutions that had happened before could happen again under a totalitarian régime which encouraged anti-Semitism.

From what was known of Communism and the Communist-inspired satellite governments of central and eastern Europe, many classes among the refugees had reasons to fear that they would be persecuted on political, racial, religious, social, or economic grounds if they returned home. Yet it was still hoped in some official quarters that the situation might change and that the larger part of the displaced persons would overcome their fears and ask for assistance in repatriation. Some people thought that the reluctance of displaced persons to return home had no justification and that in good time they would change their minds and be willing to go back to their countries. The political developments during 1946 and 1947, however, made it apparent that their fears were well founded, and that repatriation as a permanent solution would concern only the smaller part of displaced persons.

The Soviet Government and its satellites asserted[1] that assistance in repatriation should be the only aid given by the IRO to the displaced persons. The western countries insisted that each individual should decide freely whether or not to return home, without prejudicing his right to assistance. The Western policy of voluntary repatriation, based on the principle of international responsibility for refugees and those who, on conscientious grounds, were unwilling to seek the protection of their national governments or return to their jurisdiction, was embodied in the Constitution.

An attempt was made to conciliate the Soviet and other Communist view-points by declaring in the Constitution that the main task of the IRO was to encourage and assist repatriation in every way,[2] and by inserting definitions of the 'valid objections' to repatriation which would have to be advanced by refugees (and accepted by the IRO) before they could receive any assistance other than assistance in repatriation.[3] In addition, as an encouragement to repatriation, a clause was written into the Constitution providing for a three months' supply of foodstuffs to those repatriants whose countries had been damaged by the war[4]—a procedure which had been developed by UNRRA. Other features of UNRRA practices were incorporated into the Constitution: refugees should receive 'full knowledge of the facts, including adequate information from the governments of their countries of nationality or former habitual residence', and this information was to be made available by government representatives who were to be given every facility for visiting assembly centres in order to place such information before the refugees.[5]

[1] See Chapter I, p. 37.
[2] Preamble to the Constitution of the IRO.
[3] Section C of Part I of Annex I to the Constitution.
[4] Article 2. 1 (a) of the Constitution.
[5] Section 1 of Part I of Annex I to the Constitution.

Sponsors of anti-repatriation movements and leaders of movements hostile to the governments of their countries of origin were to be declared ineligible for assistance of any kind from the IRO.[1]

The principal aim of the repatriation policy laid down in the Constitution was to reduce the numbers of those in exile by securing the repatriation of those who were not in danger or exposed to injustice on account of their beliefs. The task of the IRO would be to endeavour to ensure that the vital decision on repatriation was made in the absence of unnatural and fallacious deterrents, one-sided propaganda, and tendentious information. It was a difficult and thankless task; the officers who implemented it were criticized by politicians of every shade, and by the refugees themselves—their impartiality was often not understood even by their colleagues on the staff of the Organization. The policy followed was, however, a synthesis of the spirit of the Constitution, the wishes of the member governments, and the practical realities in the areas and in the period when the IRO was operating.

It was well known from the start that many refugees, however determined they appeared not to repatriate, never completely excluded the possibility. It was suspected that clearly expressed political objections to repatriation, however understandable and even sufficient in themselves, represented in many cases an oversimplification of complex motives, among which were unwillingness to make up one's mind on an irrevocable decision and the lure of adventure and possible success in the new countries overseas where many of one's fellow countrymen had successfully emigrated before the war. Apart from that, there were many individuals normally dependent or semi-dependent for whom there was no obviously better future at home; these were the widows, old people, invalids, unmarried mothers, and so on who in any case had little hope of resettlement.

Many officials of the Organization with long training in welfare work realized that not everyone could adapt himself to an alien culture, and that not everyone was young and versatile enough to fit into the entirely different economy and civilization of the overseas resettlement countries. It was felt that on grounds of human well-being alone, many refugees would be far better off at home, whatever the political colour of the government might be. There were a multitude of social and humanitarian reasons for repatriation—keeping families together, maintaining the roots and ties of all sorts that bind people to their homes and help them to live happily and contentedly where they 'belong'. Moreover, it was known that the majority of refugees who had gone home after 1946 had previously persistently refused to do so. In view of the possibility of similar changes of mind among others, repatriation was kept before refugees as an easy and accessible form of re-establishment.

Basic principles

The Organization therefore built up its repatriation policy around three main points. First, the refugees should be able at any time to repatriate if they so desired. Secondly, the IRO would do its best to see that adequate, accurate, and impartial information was provided, so that the alternative of repatriation was kept in its

[1] Para. 6 (*b*) of Part II of Annex I to the Constitution.

proper perspective, and so that the free decision which was basic to voluntary repatriation should be an informed decision. 'Information' would be given the widest interpretation to cover the significant aspects of ordinary everyday life at home. Thus the Organization would consider it to be its duty to see that the refugees could maintain contact with their countries of origin, and to this end would organize the tracing of missing relatives and the distribution of private mail from the home countries to the refugee camps, maintaining safeguards on behalf of the refugees. Everything possible would be done to overcome unfounded prejudices among certain groups in order to counteract the herd instinct and to make the refugees' own views decisive. The material administrative arrangements would support the policy; decent trains and other travel facilities would be made available; refugees would be able to obtain information on repatriation in privacy, and so on.

Given the nature of the refugee community and their environment, carrying out this policy proved an extremely difficult matter.

When the IRO began work on 1 July 1947 the numbers of refugees repatriating from assembly centres and camps each month was still between five and ten thousand, and the necessity for continuing to assist refugee repatriation was hardly in doubt. On the other hand, the tempo of repatriation was slackening rapidly.

It was early realized that the execution of the policy of entirely voluntary repatriation involved the maintenance of adequate facilities for repatriation, regardless of whether or not they were actually used. Complicated arrangements had to be made and carried out for those willing to repatriate. Such arrangements required the provision of transportation facilities, the supply of rations, and negotiations with the countries of origin. The task of the repatriation officers in the IRO was thus felt to be as much the protection of a principle—that nothing should be allowed to stand in the way of a person who wished to go home—as the organization of refugee movements. The material aids to repatriation consisted in most cases of providing food and shelter in a collecting centre until the departure of the next available train home, transportation with family and possessions to a central point within the home country, and documentation for the journey. The Organization secured the visas, transit visas, and all other necessary permits.

The maintenance of an open door to repatriation was not a merely mechanical process. There were some very simple cases in which the job was mainly a matter of arranging transportation. But some refugees did not possess clear evidence of their nationality status, and many eastern Europeans were of uncertain nationality as the result of frontier changes and the migration of ethnic groups. Further, the governments of formerly occupied countries in general wished to prevent the return of persons of primarily German allegiance; to achieve this end, nearly all such countries imposed the requirement of individual clearance of intending repatriants. This clearance differed in form according to the country: some states issued temporary passports with entry visas, and others identity cards, permits, or repatriation certificates. It was the IRO's duty to assist refugees in these matters, and the Organization did so by helping refugees to settle individual problems of status and by establishing relations with the governments of the countries of origin.

The process of repatriation was dependent on the joint efforts of the countries of origin, the occupation authorities of the areas where the refugees were living, and the IRO itself. Clearance was not the only purpose served by establishing contacts with the home governments: information concerning current conditions in the homeland could only come from them, and close liaison with them was necessary to arrange the time-tables of the repatriation trains—provided either by the home governments or the military authorities—from the different repatriation centres and collecting and departure points which had been established. Polish repatriation centres existed at various times at Lauf, Hannover-Bucholz, Babenhausen, and Frankfurt; Yugoslav centres in Augsburg and Luitpoldkaserne, Munich; and USSR centres in Amberg in the US zone and Rastatt in the French zone of Germany, the latter being the main collecting point for Soviet nationals.

It had been hoped at first to conclude bilateral agreements for mutual assistance between the Organization and the governments interested in the return of their nationals. It was very soon evident, however, that less formal arrangements would have to suffice: for though they realized that a number of practical problems would require some kind of working relationship, at least in the initial stages, the governments under Communist guidance evinced reluctance to treat with the Organization.

Repatriation missions

In practice, individual entry clearance and the necessary personal documents were issued by the liaison officers attached to the special repatriation missions appointed at field echelon to the occupation authorities in the British, French, and US zones of Germany and Austria. It was with these missions that the IRO developed its closest co-operation, since they afforded the indispensable direct contact between the refugees and the authorities of their home countries. It had been hoped that in preference to army officers the home countries would send civilian representatives, such as consular agents, who would be acquainted with the latest laws or regulations and with the opportunities of employment in the various provinces, especially the country districts to which refugees would return. But with few exceptions the repatriation missions consisted of military personnel. The other function of the liaison officers was to convince the refugees to return home, a task which in practice was never carried out; some were unable to establish sympathetic contact with refugees whose experience had led them to distrust the military; and in turn the officers tended to regard the more vociferous refugees as undisciplined malcontents. But the presence of such officers in the occupied areas was necessary as long as refugees were to be moved home efficiently; the issue of entry clearance and practical liaison at camp level in arranging details of movements suffered greatly when the missions' activities were later restricted and finally terminated.

A number of repatriation missions had been sent out in the immediate post-war period, but the principal missions with which the IRO had to deal were those from Poland, Yugoslavia, and the Soviet Union. Contact with the missions was controlled by the occupation authorities, and matters of policy or the implementations of policy had to be handled in collaboration with them. In dealings with the Soviet mission, the British occupation authorities, for example, had to act as intermediary for every contact, because the IRO was not recognized by the Soviet mission. Repatriation missions from Yugoslavia and, in particular, Poland enjoyed some latitude as regards the visits of their officers to camps; in the British zone the missions were eventually replaced by consulates, while in the US zone the trend was to reduce the freedom of movement of the repatriation missions. A number of difficulties of a similar nature arose in Austria.

The policy of the IRO, in trying to maintain contact between prospective repatriants and the representatives of the home countries, had to be applied within the regulations of the occupation authorities who, because they were exclusively responsible for security, safety, and order in their areas, established their own rules governing the activities and safety of the liaison officers and the distribution of information material. A Hungarian mission was expelled from the US zone of Germany in April 1948, and the Soviet and Yugoslav missions were ordered to leave the same zone by 1 March 1949. Marshal V. D. Sokolovsky, Soviet Commander in Germany, was advised by General Lucius D. Clay, the US Commander-in-Chief, that sufficient time had elapsed for the completion of voluntary repatriation. The British authorities requested the Soviet mission to leave in the following year, and the Polish mission also left the British zone in December 1950. A Polish mission remained in the US zone until July 1951.

In the French zone of Germany the Soviet representatives remained until the very end of the IRO's life. When representation elsewhere had been withdrawn, the IRO was able to channel Soviet-bound repatriants through the French zone. The field staff of the Organization had persisted in their efforts to maintain informal contact with the USSR officers, so as to be able to avail themselves of their services for the return of any refugees to Estonia, Latvia, and Lithuania, though with little success.

Attitude of governments

The maintenance of an 'open-door' policy for repatriation did not depend only on the IRO and the occupation authorities. At various times the Organization had to cope with indifference on the part of the home governments. It was clear that by 1947 and 1948 most of the refugees were very reluctant to go home, but most of the home governments did not initially try to repudiate them or cut the links between the refugees and their countries of origin. In certain instances, in Rumania and Czechoslovakia, for example, refugees who had not returned by a certain time were subject to loss of citizenship; but generally speaking, and certainly for some time after the Second World War, laws for wholesale deprivation of citizenship were not enforced, and on many occasions the authorities of the countries of origin claimed that all their refugees would be made welcome. An invitation of this kind was even extended by the USSR to the pre-war Russian émigrés. The general trend of post-war nationality legislation in the eastern European states was to make provision for administrative measures for depriving emigrants of nationality, but not to make loss of nationality automatic, except in the case of small categories of people, e.g. persons of non-Bulgar stock emigrating from Bulgaria, members of the former Yugoslav army outside Yugoslavia, and certain groups of ethnic Germans

who were deemed undesirable. At all events the situation was different from that
which prevailed between the two world wars, when millions of refugees, sometimes
whole ethnic groups, had automatically been deprived of citizenship. Thus for the
greater number of prospective repatriants the legal policy on nationality practised
by their home countries was not over-rigid, and several of the countries had also
proclaimed amnesty laws for minor forms of collaboration, working in Nazi
factories, and so on. In general the wording of these laws was such as to amnesty
many political opponents of the régimes in power as well.

But although theoretically most refugees had no legal barrier to surmount if they
opted for repatriation, this is not to say that the Communist governments of the
Popular Democracies were at all times in favour of the repatriation of their refugee
nationals abroad. It was possible for these governments to give effect to their indifference on this subject by purely passive means, either by doing nothing to
facilitate the issue of individual entry clearance, or by not removing the obstacles
to the physical journey home. And towards the end of the IRO's work, more and
more restrictions or new requirements for documentation were issued for refugees
desiring to return, and a noticeable reserve became apparent about accepting persons
who had been resident too long in the west. By contrast, the Polish Government was
always willing and anxious for the repatriation of Poles, and institutional cases were
accepted even though there was a shortage of accommodation.

Entry clearance, when there was no repatriation mission to grant it, could only
be accorded by a consular or diplomatic mission, or, in their absence, upon direct
application to the home government. In the fluid conditions existing in Germany
and Austria in the post-war period, it frequently happened that refugees of several
nationalities had neither a repatriation mission nor a consular representative to
apply to. Missions were withdrawn or expelled; and often no consular or diplomatic
representation existed because governments would not appoint consuls in areas
where they were normally not needed, or because accreditation could not be provided or secured. For example, repatriation negotiations between the IRO and the
Hungarian Government had to be pursued through diplomatic channels in Paris,
Berne, Prague, Berlin, and elsewhere to solve the many and, at times, arduous
problems of organization that arose after the Hungarian repatriation mission had
been expelled from the US zone of Germany.

The case of Hungary is illustrative of the delays inherent in the working of the
national administrations with regard to repatriation. On the one hand, Hungarians
were ostensibly encouraged to return home—an amnesty law was issued comparatively late, in April 1950, suggesting that the Government had not given up
hope of further repatriation at that time. On the other hand, the Government was
anxious to prevent any Hungarian affected by the expulsion law (mainly ethnic
Germans and members of war-time German units) from returning to the country,
and accordingly each repatriant was obliged to submit a completed questionnaire
which was sent to Budapest and subjected to a lengthy screening procedure, usually
taking several months, before the repatriation certificate was issued.

The existence of these delays and difficulties made possible the repatriation
of only a few of the Hungarians who had originally wished to go home. The

circumstances surrounding Rumanian repatriation were even more unfavourable. A Rumanian repatriation mission had been withdrawn from the IRO's areas of operation on 15 May 1947 and after that date it appeared that the Government did not intend to allow their nationals to return home from the western occupation zones of Germany. So unfavourable were the repatriation prospects for Rumanians that the British Government considered the attitude of the Rumanian authorities to be one of callous indifference to the plight of their exiled compatriots, many of them Jews, and presented a strongly-worded *note verbale* through its representative in Bucharest urging the Rumanians to facilitate voluntary repatriation. One of the main obstacles was that the authorities strongly resisted the return of Rumanian nationals who had left the country prior to and during the war, contending that there was no proof that they were actually Rumanian, or that they had not since lost their nationality. The small group in Germany who finally clung to their desire to repatriate was the remnant of a large number of persons who had for some time wished to return to their homes, but had found this to be impossible owing to the absence of Rumanian representatives abroad and the complete absence of any positive action by the Rumanian Government indicating interest in the return of those of their nationals who were still abroad. No practicable method could be found for the documentation of applicants, although many left the IRO's care with the aim of returning to Rumania on foot and entering the country clandestinely.

It was clearly incumbent on the Organization to explore every possibility of getting these people home, and when it was learned that a Rumanian repatriation commission existed in east Berlin, conversations were begun there and continued with the diplomatic missions accredited to the East German Government. Nothing positive came of these talks owing to the refusal of the Rumanians to deal with repatriants except by personal interview—which was impossible owing to travel restrictions forbidding refugees to travel to Berlin and return to their respective zones afterwards. At the same time the IRO made similar approaches to the Hungarian representatives accredited to the Communist Government of Eastern Germany, in this case with slightly more success, though nothing considerable was achieved. Perseverance in these methods became increasingly undesirable. The occupation authority in the British zone pointed out that the 'East German Government', to which the Rumanian and Hungarian ministers were accredited, was not recognized by the UK Government, and that further communication with similarly accredited legations was to be deprecated and could not be agreed to. The British view was supported by doubts (later shown to be well founded) whether the two governments would do anything concrete to aid repatriation; the action of the IRO also duplicated diplomatic action between the governments concerned at a higher level, and had other undesirable implications. This objection was later modified so as to permit the IRO to continue its efforts to effect the repatriation of those wishing to go before its responsibilities for care and maintenance ceased in mid-1950; but the example is indicative of the difficulties besetting the repatriation programme and the IRO's efforts to preserve the effective opportunity of going home for the refugees in its charge.

Just as the execution of the IRO's policy in a general sense depended on many authorities, so the same is true in the physical sense—the actual material arrangements for getting people home. Although it did not become a general practice, the IRO segregated, whenever possible, those who had chosen to go home into special repatriation centres, where the necessary documentation could be dealt with, and where parties could be assembled in readiness for the next repatriation train. There was no special difficulty in providing shelter and food in centres under the Organization's supervision; but transportation was a different matter, especially in the case of movements of sizeable groups of people through the Soviet zone of Germany or Czechoslovakia towards eastern Europe. The IRO at first used trains made available by the Western Allied military authorities, and later on it used trains sent especially from the various countries of destination. Innumerable difficulties were encountered by repatriation movements to destinations behind the 'Iron Curtain', which delayed journeys often for many days. Homeward movements to other countries, though generally on a smaller scale, had other drawbacks, such as establishment of nationality or permanent residence, complicated documentation, and difficulty in reserving passages; but these, although time-consuming, were not such as to form an obstacle to repatriation.

Although it is open to question whether the countries of origin maintained their interest throughout in the return of their nationals after the majority had returned home, the countries most largely represented among the refugees, Poland, Yugoslavia, and the Soviet Union, ostensibly remained in favour of repatriation throughout the life of the IRO. Relations with the Soviet authorities were never fully satisfactory, since the USSR did not officially recognize the Organization; the other two countries for some time adopted a middle course. It has been noted that there was no possibility of concluding bilateral mutual assistance agreements for repatriation, but the return of 38,000 persons to Poland and 7,000 to Yugoslavia raised day-to-day problems of liaison between the governments and the Organization that could best be solved by the establishment of small offices in Warsaw and Belgrade, and by retaining a small office in Prague. Czechoslovakia served as a transit country for the repatriation of Hungarians, but, except for comparatively small numbers of unaccompanied Czech children, the Prague office did not have much connexion with repatriation to Czechoslovakia itself. The governments of Poland and Yugoslavia, although they maintained their disapproval of the Constitution of the IRO, agreed that the Organization should be represented in their countries 'so long as there is actual evidence that IRO is assisting in the return of refugees'.[1] In both places the IRO's delegates usually dealt personally with government officials, having little communication in writing.

The tasks of the IRO offices in Warsaw and Belgrade, both established on 1 July 1947, were similar in many respects. They assisted the local authorities to arrange adequate transport for repatriants; and they sought and obtained detailed information on specific problems such as employment opportunities for physicians and nurses, the care of unaccompanied children, opportunities for the training and employment of widows and women with dependent children, hospital facilities for TB patients and other sick, and on legal problems of all kinds. Such information,

[1] Monograph, Chief of Mission, Warsaw, 1950.

collected and disseminated by the international Organization itself, would command more attention than information suspected of propaganda bias. At the same time, the offices submitted to the governments the IRO's suggestions regarding the kind of information likely to promote repatriation among the refugees. Another important activity was tracing, in co-operation with the Red Cross and local authorities, the relatives of refugees. In some cases, the IRO was able to find relatives or friends who had been sought for several years; and quite often, when this happened, the refugee in question took the next train home. The liaison offices were also active in organizing mail services to and from the countries of origin, and assisted materially in the dispatch of information provided from governmental sources. In brief, IRO endeavoured to dispel the misunderstandings that stood as obstacles to repatriation, and tried to maintain co-operation with the governments of the home countries as far as the deteriorating international relations in Europe would permit.

The IRO worked most cordially with the Polish Government until the late autumn of 1948. During 1949 the relationship became more and more strained, and the final breach came in October of that year. The chief of the IRO's mission in Warsaw was informed by the Government on 27 September 1949 that the existence of an office of the IRO in Poland would no longer be tolerated, and he was given a fortnight in which to close it. This decision was communicated to him verbally, and in spite of a protest by the Director General of the IRO to the Minister of Foreign Affairs, the decision was not modified.

Relations between the IRO's office in Belgrade and the Yugoslav Government were conducted mostly at an unofficial level on the basis of the personal acceptability of the Chief of Mission to the Yugoslav authorities. As in Poland, much of the work consisted in arranging for information services to Yugoslav refugees abroad and the distribution of material in the assembly centres. The mission in early 1948 negotiated with the Yugoslav Government concerning an exchange of letters on repatriation matters, but before any arrangements had been completed the Ministry of Foreign Affairs informed the Chief of Mission that the 'activities of this Organization failed to provide the expected results',[1] and requested the closure of the office. This alleged failure referred to the small number of repatriants and to a divergence of opinion between the Yugoslav Government and IRO as to IRO's criteria for determining whether refugees were within its mandate, to which repeated reference had been made in discussions at the UN by Yugoslav delegates. The expulsion of the IRO's mission had been foreshadowed by the revocation on the part of the Yugoslav Government of the Bled Agreement[2] several months previously.

Supply of information

The second point of the IRO's administrative policy on repatriation, deriving from its constitutional mandate, was the provision of adequate information on the former home countries of the refugees. In Annex I to the Constitution it was further stated that information regarding conditions communicated by representatives of the governments of the home countries should normally be considered to be adequate

---

[1] Letter, Yugoslav Ministry of Foreign Affairs to Chief of Mission, Belgrade, 8 July 1948.
[2] See Chapter VII, Co-operation of Governments, p. 131.

information and that the said representatives should be given every facility for visiting camps and assembly centres in order to place such information before the refugees.

The efforts of the IRO to facilitate the provision of adequate information were at the same time an essential and a much misunderstood feature of the IRO's repatriation activities. The majority of refugees—whatever their beliefs—were at least curious to learn about the general living conditions, the labour and social security situation, and the sundry daily happenings at home; and no one doubted that the success of repatriation would depend largely on the information provided by the home countries. The information on which such decisions were based should be accurate and impartial. The Organization found that the extent to which the refugees could become informed was severely limited both by the constant insufficiency of relevant and reliable information and by the evident bias of what little was available. Thus although the IRO was not constitutionally required to do more than allow material to be distributed or to assist in distributing it, the Organization was impelled to ensure that the type of information to be diffused was in fact appropriate.

The IRO continued UNRRA's practice of distributing books, easily digested weeklies, magazines, newspapers, and posters supplied by the home countries. At the very beginning of the IRO's operations, opinions had been voiced that the material could be very much improved. In general, the daily newspapers, while of interest to the refugees, failed to provide detailed information concerning actual living conditions, and concentrated more on political propaganda which refugees did not find convincing. Illustrated magazines, technical journals, or local newspapers were of far greater interest to the refugees; but in spite of continued requests by the IRO, these were only received irregularly and in very small quantities. The countries from which the largest contingents of refugees had originated edited weekly newspapers specially for the refugee population, sometimes in large editions; the two best-known examples were *The Repatriant* published by the Polish Government and *U Domovinu*, put out by the Yugoslavs. The Polish Government, during the first three months of IRO's work, provided more than 600,000 printed leaflets and documents, including *The Repatriant*, for distribution in the British zone of Germany alone, and 500,000 during the months of October and November 1947.[1]

Another means of information employed was the showing of documentary films and, in a few cases, full-length feature films. Some forty Polish films alone were shown in Germany in the latter part of 1947 in spite of technical difficulties caused by faulty projectors or electrical equipment. The IRO thus became film operator as well as newspaper distributor and librarian; the films usually attracted a large audience[2] which in many instances recognized the scenes, not without emotion.

[1] According to a report from the IRO's Public Information Officer, in the US zone of Germany, dated 10 Mar. 1948, the usual monthly supply of newsprint distributed to the US zone was: 105,000 copies of Soviet material, 51,000 Polish, 2,650 Yugoslav. In June 1949 the Polish mission supplied the IRO with 140,000 copies of nineteen different newspapers.

[2] The Monthly Narrative Report for Austria for Dec. 1948 states: 'The extent of the attention given to the newspapers and periodicals by the displaced persons has not been determined, but the films for the most part gather a good audience, even though most of the people avoid the repatriation talk given by the Soviet officer by taking their seats after the show has started.'

But the fact that there was a good audience did not necessarily mean that the public were convinced by the facts as shown.

Since the Constitution laid down that information should be given directly to the refugees by representatives of the governments of the countries of origin, its quality and quantity were to a large extent dependent on what those countries were in a position to provide; and, where information was conveyed verbally, it was limited to what the liaison officers themselves were able to impart. In spite of the impressive amounts of publicity material disseminated, adequate, satisfactory, and credible information was not available on the matters of importance to the refugees: the value of money, prevailing wage levels, and local developments and changes. In many cases even the liaison officers themselves did not receive such information. The material that was supplied was often quite unsuitable and not of a nature to assist the refugees in making an informed decision. The tendency of these governments was to send political indoctrination rather than facts and figures; refugees who might have been swayed by objectivity were not affected by propaganda, and preferred to believe the stories of their experiences told by the refugees who were trickling through the 'Iron Curtain' towards the west. Almost certainly the inappropriate political propaganda issued by the eastern European governments prevented rather than stimulated repatriation.

The IRO's liaison offices in Belgrade and Warsaw were much concerned with the provision of information to the refugees, and they either dispatched quantities of newspapers and publications on behalf of the government or arranged for the import of such material into the occupied zones of Germany. They also assisted to some extent in providing material and suggestions for the radio broadcasts intended specially for refugees abroad; and when information material received by the IRO was shown to be decidedly unsuitable, it was through these offices that the subject was discussed with the governmental authorities. It was not always easy to convince the governments that the Organization, working directly with refugees, was in a better position to judge the type of literature needed by their own nationals. Similar approaches were made to the other countries of origin through their local representatives, liaison officers, and so on. The question of suitability was one of more than theoretical importance. The Soviet Government, for example, had provided such tendentious propaganda, amounting to an abuse of free speech in some cases, that censorship had been resorted to by the responsible occupation authorities, so that the already insufficient supplies of papers and pamphlets were also frequently subject to delay in distribution.

Of equal importance with the provision of information was the availability of representatives of the governments of origin. In fact government representatives were often few in number and unevenly distributed; they were usually army officers who had spent several years in the forces and abroad and were not well qualified to speak of present conditions of civilian life at home. In public speeches to the displaced persons they were sometimes over-emphatic, tactless, and provocative, with the result that disorderly incidents occurred; these in turn were followed in some areas by local regulations seriously restricting the activities of the liaison officers. The fault was not exclusively with the liaison officers; and, indeed, the prejudices and passions with which they and their information were sometimes received constituted a real barrier to the information programme. The military liaison officers from the countries of origin were favourite targets for hostile demonstrations, and in Austria, Germany, and Italy they had from time to time been threatened, insulted, and, in some cases, injured in the course of visits to assembly centres to encourage those whom they considered as their fellow nationals to return home. Sometimes detachments of troops were detailed to protect liaison officers from personal attack; on one occasion two liaison officers visited a centre under an escort of over 100 soldiers with fixed bayonets; on another, a Soviet general made his rounds with an escort of armoured cars. Nevertheless, liaison officers were frequently booed and cat-called; posters displayed such notices as 'Do not salute the partisan commission', 'Out with the Reds', or 'The hour of revenge is nearing'.

Some of the pamphlets supplied to the IRO by the countries of origin for distribution among their nationals in the assembly centres were propaganda attacks on the Western Allies and the countries of resettlement, although during the debates of the UN on the Constitution of the IRO delegates from the same countries had persistently urged that propaganda hostile to any member of the UN—or against repatriation—should be banned from the assembly centres. This proposal had been rejected by the majority, mainly because it was impossible to find a generally satisfactory definition of the word propaganda.[1] There was merit in the idea as far as could be applied, and it was finally decided to remove people who were leaders of anti-repatriation activities from the assembly centres. The Constitution went as far as to place such persons outside the mandate of the Organization. The intention clearly was to ensure that the refugees should make their decisions in the light of their own judgement; but the very existence of the measure was a recognition that strong political influences inimical to repatriation might be found in the refugee environment.

In some of the cases in which it was possible to prove conclusively that persons were engaged in anti-repatriation activities, the individuals concerned were referred to the eligibility officers for the appropriate action, the Constitution of the IRO, providing that '. . . sponsors of movements encouraging refugees not to return to their country of origin . . .' should not be the concern of the Organization.[2] The Administration also attempted to deal with those persons who committed acts detrimental to repatriation that constituted a breach of law and order. Provisions were made to remove such people from assembly centres, and among the misdemeanours justifying this step were active interference with the normal duties of the IRO's officials or of government representatives visiting camps, interference with the repatriation plans of other displaced persons, resistance to the distribution of information material from the countries of origin, and creating a disturbance at any film or other performance sponsored by the IRO.[3]

In the same connexion, the PCIRO, at its First Meeting in February 1947, urged the governments and authorities concerned to complete as soon as possible the

[1] UNECOSOC, *The Question of Refugees*, Documents for Special Committee on Refugees . . ., 1946, pp. 52 f.
[2] Paragraph 6 (*b*) of Part II of Annex I to the Constitution.
[3] Provisional Order 80, 8 July 1948.

screening of all displaced persons, refugees, prisoners of war, and persons of similar status, with a view to identifying all war criminals, quislings, and traitors, and, in such screening, give high priority to all persons or groups of persons who used duress or incited others to do so, in order to prevent displaced persons either from expressing the desire to return home or from approaching orally or in writing, the duly accredited representatives of the government of their country of origin.[1]

At its meeting in May 1947 the PCIRO expressed the belief that, besides ensuring the discovery of war criminals and traitors, the screening would put an end to the anti-repatriation activities, and would thus be of primary importance in repatriation. The IRO's efforts to persuade the governments to undertake such screening were not uniformly successful. It was found in actual practice that it was 'exceedingly difficult to prove'[2] whether duress had been applied in any particular instance.

Efforts were made by the IRO to continue what UNRRA had done in stimulating personal testimony—the exchange of letters between relatives and trusted friends, and the dispatch of refugee delegations to the home countries to report on conditions, and finally return visits by former refugees, already repatriated, to the camps in Austria and Germany. These efforts were considerably less successful in the IRO's period of work than they had been in UNRRA's time; the obstacles to correspondence between the home countries and the occupied areas had, if anything, increased; while, with the sole exception of a visit by former Yugoslav refugees in 1947, delays and refusals on the part of the authorities on both sides continued to prevent the movement of refugees who might have borne witness in favour of repatriation.

Aids to repatriation

In pursuance of the policy of assisting repatriation in every way possible, the Constitution of the IRO had included a provision that three months' supplies of food rations should be issued to any displaced persons returning to countries that had suffered as a result of the war.[3] As early as February 1947 the PCIRO instructed the Executive Secretary to prepare appropriate recommendations, and the sum of $1,188,000 was therefore set aside in the first quarter for the ninety-days' ration scheme, on the understanding that this expense would remain pending until the Constitution came into force. The Commission came to the conclusion that this section of the Constitution could not, for financial reasons, be implemented, and decided that the possibility of obtaining the necessary rations on loan be explored with the military authorities.[4] By October 1947, however, agreement that the latter should pay for these rations was still not reached.[5] Towards the end of the first year

[1] Paragraph 6 (b) of Part II of Annex I to the Constitution; Res. No. 8 of PCIRO which derived from Res. No. 62 (I), adopted by the UN General Assembly, 15 Dec. 1946, which embodied similar recommendations. Also E/REF/75, op. cit., p. 62.
[2] Report on the Progress and Prospect of Repatriation, Resettlement and Immigration of Refugees and Displaced Persons, submitted to the Economic and Social Council by the Secretary-General of the UN in collaboration with the Executive Secretary of the PCIRO; E/816, 10 June 1948. See Chapter XII, Eligibility, p. 207.   [3] Article 2. 1 (a).
[4] Documents PREP/39, PREP/SA/35, and PREP/83; also PREP/90 Rev. 1, 22 May 1947, and the Conference of Acting Chiefs of Mission, Geneva, 18–22 Aug. 1947.
[5] Negotiations with the Occupation Authorities for 'incentive rations for repatriants' as stated in paragraph 9 (c) 1, Section V of PCIRO/CINCEUR Agreement, which proved unsuccessful; for the text of this agreement see Appendix II (b), p. 664.

of operations it became apparent that the Organization would be able to provide some assistance of this nature, although on a more modest scale and with certain geographical limitations imposed by administrative necessity. Consequently, with effect from 1 June 1948, every refugee returning to Poland, the USSR, and Yugo-slavia from any part of Austria and Germany was given a parcel containing approximately twenty days' supply of food (40,000 calories). It was felt that this amount was adequate to tide the refugees over the period immediately following their return home and before they became re-integrated into the local economy.

In May 1947 the Executive Secretary proposed several more far-reaching measures designed to promote repatriation. At that time it was not known that the 'incentive rations' scheme would not be fully implemented, and it was proposed that the distribution should be made, as the Constitution suggested, under the auspices of the Organization after the refugees' return home. The Executive Secretary further thought it advisable to request the countries of origin to allow the IRO, through offices established on their territory, to provide such material assistance for a period not exceeding six months as might be necessary for the re-establishment of re-patriated refugees. The calculation was that the presence of the International Organization in the country of origin, and the maintenance of contact with the former refugees, would furnish a guarantee against the victimization that many of them feared.

These proposals were rejected since the representatives of the member govern-ments did not feel that the prospective numbers of repatriants were large enough to justify the establishment of a network of new offices which would entail additional financial burdens. As regards material assistance, which had been thought of in terms of cash grants, it was felt that a small allowance would be of little use and that there were no resources to make it substantial. The governments therefore confined themselves to the recommendation that those returning home be enabled to take back with them, in one form or another, the fruits of their labour, including any local currency they had saved. At the same time it was decided that, in view of the difficulties surrounding the exchange or export of goods, the problem should be referred to a technical committee of qualified experts. But this committee was never established because of the obstacles encountered in currency matters, and thus no action resulted.

In retrospect, it can be said that any broader programme than that conceived by the Administration would not have increased the repatriation figure. Refugees who wanted to return had two years in which to do so. The diminishing returns can be ascribed to various causes described in this chapter. The relationship between the western and eastern European authorities deteriorated as time went on and, as political differences came more to the foreground, there was a growing mistrust of the propaganda offered by the countries of origin. In the British zone more people at times asked for repatriation, partly because the Polish missions there were better than the Soviet missions in the US zone. When the latter complained to the autho-rities concerned about the poor response the officers pointed to the Polish success with the result merely that the Polish efforts were diminished and fewer Poles were repatriated. There was also the fact that the volume of resettlement movements grew in the course of IRO's existence, and even those who had only the remotest chance of being chosen for resettlement nurtured hopes of emigration sooner or later. This led often to the postponement of decision to return home. Camp life engendered a certain demoralization and inertia among some refugees, and doubtless there were many who hoped that the Organization would continue its programme of free assistance for an unlimited period. A counselling programme was therefore instituted examining the circumstances of each individual and making it clear to him that the Organization was a purely temporary one, and that a final choice could no longer be deferred. The expectation was that the undecided elements would be brought to make a definite choice between alternatives of which repatriation was one. When the counselling programme was carried out in the field, the Director General instructed the staff who were engaged on this programme to give their fullest support to the repatriation officers in their work with the potential residual group and institutional 'hard core' cases, considering that 'it is in this field that repatriation can be a big help in removing persons who might otherwise remain in Germany'.[1] Repatriation was to be presented as a realistic welfare solution to avoid the splitting of families by resettlement and to provide a form of re-establishment for those unable to emigrate, thereby assisting refugees whose minds were confused by political or other arguments, but for whom a return home to friends and relatives might prevent a painful separation. But the counselling programme, though valuable in other ways, was not successful in increasing repatriation.

Results achieved

The achievements of the IRO in repatriation must be judged with reference to all the complex factors which have been described, and to the principles by which its work was governed.

Many of the rules governing the physical aspects of the IRO's repatriation operation had been inherited almost intact from the predecessor agency, and both the PCIRO and the General Council made serious efforts to continue UNRRA's policy of assisting people to go home, a programme which had been written into the Constitution of the IRO as one of the Organization's primary tasks. But repatriation as a major operation was virtually finished by the time the PCIRO took over, and encouragement had ceased to produce results. The accent of the IRO's policy was therefore far more on creating an environment in which a refugee could make up his mind with the facts before him, in which he would not be harried or badgered, terrorized or propagandized into making a choice that was not in accord with the dictates of his own conscience, an environment in which there would be, both materially and morally, an open door to repatriation, but where the repatriants would be pushed neither through nor away from it. The promotion of this attitude of completely impartial detachment was in fact the IRO's most characteristic contribution to the function of repatriation.[2]

---

[1] Letter from Director General to Chief of Mission, IRO, Bad Kissingen, 20 Feb. 1950.

[2] In a statement to the General Council, Mr. Hallam Tuck, the Director General, explained the Organization's policy by stating that 'It was clear from the early days of the IRO that the great majority of willing repatriants among displaced persons had been moved during the first three years after the war and that IRO's repatriation operation would be a diminishing one. Since that time, world

The reactions of the refugees and displaced persons to the new features of the repatriation policy were at first unknown, and most of the forecasts, whether made by UNRRA officials at the UN Special Committee on Refugees in 1946, or made by the IRO officials later, tended to over-estimate the urge to return home. In the event, during the four and a half years of the Organization's lifetime, only about 5 per cent. of the refugees registered with the IRO returned to their countries of origin, whereas 65 per cent. were resettled. In 1950 the average monthly rate of repatriation fell to as low as eighty-five; during the last six months of operations only 411 people, mostly compassionate cases, went home.

At the start of the IRO's activities it was estimated that 109,000 persons would go back during the course of the first year's work; in fact only 51,000 chose to be repatriated. Political developments entirely beyond the control of the Organization were the most important cause of this small tangible result but, in view of the circumstances, the repatriation of even 51,000 so long after the war was an event of some significance. In subsequent years even fewer decided to go home, but the total ultimately achieved was 72,834. The Organization throughout did what it could, trying valiantly to promote counsels of moderation, fairness, and judgement in an atmosphere of partisan passion and hatreds.

Of the total of 72,834 refugees, 54,687 left the main areas: Austria, the three western zones of Germany, and Italy.

Area of displacement	Poles	Others	Total
Austria	1,239	3,428	4,667
Germany			
British zone	17,151	6,017	23,168
French zone	1,958	835	2,793
US zone	12,524	8,450	20,974
Italy	1,713	1,372	3,085
TOTAL	34,585	20,102	54,687

Movements to the countries of eastern Europe were the largest; next in size to the movement of Poles, which, including movements from the Middle East (3,152), totalled 37,957, came that of Yugoslavs, numbering 6,870. The balance was composed of lesser contingents, such as 3,120 to the Baltic states and less than 4,000 to the USSR, Bulgaria, Hungary, and Rumania together.[1]

The next largest movement was that of the overseas Chinese, of whom 11,122 were repatriated under the auspices of the IRO. The remainder, some 8,500, consisted of individuals or small groups of whom 2,593 went to the US and Chile, and the rest mainly to European countries.

Past experience had shown that repatriation movements were subject to considerable fluctuation; they were, for instance, higher in the warm season than in the

political developments have not been of a kind to reverse that trend. On the contrary, events have made the subject of repatriation a controversial one. In that controversy, IRO stands firmly by the letter and spirit of its constitutional mandate. Its objective is to safeguard the right of the individual displaced person to obtain information on which to base a decision about his own future and to make that decision without coercion from any source. As our operations draw to a close it may well develop that the rate of repatriation will increase . . .' (GC/SR/21, Second Session of the General Council, 19 Apr. 1949).
[1] See Annex 36, p. 363.

winter, they varied according to information received from the home countries and according to the nature of the assistance received from various quarters and also according to the expectation of future assistance.

In June 1948 the Executive Secretary noted, in a statement to the PCIRO, that the majority of willing repatriants among the displaced persons had been moved during the first three years following the end of the war. The repatriation figures for the next financial year, 1948–9, bore out this statement—there were only 10,317 repatriants, and this was not due to a sharp drop in the refugee population in camps—the repatriation figures were only 1·66 per cent. of the care and maintenance population in June 1948. In 1949–50 the percentage dropped still further to 1·07 per cent., and the total was down to 4,441 for the third financial year.

As time elapsed, therefore, movements became more and more miscellaneous and individual. And as in any humanitarian work, the daily difficulties confronting the IRO's staff did not diminish with the numbers dealt with. However small the parties, were they of Greeks, Bulgarians, or refugees from the Middle East passing through many countries en route for eastern Europe, the administration of the operation remained complex. In one case, two persons returned to Iran from the British zone of Germany; in another, a family was sent back to Brazil after an absence of ten years, and the IRO had to smooth over the difficulties arising from the fact that Brazil was not the country of origin, but merely the country of former habitual residence of the refugees concerned—the factor that had hitherto delayed their return.

The people returning to Poland formed the largest group of all, as the largest body of displaced persons originated from that country. Of the total of 37,957 Polish repatriants, 15,568 left in the first three months of operations; the figure for the ensuing quarter was less than half (7,454), while that for the third quarter of the first financial year was no more than 2,879. In the following year an average of only 400 persons monthly returned to Poland, 200 a month in 1949–50, and 25 a month in 1950–1.[1]

In 1948 there was a change in the method of transporting repatriants from the three western zones of Germany. Previously transport had been provided by the occupation authorities on the IRO's request when sufficient numbers of refugees were ready to move; later trains were provided by the Polish authorities and were regularly scheduled on a set day each month. Polish Red Cross hospital trains were used to repatriate special groups from Germany, Austria, and Italy, including unaccompanied children, hospitalized refugees, or mental cases. Such trains were also provided for similar medical cases among refugees returning from Africa and the Middle East via Italy. Special arrangements were made for the exchange of 241 insane Poles in the British zone of Germany for about 200 insane Germans in Poland. Small groups of healthy repatriants also returned from Mexico and India.

The closure of the Warsaw office of the IRO adversely affected the administrative

[1] Of the total of Poles re-established, 9·6 per cent. had chosen to go home, and 90·4 per cent. had emigrated. By contrast, former residents of Czechoslovakia and former subjects of the Soviet Socialist Republics in the present Soviet Union split 1·5 per cent. for repatriation and 98·5 per cent. for resettlement.

arrangements for repatriation to Poland. Nevertheless, co-operation with Polish representatives, then limited to consular staffs greatly reduced in numbers, was maintained, and Poles continued to form the largest body among those who decided to accept repatriation.

In four and a half years 6,870 Yugoslavs were repatriated by the Organization. This figure represents 7·7 per cent. of the total number of Yugoslavs for whom a positive re-establishment solution was found. The highest number—more than a third of the total—of Yugoslav repatriants came from the US zone of Germany; next came, in equal numbers, those from the British zone of Germany and from Austria (nearly all from the British zone of that country) and 200 were repatriated from Italy. Italy and the British zone of Austria were of course contiguous with Yugoslavia, while the US zone had the largest number of displaced persons in Germany, and was also the nearest part of Germany to Yugoslavia.

The criteria according to which the applicants for repatriation were accepted by the government authorities did not always coincide in practice with those applied by the Organization in determining eligibility, and this eligibility determination was a constant source of friction. On the one hand, the Organization could not, by a strict interpretation of its mandate, assist repatriants if they were *Volksdeutsche*, and on the other hand, the Yugoslav Government would not accept certain would-be repatriants because of their war-time activities, although they were within the IRO's mandate. The scarcity of repatriation missions did not help, and the IRO made protracted but unsuccessful negotiations to obtain a Yugoslav repatriation mission in the US zone of Austria.

The IRO assisted 1,836 people to return to the pre-1939 territory of the Soviet Union, and a further 1,909 to Latvia, 955 to Lithuania, and 256 to Estonia. One feature common to the four movements was that they were almost completely finished by the end of 1948.

The majority of the Soviet nationals went from the British zone of Germany, with an additional 490 from the US zone, 211 from the French zone, and 383 from Austria. Of the Balts a larger percentage chose repatriation from the British zone than from the US zone, although the Baltic refugee population in the latter zone was consistently somewhat higher. But, though there is a significant difference in the percentage between the two zones, the overall percentage of those in good health and able to earn a living who decided for return was only about 1·5 per cent. of the total. Unlike the Poles, who were mostly peasants and labourers, the former residents of Estonia, Latvia, and Lithuania comprised a large proportion of intellectuals, including the administrative, clerical, and commercial groups. Further, the entire Baltic group, like the refugees originating from eastern Poland, had already had some experience of incorporation into, or occupation by, the Soviet Union from 1939 onwards; this had not been the case, or only partly so, as regards the other national groups.

The homeward movement of those who had fled in the early days of the National Socialist régime from Germany and Austria was not large—3,836 persons in all. Most of the repatriants came from Shanghai, Metropolitan France, and Italy, and some 400 of them returned to Austria from the British zone of Germany.

The move of Greek displaced persons to their homeland was nearly completed in the UNRRA period, leaving the IRO only individual cases. Eight hundred and forty-two were repatriated by the Organization, mostly from Austria, Italy, and the US zone of Germany; this occurred mainly during the later months of 1947 and again towards the end of 1949. A major difficulty was obtaining recognition of the Greek citizenship of foreign-born wives who had married Greeks outside Greece and otherwise than according to the Orthodox rite.

Three hundred and thirty displaced Czechoslovak citizens were returned to their country in the first three months of the IRO's work. The usual seasonal slump was observed in the winter of 1947–8, and before the rhythm could pick up again in the spring, the Communist *coup d'état* came to discourage most of the remainder. Thereafter only sporadic, scattered individual movements took place until the expiry of the amnesty law. After the first quarter-year, an average of less than four persons a month were repatriated to Czechoslovakia during the IRO's lifetime.

There were in 1947 several thousand Hungarians[1]—many of them Jews—in Germany, many of whom wished to return home but were unable to do so; a similar situation existed in Austria. The efforts of the IRO were restricted by liaison and documentation difficulties to the movement of comparatively small bodies. A group of 115 Hungarians left the British zone of Germany in October 1947 on a Hungarian 'hospital' train. They arrived in their country after a great deal of tribulation owing to obstacles raised by the Soviet authorities to their transit through the Russian zone of Austria. A further group of 68 left in April of the following year and a third group departed from the French zone in June 1949. The total number of Hungarians repatriated amounted to 1,608, 910 of them in the first six months.

The Rumanian element among the displaced persons was also large, and in September 1947, 19,430 of them were receiving care and maintenance from the IRO. Of this figure 18,593 were Jews. It has been noted that the Rumanian Government did practically nothing to facilitate the return of its displaced citizens abroad, though several thousands of them desired to repatriate; a Rumanian repatriation mission which the Government later disowned found 1,067 willing repatriants in the course of one tour in the British zone of Germany alone. The IRO's repatriation officers noted sadly the irony of the situation: that the national groups such as Poles and Yugoslavs who could repatriate nearly all the time showed less interest in doing so than the Hungarians and the Rumanians, for example, for whom no repatriation channel could be devised. Only 185 persons were returned to Rumania in the fifty-four months of the IRO's work.

Repatriation to the US appears at first sight strange work for a refugee organization. The operation of repatriation to the US had been taken over from UNRRA (who had moved 10,000 American citizens). The persons concerned were nearly all people of Polish extraction, either born in the US and then taken back to Poland when infants, or emigrants to the US who had become naturalized and had subsequently returned to reside in Poland, or again US citizens who were caught by the Second World War when visiting relatives in eastern Europe. Again, during the processing of the emigration candidates under the provisions of the United States

---

[1] See Chapter X, Origin of the Refugees, p. 182.

Displaced Persons Act of 1948, an unexpected number of persons was discovered to have been born in the US. Where citizenship had been retained, the case was clearly no longer one of immigration; it was, so to speak, half-way between resettlement and repatriation.

Nearly all the 2,273 US citizens who went home with the assistance of the IRO did so from the US zone of Germany, 1,938 of them between 1 July 1947 and 30 June 1948. The IRO's part was mainly the provision of facilities on repayment; until December 1947, when the US Government opened its own centre adjoining, but separate from, the IRO's premises in Bremerhaven, the people concerned were lodged and fed in assembly centres for several days before being shipped home in the Organization's transports. In May 1948 it was decided that the IRO would no longer participate in arrangements for the repatriation of US nationals, but a number of miscellaneous cases continued to swell the statistics until the last month of the IRO's activity. The following arrangements were finally adopted: when the US citizen was unaccompanied, or when he was the head of a family, reimbursement to the IRO for transportation home was made prior to embarkation either by the individual, by relatives or friends in the US, or by means of money advanced by the local US consulate.

American voluntary societies assisted in this programme to a certain extent. Since, however, the cases in most instances fell within the category of individual migrants, arrangements were made with the Traveller's Aid Society to apply the usual procedure for the reception and onforwarding of non-agency cases. Many of these repatriants had no funds and no place of final destination, and their assistance was assured by departments of public welfare. The IRO's office in Washington had to notify the Federal Security Agency, the Traveller's Aid Society, and the Department of State of the imminent departure of such American nationals from Europe.

In the Far East there were, on the one hand, those Chinese who had left their homes in South-east Asia as a result of the Second World War and who had no means of going home, and, on the other hand, European refugees, victims of the Nazi régime, who had fled to China before the outbreak of the war. Some of these wished to return to their countries of origin; others wished to settle elsewhere, mostly in the US of America or, later, in Israel.

In neither case was the task of the Organization an easy one. There were numerous and often serious obstacles, lack of adequate transport and the shipping problem being not the least among them. Nevertheless, 1,809 European refugees were sent home from China during the lifetime of the IRO; they went to Austria, Czechoslovakia, Greece, Hungary, Israel, Italy, Poland, Turkey, and Yugoslavia.

The groups of overseas Chinese consisted of those whose usual place of residence had been outside China before the war and who, owing to the hostilities, were stranded in that country. Their wish was to return home. Many Chinese had lived in Burma, the Malay States, the Philippines, Indonesia, and Indo-China for a long time and had been able, owing to their trading abilities, to establish prosperous colonies there; their number is uncertain. Some of those stranded in China had been able to return to the country of their former residence by their own means; but the remainder, some 12,000 of them, were taken under the protection of UNRRA and, later, of the IRO, until such time as they could be conveyed home.[1]

The Organization met with considerable difficulties in the case of the overseas Chinese, owing mainly to the reluctance of the governments of their pre-war residence to re-admit them. An outstanding example of this was the imposition of occupational restrictions by the Burmese Government in 1948, when the admission of 3,000 Chinese, screened and approved by a Burmese deputation the previous year, was cancelled. Later, after lengthy negotiations with the IRO and strong representations from the Chinese Government, the Union of Burma agreed to admit them, and the admission of a further 3,000 was approved; but owing to Burma's internal difficulties, only 1,200 were able to enter the country in the first two years of the IRO's life. Similarly, the Government of the Philippines was consistently firm; and despite repeated interventions by the IRO, no Chinese previously resident in the Philippines were able to return thither under the auspices of the Organization.

The repatriation of the overseas Chinese involved the IRO in arranging for 11,122 people to go to their homes between 1 July 1947 and 31 December 1951. For the most part they went to Burma (6,086); the remainder went to Indonesia (1,758), Singapore (1,675), the Malayan Union (1,399), Sarawak (188), and Indo-China (16). These repatriants were accompanied on board ship by administrative and medical escorts provided by the IRO in every case where substantial groups were being moved. On arrival they were received by the local authorities, Chinese consular officials and representatives of communal associations, who arranged for their billeting, dispersal, and forwarding to their pre-war homes.

The compulsory deportations by the Nazi and similar régimes had not affected only the Poles, Yugoslavs, and other eastern Europeans whose repatriation by IRO has been described. The displacements of populations and the persecutions involved many different nationalities, and before the IRO's task had come to an end, it had arranged the return of about a thousand persons, individually or in small groups, to the Argentine, Belgium, Brazil, Canada, Chile, China, France, Iran, Italy, Luxembourg, the Netherlands, Peru, Spain, Turkey, and Venezuela.

[1] Chapter X, Origin of the Refugees, p. 187.

ANNEX 35

Repatriation

Country of destination and area of departure

Refugees repatriated from specified IRO areas, 1 July 1947–31 Dec. 1951

Country of destination	Total	Argentina	Austria	Belgium	Brazil	Chile	Czechoslovakia	Denmark	Far East — Shanghai: Europeans	Far East — Shanghai: Overseas Chinese	Far East: Philippines	France: Metropolitan	France: French North Africa	Germany: British zone	Germany: French zone	Germany: US zone	Greece	Italy	Luxembourg
TOTAL	72,834	8	4,667	125	17	3	57	32	1,809	11,122	21	745	1	23,168	2,793	20,974	4	3,085	2
Argentina	23		5											10		5		1	
Austria	2,243		..	31	5		12	1	799		3	246		419	49	3		77	
Belgium	205		28									3		71	14	85		1	
Brazil	187		158					2						22	1	4			
Bulgaria	31		6											5				13	
Canada	38		8											19		10		1	
Chile	320		12	1										117	21	189		45	
China	45		..						3									27	
Czechoslovakia	525		38						2			5		56		365			
Estonia	256		2			3						1		153		97		8	
France	243	5	11	75	12		17	9				5		74	19	2	1	133	
Germany	1,592	3	30	1			11		875		2	232		53	136	232		238	
Greece	842		271						12			157		230	2	448		237	
Hungary	1,608		345				3	1	6					2	55	18		7	
Iran	38		6	1										34					
Italy	541		146	1			7		35			8			27	252			
Latvia	1,909		11											1,334	6	536		1	
Lithuania	955		..									1		737	9	211			
Luxembourg	33		17												30	27			
Netherlands	130		6											59	27	120		7	2
Peru	126			7				19	54			25	1		120			6	
Poland	37,957		1,239				1							17,151	1,958	12,524		1,713	
Rumania	185		148						2			13		4	6	6		3	
Spain	63		7						4			18		3	13			12	
Turkey	362		29						2			5		5	4	288		18	
USSR	1,836		383	2					5		2	5		602	211	490		139	
US	2,273		8								5			84	4	2,168		7	
Venezuela	52											11				52			
Yugoslavia	6,870		1,742				5							1,806	207	2,730	1	353	
Overseas Chinese	11,122									11,122									
Burma	6,086									6,086									
Singapore	1,675									1,675									
Malayan Union	1,399									1,399									
Indo-China	16									16									
Sarawak	188									188									
Indonesia	1,758									1,758									
Miscellaneous	167		11						3			9		76	6	8	2	37	
Not reported	57			7			1		7					42					

ANNEX 35 (cont.)

Repatriation (cont.)

Country of destination and area of departure (cont.)

Refugees repatriated from specified IRO areas, 1 July 1947–31 Dec. 1951

Country of destination	Mexico*	Middle East							Not reported	Netherlands	Norway	Peru/Bolivia	Portugal	Spain	Sweden†	Switzerland	UK	US	Uruguay
		East Africa	Egypt	India	Israel	Lebanon	Syria	Turkey											
TOTAL	44	1,311	106	205	901	354	1	41	827	81	8	63	21	69	2	133	9	14	11
Argentina	1																		
Austria		14	9		448	12		18		11		36	1	1		31	5	11	
Belgium													1	1		2			
Brazil																			
Bulgaria								6											
Canada													1				1		
Chile														1					
China																			
Czechoslovakia																			
Estonia											8								
France					36	1	1	15	2	31		27	3	14		18			11
Germany						3			1	1			2	23	2	35	3	3	
Greece					8			2											
Hungary													1	1		31			
Iran																			
Italy																4			
Latvia																			
Lithuania																			
Luxembourg																			
Netherlands														1					
Peru																			
Poland	43	1,297	88	205	409	332			821	37			9			6			
Rumania										1			2	19		3			
Spain																			
Turkey																			
USSR																			
US																			
Venezuela																			
Yugoslavia			1			6										3			

* Repatriated under the auspices of the IRO Office in Washington, D.C.   † Repatriated under the auspices of the IRO Office in Denmark.

ANNEX 36

Repatriation

Country of destination

Country of destination	Total	Refugees repatriated, 1 July 1947–31 Dec. 1951								
		1 July 1947–31 Dec. 1947	1 Jan. 1948–30 June 1948	1 July 1948–31 Dec. 1948	1 Jan. 1949–30 June 1949	1 July 1949–31 Dec. 1949	1 Jan. 1950–30 June 1950	1 July 1950–31 Dec. 1950	1 Jan. 1951–30 June 1951	1 July 1951–31 Dec. 1951
TOTAL	72,834	36,856	15,049	8,880	4,709	3,284	1,476	1,541	628	411
Argentina	23	5	6	6	2	3	..	..	..	1
Austria	2,243	824	227	190	684	200	51	28	18	21
Belgium	205	43	126	7	4	8	7	5	3	2
Brazil	187	18	6	147	8	5	2	1	..	..
Bulgaria	31	5	..	..	1	13	3	3	6	..
Canada	38	8	11	12	4	3	..	..	..	..
Chile	320	304	..	8	4	..	..	4	..	..
China	45	..	45	..	..	..	..	..	..	..
Czechoslovakia	525	345	40	55	22	20	15	11	13	4
Estonia	256	127	59	42	9	5	14	..	..	..
France	243	27	99	18	16	33	16	19	7	8
Germany	1,592	575	79	112	184	231	170	133	35	73
Greece	842	283	44	62	81	235	66	19	31	21
Hungary	1,608	910	208	302	16	62	15	55	28	12
Iran	38	4	6	..	18	6	1	3	..	..
Italy	541	350	79	24	14	35	16	16	1	6
Latvia	1,909	1,243	403	165	70	16	11	..	1	..
Lithuania	955	297	476	120	46	10	4	2	..	..
Luxembourg	33	12	11	10	..	..	..	..	..	..
Netherlands	130	41	36	24	4	8	3	3	9	2
Peru	126	120	6	..	..	..	..	..	..	..
Poland	37,957	23,088	6,658	4,288	1,050	1,648	677	295	23	30
Rumania	185	145	8	6	2	4	7	10	1	2
Spain	63	7	1	8	18	14	4	5	1	5
Turkey	362	5	..	48	267	16	15	4	6	1
USSR	1,836	711	362	332	152	111	44	23	96	5
US	2,273	1,135	803	176	13	13	41	48	25	19
Venezuela	52	52	..	..	..	..	..	..	..	..
Yugoslavia	6,870	3,293	1,245	783	444	326	217	217	154	191
Overseas Chinese	11,122	2,803	3,928	1,906	1,366	248	71	633	167	..
Burma	6,086	2,017	1,106	966	1,204	142	58	464	129	..
Singapore	1,675	19	1,468	134	25	28	1	..	..	..
Malayan Union	1,399	30	1,062	206	30	71	..	..	..	..
Indo-China	16	..	1	..	..	..	..	9	6	..
Sarawak	188	3	4	137	43	1	..	..	..	..
Indonesia	1,758	734	287	463	64	6	12	160	32	..
Miscellaneous	167	76	27	29	10	11	6	4	3	1
Not reported	57	..	50	..	..	..	..	..	..	7

REPATRIATION

ANNEX 37

Repatriation

Area of departure

IRO area of departure	Total	Refugees repatriated, 1 July 1947–31 Dec. 1951								
		1 July 1947–31 Dec. 1947	1 Jan. 1948–30 June 1948	1 July 1948–31 Dec. 1948	1 Jan. 1949–30 June 1949	1 July 1949–31 Dec. 1949	1 Jan. 1950–30 June 1950	1 July 1950–31 Dec. 1950	1 Jan. 1951–30 June 1951	1 July 1951–31 Dec. 1951
TOTAL	72,834	36,856	15,049	8,880	4,709	3,284	1,476	1,541	628	411
Argentina	8	..	..	..	2	6	..	..	..	..
Austria	4,667	1,773	1,158	815	340	254	104	81	64	78
Belgium	125	6	18	8	15	25	5	16	15	17
Brazil	17	..	..	2	..	11	4	..	..	..
Chile	3	..	..	..	..	..	1	2	..	..
Czechoslovakia	57	..	9	12	13	14	9	..	..	..
Denmark	32	..	..	1	10	7	8	1	..	5
Far East	12,952	3,472	3,962	2,008	1,950	400	208	733	177	42
Shanghai:										
Europeans	1,809	669	34	102	581	144	126	101	10	42
Overseas Chinese	11,122	2,803	3,928	1,906	1,366	248	72	632	167	..
Philippines	21	..	..	..	3	8	10	..	..	..
France	746	204	106	133	134	75	33	24	12	25
Metropolitan	745	204	105	133	134	75	33	24	12	25
French North Africa	1	..	1	..	..	..	..	..	..	..
Germany	46,935	27,611	7,912	5,246	1,924	2,111	1,017	615	294	205
British zone	23,168	13,997	3,906	2,329	838	1,198	546	184	130	40
French zone	2,793	1,221	438	603	165	179	110	49	20	8
US zone	20,974	12,393	3,568	2,314	921	734	361	382	144	157
Greece	4	..	..	..	..	..	..	1	2	1
Italy	3,085	1,954	545	207	148	136	24	30	30	11
Luxembourg	2	..	..	..	..	..	..	2	..	..
Mexico*	44	..	..	44	..	..	..	..	..	..
Middle East	3,746	1,738	1,310	348	110	177	29	15	9	10
East Africa	1,311	320	756	169	21	28	16	1	..	..
Egypt	106	38	5	58	..	5	..	..	..	..
India	205	..	205	..	..	..	..	..	..	..
Israel	901	434	248	39	74	106	..	..	..	..
Lebanon	354	113	93	80	14	28	6	13	..	7
Syria	1	..	..	..	..	..	..	..	1	..
Turkey	41	6	3	2	1	10	7	1	8	3
Not reported	827	827	..	..	..	..	..	..	..	..
Netherlands	81	9	4	26	1	26	7	8	..	..
Norway	8	..	..	..	..	..	..	..	8	..
Peru/Bolivia	63	..	..	2	42	19	..	..	..	..
Portugal	21	8	4	2	2	2	3	..	..	..
Spain	69	8	13	18	2	10	5	4	4	5
Sweden†	2	..	..	..	..	..	2	..	..	..
Switzerland	133	72	8	..	8	4	12	9	12	8
UK	9	..	..	8	1	..	..	..	..	..
US	14	1	..	..	7	6	..	..	..	..
Uruguay	11	..	..	..	..	1	5	..	1	4

* Repatriated under the auspices of the IRO Office in Washington.
† Repatriated under the auspices of the IRO Office in Denmark.

CHAPTER XX

RESETTLEMENT[1]

A. PLANNED MIGRATION

THE migration for settlement of 1,038,750 persons, including individuals and families, undertaken by IRO over a period of four and a half years was its largest single operation and greatest achievement. In no earlier world migration have so many uprooted people in an organized effort been resettled in foreign countries as was accomplished by the IRO. The migration of refugees for settlement is nothing new; what was new about this migration was the fact that it was organized. The migrants were in the tradition of those English Nonconformists who landed in the new world from the *Mayflower* on 21 December 1620; of the half million English, Irish, and Scottish Catholics who followed their king into exile in the half century after 1688; of the Huguenots who so largely built up the English cloth trade; and, in more recent times, of the White Russians who left Russia after the Revolution of 1917; of the Armenians who left Turkey, and of the Germans who refused to submit to Nazism. The recent immigrants were made welcome in foreign lands in the same spirit which had inspired George Washington to express the hope that his country would increasingly become a 'more and more safe and propitious asylum for the unfortunate of other countries'. Yet, there is a difference; earlier migrations had been undertaken on the initiative of the refugees themselves, with such assistance as could be obtained from charitable sources. This new migration, on the other hand, was co-ordinated and planned to a large extent by an organization of eighteen member governments whose individual and collective resources were used to further it.

The governments, motivated primarily by humanitarian and political ideals, had sought ways of helping the refugees and displaced persons. They were just as eager to relieve human misery and suffering as they were to lessen political tension, and to counteract economic instability in the countries of refuge by an effort to settle the refugees in such a manner that they would not become an economic and social burden to either the countries of refuge or the countries of final reception. They wanted to help them become self-supporting citizens of their new homeland and to be able to contribute to its economic and social life. In other words, while the governments concerned looked upon the refugee problem as an immediate social welfare task, they were at the same time searching for a long-range solution in terms of a real economic and social integration of the refugees in their new homelands. In the late 30's and early 40's it had become apparent that the refugee problem was linked with the expansion of old and the development of new economies, and was

---

[1] IRO, *Migration from Europe*, Sept. 1951, 101 pp. A report by the Director General to the General Council of the IRO, on experience gained in the field of migration, of which extensive use has been made in this chapter.

thus part of the overall migration problem of the twentieth century. Under the leadership of President Roosevelt the US Government prepared public opinion for a new approach to the old question of immigration overseas. In October 1939, at a meeting of the IGCR, President Roosevelt pointed out that the 'geographical and economic problem of resettling several million people in new areas of the earth's surface' was a 'duty because of the pressure of need', but that it also offered an opportunity for taking part in the building of new communities for those who needed them. 'Out of the dregs of present disaster, we can distil some real achievements in human progress.'[1]

Planning immigration after the Second World War was no simple matter for the potential countries of reception. The western countries were not even sure that their demobilized soldiers could be successfully absorbed into their own post-war economies; the slumps of the early 1920's had not been forgotten, and there was no certainty that similar unemployment could be avoided after the Second World War.

At the meeting of the Special Committee on Refugees and Displaced Persons of the UN in the spring of 1946, the Australian delegate announced that his government was willing to embark on a vigorous immigration scheme, but he added cautiously that:

It will not be practicable, however, for selected immigrants to travel to Australia until our obligations to those people who are entitled to rank in priority have been met. . . . The Australian Government will not initiate any large-scale plan of immigration unless it is possible, within reasonable limits, to ensure the economic future of intending immigrants and to meet the obligations of our community. . . .[2]

The Brazilian Government, too, had plans for resettling a large number of refugees, but was anxious to protect its own national workers against competition. For the same reason the Canadian delegate pointed out that under the Canadian law immigrants had to possess sufficient means to support themselves for specified periods after their entry to Canada. In the long run, however, the western countries succeeded, and as a result of initial cautious planning the great schemes of immigration, to be described later, were realized: among these the Australian, Brazilian, and Canadian were outstanding.

At the end of 1946 and the beginning of 1947, several governments in western Europe needed man-power in specific fields of economic activity. In some cases such a need had been met before the war by immigration of labour, and the governments were now seeking for a similar solution. The IGCR joined in an agreement between the Belgian Government and the occupation authorities of the British and US zones of Germany regarding the recruitment of refugees for work as miners. Both the governments of France and the Netherlands followed with offers to admit refugee workers; and the UK Plan, 'Westward Ho!', initiated to fill a labour gap, was implemented independently although in consultation with the IGCR during the same period. Several overseas countries expressed interest in the immigration

[1] Dept. of State, *Bulletin*, i. 17, Washington, 21 Oct. 1939, pp. 398–400.
[2] E/Ref./75, op. cit., p. 87.

of refugees (some countries of Latin America). By arrangement with the IGCR, Canada began to admit small numbers of refugee workers for particular industries, such as lumber and sugar-beet workers, and girls for employment in textile mills.

While Australia, Canada, New Zealand, several countries of South America, as well as the US were embarking on programmes of industrial expansion there was a persistently low or even declining figure of unemployment. In spite of this, in some countries, fear was felt that cheap immigrant labour might prevent native labour from improving its economic position. Yet with continuing prosperity it was recognized that there was a close relationship between an expanding population and economic progress, and that increased immigration might lead to higher standards of living. This expansion of the world economy which went on during IRO's life-time created a climate favourable to the accomplishment of IRO's undertaking. The connexion between immigration and economic expansion may have been an important consideration for governments' action, yet they were definitely moved also by the humanitarian nature of IRO's task. President Truman issued a directive on 22 December 1945 instructing the Secretary of State to make quota visas available to displaced persons; under this order 41,379 persons were admitted to the US.[1] In November 1945 the British Home Secretary had announced[2] the Distressed Relatives Scheme under which certain categories of close relatives of persons already in the UK were to be admitted to that country. At first, this scheme benefited people from Germany and Austria; later it was extended to admit refugees from Shanghai. This effort was important because it was one of the first schemes expressly providing for the union of families. In November 1946 the Canadian Close Relatives Scheme was launched.[3] It was designed to bring to Canada a number of refugees nominated by close relatives who had earlier settled in that country. The IGCR contacted the refugees, and Canadian Consular representatives toured Germany and Austria to make the final selections. Other governments and peoples, at different times, and in their own ways, added their quota to the humanitarian resources that assisted the post-war migration of refugees; and in all of these efforts the voluntary societies and associations channelled the help given by those not in need to co-religionists and to members of their own national and ethnic groups.

A similar humanitarian impulse was behind the passage of the United States Displaced Persons Act of 1948, which authorized the admission of 205,000 displaced persons over a period of two years, and which was amended in 1950.[4] This Act was a departure from the principles which had dominated immigration to the US for over twenty years. It was planned specifically for meeting the needs of refugees. Under its provisions more refugees during the IRO period went to the US than to any other country.

This national legislation was mainly initiated by individual governments; in addition this legislation was supported by inter-governmental planning. Participation

[1] *Factbook*, Displaced Persons Commission, 7 Dec. 1951, p. 4.
[2] *Parl. Deb., Commons*, vol. 415, cols. 1922–7, 13 Nov. 1945; vol. 420, cols. 491–3, 7 Mar. 1946; vol. 451, cols. 1223–5, 3 June 1948.
[3] Hugh L. Keenleyside, *Canadian Immigration Policy*, Vancouver, 1948, p. 13.
[4] Displaced Persons Act of 25 June 1948 (Public Law 774, 80th Congress) with Amendments of 16 June 1950 (Public Law 555, 81st Congress), and of 29 June 1951 (Public Law 60, 82nd Congress).

by the IGCR, and encouragement given by it, paved the way for the resettlement work of the IRO.

Preparatory work

As early as 1945 the IGCR had begun assisting refugees in their immigration by paying the passages of individual refugees and family groups. This activity had been limited primarily to refugees who had found temporary asylum in western European countries. In 1946 IGCR established representatives in the British, American, and French zones of Germany and Austria. Their function was 'to assist in preparing for the emigration and permanent resettlement of those refugees who came within the jurisdiction of the Committee'. In the same year four missions were sent to South America to explore resettlement possibilities; one to Brazil, a second to Argentina, Paraguay, and Uruguay, a third to Bolivia, Peru, and Ecuador, and a fourth to Chile, Colombia, and Venezuela. Agreements regarding the immigration of refugees and displaced persons were concluded with Bolivia, Brazil, Chile, Colombia, Ecuador, Peru, and Venezuela. With this initial work IGCR had laid the foundation for the world-wide migration operations carried out on behalf of refugees and displaced persons by IRO.

When PCIRO assumed operating responsibilities, migration plans had been developed by interested European governments and by the IGCR along two principal lines: immigration under government selection schemes and emigration under normal consular procedures.

The first method, known as mass resettlement, was employed for the selection of groups and categories of immigrants, chosen by special government missions sent to the western zones of Germany and Austria. Under this procedure some 29,400 refugees and displaced persons had been moved prior to 1 July 1947.

The second procedure, individual migration, was followed in the case of those who had obtained immigration visas with the assistance of voluntary societies and known sponsors in resettlement countries, and had been transported to their destinations with the financial aid of the IGCR. In this way more than 7,500 refugees and displaced persons had been moved before 30 June 1947, including a group of 2,300 Mennonites who went to Paraguay on a colonization project initiated and executed under the sponsorship and with the active assistance of the Mennonite Central Committee.

The two main forms of migration activity developed by the IGCR were continued by the IRO and accounted for the resettlement of most of the refugees under this latter organization. Later the IRO developed a third type of procedure, based on the placement of individuals with prospective employers or sponsors whose co-operation was actively solicited on the basis of the person's specific qualifications or needs. This was called the Resettlement Placement Service.

IRO policy

All of IRO's migration activities were conducted within the framework of these three major types of approach:

(1) Emigration under government selection schemes;
(2) Emigration initiated through personal nomination by known sponsors in the resettlement country;
(3) Placement of individuals with prospective employers or sponsors on the basis of their qualifications or needs.

The implementation of each of these three schemes involved a wide variety and great complexity of procedures from the moment when a refugee applied for emigration assistance to the time when he became an integrated member of a new community in his country of adoption. These procedures and the operational techniques which were developed by the IRO in co-operation with its member governments set new standards and developed new methods for dealing with the problems involved in twentieth-century migration.

Regardless of the scheme to be adopted for each refugee, the steps involved were, more or less, as follows:

(1) Procedures in countries of emigration;
(2) Opening of resettlement opportunities;
(3) Procedures in countries of immigration;
(4) Transportation to countries of immigration.

These major aspects of resettlement operations will be described.

It must be borne in mind, however, that the entire resettlement process, from application until firm establishment overseas, was one long connected chain of clearly established procedures, a highly co-ordinated affair depending on very exact timing. It must be also realized that there was not only an overlapping of the different types at various stages but that it was sometimes difficult to determine exactly to which type belonged a particular resettlement scheme. For instance, the Canadian scheme for nominating close relatives was implemented by government selection missions in Germany, Austria, and Italy. Similarly, the special law for the immigration of displaced persons promulgated by the US Congress in 1948 provided for individual nominations on the one hand, and for a special government mission to implement it on the other. These two schemes, therefore, are a mixture of the two first types mentioned above.

In the course of years, migration schemes were often changed in essential aspects by developments in the receiving countries. A labour selection scheme, for instance, might develop into a nomination scheme and vice versa. There were in fact many instances in which the two schemes were closely linked, and in which nominated individual immigration increased in proportion to acceptances under a government selection scheme, since immigrants selected under the first scheme nominated their dependants for immigration under the second scheme once they were firmly established. Thus often two or even three different procedures were applied simultaneously for immigration to the same country. The IRO therefore had to develop a high degree of flexibility in order to adapt its policies and procedures to changing conditions.

This flexibility was all the more important since the IRO, in accordance with the essentially humanitarian task with which it was entrusted, was responsible for seeking resettlement possibilities for its total 'population'. It continuously exerted all its influence to persuade reception countries to enlarge their resettlement criteria and to adapt them to the specific task. Special schemes were developed for the disabled and the handicapped who were granted resettlement possibilities through the generosity of receiving governments which agreed to give special consideration to humanitarian projects.[1]

Procedures in countries of emigration

Administration of the resettlement operations required the construction of complicated machinery; a resettlement service at headquarters as well as delegations in the receiving countries were needed.[2]

The resettlement service working at headquarters had to prepare agreements with countries of emigration and supervise their execution; to supervise individual and collective emigration carried out by the local agents of the Organization; to supply the delegations of the IRO in the countries of residence of the refugees and displaced persons and in the receiving countries with instructions for the implementation of agreed measures; delegations of IRO were set up temporarily in receiving countries when the scale of the resettlement in hand required it. The mandate of each delegation extended over one or several countries and each delegation included one or more experts or technical advisers who were placed at the disposal of the receiving countries at request in the event of their not having organized immigration services.[3]

At headquarters a Department of Repatriation and Resettlement was established under the direction of an Assistant Executive Secretary. This administrative unit, one of the three major departments at headquarters, was divided into three divisions: (1) Repatriation; (2) Resettlement; (3) Refugee Movements. The Division of Resettlement directed operations through its three geographical branches: (1) British Commonwealth and North American; (2) Latin American; (3) Western European and French Empire. To these was added, in June 1948, a fourth, dealing with individual migration.[4]

The course of action followed by the IRO for its last three years of work was to widen the labour-recruiting schemes so that families either migrated with the breadwinner or followed him shortly afterwards. Additional schemes were initiated for those who would not normally have been admitted; some countries, e.g. New Zealand, accepted refugees who, although employable, were not normally needed in the big recruitment schemes; other countries, e.g. Norway and Sweden, took refugees suffering from particular diseases; contact between potential employers and employed was established by the Resettlement Placement Service. The US scheme, though not without restrictions, permitted the immigration of all persons (subject to the normal health and other requirements of the regular immigration law) for whom an assurance could be given that suitable employment and housing existed and that the person would not become a public charge.

The central administration, working under the direction of the governing bodies, formulated basic policy, procedure, and operational techniques to guide the field staff. In its discussions of the policies to be followed by the IRO in its resettlement

---

[1] Cf. Chapter XXIII, Hard Core, pp. 487 f.   [2] PREP/84, 20 May 1947.
[3] Ibid.   [4] PREP/161.

work, the PCIRO dealt immediately with the more technical aspects of the matter, such as transportation, reception facilities, employment, and naturalization in the receiving country, to name only a few. In regard to individual migration, the principle was established that assistance of voluntary societies should be actively sought.

The principles adopted by the PCIRO to govern the resettlement activities of the IRO were flexible enough not only to vary in their application as time went on, but also to vary in their application from country to country.

This administrative structure was maintained for nearly two years before, at the end of 1948, emigration began to increase rapidly. In March 1949, in order to effect a closer co-ordination of selection, processing, collection, movement, and shipping, the administrative structure had to be altered. The Division of Mass Resettlement then became responsible for controlling all activities, including transportation, directed towards bringing refugees to the point of embarkation, as well as for controlling the activities of the IRO's delegations in the reception countries. Thus this Division had the supervision of all IRO's work for refugees in the process of resettlement, except for the period when the refugees were on board ship. The old Division of Refugee Movements, which had been responsible *inter alia* for inland movements to the ports, concentrated its work on providing shipping and air transport for the schemes of mass resettlement. This latter work had become more technical because the rapid expansion of the IRO's fleet had involved the Organization in legal and financial questions as well as in technical problems of ships—their safety and suitability, their conversion, accommodation on board, berthing and port arrangements, and so on. The old Individual Migration Branch became a Division, responsible not only for procuring visas, but for making transit arrangements—at times a difficult task—for liaison with sponsors in receiving countries and for the procurement of passages for individual emigrants. During the first year of its work IRO had assisted more than 44,000 individually nominated migrants.

The departmental structure remained substantially the same throughout the life of the IRO. A major change external to the department was effected during 1950 as a result of the concentration of the IRO after 30 June 1950 on resettlement. All care and maintenance services for the refugees were then directed exclusively towards their migration for settlement. They were therefore taken over at head-quarters by a Department of Operations in which the technical functions of resettlement were in the charge of one division. Shipping remained in the charge of a second division; but at this stage the migration of individuals was merged with mass resettlement, since the processing of individuals became in some instances connected with that of mass resettlers; and, increasingly, individual migrants were transported on the IRO's mass resettlement ships.

The policies determined by the governing bodies and the objectives set by the central administration in Geneva were transmitted by the field missions into day-to-day practice. Instructions were sent to the operating echelons through the various combined repatriation and resettlement offices established in each field mission. Because of the number and variety of selection missions and the Organization's responsibility for supplying them with logistic support, liaison with the selection missions was everywhere important. In the US zone of Germany, for example, an Office of Governmental Liaison was established; in Austria, as elsewhere, the chief of the department assumed this responsibility himself. So far as the IRO's internal administration was concerned, the main tasks were to see that suitable refugees were chosen to put before the selection missions (a process that became known as pre-selection), that they were provided with proper documentary evidence of their background, their skill, their civil status, and so on, that they were presented to the missions in adequate and regular numbers, having been through a preliminary medical examination, and that on their acceptance they were moved forward for ultimate embarkation as expeditiously as possible.

Each receiving country supplied the IRO's central administration with particulars of the numbers of refugees it could absorb, normally classified by professions and skills as well as according to age and sex. At central headquarters in Geneva, such general requirements were allocated to the various missions in Europe and (sometimes) elsewhere. The allocations were decided by a combination of several factors. First, there was the comparison of the sort of refugees required with the known case-load in the missions; for example, a request for farmers or for refugees of a particular nationality would be transmitted to a mission where there was a large number of farmers or refugees of that nationality. Secondly, there were certain priorities; for example, the difficulties which stood[1] in the way of a satisfactory permanent establishment of refugees in Austria led the Administration to give resettlement allocations to that country whenever possible. Thirdly, in some cases certain receiving countries expressed a preference for selection in particular areas; for example, the USDP Commission preferred to begin work in the US zones because of the existence of supporting facilities; similarly, special arrangements were sometimes made by the IRO for selection in particular countries; an example is the selection of migrants for Australia from Greece and East Africa.

Allocations were sent to field missions and from there passed on to individual areas in Austria and in all zones of Germany. Each area had a number of installations in it as well as a headquarters responsible for its work. In the US zone of Germany, for example, there were seven areas.[2] It was in these operational areas that individual refugees were affected by the policies, objectives, and practices of the IRO.

At the outset of the operation, selection missions went from assembly centre to assembly centre without any organized plan. As the number of missions increased, this procedure became inadequate; assembly centres were not big enough to accommodate several at the same time, as was often necessary. Furthermore, the refugees who were living outside assembly centres had to be brought into the circuit of processing. In order to streamline the different stages of these operations, a number of special centres in which the refugees could be assembled for the purpose of selection, movements, and embarkation were established. The refugees moved

---

[1] Chapter XXII, Local Settlement, p. 477.
[2] e.g. in the Munich area the IRO had in 1950 some twenty different installations and a refugee population of 50,000.

from resettlement centres, through staging centres, to embarkation centres. The processing of refugees from one centre to another in this sequence became known as 'the pipe-line'.[1]

The task of the IRO's resettlement officers in the field was to bring available opportunities to the attention of the refugees in assembly centres and elsewhere and to select suitable applicants. The preliminary selection of refugees gave the IRO's staff an opportunity to inform each candidate about the living conditions in the receiving country, and to determine whether he matched the criteria of the particular scheme in which he was interested.

Refugees who appeared to meet the requirements laid down by the selection missions were medically examined and provided with the documents required for presentation to the mission. These documents usually included either a form of 'Application for IRO Assistance' (the CM/1 form) or an 'IRO Resettlement Registration Form' (or both) containing all relevant data on the refugee, as well as the 'IRO Medical Examination Form', a trade-test certificate, and documents concerning the refugee's civil status. Armed with this initial documentation, the refugee was sent forth with his family to a resettlement centre.[2]

Before the members of the selection mission interviewed the individual candidates, they usually reviewed their documents. Only those were interviewed who appeared to be suitable. Towards the end of the operation, the Organization was able to persuade the missions to interview all candidates in addition to looking at their papers; this change greatly enhanced the chance of acceptance.

Sometimes this routine varied, as in the case of selection for settlement in Canada. A 'labour selector' of the mission would tour the areas, study documents relating to various candidates for work in industry, and then sift them on the basis of the IRO's preliminary selection. Then each candidate was interviewed and asked whether, if he and his family were selected, he was prepared to leave his family behind until he could nominate them for call forward; he was also given details concerning work he would be expected to do and of the wages he would receive. If the selector and candidate were satisfied, the refugee and his family were sent to the resettlement processing centre for final screening and selection.

The Australian representative often operated in the same way. With documents and the refugee family in front of him, he was able, with the help of the field resettlement officer, to select the sort of family his government wanted. Often the family composition did not fit into the pattern of the selection criteria. There were grandparents who were too old, or there were too many members in the family, or the ratio of workers to dependants did not satisfy the precise requirements of the agreement. However, if the family appealed to him, if he felt that here was the type of future citizen that Australia needed, he would send the whole group on for processing.

Small initial difficulties in the relationship between the IRO's staff in the field and the government selection missions were overcome when a greater understanding was developed by experience.

Upon acceptance the candidate received a visa on a travel document which had

---

[1] Cf. Chart III, IRO's Pipeline: processing for migration.   [2] Cf. Annex 24, p. 261.

been prepared with the help of the IRO. This document was either a certificate of identity issued by the IRO or a travel document established in accordance with the Agreement of 15 October 1946 (in the British zone of Austria and in Italy) or a temporary travel document issued by the tripartite Combined Travel Board in Germany. This Board also issued the necessary exit permits from Germany.

Equipped with a visa, a refugee was normally sent back to his assembly centre or his home to wind up his affairs and await a call to one of the staging centres. Refugees in Germany and Italy went to the centre at Wildflecken in the US zone or to Seedorf and Delmenhorst in the British zone or to Naples. In Austria they were collected in a part of the resettlement centre at Salzburg before being sent by train in groups to one of the staging centres elsewhere. The staging centres were installations readily accessible to ports of embarkation, where fully processed refugees, awaiting final shipment, were assembled in adequate numbers to provide full complements for ships as they arrived. During the waiting period, which extended sometimes to two weeks, special orientation courses were made available.[1] After a refugee had been immunized, his heavy baggage was inspected by customs officers who were stationed at the staging centre.

The move to the embarkation centre took place when a sufficient number of refugees were ready for a particular sailing. Here, a last minute check was made of all documents, luggage was marked and manifested, and final immunization administered before boarding one of the IRO's ships. The main embarkation centres were at Bagnoli, near Naples, established for the Australia run and used also for most movements to New Zealand and South America, and Camp Grohn, near Bremen. In the later stages of the operation, when the rate of movement had fallen, embarkation centres were not so crowded as they had been previously; then, they fulfilled also the functions of staging centres, refugees being called forward directly to them. When their names finally appeared on the nominal roll for departure, refugees moved from the embarkation centre to the port.

The movement of individually nominated refugees required normal individual travel arrangements, and the nominated individuals were transported on commercial vessels, and often travelled in transit through one or more countries to reach their port of embarkation.

During the journey refugees could be met at stations where they had to change trains or cross borders, and they were identified by an 'Identity and Travel Authorization' which indicated the services to which they were entitled, such as daily allowance, hotel accommodation, food, rail transportation, visa, and embarkation fees.

The Identity and Travel Authorization was carried through to the IRO's office in the receiving country which, if so authorized on the document, would pay landing money and, where necessary, accommodate the refugee in the port of disembarkation and provide for his travel to his final destination.

Procedures in countries of immigration

It had become evident under IGCR, before IRO's establishment, that the maintenance of permanent missions in reception countries was a crucial factor in achiev-

[1] Cf. Chapter XVI, Adaptation to a New Life, p. 299.

ing successful resettlement. Staffed by able and experienced personnel, these missions played a big role in the development of adequate resettlement openings and the smooth implementation of migration plans. It was necessary to maintain continuous relations with the governments of receiving countries. Only representatives who were known, respected, and constantly within reach could stimulate a sense of confidence in the Organization. In many instances this was prerequisite to the conclusion of an agreement between IRO and governments covering the number and categories of persons to be admitted, their post-immigration status, and permanent settlement.

No agreement, however, whether verbal or written, could provide solutions for all problems which inevitably arose in the execution of a programme so complex and so involved with human and material imponderables as that of migration. Arrangements had to be made for the proper reception of immigrants, sometimes in co-operation with government authorities, sometimes through voluntary societies, or both. In some countries local missions found jobs for prospective immigrants, and, upon their arrival, assisted them in their initial adjustment. Visa authorizations for thousands of individually nominated cases were obtained. The movement operations also depended upon the co-operation of resident missions and local representatives who assisted in the disembarkation of immigrants, their forwarding to final destination, and frequently in the reception and transport arrangements for transients on their way to another country. All these activities called for the attention of an agent who, without representing specific national or group interests, was accredited with the authorities of the receiving country as representing the interests of immigrants as such.

PCIRO took over such offices in the UK, Belgium, France, the Netherlands, and Switzerland, countries which served for both emigration and immigration. In overseas receiving countries the PCIRO took over missions or had resident representatives as in the US, Canada, Brazil, and Venezuela. With the development of migration operations the network of missions in receiving countries had to be extended.[1]

Administrative arrangements for the selection and processing of refugee migrants depended on an agreement concluded beforehand with the receiving countries. It was on the basis of the initial contacts by visiting missions that the first resettlement agreements on behalf of refugees and displaced persons were concluded. These agreements stated in general terms that the receiving countries would accept a certain number of refugees or refugee families under specified conditions; that the immigrants would have certain obligations; that the governments would grant them certain rights; and that the IGCR would be responsible for their transportation. When concluding additional agreements in the early stages of its operations, the PCIRO went through a period of trial and error during which an attempt was made to find the most practical form. It appeared in the course of operations that agreements which were too specific with regard to all details were just as unworkable as agreements in which the respective responsibilities were inadequately defined. Operations had to be adjusted to unforeseen changes in political and economic

---

[1] Annex 38, p. 431.

conditions and had, of course, to be adapted to the various needs and habits of receiving countries. Agreements which included many details usually had to be amended later, either formally or informally; for example, the agreement with the Australian Government, originally signed in July 1947 and covering the migration of a specified number of refugees, was extended without any formality so that the final migration to Australia was far more extensive than that originally envisaged.

A formal agreement was not necessarily the basis of resettlement plans. In the case of Canada, for instance, resettlement schemes were based on verbal understandings, and operational details were usually worked out on the executive level.

Experience proved that agreements were best limited to questions of policy. Thus they were to define the general bases for selection, such as numbers, age limits, family composition (the general proportion of workers to dependants), medical standards, conditions of work, rights and duties of the immigrants, respective responsibilities of the contracting parties for transportation both overseas and inland, conditions for the admission of workers' dependants, and conditions under which undesirable immigrants could be returned to their country of origin. The understandings regarding the implementation and operational details, on the other hand, were to be worked out on the executive level; such details included specific provisions regarding occupational qualifications, legal documentation (birth and marriage certificates, travel documents, &c.), composition and rights and duties of the selection missions, facilities to be granted to the missions, procedures of selection, visaing, and transportation.

Some agreements were recorded in exchanges of letters only; for example, letters of 3 March and 23 March 1950 between a special representative of the IRO and the Ethiopian Government; or the letters of 3 July and 6 September 1948 between the Executive Secretary and the Government of Guatemala.

There were as many different types of scheme as there were countries. There was, for example, the US scheme, based on a special Act of the US Congress; under it, immigrants were, so to speak, selected by the persons in the US who would, under the terms of the Act, guarantee their work or maintenance. The aim of the Belgian scheme was the engagement of miners; details, including conditions of employment and wages, were specified in a work contract signed by each refugee before his departure. Canada, too, chose workers for specific jobs, though in a wide variety of different trades. By contrast, Australia selected with an eye to population increase, and a choice of employment was made only after the immigrants' arrival in Australia. Some governments expressed preferences for the immigration of persons of particular national or ethnic groups; Turkey, for instance, placed an emphasis on the racial and cultural background of refugees accepted, and this was particularly useful to the IRO since suitable countries for the immigration of Mohammedan refugees were rare.

In all countries the immigrant groups of displaced persons strikingly proved that the public preconceptions about them were wrong. It had been the general assumption that most displaced persons were unfit for any productive activity, an impression resulting from the facts revealed about the horrors of Hitler's concentration camps. But the displaced persons were so eager to make up for years of frustration and suffering by building new lives and settling down as useful members of their new homeland, that the original attitude toward them was soon reversed. While at the beginning of migration operations most countries had limited their selection to single workers or married couples without children, they soon realized that the satisfactory adaptation of new-comers was largely dependent upon the maintenance of family ties. Restrictions on the admission of families, in spite of the housing shortage in all receiving countries, were therefore gradually removed. The impression made by the first few hundred refugee immigrants helped the IRO to clear the way for the tens and hundreds of thousands subsequently admitted.

B. WEST EUROPEAN CONTINENTAL COUNTRIES AND TURKEY

Belgium

Towards the end of 1946 the Belgian Government began negotiations with the occupation authorities in Germany to recruit refugees for work in the Belgian coal-mines. These negotiations, to which the IGCR was a party, terminated in two tripartite agreements for the selection of refugees from the British and US zones of Germany. In the following year similar arrangements were made for the British zone of Austria.[1]

Hiring miners abroad was not a new scheme in Belgium; before the war man-power for the Belgian mines came chiefly from eastern Europe. Immediately after the liberation, as a temporary measure, German prisoners-of-war were employed in the pits; at the same time Belgium began seeking immigrant labour from other sources, turning first to Italy and Switzerland, and afterwards to the displaced persons and refugees in Germany. Some 10,000 refugees had found work in Belgian collieries under the auspices of the IGCR in April, May, and June of 1947. IRO inherited and continued this placement scheme. The 'Belgian miners scheme' was among the first, large in scope, and not over-exigent in the medical standards required.

The Belgian Government aimed at selecting 20,000 refugee miners from the US zone of Germany and 15,000 from the British zone. It was estimated that each family would include from three to four persons, and that consequently 100,000 to 125,000 refugees would be re-established. The two agreements, as well as the employment contract between the individual and the mining company, provided for a two-year period of underground work in the mines, equal treatment for foreign and Belgian workers as far as general conditions of work were concerned, and the right to social security benefits. The mining companies had to furnish living accommodation. The acquisition of Belgian citizenship by the workers was also envisaged.[2]

---

[1] Agreement between the Government of Belgium, the Occupation Authorities, US zone of Germany, and the IGCR concerning the Resettlement in Belgium of displaced persons now in the American zone of Germany, 11 Mar. 1947; Agreement between His Britannic Majesty's Government (CCG), the Belgian Government, and the IGCR for the Resettlement in Belgium of displaced persons and refugees in the British zone of Germany, 13 Feb. 1947. Agreement between the Belgian Government and the PCIRO relative to the Immigration into Belgium of displaced persons and refugees from the British zone of Austria, 11 June 1948. Also 'Memorandum of the Belgian Government on the implementation of the Agreement of March 11th, 1947, regulating the immigration of displaced persons from the United States zone'.

[2] 'The worker and his dependants will be encouraged to establish themselves in Belgium if they so desire, in that case they will be able to acquire Belgian nationality in accordance with the laws in force.'

The contract could be renewed for mine-work, but if one of the parties did not wish to renew it, the refugee settlers were allowed to seek work in the profession of their choice, with all the rights and liberties granted by Belgian law to aliens permanently established in the country, or were free to leave Belgium for any other country. Miners who broke their contract or were found to be unemployable or undesirable could be returned to the British zone of Germany within two years of their arrival in Belgium, or to the US zone of Germany as long as the US occupation authorities were responsible for refugees.

The selection of volunteers for the Belgian mines had already passed its peak when, in July 1947, the IRO took over the Belgian resettlement programme. The majority of the volunteers came forward early; in the late months of 1948 the trickle of would-be miners was negligible. At the end of 1949 nearly 32,000 refugees had gone to Belgium for resettlement under the terms of the two agreements, 21,649 of the miners and their families having been moved by the IRO.[1] By the same date 7,413 persons had returned to Germany. The total number of refugees remaining in the collieries therefore fell somewhat short of expectations, principally because the scheme, as one of the first major resettlement projects, encountered all the preliminary difficulties.

In selecting the refugees, preference was given to single men at first, but later family men were taken. Wives and minor children were allowed to follow them after the miners had completed a probation period of ninety days, and other dependants could be admitted after individual arrangements with the Belgian Government. The medical standards established by the Belgian selection mission had erred on the side of liberality at the beginning, with the result that older men and men not sufficiently robust were being chosen to perform the strenuous work of a coal-miner. Very few had been miners before; when the first volunteers were being recruited, this scheme was practically the only one open to refugees looking for resettlement opportunities. The possibility of leaving the assembly centres, of leading a free and independent life as a worker, of earning high wages, of eventually taking Belgian nationality attracted a good many refugees, and therefore many not suited mentally or physically for one of the hardest manual jobs agreed to join the scheme. Among them were a number of white-collar workers who applied in the hope of finding employment in their own professions later, or, at the conclusion of their contract, of resuming their displaced persons status in Germany.

Officials of the IRO arranged the reception of the miners and their dependants at the Belgian frontier, and, in consultation with the representatives of the mining companies, assigned them to the various mining areas; the IRO also supervised their settlement in their new home. In the early days of the scheme housing conditions were unsatisfactory; housing consisted chiefly in Nissen huts converted from their war-time use; Belgium had suffered grievously during the war, and although the Belgian authorities improved matters as soon as they could, the living conditions compared unfavourably with those in many assembly centres in Germany.

The IRO was also responsible for adjusting minor disputes between the refugee

---

[1] IRO statistical report for December 1951 shows that at the same date the total resettlement figure for Belgium was 22,183.

miners and the colliery managements. Such misunderstandings regarding rights, duties, and regulations in the mines often arose because of language difficulties. There was often a lack of mutual goodwill between Belgian miners and their refugee comrades. The IRO tried to help by securing transfers to another mine when there was cause for dissatisfaction. Some recruits were rejected on arrival by the Belgian colliery managements on the grounds of unfitness, and some did not wish to remain in Belgium, but the majority of the refugees made a serious attempt to honour their contracts; in the early months of 1947 the proportion of those returning was remarkably low—about 5 per cent. of the persons sent to Belgium. The situation, however, increased the refugees' discontent, and during the ensuing months this proportion increased to approximately 20 per cent. towards the end of September 1947. Three-quarters of the men returning were found unfit for work in the mines, while the other quarter desired to return to Germany for personal reasons, often in the hope of joining other resettlement schemes.

Returnees were assembled in Brussels in a collection centre established in one cell-block of Le Petit Château where the uncomfortable conditions prevailing were severely criticized, so that eventually, when the first refugees arrived back in Germany, their reports of life in Belgium were unfavourable. This, together with the opening of overseas resettlement projects for families, caused the scope of the programme to decrease. Finally, in December 1946, due partly to a lack of candidates and largely to less favourable employment conditions in Belgium, the Government decided to discontinue recruiting refugees for work in the mines.

Joint efforts were made by the Belgian Government, the mining corporations, and the IRO to prevent more refugees working in Belgium from returning to Germany. The Organization established five regional information and liaison offices in the main mining areas to establish closer contacts between the men and the mine managements in Liège, Charleroi, Waterschei, La Louvière, and Mons. The Belgian Government generously applied social legislation and social insurance schemes, while the mining corporations established better methods for selecting recruits in the camps in Germany, and improved their living conditions in the mining areas. The Organization in the meantime sought to inform the candidates more fully about the conditions of work before their departure from Germany.

In spite of these efforts, refugees still continued to return from Belgium voluntarily, in addition to those sent back as unfit or unsuitable. The latter were clearly still the concern of the IRO. In a 'Memorandum on policies and procedures covering returnees' issued by headquarters on 10 November 1948 IRO clarified its policies in regard to these returnees.

The firm re-establishment of refugees, the basic aim of the Organization, would not be achieved if the refugees left the countries where their settlement could have been consummated into effective and permanent establishment. Return was therefore discouraged. If a refugee returned for reasons which in the view of the Organization were inadequate, his general and legal status as a refugee would be unaffected, but he would forfeit the claim to care and maintenance and financial aid for emigration.

The Administration felt that more than the success of the Belgian scheme was at stake. By the end of 1948 some 23,000 refugees had been settled in France and thousands were due to go there during the first half of 1949. Over 80,000 refugees had also gone to the UK from the IRO's areas of operation, and more than 100,000 Polish refugees had been settled in the country through the machinery of the Polish Resettlement Corps. If it were admitted that acceptance of a work contract with the possibility of permanent residence in Belgium, France, or the UK was not a final settlement, ending the IRO's responsibility at least as far as finding opportunities and transporting refugees to them was concerned, then the Organization might be faced with over 220,000 refugees demanding a chance of establishment overseas. All governmental and intergovernmental calculations on the life-span of the IRO, on immigration, and on finance were based on the assumption that these refugees would not need further material assistance. The welfare of all refugees still not resettled depended on the same assumption.

Dissatisfaction reigned among the refugee mine-workers in Belgium, and their grievances were magnified and distorted by the deliberate action of political agitators who organized a propaganda campaign against the employment of displaced persons in Belgium. It was the Government's opinion that these individuals were attempting to disturb law and order, and to unsettle the economic equilibrium of the country. One of the most serious causes of discontent among the refugees was the feeling that serious, hard-working men were being penalized; resettlement in the US was becoming possible, under the provisions of the 'Displaced Persons Act', but recruiting was limited to those who had stayed in camps in Germany and Austria. Many of the refugees in Belgium preferred the prospects of the US scheme, and many had friends who were emigrating from assembly centres with the IRO's aid—some of them having been rejected by Belgian collieries—while the steady men who worked out their two years at the coal-face satisfactorily were not entitled to further resettlement assistance. They claimed that this was a breach of the promises made to them at the time of their recruitment, and asked why they, who had earned their own living often in hardship and discomfort and had benefited the Belgian economy, should be less privileged than others who had lived on charity for two years. At that time, in April and May 1949, the majority of the two-year contracts began to expire, and the refugees had to decide between three possibilities: to stay in the pits for an unspecified period without being bound by contract; to move to another industry in need of man-power (agriculture, building, quarrying, heavy industry, and domestic service); or to forfeit their work in the mines and seek work in another trade, where permission to work would be subordinated to prevailing economic conditions. In the latter alternative Belgian nationals would be given priority, and refugees might forgo certain entitlements by leaving the mines, such as the use of company 'tied' cottages and hostels. Finally, it was always possible to emigrate at their own expense; many miners complained that they had been unable to save, but the government authorities observed that in numerous cases men, by two or three years' work in the mines, had saved enough money to emigrate with their entire family.

Foreseeing the possible return of large numbers when the contracts ran out, the IRO mission in Belgium in January 1949 launched a publicity campaign to familiarize the refugees with the three possibilities open to them and the advantages and disadvantages of each, and to make clear the IRO's stand: the Belgian operation was a resettlement scheme, and the IRO could not resettle the same person twice; and only the most unfortunate hard cases would be accorded continued assistance after return to Germany.

The IRO's mission in Brussels investigated the case of each returnee individually, and made a recommendation to the appropriate mission in Germany as to the extent of further assistance desirable for each person going back; in most cases, assistance in care and maintenance and resettlement should cease. Nevertheless, large numbers of refugees still insisted on returning to their zone of departure—about 10 per cent. of those recruited in the British zone, and nearly 30 per cent. of those from the US zone of Germany. The military authorities in the US zone felt a growing concern because of the increasing number of refugees who were returning to live in Germany without assistance from the IRO.

At the same time the Belgian Government, desiring to keep the miners, urged the IRO to take strong action against those who wished to return. It was jointly decided that an example should be made of a few, and a group of fifty who refused to continue their work were, as a body, declared ineligible for assistance by the IRO and outside the Organization's mandate. Appeals were considered for some of them and rejected, and the entire group was returned to Germany and placed on the local economy without the benefit of refugee status.[1]

This step did not achieve the result intended. At the collection centre in Mons for refugees who refused to work, which the Government established in lieu of Le Petit Château, a second group of 300 refugees gathered and insisted on being returned with or without the IRO's assistance. They, too, were declared outside the mandate of the IRO; however, this time the military headquarters of the US zone of Germany refused to grant the re-entry permit. Many of this group succeeded in making their way back to Germany illegally, and the IRO was faced with the problem of bringing their families back from Belgium to join them. The workers had been found outside the mandate of the IRO, so that following the IRO's normal rule their families should not be the concern of the Organization. The occupation authorities proved to be compassionate and permitted the families to re-enter Germany; the IRO, equally compassionate, arranged their transportation. Further, the United States Displaced Persons Commission was of the opinion that persons who had gone to Belgium on the mining scheme were not firmly resettled within the meaning of the United States Displaced Persons Act provided they had not applied for Belgium naturalization and provided they had returned to Germany, Austria, or Italy before 1 January 1949. Such persons, judged to be not firmly resettled, would not, by reason only of their return to Germany, be excluded by the US authorities from resettlement in the US.[2]

To investigate the situation at first hand, a team was sent to Belgium, including a welfare representative and the chairman of the Review Board. They reported that some refugees in Belgium felt that they had been misled, and that they did not

---

[1] This decision was subsequently reconsidered, as were the analogous decisions mentioned below.
[2] *The DP Story, the Final Report of the US DP Commission*, Washington, 1952, p. 95.

believe that further resettlement would be impossible if they returned to Germany. In order to ease the situation, additional case-workers were assigned to the mining communities in Belgium to interview the refugees and to assist them in finding jobs other than in the mines after the expiry of their initial contract.

'Operation Black Diamond', the Belgian mine-workers scheme, had nevertheless achieved a notable measure of success in resettlement. After the elimination of the over-optimistic and the physically unfit men, over 15,000 former displaced persons are still at work today in the Belgian collieries, and are well on the way to the eight or ten years' residence in Belgium that will qualify them to apply for naturalization. Government officials point out that the majority of them do not apparently wish to leave this work in spite of the opportunities they have of obtaining working permits in other branches of industry, and at the same time call attention to the numbers of men who have amassed considerable savings from their work—one of the most favoured financially in all Belgium—on account of the inexpensive outlay on housing, now much better than in the immediate post-war period. It is not suggested that the refugees' complaints were all unjustified at the time, but in many cases their protests were directed towards the mine managements rather than the Government itself. The Government had made plans for the labour recruiting project at a very early date, and its pioneer action doubtlessly stimulated similar offers by other countries in quest of new man-power. The evidence seems to show that the scheme raised too many hopes, both through the undiscriminating selection of refugees and through the enthusiastic promotion of the project by officials of the IRO. But the intrinsic merits of the scheme were not inconsiderable, and some refugees who had abandoned work in the collieries for emigration overseas have since applied for permission to return to Belgium to work in their former occupations.

France

At the end of the Second World War France was faced with the task of reconstructing her national economy. There was an acute shortage of housing, of equipment, raw materials, foodstuffs, and textiles, and even the railway system was partially wrecked. It was in these circumstances that returning French prisoners of war and forced labourers had to be reintegrated into the French economy. Naturally the arrangements made for the reception of refugee immigrants were affected by this state of affairs, although refugee immigrant workers were not treated less well than French workers.

The post-war shortage of labour in France was met in a variety of ways. The French Government kept many German prisoners of war in France, and the National Immigration Office recruited a large number of foreign workers; Spaniards clandestinely crossing the Pyrenees and the refugees fleeing from the new Communist régimes in eastern Europe also helped to increase the country's labour resources. But still more workers were needed to help in the reconstruction and economic revival of France, particularly as the German prisoners who had not volunteered to stay in France as free workers would have to be repatriated at an early date. The French Government, whose immediate need of workers was estimated in the latter half of 1947 at from 30,000 to 40,000, was therefore willing to accept a considerable number of refugees from the assembly centres in Germany, Austria, and Italy. Centres and camps previously used by the army were converted into living quarters for the recruited workers and their families in order to offset the housing shortage.

The French Government concluded two agreements with IGCR on 10 June 1947, which provided for the recruitment of refugee immigrants in the British and US zones of Germany and Austria, and began selecting refugees without making any formal agreement with the Organization, under whose care the refugees had come on 1 July 1947. Later the scheme was covered retroactively by an Agreement concluded on 15 January 1948 providing for the recruitment of refugees for mining, farming, factory, and domestic work.[1]

Many difficulties were encountered in connexion with this scheme, especially in its primary stage. France's greatest need was for miners, and at that time, after the intensive recruiting for Belgium, few persons were left in the camps who wanted to go into mining, and none who had experience or skill in it. The French Selection Mission itself was not fully briefed, and no accurate information was given to the potential immigrants about their working and living conditions in France; in addition, the political situation did not encourage recruiting. Over 8,000 refugees settled in France in the second half of 1947, but those who went to France under the labour scheme found the reception arrangements unsatisfactory. Housing was substandard; many refugees were rejected by their employers and were left in very poor circumstances; there was delay in permitting the entry of dependants into France which caused great discontent; and in spite of protracted negotiations it was not possible to establish procedures for the return of refugees to the satisfaction of the British and US occupation authorities in Germany. A large number of those who wished to return made their own way back to Germany.

At the beginning of 1948 certain changes were introduced to improve the situation; refugees were to be interviewed in the resettlement centres in the various zones instead of in Karlsruhe, where the French selection team had been established up to that time. The French Selection Mission was reorganized and steps were taken to hasten the move of dependants to France. It never proved possible, however, to put into effect Article VIII of the Agreement of 13 January 1948, which provided that all persons who were being maintained by the IRO at the time of selection were entitled to a resettlement grant of $16.00.

The new scheme was to be an experiment in the resettlement of 1,000 agricultural workers selected from among the refugees only. These workers could bring their family with them; the children could be of any number and any age; and the work contract for the head of the family would be signed after personal negotiations with the future employer. The declaration further specified that a searching pre-selection would be undertaken by the Organization, so that only persons with real experience in agriculture would be considered. The project was welcomed as an opportunity of resettling many semi-skilled agricultural workers for whom other possibilities had not been available, particularly as it was understood that heads of families could be up to 50 years of age, and that in special cases, where the individual's physical

---

[1] Agreement concerning the Selection of Refugees and Displaced Persons for France and Algeria, PC/LEG/9, 15 Jan. 1948. See Appendix II (b), p. 613.

condition was very good, or where the children already worked, the age limit might be increased to 55.

Every effort was made by the IRO to stimulate interest in recruitment for this scheme in the assembly centres in Germany and Austria. But the refugees' response was very lukewarm; for their conception of life in France had been unfavourably influenced by the persons returning from France more than a year before. Moreover, in practice, the French Selection Missions did not interpret the selection criteria liberally. Besides, it seemed possible that the French Government might close down many of the installations erected to house refugees entering France under the farm families scheme. A delegation of refugees was invited to visit France and see conditions there at first hand. By then, in December 1948, considerable improvement in reception arrangements was noticeable, and the delegation on its return agreed to publicize the scheme in conjunction with the French publicity team.

France recruited in competition with US and Australian resettlement schemes; the overseas schemes were greatly favoured by the refugees, and this popularity was undoubtedly partly due to the more liberal supplies of adequate information made available by those countries. Some improvement in recruiting followed the visit of the displaced persons' delegation, but this increase of enthusiasm in the spring encountered a decrease in the demand for agricultural labour because of the drought. The French reduced the quota for farm families from July 1949 onwards, pointing out that the required 1,000 families had been admitted. In October 1949, owing to the seasonal unemployment in agriculture and consequent overcrowding of the refugees' reception centres, all French selection of refugee immigrants was suspended.

The French farm families scheme which began as an experiment in resettling 1,000 families in France was a success; between 11 October 1948 and 15 June 1950, 1,139 families assisted by the Organization entered France under this scheme, making a total of 3,666 persons. In many respects the plan was original, and presented a number of features ensuring firm re-establishment of the refugees who accepted it. It had the disadvantage of being started too late. More refugees might have resettled in France under its auspices had it not been that unsuccessful settlement would have rendered them ineligible for other immigration schemes. The majority preferred to wait in the assembly centres as long as there was a possibility for them of being resettled overseas.

In total, as the IRO's records show, over 38,000 refugees, nearly all of them from Austria and Germany, went for resettlement to France; this was more than to any other country except Australia, Canada, Israel, the UK, and the US. Thus France preserved her tradition of asylum and hospitality to refugees.

French Guiana

The desire for a rapid development of overseas territories was common to many governments after the war, and in 1947 the French Government announced a ten-year plan for the development of Guiana which provided for the improvement of internal and external communications and for the exploitation of the country's natural resources. According to this plan labour and skilled specialists were to be brought into the country.

After two informal meetings held in Paris between representatives of different French Ministries and of the IRO, the French Government, in a letter dated 24 August 1948, invited the IRO to participate in an economic development scheme which provided for 5,000 families to emigrate to Guiana subject to the result of an experimental settlement of 100 families. Thorough investigations were made by the IRO, and finally an Agreement was concluded with the French Government for the resettlement of 400 refugee families.[1]

The Agreement provided for a two years' employment contract between the French local authority and the immigrant; for accommodation and food-supply on arrival; for concessions of cleared land if applied for, together with farming imple-ments. The IRO undertook to pay a resettlement grant to cover the initial costs of settling, a sum which was the equivalent of $322 for each person. The French Government established a special office for the financial control of the enterprise.

The immigrants were selected mainly in the French zone of Germany. The first transport of sixty-eight refugees left Europe in June 1949, followed by a second transport of ninety-six persons in November of the same year. Further moves took place in 1950, and by the end of the IRO's operations 211 persons had been brought to French Guiana. The centre at St. Jean de Maroni served as the initial installation for the refugees for the two years from the date of arrival.

Although only a small number of refugees chose this French Guiana scheme these few constituted a community of their own; and on the whole they were reasonably well installed and accommodated.

French North Africa

The French North African resettlement scheme, which started in the summer of 1947 and included Tunisia and Morocco, was chiefly for the recruitment of skilled workers requested by industrial employers.[2]

At the beginning of the scheme there was considerable interest among refugees in emigration to North Africa;[3] family groups were accepted together and the worker had the possibility of being employed in his own occupation; further, Morocco had great possibilities for economic development and its geographical position made it attractive to refugee emigrants.

At the beginning, completed dossiers on each potential immigrant were sent to Tunis and Morocco for consideration; then, in the summer of 1948, a selection mission arrived in Europe to recruit refugees in person. By this time the Tunisian scheme was approaching completion, but interest in Morocco continued fairly high. However, this mission was interested in the selection of only a small number

[1] Special arrangement between the IRO and the Government of the French Republic concerning recruitment of displaced persons for French Guiana, dated 6 May 1949 (concluded in accordance with Article 14 of the Agreement of 13 January 1948 on the immigration of refugees into France and Algeria).
[2] Agreement between the French General Residency in Tunisia and the IGCR concerning the Immigration Scheme to Tunisia, 9 Dec. 1946, and Agreement between the Resident Commissioner General of the French Republic in Morocco and the IRO, concluded 8 July 1948. PC/LEG/30.
[3] GC/60.

of highly specialized workers, and many of the applicants were not even interviewed. The total of persons resettled in Morocco and Tunisia during the operations amounted to 1,446 and 446 persons respectively. Their re-establishment proved very satisfactory, and nearly all the refugees who moved there remained as valued members of the European community.

Luxembourg

An Agreement between the IRO and the Government of the Grand Duchy of Luxembourg concerning recruitment of single agricultural workers from Germany for work in Luxembourg was concluded on 9 March 1949. This scheme was established at a relatively late date; since single workers had been selected for many months by other missions, very few candidates were available by the beginning of 1949. Under these conditions it was not to be expected that the implementation of the plan would produce all the results that had been hoped for. In 1949 less than 200 refugees chose the Luxembourg scheme, and only about half of them remained to settle in the country. Luxembourg's agricultural conditions differ considerably from those existing in the refugees' countries of origin, and the majority of foreign agricultural workers normally have difficulty in adapting themselves to the new system. Moreover, in Luxembourg opportunities of changing from agricultural labour to some other trade were restricted by a number of factors, among them the size of the country itself.

A Luxembourg mission visited several assembly centres in Germany, and efforts were made to publicize the Luxembourg resettlement programme among the various groups of refugees. Experience showed that certain nationalities of refugees were disinclined to accept agricultural work in Europe, e.g. the Balts, while there was quite a high response from the Poles. One of the conditions of resettlement in Luxembourg was a promise by the refugee to work in agriculture for two to three years, and the authorities noted that the majority of the resettlers did not carry out this promise completely; instead they tended to enter other industries in which no real shortage of man-power existed. Many refugees found it harder than they had expected to adapt themselves; only a limited number notified the National Labour Office of their desire to return to Germany, but a somewhat larger group returned to their zone of departure by unofficial means.

The Luxembourg mass resettlement scheme fell short of the hopes felt when the Agreement was signed. Nevertheless, a fair number of young farmers chose Luxembourg as their new home; and although there were few by comparison with the vast overseas resettlement schemes, each individual case of permanent resettlement was a success, and the Luxembourg scheme was thus a modest but creditable achievement.

The Netherlands

The programme of resettlement in the Netherlands was founded on an Agreement between the Government of the Netherlands and the IGCR for the settlement in the Netherlands of displaced persons in the US zone of Germany, concluded on 5 May 1947; and an Agreement between the governments of the UK and the Netherlands and the PCIRO for the resettlement in the Netherlands of refugees from the British zone of Germany, signed on 22 October 1947. There were chiefly openings for skilled industrial workers, coal-miners, and domestic servants, and only single, unattached persons were recruited. The housing situation made it impossible to offer refugees accommodation which would meet the statutory specifications for family dwellings in the Netherlands. Had it been possible to relax this rule against the recruitment of family men, there would undoubtedly have been many more volunteers for resettlement in the Netherlands. Only one exception was made to the bar on family groups, and that was for Jewish families.

Under the Netherlands scheme 4,355 persons within the IRO's mandate were resettled, a figure considerably lower than that originally planned. This shortage was principally due to the many demands from other countries for single workers, and towards the end of 1948 it was found impossible to supply the high-grade workers required by the Netherlands selection mission; recruitment for the scheme was stopped in December 1948.

Selection of refugees had begun in August 1947, and from then on the Netherlands resettlement operations ran smoothly according to a well-organized programme. The selection mission was effective and efficient, working as a unit, so that the complete examination of applicants could be carried out in a day. Discussions open to everyone were held regularly in the camps, and thus would-be settlers were given information regarding their chances of employment and the living conditions they would find. This satisfactory co-operation between the selection mission and the Organization ensured the selection of suitable workers, and also made it possible adequately to prepare them for their future life.

The establishment of refugees in the Netherlands was accomplished without undue difficulties, and in the early months the number of those wishing to return was inconsiderable. But with the emergence of a surplus of man-power in 1948 and 1949, refugee settlers in the Netherlands found it increasingly difficult to obtain employment once they lost their original jobs, and many desired to emigrate overseas to the US, Canada, Australia, or South America. At the same time many refugees felt the urge to return to Germany because of the opportunities for family groups to emigrate overseas from there. This desire to return to Germany was also due to the fact that the 'single and unattached' resettlers had left family members in Germany, perhaps in the hope that some new policy would make family reunion possible. The IRO made it clear that its responsibility to the refugees had ended once they had been resettled for the first time, and that it would only assist in re-emigration to the extent of furnishing transportation on a reimbursable basis. In June 1949 applications for return had increased somewhat, but once it was realized that the Organization was adhering strictly to its avowed policy of giving no second opportunity to those who returned without valid reasons, the numbers of those wishing to return resumed normal proportions. About 10 per cent. of the 4,000 recruited by selection teams in Germany returned to the occupied countries at their own request, usually in order to qualify for assisted migration overseas and to meet the selection missions operating in those countries. But the majority of refugee workers stayed in the Netherlands.

Nearly two-thirds of the refugees permanently settled in the Netherlands were of Polish extraction, many of them members of the Polish army formations that liberated parts of the country in 1945, and most came within the three main categories of skilled industrial workers, miners, and domestics. There were, however, other small groups, for whom the IRO's office in The Hague secured the approval of the Government, and among them may be mentioned a party of Baltic nurse trainees, the members of a Ukrainian theological seminary, thirty specialists and engineers, and groups of Czech and Hungarian students desiring to complete their studies in the Netherlands. The inclusion of these groups spread the refugee immigrants more evenly among various classes of the population, and enabled the refugees to make a contribution to many spheres of activity in the Netherlands.

Turkey

Since it was of the utmost importance in resettlement policy to find an environment for refugees in which they could readily be assimilated, IRO always made an effort to place migrants if possible among people of the same or similar culture and denomination. For Moslems from Yugoslavia and Albania, the descendants of those left behind when the Ottoman tide had receded, and others from parts of the Soviet Union no appropriate resettlement schemes existed until the Government of Turkey and the IRO concluded an Agreement relative to the immigration of displaced persons into Turkey on 24 June 1948.[1]

Moslem refugees were to be selected in Germany, Austria, and Italy, and the Turkish Government was prepared to accept family units, allowing them to acquire Turkish nationality upon arrival and placing them in suitable employment. The implementation of this scheme was not restricted by age limits or professional qualifications; the only conditions made were medical criteria and the stipulation that the immigrant was of Moslem faith. The acquisition of Turkish nationality by the immigrants immediately secured for them full rights to work, and, in contrast to former regulations under which places of residence were assigned by the Government to immigrants, a new law enabled them to live anywhere in the Turkish Republic.

Selection of the settlers began in Italy in April 1948 on the basis of a verbal agreement, and was later extended to Austria and Germany, where the majority of the Moslem refugees were living. Many of them were illiterate and unskilled, and, until the introduction of this scheme of resettlement, had had hardly any chance of emigration. Some difficulties were encountered during the preliminary documentation of the Moslems born in Soviet territory. It was known that the Soviet Government had disapproved of the entry into Turkey of such refugees, so their eagerness to be accepted by the Turkish selection mission and their fear of being rejected because of their birth-place caused some of them to make false claims and statements and allege that they were of Turkish origin. This matter was finally straightened out and by the end of 1949 approximately 2,000 persons of Moslem faith had emigrated to Turkey.

---

[1] Agreement between the Government of the Turkish Republic and the PCIRO Relative to the Immigration of Displaced Persons into Turkey, PC/LEG/28. 25 June 1948.

A reception centre had been installed in a former quarantine station, and was administered jointly by the Turkish health authorities and the Turkish Red Crescent. The Department of Land Settlement of the Ministry of Health was in charge of settling the new-comers, an undertaking that was found to be beset with difficulties: many were unfitted for heavy work, and there were also many women with small children, persons unlikely to fit easily into any type of land settlement scheme. For this reason the Government suspended the operation of the scheme pending the solution of the difficult cases among the first group. It was not until March 1950, as a result of representations from the IRO and the Turkish Consul-General in Frankfurt-on-Main, that the Government agreed to re-open the scheme and to accept a further 777 eligible Moslems on a list of potential immigrants which had been compiled by the representative of the Turkish immigration authorities on his visit to the IRO's installations in 1948. As many of these candidates were no longer available, and as a further 400 Moslems pre-selected by the Turkish authorities were found to be outside the IRO's mandate, the selection mission agreed to accept other eligible Moslem refugees within the IRO's mandate, and in most cases wives of German (but not of Slav) origin were accepted by the Turkish authorities.

This resettlement scheme provided for the acceptance by Turkey of 2,358 persons. It made no demands regarding the refugees' labour categories, ages, sex, or family composition; instead this scheme was an expression of sympathy and understanding for the difficult problem of the Moslems, of whom many were in distress and who gladly accepted Turkey's generous offer. The experience of the Turkish authorities in the settlement of Turks returning from other Mediterranean countries was a useful guide at a time when Turkey was already feeling the effects of the expulsion of tens of thousands of men and women of Turkish ethnic origin from Bulgaria.

C. THE BRITISH COMMONWEALTH

Commonwealth countries played a leading part in the accomplishment of the vast humanitarian programme of the IRO. They contributed not only 26 per cent. towards the financing of IRO's activities, but also resettled 38·4 per cent. of the total number of refugees. 398,413 refugees were admitted to Commonwealth countries as follows: UK 86,346, Canada 123,479, Australia 182,159, New Zealand 4,837, and other Commonwealth countries (Union of South Africa, Northern and Southern Rhodesia, Ceylon, Kenya, Tanganyika) 1,592.

United Kingdom of Great Britain and Northern Ireland

Before 1933 the UK had not been a country of immigration, or a country that had ever received large groups of refugees, although it gave political asylum to many individuals fleeing from persecution in their own countries. After the Bolshevik Revolution of 1917 and after the dissolution of the Ottoman Empire somewhat larger groups of Russians and Armenians were received in Great Britain. For the first time, after Hitler came to power in 1933, a large group of refugees, mostly Jews, arrived in the country. Legally and administratively, refugees, like other foreigners, are 'aliens', and are included in more general statistics.

Some details were given in the House of Commons on 30 June 1952 regarding the numbers of refugees admitted to the UK. The Under-Secretary of State for the Home Department stated that 'In the period between the end of the war and 31 March of this year 302,396 foreigners who can be regarded as refugees either entered the United Kingdom or, having entered the United Kingdom during the war, were allowed to remain here. Well over 80,000 of these foreigners have, however, returned to their own countries or emigrated to some other country:'[1]

Poles	235,388
Latvians	14,483
Yugoslavs	9,718
Lithuanians	6,947
Estonians	5,688
Czechs	3,257
Hungarians	3,109
Stateless or uncertain . . .	22,062
Other nationalities . . .	1,774
	302,396

Therefore an exact figure of the number of refugees who came to the UK cannot be given. According to one estimate there were about 80,000 emigrants before the war, of whom 34,000 have now been naturalized (17,000 Russians and 63,000 Germans, Austrians, Czechs, and Spaniards). During the Second World War the UK gave refuge to many persons from European countries occupied by Nazi Germany; among them were many who had served in the Allied armies and who returned to their homelands after the surrender of the German armies.

After the war the UK, in common with continental western European countries, was anxious to reconstruct and rehabilitate its war-torn industry and agriculture, and as there was a shortage of man-power the UK liberalized her traditional immigration policy. In the first four post-war years nearly 200,000 displaced persons and refugees found employment under official government-sponsored schemes. The first large group consisted of 114,000 Polish service men and women (16,500 officers, 92,000 men, and 5,500 women) and members of the Polish armed forces living in camps in Britain, East Africa, and the Middle East. They enrolled into the Polish Resettlement Corps which was established by the British Government in 1946. The members of this Polish Resettlement Corps were accepted for resettlement in recognition of their war service. They were assisted either in their emigration overseas or helped to find employment in local industries which were undermanned. The Corps contained a large group of persons not suited for manual labour. Altogether, over 80,000 members of the Corps were placed in work. About 1,500 disabled members benefited from the provisions of the Disabled Persons (Employment) Act. At the end of September 1949 this military organization was disbanded and those former members who failed to obtain resettlement through no fault of their own became the responsibility of the appropriate civilian departments.

The second group consisted of displaced persons from Germany and Austria, with a few from Denmark.

---

[1] *Parl. Deb., Commons*, 1951–2, vol. 503, 10.

Under the schemes[1] 'Balt Cygnet' and 'Westward Ho!', over 84,000 'European Volunteer Workers' came to the UK from 1946 to 1948. Most of those workers were civilians of different ages and nationalities, and ranged from former farmers or unskilled workers to highly educated people in the professional classes, some of whom had been university professors.

The first recruits were 2,500 Estonian, Latvian, and Lithuanian women from assembly centres in the British zone of Germany who, in 1946, volunteered for a year's domestic work in British hospitals. This scheme, known as 'Balt Cygnet', was absorbed in the next year in the wider 'Westward Ho!' scheme, which was open to men and women from centres in Germany and Austria. Those recruited included Ukrainians, Poles, Yugoslavs, Hungarians, Czechs, Rumanians, and Bulgarians.

The 'Westward Ho!' scheme in its original form was drawn up by the British Government with the Control Commission authorities in the British zone of Germany before the beginning of the IRO's operations. The British Ministry of Labour and National Service was responsible for the recruitment and placing of the workers, and had an 'implied responsibility for looking after their welfare'.[2] When, in the summer of 1947, the number of suitable applicants in the British zone of Germany began to decrease, the scheme was extended to the US and French zones of Germany by virtue of agreements between the British and French Governments, and between the British Government and the IRO for the US zone, the latter agreement being subsequently approved by the US occupation authorities.[3]

The scheme was originally for workers only, and because of the great housing shortage dependants were expected to follow as soon as accommodation became available. At the outset the recruits included married people and people with dependants; after a while, however, acute accommodation difficulties made it necessary to restrict recruitment to single workers. Nevertheless, about 3,500 dependants of European volunteer workers were brought to Great Britain. A number of workers who applied did not disclose the fact that they were married, and were accepted for the UK. When they later announced their marital status, the British Government allowed the entry of the family group within a very narrow degree of relationship. The workers were accommodated in hostels managed by the National Service Hostels' Corporation Ltd., a non-profit-making body, and in other communal housing as well as in private billets. Many of them subsequently found their own accommodation.[4]

The agreement signed by the volunteer workers stipulated that they would accept only such employment as was selected by the Ministry of Labour and National Service, and that any change of jobs could not be made without the consent of the Ministry. Similar employment restrictions (the Control of Engagement Orders) were applicable to British workers. Some of the refugees, not fully understanding the terms of their contracts, believed that they would be free to go where they chose after one year's work in the industry in which they had been placed, and some resentment was felt when they found that this was not the case. However, the restriction

---

[1] Cmd. 7822 and 8017. Annual Reports of the Ministry of Labour and National Service 1948 and 1949, London, 1949 and 1950, p. 24, resp. 19.
[2] *Ministry of Labour Gazette*, Aug. 1949, p. 262.
[3] Ibid. [4] PC/LEG/8.

on their movements between one industry and another was gradually relaxed at the beginning of 1951.

In movements of refugees to the UK the rate of immigration was highest between December 1947 and July 1948, the peak occurring in the spring of 1948. After July the monthly departures were quite small, mainly because recruitment was still restricted to workers without dependants, because the recruitment of men was on a limited scale, and because other attractive resettlement schemes overseas had been launched. Nevertheless, a total of over 80,000 displaced persons, including 3,500 dependants, volunteered for the UK, and were brought over by the British Government. Approximately 4,000 later returned to the zones of Germany from which they had come.

Overseas resettlement schemes were being operated by selection missions in Germany, and it was discussed under what conditions those individuals who wished to do so might return from the UK to Germany in order to avail themselves of further resettlement chances. The British Government proposed that acceptance of work in the UK should not prejudice the refugee's future resettlement opportunities, while the Organization, on the other hand, maintained that once it had assisted a person to obtain employment in a country in which he could settle, no further resettlement opportunities could be afforded to him by the IRO. A statement issued by the Director General of the IRO regarding the Organization's policy was distributed to refugees throughout the UK as an attachment to a circular dated 17 January 1949.

At a later date the IRO's refusal to extend its facilities to displaced persons wishing to re-emigrate from the UK was modified to some extent, and the IRO supported further resettlement when the movement of the individual would enable a number of his or her dependants to be moved from the IRO's installations in Germany or Austria to another resettlement country, provided that such dependants could not be brought to the UK.

The British Government made arrangements for unsuitable or undesirable persons to be returned to Germany within eighteen months, where they would become the responsibility of the IRO. A few undesirable refugees were returned, and others were rejected because of their unsuitability, due in some cases to medical findings; the only persons, however, deported for health reasons were those who could not be absorbed into British institutions in which there was not sufficient accommodation for British nationals, and a few mental cases who spoke only German and who were, therefore, sent to Germany and granted institutional care by the IRO.

The resettlement scheme which Great Britain made available to such large numbers of displaced persons and refugees at a time when the country itself was experiencing a difficult period has given a high proportion of those volunteers the prospect of a secure future. The success of the scheme may be measured by the relatively small numbers who did not seek to remain in the country.

The scheme known as 'Pole Jump', under which the dependants of the ex-soldiers in the Polish Resettlement Corps were brought to the UK, was the fulfilment of a War Office obligation to reunite the men with their families who were left behind in East Africa and the Middle East. The IRO continued to be responsible for

RESETTLEMENT393

maintaining this group of Poles in the Middle East and other areas up to the time of their move, which was the responsibility of the British military authorities. The Organization adopted the policy that unreasonable refusal to take advantage of the UK's resettlement scheme would make a refugee ineligible for further assistance from the IRO.

Approximately 40,000 Polish family members were moved from Europe, India, the Middle East, and East Africa during 1947 and 1948. Figures submitted by the British War Office show that 28,997 of them were admitted to the UK under this scheme, among them numbers of hardship cases, details of which were submitted to the War Office for approval before their departure.

Some Poles in the Lebanon and East Africa, who were not eligible for the 'Pole Jump' scheme and who could not be otherwise resettled by the IRO, were later admitted to the UK under a special arrangement between the British Government and the Organization.

The UK Government's third scheme for refugee settlement was the 'Two Thousand' scheme, applicable in particular to cases with limited prospects of resettlement, including widows with children, aged persons, professional people who could not be re-trained in a trade, the blind, and individuals with relatives whom they could not leave behind.[1] Two thousand displaced persons and refugees belonging to these various groups from Germany and Austria were to be admitted to the UK, providing that accommodation and maintenance could be found for them by relatives or friends, or by voluntary organizations that were prepared to take continuing responsibility for their care. The 'Two Thousand' scheme was put into operation in the latter half of 1950, and the necessary liaison with the sponsors and the voluntary societies was maintained, not by the IRO's office in London, but by the British Council for Aid to Refugees, the members of which were representatives of the voluntary societies and which had been organized with the financial help of the IRO.

Australia

The Australian resettlement scheme came into operation in September 1947, under an Agreement between the Commonwealth and the IRO[2] regarding immigration of refugees and displaced persons into Australia. Under the terms of that Agreement a total of 4,000 workers and dependants could be admitted during 1947. The workers were accepted on the condition that they would remain at least one year in the first place of employment. The heads of family groups selected could be accompanied by all members of their immediate families and by such other relatives as were dependent upon the head of the family. Furthermore, any immigrant going to Australia under this Agreement who left his dependants or relatives behind could, after three months' residence in Australia, nominate such relatives and dependants for admission, provided that the immigrant was in a position to receive and support the dependants after their arrival in Australia. Persons to be selected were: single

[1] Cf. Home Secretary, Mr. Chuter Ede, 4 May 1950. *Parl. Deb., Commons,* vol. 474, *210–11.*
[2] Agreement between the Government of the Commonwealth of Australia and PCIRO regarding Immigration into Australia of Refugees and Displaced Persons, concluded 21 July 1947. PC/LEG/14, 16 Feb. 1948.

men up to 45 years of age, single women up to 40 years, and married couples with children where the parents were less than 50 years old. Approval was also given for the admission of aged parents or over-age dependent relatives if they formed an integral part of any family group. All migrants had to meet high medical standards and had to be screened on security grounds.

Australia wished to persist in its traditional policy of favouring the migration of north Europeans; preference was, therefore, given to Balts, and in fact only Balts were accepted at the start of the scheme.

Efforts were made by the Australian Government to make the 'New Australians' —as the refugees were officially termed—feel happy in their new surroundings, and excellent arrangements for their reception were made. From the time of arrival at the reception centre in Australia until employment was found for them, the migrants were paid a special social service benefit at a rate equivalent to the normal unemployment allowance; meals and accommodation were furnished at a nominal charge, essential clothing was supplied free of charge, and the immigrants were given instruction in the English language and in the Australian way of life.

At the time of the signature of the Australian resettlement agreement, the Organization had given assurances that adequate shipping would be available to move 4,000 migrants to Australia in 1947, but due to the budgetary position of the IRO and the scarcity of world shipping, it proved impossible to send more than one vessel. This first transport brought 840 refugees to Australia, arriving at Freemantle at the end of November 1947. The Commonwealth Government, satisfied with the early results of refugee settlement, expressed the wish to increase immigration first to 12,000 refugees annually and later to 20,000 refugees a year. However, although strenuous efforts were made to move as many as possible, only about 9,000 persons could be transported during 1948. Shipping was the main limiting factor; in July 1948, when the Government of the US announced its intention of admitting 200,000 displaced persons, the Australian Minister of Immigration declared that his government would be willing to match the US offer, providing that adequate shipping could be made available. The possibility of economizing ships by flying refugees half-way to Australia was investigated and discarded.[1] Finally, the US Government put twelve army transports at the disposal of the Organization.

Frequent representations to the Commonwealth Government by the Organization led to the extension of the selection criteria with regard to age limits, family composition, and nationality: the age limit for women nurses was raised to 45, and for single men to 50, the inclusion of parents was permitted, providing that the earning capacity of the employable members of the family was sufficient to maintain them; a number of persons were accepted for whom it was almost impossible to find other opportunities: families where one of the parents was dead or absent, deserted wives and husbands, and so on. It was specially confirmed that widows and widowers with

[1] A reconnaissance mission composed of IRO officials conversant with conditions in East Africa submitted an extensive report outlining the possibility to fly migrants from Europe to East Africa (Kenya or Eritrea) thence by sea to Australia. The passengers would land in Nairobi and continue by a twenty hours' train journey to Mombasa where they would remain about twelve days before embarking for Australia. This well-studied project of moving migrants at the rate of 2,000 persons a month with the fullest support of the Kenya Government did not materialize for lack of financial support outside the Organization.

children could come to Australia and be found suitable employment, and that their children could come as dependants. At that time selection criteria were also relaxed to permit refugees with womenfolk of German nationality to bring them to Australia and enter the country as a family group. In this way the Australian Government widened its already liberal policy of accepting as immigrants the dependants of previous immigrants who could be responsible for their welfare, and the amended regulations were in accordance with the IRO's policy of preserving the unity of families. In pursuance of this policy the Organization counted the dependants of a refugee within the mandate of the IRO as being themselves within the mandate, even though they might not otherwise be eligible for assistance. The Australian authorities also gave approval for the selection of refugees irrespective of their previous nationality.

In October 1948 the Director General of the IRO advised the Head of the Australian Military Mission in Berlin that the IRO could finance the movement of a minimum of 100,000 persons to Australia between then and 30 June 1950. This offer was accepted, and intensive preparation was made in Australia for the accommodation of the refugees upon arrival. During 1949 the movement proceeded smoothly, and during the course of the year 75,000 refugees were brought into Australia. Hostels and holding centres were built and equipped by the Government, and no great difficulty was experienced in receiving the immigrants. In 1950 some 60,000 refugees were admitted, and by the end of the year a total of 156,000 had arrived since the inception of the scheme.

As the work of the IRO progressed, and the General Council urged the governments to widen the scope of selection, the Australian Government gave admirable proof of its willingness to change and adjust its policies and to co-operate with the Organization. When the IRO's selection activities were extended to the outlying areas, where refugees tended to be somewhat neglected by the receiving countries, the Australian Government sent selection missions to interview sizeable bodies of refugees elsewhere than in Germany, Austria, and Italy. Thus, in the year 1950, 1,179 refugees were selected from East Africa, 620 from Greece, 200 Poles from the Lebanon, and 485 Yugoslavs from Egypt. In addition an Australian mission was sent to Samar in the Philippines and chose no less than 1,385 White Russians who had been evacuated there from Shanghai.

It was difficult, however, for the Australian Government to maintain refugee immigration at its highest level. Shortage of housing in the towns and country districts where immigrants were needed for work resulted in families staying in the reception camps and thus occupying accommodation that was needed for new arrivals. Socially and politically the large number of non-British immigrants caused some misgivings, both in trade union circles and elsewhere; and in the economic sphere, mass immigration was considered one of the factors which, combined with coincidental trends in world economy, were creating the inflationary pressure then causing concern in Australia. For these reasons, immigration which had been at the rate of over 6,000 a month during 1949 and the first half of 1950 dropped to less than 4,000 a month during the second half of 1950, and to an average of less than 1,000 a month in 1951.

The Australian scheme embraced 182,159 refugee immigrants. It developed into true mass resettlement, depending only on the possibilities of absorption, on the availability of shipping, and the number of selection officers, and it provided unlimited opportunities for suitable refugees. Australia, with its small population, accepted more refugees as immigrants under the IRO's auspices than any other country except the US, but whereas in the US only one person in 450 was a former IRO refugee, in Australia one person in 40 had been brought there by the IRO.

The arrival of the first group of several hundreds of individual migrants created trouble for the Australian Government, the voluntary societies, and the IRO. Although the refugees were supposed to be individually sponsored, it was found that many of those whose maintenance had been vouched for by national groups and individuals were not taken care of on arrival, that no one was prepared to receive them, and that housing and employment could not be found quickly enough. As a direct result of this confusion, the Australian Government announced in October 1947 that every landing permit granted by its Department of Immigration would be issued on the understanding that the holder would be responsible for making his own arrangements for travel to Australia, either at his own expense or at that of his nominator, and that no IRO funds were to be used to defray the cost of such transportation. This step naturally upset the plans of many of the applicants, who had made their calculations on the basis of the IRO's promise to pay for the journey to Australia.

After representations made by the IRO headquarters, the Australian Government modified and developed its policy on this point. It expected that persons in possession of work contracts or invitations from relatives would have their passage prepaid by the employer or relative. All other persons holding an individual landing permit were to be presented to the Australian selection mission for inclusion in the Mass Resettlement scheme, but persons rejected under the mass resettlement criteria could be reconsidered as hardship cases; if they were indigent or the relatives unable to pay the fare, the IRO could ship them at its own expense. The Australian Government later agreed also that candidates who had been documented before September 1948, and who had been assured that the IRO would pay their passages, could be considered as hardship cases, an arrangement that helped many people who had been waiting a long time to be moved.

Canada

In Canada PCIRO took over the arrangement originally made with IGCR and developed two main programmes: the 'Nominated Close Relatives Scheme' initiated by the Canadian Government in December 1946, and the labour selection schemes. Under the former persons residing in Canada could nominate their relatives to the Immigration Branch for their admittance, and the IRO then took the necessary steps to have them presented to a Canadian immigration team or mission. As soon as visas had been issued, the Organization arranged for the embarkation of these immigrants on chartered ships. 'Close relations' were defined as wives, husbands, brothers, sisters, sons, daughters, orphans under 21 years, and fiancées. Farmers could also apply for farm workers not related to them. Applications were investigated in Canada regarding the financial status of the nominator, his loyalty and antecedents, together with other circumstances pertinent to each case, and when these governmental inquiries were concluded satisfactorily, approval was given and the name of the prospective immigrants were forwarded to the IRO on so-called 'Master Lists'. The scheme worked well, and the machinery operated so smoothly that no less than 45,000 persons were brought to Canada under its auspices during the period from April 1947 to January 1952.

Under the second scheme the IRO in Canada received requests from Canadian labour and immigration authorities for workers belonging to various categories, such as miners, loggers, farmers, and general labourers. Selection of workers for Canada was made solely on the basis of their qualifications and without regard to their origin or religion.

Canada was the first country to send an official mission to Germany to arrange the immigration of refugees; before the start of the IRO's operations their selection team was active in Germany and Austria, primarily to arrange the admission of close relatives of persons already legally domiciled in Canada. The first selection of persons other than close relatives was a group of 100 girls for employment in a spinning mill, who were selected from assembly centres by the employer following an agreement with the Department of Mines and Resources of the Government of Canada. This move gave rise to some criticism; it was said that proper authority for the move had not been obtained. The Garment Workers' Union was critical of the contracts because they contained special provisions regarding payment rates. The matter was discussed by the Government's Labour Immigration Committee and an Order in Council was promulgated which authorized the admission of labour groups. This Order in Council remained the legal instrument under which subsequent movements of loggers, miners, farmers, domestics, and so on were made. Members of the first labour group, totalling 1,363 persons, reached their destinations in July and August 1947.

Those refugees granted visas had to sign an undertaking before entering Canada that they would remain for a certain period in the work found for them, and that they were willing to accept the prevailing rates of pay and conditions of work. The Government undertook the responsibility of finding one year's employment for them, and granted refugees the right to nominate their relatives and dependants for admission to Canada; provision was also made for language instruction and for descriptive Canadian literature in various languages to be given to refugee immigrants at the time of their selection.

IRO's obligations normally came to an end when displaced persons had legally landed in the country of reception. Although until the end of 1950 the IRO office in Canada gave funds through its port officers for railway tickets and meals *en route*, this advance made on behalf of the sponsors was subject to reimbursement. While many repaid these sums, IRO lost roughly 15 per cent. of all such advances. As early as 1951, with the end of IRO in sight, a new procedure was devised whereby inland transportation and subsistence had to be prepaid by the sponsors before their nominee could embark for Canada. This entailed close collaboration with the Canadian Passenger Association acting on behalf of both the Canadian National and the Canadian Pacific Railways. The fullest co-operation was received at all times from officials of the two companies.

On arrival at port, the IRO Port Officer met all nominated or sponsored immigrants, handed them railway tickets, gave them subsistence money, and advised the sponsor by telegram or through voluntary representatives of the date and hour of arrival of his nominee so that he could meet him at the station.

Labour groups were met by a representative of the Department of Labour and sent direct to places of employment or, when these were not immediately available, they were directed to labour hostels for eventual placement, which were maintained at the expense of the Department of Labour.

In view of the difficulties which developed when all members of a family were not thoroughly examined at the same time, the Canadian immigration authorities agreed in February 1951 to examine and visa all members of families simultaneously. This was done to make certain that each member would meet the immigration regulations before the bread-winners were allowed to depart for Canada. This procedure simplified the reunion of families to a considerable extent.

The possibilities for the resettlement of displaced persons in Canada continued to expand steadily. Many industries were applying for refugees, and the movement of not less than 3,000 a month was contemplated to bring the labour required to the employers in Canada, the Canadian Government appointing a one-man commission to deal with the vital question of shipping. For a short time refugees were moved by air, space being used on government-chartered aircraft to fly refugees from Great Britain to Canada.

In November 1947 the Canadian Government authorized the immigration of 20,000 workers and their families for specific labour opportunities, a number which was gradually augmented.[1] The reports received indicated that the employers approved of these arrangements and, except for a few misunderstandings, the refugees themselves considered their work and living conditions satisfactory. In due course, agreement was reached on projects for resettlement of suitable refugees in Canada from the Middle East, Africa, and Italy, as well as for a group of Estonian refugees domiciled in Sweden.

Because of its geographical location in the far north, Canada is subject to seasonal unemployment which inevitably had an impact on migration policies. The Government, in regulating immigration, had to take these seasonal fluctuations into account. On the part of IRO this necessitated a considerable amount of pre-selection and documentation in preparation for Canadian labour selection schemes for which no firm advance assurance could be obtained. Volunteers were often wanted at short notice for labour schemes that had ended by the time the interest of many potential immigrants was aroused and no indication could be given that this interest could be utilized for later schemes. Thus, when in the autumn of 1950 large orders were placed with IRO for workers to be available for work in Canada in the spring and

[1] The following quoted from a report of the IRO's mission in Canada illustrates the 'orders' coming forward month by month: '*Ottawa, 12 November 1947*. Total number of orders for workers received: 202 garment workers, 2,301 hard rock miners, 1,000 domestics, 2,000 hydro-electric construction workers, 50 rock tunnelling miners, 200 textile workers, 375 steel workers, 200 dress-makers, 720 track workers.'

summer of 1951, these orders could only be filled in part, and the number fell short of that required at that time. However, in the late autumn and early winter of 1951, at a time when seasonal problems of unemployment were beginning to develop, and a considerable number of these workers had arrived whom the IRO had not been able to produce when they were required, the Canadian Government accepted a considerable group of them with the full knowledge that, because of the seasonal drop in employment, it would be necessary to maintain these people at public expense until work could be found for them in the spring. Furthermore, in order to assist the closing up of IRO operations, Canada agreed to accept the dependants of all workers who had previously proceeded to Canada and maintain them at government expense until the head of the family could provide accommodation for them. Thus Canada not only took a substantial number of displaced persons in the very early stages of the IRO programme, but also at the very late stages, when most of the other immigration countries had become inactive.

The number of refugees who were moved to Canada under the 'labour quota' scheme during the year 1947 totalled approximately 2,400 persons; more than 20,000 such refugees had been brought to Canada by the end of October 1948, and their number reached 48,000 by the end of 1949. The number of persons moved to Canada declined slightly during the years 1950 and 1951, but during the whole period of the IRO's operations, 123,479 refugees were resettled in the Dominion. Workers and their dependants made up approximately 60 per cent. of the total, while nominated cases constituted the other 40 per cent.

Under the category of nominated cases, approximately 900 orphans were brought to Canada, two-thirds under the auspices of the Jewish Immigration Aid Society and one-third under the auspices of the Catholic Immigration Aid Society. These children have been treated with great human understanding since their arrival in Canada, and they all show promise of becoming happy and useful citizens. The International Student Service sponsored a group of displaced-person students, arranged free tuition in Canadian universities, and undertook to help them finish their studies and establish themselves in Canada. The Canadian National Institute for the Blind sponsored the entry of a group of blind people with their dependants, and undertook to look after them for the rest of their lives. Other voluntary agencies which have co-operated with the IRO office in Canada include: Travellers' Aid, the Ukrainian Canadian Committee, the Canadian Red Cross, Canadian Lutheran World Relief, the Canadian Welfare Council, the Canadian Citizenship Council, and the Canadian Council of Churches. Without the assistance of these voluntary bodies and the extensive co-operation of the Departments of Labour and Immigration the IRO's achievements in Canada would not have been possible.

Canadian immigration policy in common with those of the US, Australia, and New Zealand laid stress upon permanent residence and full citizenship to provide a new home country for the immigrants, thus finding a close to perfect solution for dispelling the troubles of the persecuted and the homeless, of whole groups of people in distress.[1]

---

[1] V. C. Phelan, 'Organization of Migration into Canada', *International Labour Review*, lxv. 3 Mar. 1952. Reprint, p. 25.

New Zealand

Following the first visit of a representative of the IRO to New Zealand in September 1948, the New Zealand Government agreed to accept 1,000 refugees from Europe.[1] The Agreement provided for the immigration of 300 single women under 40 years of age for domestic duties in hospitals; 50 widows or mothers up to 45 years of age with one child; 100 families of husband, wife, and one or two other dependants, not necessarily children—the wage-earners, not more than 45 years of age, were to perform heavy manual work; and finally 200 orphan children. The balance of the quota, approximately 80, was to be used for elderly persons generally fit for some light employment.

The Government of New Zealand, in a letter to the Organization, expressed a preference for the selection of Baltic people, Latvians, Lithuanians, and Estonians who, the Government believed, were more likely to be assimilated into the life of the country than were the peoples of more southerly countries. The New Zealand Government added, however, that they would be prepared to accept a reasonable proportion—up to 25 per cent.—of refugees of other nationalities. Persons selected would be required to remain at least two years in the employment to which they were directed and to join a trade union, membership of which is required in New Zealand.

The New Zealand selection team operated first in Austria and later moved to the British and US zones of Germany. As all adults were expected to be fit for employment in various capacities in the work for which they were proposed, a high standard of medical fitness was insisted upon. The first group of refugees arrived in Wellington in June 1949. The New Zealand Government had arranged for their reception in an extremely well equipped installation near the town of Pahiatua, on the North Island, about 100 miles from Wellington. This 'Reception and Training Centre' contained its own hospital, schools, church, workshops, canteens, recreation rooms, and so on, and barrack-type accommodation was provided for the single men, while the families occupied self-contained bungalows.

Following the visit to New Zealand of the Deputy Director General of the IRO in early 1950, the Government agreed to accept a further 1,000 refugees from Europe. The conditions of this acceptance were similar to those for the first scheme, except that there was no specific quota for elderly persons; the age limit for women with one child was extended to 50 years, and that for single men and women to 60, and in the case of married couples without children, the husband's age might be up to 55 years. In addition, the Government allowed refugees already resettled in New Zealand to apply for entry permits for relatives and friends still under the care of the IRO, and a number of refugees with high professional qualifications were also admitted, though the entry of persons in these two categories was subject to the availability of accommodation and employment.

There was an important aspect of both the first and second schemes: they included provisions for persons whose opportunities for resettlement, so IRO believed, were limited, and, during the later stages of the Organization's work, the satisfactory

---

[1] Department of External Affairs, Wellington, NZ, letter to the Director General, IRO, Geneva, dated 10 Nov. 1948 and the Director General's reply dated 7 Dec. 1948.

resettlement of these individuals was particularly important. The Director General of the IRO, on 25 February 1950, therefore expressed his special thanks to the people of New Zealand for their generosity.

For the year 1951 yet another scheme was initiated, providing for the selection of 2,300 persons living temporarily in Germany, Austria, Switzerland, Denmark, Greece, Italy, and Turkey, and, in all, over 4,800 refugees went to the Dominion under the aegis of the IRO. The New Zealand Government had designed its schemes on liberal and humanitarian lines, and its selection missions had applied its criteria fairly. In the end, not even the original preference for Baltic refugees had been maintained; when the final figures were collated it was found that less than a quarter of the 4,837 refugee emigrants resettled in New Zealand were of Baltic stock.

D. LATIN AMERICAN COUNTRIES

Only three Latin American countries, the Dominican Republic, Guatemala, and Venezuela, became contributing members of the IRO. Yet Latin America received 99,497 refugees, that is to say nearly 10 per cent. of the total number of refugees resettled over the globe. Of these, 78,837 persons, or about four-fifths of the refugees received in Latin America, went to Argentina, Brazil, and Venezuela; while Bolivia, Chile, Paraguay, Peru, and Uruguay accepted 17,281, that is roughly one-sixth; and Colombia, Costa Rica, Cuba, the Dominican Republic, Ecuador, Guatemala, Mexico, and Panama the rest. It is true that a need for man-power was the chief impetus behind the invitations extended to the refugees; but humanitarian factors, too, were certainly important in these countries which traditionally offer political asylum.

The Argentine

After the Second World War the Argentine, a country with a long tradition of immigration, adopted a more liberal policy than it had practised during the inter-war period. It permitted the selection of immigrants abroad for the development of rural communities. The new Constitution of 11 March 1949 stipulated that the Federal Government should encourage European immigration. Early in 1947 the Government had expressed interest in including refugees in its existing settlement schemes, and sent a representative to visit assembly centres in Germany, Austria, and Italy, at the same time authorizing its consuls to issue a large number of visas to suitable refugee applicants. The Argentine was primarily interested in obtaining agricultural labourers, particularly the type of person who, after having gained experience in the country, was likely to become a settler on a farm of his own with financial assistance from the Government. Landing permits were granted to individuals at the instigation of denominational and national groups, such as the Slovak League of America, the Holy Synod of the Orthodox Church, and the Slovene Welfare Society, all of which were represented in Buenos Aires. By the end of June 1948 some 12,000 persons, mostly from Italy, had been moved by the Organization to the Argentine.

The Organization's efforts to negotiate an overall agreement for mass and individual resettlement (and to secure the waiving or reduction of the high visa fee of $49) did not prove successful apart from a concession for the granting of free visas to Italy. Thus, on the whole, migration to the Argentine remained on an individual basis, the documentation for each application being completed in accordance with normal consular procedure. In the issue of visas, preference was given to Baltic refugees and those of Roman Catholic faith.

Conditions for individual migration to the Argentine were good. Although no formal agreement existed between the IRO and the Argentine Government, the Organization paid the cost of transport to the port of disembarkation, and provided each immigrant with a sum of $10—as landing money. Thereafter it was easy for him to obtain work, and the only drawback was an acute shortage of housing accommodation, which was particularly stringent in the capital, Buenos Aires. The Argentine received more sponsored and nominated immigrants than any other country in South America. In spite of the comparatively strict immigration regulations, a total of 32,712 refugees had entered the Argentine from the IRO's areas of operation by the end of its operations.

Brazil

After a study of the possibilities of resettlement on a large scale the Government of the United States of Brazil and the IGCR, in the autumn of 1946, concluded an Agreement for the immigration of a first experimental group of 1,000 families, totalling a maximum of 5,000 refugees.[1] The first immigrants arrived in May 1947 and were settled mainly in the state of São Paulo. By 1 July 1947, 1,923 immigrants had arrived in Brazil under the IGCR's arrangements.

Two important considerations were basic to Brazilian emigration—the need for skilled man-power in the booming industrial state of São Paulo, a state in which a long tradition of immigration from Europe facilitated the settlement of the refugees, and the desire of the Government to develop agriculture, live-stock raising, and settlement in the less advanced states. No persons in the liberal professions were selected, as Brazilian law at that time denied the right to practise their professions to foreigners who had received their training abroad. Numbers of hard-working craftsmen, bricklayers, joiners, carpenters, and other workers, were received for 'pioneer' work in rural areas. There was plenty of work in Brazil in other fields as well, e.g. several hundred displaced persons found employment in underground coal-mining near Porto Alegre. In general the emphasis in selection was for families of reasonable size in preference to single persons; unmarried refugees chosen were mainly industrial workers.

On 30 April 1948 an Administrative Agreement was signed between the Government of the United States of Brazil and the PCIRO, and was to remain in force until 31 December 1948.[2] The Agreement provided for the remainder of the initial 5,000 and a further 5,000 immigrants to be received before the end of 1948. One of its important features was the establishment of a Joint Committee of representatives of the governments and of the IRO. The Committee was called upon to study

---

[1] Agreement between the Government of the United States of Brazil and the IGCR concluded on 1 Apr. 1947, PC/LEG/24.   [2] PC/LEG/27, 21 June 1948.

colonization possibilities, conditions of welfare and employment and the legal status of the refugees, and to collaborate with international and local institutions to further the work of resettlement.

A rather exceptional situation developed. The Government of Brazil never ratified the Constitution of the IRO, upon which, in turn, the ratification of the Agreement depended. Yet the Committee, which thus functioned without any legal basis, successfully accomplished a task which was indispensable to immigration. The Committee maintained a permanent Committee Secretariat of about twenty persons in Rio de Janeiro, whose function was to assist the Brazilian Government in dealing with such matters as the reception, documentation, transportation, and placement of the refugees. In addition representatives of the Committee were appointed in the states of São Paulo, Rio Grande do Sul, Santa Catarina, Paraná, Bahia, and Goiás. In this way the influence of the Organization was brought to bear in the areas of resettlement themselves. The Brazilian immigration administrative machinery was not equipped financially or regarding personnel to deal with mass immigration and the Joint Committee took very energetic action to ensure the maintenance of adequate facilities, contributing financially to improvements of state reception centres and so on. Its action was financed by a cruzeiro contribution from the Federal Brazilian Government to the IRO, and its work helped in the successful establishment in Brazil of 9,473 refugees by the end of December 1948.

The contribution of the Joint Committee was essentially to assist the various departments and to ensure the co-ordination of services answerable to more than one Ministry. On disembarkation the immigrants were taken to the Federal Reception Centre on the Ilha das Flores, where they were lodged at the expense of the Council for Immigration and Colonization of the Ministry of Foreign Affairs; the distribution of the workers according to the placement possibilities in the various parts of Brazil was a responsibility of the National Immigration Department of the Ministry of Labour. The Ministry of Agriculture was likewise involved, since that Ministry's Department of Lands and Colonization was concerned with securing refugees with agricultural skills. The Joint Committee provided help where it was needed, and supplied the liaison indispensable in advancing projects such as the establishment of refugee Agricultural Co-operatives. Two such co-operatives were set up, in the state of Goiás, where the Joint Committee's liaison work was much needed for co-ordinating quite a few ministries and authorities interested in the projects. The Goiás scheme did not prove successful because of financial troubles. Many families left, but despite the IRO's offer of placement elsewhere, fifty-four families out of the original 200 preferred to stay on and to till their land in complete independence.

The Brazilian Government did not formally renew the Administrative Agreement, but, unofficially, friendly arrangements continued. Early in 1949 the IRO obtained the consent of the Brazilian authorities to the continuation of immigration of refugees on a large scale, and at times the flow of arrivals was considerable; during the month of May 1949 no less than 3,018 refugees arrived at the Federal Reception Centre on the Ilha das Flores, having been selected by three Brazilian selection missions which were still active in Germany, Austria, and Italy.

In May 1949 it became evident that the Government's immigration operations would shortly come to a standstill, since the appropriations voted for this purpose were exhausted. A sudden stoppage of reception, clearance, and deployment would leave many hundreds of refugees entirely stranded, without even food to eat, and advances from the IRO's cruzeiro fund were therefore made to the various official agencies.

On 25 June 1949 the President of the Federal Republic ordered the suspension of mass immigration of refugees and the recall of the Brazilian selection missions operating in Europe. At the time of this suspension many refugees were *en route* to Brazil, either at sea or in the 'pipe-line' (from the assembly centres to the ports of embarkation); upon representations by the IRO, permission was obtained to carry through the immigration in progress and even to arrange for two more ships to bring in refugees. Thus, during 1949, it was none the less possible to resettle some 13,000 displaced persons in Brazil. However, in view of the continued suspension of mass immigration and the exhaustion of the operating fund in cruzeiros, the activities of the Joint Committee was terminated on 15 December 1949 except for a small closure staff in the federal capital and in some states of the Union. Eventually the residual duties of the Joint Committee were performed by the IRO itself, and the IRO's staff became responsible for the meeting of immigrants on arrival at Rio de Janeiro, their placement in employment in the states, and the settlement of various local welfare problems.

After a change in the federal administration, about a year later, the head of the new Government recognized the merits of the scheme and signed the Agreement on 23 February 1951. Presently a Brazilian selection mission arrived in Europe to begin operations.

Chile

The Chilean resettlement scheme was intended mainly to fill vacancies in the skilled and semi-skilled industrial occupations. The Agreement between the Chilean Government and the IGCR and later the IRO did not make provision for a definite number of immigrants since immigration was based on the country's labour requirements in various trades; but the original Agreement estimated that, during 1947, Chile could absorb up to 2,000 skilled craftsmen and technicians with the members of their families.[1] There were no limitations as to age or size of family or nationality, except that preference was given to Balts and Ukrainians, and very few Jews were accepted.

Chilean resettlement was a modest undertaking, and the rate of movement was slow because of the cautious procedure in the matter of contracts between the individual and the future employer, and also because the reception centre—the Sports Stadium in Santiago—was not organized to receive and place large groups of refugees.

Though an Agreement had been signed in early 1947, it was not until 1948 that

[1] Agreement between the Government of Chile and the IGCR of 7 Feb. 1947, Article I: 'The Permanent Chilean Commission on Immigration will present to the IGCR in London, lists of the immigration requirements of Chile, by professions, that it estimates could be incorporated in that country during the year 1947.'

a Chilean mission started selection operations in Europe, choosing Austria as its field of work. The selection brought approximately 1,700 persons to Chile, of whom a fairly high proportion proved to be unsuitable. Further movements were suspended pending the arrival of a new mission to review a group of some 3,000 persons already pre-selected in Austria. In the meantime, however, as other schemes for families had become available there was less interest in this resettlement scheme. Early in 1950 the Chilean mission again returned to Europe to select potential worker immigrants, concentrating their activities in Italy and Austria. By the time IRO's operations ceased, the results of the Chilean resettlement scheme had not justified the original expectations: at the end of 1951 only 5,108 from the operational areas had emigrated to Chile; among whom the Yugoslavs with 867 persons formed the largest group. The figure included also individually nominated cases.

Dominican Republic

At the Evian conference in 1938 the Dominican Government offered, through its representative President Rafael L. Trujillo, to admit up to 100,000 refugees from Europe; the only offer of any size made by any of the countries participating in the conference.[1] In 1940 an Agreement was signed between the Government of the Dominican Republic and a Jewish sponsored American agency. This was the Dominican Republic Settlement Association. In the same year, under the auspices of IGCR, about 400 refugees were brought over to the Dominican Republic. In 1942 they were moved from the place of landing to the Sosua area, transportation costs being paid by the AJDC.

However, the high hopes entertained by the sponsors were not fulfilled, partly because of administrative difficulties, partly because the war prevented any further settlement. At the end of June 1942 no more than 457 refugees were settled.

The Dominican Republic issued a further invitation for the settlement of refugees in a statement to the General Assembly of the UN on 17 January 1946.[2] At the beginning of IRO's work a special representative of the Director General visited the Dominican Republic to explore further settlement possibilities. The Organization had no funds for large-scale colonization, and emigration to the Dominican Republic was therefore confined to small numbers of individual settlers from among the refugees.

In March 1949 the Dominican Republic, a member of the IRO, agreed to the temporary admission of up to 800 of the refugees from Shanghai who had been evacuated to Samar in the Philippines in 1949. Agriculturists were preferred; the IRO paid the costs of transportation and maintenance. In October 1949 about 200 Russian refugees had arrived at Ciudad Trujillo. They were completely unsuited and unprepared for the conditions they found. The majority were town dwellers unaccustomed to manual labour and did not adjust themselves to rural conditions on the island. In addition, some of them were suspected of Communistic views. Innocent individuals were arrested and detained on security grounds on Saona Island; subsequent investigations showed that suspicion of Communist activities

---

[1] Brookings Institution, *Refugee Settlement in the Dominican Republic*, Washington, 1942.
[2] UN Doc. A/C 3/9.

was unfounded in the majority of the cases. This attempted settlement being a failure many refugees re-emigrated elsewhere; at the beginning of 1952 some 200 refugees were living in poor conditions on the mainland while twelve were confined on Saona Island, used as a penitentiary.[1]

Colombia

Colombia had a pre-war population of Jewish refugees which numbered about 6,000. Among the 889 persons who were brought in by IRO and settled predominently in the cities were 159 Jews, and among others 400 Lithuanians, sponsored by the Lithuanian Catholic Committee. In the case of all IRO refugees Colombia waived the 1,500 pesos deposit normally required of all immigrants.

The fact that a relatively small number of refugees were received was due in part to the lack of an official immigration policy, in part to the slow development of the national economy combined with political instability.

Guatemala

Under an Agreement between the Government of Guatemala and IRO only 342 refugees were admitted to Guatemala. The majority was a group of Spanish Republicans coming from France. Although IRO granted loans and supplied them with tools and equipment, the settlement conditions were very difficult and only a few of these immigrants were able to establish a new and successful life.

Paraguay

Before the war about 10,000 Ukrainians, Balts, and Poles, most of them holders of Nansen passports, and about 3,000 Jewish refugees had settled in Paraguay. The first post-war movements of refugees to Paraguay resulted from the successful application to the Government of Paraguay of a group of several hundred Ukrainian farmers residing in various European countries. Their immigration was sponsored by the Ukrainian Relief Committee in Asunción, Paraguay, under the auspices of the IGCR.

Although Paraguay is essentially a frontier country with hard living conditions and few amenities or social services, the national groups there were most anxious to be joined by more of their countrymen, and two further groups followed, both of Ukrainian origin. However, the conditions of the country, allied with the lack of agricultural experience of the settlers, prevented the development of these beginnings into an organized programme of colonization. The IRO's normal system of mass resettlement depended on the existence of an expanding economy with jobs available, and on economic assistance to the immigrants provided by the government concerned. Paraguay was not in a position to measure up to these requirements, and consequently only individual immigration on a small scale was undertaken, with the limited help of relatives, employers, or national groups.

The Paraguayan Constitution requires that every foreigner entering the country must be in possession of a valid national passport; this was a handicap for refugees unwilling or unable to claim the protection of their national government. The

[1] Cf. Vernant, op. cit., p. 645.

Organization was able to secure a slight relaxation of this rule, authorizing consuls to visa London Travel Documents of specified refugees, a measure that enabled 275 Russian refugees from Samar to be established at the end of 1949 on a farm colony in Paraguay, where they were later joined by a further contingent of 190 refugees chosen in Germany by the Paraguayan Consul-General in Berne. Under an Agreement between the Paraguayan Agricultural Credit Bank and IRO the refugees were given 50 acres of land and a long term credit loan handed out in kind: material for building a house, a cart, a cow, and seeds. Although they were living the hard life of pioneers, they seemed to be quite successful.[1]

Under IRO's operation, 5,887 persons entered Paraguay, most of them before the end of 1948. The largest groups were made up of 2,665 Russian refugees, 1,685 Jews, and 1,433 Poles. Among the Russian émigrés were 2,000 Mennonites who joined 2,800 of their well-established co-religionists who lived in colonies that had been developed before the war with financial help from wealthy and powerful Mennonite colonies in Canada and the US.

Peru

Peru had about 2,500 pre-war Jewish refugees. Under the Agreement of 3 March 1947, concluded between the Peruvian Government and IGCR, IRO brought 2,300 refugees, mostly Yugoslavs, to Peru. About 20 per cent. of the IRO group were farm workers, while the groups of mechanics and labourers amounted to about 8 per cent. each. Most of the refugees settled in Lima and the towns. In 1949 visas for IRO refugees were suspended, since too many difficulties had been encountered in land settlement schemes and conditions were unfavourable for refugee workmen.

Uruguay

The large number of pre-war Jewish refugees (5,000 in 1939, and 7,000 in 1941) was augmented when IRO brought in 1,461 refugees, of whom nearly 50 per cent. were Jews. Of the 750 persons who were sponsored and brought in by the Mennonite Central Committee about 100 were eligible under the IRO Constitution and were provided by the Uruguayan Government with free permanent residence permits.

Venezuela

No less than 17,553 refugees were resettled in Venezuela under the auspices of the IRO up to 1 February 1952. In relation to the total population of the country, these figures represent a remarkable contribution by Venezuela to refugee welfare. The refugees, in turn, have been able to contribute to the national prosperity.

Venezuela has great economic potentialities. As in Canada, refugee immigrants benefited, with the larger number of other immigrants, from the general development of the country. Within the previous thirty years the petroleum industry had been markedly expanding, and with it other industries. Consequently industry had absorbed most of the locally available man-power. On the one hand, there had been

[1] Vernant, op. cit., p. 669.

an acute shortage of technicians and workers, and, on the other hand, the rehabilitation of the country's agriculture had been an extremely urgent task. The foundation of the Technical Institute for Immigration and Colonization (*Instituto Técnico de Immigración y Colonización*) in 1937 and the development of a strong immigration policy had opened the door for immigration.

About 10,000 to 12,000 Jews, Spaniards, Poles, and Russians had come to the country before and during the Second World War, among them about 6,000 Spaniards as the largest group.

After the Second World War, when ocean transport permitted, more than 4,000 immigrants arrived in Venezuela, most of them originating from Spain and Portugal. A considerable new impulse was given to the influx of immigrants by the signing of the Agreement between the IGCR and the Government of Venezuela,[1] in line with the latter's stated policy:

It is the definite proposal of the National Government to give a bold impulse to an immigration policy directed to improve and augment the labour force of the country, and to make use of the circumstances already favourable for the transfer of European families to American countries.[2]

Early in 1947 a Venezuelan mission began selecting refugees in Germany and Austria, choosing construction workers, mechanics, domestic servants, tractor drivers, nurses, and a small number of doctors and engineers, and giving preference to family groups rather than single persons. The first 850 refugees sailed from Bremerhaven for Venezuela on 15 June 1947. The IGCR Agreement did not provide for any specific number of immigrants to be accepted,[3] but by the end of 1947 4,250 refugees had been moved by the IGCR and the IRO, of which 2,798 were transported by the IRO.

A formal exchange of letters in April 1948[4] extended the programme, after agreement had been formulated in principle for settling 50,000 refugees in agricultural colonies. On this basis, in 1948, the number of refugees entering Venezuela as immigrants reached a total of 8,193.

On arrival, immigrants were received by representatives of the Venezuelan authorities and placed for a short time for acclimatization in a government reception centre established near the city of Maracay in the Lake Valencia region, a well-equipped installation accommodating 2,500 persons, where medical examinations and documentation could be performed. The Instituto Técnico de Immigración Colonización set up a system of farm colonies partly sponsored and financed by the Government, and established either on state-owned land or on private estates; these provided favourable resettlement conditions for several hundred farm families.

---

[1] The Agreement was signed on 17 Feb. 1947. PC/LEG/22, 15 Apr. 1948.

[2] Cables exchanged between the President of the Governing Board of the Government of Venezuela and the Venezuelan Ambassador in London, on 17 and 19 Feb. 1947.

[3] 'The Government of Venezuela will periodically present to the IGCR lists of the immigration needs of the country, determining the quantities of immigrants classified by professions and other characteristics which it estimates it will be able to absorb.' See Agreement (107) paragraph 3, Selection of Immigrants.

[4] Letter from the representative of the Government of Venezuela to the Executive Secretary of the IRO, dated 15 Apr. 1948, and letter from the Executive Secretary to the Venezuelan representative, dated 17 Apr. 1948.

Refugees with other professions were absorbed by Venezuela's growing economic development.

In November 1948 the Department of Immigration was reorganized. During this reorganization the admission of immigrants, and consequently the admission of refugees, was restricted. Furthermore, the Instituto Técnico de Immigración Colonización was replaced by the new 'Instituto Agrario Nacional', which took over such assets as were deemed appropriate for its own purposes. In consequence, the colonization projects which had already been realized between owners of private farms, refugees, and immigrants remained without official support, so that nearly all of them were bound to fail. The people concerned either did not apply to the usual sources for farm credits, as for instance the Banco Agricola y Pecuario, or were not able to produce sufficient guarantees for the credits they had requested. Over 200 refugee families were affected, and after representations by the IRO to the Government, some readjustments were made, but only 922 persons in all were received in that year.

As a result only about 1,300 refugee immigrants went to Venezuela during 1949. Later, changes in the oil industry brought a recession in trade and industry, and in 1950 and 1951 competition from other immigrants, principally Italian, Spanish, and Portuguese, who were then entering the country in large numbers, made it difficult for refugee resettlers to find satisfactory opportunities. The constant necessity for secondary aid to refugees seeking employment presented a grave problem, as the Venezuelan Government undertook to place a refugee immigrant only once on arrival and did not automatically renew this facility. If for any reason a refugee lost his first job, the Government examined the case and, if there were sufficient reasons in favour of further action, provided another job or authorized the refugee to return to the reception centre for an additional period. The refugee immigration figures for 1950 show an increase to 2,653, while during 1951, including January 1952, the number admitted was 1,535.

The final absorption of more than 17,000 people coming from different environments, having other customs and speaking other languages, could not take place without setbacks, and difficulties were only gradually overcome. Although the colonization schemes did not lead to the expected results, a certain number of refugees made their livelihood in the farm colonies under good conditions; employment possibilities in industry, commerce, and construction activities offered satisfactory working conditions to refugees, and they had opportunities of becoming economically independent and of attaining a favourable standard of living. Some of the refugees, more capable and economically more favoured than others, were especially successful, and improved their situation rapidly. Furthermore, the adaptation of the refugee children to their new environment was fostered by the generous Venezuelan legislation on education, which grants free schooling and free university tuition to foreigners as well as to the Venezuelans themselves.

Limitations on Settlement in Latin America

The limited scale of resettlement contrasts strikingly with this continent's need for man-power, its willingness to accept people, and the hospitality extended by co-religionists and co-nationalists. Financial, economic, and human factors contribute to this paradoxical situation: there is a lack of governmental and private facilities for sponsoring immigration on a larger scale; pioneer conditions still prevail which put too heavy a strain on the endurance, ability, and skill of the average settler coming from one of the older European cultures.

E. UNITED STATES OF AMERICA

Until 1948 refugee immigration into the US was not subject to special legislation but was controlled, as was all immigration, by the two basic Immigration Acts of 5 February 1917 and of 1 July 1924. This legislation provided that the number of immigrants to enter the US was limited, and a national origin quota system assigned definite quotas of immigrants to each country of origin except for the Western Hemisphere. This quota system, based on a formula of selection according to race and nationality, aimed to preserve in a general way the ethnic balance of the population of the US. The total quotas, 154,277 annually, could not be carried over from one year to the next. The size of the quotas for each country favoured countries in north and west Europe. However, immigrants from these countries had only used about a quarter of their quota. Since the early thirties an average of only 54,095 quota visas were issued annually in spite of the 154,000 visas available.

As has been seen, the US had actively participated in the formation, operation, and financing of the IRO. Realizing that, in the final solution of the refugee problem, immigration into the US was essential, the Executive and the Legislative took the necessary steps to pave the way for the reception of displaced persons. On 22 December 1945 President Truman issued a directive, according to which 90 per cent. of the regular immigration quotas for central and eastern Europe, about 39,000 annually, should be used in the US occupation zones for persons who would not or could not be returned to their pre-war homes. This was the first important emergency measure taken by the Government for the admission of refugees after the Second World War. Under this directive nearly 42,000 refugees were admitted to the US, of which about 17,000 were assisted by the IRO after the Organization had taken over the control and administration of the processing and embarkation centres.

The most important aspect of the directive was the introduction of the 'corporate affidavit', a guarantee of financial support given by voluntary organizations on behalf of the refugees in order that they would not become public charges.[1] This provision made it possible for many persons to enter the US who would otherwise have been rejected because of a lack of private means or because they had not been in a position to obtain an individual affidavit of support.

IRO's assistance did not at first include free ocean transport to refugees receiving visas. Provisions of the Immigration Act of 1917 specified that 'no corporation, association, society, municipality or foreign government' might pay for the passage of an immigrant. Voluntary societies had complied with the law by advancing

[1] Under the Commission's regulations to become a public charge meant to require 'aid at public expense for essential food, clothing or shelter, or for medical treatment for causes existing prior to entry into the US under the Act...', *The DP Commission*, First Semi-Annual Report..., 1 Feb. 1949, p. 17.

immigrants' fares as loans. The advances of voluntary societies who arranged the immigration of victims of Nazi persecution were covered by payments from the Reparations Fund administered by the IRO. Until March 1949, therefore, the IRO provided the voluntary societies with logistical support. Thus the societies were permitted to devote a maximum amount from their funds to loans. Then the Department of Justice was asked for a ruling that the quoted section should not be applicable to the IRO, so that it could furnish transport to normal quota immigrants.

While the Presidential directive was in operation, it became apparent that the available quotas were insufficient for the number of refugees who wished to enter the US. Accordingly, the President recommended, in his State of the Union message on 6 January 1947, that Congress should assist in the solution of this problem by passing appropriate legislation. This was the first of a series of recommendations from the Executive. Several interested groups, including voluntary societies, began to urge the passage of special legislation which would make it possible for their country to contribute more generously towards the solution of the refugee problem. After protracted legislative procedure, United States Public Law 774, known as the 'Displaced Persons Act of 1948', was passed by the 80th Congress on 24 June 1948 and amended in the Acts of 16 June 1950 and 29 June 1951.[1] This law provided for the admission to the US of about 400,000 refugees between 1 July 1948 and 31 December 1951.

This Act was a revolutionary decision in US history. For the first time the Government officially established an agency for implementing a planned resettlement programme for other nationals in the US. Although the law was conceived in the framework of the old immigration legislation, it provided a 'satisfactory resettlement opportunity, including a job and a home', for the immigrant, and 'a comprehensive system of public and private social service agencies was established and coordinated to help the new American adjust himself to his new homeland'.

The Quota Act of 1924 had given preference to immigrants from northern and western countries, but, in fact, only a limited quota had been granted to such northern countries as the Baltic states as the ratio of their very small populations to that of the US was unfavourable to them. The Act of 1948 counteracted a provision that had never been intended to discriminate against the Baltic countries. It stipulated that 40 per cent. of the total number of visas should be issued to persons whose place of origin or country of nationality had been 'de facto annexed by a foreign power', thus benefiting the Balts as well as the Poles.

The original Act of 1948 established criteria of selection in terms of preferences for three groups: at least 30 per cent. of the visas were to be issued to persons who had been engaged in 'agriculture before their immigration'; household, construction, and garment workers as well as persons with special professional qualifications were to be second in line; finally—in keeping with the aim of leaving the family unit intact—preference was also to be accorded to blood relatives of citizens or aliens permanently residing in the US.

A further specification determined the two priorities to be given to certain people in any of the preferred groups. The first priority benefited those who had fought

---

[1] Cf. Public Law 555, 81st Congress; Public Law 60, 82nd Congress.

against the enemies of the US during the Second World War, and included their families. The second priority was granted to persons who, on 1 January 1948, were living in refugee camps. Unfortunately the latter priority discriminated against those courageous people who had left the camps to support themselves. This priority was eliminated, therefore, by the Amendment to the Act of 1948.

The groups admitted under the DP Act, as of 30 June 1952, fell under the following categories:

Immigrants admitted under DP Act, as of 30 June 1952, by class of admission	Total	
	Per cent.	Number
All immigrants	100·0	393,542
Displaced persons	85·7	337,244
Displaced persons from Western Germany, Austria, and Italy	78·0	306,785
Recent political refugees	..	162
Venezia Giulia refugees	0·5	2,000
European displaced persons from Far East . .	0·8	3,312
Ex-Polish soldiers from Great Britain . . .	2·7	10,487
Native Greeks and preferentials	2·3	8,977
Out-of-zone refugees	1·4	5,521
German expellees	13·6	53,448
Orphans	0·7	2,838
IRO orphans	0·3	1,356

The provisions of the Immigration Law of 1917 governing contract labour were not only eliminated but reversed. Earlier American immigration legislation had excluded aliens who held labour contracts stipulating a certain period of service as a means of paying off costs for their transportation. After the passage of the Act of 1948 definite housing and employment assurances for refugee immigrants were a prerequisite of admission. Every adult or family had to have a written invitation from a sponsor in the form of a sworn assurance of adequate housing and a job that would not displace another person, as well as a guarantee that the refugee would not become a public charge. These assurances were in most cases collected by voluntary societies, from relatives of refugees, sympathizers, church groups, and civic organizations. The assurances offered by the societies were divided into two categories—'blanket' or anonymous guarantees covering a large number of refugees to be selected by the society's representative abroad, but vouched for in full by the society for resettlement; and 'individual' assurances for identified refugees, offered either by the society or by a private sponsor through the channels of the society. It was also possible for a citizen to give affidavits without the mediation of a voluntary agency. Both the IRO and the voluntary societies made great efforts to obtain the essential assurances, which were acknowledged as valid by the Displaced Persons Commission in Washington, DC, and forwarded to its headquarters in Europe.

In accordance with the terms of the Act, a three-member Displaced Persons Commission was appointed by the President on 12 August 1948 to administer the new arrangements provided by the Act. The Commission's headquarters were in Washington, DC; European headquarters were established in Frankfurt-on-Main, Germany, and field offices in IRO resettlement centres in Germany, Austria, and Italy, for selecting the persons to receive visas under the 1948 Act. Thus, representatives of all the authorities concerned with immigration to the US worked as a team inside the IRO's resettlement centres; where the Commission's representatives, consular officials, physicians of the Public Health Service, and other interested officials all worked together. The Displaced Persons Commission also maintained a senior officer at Bremen, the port of embarkation.[1]

The immigration process began when an assurance was received in Europe. In the case of an individual assurance, since the individual was known, the IRO could immediately start to prepare the documentation. In the case of anonymous assurances, documentation had to await the nomination of a candidate by the representative of the voluntary society in Germany or Austria, for the Society representative, with knowledge of his sponsor's requirements, carried out the important task of finding candidates whose qualifications matched his society's assurances. As in connexion with other schemes, technical difficulties arose: records were widely dispersed; civil status documents had to be obtained for consular action, often a time-consuming matter; dossiers had to be prepared, and finally there was the sometimes lengthy security investigation. In the last four months of 1948 a system suitable for dealing with very substantial numbers of refugees had been devised and perfected, and by January 1949 visas were being issued on a large scale. The IRO hoped to be sending 10,000 immigrants monthly to the US by June 1949.

By the end of June 1949, 54,824 refugees had been given visas, and 44,405 of them—including many persons whose opportunities for resettlement elsewhere were limited—had left Europe for the US in the IRO's ships and aeroplanes. Movements to the US reached their peak during the second half of 1949, when approximately 80,000 persons made the journey. The final statistical report shows that a total of 328,851 refugees had gone to the US by 31 December 1951; no other country received more immigrants from among the refugees under the IRO's auspices.

This increased figure was made possible by an Amendment to the Displaced Persons Act signed by the President on 16 June 1950. This amendment liberalized eligibility requirements as defined in the Act, eliminated the provision that 30 per cent. of the refugees should be farm workers or farmers—a provision that had proved impossible to fulfil—and authorized the admission to the US of a total of 313,000 refugees within the mandate of the IRO from Germany, Austria, Italy, China, and the Philippines (including the 177,000 for whom visas had already been issued) on visas granted before the final date for the issue of visas, which the amendment fixed at 30 June 1951. (This date was later extended by subsequent amendments.) The amendment to the Displaced Persons Act also gave preferential treatment to a certain number of refugees assisted by the IRO in other western European countries, and included, as a new feature, the admittance of persons of German stock who had been expelled from the countries in which they were normally

1 *The DP Story*, op. cit., p. 154.

resident. These *Volksdeutsche* were not the concern of the IRO, but, at the request of the US Government, the Organization undertook to process and transport these persons subject to reimbursement. The first group was moved during the second half of 1950.

Movements of refugees under the IRO's mandate slowed down during 1950, as fewer visas were issued because of the attempt to satisfy the percentage requirements for agriculturists laid down in the Act of 1948. After this limitation was removed by the June 1950 amendment, the operation of a new Internal Security Act of 23 September 1950 (amended on 28 March 1951)[1] seriously retarded immigration activities, which were further decreased by a deterioration of the international situation. It was not until comparatively late in 1951 that visas were again issued on a large scale.

The responsibility of IRO for the refugees ended upon their arrival at ports of entry. The reception of refugees at the ports of Boston, New York, and New Orleans was arranged by the voluntary societies, and in time reception became a routine operation, thousands of refugees being met and helped on their way every month by the voluntary societies. Refugees came ashore wearing large tags bearing the initials of the sponsoring voluntary society, whose representatives assisted them in the customs formalities, interviewed them, checked their documents, and ensured that travel arrangements for their final destination were completed. Refugees not sponsored by a voluntary society were assisted by the Travellers' Aid Society, and first-aid services were usually provided by the American Red Cross. After their arrival at their destination, the refugees were aided by their voluntary society and assisted in adapting themselves to American conditions. In the work involved in receiving and settling the refugees as well as throughout the resettlement process, the contribution of the voluntary societies was essential to the US resettlement plan.

According to careful estimates 720,296 refugees have been admitted to the US since 1933: from 1933 to 1943 285,375; under the President's directive from 1945 to 1948, 41,379; and 393,542 under the DP Act from June 1948 to 21 July 1952.[2]

The US surpassed all other countries of the world in regard to the absolute number of refugees admitted, although not in terms of the ratio to its total population. In this respect, Canada and Israel have an even higher record to their credit.

The final Report of the Displaced Persons Commission acknowledges, with all due appreciation of the generous and democratic spirit in which support was given by the nation as a whole—that 'an effort founded on purely humane grounds resulted in gains for the US that will continue for decades; that an otherwise unobtainable contribution of skills and knowledge came at a time when there was a desperate need for manpower'.[3] The report also regards the movement of refugees from the point of view of international relations, and states that: 'What started out as a movement of displaced persons, refugees, expellees, orphans, and others from Europe, to the US and other nations, also made a beginning at easing the tensions that resulted from overpopulation in Germany, Austria, Italy, Greece and other countries.'

[1] *The DP Story*, op. cit., p. 70.
[2] Jane P. C. Carey, 'The Admission and Integration of Refugees in the United States' in *Journal of International Affairs*, vii. 1, 1953, p. 68.
[3] *The DP Story*, op. cit., p. 6.

F. ISRAEL

Israel, the second largest country of immigration, accepted 132,109 displaced persons during IRO's existence. The history of immigration to Israel differs from that of any other country. Although large groups of immigrants came as refugees, not as pioneers, it was for many a 'return to the Holy Land'. Two laws gave expression to the unique situation of Israel as a country of immigration—the Law of Return, 5 July 1950, that states that 'Every Jew has the *right* to come to the country as an immigrant', and the Law of 1 April 1952 that 'Israel nationality is acquired by his return'.

Until 15 May 1948, the date of the establishment of the independent state of Israel, the immigration policy of Palestine was determined by the UK, the mandatory power. Immigration was based on selection, and the extent of immigration depended upon the economic situation. The JAFP, a Zionist organization, selected immigrants from the quota determined by the British Government. Between 1918 and May 1948 approximately 450,000 Jews entered Palestine under this scheme.[1] Only persons in possession of immigration certificates issued by the mandatory power were moved to Palestine at the expense of the IRO. After the beginning of 1947 1,500 certificates a month were issued to Jewish settlers, and the IRO paid for the immigration of about 6,000 before the withdrawal of the mandatory government. At the beginning of its existence the Government of Israel abolished the former policy and introduced a policy of a non-selective immigration *en masse*. Soon after the proclamation of the State of Israel hostilities broke out between the Arabs and the Jews, and this open warfare in Palestine presented a serious problem of policy to the IRO. The Director General issued instructions that the Organization's funds were not to be used to assist the immigration of any refugees to any of the belligerent countries in the Middle East, including Palestine, or to any area in which there was fighting. However, the delegates on the Executive Committee differed among themselves about this policy. The British Government upheld the Director General's view, while the Americans held the view that it was IRO's responsibility to get out of the camps as many displaced persons as possible, and as soon as possible, and that IRO should therefore pay the transportation. Three other governments suggested that IRO should consult the UN Conciliation Commission on Palestine, which was charged by the General Assembly with facilitating the repatriation of the Palestinians and Arabs who had become refugees as a result of the conflict in Israel. These governments felt that IRO should not facilitate or encourage a movement to Palestine if, in so doing, it would jeopardize the efforts of the Conciliation Commission to repatriate Palestinians. In order to reach a compromise the Executive Committee decided that IRO should pay for all the past movements and after 31 January 1949 IRO should consult the Conciliation Commission[2] in regard to future movements.

The suspension of the IRO's assistance did not bring about a cessation of immigration to Palestine. The JAFP and the AJDC, working in co-operation, made

---

[1] Vernant, op. cit., p. 442.
[2] The Executive Committee dealt with this matter at its Eleventh Meeting, 11 Dec. 1948 (Res. 3 and at its Nineteenth Meeting, 28 Jan. 1949 (Res. 6). Cf. Appendix III, pp. 751 and 752.

appropriate plans to expand their immigration assistance and, without the IRO's assistance, moved a considerable number of Jews to Israel, for it was the aim of these organizations that not a single Jewish refugee should be left in the assembly centres in Germany, Austria, and Italy, a plan that was encouraged by the Israel Government's four-year plan to double the country's population.

With the exception of emergency air evacuation of Jewish refugees from Shanghai to Israel, the IRO maintained its policy of taking no part in movements of Jewish refugees to Israel until 28 January 1949, when the Executive Committee authorized the Director General to reimburse the AJDC for the costs incurred in moving refugees to Israel between the end of May 1948 and the end of January 1949. A maximum of $4 million was fixed, the amount set aside for movements to Palestine in the Plan of Expenditure for the year 1948–9 approved by the General Council; the sum had been intended to cover the movement of 50,000 people.

In April 1949, when the Palestine Conciliation Commission declared that the question of the support of emigration to Israel was not within its competence, the Director General authorized a full resumption of the IRO's assistance and financial support for movements to Israel.

By April 1949 events had moved far enough for a sum of approximately $6,300,000 to be included in the plan of expenditure for the year 1949–50.[1] The exact amount to be reimbursed to the AJDC was a matter of negotiation. Agreement was reached between the IRO, the AJDC, and the JAFP in which the IRO agreed to pay the AJDC at the rate of $120 per person for the first 35,000 Jewish refugees transported to Israel after 15 May 1948, $90 for the next 30,000, and $70 and $60 per capita for the next 35,000 and 20,000 respectively. In October 1950 the IRO and the AJDC concluded a final arrangement for reimbursement of costs of emigration to Israel. A total sum of $10¼ million inclusive of previous payments was agreed upon in recognition of which the AJDC assumed full responsibility for all past and future moves to Israel and for all emigration from the Far East as of 27 October 1950; the balance did not cover the total cost to the AJDC for the movement to Israel.

Although retroactive financial help was given for the movements of refugees to Israel, the JAFP and the AJDC had originally achieved a remarkable operation by independently moving, during the second half of the year 1948, about 55,000 displaced persons and refugees, and during the first half of 1949 a further 45,000 persons to Israel, thus appreciably diminishing the IRO's case-load in Germany, Austria, and Italy by nearly 100,000 persons within a year.

The JAFP caring for displaced persons and Israel's instrument for handling matters pertaining to immigration and absorption had, in accordance with an agreement with UNRRA, sent representatives to Germany in December 1945; it continued to operate under an agreement with the IRO. The JAFP lived and worked with the Jewish refugees in assembly centres, and encouraged them to undertake productive work by urging them to take existing opportunities for vocational training. The JAFP initiated the 'Advisory Selection Boards', which were set up in the larger camps and communities for the purpose of assisting the JAFP immigrants to Israel; quotas were submitted to the Israel Government for approval. An order

[1] IEC/28, 2 Apr. 1949.

of priority was established for the countries from which immigrants were to be admitted, refugees from assembly centres in Germany, Austria, and Italy having precedence over all others.

As far as the IRO was concerned, the most important part of the movement to Israel (once the principle of payment was accepted) were the practical arrangements. Under agreement with the AJDC the IRO was to provide rations, medical supplies, and accommodation stores for the AJDC's staging and embarkation centres in Germany, Austria, and Italy; the IRO was responsible for the administration of the staging centres in Austria and of the embarkation centre in Italy. The AJDC was responsible for movements between centres and by ship, and detailed provisions were agreed upon for the certification that refugees were within the mandate of the IRO and that therefore their movement was subject to reimbursement.[1]

The majority of the refugees assisted by the AJDC with the support of the IRO were taken to their future home in Israel-owned ships, manned by Israeli crews. The present Israel merchant line is a natural outgrowth of 'Immigration B', as the unauthorized Jewish immigration to Palestine was called. Many of the ships used for this transportation of refugees to the Jewish state had formerly, during the British mandate, conveyed illegal entrants.

On arrival at the port of Haifa, the immigrants were brought to the clearing camp, from where they were moved to one of the reception camps until they could be provided with housing. They were at liberty to leave the camps or to accept employment. No deductions were made for food or lodging during their stay in the camps, but each immigrant was expected to give one day's work a week in order to help in the proper maintenance of the camp. The steady inflow of immigrants and the housing shortage in Israel caused the period of their residence in reception camps to lengthen, and the 'Department for the Absorption of Immigrants' had to modify the living conditions in these reception camps to fit them for a prolonged stay of the immigrants. The various social welfare institutions of the country, with a long tradition of immigrant aid and training, co-operated in the assistance given immigrants to overcome the difficulties and hardships of this interim period.

Israel's open-door policy confronted the young state with an absorption problem of some complexity. The admission of immigrants was not determined by economic needs or financial criteria. All Jews were welcomed, and a heterogeneous throng of migrants from all parts of the world poured into Israel; they came from the displaced persons' camps, the Balkans, and North Africa; from Shanghai, and as immigrants from Bulgaria, Iraq, Iran, and the Yemen. The national authorities of the new state confronted not only the task of welding these diversified elements into one population, but also the task of developing and reclaiming a country which, by European standards, was under-developed. The refugees entering the country after 1948 differed from the trained pioneer settlers, with skills specially adapted to their new homes, who had been admitted under the British mandate; these later refugees were a mass of uprooted people, with little in common apart from faith and hope. The contribution of Israel to the resettlement of refugees must be considered in

---

[1] Exchange of letters, 30 Aug. 1949 and 8 Sept. 1949 between Assistant Director General of the IRO and vice-chairman, European Executive Council, AJDC. IRO/HCM/VOL/21.

the light of these facts. Proportionately to its total population, a far larger number of refugees was absorbed into Israel than into any other country, and finally one person in every ten of Israel's population was a former inmate of an assembly centre who had been able to settle in a free country thanks to the sacrifice and great generosity of his co-religionists and to the help of the IRO.

G. RESETTLEMENT FROM OUTLYING AREAS OF FIRST REFUGE

The three other extensive areas, although harbouring only a minority of IRO's refugees, were the Middle East, East Africa, and the Far East. These outlying areas, far apart from the war-torn countries and far apart from one another, served as countries of temporary refuge only and hardly offered any opportunities for local settlement. For the refugees they were at best one of the many preliminary stopping points on their long and uncertain journey to new homes.

The enormous area known as the Middle East theatre of operations of UNRRA and subsequently of IRO had its headquarters at Cairo. It covered countries as far apart as India and East Africa, as well as Palestine, Turkey, the Lebanon, and Syria; and negotiations for the accommodation or movement of refugees, whether routine business or emergencies, necessitated visits of the mission's officials to Cyprus, Eritrea, and many other places not normally connected in the public mind with the problem of European refugees.

The operational characteristics of the Middle East, apart from Turkey, were first the gradual British withdrawal from the area; secondly the presence of large numbers of Poles; and thirdly the effect of the Jewish exodus through Austria, Germany, and Italy to Palestine.

IRO continued UNRRA's activities and wound them up in Palestine, the Lebanon, East Africa, and India. UNRRA's operational activities in Egypt had been confined to the direct administration of El Shatt camp, which has already been mentioned, and which was subsequently taken over by IRO. The camp was maintained with the consent of the Egyptian Government. When all inmates were either resettled or repatriated the camp was closed in 1948.

The withdrawal of the British in 1947 from India and in 1948 from Palestine made it necessary for the IRO to take emergency measures, and the division of the Indian sub-continent into India and Pakistan resulted in major movements of populations.

The last of the British troops were scheduled to leave India on 28 February 1948. The IRO's operations in India entailed responsibility for Poles accommodated in a camp at Kolhapur under the dual control of the British High Commissioner and the new Indian Government, and this camp, at the request of the Indian Government and under the pressure of rapidly deteriorating conditions, had to be liquidated quickly. The bulk of Poles were therefore evacuated from Kolhapur camp at the end of February and moved from India. Most of them went to East Africa and some to the French zone of Germany.

With the assistance of the British and Indian authorities, this evacuation was successful; only a small number, 150, remained at the camp, and they were removed later.

Palestine was still under the British mandate when IRO began its operation. The problem of Polish refugees in Palestine eligible for IRO assistance was obviously a matter of increasing concern, even before the announcement of the partition of Palestine on 30 November 1947 intensified the situation. Some of these were Jews, but the majority were not, and as their position was increasingly dangerous, their evacuation from Palestine was arranged.

Conditions under which preparations for this evacuation, and the evacuation itself, were carried out seemed completely unreal at the time and appear even more unreal in retrospect. In Jerusalem, where the IRO office was located, conditions were extremely unstable; security, mail, telephone, and transport were almost non-existent; Arab and Jewish convoys were attacked by the opposing side on roads connecting the two spheres of influence; and IRO officials, attempting to make contact with widely scattered settlements and individuals, did so at great personal risk.

An IRO official from Middle East headquarters was sent to Jerusalem in order to arrange an early evacuation from Palestine of all eligible refugees. In conjunction with the Polish Committee of the Palestine Government the IRO decided to inform all refugees that it would no longer be possible to afford them cash assistance after 1 January 1948. They would have to choose between repatriation, the Polish Resettlement Corps (if eligible under its criteria), absorption into Palestine, or they could remain under IRO's care and be evacuated in the near future. The joint convoy of nearly 500 refugees finally left for El Shatt camp in Egypt with the permission of the Egyptian Government. The French zone of Germany was their destination until they could be established elsewhere.

The removal of Poles of Jewish faith by boat from Haifa entailed even greater difficulties than the evacuation of Christians, as any appearance of forcing these Polish Jews to leave had to be avoided. Embarkation on two ships was finally completed and the rest of the refugees were ultimately evacuated over land to the Lebanon.

On 15 May 1948 the British Mandate in Palestine ended; at midnight on 14 May 1948 the Provisional Government of the state of Israel was established; on 15 May 1948 Arab intervention in Palestine began, and war broke out.

There were immediate repercussions. The problem of the residual group of IRO refugees left behind in Palestine was dwarfed by the mass flight of Arab refugees whose traditional home had become a battlefield. On 18 May 1948 IRO suspended all assistance in emigration to countries in the Middle East involved in the Palestine war.

The Lebanon

When the IRO began work there were nearly 4,000 Poles in the Lebanon. They had been settled in villages, and given maintenance allowances administered by the British Legation and a local Polish organization. The latter was strong; for the Lebanese Government had not recognized the new (Warsaw) Polish Government and continued to grant diplomatic privileges to the 'London' Polish Minister in Beirut who therefore continued to act as the official Polish diplomatic representative.

They were later joined by the Poles moved from Palestine, making a total of about 6,000, of which nearly 3,000 were resettled before the end of 1947 and another 1,000 by the middle of 1948; these moves had been made mostly to the UK under the British Government's arrangements for accepting dependants of members of the Polish forces. The majority of the remaining Poles were people living in relative comfort on pensions, who made little effort to move. By persuasion and by the efforts of Australian and Canadian selection missions, most of the Poles were found new homes by the end of 1950; the balance went to Argentina or was accepted by the British Government.

East Africa (Kenya, Nyasaland, Tanganyika, the Rhodesias, and Uganda)

The internees and refugees brought to East Africa during and after the war were accepted by the colonial governments concerned; extensive arrangements were made for their accommodation and general administration; but their permanent stay was not envisaged and their removal remained the ultimate responsibility of the British Government.

It was not possible for selection missions to visit East Africa, and therefore a pre-selected group of between 650 and 800 persons from India and East Africa was sent to Europe and was visited in Marseilles by resettlement missions representing the French, Canadian, and British Governments.

IRO's efforts in East Africa were almost entirely successful. The total number of refugees in the sixteen centres in East and Central Africa on 1 July 1947 was 16,519; nearly 1,000 additional refugees received assistance after that date including a residue of 720 Poles from India, former officials of the London Polish Government from other parts of Africa, and a group of former internees. The total number of refugees in East Africa assisted by the IRO was thus about 17,500. More than half of these refugees were dependants of Polish military personnel demobilized in the UK and were resettled in the UK by the British authorities. Movements to the UK of over 7,000 individuals took place in the first half of 1948 and were followed by smaller moves later. At the same time, final efforts to encourage repatriation included a visit arranged by IRO of representative refugees to Poland, and over 1,000 refugees went home during the first year of IRO's operations.

About 4,000 who were left after the main exodus, at the end of 1948, continued to live in favourable conditions in a European though colonial environment, 5,000 miles from European problems and unconcerned about their future. This psychological factor was one of the reasons that made their ultimate resettlement more difficult than had been expected.

The resettling of refugees depended upon contact between them and the selectors, and 545 persons were accordingly transferred to France for presentation to selection missions. Refugees in East Africa were, however, well established; and though they could not remain indefinitely, they had so often been threatened by eviction or a withdrawal of their eligibility status because of their refusal of re-establishment opportunities that new threats had little effect. They were sure that neither IRO nor the territorial governments concerned would ever forcibly repatriate them, and no other method of removing them seemed possible.

A case is on record of a Canadian selection mission being invited to an elaborate banquet, offered by refugees to a departing camp commandant. The impression made on the Canadians by these refugees was so unfavourable that for a time it looked as if a proposed movement to Canada would be jeopardized. Only after some of the camps were closed and the inmates sent to other surroundings did certain refugees realize that conditions would not continue indefinitely as they were, and that they must decide about their future without delay.

The only countries which sent selection missions for mass resettlement schemes to Africa were Australia, Canada, and the UK; the Australian mission issued entry visas to almost 1,200 people, and the Canadian selected some 400 young people, many of whom managed subsequently to send for their relatives. A British mission to select persons for work in the UK under the 'Westward Ho!' scheme had already visited the area; and after everything possible had been done by IRO to resettle the remainder, another British mission visited East Africa at the very end of the IRO's operation to accept 1,300 persons, some of them institutional cases, for maintenance in the hostels of the National Assistance Board.

When the IRO withdrew, only about 250 refugees were left in the area, most of them with some hope of later settlement. The number of refugees remaining in mid-1952 was thirty-one.

The East African governments were persuaded to accept, for permanent settlement in Africa, only a small number of Polish refugees. Suitable employment was scarce, except for technicians, and the laws governing immigration into the various East African territories were very severe, chiefly to prevent the growth of a 'poor white' population. The protectorates in any case offered little scope for white settlement, and elsewhere there was a strong preference for immigrants of British stock. Southern Rhodesia practised a quota system similar to that of the US. About 7 per cent. of Kenya's white population were already of refugee origin, and had come to the colony before the war to escape Nazism. All in all some 1,500 Polish refugees were settled in the six British mainland territories.

There was one aspect of integration within East Africa which was not solely the result of the local governments' generosity. Fifty per cent. of the refugee population consisted of women of 14 years and over, and the territories have a good record of successful marriages, believed to be over 300. For example, in Southern Rhodesia local prospectors used often to write to the IRO Camp Commandant in the territory, proposing marriage to any suitable girl who was prepared to share their life. These proposals were posted, without IRO comment, on the camp's notice boards, and a number of successful cases of local resettlement resulted.

The Far East

The background to the IRO's work in the Far East was the struggle between the Chinese Nationalists and Communists which ended with a Communist victory in 1949 and the escape of General Chiang Kai Shek to the island of Formosa.

The distinct groups with which the IRO was concerned in the Far East were European Jews, pre-war Russian émigrés, and overseas Chinese. The Jews had arrived in Shanghai during the late 1930's when other refuge could not be found. Over 16,000 had been maintained by UNRRA after the war; but thanks to the activities of the AJDC in arranging individual resettlement, to which the IGCR also contributed, only about 9,000 required maintenance by the time IRO began. The Russians were the remnants of many tens of thousands of refugees who had arrived fifteen years earlier; their somewhat artificial life in the Orient forced them to live by their wits if they were to survive in a non-European society where only a limited number of trades and professions were open to foreigners. Nevertheless, being more or less self-supporting, they were no problem for the IRO until the Communist advance in 1948, although as early as 1947 certain requests for protection had been dealt with by the Shanghai office on orders from Geneva headquarters. The Chinese, members of groups normally resident in south Asiatic countries, were only a commitment for repatriation to these countries.

For the Jewish group, free maintenance was continued; there was a steady small repatriation of a few hundreds each year, but resettlement only became important with the opening of Israel and the US for immigration. For the Russian group emergency evacuations, similar to those earlier arranged from India and Palestine, were carried out by air and sea. The Chinese repatriation continued for two years, and was largely concluded by the middle of 1949. Both the Nationalist and subsequently the Communist governments in China were anxious to be rid of the European refugees; but the group whose removal was of secondary importance during the Nationalist régime was the one which was in greatest danger when the Communists approached Shanghai.

To deal with this work, offices were established not only in Shanghai but also in Hong Kong (which assumed increasing importance as the result of subsequent political changes), Amoy, Canton, Foochow, Swatow, and Tientsin.

IRO also negotiated with the Government to regularize the work of its missions. Although in view of the Chinese Nationalist Government's other preoccupations, the formal agreement did not develop past the draft stage, its spirit was honoured to the maximum extent. Under the draft agreement the Organization was to be responsible for the provision of such facilities and supplies as were locally available, including the cost (not involving foreign currency) of the care and maintenance for refugees.

In the middle of 1948 the Israeli Government sent a representative with consular powers to Shanghai, issuing entry visas for Israel to Jews who wished to go there and who fulfilled the conditions laid down by the immigration authorities.

By the beginning of October 1948 a total of approximately 3,000 Jews had been evacuated from Shanghai through the IRO. Of these approximately 2,800 had been sent on their way to Israel and 200 repatriated to Germany and Austria. A further convoy of approximately 500 persons was being organized. After this convoy left it was estimated that 1,500 Jews remained in Shanghai. It was thought that 800 of those would remain in Shanghai either because they did not want to leave, or because they were unable to travel. A further 700 Jewish refugees were awaiting Australian, Canadian, US, or other visas and expressed the wish to remain in Shanghai until these visas were obtained.

Evacuation of Russians

Political and military events of 1948 caused many refugees living in other Chinese towns to come to Shanghai where they often arrived destitute, so that an assistance programme had to be organized. They were also panic stricken by the speed of events. The IRO Office in Shanghai realized that no time should be lost in evacuating persons of Russian origin because of the risk of forced repatriation; and a personal representative of the Director General decided that at least four to five thousand should be evacuated without delay.

The Director General appealed to various countries for temporary or permanent asylum for these refugees but only one offer was made: the Government of the Philippines agreed to admit 6,000 refugees temporarily on condition that the IRO should meet the expenses of their stay in the Philippines, and that they would not remain more than four months. This offer was gratefully accepted by the Director General. A camp to accommodate the 6,000 refugees was set up at Samar, with the co-operation of the Philippine Government and with the help of the American army; some IRO stocks of food and equipment from Shanghai were also sent to the camp. The evacuation of these refugees from Shanghai began on 13 January 1949. On 26 January 1949 a decision of the Executive Committee of the IRO[1] provided for the evacuation of all European refugees whose lives or well-being were in serious danger, subject to a careful control of their eligibility and an assessment of the degree of their danger.[2] By the end of March 1949 5,000 non-Jewish refugees had left Shanghai.

The first stage of the evacuation was their temporary reception in the Philippines. The second stage was intended to be their establishment in other countries of permanent or temporary reception; and an urgent approach was made to member governments of IRO and other governments of goodwill to provide opportunities for permanent (or, if this should prove necessary, temporary) resettlement.

In April 1949 IRO officially opened an office in the Philippines, and on 25 May 1949 Communist forces entered Shanghai. IRO's head office for the Far East and China was still located in Shanghai but arrangements had been made to transfer certain of its functions to Hong Kong.

Remaining work in China

Although many Jews and Russians were thus evacuated, the future of European refugees in China became increasingly uncertain, and additional application continued to be made to the IRO Office from persons who had not previously approached the Organization. These included applications from White Russians in Harbin who requested IRO assistance.[3]

During the summer of 1949 the possibility of arranging a mass evacuation to Germany was discussed.[4] In November 1949 more than 600 refugees were evacuated by ship from China and taken to Italy, most of them for transhipment to Israel. In May 1950, after various changes of plans due to unsettled conditions, the IRO Office in the Far East succeeded in embarking 260 persons from Tientsin for San

[1] EC/37, Res. No. 5.   [2] GC/60.
[3] EC/32.   [4] Ibid.

Francisco, the majority of whom were immigrants destined for the US, while others were going to Latin America and Canada, and the remainder were repatriants on their way to Europe and immigrants for Israel. Later more refugees were moved to Israel, Australia, the US, and other destinations. About 200 of them were moved under a special arrangement between AJDC and IRO, whereby the AJDC undertook to move resettlers to Israel from Tientsin to Hong Kong by ship, and from Hong Kong to Israel by air, against reimbursement by the IRO. Early in 1951 evacuation to Germany was again considered and about 450 refugees were transferred there; the majority, after considerable delay, received visas for the US.[1]

At the end of December 1951 4,917 refugees remained in Shanghai of whom 3,196 were entitled to resettlement and repatriation assistance, while 2,114 were receiving care and maintenance. Of the total refugees assisted by the IRO, over 1,500 had been classified as requiring institutional care; the cases of 333, however, remained unsolved on 31 December 1951. It was expected that a further group of twenty aged persons would be moved to Belgium under a scheme negotiated with the World Council of Churches.

As IRO operations came to a halt, the number of persons who could have been resettled from China showed a constant increase. The Organization therefore gave funds to the UNHCR and to the PICMME (later ICEM) to permit the continuation of both maintenance and evacuation for some time.

Samar

Before the evacuation of refugees to the Philippines, certain misgivings regarding this move were expressed during meetings of the Executive Committee of the IRO. The Chinese delegate advocated extreme caution in embarking on a large movement of refugees from China without having found for them a place of permanent settlement;[2] the American delegate also urged that careful consideration be given to the degree of actual danger to which the refugees in China were exposed, and stressed the risk of moving more persons to the Philippine Republic than could be transferred elsewhere within the four months stipulated.[3] The delegate of Belgium wished to be sure that the White Russian refugees were thoroughly screened and found to be eligible for IRO care, and that the reasons for the relinquishment by refugees of Soviet passports were political and not merely economic.[4] In reply, the Director General said that most of the Soviet passports issued to White Russian refugees in China had been granted shortly after the end of the Second World War; in many cases these had been the first official documents received from the USSR by such persons for two or three generations. The passports had been turned in at various times over the past two or three years as reports had filtered through from passport holders who had returned to Russia and met with unacceptable conditions. Persons who had relinquished their passports had thus demonstrated their unwillingness to accept the protection of the Soviet Government.[5]

In 1949 1 million, out of a total population of 22 million, people in the Philippines were registered as unemployed. Manila, the capital, has a population of over

[1] GC/227/Ref. 1, 30 Oct. 1951.   [2] EC/SR/12, p. 4.
[3] Ibid., p. 6.   [4] EC/SR/13, p. 3.   [5] Ibid., p. 4.

2 million, and is some three hours' flight, or three days' voyage by boat, from the camp at Guiuan where the refugees were accommodated. Guiuan is on the southern tip of Samar, one of the 7,000 Philippine islands, and was formerly joined to the island of Tubabao by a bridge which was destroyed by the typhoon of December 1951. The Guiuan area is approximately 10 miles square, and the camp was surrounded by what is locally known as jungle: mainly scrub and coco-nut trees. Guiuan was chosen as a camp because the refugees could be kept there without contact with the local people, and their movements could be controlled.

When the Agreement for the reception of Shanghai refugees was concluded, the country was still in an extremely troubled and unsettled state. Bandits were ravaging the country, and it was unsafe to travel even 20 or 30 miles away from Manila. In spite of eligibility screening in Shanghai, the Philippine Government was never entirely sure of the political views of the IRO refugees, and a pass issued by the Philippine Police Security Office was required by anyone wishing to leave the camp.

Nearly all the refugees were White Russians who had been in China since the Russian revolution. In China they had been government officials, police officials, and so forth; most were white-collar workers. Their composition and antecedents made them one of the most difficult groups IRO was called upon to handle. They included 150 prostitutes and dozens of drug addicts and alcoholics; and few of the others worked willingly or helped to keep the camp clean without payment. Psychologically they had remained refugees; conditions in China had effectively prevented their assimilation into a normal life. The older ones amongst them still retained the hope of a victorious return to Russia; and the idea was common that, as they were the earliest refugees from the Bolsheviks, the world owed them something.

The permanent settlement of these refugees progressed far more slowly than had been hoped; and the IRO's undertaking to the Philippine Government that all of them would be moved in four months could not be fulfilled. Only 400 departed by the middle of 1949, and only 2,000 by the end of the year. Relations with the Philippine Government were naturally somewhat difficult for the IRO staff members on the spot. But movements continued; during 1950 1,000 left. And gradually, as the Government saw that IRO was moving people from the Philippines, though much later and more slowly than had been hoped, relations became more cordial.

The Government was kept fully informed of all movements of refugees within the Philippines and of all departures, and at a later stage refugees were permitted to go to Manila to see consuls, permission for such travel having earlier been refused. Later, when selection missions visited the Philippines under IRO auspices, it was no longer necessary for refugees to go to Manila for this purpose. In 1951 nearly 2,000 left.

As the result of conditions in the Philippines, and, no doubt, because of the composition of the refugees in question, it had been impossible to persuade the Government to allow any of the refugees to remain permanently in the Philippines. Requests of this nature, even if they only concerned one or two persons, were invariably refused on the grounds that if permission was granted to one person, the rest would claim the same privileges. For similar reasons, refugees were not permitted to work while they were in the Philippines, even on a temporary basis.

The camp itself, which was selected on the assumption that accommodation was required for four months only, and that suitable equipment would be provided by the US army, was hardly suitable as a semi-permanent establishment; and as a result of this initial optimism the operation was very expensive. The mission had to find and pump its own water and to generate its own electricity for power and light. The climate was bad, and the camp was located in the typhoon belt. During the first week of December 1951 the camp was struck by the worst typhoon experienced in twenty years. Fortunately, only two refugees were killed as the majority had left by then. A fully equipped hundred-bed hospital was completely destroyed during the typhoon; but most of the patients (TB cases) had been sent to France two weeks earlier. The few who remained were flown out by two specially chartered planes, some to the mainland and some to Tacloban on the neighbouring island of Leyte.

Refugees who had been admitted for a period of four months stayed in the Philippines for nearly three years. Nevertheless, thanks to the reasonable attitude adopted by the Philippine Government, and to the generosity of reception countries, above all the US, France, Australia, Paraguay, and the Dominican Republic, the problem was practically solved when IRO operations ceased.

H. MIGRATION OF SPECIALISTS

Of the total number of refugees to be re-established about 10 per cent. were intellectuals or professional persons. They constituted a special problem, since the demands of resettlement countries were largely confined to manual labourers and agricultural workers, with the exception of a few categories of technicians, engineers, and the like. Difficulties in connexion with the resettlement of professional refugees were not new. After the First World War, for example, some Russian and Armenian refugees had not been easy to place, and Dr. Fridtjof Nansen, therefore, in 1922, had made a special effort on behalf of the students among the refugees for whom he was responsible. The numbers of displaced intellectuals increased greatly after 1933, when the National Socialist régime in Germany deprived many intellectuals of their posts, and forced them to become refugees because of racial discrimination or political persecution. Much valuable work was done for them by the Academic Assistance Council which was set up in England in May 1933, by the Comité International pour le Placement d'Intellectuels Réfugiés in France, by relief committees for refugee physicians and scholars in the US, and by many other organizations elsewhere which assisted displaced professional people in the preservation of their special skills, and helped them find professional employment.[1]

Early in 1947 the IGCR initiated a special registration of twenty-two categories of professional workers to ascertain their numbers and to obtain detailed information concerning their personal history, qualifications, and experience. With the transfer of the IGCR's responsibilities to the IRO, an Advisory Committee on Resettlement of Specialists, composed of representatives of various international organizations and voluntary societies and a number of special advisers, was appointed at the Geneva headquarters to co-ordinate all the efforts being made.

[1] Stephen Duggan, *The Rescue of Science and Learning*, N.Y., 1948; Norman Bentwich, *The Rescue and Achievement of Refugee Scholars*, The Hague, 1953.

Special professional boards were set up, composed of well-known and fully qualified refugee experts in the various fields, to verify the qualifications claimed by refugee intellectuals. Medical specialists were interrogated by 'special qualification boards', supervised by medical officers and nurses on the IRO's staff.[1] Once the refugee specialist had satisfied the board as to his professional standing, and had substantiated his qualifications, he was given a Certificate of Professional Status— a document indispensable to people whose diplomas and certificates had been lost or destroyed. The information obtained during interviews with professional refugees was recorded, and eventually incorporated in a Professional Register of the refugee population. This catalogue, compiled at the Geneva headquarters, was distributed to the representatives of the IRO in all receiving countries, and enabled them to present appropriate cases for consideration to local employment officials, heads of educational institutions, research organizations, and other potential employers.

There were also some 10,000 students, some of whom attempted to continue their studies at German and Austrian universities, while others attended courses in special refugee universities established for them at Penneburg, Munich, Ravensburg, and Esslingen. Some categories of specialists were much easier to resettle than others, and it was the IRO's policy to encourage students of technical sciences, because the study of one of the scientific or technical professions would lead to a better and more stable resettlement than would otherwise be possible. But in order to achieve resettlement during the IRO's lifetime, all studies sponsored by the IRO were to be completed by October 1949, except in specific cases where a firm re-establishment was guaranteed and studies could be completed by June 1950.

The efforts of the IRO to find far-reaching solutions for the future of its 'Forgotten Elite' were not successful. The PCIRO had appealed to the governments of potential reception countries to accept a certain number of professional refugees, but most of these countries showed little interest. An attempt was also made to attract the attention of prominent members of the professions all over the world to the distress of their displaced colleagues, but, unfortunately, professional associations were reluctant to recognize the qualifications of their foreign confrères, whose potential competition was not welcomed. The Director General of the Organization, in the opening speech at the Conference on the Resettlement of Refugee Specialists in April 1948, declared: 'The attitude of the professional associations is one of the greatest obstacles as far as specialists are concerned . . . the government members of the IRO have demonstrated their concern. However, there are international and political difficulties with which those governments are contending at the present time which have to be taken into account.'

Although comprehensive schemes were not forthcoming, some results were obtained on an individual basis and through nominations and sponsorships—such as the USDP Act which provided for the emigration of a number of intellectuals— and a few offers of work for highly qualified experts were received. Thanks to the initiative of private persons and organizations some scholars and professors were placed in universities. The 'Lady Davis Foundation' in Montreal, for example, a

---

[1] Cf. Chapter XVI, Adaptation to a New Life, p. 303.

private organization, granted about thirty fellowships to refugees, and in most cases succeeded in placing them in Canadian universities. And the 'British Universities Bureau' in Great Britain sent a mission to the assembly centres in January 1948 for the purpose of interviewing and placing refugee professors in universities of the UK and the Dominions. The presence of highly skilled specialists of all categories in the assembly centres was also brought to the attention of the various selection missions from the South American countries. However, the IRO realized that individual efforts would not suffice to resettle all the refugees in the 'professional' classification, and it therefore encouraged them to accept resettlement offers as manual workers in the hope that they would later be able to resume their former professions. In the first two years of the IRO's operations some 4,000 professional people were resettled as manual workers or in some other calling in which their years of experience and specialized knowledge was not used. Only for nurses were mass schemes available, and some 2,000 emigrated. In the same period, 225 specialists were able to obtain visas for immigration through the efforts of friends, relatives, and sponsoring voluntary societies.

In order to place refugees from the intellectual classes an active campaign was launched. A few Special Representatives of the Director General, acting as roving ambassadors, stimulated employment possibilities for the 'Forgotten Élite'. These Special Representatives worked in conjunction with IRO's resident missions where they existed, but also explored countries in which the Organization had not hitherto been represented. The new scheme was preceded by an appeal by the Director General, who asked all members of the Organization to give their full support to the forthcoming campaign. Meanwhile, to co-ordinate all the activities related to the preparation of individual dossiers, obtaining nominations, sponsorships, and employment offers, a Resettlement Placement Service was created in October 1949.

Resettlement Placement Service

This service was in effect an international labour exchange where an attempt was made to place the qualifications of individual refugees before potential employers, and to report the requirements of those employers to the refugees who might be able to fill them. The Resettlement Placement Service (RPS) included in its scope not only the intellectuals but also as great a number as possible of those refugees classified as having limited opportunities for resettlement. In each zone headquarters in Germany, and at the Vienna and Rome headquarters, a special unit was created in the Department of Repatriation and Resettlement, corresponding to the Resettlement Placement Service at the Geneva headquarters.

The RPS officers in the field compiled a dossier on each refugee of the type to be dealt with, giving a complete professional history of the head of the family as well as all relevant information about each member. The dossier also included photostatic copies of diplomas, testimonials of former employers, the IRO's trade-test certificate,[1] a curriculum vitae, and complete medical report on any member of the family who was disabled or handicapped. The interviewing officer prepared a case summary and made recommendations concerning employability; he also recorded

[1] Provisional Order No. 95 of 24 Jan. 1949.

his general impressions regarding the family's adaptability to new conditions in the prospective country of immigration.

These dossiers were sent through mission headquarters to Geneva, were passed on from there to the branches of the Division of Resettlement and Repatriation, and finally forwarded by them to the special representatives touring various countries. In the course of their negotiations with governments and private employers these representatives made an effort to secure employment for the persons referred to in the dossiers. Voluntary societies and other organizations, too, in the prospective countries of immigration, received such dossiers either to promote the refugees' cause or to find employers for specific refugees. The placement dossiers were favourably regarded, and certain countries used them as a model for their national employment services.

By June 1950 a total of 1,114 employment or sponsorship offers had been received, and over 1,000 refugees resettled as a result of these efforts.[1] The 'specialists' constituted an important section of this group, but were not the whole of it, since, as has been said, other categories such as domestics, agricultural, and industrial workers as well as physically handicapped persons were included in this scheme.

Offers of employment and of possibilities for rehabilitation came from all over the world. The countries of South Asia and the Middle East were chiefly interested in accepting refugees with high academic qualifications (university professors, doctors, and engineers); Canada, Ethiopia, South America, and the UK accepted refugees up to a certain age limit for placement in the manufacturing industries, or the higher grade of agriculture, with no limitation regarding family composition provided strict health standards were met. Eire, Norway, and Sweden accepted even more difficult cases—such as families with members who were physically handicapped or ill—as long as one or more members of the family were able to work.

This scheme later experienced difficulties because many refugees registered by the Resettlement Placement Service had naturally continued to search for other emigration possibilities, so that they were not always available when they received a specific employment offer. Certain other candidates declined offers from a country because they preferred to go to another country. Some of the employers, on the other hand, found the necessary delay too long between the time the choice was made and the date of the candidate's arrival at his destination.

Because of these difficulties, and because this scheme was not introduced until the third year of the IRO's existence when the Organization was already beginning to end its work, it did not have the success that had been expected. As a result, by the spring of 1951 only some 3,000 persons had been moved under this scheme.[2] Both the compilation of individual dossiers and the discussion with prospective employers had been very expensive in terms of staff-time. It was, however, taken into consideration that emigration through the RPS was the only chance for many refugees to have their plight ended, and that according to the views of the Western world men have a fundamental value which outweighs any costs incurred in salvaging them from their status as refugees.

[1] GC/166 of 23 Aug. 1950, p. 23.   [2] GC/199 of 5 Mar. 1951.

I. CONCLUSION

The migration for permanent settlement of over 1 million refugees in the four and a half years after 1 July 1947 was a combined operation between the IRO, its member governments acting both within its framework and outside it, other governments, private charities, and people of goodwill everywhere.

The administrative complication of the work is indicated by the fact that refugees were settled in forty-eight recorded countries, ranging from the US which accepted 328,851 to Panama which accepted 63. The IRO participated to some extent in all these moves, either by arranging the selection of refugees, by obtaining visas for them, by paying for their transport, or just by providing the facilities of its resettlement centres. The work did not become simpler with the passage of time; in 1951 twenty-one countries received more than 100 refugees each, and a total of 635 refugees were accepted in twenty-five others.

The programme was based on the assumption that the majority of refugees not already established would be either acceptable or definitely wanted as immigrants. The connexion thus established between the welfare of refugees and normal migration was the new and original contribution made by the IGCR and the IRO to the solution of the refugee problem, and the outstanding achievement of the IRO was the development of a procedure for the processing of large numbers of refugee migrants. In the past, there had been no such systematized procedure, but by the time the IRO reached the peak of its activity the machine was capable of handling over 1,000 visas daily.[1] And before the IRO had finished its work, a slightly different group of governments had decided to continue the method in the interests of organized migration of normal citizens as well as of refugees.[2]

---

[1] In the peak year, 1949, 345,321 refugees were resettled; the numbers ready for movement at the beginning and at the end of the year would not have been very different; assuming a $5\frac{1}{2}$-day working week the rate of processing would be nearly 1,200 a day.

[2] The Intergovernmental Committee for European Migration.

ANNEX 38

IRO missions in receiving countries (on 31 December 1950)

Location of office	Number of personnel*
Europe	
†Belgium (Brussels)	17 (4)
†France (Paris)	56 (8)
Eire (Dublin)	3
†Luxembourg	3 (1)
†The Netherlands (The Hague)	5 (2)
Norway (Oslo)	4
†Switzerland (Geneva)	8 (1)
†United Kingdom (London)	15 (8)
Overseas	
Argentina (Buenos Aires)	6
Australia (Canberra; with port officers in Melbourne and Sydney)	3
Bolivia (La Paz; IRO correspondent)	1
Brazil (Rio de Janeiro)	16
Canada (Hull, Quebec; with port officer in Halifax) . .	30
Chile (*see* Peru)	1
Colombia (Bogota; IRO correspondent)	1
Ecuador (*see* Peru)	1
Ethiopia (Addis Ababa)	4
Guatemala (Guatemala City)	6
Mexico (Mexico City; IRO correspondent)	1
New Zealand (Wellington)	3
Paraguay (Asuncion)	4
Peru (Lima; also covering Chile and Ecuador) . . .	3
US (Washington, DC; with port officer in New York) . .	26 (11)
Uruguay (Montevideo)	8
Venezuela (Caracas)	7
India (New Delhi; IRO correspondent)	1
Pakistan (Karachi; IRO correspondent)	1
Ceylon (Colombo; IRO correspondent)	1
Iran (Teheran; IRO correspondent)	2

* These figures include locally-recruited staff. Figures in 'parentheses indicate the personnel directly concerned with immigration.

† These countries were both immigration and emigration countries, and an important proportion of the personnel was, therefore, concerned with problems other than those of immigration, such as care and maintenance and emigration.

ANNEX 39

European volunteer workers and dependants in the UK

Recorded as at 31 May 1951

Nationality	European volunteer workers			Dependants arrived	Total in the UK		
	Arrived	Returned*	Balance in the UK		Male	Female	Total
Latvian	12,920	558	12,362	1,321	9,790	3,893	13,683
Lithuanian	6,186	439	5,747	741	4,741	1,747	6,488
Estonian	5,154	333	4,821	496	2,926	2,391	5,317
Polish	13,632	792	12,840	88	8,495	4,433	12,928
Polish-Ukrainian	12,893	424	12,469	473	9,920	3,022	12,942
Ukrainian	8,019	270	7,749	389	5,962	2,176	8,138
Yugoslav	9,626	381	9,245	30	8,546	729	9,275
Hungarian	2,539	201	2,338	15	1,956	397	2,353
Greek	75	11	64	..	49	15	64
Czechoslovak	1,263	132	1,131	9	998	142	1,140
Volksdeutsche	1,378	10	1,368	..	738	630	1,368
Sudeten Germans	1,304	73	1,231	..	..	1,231	1,231
Stateless	389	48	341	84	245	180	425
Undetermined	699	92	607	26	471	162	633
Others	911	121	790	35	692	133	825
Ukrainian ex-prisoners of war	8,128	67	8,061	..	8,061	..	8,061
TOTAL	85,116	3,952	81,164	3,707	63,590	21,281	84,871

Included in the figures above are 2,572 'Balt cygnets'.

* Including 613 deportees.

ANNEX 40

Resettlement

Country of destination and area of departure

Country of destination	Refugees departed for resettlement from specified IRO areas, 1 July 1947–31 Dec. 1951					Far East	
	Total	Austria	Belgium	Czecho-slovakia	Denmark	Philip-pines	Shanghai
TOTAL	1,038,750	145,233	8,672	3,226	2,034	5,308	13,957
Argentina	32,712	8,772	663	99	206	29	159
Australia	182,159	18,588	1,173	84	814	1,669	1,239
Belgium	22,477	311	..	30	..	1	7
Bolivia	2,485	186	256	34	..	1	61
Brazil	28,848	6,666	92	2	5	67	522
Canada	123,479	19,644	3,238	65	609	24	640
Chile	5,108	2,393	46	14	1	8	53
Colombia	889	62	18	5	..	8	25
Costa Rica	198	58	2	9	4	..	10
Cuba	432	60	7	17	..	4	11
Dominican Republic . .	413	40	52	..	..	196	14
Ecuador	394	54	11	4	..	..	35
Egypt	169	8	..	..	..	..	..
Eire	224	27	1	..	2	..	..
Ethiopia	243	23	..	..	..	..	..
France	38,455	14,199	41	133	1	117	75
French Guiana . . .	211	..	..	..	..	..	..
French Morocco . . .	1,446	73	12	..	..	..	6
Germany	344	70	27	11	140	6	8
Guatemala	342	29	1	3	..	..	..
Hong Kong	78	1	..	..	..	5	69
Israel	132,109	21,865	1,658	2,398	16	1	5,112
Italy	235	91	3	8	1	..	47
Kenya	233	6	3	..	..	..	..
Luxembourg	198	..	2	3	..	..	5
Mexico	437	3	..	..	..	..	2
Netherlands	4,355	46	1	15	..	..	6
New Zealand	4,837	649	5	5	104	10	27
Northern Rhodesia . . .	312	..	..	..	..	..	..
Norway	1,105	100	2	1	5	..	1
Pakistan	78	16	..	..	..	..	1
Panama	63	2	1	3	..	6	6
Paraguay	5,887	615	6	148	..	281	76
Peru	2,340	57	..	25	..	..	6
Philippines	68	1	..	..	..	8	54
Southern Rhodesia . . .	135	..	..	4	..	..	..
Spain	120	37	..	..	..	..	..
Sweden	4,330	1,408	4	..	25	..	19
Switzerland	589	190	1	..	..	..	18
Syria	280	18	..	..	..	..	1
Tanganyika	300	1	..	..	..	..	..
Tunisia	446	187	..	3	..	..	..
Turkey	2,358	589	..	..	..	31	66
Union of S. Africa . . .	457	54	10	..	1	..	31
UK	86,346	11,561	24	18	28	9	185
US	328,851	31,462	1,061	8	67	2,740	4,837
Uruguay	1,461	115	7	25	..	..	27
Venezuela	17,277	4,731	163	28	3	7	94
Miscellaneous	968	107	45	14	2	80	159
Not reported	1,469	58	36	10	..	..	243

ANNEX 40 (cont.)

Resettlement (cont.)

Country of destination and area of departure (cont.)

| Country of destination | France | Germany | | | | Greece | Italy | Luxem-bourg |
		British zone	French zone	US zone	Not reported			
TOTAL	31,434	224,261	38,087	450,163	7,025	3,137	70,535	200
Argentina	4,687	861	337	2,242	..	214	13,394	14
Australia	3,526	58,657	9,789	67,803	..	665	14,079	100
Belgium	3	3,942	51	18,081	..	..	18	..
Bolivia	1,169	22	..	553	..	..	149	1
Brazil	1,836	7,900	2,934	5,831	..	806	1,843	7
Canada	4,936	32,297	3,284	47,850	..	49	7,839	54
Chile	912	239	102	454	..	..	764	3
Colombia	121	92	130	323	..	..	51	3
Costa Rica	33	..	2	54	..	..	25	..
Cuba	94	3	..	144	..	..	83	..
Dominican Republic	24	5	11	23	..	..	18	..
Ecuador	65	19	2	56	..	..	137	..
Egypt	1	2	1	17	..	..	138	..
Eire	39	37	9	46	..	..	61	..
Ethiopia	6	35	25	148	..	..	1	..
France	..	8,115	6,330	8,941	..	17	319	1
French Guiana	..	..	198	12	..	..	..	1
French Morocco	336	145	143	696	..	..	18	..
Germany	32	..	..	..	..	10	23	1
Guatemala	244	..	..	13	..	..	24	..
Hong Kong	1	..	..	1	..	..	..	..
Israel	5,671	6,585	19	63,447	7,025	50	14,277	1
Italy	3	13	4	36	..	11	..	..
Kenya	..	3	..	6	..	..	2	..
Luxembourg	..	128	5	55	..	..	..	..
Mexico	281	2	..	17	..	..	13	..
Netherlands	..	217	11	4,048	..	..	5	..
New Zealand	113	1,317	70	745	..	1,211	378	1
Northern Rhodesia	..	7	..	1	..	..	3	..
Norway	5	323	65	407	..	31	161	..
Pakistan	1	22	3	31	..	..	4	..
Panama	8	1	..	19	..	..	12	..
Paraguay	190	2,560	22	1,033	..	..	901	..
Peru	68	22	9	71	..	1	2,047	..
Philippines	2	..	1	2	..	..	..	..
Southern Rhodesia	1	2	..	20	..	..	4	..
Spain	..	5	6	36	..	3	22	..
Sweden	12	1,229	35	1,383	..	..	191	1
Switzerland	1	70	48	206	..	5	44	1
Syria	4	3	..	..	..	..	245	..
Tanganyika	..	5	..	..	..	..	5	..
Tunisia	18	4	106	109	..	2	15	..
Turkey	14	22	..	988	..	20	625	..
Union of S. Africa	40	32	3	99	..	..	111	..
UK	136	36,175	2,770	16,506	..	2	173	..
US	3,094	62,639	10,542	200,320	..	18	10,648	6
Uruguay	400	69	2	208	..	..	583	..
Venezuela	2,815	346	970	6,995	..	21	857	5
Miscellaneous	106	89	47	87	..	..	108	..
Not reported	386	..	1	..	..	1	117	..

Refugees departed for resettlement from specified IRO areas, 1 July 1947–31 Dec. 1951

ANNEX 40 (cont.)

Resettlement (cont.)

Country of destination and area of departure (cont.)

	Refugees departed for resettlement from specified IRO areas, 1 July 1947–31 Dec. 1951							
	Middle East							
Country of destination	East Africa	Egypt	India	Israel	Lebanon	Syria	Turkey	Not reported
TOTAL	14,044	820	3,082	11	5,857	71	405	21
Argentina	124	116	..	..	233	..	25	2
Australia	1,234	594	..	2	283	31	21	2
Belgium	4	..	..	..	11	..	..	..
Bolivia	..	5	..	..	..	..	..	2
Brazil	4	18	..	..	4	..	118	9
Canada	627	6	..	..	374	8	16	..
Chile	..	25	..	..	..	..	..	..
Colombia	..	..	..	..	..	..	..	..
Costa Rica	..	..	..	..	..	..	..	..
Cuba	..	..	..	..	..	..	..	..
Dominican Republic	2	8	..	..	..	..	..	2
Ecuador	1	..	..	..	..	..	..	..
Egypt	..	..	1	..	..	..	1	..
Eire	2	..	..	..	..	..	..	..
Ethiopia	..	2	..	..	..	..	..	..
France	23	5	..	1	13	4	62	..
French Guiana	..	..	..	..	..	..	..	..
French Morocco	2	..	..	..	..	..	1	..
Germany	3	..	..	..	..	..	2	..
Guatemala	..	..	..	..	..	..	..	..
Hong Kong	..	..	..	..	..	..	..	..
Israel	8	3	..	..	6	..	3	..
Italy	3	1	..	..	3	1	4	..
Kenya	211	..	..	..	..	..	..	..
Luxembourg	..	..	..	..	..	..	..	..
Mexico	1	..	..	..	..	..	..	..
Netherlands	2	..	..	..	..	..	..	..
New Zealand	10	2	..	..	8	..	115	..
Northern Rhodesia	300	..	..	..	1	..	..	..
Norway	..	..	..	..	..	..	..	..
Pakistan	..	..	..	..	..	..	..	..
Panama	..	..	..	..	..	..	..	..
Paraguay	..	..	..	5	2	..	..	..
Peru	..	..	..	..	..	..	..	..
Philippines	..	..	..	..	..	..	..	..
Southern Rhodesia	100	..	..	..	..	..	..	..
Spain	..	..	..	..	4	..	3	..
Sweden	2	..	..	..	..	..	..	..
Switzerland	..	..	..	..	2	..	..	..
Syria	..	3	..	..	..	..	6	..
Tanganyika	289	..	..	..	..	..	..	..
Tunisia	..	2	..	..	..	..	..	..
Turkey	..	1	..	..	1	1	..	..
Union of S. Africa	33	9	3	..	1	..	2	..
UK	10,829	1	3,078	2	4,819	..	2	3
US	139	10	..	..	81	24	18	..
Uruguay	..	..	..	..	..	..	..	..
Venezuela	9	..	..	..	..	..	3	..
Miscellaneous	74	9	..	1	5	2	3	1
Not reported	8	..	..	..	6	..	..	..

RESETTLEMENT
ANNEX 40 (cont.)

Resettlement (cont.)

Country of destination and area of departure (cont.)

Country of destination	Refugees departed for resettlement from specified IRO areas, 1 July 1947–31 Dec. 1951								
	Nether-lands	Norway	Portugal	Spain	Sweden*	Switzer-land	Union of S. Africa	UK	Not reported
TOTAL	1,691	138	348	319	1,539	3,919	4	446	2,763
Argentina	27	..	9	61	9	396	3	30	..
Australia	116	82	4	6	100	1,347	..	151	..
Belgium	..	..	..	1	..	17	..	..	..
Bolivia	21	..	..	9	2	12	..	2	..
Brazil	21	..	3	24	8	109	..	19	..
Canada	164	54	5	12	1,035	607	1	41	..
Chile	17	..	7	11	..	59	..	..	..
Colombia	13	..	..	19	..	18	..	1	..
Costa Rica	1	..	..	..	..	..	..	..	..
Cuba	1	..	4	..	..	4	..	..	..
Dominican Republic	14	..	1	..	..	..	..	3	..
Ecuador	5	..	..	1	..	4	..	..	..
Egypt	..	..	..	..	..	..	..	..	..
Eire	..	..	..	..	..	..	..	..	..
Ethiopia	..	..	..	..	..	2	..	1	..
France	..	..	10	24	..	24	..	..	..
French Guiana	..	..	..	..	..	..	..	..	..
French Morocco	..	..	12	..	..	2	..	..	..
Germany	..	..	..	1	..	9	..	1	..
Guatemala	6	..	22	..	..	..	..	..	..
Hong Kong	..	..	..	..	..	1	..	..	..
Israel	777	..	7	16	106	193	..	102	2,763
Italy	..	..	..	..	..	5	..	1	..
Kenya	..	..	..	..	..	..	..	2	..
Luxembourg	..	..	..	..	..	..	..	..	..
Mexico	1	..	109	6	..	1	..	1	..
Netherlands	..	..	..	1	..	3	..	..	..
New Zealand	7	..	..	..	9	46	..	5	..
Northern Rhodesia	..	..	..	..	..	..	..	..	..
Norway	..	..	..	..	..	4	..	..	..
Pakistan	..	..	..	..	..	..	..	..	..
Panama	4	..	1	..	..	..	..	..	..
Paraguay	12	..	..	3	..	28	..	5	..
Peru	2	..	..	..	1	30	..	1	..
Philippines	..	..	..	..	..	..	..	..	..
Southern Rhodesia	..	..	..	..	..	3	..	1	..
Spain	4	..	..	..	..	..	..	..	..
Sweden	..	..	..	..	..	21	..	..	..
Switzerland	..	..	..	3	..	..	..	..	..
Syria	..	..	..	..	..	..	..	..	..
Tanganyika	..	..	..	..	..	..	..	..	..
Tunisia	..	..	..	..	..	..	..	..	..
Turkey	..	..	..	..	..	..	..	..	..
Union of S. Africa	4	..	1	..	..	21	..	2	..
UK	6	..	..	3	..	16	..	..	..
US	451	2	29	45	261	293	..	56	..
Uruguay	4	..	2	3	8	8	..	..	..
Venezuela	8	..	119	53	..	30	..	20	..
Miscellaneous	5	..	2	15	..	6	..	1	..
Not reported	..	..	1	2	..	600	..	..	..

* Resettled under the auspices of the IRO Office in Denmark.

ANNEX 41

Resettlement

Country of destination and country of citizenship

Country of destination	Refugees of specified country of citizenship, last habitual residence, or ethnic group departed for resettlement, 1 July 1947–31 Dec. 1951						
	Total	Albania	Austria	Belgium	Bulgaria	Byelo-russia	Czecho-slovakia
TOTAL	1,038,750	1,104	5,129	130	3,068	2,517	34,450
Argentina	32,712	16	102	5	40	..	603
Australia	182,159	260	659	2	854	670	9,884
Belgium	22,477	1	15	..	..	30	133
Bolivia	2,485	..	52	..	5	..	98
Brazil.	28,848	60	78	..	357	336	1,499
Canada	123,479	134	565	6	565	152	5,916
Chile	5,108	7	36	5	30	..	289
Colombia	889	..	19	..	5	..	57
Costa Rica	198	..	2	..	..	..	6
Cuba	432	..	9	8	1	..	8
Dominican Republic . .	413	..	14	..	..	..	4
Ecuador	394	..	4	..	2	..	41
Egypt	169	2	..	..	..	..	10
Eire	224	1	..	..	1	..	19
Ethiopia	243	..	..	..	4	..	47
France	38,455	2	58	16	237	56	1,068
French Guiana . . .	211	..	..	..	..	..	16
French Morocco . . .	1,446	2	5	..	2	..	95
Germany	344	10	4	..	1	..	27
Guatemala	342	..	..	..	..	..	7
Hong Kong	78	..	5	..	..	..	1
Israel	132,109	..	1,200	..	7	44	1,960
Italy	235	10	6	..	2	..	37
Kenya	233	1	17	..	..	..	3
Luxembourg	198	..	..	..	1	..	37
Mexico	437	..	4	..	..	..	2
Netherlands	4,355	..	4	..	2	..	365
New Zealand . . .	4,837	29	31	..	199	12	336
Northern Rhodesia . .	312	..	..	..	..	..	..
Norway	1,105	4	2	..	5	4	290
Pakistan	78	..	2	..	2	..	8
Panama	63	..	..	..	..	..	2
Paraguay	5,887	..	25	..	..	..	134
Peru	2,340	9	18	2	10	..	148
Philippines	68	..	..	..	..	..	..
Southern Rhodesia . .	135	..	..	..	..	..	4
Spain	120	..	..	..	1	..	8
Sweden	4,330	3	30	..	6	2	287
Switzerland	589	..	4	..	1	..	41
Syria	280	93	1	..	..	..	2
Tanganyika. . . .	300	..	2	..	..	..	..
Tunisia	446	..	..	..	..	..	6
Turkey	2,358	100	..	..	3	..	..
Union of S. Africa . .	457	..	13	..	2	..	9
UK	86,346	3	171	69	26	29	1,956
US	328,851	292	1,844	6	593	1,135	8,057
Uruguay	1,461	5	24	..	4	..	54
Venezuela	17,277	29	55	11	93	47	816
Miscellaneous . . .	968	31	19	..	3	..	60
Not reported . . .	1,469	..	30	..	4	..	..

ANNEX 41 (cont.)

Resettlement (cont.)

Country of destination and country of citizenship (cont.)

Country of destination	Refugees of specified country of citizenship, last habitual residence, or ethnic group departed for resettlement, 1 July 1947–31 Dec. 1951						
	Estonia	Germany	Greece	Hungary	Latvia	Lithuania	Poland
TOTAL	27,096	21,481	651	62,871	81,215	55,165	357,635
Argentina	201	99	28	3,067	640	603	6,563
Australia	5,958	1,826	68	13,320	19,601	10,136	60,308
Belgium	270	116	2	450	882	720	10,378
Bolivia	3	109	1	177	7	18	510
Brazil	158	138	166	3,146	794	398	7,770
Canada	4,118	471	28	7,479	8,619	8,559	46,961
Chile	26	82	52	574	134	56	516
Colombia	8	24	..	66	4	436	31
Costa Rica	..	3	..	33	..	..	41
Cuba	..	11	..	22	2	6	148
Dominican Republic . . .	2	7	..	130	2	..	31
Ecuador	1	34	..	38	..	..	66
Egypt	..	..	..	8	1	..	..
Eire	6	1	..	10	12	6	32
Ethiopia	10	13	..	23	9	6	46
France	179	140	40	3,655	925	434	11,882
French Guiana	..	6	..	67	2	..	62
French Morocco . . .	11	2	..	106	53	24	166
Germany	5	..	..	32	22	58	46
Guatemala	..	4	..	20	..	..	16
Hong Kong	..	8	..	..	..	..	2
Israel	2	4,535	27	7,191	58	1,178	54,904
Italy	9	12	1	38	3	5	27
Kenya	..	9	..	1	..	..	184
Luxembourg	..	5	..	13	2	6	77
Mexico	..	1	..	4	..	..	15
Netherlands	110	33	2	188	117	37	2,969
New Zealand	189	21	..	280	545	242	847
Northern Rhodesia . . .	..	..	..	..	..	1	310
Norway	37	3	..	55	130	9	232
Pakistan	2	1	..	16	17	4	3
Panama	3	..	..	1	1	3	8
Paraguay	19	85	1	166	33	19	1,433
Peru	4	19	25	117	6	4	103
Philippines	2	7	2	3	2	..	1
Southern Rhodesia . . .	..	1	..	1	1	11	97
Spain	..	..	..	34	13	2	9
Sweden	1,089	62	1	155	611	37	563
Switzerland	32	28	1	86	75	15	76
Syria	..	..	..	..	..	..	4
Tanganyika	5	..	..	..	..	..	280
Tunisia	1	..	..	51	3	5	167
Turkey	6	18	..	4	1	..	8
Union of S. Africa . . .	8	41	..	49	16	26	111
UK	3,418	118	..	3,013	8,447	3,407	35,780
US	10,992	13,096	170	16,718	38,637	27,825	110,566
Uruguay	..	32	..	139	2	17	241
Venezuela	192	171	23	1,999	731	826	2,814
Miscellaneous	16	44	12	81	51	25	177
Not reported	4	45	1	45	4	1	54

ANNEX 41 (cont.)

Resettlement (cont.)

Country of destination and country of citizenship (cont.)

Country of destination	Refugees of specified country of citizenship, last habitual residence, or ethnic group departed for resettlement, 1 July 1947–31 Dec. 1951						
	Rumania	Spain	Turkey	Ukrainian	USSR	Venezia Giulian	Yugo-slavia
TOTAL	23,010	9,988	362	113,677	41,325	3,167	82,090
Argentina	639	2,951	6	2,283	2,071	44	10,105
Australia	2,190	84	49	19,607	4,944	275	23,350
Belgium	80	..	5	5,650	1,826	..	849
Bolivia	111	920	2	..	9	5	111
Brazil	1,365	714	11	4,609	1,427	33	2,587
Canada	2,536	434	5	14,877	8,158	389	9,828
Chile	245	776	14	319	320	85	867
Colombia	67	49	..	3	9	..	20
Costa Rica	38	18	..	..	..	..	..
Cuba	36	61	..	1	5	..	16
Dominican Republic . . .	5	9	..	8	169	..	8
Ecuador	19	7	..	..	5	..	34
Egypt	..	..	..	..	1	..	4
Eire	1	..	..	16	9	26	38
Ethiopia	..	..	..	..	9	..	27
France	1,558	27	62	3,342	735	..	2,085
French Guiana . . .	18	7	..	4	..	..	6
French Morocco . . .	7	8	..	57	67	..	40
Germany	19	33	..	7	17	..	9
Guatemala	26	232	..	..	3	..	..
Hong Kong	..	..	..	1	3	..	1
Israel	7,260	3	2	35	1,689	..	83
Italy	32	1	2	3	14	..	9
Kenya	..	..	..	..	5	..	..
Luxembourg	7	..	..	16	2	..	25
Mexico	11	327	..	..	..	1	2
Netherlands	19	..	1	118	63	..	57
New Zealand . . .	918	2	47	179	275	9	504
Northern Rhodesia . . .	..	..	..	..	..	..	..
Norway	27	3	4	58	41	37	121
Pakistan	2	1	4	1	6	..	2
Panama	3	5	..	..	5	..	6
Paraguay	353	21	10	146	2,665	..	68
Peru	91	72	..	86	33	11	1,492
Philippines	..	..	..	..	5	..	2
Southern Rhodesia . . .	3	..	..	1	..	..	5
Spain	11	..	..	7	4	..	26
Sweden	52	..	..	46	12	4	168
Switzerland	11	..	1	25	45	1	58
Syria	..	..	4	2	..	..	114
Tanganyika	..	..	..	..	..	..	..
Tunisia	8	..	..	138	9	..	33
Turkey	27	1	1	12	749	..	107
Union of S. Africa . . .	1	..	..	..	2	..	80
UK	501	10	14	15,001	459	..	9,817
US	4,249	24	105	45,044	14,506	1,971	17,213
Uruguay	149	237	1	5	58	20	76
Venezuela	257	2,623	10	1,887	786	256	1,997
Miscellaneous	47	33	2	9	91	..	39
Not reported . . .	11	295	..	74	14	..	1

RESETTLEMENT

ANNEX 41 (*cont.*)

Resettlement (*cont.*)

Country of destination and country of citizenship (*cont.*)

Country of destination	Refugees of specified country of citizenship, last habitual residence, or ethnic group departed for resettlement, 1 July 1947–31 Dec. 1951						Jewish refugees included*
	Nansen status	Stateless	Volks-deutsche	Unde-termined	Miscel-laneous	Not reported	
TOTAL	20,196	6,127	986	12,799	1,436	71,075	231,548
Argentina	1,461	330	6	164	148	537	736
Australia	2,383	1,513	..	427	94	3,697	8,172
Belgium	823	3	..	73	84	87	228
Bolivia	15	56	..	20	6	250	912
Brazil	1,549	963	..	329	52	309	803
Canada	825	441	218	809	107	1,279	16,021
Chile	404	62	..	48	11	150	388
Colombia	14	19	..	7	1	50	159
Costa Rica	7	..	..	9	..	41	115
Cuba	2	..	..	11	1	84	278
Dominican Republic	1	..	..	2	1	20	58
Ecuador	11	5	..	4	..	123	201
Egypt	4	1	..	..	4	134	..
Eire	5	7	..	..	..	34	5
Ethiopia	28	8	..	13	..	..	..
France	1,013	103	10	805	141	9,882	2,220
French Guiana	..	7	..	3	..	13	6
French Morocco	461	44	..	2	1	293	12
Germany	13	2	..	1	7	31	21
Guatemala	7	..	..	2	..	25	17
Hong Kong	54	..	..	2	..	1	..
Israel	627	156	..	3,444	146	47,558	130,408
Italy	14	2	..	1	2	5	14
Kenya	..	2	..	7	..	4	5
Luxembourg	..	3	..	1	1	2	..
Mexico	3	1	..	1	..	65	19
Netherlands	94	8	..	110	4	54	616
New Zealand	67	58	..	5	9	33	104
Northern Rhodesia	..	..	..	..	..	1	8
Norway	15	20	..	3	4	1	30
Pakistan	3	4	..	..	..	..	..
Panama	..	..	..	..	..	26	11
Paraguay	89	24	..	95	14	487	1,685
Peru	35	11	..	4	5	35	98
Philippines	37	..	..	2	..	5	..
Southern Rhodesia	..	4	..	2	..	5	14
Spain	1	2	..	..	2	..	..
Sweden	85	14	751	119	5	228	558
Switzerland	16	12	1	5	1	54	105
Syria	2	37	..	..	21	..	2
Tanganyika	..	..	..	..	..	13	..
Tunisia	15	2	..	..	2	6	4
Turkey	248	8	..	8	18	1,039	4
Union of S. Africa	12	6	..	6	7	68	169
UK	217	45	..	2,679	139	1,027	586
US	8,357	1,975	..	3,163	312	2,001	64,930
Uruguay	8	21	..	22	6	340	699
Venezuela	947	118	..	368	41	180	417
Miscellaneous	112	30	..	23	29	34	230
Not reported	112	..	..	..	10	764	480

* Jewish refugees are included in the preceding columns under their country of citizenship or last habitual residence.

ANNEX 42

Resettlement

Area of departure

IRO area of departure	Refugees departed from specified IRO areas for resettlement, 1 July 1947–31 Dec. 1951									
	Total	1 July 1947–31 Dec. 1947	1 Jan. 1948–30 June 1948	1 July 1948–31 Dec. 1948	1 Jan. 1949–30 June 1949	1 July 1949–31 Dec. 1949	1 Jan. 1950–30 June 1950	1 July 1950–31 Dec. 1950	1 Jan. 1951–30 June 1951	1 July 1951–31 Dec. 1951
TOTAL	1,038,750	95,147	113,531	142,383	180,774	164,547	99,818	91,729	74,320	76,501
Austria	145,233	10,561	15,589	27,581	32,512	19,260	10,421	11,423	8,510	9,376
Belgium	8,672	117	440	885	1,268	945	533	613	1,343	2,528
Czechoslovakia	3,226	113	255	511	1,130	1,203	14	..	..	..
Denmark	2,034	..	..	144	275	683	214	416	156	146
Far East	19,265	1,896	1,816	2,369	3,713	3,099	1,114	2,197	2,138	923
Philippines	5,308	..	..	..	416	1,772	260	872	1,761	227
Shanghai	13,957	1,896	1,816	2,369	3,297	1,327	854	1,325	377	696
France	31,434	1,142	2,773	5,311	4,333	2,022	2,569	3,927	3,946	5,411
Germany	719,536	70,736	68,671	83,870	131,489	127,596	74,933	65,222	49,538	47,481
British zone	224,261	26,283	28,340	21,113	27,554	36,847	26,788	23,793	17,849	15,694
French zone	38,087	3,480	3,711	3,237	6,094	7,552	3,927	3,877	3,024	3,185
US zone	450,163	40,973	36,620	52,849	97,487	83,197	44,218	37,552	28,665	28,602
Not reported	7,025	..	..	6,671	354	..	..	..	..	..
Greece	3,137	..	..	..	..	..	679	48	968	1,442
Italy	70,535	3,892	11,613	16,624	5,045	7,547	6,790	4,349	6,483	8,192
Luxembourg	200	..	..	16	8	69	35	10	24	38
Middle East	24,311	5,595	8,997	3,917	475	1,334	1,511	2,185	159	138
East Africa	14,044	252	7,047	2,950	333	730	1,339	1,369	19	5
Egypt	820	47	104	616	11	28	14	..	..	..
India	3,082	2,409	673	..	..	..	..	..	..	..
Israel	11	1	7	2	1	..	..	..	..	..
Lebanon	5,857	2,862	1,161	334	104	513	131	736	9	7
Syria	71	..	..	..	..	16	22	10	4	19
Turkey	405	3	5	15	26	47	5	70	127	107
Not reported	21	21	..	..	..	..	..	..	..	..
Netherlands	1,691	228	187	684	175	93	65	81	118	60
Norway	138	..	..	..	..	..	17	76	11	34
Portugal	348	82	60	118	30	22	13	4	17	2
Spain	319	56	32	32	65	26	9	31	33	35
Sweden*	1,539	..	..	..	..	98	175	481	384	401
Switzerland	3,919	719	312	281	199	500	647	561	407	293
Union of S. Africa	4	..	..	..	..	..	..	..	3	1
UK	446	10	23	40	57	50	79	105	82	..
Not reported	2,763	..	2,763	..	..	..	..	..	..	..

* Resettled under the auspices of the IRO Office in Denmark.

ANNEX 43

Resettlement

Country of destination

Country of destination	Total	Refugees departed from IRO areas for resettlement, 1 July 1947–31 Dec. 1951								
		1 July 1947–31 Dec. 1947	1 Jan. 1948–30 June 1948	1 July 1948–31 Dec. 1948	1 Jan. 1949–30 June 1949	1 July 1949–31 Dec. 1949	1 Jan. 1950–30 June 1950	1 July 1950–31 Dec. 1950	1 Jan. 1951–30 June 1951	1 July 1951–31 Dec. 1951
TOTAL. .	1,038,750	95,147	113,531	142,383	180,774	164,547	99,818	91,729	74,320	76,501
Argentina .	32,712	3,332	8,880	9,424	5,348	1,099	1,358	1,574	727	970
Australia. .	182,159	1,325	4,377	9,940	38,983	50,691	40,083	25,115	6,761	4,884
Belgium . .	22,477	15,894	3,253	2,615	292	129	112	75	66	41
Bolivia . .	2,485	255	164	155	185	83	145	406	751	341
Brazil . .	28,848	1,804	1,722	5,949	10,349	3,481	530	813	1,327	2,873
Canada . .	123,479	7,721	17,592	23,212	17,498	11,096	8,897	7,015	14,110	16,338
Chile . .	5,108	193	1,293	210	182	1,708	231	585	197	509
Colombia .	889	75	76	196	73	78	51	209	69	62
Costa Rica .	198	25	51	36	36	21	13	10	..	6
Cuba . .	432	80	196	46	33	35	13	10	5	14
Dominican Republic .	413	41	27	25	41	200	10	63	4	2
Ecuador . .	394	71	27	107	77	27	16	36	26	6
Egypt . .	169	137	10	4	2	4	5	3	4	..
Eire . .	224	..	..	41	7	6	10	18	69	73
Ethiopia . .	243	..	1	2	10	32	16	176	4	2
France . .	38,455	8,637	7,581	8,441	10,356	1,856	538	698	125	223
French Guiana	211	..	..	..	66	113	1	19	12	..
French Morocco .	1,446	701	28	176	268	93	73	55	36	16
Germany .	344	21	5	8	136	32	24	35	45	38
Guatemala .	342	7	144	80	29	28	6	14	24	10
Hong Kong .	78	2	..	1	22	36	9	6	2	..
Israel . .	132,109	7,481	9,410	54,439	45,087	8,640	2,128	3,234	1,142	548
Italy . .	235	15	35	10	43	36	37	31	15	13
Kenya . .	233	..	7	22	120	52	20	10	2	..
Luxembourg .	198	1	5	10	174	2	1	..	..	5
Mexico . .	437	123	59	63	68	12	24	26	17	45
Netherlands .	4,355	2,359	1,129	532	27	21	8	184	28	67
New Zealand .	4,837	9	28	38	1,027	20	46	1,020	1,492	1,157
Northern Rhodesia .	312	..	21	268	7	10	3	3	..	..
Norway .	1,105	2	12	22	154	77	110	39	117	572
Pakistan . .	78	..	..	..	..	56	4	14	3	1
Panama . .	63	33	6	6	6	10	2	..	..	..
Paraguay .	5,887	495	2,552	1,791	136	370	276	87	70	110
Peru . .	2,340	25	1,258	617	227	56	54	54	41	8
Philippines .	68	3	2	5	10	14	30	..	4	..
Southern Rhodesia .	135	10	34	49	21	5	5	8	3	..
Spain . .	120	13	14	9	22	16	12	11	9	14
Sweden . .	4,330	884	1,071	922	225	174	126	451	135	342
Switzerland .	589	61	131	57	45	16	14	9	203	53
Syria . .	280	44	215	16	..	..	..	..	..	5
Tanganyika .	300	4	89	53	26	90	24	13	..	1
Tunisia . .	446	69	188	126	42	11	3	3	2	2
Turkey . .	2,358	..	519	908	512	31	10	182	162	34
Union of S. Africa . .	457	79	87	77	67	17	28	45	36	21
UK . .	86,346	29,471	39,986	10,919	1,344	754	488	2,305	606	473
US . .	328,851	9,320	7,925	4,413	46,721	81,592	42,941	45,120	44,793	46,026
Uruguay . .	1,461	199	160	200	221	224	172	90	53	142
Venezuela .	17,277	2,798	2,925	6,055	317	1,181	968	1,751	979	303
Miscellaneous .	968	109	134	88	124	182	127	104	44	56
Not reported .	1,469	1,218	102	..	8	30	16	..	..	95

CHAPTER XXI

MOVEMENTS

INTERNATIONAL agencies, acting on behalf of refugees in the decades following the First World War, were unable to resettle large groups of refugees in other countries mainly because of a lack of transport facilities, especially shipping, with which to bring their beneficiaries to their destinations. Neither the agencies nor the individual national governments concerned had at their disposal adequate funds to meet the large costs of transportation for mass emigration. When IRO's Constitution was drawn up, transportation which would assure the repatriation or resettlement of the refugees and displaced persons was clearly defined as one of the functions of the Organization, together with the stipulation that the member governments would provide the necessary funds. For the first time, therefore, it was possible, on an international level, to transport masses of people stranded in one part of the globe to another area which held out the promise of better life or at least survival.

In terms of numbers, people had to be moved either in mass, in groups, or as individuals. Movements might be either inland or overseas; the former would be local within a single country, or from one country to another on the same continent, primarily requiring rail transportation, but also resorting to air travel if necessary; the latter would involve movements chiefly from Europe to other countries throughout the world, mostly by sea but also, to a more limited degree, by air. Movements were to be paid for either entirely by the Organization, or were to be paid partly by the refugees or their sponsors, or financed by the Organization on a reimbursable basis. Further, there would be movements of non-eligibles, who would be transported by the Organization's transportation facilities, chiefly on return trips or backhauls of empty ships of the Organization, against payment by the governments or others using these facilities.

During its first year, the IRO planned its policies and developed a procedure for the movements of refugees. In September 1947 the Administration directed the Division of Refugee Movements in Geneva to procure shipping on a long-term hire basis. Space for groups or individual movements was to be secured either by the Headquarters Movements Office or by field offices,[1] who were to make arrangements to fill the boats as directed.

In accordance with a specific order, the Organization would provide, in normal cases, free transportation of baggage up to 100 kg. for each traveller. A limit on the amount of baggage per individual was fixed at 250 kg., provided that the traveller would pay the transportation charges for any excess baggage over the basic 100 kg., unless his baggage contained material certified as tools of his trade. Travellers were advised to insure their baggage, even though the Organization accepted no responsibility for the payment of the premiums involved.[2]

[1] Provisional Order No. 11, 29 Sept. 1947.
[2] Provisional Order No. 22, 23 Oct. 1947: Baggage and Excess Baggage on Refugee Movements.

Early in November 1947 the Organization laid down as a rule that escort officers, whose functions were defined in this order, would be provided for refugee movements. Health standards were established for all movements of refugees by road, rail, sea, and air.[1] At the close of the first year of operations, the Organization defined the policy and procedures relating to individual resettlement.[2]

At the same time the IRO was developing its administrative machinery for its vast transportation task. After some four months of planning and experience, the Division of Refugee Movements was established in the Department of Repatriation and Resettlement at headquarters in Geneva. Its main functions were to establish policy in all matters concerning the movement of refugees, to negotiate for all needs of transportation, to co-ordinate all movements, to control budgetary matters, to establish certain sub-offices, and to supervise escort officers appointed in connexion with sea movements.

One sub-office established by the new Division was the Shipping Liaison Office in London whose functions were to negotiate for shipping space, to maintain liaison with the Ministry of Transport, and to supervise and control refugee movements via the UK. The Washington Office of the IRO became an important link between the Central Shipping Office and the US army and navy authorities. Further inter-zonal movements offices were opened in the British zone of Germany and Italy; the former at Diepholz, the latter for a time in Rome, but ultimately in Genoa. The inter-zonal movements officers at these places were responsible for embarkation and disembarkation including documentation, for the maintenance of liaison with field officers and with port authorities, for detailed sailing schedules, and for procuring offers of suitable sea transportation from shipping owners and agents.[3]

An American and a British shipping expert were temporarily appointed to review jointly the methods of chartering ships and of booking spaces on ships, and to survey the organization and administration of the Movements Division at headquarters and in the field. The immediate concern of PCIRO was necessarily to procure transportation facilities especially shipping space. PCIRO was helped by the experience of the IGCR.

In the latter part of 1946 it became evident that non-repatriable European refugees in any substantial numbers could be carried overseas only if adequate shipping facilities were available to ensure the transport of these persons to their destinations. If shipping could be secured, then it would be possible to take steps in Europe to select and process candidates for resettlement, and to conclude agreements with countries of reception. The IGCR responsible for resettlement at that time therefore investigated the possibilities of acquiring shipping. Suitable shipping, however, was not only extremely short in world supply, but, besides, many factors were involved which complicated the situation: safety regulations pertaining to passenger vessels at sea, amortization of cost of repairs and conversions, duration of contracts, availability of vessels, the question of an operating agency for the transport, all these factors had to be taken into account when agreements were made with private

[1] Provisional Orders No. 26 (12 Nov. 1947) and No. 26.1 (18 Nov. 1948): Escort Officers on Refugee Movements. PREP/SR/77, 8 May 1948.
[2] Provisional Orders No. 70 (11 May 1948) and No. 70.1 (8 Nov. 1948).
[3] Provisional Order No. 28, 12 Nov. 1947.

operators. Although private companies were generally interested in any proposals promising long-term contracts and definite profits, no company was able to provide specific ships for specific periods and routings at specific rates because of a lack of suitable ships. The only vessels suitable and available for the purpose were US Government vessels of the Victory Class (Atlantic Conversion), and C4SA3 types of ships which had been built during the war as fast cargo vessels.[1] Most of them were under the control of the US War Department or the US Maritime Commission.

In 1946 the IGCR had presented a complete plan through the US State Department to the US Interdepartmental Co-ordinating Committee on Shipping (US Departments of State, War, Navy, Maritime, Budget, Coastguard, and Treasury). In March 1947 an agreement had been concluded, on the basis of this proposal, between IGCR and the War Department according to which the operations of three ships were scheduled with the first sailing on 1 May 1947, the second on 1 June, and the third on 1 July. Under this agreement the Transportation Corps of the US army supervised all repairs, conversions, crewing, stocking, and operating of the vessels on a cost of operation basis for the IGCR or its successor. The latter appropriated advances in US dollars into a receipt and expenditure account to the credit of the War Department. The initial advance of $759,500 paid by IGCR covered the estimated costs for the preparation and operation of two vessels to 30 June 1947.

On 1 July 1947, when the IRO assumed the responsibility for the continuation of the IGCR–US Army Shipping Programme, the IGCR's plan had been realized to a certain extent: two US Government vessels had been obtained, and 1,722 refugees had been transported to Brazil and 859 to Venezuela.[2] Thus a foundation had been laid for world-wide migration.

Although each of these ships had a capacity of about 900 passengers, they were not able, on their various journeys to South American countries, to carry more than 13,000 persons altogether of the 20,000 tentatively scheduled in earlier IGCR programmes, thus providing only about 40 per cent. of the tonnage required to meet the tentative goal of 68,000 refugees to be resettled by overseas movements in the first year of operation. Additional ships of a similar type were therefore required.[3] In October an offer of two British-owned vessels for the Australia route was accepted; and in the following month the fleet was increased to eight ships.

The rapid rise in the need for ships occurred during a desperate world shortage of shipping. Passenger ships of reasonable size were engaged in transporting troops and dependants, or were being converted from war to peace use, or were fully occupied in normal business. The suspension of normal travel during the war led to such a great demand after the war that hundreds of thousands of persons were unable to obtain passages despite their willingness to pay high fares. The Organization

[1] These types became known as United States Army Transports (USATs) and were operated as part of the Military Sea Transportation Service (MSTS). The information of the IGCR–War Department Agreement is taken from the memorandum of 15 Apr. 1947 on IGCR Shipping Negotiations and Agreements by Major-General W. A. Wood, Jr., who was Assistant Director of IGCR at that time and became the Chief of the IRO Office in Washington.

[2] Monograph: W. A. Wood, *History of the IRO US Office, Part II: Shipping Accomplished in US Vessels in IRO Service*, p. 19.

[3] GC/199/Rev. 1, Sept. 1951; PREP/SA/17/10, May 1947.

made every effort to charter vessels, and to utilize small blocks of space on regular sailings for groups of one hundred or so refugees, but this method of transportation was very expensive. Only the development of the IRO–US Army–Navy Shipping Programme made it possible to carry out a successful large-scale resettlement operation.[1]

As a rule the US commercial shipping agencies did not favour the use of military ships by the Organization. Nevertheless the US Government agreed to make these ships available primarily because it was justified to render assistance to an international organization engaged in a vast humanitarian endeavour which placed it beyond the realm of a commercial shipping enterprise. Besides, this arrangement would help relieve the army, by bringing more rapidly to an end its responsibilities for displaced persons in Germany and Austria.

In June 1948 only sixteen ships were in IRO service. Of these five were USATs with an average capacity of 875 persons, five were USMC vessels with accommodation for 550 refugees on each ship, and six were commercial vessels chartered by IRO with an average capacity of 800. Thus, approximately only 11,900 bookings were available on IRO ships at the end of the first year of its operations. At the end of its second operational year, thirty-six vessels were engaged in carrying 30,000 refugees per month to overseas countries. On an average one IRO ship left European ports once a day. The IRO shipping programme reached its peak during the first quarter of the third year when forty vessels, including twenty USATs, were in constant operation. From that time on until the end of operations in February 1952 the fleet was gradually reduced.

In addition to mass movements in IRO vessels individual refugees were transported overseas on blocked space of commercial sailings to destinations all over the world. To give an example, during the fiscal year 1949–50, 10,448 refugees were transported on an average of fifty ships each month.

Mass movements by sea, 1947–52

From small beginnings IRO developed the largest mass transportation scheme in the world. It had grown gradually to meet the needs of the resettlement programme in spite of such obstacles as the world-wide post-war shipping shortage and IRO's lack of freely convertible currencies.[2]

The majority of the more than 1 million refugees moved were transported by facilities of the IRO, or with the Organization's budgetary or operational assistance, more than 600,000 were transported by sea alone; and additional passengers carried in backhaul movements and by special arrangements brought the total number of sea passages to more than 700,000.[3]

Throughout the first year 1947–8 a consistent shortage of shipping prevailed and created a substantial backlog of refugees awaiting transportation. In addition to the basic difficulty of finding ships, uncertainty as to funds available to charter tonnage or procure space complicated the planning for movements *en masse*.

The Organization had been unable, on several occasions, to charter ships for lack

[1] PREP/C/26, 22 Jan. and PREP/SR/61, 26 Jan. 1948.
[2] Chapter VI, Finances, p. 111.
                                                                    [3] Annex 44, p. 470.

of funds, and other shipping operations had been greatly hampered for lack of capital.[1] Therefore, primarily to advance the shipping position of the Organization by three months, a Special Fund for Ocean Transport was created in January 1948. It was limited to $10 million and was to consist of moneys from contributions of governments for the fiscal year 1948–9 which might be made available in the previous fiscal year.[2] New Zealand was the only government able to pay in advance the contribution for the fiscal year 1949, but as this payment was made in non-convertible sterling, its use was problematical.[3] As a result of insufficient shipping, refugees already selected for resettlement were forced to remain in camps, thus increasing costs for care and maintenance and reducing funds which otherwise might have been available for transportation.[4] This situation was a matter of particular concern to various member governments: the US was primarily concerned about the resultant high cost of care and maintenance, whereas Canada, Australia, and other governments were displeased because they did not receive the anticipated numbers of refugees.[5]

By the spring of 1948 Canada had received some 18,000 refugees, yet this total could have been higher had it not been for the shipping shortage. While the total overseas movement by the Organization was necessarily limited to around 4,000 to 5,000 monthly, Canada alone was prepared to accept a monthly total of 4,000;[6] processing had reached the rate of 6,000 monthly and some 3,000 refugees were awaiting ships.

Australia also was most anxious to receive refugees in increasing numbers and believed that the shipping arrangements for Australia were inadequate; accordingly, the Organization was making every effort to increase movements to this country and was contemplating large-scale movements by air.[7]

The field offices of the Organization felt the full impact of these difficulties. In November 1947 the Italian mission complained that there had been no sailings from their country since July, and that a total of only 1,000 had been moved out in groups; further, that despite the Organization's intention to clear out high cost areas such as Italy, more shipping was being made available to Germany where costs were lower and the political situation less combustible. At the time, some 3,500 refugees in Italy were ready to sail; moreover, many visas dating back to the early spring of 1947 would soon lapse. By December it was estimated that at least 4,000 persons would be waiting, and that only 1,000 places were expected to be available. The mission suggested that the development of reserves of refugees ready to sail had proved to be a questionable method, and that Peru, in particular, was disheartened by the lack of shipping.

In the Middle East similar problems were experienced because of the difficulties in providing shipping to the Argentine for people in the El Shatt camp. Normal unchartered shipping in the Middle East to the Argentine was available only for

[1] PREP/SR/61, 26 Jan. 1948.   [2] Ibid.
[3] Memorandum, PCIRO Geneva, Comptroller to Asst. Executive Secretary for Repatriation and Resettlement, 19 July 1948.
[4] Annual Report to the Genera Council, Fisca Year 1947/8. GC/7, op. cit., p. 38.
[5] PREP/SR/78, 10 May 1948.   [6] Ibid.
[7] PREP/SR/77, 8 May 1948; cf. also Chapter XX, Resettlement, p. 344.

exorbitant fares, and budget restrictions forced Geneva to establish ceilings on such movements; further, most shipowners demanded payment in dollars, whereas the Organization was obliged to utilize other currencies also as extensively as possible. The Middle East Office was accorded priorities by dates when visas were obtained; unless there was an actual charter there was little control over cancellation of space by shipowners. The mission was able to get space only in Italy or in France, but the former refused transit visas except under very precise arrangements and the latter required too long a time in furnishing visas.

While engaging in active negotiations to increase shipping capacity, the Organization took steps to accommodate a large fleet when it should become available. As early as November 1947 efforts were made to secure increased berthing accommodation at Bremerhaven, but it was foreseen that some of the additional vessels might, of necessity, be channelled to Italy.

At the same time, plans were made to speed up documentation and administration in Germany and Italy in order to utilize fully the increased fleet.[1]

Primarily due to the shortage of shipping during the first year, movements were extremely uncertain and necessitated constant revisions in estimates and planning. In the first six months Australia had been able to receive no more than 1,700 refugees out of 5,000 hoped for,[2] yet the shipping capacity for the Australian run had been increased to 3,500 monthly.[3]

Canada was requesting as many as 15,500 workers, to be received at the rate of 3,000 monthly, with an additional 25,600 to be received under the close relatives scheme. By October 1947 less than 4,000 had been transported, and for the period October–December a schedule of eight ships was planned which was to carry almost 7,000 persons. But the three Canadian selection teams, then working in the field, were unable to keep pace with the schedule and it became necessary to cancel sailings. As a result efforts were made to arrange for an additional one or two selection teams. At the time, in addition to regular USAT sailings to Canada, the US Maritime Commission ships began in March to make available a monthly lift of from 1,000 to 1,800 passengers,[4] and block space had been obtained on a commercial vessel to carry from 40 to 200 refugees on every sailing to Canada.[5]

In addition to the regular runs of the IRO's chartered fleet mainly to Australia, Canada, and South America, other shipping was arranged for special purposes.

In the Far East shipping continued to be very scarce for long hauls, thus small numbers had to be moved by regular commercial transport. The movement of overseas Chinese to nearby countries was steady, and was accomplished largely by space procured locally.[6] In the autumn of 1947 it was expected that many opportunities for settlement would open up in North Africa; plans were made to ship 800 refugees a month for six months from Italian ports, but the opportunities proved to be non-existent and the arrangements thus proved to have been largely unnecessary.[7] The non-chartered steamer *Santa Cruz* carried to Argentina two groups of between 900 and 1,000 persons; the first sailing from Naples on 31 December 1947.[8] Poles

[1] PREP/161, 5 Jan. 1948; PREP/130, 19 Oct. 1947; PREP/209, 30 Apr. 1948.
[2] PREP/C/26, 22 Jan. 1948.   [3] PREP/130, op. cit.
[4] PREP/209, op. cit.   [5] PREP/161, 5 Jan. 1948.
[6] Ibid.   [7] PREP/130, op. cit.   [8] PREP/161, op. cit.

were repatriated from Africa to Poland in vessels returning from Australia,[1] and in small commercial ships; they were entrained at the port of entry, either Genoa or Naples, and moved directly to Poland.

There was, however, no uniform or even flow of movements from month to month; for example, in the three-month period from 1 January to 8 April 1948 slightly more than 11,000 refugees were carried in nineteen voyages—whereas the firm shipping schedule for the single month following provided for a lift of over 18,000 persons in twenty-six voyages. For the nineteen voyages in the 100-day schedule, departures were eleven from Germany, five from England, and three from Italy, while destinations were fourteen to Canada, three to Argentina, and two to Australia. Of the twenty-six voyages in the thirty-day schedule, there were eighteen departing from Germany, four from Italy, two from France, and one from England; and of these thirteen were destined for Canada, four for Argentina, three for Australia, three for Venezuela, two for Brazil, and one for Chile, Colombia, and Peru together.[2]

Despite the numerous problems and set-backs encountered in the first twelve months of operations, certain goals set in November 1947 for the fiscal year 1947–8 were more than realized, as the following figures indicate:

	Anticipated	Realized
Australia	5,000	5,700
Canada	20,000	25,313
South America	12,000	28,000 plus

In addition a total repatriation movement of almost 52,000 persons took place, which involved transportation provided or arranged for by the Organization.

A relatively large percentage of the total numbers of refugees resettled in the first twelve months travelled on transportation not provided by the Organization. Of a total movement of more than 98,000 to overseas countries, the major movements which IRO did not handle were 17,000 to Israel. Nor did the IRO—of a grand total of more than 110,000 persons resettled in European countries—take any appreciable part in the movement of some 69,000 persons to the UK.

At the end of the year the fleet of the Organization was capable of a monthly lift averaging 10,000 persons.[3] The goal set by the Organization at an earlier date had, to a great extent, been realized; for, at the end of the first six months, when the monthly lift had reached about 5,000, it had been hoped that a figure of 12,000 might be achieved by the start of the second year.[4]

1948–9

At the beginning of the second year a clear need for additional shipping capacity was apparent. The most careful study and planning were necessary if shipping facilities were to be adequate and sufficiently flexible. Apart from financial considerations

[1] PREP/130, op. cit.   [2] PREP/209, op. cit.
[3] GC/7, op. cit., p. 37.   [4] PREP/161, op. cit.; PREP/SR/77, op. cit.

and the availability of shipping, the determining factor was the probable number of refugees to be moved. This figure would be subject to constant change and could not be foreseen with accuracy.

Nevertheless, as resettlement agreements were negotiated with reception countries and the earlier difficulties were overcome, a more definite pattern of movement became discernible. Overseas movements would consist largely of resettlement in the US, Australia, Canada, and South America, probably in that order numerically; areas of departure of these movements, in the same order, would probably be Germany, Austria, Italy, and France. The largest movements to European countries were anticipated for France, the UK, and Belgium.

After the first year, repatriation movements were expected to decrease, then to decline from year to year, and it was thought that they would consist chiefly of travel from Germany to Poland, Yugoslavia, and the USSR; and from Shanghai to Far Eastern countries.

With arrangements well in hand for procuring additional shipping space, the major problem anticipated was the speeding up of screening and processing of refugees for travel. To accomplish the monthly movement of 30,000 persons, a reserve of fully processed resettlement candidates assembled for speedy embarkation was foreseen as a primary prerequisite. This meant that about 1,200 persons had to be processed each working day. Since it was expected that the Organization's investment in ships alone would cost about $100,000 per day by the fourth month of the year, this investment had to be safeguarded by making sure that refugees were available and ready to sail, and that ships would not have to wait for refugees.

It was estimated that available chartered shipping would be able to transport between 185,000 to 230,000 refugees overseas during the second year, with an additional 15,000 to 52,000 sailing by other means.[1] Early in the year the backlog was insufficient, and it was not always possible to achieve complete co-operation from the various resettlement missions, who either were not able to accomplish what was desired or were reluctant to develop backlogs which they doubted could be moved on schedule. Movements to Australia had expanded rapidly with a total of some 8,000 shipped in the first four months, and selection teams were unable to get ahead of sailings. Canada had developed a reserve of some 8,000 refugees selected, but was dissatisfied because this backlog was being used also for shipments to the US. There were in fact too many ships for the US programme, and the need for a substantial backlog was of the utmost importance. Processing for Argentina in Italy was decreasing, the high cost of visas being an important factor. Movements to Chile and Peru had been temporarily held up because of inadequate reception arrangements; while there was a backlog of 4,000 for the former, acceptances could not exceed some 450 monthly. Important movements to Venezuela had just started, and processing had been just able to keep up with the movement of some 5,000 during the first three months.

Meanwhile, arrangements were made for the Organization to acquire additional military ships, and by the end of 1948 it had contracted for all of these which were regularly to enter into its service, adding a total of eight new MSTS vessels,

[1] GC/7, op. cit.

namely: *General Ballou, General Howze, General Hersey, General Taylor, General Muir, General McRae, General Blatchford,* and *General Greeley.* The six vessels of the US Maritime Commission which had transported refugees in the first year continued regular sailings up to April 1949, and during a total of thirty-six voyages had carried slightly more than 18,000 refugees to either Canada or the US. At that time four of the USMC ships became unavailable, but the S.S.s *Marine Marlin* and *Jumper* were turned over to the army by the USMC and continued in IRO service throughout the second year.[1]

The Organization also chartered additional commercial ships, and attained the peak total of thirty-five vessels actively in service in a single month. All these vessels were not on the high seas at the same time, and a few were chartered for one voyage only, but during the year the Organization had more than forty vessels under charter; at the peak a total of nineteen USATS and USMC vessels were in active service.[2]

As early as September 1948 the Organization suffered losses beyond its control in a scheduled lift up to some 25,000—partly as a result of delays in availability of chartered vessels, mishaps to these ships, and the non-materialization of plans such as a substantial air lift to Canada. A more important factor, however, contributing to the relatively small lift in the early months, was the difficulty in preparing sufficient numbers of refugees for embarkation—particularly for sailings to the US, Argentina, and Brazil—which necessitated cancellations of scheduled sailings.

But these set-backs had been offset by the spring of 1949 when a record monthly movement of some 34,500 refugees was achieved with a total shipping capacity of less than 37,500. It was expected then that mass movements to the US would soon reach a total of 15,000 monthly, and a lift of 10,000 to Australia was foreseen.[3] In May a movement of almost 11,500 had been achieved to the US and the backlog for this scheme had been almost completely absorbed; accordingly, each mission concerned was instructed to use all rail and other resources to get sufficient numbers of refugees ready for scheduled sailings in order to meet a serious crisis. By the end of the fiscal year thirty-five IRO vessels were actively engaged in accomplishing a lift of some 30,000 refugees monthly, and throughout the year the Organization had moved by its own ships and aircraft more than 138,500 by sea and 9,400 by air.[4]

In the fiscal year total resettlement movements to overseas countries numbered more than 280,000, including movements of almost 51,000 to the US, 49,000 to Australia, and 41,000 to Canada; the largest movement, however, was that of some 93,000 refugees to Israel. Some of the movements to Israel were accomplished by voluntary societies and others without the use of transportation facilities, chartered or otherwise, arranged by the Organization.[5]

Repatriation movements for the year declined to some 13,600 from the total of 52,000 achieved in the previous year; the largest movements consisted of 7,200 from Germany, mostly destined for Poland, and 3,300 overseas Chinese departing from Shanghai to other Far Eastern countries, of which Burma received some 2,200.

[1] Wood, op. cit., Section II, pp. 10–14.
[2] GC/199/Rev. 1: *Migration from Europe,* p. 63.   [3] GC/SR/21, 19 Apr. 1949.
[4] GC/100, p. 51.   [5] GC/199/Rev. 1, 1 Sept. 1951.

1949–50

For the third year, total overseas movements of some 285,000 were planned for the IRO fleet as follows: US 175,000, using seventeen MSTS vessels with a monthly capacity of 14,500; Australia 70,000, using thirteen ships with a capacity of 14,000 in five voyages; Canada 15,000, using two ships; and South America 25,500, using three MSTS vessels with a monthly capacity of 2,100.[1] Now that earlier difficulties had been largely overcome in obtaining shipping space under contract and space bookings for individual migration, it seemed likely that the shipping facilities of the Organization might be excessive in the months ahead.[2] This proved to be the case. In the first quarter of the year resettlement reached a peak of 32,500 in August; but by January 1950 it had declined to around 16,300.[3]

Early in September 1949 it was foreseen that there might be a serious surplus of shipping to the US unless assurances were issued at an increased rate. At about the same time an agreement was reached with the Australian Government to stop, for a period of six weeks, all movements to Australia of families having a child under 1 year of age. This move was taken to prevent a further high mortality of infants on this voyage due to the excessive heat of the Red Sea. Apart from this decision made for health reasons, there was a decline in the numbers going to Australia, a reduction in the numbers being accepted for Brazil, and a slackening of the numbers being processed to the US. Thus IRO had more shipping than it could use and a decision was reached to get rid at once of at least eight ships.

Throughout the second quarter the movement to the US declined rapidly, mass resettlement to Brazil ceased, and certain Latin-American prospects failed.[4] In December it was feared that movement to the US might be reduced to as low a number as 6,000 monthly, and by the end of the calendar year the IRO fleet had been reduced by ten vessels, half of them USATs.[5]

In the third quarter delays in producing visas for the US precipitated a grave shipping crisis. Serious consequences were avoided, however, partly because Australia had agreed to take 10,000 refugees each month during February and March, although originally this Government had wished to decrease its reception at that time.[6] While movements to the US increased in the final three months of the year, movements to Australia dropped sharply in this period and it was necessary to reduce further the shipping facilities.[7] Nevertheless, both of these countries attained higher totals in this year than in any other year of reception and, some time before the year ended, the US celebrated the arrival of the 150,000th refugee on the ship *General Ballou*.

As a means towards avoiding serious losses in connexion with its contractual obligations for surplus shipping, the Organization successfully carried out a satisfactory charter cancellation programme and arranged sub-chartering of excess tonnage.[8] There was a constant and sharp reduction in the number of commercial

[1] GC/60/Add. 1, 28 Mar. 1949.   [2] GC/60, 22 Mar. 1949.
[3] GC/SR/65, 15 Mar. 1950.   [4] GC/166, op. cit., p. 24.
[5] Ibid.   [6] GC/SR/65, 15 Mar. 1950.
[7] GC/166, op. cit., p. 24.
[8] GC/140, 7 Feb. 1950, and GC/SR/65, 15 Mar. 1950.

vessels under charter up to the end of the year, when only six of the latter were left in active operation.[1]

But the adjustment of shipping capacity to movement needs, substantially reduced by unpredictable changes in the policies of certain resettlement countries, was accomplished chiefly by drastic reductions in the US vessels.[2]

All MSTS vessels had been transferred from the army to the navy as of 1 March 1950, but seven continued in IRO service under navy control. A month or so later the Organization decided to employ after 30 June 1950 non-commercial vessels only, that is, the ships first known as USATs and operated first by the US army and now by the US navy as part of the US military sea transportation service. These vessels had been found to provide standards and economies more favourable than most of the Organization's other shipping, and it was believed possible to continue this arrangement, which was in many respects unique.

Supplementary and closure period

Formerly the Organization had budgeted for the twelve months of the fiscal year ahead, but as it was expected that it would achieve final closure by October 1951, a budget was prepared to cover a supplementary and closure period beginning 1 July 1950 and ending 30 September 1951; almost $32 million was reserved for sea and air transportation for 185,000 refugees as follows: Australia 35,000, Canada 100,000, US 140,000.[3]

The US amended DP Act became law on 16 June 1950, imposing certain changes which would slow down the movements to the US;[4] consequently, no additional shipping was taken on despite heavy short time requirements.

In September the Australian Government expressed concern regarding the anticipated rate of movement to that country, and during November shipping to Australia was increased in deference to that Government's wishes to receive as many refugees as possible by the end of the calendar year. To meet this request the Organization took up four extra commercial vessels and arranged for sixteen extra air flights.[5] A total of nearly 156,000 migrants had departed from Europe for Australia; by the end of the calendar year an additional 3,000 were scheduled to leave from Europe, and another 2,300 from Samar and the Far East to achieve a grand total of over 161,000 against the overall commitment of 167,000 with Australia. Of those already moved, almost 1,700 had been transported in twenty-nine separate air flights and the balance in 142 sea voyages under mass resettlement schemes.

Although the decision had been taken earlier to rely increasingly on MSTS vessels and to scale down dollar commercial vessels, it proved necessary to reverse this stand. The outbreak of hostilities in Korea, which affected the availability of MSTS vessels, and heavy short-term requirements necessitated the use of commercial vessels; and it was also necessary to use available soft currencies for the shipping programme.[6]

---

[1] GC/166, op. cit., p. 24.   [2] Wood, op. cit., Section II, pp. 1 and 11.
[3] GC/50, 22 Oct. 1950.
[4] Wood, op. cit., Section I, p. 17; GC/167, 30 Aug. 1950.
[5] GC/197, 28 Feb. 1951.
[6] GC/167, 30 Aug. 1950. Wood, op. cit., Part I, p. 16.

Because of the Korean War the US military authorities asked for the return of the four vessels which the Organization had just placed in a standby status. This requisitioning by the US navy saved the Organization standby expenses which were estimated to be $3,200 per ship per day for the first ten days and $1,800 per ship per day thereafter, but the loss of these standby vessels also necessitated the renegotiation of certain commercial contracts which had just been cancelled.

By the middle of the year, all transportation to Latin America, except Venezuela, was carried out by commercial vessels and planes—flights for which the Organization obtained favourable rates, mostly payable in soft currencies.[1] During the same period, large movements of children and infants to Australia necessitated modifications and improvements in accommodation on chartered ships.[2]

In January 1951 instructions were released for the processing and transportation of persons of German ethnic origin under Section 12 of the amended US Displaced Persons Act. Agreements for such transportation had been concluded early in November to afford the Organization greater flexibility in its facilities.[3]

During the year the number of MSTS vessels in IRO service fluctuated between seven and nine, in accordance with the needs of the Organization and arrangements with the military authorities. By the end of the year, and through January 1952, when IRO ceased operations, only five of these carriers remained in IRO service. Also several westbound passages on ships regularly in navy service were made available for IRO use as required.[4] As of 1 July 1951 the Organization still retained five commercial vessels.[5]

During the year almost 129,000 persons were transported on IRO chartered vessels, and IRO chartered planes flew 6,000 refugees to the US and Australia. In addition, transportation was arranged for more than 13,000 individual migrants, 600 of whom travelled by air.[6]

In the last quarter of the fiscal year 1950–1 the Organization raised its estimates of overseas transportation by some 37,400 passages; and by October 1951 this estimate had again been raised by an additional 9,000, that is to say, the total number was estimated at 231,400 passages for the final supplementary and closure period from 30 June 1950 to 31 December 1951.

At the end of September all IRO offices connected with movements were instructed to meet specified dates for the final selection and processing of refugees and for their final transportation: with few exceptions all refugees were to be made ready during the month of November for final movement during December.

Final overseas resettlement movements were outlined for Australia, Canada, and the US and several Latin American countries. Resettlement to European countries was restricted to the UK, Norway, Sweden, and institutional hard core movements to various countries. Small repatriation moves, both overseas and to European countries, also were outlined.

In the period July–December 1951 almost 60,000 persons were transported on IRO chartered vessels, while an additional 4,500 were carried to the US and Canada

[1] GC/197, op. cit.   [2] GC/227/Rev. 1, 30 Oct. 1951.
[3] USA Branch Instruction No. 23, Resettlement and Repatriation Division, 17 Jan. 1951.
[4] Wood, op. cit., Section II.   [5] GC/227/Rev. 1, op. cit.
[6] Ibid.

by IRO chartered planes; in addition, transport was arranged for some 8,500 individual refugees to travel by sea, and 400 by air.[1] In the final month of movements, January 1952, a further 10,800 refugees were resettled and a final fifteen persons were repatriated.

The IRO–MSTS shipping programme ended with the last sailings in January of the remaining five vessels from Bremerhaven and the debarkation of passengers and baggage in the US.[2] The last boatload of refugees transported in military ships regularly in navy service arrived in New York on 9 February with 1,272 passengers; this was the final westward voyage of refugees in military ships not regularly in IRO service, and brought the total carried by them to almost 25,000 in the period of slightly more than a year during which these special movements were made.

Individual migration

Refugees chosen by selection missions for mass resettlement schemes travelled, with few exceptions, by mass movement arrangements. On the other hand, persons selected for special schemes or nominated or sponsored by individuals or voluntary societies, apart from mass schemes, were normally moved by individual migration methods. Mass transportation, however, notably in the case of the US, often included persons travelling under individual schemes; conversely, some persons resettling under mass schemes were transported by individual migration arrangements.

At times, a not insignificant number of travellers who were not the responsibility of the Organization were transported in mass movements by special arrangements against reimbursement. Such transportation was provided mostly on behalf of governments and voluntary societies and, since these passages usually occupied space which otherwise might have been vacant, they constituted an important source of income to the Organization.

Apart from the relatively few individual migrants who were transported by mass facilities, most individual movements were accomplished by normal individual travel arrangements. This method was not only practicable, it also suited some countries which insisted that refugees travel by commercial vessels rather than by IRO mass transport.

When travel facilities were still disrupted as a result of the war, the Organization utilized government channels in obtaining reservations, partly because financial limitations made it difficult to compete for scarce passages, and delays might mean cancellation of visas and loss of emigration possibilities. Before long, however, the Organization itself obtained passages, for its importance as a purchaser of travel accommodation was recognized.

It was the duty of Geneva headquarters to negotiate and complete contracts for transportation by road, rail, sea, or air of individual migrants; however, field offices were asked to negotiate for passages as required. In obtaining space on all shipping lines to main destinations, the Organization contributed substantially to improving transportation standards for low-fare passengers. Single bookings often were made by land, sea, and air to comparatively inaccessible regions, and the

---

[1] GC/256, 29 Jan. 1952.
[2] Wood, op. cit., Section II, p. 5.

passage procurement service of the Organization served more than fifty countries.[1] The individual movements office at Genoa, together with field offices in embarkation countries, was responsible for arranging the reception of refugees in transit, for completing formalities prior to embarkation, and for the negotiation of passages as instructed by Geneva.

As far as possible individual or groups of refugees were met at stations and aided in any required change of trains, dealing with customs, or transportation to hotels or embarkation points. On movements of large groups of individual migrants, escort service was provided wherever possible, and for movements of 100 or more the reception countries were advised in time to arrange suitable reception facilities. Officers of the Organization in receiving countries were not only responsible for the reception and disembarkation of individual immigrants, but were also given the task of paying landing money where applicable, of arranging accommodation for refugees on arrival, and their onward transportation to final destinations.[2] Rates for landing money and subsistence *en route* were fixed towards the end of the first six months of operation; and while, preferably, landing money was not paid before the refugee's arrival at his destination, it was sometimes necessary to make other arrangements.

Before the end of the first year the policy covering fare contributions was determined: the emigration and resettlement of an individual refugee was not to depend on his ability to pay for the passage, nor on a sponsor's contribution towards the costs; but the costs or a contribution towards them were to be collected where possible from the sponsor, a voluntary society, or the refugee himself.[3] The payment of contributions by refugees or their sponsors was particularly significant in certain cases because the immigration laws of certain countries barred refugees from entry if passage was paid by IRO.

For the first two months of the second year a proposed shipping schedule showed movements to six or seven different countries on six ships carrying 960 individual migrants. But by January 1949 the actual sailings under this programme for the month involved twenty-two different ships carrying a total of 3,049 individual migrants, 2,733 of whom travelled on three mass movements by IRO chartered vessels; in addition, there were three air flights to Buenos Aires, Quebec, and Mexico carrying six passengers.

For the first eight months of fiscal year 1948–9 a total of 31,400 were resettled under the IRO individual migration scheme, including almost 12,500 transported overseas by the Organization; of these almost 7,400 moved on chartered tonnage and more than 5,100 on commercial vessels. In addition, others were moved by voluntary societies on a reimbursable basis. In the same period eighty-one persons were repatriated individually from overseas.[4]

During the calendar year 1949 the individual migration office handled more than 9,500 individual movements for resettlement and 800 for repatriation on a total of 194 vessels.

Practically all countries maintained a consular representative in Genoa, and during

[1] GC/199/Rev. 1, op. cit.
[2] Ibid., and Provisional Order No. 119, 11 Nov. 1949.
[3] Provisional Order No. 70, 11 May 1948; ibid., No. 701, 8 Nov. 1948.
[4] GC/60, 22 Mar. 1949.

1950 the office was called upon to arrange for more than 200 visas, mostly for Vene-zuela and Argentina; transit visas were also obtained, mostly for movements from Brazil to Paraguay and from France to England, to a total exceeding 500. In March 1950 transfer of embarkation operations from Naples to Bremerhaven had been effected, and the Genoa office was in the future considered as an international move-ments office rather than the individual migration office. But in the calendar year of 1950 this office serviced a total of almost 6,900 individual migrants for resettlement and some 154 for repatriation on a total of 198 vessels.

Costs of individual resettlement which had totalled almost $9 million for the second year of operations had fallen to some $3,600,000 for the third fiscal year, 1949–50.

During the last six months of the calendar year 1950 transportation was arranged for almost 6,700 individual refugees, almost 300 by air; but for the same period a year later the figures had increased to almost 8,500 and 400 respectively.[1] In January 1952, the last month in which these movements were arranged, a total of 438 individual migration passengers were transported, sixty-eight by air.

Reimbursable movements

In the first months of operation the Australian Government had asked the Organization to repatriate 600 prisoners of war from Australia on the return journey of a ship sailing from that country; arrangements had also been made for the picking up of Polish nationals who were repatriating from East Africa, and some 700 were carried at a time by vessels returning from Australia.[2] Resettlement movements in-volved the voyages of filled ships to destinations and of empty ships on the return trip; therefore it was financially desirable that arrangements be made for the paid use of the available space on return voyages.

To arrange such backhauls of both passengers and freight[3] entailed certain diffi-culties. Because there was a certain resistance by Main Conference Lines to new owners on regular trading routes, IRO ships had been classed as emigrant ships, and this made it difficult to divert and to use them for fare-paying passengers. As the result, backhauls of non-refugees were made only from areas with emigrants who could be handled in the same way as refugees, and only upon the request of a government. By agreement, the use of MSTS vessels was restricted to the movement of eligible refugees,[4] except when special approval was given for the unprecedented transport of foreign troops by US military vessels in time of peace.

By November 1947 the British Ministry of Transport had agreed to arrange back-hauls so far as possible, providing the Organization presented a twelve-month sailing schedule; to avoid the dislocation of schedules the Organization, on the other hand, made the condition that backloading must not delay sailings more than forty-eight hours.

By January 1950 the Organization had reached agreement to undertake a back-haul of some 25,000 Dutch troops and dependants from Indonesia to the Nether-lands in ships returning empty from Australia.[5] This movement involved eight

[1] GC/199/Rev. 1.   [2] Ibid.   [3] PREP/161, 5 Jan. 1948.
[4] PREP/209, 30 Apr. 1948.   [5] GC/25, 23 Aug. 1950.

MSTS and eight commercial vessels, and was intended primarily to integrate the backhaul into general movement operations so that all large embarkations of the Organization were shifted, in April 1950, from Italy to Bremerhaven.[1] By the close of 1950 a total of 42,500 Dutch civilians and soldiers had been evacuated from Indonesia;[2] and subsequent smaller carriers brought this total to some 45,000.

Negotiations for the transport of Canadian troops to Europe resulted in the movement of 2,442 officers and men by two voyages of an IRO vessel late in 1951.

At times the US military had lift requirements on return voyages from the US to Europe, as well as on westbound passages and even on voyages requiring temporary diversion of the vessels from their normal routes. In 1951 the policy was established in the US Defence Department to utilize to the maximum all eastbound passages of the five ships regularly in IRO service.[3] Such utilization of MSTS vessels for backhauls and other transportation resulted in substantial savings inasmuch as certain costs that otherwise would accrue to the Organization were borne in whole or part by the US military.[4]

Apart from backhaul transportation, there were other reimbursable movements. The IGCR had granted loans to France for transportation which had been almost entirely reimbursed; later, the IRO had arranged for the transportation to Canada, under the Close Relatives Scheme, of the relatives of refugees who had resettled in that country, obtaining reimbursement of upward of 90 per cent. of expenditures.[5] Before the second year of operations ended, almost 4,000 other refugees had been transported by IRO on a reimbursable basis under the sponsorship of voluntary societies (excluding movements to Israel).[6]

MSTS vessels moved a backhaul of prisoners of war, of Dutch troops and their dependants, refugees from Mombasa, Beirut, Shanghai, Samar, and other places, and in addition, on one occasion, Australian camp equipment from Sydney and Melbourne to Fremantle. IRO employees and their dependants also were moved on the eastward voyages of these ships.[7]

During the first three years of operation the Organization was reimbursed by more than $7½ million for various movements: movements from Australia, $3,700,000; movement of close relatives to Canada, $3½ million; payments by other sponsors, $300,000.

In October 1950 the Organization agreed to handle the transportation of some 45,000 ethnic Germans under the newly amended US Displaced Persons Act, with all transportation costs to be paid by the US Government. This arrangement had the advantage of smoothing out shipping operation and helping towards the maintenance of a refugee fleet.[8]

Organization and administration

In view of the constant changes in both the demand for and the availability of transportation facilities, the Organization's machinery and working procedures for

[1] GC/166, 23 Aug. 1950.   [2] GC/199/Rev. 1, Sept. 1951, op. cit.
[3] Wood, op. cit., Section II.   [4] Ibid., Part I, p. 24.
[5] PREP/SR/48, 28 Oct. 1947.   [6] GC/SR/21, 19 Apr. 1949.
[7] Wood, op. cit., Section I, p. 102.
[8] IRO Press Release No. 193, 6 Oct. 1950. (31/7.)

transportation had to be as flexible as possible. They were planned so that a speedy adaptation to the diverse and complex transportation operations was ensured.

When the Division of Refugee Movements had been in existence for about a year, Geneva headquarters issued a detailed description of this important organizational unit and of its functions.[1] About nine months later the Department of Repatriation and Resettlement was reorganized.[2] The Division of Refugee Movements was dissolved and the newly organized Department included the Divisions of Repatriation, Mass Resettlement, Individual Migration, Shipping, and international movement offices at Bremen and Naples. This change separated land and sea movements, and the new shipping division assumed the clearly defined responsibility for the sea-transportation of refugees.

Subdivisions of the newly created Shipping Division were the port superintendent's branch, shipping control branch, air branch, and legal adviser on sea and air movements; in addition, liaison was maintained with the shipping liaison office in London and with the international movements offices at Grohn near Bremen and Naples.

The principal functions of the port superintendent's branch were the supervision and direction of all technical matters pertaining to the management and operation of ships, the supervision of port activities, the responsibility for escort staff, the inspection of ships, and provision for all professional and technical shipping matters. The shipping control branch planned shipping programmes, maintained current schedules, charted daily positions, and kept a check on the speed of vessels in coordination with the office of port superintendent. The functions of the air branch were the supervision and direction of all matters pertaining to the management and operation of chartered aircraft and the final authority on all matters affecting their departure, arrival, load, and capacity. The legal adviser was given the supervision of all legal aspects of negotiation, preparation, and execution of all commitments for mass air and sea movements.[3]

In addition to the Shipping Division, the other divisions of the reorganized department, too, had certain responsibilities in connexion with the movement of refugees. It was the function of the division of individual migration to initiate and arrange all stages of movements for persons not emigrating on government-sponsored schemes. The division of mass resettlement shared the responsibility with the division of shipping for arranging mass resettlement movement; it was also the duty of the former to arrange all sea and air transportation for mass resettlement movements and, through its traffic office, all overland mass resettlement movements and all other aspects of traffic operations. Responsibility for a complete mass resettlement movement was divided as follows: the division of mass resettlement undertook delivery of the emigrant, fully processed, together with his baggage and documents to the division of shipping at the embarkation point; actual embarkation was carried out by the international movements office; the division of shipping was responsible for moving the emigrant, his baggage and documents from the embarkation point

---

[1] Provisional Order No. 90, 25 Nov. 1948.
[2] Provisional Order No. 114, 27 Aug. 1949; see Chapter XX, Resettlement, p. 370.
[3] Provisional Order No. 177, 15 Oct. 1949.

to the disembarkation point; and, finally, disembarkation was accomplished under the direction of the IRO representatives in the country of destination.[1]

This reorganization indicated, among other things, the development of control technique necessary for the efficient operation of the fleet, the effective planning of transportation movements, and the co-ordination of availability of passengers and of shipping space. Arrangements could now be made so that shipping could be adjusted more readily to the development of resettlement schemes; tentative shipping schedules could be developed several months in advance so that officers responsible for processing and overland movements could take the necessary steps towards filling the vessels or forewarn the shipping office of any necessary reductions.[2]

Vital links in the total transportation operation were the staging and embarkation centres. In the first part of the second year the increasing movement of refugees to port areas accelerated the plans to expand staging centres and develop the capacity of port embarkation centres. It was foreseen that with staging centres working to capacity, many operational problems would be solved. Sizeable backlogs could then be accumulated for major resettlement programmes—in order to simplify the control of the shipping programme and increase its flexibility. Expansion of staging centres made it possible to eliminate overcrowding in resettlement centres and facilitated camp closure plans by accelerating the movement of fully processed emigrants from basic camps to staging centres.

By the spring of 1949 movements for Canada and the US left north German ports, while those for Australia and South America left from Naples; this change was favourable to inland train movements and reduced turn-round time on each voyage meant a considerable saving for the Organization. It was planned, at that time, to increase by 27,000 the existing capacity for 10,000 persons in staging centres.[3]

Although conditions for IRO's operations in and to the port of Naples were unsatisfactory, embarkation of refugees from there was not discontinued before April 1950, when all major embarkation was transferred from Italy to Bremerhaven, and the staging and embarkation centres in Naples were closed. One important objective of the switch to Bremen was to integrate into general shipping operations the backhaul of Dutch troops and their dependants from Indonesia to the Netherlands; another objective was to achieve substantial economies by concentrating movement and shipping operations, and eliminating long and costly train journeys to Italy. By reducing these arduous train journeys this change also benefited the health of refugees.[4]

Continuous negotiations with shipowners and US military authorities were necessary to ensure that chartered space would be available as needed. The movement of USNS, for example, had to be adjusted to requirements for complete review and refit after ninety days of steaming at sea, and a further strict examination at the end of each year, in order to obtain renewal of safety certificates for the carrying of passengers.[5] When the operation of the US ships had reached substantial

[1] Provisional Order No. 125, 12 Dec. 1949.
[2] GC/199/Rev. 1, op. cit.
[3] GC/SR/21, 19 Apr. 1949 and GC/60, 22 Mar. 1949.
[4] GC/166, op. cit., p. 166.   [5] GC/199/Rev. 1, op. cit.

proportions during the third year of operations, it was found advisable to develop, with the military authorities, a formal 'standing operation procedure' to outline in detail all major technical and other aspects of the operation of these ships.[1]

At about the same time a shipping inspector was appointed for the purpose of making short trips on IRO chartered vessels. He briefed escort staff members and made suggestions for the improvement of the passengers' life on board.[2]

Budget and finance

The financial importance of the shipping programme is reflected in the following costs: costs for necessary conversion and repairs and placing on berth of the third vessel to enter the service of the Organization totalled more than $250,000;[3] total costs of placing this and two other ships on berth was $550,000 amortized over a period of six months; daily operating costs of chartered commercial vessels amounted to upward of $5,000 in the early days,[4] and these costs for one MSTS vessel in the calendar year 1948 were estimated at $3,500.

Throughout the entire shipping programme financial matters demanded close attention. In November 1947 the Executive Secretary decided that every effort should be made to provide necessary shipping in spite of the financial risks involved. Accordingly, possibilities were explored for obtaining supplies for care and maintenance on credit, and other methods were studied for releasing funds from this and other programmes for shipping needs.

The creation of the Ocean Transport Fund towards the close of the first year had been an attempt to meet the need for funds and appropriate currencies, but when this plan proved difficult, it was possible to make appropriate currency provisions by other means in certain shipping contracts.

At the end of the second year it proved possible to convert some sterling into kroner to pay for shipping commitments made with Scandinavian countries; but some six months later shipping costs were still charged mainly against dollar and sterling resources. From 1 July 1950 to 30 June 1951 more than 95 per cent. of estimated ocean transportation costs were in US dollars and non-convertible sterling.

Budget allocations for shipping in the second year were in the following currencies: $43,300,000 in dollars, $17½ million in non-convertible sterling, $1,600,000 in Belgian francs, $200,000 in French francs, $900,000 in Italian lire, $50,000 in Canadian dollars. This budgeting accounted for approximately 55 per cent. of total funds allocated to the Organization's plan of expenditure.[5]

Actual ocean mass transportation expenditures for the year, however, were about $43 million and this figure had risen to more than $61 million for the third year. These mass ocean transport expenses of approximately $105 million represented 80 per cent. of the total resettlement costs of $132,700,000. In turn, resettlement and repatriation expenses for the first three years accounted for more than 45 per cent. of all budgeted funds. The Organization had adopted the policy of scaling down

[1] Wood, op. cit., Section I, p. 23.   [2] IRO/SHP/20.
[3] PREP/SR/17, 10 May 1947.   [4] PREP/161, 5 Jan. 1948.
[5] GC/140, 7 Feb. 1950.

commercial dollar charges so far as possible,[1] and when sterling was devalued, on 19 September 1949, total costs during the fiscal year were reduced by several million dollars.

While the shipping budget for the supplementary period (1 July 1950 to 30 September 1951) provided $33,350,000 for the movement of 200,000 refugees, more than $21,200,000 had been spent at the end of 1950, leaving a balance of $12,100,000 for the transportation of almost 111,500 refugees. The main reasons for this disparity were the unforeseen costs of an emergency movement from China to Europe, the accelerated and increased movement to Australia, and the fact that the costs of the special air lift to that country were higher than expected. At the time it was suggested that the Organization might arrange a loan from the UN or from the UN Agent-General for Korea which could be secured by frozen assets in the US Military–IRO shipping programmes. These assets were believed to amount to between $200,000 and $500,000. Another alternative was that the UN Agent-General for Korea might require some ships, and might take over certain MSTS on a reimbursable basis against advance payments.

In all, additional shipping funds of some $10 million were needed to cover this supplementary period and the subsequent months until the final closure. Almost 36,000 more refugees than originally planned for the supplementary period were transported. These funds were provided chiefly by returns from disposal of surplus properties and through the liquidation of various financial reserves which the Organization no longer needed to maintain.

Contractual arrangements for shipping

As early as November 1947 all commercial contracts included a clause permitting sub-letting, should budget appropriation matters make it necessary to do so in later months. Another clause permitted the Organization to cancel contracts, should circumstances arise beyond the control of the owners or the charterers, at a probable loss to the Organization of only the cost of repairs and one month's hire as notice of cancellation. While these and other aspects of the contracts were considered suitable, certain aspects of the contracts were still being questioned, and an American shipping expert, at the beginning of the second year of operations, was asked to review the existing charters.

This expert stated in his report that, with certain exceptions, the charters were in accordance with sound commercial practice. He recommended that all future contracts should be submitted to an Admiralty lawyer and that a shipping expert should be attached to headquarters to provide sound technical advice on shipping contracts.

Consultants also suggested changes in chartering procedures and control of chartered tonnage. At the start, commercial ships were obtained on a time charter basis, and the charterer was responsible for numerous technical details such as bunkering, port charges, canal tolls, victualling, and so forth. This type of charter, requiring administrative and technical staffs, was unsuited to the Organization's operation. A time charter also was potentially costly in the event of delays for which

[1] GC/167, 30 Aug. 1950.

the Organization might be held responsible, and such a charter often entailed disputes and negotiations to fix responsibilities and to settle accounts.

When the American shipping expert was appointed chief of the shipping division in 1949, it was decided to prepare a new type of contract according to which the owner assumed full responsibility for technical details in meeting the standards of the Organization. The contract also provided for a flat daily rate, which covered all costs of running the ships at full passenger capacity. Subsequently, as the shipping market improved, this contract was replaced by yet another type of agreement, known as 'bulk booking note'. This covered single voyages, with the charterer paying a fixed price for the full ship's capacity at a fixed *per capita* cost, while the owner assumed all operational responsibility.[1]

Commercial vessels were usually chartered on resettlement runs from Italian ports to Australia and South America; and, while these included some modern ships with speeds up to almost 20 knots and capacity for 1,500 passengers, others secured by emergency agreements were less desirable, and caused the Organization most of the difficulties it experienced under contractual arrangements. But from the start the Organization was protected by bank guarantees and liens on vessels, as well as hull insurance or off-hire and total loss insurance—which afforded protection against lost operational time or financial losses due to the failure of shipowners to carry out their commitments or to have ships ready for service at given dates.[2]

Despite protective measures, certain contracts made in the earlier days resulted in some financial loss. But such losses, to be expected even in normal shipping transactions, were largely unavoidable in view of the extraordinary circumstances which had prevailed. On the other hand, the devaluation of the pound sterling substantially reduced total operating costs in the third year. This change in currency values necessitated a revision of financial clauses in shipping contracts, but resulted in considerable savings; for example, the cost of a passage to Australia was generally reduced by one-third.

When it became necessary to cancel chartered ships because of surplus shipping, it was often possible to negotiate favourable arrangements with the owners. In December 1949, for example, it was estimated that the cancellation of contracts for five commercial vessels would result in an interim cost to the Organization of some $300,000, but that estimated savings effected by using MSTS instead of the commercial vessels would amount to more than $1,400,000; as a result the Organization achieved a total net saving of about $1,100,000 through the cancellation. Some six months later the Organization decided to terminate all contracts on commercial vessels for mass movements by exercising cancellation options, and by January 1951 the last notices of cancellation had been sent out.

In that month the principles adopted for the negotiation or re-negotiation of commercial shipping contracts stipulated that payments should be made in soft currencies, fares should not be higher than the cost of USNS plus 10 per cent. maximum, that all contracts should have a cancellation clause and no firm commitments should be made after May, and that all commitments beyond $100,000 were to be approved by the director of the department of repatriation and resettlement.

[1] GC/199/Rev. 1, op. cit.   [2] GC/100, op. cit.

Expert and constant vigilance during the last two years or so of operations kept contractual difficulties and losses at a minimum; because of these later efforts many difficulties were avoided which might have resulted from unsatisfactory contractual obligations assumed, often unavoidably, in the earlier stage of operations.

In the chartering of MSTS ships there were no formal agreements, and terms were agreed upon in an exchange of letters. The Organization had decided early that further formalities were neither essential nor desirable. Then, in the second year of operations, the external auditors for the Organization pointed out that such letters did not cover certain important points of principle such as liability in the event of damage to or loss of a ship, and that difficulties might arise in contingencies not covered by a written agreement. Until that time, the Organization had faced the possibility of liabilities in the event of accident or loss to MSTS ships as a calculated risk against which the Organization was self-insured. Then, for almost a year, this question was explored from every possible point of view before it was finally decided to continue the calculated risk. This proved to be a profitable decision and saved the Organization several millions of dollars as the cost of insurance for each MSTS would have been about $78,000 yearly.

The Organization accepted no liability for the death or injury to refugees during or as the result of their transportation, and required all persons in transit to sign a waiver of all rights, claims, or demands against the Organization; the Organization was willing nevertheless to make *ex gratia* payments as desirable in individual cases to refugees who suffered injury while actually in transit, and to nominees of refugees who died as the result of injuries received while actually in transit.[1] For the further protection of refugees the Organization carried commercial insurance policies covering them in the event of a maritime disaster. This insurance applied to a disaster experienced by any one vessel carrying fifty or more refugees at any one time at any place. Under the terms of this insurance only the wage-earner in a refugee family was covered up to the amount of $4,000 for each refugee, up to a total of $4 million for a single disaster. The cost of this insurance was low, and fortunately it was never necessary to claim against it.

As a rule transportation by rail, air, and sea was an integrated operation, with a single movement often involving two and sometimes three means of travel. The procurement of vessels and shipping space was one of the most urgent and most difficult tasks during the entire period of operation, yet the carrying out of actual movements was almost equally demanding.

Transportation by rail

The importance of transport by sea and air overshadows in magnitude, scope, and expense that by rail although the latter is important as a link between other means of transportation. Trains were used to transport most refugees from assembly centres or residences to resettlement centres and to ship-side. Not only was train travel the first stage in virtually all overseas movements, but most inland resettlement and repatriation movements as well were accomplished by rail.

In the three zones of Germany and in Austria the Allied military authorities gave

---

[1] *Operational Manual*, Appendix X, p. 81.

most valuable co-operation and nearly all rail needs were met in these areas by military trains, at no expense to the Organization except for the cost of rations and escort staff. Equal co-operation was received from the Italian State Railways, particularly in providing rolling stock for use on Italian soil which permitted a more rapid and economical turn-round of trains belonging to the occupied zones of Germany; trains were also supplied for destinations as far as north-west Germany and Poland. Their safe return was guaranteed at the start by the Italian Ministry of Foreign Affairs. Certain repayments of costs by refugees (98 per cent. of the costs) were made for rail facilities provided by France and Italy.

At the start of operations, available rolling stock was scarce and generally in very poor condition as the result of the war; much of it was obsolete, damaged, and dirty. To assure a minimum of comfort and well-being in rail travel, the Director of Health recommended in September 1947 minimum standards to be achieved.[1]

There was some early difficulty in obtaining decent rolling stock for use during winter months, but promises for such facilities were fulfilled later and most requirements were ultimately met including those for special dining cars and ambulance coaches.

Apart from rail movements within a country, there was considerable railway travel from country to country in Europe. Because of difficulties of transit through the Russian zone of Germany it became necessary to route trains to other countries such as Czechoslovakia.[2] An average of twenty-seven special trains monthly was maintained for the entire year of 1947–8; of these the Allied military authorities provided an average of seventeen trains monthly for repatriation movements to eastern Europe and for resettlement to staging centres and ports; in addition, the Organization chartered an average of ten international trains monthly for resettlement movement to western Europe.

In the early months the Polish Government supplied five trains varying in capacity from 350 to 700 each, chiefly for the repatriation of Poles from East Africa through Italy and for the repatriation of Polish nationals in Germany who were ill and for whom special train facilities had to be provided. These special trains and hospital trains often comprised as many as forty-five coaches with crews of thirty-five persons including medical and technical railway staff. As repatriation movements slackened the need for these trains decreased. By the spring of 1948 the Polish Government was providing only one train for permanent use.[3]

In Germany rail transportation was largely without cost for IRO. In the US zone the Organization assumed responsibility for rail transportation with the full co-operation of the Occupation Authorities who took steps to ensure that facilities were adequate and satisfactory. The Occupation Authorities in the British and the French zones were responsible for actual movements, with the Organization serving largely as a co-ordinator; in January 1951, however, the IRO assumed responsibility for rail transportation in the British zone.

In Italy freight vans had to be used because a serious shortage of rolling stock existed to the end of 1948. Special trains for Bremen, for the major rail movements

---

[1] GC/199/Rev. 1.　　　　　　　　　　　　　[2] PREP/SL/49, 27 Oct. 1947.
[3] PREP/209, 5 May 1948.

　　　　　　　　　H h

from Italy, were composed at specially reduced rates by the railway authorities on forty-eight hours' notice for a minimum of 350 passengers. For individual movements, the Organization made formal requests to the Italian State Railways to issue a ticket in the name of an individual traveller. Ticket inspectors demanded identification of persons holding tickets marked 'Transport IRO', as was the case for Italian citizens obtaining concessions. Because of that country's determination that people in transit should not remain in Italy, authorities later took extreme precautions in mass movements to Italy by maintaining better guards, finger-printing travellers, and issuing to them special identification cards.

In Austria, at first, only freight vans were available. In February 1948, however, the Minister of the Interior and the Federal Railways approved the release of ten miscellaneous cars to the Organization. The IRO made up its own trains in this way, which were used by IRO only and ran on special train schedules arranged with foreign railway administrators. Major runs of these trains were to Bremen, Turin, Genoa, Naples, and Senegallia up to May 1950. By June of that year only one of the trains was still in operation; it left regularly every Thursday for Bremen, making its last trip on 24 January 1952 carrying 1,001 persons. Then the train which bore the insignia of the IRO was turned over to the Austrian authorities for transportation of *Volksdeutsche* going to the US and for refugees leaving on resettlement plans after the closure of operations. A grand total of more than 147,000 were moved from Austria, 95,000 of whom travelled on IRO trains.

Apart from basic logistical problems, rail movements had been relatively uncomplicated up to the end of 1949, with the exception of a difficulty in early repatriation movements to Berlin in military trains. But then an excessive amount of illness during transportation to Australia led to an investigation of both overland and sea transportation arrangements and steps were taken for improving conditions. The corrective measures combined with increased movement of aged and incapacitated refugees on hard core schemes made rail movements more difficult than they had been earlier.

Train movements to fill chartered ships and aircraft to capacity at scheduled departure times was a very complex operation, the more so as 50–60 special trains per month moved between various processing centres, staging areas, and embarkation camps. The operation of these trains involved the allocation of rolling stock, setting up of watering points, and halts for meals, provision of food supplies, and medical escort staff, and, at the same time, maintenance of an intricate and flexible schedule to meet constantly changing shipping availability and the limited capacities of embarkation centres.

Transportation by air

The Organization also used air travel extensively, and at times explored the possibility of an even greater use. The numbers of refugees, however, moved by air constituted only a small percentage of total overseas transportation. More than 35,000 persons were flown to Australia, Canada, the US, South America, and a variety of other overseas destinations. Air flights were resorted to at times to speed up the reception of refugees in certain countries, but were chiefly reserved for refugees who could be transported by air most comfortably and most suitably from the point of view of health: the aged and the ill, children under 6 months of age; women who on the day of embarkation would have passed the sixth month of pregnancy, and children under 3 years of age for whom sea travel to Australia during the hot summer months was discontinued. To avoid the separating of families, close relatives of these persons were also transported by air. The baggage of air travellers followed by boat, a reason why many refugees resisted air travel.

On 23 July 1947 the first aircraft under contract to the Organization arrived at Caracas with nineteen mothers, one female escort, and twenty-four infants and children aboard. Substantial movements by air, however, did not begin until May of the following year, when it soon increased in importance.

The Organization entered into special arrangements for a movement of some 2,400 refugees to the US with Youth Argosy, Inc., an educational and non-profit-making organization arranging world-wide travel opportunities for student groups. This organization had contracted to fly some 2,400 students eastward to Europe, and the return westbound spaces were to be used by the Organization, thus providing a balanced trip for the air carriers. The IRO, on the other hand, provided chartered shipping space for westbound returning students. Under this arrangement some fifty flights of refugees took place, leaving from the British and US zones of Austria and Germany. Most of the passengers were compassionate cases (pregnant women, infants, orphans, the aged, and the unfit) with lower priority than given to agency-sponsored cases, and lastly, persons not sponsored by voluntary agencies.

MSTS vessels did not usually accept more than forty infants per ship, and since this figure was often insufficient to deal with the high percentage of infants among families emigrating to South America, aircraft proved a particularly helpful means of transportation for such trips. In less than eight months of the first year's operation the air organization had accomplished an air lift of some 5,500 people.

During the entire second year the Organization had transported by air a total of more than 9,400 persons, mostly compassionate cases, to Canada, the US, Brazil, Venezuela, and Morocco. From Munich alone more than 7,900 persons were flown to new homes during a period of somewhat more than a year up to September 1949; including 80 flights to Venezuela, 8 to Morocco, 30 to Canada, and 65 to the US.

At the beginning of the third year (1949–50), the US Displaced Persons Commission urged continuation of the air lift for compassionate cases. Such flights were maintained between Germany (from Munich and Bremen) and the US, carrying more than 7,500 refugees in a total of 104 flights. In addition there were three chartered flights from Italy to Australia and from Samar to Australia and Paraguay. Individual migrants were also booked on a large number of the air routes to various otherwise inaccessible destinations.[1]

By August 1950 difficulties of obtaining air-space were foreseen. The three non-scheduled carriers formerly used for compassionate air lifts from Europe to the US were taken back by the US defence forces for the Korean lift after providing a few flights only, and efforts to obtain space from American scheduled carriers at satisfactory rates were unsuccessful. Nevertheless, in the first six months of the

[1] GC/166, 23 Aug. 1950, p. 25.

fourth year nearly 3,300 refugees were carried by chartered planes to Australia and to the US, and arrangements were made for an additional 300 individual migrants. During this period the Organization arranged for fifteen extra air flights to Australia to meet the wishes of the Australian Government in speeding up early reception, which was difficult to arrange at short notice. When these additional air lifts had been completed total air flights to Australia had carried almost 1,700 passengers in twenty-nine flights by December 1950. While the *per capita* cost of the special air lift of some 1,000 refugees to Australia had been budgeted at some $300, the actual cost was more than twice that amount.

At the start of the final six months' period of operation there had been an acute shortage of aircraft for several months, but the Organization was able to charter planes by which, up to 31 December 1951, almost 4,500 persons were carried to the US and Canada. In this final period air transportation was also provided for nearly 400 individual migrants.

While throughout the entire air transportation programme mishaps, problems, and difficulties were unavoidable, they were fortunately of a minor character and did not blur the outstandingly successful contribution of air transportation to the total air movement of more than 35,000 persons to Australia, Canada, the US, South America, and a variety of other overseas destinations.

Importance of the Transport Operations

The magnitude and scope of the whole transportation operation are indicated by the fact that during the period from 30 June 1947 to 31 January 1952 the Organization completely accomplished or materially aided the resettlement of more than 1,049,500 refugees and the repatriation of an additional 72,850. Each of these types of movements originated in some thirty IRO areas of departure and were made to some fifty countries of destination.

During the life of the IRO more than 436,000 refugees, including those transported by vessels of the US Maritime Commission, were carried under arrangements made between the IRO and the appropriate US governmental agencies, more than 260,000 of them in the supplementary and closure period of only nineteen months. In addition almost 2,600 had been transported under similar arrangements made by the IGCR before the Organization began to operate; and beyond these movements US military ships transported 400 prisoners of war, 3,000 displaced persons on backhauls and special voyages, and more than 20,000 Dutch troops and dependants from Indonesia to the Netherlands.[1]

US military transports made the greatest contribution towards the success of the IRO's shipping activities and produced positive results in regard to economy, safety, professional management, high sanitation and health standards, and reliability. On the other hand, the use by the IRO of vessels temporarily not in military demand was advantageous to the US Department of Defence, for it ensured that the ships could be returned to military control at short notice—fully crewed, stocked, and in operational condition. Otherwise the vessels would have had to be

[1] Wood, op. cit., Section II, p. 6.

decommissioned and stripped, and crews released, which would have resulted in higher costs and greater depreciation of the ships.[1]

The final record proved that the MSTS shipping arrangement was the best and the cheapest possible. While a variety of conditions tended to make the immigration of refugees more costly than normal international migration, the overall costs on MSTS vessels ranged from slightly more than $100 *per capita* to Canada and the US, to almost $350 *per capita* to Australia; *per capita* costs to Chile amounted to almost $250, whereas costs to other South American countries except Peru were substantially lower.[2]

The use of US military vessels brought about various savings: government-operated vessels paid no insurance or bare boat charter fees, a saving of approximately $900 daily; transportation agents aboard the ships were competent to save much of the normal expenditure of $2,500 in agents' fees in foreign ports; in the majority of foreign ports government vessels were not charged port entry fees; planned army menus effected substantial savings in food costs, and advantage was taken of the large army purchasing contracts for subsistence; and special maintenance and repair facilities in ports ensured a short turn-round of the vessels. Also the use of an army vessel with an army representative on board reduced the usual cost of about $7,000 paid to civilian agents for a typical three-day turn-round to less than $200.

In the second year of operation it developed that the provision of additional nests of lifeboats, at a cost of some $75,000 per ship, made it possible to increase the average passenger list of each by some 400 passengers; in this way the already low *per capita* costs of movements on these vessels was substantially decreased. The use of appropriate passengers for certain shipboard duties not only reduced costs and crews directly, but also permitted a larger number of refugees to be carried on each ship. In addition to the considerable savings realized from the backhauls of passengers, the IRO saved more than $137,000 by moving IRO cargo from the US to Bremerhaven on US military vessels. During the operations of the Organization it received $8–9 million in refunds and payments for sublet shipping. Other important savings were the policy of self-insurance and the unforeseen advantages deriving from the devaluation of sterling.

Financially the sea transportation programme of the Organization was one involving large expenditures for which most excellent value was generally realized. Even more important from a humanitarian point of view was the fact that this vast movement by sea was successfully carried out without any disaster or catastrophy.

When the IRO–MSTS programme came to an end with the last sailing in January 1952, five vessels having accomplished debarkation of refugees in the US were transferred to the Provisional Intergovernmental Committee for the Movement of Migrants from Europe (PICMME) on the day after their arrival.

In carrying out what was probably the greatest organized transoceanic exodus in history, the IRO not only achieved complete success as far as the total numbers transported, economy, and savings were concerned, but also established precedents

---

[1] Ibid., p. 28.
[2] See Annex 44, Overseas Transportation of Refugees (by fiscal year), p. 470, and Annex 45, Costs and Numbers moved in USMTs, p. 471.

and developed methods of great interest and value to any future sea transportation of a similar nature.

The flexibility which the programme achieved was the key to the great attainment of the migration operation, which could operate efficiently and at low costs only as it carried out simultaneously and co-ordinated a number of different migration plans. The MSTS shipping programme, the first large scale use of government-owned military vessels for other than strictly military purposes in time of peace, resulted in an all-round benefit not only to the Organization but also to the army, and established a new pattern for the use of such vessels in peace-time on secondary missions undertaken in connexion with endeavours of international or national interest and importance.

ANNEX 44

Overseas transportation of refugees (by fiscal year 1 July to 30 June)

Country of destination	Total	1947–8	1948–9	1949–50	1950–1	1951–2 (7 months)
1. US . . .	338,144	17,245	51,134	124,533	89,913	55,319
2. Australia . .	182,212	5,702	48,923	90,774	31,876	4,937
3. Canada . .	123,738	25,313	40,710	19,993	21,125	16,597
4. Latin America .	100,465	29,097	42,354	12,596	10,049	6,369
Transported overseas chiefly by IRO arrangements . .	744,559	77,357	183,121	247,896	152,963	83,222
Transported inland or overseas to other countries chiefly by non-IRO shipping arrangements .	304,978*	131,321	140,036	16,469	13,086	4,066
TOTAL RESETTLED . .	1,049,537	208,678	323,157	264,365	166,049	87,288

* Includes more than 158,000 resettled to European countries and 122,000 resettled to Israel.

ANNEX 45

Average per capita and total net operational and overall costs and numbers moved in US military transports* (May 1947 to February 1952)

Movement	Numbers moved	Per capita costs net operational†	Per capita costs overall‡
Europe to:		$	$
Argentine	10,784	176·15	191·50
Australia	44,187	315·47	340·75
Brazil	16,623	145·06	157·70
Canada	37,868	93·25	101·38
Chile	2,618	227·96	247·82
Paraguay	882	165·79	180·23
Peru	1,563	207·23	225·29
Boston or New York . . .	271,805	103·62	112·65
New Orleans	27,129	145·06	157·70
Venezuela	7,315	124·34	135·17
Total	420,774§	$55,857,238·63	$60,627,262·65
Samar to:			
San Francisco	2,223	155·42	168·97
Naples	442	259·04	281·61
Total	2,665	$460,003·18	$500,889·70
New York to:			
Bremerhaven	106	103·62	112·65
Naples	486	124·34	135·17
Total	592	$71,412·13	$77,635·28
Grand Total	424,031	$56,388,653·94‖	$61,204,987·62‖

* Submitted by Major-General W. A. Wood, Washington, DC.

† Net operational costs are overall water transport costs except for the IRO escort and staff wages and Bremerhaven Port Charges paid for in DM less initial repairs and conversion costs.

‡ Overall costs include all costs attributable to the water transportation provided in USMTs to include cost of operations, maintenance, initial repairs, conversion and termination costs, customs, pilot, public health, post exchange, and port charges, but exclude port charges at Bremerhaven paid in DM and wages of IRO escort staff.

§ Includes 2,581 (1,722 to Brazil, 859 to Venezuela) moved by IGCR. Excludes 18,048 (9,871 to Canada, 8,177 to the US) moved by IRO on USMC vessels operated by US lines for the IRO.

‖

Total paid by IGCR and IRO . . .	$64,099,037[1]
Revenues paid IRO	2,894,043[2]
Net overall cost	$61,204,994[3]
Initial repairs and conversion and liquidation .	4,816,340
Net operational cost	$56,388,654

[1] Includes $250,000 estimated final liquidation liability on termination of programme.

[2] Comprises $2,697,930·00 paid to the IRO by Dutch Government for Dutch troop lift.
    894·76 paid by Dutch for lost US property.
    188,330·00 paid IRO by Australia for POW lift.
    6,888·00 paid IRO by British for POW lift.

  $2,894,042·76 Total revenues.

[3] Includes approximately $1,120,000 Suez tolls for forty round trips through canal.

CHAPTER XXII

LOCAL SETTLEMENT

THROUGHOUT its period of operations IRO made every possible effort to provide emigration, resettlement, and re-establishment possibilities in other countries for those individuals or family units who did not want to repatriate or could not do so. When the receiving countries gradually liberalized their immigration policies, the Organization succeeded in resettling large numbers of migrants. But at no time was resettlement considered the only solution, and from the beginning the Constitution contained a provision for 're-establishment in countries of temporary residence'. In fact it became apparent by the summer of 1948 that many refugees desiring resettlement were unable to fulfil the requirements of the countries of immigration or, for one reason or another, could not meet the criteria which the selection teams had to apply. A group of 'rejects' developed and this was an anxiety for the IRO. As a short-lived organization IRO was faced with the grave situation of having a residuum of refugees and displaced persons within their mandate who were in danger of being left behind as undesirables in places where no care would be available to them once the IRO had ceased to exist. This was a matter of serious concern to the General Council and the Executive, and it was brought up for discussion at many sessions, from the very first session onwards. Solutions to this formidable problem were found under the vigorous and imaginative leadership of the Director General, Mr. J. Donald Kingsley, supported by governments and voluntary agencies.

When hostilities ended in May 1945 a number of refugees were found to be well on their way to being absorbed in their respective country of first asylum. In recommending such local settlement PCIRO had in mind the kind of work that had already been successfully undertaken in Belgium, France, the Netherlands, and the UK.[1]

Some refugees remained in the country of refuge and never called upon the services of an international organization as they were able to adapt themselves to conditions as they found them. Others, impatient and disappointed because of the long periods of waiting and delay in connexion with resettlement, left the assembly centres and/or relinquished their refugee status and began to make their way into the local economy of the country in which they happened to be living. The latter, though relying chiefly on their own initiative, sometimes submitted their problems to the Organization in order to obtain some kind of assistance while they were in the process of local integration. Their establishment in the country of refuge, called 'local settlement', was comparable to individual migration, for it depended mainly on the efforts of the refugees themselves, while the Organization was more concerned with individual case work. The IRO welcomed and strongly supported the initiative of these individuals, but it soon became apparent that the Organization had to plan for and to give financial support to larger groups of other individuals

---

[1] PCIRO, First Session, Second Part (PREP/84, 20 May 1947, p. 2).

who had no chance to emigrate yet had no opportunity to help themselves. Neither repatriation nor resettlement could be looked upon as final solutions of IRO's task. If this task was ever to be completed systematic planning for local settlement of larger numbers had to be included in the work. The impending closure of the IRO caused these plans to become urgent, and they involved a transfer of responsibilities to national governments.

As has been stated, the General Council during its Second and Third Sessions in May and July 1949 was concerned with the termination of the IRO programme. It outlined further operations and came to decisions in regard to the orderly termination of IRO's activities. Date-lines were set up fixing a last possible time for accepting applications for assistance or services from IRO (1 October 1949); for admission to care and maintenance (31 March 1950); and for the termination of the care and maintenance programme. Resettlement activities were to be speeded up, and refugees who registered for IRO care or services were required to choose a specific form of re-establishment by 31 December 1949 at the latest.[1]

In July 1949 the General Council set 30 June 1950 as the final date for the transfer of responsibility to the national governments for care and maintenance of refugees, except for those who were already in the process of being resettled or repatriated, for those who required permanent assistance such as institutional care, and for unaccompanied children. Simultaneously the Administration was to make plans for this group who needed permanent assistance, and who were called the 'hard core'.

The decision taken by the General Council in regard to the termination of the IRO operations projected the programme of local establishment into the foreground of the Organization's activity; and, with the completion of the counselling programme, the particular groups involved were classified so that definite arrangements could be made for their final care.

Because of this close connexion between the closure of the IRO's operations and the efforts towards a final absorption of the residual groups in the countries of first refuge, arrangements had to be made for a continuation of protection and for maintenance after 30 June 1950, at the expense of the respective national governments, of those persons who had so far been maintained at the joint expense of governments through their contributions to the IRO. As this transfer of responsibility made necessary financial and other adjustments, the Director General and the Deputy Director General negotiated with various European governments concerning the future activities of the IRO in their countries, and the questions of contribution, 'hard core', protection, and welfare services.

The transfer of responsibility for the maintenance of refugees needing assistance presented no major difficulty in western European countries where negotiations were carried out under the most favourable conditions. These countries again showed their willingness to make arrangements to assist those refugees who, in the majority, belonged to the residual group, but who differed from members of the residual group in Germany and Austria in that, in the main, they wanted to stay where they were while nearly all those in Germany and Austria wished to leave.

GC/W/3; GC/80, 9 May 1949, and GC/242, 23 Oct. 1951, and GC/Res. 36 and 39, Appendix III, pp. 724 and 725.

France, Belgium, Luxembourg, the Netherlands, and Switzerland by agreement with IRO undertook to accept responsibility for their care and maintenance on 1 July 1950; in Denmark the transfer of such cases was effected on 31 March 1951. To assist the governments in meeting expenses during the period of transition the Organization returned to them a portion of their earlier contributions.

France

Of all the western European countries France had the largest share of refugees settled 'sur place'. As of 30 June 1950 a total of 24,693 refugees in France received care and maintenance from IRO, including 260 persons in French North Africa. IRO's responsibilities for the care and maintenance of refugees in France, including institutional care for those requiring it, were transferred to the Government as of 1 July 1950, in accordance with an Agreement between the French Government and the IRO signed on 28 February 1950. Under the terms of this Agreement the French Government assisted needy refugees, while IRO returned a considerable portion of the French Government's contribution to the IRO to cover those expenses which had hitherto been met by IRO through the medium of voluntary societies. These activities were to be delegated to the SSAE (Service Social d'Aide aux Émigrants). The French Government was to take over the legal and political protection of refugees and, on 29 November 1950, the Government introduced a draft law 'to create a French Office for the Protection of Refugees and Stateless Aliens' (Office Français de Protection des Réfugiés et Apatrides). Since the Bill did not become law until July 1952, the French Government requested IRO to review the basic agreement of 13 January 1948 on a month to month basis. IRO continued, therefore, to be responsible for protection until the end of its work in France. According to IRO statistics for the period from 1 July 1947 to 31 December 1951 a total of 224,890 refugees had registered with and had been assisted by the Organization in France. Of these 32,080 were resettled in other countries or were repatriated (764); the remaining 192,710 refugees were still in Metropolitan France, 181,110 of whom received legal and political protection only.[1]

The UK

In the United Kingdom the Government had always regarded the displaced persons brought to the country as being permanently settled under the various resettlement schemes already described. On 11 November 1948, in the House of Commons, the Minister of Labour, referring to the 'Westward Ho!' scheme, stated that this settlement was permanent in character and that these people had come to the country 'working their passage to British citizenship'.[2]

No material or financial assistance had been given by the IRO in the UK to persons within its mandate. Since, as a general rule, refugees enjoyed in that country the same rights as other aliens, and their interests were carefully guarded by the competent government departments, the only assistance given by the IRO

[1] Cf. Summary of IRO Statistics, Annex 17, p. 186. Refugee statistics in France were not standardized. See Vernant, op. cit., p. 282.

[2] Report by the Chief of Mission, IRO, London, on 'Operations in the UK on Behalf of Refugees and Displaced Persons' (1 July 1947 to 30 June 1950), p. 17. MR/3/51.

was advice and information concerning repatriation, resettlement, and the legal rights which a refugee could obtain in the country.

Austria, Germany, and Italy

It was much more difficult for the IRO to work out acceptable local establishment programmes in Austria, Germany, and Italy. Austria, burdened with a large population of German refugees, laboured under poor economic conditions which were aggravated by a diminishing chance of ending its division into four occupied zones. Germany was faced with widespread unemployment and a considerable housing shortage which was intensified by the presence of large numbers of German refugees. The tension separating the German population from the non-German refugees presented a severe obstacle to a local settlement programme. Italy, because of demographic and financial difficulties, had frankly advocated the removal of all refugees from the country.

Even during the preliminary planning period, therefore, a distinction was made between 'desirable' and 'undesirable' countries for local settlement. In these latter countries IRO made every effort to use local settlement as a last resort only, and to do everything in its power to facilitate resettlement of as many refugees as possible before winding up its operations. On the other hand, in December 1949, the Director General stated, in a message to the chiefs of field offices that many thousands of refugees in Germany, Austria, and some in Italy had no opportunity for overseas settlement, and that IRO was compelled to deal with the problems of local establishment. A positive programme to be put into operation progressively was needed, he pointed out, in order to help the refugees by securing their status with the local authorities and by providing necessary clothing and household equipment.[1]

Subsequently, in accordance with the General Council resolution of 22 March 1950,[2] the Executive gave 'a liberal interpretation' of the 'pipe-line'[3] on the basis of 'reasonably predictable resettlement opportunities' and, at the same time, tried to make the most satisfactory arrangements with the Allied High Commissioners for those refugees who would have no choice but to stay in Germany after the termination of IRO. The interpretation of the 'pipe-line' was not the same in the various zones. A broad interpretation applied in the French and US zones was based on an agreement concluded with the respective occupying authorities. All refugees considered eligible for resettlement were maintained in those zones by IRO, in camps or under cash assistance, until their final resettlement. In the British zone, mainly because of an acute shortage of accommodation, it was agreed with the British High Commissioner to establish as a ceiling for the 'pipe-line' 24,000 at any given time.[4]

According to GC Resolution 39 and on the basis of further instructions[5] from the General Council, the Director General conducted negotiations with the Allied High Commission both regarding the status of residual cases in Germany and the actual transfer of residual camps to the local authorities.

[1] IRO/FM/22, 21 Jan. 1950: Summary Records of the Conference of Chiefs of Field Offices, Geneva, 12–17 Dec. 1949.   [2] GC/Res. 64, Appendix III, p. 737.
[3] Cf. 347.   [4] GC/166, p. 29.
[5] GC/Res. 63 of the Fifth Session, Appendix III, p. 736.

The Allied High Commission agreed with the suggestions of the General Council that the German Federal Government should be induced to safeguard the rights of refugees and displaced persons on its territory. The Commission, in a letter of 10 February 1950, informed the Chancellor of the Federal Republic of Germany that, as from 30 June 1950, all refugees and displaced persons other than those in process of repatriation or resettlement would become the responsibility of the Federal Government, both financially and administratively, subject to the overriding powers reserved to the Allied High Commission, and requested that the Federal Government should undertake the enactment of suitable legislation defining the legal, political, social, and economic status of such persons.

Subsequently, the Federal Government of Germany guaranteed the refugees the rights referred to in Articles 1–19 of the Basic Law of the Federal Republic, and assured them that every provision would be given for their integration into the German community. Later these assurances were laid down in the Law on Homeless Foreigners of 25 April 1951. This Law followed the main provisions of the UN Convention Relating to the Status of Refugees which had been signed in July 1951.[1] It should be mentioned that the Federal Government was one of the first governments to ratify this Convention.

In the actual transfer of residual camps to the local authorities, these authorities and the German Federal Government co-operated fully to ensure the maintenance of standards of care for those refugees who became their responsibility.

Although the transfer of care and maintenance responsibilities was to become effective on 1 July 1950, arrangements were made so that this transfer could take place gradually, and in such a way that by 1 July 1950 all residual cases would already have been transferred to the German authorities. In principle an effort was made to bring the residual cases together in special centres where living conditions were satisfactory, and to arrange that those centres were situated in areas where the chances of finding employment were favourable.

The conditions in which the transfer was carried out varied from one zone to another and, within each zone, from one *Land* to another.

In the US zone of Germany the transfer was carried out in consultation with the occupation authorities and with German officials. All institutional 'hard core' cases and their dependants, unaccompanied children, and all refugees with prospects of resettlement were excluded from the plan and remained under the IRO's administration. The actual transfer of the residual group was concluded smoothly; the German authorities provided the refugees with identity cards, arranged for housing, and placed the unemployed on welfare lists as persons eligible for public assistance. Naturally, opportunities for the employment of refugees were seriously limited by the widespread unemployment in Germany which affected all classes of the population.

In the British zone the transfer was based on a different principle, but was similar in practice. The administrative responsibility was transferred from the British authorities to the German, the IRO ceasing to pay except for persons in process of resettlement, the phrase being strictly interpreted so as not to include all those with

---

[1] Cf. Chapter XVII, Legal and Political Protection, p. 327.

chances of resettlement. The aim in the British zone as elsewhere was to provide individual private accommodation for refugees wherever possible so as to encourage their integration into the life of the normal community. A particularly good example of the possibilities of this method was a project instituted in the British zone. With the encouragement of the British Land Commissioner, the German authorities undertook to provide individual houses for 1,000 refugee families including 4,500 persons, the entire cost to be borne by the *Land* government. At the time of the transfer from IRO's responsibility, refugees were given an allocation of furniture and household goods. All these arrangements for the transfer of responsibilities in the British zone of Germany to the Federal authorities were initiated, planned, and executed by the British authorities.

In the French zone, too, the transfer of responsibility for the administration of centres was shared by the occupation and the German authorities. But as the majority of refugees in the French zone had always lived privately the task was much smaller. As was the case in the US zone, however, the IRO in the French zone remained financially responsible for persons with chances of resettlement.

In an effort to provide further assistance to the residual group and to enable some of these people to become self-supporting, the IRO, in co-operation with the Allied High Commissions, negotiated an agreement with the Expellee Bank in Germany whereby a Displaced Persons Fund was established to grant loans to eligible refugees to help them to establish or expand small businesses. An initial payment of $1\frac{1}{2}$ million DM was made by the IRO to start the fund with the understanding that the IRO might, if it so decided, make a further payment of 1 million DM at a later date.

In order further to help the process of integration, the Organization made arrangements with the NCWC, the LWF, and the WCC, whereby those voluntary societies were to assist refugees with their personal difficulties and were also to co-operate in long-term plans for the residual group. This was done through the respective German counterpart agencies of these societies—Caritas, Innere Mission, and the Evangelisches Hilfswerk. The welfare workers of these societies were sufficiently familiar with the resources available in Germany to assist each family individually and to help each of them to make the best possible long-term re-establishment plan.

In Austria the actual transfer of responsibility for the residual group took place on 1 July 1950 according to a schedule which varied in the three zones. In the French zone of Austria the French authorities continued to administer the camps for the residual group, but the Organization ceased to be financially responsible. In the British zone the British authorities gradually transferred to the Austrian authorities the responsibility for finance, administration, and supervision of the centres, whose conditions were improved in order to convert them into settlements. In the US zone the IRO transferred to the US High Commissioner responsibility for the care and maintenance of all refugees in the IRO's installations, except those in a resettlement transit centre, in medical rehabilitation centres, hospitals and institutions for the chronic sick and aged, and in a children's home. All refugees were provided with a three months' issue of supplementary food, clothing, and amenity supplies before their transfer occurred. Children in vulnerable age groups continued to receive supplementary food from UNICEF on the same basis as other children in Austria.

In general the problem of integrating the residual group in Austria was the same as in Germany; but the housing shortage and unemployment were more serious, and consequently most of the refugees of the residual group were in need of outside assistance.

As has been mentioned previously, provision was made for refugees to obtain residence permits for an indeterminate period; but in actual practice they found it extremely difficult to do so. In principle this permit, when obtained, entitled the holder to seek employment; but employment was only available to a refugee if the vacancy could not be filled by an Austrian worker. The right to public relief benefits was dependent upon the right to work. The Austrian Government later signed the Convention on the Status of Refugees, but with reservations regarding those articles dealing with the right to remunerative employment and public relief.[1]

As a result of these conditions, refugees in Austria were in a most unsatisfactory position. Nor could anything be done about it, for local settlement implied the integration of refugees into the Austrian community. The transfer of assembly centres to the Austrian administration caused the deterioration of many of them, as funds for their upkeep were inadequate; similarly, the amount and standard of food available to refugees was reduced, and the public assistance without supplements was admittedly inadequate to support normal life. But in both respects the position of other refugees (such as the *Volksdeutsche*) for whose welfare the Austrian Government was responsible and of unemployed Austrian citizens was substantially the same.

In planning the termination of the Organization's programme in Italy, the General Council had advised the Director General[2] 'to take into account to the greatest possible extent the special situation of Italy when implementing the Organization's resettlement policies'. Therefore, because of Italy's extremely difficult economic and financial problems, the Organization continued after 30 June 1950 to provide care and maintenance for all refugees under its mandate in that country.

According to an agreement reached in November 1950, however, Italy agreed to accept responsibility for a maximum of 9,500 (including 1,000 institutional 'hard core' cases) residual refugees either by maintaining them in camps or by providing out-of-camp cash assistance. The Organization agreed at the same time to move 20,000 refugees out of Italy if that number was found to require resettlement assistance and the individuals could meet existing selection criteria.

By 1 July 1950 the case-load of IRO was considerably diminished. Its efforts to settle refugees locally in countries of first refuge had brought more than 110,000 refugees under the responsibility of the local authorities of western Europe, Germany, and Austria, among them 65,615 persons classified as those 'with limited opportunities' for resettlement. Nearly 40,000 of these persons were still in Germany, approximately 7,500 in Austria, over 7,000 in Italy, and 4,900 in France. Those refugees who were 'potentially resettleable' but transferred to local administrations

---

[1] GC/229/Rev. 1, 9 Oct. 1951. [2] GC/Res. 66, 22 Mar. 1950.

were assured that they had not lost their chance of being resettled, and that—if they should have any opportunity for emigration later—they would be returned to the resettlement 'pipe-line' (in processing, staging, and embarkation centres). There were approximately 137,000 other refugees, either still in the 'pipe-line' or belonging to the institutional hard core and residual non-institutional group, who continued to receive care and maintenance from the Organization.

ANNEX 46

Refugees with limited opportunities for resettlement

	30 June 1950	1 July 1950
TOTAL	65,615	65,615
Care and maintenance	51,811	14,453*
1. Central European countries:		
Austria	4,563	800
Germany:		
British zone	12,085	700
French zone	2,736	200
US zone	15,242	1,000
Italy	6,593	6,593
2. Western European countries:		
Belgium	243	..
Denmark	503	503
France	4,905	..
Greece	148	148
Luxembourg	24	
Netherlands	20	..
Portugal	14	14
Spain	8	8
3. Middle East:		
East Africa	1,146	906
Lebanon	624	624
Syria	68	68
Turkey	13	13
4. Far East:		
Shanghai	849	849
Philippines	2,027	2,027
Registered but not receiving care and maintenance	13,804	51,162
1. Central European countries:		
Austria	2,937	6,700
Germany:		
British zone	1,938	13,323
French zone	2,304	4,840
US zone	5,685	19,927
Italy	729	729
2. Western European countries:		
Belgium	..	243
Denmark	..	..
France	..	4,905
Greece	100	100
Luxembourg	..	24
Netherlands	..	20
Portugal	1	1
Spain	..	..
3. Middle East:		
East Africa	..	240
Lebanon	4	4
Syria	1	1
Turkey	1	1
4. Far East:		
Shanghai	104	104
Philippines	..	..

* Includes persons in medical rehabilitation centres:

Austria	. .	800
Germany:		
British zone	.	700
French zone	.	200
US zone	.	1,000
Italy	. .	450
		3,150

CHAPTER XXIII

THE HARD CORE[1]

A T the time the establishment of IRO was in the planning stage it had never been the intention of the representatives of the UN to make the Organization a permanent custodian of the sick and destitute and other groups belonging to the 'hard core'. However, at the Third Session of the General Council the Director General emphasized his belief that the Organization had the responsibility to find a solution for the problems of the persons under its care prior to the time it would cease operating.[2] Whenever it would prove impossible to find an immediate solution, it should at least, he suggested, do its best to plan for the future of those persons who could not be satisfactorily re-established. It was essential to make specific plans for the people constituting the hard core lest they had to look forward to a hopeless existence.

A 'working group' composed of members of headquarters staff and representatives of voluntary societies was established in Geneva by the Administration. On the basis of information from the operational areas and personal experience of several of its members in resettlement matters, this commission drew up a list of possible handicaps of refugees which might diminish their chance of being accepted by a selection board. The chief deterrents mentioned were adverse health conditions, advanced age (i.e. unattached men over 45 or unattached women over 40), family composition (i.e. widows and unmarried mothers with young children, or other family groups with little prospect of self-support), difficulty or impossibility of procuring adequate documents regarding nationality, birth, marriage, divorce, &c., unsolved personal problems (e.g. criminal record, undesirable security risks, members of special groups, such as Asiatics and non-Turkish speaking Moslems), and finally membership of people over 35 in a professional or intellectual class. These different handicaps, although not always representing a physical defect or a grave social stigma, were sufficient to jeopardize the future of individuals who in a normal community would not have been considered unfit to play a useful part in society. It can well be understood that those whom old age, infirmity, or sickness put at a real disadvantage were not likely to be considered as candidates by missions instructed to recruit man-power.

On the basis of the list drawn up by the Commission a census was taken of those refugees likely to remain in the residual group and of the size of the groups classified according to the categories of the list. This inquiry, completed by 1 November 1949, showed some interesting facts about the composition of the residual group.

The majority of hard core refugees in the medical group were people from the Baltic countries. More than 10 per cent. of all Baltic refugees in receipt of care and

[1] Marie Dresden Lane, '"Who Share our Concern for these People." The Resettlement of Unwanted Refugees by the IRO', *Social Service Review*, Sept. 1952, pp. 270–83. Mrs. Lane was chief of the Welfare Division, Department of Health, Care and Maintenance, IRO.

[2] GC/80, 9 May 1949, p. 12.

[3] Cf. Chapter XV, Counselling, p. 270, and GC Res. No. 39.

maintenance were classified as institutional cases. Tuberculosis was the leading clinical factor. Chronic medical disorders and miscellaneous medical conditions were responsible for the next largest number of institutional cases. Psychosis cases formed a significant part of the total, undoubtedly an after-effect of the war years, and a result of uncertainty about the future. The number of really unemployable persons, however, those who were helpless through age or ill health, who needed special care or the shelter of asylums or other appropriate institutions, was far lower than had been anticipated.

According to estimates an institutionalized group of some 16,900 persons accompanied by 8,400 family members would still exist by 30 June 1950. This was the group that from November 1949 onwards was called the 'hard core'. At last a precise meaning was given to a somewhat ill-chosen expression that had been used indiscriminately for all sorts of refugee categories, and had been a cause of confusion in working out the relief programme.[1]

Thus a distinction was made between those refugees who, for reasons of old age or ill health, would require continuing institutional care, plus the members of their immediate families, and those who, because they did not possess the qualifications which would have made them acceptable to the countries of immigration, were considered to have only 'limited opportunities for resettlement'. The members of the former group, the 'hard core' proper, had little or no chance of becoming financially independent and of engaging in some useful calling that would prevent them from becoming a public charge in the country that might accept them. At the end of the Organization's activities they would be in the residual group unless some solution motivated by charity tipped the scales in their favour.

The remainder of refugees who did not possess the qualifications required for emigration under the mass resettlement schemes had among them specialists and intellectuals who could with special effort be resettled as self-supporting individuals. The chapters devoted to migration for settlement relate the Organization's efforts to bring about a gradual reduction in the numbers of this group: appeals by the Director General to governments to persuade them to adopt a more liberal immigration policy, campaigns in favour of the intellectuals, development of individual migration schemes that enabled, usually through the support of sponsors in the resettlement countries, a good number of people to emigrate even after rejection by the selection missions.

In contrast to the practice in a normal society, aged or sick refugees could not expect any lasting relief from the community to which they belonged, since its members were all temporarily in the same state of exile and/or destitution, and since the more robust among them, those best fitted for the battle of life, were being slowly dispersed as the result of emigration, and were being forced to leave behind their weaker brethren.

[1] In 1945 the term 'hard core' covered all non-repatriable refugees. In 1948 the IRO applied the same term to those refugees only whom it could neither repatriate nor resettle abroad. But the composition of this group was constantly being modified; today a given category of refugees might be passed over by the selection missions, but tomorrow they might find a chance to emigrate through the liberalization of legislation in one of the receiving countries, or the inauguration of a resettlement plan in a new country.

The task of offering relief to the helpless was therefore bound to fall on the government or the public of the countries of first refuge, or on members of the public of other countries acting through the churches and the voluntary societies. To quote a few examples, the Ukrainians in the New World were able to help their fellow countrymen in Europe through societies such as the Ukrainian Canadian Relief Fund or the United Ukrainian American Relief Committee; the unity of the Jewish people found expression in the AJDC, the JCRA, HIAS, or the World ORT Union; and the Lutherans throughout the world were able, through the good offices of the Lutheran World Federation, to sustain their co-religionists among the émigrés from the Baltic countries. Sometimes, too, the refugees of like nationality in a given country banded together in mutual aid associations such as the Union of Russian War Invalids in Belgium or the Self Help of Émigrés from Central Europe in France and in the United States. But associations of this nature did not usually have sufficient resources to alleviate all the cases of distress and assure the future of those who were incapable of fending for themselves.

The aid that refugees could expect from the governments of the countries of refuge differed widely from one country to another according to national legislation and resources, as some were already burdened with a relatively large charge of other refugees.

At the end of 1949 the hard core survey carried out by health and welfare officials of the IRO gave the following figures:

Situation at	Total hard core	Institutional cases	Family members
31 Oct. 1949	23,087	15,249	7,838
31 Dec. 1949	24,877	16,150	8,727
30 June 1950 (estimated) . . .	25,300	16,900	8,400

The geographical distribution showed that of the persons included in the survey of 31 December 1949, 14,015 were living in Germany, 1,644 in Austria, and 948 in Italy. More than 80 per cent. of the 8,270 remaining were living in France, and sizeable groups were found in Denmark (454), the Philippines (286), and the Lebanon (271). In every other country the number of hard core refugees was very low.

Proposed solutions

In 1948 the Director General had proposed that the resettlement countries or, failing that, the individual member states of the Organization, were to accept a quota of refugees including some physically handicapped, sick, and aged people, as well as the refugees who were able to work and make a useful contribution to the country's economic development. However, this 'fair share plan' was unworkable, because not only the immigration laws but also the hospital accommodation available and the number of infirm refugees already there differed greatly from country to country. Further, governments approached by the Administration were unwilling to accept quotas of refugees determined by majority vote.

At the Third Session of the General Council the Director General brought up for discussion the following four alternatives:

(1) The various governments throughout the world would accept into their countries a 'fair share' of these refugees, the individual countries determining the form of care and the method of providing for it, or

(2) they might assume financial responsibility for providing care for a stated number of refugees in the country of residence, or

(3) the responsibility for continued care and maintenance would be divided between the IRO, the local authorities of the country of residence and other interested agencies or governments, or

(4) the local authorities of the countries of residence would assume complete responsibility.[1]

These proposals were thoroughly and very sympathetically discussed by the delegates of the General Council at several sessions. Several members of the General Council were of the opinion that responsibility for assisting the hard core refugees should be shared by other members of the UN. Others advocated immediate negotiations with the occupation authorities, the German Government, and the voluntary societies with a view to securing the future of the hard core refugees who would have to remain in Germany after the IRO's activities came to an end. Certain delegates intimated that their governments might on certain conditions take care of the hard core refugees already on their soil, or that they would take in a fair share of those who could not remain in their country of present residence, or that they would be prepared to make a special contribution towards specified projects in favour of the hard core. Usually a plan was worked out for persons who would require special care and possibly financial aid for some years to come, no matter where they were, and persons who needed institutionalized care.

These decisions meant that very large sums of money had to be allocated by the Organization to allow grants to be made to authorities, societies, or institutions that agreed to provide care and shelter for sick and aged refugees. With this end in view the General Council decided to allocate a total amount of $22 million leaving the Administration to employ it not by making grants on the basis of a rigid tariff, but in seeking to subsidize the projects that seemed likely to afford the best and most economical solution of the problem. The General Council suggested that the Director General should appeal to all governments to accept as many refugees as possible and then to determine the actual number and type to be accepted in separate negotiations with each government.

The Administration left no stone unturned to perfect the various schemes for assisting the hard core refugees and to enrol help from every possible side in this cause. After the working group formed in Geneva with the participation of the voluntary societies, other joint committees of the same kind examined the problem in the principal operational areas. In January 1949 the question of the hard core refugees was discussed at a joint conference in Geneva of the IRO and the voluntary societies. At a conference held in Frankfurt in May 1949 the IRO's mission chiefs in the three zones of Germany considered the aspects of the problem in their respective zones with representatives of headquarters.

It was clear that the Organization did not possess the resources to settle sums of

[1] GC/80, 9 May 1949, p. 28; GC/77, Res. 1, p. 8.

money to cover costs of the lifelong institutional care of hard core refugees which worked out at some $4,000 *per capita* on the average. The solution adopted was to offer any government, organization, or institution that was willing to assume responsibility for a handicapped refugee a sum that would both contribute towards the cost of installing the necessary equipment for the refugee's accommodation in a new or existing institution, and also defray the cost of his maintenance until 30 June 1950. When the IRO's mandate was extended, some other basis had to be found to calculate the grants payable in respect of hard core cases that had not been resettled before this date.

The Director General was instructed to develop schemes for dealing with the hard core, taking into account the attitude of governments in the countries of present residence. Refugees who were located in Germany, Austria, Italy, Lebanon, East Africa, Shanghai, Samar, Spain, and Portugal and required continuing institutional care were to be moved, to the extent possible, to countries willing to receive them. Refugees in the same category who were already residing in France, Belgium, the Netherlands, Italy, Luxembourg, and Switzerland were to remain in these countries on the basis of specific projects to be agreed between the IRO and the respective national governments.

Finally, the institutional cases then resident in Germany and Austria who could not be moved were to be established on the basis of specific projects to be agreed between the IRO and either the High Commissions or, with their approval, the Federal authorities of Germany and of Austria.

On the basis of agreements between headquarters and governments of occupation authorities, the IRO concluded agreements with local authorities. The IRO offered its expert services in regard to the planning of projects designed for providing institutional care; it vouched for the cost of transportation, and, in its discretion and in accordance with the resolution of the General Council, it pledged to pay to the government or authority the sums budgeted by the IRO up to 30 June 1950 for the care and maintenance of refugees. In its discretion the IRO also might make to the government or authority a grant towards the permanent maintenance of hard core cases requiring institutional care, either in the form of cash or equipment or supplies. The governments, on their part, guaranteed to grant permanent residence permits, thus providing permanent rights of settlement.

The end of 1949 saw the first favourable responses to the IRO's efforts to bring about the resettlement of sick and aged refugees. The first move in favour of the hard core was made by Norway, who declared itself ready to provide care for 200 refugees, including at least fifty blind persons and their families;[1] selection of cases would be carried out by Norwegian officials in Germany and Austria, documentation and movement being the IRO's responsibility. Also Belgium, at the instigation of the *Secours international*, settled nearly eighty old people, mostly from Austria and Lebanon, who were spread over the establishments attached to the *Fédération des Œuvres Hospitalières de Caritas Catholics*. In the Netherlands subsidies given jointly by the IRO and the AJDC (with the approval of the Netherlands Government) enabled annuities to be purchased in favour of forty aged Jewish refugees.

---

[1] Agreement of 17 Sept. 1949.

The most important agreement was concluded at the end of 1949 with the Government of Israel, in which it undertook to construct institutions for the care and shelter of 800 TB cases, 300 persons with chronic illnesses, 100 mental patients, and 400 old people or invalids, a total of 1,600 people within the mandate of the Organization. For its part the Organization agreed to contribute a grant of $2½ million towards the construction and equipment of the necessary installations.

Negotiations about local settlement of refugees in the old-age home at Berchtesgaden-Strub were conducted in Germany between the Bavarian authorities, the Bavarian Lutheran Church, the Lutheran World Federation, and the IRO.

These early results were extremely encouraging. They showed, on the one hand, that the governments were willing to entertain the purely humanitarian considerations that alone could induce them to shoulder responsibility for the maintenance of uneconomic refugees. On the other hand, they showed that the voluntary societies, both by their influence on the governments of receiving countries and by their own resources, were able to play a most effective part in solving the problem.

At the beginning of 1950 the Director General paid visits to the various European member governments of the IRO to review the hard core question with them. Furthermore, the Director General launched a fresh appeal in February 1950 to the governments, churches, and voluntary societies in all resettlement countries in compliance with the directives of the General Council. In accordance with the principles adopted by the General Council this appeal specified that the Organization was ready to grant certain subsidies to encourage schemes for the acceptance of aged and sick refugees; these grants would be limited by the relatively modest amount of money available, however, and would not constitute much more than an initial contribution to the costs of the task to be accomplished. The final aim was to settle the 26,000 people in the hard core, one by one or in small groups, in thousands of communities, so that their future could be assured without severely taxing charitable enterprise anywhere. Institutional care was not the only arrangement visualized, and it was suggested that those refugees whose health permitted it could be sponsored by individuals and family groups who would provide them with a home, subsistence, and the necessary treatment. Such 'adoption' would have to be arranged through the medium of a competent public service or recognized voluntary society which was prepared to assume responsibility. The Organization's contributory grants to the resettlement of each hard core refugee were to be paid on the following scale:

	$
Tuberculous cases	1,000
Chronically ill	800
Mental cases	700
Blind (totally or partially)	650
Persons without the use of one or more limbs . .	650
Old-age cases	500
Dependants of persons in each of the above categories .	250

The group on whose behalf these grants could be paid was described as follows:

Persons in institutions or awaiting an opening in an institution or persons who, due to old age, mental or other illness are not competent to live and compete in the normal economy without the social and economic aid which can be supplied by a family or institution.

Sent out to every voluntary society that the IRO had any direct or indirect connexion with, and repeated in every operational area and every resettlement country by the IRO's representatives, the Director General's appeal was successful beyond all hopes.[1] The years 1950 and 1951 witnessed the fruition of a series of resettlement plans that had the patronage of the voluntary societies and the approval of the governments concerned, and through which permanent arrangements were made for several thousand hard core refugees.

A great willingness to help led voluntary agencies, governments, individual sponsors, and the IRO to join hands in a co-operative enterprise and to develop schemes adapted to the capability of various countries around the world. In regard to their attitude towards help for the hard core, there were four different groups of countries: first, the European countries of first refuge which for the most part showed goodwill: France, the Netherlands, Belgium, Switzerland, Greece, Norway, and Sweden. They retained those who had originally found refuge in their country and were ready, over and beyond this, to receive their share of the residual group.

France

The Agreement with France on behalf of the 'Institutional Hard Core' was based on a wider Agreement between IRO and the French Government[2] regarding the transfer to the French Government of IRO's responsibilities on the termination of IRO. The Agreement in question contained the following provision on the subject of the hard core (Article 5):

In accordance with the decisions of the General Council, the IRO shall pay to the French Government or to the organizations designated by it, for the refugees who have been placed by the IRO in the special category of 'Institutional Hard Core', a share of funds in keeping with their numbers and their special circumstances. The sum in question shall be handed over by the IRO as soon as both Parties have approved a general programme on the subject, or on the several sections thereof, to be drawn up by mutual agreement. The responsibility for drawing up this programme shall rest with a working party consisting of representatives of the IRO, the French Ministries concerned (Foreign Affairs, Health, Interior, Labour) and of the SSAE, which shall be convened by the IRO.

The programme itself was elaborated by a planning group formed of officials of the IRO and of French voluntary societies, foremost among them the very active Social Service Aid to Emigrants (SSAE),[3] the French branch of the International Social Service, the *Secours Catholique*, the Protestant CIMADE, and the Jewish OSE.[4]

[1] Res. No. 54 adopted at the meeting of the General Council on 20 Oct. 1949 authorized the Director General 'to continue to seek solutions for the continuing care and permanent settlement of refugees proven to be institutional cases, by means of direct negotiations with governments and interested agencies'.

[2] Agreement between the French Government and the IRO Regarding the Transfer to the French Government of the Care and Maintenance of Responsibilities of the IRO, signed 28 Feb. 1950. IRO/LEG/GOV/30, 14 Mar. 1950.

[3] Annual Reports on the activity of Service d'Aide aux Émigrants (SSAE), 39 rue de Vangirard, Paris.

[4] Cf. George W. Davis, 'Handling of Refugees and Displaced Persons by the French MMLA (Section Féminine)', *Social Service Review* (Chicago), xxii (1948), 34–39.

The fund in question, amounting to 1,575 million francs, was managed by IRO as long as it was in function, and then by an independent private society, the Association for the Establishment of Foreign Refugees (Association pour l'Établissement des Réfugiés Étrangers—AERE) nominated by the French Government, which retained the financial supervision and appointed an Inter-ministerial Commission, consisting of a representative of the Ministries of Foreign Affairs, of the Interior, of Finance, of Public Health and Population, and of Labour and Social Security, with a representative of the SSAE, to carry this out.

Dating back to the Russian and Spanish revolutions, a large number of sick and aged people had sought refuge and resided in France, 'traditional haven of refugees'. Their number had been increased by the many refugees created by the Second World War. An analysis made by the *Service Social Aide des Émigrés* showed that the total number of hard core cases residing in France amounted to 7,618. Of these 800 were resettled to other countries, and 6,818 settled *sur place*. In addition France received 670 new institutional hard core cases. The IRO created new establishments, asylums, sanatoria, hospitals, orphanages, re-education centres, some of them reserved to special categories such as Russian, Armenian, Jewish; while others, such as the retreat at Hyères (125 places), was open to persons of different origin.[1]

Under French social security legislation the majority of refugees were entitled to the same benefits as French citizens. However, the number of available openings in state-run welfare homes and sanatoria was limited. Therefore, the programme agreed upon aimed mainly at establishing new institutions or increasing the capacity of existing institutions by means of the funds supplied by the IRO. Provision was made in the covenants signed with the French Government for the installation thus created to revert to the state when no longer needed for refugees. Priority in the use of each bed endowed by the IRO's funds was reserved for another refugee when the original occupant no longer required it. Elsewhere, when the IRO granted $1,000 to a voluntary society or an authority that took charge of a tubercular refugee, only one individual case had been solved, whereas in France the sum used to endow a sanatorium bed provided accommodation for an indefinite number of TB refugees in the future.

Thanks to the understanding attitude and the support of the public authorities, the refugees were provided with quarters that were outstanding for comfort and pleasant surroundings. On the eve of closure of the IRO mission in France, the hard core programme had resulted in the endowment of 2,418 beds, covering 63 per cent. of the requirements for the institutional cases reported in the SSAE survey.[2]

Arrangements for assistance were made to the remaining 37 per cent. of the institutional cases who could not be immediately hospitalized, and also to certain refugees who, while not absolutely in need of institutional care, were, nevertheless, unable to provide for themselves. A special committee of representatives of the IRO and the voluntary societies was formed in liaison with the Ministry of Health to decide how these funds were to be used and to examine the individual applications for assistance.

With the hard core funds and the good offices of the SSAE and of other voluntary

---

[1] See *Un aspect de l'œuvre de l'OIR en France*, illustrated pamphlet of 62 pp. (Paris, 1952).
[2] Ibid.

societies, it often proved possible to find satisfactory solutions for such diversified problems. Since the IRO has ceased to function, this special kind of welfare work and the supervision of hard core funds are in the hands of AERE.

The Netherlands, Belgium, Denmark, Luxembourg

In the Netherlands, Belgium, Denmark, and Luxembourg, as in France, local settlement of institutional cases was arranged on pursuance of agreements reached by the IRO and the governments concerned. One hundred and twenty-eight institutional hard core cases resided in the Netherlands, of which 124 were settled *sur place*, and an additional 221 received, who came from Germany and Austria. Participating agencies were Protestant and Catholic church groups, the Jewish Agency, and a number of individual citizens.

In Belgium the Government and the local and international voluntary agencies formed a central committee to plan for the hard core refugees; 91 of them resided in Belgium (27 resettled and 58 settled *sur place*) and 199 additional who came from Italy, Germany, Austria, and the Middle East found a sanctuary there. Among these were 43 unaccompanied children who were mentally deficient. A number of Belgians 'adopted', without help from an organization, 68 aged refugees from Austria. They bought a home for them and assumed care and maintenance after the IRO grant had been exhausted.

The governments of Denmark and Luxembourg assumed full responsibility, including financial, for the support of the hard core cases residing within their borders after IRO's contributions were exhausted. Denmark settled *sur place* 430 of its 466 residing cases and Luxembourg its 3 cases.

Switzerland

When IRO had come into being about 25,000 refugees lived in Switzerland, many of them on public charge. Since the Swiss Government assumed full responsibility for all refugees remaining in the country, hard core cases were not separately counted. Of those 25,900 refugees residing in Switzerland in 1949, 4,819 were resettled, 133 repatriated, and 20,948 settled *sur place* (including institutional hard core cases). In addition the Government provided care and maintenance for 240 hard core cases through the Swiss Aid to Europe.

Greece

In Greece 85 cases were in need of institutional care. A Refugee Service Committee was set up and, under the auspices of IRO, a house for 100 aged persons was established.

Norway and Sweden

Norway and Sweden responded very generously to the appeal of the Director General. Both offered to receive, in Norway's own words, 'hard core refugees most difficult to place'. Norway accepted 63 blind and 112 tubercular cases with the members of their families, providing not only care but also necessary training and job placement. In addition to this governmental aid, religious groups received 50 aged refugees with their families for permanent care. Sweden made individual case plans for 462 tubercular refugees with their families and dependants including a large number of children in need of hospitalization.

Spain and Portugal

While in the previously mentioned countries willingness and co-operation of the governments concerned helped the completion of IRO's endeavours on behalf of hard core cases, a second group posed a nearly unsurmountable problem. Countries in which refugees were driven as a result of forced migration or stranded *en route* to possible asylum offered no assistance. The mutual disinclination between the countries who did not want the refugees, and the refugees who were set to leave, weighed heavily on the most helpless cases.

Spain and Portugal neither accepted refugees legally nor granted them residence rights or labour permits. But international voluntary and religious agencies, who joined efforts with those of various embassies, were successful in raising money, so that 39 institutional cases in Portugal and 33 cases in Spain could receive a lump sum to cover their institutional care, a sum given either directly or to the agency representatives. When IRO was dissolved only 32 cases in both countries taken together could be considered as being properly cared for, since AJDC had taken over responsibility for them.

Turkey

In Turkey were 53 refugees classified as institutional cases. The Turkish Red Crescent in co-operation with a Refugee Service Committee had assumed responsibility. But no provisions were available for long-term plans once IRO funds would be exhausted.

East Africa and Lebanon

Those refugees, a residue of the masses who, during the war, had been evacuated to East Africa and Lebanon, were in a most difficult situation. The countries had granted them temporary asylum under the UK's pledge that they would not become 'a permanent charge upon' them. Many of the original group were settled in the UK, Canada, Australia, and New Zealand during the period when IRO was still in function. Of a small group remaining in 1950, 358 were classified as institutional hard core. Of 77 cases in East Africa 52 were resettled and of 281 in Lebanon 39 were settled *sur place*, and 63 resettled. However, 25 in East Africa and 179 in Lebanon had not found permanent settlement when IRO closed its activities and continued to be maintained by the UK Government.

White Russians

When the Communist Chinese entered Shanghai IRO evacuated 5,500 of 9,000 White Russians to Samar in the Philippines and promised the Philippine Government to resettle these refugees in other countries. Six hundred and twelve institutional hard core cases were accepted by the US, 219 under the auspices of voluntary societies, by France 72, Argentina 11, Australia 30, Paraguay 14, Brazil 2, and 11 by other countries; 240 cases were left unsolved.[1]

Of those White Russian refugees left in China 1,539 were institutional hard core cases. In spite of IRO's efforts to make arrangements for them, only 451 could be resettled, 41 repatriated, and 67 transferred to voluntary agencies, while for 421 plans had to be left unsolved and the fate of 59 cases is unknown.

Sponsored cases

The resettlement countries which had accepted large groups of migrants, such as the US, Canada, and Australia, constituted a third group. Throughout the period in which IRO was in operation these migrants who, in the overwhelming majority of cases, were healthy and 'self-supporting had sponsored and sent for their old and sick and dependant who thereupon left as sponsored cases; and hence no record was made that would identify them as of the hard core type'.[2] Payments by IRO were made to individual cases through international voluntary and religious agencies such as the AJDC, the LWF, and the WCC. Under the UK 'Two Thousand' scheme, sponsored by the British Council for Aid to Refugees, a number of hard core cases received permanent care in Great Britain.[3]

Residual groups

It was recognized in 1949 that notwithstanding all efforts of IRO and in spite of the goodwill of western European and overseas countries, there would be left many aged, chronic sick, tuberculous, and other persons in need of permanent institutional care who had to remain where they were staying in Germany, Austria, and Italy. German Government officials, with the fullest co-operation of the occupying authorities, made arrangements with voluntary agencies and the IRO, which guaranteed satisfactory care for residual displaced persons. IRO financed the establishment and maintenance of old-age homes, sanatoria, hospitals, and other institutions to provide a permanent home for them, at the same time aiding Germany in increasing its institutional resources.

Typical of these arrangements are provisions in the American zone. The first home for the aged was established at Berchtesgaden-Strub, a former *Wehrmacht* caserne, confiscated by the occupying authorities and used by IRO to house displaced persons. This building was released by EUCOM to *Land* Bavaria which agreed to lease it without cost for fifty years to the 'Inner Mission', the German Protestant charitable organization. IRO, using its Blocked DM Funds, released for the purpose by HICOG, spent nearly 2 million DM for structural changes and suitable equipment to make it a home for 450 old people. The Bavarian authorities, assisted by the Federal Government, furnishes basic maintenance on a *per diem per capita* plan which enables the Inner Mission to operate the home. The LWF, a voluntary agency affiliated with IRO, keeps a continuing interest in the home, meeting certain special needs. The home is not established exclusively for displaced persons. Ninety per cent. of the spaces are granted to hard core cases as long as there are sufficient

[1] Chapter X, Origin of the Refugees, p. 186.
[2] Lane, op. cit., p. 282.   [3] Cf. Chapter XX, Resettlement, p. 393.

applications. Gradually the home will serve the care of aged Germans. A Management Agreement, signed by all parties and endorsed by the US High Commissioner for Germany, incorporates all provisions.[1] There were three other homes for the aged with a capacity of altogether 980 places. The problems of the residual tuberculous were solved by the refurnishing of the former TB sanatorium at Gauting with 1,200 places and its transfer to the German administration. Mental cases were cared for at Wiesloch in Württemberg-Baden and in institutions in Bavaria. Continuing care is given for mentally deficient children in a newly constructed wing of Goddelau Hospital in Hesse. In most of these installations IRO made available confiscated property formerly under the control of IRO, a considerable inventory of equipment, supplies, and furnishings, and in many cases considerable sums of money from the Blocked Account for necessary improvements.

Since it was difficult to make provision for hard core cases in Austria, special priority was given to the resettlement of such cases from that country.

In November 1950 the IRO concluded an Agreement with the Italian Government, according to which the Organization undertook to resettle as many as possible of the refugees in the hard core group, while the Government undertook financial assistance in the permanent care of the remaining case-load up to a total of 1,000 refugees, including dependants.

The numbers quoted in the final report of the ECOSOC tell the unusual story of an international organization which, through its persistent efforts, conquered the difficulties of a truly formidable task:[2] 'The total number of institutionalized cases and their dependants who were the responsibility of IRO was about 32,000. By the beginning of 1951 the known number of institutional cases and their dependants had been reduced to about 11,000 persons, and by the end of the year there were only 362 cases for whom no satisfactory arrangements had been made.' This result would not have been reached were it not for the human interest and co-operation of the governments, voluntary agencies, and church organizations concerned.

[1] Report to the US HICOG on the IRO, US zone of Germany, 22 Oct. 1951, p. 4 and Annex III, B.
[2] UN, ECOSOC, Fourteenth Session, E/2211, 23 Apr. 1952, p. 17.

CHAPTER XXIV

UNACCOMPANIED CHILDREN

ONE of the greatest tragedies of the Second World War was the forcible separation of children from their families by the Nazi régime in pursuance of its policy of depleting the population of non-Germanic national communities and of replenishing and increasing the German race. To this end, a large-scale plan was executed with the greatest ruthlessness and thoroughness, particularly in the eastern European countries; children with physical and mental behaviour 'desirable' according to the Nazi ideals of the Aryan race were sent to special institutions for Germanization. After a period in the institutions they were sent to German families for foster placement and eventually adoption. The records of the places of birth and the names of the children were changed, and contact with their own families was forbidden. The Nazi organization, *Der Lebensborn*, which dealt with the selected children, was concerned not only with children of the indigenous population in German-occupied countries but also with children of German fathers and foreign mothers, children of parents executed for anti-German activities—for instance the children from the Czech village of Lidice, burned in reprisal for the assassination of the Nazi Governor of Bohemia, Heydrich—and children born to persons doing forced labour in Germany and torn from their mothers at an early age.

It is difficult to estimate the number of children kidnapped by the Nazis. Not all were accorded the privilege of Germanization. A large number died in concentration camps from disease and maltreatment, and many of those who were adopted were never identified. Figures suggested by Polish sources for missing Polish children alone vary between 20,000 and 200,000—the Polish Cabinet Minister Wolski put their number at 150,000.[1] Smaller but nevertheless considerable numbers of missing children were of Baltic, Ukrainian, and Yugoslav origin; the numbers of children from other countries opposed to Germany were more limited.

Besides those deliberately separated from their families by the Nazis, other children were separated by the vicissitudes of war—the deportation of whole groups of the indigenous population, the mass executions that resulted in children roaming about Europe with relatives or neighbours from the same village, the evacuation of territories for military reasons, the headlong flight of the population before an advancing army, the death of parents and relatives in air raids. There were also the children of women who had been deported for forced labour to Germany, children whose fathers were often members of the armed forces in occupied territories. In many cases these children were abandoned by their mothers or placed by them in German families, often with the family of the child's natural father. Thus, of the children living with German foster parents, a distinction must be made between those kidnapped by the SS and those voluntarily left by their mothers.

Naturally, after the war, the governments of the countries to which the children

[1] Report by the Polish Ministry of Labour and Social Welfare, spring, 1948.

or their parents belonged—and the families of the children themselves—were anxious to trace them and provide for their welfare. This was a difficult task. It was entrusted to UNRRA and then to the IRO. The work fell into four main parts: finding the children, housing and caring for them, re-uniting them with their relatives, and establishing permanently those for whom no relations could be found.

Under the UNRRA's administration, 12,843 children were given care in separate camps as well as in special sections in normal camps. Special attention under the direction of specialists was given to their health and nutrition, education, and vocational training. The same procedure of eligibility was applied as for adult displaced persons. 1,016 children were reunited with their families, 2,703 repatriated, and 1,889 resettled. A special Child Search Service was set up, working in collaboration with the military authorities.

In the French zone of Germany an ordinance of the French Commander-in-Chief provided for the registration of all children one of whose parents was a UN national, as a result of which 18,000 children were indexed. In the French zone the military government itself was responsible for child search, whereas in the British and US zones UNRRA was responsible for the location and identification of UN children living in German institutions and with German families. By directives issued in January and March 1946, the Allied control authorities called upon German officials to submit lists of identified non-German children living in German communities.

The results of this search work were not fully comprehensive; children had often been taken away from home when they were very young and had no memory of their former language, their family, or their place of birth; records had been partly destroyed by the Nazi organizations, and frequently individual families concealed the identity of children, while local authorities were reluctant to elucidate the facts.

A similar situation prevailed in Austria. In the British zone of Austria UNRRA child welfare workers were empowered by military government ordinance to enter any premises where they had reason to believe an unaccompanied child might be found and to remove him or her into the custody and care of UNRRA whenever it appeared to be in the interests of the child to do so.

Thus the PCIRO took over a well-established pattern of child welfare and child search activities. Thirty-five children's centres were in existence when the IRO assumed responsibility. Maintenance in centres was supplemented by temporary care outside Germany for the children found after the liberation of the concentration camps in extremely low conditions of health. From May 1946 until June 1947 nearly 1,000 children were sent from the US zone of Germany to the United States of America under the sponsorship of the Committee for the Care of European Children whose resettlement work at this period was limited, however, by the national quota restrictions on immigration. Three hundred and fifty Jewish young people, mostly children, were removed from Buchenwald in 1945 and sent to Switzerland for six months' care, and the Swiss authorities permitted them to remain in Switzerland beyond the period originally planned. After one year they assumed the cost of maintaining these young people, the larger part of whom were able to learn a trade and remain in Switzerland several years. Many obtained permission to establish themselves in the country. In addition, 150 non-Jewish children were taken care of in Switzerland for six months and repatriated directly afterwards to their home countries. Five hundred and thirty-five children came to France, and Sweden took 900, while the UK took in a number of Jewish children variously estimated at between 700 and 800 during the years 1945-7. Other welfare work among the children was done by the JAFP and the Canadian Jewish Congress.

There was an estimated total of 4,090 unaccompanied children taken over by PCIRO on 1 July 1947. Of this number, 1,417 were recorded as of Polish nationality, about 400 were classed as 'stateless', another 123 were of undetermined nationality, thirty other nationalities accounted for the remaining 1,119. Of the total, 728 were in the US zone of Germany, 633 in the British, and 82 in the French zone. One hundred and fifty-nine were in the three western zones of Austria, 427 in Italy, 304 in Belgium, 277 in France, and 381 in East Africa. The last group, of Polish nationality, had come from Siberia by way of Iran to Bombay from whence they were shipped to East Africa.[1]

Annex 1, Part 1, paragraph 4 of the Constitution established a priority obligation on the IRO to render all possible assistance, including repatriation, to unaccompanied children. War orphans and those children whose parents had disappeared, living outside their countries of origin and being 16 years of age or under, were defined as unaccompanied children. It was not always possible to adhere to the above principle of the Constitution and the disposal of children by the IRO and/or governmental authorities was one of the most politically contested tasks of the IRO. The divergencies of opinion between governments on the subject of repatriation extended to children had already become evident in the deliberations of the Special Committee on Refugees and Displaced Persons of the UN in 1946. While adults were responsible for their own decision in regard to repatriation, this matter was complicated in the case of children under age, since the IRO did not stand *in loco parentis*, able to make a binding decision. It had to take into account the wishes of the country of origin, of the country of residence, of the remaining members of the family, and of the child itself, at least if it had reached years of discretion. In addition to the truly unaccompanied children, the waifs and orphans, there were those who were temporarily unaccompanied because they were deprived of parental care for a period, and had to be admitted to care and maintenance and receive the same welfare services as unaccompanied children. The functions of the Organization in relation to unaccompanied children were the same as those applicable to adults: identification; registration and classification; care and assistance; legal and other protection; transport; re-establishment by repatriation and resettlement. The carrying out of the functions, however, raised serious difficulties of which the greatest was to determine who was competent to dispose of the child. Was it the international organization whose Constitution, approved by the UN in General Assembly, contained special provisions? Was it the government of the child's country of origin, or that of its country of residence? Or was it the family—a particularly difficult question if the parents were dead? And to what extent should the wishes of the children themselves, who very often had strong views of their own, be taken into account?

[1] UN, ECOSOC, E/816: Report on the Progress of Repatriation, Resettlement and Immigration of Refugees and Displaced Persons, p. 51.

The parties claiming an interest in any decision, on even an individual case, were the governments of the countries of origin and of the country of residence (the latter were in most cases the occupying authorities in Germany and Austria), the national committees of refugees (to whose care some refugees had been entrusted), and religious agencies. It was in general the wish of governments that children separated from their families, whether by the programme of Germanization implemented by the Nazi régime, by deportation, or by war events should be reunited with their families in the homeland. Beyond this, certain governments, chiefly those of the USSR, of Byelo-Russia, and of Poland, claimed that all children should be repatriated regardless of whether the parents were living in the homeland or not. They took the view that the country of nationality was entitled to dispose of children of that nationality and to confirm or deny the nationality of individual children; that that country only could appoint legal guardians, and only a guardian so appointed could make valid statements and decisions in the name of a person under age. As the law of the country was applicable in the matter, it would be a violation of international law to take into account the will of a minor. Besides these legal arguments, the governments emphasized that repatriation had been approved by a number of political decisions, from Potsdam onwards, and that the separation of children from their families, deportation, and Germanization were alike considered as crimes against humanity. The return of the stolen children was taken for granted.[1]

Legal position

According to the law of the great majority of continental European countries, the government of the country of origin was entitled to appoint guardians for children living abroad. The Hague Convention of 12 June 1902, to regulate the conflict of laws and jurisdiction in regard to guardianship of minors, followed this principle. When the Second World War broke out, this Convention was in force between Belgium, Danzig, Germany, Hungary, Italy, Luxembourg, the Netherlands, Poland, Portugal, Rumania, Spain, Sweden, and Switzerland.[2] However, states with the tradition of common law did not apply the same principle. For them the authorities of the country of residence of the child were entitled to appoint guardians who would legally represent the child in that territory.

The British and American occupation authorities took the view that the relationship between ward and guardian constituted a domestic status, governed by the law of domicile, and that in all questions concerning children, the best interests of the child should be the guiding consideration. Therefore all children living in the territory were within the jurisdiction of that country. If they were foreign nationals a guardian could be appointed for them, though there might also be a fully appointed

---

[1] Speech of Mr. Modzelevsky, Polish Minister for Foreign Affairs, on 23 Sept. 1948 at the Plenary Session of the UN General Assembly, Paris, 1948. (U.N. General Assembly, Third Session, Part I, *Official Records*, Plenary Meetings, Sept.–Dec. 1948, pp. 52–53.)

[2] After the war, the Convention was no longer valid between Germany and the states with which she had been at war, as all international treaties were invalidated by the outbreak of war. This is the opinion of the Allied Powers, of the Government of the German Federal Republic, and of the German courts; it is also prevalent in doctrine.

foreign guardian. In either case, the removal of the child to its homeland could be ordered by the court on the desire of the guardian, but such order would not be given if the paramount consideration, the welfare of the child, seemed to oppose repatriation and call for resettlement or local settlement.

This view was followed by other countries where the common law, or principles derived from it, prevailed. For instance, the authorities in India, in the Union of South Africa, and in territories in Africa under the international responsibility of the UK, appointed guardians for refugee children of foreign, chiefly Polish, nationality living in their territory.

The attitude of national committees and voluntary agencies was dictated by the political or religious point of view of the body concerned. National committees of refugees were inclined against repatriation to a country from which they had fled, and certainly against forcible repatriation. They claimed the right to represent children of their group at least morally, if not legally. Welfare agencies would have in mind primarily the welfare of the child, and agencies of a religious tendency would demand resettlement of the child in a country where they could take care of its religious education, and were opposed to the return of the child to a country where education in its own faith was not guaranteed.

As regards the family, there was a distinction between the legal rights of parents having parental power over the child and other members of the family. There was no doubt that the will of a parent of the child carried more weight than that of another member of the family, which has the importance only when the possibility was offered of reuniting the child with a member of the family and the other conditions (welfare and education) were satisfactory.

In general, the wishes of the parent, the natural and legal representative of the child, had to be respected. However, there was the delicate question whether it was permissible to override those wishes if the best interest of the child did not coincide with them. It was possible to defend the strong legal argument that as long as the father or the mother had not been deprived of their power by the competent authorities, they were entitled to dispose of the child. On the other hand, it was defensible for human reasons to decide the fate of the child in its own interest against the legal position in national law.

The IRO, entrusted by the UN with the protection of refugees and with the special duty of giving all possible priority assistance to unaccompanied children, had to carry out this task amidst the contradictory attitudes and opinions of governments and non-governmental organizations. The Organization tried to steer a middle course. The Director General declared: 'It is not easy to navigate an international ship in the turbulent cross-currents of ideological conflicts. Mistakes can be made and what, from one point of view, looks to be failure can be equally acclaimed as success when viewed differently.'[1]

Although the IRO had, from the international point of view, the responsibility for unaccompanied children and their custody, it could not assume the position of a legal guardian. But for children, adequate status pre-supposed guardianship, and therefore Provisional Order No. 33 in 1947 prescribed that unaccompanied children

---

[1] Press release PM/1550, 10 Nov. 1949, Lake Success.

should be provided with a legal guardian as soon as possible. The policy applicable to the temporary stay of a child in a country of first asylum was essential for all cases of permanent establishment, including those of local settlement. For those who were resettled, the sponsoring agencies were given the responsibility for the early appointment of a guardian; in cases of local settlement, the IRO generally followed the case through until legal guardians had been appointed or adoption effected.[1]

There were no further difficulties in Germany after promulgation of Law No. 23 by the Allied High Commission, as the German courts became competent to appoint guardians for refugee children and the *Jugendamt* (the official German authority) to exercise tutelage over refugee children born out of wedlock. In Austria and in Italy similar legislation did not exist, but the Allied authorities in Austria and the courts and the national authorities in both countries co-operated with the IRO to find a satisfactory solution for the protection of unaccompanied children who had not been resettled.

Beyond this, the IRO was anxious to improve the status of children living with foster-families by arranging their adoption. Here, too, Law No. 23 was useful in Germany; and a special law authorizing adoption by parents having legitimate children gave a further basis for the settlement of cases. Finally, owing to Law No. 23, marriages of refugees which had not been valid in Germany because they had not been solemnized in the form prescribed by German law, were validated and the children became legitimate.

In Austria legal guardianship and adoption of children within the mandate were subjects reserved to the occupation authorities under the control agreement. Thus, in the case of local settlement, the Austrian authorities made the decisions, but had to apply to the Allied authorities[2] for approval of the appointment of a guardian or the granting of adoption rights to Austrian citizens.

Political problems

At the request of the UN Assembly on 17 November 1947 and the ECOSOC in March 1948[3] the Secretary General, in collaboration with the Executive Secretary of the PCIRO, submitted in a report to the Eleventh Session of ECOSOC in August 1948 'a specific account of the situation of children removed from their country of origin during the course of the war, and on measures taken or contemplated on their behalf as provided' by the Constitution and recommendations on what could be done to accelerate a final solution.

In this report the difficulties with which PCIRO was confronted were clearly set forth; the delay in decision caused by following the procedure of the governments of countries of origin was explained, and the difficulty which PCIRO

---

[1] GC/197, Semi-Annual Report of Director General, 28 Feb. 1951, p. 36.

[2] The Allied Commission for Austria (British Element), Displaced Persons Branch, stated in May 1950 that due weight would be given to the feeling of the child, where it was mature enough to have an opinion of its own, regarding the future, and that normally a child which had been in a foster-home for five years or more should not be removed unless there were legal impediments to the child being adopted.

[3] ECOSOC, Res. 122 (VI), adopted on 1 Mar. 1948.

encountered when it recommended repatriation, but permission was not granted by the military authorities when they found out that repatriation was not in the best interest of the child. A further problem arose in connexion with those children whose country of origin was not known and those where there had been a change of status or sovereignty which was not recognized by the countries represented by the occupying authorities. Also certain religious or national groups exerted their influence to hinder re-establishment of the children in accordance with PCIRO policy. Therefore the mission urged above all other suggestions the member governments of the UN to lay down the principles of policy which the PCIRO should follow and thus to make its task less complicated.

In the discussions of ECOSOC in August 1948 the conflicting opinions over repatriation of unaccompanied children came to the fore when the Polish delegate stated that no progress had been made in repatriation and that 80,000 Polish children who had been taken from their country and separated from their parents were still in Western Germany.[1] He was of the opinion that neither the military authorities of the western occupation zones of Germany nor the IRO had made any attempt to solve the tragic problem of such children. The delegates for the Soviet Union and for Byelo-Russia stated that children were still not allowed to return even when all the appropriate documents and the requests of the parents themselves were available. He asked that the words 'always providing that the best interests of the individual child shall be the determining factor' be deleted in the resolution under consideration.

The delegate for the US stated that this phrase was of the utmost importance, emphasizing that: 'The competent authorities would be dealing with defenceless and feeble human beings, and in the settlement of their fate the best interest of the children should be constantly borne in mind.' The delegate for Soviet Russia answered that the best interests of any child would clearly be served by its return to the country from which it had originated. The delegate for Brazil maintained that the only criteria to be observed as regards unaccompanied children were the kinship, physical comfort, and welfare of the children. This discussion ended with the adoption of a resolution expressing the view of the ECOSOC:[2]

'That the policy which should be followed with regard to unaccompanied children is:
  (1) to unite children with their parents wherever the latter may be; and
  (2) in the case of orphans or unaccompanied children whose nationality has been established beyond doubt, to return them to their country, always providing that the best interests of the individual child shall be the determining factor.'[3]

Basing its policy on this resolution, the IRO promoted repatriation when it was not counter to the best interests of the individual child, and in other cases arranged resettlement or local settlement.

[1] At a meeting of the Social Committee of ECOSOC the figures presented by the Polish Red Cross were contested by the Director of the ITS, see document E/AC, 7/SR/57.

[2] For details of this discussion see Summary Records of the Fifty-seventh, Fifty-eighth, and Sixtieth Meetings of the ECOSOC, Docs. E/AC. 7/SR/57, 58, and 60.

[3] Res. No. 157 (VII) of 24 Aug. 1948 (E/1027). Other recommendations were that member governments of the UN should instruct their occupying authorities to facilitate plans made for the permanent establishment of the children by the PCIRO; official representatives of the countries of origin should take prompt action on cases submitted for certification of nationality; and sufficient qualified child welfare staff should be employed to make possible individual planning in the best interest of the child.

IRO policy

The first provision of the resolution confirmed the Organization's policy that the natural unit for human beings was the family, and that its primary task, in planning the future of children, was to reunite members of the family if they were to be found and to keep them together in the mode of re-establishment which they chose—repatriation, resettlement, or local settlement. The Organization's policy was that it would not be prepared to grant resettlement services to people intending to resettle without taking their children with them. Experience showed, however, that it was not always possible to apply this rule in all cases, and that sometimes a child had to be left in the country of residence for medical or other reasons, while the other members of the family accepted opportunities to be resettled. The Organization laid down that this arrangement should be resorted to only if every other solution had been examined and rejected as impracticable.

When a child was located and his identity established, it was necessary to decide on his removal from the institution or the family he was living in before any positive action could be taken by the Organization towards family reunion or resettlement. This removal needed the approval of the government of the country concerned or, in occupied territories, of the occupation authorities.

During most of the IRO's operation permission for the removal of unaccompanied children from Germany either for repatriation or resettlement was obtained through OMGUS and HICOG administrative channels in the US zone as in other zones under the control of the Allied Powers. In October 1950, however, this responsibility was delegated to HICOG courts through HICOG Law No. 11. While this resulted 'in some slowdown of the movement of children', it established 'a more normal legal machinery for determination of the best interests of the children'.[1]

Legal proceedings

The first cases were heard in public so as to demonstrate the correctness of the procedure adopted, but this had serious effects upon some of the children involved and the practice was stopped. The hearings became informal; the child was usually not present in court and was interviewed by the judge in his own chambers. In general, interested parties only (officials of the IRO, representatives of the *Jugendamt*, and so on) were present. In order to accelerate the procedure, the court increased the number of hearings and the IRO improved the preparatory work in order to process the cases completely and present them effectively. A case worker was designated in each case to prepare a pre-hearing summary based on the case record and to transfer it with the complete case history to the legal officer. The legal office had to arrange a steady flow of cases, collecting all pertinent information and documents available. The supervision of the whole operation by an international legal officer of the IRO ensured that no case was brought before the court without the documents essential to the support of the IRO petition.

The total case-load of unaccompanied children in May 1951 was 476. By 25 May 1951, 216 cases had been referred to the responsible legal officer, 150 petitions

---

[1] Report to US HICOG on IRO, US zone of Germany, 22 Oct. 1951, p. 10. The Law was improved by an Amendment Law No. 18, effective 27 Feb. 1951.

had been filed by the IRO, and 46 finally decided. By 19 September 1951, 271 cases had been received. Of this number 52 were not filed, 219 were filed (114 for resettlement outside Germany, 42 for repatriation, 31 for settlement in Germany). At this date 121 final decisions had been pronounced and 52 cases had still to be heard from the beginning, others being heard but not finished. Thus, thanks to co-operation between the court and the IRO, the procedure became more satisfactory.

The law was based on the principles of similar legislation and courts in the US and was designed for the protection of the children. The court determined whether or not the child was in fact an unaccompanied displaced child and whether the child's interest could best be served by his settlement in Germany or whether he required repatriation or resettlement elsewhere. The Polish Government protested to the US Department against the American jurisdiction in the matter.

In determining the child's best interests the court, pursuant to Article 14 of the law, was to be guided by the following factors:

(a) the existence or absence of a wholesome relationship between the child and its foster-parents or other persons,
(b) the likelihood that the child would secure an adequate education,
(c) the physical and moral welfare of the child including the probability of its obtaining adequate food, clothing, medical care and a desirable home atmosphere,
(d) the legal and economic protection of the child in the relation to rights of citizenship, rights to future public care and maintenance including medical and nursing care, opportunity to earn a livelihood, and the likelihood of discrimination or bias,
(e) the wishes of the child if it had sufficient maturity and had formed its wishes without coercion,[1]
(f) the desires of a natural parent, foster-parent, or other near relative by consanguinity.

If the child had to be removed from German custody (either in an institution or private home or in some other such place) the judgement included an order for the removal and designated a guardian for the person and the property of the child.

The British authorities followed a different method of safeguarding the interests of these children. At the beginning of the operation, child search officers had almost complete power of individual decision concerning the future placement of an unaccompanied child. In all cases their recommendations on this subject were referred to the local military official (Relief Detachment Commander) for decision; but in many cases the representative of the occupation authorities had little opportunity, because of pressure of work and time limitations, to study the scores of individual cases submitted. In consequence a child's future was almost wholly dependent on the attitude of the individual IRO officer towards repatriation and German foster-care, and the officers varied considerably in their interpretation of policy. To achieve a more uniform policy, a Child Welfare Board, composed of

---

[1] Decision of the American Court of Appeal with respect to a 13-year-old Czech child. On 4 June 1949 the Supreme Court of Sweden decided that a Finnish child which was placed with foster-parents in Sweden during the war and expressly stated that it did not want to return to its parents in Finland should not be forced to return.

representatives of the occupying power and of the IRO, was established in August 1947, which worked until its termination on 31 December 1951.

The main function of the Board was to make recommendations for the future of the child on humanitarian grounds without considerations of a political nature, so that the welfare of the child became the primary aim within the agreed policy. Child welfare officers submitted cases with their recommendations to the Board, which, upon making findings and further recommendations, forwarded the cases for confirmation and final approval to the Chief, PW and DP Division, of the British Element of the Control Commission for Germany (later to the UK High Commissioner who was the final authority for approving repatriation and resettlement overseas or local settlement). 2,500 children were repatriated and 1,200 resettled in Europe and overseas during the period 1 July 1947 to 31 December 1951, and 57 uncompleted cases were handed over to the International Social Service in Geneva.

The work of the British Child Welfare Board was an outstanding example of successful liaison between the IRO and the occupation authorities and was described as such by the IRO Chief of Mission in his final Report in December 1951 to the IRO headquarters in Geneva. In retrospect it can be said that the British procedure was preferable to the court system in the US zone. The latter might have been more 'legal', but in practice could often not avoid delay and harmful publicity of the case which were contrary to the best interest of the child.

Child search

The search for unaccompanied children taken to Germany and Austria for purposes of Germanization, begun by UNRRA, was carried on by the IRO, but with significant changes in the method previously used, so that a final intensive effort could be made to find the maximum number of missing UN children in the minimum of time. Child searching[1] was delegated to the ITS, to which was added a Central Child Search Branch, with its headquarters at Esslingen. Its task was to find children kidnapped by the Nazis, and all other non-German children who had become displaced persons and unaccompanied as the result of the war; to identify these children, establish their citizenship, and provide them with documents; and to bring them into communication with their parents or relatives. Child search officers were appointed in the three zones of Germany to be responsible for the field operations and to direct the search teams which carried out all the necessary investigations and interrogations. For financial and administrative reasons only a 'Limited Registration Plan' was adopted and was inaugurated in the French zone at the end of 1948, early in 1949 in the two other western zones,[2] and shortly afterwards in the western sectors of Berlin. This plan involved a systematic investigation of the records of German institutions, foster families, and of adoption courts. The total number of

---

[1] Child search was defined as the process of looking for and locating children believed to be in occupied areas and whose names and particulars were not known. By tracing was meant the process of locating a child at the request of someone who could give particulars about him and of locating relatives of a child found without his family. See GC/198.

[2] In the US zone instructions were sent by the military government to the Prime Ministers of the German *Länder*. In the British zone the representative of the Child Search Branch was empowered to deal directly with the German officials.

children's cases reported amounted to 343,057 (191,199 in institutions, 130,682 in foster homes, 21,176 adopted).[1]

The next step was to register those children likely to be eligible for the IRO services, establish their identity and nationality if possible, and initiate tracing for their relatives if no inquiry was held on file in the children's master index. Upon further investigation many children were found to be German, while the nationality of others was not determinable.

The 'Germanized' children were difficult to discover as their names, birth-dates, and nationalities had usually been completely obliterated. They had been subjected to intensive German doctrinization and, in the case of smaller children, no longer remembered their rightful parents nor the country of their origin. Such children could only be found by detective search for documents which might reveal the identity and subsequent disposal made of these children during the Nazi régime. After further investigation and screening, a total of 4,000 children were finally registered by Child Search, their cases being passed to the IRO field offices for determination of eligibility. When accepted by the IRO the children became the responsibility of the IRO child welfare officers, who initiated social investigations preparatory to making final plans for their future permanent establishment.

At the same time as the Limited Registration Plan was being carried out individual inquiries were still being received. These amounted to 5,576, comprising forty-six nationalities and emanating from twenty-seven different countries, from 1 January 1949 to 1 January 1951. They were handled in the same way as adult inquiries. Altogether a total of 4,808 cases were solved by Child Search and Child Tracing during 1949–50.

On 1 January 1948 the total Child Search/Tracing staff amounted to 11 (2 international); by 1 January 1950, 386 (59 international); and by 1 January 1951 it had been reduced to 20 (1 international).

This search and registration applied only to Germany. In Austria, where the ITS did not operate, children were traced by local child welfare officers who followed up the cases themselves.

The determination of eligibility for the IRO assistance followed the Constitutional provisions which differed from those for adults in so far as it was officially stated: 'the unaccompanied children were eligible irrespective of any other conditions or requirements; the mere fact that they were unaccompanied children as defined' in the Constitution was 'enough to make them eligible'.

Thus no valid objections to repatriation and other conditions relevant to adults, e.g. exclusion of persons of German ethnic origin, needed to be taken into account. The definition of unaccompanied children was interpreted by the Administration in November 1947 to mean children who fulfilled the six following conditions:

(a) 16 years of age or under (i.e. a child who has not attained his or her seventeenth birthday);
(b) outside of their countries of origin or of that of their parents;
(c) orphans, or children whose parents have disappeared or whose parents are unattainable, or who have been abandoned;

[1] GC/198.

(d) not provided with a legal guardian, or children whose guardian has disappeared or abandoned them, or who is unobtainable;

(e) not accompanied by a close relative (adult brother, sister, uncle, aunt, or grand-parents);

(f) children in respect of whom there exists a presumption that they belong to one of the categories of refugees or displaced persons on whose account the IRO was established.[1]

Thus Arab children were not within the mandate; the question of the eligibility of Jewish children from Tripolitania was dealt with.

A number of *Volksdeutsche* children, however, were assisted by the IRO in Austria. Most of them had left Yugoslavia after the war and had been accepted into a children's home on humanitarian grounds and for the examination of their cases, before their origin was known. Later it was not easy to assist them once they were over 16 years old and the normal clauses of the Constitution operated.

Nationality was a factor in the decision on eligibility. In particular, plans for re-patriation and resettlement could be made only after the child's nationality had been determined. As a general rule, citizenship had to be certified by the representative designated by the government of origin. This was often a slow process, delaying an action sometimes as long as ten months. For the guidance of eligibility officers, certain presumptions were established: a child of legally married parents would be presumed to possess the nationality of his father; and a child of unmarried parents would be presumed to possess the nationality of his mother.

The dependency of some accompanied children raised equally complex points. Especially as regards children of the first husband after the remarriage of the mother. If the stepfather accepted the child as a member of the family, the child would con-tinue to be accompanied. A second marriage of the mother, however, had no in-fluence on the nationality of the child. The child could still be a refugee even if the mother lost that status, having acquired a nationality by marriage.

Misunderstandings sometimes arose as some officials thought that the principle of *jus soli* applied, and that children born in the territory of a state were nationals of that state by birth, although under some continental law (e.g. Italian, Austrian, and German) this was not the case. Children whose parents' nationality could not be determined possessed the nationality of the territory in which they were found or were deemed, for the purposes of the Organization, to have an undetermined or no nationality. The Baltic unaccompanied children were claimed by the Soviet Union. The military authorities which did not recognize the annexation of the Baltic states, however, refused permission for the referral of such cases to the repre-sentatives of the USSR, and did not grant exit releases from the zones concerned. Further, *Volksdeutsche* unaccompanied children outside their country of origin were, as already indicated, within the mandate of the Organization, as the provisions of the Constitution on exclusion of refugees of German ethnic origin were not applicable to unaccompanied children. This was, however, only the case as long as they were not protected by a national government. For this reason, unaccompanied children of German ethnic origin residing in Germany were not within the mandate

---

[1] UN, ECOSOC Doc. E/816, p. 49 and IRO *Operational Manual*.

of the Organization as they were protected by the Government of the German Federal Republic pursuant to Article 16 of the Bonn Constitution. Likewise, unaccompanied children of south Tyrolean origin transferred to Austria were not within the mandate of the Organization, as they were transferred under an international agreement and firmly established in Austria. As regards children from Venezia Giulia, it had to be assured that they were really refugees and not Italian citizens during the time they were under the Yugoslav régime. Children of this group often had an Italian legal guardian who opted in their name for Italian citizenship. It had to be found out whether this declaration was legally justified or not.

Unaccompanied children, boys and girls, were the particular concern of the child welfare officers. Once basic eligibility was determined they made the important initial decision as to whether it was advisable for a given child to stay in an institution or foster-home or be removed to a children's centre. A gift of $2 million by UNRRA for child welfare purposes enabled the IRO to engage a larger child welfare staff than would otherwise have been possible. The Organization made speedy plans to re-establish the children and to provide a supplementary food ration, which furnished approximately 350 calories a day from 1 January 1948 to each child.

Children's centres

In occupied Germany, following the removal of children from German communities, centres exclusively for children were needed—establishments where the children could be physically rehabilitated if they were undernourished, and psychologically adapted to a new life. Children who could be repatriated were kept in these centres only long enough to prepare them for their return home, thus the turn-over in the camps was fairly high and had to be taken into account in the organization of the children's centres.

The numbers of centres for the accommodation of children in the zones varied in the different periods of the IRO's activities, since the tendency was to consolidate them whenever possible. In the US zone there were, in July 1947, 2,814 unaccompanied children in the IRO's charge. 1,792 of them were cared for in thirteen children's centres having a total capacity of 4,515 children, and the remaining 1,022 were sheltered in regular assembly centres. In November 1948 a single children's village was established at Bad Aibling, in which were assembled children from other centres at Aglasterhausen, Prien, and Wartenberg. It had a maximum capacity of 525, and the peak figure reached there, in June 1949, was 486 residents—290 unaccompanied children, 125 unaccompanied young people, and 71 temporarily unaccompanied children. The figures were constantly fluctuating with large numbers entering for temporary care, and equally large numbers leaving for some form of re-establishment. In the planning of this village, voluntary societies such as the American Friends Service Committee, the World's YMCA/YWCA, and ORT were particularly helpful, not only as regards general policy, but also in arranging camp activities, counselling children, working in kindergartens and in pre-primary schools. At the end of the IRO's operations a small residual group of about 100 unaccompanied children (because of legal and other complications) were placed in the children's centre at Feld Afing, near Munich, on 1 November 1951. Other services to children in the US zone were a children's psychiatric service for difficult children who required expert diagnosis, therapy, and psychological testing, and a hospital and centre for the rehabilitation of forty physically handicapped boys and girls at Dorfen, near Munich. Both of them afforded treatment by specialists, and the latter was turned over to the Bavarian State, at the end of the IRO's operations, to be administered by the *Arbeiter-Wohlfahrt*, a German voluntary society which agreed to continue to supply services to displaced persons' children as long as required.

In the British zone the administration of children's centres was the responsibility of the occupation authorities. In July 1947 there were sixteen such installations with a total capacity of 843 children and an actual population of 573 children. The policy was also to concentrate the work, with the result that in July 1949 there were only nine centres, in November 1949 three, and in January 1950 two. One of these two remaining in 1950, Klinkberg, was specially maintained for children who were to be resettled in the US. When Klinkberg was closed another centre was opened by the occupation authorities in the Wentorf assembly centre.

In the French zone the children's centres were in Hinterzarten (Baden), replaced later in July 1949 by the Aeriom Donaueschingen, with 120 beds, and in Unterhausen (Württemberg) with 81 beds.

In Austria there was a children's home at Bad Schallerbach in the US zone, and at Leoben in the British zone.

In Italy the children's centres were usually established by voluntary societies, such as the Jewish Hachshara, the vocational training groups that were supported by the IRO and later extended to children. Centres for children of Catholic or Orthodox faith were gradually set up, especially through the work of the NCWC also supported by the IRO. The only children's centre operated by the IRO itself was that at Mercatello, Salerno, established in March 1949. It was used in the spring of 1949 by a group of Tripolitanian Jewish children who left for Israel, and later by a group of Polish children who came to Italy from East Africa in June 1949 and stayed in the centre until October 1949. Afterwards it was used as a processing centre for small groups of 15–20 unaccompanied children being resettled in the US. The equipping, supplying, and supervising of this centre was difficult.

In other countries the IRO did not maintain refugees directly, and the voluntary societies to which the Organization granted financial aid placed their existing children's homes at the disposal of the IRO's unaccompanied children, and even in some cases created new homes, e.g. in France, Belgium, and the Netherlands. Nurseries and kindergartens were also established by voluntary societies with the participation of the IRO in many parts of the world, for instance in Shanghai.

Temporary care

Temporarily unaccompanied children, i.e. those who normally lived with their family but needed temporary care during the family's illness or absence, were admitted to the IRO's children's homes until 30 June 1950 and received the same welfare services as unaccompanied children. Towards the end of operations, temporarily unaccompanied children remained the responsibility of the IRO only if they were in the process of being resettled, while responsibility for children with no expectation of being resettled would be transferred to the local authorities, and case records given to an appropriate agency (NCWC, CWS, LWF).[1]

Offers of temporary care for children in countries outside the country of residence were accepted only if this meant an opportunity to give them better care than was available in the country of residence. Such a scheme had to be sponsored by a recognized agency or organization and approved by the IRO's Geneva headquarters; the sponsoring agency had to assume full moral, physical, and financial responsibility for the child during the time it was under the care of the agency; provision for transportation to and from the place of temporary care had to be made; and contact with the child's family had to be ensured, if possible, by an exchange of correspondence. The selection of children for such care was carried out by child welfare and medical officers at the IRO's field headquarters.

Settlement

After every attempt to keep or reunite the child with its own family had proved fruitless, the child was placed into a foster home. Foster-homes were family homes in which a child under 17 years of age who was unrelated to the family received care. They were approved when their standards were equal to or above the average prevailing in the community. There had to be a written agreement covering details. The child, provided with clothing, was placed in the foster-home after medical and dental examination. Periodic inspection of the home was prescribed to safeguard the child and help the foster-family. In occupied areas, placement in a home of the indigenous population was not the normal practice. However, when a child had been found in a foster-home, the decision might be taken to leave it there if that were in its best interest. Procedure for legal guardianship or adoption might be instituted. If there were relatives, a foster-home record was forwarded to them.

The IRO gave assistance in repatriation to unaccompanied children whose nationality had been determined. The figures were rather small. In all cases where children or young people were prepared to return, the IRO gave them facilities for doing so, but did not take any measures of coercion.

Repatriation from Germany and Austria was effected continuously, usually by rail after approval by the occupation authorities. On the Polish side, a reception centre was established in Katowicz, where the children were cared for and received identity cards. Sometimes, delays in repatriation arose through the attitude of the other countries of origin, as the national liaison officers or repatriation missions received rather lengthy instructions from their governments, or the authorities hesitated to repatriate children or the repatriation was delayed because of lack of escorts. Minor groups were repatriated from other European countries, as, for instance, several Polish children from Spain.

The repatriation of children who were in far distant countries was also arranged. For instance, children who went in 1944 from Persia to New Zealand with the approval of the Polish Government returned if they wished; and children who

---

[1] Report of the Director General on the Plan of the IRO's Operation for the Supplementary Period, 30 Aug. 1950, p. 29.

were living in the Union of South Africa either remained there, or were removed for repatriation or resettlement in accordance with their wishes.

The most difficult case was the group of Polish children who had been in India, were transferred to East Africa, and thence were to be in part repatriated and in part resettled to Canada. When they were in India, all the children had legal guardians appointed by the local courts[1] although the Polish Government considered itself exclusively entitled to make such appointments. In early spring of 1948 the children were moved with the adult group of Polish refugees from India to East Africa: 329 of them were in Tanganyika, 52 in Uganda, and 29 in Southern Rhodesia. The high courts of the territories concerned appointed boards of guardians according to the local laws to be responsible for the welfare of the children. These boards were opposed to the repatriation of the children, chiefly because they feared that no religious education would be tolerated. They were even reluctant to give their approval for resettlement purposes without being fully informed about the plans and the persons likely to be appointed as guardians.

Thus the IRO, in seeking the best interests of the children, had to steer between the strong view of the Polish Government in favour of repatriation of all children regardless of their personal wishes and the attitude of the boards of guardians.

Resettlement in Canada was proposed finally for those children who were prepared to be resettled. The children were moved, with the approval of the boards of guardians, in transit to Italy. One hundred and fifty persons (93 children, 54 young people, and 3 who had just passed their twenty-first birthday) moved via Mombasa to Bari with 7 adult refugees and 1 international member of the IRO's escort staff. Arriving on 19 June 1949 they were transported from the port of debarkation to a centre at Salerno, where they were met by a welfare officer sent from Germany. A repatriation officer, speaking Polish, was sent to this camp, staying there three weeks to give information on repatriation in an objective manner; instructions were given that repatriation had priority over resettlement. As the Polish Embassy in Rome wanted its staff to meet the children, the wish was complied with by the IRO.

From Salerno the children were transported to a centre near Bremen to be resettled in Canada. Here, the delegation of the Polish Red Cross claimed that all the children should be repatriated and protested against their resettlement. The Polish Minister for Foreign Affairs requested the IRO's office in Warsaw to inform Geneva that the IRO's staff in Germany refused information, and asked for the repatriation of the group. The IRO's Geneva headquarters proposed that a representative be sent to discuss the matter. The Polish Government did not send a representative to Geneva and the Polish Red Cross representative in Germany asked for the nominal rolls of all children and an opportunity to see their individual documents. In accordance with the attitude of the ECOSOC in this matter, the IRO could not meet this wish. The children were transported to Canada, and the Polish Government requested the closure of the IRO's mission in Warsaw. The Director

---

[1] Guardians were persons residing within the local limits of the jurisdiction of the court: the guardians might not remove the ward, without the leave of the court, outside the limits of the jurisdiction.

General made a statement on the matter before the Third Committee of the General Assembly of the UN on 10 November 1949.[1]

The policy on resettlement was laid down in Provisional Order No. 33 which stated:

No plan for resettlement of unaccompanied children will be considered unless the plan has been approved by headquarters Geneva and information concerning it has been issued to the Field. The only exception will be children reunited with parents or close relatives in other countries.

A later order defined the conditions under which proposed resettlement schemes for unaccompanied children and young people under 18 years of age would be acceptable to the Organization. The main conditions were the appointment of a guardian (individual or responsible agency) and supervision by him as regards adjustment to the new surroundings, opportunity to become a citizen, opportunities of education as for citizens, protection by child labour laws, and sound financial position of the sponsor bearing the costs of maintenance, education, and medical care until the young person could become self-supporting.

According to these principles the IRO as a general rule did not deal directly with individual offers. The Organization prepared general schemes on resettlement and forwarded individual offers of homes for children to the appropriate voluntary societies. Altogether 4,053 children were resettled.[2]

As regards resettlement in various countries, there were schemes for the resettlement of children in general and special agreements for the benefit of physically or mentally handicapped children. The main resettlement countries for normal children were the US, Canada, Australia, Sweden, and Israel.

Resettlement in the US was regulated by the Displaced Persons Act of 25 June 1948, section 2e of which provided for the immigration of 3,000 displaced orphans in accordance with certain eligibility requirements: they were to be children eligible for the IRO's assistance, under the age of 16 years who were orphans because of the death or disappearance of both parents and who, on 25 June 1948, were in the three western zones of Germany or Austria or in the western sectors of Berlin or in Italy.

This provision was later amended. First it was provided that a displaced orphan was eligible if he or she were 16 years of age or under on 25 June 1948, so that it was possible to resettle even a person who was more than 16 years of age at the date of resettlement. Secondly, the residence date was changed from 25 June 1948 to 16 June 1950 so that resettlement opportunities were made available to 'unaccompanied youth' who had come after 25 June 1948 from eastern European countries.

The two committees which dealt especially with the resettlement of children in the US in co-operation with the IRO were the United States Committee for the Care of European Children and the War Relief Service of the NCWC. The former committee operated initially in the US zones of Germany and Austria, and accepted children up to 18 years of age of any religion. The committee ran a home in the Bronx, New York, from which children were sent into foster homes or institutions according to their religion. The activity of the committee was extended to the British

---

[1] UN General Assembly, Fourth Session, *Summary Records*, Third Committee, Sept.–Nov. 1949, pp. 120–1.   [2] Annex 48, p. 514.

zones from which a first group of sixty-seven children who, for five years had looked forward to the possibility of immigration to the US, were resettled in March 1949. A total of 1,866 orphans and unaccompanied children were admitted to the US under the sponsorship of the committee during the lifetime of the IRO.

The second committee dealt with Catholic children, particularly those located in Italy. From August 1950 onwards a representative of that office was attached to the Child Resettlement Branch in Italy, and afterwards a special NCWC office was established. Catholic immigration to Canada, on the other hand, was regulated by an agreement between the Catholic Emigrants' Aid Society and the IRO, concluded in December 1948. This society was authorized by Canadian Order-in-Council, P.C. 3396 of 3 August 1948, to sponsor the immigration, reception, maintenance, and placement of 1,000 unaccompanied and orphan Catholic children aged from 5 to 16 years, to be selected in the US, French, and British zones of Germany and Austria. The society sent to Europe a trained social worker to supervise the selection of the children in collaboration with the Canadian selection officers and the occupation authorities. The children remained in reception centres in Canada pending their placement in suitable private homes.

Another Canadian Order-in-Council[1] authorized the Canadian Jewish Congress to accept 1,000 orphan children for placement. The selection was made by the IRO's child welfare staff, working in conjunction with a representative of the Jewish Congress in the three western zones of Germany and Austria, in France, and Italy. The children were received by the Jewish Congress in reception centres, and their placement in foster-homes and their supervision was arranged with the provincial government authorities responsible for child care and protection.

The IRO's Resettlement Division suggested that the Australian military mission in Berlin should consider the allocation of a part of its immigration requirements to the adolescent group. The Commonwealth of Australia decided to accept under the terms of its agreement with the IRO a number of juveniles of 16–18 years. It was agreed that the legal guardianship of them would be vested in the Ministry for Immigration and that supervision over them would be exercised by the State Child Welfare departments. The young people would be received in reception centres in the charge of that department, which would be responsible for accommodation and training, medical, dental, and optical treatment, and for suitable employment after the period in the centre.

As regards employment, difficulties arose because the Australian Government decided that adolescents should be warned before selection that they would be directed mainly to rural and domestic employment for a period of two years with the understanding that efforts would later be made to assist any selected juveniles to take up occupations for which they might appear better suited. The IRO Welfare Division had thought it was understood that apprenticeship and the continuance of technical education would be encouraged and consideration be given to choice of occupation. Many young people were unwilling to accept the conditions; but, finally, a number were selected, documented, and sent to Australia, the special scheme closing in June 1950.

---

[1] P.C. 1647 approved by the Governor General on 29 Apr. 1947.

One hundred and twenty unaccompanied children of undetermined nationality, under 12 years of age, and of Protestant faith were authorized by the Swedish Government to resettle permanently in that country. The children were sent first to an excellent children's centre operated by the Swedish Save the Children Fund. Foster-home placements were made with a view to adoption; the same educational opportunities were available as for Swedish citizens. Officials of the Save the Children Fund were appointed as legal guardians. The scheme, which was first drawn up for the British zone of Germany and was put into operation there in September 1947, was extended in September 1948 to the three zones of Germany and Austria. The IRO paid for travel while the Swedish Save the Children Fund provided the travel documents, visas, and escort.

The Jewish Agency for Palestine which operated in Germany and Austria on the basis of an agreement with UNRRA and without formal agreement with the IRO arranged for the selection of unaccompanied children to be resettled in Palestine.

Beside the agreements on unaccompanied children as such, special agreements were concluded on mentally or physically handicapped or tuberculous children, who were in general prevented from immigrating by restrictions in the legislation concerned. Thus, handicapped children were established in Belgium, Ireland, Sweden, Switzerland, the US, and elsewhere. The IRO contributed either by the payment of a lump sum or with an amount for each child in the various schemes.

In the early years of the IRO's activities it was hoped to avoid the necessity of local settlement. While it had been possible to extend the time-limits more than once, the Administration had to decide that the final plans for all children should be completed by 31 October 1951, and that new cases would not be accepted after 30 June 1951. Although visas for children were issued in accordance with the extension of the US Displaced Persons Act until June 1952, officers were urged not to consider resettlement as definite without the actual promise of a visa or acceptance by a selection mission. For children who had not yet been accepted by countries or agencies, it was agreed to complete plans of local settlement. The IRO child care branch arranged for such cases to be referred to voluntary agencies who would see to their care in foster homes or institutions. Agreements were concluded with the governments of the countries of residence, with the German *Länder* governments, and national welfare agencies in order to assure the welfare of the small residual group of unaccompanied children in Germany, Austria, and Italy. In August 1951 520 children were settled in Germany, 269 in Austria, and 45 in Italy; all were placed with families except for the handicapped children who had been placed in institutions.

The action taken in connexion with the transfer of responsibilities can be illustrated by the example of the US zone of Germany. Here the NCWC accepted all cases of Catholic children referred to it by the IRO for possible resettlement in the US. This organization undertook to arrange with the Caritas organization for the care of the children during the period of waiting for transportation to the US, and also for the preparation and filing of petitions with the childrens' courts and the completion of pending cases. The United States Committee for the Care of European Children, European Headquarters, dealt with other children nominated for the

Committee's assurances. The International Social Service (ISS) accepted responsibility for all new cases appearing after November 1951 which would have been within the responsibility of the Child Welfare Division of the IRO, referring the cases to the appropriate sponsoring agency in the US if resettlement in that country seemed to be in the child's best interest. Furthermore, the ISS accepted responsibility for children on behalf of whom plans for resettlement or repatriation had not been completed, and for children who were remaining in Germany whose cases required following up by the German Branch of the ISS until adoption and if possible naturalization. Finally, negotiations were initiated with the CWS and the LWF with a view to their acceptance of residual children in co-operation with their local agencies. Nominal rolls of children remaining within the IRO mandate after 30 June 1950 and not established outside Germany were transferred to the Allied High Commission in Germany and the German *Jugendamt*.

In the British zone legal guardianship or adoption was arranged for the normal children who remained, and institutional care was provided for mental deficient and handicapped children. Similar arrangements were made in the French zone of Germany. The children left in France, Belgium, and the Netherlands were under the supervision of voluntary societies; permanent and social assistance were furnished by the governments concerned.

The IRO was entrusted by its constitution with a tremendous task. The priority protection and assistance for unaccompanied children meant, both in the minds of those who had drafted the Article and in the minds of those who had to interpret it, that the Organization would act in almost every respect as a kindly parent to the children, providing for their care and shelter, their education, vocational training, their physical health, and their moral guidance. The IRO laboured under several handicaps in performing its obligations to its little charges. It did not have the legal status of a guardian or the confidence of the countries of nationality of the children or the right to make final decisions on re-establishment. Moreover, in order to carry out its mandate completely, the Organization had to search for those who had disappeared as a result of deportation or war events, to trace families, to reunite children with their families—in a word, to try to remedy, during its temporary existence, the evils brought about by a deliberate, painstaking, and thoroughly ruthless Nazi plan to kidnap foreign children and conceal their whereabouts. The humanitarian claims of social assistance were often such as to oppose restitution of the child to its original country, and the child welfare workers of the Organization often had to assist in evaluating the relative merits of foster-parents who loved the children and surviving relatives who hardly knew them. The fact that this part of the Organization's programme was carried out with such substantial success in the face of overwhelming difficulties reflects most creditably on the individual child search and child welfare officers of the IRO and the ITS whose devotion to the well-being of the children in their charge went far beyond the normal call of duty.

ANNEX 47

Unaccompanied children repatriated by IRO

Unaccompanied children, 16 years and under, within the IRO Mandate repatriated from specified IRO areas
1 July 1947–31 Dec. 1951

Country of destination	Total	Austria	Czechoslovakia	Far East		France	Germany			Italy	Middle East
				Philippines	Shanghai		British zone	French zone	US zone		East Africa
TOTAL	1,898	585	1	2	3	21	617	85	573	3	8
Algeria	1						1				
Argentina	2					2					
Austria	41					1	4	1	33	2	
Belgium	41	1				1	23	4	12		
Bulgaria	1	1									
Burma	1				1						
Chile	4	4									
Czechoslovakia	83	4					15	2	62		
Denmark	4						4				
Eire	1								1		
Finland	1					5	1		1	1	
France	47						17		30		
Germany	9	1					1	1			
Greece	6	1			2		1	1			
Hungary	26	2				8	2	1	4		
Italy	18	1					5	3	13		
Latvia	10						10	3	9		
Lithuania	3						3				
Luxembourg	3						1	1	1		
Netherlands	73					1	1	2	29		
Norway	14						41		10		8
Poland	836	5					452	53	315		
Rumania	17	9				3	3		5		
US	6			2			2		2		
USSR	45	1					23	9	12		
Yugoslavia	80	30	1				5	9	35		
Not reported	525	525									

L l

ANNEX 48

Unaccompanied children resettled by IRO

Unaccompanied children, 16 years and under, within the IRO Mandate resettled from specified IRO areas
1 July 1947–31 Dec. 1951

Country of destination	Total	Austria	Belgium	Denmark	Far East — Philippines	Far East — Shanghai	France	Germany — British zone	Germany — French zone	Germany — US zone	Italy	Middle East — East Africa	Middle East — Lebanon	Middle East — Turkey	Netherlands	Spain
TOTAL	4,053	559	10	1	20	22	381	1,102	53	1,628	205	62	1	1	5	3
Algeria	2						2									
Argentina	5	1					2				2					
Australia	192	26					27	55	7	54	23					
Austria	5						1	4								
Belgium	35	7					1	8		19						
Bolivia	1							1								
Brazil	11						1	4	1	3	1	1				
Canada	447	28					16	61	2	318	21					
Chile	4	1							2	2	1					
Eire	12							2		10						
France	70	3	4				43	8			10					
Germany	5					5										
Israel	952	8	5				201	475	6	215	43				5	
Italy	2						1									
Netherlands	2															2
New Zealand	27	7						3		5	10	1		1		
Norway	3							3								
Paraguay	4	1						1		2						
Sweden	60	6						44		6	4					
Switzerland	2									2						
UK	137	9	1	1			4	37	1	21	1	60	1			1
US	1,717	139			20		81	397	24	963	88					
Uruguay	3									3						
Venezuela	8	3								5						
Not reported	347	320				17			10							

Israeli Government authorities claim that the Children's and Youth Department of the Jewish Agency were instrumental in bringing 12,592 young people to Israel in the period 1 Sept. 1945 to 1 July 1951 (7,713 from Germany, 3,680 from Italy, and 1,199 from Austria). They observe that it is obvious that most of these children arrived in Israel after the beginning of the IRO's operations on 1 July 1947, and were unaccompanied.

CHAPTER XXV

SUPPORTING SERVICES

A. SUPPLY AND VEHICLES

ON 1 July 1947 IRO was responsible for providing clothing, food, and the basic necessities for approximately 713,000 persons. Some 28,000 were in the Middle East, 10,000 in the Far East, and more than 675,000 in eight countries of Europe. Most of them, however, were concentrated in Germany where there were more than 604,000, almost 85 per cent. of all refugees receiving care and maintenance.[1]

The main pattern and course of the Organization's supply operation was greatly influenced by the fact that the majority of refugees materially supported by the IRO were located in a single country. Primarily because these refugees lived in an occupied country, all supply efforts of the Organization on their behalf were required to be in co-ordination and co-operation with the Occupation Authorities of three Allied Powers. In all activities the Organization sought to avoid, so far as possible, any conflicts with the plans, arrangements, and activities of the Occupation Authorities for the control of Germany and its rehabilitation and recovery.

Beyond this, early supply operations were greatly influenced by the fact that they were carried out in war-ravaged areas whose economies were seriously crippled. As the result of recent hostilities, industrial and agricultural production was at abnormally low levels; and indigenous facilities for carrying goods and passengers were either inadequate or non-existent. Germany in 1947 lacked the basic economic resources essential for the livelihood of even its own population apart from the refugees who had found asylum there: and it seemed then that this condition could not be repaired for years to come.

To counteract vital deficiencies and to start the country toward ultimate economic recovery, the occupying countries buttressed the German economy according to their respective capacities. Largely because of the greater impact which the war had had on their own economies, France and Great Britain were unable to aid Germany in a material way to the same extent as the US. When hostilities had ceased, the US alone was in a position to export food to Germany. As the US army and its auxiliary services were able to supplement the German food ration as early as 1945, the US zone of occupation became a preferred haven for hungry refugees.

Throughout the entire operation, the refugee population receiving care and maintenance in the US zone of Germany comprised more than half of the grand total for all countries; and as the supply activities for this area related significantly to the other zones of Germany and elsewhere as well, the total supply effort of the Organization was carried out largely through the section of Germany controlled by the US occupation authorities. Inevitably, as the economic reconstruction of Germany

---

[1] PREP/130, 25 Oct. 1947, p. 14.

progressed throughout the years, the supply programme of the Organization was adapted in line with these changes.

But even in normal and full functioning economies, the care and maintenance of large refugee populations would present a special supply problem. The vast majority of refugees were forced by circumstances to live apart from the normal community, with little or no access to the life of the surrounding economy. Lacking an economic basis of its own, the refugee community was dependent for its bare existence on aid from the outside, and on the special and unusual arrangements which must be made to provide this help.

The basic supply task of the Organization was thus to develop suitable means of a special nature for providing the material assistance needed by refugees. In meeting this responsibility the closest co-operation and co-ordination with the Occupation Authorities was indicated, particularly in the US zone of Germany where such a large part of the total refugee population was concentrated, and where the Occupation Authorities in earlier days had established exceptional measures to improve the welfare of the refugee as well as that of the local population.

In Germany the supply task of the new organization could have been considerably larger had it not been for actions and decisions of the past. In April 1945 General Eisenhower named the care of UN displaced persons as a major Allied objective. Subsequent staff planning on the supply programme for the care of displaced persons followed the basic principle that the German economy had been responsible for the importation of slave labour and therefore was responsible for continued care and maintenance of the victims until such time as they could be repatriated or otherwise re-established.

A most significant limitation was put on this responsibility, however, by the Byrnes–Bevin Agreement for the economic fusion of the US and UK zones in Germany which became effective 1 January 1947, and provided that the maintenance of displaced persons within both zones from the German economy should equal but not exceed the maintenance German citizens received from this economy.

The Byrnes–Bevin Agreement confirmed the earlier advantages to the Organization of deriving material support for refugees from the German economy. But it served also to restrict this support and to give the Organization the burden of payment for supplies, in excess of those to be provided by the German economy, which might be needed to bring the care of refugees up to the minimum standard of the Organization. Consequently, from the beginning, the Organization had to provide large quantities of supplies to supplement those drawn from the German economy without cost.

The implementation of the Byrnes–Bevin Agreement proved most complex and difficult. First, there was the problem of determining the ever-changing level of maintenance available to the Organization; this essentially was the responsibility of OMGUS whose findings were approved by the Organization. There was the further problem of agreement as to the method for drawing from the German economy; this was accomplished by calculations on the average level available to the German population rather than by item-by-item or group-by-group analysis.

Finally, there was the task of computing excessive drawings and arranging for satisfactory replacements to the German economy; this aspect chiefly concerned food supplies, and the Organization reached agreement with OMGUS on replacement items to be imported, largely those most needed by the German economy and, at the same time, advantageously procurable by the Organization.

One of the main factors which complicated calculations was the need for computing the ever-changing average population figures for both the refugee and the German populations. But despite frequent preliminary disagreements, differences, and negotiations, the Organization usually was able to reach agreement with the Occupation Authorities as to the average German level of maintenance. For the third year of operation the entitlement of the Organization from the German economy was estimated at around 1,060 DM *per capita* for the year; this total included 120 DM for food, 560 DM for other direct care items, and 380 DM for costs of administration and resettlement.

While the two predecessor organizations had received virtually all basic requirements from the Allied military governments, PCIRO was faced with the huge responsibility of providing all supplies and means of transport other than those obtained from indigenous sources under the terms of the Byrnes–Bevin Agreement. This enormously increased responsibility was particularly heavy in the US zones of Germany and Austria and also in Italy and, to a minor degree, in Egypt where the responsibility included a complete operation of supply and transport agencies.

Apart from financial considerations there was not sufficient time to establish fully the supply facilities required, and it was physically impossible for the new organization to supply camps immediately through its own resources; the PCIRO had decided only in May. 1947 to become operationally responsible on 1 July. The only way toward meeting responsibilities at the start was to attempt to consolidate and use fully the services, supplies, equipment, and supply lines of UNRRA, IGCR, and the three Allied armies.[1]

Faced with the necessity for making long-term arrangements to ensure a continuous flow of needed supplies throughout the years ahead, PCIRO first was anxious to conclude immediate measures to prevent any early breakdown in the provision of basic necessities to refugees. In the US zone of Germany this was achieved in an early agreement that Occupation Authorities would continue in 1947, from current military stock on repayment, the same support refugees had received under UNRRA. In other areas as well, military authorities were most helpful in providing needed help. Whenever possible the Organization assisted by lending PCIRO-owned property for use in carrying out duties previously performed by UNRRA.

Under the agreement in the US zone of Germany[2] PCIRO undertook to care for physically and maintain refugees, and to provide supplementary supplies and facilities. In the British zone of Germany[3] these functions were delegated to the Occupation Authorities who were to perform them under the supervision of PCIRO.

[1] PREP/161, 5 Jan. 1948.
[2] IRO–CINCEUR, 9 July 1947, cf. Chapter VII, p. 128, and Appendix II, pp. 662 f.
[3] IRO, 28 June 1947, cf. Chapter VII, p. 129, and Appendix II, p. 656.

The agreement with the Occupation Authorities for the US zone of Austria[1] conformed essentially with that for the US zone of Germany; while agreements with the French zone of Austria[2] and with the British zone of Austria[3] were essentially similar to the agreements in the British and French zones of Germany.[4] The new organization was in the peculiar position of supervising the provision and distribution of supplies in the British and French areas of control, but of actually performing administrative and operational duties in these respects in the zones under American control where these responsibilities had been declined by the military authorities.

In China, Italy, and the Middle East necessary agreements dealing with the problem of actual supplies were concluded with the appropriate authorities, which also covered supply services and facilities to be provided by both parties to the agreements.

The agreements served to organize and regularize the supply job to be carried out jointly with the Occupation Authorities in Germany; generally, the authorities agreed to make available for refugees those needed supplies which could be drawn from the local economy; and there was to be no cost to PCIRO for these indigenous supplies up to the level available to Germans.

In the US zone of Germany the Organization imported supplies needed to supplement German supplies or to replace those supplies drawn from the German economy which were in excess of the level available to the indigenous population. In the British zone of Germany the Occupation Authorities at first undertook to make available the supplies which were above the indigenous level, and obtain repayment from PCIRO through a *per capita* charge; but the agreement later was amended so that the Organization would assume the task of procuring these supplies. In the French zone of Germany costs of supplies were included in a similar *per capita* charge, but this arrangement was changed later so that the Occupation Authorities obtained the supplies against repayment of actual costs.

In Austria the Government agreed to make available indigenous supplies up to the Austrian level and PCIRO imported and paid for additional supplies as required; in China and Italy the Organization procured and paid for all needed supplies; though when food shortages were critical in Italy in 1947 the Government made special deliveries direct from mills for needed pasta and flour; and loans of needed supplies, with all attendant difficulties, were necessary from the Italian Government until 1949.

In these days PCIRO made general agreements also with voluntary societies for the importation, handling, and distribution of supplies. The imported relief materials provided by voluntary societies had made a very substantial contribution to the care and well-being of displaced persons since 1946 and this assistance was regarded as an important asset for the future. Throughout the years, basic provisions of the early agreements on supply matters remained substantially the same. Later revisions and amendments pertained mostly to changes in the more technical aspects of co-operative efforts, and to methods of accounting and repayment to occupation

---

[1] 12 Sept. 1947, cf. Chapter VII, p. 128, and Appendix II, pp. 670–4.
[2] 6 Sept. 1947, cf. Chapter VII, p. 129, and Appendix II, pp. 605–12.
[3] 7 Nov. 1947, cf. Chapter VII, p. 129, and Appendix II, pp. 653–61.
[4] PREP/130, 25 Oct. 1947, p. 8.

authorities for their share of the refugee supply operation undertaken on behalf of IRO.

The early supply operation of PCIRO benefited greatly not only from the advance planning and efforts of the staff of UNRRA and IGCR, but also from the continued services of this staff; for, on the morning of 1 July 1947, most of the staff then remaining in the work of supply merely changed shoulder patches and continued to make available, as PCIRO employees, their earlier acquired skills and experience.

Temporary arrangements and development of the later supply operation were facilitated greatly by the earlier efforts of UNRRA. By February 1947 the UNRRA supply system had undergone numerous changes and reorganizations until finally it operated effectively through area team supply officers, each serving anywhere from 5,000 to 30,000 refugees; this staff worked through refugees in assembly centres who assumed responsibility for supply indenting, receipt, storage, and accounting. All planning by UNRRA supply division and EUCOM supply control branch prepared for the time when IRO would come into being, and when the programme would need to be paid for, in large measure, in hard currency.

In order to close UNRRA with an accurate transfer of all supplies, commodity accountants were appointed to each area team and accounting staff at US zone headquarters increased from one to seventy-five in the period 1 January to 1 July 1947. In every way possible a programme was prepared which could operate even if IRO did not have sufficient funds to commence field operations by 1 July. This forward planning, known as Operation Handout, was a working scheme which had the objective of effecting a competent supply organization to continue care and maintenance for refugees for the period from 1 July to 30 September 1947. Individual military and UNRRA officers assumed the responsibility for basic policy decisions; jointly they overcame vast difficulties to develop the machinery which provided for the continuation through the first three months of PCIRO operations of the earlier displaced persons' relief programme in the US zone of Germany.

In addition to such non-material aid, PCIRO also received goods from its predecessors. UNRRA gave the Organization supplies worth about 13 million appraised on the basis of actual costs. During the first six months of 1947 UNRRA had provided large quantities of materials for educational and employment programmes, and medical supplies and clothing to help the military meet its obligations; in the American zone of Germany alone, funds, equipment, and medical supplies worth almost $1,800,000, apart from motor vehicles and other assets, were turned over. The IGCR material assets, consisting mostly of inventories and reserves for USATS ships under contract, were valued at more than $400,000.

The UNRRA turnover comprised all property—including PX supplies[1] to which UNRRA had a clear title of ownership—which had not been declared surplus, and was held on charge for displaced persons operations as at 30 June 1947. Provisions also were made to ensure the continued use by IRO of properties and facilities formerly loaned to, leased by, or requisitioned on behalf of UNRRA. Previously existing contracts for the shipment of supplies and other essential facilities of this

[1] Amenity supplies issued through the military store or Post-Exchange (PX).

sort also were turned over to PCIRO which acquired from UNRRA virtually a complete supply organization in Germany.

In Italy UNRRA turned over food supplies estimated as sufficient for ninety days. Several hundred tons of canned food, medical supplies, and clothing worth millions of dollars were inherited by PCIRO in China, and proved to be adequate for more than the first six months of operation in that country.[1]

The complexities and far-flung nature of the UNRRA operation made impossible any precise evaluation of the vast amount of supplies transferred to PCIRO. Only one of the complicating factors, particularly in Italy and China, was the fact that PCIRO not only acquired supplies already delivered, but also those which were in the pipe-line at the time UNRRA ceased active operations; a reimbursable value of almost $385,000 was placed on these supplies alone.

During the first twelve months of the Organization's existence the procurement of supplies was one of its crucial functions, and the results and methods achieved in that period markedly affected not only the future of the Organization but, more important still, the welfare of hundreds of thousands of refugees. The achievements during these early months met immediate demands, and developed services of supply and transport necessary to the Organization's future success: services were combined and consolidated; supplies and equipment were effectively taken over from two predecessor organizations and from three allied armies; and earlier arrangements to support operations were maintained until new procedures could be developed and established. The Organization was thus able to carry out substantial economies needed and to solve problems which threatened its operations.

As a rule activities were decentralized and taken over by the field offices, while headquarters assumed the general supervisory responsibilities, directed policy-making and administration, and controlled the large-scale procurement of imported supplies.

Supply organization

The various missions submitted budgets and procurement requests for headquarters' approval, and made local purchases as authorized. The missions also distributed and handled supplies, though later headquarters controlled transfers of excess supplies from one mission to another. After the first year of operation, commodity accounting control was decentralized from headquarters; but in the final period Geneva organized the disposal of surplus properties.

During the first year it became evident that a clarification of internal responsibilities and procedures was needed; besides, the relatively small staff directing earlier operations found it difficult to cope with increased operations, and there were also occasional controversies at headquarters regarding supply matters. In the spring of 1948, therefore, definite and detailed official procurement instructions were released and issued to field offices by headquarters. This defined the procedure to be followed in the field offices for the programmes, procurement, and budgeting of all supplies and equipment (other than motor vehicles). The object of these instructions was to ensure that requirements in the field would be known to Geneva

[1] PREP/SR/76, p. 6.

early enough for goods to be bought and distributed before they were actually needed. Field offices, according to these instructions, had to submit a detailed list of all supplies and equipment required; Geneva headquarters then approved these procurement requests and arranged imports of some of the articles required, while field offices were empowered to purchase those goods which could be locally obtained. Under normal conditions field offices were instructed to maintain stocks of all expendable items including perishable goods, sufficient to cover four months' requirements. Any emergency procurement was undertaken by Geneva, and by field offices only in critical circumstances.

Transport

The procurement of motor vehicles presented special problems. Towards the end of 1947 instructions had been released covering the procurement of motor transport spares through the London Office, and almost a year later this was followed by further instructions outlining the procedure for the uniform requisitioning of motor transport supplies and equipment through the division of transport at headquarters in Geneva.

In the field of transport IRO began its operation with a total of 2,535 vehicles taken over from predecessor organizations. In addition IRO was allotted a large number of captured enemy vehicles plus 100 cars in the British zone, and 600 military vehicles and 1,558 trucking vehicles in the US zone of Germany. In all, seventy-seven different types of vehicle were received, many of them in their last stages of usefulness. This multiplicity of types and conditions of repair presented an extremely difficult problem of maintenance and provision of spare parts.

During this first year it proved possible to replace many of these vehicles through the purchase of 1,933 new commercial and military passenger and load-carrying units. In this way important steps toward standardization, which would drastically reduce maintenance and replacement costs, were taken.

In general the division of the transport function between IRO and the Occupation Authorities in Germany and Austria followed the same pattern as described above for the supply function. That is, in the US zones of both countries IRO was responsible for the movement of supplies at all levels, whereas, in the British and French zones this service was performed largely by the Occupation Authorities. IRO transport in these latter zones was largely limited to passenger vehicles for administrative staff. In other areas IRO operated administrative vehicles, obtaining most load-carrying vehicles from civilian sources.

Allocation of supplies

From the outset resources affected supplies; and in the years ahead much attention was directed to finance and accounting. In order to prepare a budget a rough computation of estimated *per capita* costs of care and maintenance was calculated. But there was the need to determine as soon as possible definite standards for the care to be provided by PCIRO; and to ascertain actual costs of supplies required to provide it. Headquarters in the US zone of Germany in the first days of operation advised that they needed definite instructions on standards of care in order to cope with daily problems and to avoid over-expenditures. EUCOM was pressing for official basic tables of allowances of supplies including food, clothing, medical stores, and household equipment. Voluntary societies, too, which had established earlier working arrangements, were pressing for information regarding their situation in the future.

When, in the first year, standards of health, care, and maintenance of refugees had been defined, the procurement of supplies was simplified; and efforts were made to implement these standards by overcoming circumstances which, at the start, had prevented refugees in some areas from receiving sufficient food and clothing. Costs of required supplies and services were ascertained in the early months, so that later supply budgets could be based on actual figures rather than on estimates.[1]

To meet immediate supply requirements, approximately 70 per cent. of the Organization's revised budget was allocated to the costs of the essential care and maintenance programme[2] and made available to the chief of the Office of Supply and Transport to enable him to procure ship transport and distribute supplies; new supply lines had to be established when necessary. The anticipated cost of maintaining the refugee population would leave very limited funds available for repatriation and resettlement, and it was abundantly clear that considerable economies must be effected if the Organization was to survive its first year of operation.

In view of this need for stringent economies, the Organization greatly reduced estimated costs so that considerable sums could be released from the direct supply budget to assist resettlement activities; and as a result of these savings a balanced budget was submitted for the following fiscal year.[3]

While expenditures for direct care, consisting mostly of supplies, remained at about the same level during the first two years—about $28 million—this total had dropped to $11,350,000 for the third year. Funds required for transport were budgeted directly to the organizational unit responsible for it, but the moneys needed for the procurement of supplies were charged to the budgets of the respective programmes which utilized these supplies.

The supply operation provided the chief means of utilizing non-convertible currencies received by the Organization as contributions from member nations, and this had an important effect on procurement sources, policies, and procedures. It was impossible, in the early days, to purchase basic supplies in large quantities with currencies not freely convertible,[4] but later such currencies amounted to 35 per cent. of the total procurement in the fiscal year 1948–9, with a record of 43 per cent. in the last six months of this year, as compared with only 8 per cent. in the first year of operations.[5]

To a certain extent this problem was solved by accepting, when possible and practicable, contributions from member governments in kind rather than in funds; for example, herrings, dehydrated vegetables, and other commodities were delivered by the governments of the Netherlands and Norway.[6] A general solution of the problem, however, was the development of procurement sources which would

[1] PREP/209, 30 Apr. 1948, p. 33.   [2] PREP/130, 25 Oct. 1947.
[3] Cf. Chapter VI, Finances, p. 103.   [4] GC/7, 7 Sept. 1948.
[5] GC/60, 22 Mar. 1949, p. 34.   [6] PREP/209, 30 Apr. 1948, p. 34.

accept non-convertible currencies, and in this effort the Organization was fairly successful. The expenditure of sterling was always a pressing problem, and the generous offer of the British Government to supply urgently needed motor vehicles was a welcome opportunity to expend soft currencies. Local procurement in non-occupied countries also was a partial solution of the problem, but the great expenditure necessary for food was never financed to any appreciable extent in soft currencies despite repeated efforts to do so.

Financial dealings connected with the purchase of supplies were greatly simplified because, necessarily, large quantities of supplies were purchased in the US and were handled by the Washington Office. Procurement in the US was financed largely from a trust account established to pay the US army for purchases most of which replaced supplies drawn from occupied areas so as to place the consumption of refugees above the indigenous level, and partly from a separate account established to pay for supplies otherwise obtained.[1]

Accounting

The complexity and financial significance of the supply operation called for an effective system of controls, reports, and accounting.[2] Originally, a budgetary control and commodity accounting branch was established in the office of supply and transport, Geneva, but it became evident after twelve months that this arrangement was not practicable, so the branch was abolished and the field missions undertook this work, and quantitative control was decentralized with responsibilities vested in the chiefs of office.

The principles, procedures, and methods of accounting for the property of the Organization and for the protection of such property was outlined fully at the time of the change. The new instruction defined IRO property, and placed responsibility for such property and its protection entirely upon the staff of the Organization; it required a continuous system of internal control, records, inventories, and inspections; it outlined methods for reporting losses and for investigations and action by survey officers and boards of survey.

Another comprehensive order covered the submission by field offices of inventories and reports on stock.[3] In the third year the Executive Committee requested regular reports to headquarters concerning the total stocks of supplies, equipment, and vehicles on hand at the end of each quarter of the fiscal year. On the basis of these reports, it was possible to include in quarterly financial statements estimates of values and forecasts of proceeds to be realized from the sale of surplus property.[4] The estimated value of stocks in hand on 30 September 1949 was more than $7\frac{3}{4}$ million;[5] by 30 June 1951 this figure had decreased to a total of less than $3,300,000.

The task of accounting for food supplies was particularly onerous as related to

---

[1] Monograph: Wood, *History of the IRO United States Office, Section I, Functions and Activities*, pp. 68–78.
[2] Provisional Order No. 67, 10 May 1948.
[3] Provisional Order No. 68, 6 July 1948.
[4] Annual Report to the General Council, 1949–50, p. 77.
[5] Half-yearly Report to the General Council, July–Dec. 1949.

support from the German economy. In the French zone of Germany, where economic integration with the other two zones had been delayed for two years, food drawings and accounting was complicated by the lack of early controls; and in the British zone of Germany there was considerable controversy at first regarding methods of accounting and systems of control.

Voluntary assistance

The close co-operation and reciprocity of aid which characterized all relationships with voluntary societies was well exemplified in matters of supply. Things such as toys, games, sports equipment, and books were given by voluntary societies and private donors, who also made gifts of food, clothing, and amenity items.

The Jewish population, in particular, benefited greatly from supplementary foods furnished by voluntary societies, chiefly AJDC. This agency was the only voluntary society which continued to bring into Germany increasing amounts of supplies after the advent of IRO; the supplies contributed by other societies steadily declined as their resources became more limited. For the period 1946–51 AJDC reported shipments of more than 100 million pounds of commodities to areas of refugee operations; and a further 15 million pounds to Belgium, France, Greece, and the Netherlands for refugees and others. Particularly in the earlier days, AJDC used rations to remunerate persons fulfilling useful functions in refugee committees. The political, cultural, and religious life of Jewish refugees would not have been possible without such use of AJDC rations.

AJDC brought in supplies of all kinds for Jewish refugees, and other agencies also limited their distribution to certain projects or to certain categories of refugees. The YMCA emphasized support for its recreational programmes; Vaad Hatzala supplied kosher foods and religious books; CWS furnished items for its vocational training schools, employment, and production projects; ORT brought in materials in direct support of its vocational training activities, and other societies made available a variety of amenity and other items.

IRO required that cigarettes and personal and household items contributed by voluntary societies should be utilized and distributed in accordance with mutual agreements concluded between the contributing organizations and the appropriate IRO authorities. In the beginning it was often possible to make general distribution in assembly centres of amenity supplies from voluntary societies; but as the amounts of these supplies decreased it was necessary to make distribution only according to need, and the voluntary societies were usually obliged to channel the distribution of their supplies according to conditions specified by donors.

The Organization made no charge for the transport of voluntary societies' supplies within Germany—the same arrangement had previously been made by UNRRA. For the importation of supplies by voluntary societies IRO obtained a general licence from JEIA under which it acted as receiving and distributing agent for approved imports by agencies exempted from the payment of taxes, customs duties, and other fees.

In Italy IRO obtained customs clearance for goods shipped to voluntary societies, but as this arrangement proved too difficult and costly, all voluntary societies' shipments were later addressed directly to IRO, Rome. In addition to facilitating imports, IRO also intervened successfully with Occupation Authorities on behalf of voluntary societies which had experienced difficulties in Germany, such as delays and complications in drawing their own supplies from CCG warehouses in the British zone. Again, late in 1947, when voluntary societies wished to buy surplus army stocks, IRO permitted the transactions to be billed to the Organization, as required, and undertook in turn to collect payment from the voluntary societies concerned.

Mutual benefit was also derived by IRO and the voluntary societies from the material support which the Organization gave to societies; IRO, for example, during the first year, supplied food for children's summer camps in Austria, Germany, and Italy. Most important, logistical support was given to voluntary societies particularly by the provision of vehicles, and by the loan from IRO of office furniture, machines, and equipment; of musical instruments, photographic items, and language training materials; of tools and other things. When IRO ended its operations, voluntary societies were able either to purchase or to obtain free of charge certain surplus stocks of the Organization. In other instances, gifts of such supplies also were made to certain societies in consideration of their past or future efforts on behalf of hard core and residual cases.

Sources of supply

The supplies dealt with by the IRO consisted chiefly of food, clothing, fuel, medical, training, and miscellaneous items. Supplies which were obtained locally, where used, were largely obtained in the early days from predecessor organizations and from military stocks; but local procurement was chiefly made by purchase from indigenous sources, and in Austria and Germany from drawings against the local economies under the terms of the Byrnes–Bevin Agreement. Imported supplies were obtained largely from the US through the US army, but purchases were made in many countries both in the open market and from governments; imported supplies were also received through voluntary societies and other contributors.

Even before the Organization had begun field operations, the Executive Secretary was directed to investigate the possibilities of obtaining supplies from governments who were not members of the Organization, and was also given discretion to recommend direct procurement and shipments as required by the Organization.[1] The practice of the Organization was to obtain necessary supplies, as far as possible, from indigenous sources, and to purchase supplementary imported supplies required wherever they could be purchased most economically and for currencies available to the Organization.[2]

In the first year of operations, slightly less than $22 million was spent on commodities. During the second year expenditure increased by about 10 per cent. to $24,162,697; this increase resulted from the depletion of former UNRRA and military stocks, anticipated restrictions on drawings from the German economy, development of a ninety-day reserve supply of non-perishable goods for European operations, and a large-scale procurement of vocational training, medical, and dental

[1] PREP/27, 21 Feb. 1947.   [2] GC/7, 7 Sept. 1948.

supplies; also, certain existing stores of clothing, considered unsuitable for issue, were replaced. Total procurement was much reduced in the following year, and the fourth year showed a further reduction of 70 per cent. in the value of procurements, chiefly because of the relinquishment of responsibility for maintaining most refugees after 30 June 1950.

During the first three months of operation the Organization received supplies of US army origin and services valued at more than $5,270,000, including $3½ million for food and other fixed daily issues to refugees, and $1,400,000 for such items as clothes and bedding; in addition, reserve stores in assembly centres of food, clothing, and medical supplies turned over to the Organization without reimbursement were valued at $350,000. The Organization bought from the US army the contents of the Augsburg Quartermaster's Depot, and other purchases from military sources of clothing, blankets, and other needed items further reduced expenditures.

During the first year the London Office also began making plans for purchases, and a commercial procurement and forwarding agent was appointed.

The US Office of Supply and Transport was established in Washington on 11 August 1947 to arrange procurement, storage, and shipment of supplies and equipment obtained in the US and Canada. Most of the work was done through US War Department agencies which had originally undertaken to give the Organization logistical services and support through 1947, but subsequently agreed to continue the work provided funds were available in advance to cover expenditures.

Early methods of dealing with these accounts required excessive paper work with the War, State, and Treasury Departments, and also piecemeal allocations of funds by the Organization. But on 23 April 1948 a Trust Fund Receipt and Expenditure Account was established with the Treasurer of the US through blanket deposits by the Organization to cover these services.[1]

For the period 11 August 1947 to 30 June 1950 expenditures totalled $25,291,640·77 for procurement and $2,496,606·83 for freight and handling. But when the Trust Account was closed on 30 November 1951 cancellations and adjustments during the later period of operations caused the totals to be below earlier figures, and the final totals for this account showed decreases of $135,754·91 and of $22,213·94 respectively.

The Washington Office also developed particularly favourable sources of supply by co-operating with other US Government agencies, especially in connexion with direct purchases of various items of food, and bought, in addition, other items directly from primary commercial sources. To finance these purchases, a part of the US contribution to IRO was used to establish with a Washington bank what was to be known as the 'A' Account. For the same period (August 1947 to June 1950) expenditures for this account amounted to $4,912,094·95 for procurement and $5,861·08 for freight. During the nineteen months which followed, up to 31 January 1952 when the 'A' Account was closed, additional expenditures amounted to only $52,797·98 and $4,981·50 respectively.

Efforts to utilize the contributions of the Canadian Government for supplies

[1] Monograph: Wood, op. cit.

resulted in the expenditure during this same period of $360,227·32 for procurement and $19,464·20 for freight.

Local procurement was usually difficult and invited irregularities. Costs were often high, as in Italy, where, in the first year, unsuitable procurement resulted in large surplus stores of potatoes and fuel wood, and unsatisfactory deliveries of medical supplies. At times, local procurement plans were upset by over-issue of supplies in certain areas; and occasionally special problems arose, e.g. in the case of Iceland, which wanted to pay in fish its annual contribution to IRO amounting to $22,179·00.

But perhaps the greatest difficulty was involved in ascertaining exactly what quantity of indigenous supplies would be provided by the German economy in support of refugees. Estimates or informed guesses had to be made regarding the quantities of imported materials, primarily food and clothing, which would ultimately be needed to replace drawings on the German economy over and above those drawings which represented the 'average' level available to Germans.

Food

Procurement of food was related directly to the standards or ration scales adopted by the Organization; and as scales were increased it became necessary to obtain more food for each refugee. In the earlier days it was not possible for all refugees in all areas to be fed according to IRO's standards, but the Organization was gradually able to make diets adequate.

For the first three months EUCOM continued to be responsible for supplying food on the same basis as had previously been done by UNRRA. This responsibility, taken from EUCOM and assigned jointly to PCIRO and OMGUS, on 1 October 1947, led to the food replacement plan which resolved many of the past difficulties by providing that all of IRO's requirements would be supplied from indigenous sources by OMGUS, subject to reimbursement or replacement by IRO of the issues above the calory level of the German population. Previously, food issues in the British zone of Germany varied widely from period to period according to the German issues, and in the French zone of Germany issues were not readily ascertainable; but by the new plan these problems were gradually solved by ensuring that requirements would be met fully from the local economy, with IRO making replacements three months in advance of each ninety-day consumption period.

In preparation for this plan the director of supply and transport at IRO headquarters went to the US to ensure that total requirements from indigenous sources would be allotted by the army. At about the same time the mission in the US zone had requested that food distribution should be integrated into the German food supply organization, as the existing system of utilizing a separate chain of depots exclusively for refugees was believed to be uneconomical.

When OMGUS assumed final responsibility for the provision of food for refugees, it thereupon gave the assurances that German authorities would provide warehousing of a forty-five-day reserve of foodstuffs; transport for this material; priorities for procurement, quality, and delivery of food from indigenous sources; storage of fresh fruits and vegetables; and breadmaking facilities. The Organization, on the other hand, was made responsible for a weekly headcount, transport as required for internal distribution of indigenous supplies, and for the maintenance of a seven-day reserve of non-perishable items in all assembly centres.

Refugees, at first satisfied with this increase in fresh food provided by the new programme, later complained of the monotony of the diet and the poor quality of the flour supplied. During the first month of the new plan's operation, shortages in indigenous deliveries amounting to more than 25 per cent. had been reported and although they were speedily rectified IRO food liaison officers, assigned for special duty to OMGUS, were instructed to prevent further difficulties regarding deliveries.

Despite these early difficulties, the food replacement plan brought about great financial savings for the Organization. In the US zone of Germany the daily *per capita* cost of the imported procurements was reduced from an estimated 18 cents to less than 10 cents; and in the British zone from 14 cents to 8 cents. These savings were achieved largely by the use of less expensive ration components and by the elimination of special depots and distribution systems in Germany. During the first year of operations the food replacement plan involved the importation of more than 75,000 tons of foodstuffs for the two zones. During the first quarter of 1948–9 tentative food requirements to be met by procurement arranged by IRO's Washington Office amounted to some 13,600 long tons for the US zone; 5,100 for the British zone of Germany; 1,300 for Italy; and 200 for Austria; wheat accounted for the major part of all these shipments except in Austria, where flour constituted the bulk.

The Byrnes–Bevin Agreement was difficult to implement. It was hard not only to estimate the indigenous level, but also to interpret it for purposes of accounting. At the start, it was agreed that food would not be calculated item by item but according to the caloric content of foodstuffs. There was the further problem as to whether the level should be calculated on the basis of amounts actually received by the local population or on amounts available; the latter method was adopted. Accordingly, it was necessary to know the total calories available to the entire indigenous population, *per capita*; this figure represented the amount of food to be obtained without charge from the local economy for the individual refugee.

For the period 1 July–30 September 1947 the German indigenous level had been estimated by the occupation authorities at 1,014 calories, and the Organization made plans for the fiscal year 1947–8 on that basis; but it later was established that the level for that year had actually been only 800. For the following fiscal year IRO imported food on an estimate of 1,032 calories; but not until 11 May 1950 did the occupation authorities finally establish that the actual level had been 1,393 calories for the period.

The effect of these miscalculations was that the Organization imported and replaced far more food than should have been required. Further importation of food was stopped, but when the account was settled for the first two years there remained a credit to the Organization of more than $6 million. This credit was utilized in lieu of imports up to the end of operations, after which, in June 1952, the remaining debt of the German economy was settled by a payment of 12 million DM by the German Federal Republic.

In Austria IRO was not permitted to issue more food than was available to the

Austrians, except to people in particular categories such as children and hospital patients. The entire food programme in this country was made easier by the fact that refugees who were employed outside camps for schilling wages were entitled to an Austrian ration card and obtained their food in the open market. For refugees without ration cards, food, on the Austrian level, was made available without reimbursement by the Austrian Government according to a scale based on schilling expenditures per day. This basic ration was usually purchased by IRO at the area or assembly-camp level from local suppliers, and bills were sent to the *Land* Government for payment. Supplementary foods for the special categories of higher rations were procured locally or imported six months in advance. But for almost a year, until these methods were well established, the Organization was forced to obtain food supplies by borrowing from the armies and from various voluntary societies.

For the Organization's work in Italy it purchased most of the food required in the country independently, except at the very beginning when certain items were obtained from the Italian Government on loan. Later, rising prices caused the Organization to resort increasingly to world markets.[1] Early procurement outside of Italy took the form of *ad hoc* purchases from the Continent and were often of an emergency nature and expensive; on one occasion an expenditure of nearly $245,000 was necessary for a badly needed eight months' supply of milk. But eventually most food supplies, apart from fresh meat and vegetables, were obtained from the US, and the ration scale was about the same as that prevailing in the US zone of Germany.

In China, too, local procurement was at first resorted to when food, originally received through UNRRA and CNRRA, had been exhausted to a considerable degree by spoilage. When commodity prices in China rose steeply during the fiscal year 1948–9, certain food items were procured from US markets; later, international hostilities made it necessary to cancel all procurement of imported foods, and cash grants in lieu of food were given to refugees when requirements could not be met through local procurement. When the National Government armies retreated from the areas of the IRO operation, some food supplies were transported to Samar to maintain the refugees transferred to that area from China. But most procurement for Samar was done on the mainland of Guiuan after an attempt to utilize army sources had failed.

On occasions when the constitutional recommendation to provide an extra ration to repatriants was implemented, the Organization issued army dry rations whenever indigenous food appropriate for travel was not available; the same arrangement was established for transit rations in resettlement or other movements until the supply of these rations was exhausted. Up to 1949, until a sound accounting system could be implemented, IRO had been required to replace in the German economy all items issued as transit rations; then, transit rations were given out on the same basis from the German economy as normal daily rations.

Other special food requirements were introduced by the Child Supplementary Feeding Programme which necessitated additional amounts of appropriate items

[1] GC/7, 7 Sept. 1948.

such as cocoa, sugar, tinned fruit juices, dried milk, and flour. For all areas food supplies under this programme were imported and distributed by the Organization through its own channels; an exception was made when certain items in repatriation incentive parcels were made up of foods provided by this programme.

Clothing

Under the Byrnes–Bevin Agreement eligible refugees were entitled to receive from the German economy, at no cost to IRO, the same allowance of clothing and footwear as the average German citizen; but this clause in the Agreement could be implemented to only a very limited extent because of the acute shortages of essential items of wearing apparel and related raw materials both in Germany and in supplier nations. As a result, emergency and extraordinary measures had often to be taken for providing suitable clothing to refugees.

In the US zone of Germany PCIRO arranged through the occupation authorities to purchase clothing from military government depots. Further procurement was hindered not only by the virtually world-wide shortage of clothing but also by the likelihood that, if IRO utilized goods available from the German economy, it might be required to pay the full export value of finished articles containing imported raw materials, as most of them did. Negotiations were completed with the occupying authorities for the manufacture of clothing and footwear. Under this programme the Organization purchased from world markets and made available to the German economy raw materials which were processed into finished articles, at no additional cost to IRO, the manufacturing costs being borne by the German budgets.

In the British zone of Germany the occupational authorities were unable, in the early period, to meet their obligations for providing the basic clothing items to refugees under their jurisdiction; and little or no clothing was issued during the first nine months. IRO imported through the Joint Export–Import Agency some $1 million worth of raw materials to be processed into finished garments by German manufacturers at no cost to the Organization. By the end of June 1948, however, when less than 10 per cent. of the total orders placed had progressed to the manufacturing stage, CCG finally took the necessary steps to speed up the manufacture and delivery of the clothing required. Subsequently, a second manufacturing programme, more strictly controlled by CCG, was carried out and clothing standards were eventually met. The clothing situation in the French zone, too, was unsatisfactory during the first six months, but later improved greatly.

In Austria, Italy, and other areas of operation in Europe clothing items were imported or purchased locally or procured from surplus army stocks, or manufactured by the refugees themselves under the work projects programme. At times clothing needs were met by transfers between areas of operations, and the Italian mission was made responsible for supplying the Greek mission.

In Italy the voluntary societies assisted the Organization in the early days by loans of essential items; and societies of this kind aided the clothing programme elsewhere as well. In Austria five voluntary societies jointly distributed clothing to needy resettlers in the period from June to December 1951, with IRO supplying the clothing and a nominal assistance grant for this valuable service, which otherwise might not have been possible in the final closure period. One of these agencies, AJDC, had earlier helped by selling to the Organization clothes produced in its manufacturing projects which were co-ordinated closely with the IRO work projects programme.

Fuel

As in the case of food, it was difficult to determine the amount of fuel available to the average German, but this figure, when finally ascertained, showed that the average refugee had consumed more coal in both the British and US zones of Germany. As a result, the military authorities in each zone at first charged IRO for this extra fuel, but later this account was cancelled.

In the British zone coal was in short supply during the exceptionally severe winter of 1947, and the *per capita* quantity issued to refugees necessarily exceeded the amount normally provided. The IRO argued that during this period much more fuel was available to the average German than to the refugee, whose total needs for fuel were greater. It was also pointed out that savings by refugees on the German economy for other items should reasonably offset their increased fuel demands. These considerations finally led to the cancellation of the charge against IRO in the British zone of Germany of more than $1 million.

The situation in the US zone was somewhat different because a wood-cutting programme by refugees resulted in a lower consumption of coal than in the British zone where similar schemes produced insignificant results. Coal consumption in the British zone had been no higher under IRO than previously, and this fact was a major consideration in the speedy withdrawal of the US zone's claim. In later months, as the fuel situation improved in Germany, there were no further over-issues by IRO.

In Austria IRO-controlled camps received hard fuel from the Austrian Government; in one area the basis of issue during April was 1 kg. per person per day except that camp hospitals were issued 1·5 kg. per bed per day.

Medical supplies

Essential medical and dental supplies were at first most difficult to get, because of the range and multiplicity of the items required, the world shortages, currency difficulties, and cumbersome procedures which later were revised.

Technically, the supply of medical items for needs in Germany was the responsibility of the German economy, but this source was not completely adequate. For the first nine months the Organization used largely former UNRRA stocks; but in August 1948 deficiencies in medical supplies threatened care and maintenance as well as the resettlement programme.

The largest procurement orders had been placed in the UK, but deliveries were held up by the Treasury as there was a long delay in deciding what currencies would be required for these purchases. While this matter was pending, other procurements in the UK were made on the basis of delivery without regard to the types of funds to be expended, and other steps were taken to simplify procedures for procurement.

As the result of these measures, and of emergency arrangements for express deliveries by air, the Organization was able to carry on its work in this connexion by utilizing the limited medical supplies previously procured without undue delay from America, Belgium, France, Switzerland, and other sources. At about the same time, the Organization also purchased from the US army some $250,000 worth of medical supplies which had been stored in Fürth in the US zone of Germany.

The procedure for procurement of medical supplies and equipment followed the same pattern as for all other types of supplies. While all possible steps were taken to obtain with the utmost speed any items urgently needed, even such procurement was at times delayed, though fortunately without any regrettable consequences.

Apart from procurement, valuable contributions of medical supplies were received from voluntary and unexpected sources.

Equipment and Amenities

Beyond meeting the primary human needs, the IRO also provided building maintenance materials, office equipment, personal and sanitary supplies and cigarettes, amenities, and recreational items; and a substantial programme was carried out to provide supplies and equipment for education, vocational and language training, and allied activities for which the initial supplies were taken over from UNRRA.[1]

Since IRO had inherited most of the office equipment needed from predecessor organizations, its additional needs were slight. The Occupation Authorities had primary responsibility for repair and maintenance of assembly-centre installations as well as that of office accommodations, warehouses, garages, and other facilities made available to the Organization, and few costs were subject to reimbursement by IRO. In Austria maintenance was carried out either by control units of refugee workers, or on contract by established Austrian firms.

In the early autumn of 1945 UNRRA had instituted its amenity supply programme with a budget of about $5 million for the fiscal year 1945–6, of which half was allocated to the US zone of Germany. IRO continued the issue to refugees of amenity items such as cigarettes, razor blades, and other personal essentials according to standard scales. Amenities were also supplied to the staff of IRO in the five major areas where, at first, civilian supplies were inadequate.

The needs of training activities increased greatly as these programmes were expanded. Large quantities of machines, tools, and supplies were made available for early vocational training classes from UNRRA stock, the army, and indigenous sources. But the later development of numerous vocational training and rehabilitation centres necessitated substantial procurement in world markets. It was difficult to obtain the materials for delivery when needed at satisfactory prices in available currencies; long delays, in most instances unavoidable, were finally overcome, and delivery obtained by personal visits of buyers to supplier countries in western Europe.

For the extensive programme of language training, large-scale purchases were made of gramophones, language textbooks, and related language disks; and in the

[1] GC/7, 7 Sept. 1948.

later days of operations a limited procurement was carried out in connexion with the closely related programme of orientation for resettlement.

During the first year the Organization envisaged the possibility of supplying food for ships in its service, but, instead, this was done by the shipowners. Nevertheless, the Organization did supply supplementary medical supplies and clothes suitable for work on shipboard. IRO also provided welfare kits of games and other recreational materials for longer voyages.

Movement of supplies

The task of bringing supplies from the supplier to the ultimate user or consumer had two main aspects: first, movement of imported supplies to the country of use; and secondly, the movement of supplies within that country. A third more limited aspect was the transfer of supplies among field offices in different countries in order to cancel out excesses and shortages which developed later in the operation; also, emergency transfers, such as the movement of supplies from China to Samar, were made.

For import movements by sea the Organization was required to arrange for shipping routes and schedules, for shipping facilities, for payment of port charges, for meeting customs requirements, and, finally, for the unloading of the ships. As far as possible freight was shipped in US military vessels in the service of the Organization, and a total of almost 3,400 tons of freight was thus moved from the US to Bremerhaven at a rate substantially lower than commercial rates.

Imported supplies destined for replacement to the German economy were turned over directly to a German agent at the port of unloading for delivery into the German supply system, and the Organization had no further responsibility. Imports for the direct use of the Organization involved additional activities: arrangements were necessary with the Joint Export and Import Authority and the customs authorities; the Organization or Occupation Authorities furthermore were responsible for routing the supplies to central warehouses and, later, to ultimate consignees.

In May 1948 the Organization began to utilize the services of a London firm as procurement and forwarding agent for the UK. Hamburg was closed as a base supply depot; the new route from the UK was to Antwerp and thence overland into Germany. In shipments to Austria imported supplies were landed at Trieste and forwarded to the Organization's main warehouse by the US Occupation Authorities.

The transportation of supplies within a country was of two kinds: one, the movement of materials drawn from the local economies of Austria and Germany, and, the other, the movement in these and other countries of all other supplies. The movement of indigenous supplies in Austria and Germany was performed usually by indigenous suppliers who made deliveries either to central points or directly to assembly centres. But the other task of transporting non-indigenous supplies in occupied countries was undertaken largely by the Organization itself; in non-occupied countries either the suppliers made direct delivery or the Organization used its own or commercial transport.[1]

Arrangements for the turning over of imported replacement supplies to the

[1] Ibid.

German economy at the ports—as well as arrangements for direct delivery by suppliers of indigenous supplies—eliminated the necessity of maintaining costly depot and delivery systems. But the Organization did need warehousing facilities for clothing, medical supplies, machinery, tools, and other items apart from those drawn from indigenous sources. In developing a warehousing system in the US zone of Germany, the Organization took over certain military government warehouses and depended on a few large zonal warehouses with numerous area and sub-area depots; these smaller facilities were later consolidated and eliminated as far as possible in the interests of economy and operational efficiency.

In these and in other aspects of supply the Organization had almost continuous dealings with voluntary societies. In China the actual distribution of supplies in the Far East was originally undertaken on its behalf by AJDC until the Organization was prepared to assume this responsibility.[1]

Transport

Vehicles were required for transportation of supplies and goods within a zone or country, and for the road transport of refugees within similar boundaries as necessary for internal movements related to assembly-centre operations, repatriation or resettlement, and of IRO staff in administrative, operational, and recreational travel within specified areas.

For these purposes the IRO had motor vehicles and provided maintenance, fuel, and spare parts. Budgetary provision of more than $3,760,000 was made for this work for the first fiscal year 1947–8.

In connexion with motor transport the Organization faced two main tasks. The first was the consolidation and reconditioning of inherited vehicles and the development of operating methods and controls, mostly for assembly-centre operation; the second was the unification of the vehicle fleet, the weeding out of miscellaneous types of vehicles, and the procurement of vehicles and supplies required —all with the aim of reducing operational and administrative costs—as the resettlement programme brought greater demands upon transport services.

Some six months before the Organization began operations, it was estimated that 3,405 vehicles, including passenger vehicles, trucks, ambulances, and technical vehicles, were required to meet needs in Austria, Germany, Italy, and the Middle East. In addition, vehicles would be required by the staffs of voluntary societies. At first, to meet these demands, many captured enemy vehicles were placed at the disposal of the Organization, and large numbers of cars and trucks were loaned by military authorities, but the Organization's chief transport assets at the time were vehicles turned over to it by UNRRA. These former UNRRA vehicles were valued at more than $3 million, and comprised 2,535 vehicles of various types, but most of them were in the last stages of usefulness, and the multiplicity of types and condition presented an extremely difficult problem of maintenance and provision of spare parts. Spare parts received from UNRRA, however, were adequate to meet requirements for many months in the earliest period.

At the end of the first six months the vehicle situation had so deteriorated that it

[1] GC/7, 7 Sept. 1948.

was imperative that procurement of a considerable number of new vehicles, long postponed for reasons of economy, should be carried out without delay. When the trucking company operated in the US zone of Germany by the US army was liquidated in December 1947, the Organization was able to purchase nearly 1,600 vehicles which it had rented up to then for about $500,000. Later, arrangements by which PCIRO held vehicles on loan were terminated, partly because of difficulties in obtaining replacements.[1]

From the US army again, seventy-one surplus vehicles and large quantities of spare parts were purchased for use in Italy. The problem of cargo vehicles in Austria was temporarily solved when US military authorities were persuaded to sell to the Organization urgently needed ambulances and quarter-ton trucks, but the captured enemy passenger vehicles continued to be entirely inadequate.

At a time when new motor-cars were unavailable, the PCIRO procurement office in Washington obtained the assistance of the US Department of the Army in procuring 250 new passenger units for delivery by the end of 1948. Subsequently, an additional 375 new passenger vehicles were purchased for use in Austria, Italy, and the three zones of Germany and the Paris mission. During the first year a total of 1,933 vehicles was purchased for somewhat less than $1 million.

Toward the end of the second year all vehicles on loan to PCIRO from the US army became the property of the Organization through a cash settlement. The vehicle procurement programme was then virtually completed, and the operational IRO fleet of vehicles, after reaching an even higher total, had been consolidated to a figure of 3,900 in more than twenty different countries. A few months later operational establishments totalled 3,565 vehicles out of 5,125 total holdings, and it was estimated that 3,965 surplus vehicles would be disposable before the end of the third year. At the end of the fourth year the vehicle establishment in Austria, Germany, and Italy totalled less than 1,000 units.

Procurement of needed spare parts and supplies was an equally difficult problem, primarily because of the shortage of these items in western Europe. Such purchases from the US army excessively increased the high expenditure of US dollars needed for motor fuels and supplies for American vehicles; and the Organization explored other markets unsuccessfully until the British Government, at a sacrifice to its economic recovery, made available for non-convertible sterling all the automotive supplies it could possibly spare. Largely as the result of this step, and by installing a motor transport procurement officer in the IRO office in London, it was possible to obtain more than $800,000 worth of automotive supplies, 90 per cent. of which were paid for in non-convertible currencies.[2]

In Germany and Austria arrangements between IRO and the Occupation Authorities for transport generally followed the same pattern as for supply. In the US zone of Germany IRO was responsible not only for administrative transport but also for the movement by vehicles of supplies, apart from indigenous deliveries, and of refugees among some 300 installations and to distant railheads. In the other two zones of Germany the Organization was only responsible for the transportation required by the Administration, while the military authorities operated transport for

---

[1] PREP/209, 30 Apr. 1948, p. 35.   [2] Ibid.

actual assembly-centre operations and for the movement of supplies and refugees. Separate and different agreements existed for the three zones of Austria, but transport was entirely dependent upon PCIRO and indigenous vehicles.

Transport in other areas of operation was entirely the responsibility of IRO. In these areas IRO operated its own administrative vehicles and obtained most load-carrying vehicles and services from civilian sources. At the close of the first year holdings totalled some 4,000 vehicles: 2,850 in the US zone, 475 in the British zone, 75 in the French zone of Germany; 285 in Austria, 250 in Italy, and some 100 in a dozen or so other countries.

At first, in accordance with contracts between voluntary societies and UNRRA, the Organization furnished logistical support for approved vehicle establishments of these agencies. This assistance included procurement services, loan of vehicles, provision of fuels, and often such services as repairs and provision of spare parts, tyres, and tools. Initially, voluntary agencies operated 314 vehicles, but this figure had increased to more than 800 before the end of the first financial year; even so, it had not been possible at all times to furnish vehicles to which voluntary societies were entitled under the UNRRA contracts. A similar policy regarding voluntary society vehicles was continued throughout, as budgets permitted, and during the closure period 190 vehicles were transferred to voluntary societies which had, on behalf of IRO, undertaken certain projects previously carried out by the Organization.

The Occupation Authorities in Austria and Germany were responsible, under terms of agreements, for providing maintenance in their workshops for the majority of the Organization's vehicles; but as they were unable to obtain essential equipment, tools, and spare parts for this enormous task, IRO established its own workshops, to rebuild badly worn motor units and for maintenance of newly purchased vehicles.

These shops, which constituted large central motor depots, undertook an extensive rebuilding programme in the US zone of Germany, and a sufficient number of vehicles were completely reconditioned to meet needs in Austria, Germany, and Italy. In this task, the spare parts obtained from military depots were of indispensable value.

For the early maintenance and operation of vehicles, more than 800,000 gallons of petrol and almost 30,000 gallons of oil had been turned over by UNRRA. Further supplies were obtained chiefly from occupation sources, and continuous efforts were made to reduce consumption rates which had been high at the start because of the necessary use of old vehicles which were in lamentable disrepair; later, achievements proved to be exceptionally good in this respect.

To make full use of available vehicles, to cut vehicle establishments, and to reduce operating costs, all passenger vehicles attached to a field office were pooled. This rule had always been followed at Geneva where even the Director General did not have a special vehicle.

When many of the best drivers were lost to IRO employment by their resettlement, particularly in the US zone of Germany, the Organization set up training schools to train replacements. Drivers were required to be not only licensed drivers but also qualified mechanics, and were held directly responsible to the Organization for vehicles assigned to them.

In an early effort towards savings, the transport administration inaugurated an economy drive to conserve funds for building up an improved fleet of vehicles. In the second year the cost of vehicle transportation had been cut considerably and expenditures were some $270,000 less than the original budget allotment. Economies resulted chiefly from the consolidation and liquidation of operations; but other factors contributing to economy were the increased use of rail transport, more effective procurement procedures and supply channels, the purchase of new passenger vehicles, and the withdrawal of obsolete units.

In the following year consolidation was accelerated further and a reduction by more than 50 per cent. in supply and transport installations in Austria, Germany, and Italy was achieved, as well as a 52 per cent. decrease in the number of vehicles required. As a result, the budget was reduced from $3,600,000 to $2,200,000, and estimated operating costs of the working fleet of IRO vehicles was reduced from $900 per vehicle to $760.

Other leading factors in reducing costs were the standardization of vehicle types from over 70 to 20; exceptionally effective maintenance work; the substantial use of soft currency in procurement; advantageous purchases of vehicles; and the economies realized by a central dispatch or pool utilization of vehicles instead of individual allocations.

By the middle of 1948 the Organization operated throughout the three zones of Germany and ten other countries in all parts of the world, with a total fleet of some 3,400 vehicles, including one motor boat; in addition, added responsibilities were involved in the more than 600 vehicles operated by voluntary societies in Austria and Germany. As the transport operation continued, the Organization coped successfully with problems ranging anywhere from the unsuitability of IRO vehicles for selection missions and visiting dignitaries to the lack of ambulance transportation for Samar.

The disposal of surplus property

The procurement of supplies and equipment was controlled in such a manner that the quantities of stocks on hand at any given time were consistent with the forecast rundown operation, and current procurement covered only known requirements for consumption. Furthermore, the examination of stocks on hand was consistently directed toward the identification of items no longer necessary to the IRO programme. Planning for the disposal of surplus property began early in 1949 in preparation for the closure of camps by 30 June 1950.

In January 1949 headquarters issued instructions regarding the disposal of surplus property[1] which proved to be too general in character, and was replaced by more comprehensive instructions to the field in October 1949.[2]

By then the procedure had been established for determining property in excess of needs where it was held, for determining what property was surplus to the require-

---

[1] Provisional Order No. 96, 28 Jan. 1949.
[2] Provisional Order No. 96.2, 4 Oct. 1949.

ments of IRO as a whole, and for the disposition of such property by donation, sale, or otherwise. Two principal means of sale were established: one, the holding field office was to be given appropriate instructions to effect sales locally; two, Geneva headquarters were to undertake sales by advertising the property as widely as possible, issuing invitations to bid to interested parties. Procedures were also clarified for disposition of unserviceable and scrap property, primarily by giving authority to chiefs of field offices to handle disposals where survey action had been completed or the survey board had decided the property to be unserviceable or scrap, but only up to an original cost value of $800. Methods were also outlined for the canvassing of bids, for the making of awards, and for delivery.

In February 1950 the policy was adopted of giving voluntary societies a prior claim on surplus supplies which could not be profitably sold; the agencies were to make formal requests for supplies and list specific requirements with justifications for their reasons for desiring these acquisitions.

By June 1950 responsibility for disposal of surplus properties was centralized in a surplus property branch at headquarters. Efforts were largely related to the determination and segregation of surplus items, a task complicated by constant uncertainty as to closure dates, not only for particular programmes but also for the entire organization.

A few months earlier the Director General had stressed the objections to ending operations with a colossal amount of supplies and property on hand, as had been the experience of UNRRA; in turn, the General Council had recently requested a continuing review of all contracts for supplies and other commitments of the Organization; to ensure prompt cancellation or such other appropriate action as might be necessary to avoid accumulation of supplies and services which would not be delivered in time for effective utilization in the programme. And early in October 1950 new instructions outlining the disposal policy: first, of maximum consumption; second, of assistance to other agencies; and, third, disposal by competitive or negotiated sale.

When the time came for arranging substantial sales, the situation was made difficult in Germany by a ruling of the Allied High Commissioner that local sales must be made through a single German agency; IRO protested against this ruling and eventually obtained permission to sell surplus items through the sealed bid method. In Austria laws and ordinances made it possible to sell surplus items only to the Government and, consequently, it was necessary to transfer surplus items to the US zone of Germany for disposal there. Problems of duties and taxes postponed local sales in Italy, but finally the Government modified its rulings so that the buyer in Italy paid whatever taxes or duties were involved. At times it was necessary to negotiate with governments on currency restrictions placed upon the potential buyer of surplus items: when the Organization needed sterling funds, the UK arranged for purchasers to use this currency in obtaining surplus items; but in France official regulations made it virtually impossible for French firms to purchase surplus items.

From the beginning it was clear that surpluses would be of two kinds; on the one hand, non-consumable goods which would not be required after the closure of certain programmes, i.e. vocational training equipment and vehicles; and, on the other hand, consumable goods which were unsuitable for, or in excess of, the needs of the Organization up to the time of closure—such items as raw materials, clothing, foodstuffs, and so forth.

It was also foreseen that the final disposal of surplus goods might be accomplished in different ways: first, the return to proper authorities of requisitioned property; second, return to owners of hired or borrowed property; third, donations to UN agencies or other organizations, governments, and voluntary societies; fourth, special sales, negotiated or otherwise, to governments or voluntary societies; fifth, regular open sales to the highest bidder; and, where none of these methods had proved to be suitable, destruction of items which could not be sold for scrap.

Disposal in fact started as early as the second year of operations. At the time the IRO operation ended in the Middle East, supplies already on hand there were transferred without charge in December 1948 to the United Nations Relief for Palestine Refugees. At about the same time, unsuitable vehicles were being disposed of and the proceeds reserved for vehicle replacement. As newer vehicles were procured, some 732 less serviceable units were sold, 387 as scrap, and it was foreseen then that vehicle disposal would increase with the rundown of operations, ultimately involving some 5,000 units.

For the following year, disposal of surpluses was a point of emphasis, not only for the supply organization but for the entire IRO. Increased attention was given to the identification, segregation, and disposal by sale and donation of supplies which had been carefully screened, and reported to headquarters as surplus to needs.

As a preliminary step in segregation of surplus items, the Organization returned large quantities of supplies and equipment which originally had been obtained from US army stocks and from the German economy. Concurrently, actual sales produced more than $725,000 to bring the grand total to some $933,000. At that time, it was estimated that further disposals would realize about $3,100,000.[1]

By the end of June 1950 surplus stocks to the value of almost $707,000 had been given to the UN Relief for Palestine Refugees under the terms of Resolution No. 9 of the Executive Committee. These items consisted of hand tools and other equipment transferred by UNRRA without charge, various items such as blankets and bedding which had accrued as the result of reduction in the Organization's programme of care and maintenance, and certain equipment obtained through the purchase of the Augsburg depot in June 1948.

At the start of fiscal year 1950–1 it was estimated that if closure were accomplished on 31 March 1951, there would be surplus equipment and supplies worth approximately $3,400,000 and $3 million respectively. Almost half of the value of equipment items was represented by some 3,400 motor vehicles, while the balance consisted mostly of vocational and rehabilitation training items, camp equipment, and medical and dental supplies. Of the supply items visualized as surplus, approximately 60 per cent. were made up of raw wool and cotton and of finished garments and footwear.[2] But by April 1951 the estimate of supplies considered surplus was reduced by almost $800,000, partly because of sales or donations accomplished

---

[1] GC/175, 6 Oct. 1950.   [2] Ibid., p. 2.

and partly by transfer back to active stocks of items previously considered surplus to requirements.[1]

During this fiscal year substantial gifts of tents, blankets, clothing, and other items had been made for the relief of victims of the Korean War. Further gifts had been made to UNWRA, to charitable relief organizations in China, and to the Kenya Government, while other substantial transfers had been made to accredited voluntary agencies engaged in programmes of the Organization. As early as January 1951 the total of all such gifts had reached $1½ million, and the question arose as to whether gifts should continue or the Organization should attempt to realize a more substantial monetary return for surpluses. The decision was taken to continue the donation of supplies with little cash value but with high use value to voluntary societies, giving, however, increased emphasis to the sale of other items.

During the twelve months of the fiscal period, more than $2 million had been received through sales, bringing the grand total of such receipts beyond the $3 million mark; up to this time the monetary return from sales had proved to be almost 40 per cent. higher than expected, partly because of favourable market fluctuations. All sales during this period, with the exception of negotiated sales with sovereign powers, had been conducted by the closed bid method, with formal public opening of bids.

During the last half of the calendar year 1951, sales were accelerated, and the grand total of receipts from sales surpassed the $4 million mark in this period. By the time the final sales had been held in July 1952, an additional $2 million had been realized, bringing the grand total of monetary receipts to a final figure of more than $6 million.[2]

B. PUBLIC INFORMATION

The success of IRO depended to a large extent on public support, whether through payment of taxes, through toleration of refugees as temporary neighbours, or sponsoring their permanent settlement. The public had to be kept informed of IRO's work by all possible means: books, films, the press, radio, and television. Besides supplying information through the normal channels IRO undertook its own publicity when necessary.

The object of the public information programme was to stimulate public interest in the work of the Organization and to promote re-establishment opportunities.[3] It tried to appeal to as many people as possible and to interest many different groups: local officials whose private views might conflict with the official directives they received; the ordinary taxpayers, whose knowledge of refugees, of high government policy, and of the IRO was limited; government circles in countries giving refugees temporary asylum. It was important to interest potential financial backers, private philanthropic bodies, governments who might contribute to the IRO budget, or those contemplating considerable expenditure for the reception of refugee

---

[1] GC/204, 4 Apr. 1951, p. 2.
[2] For nature and kind of disposal cf. Annex 49, p. 558.
[3] *Operational Manual*, p. 19.

immigrants; equally that people in countries which might at some stage offer permanent shelter to refugees should become aware of the objects and work of the Organization and of the living conditions of these less fortunate people, so that public opinion might be organized in support of the IRO and its beneficiaries. It was further necessary that the refugees and the displaced persons themselves should understand the Organization's services and methods so as to take full advantage of its assistance. It was hoped, too, that the countries in which refugees temporarily found themselves might open their hearts to the exiles and help them to forget past sufferings and bitterness and start a new life. Such a hope could only be realized if the public information services managed to dispel deep-seated prejudices on both sides, among the indigenous population and the refugees. Unfortunately, hostility between the refugees and the local population made itself felt quite often. IRO had to counteract rumours of misdeeds on the part of the refugees or abuses on the part of the local authorities.

In a wider context, the publicity programme was designed to broadcast to the world the simple facts about the refugees, their background, qualifications, and will to work so that countries hitherto closed would be opened to them in a spirit of Christian brotherhood. The immigration countries had to be convinced that in time the refugees would become useful citizens and contribute to the country's prosperity, and that those who were no longer fit, because of age or ill-health, were also entitled to be treated humanely. Finally, in order that the Organization could be certain of receiving financial contributions from the governments it was necessary to prove not only to officialdom, but also to the public, that its efforts were fruitful.

Publicity was concerned with every part of IRO's world-wide operation. It was necessary to give a complete picture of the task accomplished, the attacks to which IRO was subjected, its defence, and the changes brought about by political upheavals. Unlike most other branches of its work the public information programme of IRO did not derive from the experience of predecessor organizations. The IGCR had been little interested in publicity and UNRRA was mostly concerned with the distribution of supplies. During the autumn of 1947 a programme was drawn up, the chief aim of which was to break down the hostility of public opinion to financial backing for the Organization and to create a public opinion favourable to increased migration of refugees for permanent settlement. At this early period there was a tendency to believe that nearly all the displaced persons were Jews, that many of those coming from Central Europe were Communists, that most of the Yugoslavs and Poles were fascists or collaborators, that many were human wreckage found in the concentration camps, and that others again, weakened by age and privation and demoralized by camp life, would never be of use to the community.

The first aim therefore was to combat these ideas by putting the real facts before the public eye. Emphasis was placed on obtaining publicity through existing channels. IRO had neither the time nor the money to organize permanent contacts with the public. From the beginning, however, there was a close collaboration between IRO and public and private agencies, including various citizen groups and UN information centres.

The IRO used all the media of publicity that were open to it. Its high officials held press conferences; its public information officers met officially and unofficially the correspondents of the world press; press releases were issued, books and reports were written and pamphlets published; live and recorded broadcasts of refugees and officials were arranged and even a set of gramophone records of refugee choirs made; films were commissioned. No means were overlooked which were likely to publicize the IRO, whether as a single news item or in connexion with some other items of interest, e.g. the personal history of staff members was placed in the individual's home-town newspapers so that the distant organization might be more real to the man in the street; and many staff members on leave gave lectures on their own work or on that of the Organization as a whole.

In order to dispel public misconceptions the concise and non-technical pamphlet *Facts about the Refugees* was published by the end of September 1948 which provided a firm statistical and historical picture of the operation and was available in English, French, and Spanish for public officials, press correspondents, and the general public. With the same object, arrangements were made for exhibitions of refugees' traditional handicrafts, and things made by displaced persons in vocational training centres and camp workshops, to be shown in countries of potential emigration and elsewhere, as opportunity arose.

Generally the press was most sympathetic. It was given every facility by the IRO. Several tours by top-ranking journalists who came to Europe specially to study the refugee problem were carried out successfully, and numerous individual tours by journalists, including voyages on the IRO's transports, created goodwill for the Organization; one American journalist made a round-trip, coming to Europe with a shipload of American troops and returning with a shipload of former refugees. Press releases reached every corner of the world, and news, simultaneously released in Geneva and New York, was teletyped or otherwise communicated to the IRO's offices everywhere. UN headquarters, as part of the agreement between the UN and the IRO, were instrumental in distributing certain releases to international agencies and governments. More than 300 such releases were issued in Geneva, the distribution lists of UN and the IRO totalling about 2,000 addresses. The more important missions issued their own releases; the Washington Office's numbered 350; those issued in the US zone of Germany 440; in the British zone of Germany 120; in Austria 100; and in Italy 90. Photographs for newspapers were particularly the concern of the Washington Office, where 3,850 were issued; and various news reports in addition to normal press releases were also put out—2,500 by the Washington Office; in Austria 200 in English and 125 in German; in Italy 90; and in Poland 15. Considerable emphasis was placed on distribution to magazines which required material carefully prepared to fit the needs of particular publications.

The annual reports of the Director General, being technical reports for the use of the governing bodies, were not printed documents published for a wide public. The 1948–9 Report, however, had this double purpose and was printed as an illustrated booklet. Certain publications dealt with special problems, such as the 'Forgotten Elite'—specialists, intellectuals, and musicians; or 'S.O.S.'—hard core; and finally, the 'Displaced Persons Professional Medical Register', containing the names of refugees in the medical field. An important booklet, published in the autumn of

1951, was *Migration from Europe*, a report on experience gained by the IRO in the field of migration through the processing and transportation for resettlement of more than 1 million refugees and other migrants. This report, written and published at the direction of the General Council, was printed in English, French, Spanish, and, an innovation, in German. Its conclusions, advocating solution of the problem of European over-population through the maintenance of an international agency in which all governments concerned would co-operate, received considerable governmental attention. The Intergovernmental Committee for European Migration (ICEM) partly owes its existence to this work.

The IRO was associated with publications produced by other organizations or individuals, for instance, the UN publications *IRO—What is it?* and *What the U.N. is doing for Refugees and Displaced Persons*,[1] René Ristelhueber's *Au secours des réfugiés* (a digest of which was issued by the Carnegie Endowment) which received a French Academy award in June 1952. Numerous articles were specially written by the Director General and other officials for a variety of publications, and the IRO contributed also to the UN year-book.

It would be impossible to enumerate all the stories or news items circulated under the auspices of the Public Information Office, nor to mention every tour of visiting Congressmen and other celebrities, journalists or scriptwriters, broadcasters, photographers, commentators, or talent-seeking impresarios. Radio was used to the fullest extent to bring the refugee story before a world-wide public.

The IRO enlisted the aid of the cinema for both internal and external publicity, for refugee audiences, and for the general public. The Organization produced—or took a hand in producing—numerous training films of a more technical nature, concerning health, physical rehabilitation, community hygiene and repatriation, and, for those refugees whose resettlement was imminent, a series of documentaries showing life aboard ship. For the general public the Organization made two films which were given a showing around the world, they reached the television as well as the cinema audience: a ten-minute sound film entitled 'Home of the Homeless', showing life in a displaced persons' camp from dawn to dusk, including such phases as vocational training, resettlement, and movements, and a thirteen-minute sound film under the title 'The Hard Core', describing the plight of those refugees whose resettlement was most difficult.

Numerous film companies made feature films or documentaries about the refugee problem and used background information supplied by the IRO. One, 'The Search', was made in assembly centres with Hollywood backing. The Australian Department of Information produced a full-length sound film about the resettlement of refugees in Australia. It covered the selection, transport, and reception of refugees, dealing with the subject through the story of one individual family. The film was shot in 1949 and 1950 by one of Australia's foremost producers of documentary films in Germany on an IRO ship and in Australia. The IRO's Office of Public Information gave its services, and the Organization contributed toward the cost of the film. At the request of, and in collaboration with, the Brazilian Government, the IRO had to film at short notice the selection, orientation, and shipment of refugees to Brazil.

[1] UN Publications, 1948, l. 13 (1), 2nd edition, Dec. 1949, 19 pp.

The film was shipped to Brazil, there to be combined with other sequences following the refugees through to final settlement.

In making the truth about the refugees known, IRO became known itself. Monthly digests of its work and plans for the future were published in English and French and were circulated through official channels, international organizations, and IRO's local offices. These in turn translated them into other languages and distributed them to their own operational zones in order to give them as wide a circulation as possible so that both the local authorities and the refugees themselves should be informed of the aims and the results achieved. Weekly information bulletins in English and French, distributed inside the Organization, kept staff members informed of current events outside their own immediate sphere of activity.

There was also need for publicity to help local operations. It was important that the Organization should be known and understood in the countries where the refugees actually found themselves, and that their period of waiting, until satisfactory arrangements for their re-establishment were made, should be spent in a reasonably good atmosphere. The information officers who were attached to the IRO missions in Germany, Austria, and Italy helped to create an atmosphere of confidence and reciprocal goodwill between IRO and the local authorities and the occupation forces. Relations with the local press had to be maintained also, to make known the benefits to the country itself resulting from IRO's assistance to the refugees on its territory. This was particularly the case in Austria where the authorities had to be convinced that when IRO desired that its protégés be put to some useful employment, this would also prevent them from being a burden on the country. Attacks against the refugees were bad propaganda for the immigration countries, and it was in Austria's own interest not to hinder their departure. This theme was developed by influential Austrian journalists and eventually bore fruit. Very soon the tone of Press comments and public utterances of Austrian officials noticeably improved.

A similar problem arose when Italy regained her independence. The Organization succeeded in getting the Press to present a favourable picture of its work and of the refugees. Close collaboration developed during the following years. The Christmas message of the Pope in 1947 aided the people in a better understanding of the refugees' plight and needs.

As the practical aim of IRO's work was to find new homes for the refugees the main efforts were directed to combating prejudices which might hinder emigration. The refugees had to be presented as what in truth they were, persons who could make themselves useful. The local officers furnished material for articles and illustrations. The emphasis in the stories was to show the refugees as decent and intelligent people, by describing their skill, their work, their democratic spirit, and presenting their self-government in the camps, telling of families resettled, and quoting correspondence between refugees in the camps and relatives overseas.

During the period of increasing migration to the US and Canada the aim of publicity was to awaken the interest of local communities in refugees and thus to encourage individual citizens to offer shelter and work to refugees, since without such sponsorship immigration was not permitted. With shipload upon shipload of refugees sailing to North America, case histories or stories of refugee families were prepared well before their departure and distributed with pictures through the Washington Office to the local newspapers concerned before their arrival. These stories, widely used, brought about increased interest in the IRO and its protégés. They were of considerable help to the voluntary societies in developing further sponsorships and securing a sympathetic welcome for the resettled refugees in their new home-towns. During this campaign, IRO's office in Washington released about 2,500 separate stories and 500 photographs.

Although IRO's publicity was largely directed to people of the countries where refugees lived and where they hoped to go, public information officers had to keep close contact with the refugees themselves, and to supply them with information about countries of resettlement. The publication of letters from those refugees already overseas were the surest means of inspiring confidence in those who still hesitated to migrate.

It was difficult to circulate information to refugees living outside camps since they were widely scattered. A special official kept in touch with them through their national groups or private organizations.

The 'DP Press', not part of the IRO nor organized by its Public Information Office, was another noteworthy channel of information and comment. There were many national newspapers in the American zone and four or five in the British zone. The refugees were glad to publish a newspaper, or a news bulletin, in their own language. These newspapers had a wide circulation in Germany. Among IRO's protégés were many hundreds of journalists from eastern Europe and they published more than fifty national papers and magazines. Between 1945 and 1947, therefore, there were a great many news bulletins in the camps. They gradually improved in quality and they were recognized and authorized by the occupation authorities, UNRRA, and by IRO. It was stipulated that these papers could only be published under a licence by the occupation officials and on IRO's recommendation[1] who furnished them with 75 tons of paper paid for in dollars, at that time a scarce commodity.

These publications were not permitted to print articles of a political or internationally controversial nature. Nor were they allowed to criticize the policy or the personnel of the occupation forces. Following the publication of several rather ill-inspired editorials—one of which circulated rumours of another war—which flagrantly violated IRO's rulings, Public Information reminded the editors that any articles of a political nature likely to harm IRO's relations with the UN would mean that their licence would be cancelled and the supply of paper stopped. This aroused some protestations. In answer to a request for information by the US State Department on behalf of a Senator who inquired whether such instructions implied both censorship by IRO and a curtailment of freedom of speech, the Organization pointed out that censorship was not its purpose, but that publications licensed under its sponsorship could not be permitted to attack the occupation authorities or members of the UN, to publish unfounded stories or rumours which would tend to create unrest among the displaced persons, or to publish non-factual material which either advocated war or would tend to increase the fear of war.[2]

It has been noted that all refugees who had not previously registered with the

---

[1] EUCOM Circular No. 100, 22 Sept. 1948. [2] Press Release No. 5, 18 Apr. 1950.

Organization had to do so by 31 July 1949 at the latest, or forfeit the right to any assistance other than legal protection. The information service tried to reach those who came under this category with the help of the local authorities. Notices appeared in the press, broadcasts and posters publicized the forthcoming closing of IRO. Announcements were made in churches, and farmers and other employers were told to warn their refugee employees to register.

Every refugee resettled was in a sense an ambassador for those left behind, and for the IRO. With this in mind, a 'bon voyage' letter was drafted, on the initiative of the Director General, and a copy handed to every refugee as he left Europe for final settlement. The letter congratulated the recipient and wished him God-speed on this great day for which he had waited and suffered and prayed for so long. It went on to ask for his help in opening the door of opportunity to those still left behind; first, by setting an example of hard work, tolerance, and fairness, so that his new countrymen would find him a good neighbour; second, by spreading news of the work the IRO was doing. A postcard was attached to the letter, which the former refugee was invited to send back when he reached his destination, telling the IRO of his experiences on the journey, of his new environment, and future plans. Many thousands of these postcards reached Geneva. With their happy news and messages of appreciation, they became one of the Organization's most touching and most treasured signs that a difficult job had been brought to a successful end.

No organization with a large staff and complex operations is immune from criticism. The IRO was attacked, sometimes justifiably for specific faults, often unjustifiably, and sometimes even for its successes. Its invariable practice was to examine the facts carefully, to take corrective action when necessary, and not to argue in public. Frequently what appeared to be an attack was only a distortion in the transmission of news requiring simple correction; at times, however, the publication of adverse information required demands for retraction or an explanation of the facts. Adverse publicity was sometimes provoked by circumstances which the IRO had already become aware of, and had taken steps to rectify. However, distortion of the truth, and prejudiced or ill-natured reports were comparatively rare. The editorial support given by leading newspapers contributed much to establishing IRO's reputation. A small group of correspondents remained hostile and did not cease to represent the refugees as a group of undesirables, and IRO personnel as incompetent and with communistic leanings. Amongst the $1\frac{1}{2}$ million individuals under IRO, examples could always be found to support this theory. More disconcerting were the allegations in Soviet-controlled newspapers and broadcasts that IRO carried out wholesale kidnapping of children, and that its resettlement operations amounted to nothing more than a slave market. Against such deliberate and malicious misrepresentation the IRO was content to publish truthful and unsensational news confident that in the long run the human fairness of ordinary people would vindicate it.

C. PROTECTIVE SERVICES

As in all large organizations, IRO had to take the necessary measures to protect its property and funds from loss by fire or theft. This was all the more necessary in that the Organization operated in those countries where social conditions were most disturbed, and very often police and other security services had been most disorganized. It was not practicable to insure all IRO property. The Organization had to be content with evolving a system of preventive measures, making careful inquiries each time there was any material loss, and prosecuting the delinquents. It was the duty of the Protective Services to minimize the risks.

IRO took over the Protective Service Organization instituted by UNRRA in October 1945, making only minor changes. In January 1946 UNRRA had clearly defined the duties of the Services: liaison with the police authorities, check on personnel activities, and advising on safeguards for the Administration's property. During IRO's period of operations general conditions became more stable than they had been during UNRRA's activities. Economic improvements eliminated opportunities for 'getting rich quick'. Though some displaced persons or local employees continued to practise minor irregularities, these became rarer. Anxiety as to the future and lawless habits acquired during the war can explain, though not excuse, these practices. IRO realized that employees, normally honest, might be exposed to temptation if there were not a strict check on funds and stores. Thus the Organization took every precaution to prevent fraud. The Protective Service did not regard its duties as purely punitive, and its activities were based on the best principles of the police forces in which many of the senior protective officers had served.

The preventive measures fell into two main categories: fire precautions and operation security. Installations were frequently inspected, and though fire-fighting equipment was inadequate, it was put to the best use by means of fire posts. Buildings which might catch fire easily were progressively abandoned or improved.

As regards the security of operation, the most efficient preventive measure was the existence of this service, staffed by experienced personnel who were regarded with fear and respect. Frequent inspections and checks were made in many branches, particularly in the various parts of the supply operation, where large numbers of refugees and local employees were working, and close liaison was maintained with commodity accountants to ensure that the systems used were effective and adequate. Many of the improvements recommended by the officers of the Protective Service arose out of actual losses or irregularities that occurred, but undoubtedly much wrong-doing was obviated by the vigilance of the officers.

At the base of all operational security was a need for employing only persons of high integrity. Protective Service was responsible for security checks and screening when it was required. In the case of international personnel, recruited abroad, the recruitment procedure was in itself a reasonable guarantee, but this was not always so with the personnel engaged by local offices. If the inquiries carried out by the Protective Service did not always prove a person's guilt, they were sometimes sufficient to warrant his removal from his job or even from IRO.

Inevitably the investigation work of the officers was the most conspicuous part of their activities. Complaints or reports were received from official sources, from zone officials, area directors, and security officers, on occasions from police or military authorities external to IRO, unofficial complaints were received also from informants and disgruntled employees, and by means of anonymous letters, sensational

Press reports, and even rumours. Many complaints of this kind were lodged from base motives, and mostly turned out to be unfounded. A monthly digest of these inquiries was sent to the Special Adviser to the Director General and complete reports to the chiefs of the mission concerned.

Protective Service in field offices maintained close collaboration with Military Police and Public Safety Authorities in the British and American zones of Germany, with the Criminal Investigation Division, the Counter Intelligence Corps, and the US constabulary in order to further the investigations. Similar relations were established with the civilian police in Italy, Austria, and Germany. These authorities were very helpful in giving complementary information, making analyses in laboratories, or putting their records and their knowledge of local conditions at the disposal of the inquirer. In exchange, the Organization investigated complaints lodged by these authorities against IRO employees, in particular with regard to customs violations.

The resettlement countries laid down strict rulings concerning not only the health, but the moral and social qualifications of the candidates for immigration. Persons convicted of serious offences were excluded and, in general, also unmarried couples were not accepted. Here many attempts at fraud were discovered: substitution of radiographs, analyses, or even of persons; forgery or theft of identity papers, &c. Most of these abuses were accompanied by attempts at bribery and corruption. Sometimes IRO employees blackmailed their fellow refugees with the threat of using their influence to secure the applicant's rejection. Protective Service made investigations into these and other offences, which resulted in excluding from IRO help ex-enemy nationals, criminals, and common adventurers who sought to exploit the Organization. The name and prestige of the Organization were frequently misused for illegal purposes. As an official international agency it had the right of importing its stores free of customs duty, and its personnel enjoyed privileges and special status. In this field investigations ranged from such trivial offences as obtaining hotel rooms by posing as an IRO employee to attempts to smuggle black market commodities into Germany in car-load lots. Freight cars would be consigned to an IRO installation and an accomplice on the IRO pay-roll would forge documents for releasing the property which found its way then on to the black market. IRO might not suffer any financial loss by these misdeeds, but energetic action was taken by Protective Service to secure the dismissal of any IRO employees involved and the prosecution of the offenders.

The most numerous cases were thefts, larcenies, and burglaries of IRO property. In Germany, Austria, and Italy, where the largest numbers of refugees lived, there was considerable shortage of consumer goods. IRO clothing, foodstuffs, petrol, solid fuel, office machinery, and the like were stolen or pilfered. When the losses were immediately discovered the return of the property usually could be secured and the offenders convicted. But the supply operation was so ramified, and the stock so large, that many deficiencies were not discovered until long after when accounts were checked, or an inventory was made; by that time it was too late to open an inquiry as often the witnesses had emigrated. Sometimes losses were due to embezzlement by use of false inventories or requisition slips. The biggest investigation of stock losses was the 'textile affair'. A small irregularity discovered in the British zone of Germany led to a comprehensive investigation of the whole programme of clothing manufacture. Raw cotton and raw wool was imported by IRO into Germany and made up into clothing by German firms, the entire processing being borne by the German economy. One branch of the British Control Commission for Germany placed orders with the spinners who sent back an estimate of the raw material needed. This was checked by a person with some knowledge of textiles in another branch of the military government. Then the stocks were released from warehouses on the orders of the appropriate division of CCG. The same process of orders and estimates was followed with the weavers and the garment makers. Materials were delivered direct from spinner to weaver to garment maker without being examined by either IRO or the Control Commission Authorities. The system probably produced as much clothing as the outlay of hard currency would have bought in the world markets. Nearly all the 250 German firms involved, however, greatly overestimated their requirements of materials in order to obtain scarce raw materials for their own use, not returning the valuable waste and by-products. As a result of the Protective Service investigation, raw materials and waste products owned by IRO were located and returned to IRO control, to a value of more than a quarter of that of the original raw material, which had cost $2,159,284.

In the US zone of Germany IRO similarly bought raw material and the German economy was responsible for paying for the manufacture. An inquiry showed that here, too, some irregularities had occurred.

These cases did not reveal any evidence of dishonesty on the part of IRO officials except the small lapse of one official which led to the inquiry. The mismanagement of the programme was apparently caused by the lack of a proper accounting system, by the absence of technical knowledge among the responsible officials, and by the number of agencies involved. In Germany the fact that goods and services rendered to IRO by German firms were paid for from occupation costs made certain forms of embezzlement relatively easy; the budget for occupation costs was large, and accounting procedures lax. A grave misdemeanour was committed by a person in charge of medical supplies who by means of false bills and permits perpetrated a swindle to the amount of some 40,000 DM.

In the US zone of Germany the IRO had the additional function of assisting the military authorities in maintaining law and order among the refugees in assembly centres. In the UNRRA time a force of more than 10,000 refugee policemen had been organized. IRO continued to administer this force on a smaller scale, but in November 1947 the responsibility for the police was given to local and area security officers, and the central Protective Service gave advice only on organization and training. As a result of this reorganization of the DP police, a certain slackness spread throughout the force because of faulty command and supervision. The Protective Service made suggestions in May 1950 for the improvement of discipline and administration. Upon the reorganization of the US zone headquarters in July 1950 a DP police force was placed under the direct command of the experienced former police officers who were then at the head of Protective Service. In spite of the perennial difficulties, lack of training facilities and the departure of the best personnel through emigration, the DP police performed highly valuable work in guarding IRO warehouses and installations, keeping law and order in the camps and assembly centres, fighting fires, and carrying through preliminary investigations of crimes and thefts in conjunction with the Protective Service. During the spring of 1951 large numbers of the police were emigrating and it was necessary to employ the services of a civilian protection agency which gradually took over the protective functions of the former DP police. Most of the remaining DP police were taken over by this agency. This arrangement proved to be so satisfactory that at the end of 1951 only the units of the DP police in the Bremen Enclave camps remained under the direct control of IRO.

There is no doubt as to the efficiency of the preventive measures applied by the Protective Service; there were never any major disasters or conflagrations during the existence of IRO. No claim was made on the calamity insurance carried on warehouses and similar installations. The insurance criterion was a means of appraising the work done by the Protective Service. The satisfactory results obtained in retrieving stolen goods and finding guilty persons allowed IRO to obtain very favourable rates for the fidelity and forgery insurance policies taken out on the staff.

D. ADMINISTRATIVE SERVICES

The function of the Division Administrative Services, the 'housekeeping' services at headquarters and in the field offices, was to provide the essential ancillary services required for the smooth running of the various offices. Since the conditions of work varied widely from country to country, Administrative Services offices in the missions were operationally responsible at first to the Chief of Mission and were not under direct control of the headquarters division, which issued only directives on general policy and procedure. However, in certain aspects of the work, notably in travel arrangements, the need for uniform standards and interpretation of policy was felt, and the Chief of Administrative Services at headquarters was given general supervision in March 1948 over the procedure to be followed in the field.

Travel arrangements

IRO operations extended over a large part of the globe, and the need for effective supervision and liaison in the work, and for consultations between senior executives and the national governments participating in assistance to refugees, entailed a great deal of travel for members of the international staff. In addition, IRO had to arrange for the journeys necessitated by its international recruitment—initial travel to duty stations, passage paid leave, and the repatriation of staff members and their dependants at the end of the employees' service. In order to handle this large volume of staff travel efficiently and economically, IRO set up what amounted to a private travel agency, with travel branches at headquarters and in the larger missions, while in the smaller field offices travel was dealt with by the local Administrative Services officer as part of his general duties.

The task of the travel branches was by no means easy. Most of the journeys were arranged at very short notice, and the schedules had to be arranged to reduce the time spent in travelling to the minimum, so that the journey could be made at the least cost to the Organization. The funding position of the Organization made it necessary to save dollar exchange and to utilize soft currencies as far as possible in payment of travel services.

The IRO travel officers worked in close collaboration with the local agencies and achieved outstanding results. In September 1951 the Assistant Director General for Operations had to meet the chiefs of the IRO missions in North and South America. His itinerary was from Geneva—Rio de Janeiro—Caracas—New York—Washington —New York and back to Geneva. The travel branch in Geneva made all the necessary arrangements within three hours of the receipt of the travel order, although plane bookings at the time were very heavy, and the Director of Operations was able to hold extensive conferences and review the entire IRO operation in the two Americas in nine days in accordance with the original schedule drawn up in Geneva. Similar *tours de force* were the rule rather than the exception, although the journeys themselves were not always so long or spectacular. IRO duty journeys were often urgent and sometimes had to be arranged within an hour or two—making out the itinerary, securing reservations, fetching the tickets, reserving hotel accommodation at the destination, typing the travel authorizations and having them signed, drawing up a written 'briefing' for the journey showing departure and arrival times, telephoning members of offices, hotels, &c., checking visas, and drawing the fixed travel allowance on behalf of the traveller from the Finance Department. In the case of journeys in Germany, there were special rail warrants and military duty authorizations to be issued as well.

More than $3 million were spent on travel costs and travel subsistence for members of the international staff. At headquarters alone 5,000 separate journeys, many of them to other continents, were arranged during the three years from 1948 to 1950. IRO received preferential treatment from the travel agencies at a time when reservations were hard to obtain. Good relations were also established with the military transportation offices in Germany and Austria. These circumstances, put to good use by ingenious travel officers, saved many man-hours and resulted in efficient performance.

The travel branches also had to obtain visas and military entry permits. The latter were required for every journey in the occupied zones of Germany until the time the German consulates reopened in 1951 and issued visas. Requests for military entry permits passed through several offices—from Geneva to the IRO Office in the zone of Germany to the Allied Combined Travel Board—for intelligence scrutiny. When approval was given and sent back to Germany after a delay of perhaps six weeks, the passport of the person concerned was sent to the Military Permit Office in London, Paris, or Berne for the permit to be inserted. During the first two years the Military Permit Office in Berne, which dealt with permits for the Geneva headquarters, was empowered to issue a permit for only one zone at a time, and valid only for six months, and then a year, so that renewals were constantly needed. The permit offices also dealt with permits and visas for Austria, and while the procedure was not the same, the results were not appreciably different.

By comparison, visas for other countries were easy to obtain. In the bigger cities, with wide consular representation, the only visas difficult to get were for Abyssinia, Thailand, Iraq, the Philippines, and others. The Arab states insisted on a certificate of religion before issuing a visa.

As a specialized agency of the UN the IRO obtained nearly all the visas required for duty journeys without payment of the customary visa fees, and many countries extended to IRO officials the additional courtesy of service or diplomatic visas. IRO was also entitled to issue UN *laissez-passer* to certain members of its staff.

At headquarters in Geneva and in those countries that were not under military occupation the individual staff member had to find his own living accommodation. On the arrival of a staff member recruited elsewhere, the travel branch reserved rooms in pensions or hotels and assistance was given in moving luggage in an official car; but thereafter the employee could suit himself in the matter of lodging. In the three zones of Germany and Austria, however, requisitioned billets were obtained from the military authorities in the early stages of the operation. In most cases there was a great shortage of suitable accommodation, since billets had to be found for IRO international and local personnel, and also the personnel of the voluntary agencies, in spite of a scarcity of housing due to war-time destruction. Whenever possible IRO obtained the use of requisitioned hotels, as in the US zone of Germany, but flats were sometimes available for senior officials with dependants. IRO did not provide billets free of charge after the initial take-over from UNRRA had been completed, and the cost of billets was collected by IRO and paid to the military authorities by zone headquarters. Transient accommodation was the responsibility of the travel branches in Administrative Services, who automatically reserved hotel rooms for staff members at their destination. Conferences were sometimes difficult to accommodate.

Office accommodation

The Division of Administrative Services was responsible for obtaining suitable office accommodation. At headquarters in Geneva the problem was never satisfactorily solved. No empty building was available to accommodate the whole of the Secretariat when it assembled in the second half of 1947. Some offices had been allotted by the UN to the IRO in the Palais des Nations,[1] and to supplement this the top floor in the old Palais Wilson—the original home of the League of Nations— was made available, together with other neighbouring accommodation, through the courtesy of the Swiss Cantonal and Federal authorities. A distance of 2 kilometres separated the units in the Palais des Nations from those around the Palais Wilson, and since a substantial rental was payable for the offices in the UN building, efforts were made to concentrate as many offices as possible near the Palais Wilson. By the acquisition of an old house, by the transfer from Berne to Geneva (by the Swiss Federal Government) of a large prefabricated office building, and by the purchase by IRO of a smaller prefabricated structure which the Canton of Geneva agreed to buy on or before 31 December 1952, the whole headquarters administration was by July 1949, after two years' work, concentrated in five buildings within a 100-yard

---

[1] The building was erected as headquarters for the League of Nations, and subsequently used as the European office of the UN and the headquarters of several specialized agencies of the UN.

radius. Administration was greatly simplified and the frequent motor courier service that had been needed to transport staff, mail, and inter-office communications was reduced.

In the occupied zones office and warehouse accommodation were provided under the terms of agreements between IRO and the military authorities. In general adequate facilities were available, often in German military barracks. Zone headquarters were, however, not always conveniently located; Bad Kissingen in the US zone, to which IRO had been forced to move because the military required space in Heidelberg, was not easy of access, and was removed from the main concentrations of refugees in the zone; the same was true of Lemgo in the British zone. By the end of 1948, after eighteen months' work, quite a few missions and operational areas in Germany and Austria were yet to be provided with an adequate number and an even distribution of offices. In renting office premises in other countries IRO could often take advantage of special governmental facilities, such as the use of premises under requisition.

The Administrative Services Division in the various offices undertook a variety of other services. Some were common to every office, such as the provision of stationery, office machinery and furniture, and accountancy for such items as were not expendable; others arose from purely local conditions, for instance, the provision and management of messing facilities in Germany, the issue of PX and NAAFI military rations of amenity supplies and food rations in Germany, Austria, and Italy at various times, or the provision of local transport for the official needs of IRO employees. Where good public transport facilities were available, the transport requirements were not large; but in the occupied countries big fleets of cars had to be maintained, both for official journeys and for recreational transport (on repayment) of the staff. Administrative Services also arranged for the issue of identity cards, PX cards, and the documentation of personal vehicles of the IRO staff.

Insurance

The question of insurance was transferred in 1948 from the Comptroller's Office to the Administrative Services. This latter had to take out insurance policies to cover risks common to every organization for headquarters and the delegations when it was considered necessary to utilize hard currency. It also gave advice on matters connected with insurance to the chiefs of missions, each of whom was responsible for risks concerning his own delegation and, where it was possible, for the premiums and payments to be paid in local currency.

The size of the Organization enabled it to rely mainly on self-insurance for the 'usual' risks, such as thefts and pilferage, and financial reserves were established for this purpose. The cover provided by commercial underwriters was in the main calamity insurance—risks that would have been too great for the IRO to handle alone. An example was the insurance on the movement of refugees by sea or air; the Organization insured itself against liabilities which might arise out of loss of life in shipping or aircraft disasters involving refugees. Fortunately no claim had to be made under this heading, and the precise degree of liability borne by the IRO when it arranged the transportation of refugees was never exactly determined. However, although each immigrant had to sign a waiver of claim before embarking, a major disaster could have involved IRO in tremendous liabilities, if only for the *ex gratia* payments that IRO customarily made in the rare cases where the death of a refugee wage-earner occurred during the journey. A self-insurance reserve of $50,000 was established for similar risks on road or rail journeys, and another reserve of $10,000 against pilferage of refugees' baggage in transit. Separate commercial insurance was taken out for unaccompanied luggage to an amount of $200 per adult refugee traveller, and public liability insurance was also effected commercially for damage over $50 caused by refugees transported on vessels under charter to IRO. On the other hand, refugees were not insured in camps, institutions, or static installations, although IRO kept a self-insurance reserve of $100,000 to cover cases of death or disability arising from fire.

Stocks in warehouses were also self-insured against fire (the first $100,000 of each loss being borne by IRO), while stores elsewhere were self-insured, the only exceptions being highly valuable items such as X-ray apparatus, electrocardiographs, generators, and the like, valued at $4,000 each or more. These were covered by comprehensive commercial insurance, usually arranged by headquarters, since many of these items could only be replaced from hard-currency markets.

Special commercial cover was obtained for vulnerable assets such as cash and securities, which were insured against theft and fire while in safes, in offices, or in transit. This insurance was negotiated by headquarters for all dollar and dollar-based funds throughout the Organization, and chiefs of missions took out policies locally to provide equivalent safeguards for their holdings of local currencies. A similar division of responsibility between headquarters and the field existed for the third-party insurance of vehicles, chiefs of missions being responsible for compliance with the relevant local legislation; here again only the legal minimum amount was commercially underwritten, the balance of the risk being covered by self-insurance. IRO vehicles were not insured against other risks, except for the highly valuable vehicles such as mobile radiography vans.

The experience of the Organization in self-insuring the selected risks was very satisfactory, since the losses from such risks amounted to substantially less than the cost of commercial insurance to cover them. IRO was justified in embarking on such a large self-insurance programme—$463,940 had been segregated for such contingencies by the end of 1950—by the fact that commercial underwriters' rates include factors for risks that in IRO were minimized by the existence of an effective protective service and security organization, or were covered to some extent by the fidelity insurance on the staff.

Early in its operations IRO had taken out a comprehensive fidelity and forgery bond covering all persons gainfully employed by the Organization, whether international or local staff, or indigenous employees, and was thus protected against theft or misappropriation of IRO material and funds, and falsification of documents, up to an amount of $500,000 in respect of any one loss. This type of insurance, for which the annual premium amounted to some $9,500, seemed somewhat costly in the beginning, although the underwriters' appraisal of the work of Protective Services had secured very favourable rates for the Organization, but as the operations progressed and losses were discovered mainly by accounting, the policy became more and more profitable for IRO. The very thorough investigations and prosecutions that were undertaken in cases of loss under this bond undoubtedly deterred many would-be thieves and swindlers, but even so nearly 200 claims were initiated under this insurance. In the main the claims were for a few dollars only, but one case involved 40,000 DM, which were embezzled as a result of collusion between an IRO local employee and a German supplier.

For the international staff, employer's liability and occupational accident insurance was provided under the Staff Compensation Plan, the Organization's liability being commercially underwritten for 80 per cent. of each claim exceeding $500. For the remainder of the risks, including war risks, the Organization maintained reserves of some $200,000. The international employees were covered as regards ordinary sickness insurance by a contributory mutual health scheme for which no supplementary cover was underwritten.[1] Each Chief of Mission was required to take out in respect of his local employees commercial insurance against occupational accidents and sickness in accordance with the legal requirements and usages of the country concerned, and to afford the local employees cover in health insurance comparable to that enjoyed by the international staff under the IRO Medical Plan, subject to the modifications of local practice. Local staff employed as maritime escorts and train escorts beyond the country of which they were nationals were also insured and received approximately the same social security benefits that they would have been entitled to under their national schemes.

In addition to the continuing insurance contracts, special policies were obtained to underwrite non-recurrent risks; an example of these was the insurance against possible loss of hire of the SS *Anna Salen* when chartered for duty in a war-risk area in the Far East to move refugees from China. Special provision was made for staff members undertaking transoceanic air journeys, or entering areas of special risk, as, for example, Korea.

Communications

The establishment of fast and efficient communications had been one of the more important administrative problems facing the UNRRA Administration, and it was solved largely by using the diplomatic and military channels of communication of the Allied Powers. In IRO, communications were no less important to the operation, but except for the continued use of military communications facilities in Germany and Austria, IRO was obliged to develop a system based on civilian communications services. At the Geneva headquarters the full peace-time services were available, but communications with the zones of Germany left much to be desired, and in France and Italy it was some time before war damage to cables and installations could be repaired and normal service restored.

After the initial take-over period from UNRRA, during which IRO continued the use of the UNRRA cable, mail, and telephone systems in Paris, the headquarters obtained cable and mail service through the UN post office in Geneva. Owing to the

[1] See Chapter V, Personnel, p. 93.

volume of cable and telephone traffic between Geneva and Paris, a direct teleprinter circuit was rented for the period from 29 July to 14 September 1947.

The cable procedure did not differ materially from that of the other UN Specialized Agencies or large administrations throughout the world, except that the operational aspects of the work—particularly the shipping and the resettlement programme—made the Organization's traffic particularly heavy; during the peak working periods cable expenditure at headquarters alone amounted to some $10,000 a month. The Organization adopted a standard cable address, INOREFUG, for all its offices, and was admitted to the privilege of governmental priority, ETAT, in countries where its cable correspondence was sufficient to warrant it. Normally the postal telegraph facilities were used, but in Germany special arrangements with the military authorities remained in force for some time after the hand-over from UNRRA. Thus, in the US zone, PCIRO enjoyed the free use of the US army teletype (TWX) system until August 1947, on which it was possible to cable Washington and Paris without charge. In September 1947 authority was given to use the German Postal Telegraph. This cut delivery time from a matter of days to two or three hours for messages within Germany, and efficiency was improved when a branch post office was installed in the US zone headquarters in June 1948. As in the British zone, external telegrams were paid for in contributed currency (dollars or sterling), while the domestic traffic was a charge on the German economy.

The use of cables had to be carefully controlled as circularizing the numerous missions could be very costly. For example, in 1949 the cost of sending one important message based on the Director General's instructions to all missions amounted to $4,200. At the end of 1948 it was noticed that the embarkation preparations in Bremen and Genoa necessitated a very costly system of communications. Telephonic relations between Geneva and these two ports were very slow, and the boats were often held up, all of which led to further expense.

At each departure there were long lists of names—often of complicated Slav origin—which had to be communicated by telegram. Two private teleprinter circuits were hired. By making arrangements locally IRO was able to utilize a teleprinter communication circuit direct from Naples to Rome when Naples replaced Genoa in March 1949, and another from Bremen to Lemgo. With direct lines of communication thus established, expenses were reduced by 60 per cent. for the first circuit and 75 per cent. for the second, and communications were greatly speeded up.

These experiments succeeded so well that the teleprinter system was extended to other regions, especially in Germany. There was a direct line between the embarkation camp at Grohn near Bremen to the neighbouring one of Aurich in conjunction with the international Telex network. In this way, at the end of 1950, IRO enjoyed rapid and excellent communications between Geneva, Grohn, Aurich, Hamburg, Frankfurt, Munich, the three delegations in the US zone of Germany, and Washington. The Organization could also communicate with the other users of Telex, including the London and Paris banks, and the airline companies of all Europe. Three operators sent up to 12,500 words a day to headquarters.

Initially the switchboard of the Palais des Nations in Geneva handled nearly all the IRO telephone communications. But in 1950 the latter had its own switchboard with 220 internal lines, 13 attached to the local switchboard, 9 to the international switchboard, and 5 to the Palais des Nations. The operators had to know at least three languages in order to obtain communications via the German, English, French, and Italian exchanges. At the end of 1950 the cost of international communications for headquarters alone was about $6,500 per month. Similar measures operated in all the IRO offices in Europe and Washington.

In Germany international telephone calls were paid by the Organization, while internal calls were charged to the German budget under arrangements that differed from zone to zone. There was no difficulty in the French and British zones where IRO did not administer the camps, but in the American zone the question of telephone communications did not receive a satisfactory solution until October 1950. Until April 1948 PCIRO officials used the first telephone that came to hand, and this entailed considerable expense. After, the army installed category A telephones for inland communications and category C for local calls, both were gratis at the disposal of IRO, and were charged to occupation expenses. After the autumn of 1950 the service was paid for out of IRO's own Deutschmark budget. International calls were made with a category B telephone and invoiced in dollars.

From 1947 to 1949 Germany and Austria were not capable of handling bulk international mail; consequently IRO used the services of forwarding agents to send correspondence by train. Mail from Geneva for Germany was sent to the IRO Communications Centre in Frankfurt, whence it was distributed to the three zones by courier services provided by the US Army Signal Service, the British Control Commission, and, in the French zone, by the IRO itself. The same means were used for the return journey, even after headquarters had begun in 1950 to send letters by normal German postal facilities; the reason for this was the difficulty experienced in procuring German stamps from the Care and Maintenance budget allocation. Mail for Vienna was sent first by train through the US Army Post Office and later by air.

At headquarters the postage on outgoing mail alone amounted to $3,500 a month in late 1950. To record and file copies and deal with the even heavier incoming mail a central registry system was evolved. This obviated the necessity for separate files kept by each branch or division, and it undoubtedly made for efficiency. At the peak period the central registry was handling 45,000 items a week, and at the end of 1951 an estimated 50,000 files were in use, in addition to the 5,000 personal files of staff members and the files of appeals to the Review Board.

ANNEX 49

Disposal of surplus supplies and equipment

Sales	1948–50 (up to 1.4.50)	1950 (Apr. to Dec.)	1951	1952 (up to 1.7.52)	Total
	$	$	$	$	$
Conducted by Geneva headquarters	..	2,491,198	1,408,471	1,516,929	5,416,598
Conducted by field offices .	236	113,958	268,931	216,783	599,908
Total sales . . .	$236	$2,605,156	$1,677,402	$1,733,712	$6,016,506*
Donations					
Governments . .	10,994	3,637	7,115	52,176	73,922
Voluntary agencies, Europe . . .	900	122,395	224,870	56,471	404,636
Korea	..	125,805	48,003	..	173,808
UNRPR/UNRWA .	674,543	133,902	3,421	..	811,866
Local authorities .	..	..	475,941	133,445	609,386
Far East . . .	..	2,960	143,942	2,950	149,852
Various . . .	..	..	12,280	12,160	24,440
Total value of donations .	$686,437	$388,699	$915,572	$257,202	$2,247,910
TOTAL DISPOSAL VALUE .	$686,673	$2,993,855	$2,592,974	$1,990,914	$8,264,416

* Including sales to: governments $610,000; voluntary societies $285,000; UN agencies $100,000 (approximate figures).

CHAPTER XXVI

FINAL TRANSFER OF RESPONSIBILITIES
AND LIQUIDATION

THE preceding chapters described how the Organization's imminent closure, coupled with the need to make available all resources to the primary task of resettlement, caused the General Council in June 1949 to direct the Executive to discontinue care and maintenance of refugees by 30 June 1950 except of those who were in the process of repatriation or resettlement and of those who required permanent assistance such as institutional cases and unaccompanied children. In addition, refugees and displaced persons in need of the legal and political protection offered by the Organization could still apply for a declaration of eligibility 'for the sole purpose of receiving this form of assistance'. The final establishment of the 'hard core' and of the groups of unaccompanied children has been dealt with in earlier chapters.

The ultimate transfer of responsibilities to international and national bodies arranged so that the IRO could be liquidated 'at the earliest possible date after 1 July 1950' had been determined at an early stage: at the Second Session of the General Council.[1] However, at its Sixth Session, the General Council rescinded the 31 March 1951 dead-line for IRO operations, and its operational programme was extended to 30 September 1951; the former resettlement dead-line for new refugees was also abolished, and 1 October 1950 was fixed as a new date-line.[2]

During this so-called supplementary period, lasting finally until 28 February 1952, the Organization concentrated its efforts on resettling such refugees as could be resettled, and on developing possibilities for those with 'limited opportunities' and those in need of continued institutional care.

At the beginning of July 1950 refugees classified as 'potentially resettleable' numbered 235,892. By the end of December their number had been reduced to 167,883, but to them were added approximately 10,000 as a result of the above decision to extend resettlement services to refugees who had arrived in areas of IRO operations in Europe and the Middle East before 1 October 1950.

Temporary character of IRO

At no time during IRO's operations did the General Council or the UN lose sight of the Organization's temporary character. At the Seventh Session of ECOSOC, in the summer of 1948, after IRO had been in existence for only one year, the Hambro Report came up for discussion. The point of view was accepted that the initiative regarding the process of liquidation should be taken by the Organization itself, and the Report urged the IRO to prepare its own plan of action instead of leaving

[1] GC/77/Res. 1, p. 20.
[2] GC/Res. 71 and 78, 11 and 12 Oct. 1950.

this to the haphazard and piecemeal efforts of individual governments.[1] On this basis the ECOSOC did not envisage a continuation of the IRO for more than the two following years.

Expressing their governments' policy some delegates to the General Council, too, urged the early preparation of plans to liquidate IRO, for the temporary nature of the Organization was borne in mind, as was the fact that it had been created only to meet an emergency situation, and to prepare for an unimpeded and gradual transfer of responsibilities to whatever organizations might eventually succeed the IRO. The adverse circumstances prevailing at the beginning of IRO's work, which were due to a lack of timely provisions by its predecessor organizations, were not forgotten. But, above all, those governments carrying the heaviest burden in contributions did not wish to give further funds for material assistance after the basic emergency problem had been solved.

At the request of the Executive Committee, therefore, the Director General submitted preliminary recommendations for the termination of the IRO programme to the Second Session of the General Council in March 1949.[2] Foreseeing the problems that would remain unresolved after the closure of IRO, he added to his recommendations suggestions for future international action on behalf of refugees. On the basis of a further study,[3] discussed at the Third Session in July 1949, the General Council adopted a memorandum for transmission to the ECOSOC.[4]

As the Council reckoned with a certain number of refugees and displaced persons who would remain in Europe after the termination of IRO and would require legal protection, it advocated continuous international assistance to be given by an organization to be created within the framework of the UN. The members of the Council were not in agreement concerning the choice of such an organ: some proposed the appointment of a High Commissioner for Refugees under the UN and the establishment of an international fund; others wished to leave the decisions regarding such plans to the ECOSOC and the General Assembly of the UN.

When ECOSOC, at its Ninth Session in July 1949, considered this communication in conjunction with a discussion of a Study of Statelessness prepared by the Secretary General,[5] it adopted a resolution[6] requesting him to prepare a plan for an international organization within the framework of the UN. The main task of this organization was to discharge the function of international protection of refugees. In response to this request, at its Fourth Session in the winter of 1949, the General Assembly decided upon the establishment of a new body, the UN High Commissioner's Office for Refugees, which was to provide international protection for refugees after IRO's closure.[7]

The Director General of the IRO submitted to the General Council at its Fourth Session in October 1949 financial and statistical data which verified the need for sontinuance of IRO operations after 30 June 1950. It was obvious that further

[1] UN, E/816, June 1948, op. cit., p. 60.   [2] GC/W3 and GC/80.
[3] GC/81.   [4] GC/Res. 40, Appendix III, p. 727.
[5] Cf. above, p. 326.
[6] Res. 248A, 6 Aug. 1949. It also adopted Res. 248B (IX) which provided for an *ad hoc* committee to consider the solution of the problems relating to the international status of refugees and stateless persons.
[7] GA/Res. 428 (V).

provisions had to be made for non-resettleable refugees, and that the movement of those refugees who possessed settlement opportunities had to be completed. In the same year, when the Fourth General Assembly of the UN included on its agenda a discussion of the protection of refugees after the termination of the IRO, the Council informed[1] the Assembly that, in its opinion, the establishment of services of protection under the auspices of the UN should take place not later than 1 January 1951.

The various UN bodies and the General Council of the IRO brought up for discussion both problems, the international protection of refugees and the maintenance of international funds needed for the direct assistance of refugees remaining in the countries of residence. There was a consensus of opinion that legal and political protection of refugees was a matter of international concern. A difference of opinion, however, prevailed in regard to the need for further international material assistance. The US representative disclosed at the Fifth Session of the General Council, in March 1950, that his government would not find it possible to continue contributions to the IRO beyond those appropriated for the supplementary period from 30 June 1950 to 20 March 1951. In the opinion of his government there would be no need of funds for direct material aid to refugees after the termination of IRO, because the refugees remaining in any country would no longer constitute more than a normal burden on that country.

Establishment of a UN High Commissioner for Refugees

At its Fifth Session, on 14 December 1950, the General Assembly adopted the Statute of the Office of the United Nations High Commissioner's Office for Refugees, and appointed Dr. G. J. van Heuven Goedhart, of the Netherlands, as High Commissioner.[2] The primary function of his office was to provide legal and political protection for refugees. The question of material assistance, postponed for decision by the Fourth Session, came up for discussion at the Fifth Session and was vigorously debated by both sides. Supported by several other members, the American delegate reiterated his point of view that the period of large-scale operations under the auspices of the UN would be concluded upon the termination of the IRO, while others, chiefly the members representing western European countries—most outspoken of whom were the French and Belgian members—argued that the concluding operations of the IRO would not completely solve the problems of material assistance, and that the functions of protection and material assistance were so inextricably bound together as to make it unpracticable to establish a UN High Commission Office without operational funds. According to the final decision, however, representing the former point of view, only administrative expenses relating to the functioning of the Office were to be met by the budget of the UN.

Although the UN had decided against international refunding of material assistance on a large scale, the needs for social and welfare assistance of refugees who had

---

[1] GC/54, Appendix III, p. 730.
[2] GA/Res. 428 (V), 14 Dec. 1950.

been resettled but were not yet 'firmly established',[1] were recognized in the discussions before all three forums, the General Council of the IRO, the ECOSOC, and the General Assembly of the UN. The UNHCR was entrusted, therefore, with the co-ordination of the efforts of private organizations concerned with the welfare of refugees, when his main functions, concerned with legal and political protection, were transferred to him in January 1951.

Refugee Service Committees

As part of the general plan for the transfer of responsibilities to local authorities and in anticipation of the end of IRO's activities, steps were taken to encourage the formation, wherever feasible, of local committees which would concern themselves with the firm establishment of the refugees whether in the country of emigration or in that of local settlement. The IRO promoted the formation of groups, or designated suitable existing private organizations, which were to continue to render assistance to refugees in their day-to-day needs; such organizations were then eligible to receive the assistance from the UNHCR. Local committees established in various countries consisted of representatives of governments, of voluntary societies, of public groups in a position to assist the refugees, and of international and local agencies with a social service or welfare purpose. To implement this programme, a 'Guide for the Formation of Refugee Service Committees' was prepared, advising the chiefs of the IRO's missions in western Europe and Latin America about the desirable composition, functions, and funding of the committees.

The primary aim was to see that any committee, whether newly formed or an existing group adapting itself to this purpose, should be established before the IRO's closure, so that it might gradually take over the provision of the services to refugees previously provided by the IRO. The IRO made limited cash grants for administrative purposes during the initial stages, or contributed by the transfer of office equipment and other local assets.

Initial meetings with governments and voluntary societies in some countries began early in 1950, and the planning and formation of committees progressed during the last phase of the IRO's operations. Headquarters provided guidance and encouragement but did not attempt to impose a uniform pattern. With the variations in the law and administrative pattern and the various backgrounds and needs of refugees the traditions and results of these voluntary activities were widely dissimilar.

Accordingly, there was great variation in the structure, composition, and functions of the committees which were formed. Such refugee committees were not needed in those countries where existing government departments and voluntary societies generally satisfied the need, as, for instance, in France. Some countries expressed their wish to wait until the future plans of the UNHC's Office became known. In some areas there were too few refugees to justify the formation of a committee, while in other countries the lack of organized voluntary societies and similar groups precluded the formation of any effective committee.

---

[1] The term 'firm establishment' was used to indicate that a new citizenship had been obtained, or that permanent legal residence rights and a legal status equal to that of a citizen in the country of resettlement had been acquired.

Creation of an intergovernmental organization for migration from Europe

An important link was provided by a new intergovernmental organization for resettlement. It appeared that upon the termination of resettlement operations by the IRO on 31 January 1951 there would remain in Europe of the refugees eligible for assistance under the IRO Constitution about 12,000 already visaed and able to emigrate. In addition, there were some 25,000 ethnic Germans eligible for admission to the US under the Displaced Persons Act (Section 12) but without means of transportation. On the suggestion of the US Government a conference on Migration, convened by the Belgian Government, was held at Brussels from 26 November to 5 December 1951. Representatives of nineteen governments attended the conference,[1] while eight governments were represented by observers.[2]

On the suggestion of the US a provisional intergovernmental committee on migration was established to facilitate the movement of migrants from Europe. This Committee, PICMME, which subsequently became the International Committee for European Migration (ICEM) with twenty-four members, carried on the planned migration operations of the IRO though on a somewhat different basis.[3]

ICEM's purpose is:

to make arrangements for the transport of migrants, for whom existing facilities are inadequate and who could not otherwise be moved, from certain European countries having surplus population to countries overseas which offer opportunities for orderly immigration, consistent with the policies of the countries concerned; . . . that among the migrants with whom the Committee will be concerned are included refugees and new refugees for whose migration arrangements may be made between the Committee and the Governments of the countries affording asylum; that membership in the Committee will be open to Governments with a demonstrated interest in the principle of the free movement of persons. . . .

The Committee established its headquarters at Geneva and began its operations on 1 February 1952 when IRO's resettlement activities ceased. IRO turned over to PICMME the charters of its twelve-ship migration fleet as well as $2,737,096 toward the completion of the final resettlement of the 12,000 refugees already mentioned who had completed the formalities of pre-embarkation processing; most of them holding visas for US, Canada, or Australia. The Committee not only inherited the fleet but also some of the experienced personnel of IRO as well as its experience in planned migration: the selecting of candidates, vocational training, language courses, reorientation before migration, and also reception and adaptation procedures in the receiving countries.

Operational closure period

During the closure period the operational efforts concentrated on resettlement and hard core cases, and on the intricate problems posed by some residual groups in

[1] Australia, Austria, Belgium, Bolivia, Brazil, Canada, Chile, Colombia, France, German Federal Republic, Greece, Italy, Luxembourg, Netherlands, Switzerland, Turkey, the UK, the US, and Venezuela.
[2] Argentina, Denmark, Guatemala, Israel, Norway, Paraguay, Peru, and Sweden. Also in attendance were observers from the Vatican, the UN, ILO, IRO, OEEC, ICFTU, ICCTU, Standing Conference of Voluntary Agencies, ISS, and the UNHCR.
[3] For details cf. *The World Today*, Oct. 1953, p. 453.

the outlying areas. The governments of the western European countries, as well as Germany and Austria, where refugees had been maintained by IRO, took over their care and maintenance in July 1950, and early in 1951 turnover of responsibility was completed in Italy.

After the transfer had been effected the administrative activities of IRO were geared to the impending closure. A Surplus Property Branch was established at headquarters in July 1950; with the disposal of considerable quantities of surplus property by sale, the cash resources of the Organization increased. The gradual winding up of IRO entailed the closure of offices and the reduction of staff and field officers.

At its Seventh Session in April 1951 the General Council decided that the operations of the Organization might continue beyond 30 September 1951 for as long a period as resources permitted and for any eligible refugees who still required resettlement assistance and for whom resettlement opportunities could be found. Actually there was still a considerable number of such opportunities particularly under the US Displaced Persons Act. In view of these prospects it was hoped that the Organization would be able to move nearly all the 300,000 refugees whose admission was authorized under the Amended Act. The date at which mass shipments would be completed and funds exhausted was expected to be somewhere around January 1952 and to coincide approximately with the date of completion of resettlement activities.

During the closure period the problem of the hard core was brought to a relatively successful solution; however, in spite of the impressive number of 25,000 cases being taken care of, a group of 362 remained for whom no final settlement had yet been found.

The Organization continued to make every effort to solve the difficult problems presented in the outlying areas, and made some progress even in the face of nearly unsurmountable obstacles. The greatest difficulties were confronted in Shanghai, the Philippines, and Trieste, and to a lesser degree problems were encountered in Syria, Lebanon, Greece, Spain, and Portugal.

In February 1947 the Organization had begun as a 'Preparatory Commission for IRO', and it ended its operational phase on 31 January 1952. During the fifty-five months of its operations 1,038,750 refugees had been resettled; 72,834 had been helped to return to their homelands, and a further 500,000 had received some form of aid from the Organization.

At its Ninth and last Session in February 1952 the General Council adopted the Final Plan of Expenditure for the Supplementary and Closure Periods beginning 1 July 1950 to the amount of $102,827,440.

The Final Plan of Expenditure provided for the care and transfer of 100 TB cases from Trieste to Italy; the continued administration for six months of the Hong Kong and Shanghai offices; the care and maintenance of refugees in Shanghai for an additional six months after 31 January 1952. On 1 March 1952 this fund, $217,000, was turned over to the UNHCR for administration. A further sum of $500,000 was set aside to comprise a trust fund to be administered by the Provisional Intergovernmental Committee for the Movement of Migrants (PICMME) for the future movement of IRO refugees out of Shanghai who might obtain immigration visas. Yet another sum of $950,000 was to constitute an initial payment to PICMME for the movement of 12,205 refugees in Europe who had received their visas and were awaiting transportation on 1 February 1952; additional provision was also made for the care of the residual group in Samar, and for grants to voluntary societies and refugee service committees for furthering assistance to residual refugees in Germany, Greece, the Lebanon, and Turkey. $1,137,000 were earmarked for liquidation expenditures, including $400,000 for the payment of all sums owing to staff which were set aside in the Final Plan of Expenditure. Furthermore, on 15 February 1952 the General Council approved plans for the final liquidation of the Organization, which had been tentatively considered in the previous session, and resolved that the Organization would go into liquidation on 1 March 1952, accepting the resignation of the General Director, J. Donald Kingsley, as of that date.

IRO in liquidation

The final session of the General Council, ending on 16 February, terminated the IRO as such. Its active operations on behalf of refugees and displaced persons were concluded on 31 January 1952, and the Organization went into liquidation on 1 March 1952. Colonel Oliver E. Cound (American), former Chief of the IRO Office in Italy, was appointed Liquidator; the Deputy Liquidator was Brigadier Francis H. Dallison of British nationality, former Chief of Administrative Services at headquarters; M. Henri Ponsot, Ambassador of France, was made Councillor. The liquidation was carried out under the astute and efficient leadership of the indefatigable Liquidator; his transactions were subject to the control of the Liquidation Board which consisted of representatives of the three member governments, the UK, France, and Venezuela. The Board of Liquidation was vested by the General Council 'with all the powers necessary to carry on and complete the work of the liquidation and dissolution of the Organization'.[1]

The Liquidator was designated as the Chief Administrative Officer of the Organization, responsible to the Board of Liquidation. He had the same authority and powers as were formerly held by the Director General, limited, however, to liquidation operations.

The liquidation of most organizations such as IRO is made relatively easy because, as a rule, some of the activities and assets of such bodies are passed on to a successor organization. In the case of IRO, however, there was complete liquidation. Besides, many complicated claims connected with the operational period had to be met, and entirely new ones, such as reimbursement of US income tax, had to be taken into consideration. The distribution of large residual funds also necessitated serious study and planning.

When the General Council considered and accepted the plans for liquidation the full scope and diversity of the problems could not be foreseen,[2] as the financial returns were much larger than had originally been taken into account or assumed.

It was the task of the Liquidator to complete the liquidation of the Organization

[1] GC/Res. 108, Appendix III, p. 748.
[2] The IRO in Liquidation. Report of the Liquidator, 31 July 1953, p. 26.

'at minimum cost and in the shortest time consistent with creditable, efficient and thorough performance, thereby leaving available the maximum possible funds for the purposes determined by the GC'.[1] All outstanding liabilities had to be settled by the Liquidator who realized the assets.

The General Council had set up a schedule of priorities according to which the assets were to be utilized.

The first charge was to meet unforeseen claims against the Organization and to be responsible for any additional costs of liquidation beyond those provided for in the Final Plan of Expenditure. The second charge was to reimburse PICMME for the costs of moving IRO eligible refugees after 1 February 1952. The third charge was to use any assets realized from the Food Replacement Account in Germany or from Deutschmark assets for the assistance of various residual refugees by way of the Displaced Persons Department of the Expellee Bank, the Voluntary Societies, and the Refugee Service Committees. The fourth charge was the establishment of a revolving trust fund to be managed by PICMME.

The major steps necessary to the achievement of a quick and efficient liquidation were as follows:

Closure of field installations; realization of the Organization's assets; settlement of liabilities and claims; disposal of residual assets and the disposition of archives and financial records.

The diversity and geographical scope of IRO operations made the liquidation complicated and difficult, particularly the settlement of the Organization's financial and contractual obligations. Operations of a limited character had continued until 31 January 1952, thus closure and return of installations, together with the adjudication of claims, documentation, and disposal of property were left to the Liquidator. Field offices in all areas except Germany and Italy were closed by the end of March 1952. Operations in Germany, consisting mainly of the disposal of surplus equipment and settlement of outstanding claims, were centralized in the Munich area. Property available for disposal was assembled in Munich for subsequent sale. The Munich office was closed in July 1952. The volume of outstanding claims in Italy required the maintenance of a small office in Rome until the middle of June 1952. In Austria all installations were closed before 31 March 1952, while sales of surplus equipment continued, and were carried out by the government auctioneers on behalf of the Organization.

Realization of assets

When liquidation was begun there were still bank accounts in more than thirty different currencies in some twenty areas. These consisted of balances for reimbursable migration schemes which had been financed by the Organization on behalf of governments or government-sponsored agencies. Other assets to be realized consisted of stores and equipment which proved to be a very valuable financial resource.

Another type of asset which caused the Liquidator and his staff considerable effort were the so-called unrecorded assets such as the Food Replacement Account in Germany, the reimbursement of US income tax, and the shipping claims. As has

[1] *The IRO in Liquidation. Report of the Liquidator*, 31 July 1953, p. 2.

been said,[1] the Organization assumed the responsibility for replacing in kind the imported foods issued to eligible refugees in Germany. It was not until the early part of 1950 that realistic figures of the indigenous food production during the fiscal year 1948–9 were obtained. As a result of the retroactive calorific revision which reduced the quantities of food required to be supplied by the IRO, the Organization claimed reimbursement of costs for excess food which it had provided. In May 1952 payment in Deutschmarks of the equivalent of $2,857,143 was received from the German Federal Government. This made it possible to use these funds according to the instructions of the General Council regarding the allocation of residual assets.

In common with other specialized agencies of the UN, IRO had remunerated their staff on a free of national tax basis. Since under US Federal Laws American members of the staff were subject to taxation, the IRO reimbursed them for such taxes by quarterly payments. In October 1951 the US Revenue Act was amended so as to exclude from gross income and exempt from taxation earned income received outside the US. This new American legislation resulted in reimbursements to IRO amounting to more than $75,000.

In the end, the total of realized assets was over $5 million.[2]

Settlement of liabilities and claims

The settlement of the Organization's liabilities was carried through with extraordinary success due both to the painstaking efforts of the Liquidator in personally investigating and negotiating claims, and the fair-minded attitude of the governments and other agencies to which the Organization was a debtor. The claims of the French and Italian governments were ultimately settled with a net saving over the original estimate. The same became true of the settlement with the US navy for operating costs during the final period of operation. Though at one time it appeared that the Organization might have to meet a charge of some $400,000 over and above expectations, the untiring efforts of Major-General Wood, former chief of the IRO Washington Office, and excellent co-operation of American naval authorities resulted in an agreement that the Organization had no further liabilities but, on the contrary, received the sum of $119,412.

Among sundry claims raised by different governments, by far the most significant was that for transporting displaced persons by train through Germany to the port of Bremerhaven from which the majority of refugees were moved overseas in the later period of operations. These costs were met originally by the occupation costs budget, but claims were filed for all such costs after April 1950, amounting to over $500,000. After long negotiations, however, in which the Liquidator pointed out the advantages to the German economy of being relieved of the pressure of refugees, the claim was generously waived.

The net result of the settlement of liabilities[3] was that savings of $724,045 were achieved. Equally impressive is the fact that of liabilities amounting to $10,343,226 on 31 January 1952, all that remained outstanding by the end of 1952 were $63,000

---

[1] Cf. Chapter XXV, p. 518.   [2] Annex 51, p. 573.
[3] Ibid.

Disposal of assets

The final disposal of the Organization's assets was made in such a way as to aid as far as possible the areas in Europe which still had substantial residual groups of refugees, and those, particularly in the Far East, where refugees were in a critical position. By far the largest amount was handed over to PICMME which received $2,237,096 to aid some 12,000 refugees visaed prior to 1 February 1952, and by 10 July 1953, $1¾ million in a revolving trust fund for refugees visaed after that date.[1] Among the amounts granted to other European organizations, as noted in Annex 52,[2] special mention may be made of $805,761 to the Displaced Persons Department of the Expellee Bank, Bonn, to enable former refugees in Germany to establish themselves as self-supporting members of the community, and various grants to voluntary societies.

To aid refugees in the Far East and Middle East, smaller grants were made to the World Council of Churches and the National Catholic Welfare Conference.

Writing of the history, and disposition of archives

Already during the operational period of the Organization it had been decided to publish an official history of its work. A History Unit was set up under Mr. Hacking to organize the archives and lay the groundwork for a two-volume history of the IRO and a third volume of documents. Subsequently, the Liquidation Board decided to go outside the Organization and entrust the preparation of a one-volume history to an American professor of political science, Dr. Louise W. Holborn. A veteran French diplomat, M. René Ristelhueber, was chosen to collaborate with her and to adapt the English text to the French edition.

The archives of the IRO were moved to Paris where the Archives Nationales offered to assume custodianship without charge. They will not be open to the public for a period of ten years and then only under such conditions as the Archives Nationales determine.

Personnel

In carrying out the difficult work of liquidation, the Liquidator received the loyal and devoted service of those staff members retained during this period. Staff was reduced as quickly as possible, and this, and other economies, made it possible for the Liquidator to show a balance of some $80,000 at the end of liquidation. In the Foreword to his official report the Liquidator has borne testimony to the exceptional services rendered by those who aided him in the final task of winding up the affairs of the Organization.

Conclusion

The task of the IRO was a specific and, in a sense, limited one. Its dimensions were determined by what other agencies working for refugees and displaced persons

---

[1] This was not the final figure. In addition, three notes for lire 10,000,000 each, maturing in 1954–5, were conveyed to ICEM for credit of the Trust Fund; more than $75,000 was deposited in IRO Fund no. 2 with the Chase National Bank, which will be placed in the Trust Fund on 1 Oct. 1955. Further tax reimbursements have been realized. Ibid., p. 21.

[2] Annex 52, p. 573.

—the Allied military authorities, UNRRA, and IGCR—had been unable to accomplish. In other words, IRO was set up to deal with the residue of the problem of refugees and displaced persons as it existed at the end of the Second World War. If the $1\frac{1}{2}$ million persons handled by IRO may seem, at first sight, less impressive than the far greater numbers repatriated by the Allied authorities, it must be remembered that the responsibilities of IRO were for persons who could not be handled by these authorities because their problems were of such great complexity.

It is in this perspective that a distinguished international lawyer, Professor Wolfgang Friedmann, has evaluated the work of IRO. 'The achievement of the IRO has been as magnificent as it has been unspectacular', he wrote in an article entitled 'Migration and World Politics'.[1] 'It has selected, trained and counselled a particularly difficult and heterogeneous collection of people left uprooted, poor and embittered in [Central Europe] after the collapse, . . . and had the lion's share in solving at least one of the major problems of Central Europe. Its record is magnificent proof of what an international agency can do, if it is given a task and inspired with a sense of purpose.'[2]

The achievements of IRO also bear testimony to what a limited number of governments can accomplish through joint effort. Although only eighteen governments, out of the fifty-four of the UN, participated in establishing and financing IRO, they contributed more than $400 million over a period of four and a half years, marking a new level in the assumption of official governmental responsibilities for refugees. The co-operation of governments and voluntary organizations also reached a high point during the operational period of IRO, a fact contributing immeasurably to the success of its efforts. In fact, it was the admirable team work developed between the General Council of IRO, the voluntary agencies, individual governments, and the IRO staff to which must be attributed much of the Organization's achievements, not to mention the support of the people who accepted the obligation of paying higher taxes and urged their governments to support this unusual enterprise.

It is, of course, easy either to over-estimate, or under-estimate, what IRO accomplished. The basic pattern for its activities had long been set by the character of the refugee problem. Earlier agencies working for refugees had also seen their work fall into three main phases: temporary relief action of care and maintenance; the movement of refugees from the country of temporary hospitality through repatriation or resettlement; and the full re-establishment of the refugee as a person possessing full citizenship, and thus adequate legal protection, and means of earning his livelihood. This latter process of integration was facilitated by the temporary legal status afforded through special arrangements like the Nansen passport, deriving from international conventions and agreements.

In all three phases of international activities for refugees, however, IRO devised better methods of dealing with the problems. In addition to complete maintenance—food, shelter, and medical care—the basic relief programme of IRO comprised the

---

[1] *International Journal*, Summer 1952, p. 197.
[2] For other evaluations of IRO's work see the speeches by members of the General Council, the Director General, and others at the celebration for the one millionth IRO refugee on 22 Oct. 1951 at Geneva (GC/Inf/36, 26 Oct. 1951), and also at the Eleventh Executive Committee, held at Geneva on 13 Feb. 1952 (EC/SR/87, 4 Mar. 1952, pp. 9–17).

whole range of social activities developed in any normal community. In so doing, IRO sought to rehabilitate the uprooted people and make it possible for them to be useful citizens in whatever country they were destined to live.

Beyond this, IRO developed a new pattern of emigration. Never before had it been planned so carefully, so humanely, and on such a scale. Three main types of migration plans were developed: group emigration under governmental selective schemes; individual emigration under normal consular procedures, initiated through personal nomination by relatives or friends in the country of resettlement; and individual emigration by placement of individuals with prospective employers or sponsors on the basis of their qualifications. To carry out each of these three schemes involved a wide variety and great complexity of procedures from the moment when the refugee first applied for emigration assistance until he became an integrated member of a new community in his country of adoption. Group resettlement, in particular, required the exploration and opening of resettlement opportunities, developing procedures in countries of emigration, transporting to countries of immigration, and organizing reception in these countries.

A significant feature of IRO policy was that emigration was never compulsory. The task of the organization was to facilitate it through liberalizing, and even humanizing, opportunities for emigration. Thus there was a progressive widening of selection criteria until, in the end, there was an emphasis on accepting families as a unit, and even hard core cases were accepted for immigration. This required whole-hearted co-operation of all concerned.

For the residual category of those unable to emigrate, integration programmes were developed with the countries of residence. In this field, new ways were found through the so-called hard core programme to help the aged, and chronically ill, to secure institutional care.

Lastly, IRO helped to prepare the Convention relating to the Status of Refugees of 1951 which consolidated, for the first time, all previous international instruments for the benefit of refugees, and established a uniform status for practically all existing groups of refugees. This convention supplanted all previous ones referring to particular groups, e.g. that of 1933 referring to Nansen refugees.

These tasks were performed for more than $1\frac{1}{2}$ million persons, almost none of whom were willing to accept repatriation to their country of origin, and few of whom could be absorbed in the countries in which they were then domiciled. Moreover, the task was undertaken in a period when hate and bitterness were still rampant, and Central Europe still stricken by war devastation. Admittedly, the opportunities for resettlement abroad were particularly good in the period from 1948 to 1952 when overseas countries were building their economies still further. None the less, the work of IRO stands as 'a landmark in international experience,' as has been said, because of the comprehensiveness of its approach and the magnitude and speed of its operations.

Yet this work of IRO was not without criticism. Two charges, in particular, were levied, which in effect did much to cancel out each other. The one charge was that IRO did not do enough for refugees, partly because it helped only special groups of refugees, and partly because it did not act quickly and long enough. The other charge is that IRO spent too much money, was extravagant in its administrative methods and operational activities.

No one studying IRO can be unaware that to a certain extent these criticisms can be supported. It seems still more important, however, to recognize that because IRO was responsible for such vast numbers of people, hard necessity and even the requirements of justice often meant thinking in terms of abstract figures. To institutionalize care means to set up impersonal standards and establish certain criteria which may seem to fit individuals into a Procrustean bed. Yet without such an organization, large-scale international co-operation for humanitarian purposes cannot be secured. Moreover, the Directors General, Mr. Hallam Tuck and Mr. J. Donald Kingsley, the Deputy General, Sir Arthur Rucker, and the IRO staff kept to the fore to a remarkable degree the humanitarian motive which had led the governments in the first place to establish IRO. The very difficulties of dealing under pressure with such overwhelming tasks welded the staff together and created common techniques, common plans of action, and procedures which were truly international in character, and often infused by that sense for individual needs which institutionalized care too often lacks.

All in all, the work of IRO demonstrates a great development in international responsibility. While it was a costly operation, an analysis of the operations shows that the funds were generally spent constructively. Because of widespread co-operation within and outside the Organization, duplication of effort was avoided, and existing facilities used. Through IRO, governmental and non-governmental organizations were able to pool their resources, and contribute their experience, vision, and imagination towards a common purpose. In this way, their efforts were far more effective than they could have been operating individually.

IRO was set up to perform a particular task, as has been said, and when that work was finished, IRO naturally went out of existence. Its techniques and organization were no longer suitable to the task which remained after it had coped with the $1\frac{1}{2}$ million refugees entrusted to it. IRO's experience, and pattern of action, remain, however, as an example for any future international action for refugees.

Perhaps the best epitaph for IRO lies in the answer of Mr. Peter Fraser, Prime Minister of New Zealand, to Mr. Andrei Vishinsky, the Soviet Russian delegate, who maintained that refugees should be compulsorily repatriated. In opposing this view with the one for which the Western countries had fought, the right of individuals to seek the conditions under which they wished to live, Mr. Fraser used the words of Ralph Waldo Emerson:[1]

> What avail
> The plough or sail
> Or land or life
> If Freedom fail?

The keynote of the resolution under which IRO was established, individual freedom and mutual responsibility are at one and the same time the achievement and the justification of IRO.

[1] UN, First General Assembly, Thirtieth Plenary Meeting, 12 Feb. 1946. (*Official Records*, op. cit., p. 429.)

ANNEX 50

*Liabilities outstanding as at 31 January 1952**

(Expressed in terms of US dollars)

Care and maintenance	Total
French Government	233,905
US zone	151,870
Miscellaneous	150,027
	$535,802

Residual cases	
French Government	2,406,430
UNHCR	185,869
Institutional grants	1,137,615
	$3,729,914

Maintenance of vehicles	
EUCOM	41,798
Miscellaneous	18,517
	$60,315

Repatriation and resettlement	
MSTS Programme	789,600
Dundalk Bay	99,597
Migration Committee	1,326,422
Resettlement agreements	586,179
Flying tigers	176,856
Miscellaneous	493,005
	$3,471,659

Other liabilities and provisions	
Administrative grant UNHCR . . .	50,000
Administrative grant ICEM	21,154
Peat, Marwick, Mitchell & Co. . . .	52,975
Miscellaneous	484,815
	$608,944

Pertaining to staff members	
Provident Fund and Medical Service Plan .	858,162
Terminal emoluments	989,298
National tax	50,000
Staff Compensation Plan	33,792
Miscellaneous	5,340
	$1,936,592
GRAND TOTAL	$10,343,226

Grant to AMG, Trieste, outstanding as at Dec. 1952 $75,000

* *Report of the Liquidator*, Exhibit IV.

ANNEX 51

Income during period of liquidation (1 March 1952 to 31 July 1953)*

(Expressed in terms of US dollars)

	Total for period
Miscellaneous income	
Food Replacement Account Germany	2,857,143
Sales of surplus stores and equipment	1,439,761
Proceeds of investment of funds, including bank interest . . .	57,970
Refunds against resettlement expenses	15,682
Refunds of shipping expenses	32,485
SITMAR shipping claims	150,000
MSTS programme	119,412
Staff compensation insurance	21,891
Miscellaneous	41,420
	$4,735,764

Settlement with creditors for previous financial periods representing a net reduction
of costs 724,045

$5,459,809

Deduct: Disbursements made and provisions established to meet claims for which
no specific provision had been established 261,964

$5,197,845†

* *Report of the Liquidator*, op. cit., Exhibit III.
† In addition Promissory Notes to the value of $48,000 were accepted during July 1953 in settlement of the 'Liguria' shipping claim.

ANNEX 52

Distribution of Assets from 1 March 1952 to 31 July 1953*

(Expressed in terms of US dollars)

	Total
Charge 2	
ICEM Balance due under GC Resolution No. 106 . .	$1,287,841
Charge 3	
Expellee Bank	805,761
NCWC	390,500
WCC	419,900
AJDC	102,750
LWF	72,450
YMCA	54,975
ISS	50,000
BCAR	25,000
Association for Settlement of Foreign Refugees (France) .	50,000
Allied Military Government (Trieste)	200,000
	$2,171,336
Charge 4	
Trust Fund for ICEM	$1,750,000†
Other Expenditures	
Ex gratia payment to UK	$75,000

* *Report of the Liquidator*, Exhibit II.
† Promissory notes for lire 30,000,000, tax refunds and substantial balance remaining for transfer at close of liquidation, are not included.

MIGRATION FROM EUROPE

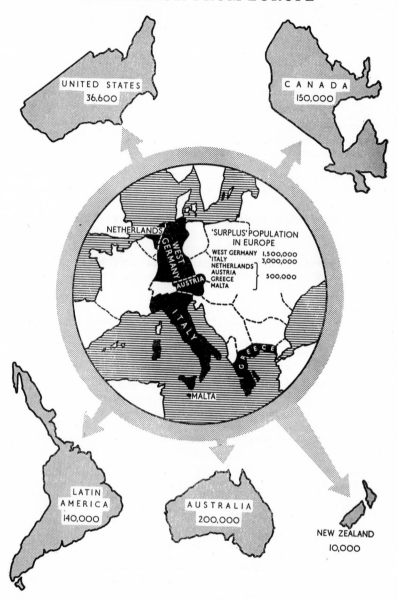

Chart prepared by the IRO in 1951 showing six areas on the continent of Europe from which, according to estimates, 5 million persons (including new refugees constantly arriving) should emigrate during the next ten years; and the estimated annual capacity of overseas countries for absorbing European immigrants.

Source: *Migration from Europe*, a Report by the Director General to the General Council of the International ¡Refugee Organization on experience gained in the field of migration through the processing and transportation for resettlement of more than one million refugees and other migrants (GC/199/Rev. 1, p. 15). Reproduced with permission of the Printer, Editions du Rocher, Monaco.

APPENDIXES

APPENDIX I

CONSTITUTION OF THE INTERNATIONAL REFUGEE ORGANIZATION

PREAMBLE

The Governments accepting this Constitution,

RECOGNIZING: that genuine refugees and displaced persons constitute an urgent problem which is international in scope and character;

that as regards displaced persons, the main task to be performed is to encourage and assist in every way possible their early return to their country of origin;

that genuine refugees and displaced persons should be assisted by international action, either to return to their countries of nationality or former habitual residence, or to find new homes elsewhere, under the conditions provided for in this Constitution; or in the case of Spanish Republicans, to establish themselves temporarily in order to enable them to return to Spain when the present Falangist regime is succeeded by a democratic regime;

that re-settlement and re-establishment of refugees and displaced persons be contemplated only in cases indicated clearly in the Constitution;

that genuine refugees and displaced persons, until such time as their repatriation or re-settlement and re-establishment is effectively completed, should be protected in their rights and legitimate interests, should receive care and assistance and, as far as possible, should be put to useful employment in order to avoid the evil and anti-social consequences of continued idleness; and

that the expenses of repatriation to the extent practicable should be charged to Germany and Japan for persons displaced by those Powers from countries occupied by them:

HAVE AGREED: for the accomplishment of the foregoing purposes in the shortest possible time, to establish and do hereby establish a non-permanent organization to be called the International Refugee Organization, a specialized agency to be brought into relationship with the United Nations, and accordingly

HAVE ACCEPTED THE FOLLOWING ARTICLES:

Article 1. MANDATE

The mandate of the Organization shall extend to refugees and displaced persons in accordance with the principles, definitions and conditions set forth in Annex I, which is attached to and made an integral part of this Constitution.

Article 2. FUNCTIONS AND POWERS

1. The functions of the Organization to be carried out in accordance with the purposes and the principles of the Charter of the United Nations, shall be: the

repatriation; the identification, registration and classification; the care and assistance; the legal and political protection; the transport; and the re-settlement and re-establishment, in countries able and willing to receive them, of persons who are the concern of the Organization under the provisions of Annex I. Such functions shall be exercised with a view:

(*a*) to encouraging and assisting in every way possible the early return to their country of nationality, or former habitual residence, of those persons who are the concern of the Organization, having regard to the principles laid down in the resolution on refugees and displaced persons adopted by the General Assembly of the United Nations on 12 February 1946 (Annex III) and to the principles set forth in the Preamble, and to promoting this by all possible means, in particular by providing them with material assistance, adequate food for a period of three months from the time of their departure from their present places of residence provided they are returning to a country suffering as a result of enemy occupation during the war, and provided such food shall be distributed under the auspices of the Organization; and the necessary clothing and means of transportation; and

(*b*) with respect to persons for whom repatriation does not take place under paragraph 1 (*a*) of this Article to facilitating:

(i) their re-establishment in countries of temporary residence;

(ii) the emigration to, re-settlement and re-establishment in other countries of individuals or family units; and

(iii) as may be necessary and practicable, within available resources and subject to the relevant financial regulations, the investigation, promotion or execution of projects of group re-settlement or large-scale re-settlement.

(*c*) with respect to Spanish Republicans to assisting them to establish themselves temporarily until the time when a democratic regime in Spain is established.

2. For the purpose of carrying out its functions, the Organization may engage in all appropriate activities, and to this end, shall have power:

(*a*) to receive and disburse private and public funds;

(*b*) as necessary to acquire land and buildings by lease, gift, or in exceptional circumstances only, by purchase; and to hold such land and buildings or to dispose of them by lease, sale or otherwise;

(*c*) to acquire, hold and convey other necessary property;

(*d*) to enter into contracts, and undertake obligations; including contracts with Governments or with occupation or control authorities, whereby such authorities would continue, or undertake, in part or in whole, the care and maintenance of refugees and displaced persons in territories under their authority, under the supervision of the Organization;

(*e*) to conduct negotiations and conclude agreements with Governments;

(*f*) to consult and co-operate with public and private organizations whenever it is deemed advisable, in so far as such organizations share the purpose of the Organization and observe the principles of the United Nations;

(*g*) to promote the conclusion of bilateral arrangements for mutual assistance in the repatriation of displaced persons, having regard to the principles laid down in paragraph (*c*) (ii) of the resolution adopted by the General Assembly of the United Nations on 12 February 1946 regarding the problem of refugees (Annex III);

(*h*) to appoint staff, subject to the provisions of Article 9 of this Constitution;

(*i*) to undertake any project appropriate to the accomplishment of the purposes of this Organization;

(*j*) to conclude agreements with countries able and willing to receive refugees and displaced persons for the purpose of ensuring the protection of their legitimate rights and interests in so far as this may be necessary; and

(k) in general, to perform any other legal act appropriate to its purposes.

Article 3. RELATIONSHIP TO THE UNITED NATIONS

The relationship between the Organization and the United Nations shall be established in an agreement between the Organization and the United Nations as provided in Articles 57 and 63 of the Charter of the United Nations.

Article 4. MEMBERSHIP

1. Membership in the Organization is open to Members of the United Nations. Membership is also open to any other peace-loving States, not members of the United Nations, upon recommendation of the Executive Committee, by a two-thirds majority vote of members of the General Council present and voting, subject to the conditions of the agreement between the Organization and the United Nations approved pursuant to Article 3 of this Constitution.

2. Subject to the provisions of paragraph 1 of this article, the members of the Organization shall be those States whose duly authorized representatives sign this Constitution without reservation as to subsequent acceptance, and those States which deposit with the Secretary-General of the United Nations their instruments of acceptance after their duly authorized representatives have signed this Constitution with such reservation.

3. Subject to the provisions of paragraph 1 of this article, those States, whose representatives have not signed the Constitution referred to in the previous paragraph, or which, having signed it, have not deposited the relevant instrument of acceptance within the following six months, may, however, be admitted as members of the Organization in the following cases:

(a) if they undertake to liquidate any outstanding contributions in accordance with the relevant scale; or

(b) if they submit to the Organization a plan for the admission to their territory, as immigrants, refugees or displaced persons in such numbers, and on such settlement conditions as shall, in the opinion of the Organization, require from the applicant State an expenditure or investment equivalent, or approximately equivalent, to the contribution that they would be called upon, in accordance with the relevant scale, to make to the budget of the Organization.

4. Those States which, on signing the Constitution, express their intention to avail themselves of clause (b) of paragraph 3 of this article may submit the plan referred to in that paragraph within the following three months, without prejudice to the presentation within six months of the relevant instrument of acceptance.

5. Members of the Organization which are suspended from the exercise of the rights and privileges of Membership of the United Nations shall, upon request of the latter, be suspended from the rights and privileges of this Organization.

6. Members of the Organization which are expelled from the United Nations shall automatically cease to be members of this Organization.

7. With the approval of the General Assembly of the United Nations, members of the Organization which are not members of the United Nations, and which have persistently violated the principles of the Charter of the United Nations may be suspended from the rights and privileges of the Organization, or expelled from its membership by the General Council.

8. A member of the Organization which has persistently violated the principles contained in the present Constitution, may be suspended from the rights and privileges

of the Organization by the General Council, and with the approval of the General Assembly of the United Nations, may be expelled from the Organization.

9. A member of the Organization undertakes to afford its general support to the work of the Organization.

10. Any member may at any time give written notice of withdrawal to the Chairman of the Executive Committee. Such notice shall take effect one year after the date of its receipt by the Chairman of the Executive Committee.

Article 5. ORGANS

There are established as the principal organs of the Organization: a General Council, and Executive Committee and a Secretariat.

Article 6. THE GENERAL COUNCIL

1. The ultimate policy-making body of the Organization shall be the General Council in which each member shall have one representative and such alternates and advisers as may be necessary. Each member shall have one vote in the General Council.

2. The General Council shall be convened in regular session not less than once a year by the Executive Committee provided, however, that for three years after the Organization comes into being the General Council shall be convened in regular session not less than twice a year. It may be convened in special session whenever the Executive Committee shall deem necessary; and it shall be convened in special session by the Director-General within thirty days after a request for such a special session is received by the Director-General from one-third of the members of the Council.

3. At the opening meeting of each session of the General Council, the Chairman of the Executive Committee shall preside until the General Council has elected one of its members as Chairman for the session.

4. The General Council shall thereupon proceed to elect from among its members a first Vice-Chairman and a second Vice-Chairman, and such other officers as it may deem necessary.

Article 7. EXECUTIVE COMMITTEE

1. The Executive Committee shall perform such functions as may be necessary to give effect to the policies of the General Council, and may make, between sessions of the General Council, policy decisions of an emergency nature which it shall pass on to the Director-General, who shall be guided thereby, and shall report to the Executive Committee on the action which he has taken thereon. These decisions shall be subject to reconsideration by the General Council.

2. The Executive Committee of the General Council shall consist of the representatives of nine members of the Organization. Each member of the Executive Committee shall be elected for a two-year term by the General Council at a regular session of the Council. A member may continue to hold office on the Executive Committee during any such period as may intervene between the conclusion of its term of office and the first succeeding meeting of the General Council at which an election takes place. A member shall be at all times eligible for re-election to the Executive Committee. If a vacancy occurs in the membership of the Executive Committee between two sessions of the General Council, the Executive Committee may fill the vacancy by itself appointing another member to hold office until the next meeting of the Council.

3. The Executive Committee shall elect a Chairman and a Vice-Chairman from among its members, the terms of office to be determined by the General Council.

4. Meetings of the Executive Committee shall be convened:

(a) at the call of the Chairman, normally twice a month;

(*b*) whenever any representative of a member of the Executive Committee shall request the convening of a meeting, by a letter addressed to the Director-General, in which case the meeting shall be convened within seven days of the date of the receipt of the request;

(*c*) in the case of a vacancy occurring in the Chairmanship, the Director-General shall convene a meeting at which the first item on the agenda shall be the election of a Chairman.

5. The Executive Committee may, in order to investigate the situation in the field, either as a body or through a delegation of its members, visit camps, hostels or assembly points within the control of the Organization, and may give instructions to the Director-General in consequence of the reports of such visits.

6. The Executive Committee shall receive the reports of the Director-General as provided in paragraph 6 of Article 8 of this Constitution, and, after consideration thereof, shall request the Director-General to transmit these reports to the General Council with such comments as the Executive Committee may consider appropriate. These reports and such comments shall be transmitted to all members of the General Council before its next regular session and shall be published. The Executive Committee may request the Director-General to submit such further reports as may be deemed necessary.

Article 8. ADMINISTRATION

1. The chief administrative officer of the Organization shall be the Director-General. He shall be responsible to the General Council and the Executive Committee and shall carry out the administrative and executive functions of the Organization in accordance with the decisions of the General Council and the Executive Committee, and shall report on the action taken thereon.

2. The Director-General shall be nominated by the Executive Committee and appointed by the General Council. If no person acceptable to the General Council is nominated by the Executive Committee, the General Council may proceed to appoint a person who has not been nominated by the Committee. When a vacancy occurs in the office of the Director-General the Executive Committee may appoint an Acting Director-General to assume all the duties and functions of the office until a Director-General can be appointed by the General Council.

3. The Director-General shall serve under a contract which shall be signed on behalf of the Organization by the Chairman of the Executive Committee and it shall be a clause of such contract that six months' notice of termination can be given on either side. In exceptional circumstances, the Executive Committee, subject to subsequent confirmation by the General Council, has the power to relieve the Director-General of his duties by a two-thirds majority vote of the members if, in the Committee's opinion, his conduct is such as to warrant such action.

4. The staff of the Organization shall be appointed by the Director-General under regulations to be established by the General Council.

5. The Director-General shall be present, or be represented by one of his subordinate officers, at all meetings of the General Council, or the Executive Committee and of all other committees and sub-committees. He or his representatives may participate in any such meeting but shall have no vote.

6. (*a*) The Director-General shall prepare at the end of each half-year period a report on the work of the Organization. The report prepared at the end of each alternate period of six months shall relate to the work of the Organization during the preceding year and shall give a full account of the activities of the Organization during that period. These reports shall be submitted to the Executive Committee for

consideration, and thereafter shall be transmitted to the General Council together with any comments of the Executive Committee thereon, as provided by paragraph 6 of Article 7 of this Constitution.

(b) At every special session of the General Council the Director-General shall present a statement of the work of the Organization since the last meeting.

Article 9. STAFF

1. The paramount consideration in the employment of the staff and in the determination of the conditions of service shall be the necessity of securing the highest standards of efficiency, competence and integrity. A further consideration in the employment of the staff shall be adherence to the principles laid down in the present Constitution. Due regard shall be paid to the importance of recruiting staff on an appropriate geographical basis, and of employing an adequate number of persons from the countries of origin of the displaced persons.

2. No person shall be employed by the Organization who is excluded under Part II, other than paragraph 5, of Annex I to this Constitution, from becoming the concern of the Organization.

3. In the performance of their duties, the Director-General and the staff shall not seek or receive instructions from any Government or from any other authority external to the Organization. They shall refrain from any action which might reflect on their position as international officials responsible only to the Organization. Each member of the Organization undertakes to respect the exclusively international character of the responsibilities of the Director-General and the staff and not to seek to influence them in the discharge of their responsibilities.

Article 10. FINANCE

1. The Director-General shall submit, through the Executive Committee, to the General Council an annual budget, covering the necessary administrative, operational and large-scale re-settlement expenditures of the Organization, and from time to time such supplementary budgets as may be required. The Executive Committee shall transmit the budget to the General Council with any remarks it may deem appropriate. Upon final approval of a budget by the General Council, the total under each of these three headings—to wit, 'administrative', 'operational' and 'large-scale re-settlement'—shall be allocated to the members in proportions for each heading to be determined from time to time by a two-thirds majority vote of the members of the General Council present and voting.

2. Contributions shall be payable, as a result of negotiations undertaken at the request of members between the Organization and such members, in kind or in such currency as may be provided for in a decision by the General Council, having regard to currencies in which the anticipated expenditure of the Organization will be effected from time to time, regardless of the currency in which the budget is expressed.

3. Each member undertakes to contribute to the Organization its share of the administrative expenses as determined and allocated under paragraphs 1 and 2 of this article.

4. Each member shall contribute to the operational expenditures—except for large-scale re-settlement expenditures—as determined and allocated under paragraphs 1 and 2 of this article, subject to the requirements of the constitutional procedure of such members. The members undertake to contribute to the large-scale re-settlement expenditures on a voluntary basis and subject to the requirements of their constitutional procedure.

5. A member of the Organization, which, after the expiration of a period of three months following the date of the coming into force of this Constitution, has not paid

its financial contribution to the Organization for the first financial year, shall have no vote in the General Council or the Executive Committee until such contribution has been paid.

6. Subject to the provisions of paragraph 5 of this article, a member of the Organization which is in arrears in the payment of its financial contributions to the Organization shall have no vote in the General Council or the Executive Committee if the amount of its arrears equals or exceeds the amount of the contributions due from it for the preceding one full year.

7. The General Council may, nevertheless, permit such members to vote if it is satisfied that the failure to pay is due to conditions beyond the control of such members.

8. The administrative budget of the Organization shall be submitted annually to the General Assembly of the United Nations for such review and recommendation as the General Assembly may deem appropriate. The agreement under which the Organization shall be brought into relationship with the United Nations under Article 3 of this Constitution may provide, *inter alia*, for the approval of the administrative budget of the Organization by the General Assembly of the United Nations.

9. Without prejudice to the provisions concerning supplementary budgets in paragraph 1 of this article the following exceptional arrangements shall apply in respect of the financial year in which this Constitution comes into force:

(*a*) the budget shall be the provisional budget set forth in Annex II to this Constitution; and

(*b*) the amounts to be contributed by the members shall be in the proportions set forth in Annex II to this Constitution.

Article 11. HEADQUARTERS AND OTHER OFFICES

1. The Organization shall establish its headquarters at Paris or at Geneva, as the General Council shall decide, and all meetings of the General Council and the Executive Committee shall be held at this headquarters, unless a majority of the members of the General Council or the Executive Committee have agreed, at a previous meeting or by correspondence with Director-General to meet elsewhere.

2. The Executive Committee may establish such regional and other offices and representations as may be necessary.

3. All offices and representations shall be established only with the consent of the Government in authority in the place of establishment.

Article 12. PROCEDURE

1. The General Council shall adopt its own rules of procedure, following in general, the rules of procedure of the Economic and Social Council of the United Nations, wherever appropriate, and with such modifications as the General Council shall deem desirable. The Executive Committee shall regulate its own procedure subject to any decisions of the General Council in respect thereto.

2. Unless otherwise provided in the Constitution or by action of the General Council, motions shall be carried by simple majority of the members present and voting in the General Council and the Executive Committee.

Article 13. STATUS, IMMUNITIES AND PRIVILEGES

1. The Organization shall enjoy in the territory of each of its members such legal capacity as may be necessary for the exercise of its functions and the fulfilment of its objectives.

2. (*a*) The Organization shall enjoy in the territory of each of its members such privileges and immunities as may be necessary for the exercise of its functions and the fulfilment of its objectives.

(*b*) Representatives of members, officials and administrative personnel of the Organization shall similarly enjoy such privileges and immunities as are necessary for the independent exercise of their functions in connection with the Organization.

3. Such legal status, privileges and immunities shall be defined in an agreement to be prepared by the Organization after consultation with the Secretary-General of the United Nations. The agreement shall be open to accession by all members and shall continue in force as between the Organization and every member which accedes to the agreement.

Article 14. RELATIONS WITH OTHER ORGANIZATIONS

1. Subject to the provisions of the agreement to be negotiated with the United Nations, pursuant to Article 3 of this Constitution, the Organization may establish such effective relationships as may be desirable with other international organizations.

2. The Organization may assume all or part of the functions, and acquire all or part of the resources, assets and liabilities of any inter-governmental organization or agency, the purposes and functions of which lie within the scope of the Organization. Such action may be taken either through mutually acceptable arrangements with the competent authorities of such organizations or agencies, or pursuant to authority conferred upon the Organization by international convention or agreement.

Article 15. RELATIONSHIP WITH AUTHORITIES OF COUNTRIES OF LOCATION OF REFUGEES AND DISPLACED PERSONS

The relationship of the Organization with the Governments or administrations of countries in which displaced persons or refugees are located, and the conditions under which it will operate in such countries, shall be determined by agreements to be negotiated by it with such Governments or administrations in accordance with the terms of this Constitution.

Article 16. AMENDMENT OF CONSTITUTION

Texts of proposed amendments to this Constitution shall be communicated by the Director-General to members at least three months in advance of their consideration by the General Council. Amendments shall come into effect when adopted by a two-thirds majority of the members of the General Council present and voting and accepted by two-thirds of the members in accordance with their respective constitutional processes, provided, however, that amendments involving new obligations for members shall come into force in respect of each member only on acceptance by it.

Article 17. INTERPRETATION

1. The Chinese, English, French, Russian and Spanish texts of this Constitution shall be regarded as equally authentic.

2. Subject to Article 96 of the Charter of the United Nations and of Chapter II of the Statute of the International Court of Justice, any question or dispute concerning the interpretation or application of this Constitution shall be referred to the International Court of Justice, unless the General Council or the parties to such dispute agree to another mode of settlement.

Article 18. ENTRY INTO FORCE

1. (*a*) States may become parties to this Constitution by:
    (i) signature without reservation as to approval;
    (ii) signature subject to approval followed by acceptance;
    (iii) acceptance.

(b) Acceptance shall be effected by the deposit of a formal instrument with the Secretary-General of the United Nations.

2. This Constitution shall come into force when at least fifteen States, whose required contributions to Part I of the operational budget as set forth in Annex II of this Constitution amount to not less than seventy-five per cent of the total thereof, have become parties to it.

3. In accordance with Article 102 of the Charter of the United Nations, the Secretary-General of the United Nations will register this Constitution, when it has been signed, without reservation as to approval, on behalf of one State or upon deposit of the first instrument of acceptance.

4. The Secretary-General of the United Nations will inform States parties to this Constitution, of the date when it has come into force; he will also inform them of the dates when other States have become parties to this Constitution.

IN FAITH WHEREOF the undersigned, duly authorized for that purpose, have signed this Constitution.

DONE at Flushing Meadow, New York, this fifteenth day of December, one thousand nine hundred and forty-six, in a single copy in the Chinese, English, French, Russian and Spanish languages. The original texts shall be deposited in the archives of the United Nations. The Secretary-General of the United Nations will send certified copies of the texts to each of the signatory Governments and, upon the coming into force of the Constitution and the election of a Director-General, to the Director-General of the Organization.

ANNEX I

DEFINITIONS

GENERAL PRINCIPLES

1. The following general principles constitute an integral part of the definitions as laid down in Parts I and II of this Annex.

(a) The main object of the Organization will be to bring about a rapid and positive solution of the problem of *bona fide* refugees and displaced persons, which shall be just and equitable to all concerned.

(b) The main task concerning displaced persons is to encourage and assist in every way possible their early return to their countries of origin, having regard to the principles laid down in paragraph (c) (ii) of the resolution adopted by the General Assembly of the United Nations on 12 February 1946 regarding the problem of refugees (Annex III).

(c) As laid down in the resolution adopted by the Economic and Social Council on 16 February 1946, no international assistance should be given to traitors, quislings and war criminals, and nothing should be done to prevent in any way their surrender and punishment.

(d) It should be the concern of the Organization to ensure that its assistance is not exploited in order to encourage subversive or hostile activities directed against the Government of any of the United Nations.

(e) It should be the concern of the Organization to ensure that its assistance is not exploited by persons in the case of whom it is clear that they are unwilling to return to their countries of origin because they prefer idleness to facing the hardships of helping in the reconstruction of their countries, or by persons who intend to settle in other countries for purely economic reasons, thus qualifying as emigrants.

(f) On the other hand it should equally be the concern of the Organization to ensure that no *bona fide* and deserving refugee or displaced person is deprived of such assistance as it may be in a position to offer.

(*g*) The Organization should endeavour to carry out its functions in such a way as to avoid disturbing friendly relations between nations. In the pursuit of this objective, the Organization should exercise special care in cases in which the re-establishment or re-settlement of refugees or displaced persons might be contemplated, either in countries contiguous to their respective countries of origin or in non-self-governing countries. The Organization should give due weight, among other factors, to any evidence of genuine apprehension and concern felt in regard to such plans, in the former case, by the country of origin of the persons involved, or, in the latter case, by the indigenous population of the non-self-governing country in question.

2. To ensure the impartial and equitable application of the above principles and of the terms of the definition which follows, some special system of semi-judicial machinery should be created, with appropriate constitution, procedure and terms of reference.

PART I

Refugees and Displaced Persons within the Meaning of the Resolution adopted by the Economic and Social Council of the United Nations on 16 February 1946

Section A. *Definition of Refugees*

1. Subject to the provisions of sections C and D and of Part II of this Annex, the term 'refugee' applies to a person who has left, or who is outside of, his country of nationality or of former habitual residence, and who, whether or not he had retained his nationality, belongs to one of the following categories:

(*a*) victims of the nazi or fascist regimes or of regimes which took part on their side in the second world war, or of the quisling or similar regimes which assisted them against the United Nations, whether enjoying international status as refugees or not;

(*b*) Spanish Republicans and other victims of the Falangist regime in Spain, whether enjoying international status as refugees or not;

(*c*) persons who were considered 'refugees' before the outbreak of the second world war, for reasons of race, religion, nationality or political opinion.

2. Subject to the provisions of sections C and D and of Part II of this Annex regarding the exclusion of certain categories of persons, including war criminals, quislings and traitors, from the benefits of the Organization, the term 'refugee' also applies to a person, other than a displaced person as defined in Section B of this Annex, who is outside of his country of nationality or former habitual residence, and who, as a result of events subsequent to the outbreak of the second world war, is unable or unwilling to avail himself of the protection of the Government of his country of nationality or former nationality.

3. Subject to the provisions of section D and of Part II of this Annex, the term 'refugee' also applies to persons who, having resided in Germany or Austria, and being of Jewish origin or foreigners or stateless persons, were victims of nazi persecution and were detained in, or were obliged to flee from, and were subsequently returned to, one of those countries as a result of enemy action, or of war circumstances, and have not yet been firmly re-settled therein.

4. The term 'refugee' also applies to unaccompanied children who are war orphans

or whose parents have disappeared, and who are outside their countries of origin. Such children, 16 years of age or under, shall be given all possible priority assistance, including, normally, assistance in repatriation in the case of those whose nationality can be determined.

Section B. *Definition of Displaced Persons*

The term 'displaced person' applies to a person who, as a result of the actions of the authorities of the regimes mentioned in Part I, section A, paragraph 1 (*a*) of this Annex has been deported from, or has been obliged to leave his country of nationality or of former habitual residence, such as persons who were compelled to undertake forced labour or who were deported for racial, religious or political reasons. Displaced persons will only fall within the mandate of the Organization subject to the provisions of sections C and D of Part I and to the provisions of Part II of this Annex. If the reasons for their displacement have ceased to exist, they should be repatriated as soon as possible in accordance with Article 2, paragraph 1 (*a*) of this Constitution, and subject to the provision of paragraph (*c*), sub-paragraphs (ii) and (iii) of the General Assembly resolution of 12 February 1946 regarding the problem of refugees (Annex III).

Section C. *Conditions under which 'Refugees' and 'Displaced Persons' will become the Concern of the Organization*

1. In the case of all the above categories except those mentioned in section A, paragraphs 1 (*b*) and 3 of this Annex, persons will become the concern of the Organization in the sense of the resolution adopted by the Economic and Social Council on 16 February 1946 if they can be repatriated, and the help of the Organization is required in order to provide for their repatriation, or if they have definitely, in complete freedom and after receiving full knowledge of the facts, including adequate information from the Governments of their countries of nationality or former habitual residence, expressed valid objections to returning to those countries.

(*a*) The following shall be considered as valid objections:

    (i) Persecution, or fear based on reasonable grounds of persecution because of race, religion, nationality or political opinions, provided these opinions are not in conflict with the principles of the United Nations, as laid down in the Preamble of the Charter of the United Nations;

    (ii) objections of a political nature judged by the Organization to be 'valid', as contemplated in paragraph 8 (*a*)[1] of the report of the Third Committee of the General Assembly as adopted by the Assembly on 12 February 1946;

    (iii) in the case of persons falling within the category mentioned in section A, paragraphs 1 (*a*) and 1 (*c*) compelling family reasons arising out of previous persecution, or, compelling reasons of infirmity or illness.

(*b*) The following shall normally be considered 'adequate information': information regarding conditions in the countries of nationality of the refugees and displaced persons concerned, communicated to them directly by representatives of the Governments of these countries, who shall be given every facility for visiting camps and assembly centres of refugees and displaced persons in order to place such information before them.

2. In the case of all refugees falling within the terms of section A, paragraph 1 (*b*) of this Annex, persons will become the concern of the Organization in the sense of

---

[1] *Paragraph 8 (a)*: 'In answering the representative of Belgium, the Chairman stated that it was implied that the international body would judge what were, or what were not, "valid objections"; and that such objections clearly might be of a political nature.'

the resolution adopted by the Economic and Social Council of the United Nations on 16 February 1946, so long as the Falangist regime in Spain continues. Should that regime be replaced by a democratic regime they will have to produce valid objections against returning to Spain corresponding to those indicated in paragraph 1 (a) of this section.

Section D. *Circumstances in which Refugees and Displaced Persons will cease to be the Concern of the Organization*

Refugees or displaced persons will cease to be the concern of the Organization:

(a) when they have returned to the countries of their nationality in United Nations territory, unless their former habitual residence to which they wish to return is outside their country of nationality; or

(b) when they have acquired a new nationality; or

(c) when they have, in the determination of the Organization become otherwise firmly established; or

(d) when they have unreasonably refused to accept the proposals of the Organization for their re-settlement or repatriation; or

(e) when they are making no substantial effort towards earning their living when it is possible for them to do so, or when they are exploiting the assistance of the Organization.

PART II

PERSONS WHO WILL NOT BE THE CONCERN OF THE ORGANIZATION

1. War criminals, quislings and traitors.

2. Any other persons who can be shown:

(a) to have assisted the enemy in persecuting civil populations of countries, Members of the United Nations; or

(b) to have voluntarily assisted the enemy forces since the outbreak of the second world war in their operations against the United Nations.[1]

3. Ordinary criminals who are extraditable by treaty.

4. Persons of German ethnic origin, whether German nationals or members of German minorities in other countries, who:

(a) have been or may be transferred to Germany from other countries;

(b) have been, during the second world war, evacuated from Germany to other countries;

(c) have fled from, or into, Germany, or from their places of residence into countries other than Germany in order to avoid falling into the hands of Allied armies.

5. Persons who are in receipt of financial support and protection from their country of nationality, unless their country of nationality requests international assistance for them.

6. Persons who, since the end of hostilities in the second world war:

(a) have participated in any organization having as one of its purposes the overthrow by armed force of the Government of their country of origin, being a

---

[1] Mere continuance of normal and peaceful duties, not performed with the specific purpose of aiding the enemy against the Allies or against the civil population of territory in enemy occupation, shall not be considered to constitute 'voluntary assistance'. Nor shall acts of general humanity, such as care of wounded or dying, be so considered except in cases where help of this nature given to enemy nationals could equally well have been given to Allied nationals and was purposely withheld from them.

Member of the United Nations; or the overthrow by armed force of the Government of any other Member of the United Nations, or have participated in any terrorist organization;

(b) have become leaders of movements hostile to the Government of their country of origin being a Member of the United Nations or sponsors of movements encouraging refugees not to return to their country of origin;

(c) at the time of application for assistance, are in the military or civil service of a foreign State.

ANNEX II

BUDGET AND CONTRIBUTIONS FOR THE FIRST FINANCIAL YEAR

1. The provisional budget for the first financial year shall be the sum of 4,800,000 United States dollars for administrative expenses, and a sum of 151,060,500 United States dollars for operational expenses (except for large-scale re-settlement expenses), and a sum of 5,000,000 United States dollars for large-scale re-settlement expenses. Any unspent balance under these headings shall be carried over to the corresponding heading as a credit in the budget of the next financial year.

2. These sums, (except for large-scale re-settlement expenses), shall be contributed by the members in the following proportions:

A. FOR ADMINISTRATIVE EXPENSES

Country	Percentage	Country	Percentage
Afghanistan	0·05	Iraq	0·17
Argentina	1·85	Lebanon	0·06
Australia	1·97	Liberia	0·04
Belgium	1·35	Luxemburg	0·05
Bolivia	0·08	Mexico	0·63
Brazil	1·85	Netherlands	1·40
Byelorussian Soviet Socialist Republic	0·22	New Zealand	0·50
Canada	3·20	Nicaragua	0·04
Chile	0·45	Norway	0·50
China	6·00	Panama	0·05
Colombia	0·37	Paraguay	0·04
Costa Rica	0·04	Peru	0·20
Cuba	0·29	Philippine Republic	0·29
Czechoslovakia	0·90	Poland	0·95
Denmark	0·79	Saudi Arabia	0·08
Dominican Republic	0·05	Sweden	2·35
Ecuador	0·05	Syria	0·12
Egypt	0·79	Turkey	0·91
El Salvador	0·05	Ukrainian Soviet Socialist Republic	0·84
Ethiopia	0·08	Union of South Africa	1·12
France	6·00	Union of Soviet Socialist Republics	6·34
Greece	0·17	United Kingdom	11·48
Guatemala	0·05	United States of America	39·89
Haiti	0·04	Uruguay	0·18
Honduras	0·04	Venezuela	0·27
Iceland	0·04	Yugoslavia	0·33
India	3·95		100·00
Iran	0·45		

B. FOR OPERATIONAL EXPENSES (EXCEPT FOR LARGE-SCALE RE-SETTLEMENT)

Country	Percentage	Country	Percentage
Afghanistan	0·03	Iraq	0·15
Argentina	1·50	Lebanon	0·05
Australia	1·76	Liberia	0·02
Belgium	1·00	Luxemburg . . .	0·04
Bolivia	0·07	Mexico	0·54
Brazil	1·50	Netherlands . . .	0·90
Byelorussian Soviet Socialist Re-		New Zealand . . .	0·44
public	0·16	Nicaragua	0·02
Canada	3·50	Norway	0·44
Chile	0·39	Panama	0·04
China	2·50	Paraguay	0·02
Colombia	0·32	Peru	0·17
Costa Rica	0·02	Philippine Republic . .	0·24
Cuba	0·24	Poland	0·61
Czechoslovakia . . .	0·80	Saudi Arabia . . .	0·07
Denmark	0·68	Sweden	2·20
Dominican Republic . .	0·04	Syria	0·10
Ecuador	0·04	Turkey	0·88
Egypt	0·68	Ukrainian Soviet Socialist Republic .	0·62
El Salvador	0·03	Union of South Africa . .	1·00
Ethiopia	0·07	Union of Soviet Socialist Republics .	4·69
France	4·10	United Kingdom . . .	14·75
Greece	0·15	United States of America .	45·75
Guatemala	0·04	Uruguay	0·15
Haiti	0·02	Venezuela	0·23
Honduras	0·02	Yugoslavia	0·23
Iceland	0·02	New Members . . .	1·92
India	3·66		
Iran	0·39		100·00

3. Contributions to large-scale re-settlement expenses shall be governed by the provisions of Article 10, paragraph 4 of this Constitution.

ANNEX III

RESOLUTION ADOPTED BY THE GENERAL ASSEMBLY ON 12 FEBRUARY 1946
(Document A/45)

THE GENERAL ASSEMBLY,

RECOGNIZING that the problem of refugees and displaced persons of all categories is one of immediate urgency and recognizing the necessity of clearly distinguishing between genuine refugees and displaced persons on the one hand, and the war criminals, quislings and traitors referred to in paragraph (d) below, on the other:

(a) DECIDES to refer this problem to the Economic and Social Council for thorough examination in all its aspects under item 10 of the agenda for the first session of the Council and for report to the second part of the first session of the General Assembly;

(b) RECOMMENDS to the Economic and Social Council that it establish a special committee for the purpose of carrying out promptly the examination and preparation of the report referred to in paragraph (a); and (*c*) RECOMMENDS to the Economic and Social Council that it take into consideration in this matter the following principles:

(i) this problem is international in scope and nature;

(ii) no refugees or displaced persons who have finally and definitely, in complete freedom and after receiving full knowledge of the facts, including adequate information from the Governments of their countries of origin, expressed valid objections to returning to their countries of origin and do not come within the provisions of (*d*) below, shall be compelled to return to their country of origin. The future of such refugees or displaced persons shall become the concern of whatever international body may be recognized or established as a result of the report referred to in paragraphs (*a*) and (*b*) above, except in cases where the Government of the country where they are established has made an arrangement with this body to assume the complete cost of their maintenance and the responsibility for their protection;

(iii) the main task concerning displaced persons is to encourage and assist in every way possible their early return to their countries of origin. Such assistance may take the form of promoting the conclusion of bilateral arrangements for mutual assistance in the repatriation of such persons, having regard to the principles laid down in paragraph (*c*) (ii) above;

(*d*) CONSIDERS that no action taken as a result of this resolution shall be of such a character as to interfere in any way with the surrender and punishment of war criminals, quislings and traitors, in conformity with present or future international arrangements or agreements;

(*e*) CONSIDERS that Germans being transferred to Germany from other States or who fled to other States from Allied troops, do not fall under the action of this declaration in so far as their situation may be decided by Allied forces of occupation in Germany, in agreement with the Governments of the respective countries.

AGREEMENT ON INTERIM MEASURES TO BE TAKEN IN RESPECT OF REFUGEES AND DISPLACED PERSONS

THE GOVERNMENTS which have signed the Constitution of the International Refugee Organization,

having determined that they will take all measures possible to accomplish expeditiously the entry into effective operation of that Organization, and to provide for an orderly transfer to it of the functions and assets of existing organizations;

having decided that, pending the entry into force of the Constitution of the Organization, a Preparatory Commission for the International Refugee Organization should be established for the performance of certain functions and duties;

AGREE to the following measures:

1. There is hereby established a Preparatory Commission for the International Refugee Organization, which shall consist of one representative from each Government signatory to the Constitution. The Director of the Inter-governmental Committee on Refugees, the Director-General of UNRRA and the Director of the International Labour Organization, or their representatives, shall be invited to sit with the Commission in a consultative capacity.

2. The Commission shall:

(*a*) take all necessary and practicable measures for the purpose of bringing the Organization into effective operation as soon as possible;

(*b*) arrange for the convening of the General Councils in its first session at the earliest practicable date following the entry into force of the Constitution of the Organization;

(*c*) prepare the provisional agenda for this first session as well as documents and recommendations relating thereto;

(*d*) suggest plans, in consultation with existing organizations and the control authorities, for the programme for the first year of the Organization;

(*e*) prepare draft financial and staff regulations, and draft rules of procedure for the General Council and the Executive Committee.

Dates of signatures to the Constitution and their ratification

Country	Date of signature	Date of ratification
Argentine	10 June 1947	..
Australia	13 May 1947	★
Belgium	1 May 1947	30 Mar. 1948
Bolivia	5 June 1947	..
Brazil	1 July 1947	
Canada	16 Dec. 1946	7 Aug. 1947
China	29 Apr. 1947	★
Denmark	20 Aug. 1948	★
Dominican Republic . .	17 Dec. 1946	22 Oct. 1947
France	17 Dec. 1946	3 Mar. 1948
Guatemala	16 Dec. 1946	28 July 1947
Honduras	18 Dec. 1946	..
Iceland	12 May 1947	★
Italy	24 Mar. 1949	★
Liberia	31 Dec. 1946	..
Luxembourg . . .	2 Aug. 1948	★
Netherlands . . .	28 Jan. 1947	11 Aug. 1947
New Zealand . . .	17 Mar. 1947	★
Norway	4 Feb. 1947	18 Aug. 1947
Peru	25 July 1947	..
Philippine Republic . .	18 Dec. 1946	..
Panama	23 June 1947	..
Switzerland . . .	28 Mar. 1949	★
United Kingdom . .	5 Feb. 1947	★
United States . . .	16 Dec. 1946	3 July 1947
Venezuela	4 June 1948	★

★ Signatures without reservation.

3. The Commission may, in its discretion and after agreement with existing organizations dealing with refugees and displaced persons, take over any of the functions, activities, assets and personnel of such organizations, provided that the Commission is satisfied that this is essential in order to accomplish the orderly transfer to the International Refugee Organization of such functions or activities.

4. The Commission shall be governed by the rules of procedure of the Economic and Social Council of the United Nations so far as these are applicable.

5. The Commission shall appoint an Executive Secretary, who shall serve the Commission in that capacity and perform such duties as the Commission may determine. He shall be responsible for the appointment and direction of such staff as may be required for the work of the Commission.

6. The expenses of the Commission may be met by advances from such Governments as choose to make advance contributions, which shall be deductible from their first contributions to the Organization; and from such funds and assets as may be transferred from existing organizations to meet the cases provided for in paragraph 3 of this Agreement.

7. The first meeting of the Commission shall be convened as soon as practicable by the Secretary-General of the United Nations.

8. The Commission shall cease to exist upon the election of the Director-General of the Organization, at which time its property, assets and records shall be transferred to the Organization.

9. This Agreement shall come into force as soon as it has been signed by the representatives of eight Governments signatories to the Constitution of the International Refugee Organization and shall remain open for signature by Members of the United Nations which sign the Constitution of the International Refugee Organization until the Commission is dissolved in accordance with paragraph 8 of this Agreement.

IN FAITH WHEREOF, the undersigned representatives, having been duly authorized for that purpose, sign this Agreement in the Chinese, English, French, Russian and Spanish languages, all five texts being equally authentic.

DONE at Flushing Meadow, New York, this fifteenth day of December, one thousand nine hundred and forty-six.

APPENDIX II (a)

AGREEMENT BETWEEN THE IGCR AND THE PCIRO,
27 JUNE 1947

THE INTERGOVERNMENTAL COMMITTEE ON REFUGEES (hereinafter referred to as 'the Committee') represented by THE DIRECTOR, SIR HERBERT EMERSON, acting pursuant to Resolution IC/Pl. VII/8 (i), adopted by the Committee in plenary session on 3rd June 1947, and

THE PCIRO (hereinafter referred to as 'the Commission') represented by THE EXECUTIVE SECRETARY, MR. ARTHUR J. ALTMEYER acting pursuant to the Agreement on Interim Measures to be Taken in Respect of Refugees and Displaced Persons approved by the UN on 15 December 1946, and in particular to Resolution PREP/ 65 Rev. 1 enacted at the Second Part of the First Session of the PCIRO.

HAVING IN MIND that with effect from 1st July, 1947, the Committee will not undertake any further activities but will proceed to the liquidation of its affairs,

TAKING NOTE THAT the Commission has determined, under Resolution PREP/65 Rev. 1 approved 13th May, 1947, to assume responsibility for Displaced Persons operations as from 1st July, 1947, pending the establishment of the IRO

HEREBY AGREE AS FOLLOWS: 1. The Commission undertakes to carry out so far as practicable and within the limits of available resources the functions heretofore performed by the Committee with regard to Refugees and Displaced Persons in accordance with the provisions of the IRO Constitution.

2. The Committee, in accordance with the provisions of IC/Pl. VII/8 (i), dated 3rd June, 1947, adopted in plenary session will arrange through the Executive Committee prior to 1st July 1947, and thereafter through the Board of Liquidation, for the transfer to the Commission of such surplus funds as are found to be available.

3. The Committee will transfer free of charge to the Commission of all office equipment, motor vehicles and other stocks and stores as and when they become available

for transfer. Documentation with regard to such assets shall be provided in accordance with arrangements to be made between the Committee and the Commission.

4. The Committee will transfer to the Commission its rights to all outstanding balances as on 1st July, 1947, on account of short-term loans granted by the Committee to individual refugees for purposes of rehabilitation.

5. Subject to the retention of records required for its accounting, audit and other purposes, the Committee will transfer to the Commission as of 30th June, 1947, its records and will give access to, or to the extent practicable, summaries or copies of any records which it may find necessary to retain.

6. The Committee shall, when so requested by the Executive Secretary of the Commission, assist wherever possible, and appropriate to secure for the Commission the benefits of any immunities, privileges, agreements or contracts outstanding in favour of the Committee on 30th June, 1947.

7. The Commission accepts responsibility for any obligations under agreements entered into by the Committee before the signing of this agreement for benefits accruing after 30th June, 1947, in connection with its Displaced Persons Operations in so far as such obligations have not matured before 1st July, 1947, as well as for any specific obligations accepted by the Executive Secretary. The Committee and the Commission will also agree on detailed accounting procedures for the implementation of this agreement.

8. The Commission shall take over as from 1st July, 1947, the personnel of the Committee employed on 30th June, 1947, for whom letters of appointment have been authorised by the Executive Secretary. Employees so taken over shall during the first three months of their employment receive from the Commission basic salaries, including increments granted previous to 1st July, 1947, at least as favourable as those which they were receiving at the time at which they were transferred. The conditions of service will be continued in accordance with the Staff Regulations and Provident Fund rules of the Committee prevailing on 30th June, 1947, until such time as revised regulations are issued by the Executive Secretary. Subject to the administrative requirements of the Commission, it undertakes to bear the travel costs of home leave on the same terms that prevailed under regulations of the Committee for employees entitled to home leave as of 30th June 1947. The Committee undertakes to meet the expenses of repatriation of such personnel as are transferred by the Committee to the Commission on 30th June, 1947, and whose services with the Commission are terminated previous to 1st October, 1947, by resignation or any other cause. The Commission undertakes to meet the expenses of repatriation of personnel transferred by the Committee to the Commission on 30th June, 1947, and whose services with the Commission terminates after 30th September, 1947.

9. The Commission undertakes to assist, subject to reimbursement by the Committee, in the repatriation of any personnel of the Committee whose services are not transferred to the Commission, in so far as such personnel have not been repatriated previous to 1st July, 1947.

AGREEMENT BETWEEN THE PCIRO AND UNRRA,
29 JUNE 1947

The UNITED NATIONS RELIEF AND REHABILITATION ADMINISTRATION (hereinafter referred to as 'the Administration') represented by Lowell W. Rooks, Director General, acting pursuant to the Agreement of UNRRA signed on 9 November 1943, and in particular Resolution 99 enacted at the Fifth Session of the UNRRA Council and the

PCIRO (hereinafter referred to as 'the Commission') represented by A. J. Altmeyer, Executive Secretary acting pursuant to the Agreement on Interim Measures to be taken in Respect of Refugees and Displaced Persons approved by the UN on 15 December, 1946, and in particular Resolution NO/3 enacted at the Second Part of the First Session of the PCIRO,

HAVING IN MIND that the authority of the Administration to undertake Displaced Persons Operations terminates on 30th June 1947, and that under Resolution 99 it was contemplated that the Administration would transfer to the IRO or an appropriate Interim Commission its records, files, equipment and other property, as well as its personnel and, with the approval of the Central Committee, any remaining part of the funds set aside relating to its operations with respect to displaced persons.

TAKING NOTE THAT the Commission has determined, under Resolution NO/1 approved 13 May 1947 to assume responsibility for Displaced Persons operations as from 1 July 1947, pending the establishment of the IRO

HEREBY AGREE AS FOLLOWS: 1. The Administration agrees to transfer to the Commission the functions heretofore performed by the Administration with regard to Displaced Persons under the UNRRA Resolutions, and the Commission undertakes to carry out the functions in accordance with the Provisions of the IRO Constitution, as from 30 June 1947.

2. The Administration will transfer to the Commission, as of 30 June 1947, its equipment, supplies and other property relating to its Displaced Persons operations. Documentation with regard to the transfer thereof shall be provided in accordance with arrangements to be made between the Administration and the Commission. The Commission undertakes, where practicable, to safeguard in areas where it is operating any property of the Administration designated by the Administration as surplus. Where this is impracticable, the Commission shall immediately notify the Administration.

3. Subject to the retention of records and files required for its accounting, audit, historical and other purposes, the Administration will transfer to the Commission as of 30 June 1947 its records and files relating to Displaced Persons operations, and will give access to, or to the extent practical summaries or copies of, any records and files which it may find necessary to retain.

4. The Administration will also transfer to the Commission such funds as are authorized by the Central Committee under Resolution 99 of the Council of the Administration.

5. The Administration shall, when so requested by the Executive Secretary of the Commission, assist wherever possible and appropriate to secure for the Commission the benefits of any immunities, privileges, agreements or contracts outstanding in favour of the Administration on 30 June 1947.

6. The Commission accepts responsibility for any obligations under agreements entered into by the Administration before the signing of this Agreement for benefits accruing after 30 June 1947, in connection with its displaced persons operations in so far as such obligations have not matured before 1 July 1947, as well as for any specific obligations accepted by the Executive Secretary. The Commission likewise accepts responsibility for any obligations entered into by the Administration with the agreement of the Commission after the signature of this Agreement and prior to 1 July 1947, in so far as such obligations have not matured prior to 1 July 1947. The Administration and the Commission will also agree upon detailed accounting procedures in implementation of this Agreement.

7. The Commission shall take over as from 1 July 1947 the personnel of the Administration employed on 30 June 1947 in Displaced Persons operations for whom letters

of appointment have been authorized by the Executive Secretary. Employees so taken over shall, during the first three months of their employment, receive from the Commission basic salaries including increments to 1 July 1947 at least as favourable as those which they were receiving at the time at which they were transferred. The conditions of service will be continued by the Commission in accordance with the regulations of the Administration prevailing on 30 June 1947 until such time as revised regulations are issued by the Executive Secretary. The Commission undertakes to meet, on behalf of and from funds provided by the Administration, the expenses of repatriation on termination of such personnel as are transferred by the Administration to the Commission on 30 June 1947, and the travel costs of home leave on the same terms, subject to the administrative requirements of the Commission, as prevailed under regulations of the Administration for employees entitled to home leave as of 30 June 1947.

8. The Commission undertakes to assist, subject to reimbursement by the Administration, in the repatriation of any personnel of the Administration, engaged in Displaced Persons operations terminated on 30 June 1947, but not transferred to the Commission, in so far as such personnel have not been repatriated by 1 July 1947, and to make its facilities available to personnel of the Administration engaged in closure activities.

APPENDIX II (b)

AGREEMENTS WITH GOVERNMENTS AND MILITARY AUTHORITIES IN EUROPE

Denmark

IRO/LEG/GOV/1 22 Nov. 1948	Agreement between the Danish Government and the IRO on operations in Denmark, concluded 19 November 1948.
IRO/LEG/GOV/19 1 Aug. 1949, and corr. 1, 31 Aug. 1949	Protocol to amend the above Agreement, dated 1 August 1949.
IRO/LEG/GOV/37 10 July 1950	Protocol to amend the above Agreement, signed 30 June 1950.

France

PC/LEG/2 6 Sept. 1947	Agreement between the French Government and the PCIRO relating to operations in the French zone of Austria.
PC/LEG/7 29 Dec. 1947	Agreement between the French Government and the PCIRO relating to operations in the French zone of Germany. (Superseded PC/LEG/3.)
PC/LEG/7, Add. 1 and 2, 4 Mar. 1948 and 31 Oct. 1949	Codicils to above Agreement.
PC/LEG/9 15 Jan. 1948	Agreement between the French Government and the PCIRO concerning the selection of refugees and displaced persons for France (Home Territory) and Algeria.

IRO/LEG/GOV/9 and corr. 1, 5 Nov. 1948, 28 Apr. 1949	Technical Agreement for implementation of above Agreement (French only).
PC/LEG/10 15 Jan. 1948	Agreement between the French Government and the PCIRO concerning privileges and immunities.
PC/LEG/11 15 Jan. 1948 (no text)	Agreement between the French Government and the PCIRO concerning the protection of refugees and displaced persons coming within the mandate of the IRO and the quasi-consular functions of the representatives in France of the PCIRO.
PC/LEG/12 15 Jan. 1948	Agreement between the French Government and the PCIRO concerning the establishment and the activities of the PCIRO office in France.
IRO/LEG/GOV/2 16 Dec. 1948	Joint Statement by the French Government and the PCIRO on an experiment in the resettlement of 1,000 families of agricultural workers selected among displaced persons.
IRO/LEG/GOV/2/Add. 1 14 Dec. 1948	Supplementary Agreement between the French Government and the IRO concerning an experiment in resettlement of 1,000 families of agricultural workers selected among displaced persons.
IRO/LEG/GOV/14 6 May 1949, and corr. 1, 16 Sept. 1949, and corr. 2, 22 July 1950	Special Arrangement between the IRO and the French Government concerning recruitment of displaced persons for French Guiana.
IRO/LEG/GOV/28 21 Feb. 1950 (no text)	Protocol between the French Government and the IRO on immigration to Morocco under the auspices of the IRO of skilled workers recruited among displaced persons, signed 2 February 1950 (see also PC/LEG/30, 8 July 1948).
IRO/LEG/GOV/30 14 Mar. 1950	Agreement between the French Government and the IRO regarding to the transfer to the French Government of the care and maintenance and responsibilities of the IRO (and protections).

Italy

PC/LEG/4 28 Oct. 1947	Agreement between the Italian Government and the IRO, signed 24 October 1947.
IRO/LEG/GOV/45 9 Mar. 1951	Supplementary Agreement between the Italian Government and the IRO operations in Italy during supplementary period 1950–1, concluded 14 November 1950.
IRO/LEG/GOV/45.1 19 Feb. 1953	Additional Protocol, signed 31 December 1952.

Luxembourg

IRO/LEG/GOV/11
17 Mar. 1949

Agreement between the Government of Luxembourg concerning the selection of refugees and displaced persons for Luxembourg, signed 9 March 1949.

The Netherlands

PC/LEG/21
15 Apr. 1948

Agreement between His Britannic Majesty's Government, the Royal Netherlands Government, and the PCIRO for the resettlement in the Netherlands of displaced persons and refugees in the British zone of Germany, signed 22 October 1947.

IRO/LEG/GOV/38
10 July 1950

Agreement between the IRO and the Netherlands Government, concluded 20 June 1950.

Norway

IRO/LEG/GOV/23
8 Nov. 1949

Memorandum of Understanding (*Aide Memoire*) agreed by the Norwegian Government and the IRO, signed 17 September 1949.

Sweden

IRO/LEG/GOV/34
4 June 1950

Agreement between the IRO and the Swedish Government concerning the admission of refugees, classified as tubercular cases, and members of their families, signed 27 May 1950.

Switzerland

IRO/LEG/GOV/4
29 Jan. 1949

Agreement between the Swiss Federal Council and the IRO concerning the legal status of the IRO in Switzerland, signed 15 September 1948.

IRO/LEG/GOV/5
29 Jan. 1949
(no text)

Arrangement for the execution of the above Agreement, signed 15 September 1948.

United Kingdom

PC/LEG/
28 June 1947
(Annex to IRO/LEG/GOV/44)

Agreement between the Control Commission for Germany (British Element) and the PCIRO concerning the IRO operation in the British zone of Germany, effective 1 July 1947.

PC/LEG/5
7 Nov. 1947
(no text)[1]

Agreement between the Allied Commission for Austria (British Element) and the PCIRO, signed 7 November 1947.

PC/LEG/8
14 Jan. 1948
(no text)

Agreement between the British Government and PCIRO relative to recruitment for employment in Great Britain of displaced persons resident in the US zone of Germany, signed 26 September 1947.

[1] See footnote, p. 656.

IRO/LEG/GOV/44   Agreed definition of responsibilities between
13 Feb. 1951   the Control Commission for Germany
                                             (British Element) and the IRO concern-
                                             ing the IRO operation in the British zone
                                             of Germany, effective 1 January 1951.
                                             (Annex: PC/LEG, 28 June 1947.)

United States of America
PC/LEG/29   Agreement between the Commander-in-Chief,
21 Aug. 1948   European Command, and the IRO as to
                                             IRO's operation in the US area of control
                                             in Germany, signed 28 July 1948.

PC/LEG/31   Agreement between the US HC for Austria
24 Aug. 1948   and the PCIRO, signed 11 August 1948.

AGREEMENT BETWEEN THE DANISH GOVERNMENT AND THE IRO, 19 NOVEMBER 1948[1]

Desirous of reaching rapid and constructive solutions to the problem of refugees and displaced persons in Denmark, and wishing to establish a basis for close co-operation in a common effort to achieve this objective, the Danish Government (hereinafter referred to as 'the Government') and the International Refugee Organization (hereinafter referred to as 'IRO') have agreed as follows:

Article I. SCOPE OF THE AGREEMENT

1. As used in this Agreement, the term 'refugees' refers to displaced persons and refugees in Denmark on 1 July 1948 who may be determined by IRO as falling within the IRO mandate as it is defined in Annex I to the IRO Constitution.

Article II. STATUS AND FUNCTIONS OF IRO

2. The Government recognizes the status and powers of IRO as an international organization which is a specialized agency of the United Nations authorized to perform the following principal functions in accordance with the provisions of the IRO Constitution and the Resolutions of the IRO General Council and Executive Committee:
   (a) Determination of the persons who fall within the mandate of IRO as it is defined in Annex I to the IRO Constitution.
   (b) Encouraging the return of refugees to their countries of origin and assisting with the return of those who voluntarily choose to be repatriated.
   (c) The re-establishment or resettlement of refugees who have valid reasons for not returning to their countries of origin.
   (d) Pending their repatriation, re-establishment or resettlement, assistance with the care and maintenance of refugees.
   (e) Legal and political protection of refugees.

Article III. RELATIONSHIP BETWEEN THE GOVERNMENT AND IRO

3. The Government invites the assistance of IRO in providing for the care, maintenance and legal protection of refugees in Denmark, and in facilitating their early re-establishment.

[1] IRO/LEG/GOV/1, 22 Nov. 1948.

4. IRO undertakes to assist with the performance of these tasks to the fullest extent possible within its constitutional powers and available resources, and in particular to perform the functions described in Articles IV, V, VI and VII of this Agreement.

5. The Government and IRO will extend to each other the fullest possible assistance in the solution of questions concerning persons within the mandate of IRO in Denmark, and will maintain close liaison with each other through an IRO Representative in Denmark, who will be selected in agreement with the Government. In particular, the Government and IRO will keep each other informed in advance of measures to be taken which may affect the conditions or status of the refugees.

Article IV. REPATRIATION OF REFUGEES

6. While preserving freedom of decision by refugees, in accordance with the principles expressed in its Constitution, IRO will encourage and assist in every way possible with their return to their countries of origin.

7. IRO will pay or arrange for the payment of expenses incidental to the voluntary return of refugees to their countries of origin. Such costs will not, in any event, be chargeable to the Government.

8. The Government agrees to permit refugees who are being repatriated from Denmark to take with them all of their personal belongings, including professional equipment for the transport of which IRO is able to make provision; and the Government agrees to exempt such articles from any form of export taxes or customs duties.

Article V. CARE AND MAINTENANCE OF REFUGEES

9. The Government will continue, under the general supervision of IRO, the direct operation of refugee camps and the direct administration of care and maintenance of refugees whether inside or outside camps. The Government agrees to perform these functions in accordance with the principles established by the IRO Constitution and defined in Resolutions of the IRO General Council and Executive Committee.

10. IRO undertakes financial responsibility for the actual and reasonable cost of care and maintenance for refugees at standards to be agreed upon. The caloric diet for refugees under IRO care will be no higher than that prevailing in Denmark.

11. Such refugees as may be employed during their stay in Denmark will be required by IRO to pay sums to be agreed between the Government and IRO which will be applied against the cost of their care and maintenance in Denmark. Such sums will be deducted from payments to be made by IRO under the preceding paragraph for the costs of care and maintenance.

12. The Government agrees to render periodic reports to IRO in a form which will enable IRO to consolidate the reports of the refugee program in Denmark with similar reports of IRO operations elsewhere.

Article VI. RESETTLEMENT OF REFUGEES

13. IRO will take immediate steps to assist with the repatriation or resettlement of as many refugees from Denmark as possible within a minimum delay, and will establish as its first target the repatriation or resettlement within the year ending 30 June 1949 of not less than between 2,000 and 2,500 refugees.

14. IRO will arrange contacts with refugees by Missions from countries of resettlement who are charged with the selection of refugees for admission into such countries. The Government undertakes to facilitate such contacts.

15. IRO will pay or make arrangements for the payment of expenses incidental to the transport of refugees from their places of residence in Denmark to the countries of

resettlement. These transport charges will not, in any event, be chargeable to the Government.

16. The Government agrees to grant exemption from all port charges in Danish State ports on vessels chartered or owned by IRO which are used for the transport of refugees being resettled or repatriated.

17. The provisions of Article IV, paragraph 8, concerning the removal by refugees of their personal belongings and equipment will apply equally to refugees resettled under this Agreement.

Article VII. LEGAL AND POLITICAL PROTECTION TO REFUGEES

18. The Government recognizes that the right of protection pertaining to nations with regard to their nationals will be exercised in Denmark by IRO, in accordance with the IRO Constitution, with regard to persons within the IRO mandate who do not enjoy in law or in fact the protection of any Government. IRO will accordingly take appropriate measures, in accordance with the arrangements to be worked out with the Government Departments concerned, to safeguard the legitimate interests of refugees, and the Government will give IRO every assistance to this end.

19. The Government recognizes that the function of legal and political protection includes, and will, with due regard to the principles of Danish Law, take appropriate steps towards establishing the authority of the IRO Representative in Denmark to exercise, when the need exists, the following quasiconsular functions on behalf of refugees who do not in law or in fact enjoy the protection of any Government:

(a) certifying the identity and the position of the refugees;

(b) certifying their family position and civil status, in so far as these are based on documents issued or action taken in the refugees' country of origin;

(c) testifying to the regularity, validity, and conformity with the previous law of their country of origin, of documents issued in such country;

(d) certifying the signature of refugees and copies and translations of documents drawn up in their own language;

(e) testifying before the authorities of the country to the good character and conduct of the individual refugee, to his previous record, to his professional qualifications, and to his university or academic standing;

(f) recommending the individual refugee to the competent authorities, particularly with a view to his obtaining visas, permits to reside in the country, and admission to schools, libraries, etc.

20. In particular, the Government will take measures to facilitate the employment of refugees, in accordance with the requirements of Danish employment regulations.

Article VIII. FINANCE

21. The contribution of the Government as a Member of IRO will be paid partly in goods and services for the maintenance, on essentially the same line as hitherto, of refugees in Denmark, and partly—insofar as the contribution is not required for such goods and services—in non-convertible Danish kroner. Such payments will be made in accordance with paragraphs 22, 23 and 24 of this Article.

22. The Government will, within thirty days after the signing of this Agreement, establish a credit in favour of IRO in the full amount of its contribution, as a Member Government, to the IRO administrative budget for the financial year 1 July 1948 to 30 June 1949 (the equivalent in Danish kroner of $37,902.62). IRO will have the right to draw against this credit at such times and in such amounts as may be required to meet its administrative expenses.

23. The Government will similarly, within thirty days after the signing of this

Agreement, establish a credit in favour of IRO in the full amount of its contribution to the IRO operational budget for the financial year 1 July 1948 to 30 June 1949 (the equivalent in Danish kroner of $1,021,558.95). This credit may be drawn upon by IRO for the purpose of making payments due to the Government under this Agreement. Such portion of this credit as is not required for payments to the Government under this Agreement may be drawn by IRO at such times and in such sums as IRO may require.

24. Drawings by IRO on the credits established under paragraphs 22 and 23 of this Article will be made at the official rate of exchange prevailing between Danish Kroner and US dollars on the date of such drawings. It is understood that the official rate of exchange is the par value agreed between the Danish Government and the International Monetary Fund, this value being at present 4.79901 kroner to one US dollar.

25. The establishment of credits under the Government's contributions to IRO for the financial year 1 July 1949 to 30 June 1950, and IRO drawings against such credits, will be governed by the provisions of paragraphs 22, 23 and 24.

26. Negotiations will be undertaken immediately between the Government and IRO with the object of establishing as soon as possible the basis for calculating the specific sums to be paid to the Government by IRO under this Agreement in respect of the care and maintenance of refugees.

27. In view of the fact that IRO will have only a limited staff in Denmark who will be charged with carrying out the IRO functions described in Article II, the Government agrees to handle and settle claims against or on behalf of IRO arising in the course of official business. The sums paid by the Government in the implementation of this paragraph will be reimbursable to the Government in Danish kroner.

Article IX

28. This Agreement shall come into force on the date of its signature by representatives of the Government and IRO, and shall remain in force until 30 June 1950 or the expiration of 90 days from the date upon which either Party shall have given notice in writing of its intention to terminate the Agreement.

29. The provisions of Article IV, paragraph 7; Article V, paragraph 10; and Article VI, paragraph 15, will be given effect as from 1 July 1948 with regard to repatriation, care and maintenance, and resettlement costs to be agreed between the Government and IRO.

30. This Agreement may be amended by mutual agreement at any time.

PROTOCOL BETWEEN THE DANISH GOVERNMENT AND THE IRO TO AMEND THE AGREEMENT OF 19 NOVEMBER 1948, DATED 1 AUGUST 1949[1]

The Danish Government and the IRO, desirous of effecting every economy in the IRO programme in Denmark consistent with administrative efficiency and the welfare of the refugees and displaced persons, agree hereby to amend their Agreement of 19 November 1948 as follows:

A. Article V shall be deleted and the following substituted:

Article V. CARE AND MAINTENANCE OF REFUGEES

1. IRO undertakes to carry out with effect from 1 August 1949 the direct operation of refugee camps and the administration of care and maintenance of refugees whether

[1] IRO/LEG/GOV/19/and Corr. 1, 31 Aug. 1949.

inside or outside camps, in accordance with the principles established by the IRO Constitution and defined in Resolutions of the General Council and Executive Committee of IRO. The caloric diet for refugees under IRO care will be no higher than that prevailing in Denmark.

2. The Government undertakes to turn over to IRO by 1 August 1949, to the same extent as at present engaged in the care and maintenance programme, the camps, camp facilities and equipment, necessary office and storage space, and transport and administrative equipment. IRO agrees to return all such properties to the Government, periodically as the reduction of its programme in Denmark permits, in the same condition as received, normal depreciation excepted.

3. Such refugees as may be employed during their stay in Denmark will be required by IRO to pay the cost of their care and maintenance in Denmark.

B. Article VIII shall be deleted and the following substituted:

Article VIII. FINANCE

1. The contribution of the Government as a Member of IRO will be paid in non-convertible Danish kroner, or partly in kind in such manner as may be agreed between the Government and IRO.

2. The Government will by 1 August 1949 establish a credit in favour of IRO in the full amount of its contributions to the administrative and operational budgets of IRO for the financial year 1 July 1949 to 30 June 1950. IRO will have the right to draw against this credit at such times and in such amounts as may be required to meet its administrative and operational expenses in Denmark and such other of its expenses as may be agreed with the Government.

3. Drawings by IRO on the credit established under paragraph 2 of this Article will be made at the official rate of exchange prevailing between Danish kroner and US dollars on the date of such drawings. It is understood that the official rate of exchange is the par value agreed between the Danish Government and the International Monetary Fund, this value being at present 4.79901 kroner to one US dollar.

4. Negotiations may be undertaken at any time between the Government and IRO concerning the sums to be paid to the Government by IRO under this Agreement in respect of the properties and facilities made available to IRO by the Government under the provisions of Article V as amended.

5. For the period between 1 July 1949 and the earliest date by which direct operation of the camps can be transferred from the Government to IRO, reimbursement will be made by IRO to the Government of the actual and reasonable cost of care and maintenance in the manner and at the rates heretofore established under Articles V and VIII of this Agreement for the period 1 July 1948 to 30 June 1949.

6. In view of the fact that IRO will have only a limited staff in Denmark who will be charged with carrying out the IRO functions described in Article II, the Government agrees to handle and settle claims against or on behalf of IRO arising in the course of official business. The sums paid by the Government in the implementation of this paragraph will be reimbursable to the Government in Danish kroner.

PROTOCOL BETWEEN THE IRO AND THE DANISH GOVERNMENT TO AMEND THE AGREEMENT OF 19 NOVEMBER 1948, DATED 30 JUNE 1950[1]

The Danish Government and the IRO, recognizing the need for modification and termination of the IRO program in Denmark during the IRO Supplementary Period

[1] IRO/LEG/GOV/37, 10 July 1950.

1950/51, agree hereby to amend their Agreement of 19 November 1948 as follows, with effect from 1 July 1950:

A. Article V as previously amended by the Protocol of 1 August 1949 shall be deleted and the following substituted:

Article V. CARE AND MAINTENANCE OF REFUGEES

1. The Government and IRO agree to the following provisions for the discontinuance of care and maintenance of refugees by IRO:

(a) The Government will, as rapidly as possible after 30 June 1950 assume progressively full responsibility for the care and maintenance of refugees requiring institutional care. The transfer of responsibility for care and maintenance of such refugees will be completed in any event no later than 31 December 1950. IRO will continue to provide care and maintenance for such refugees until their transfer to the Government and will contribute the sum provided for in Article VIII toward the cost of the required institutional care of these refugees and their dependents after their transfer.

(b) Between 1 July 1950 and 31 March 1951 or such earlier dates as they may be resettled IRO will, as heretofore, provide for the care and maintenance of refugees for whom there are reasonable prospects of resettlement by the Organization. Care and maintenance of such refugees by IRO will not in any event be continued beyond 31 March 1951, and the Government undertakes to make provision for them beyond that date.

2. Until the transfer of care and maintenance responsibilities to the Government under paragraph 1 of this Article IRO will continue the direct operation of refugee camps to the extent required, and the administration of care and maintenance of refugees whether inside or outside camps, in accordance with the principles established by the IRO Constitution and defined in Resolutions of the General Council and Executive Committee of IRO. The caloric diet for refugees under IRO care will be no higher than that prevailing in Denmark.

3. The Government agrees that IRO shall retain, so long as necessary, the required camps, camp facilities and equipment, necessary office and storage space, and transport and administrative equipment. IRO agrees to return all such properties to the Government, progressively, as the reduction of its program in Denmark permits, in the same condition as received, normal depreciation excepted.

B. Article VI, paragraph 13 shall be deleted and the following substituted:

'IRO will continue its effort to assist with the repatriation and resettlement of as many refugees from Denmark as possible within the remaining period of its operations as authorized by the IRO General Council.'

C. Article VII, LEGAL AND POLITICAL PROTECTION OF REFUGEES. Paragraph 19 shall be deleted and the following substituted:

'The exercise by IRO of its constitutional function of legal and political protection of refugees in Denmark will continue till 31 March 1951 or till such earlier date on which arrangements may have been completed for the transfer of this responsibility to the UN High Commissioner for Refugees who is to be appointed under the terms of Resolution 319A (N) of the UN General Assembly dated 3 December 1949.'

D. Article VIII as previously amended by the Protocol of 1 August 1949 shall be deleted and the following substituted:

'IRO agrees that the total contribution by the Government to the Organization for the Supplementary Period 1950/51, which has been fixed by the IRO General Council at $19,804.00 for the administrative budget and $356,721.00 for the operational budget, a total of $376,525.00, will, subject to approval by the General Council under Article 10, paragraph 2 of the IRO Constitution, be credited to the Government as of 1 July 1950 on account of:

(i) Adjustment of the Government's Contribution for the fiscal year 1949/50 in the amount of Kroner 487.913.00 ($70,638.93).

(ii) Payment in full of IRO's agreed contribution toward the costs of institutional care of refugees referred to in Article V, paragraph 1 (a) ($305,886.07).'

E. In derogation of the terminal date (30 June 1950) previously established in paragraph 28, this Agreement will remain in force until 31 March 1951, subject to earlier termination of particular aspects of the IRO program in Denmark as provided in the foregoing Amendments.

AGREEMENT BETWEEN PCIRO AND THE FRENCH GOVERNMENT RELATING TO OPERATIONS IN THE FRENCH ZONE OF AUSTRIA, 6 SEPTEMBER 1947[1]

[*Sections I–V and IX–XI are identical in content and in most of the wording with the Agreement for the French zone of Germany (PC/LEG/7, 29 December 1947).*]

Section VI. FACILITIES AND SERVICES TO BE PROVIDED FOR THE IRO BY THE FRENCH AUTHORITIES

The French Authorities

1. shall supply to the IRO, subject to reimbursement in francs, or failing this, in any other currency acceptable to the French Government, the occupation francs required;

2. shall arrange that refugees and displaced persons employed by the IRO in the French Zone of occupation in Austria shall be paid by the appropriate Austrian agencies;

3. shall arrange that Austrians employed by the IRO shall be paid by the appropriate Austrian agencies;

4. shall provide office and living accommodation free of charge for the staff of the IRO employed in the French Zone of Austria under as favourable conditions as apply to the French staff;

5. shall supply to the IRO the petrol, oil and lubricants required for IRO vehicles, subject to reimbursement except for local currency costs as provided in Section VII, Article 5;

6. shall provide maintenance and repair facilities for IRO vehicles against reimbursement except for local currency costs as provided in Section VII, Article 5;

7. shall supply rations for IRO staff similar to those supplied to the French occupation staff, subject to reimbursement except for local currency costs as provided in Section VII, Article 5;

[1] PC/LEG/2: original French, 6 Sept. 1947. (Amendments to an earlier text, which were agreed in a letter addressed to the Executive Secretary by the French Ministry of Foreign Affairs on 6 Sept. 1947, are incorporated in the following text.)

8. shall extend to IRO staff the use of clubs, messes, cultural, recreational and other facilities provided for the French occupation staff, on the same bases and subject to the same restrictions;

9. shall allow the IRO to use for its official communications the communications system established by the French Authorities, subject to reimbursement except in respect of internal communications in Austria;

10. shall authorize IRO staff to use the same facilities for personal correspondence as are available to French occupation staff, and on the same conditions;

11. shall provide housing accommodation for families of IRO staff on the same scale and subject to the same conditions and priorities as are enjoyed by French occupation staff;

12. shall provide free of charge for IRO staff travelling on official business in the French Zone of Austria, the necessary railway facilities. In that connection, IRO staff going on leave shall enjoy the same facilities and be subject to the same charges as the French occupation staff;

13. shall provide for the IRO staff, the same medical and dental services as are provided for the French occupation staff, subject to repayment;

14. shall lend free of charge to the IRO the military or indigenous equipment (including captured enemy equipment, vehicles and administrative supplies) put at the disposal of UNRRA. For its part the IRO shall lend to the French Authorities, free of charge, such of its facilities and equipment (including vehicles) as may be considered necessary for the operation of camps and assembly centres;

15. shall process claims against the IRO or its personnel for compensation of damage occurring in the execution of their official duties, under the procedures used for French personnel, IRO being, as far as possible, responsible for the payment of such indemnities as might be fixed as a result of this procedure; failing this, such payment will remain a charge on the French Authorities.

Section VII. MAINTENANCE OF DISPLACED PERSONS

1. The French Authorities shall be responsible for ensuring the provision to refugees and displaced persons by the Austrian Authorities of necessary accommodation, food and other supplies.

2. The French Authorities shall be responsible for ensuring the provision by the Austrian Authorities without charge to IRO of basic supplies for the maintenance of refugees and displaced persons eligible for IRO care and maintenance, at the same level as are available to the Austrian population in the French Zone.

3. The French Authorities shall further provide within the limits of available resources, and subject to repayment, the additional supplies required by IRO, including food necessary to bring the ration up to a level to be determined by the IRO after consultation with the French Authorities.

4. The IRO shall pay to the French Authorities, in French francs, (or, in any other currency acceptable to both parties), an agreed allowance, based on an estimate per head of the expenses incurred by the French Authorities for the maintenance of refugees and displaced persons eligible for IRO assistance. This sum shall include the payment of the staff required for the administration, the maintenance of transport and equipment and any other expenses, inter alia the additional supplies provided by the French Authorities to special groups.

5. The French Authorities shall ensure provision to the IRO, free of charge, by the Austrian Authorities of such Austrian currency as may be agreed between IRO and the French Authorities to be necessary for IRO to carry out its responsibilities under this Agreement.

Section VIII. ACCOUNTING AND FINANCIAL PROVISIONS

(a) The French Authorities and the IRO shall maintain proper accounting records of all supplies delivered and services rendered to the IRO in accordance with this Agreement;

(b) The prices fixed in respect of such supplies and services may include a supplement to cover transport and accessory charges;

(c) The exact form of the accounting records and the method of calculating prices and additional charges shall be agreed upon between the IRO and the French Authorities.

2. The payments to be made by IRO to the French Authorities shall be settled by arrangement between the French Government and IRO Headquarters, the settlement to be made either by way of direct payment or by deduction from the French contribution.

3. The IRO shall not be called upon to make any payment or reimbursement in respect of any item not specifically stated in this Agreement to be subject to payment or reimbursement.

AGREEMENT BETWEEN PCIRO AND THE FRENCH GOVERNMENT RELATING TO OPERATIONS IN THE FRENCH ZONE OF GERMANY, 6 SEPTEMBER 1947[1]

Section I. OBJECT

The French Authorities and IRO agree that it is their common objective in accordance with the principles of the Constitution of the IRO to ensure as soon as possible the repatriation or the resettlement in other countries of refugees and displaced persons now in the French Zone of Germany. In furnishing care and maintenance to such persons pending their repatriation or resettlement the French Authorities and IRO shall keep that objective in view.

Section II. GENERAL PROVISIONS

1. IRO shall carry out its activities as authorized and required by its Constitution and shall operate subject to the military regulations, general laws and military government enactments in force in the French Zone of Germany.

2. The IRO shall establish such offices and bring into the French Zone of Germany such staff as it may require. The number of such staff shall be settled in agreement with the French Authorities and be such as will ensure that the tasks entrusted to it will be carried out with the maximum efficiency. Appointments to the more responsible positions in IRO in the French Zone of Germany shall be made in consultation with the French Authorities.

3. Consultation shall take place at all levels between the IRO staff and the French Authorities regarding the implementation of IRO policy concerning displaced persons and refugees in the French Zone of Germany. In particular, consultation shall take place between the Zone Director of IRO and the representatives of the French Authorities with a view to reaching agreement on the instructions they will respectively issue for the effective implementation of such policies in accordance with the general administrative and economic requirements of the French Zone of Germany.

4. Having regard to the provisions of Article 2, paragraph 2 (d) of its Constitution

[1] PC/LEG/7: original French, 29 Dec. 1947. This text corrects and supersedes the text published on 6 Sept. 1947 as PC/LEG/3.

the IRO agrees to entrust to the French Authorities the execution of IRO policy with respect to care and maintenance, under its supervision, of refugees and displaced persons in the French Zone of Germany, whether inside or outside the camps pending their repatriation or resettlement, including the operation of camps and assembly centres.

Section III. RESPONSIBILITIES OF THE IRO

The IRO is responsible for:

1. supervising at every level the carrying out of IRO policy by the French Authorities concerning care and maintenance of refugees and displaced persons in the French Zone of Germany, subject to the overriding needs of the maintenance of law, order, security and public health;

2. determining the eligibility of refugees and displaced persons for IRO assistance according to its Constitution. The IRO shall keep the French Authorities informed as to the methods and machinery it establishes for this purpose as well as the manner in which this task will be carried out (cf. Section V);

3. the classification and the registration of refugees and displaced persons in close cooperation with the French Authorities and the issue to them of documents showing that those formalities have been fulfilled;

4. maintenance in conformity with its general reporting procedures of general statistical records of refugees and displaced persons. The statistics shall be communicated to the French Authorities in a form to be agreed upon; and those statistics may be utilised inter alia in connection with financial transactions provided for in Section VII, article 4;

5. the measures to be taken in cooperation with the French Authorities to encourage and organise repatriation. To that end, IRO representatives shall have access to and keep in close touch with the national repatriation representatives accredited to the French Authorities;

6. ensuring that, subject to the general control of the French Authorities in regard to law, order and security, the national repatriation representatives will be able to inform refugees and displaced persons about the conditions existing in their countries of nationality or former habitual residence;

7. providing for the resettlement, including the selection of refugees and displaced persons who are to be resettled, and making for them all the necessary preparations;

8. negotiations with the representatives of the governments of countries of reception and arrangements for the transport of refugees and displaced persons who are to be resettled;

9. providing, where necessary, staff to accompany repatriation or resettlement convoys;

10. plans for the rehabilitation and vocational training of refugees and displaced persons with a view to their ultimate repatriation or resettlement;

11. reuniting families whose members are scattered, alleviation of other cases of individual distress, and the search for and the repatriation of unaccompanied children;

12. protection of the legitimate interests of refugees and displaced persons;

13. cooperation with the French Authorities in the development and implementation of an employment program for the provision of suitable work for refugees and displaced persons in accordance with the provisions of the IRO Constitution so that IRO shall not be concerned with any refugees or displaced persons who make no substantial effort towards earning their living where it is practicable for them to do so;

14. providing means of transport for its staff moving within the French Zone of Germany;

15. coordinating and supervising in agreement with the French Authorities, as provided inter alia in Section IV, the activities of all voluntary societies working with refugees and displaced persons and participating in the agreements to be concluded by the French Authorities with the voluntary societies insofar as the activities of those societies are in conformity with IRO's responsibilities under this agreement.

Section IV. RESPONSIBILITIES OF THE FRENCH AUTHORITIES

The French Authorities shall be responsible for:

1. putting into effect as far as possible the general policies laid down in Resolutions of the PCIRO or of the General Council of the IRO or embodied in the instructions of the Executive Secretary or the Director General concerning the care and maintenance of refugees and displaced persons, having regard to the overriding requirements of law, order and security and to the practical difficulties that may arise in the provision of accommodation, supplies, food and transport;

2. the maintenance of law, order and security, including the enforcement of military regulations and laws and decrees in force in the French Zone of Germany;

3. the provision of food, clothing, fuel, medical supplies, and household materials such as furniture, bedding, household and kitchen utensils and amenity supplies for refugees and displaced persons in the French Zone of Germany, in accordance as far as possible with the standards laid down by the IRO after consultation with the French Authorities;

4. providing, under the supervision of the IRO, for the operation of all camps and assembly centres for refugees and displaced persons. The housing accommodation should as far as possible permit:

(a) grouping the refugees and displaced persons in such a way as to facilitate their repatriation and resettlement as well as the administration of the camps and assembly centres,

(b) getting suitable work for them,

(c) combining camps and centres so as to reduce administration costs;

5. granting IRO personnel free access to all refugees and displaced persons whether inside or outside the camps or assembly centres;

6. providing public health services, and making available for refugees and displaced persons medical care and hospital facilities at least as good as that provided for the local population, and arranging, wherever possible, in consultation with the IRO that the medical care for refugees and displaced persons is separate from that for the Germans;

7. providing for refugees and displaced persons educational facilities and religious services;

8. implementing, at the request of the IRO, the program drawn up by it to accomplish the tasks laid down in Section III of this Agreement;

9. providing to the maximum extent possible employment for refugees and displaced persons, pending their repatriation and resettlement;

10. cooperation with the IRO in carrying out repatriation and resettlement plans, including the provision of transport for movements of refugees and displaced persons within the French Zone of Germany;

11. providing guards, where necessary, to escort repatriation and resettlement convoys;

12. arranging for the issue of travel documents to refugees being resettled and permitting the movement out of the French Zone of Germany of refugees and displaced persons being repatriated or resettled.

Section V. SPECIAL PROVISIONS WITH RESPECT TO THE ELIGIBILITY OF REFUGEES AND DISPLACED PERSONS

1. The French Authorities shall alone be responsible for action (other than determination of eligibility) to be taken with regard to persons suspected of being war criminals, quislings or traitors. The IRO shall cooperate as closely as possible with the French Authorities to avoid conflicting decisions in this matter.

2. In any case in which the French Authorities are apprehensive that a determination of eligibility by the IRO in accordance with Section III, Article 2 of this Agreement, would create a situation prejudicial to law and the maintenance of order and security, they shall take whatever action they deem appropriate.

3. The French Authorities shall be responsible for taking such measures as may be necessary to prevent persons determined ineligible by the IRO from receiving its assistance. To this end they shall arrange for the removal from camps and assembly centres, entrusted by the IRO to the French Authorities for administration, of all persons determined by the IRO to be ineligible.

Section VI. FACILITIES AND SERVICES TO BE PROVIDED FOR THE IRO BY THE FRENCH AUTHORITIES

The French Authorities

1. shall supply to the IRO, free of charge, the local German currency required for the settlement of costs to be paid in cash, in accordance with a budget which shall be mutually agreed;

2. shall supply to the IRO, subject to reimbursement, the occupation francs required;

3. shall arrange that refugees and displaced persons employed by the IRO in the French Zone of occupation in Germany, shall be paid by the Burgermeister or other qualified German official;

4. shall arrange that Germans employed by the IRO shall be paid by the Burgermeister or other qualified German official;

5. shall provide office and living accommodation, free of charge, for the staff of the IRO employed in the French Zone of Germany under as favourable conditions as apply to the staff of the French occupying Authorities;

6. shall supply to the IRO the petrol, oil and lubricants required for IRO vehicles, subject to reimbursement, except in respect of costs incurred in Reichsmarks;

7. shall provide maintenance and repair facilities for IRO vehicles, against reimbursement, except in respect of costs incurred in Reichsmarks. The French Authorities shall make use as far as possible of German resources for which no reimbursement shall be required;

8. shall supply rations for IRO staff similar to those supplied to French occupation staff, subject to reimbursement, except in respect of costs incurred in Reichsmarks;

9. shall extend to IRO staff the use of clubs, messes, cultural, recreational and other facilities provided for the French occupation staff, on the same basis and subject to the same restrictions;

10. shall allow the IRO to use for its official communications the communications system established by the French Authorities, subject to reimbursement except in respect of costs incurred in Reichsmarks;

11. shall authorize IRO staff to use the same facilities for personal correspondence as are available to French occupation staff;

12. shall provide housing accommodation for families of IRO staff on the same scale and subject to the same conditions and priorities as are enjoyed by French occupation staff;

13. shall provide, free of charge, for IRO staff travelling on official business in the French Zone of Germany, the necessary railway facilities under the same conditions as apply to the French occupation staff. IRO staff proceeding on leave shall enjoy the same facilities and pay the same fares as the French occupation staff;

14. shall provide for the IRO staff, the same medical and dental services as are provided for the French occupation staff, subject to repayment except in respect of costs incurred in Reichsmarks;

15. shall lend free of charge to the IRO the military or indigenous equipment (including captured enemy equipment, vehicles and administrative supplies) put at the disposal of UNRRA. For its part the IRO shall lend to the French Authorities, free of charge, such of its available facilities and equipment (including vehicles) which are at present in the French Zone and are not required for its operations in the French Zone of Germany and are considered necessary for the operation of camps and assembly centres;

16. shall process claims against IRO and its personnel for compensation of damage occurring in the execution of their official duties in the same way as for French occupation staff.

Section VII. MAINTENANCE OF DISPLACED PERSONS

1. The French Authorities shall be responsible for providing refugees and displaced persons with living accommodation, food and necessary services—as far as possible from German resources.

2. The French Authorities shall provide without charge to IRO from the German economy indigenous produce for the maintenance of refugees and displaced persons so that the rations issued to refugees and displaced persons from the German economy shall be at the same level and of the same composition as the average rations issued to the local population and provided from the production of the Zone.

3. The French Authorities shall further provide within the limits of available resources, and subject to repayment, the additional supplies necessary to bring the ration up to a level to be determined by the IRO after consultation with the French Authorities.

4. The IRO shall pay to the French Authorities an allowance, to be revised periodically, for each refugee and displaced person maintained on behalf of the IRO by the French Authorities in the French Zone of Germany. This sum multiplied by the number of eligible refugees and displaced persons receiving care and maintenance shall include the following expenses:

(a) payment of the staff required for the administration of refugees and displaced persons (not including the staff of the Zone Tracing Bureau—see Section X) as well as administrative costs,

(b) the cost of supplies required in order to bring the standard of living of refugees and displaced persons, such as it would be if the French Zone of occupation had to live on its own resources, up to the level fixed by the IRO after consultation with the French Authorities and within the limits of available supplies.

5. The French Authorities shall not require repayment of any German currency supplied by them in implementation of Article 1 of Section VII above.

6. For the period of three months from the 1st July 1947, the sum referred to in paragraph 4 above shall be 35 cents (US). During that three months' period the IRO and the French Authorities shall examine information relative to supplies and costs and agree upon a per capita sum for the period after 1st October 1947. The figure of 35 cents is established for the three months' period on the basis that the ration received by the refugees and displaced persons will correspond to an average ration of 1,900

calories with the necessary allowances for special groups in accordance with the minimum emergency ration standard recommended by the Food and Agricultural Organization.

Section VIII. ACCOUNTING AND FINANCIAL PROVISIONS

1. (a) The French Authorities and the IRO shall maintain proper accounting records of all supplies delivered and services rendered to the IRO in accordance with this Agreement;

(b) The prices fixed in respect of such supplies and services may include a supplement to cover transport and accessory charges;

(c) The exact form of the accounting records and the method of calculating prices and additional charges shall be agreed upon between the IRO and the French Authorities.

2. The payments to be made by IRO to the French Authorities shall be settled by arrangement between the French Government and IRO Headquarters, the settlement to be made either by way of direct payment or by deduction from the French contribution. No repayment shall be made in Germany except for sums due from individuals for personal purchases or services.

3. The IRO shall not be called upon to make any payment or reimbursement in respect of any item not specifically stated in this agreement to be subject to payment or reimbursement.

Section IX. STATUS

1. IRO staff shall be subject to military government laws and tribunals in respect of any offence committed by them in the French Zone of occupation in Germany.

2. IRO staff, other than refugees and displaced persons employed by the IRO, shall enjoy the same legal status and the same rights as civilian staff of the Occupation Authorities.

3. IRO staff shall be subject to financial regulations to be agreed between the French Authorities and the IRO.

4. Refugees and displaced persons eligible for IRO assistance in the French Zone of Germany shall have the same legal status and be subject to the same laws and tribunals as UN nationals having no official relations with the occupation Authorities.

Section X. TRACING BUREAU IN THE FRENCH ZONE OF OCCUPATION

The Zonal Bureau for tracing refugees and displaced persons shall be under the supervision of the Central Tracing Bureau of IRO. Its staff shall continue as part of the French occupation services. The numbers of such personnel shall be fixed by agreement between the French Authorities and IRO. The salaries of the staff and the operating expenses of the Bureau shall be paid by IRO and shall be the subject of an agreement between the two contracting parties.

Section XI. DURATION OF VALIDITY

The Present agreement which replaces and annuls the agreement concluded on 18 February 1946 by the French Commander in Chief in Germany and the Director General of UNRRA shall come into force on 1 July 1947 and shall remain in force for a period of six months. After the expiration of that period it may, subject to three months' notice by either of the contracting parties, cease to have effect. If one or other of the parties so requests, discussions may take place at any time with a view to revising the provisions of this Agreement.

CODICIL TO THE AGREEMENT OF 6 SEPTEMBER 1947 CONCERNING THE FRENCH ZONE OF GERMANY, 2 MARCH 1948[1]

In accordance with the Agreement signed on 6 September 1947 between the French Government and PCIRO concerning the French Zone of Germany, the accounts submitted by the French authorities to the Organization for repayment under the terms of Section VII, para. 4 of the Agreement have been checked.

Following this examination, the decisions indicated below have been reached:

1. *Expenses.* It has been agreed that for the period 1 July 1947 to 1 April 1948 the sum to be repaid by the Organization to the French Government shall be

25 cents per day for each full rationnaire;
15 cents per day for each partial rationnaire.

Before 1 April 1948, the French authorities will submit a detailed estimate of expenditure to be jointly examined for the purpose of establishing a new sum, which may be different from the sum indicated above, and which will represent the cost of supplies imported by the French authorities for eligible refugees, and administrative costs. This new financial settlement shall come into effect as from 1 April 1948.

2. *Number of eligible persons*

(*a*) for the period 1 July 1947–31 December 1947:

   (i) the number of full rationnaires in the French Zone of Germany who are considered as eligible for PCIRO assistance has been fixed at 33,756;

   (ii) the number of partial rationnaires in the French Zone of Germany who are considered as eligible for PCIRO assistance has been provisionally fixed at 11,310.

(*b*) as from 1 January 1948, the number of persons considered as eligible in the French Zone of Germany has been provisionally fixed at:

   29,201 (full rationnaires);
   13,310 (partial rationnaires).

(*c*) the eligibility of persons in the French Zone of Germany shall be determined by PCIRO in accordance with the Constitution and the terms of the Agreement of 6 September 1947 between PCIRO and the French Government.

   Before applying eligibility determination to the calculations provided for in paragraph 2 (*d*) of this Agreement, PCIRO shall consult the French authorities and shall take into account any remarks which may be submitted by the latter, in particular regarding the lists of refugees which have been or will be handed over to them by PCIRO in the French Zone.

(*d*) (i) If any of the full rationnaires referred to in paragraph 2 (*b*) are found to be ineligible, the French Government shall pay back to PCIRO all the sums it has received for these persons during the period following the date on which the right to appeal expires (if no appeal has been lodged), or (if an appeal has been lodged) following the date on which a decision is reached regarding the appeal.

   (ii) If any of the partial rationnaires referred to in paragraph 2 (*b*) are found to be ineligible, the French Government shall pay back to PCIRO all sums it has received for these persons during the period subsequent to 1 January 1948.

(*e*) The figures obtained as a result of the application of subparagraph 2 (*d*) will be

---

[1] PC/LEG/7/Add. 1, 4 Mar. 1948: original French.

adjusted henceforth according to the number of departures from the Zone (repatriation or resettlement) and the number of new admissions (families being reunited, hardship cases, workers sent back from reception countries, etc.).

(f) PCIRO is determining the eligibility of all refugees in the French Zone in January 1948. The number of partial rationnaires mentioned in paragraph 2 (a) (11,310) shall be reduced by the percentage of persons found so to be ineligible; but it is agreed that if this percentage exceeds 10%, not more than 10% shall be deducted from the 11,310 partial rationnaires. The French Government shall pay back to PCIRO all sums which have been paid to it for the partial rationnaires thus determined ineligible.

3. *Facilities and services provided by the French authorities.* The facilities and services provided to PCIRO for the French Zone of Germany by the French authorities subject to reimbursement (in accordance with Section VI of the Agreement of 6 September 1947) shall be paid for by PCIRO in cash.

4. *Supply of German marks to PCIRO.* The total requirements in marks, which, under the terms of Section VI of the Agreement of 6 September 1947, the French occupation authorities in Germany provide free of charge to PCIRO, shall be fixed for each quarter by an agreement to be reached beforehand between the French occupation authorities and PCIRO representatives.

CODICIL TO THE AGREEMENT CONCLUDED ON 6 SEPTEMBER 1947 BETWEEN THE PCIRO AND THE FRENCH GOVERNMENT RELATING TO OPERATIONS IN THE FRENCH ZONE OF GERMANY, 22 OCTOBER 1949[1]

The Agreement concluded on 6 September 1947 between the PCIRO and the French Government concerning the French Zone of Germany shall be amended as follows, with effect from 18 October 1948:

Section VII. MAINTENANCE OF DISPLACED PERSONS

Paragraph 4 of Section VII:

'(a) IRO shall make settlement with the German Economy, through the appropriate Allied departments in Germany, for food supplied to the eligible displaced persons maintained on behalf of IRO in the French Zone of Germany, in accordance with Paragraphs 2 and 3 above. Agreement of the accounts of food supplied to the displaced persons, and the actual number of eligible displaced persons maintained on behalf of IRO, shall be made quarterly.

'(b) The IRO shall reimburse to the French Authorities the reasonable and necessary expenses of their administration of refugees maintained on behalf of IRO in the French Zone. These expenses include the payment of salaries of the persons necessary for the administration of refugees and displaced persons (not including the Zone Tracing Bureau) as well as the running costs of that administration. Reimbursement shall be effected promptly on the basis of the quarterly figures submitted by the French Authorities and approved by the IRO.'

Paragraph 6 of Section VII:

'The refugees and displaced persons shall receive the IRO ration scale for Germany, the caloric value of which shall be no higher than that available to the indigenous population.'

[1] PC/LEG/7/Add. 2, 31 Oct. 1949: original French.

AGREEMENT BETWEEN THE GOVERNMENT OF THE FRENCH REPUBLIC AND THE PCIRO CONCERNING THE SELECTION OF REFUGEES AND DISPLACED PERSONS FOR FRANCE (HOME TERRITORY) AND ALGERIA, 13 JANUARY 1948[1]

The Government of the French Republic (hereinafter referred to as 'the Government'), and the Preparatory Commission of the International Refugee Organization (hereinafter referred to as 'PCIRO') have agreed as follows concerning the immigration into France (Home Territory) and Algeria, of eligible refugees and displaced persons (hereinafter referred to as 'refugees'), as defined by the IRO Constitution.

Article 1. NUMBER AND TYPES OF IMMIGRANTS

(a) The Government agrees to receive as large a number as possible of 'refugees' eligible under the IRO Constitution and PCIRO resolutions, during the period 1 July 1947 to 30 June 1948, under the conditions specified below, but reserves the right to fix that number.

(b) The Government and PCIRO shall agree on the numbers and categories of immigrants which the Government wishes to receive.

The Government Missions in the zones of Germany and in Austria shall supply the representatives of PCIRO in the zones with all relevant information concerning the number of immigrants and the qualifications required.

(c) The Government undertakes to establish on its territory the refugees' families.

Article 2. SELECTION OF IMMIGRANTS

(a) The Government reserves the exclusive right to arrange for immigrants to be selected by representatives of its own choosing; and it shall inform the PCIRO beforehand of the names and titles of these representatives. The latter shall have access to displaced persons camps and shall be granted every facility for informing possible applicants about working conditions in France. The PCIRO shall give the representatives of the Government any assistance they may require in carrying out their task.

(b) The Government guarantees that selection of immigrants will be carried out without distinction as to race or religion.

(c) PCIRO shall make preliminary arrangements as requested by the Government.

Article 3. RELATIVES AND DEPENDANTS

(a) Workers who have obtained an employment contract may be accompanied, or joined within three months, by their wives and minor children. Parents of workers may be admitted to France provided they can be supported by them and live with them.

(b) Individual cases involving humanitarian considerations shall be specially examined by the Government.

Article 4. TRANSPORT

(a) The Government shall not be liable for the cost of transporting 'refugees' as far as the French frontier, subject to Section 4, paragraph 10 of the Agreement concluded on 6 September 1947 between the French Government and PCIRO. The Government shall assume administrative responsibility for transport from the staging centre to the French frontier.

[1] PC/LEG/9: original French, 15 Jan. 1948.

(b) The Government shall be entirely responsible for transport from the frontier to the place of final destination.

(c) PCIRO shall pay to the Government, as reimbursement of costs of transport in France, a sum equivalent to $8 for each worker already recruited or who may be recruited, and for each member of his family.

(d) The Government agrees that these sums should not be refunded by the PCIRO until after 1 July 1948.

(e) The Government shall undertake to transport from the staging centre to the place of final destination all the luggage of persons recruited for France under the terms of this Agreement namely: their professional equipment and all the articles which they own.

Article 5. RECEPTION AND PLACING OF IMMIGRANTS

In so far as the expenses incurred for the maintenance of staging centres and of the refugees in these centres are not a responsibility of the occupation authorities, such expenses shall be paid by PCIRO. The choice of the staging centre for the selection zones shall be a matter for agreement between the Government, the occupation authorities and PCIRO.

Article 6. LEGAL STATUS

The provisions of articles 4 to 6 inclusive and article 8 of the Convention of 28 October 1933 and of articles 6 to 8 inclusive and article 10 of the Convention of 10 February 1938 shall apply to refugees coming within the terms of this Agreement as long as they reside in French territory. As regards social security, they will be treated in the same way as ordinary or privileged resident foreigners, not enjoying the benefit of a convention. While residing in France they will enjoy the legal and administrative protection of PCIRO.

Article 7. CONDITIONS OF EMPLOYMENT

(a) The Government shall provide each worker before his departure with a formal employment contract, and on his arrival on French territory, with a 'Foreign worker's card'. This card may be renewed at the request of the worker.

(b) Refugees employed in France shall receive the same wages and enjoy the same advantages as French workers employed in the same occupation and in the same area.

They shall be free to join whatever trade union they may choose.

The Government guarantees to refugees who have obtained the employment contract mentioned above all the rights and liberties which French law accords to aliens who have been authorized to live in France.

(c) The Government undertakes to find other employment, within the framework of the national economy, for any refugee who, through no fault of his own, proves unsuited for the work for which he was recruited by the French selection missions.

Article 8. RESETTLEMENT GRANT

(a) The Government shall pay to each eligible refugee already recruited or who may be recruited and to each member of his family, in the case of refugees who at the time of their recruitment are receiving care and maintenance from PCIRO, a sum equivalent to $16, which PCIRO undertakes to refund.

(b) The Government agrees that the total amount of these grants shall not be refunded by PCIRO until 1 July 1948.

(c) PCIRO undertakes to reconsider at the Government's request, as soon as circumstances permit, and not later than 1 July 1948 the possibility of paying resettlement grants to all the refugees, whether or not they are receiving care and maintenance from PCIRO.

Article 9. CONDITIONS OF ENTRY

(a) The Government undertakes to issue visas and entry permits without cost to PCIRO or to the refugees.

(b) The Government undertakes to exempt from all duties articles, including professional equipment, belonging to refugees recruited for work, or to their dependants, on their arrival in France.

Article 10. CONDITIONS OF EXPULSION AND RETURN TO ZONE OF ORIGIN

(a) *Expulsion*—Chapter IV of the Order of 2 November 1945 is applicable to all refugees who enter France under the terms of this Agreement.

(b) *Return to zones*—Any refugee admitted into France under this Agreement, who proves to be unsuited to the French economy, may be sent back to the zone from which he came. This provision applies to:

(1) refugees who break their contract without valid reason,
(2) refugees who, after several attempts at re-employment, in accordance with article 7 (c) above, prove unsuited to any work in France.

(c) PCIRO agrees to make itself responsible again for refugees and displaced persons expelled or returned from French territory, provided their expulsion or return is in accordance with the provisions of the foregoing paragraphs (a) and (b) and takes place within 15 months from the date of their admission into French territory.

If British or American occupation authorities refuse to allow such expelled persons to re-enter their respective zones within the foregoing time-limit, the persons concerned would be moved to the French zone of occupation and allowed to remain there.

(d) The Government shall be liable for all expenses which may be incurred in the course of the expulsion or return, as far as the French frontier, of the persons mentioned in the foregoing paragraphs.

(e) The refugees to whom this Agreement applies shall in no case be repatriated to their countries of origin unless they formally express a wish to that effect by making application in writing to the French authorities or to the PCIRO office in France.

Article 11. EXPENSES OF SELECTION MISSIONS

(a) Salaries and travelling expenses of the French selection missions shall be paid by the Government.

(b) Subject to provisions in force in occupied territory, PCIRO shall, at the request of the Chief of the selection missions and under his responsibility, make advances of funds to members of the selection missions. Those sums shall be refunded by the Government to PCIRO in the currency in which the advances were originally made.

(c) PCIRO will provide, without charge, to the French selection missions:

1. the petrol and oil they require for their motor vehicles in carrying out their duties within the selection zones, and
2. as far as practicable, the machine tools and technical equipment required for the vocational testing of candidates as well as the medical equipment for their health examination.

Article 12. PROVISION OF CLOTHING

PCIRO shall provide refugees, free of charge, with the clothes and shoes they normally wear.

Article 13. COMING INTO FORCE

This Agreement shall come into force as soon as it has been approved by the Preparatory Commission and the French Government.

Article 14. APPLICABILITY OF THE AGREEMENT

The French Protectorates of Morocco and Tunisia and the French overseas departments and territories may, through special implementation arrangements, be included among the territories to which this Agreement shall apply.

Article 15. PERIOD OF VALIDITY

This Agreement shall remain in force until 1 July 1948. It may be renewed by mutual consent of the two Parties.

Article 16

This Agreement may be taken over by the International Refugee Organization when its Constitution comes into force, after the Government has been duly notified.

AGREEMENT BETWEEN THE GOVERNMENT OF THE FRENCH REPUBLIC AND THE PCIRO CONCERNING PRIVILEGES AND IMMUNITIES, 13 JANUARY 1948[1]

In order that the Preparatory Commission for the International Refugee Organization (hereinafter referred to as 'the Preparatory Commission'), and in particular its Office in France, may enjoy the privileges, immunities and facilities necessary to enable them to carry on their work on French territory, the Government of the French Republic and the PCIRO have agreed to the following provisions:

Article 1. The PCIRO has full juridical personality. For the attainment of its ends and the execution of its duties, it has the capacity to:

(*a*) contract;

(*b*) acquire and dispose of immovable and movable property;

(*c*) institute legal proceedings.

Article 2. The PCIRO enjoys immunity from jurisdiction. No action may be brought against it in a court of law, unless it expressly waives its immunity for the purpose of any particular proceedings or by the terms of any particular contract.

Article 3. The premises on which the PCIRO carries on its work, its records, and in general all papers belonging to it or held by it, are inviolable.

The PCIRO shall not, however, permit its premises to be used to shelter any persons for whose arrest a warrant has been issued by the French authorities.

Article 4. The property of the PCIRO is immune from seizure. It cannot be subject to requisition.

It cannot be subject to expropriation except for public purposes and after agreement has been reached between the PCIRO and the Government.

[1] PC/LEG/10, 15 Jan. 1948: original French.

Article 5. Without being restricted by financial controls, regulations or moratoria of any kind, the PCIRO may receive and freely dispose of any sums or securities of any kind, made payable in any currency.

Article 6. The PCIRO is exempt from all direct taxation. It shall, however, pay the usual charges for services rendered.

The PCIRO is exempt from all customs duties in respect of subjects imported by it for its official use and in respect of publications, cinematograph films, slides and photographic documents issued by it, and of paper it may import into France.

It is understood, however, that articles imported free of customs duty will not be sold on French territory except under conditions agreed upon with the French authorities.

Article 7. The PCIRO shall pay in accordance with law any indirect taxes forming part of the price of articles sold.

Article 8. The French Government accords to the PCIRO treatment not less favourable than it accords or may accord to diplomatic representatives accredited to it, in the matter of postal, telephone, telegraphic and radio-telegraphic communications, and particularly as regards franking privileges, postal rates and taxes, priorities, use of codes.

It shall do all in its power to facilitate any communication the Director of the Paris Office or his principal officers may wish to make through the press and the radio.

The correspondence and communications of the PCIRO shall not be subject to delays except where this is unavoidable.

Article 9. The delegates of Member-Governments to conferences convened by the PCIRO shall enjoy, in the exercise of their duties and during their journey to and from the place of meeting, the same facilities, privileges and immunities as are accorded to members of diplomatic missions accredited to the French Government it being understood that the PCIRO shall forward to the French authorities in due time, the list of delegates attending the Conference.

The facilities, privileges and immunities mentioned in the foregoing paragraph shall be enjoyed by the representatives of Member Governments, their substitutes, advisers, technical advisers and experts.

Article 10. The officials of the PCIRO:

1. shall be immune from legal process with respect to acts performed by them in their official capacity;
2. shall be exempt from all direct taxation on the salaries and emoluments paid to them by the PCIRO;
3. shall be exempt, together with their spouses or children under age, from the provisions of common law contained in legislation concerning aliens;
4. shall enjoy the same exchange facilities as are accorded to members of diplomatic missions accredited to the French Government;
5. shall enjoy, together with their spouses and children under age, the same repatriation facilities as are accorded to members of diplomatic missions accredited to the French Government, in times of international crises.
6. The PCIRO shall submit to the French Government a list of the officials entitled to enjoy the benefit of the provisions of this article. This list shall be subject to approval by the French Government.

Article 11. The PCIRO Representative in France, his deputy and their spouses and children under age, shall enjoy the privileges, immunities, exemptions and facilities granted to members of diplomatic missions accredited to the French Government and to their spouses and children under age, in accordance with international law and practice. They shall not, however, be entitled to invoke before the courts of the state of which they are nationals immunity from legal process in respect of matters not connected with their official duties.

Article 12. These privileges and immunities are granted to officials in the interests of the PCIRO and not for the benefit of the officials themselves. The Executive Secretary of the PCIRO may waive the immunity of any official if, in his opinion, this can be done without prejudice to the interests of the PCIRO.

Article 13. The French Government shall take all measures required in order:

(a) to ensure at any time the movement, between the headquarters of the Organization and the frontiers of French territory, of persons called upon to participate in the work of, or invited by, the PCIRO;

(b) to dispatch mail or telegrams;

(c) to ensure the transportation of supplies sent to the PCIRO.

Article 14. The PCIRO and the French Government shall agree on the procedure and conditions under which admission to or exit from French territory, sojourn in French territory or transit through French territory shall at any time be facilitated for persons called upon to participate in the work of, or invited by the PCIRO.

Article 15. In so far as such measures do not interfere with the independence or efficiency of the PCIRO, the French Government shall be free to take all precautions required on grounds of national security.

Article 16. The PCIRO shall, in the premises put at its disposal, be provided with electricity, water and gas, as well as with general utility services.

If owing to circumstances outside the control of French authorities, those services were interrupted, either partly or completely, the needs of the PCIRO would be considered by the French Government as equal in importance to those of its own official departments.

Article 17. The French Government shall take all police measures required for the protection of the PCIRO's headquarters in France, and for the maintenance of law and order in their immediate vicinity.

At the request of the PCIRO Chief Representative in France, the French Government shall provide such police forces as may be necessary for the maintenance of order within the premises.

Article 18. The PCIRO shall constantly co-operate with the competent French authorities in order to facilitate the smooth administration of justice, to ensure the application of police regulations, and to prevent unlawful use being made of the privileges and facilities provided for in this Agreement.

Article 19. The PCIRO shall take steps with a view to establishing procedures for the settlement:

1. of any disputes arising from contracts or any other dispute, concerning matters of private law, in which the PCIRO might be involved;

2. of disputes in which a member of the staff of the PCIRO might be involved, if this person enjoys immunity owing to his official position, and if his immunity has not been suspended by the Executive Secretary of the PCIRO.

Article 20. Any disagreement arising between the PCIRO and the French Government as to the interpretation or implementation of this Agreement, or of any additional convention or agreement shall, if it is not settled through negotiation, be referred for decision to an arbitrator jointly chosen by the two Parties or, failing agreement to this effect, chosen by the President of the International Court of Justice.

Article 21. This Agreement shall take effect from the day when it has been approved by the PCIRO and by the French Government. It can be denounced by either of the contracting Parties subject to six months' notice.

Article 22. This Agreement can be amended at the request of the contracting Parties, who shall consult together with regard to any amendment that might prove desirable.

Article 23. The IRO may, on coming into existence, take over this Agreement with the PCIRO after due notification to the Government.

AGREEMENT BETWEEN PCIRO AND THE FRENCH GOVERNMENT CONCERNING THE ESTABLISHMENT AND THE ACTIVITY OF THE PCIRO OFFICE IN FRANCE: PARIS, 13 JANUARY 1948[1]

Section I. PURPOSE OF THE AGREEMENT

The French Government (hereinafter referred to as the 'Government') and the Preparatory Commission for the International Refugee Organization (hereinafter referred to as 'PCIRO') recognize that their common aim is to implement the principles embodied in the Constitution of IRO.

With this aim in view, and in order to determine the methods by which they will cooperate, they have agreed as follows.

Section II. GENERAL PROVISIONS

1. PCIRO shall fulfil the functions assigned to it and authorized under its Constitution, and shall, in the discharge of such duties, be subject to the laws and regulations in force in French home territory.

2. The Government and PCIRO will extend to each other the greatest possible assistance in the solution of all questions concerning those refugees in France who are the concern of PCIRO. In particular, the Parties will keep each other informed, in advance, of measures to be taken which may affect the conditions or status of such refugees.

3. It is agreed that PCIRO will maintain an Office in Paris, entrusted, in accordance with this agreement, with the protection, the care and assistance and the re-establishment of refugees and displaced persons coming under its mandate. It is also agreed that PCIRO will, in consultation with the Government, establish such subsidiary offices as may be necessary for carrying out its programme.

4. It is agreed that PCIRO shall maintain in France the staff necessary to carry out its programme.

5. The appointment of the Chief Representative and the Deputy Chief in France shall be made by PCIRO with the previous approval of the Government.

6. PCIRO shall be responsible for determining the eligibility of refugees and displaced persons in accordance with Annex I to the Constitution of IRO, as approved by the General Assembly of the United Nations on 15 December 1946.

Section III. RESPONSIBILITIES OF PCIRO

A. *Legal and Social Protection*

7. PCIRO shall be responsible for the legal and social protection of all refugees and displaced persons coming under its mandate, who are at present in France or who may come to reside in France during the period of validity of this Agreement.

[1] PC/LEG/12, 15 Jan. 1948: original French.

8. At the request of the Government, PCIRO undertakes to maintain, in favour of the so-called 'Statutory refugees', the advantages granted to them under international arrangements, including the Agreements of 5 July 1922, 31 May 1924, 12 May 1926, 30 June 1928 and the International Conventions of 28 October 1933 and 10 February 1938, and under the laws and Regulations in force in France with regard to the above-mentioned categories, including the Decree dated 27 August 1935.

9. Under the foregoing paragraph, the PCIRO Office in France shall maintain general administrative and financial supervision of the Refugee Offices. PCIRO will keep the Government informed of the activities of these Offices. The Directors of those offices shall be appointed by the PCIRO with the approval of the Government.

B. *Care and Maintenance*

10. PCIRO shall assume, within the limits of its financial resources, the care and maintenance of those refugees and displaced persons who are its concern and who cannot enjoy the benefit of the provisions mentioned in paragraph 13 below.

C. *Transit, Repatriation and Resettlement Functions*

11. It is agreed that PCIRO will perform such transit, repatriation and resettlement functions as may be necessary under its programme.

Section *IV*. RESPONSIBILITIES OF THE GOVERNMENT

12. The Government shall accredit the PCIRO Representative in France to the French Administrations concerned and shall confer upon him the exequatur. The Government shall recommend all legislative measures and shall take all necessary steps with a view to enabling the PCIRO representative in France to carry out for the benefit of all refugees and displaced persons coming under PCIRO mandate, the quasi-consular functions mentioned in article I of the International Agreement of 30 June 1928.

13. The Government undertakes to make applicable to refugees and displaced persons under PCIRO mandate, the provisions of the laws and decrees concerning social security in the same way and under the same conditions as to other foreigners resident or domiciled in French territory and not covered by a Convention.

The so-called 'statutory refugees' will continue as in the past, to enjoy in that respect the benefit of the provisions of the Conventions of 28 October 1933 and 10 February 1938.

14. The Government recognizes the international status of PCIRO and will grant the customary facilities and diplomatic immunities in accordance with rules to be established.

Section *V*. APPLICABILITY OF THE AGREEMENT TO FRENCH OVERSEAS TERRITORIES

15. The offices which the PCIRO may consider necessary to establish in the French Overseas Territories, including the Protectorates of Morocco and Tunisia shall be placed under the authority of the PCIRO office in France.

The provisions of this Agreement shall be applicable to the above-mentioned territories insofar as they do not conflict with international agreements already entered into by France, or with the laws and regulations in force in the aforenamed territories.

Section *VI*. DURATION OF THE AGREEMENT

16. This Agreement shall be considered as having come into force on 1 July 1947 and shall remain in force until 30 June 1948. After that date it shall be extended by

tacit agreement, unless it has been denounced subject to six months' notice by either of the two contracting Parties.

The IRO may, on coming into existence, take over this Agreement with the Preparatory Commission, after due notification to the Government.

Subject to previous consultation, the two contracting Parties reserve the right to amend or add to this Agreement.

JOINT STATEMENT ISSUED BY THE FRENCH GOVERNMENT AND PCIRO ON AN EXPERIMENT IN THE RESETTLEMENT OF 1,000 FAMILIES OF AGRICULTURAL WORKERS SELECTED AMONG DISPLACED PERSONS, 17 AUGUST 1948[1]

The French Government and PCIRO, having taken note of the conditions in which the Agreement of 13 January 1948, concerning the recruiting of refugees and displaced persons for metropolitan France and Algeria is being put into effect, of the results obtained and of the difficulties experienced in finding employment for workers with families, have agreed to try out as soon as possible the experiment of admitting into France 1,000 agricultural workers, accompanied by their families.

The provisions of the Agreement of 13 January 1948 apply to the persons referred to in this joint statement, except as regards the methods of implementation set forth below.

Before carrying out this experiment, the French Government and PCIRO have issued the following statement, by mutual agreement.

I. OPERATIONS IN THE ZONES OF GERMANY AND AUSTRIA

Concurrently with the present recruiting, selection operations will be carried out among eligible displaced persons and refugees as defined by the IRO Constitution, who volunteer for paid work in France, and giving priority to displaced persons from the Banates who are at present in the French Occupation Zone of Germany, and, in so far as they receive financial aid from IRO, to displaced persons from the Banates now living in Austria.

The term 'family' should in general be taken to mean the spouse and minor children but in exceptional cases it may include the parents and grand-parents.

(a) *Professional and medical preliminary selection.* PCIRO will carry out strict professional and medical preliminary selection. Only volunteer workers who have actual experience of agricultural work and have undergone preliminary selection will be transferred, with their families, to the Emigration Centres, where they will be interviewed by the National Immigration Office Selection Mission. Not only the worker, but every member of his family will be medically examined by PCIRO before being sent before the NIO Mission.

The preliminary medical examination will be carried out in accordance with the criteria established by the French Government, which have already been communicated to PCIRO.

(b) *Final selection.* Preliminary selection will be followed:
— by security screening not only of the worker, but also of the members of his family;
— by professional selection of the worker by the officials of the NIO Mission;

[1] IRO/LEG/GOV/2, 16 Dec. 1948: original French.

— by a thorough medical examination by the NIO to check the preliminary examination carried out on the worker and his family.

Five selection missions will be designated for this work. They will be assigned as follows:

  3 missions to the French, British and American Zones of Germany,
  2 missions to the French, British and American Zones of Austria.

Each Mission will in theory be composed as follows:

  1 Head of Mission, responsible for directing the work of the Mission,
  1 Doctor,
  1 Representative of the Security authorities.

In addition:

  1 Representative of the CGA will be allowed to take part in the selection operations, under the authority of the NIO representative.

(c) The selection operations will be so organized that the workers will be admitted into France at the rate of 10 workers, with their families, per day for each Mission, giving a total of 50 workers per day for all five Missions together.

II. OPERATIONS IN FRANCE

1. *Liaison at local and central levels.* So that a check may be kept on the use made of the financial contribution from IRO which is provided for in paragraph IV below, and in order to establish liaison between the officials dealing with selection and the PCIRO representatives in France, the following measures have been decided upon:

  (a) Close liaison will be ensured at the Departmental level by a joint inter-Departmental Committee, composed (of the delegates) of the Directors of the Departmental Labour and Population Offices, and of a representative of the CGA, in an advisory capacity, so that all relevant information can be obtained concerning the admission of workers and their placing in employment and resettlement.

  The PCIRO representative may take part in the meetings of the Joint Departmental Committees.

  (b) A central joint Committee, composed of PCIRO and French Government representatives and of a CGA representative, in an advisory capacity, will meet periodically in Paris, in order to examine jointly any suggestions or criticisms arising out of the application of the foregoing measures. It will also supervise the administration of the funds provided for in Art. IV, paragraph 2, below.

2. *Reception Centres.* The NIO will be responsible for providing lodging.

The Departmental Labour and Man-Power Offices will be responsible for placing in employment, transfer to other employment, and for completion of the various administrative formalities (employment contract, employment cards, etc.)

A copy of the employment contract will be given to each party after it has been signed. This contract will include a clause stating that accommodation for the whole family is guaranteed or that the employer undertakes to provide such accommodation.

In so far as circumstances permit, use may be made of hotels, in addition to the reception centres, to provide temporary accommodation at a moderate price for displaced persons, in order to bring applicants for employment into closer contact with employers.

Employers will be permitted to interview the displaced persons and their families with a view to engaging them, in the presence of the representatives of the Departmental Labour Office (in liaison with the CGA representatives).

III. Rejections (Return to Zones)

The French Government will endeavour to find other employment, either with another employer in the same type of work, or in occupations where there is a shortage of manpower, for workers who have proved unsuitable, through no fault of their own.

If transfer to other employment proves impossible or unsuccessful, or if the contract is broken for no good reason, or because the displaced person has proved undesirable on French territory, the latter will be sent back to his zone of origin, within six months at the most from the date of his admission into France.

On the departure of each convoy from the zone of origin, local PCIRO officials will provide the competent zonal authorities with a complete list, indicating the civil status of the persons in the convoy. When this list of the displaced persons is handed over to the authorities of the zone of origin, it will contain a reference to the above-mentioned provisions of this article, so that the said authorities may be fully informed of the conditions on which the displaced persons in question may be returned to their zone of origin within the above-mentioned period of six months. The cost of the return journey as far as the French frontier will be met from the balance resulting from the difference between the expenditure and receipts entered in the special account provided for in paragraph IV below.

IV. Financial Arrangements

1. (a) Expenses of every kind incurred in the preliminary selection of workers and their families in the occupation zones as far as the Emigration Centre are to be met by PCIRO. The same applies to the food for the journey between the zone of origin and the Reception Centre.

(b) The staff expenses involved in the final selection (security, professional, medical) will be met from NIO funds.

(c) Transport expenses between the Emigration Centre and the French frontier will not be defrayed by the French Government.

(d) The cost of the transport in France of the workers, their families and luggage, escort and propaganda expenses, the cost of lodging the displaced persons in the Reception Centres and the administrative, secretariat and travelling expenses of the members of the Joint Committee will be entered in a *special account* which will be described below.

2. *Special Account.* (a) A special account has been opened.

All the expenses referred to in paragraph 1 (d) above are entered in this account.

The contributions of the French Government and PCIRO, which will be equal and will amount to the equivalent in French francs of $24 per person, will be entered as receipts.

Within the first fortnight of the proposed experiment, the Joint Central Committee will examine the state of the special account.

(b) The repatriation costs of any workers rejected, and their families, and any unforeseen expenses, will be deducted from the surplus of receipts over expenditures.

In the event of a balance remaining after the deduction of these expenses, the remainder will be distributed between the workers and their families as resettlement grants in proportion to the number of dependants.

3. *Treasury.* An advance equal to the total amount of the PCIRO contribution, i.e. 15,444,000 francs, will be paid immediately into the above-mentioned Special Account.

The French Government will also pay in an equivalent sum before 31 August 1948.

4. *Resettlement grants.* Notwithstanding Article VIII of the Agreement of 13 January

1948, the grant of $16 will not be paid by the French Government to refugees re-cruited under the terms of the present agreement.

V. DATE OF ENTRY INTO FORCE

This agreement shall come into force immediately, as from the date of signature.

VI. TAKING OVER BY IRO

When the Constitution of the IRO comes into force, the Organization may take over the present agreement after duly notifying the Government to this effect.

AGREEMENT SUPPLEMENTING THE JOINT STATEMENT ISSUED BY THE FRENCH GOVERNMENT AND THE PCIRO ON 17 AUGUST 1948 CONCERNING AN EXPERIMENT IN THE RESETTLEMENT OF 1,000 FAMILIES OF AGRICULTURAL WORKERS SELECTED AMONG DISPLACED PERSONS, 5 NOVEMBER 1948[1]

The French Government, on the one hand, and the IRO on the other, have come to the following agreement:

1. The IRO undertakes to pay into the Special Account provided for in the Joint Statement of 17 August 1948 a sum not exceeding 30,000,000 francs (THIRTY MILLION FRANCS), of which 15,444,000 francs (FIFTEEN MILLION FOUR HUNDRED AND FORTY-FOUR THOUSAND FRANCS) have already been paid, for the purpose of carrying out the scheme for the admission into France of not less than 1,000 families of agricultural workers recruited among displaced persons who are the concern of the IRO.

2. The French Government, for its part, undertakes to make available for the same Special Account a sum of not less than 30,000,000 francs (THIRTY MILLION FRANCS).

3. The payments to be made by the IRO, the total of which shall not exceed 30,000,000 francs (THIRTY MILLION FRANCS), shall be effected at the request of the Joint Committee, as the scheme is put into execution.

At no time shall the total of payments made by the IRO in implementation of this Agreement exceed the total of payments made by the French Government.

4. The French Government shall be entirely responsible for the cost of setting up and equipping the reception centres established in France.

5. The clauses of the Joint Statement of 17 August 1948 remain in force, in so far as they are not altered by this Agreement, except as regards Section IV, 2, Special Account, (a), sub-para. 2, which provides for $24 per head to be credited to the Account.

This sum will be altered to correspond to the cost of admitting a displaced person to France and placing that person in employment, as it is determined by the Joint Committee on the basis of the financial data obtained from the experiment.

6. In the event of this Agreement having been fully implemented, either on 28 February 1949 or at a later date, by the actual admission to France of the minimum number of 1,000 families provided for in the Agreement, the IRO authorities and the appropriate French departments shall by common consent study the possibility of either concluding another agreement on the same basis, or beginning conversations with a view to concluding an agreement providing for a larger number and containing financial provisions adequate to ensure the resettlement of this new group.

[1] IRO/LEG/GOV/2/Add. 1, 14 Dec. 1948: original French.

SPECIAL ARRANGEMENT BETWEEN THE IRO AND THE FRENCH GOVERNMENT CONCERNING RECRUITMENT OF DISPLACED PERSONS FOR FRENCH GUIANA, CONCLUDED 21 APRIL 1949[1]

The Government of the French Republic (hereafter referred to as 'the Government') and the International Refugee Organization (hereafter referred to by the initials 'IRO') have agreed upon the following provisions regarding the immigration into the Department of French Guiana of refugees and displaced persons coming under the IRO mandate (hereafter referred to as 'refugees'):

Article I. NUMBER AND TYPE OF IMMIGRANTS

The Government undertakes to transport to and receive in Guiana 100 families of refugees, during the period 1 January 1949–31 December 1949, in the conditions indicated below.

The Government's Missions in the Zones of Germany and Austria shall supply the IRO Representatives in the Zones with all information of a practical nature regarding the qualifications of the immigrants to be recruited, the order in which they are to be sent and the dates.

The Government undertakes to receive and settle the workers recruited, and their families at the same time, on the territory of the French Department of Guiana.

Article II. SELECTION OF THE IMMIGRANTS

The IRO undertakes to bring before the Selection Missions candidates who fulfil the medical and occupational requirements specified by the Missions.

The Government reserves to itself the exclusive right to have the final selection of immigrants carried out by representatives of its own choosing. The latter shall have access to the displaced persons camps and must be given every facility for informing possible candidates of the conditions offered them in Guiana.

The IRO undertakes to distribute beforehand the propaganda booklets and leaflets offered by the Government.

Article III. EMPLOYMENT CONTRACT

The Selection Missions shall have signed by the workers a two-year employment contract, in French and translated into the refugee's own language, a specimen of which is attached.

Article IV. RECEPTION AND SETTLING IN

(a) The refugees shall be engaged by the Prefectorial Authority, which shall employ them in accordance with the terms of the contract signed.

(b) The Government undertakes to provide the refugees on arrival in Guiana with the means to ensure that they have accommodation and food supplies.

(c) The Government undertakes to make available to the refugees, at cost price, which shall not at any time exceed the average departmental price, food and articles of everyday use (household utensils—cloth—footwear—clothing).

Article V. RESETTLEMENT

On the expiry of the contract mentioned in Article III, the Prefectorial Authority shall make available to the refugees, who apply for them concessions of cleared land

---

[1] IRO/LEG/GOV/14, 6 May 1949: original French. In accordance with Article 14 of the Agreement of 13 Jan. 1948 . . . into France and Algeria.

with sanitary dwellings and a supply of drinking water, together with farming implements on a collective basis. The others shall be settled, according to the needs of the Department, at their own occupations, as a general rule as craftsmen.

The terms on which the concessions will be granted shall be those which apply to French nationals and which were laid down in Decree No. 48–2028 of 27 December 1948 (Official Gazette of 3 January 1949).

Article VI. CONDITIONS OF EMPLOYMENT

(*a*) Refugees authorised to work in Guiana shall receive the same wages and enjoy the same advantages as French workers in the same occupations in the Department of Guiana.

(*b*) The Government guarantees to refugees who have signed an employment contract, and to the members of their families, all the rights and liberties granted by French law to foreigners authorised to live in Guiana.

Article VII. SOCIAL LEGISLATION AND LEGAL STATUS

The provisions regarding legal status and social legislation contained in Articles 6 and 7 of the Agreement signed on 13 January 1948 between the PCIRO and the Government of the French Republic concerning the selection of refugees and displaced persons for France and Algeria, are extended to the Department of Guiana, in application of Article 14 of the said Agreement, with the following changes:

With regard to labour regulations, social security and family allowances, refugees who have signed an employment contract shall receive the same treatment as French workers receive under French laws which apply in the Department of Guiana.

Refugees admitted to Guiana under this Agreement shall enjoy the protection of the IRO, which shall be exercised either by the IRO Office in France or by a person appointed by that Office and approved by the Prefect.

The Office may exercise the functions specified in the Agreement of 13 January 1948 concerning quasi-consular services, and may issue the document referred to in Article I of the Arrangement concluded in Geneva on 30 June 1948. Documents issued by the Office or its Representative shall be recognised as authentic in the same way as similar documents issued to their nationals by foreign consuls.

The Government shall encourage and facilitate, as far as is compatible with French law, the naturalization of immigrants and members of their families. Particularly favourable consideration shall be given to applications submitted by immigrants who have fulfilled the terms of their engagement.

The Government shall accord to refugees and members of their families the same treatment as it gives to its own nationals with regard to admission to trade schools, vocational training courses and the universities.

Refugees who have been recognised as unfit or who have fulfilled their contractual obligations, and the members of their families, may obtain, at their request, travel documents which will enable them to leave Guiana.

Article VIII. FINANCIAL ARRANGEMENTS

The IRO undertakes to pay to the French Government the sums required for transporting the refugees from their present place of residence to Guiana, and a resettlement grant intended to cover the initial costs of settling in.

This sum shall be the equivalent of 322 US dollars per head.[1]

---

[1] Amended as follows: 'This sum shall be the equivalent of *332* US dollars per head.' (IRO/LEG/GOV/14/Corr. 2, 22 July 1950.)

To facilitate the financing of the operation, the IRO undertakes to pay a sum equivalent to 132,800 US dollars, i.e. the sum required for the resettlement of 400 persons; this sum shall be subject to readjustment on 1 January 1950, so that it will correspond to the actual number of refugees who have left for Guiana.

Article IX. CONDITIONS OF ADMISSION

(a) The Government undertakes to issue visas and entry permits without cost to the IRO or to the refugees.

(b) The Government undertakes to exempt from all duties and formalities, on arrival in Guiana, the personal effects and professional equipment owned by the refugees recruited and their dependants.

Article X. CONDITIONS OF EXPULSION AND RETURN[1]

In accordance with the terms of the Agreement of 13 January 1948, the conditions of expulsion and return shall be as follows:

(a) *Expulsion*—Chapter 4 of the Order of 2 November 1945 shall apply to all refugees covered by this Agreement.

(b) *Return*—Any refugee admitted to Guiana under this Agreement who is recognised by the representative of the Factory Inspection Department as unfit for any kind of work, or against whom an expulsion order is issued, shall be sent back to France.

(c) The expenditure which may be necessitated by expulsion or return operations involving the persons referred to in the previous paragraphs, namely the cost of transporting the person concerned, and the members of his family, to French home territory, shall be the entire responsibility of the Government, including the cost of transporting the refugee's personal effects and professional equipment.

Article XI. EXPENSES OF THE SELECTION MISSIONS

The salaries and travelling expenses of the Selection Missions shall be payable by the Government.

Article XII

Subject to any international agreements which the French Government may later sign concerning refugees, those refugees who are admitted to Guiana before the liquidation of the IRO or the termination of this Agreement shall continue to enjoy the advantages specified in the Agreement.

The services the IRO is empowered to provide for the refugees under paragraph 4 of Article VII of the Agreement may, if necessary, be taken over by the Organization which succeeds the IRO.

Article XIII. ENTRY INTO FORCE

This Agreement shall come into force when it has been signed by the IRO and by the French Government. It may be denounced at three months' notice on either side. It may be revised at the request of either of the parties, who shall consult together as to the changes to be made in it.

[1] Corrected by IRO/LEG/GOV/14/Corr. 1, 16 Sept. 1949: original English.

ANNEX

EMPLOYMENT CONTRACT FOR FOREIGN WORKER IMMIGRATING INTO GUIANA

The Prefect of Guiana, represented by the Head of the Labour Department, and Mr. . . .

Have come to the following agreement:

I. The employer undertakes:

   (1) to provide Mr. . . . with regular employment for a period of two years, dating from the day of his arrival in Guiana, . . .,
   (2) to employ Mr. . . . on work which is in keeping, as far as possible, with his physical and professional abilities,
   (3) to ensure that Mr. . . .'s conditions of employment are identical with those of French workers.

It follows that Mr. . . . will enjoy, in addition to the special advantages granted under this contract, all the moral and material advantages provided for the wage-earner by French social legislation: regulation working hours—holidays with pay—family allowances and wages.

Mr. . . . will receive the Category IV wage per hour, at the present rate . . . per hour.

   (4) to provide for Mr. . . . and his family, consisting of . . ., private accommodation, with essential furnishings,
   (5) to provide the immigrants and their families with free medical treatment and medicine, until such time as the social security scheme is effectively applied in Guiana,
   (6) to facilitate the establishment of Mr. . . . as an independent agricultural or forestry worker or craftsman, upon the expiry of this contract.

II. Mr. . . . undertakes:

   (1) to agree to do all work compatible with his physical strength which may be asked of him in the reconditioning and running of the St. Jean centre,
   (2) to maintain in the best possible state the premises, furniture and tools entrusted to him.

III. *General provisions*

   (1) Any difficulties arising out of the implementation of this contract shall be submitted to the Inspector of Labour and Man-power for conciliation, before being brought before the appropriate legal authority of the Department of Guiana.
   (2) This contract may be cancelled before the end of the two-year period stipulated in Paragraph I above, provided that the two parties are agreed, and that the immigrant can produce evidence either of sufficient means of livelihood or of the offer of a new employment contract presenting adequate guarantees.

The two contracting parties acknowledge the Inspector of Labour and Man-power as final judge of the guarantees offered.

   (3) If a public institution or a company recognised as acting in the public interest takes over responsibility for immigration questions in Guiana in place of the Prefectorial Authority, the new body shall take the place of that Authority in carrying out this contract.

DONE AT . . . on . . .

The Immigrant:

The Representative
of the Prefect
of Guiana:

AGREEMENT BETWEEN THE FRENCH GOVERNMENT AND THE IRO REGARDING THE TRANSFER TO THE FRENCH GOVERNMENT OF THE CARE AND MAINTENANCE RESPONSIBILITIES OF THE IRO, 28 FEBRUARY 1950[1]

Whereas, in accordance with the decisions of the General Council of the IRO, the latter will cease to accept care and maintenance responsibilities as from 1 July 1950, and at the same time does not contemplate carrying on its legal protection work beyond that date.

Whereas, in view of the importance of the work being done in this field by the IRO on French territory, it is advisable that the French body which is to take over care and maintenance duties from it should do so as soon as possible before 1 July 1950, in order that it may act in concert with the IRO during this period of transition, so as to be in full working order on 1 July 1950.

The High Contracting Parties (the International Refugee Organization being hereafter indicated by the initials 'IRO') have reached agreement on the following provisions.

Heading I. CARE AND MAINTENANCE

Article 1. The IRO shall proceed to transfer gradually to the French Government all its care and maintenance responsibilities in France as soon as this Agreement comes into force, so that the transfer may be completed by 30 June at the latest.

Article 2. The French Government has stated that it has entrusted the work of refugee care and maintenance to the Service Social d'Aide aux Emigrants (hereafter indicated by the initials 'SSAE') the latter to begin gradually to carry out these duties with the entry into force of this Agreement.

Article 3. The IRO shall hand over to the SSAE:

  (a) the files required for individual care and maintenance work;

  (b) the sums at present earmarked in its budget for carrying out the current programme, and a fair share of the sums allocated for administrative expenses.

The exact amount shall depend on the length of time which will still have to elapse between the dates of the successive transfers and 30 June 1950.

Article 4. (a) Up to 30 June 1950, the IRO, in close collaboration with the French Government, shall ensure that the SSAE carries out the care and maintenance programme in accordance with IRO regulations.

(b) After 30 June 1950, the SSAE shall use the funds allocated to it for care and maintenance on behalf of refugees according to the directives issued by the French Government.

Article 5. In accordance with the decisions of the General Council, the IRO shall pay to the French Government or to the organizations designated by it, for the refugees who have been placed by the IRO in the special category of 'Institutional Hard Core', a share of funds in keeping with their numbers and their special circumstances. The sum in question shall be handed over by the IRO as soon as both Parties have approved a general programme on the subject, or on the several sections thereof, to be drawn up by mutual agreement.

The responsibility for drawing up this programme shall rest with a working party consisting of representatives of the IRO, the French Ministries concerned (Foreign Affairs, Health, Interior, Labour) and of the SSAE, which shall be convened by the IRO.

[1] IRO/LEG/GOV/30, 14 Mar. 1950: original French.

Heading II. LEGAL PROTECTION

Article 6. The French Government shall inform the IRO as soon as possible, and at all events before 30 June 1950, of the date on which it proposes to take over responsibility for the work of legal protection.

Heading III. GENERAL PROVISIONS

Article 7. For the period following 30 June 1950, the IRO shall return to the French Government a fair and substantial share of its contribution, to enable it to meet the responsibilities transferred to it.

Article 8. As soon as the French Government has approved its contribution to the IRO budget for the supplementary period 1950–1951, the IRO shall arrange with the Government, at the latter's request, to advance to it before 30 June 1950 some of the funds to be returned under Article 7.

The purpose of this advance will be to help the French Government to draw up a long-term programme of refugee establishment.

Article 9. This Agreement, which takes the place of the text signed on 12 July 1949 (but not put into force), shall become effective on the day of signature.

The time-limits for denunciation of the Agreement of 13 January 1948 on the protection of refugees and displaced persons coming under the IRO mandate and the quasi-consular functions of the IRO Representative in France, and of the Agreement of the same date on the establishment and activity of the IRO Office in France, are hereby cancelled (in the latter case only as regards the questions covered by this Agreement).

AGREEMENT BETWEEN THE ITALIAN GOVERNMENT AND THE PCIRO, 24 OCTOBER 1947[1]

WHEREAS, the Preparatory Commission for the International Refugee Organization (hereinafter referred to as the PCIRO) has assumed from 1 July 1947 operating responsibility for a programme of care, maintenance, resettlement and repatriation of certain refugees who are the concern of the PCIRO and who are at present located in Italy: and

WHEREAS, the Italian Government (hereinafter referred to as the Government) has agreed to cooperate in such programme within the limits of its jurisdiction:

The Government and the PCIRO have agreed as follows:

Article I. RECOGNITION OF THE PCIRO AND ITS ADMINISTRATION IN ITALY

1. The Government recognises the establishment of the PCIRO and its possession of the status and powers conferred upon it by the Constitution, the Agreement on Interim Measures and by the Resolutions and Decisions adopted by the Preparatory Commission for IRO.

2. The Government authorises the PCIRO to operate in Italy in accordance with its Constitution and Resolutions, and to establish in Italy an administration for the purpose of carrying out its programme in Italy. In the implementation of such programme the PCIRO may avail itself of the collaboration of Italian and non-Italian Voluntary Societies operating in Italy.

[1] PC/LEG/4: original English, 28 Oct. 1947.

Article II. RESPONSIBILITIES OF THE PCIRO

1. The PCIRO will be responsible for carrying out, within the limits of its available resources, the functions laid down in the Constitution in respect of eligible refugees in Italy, including the following:

(*a*) The operation and administration of camps for the care and maintenance of refugees.

(*b*) The determination of which refugees are eligible for its assistance, and the establishment and operation of whatever machinery and procedure may be required for this purpose.

(*c*) Encouraging and arranging for the repatriation of refugees, and for this purpose maintaining contact with the representatives of the countries of origin of the refugees.

(*d*) Arranging for the resettlement or emigration of refugees who are unable or unwilling to be repatriated, and for this purpose maintaining close contact with the representatives of the countries of resettlement.

(*e*) Arranging, in accordance with a procedure to be agreed upon with the appropriate officials of the Government, for the movement of refugees and for the transport of those who are being resettled or repatriated.

(*f*) Protection of the legitimate interests of such refugees in Italy as may request its assistance.

2. The functions and activities of the PCIRO in Italy will be carried out in conformity with Italian laws and with international undertakings which Italy has assumed or may assume.

3. The Government and the PCIRO will extend to each other the greatest possible assistance in the solution of all questions concerning refugees in Italy who are the concern of the PCIRO. In particular, the Parties will keep each other informed in advance of measures to be taken which may affect the conditions or status of such refugees.

Article III. RESPONSIBILITIES OF THE GOVERNMENT—FACILITIES AND SERVICES

1. As an evidence of its sympathy with the humanitarian task pursued by the PCIRO, and in consideration of the fact that the PCIRO has assumed as from 1 July 1947 the continuation of the programme on behalf of refugees previously carried out by other international agencies, the Government shall:

(*a*) Grant to the PCIRO the free use of all the real and movable property which may be considered by the Joint Committee established under Article VII below to be necessary to carry out the programme of assistance to refugees in Italy.

The Government shall assume the expenses connected with the maintenance, repairs and improvements of such real and movable property, within the limits of the running expenses for the use of the property.

Furthermore, the Government shall assume the defense against, and liability under, all claims asserted on account of the use of the property or its damage, deterioration, consumption, or loss. However, the PCIRO shall assume financial liability for damages which, in accordance with Italian law, are based upon the wilful acts or gross negligence of its personnel or the refugees. The PCIRO shall return to the Government all such property as the PCIRO no longer requires for the implementation of its programme.

(*b*) Take into consideration, in the free distribution of UNRRA TESSILE products and medical supplies imported by UNRRA, the requirements of the refugees assisted in camps operated by the PCIRO; such requirements will be presented by the Preparatory Commission for IRO at the Joint Committee under Article VII of this Agreement.

(c) Grant to the PCIRO, for the operations strictly necessary for the implementation of its programme, immunity from taxation, except for the general sales tax, the communal excise tax and the special tax established by Communes on some goods of large local production.

The Government will agree with the PCIRO on the procedure for reimbursement.

Such immunity is also applied to the salaries and remunerations paid to the personnel of the PCIRO of non-Italian nationality and not permanently resident in Italy. Furthermore, the Government will grant to the PCIRO exemption from custom duties (including license and general sales tax) for the goods—except for tobacco goods and other products subject to State Monopoly—imported to be distributed to refugees in Italy or needed for the equipment and functioning of the offices of the PCIRO and of the refugee camps, in implementation of the assistance programme under this Agreement, and also for the fuel and lubricants required for such purpose, within an amount to be fixed by the Joint Committee under Article VII below.

The documentation regarding the goods which will be granted the above exemptions, is subject to audit by the Joint Committee under Article VII below.

The vehicles to be used for the operation of the PCIRO in Italy will be granted temporary import license.

The above immunities from taxation are effective from 1 July 1947.

(d) Grant facilities, including adequate transportation priority, for the purpose of ensuring the procurement and distribution of the supplies necessary for carrying out the programme of the PCIRO in Italy.

(e) Grant appropriate rail facilities to the PCIRO for the transportation of refugees in necessary movements between camps and to the point of exit in repatriation or resettlement.

(f) Grant priority for official journeys on railways, motorbuses, sea and airlines for personnel of the PCIRO in Italy.

2. The Joint Committee under Article VII below will agree on the measures necessary to ensure the maintenance of law, public order, security and public health in the camps operated by the PCIRO.

Article IV. IMMUNITIES

1. The Government shall accord to the Chief of Operations of the PCIRO and its principal officials of non-Italian nationality and not permanently resident in Italy, the immunities, facilities, privileges and exemptions—including custom exemptions—which are normally granted to diplomatic representatives. The list of officials entitled to such immunities will be agreed upon between the Government and the PCIRO.

2. The appointment of the Chief of Operations is subject to the agreement of the Government.

3. The PCIRO will communicate to the Government an official list of all its non-Italian personnel, and will inform the Government of any changes to such list.

Article V. PERSONNEL AND INSURANCE

1. The Government shall facilitate the admission into and the movement within Italy of the personnel of the PCIRO indicated in the official list under Article IV (3)

above, and shall furnish all practicable assistance to enable the PCIRO to select and employ qualified Italian citizens for its operations under this Agreement.

2. The Government shall provide to all employees concerned of the PCIRO, all the social insurance coverage which under Italian law is provided to the employees of Italian private firms.

3. The Government shall assume the handling and settlement of claims against or on behalf of the PCIRO and against or on behalf of its personnel in Italy arising in the course of official business.

4. The sums paid by the Government in the implementation of the provisions of paragraph 2 and 3 above shall be reimbursed to the Government by the PCIRO, in a manner to be agreed between the Parties.

5. The PCIRO will assure the good conduct, integrity and moral character of its employees, and will discharge or recall any of its personnel who violates these standards.

Article VI. FINANCIAL PROVISIONS

1. Subject to the provisions of paragraph 2 of this Article and paragraph 1 of Article II, the PCIRO undertakes to meet in dollars, sterling, Swiss francs or any freely convertible currency, at its own choice, the expenditures for the operation of its programme of activities under this Agreement, including the cost of repatriation and resettlement of refugees under its mandate who are at present in Italy.

The Government shall issue instructions to the Bank of Italy to supply to the PCIRO the amount of Lire required to meet its expenditures in Italy and to maintain an adequate working balance, against simultaneous payment by the PCIRO of equivalent amounts in dollars, sterling, Swiss francs or any freely convertible currency, at the choice of the PCIRO, at the rate of exchange fixed for the diplomatic representatives in Italy of the United States, United Kingdom and Switzerland.

2. In order to facilitate the programme undertaken under this Agreement by the PCIRO, the Government agrees to extend an interest free loan from the UNRRA Lire Fund of one milliard lire to the PCIRO to be drawn as required, during the period from 1 July 1947 to 31 December 1947. The sums drawn shall be repaid in dollars, sterling, Swiss francs or any freely convertible currency six months from the date of drawing of each amount, at the rate of exchange, as determined under paragraph 1 above, prevailing on the date of the drawing.

Article VII. JOINT COMMITTEE

1. A Joint Committee shall be established and shall be composed of representatives of the Government and the PCIRO.

2. The Government Delegation shall be composed of representatives of the following Agencies and experts whom the Government may designate from time to time:

Presidency of the Council of Ministers, Ministries of Foreign Affairs, of the Interior, of the Treasury (Ragioneria Generale dello Stato), of Finance, of Transport, of Industry and Commerce, of Foreign Trade, High Commissariat for Food, Administration for International Aid.

3. The Delegation of the PCIRO shall be composed of the chief of Operations and such additional representatives as he may designate.

4. The Joint Committee shall meet at the Ministry of Foreign Affairs and its meetings shall be chaired alternatively by a representative of the Government and of the PCIRO.

5. The functions of the Joint Committee shall be as follows:

(a) To provide the normal channel of communication and exchange of information between the Government and the PCIRO. In particular, the Joint Committee will be the channel through which the PCIRO will keep the Government informed about the records concerning refugees, their location, movements in Italy, and departure for other countries.

(b) To examine, discuss and decide by common agreement on matters pertaining to the implementation of such provisions of this Agreement, as require joint action by the Government and the PCIRO, including the following:

    (i) Rules and regulations relating to public order, sanitation, public health, etc.

   (ii) Methods of supply of fuel, lubricants, foodstuffs and other goods.

  (iii) Transportation.

  (iv) Redistribution of refugees in camps other than the existing ones; measures to encourage voluntary repatriation; schemes for the resettlement of refugees in other countries; and other matters in which the assistance of the Italian Government may be needed.

(c) To study, draft and recommend any supplementary agreements which the Government and the PCIRO may from time to time consider necessary.

Article VIII. LEGISLATION

The Government shall promulgate such legislation as may be deemed necessary for the implementation of the Agreement.

Article IX. DURATION OF AGREEMENT

This Agreement shall be considered as having come into force on 1 July 1947, and shall remain in force until such time as the Government and the PCIRO may decide to enter into a new Agreement, or until the expiration of 90 days from the date upon which either of the Parties shall have given notice in writing of its intention to terminate it.

The IRO may, on coming into existence, take over this Agreement from the PCIRO after due notification to the Government.

Both English and Italian texts shall be authoritative.

SUPPLEMENTARY AGREEMENT BETWEEN THE ITALIAN GOVERNMENT AND THE IRO RELATING TO IRO OPERATIONS IN ITALY DURING THE SUPPLEMENTARY PERIOD 1950-51, 14 NOVEMBER 1950[1]

The Italian Government and the IRO,

CONSIDERING the recommendation dated November 10th, 1950, by the Joint Committee of the Italian Government and IRO, set up according to Article VII of the Agreement between the Italian Government and IRO of 24th October 1947;

CONSIDERING the approach of the date-line set for the conclusion of IRO operations and the necessity deriving therefrom to concentrate every effort and material resource of IRO during the residual period on the resettlement of refugees abroad;

CONSIDERING the necessity that to this end the Italian Government contribute to relieving IRO of the burden of material assistance to refugees, thus adhering to the request made by the above mentioned Organization;

HAVE AGREED as follows:

IRO/LEG/GOV/45: original English and Italian, 9 Mar. 1951.

Article I. IRO shall intensify as much as possible the resettlement abroad of refugees coming within the mandate of IRO's Mission in Italy on September 30th 1950, in order that all the refugees, for whom a possibility of resettlement abroad is found, be actually transferred abroad before the end of operations.

The number of refugees resettled during the Supplementary Period will be not less than 20,000 provided the Italian Government, on its part, in cooperation with the IRO Mission in Italy, will endeavour by the most appropriate and effective means to produce the number of refugees required to complete the number of 20,000 quoted above.

These refugees will have to come within IRO's mandate and will have to be offered adequate resettlement possibilities by the Selection Commissions.

It is also agreed that the refugees for whom, according to the present Agreement, material assistance will be transferred from IRO to the Italian Government shall not exceed about 9,500 in number. This number will include:

(a) 3,600 refugees receiving any form of out-of-camp assistance and 4,200 assisted in the camps of Aversa, Capua, Salerno and S. Antonio a Pontecagnano;

(b) the institutional hard-core cases—not exceeding 1,000 in number (including dependants)—whom, for purposes of financial aid, the Italian Government shall consider as assisted in the camps.

In arranging its plans for resettlement and shipping, IRO Authorities shall avail themselves of the cooperation of the Italian Authorities and will keep the latter timely informed of operations in order to allow them to follow the general movement of refugees and submit suggestions thereon.

Article II. At the date of 1st February 1951, IRO will transfer to the Italian Government the responsibility of furnishing cash assistance to the refugees who at that time will be receiving such assistance from IRO, i.e. no more than 3,600 refugees at present out of camp.

Such assistance will be provided under the same conditions and in the same measure as is granted to the Italian refugees.

From the date of the signature of the present Supplementary Agreement until 1st February 1951, IRO will endeavour to have the said number of refugees at present receiving out of camp assistance reduced as much as possible.

Article III. At the date of 1st February 1951, IRO will concentrate in Bagnoli the refugees in process of resettlement abroad at present assisted in the other IRO camps endeavouring that their number be as great as possible.

At the same date IRO will transfer to the Italian Government the administration of the 4 remaining camps, namely: Aversa, Capua, Salerno and S. Antonio a Pontecagnano, for a maximum total population of 4,200.

The cost of maintenance of the refugees living in such camps will continue to be borne by IRO until 31st March 1951, on the basis of a daily 'pro capite' quota of 350 Lire.

These camps will be transferred to the Italian Government with complete installations and assets, including such hospital equipment as will assure the full operation of such camps.

Furthermore, IRO will terminate employment and labour contracts and pay termination emoluments to the staff before the transfer of the administration is effected.

Article IV. Not later than 15th January 1951, IRO will transmit to the Italian Government 2 distinct nominal rolls of refugees whose assistance—in camp or out of camp—will be transferred to the Italian Government under the previous Articles of the present Agreement.

A nominal roll of any institutional hard-core cases to be transferred from IRO will be furnished at least 30 days before the date of transfer.

Article V. The Italian Government reserves the right to negotiate with the UN High Commissioner for Refugees, when appointed, any kind of cooperation which may alleviate the burden deriving to it from the present Agreement.

Article VI. The Italian Government reserves the right to entrust—under the terms of para. (*c*) of Article II of the Law No. 1006 of September 19th, 1947—the administration of the above camps to a new section of the International Aid Administration to be set up under the name of 'Assistenza Profughi Stranieri' (APS).

The treatment and the disciplinary regulations of the refugees living in camps under A.P.S. administration will be entirely identical to those in force for Italian refugees.

Any question that may arise regarding disciplinary regulations for refugees and their treatment will be submitted to an Interministerial Committee, presided over by a representative of the Ministry for Foreign Affairs and made up of representatives of the Administrations concerned, to which representatives of IRO may be invited to attend with consulting powers.

Article VII. Until September 30th 1951 the date on which IRO will cease operations, the Organization will provide the refugees whose assistance is transferred to the Italian Government, under the terms of the present Agreement, and who will be protected by the Italian Government, with the assistance required for their repatriation and resettlement in the receiving countries.

It is also agreed that IRO may continue, without burden to the Italian Government, to counsel refugees and furnish them with any required documentation, certificates and legal assistance.

IRO may also make suggestions to the Italian Government on any matter affecting the legitimate interests of the refugees.

Article VIII. The Italian Government will welcome any form of assistance that Voluntary Societies of any nature or religion duly recognized by the Italian Government may be able to offer refugees, it being understood that such assistance will not affect the kind and measure of care and maintenance granted by the Italian Government, and the latter will grant their representatives reasonable permission to visit the camps.

Article IX. As a counterpart to the burden undertaken by the Italian Government, IRO renounces the cash contribution due to it by Italy for the Supplementary Period.

It is agreed, however, that in providing IRO with the services and facilities under Article III of the Agreement of 24th October 1947, and the appended letter of the same date, for the period April 1st–September 30th, 1951:

(1) The Italian Government will provide to the expenses for rail and road transport up to the amount of 50,000,000 Lire.

(2) The cost of rent and repairs for the properties occupied by IRO during that period shall be a matter for discussion between IRO and the Italian Government, it being understood, however, that the Italian Government is not committed to a payment of more than 20,000,000 Lire.

Article X. In order to face the expenses necessary to carry out the program of operations in Italy for the Supplementary Period, the Italian Government will accept from IRO one million and a hundred thousand Canadian Dollars and one million seventy thousand four hundred and twenty-eight Pounds Sterling in exchange for Italian Lire at the rate of exchange on the date when exchange of these sums is effected.

Article XI. The solution of the problem relating to institutional hard-core cases which shall have to remain in Italy will be the subject of a special Agreement between the Parties concerned

IRO on its part will endeavour by the most effective means to reduce to a minimum the number of such cases at the end of its activities in Italy.

Article XII. The present Agreement, which will become effective on December 1st, 1950, shall enter into force definitively as soon as approved by the competent constitutional bodies of the Italian Republic.

Immediate notification of the fulfilment of its constitutional requirements shall be given by the Italian Government to IRO.

IN WITNESS whereof the undersigned plenipotentiaries, being duly empowered, have signed the present Agreement and affixed thereto their seals.

ADDITIONAL PROTOCOL TO THE SUPPLEMENTARY AGREEMENT BETWEEN THE ITALIAN GOVERNMENT AND THE IRO STIPULATED IN ROME ON 14 NOVEMBER 1950, SIGNED 31 DECEMBER 1952[1]

CONSIDERING the necessity of completing by all possible means the resettlement abroad of refugees still in Italy, the Italian Government and the IRO;

WHEREAS IRO's General Council in its Resolution No. 84, adopted on April 11th, 1951 at Geneva, has authorized the Director-General of IRO to continue—within the financial means at his disposal—the implementation of refugee assistance and resettlement plans beyond the date limit of September 30th, 1951;

HAVE AGREED as follows:

Article 1. The provisions of Article IX of the Supplementary Agreement of 14 November 1950 will be effective until such date as the activities of IRO in Italy will cease, and in any case not later than March 31st, 1952.

Article 2. IRO undertakes to further resettle abroad the greatest possible number of refugees up to the maximum number that its financial resources will allow.

Article 3. The better to specify what is provided under Article IX of the Supplementary Agreement quoted above, it is agreed that for the period subsequent to 30th September 1951:

(1) The Italian Government will undertake to pay expenses incurred on account of railway transport up to a quarterly amount not exceeding 25,000,000 Lire.

(2) As regards leases and cost of repairs to property occupied by IRO, the Italian Government is under obligation to pay in cash an amount not exceeding 10,000,000 Lire per quarter.

(3) All other expenditure over and above the limits laid down in paragraphs 1 and 2 above, will be a total charge to IRO.

Article 4. In payment of the amounts due under the terms of Article III (*a*) and (*c*) para. 2, of the Agreement of 24 October 1947, the Italian Government will undertake to pay 329,807,887 Lire, viz.:

L. 140,000,000 for repairs affected to the whole of the real property owned by the 'Fondazione del Banco di Napoli' at Bagnoli. This latter payment is subject, however, to the result of the law suit started at the request of the above named 'Fondazione' with the Naples Courts for the payment of lease and damage suffered during the occupation of the property by IRO.

[1] IRO/LEG/GOV/45/1, 19 Feb. 1953.

L. 111,242,678 as a reimbursement of General Sales Tax.

,, 78,565,209 as a reimbursement of Communal Excise Tax.

The present Protocol will be embodied in the Supplementary Agreement of 14 November 1950 which will enter into force definitively as soon as parliamentary approval has been obtained.

For the above purpose the undersigned Plenipotentiaries, duly authorized to do so, have signed and sealed the present Protocol.

AGREEMENT BETWEEN THE IRO AND THE GOVERNMENT OF LUXEMBURG CONCERNING THE SELECTION OF REFUGEES AND DISPLACED PERSONS FOR LUXEMBURG, 9 MARCH 1949[1]

THE INTERNATIONAL REFUGEE ORGANIZATION (hereinafter referred to as the IRO) and the GOVERNMENT OF THE GRAND DUCHY OF LUXEMBURG (hereafter referred to as the Government) have agreed upon the following provisions regarding the immigration into Luxemburg of refugees and displaced persons (hereinafter referred to as refugees) as defined in Annex I of the IRO Constitution.

Article I. NUMBER AND TYPES OF IMMIGRANTS

1. The Government agrees to admit into Luxemburg refugees selected from the Allied Zones of Occupation in Germany.

2. The Government shall provide the IRO in due time with all particulars concerning the immigrants it is prepared to admit to its territory: number, professional qualifications, sex, family circumstances, etc.

Article II. SELECTION OF CANDIDATES

3. The IRO shall be responsible for determining which refugees come within its mandate.

4. The Government reserves to itself the exclusive right to carry out the final selection of the candidates of its choice on its own responsibility. The Government further undertakes that the selection of immigrants will be carried out without discrimination as to race, religion or nationality.

5. The Government shall inform the IRO beforehand of the names, titles and respective duties of the persons appointed as its representatives to select and recruit refugees.

6. The IRO shall supply the Luxemburg Selection Mission free of charge with:

(a) The petrol and oil required for its motor vehicles to enable it to carry out its duties within the limits of the zone of selection;

(b) telephone calls and any other communication facilities that Field Offices may be able to offer; the cost of international communications shall be met by the Government;

(c) wherever available, machine tools and technical equipment for testing the candidates' professional qualifications;

(d) the medical equipment needed for their medical examination.

7. The expenses incurred by the Luxemburg Mission shall be payable in their entirety by the Government. At the request of the Chief of the Selection Mission, who

---

[1] IRO/LEG/GOV/11, 17 Mar. 1949: original French.

shall be held responsible, and subject to the texts and regulations in force in the occupied territories, the IRO shall make financial advances. The Government shall reimburse the IRO in the currency in which the advances were made.

8. The IRO shall bring before the Selection Mission refugees volunteering for resettlement in Luxemburg who have the qualifications required by the Government, without, however, assuming any responsibility for their final selection.

9. The representatives of the Government shall have access to the refugee camps and shall be granted every facility for informing the refugees about working and living conditions in Luxemburg. The IRO undertakes to distribute among the refugees all the propaganda material with which the Government supplies it for the purpose.

10. The IRO shall assist wherever possible with registration and with the administrative work of the Selection Mission.

11. Medical officers of the IRO shall carry out a preliminary medical examination in accordance with the standards of the Organization. This examination shall consist of

a clinical examination,

an X-ray examination (screening or radiography of the lungs),

a blood test (Kahn or Wassermann test).

A medical file indicating the results of this examination shall be supplied for each candidate brought before the Luxemburg Selection Mission, although the IRO shall not be held responsible.

12. The Luxemburg Selection Mission shall inform the Field officers of the IRO of its reasons for rejecting any of the candidates brought forward.

13. The IRO reserves the right to allocate quotas to the zones on the basis of the needs stated by the Government.

14. The itinerary of the Selection Mission visiting IRO camps and centres shall be planned in collaboration with the services in the respective zones.

Article III. WORKERS' FAMILIES

15. The Government undertakes to accept at the same time as the worker who has been selected, members of his family who were brought before the Luxemburg Selection Mission at the same time.

16. The Government undertakes to allow refugees resettled in Luxemburg under the terms of this agreement to go temporarily to the occupation zones when circumstances beyond their control make this necessary or for humanitarian reasons.

The IRO shall be responsible for helping them to complete the requisite formalities.

Article IV. TRANSPORT

17. The Government shall not be responsible for the cost of transporting refugees and their luggage, or for the coordination of movements from their place of residence to the Luxemburg frontier.

18. The Government shall accept administrative responsibility for and meet the cost of transporting refugees and their luggage from the Luxemburg frontier to their final destination.

Article V. ADMISSION TO LUXEMBURG AND RECEPTION

19. The Government undertakes to issue visas and entry permits without cost to the IRO or to the refugees.

20. The Government agrees to admit to Luxemburg, duty free, all articles, including the tools of their trade, legally owned by the refugees selected and their dependants.

21. The Government shall meet all costs of reception, housing and maintenance

of the refugees, until such time as they have obtained employment in normal conditions.

22. Under the terms of this Agreement the IRO shall pay to each refugee resettled in Luxemburg a resettlement grant in Luxemburg francs equivalent to the sum of $16.

Article VI. LEGAL STATUS

23. The Government shall guarantee to all refugees admitted under this Agreement all rights and liberties granted by Luxemburg law to aliens resident in Luxemburg.

24. As regards social security, wage-scales and various forms of taxation, they shall receive the same treatment as other aliens resident in Luxemburg and shall be subject to Luxemburg law.

Article VII. CONDITIONS OF EMPLOYMENT

25. Prior to his departure for Luxemburg each worker shall receive an employment contract.

26. Refugees accepted for work in Luxemburg shall receive the same wages as are paid to Luxemburg workers with similar professional qualifications, and the whole body of labour and social security legislation in the Grand Duchy shall be applicable to them.

27. The Government shall endeavour to find work with another employer in the same industry, or in other industries where there is a shortage of manpower, for workers who prove unfit, through no fault of their own, for the work for which they were originally chosen by the Luxemburg Selection Mission.

Article VIII. LEGAL AND POLITICAL PROTECTION

28. The Government recognizes the IRO as having the same rights as are granted to nations with regard to their nationals, in the matter of the legal and political protection of persons coming within its mandate who do not, in law or in fact, enjoy the protection of any government.

The IRO shall therefore take all necessary steps to safeguard the interests of the refugees, in agreement with the competent departments of the Government, which shall give it every possible assistance to that end.

Article IX. CONDITIONS OF EXPULSION AND RETURN TO ZONES

29. Any refugee admitted into Luxemburg under this Agreement who cannot be absorbed into the economic structure of the country, may be returned to the Zone from which he came within 6 months of the date of his entry into the country. This condition applies only to:
  (a) those refugees who have broken their contract for no valid reason;
  (b) those refugees who, after several attempts to place them in other employment, in accordance with para. 27 above, prove unsuited to any work in Luxemburg;
  (c) those refugees who, by their presence, their acts or their propaganda, constitute a danger to public order and safety;
  (d) refugees suffering from an infectious or contagious disease, contracted in the zones before their departure for Luxemburg.

30. The Government shall be responsible for the expenses involved in expulsion or return operations in accordance with para. 29 above, as far as the Luxemburg frontier.

31. The refugees referred to in this Agreement shall in no case be repatriated to their countries of origin, unless they express a formal wish for this by submitting an application in writing to the IRO Mission in Luxemburg.

32. The case of each refugee whom the Government proposes to send back to Germany shall be submitted to the IRO Mission in Luxemburg, who, in accordance with paras. 28 and 29 above, shall be at liberty to intervene, whenever that is possible, on behalf of the refugee in question.

Where it proves impossible to come to any arrangement, an individual file, indicating as far as possible the reasons for the return and the attempts made to find other employment for the person concerned; shall be sent direct by the Luxemburg Office of the IRO to the IRO Headquarters in the refugee's zone of origin.

Article X. ENTRY INTO FORCE

33. This Agreement shall take effect from the date of signature by the duly qualified representatives of the Government and the IRO and shall come into operation as soon as the military authorities of each zone of occupation, where selection is to be carried out, have signified their approval.

Article XI. PERIOD OF VALIDITY OF THE AGREEMENT

34. This Agreement shall remain in force as long as it is not denounced by one or other party after 2 months' notice on either side.

When this period of 2 months has elapsed, the Articles of this Agreement concerning immigration operations into the Grand Duchy shall become null and void. The Articles concerning legal status, the rights and duties of the IRO and the Government respectively with reference to the refugees residing in Luxemburg under the terms of this Agreement, namely Articles 6, 7, 8 and 9, shall remain in force for an indefinite period.

AGREEMENT BETWEEN HIS BRITANNIC MAJESTY'S GOVERNMENT, THE ROYAL NETHERLANDS GOVERNMENT AND THE PCIRO FOR THE RESETTLEMENT IN THE NETHERLANDS OF DISPLACED PERSONS AND REFUGEES IN THE BRITISH ZONE OF GERMANY, 22 OCTOBER 1947[1]

His Britannic Majesty's Government, the Royal Netherlands Government (hereinafter referred to as 'the Government') and the PCIRO have agreed as follows regarding the immigration to the Netherlands from the British Zone of Germany of refugees and displaced persons as defined in Annex I to the Constitution of the International Refugee Organization.

1. *Persons Eligible for Immigration*

(a) The Government agrees, subject to the provisions of this Agreement, to admit into the Netherlands, as workers, displaced persons and refugees who have never collaborated in any way with the Nazi regime, who are acceptable to accredited representatives of the Government and to PCIRO.

(b) The admission of dependent relatives of the workers entering the Netherlands under this Agreement will be governed by Section 7 hereof.

(c) In the event of the deportation of immigrants from the Netherlands under Section 4 (e) hereof, the Government will permit the immigration of an equal number of refugees or displaced persons in their place.

2. *Selection of Immigrants*

(a) PCIRO will be responsible for the determination as to which persons will be

---

[1] PC/LEG/21, 15 Apr. 1948: original English.

the concern of the International Refugee Organization under Annex I to the IRO Constitution.

(b) The Government will be responsible for selecting from the group referred to in Section 2 (a) above, those persons whom it considers qualified for immigration to the Netherlands under this Agreement.

(c) The Government agrees that the selection of immigrants will be carried out without discrimination as to race or religion.

(d) PCIRO will assist as far as possible in establishing contact between representatives of the Government and refugees and displaced persons who appear to meet the requirements of the Government, without, however, assuming any responsibility for their eventual selection by the Government.

(e) The Government will inform PCIRO with the minimum of delay the particulars of the numbers and qualifications of immigrants to be admitted under this Agreement.

(f) The Government will also inform PCIRO the names and functions of officers nominated to perform the selection of immigrants, and of their procedural requirements. The salaries, travelling and other expenses of the Government's representatives will be paid by the Government.

3. *Transportation and Reception of Immigrants*

(a) The immigrants to be admitted into the Netherlands under this Agreement will be transported to the Netherlands border by the Control Authorities in the British Zone of Germany without cost to the Government, PCIRO or the immigrants.

(b) The Government is responsible for reception and transportation of the immigrants within the Netherlands.

(c) The Government agrees to issue visas and entry permits without cost to the immigrants or to PCIRO.

(d) The Government agrees to admit to the Netherlands duty free all the personal belongings, including tools of trade, of selected immigrants, and of their dependent relatives who are permitted to join them in the Netherlands under Section 7 of this Agreement.

4. *Rights of Immigrants*

(a) Immigrants admitted into the Netherlands under this Agreement will, after five years continuous residence, be given an opportunity to apply for Netherlands citizenship in accordance with the requirements of the Netherlands law.

(b) The Government guarantees to immigrants all rights and liberties granted by law to foreigners resident in the Netherlands. The enjoyment of certain rights and the benefit of certain favours accorded to foreigners subject to reciprocity shall not be refused to the immigrants in the absence of reciprocity.

(c) The Government will provide maintenance for immigrants admitted into the Netherlands under this Agreement until such time as they have obtained employment, without cost to the other Parties to this Agreement, or to the immigrants.

(d) The Government agrees that should an immigrant under this Agreement, owing to reasons other than his misbehaviour, find it impossible to earn his living or to support his dependants, and therefore finds himself in need of material assistance, such immigrants will not be deported from the Netherlands; and that PCIRO will be given an opportunity to make representations to the Government concerning the solution of the difficulty.

(e) Apart from the provisions of Section 4 (d) hereof, the Government agrees that immigrants admitted under this Agreement will not be deported under any other circumstances except those normally applying under Netherlands law to foreigners resident in the Netherlands. In the event of deportation proceedings against any immigrants admitted under this Agreement, the Netherlands Government will notify PCIRO and will give PCIRO an opportunity to make representations to the appropriate governmental authorities within 15 days of such notification.

(*f*) In case of the deportation of immigrants admitted under this Agreement, they may be returned to the British Zone of Germany within two years from the date of departure, and they will in no case be unwillingly deported to their countries of origin. They shall also be allowed a reasonable period of time during which they may obtain permission and make necessary arrangements for proceeding to any other territory they may elect. Should the immigrants fail to make such arrangements within a period of three months after receiving notice of final deportation orders, they may be deported to the British Zone of Germany. Immigrants who by their actions or propaganda seriously endanger or have seriously endangered public order and safety in the Netherlands may be deported to the British Zone of Germany only without enjoying the right to three months' time in which to make alternative arrangements.

(*g*) The Control Authorities will readmit any immigrants deported to the British Zone of Germany from the Netherlands under Section 4 (*e*) and 4 (*f*) hereof under the same conditions as apply generally to refugees and displaced persons in the British Zone of Germany at the time of deportation.

(*h*) Immigrants under this Agreement will be permitted to terminate their employment in accordance with the requirements of Netherlands law and may thereupon obtain from the Government permission and documents necessary to leave the Netherlands.

(*i*) Subject to the provisions under Section 3 (*d*), the Government undertakes not to impose upon the immigrants duties, charges or taxes, under any denomination whatsoever, other or higher than those which are or may be levied on their nationals in similar situations.

(*j*) Immigrants shall have, in the territory of the Netherlands, free and ready access to the courts of law. They shall enjoy, in this respect, all rights and privileges which it may be possible to grant them under Netherlands law.

(*k*) The Government undertakes to apply to immigrants, as regards the social insurance laws at present in force or which may subsequently be established, the most favourable treatment applicable under Netherlands law.

(*l*) Children of immigrants shall enjoy, in the schools, treatment as favourable as that accorded to other foreigners in general. They shall benefit in particular to the same extent as the latter by the total or partial remission of fees and charges and award of scholarships.

5. *Conditions of Employment*

(*a*) The Government will provide regular employment for the immigrants entering the Netherlands under Section 1 hereof and will insofar as possible provide employment for dependent relatives who may be admitted to join the immigrants in the Netherlands under Section 7.

(*b*) Immigrants who have shown willingness to perform the work originally chosen, but who are found unsuitable for that work will be assisted by the Government to secure other work in the Netherlands for which they are fitted.

(*c*) Immigrants admitted under this Agreement will enjoy the same working and living conditions and wages as Netherlands workers in similar categories and will be treated in the same manner and without discrimination in case of unemployment. They will be allowed to join trade unions in the same manner as Netherlands citizens.

(*d*) Prior to the departure of the immigrants from the British Zone of Germany, contracts of employment will be signed with them in conformity with the contract annexed to this Agreement.

(*e*) The Government undertakes to accord to immigrants who may be victims of industrial accidents in its territory, or to their beneficiaries, the most favourable treatment applicable under Netherlands law.

6. *Legal and Other Protection by PCIRO*

(*a*) The legal and other appropriate protection of immigrants will be assumed by PCIRO acting under the provisions of the Constitution of the IRO in such matters.

(*b*) The Government will grant such reasonable facilities as will enable PCIRO to assume the above-mentioned legal and other protection.

7. *Admission of Dependent Relatives*

(*a*) Dependent relatives of workers admitted into the Netherlands under this Agreement will be permitted to join the workers in the Netherlands as soon as the following conditions are satisfied:

(i) their support is assured either by the workers whom they join or, where possible, by employment of the relatives themselves; and

(ii) adequate housing facilities are available.

(*b*) Similarly, the Government will admit other persons who should be permitted from a humanitarian standpoint to join immigrants, each such case being for individual determination by the Government.

(*c*) The Government will take all possible steps to provide housing facilities for dependent relatives with the least possible delay.

This Agreement shall become effective on the date of signature by the three Parties.

ANNEX TO AGREEMENT CONCLUDED BETWEEN HIS BRITANNIC MAJESTY'S GOVERNMENT, THE ROYAL NETHERLANDS GOVERNMENT AND THE PCIRO FOR THE RESETTLEMENT OF DISPLACED PERSONS AND REFUGEES IN THE NETHERLANDS

WORK CONTRACT FOR REFUGEES AND DISPLACED PERSONS FROM THE BRITISH ZONE OF GERMANY TO BE EMPLOYED IN THE NETHERLANDS

1. Enterprise (person, firm, or company):
2. Place of work:
3. Name:
4. Birthplace and birthdate, or date of incorporation:
5. Nationality:
6. Residence, or registered office:
7. Status:

Article I. (*a*) The above-mentioned employer undertakes to employ the undersigned worker permanently during a period of not less than 24 months from the date of his initial employment.

Upon the worker's request, this contract will be automatically renewed for a further period of one calendar year (and so on from year to year), providing his work has in the meantime been satisfactory.

(*b*) During the period of this contract, the undersigned worker agrees to remain in the sole employment of the undersigned employer, to perform the assigned work in a satisfactory manner and to observe all legal regulations of employment brought to his attention.

Article II. (*a*) The Royal Netherlands Government represented by its appropriate officials shall supervise the observance of all working contracts.

(*b*) The undersigned worker certifies that he is engaged for employment as a . . . .

The location and type of his employment will be specified after his arrival in the Netherlands. He agrees to remain in this employment during the period of his contract. In certain circumstances, transfers to other employment are permitted, and expenses of such transfer, if considered justified, shall be borne by the Royal Netherlands Government. Upon termination of this contract the worker is free of any obligation provided the equipment, tools and furniture issued at the time of his employment are returned in satisfactory condition, with due consideration for normal depreciation, or that compensation is paid for their misuse.

Article III. (*a*) The employer will provide adequate living quarters for the worker under the supervision of the Royal Netherlands Government.

(*b*) The worker admitted to the Netherlands will be permitted to remain in the Netherlands permanently if he desires and if his conduct is satisfactory and will be given an opportunity to acquire Netherlands citizenship according to Netherlands law.

Article IV. The normal work-week is 6 days or 48 hours. All Sundays, Easter Monday, Ascension Day, New Year's Day, and all other National holidays will be recognised as non-working days. The workers will receive holidays on other days as established by the conditions of his contract with his employer.

Normal work-hours will be 8 hours per day.

Supplementary bonuses and overtime will be paid according to regulations approved by the Royal Netherlands Government.

Article V. (*a*) The undersigned worker will enjoy the same working and living conditions and wages as Netherlands workers performing the same work for the same employer.

Guaranteed minimum wages for the mining industry have been established and are enforced by the Royal Netherlands Government. The undersigned worker will receive premiums on the same basis as Netherlands workers. The worker is subject to the same deductions from his salary in the same manner as Netherlands workers in accordance with Netherlands law.

(*b*) The minimum wages rate at the time of entering into the contract is . . . .

(*c*) Salaries will be paid weekly (monthly).

Fluctuation of salaries will affect the undersigned worker in the same manner as Netherlands workers.

(*d*) Displaced persons performing the same work as Netherlands workers but who do not speak the Dutch language will not be discriminated against in the matter of wages, living conditions, type of conditions of employment or any other manner.

Article VI. (*a*) The undersigned worker will be entitled to receive supplementary items of the same quality and quantity as Netherlands workers receive.

(*b*) He is authorized a paid furlough once a year in the same manner as Netherlands workers receive, according to the terms of his contract and to the regulations in force.

Article VII. (*a*) In the event of repatriation, the worker signing this contract who works thereunder for a period of not less than 5 years, will receive payment to cover expenses for his travel to the frontier of his country.

(*b*) In the event the worker wishes to leave the Netherlands to enter a country other than his home land, payment covering the costs of transportation of the worker to the Netherlands frontier will be made, providing he has been employed as described herein for a period of at least 5 years.

(c) The worker leaving the Netherlands under sub-paragraphs (a) and (b) above, will be entitled to take with him all personal possessions (or replacements thereof) which he originally brought to the Netherlands. Export facilities for such articles and freight payable thereon shall be paid by the Royal Netherlands Government.

Article VIII. (a) The undersigned worker will be assessed for social insurance by deduction from his wages in the same manner as Netherlands workers, according to Netherlands law.

(b) The undersigned worker will receive the same advantages of pension as are accorded Netherlands workers for performing the same work for the same employer.

(c) The undersigned worker will be permitted to join the trade unions of his choice and he will enjoy the same status as Netherlands workers, according to Netherlands law.

Article IX. In the event of illness, the undersigned worker will receive the assistance granted by Netherlands law.

Article X. In case of accident during employment, the undersigned worker will receive compensation, medical and pharmaceutical treatment in the same manner as Netherlands workers under similar conditions under Netherlands law.

Article XI. In the event of death due to accident during employment, disease or sickness directly attributable to the employment, dependants will receive compensation according to the Netherlands law. The employer will immediately inform the International Refugee Organization of the death of the undersigned worker.

Article XII. (a) The contract may be cancelled by the employer if:

1. The worker disobeys instructions addressed to him by duly authorized superiors; or

    persists in breaches of his contract or of local employment regulations.

2. The behaviour of the worker is subversive to order and discipline in his employment.

3. The worker refuses to be medically treated when infectiously ill.

(b) The contract may be cancelled by the worker if:

1. He becomes unable to work as a result of accident or illness.

2. The employer retains and refuses to return his personal documents such as identity card, pass, work permit, work contract, registration certificate, on demand.

3. The employer fails to comply with the terms of his contract with the worker.

4. It is found by the competent officials of the Royal Netherlands Government that the worker has been maltreated or the terms of his contract abused and the worker so demands.

(c) In case of cancellation, notice must be served by either party, at least two months in advance.

Article XIII. At the expiration of the above-mentioned period of 24 months and at the expiration of any subsequent calendar year, the employer may terminate his contract with the worker on giving two months' notice in writing, expiring at the end of such period of 24 months or of such calendar year. If the worker shall not give the notice prescribed in Article I (a) of his desire to continue the contract, the contract shall terminate at the end of such period of 24 months or of any subsequent calendar year as the case may be.

Article XIV. SIGNATURE OF THE EMPLOYER: . . . .
SIGNATURE OF THE WORKER: . . . .

AGREEMENT BETWEEN THE IRO AND THE
NETHERLANDS GOVERNMENT, 20 JUNE 1950[1]

Article 1. The IRO and the Netherlands Government, desiring to conclude arrangements for their assistance to aged refugees under the mandate of the IRO, and to their dependants, agree as follows concerning the permanent care and financial support of the thirty aged refugees and their ten dependants, who are beneficiaries under the attached annuity insurance policies issued by the Life Assurance Company of the Netherlands Insurance Company.

Article 2. The Netherlands Government: (*a*) Approves the adoption of this annuity scheme to provide supplementary assistance, on a life-time basis, to the forty refugees referred to in Article 1.

(*b*) Agrees to accept these refugees as permanent residents of the Netherlands, that is to say, as aliens who have been granted a permit of residence in the Netherlands for an indefinite period and who are not subject to measures of expulsion, exclusively on the ground of indigency.

(*c*) Agrees to grant these refugees as far as possible (especially with respect to public relief and assistance and social security) a legal status as envisaged within the framework of the Convention Relating to the Status of Refugees as prepared by the United Nations.

(*d*) Agrees to permit grants of public assistance, as needed by this group, without requiring deductions of the supplementary amounts provided by the annuities under this policy.

(*e*) Agrees to the principle of direct payment of the annuities to the refugees concerned.

Article 3. The IRO: (*a*) Agrees to pay the total cost of the premium, or Dutch guilders 110,415 (hundred and ten thousand four hundred and fifteen) for lifetime annuities for the refugees concerned.

MEMORANDUM OF UNDERSTANDING (*AIDE MÉMOIRE*)
AGREED BY THE NORWEGIAN GOVERNMENT AND THE
IRO, 17 SEPTEMBER 1949[2]

1. In accordance with the decision of the Government of Norway to accept 200 Refugees, of whom 100 are to be Hard Core or 'Minus' Refugees, it is agreed that 50 Blind and 50 Dependants of these Blind will be received in Norway.

2. The 50 Blind and 50 Dependants will be selected individually by representatives of the Government, with the assistance of the IRO. Selection will start at the earliest possible date and movement will be completed by April 1, 1950.

3. Refugees accepted into Norway under this agreement will be permitted to apply for Norwegian citizenship, in accordance with the established regulations of the Government.

4. The IRO will:

A. Reimburse the Norwegian Government for the actual costs of care and maintenance of these refugees from the date of their arrival in Norway until 30 June

---

[1] IRO/LEG/GOV/38, 10 July 1950: original English.

[2] In accordance with paragraph 6 of the Memorandum of Understanding formal approval was signified by the Norwegian Government by telegram of the Minister of Social Affairs, dated 28 Sept. 1949. IRO/LEG/GOV/23, 8 Nov. 1949: original English.

1950. The actual cost of care and maintenance for refugees receiving full care and maintenance in institutions in Norway is 8,50 Kr. per day.

B. Grant the sum of $50,000 to the Norwegian Government to be used for the construction and equipping of a Rehabilitation Training Centre (Workshop) for the Blind.

C. Provide funds, not to exceed $10,000 for the salaries of several supervisory staff members for the Rehabilitation Training Centre and/or Home for the Blind.

D. Grant as a contribution toward the permanent care of these refugees, the sum of $50,000 to the Norwegian Government.

E. Pay the Transportation costs to Norway of these Refugees.

F. The IRO will turn over to the Government one Jeep Station Wagon for use at Konnerudkollen.

5. The funds referred to in 4A and 4D will be paid in Norwegian Kroner. The IRO will provide the funds under 4B and 4C, either in Norwegian Kroner, or in hard currency, as requested by the Norwegian Government.

Funding for 4E will depend on transportation arrangements.

6. The above Memorandum of Understanding is subject to formal approval by the Norwegian Government.

AGREEMENT BETWEEN THE IRO AND THE SWEDISH GOVERNMENT CONCERNING THE ADMISSION OF REFUGEES CLASSIFIED AS TUBERCULAR CASES AND MEMBERS OF THEIR FAMILIES, 27 MAY 1950[1]

The International Refugee Organization (IRO; hereinafter referred to as the Organization) and the Swedish Government (hereinafter referred to as the Government),

Jointly recognizing that the problem of refugees and displaced persons of all categories, as that problem has been defined by the General Assembly of the UN, continues to be one of immediate urgency and of international character; and

Recognizing in particular the importance of making future provision for refugees and displaced persons, who require permanent assistance such as institutional care, have agreed as follows:

Article 1. The Government will receive for permanent residence and for institutional or similar care in Sweden 150 refugees at present under IRO care, who have been classified by the Organization as tubercular cases; and will receive for permanent residence the members of their immediate families or their dependants, totalling approximately 150 such additional persons.

Article 2. The Organization will provide the Government with basic information on the location and description of tubercular cases and of their dependants.

Article 3. The Government will send to the IRO installations a selection mission, which shall have full responsibility for the final decision as to the cases to be selected. The Organization will provide any necessary technical assistance in this process.

The Organization will arrange for the transportation of the mission in the areas where the selection is to take place and assist the mission in obtaining all facilities during their stay in areas where such facilities are granted.

Article 4. The Organization will provide transport to the port of Malmö, together with care and maintenance in transit, for all persons selected.

Article 5. The Organization will make a contribution toward the costs of the perm-

---

[1] IRO/LEG/GOV/34, 4 June 1950: original English and Swedish.

anent care of such refugees in the amount of $1,200 per capita for each tubercular case received in Sweden and $250 for each dependant, payments to be made in one-half in US dollars and one-half in Swedish crowns.

Article 6. Refugees received in Sweden under the stipulations of this Agreement will be entitled to make application for Swedish citizenship and to have their applications considered on the same terms as other foreigners in corresponding circumstances. They will likewise enjoy the same social assistance benefits under Swedish law as other foreigners resident in Sweden. Tubercular cases admitted to institutions will receive the same standards of care as Swedish nationals in similar circumstances.

Article 7. The present Agreement shall come into force on the date of signature.

AGREEMENT BETWEEN THE SWISS FEDERAL COUNCIL AND THE IRO CONCERNING THE LEGAL STATUS OF THE IRO IN SWITZERLAND, 15 SEPTEMBER 1948[1]

THE SWISS FEDERAL COUNCIL, of the one part, and THE IRO, of the other wishing to conclude an agreement to regulate the legal status of the IRO in Switzerland, have agreed on the following provisions:

Article 1. FREEDOM OF ACTION OF THE IRO

The Swiss Federal Council guarantees to the IRO the independence and freedom of action belonging to it as an international institution.

Article 2. PERSONALITY OF THE IRO

The Swiss Federal Council recognizes the international personality and legal capacity in Switzerland of the IRO.

Article 3. IMMUNITIES OF THE IRO

The IRO enjoys the immunities known in international law as diplomatic immunities.

Article 4. EXTERRITORIALITY OF THE GROUNDS AND BUILDINGS

The Swiss Federal Council recognizes the exterritoriality of the grounds and buildings of the IRO and of all buildings occupied by it in connection with meetings of the IRO or any other meeting convened in Switzerland by the IRO.

Article 5. FREEDOM OF MEETING

The Swiss Federal Council recognizes that the IRO and its members in their relations with the Organization enjoy absolute freedom of meeting, including freedom of discussion and decision.

Article 6. IMMUNITY FROM LEGAL PROCESS AND IMMUNITY FROM OTHER MEASURES

1. The IRO, its properties and assets, wherever they may be or by whomsoever they may be held, shall enjoy immunity from every form of legal process except in so far as this immunity is formally waived by the Director-General of the IRO or his duly authorized representative.

2. The property and assets of the IRO, wherever they may be and by whomsoever

[1] IRO/LEG/GOV/4, 29 Jan. 1949: original French.

they may be held, shall enjoy immunity from every measure of perquisition, requisition, confiscation, expropriation or any other form of seizure or interference by any public authority, whatsoever its nature.

Article 7. INVIOLABILITY OF GROUNDS AND BUILDINGS

The grounds and buildings of the IRO are inviolable. No agent of the Swiss public authority may enter them without the express consent of the IRO.

Article 8. INVIOLABILITY OF THE ARCHIVES

The archives of the IRO and all documents belonging to it or in its possession are inviolable.

Article 9. PUBLICATIONS

The export and import of the publications of the IRO shall not be subject to any restrictive measures.

Article 10. FISCAL POSITION OF THE IRO

The IRO is exonerated from direct and indirect taxes, federal, cantonal and communal, on buildings of which it is the owner and which are occupied by its services, as well as on its movable property, it being understood that the IRO does not claim exemption from charges corresponding to a service rendered by a public authority.

Article 11. FREE DISPOSAL OF FUNDS

1. The IRO may receive and hold funds, notes, coins and securities of any kind and may dispose of them freely both within Switzerland and in its relations with other countries.

2. The present article also applies to members of the IRO in their relations with the Organization.

Article 12. OFFICIAL COMMUNICATIONS

The IRO shall enjoy for its official communications treatment not less favourable than that accorded to diplomatic missions in Switzerland in respect of:

(a) All priorities for communications and transport;
(b) Postal, telegraphic, radio-telegraphic, telephonic, radio-telephonic and telephotographic tariffs; etc.

Article 13. EXEMPTION FROM CENSORSHIP

No censorship shall be applied to the duly authenticated official communications of the IRO, whatever the means of communication employed.

Article 14. FREEDOM OF ACCESS AND SOJOURN

1. The Swiss Authorities shall take the necessary measures to facilitate the entry into, sojourn in, and departure from Swiss territory of all persons having official business with the IRO, that is to say:

(a) Representatives of Member States, whatever may be the relations between Switzerland and the said States;
(b) Members of the General Council and the Executive Committee of the IRO, irrespective of nationality;
(c) Agents and officials of the IRO;
(d) Other persons, irrespective of nationality, summoned by the IRO.

2. Any police regulations tending to restrict the entry of foreigners into Switzerland

or to regulate the conditions of their sojourn shall not apply to the persons covered by the present article.

Article 15. IMMUNITIES OF THE REPRESENTATIVES OF MEMBERS OF THE GENERAL COUNCIL AND OF THE EXECUTIVE COMMITTEE

The representatives of the Members of the IRO and members of the General Council and of the Executive Committee who are in Switzerland on official business shall enjoy the following privileges and immunities:

(*a*) Inviolability of the person, place of residence and all objects belonging to the person concerned;

(*b*) Immunity from jurisdiction;

(*c*) Fiscal immunity corresponding to that accorded to diplomatic agents in accordance with international usage as accepted in Switzerland;

(*d*) Customs facilities corresponding to those accorded to diplomatic agents in accordance with international usage as accepted in Switzerland;

(*e*) The right to use cyphers in official communications and to receive and send documents and correspondence by courier or duly sealed diplomatic bags;

(*f*) Exemption from exchange restrictions under conditions identical to those accorded to diplomatic agents of foreign Governments on temporary mission.

Article 16. DIPLOMATIC IMMUNITIES OF THE DIRECTOR-GENERAL AND CERTAIN OFFICIALS

The Director-General of the IRO and certain officials of the categories designated by him and agreed to by the Swiss Federal Council shall enjoy the privileges, immunities, exemptions and facilities granted to diplomatic agents in accordance with international law and custom.

Article 17. IMMUNITIES AND FACILITIES ACCORDED TO ALL OFFICIALS

All officials of the IRO, irrespective of nationality, shall enjoy the following immunities and facilities:

(*a*) Exemption from jurisdiction for all acts performed in the discharge of their duties;

(*b*) Exoneration from all federal, cantonal and communal taxes on salaries, emoluments and indemnities paid to them by the IRO.

Article 18. EXEMPTIONS AND FACILITIES ACCORDED TO OFFICIALS NOT OF SWISS NATIONALITY

Officials of the IRO who are not of Swiss nationality shall enjoy the immunities, exemptions and facilities enumerated in the Arrangement for the execution of the present Agreement.

Article 19. PENSIONS FUND, ETC.

1. Any pensions fund or provident fund conducted under the authority of the IRO shall enjoy legal capacity in Switzerland, if it so requests, and shall enjoy the same exemptions, immunities and privileges as the Organization itself.

2. Funds and foundations with or without separate legal status, administered under the auspices of the IRO and devoted to its official objectives, are given the benefit of the same exemptions, immunities and privileges as the Organization itself, with regard to their movable property.

Article 20. FORMER ARRANGEMENTS

In so far as they are not modified by the present Agreement, the *Modus vivendi* of 1921 and 1926 and the supplementary arrangements concluded between the Federal Political Department and the League of Nations shall continue to apply mutatis mutandis to the IRO.

Article 21. OBJECT OF THE IMMUNITIES AND WAIVING OF IMMUNITIES

1. The immunities provided for in the present Agreement in respect of officials of the IRO are not designed for the personal benefit of those officials but solely to ensure the free functioning of the IRO and the complete independence of its agents in all circumstances.

2. The Director-General of the IRO has the right and duty to waive the immunity of any official in any case in which he considers that such immunity would impede the course of justice and could be waived without prejudice to the interests of the IRO.

Article 22. PREVENTION OF ABUSES

The IRO shall co-operate at all times with the Swiss Authorities to facilitate the proper administration of justice, secure the observance of police regulations and prevent any abuse in connection with the privileges, immunities and facilities provided for in this Agreement.

Article 23. DISPUTES OF A PRIVATE NATURE

The IRO shall make provisions for appropriate methods of settlement of:
(a) disputes arising out of contracts and disputes of a private law character to which the IRO is a party;
(b) disputes involving an official of the IRO who by reason of his official position enjoys immunity, if such immunity has not been waived by the Director-General.

Article 24. NON-RESPONSIBILITY OF SWITZERLAND

Switzerland shall not incur by reason of the activity of the IRO on its territory any international responsibility for acts or omissions of the Organization or of its agents acting or abstaining from acting within the limits of their functions.

Article 25. SECURITY OF SWITZERLAND

1. Nothing in the present Agreement shall affect the right of the Swiss Federal Council to take the precautions necessary for the security of Switzerland.

2. If the Swiss Federal Council considers it necessary to apply the first paragraph of this article, it shall approach the IRO as rapidly as circumstances allow in order to determine by mutual agreement the measures necessary to protect the interests of the IRO.

3. The IRO shall collaborate with the Swiss authorities to avoid any prejudice to the security of Switzerland resulting from its activity.

Article 26. EXECUTION OF THE AGREEMENT BY SWITZERLAND

The Federal Political Department is entrusted with the execution by the Swiss Confederation of this Agreement and the Arrangement for its execution.

Article 27. JURISDICTION

1. Any divergence of opinion concerning the application or interpretation of this Agreement or the Arrangement for its execution which has not been settled by direct conversations between the parties may be submitted by either party to a tribunal of

three members, which shall be established on the coming into force of this Agreement.

2. The Swiss Federal Council and the IRO shall each choose one member of the tribunal.

3. The judges so appointed shall choose their president.

4. In the event of disagreement between the judges on the choice of president, the president shall be chosen by the President of the International Court of Justice at the request of the members of the tribunal.

5. The tribunal may be seized of an application by either party.

6. The tribunal shall determine its own procedure.

Article 28. COMING INTO FORCE

This Agreement shall come into force as soon as it has been approved by the Swiss Federal Council and the competent authority of the IRO.

Article 29. MODIFICATION OF THE AGREEMENT

1. This Agreement may be revised at the request of either party.

2. In this event, the two parties shall consult each other concerning the modifications to be made in its provisions.

3. If the negotiations do not result in an understanding within one year, the Agreement may be denounced by either party giving two years' notice.

Article 30. ARRANGEMENT FOR EXECUTION

The provisions of this Agreement are completed by the Arrangement for its execution.[1]

AGREED DEFINITION OF RESPONSIBILITIES BETWEEN THE CONTROL COMMISSION FOR GERMANY (BRITISH ELEMENT) AND THE IRO CONCERNING THE IRO OPERATION IN THE BRITISH ZONE OF GERMANY, EFFECTIVE FROM 1 JANUARY 1951[2]

This agreed definition of responsibilities between the Control Commission for Germany (British Element) and the IRO amends the original agreement between the CCG (BE) and PCIRO of 28 June 1947,[3] by providing for IRO's assumption of certain operating responsibilities hitherto performed by CCG (BE). Insofar as it is not amended by this statement, the former agreement remains effective.

1. *Operation*

(a) IRO will take over from Displaced Persons Branch the executive responsibilities previously exercised by that Branch with regard to the Repatriation and Resettlement Programme operation and camp administration.

(b) CCG will provide IRO with the installations necessary for this operation which

[1] Arrangement for the Execution of the Agreement (IRO/LEG/GOV/5, 29 Jan. 1949: original French).
[2] IRO/LEG/GOV/44, 13 Feb. 1951.
[3] See Annex to this document, p. 656.

will remain on the requisition of CCG. If overriding considerations necessitate the release of any of these installations, CCG will furnish suitable alternative installations if available. IRO will be given reasonable advance notice of any such change.

(c) IRO will not vacate any camp until the camp has been handed over to the CCG which, in any case, will take place within reasonable time after notification has been given.

(d) No camp may be allocated a basically new function without the consent of the CCG and in particular, no displaced persons except those originating from the British Zone may be directed to any camp other than those designated as Staging or Embarkation Centres, without the prior sanction of CCG.

(e) No person who is not within the Mandate of the IRO may be accommodated in the IRO administered camps without the prior sanction of the CCG.

(f) The IRO will be responsible for ensuring that all displaced persons in the Repatriation/Resettlement Camps who do not originate from the British Zone of Germany will be cleared from that Zone.

(g) The IRO will make detailed arrangements with the appropriate German Authorities for the placement of all displaced persons rejected for resettlement. The CCG will keep the IRO informed of policies agreed with the German Authorities for their reception.

(h) The IRO will arrange the detailed travel documentation direct with the Combined Travel Board or other appropriate Authority designated by CCG.

(i) The CCG will continue to provide road transport for the IRO operation in the British Zone of Germany in accordance with existing practice. Such transport will be restricted to load-carrying vehicles and ambulances. The IRO will make demands for vehicle requirements direct to Road Transport CCG (BE).

(j) The IRO will be responsible for making arrangements for all movements by rail in connection with the IRO operation in the British Zone direct with the Bundesbahn and Combined Repatriation Executive (CRX).

(k) The IRO will make detailed arrangements with Frontier Control CCG (BE) and the German Customs Authorities for the customs clearance of all baggage and personal belongings of displaced persons leaving the British Zone of Germany on repatriation or resettlement.

(l) The IRO will be responsible for all medical and dental care, treatment, sanitation and general public health in IRO administered camps. The IRO agrees to observe the German Public Health Regulations. The IRO may arrange direct with the local German Authorities for the admission of displaced persons to German hospitals for any treatment, tests, examinations, etc., when necessary. The IRO will ensure that full advantage is taken of the Krankenkasse benefits to which many displaced persons are entitled. Payment of approved charges accruing will be effected through Displaced Persons Branch. IRO may liaise with the German Medical Authorities on matters affecting resettlement medical examination of displaced persons outside the IRO camps, and may request any medical information if required.

(m) Fixed establishments for DP/German labour will be provided by the CCG and the IRO shall not vary these establishments without the CCG approval. Engagements and dismissals within establishment may be settled direct with local authorities under the normal German regulations.

(n) Displaced Persons Branch is the agency of the High Commissioner's Office appointed to coordinate all matters appertaining to displaced persons and refugees. The normal channel of communication between the IRO and the Office of the UK High Commissioner will therefore be Displaced Persons Branch. On routine matters the IRO may deal direct with the appropriate CCG authority, DP Branch being kept informed of the scope of the negotiations. (Nothing herein stated limits in any way the right of the Chief of Mission of IRO to direct access to the UK High Commissioner.)

2. *Administration*

(*a*) The IRO will be responsible for the distribution of food supplies in camps which will be indented for through the appropriate German Land Food Ministry in accordance with the procedures laid down by the CCG.

(*b*) The CCG will hand over on charge to the IRO accommodation stores and equipment, the property of CCG for the running of IRO administered camps. The IRO will take appropriate measures for their safe custody, for their accounting and for their ultimate return. Stores will not be moved from camp to camp without prior approval of CCG.

(*c*) IRO and/or CCG may be held liable to make good to each other, any loss or damage to (excluding fair wear and tear), or misappropriation of, supplies, stores or accommodation, which is proved to have been caused by the lack of due care or the wilful misconduct of their officials.

(*d*) The CCG will procure and provide supplies to IRO camps on agreed scales. The IRO will be responsible for the correct distribution of these supplies including medical supplies in IRO administered camps. (As a general principle, not more than one month's supply will be held in camps.) An accounting system will be maintained and all accounts subject to inspection and audit by CCG. IRO owned property in CCG warehouses will likewise be accounted for by CCG and be subject to audit, inspection and disposal by the IRO.

(*e*) The IRO will be responsible for normal running repairs and works services in IRO administered camps with materials supplied by Displaced Persons Branch at fixed scales.

(*f*) The use of gas, water and electricity in IRO administered camps will be in accordance with permitted scales of consumption. IRO camp administrators will certify bills before presentation to CCG for payment.

(*g*) With the exception of displaced persons in the process of repatriation/resettlement, only those persons actively engaged in the programme of resettlement/repatriation and entitled to Category 1 facilities, may be permitted to use accommodation within the camps.

(*h*) The IRO Camp Administrator may establish relations with local German Authorities or private individuals as necessary to further the good administration of individual camps. All interested German authorities will be assisted to carry out their functions within camps in an appropriate manner.

3. *Finance*

CCG will obtain from the Federal German Government an adequate Deutschemark budget for the continued support of the IRO operation in the British Zone of Germany. Expenditure against this budget will be for the provision of essential basic indigenous supplies and services without charge to IRO Control of expenditure against this budget will be vested in CCG, and IRO agrees that CCG has the right to examine such expenditures against the budget to ensure that maximums are not exceeded and that expenditures are in accordance with agreed policies and scales.

4. *Procedures*

CCG (BE) and IRO will, during the transfer period, agree on the measures necessary to effect the changes in operational responsibility outlined in the preceding paragraphs.

ANNEX

AGREEMENT BETWEEN THE IRO AND THE CONTROL COMMISSION FOR GERMANY (CCG) WITH RESPECT TO IRO OPERATIONS IN THE BRITISH ZONE OF GERMANY, EFFECTIVE 1 JULY 1947[1]

Article I. OBJECT

The object of this agreement is to define the relative functions and responsibilities of IRO and the CCG.

CCG and IRO agree that it is their common objective in accordance with the principles of the Constitution of IRO, to effect as soon as possible the repatriation, or the resettlement in other countries, of displaced persons and refugees now in the British Zone of Germany. Their actions in matters relating to the care and maintenance of such persons pending their repatriation or resettlement will be directed towards the achievement of this objective.

Article II. PERSONS TO WHOM THIS AGREEMENT RELATES

1. This agreement relates only to all persons eligible for the care and assistance of IRO under its Constitution.

2. The IRO shall be responsible for determining eligibility under the IRO Constitution (IRO shall keep CCG informed as to the methods and machinery it establishes for this purpose).

3. IRO recognises that it is the function of CCG to adjudicate in cases of suspected war criminals, traitors and quislings who may thus be ineligible for IRO assistance. IRO has the right to make representations in such cases.

4. IRO agrees that CCG may take such action as it may deem appropriate, including the arrest, deportation or prevention of entry into camps of any persons whom it has good reason to regard as illegal entrants to the Zone. The CCG in turn recognises that it is the obligation of IRO to make such representations as it deems necessary on behalf of bona fide refugees and displaced persons in order to fulfil its responsibilities under its Constitution.

5. The CCG will be responsible for taking such action as may be necessary in order to prevent persons whom the IRO has determined to be ineligible from receiving assistance from the IRO. For this purpose, the CCG will be responsible for removing from camps and assembly centres maintained on behalf of IRO such persons as the IRO may determine to be ineligible.

Article III. RELATIONSHIP BETWEEN IRO AND CCG

1. The IRO will operate in the British Zone of Germany in accordance with the general laws and Military Government ordinances applicable throughout the Zone, and recognises that the Commander-in-Chief has sovereign authority in the Zone and full and complete responsibilities over law, order and all aspects of security, including the entry and continued presence in the Zone of IRO staff.

2. Under the provisions of Article 2, paragraph 2 (*d*) of its Constitution, IRO agrees to entrust to CCG the execution of IRO policy in regard to the material care and maintenance of displaced persons and refugees pending their repatriation or re-

[1] The Agreement between PCIRO and the Allied Commission for Austria (British Element), concluded 7 Nov. 1947, was in content and most of its wording identical with the Agreement for the British Zone of Germany, with the exception of the financial arrangements. Article XI provided for a separate Agreement to determine the financial responsibility of the PCIRO. (PC/LEG/5, 7 Nov. 1947.)

settlement, including the operation of camps and assembly centres, under the supervision of IRO.

3. CCG will put into effect the policies decided on by resolution of Preparatory Commission or the General Council of IRO as contained in the instructions of the Director General in regard to material care and maintenance to the greatest extent possible having regard to the over-riding requirements of law, order and security and practical difficulties in regard to the provisions of accommodation, transport, food and other supplies.

4. Consultation will take place in regard to the implementation of IRO policies in regard to displaced persons and refugees at all appropriate levels. In particular consultation shall take place between the Zone Director of IRO and the representatives of the C-in-C with a view to agreement on respective instructions to be issued for the effective implementation of such policies in harmony with the general requirements of the government and economy of the Zone. The Zone Director, IRO, has the right of personal access to the C-in-C to make representations where he deems it necessary.

5. IRO may maintain a staff in the Zone, subject to Article VIII below. The IRO staff can supervise at every appropriate level the execution of IRO policy by CCG with regard to material care and maintenance, subject to the over-riding needs of the maintenance of law, order, security and public health.

6. Should it be agreed that IRO requires to maintain a staff or to employ personnel also in the British Sector of Berlin, the words 'in the British Zone' used in this agreement shall be deemed to include the British Sector of Berlin.

Article IV. RESPONSIBILITIES OF IRO

IRO shall be responsible for:

1. The supervision of the care and maintenance of displaced persons and refugees in accordance with Article III;

2. The determination of eligibility under the IRO Constitution in accordance with Article II;

3. Classification of displaced persons and refugees, in close cooperation with CCG and with a view to the issue to them of appropriate document to show that such classification has taken place;

4. Measures to be taken in cooperation with CCG for the encouragement and organisation of repatriation. IRO representatives shall have access to, and maintain close touch with, the National Liaison Officers and Repatriation Missions accredited to the C-in-C and for this purpose will work in cooperation with the Allied Liaison Branch of CCG;

5. The arrangements, subject to general control by the C-in-C in the interests of law, order and security, whereby the national liaison officers and repatriation missions may give information to displaced persons and refugees about the conditions existing in countries of nationality or former habitual residence;

6. Resettlement, including the selection and preparation of displaced persons and refugees for resettlement, negotiations with representatives and Governments of countries of eventual reception and notification to CCG of arrangements required for movement;

7. Providing, where required, Staff to accompany repatriation or resettlement convoys;

8. Schemes for rehabilitation and special training with a view to eventual repatriation or resettlement;

9. Plans for the benefit of unaccompanied children, for the reuniting of separated families and for the alleviation of other similar cases of individual distress. Such

plans will be formulated solely in the humanitarian interests of the persons concerned, and without regard to considerations of a political nature;

10. Protection of the legitimate interests of stateless displaced persons and refugees and of those who do not enjoy the protection of their Government of nationality and of such other persons as may be agreed upon;

11. Providing means of transport for its staff;

12. Notifying CCG of its requirements for German Labour with a view to the recruitment of Germans through the appropriate machinery subject to the approval of CCG of the numbers and categories involved.

Article V. RESPONSIBILITIES OF CCG

CCG shall be responsible for:

1. The maintenance of law, order and security, including the enforcement of administrative ordinances and regulations in the Zone;

2. Putting into effect the policies of IRO in accordance with Article III;

3. The provision and distribution of food, clothing, accommodation and other necessaries, including necessary amenity supplies for displaced persons and refugees in accordance with the standards laid down by IRO insofar as this may be practicable and within the resources made available to CCG;

4. The control and operation of all camps and assembly centres;

5. Providing IRO personnel with free access to all displaced persons and refugees;

6. Public Health, medical and dental care and hospital facilities;

7. Provision of religious and educational services and facilities;

8. The implementation, on request by IRO and where practicable, of plans prepared by IRO in connection with their responsibilities under Article IV;

9. Ensuring the employment to the maximum extent possible of displaced persons and refugees, pending their eventual repatriation or resettlement;

10. Keeping IRO informed regarding the development of CCG's employment policy and considering any representations or proposals put forward by IRO in this connection;

11. Cooperation with IRO in the execution of plans for repatriation and resettlement, including provision and control of internal movement in Germany;

12. Providing, where necessary, guards to escort repatriation and resettlement convoys within the British Zone;

13. Arranging for the issue of exit permits to refugees being resettled and permitting the movement out of the Zone of refugees and displaced persons being repatriated or resettled;

14. Taking such action as may be necessary or appropriate in accordance with Article II in regard to displaced persons and refugees who are determined by IRO to be ineligible for assistance or who are deemed to be illegal entrants into the Zone.

Article VI. FACILITIES AND SERVICES TO BE PROVIDED FOR IRO BY CCG

CCG shall:

1. Make arrangements whereby IRO shall not be liable for any charge arising from expenditure incurred by IRO in German currency in accordance with arrangements to be agreed;

2. Arrange for the payment of refugees or displaced persons officially employed by IRO in the British Zone of Germany;

3. Arrange for the payment of Germans officially employed by IRO in the British Zone of Germany;

4. Provide adequate heated and lighted office and living accommodation free of charge for the staff of IRO employed in the British Zone on the same scales as those in force for the staff of CCG, subject to agreement with the C-in-C in regard to numbers to be accommodated and their location;

5. Provide on repayment petrol, oil and lubricants for official vehicles held by IRO;

6. Arrange for the repair of official vehicles subject to repayment of costs incurred in currency other than Reichsmarks. CCG shall, therefore, make use as far as possible of German resources for which no reimbursement shall be required;

7. Provide on repayment for members of the staff of IRO, rations on the same scales as are in force for CCG, and NAAFI supplies on the same basis as provided to UNRRA personnel up to the 30th June, 1947.

8. Permit the use by the staff of IRO, of CCG clubs and messes and of cultural and recreational facilities on the same terms as CCG personnel;

9. Permit the use of CCG communications systems for IRO official communications. Internal communications will be free of charge. External communications will be subject to repayment;

10. Provide for the staff of IRO the same facilities for personal mail as are available to civilian personnel of CCG;

11. Provide without charge to IRO rail and transport facilities within the British Zone of Germany for IRO personnel on official business. For leave purposes such facilities will be provided on repayment on a similar basis as for personnel of the British Authorities;

12. Provide for IRO staff and their families, on repayment, medical and dental facilities, subject to the same conditions as for CCG personnel;

13. Provide, on repayment, accommodation and facilities for families of IRO personnel on the same scale and subject to the same conditions and priorities as for CCG personnel;

14. Consult with IRO regarding the distribution of UNRRA equipment in accordance with Article X;

15. Process claims for damages against IRO or its personnel arising out of the execution of their official duties.

Article VII. FINANCE

1. CCG shall provide from indigenous resources without charge to IRO basic supplies (including food, fuel, clothing, and agreed scale of personal necessaries, medical supplies and accommodation stores, such as furniture, bedding and household equipment) for use at places where displaced persons and refugees are living under control of CCG and for incentive rations for repatriates, for the maintenance of displaced persons and refugees up to the same level, and with the same composition, as are provided from indigenous resources on the average for general distribution to the German population of the Combined Areas of Occupation.

2. IRO shall make payment or an allowance deductible from contribution due from HMG in UK, in accordance with the decisions to be reached under Article X (2) of the IRO Constitution, of a sum based on a per capita assessment of the cost incurred by CCG in respect of the care and maintenance of eligible displaced persons and refugees, which shall include the cost of imported supplies, the cost of the staff necessary for the administration and the cost of necessary administrative services incurred in currencies other than Reichsmarks.

3. For the period commencing 1st July 1947, and until such time as it is revised by Agreement, the per capita assessment shall be fixed at 20 cents (US) per person per day. (The figure of 20 cents relates to maintenance at the existing level of

consumption by Germans in Germany and shall be deemed attributable to sterling expenditure the equivalent of 6 cents and to expenditure of 14 cents in US dollars.) Negotiations for a revision may be initiated by either party at any time on a change of circumstances such as an alteration in the level or composition of the rations supplies, a substantial alteration in the number of eligible persons in the British Zone, changes in prices or other relevant factors.

4. The per capita assessment shall not include any sum in respect of the cost of services carried out by voluntary societies in the British Zone which may be subject of a separate agreement under Article IX.

5. IRO shall make separate payment for amenity supplies (i.e. those additional to basic supplies referred to in para 1 above) provided by CCG.

6. The provision of maintenance above the existing level of consumption by Germans in Germany shall, in so far as it is supplied by procurement within Germany, be deemed to constitute a (dollar) export from the German economy, and IRO shall make payment or an allowance deductible from contributions.

7. The IRO shall not be called upon to make any payment therefore or reimbursement in respect of any item which is not either specially stated by this agreement or subsequently agreed to be subject to payment of reimbursement.

8. A subsidiary agreement shall be made between the IRO Zone Director and CCG covering the technical method of implementing this agreement.

9. It is agreed that paragraph 3 and 6 of this Article involve no commitment as to the currency in which payment shall be made. This must finally depend on the decision reached under Article X of the IRO Constitution and on the agreed method of use of the contribution of HMG in the UK. It is, however, also agreed that in considering action under Article X of the IRO Constitution IRO will take account of the dollar liabilities referred to in paragraph 3 and 6 which HMG will be incurring on its behalf and to the extent that contributions by governments to the IRO and other dollar liabilities will permit IRO will endeavour to make reimbursement in dollars for the dollar liabilities incurred on its behalf by HMG.

Article VIII. CONDITIONS RELATING TO IRO PERSONNEL

1. (a) IRO personnel will be subject to Control Council Law, Military Government Law and such Routine Orders and Instructions issued by Military Government as are applicable to Civilian Members of the Control Commission. IRO personnel will be subject to the jurisdiction of Control Commission Courts in respect of offences committed by them in the British Zone or the British Sector of the Greater Berlin Area.

(b) Each member of IRO entering the British Zone or the British Sector of the Greater Berlin Area shall sign a certificate that he or she acknowledges to be bound by the terms contained in Article VIII Section (1) (a) herein.

2. IRO personnel, other than Displaced Persons and Refugees and Ex-enemy nationals, shall have the same legal status and immunities as civilian personnel of CCG.

3. Displaced Persons and Refugees employed by IRO shall be subject to the same Courts as other UN nationals who have no official relation with the occupation authorities.

4. IRO personnel shall be subject to the same financial regulations as are applicable to the civilian personnel of the CCG.

5. IRO agrees that the number of IRO personnel employed in the Zone shall be the minimum consistent with the efficient discharge of its functions.

6. Appointments of senior IRO personnel to posts of responsibility in the British Zone, shall be made in consultation with CCG.

Article IX. AGREEMENT WITH VOLUNTARY SOCIETIES

IRO and CCG shall be jointly associated in tripartite agreements to be reached with voluntary societies in regard to activities to be undertaken by the societies in connection with eligible displaced persons and refugees pending their repatriation or resettlement and in regard to the provision of any amenities supplied, or to be supplied, to displaced persons or refugees by such societies.

Article X. TRANSFER OF UNRRA EQUIPMENT

1. IRO and CCG shall consult together with a view to agreeing as to the distribution between them of equipment (including captured enemy equipment, vehicles and administrative supplies) to be transferred by UNRRA, having regard to their respective responsibilities under this Agreement.

2. Any equipment owned by or appertaining to one party which under paragraph 1 above is made available to the other party shall be lent free of charge.

Article XI. DURATION AND REVIEW

This Agreement shall come into force on the 1st July, 1947, and remain in force for a period of six months. After the expiry of that period it will be subject to termination on three months' notice given by either party. Discussions for the purpose of reviewing these provisions may be undertaken at any time at the request of either party.

This Agreement shall be interpreted in accordance with English Law.

AGREEMENT BETWEEN THE IRO AND THE COMMANDER-IN-CHIEF, EUROPEAN COMMAND, AS TO IRO'S OPERATION IN THE US AREA OF CONTROL IN GERMANY, 28 JULY 1948[1]

Section I. PREAMBLE

1. IN RECOGNITION OF AND SUBJECT TO:

   a. the responsibility of the IRO in regard to refugees and displaced persons (hereinafter termed 'refugees') in the US area of control in Germany as provided by its Constitution;

   b. the supreme authority of the Commander-in-Chief, European Command, as the Occupation Authority, and his responsibility for the maintenance of law order, security and the economy in the US area of control;

   c. the practical situation, and with the object of relieving, to the maximum extent practicable the occupation authority from support or participation in the refugee program in that area,

   THE FOLLOWING AGREEMENT IS MADE between the Commander-in-Chief, European Command, US Army (hereinafter referred to as CINCEUR) and the Director General of the International Refugee Organization (hereinafter referred to as IRO).

Section II. OBJECT

2. The object of this agreement is to:

   a. continue IRO on an operating basis in the US area of control in Germany; and

   b. continue the relationship between the IRO and the US occupation authority and to define their respective responsibilities for refugees.

[1] PC/LEG/29, 21 Aug. 1948. This Agreement was effective from 1 Jan. 1948 and supersedes the Agreement contained in Document PC/LEG/13.

Section III. GENERAL

3. IRO will carry out its activities as authorized and required by its Constitution subject to the terms of this agreement. It will operate in accordance with military regulations, military government enactments and general laws in force in the US area of control, but will not be subject to specific military or military government direction in regard to its routine activities, except as provided in paragraph 1. *b.*

4. Subject to provisions of paragraph 1, IRO will establish such offices and bring into the US area of control such personnel as it may require. CINCEUR will retain his authority to control for security purposes the entry of such personnel, including voluntary societies and their personnel and their continued presence in the area.

5. *a.* Reference to IRO and IRO personnel will, subject to provisions of paragraph 1, and where the context permits, include voluntary agencies, repatriation and resettlement agencies or missions and their personnel where such agencies are operating under the auspices of IRO.

b. The term IRO as used herein shall include the PCIRO except as used in paragraph 13. *a.*

6. IRO will not be responsible for refugees for whom CINCEUR accepts specific responsibility under any intergovernmental arrangements.

7. Liaison will be maintained at each appropriate level of operation by the IRO and the occupation authority.

Section IV. RESPONSIBILITIES OF IRO

8. IRO will be responsible subject to the terms of this agreement for:

a. the carrying out of the functions laid down in its Constitution with respect to all eligible refugees in the US area of control whether or not they are in assembly centers;

b. the operation of assembly centers in the US area of control. Within assembly centers IRO will provide care and maintenance to refugees in accordance with standards agreed to between IRO and CINCEUR, and will be responsible for the control and the administration of such assembly centers. However, assembly center care will be limited to those refugees contemplated in and specifically authorized under the provisions of cable directive No. SX–4301, Headquarters, European Command, dated 21 April 1947 as amended by SX–5696, dated 19 June 1947 and SX–5885, dated 26 June 1947 (Annexes II, III, and IV to this agreement);

c. the refugees determined eligible under the definitions contained in Annex I to the Constitution of the IRO, which definitions are attached as Annex I to this agreement. In this agreement the term 'refugees' shall be read as meaning a 'refugee' or 'displaced person' as defined in such definition;

d. the coordination and supervision of the activities of all voluntary societies working with refugees determined eligible for IRO assistance in the area and will make agreements subject to approval of CINCEUR, with such voluntary societies wishing to undertake work in connection with the refugee program. In addition, and as agreed with IRO, CINCEUR may make direct agreements or arrangements with the American Red Cross and with other voluntary societies working with refugees;

e. determination of the persons who are the concern of IRO under Annex I to the IRO Constitution, and the establishment and operation of procedures for such determination. IRO will keep the Occupation Authority informed regarding such procedures and their operation;

f. the maintenance, in conformity with its general reporting procedures, of statistical records of refugees under its care. Reports will be submitted to CINCEUR in the form to be agreed upon;

g. providing or arranging for medical care for refugees within assembly centers and operating established IRO refugee hospitals and facilities; (See also para. 9. *g.*)

h. arranging for appropriate contacts with refugees by special civilian or military repatriation representatives of the countries of origin of the refugees, authorized by CINCEUR to perform functions limited to activities in respect to voluntary repatriation. Subject to security and to the availability of facilities, CINCEUR will authorize the entry and continued presence of such representatives in the occupied area;

i. arranging, in coordination with CRX, subject to the provisions of paragraph 9. *b* for repatriation movements in accordance with a procedure to be agreed with the appropriate officer or officers of the occupation authority;

j. providing accompanying staff on repatriation transport where required;

k. negotiating with countries of resettlement and their representatives and with voluntary societies interested in resettlement with a view to arranging such resettlement IRO will keep CINCEUR currently informed of the progress of such agreements;

l. accrediting and administering representatives of voluntary societies, and arranging for appropriate contacts with refugees by governments of countries of resettlement authorized by CINCEUR to assist in programs of resettlement. Subject to security and the availability of facilities, CINCEUR will authorize the entry and continued presence of such representatives or missions in the US area of control;

m. arranging, in accordance with the same procedure as for repatriation transportation, transport within Germany for refugees being resettled;

n. providing accompanying staff on resettlement transport where required;

o. providing vehicles for all motor transportation requirements; (This does not affect provisions of paragraph 9. *j.* (1) Section V.)

p. developing, in cooperation with the occupation authority, an employment program to provide work opportunity for employable refugees to the end that, in accordance with its Constitution, IRO will not be concerned with refugees who are making no substantial effort towards earning their living where it is practicable for them to do so. To this end IRO will not employ indigenous personnel ineligible for IRO care and maintenance except in the case where technically qualified refugees are not available; further, IRO will cooperate with the occupation authority in providing workers required by it;

q. maintaining contact with refugees where their work results in their living away from assembly centers;

r. the operation of an inquiry and tracing service in and for the US area of control for determining the locations and conditions of displaced persons and refugees, including child search.

Section V. RESPONSIBILITIES OF THE OCCUPATION AUTHORITY WITH REGARD TO REFUGEES

9. The occupation authority will be responsible, subject to availability as determined by CINCEUR, for:

a. continuing to provide assembly center accommodations, to include fuel and the usual utilities (water, electricity, gas, sewage disposal etc.) for those refugees authorized such care by CINCEUR or admitted to such care under the provisions of paragraph 8. *b.* of this agreement. The cost of repair and maintenance of such installations will be furnished to the maximum extent practicable from the German economy. Only such cost which involves US appropriated funds will be subject to reimbursement by IRO in accordance with paragraph 11. The accommodations will be provided where practicable by the occupation authority in agreement with IRO with a view to making possible:

(1) suitable groupings of refugees in order to assist repatriation, resettlement and the proper administration of assembly centers,

(2) the provision of suitable work for refugees, when, as and if available, and

(3) consolidation of assembly centers so as to reduce administrative costs;

b. providing, without charge to IRO, necessary rail transportation within the US area of control for refugees being shifted, repatriated or resettled within or without such area of control. Movements outside the US area of control will be subject to reimbursement in accordance with paragraph 11, c. (6):

(1) Such transportation will be given appropriate priorities in order to facilitate the work of repatriation and resettlement,

(2) Where necessary, train guards for repatriation and resettlement movements will be provided by the occupation authority;

c. (1) providing, without charge to IRO, basic supplies, including food, fuel, clothing, medical supplies and accommodation stores such as furniture, bedding, and household equipment for use within assembly centers, and for the incentive rations for repatriates, from the German economy for the maintenance of refugees up to the same level and with the same composition as are provided on the average for general distribution for the combined German population of the US/UK areas of control from agriculture and other basic supplies available for such distribution in the US/UK areas of control from whatever source with the exception of items procured from US or UK appropriated funds or other foreign exchange. Procurement within Germany above the German level will be chargeable to IRO as constituting a dollar export from the German economy. Articles manufactured from imports paid for with the proceeds of German exports will be available to IRO only through payment of the export value of the manufactured article. Further, provisions with respect to drawing supplies from the German economy are subject to approval of the Bi-Partite Board for the US/UK Zone. Modification of this agreement is subject to confirmation of the Bi-Partite Board;

(2) providing, subject to advance payment or reimbursement for expenditures of appropriated funds, in the manner provided in paragraph 11 and in accordance with procedures and schedules agreed upon, such additional basic supplies, from stocks including new procurement or from such stocks maintained by the occupation authority, as are required to bring the supplies and incentive rations indicated in (1), above, up to a level and a composition established by IRO within the limits of its available resources. IRO will be given every consideration as a purchaser of supplies allocated for export and US Army surplus property;

d. upon request by IRO, procuring and shipping to the US area of control in Germany, against reimbursement by IRO as provided in paragraph 11 of this agreement, such amenity and additional supplies as IRO may require for essential operations;

e. (1) overall maintenance of law, order, security and public health, but within assembly centers IRO will assist in discharging these responsibilities; in the execution of these responsibilities within assembly centers, the appropriate officers of the occupation authority and IRO will consult with each other and coordinate their activities;

(2) occupation authorities shall have such access to assembly centers as may be necessary in the exercise of their occupational missions;

(3) for the apprehension and appropriate disposition of wanted persons and witnesses and for check and search operations which will be carried out under current occupational authority policies and directives with due regard to the safety and preservation of IRO files and documents. IRO will provide any information available to it in order to assist in carrying out this responsibility;

f. in the event of an emergency which might be considered a threat to the security of the locality or the zone and upon request by IRO, removing from IRO assembly centers such persons as IRO may determine to be ineligible for IRO assistance and whom IRO cannot cause to be removed through use of the camp police. Those persons refusing to leave or who return without authority after expulsion will be subject to punishment according to law;

g. (1) requisitioning from local German resources facilities for medical care for IRO to provide refugees within assembly centers with a standard of care at least equal to that of the local German population;

(2) in consultation with IRO, the occupation authority will, wherever practicable, arrange for the provision of segregated medical facilities for refugees apart from Germans;

h. (1) employing the maximum number of refugees practicable and advisable on work for and under the control of the occupation authority;

(2) making arrangements in cooperation with IRO to protect the interests of refugees as to provision of work and to prevent in every practical way any discrimination against refugees who may be working under German supervision;

i. (1) requiring the payment of refugees employed by IRO on work in assembly centers or elsewhere by the Burgermeister or other appropriate German office subject to ceilings as to numbers, rates of pay, etc., to be established by CINCEUR in consultation with IRO;

(2) where it is necessary for IRO to employ Germans, as authorized in paragraph 8. *p*, their payment will be effected in the same manner;

j. (1) continuing to provide to IRO on loan US Army and indigenous property, including vehicles and administrative equipment which was on loan to UNRRA on 30 June 1947 and available unless and until an alternative arrangement is agreed between the occupation authority and IRO. Similarly, any facilities, supplies and equipment now provided without charge not within the scope of paragraph 9. *c* will continue to be provided to IRO without charge unless and until a new arrangement is agreed between them;

(2) IRO will be both responsible and accountable for all facilities and equipment loaned by CINCEUR;

k. arranging for the issuance of travel documents subject to inter-governmental and inter-zonal agreements and security, to refugees being resettled, and permitting the movement out of the US area of control in Germany of refugees being repatriated or resettled by IRO,

l. providing to IRO access to all pertinent unclassified files and records concerning refugees in the US area of control and giving IRO access to all pertinent unclassified information, statistical data and records which the occupation authority may have relevant to IRO operations.

Section VI. RESPONSIBILITIES OF THE OCCUPATION AUTHORITY FOR
PROVISION OF FACILITIES FOR IRO AND IRO PERSONNEL

10. The occupation authority will:

a. make arrangements whereby IRO will not be liable for any charge arising from previously agreed legitimate costs chargeable to the German economy;

b. (1) provide, without charge to IRO (except where chargeable against appropriated funds in accordance with para. 11) office accommodations, fuel and maintenance therefor at all levels;

(2) provide, without charge to IRO, such warehouses, garages and like facilities as may be required for storage of IRO property and supplies, together with necessary building maintenance (except where chargeable against appropriated funds);

c. (1) provide suitable living accommodations for IRO personnel including author-ized dependants in accordance with regulations and scales prescribed by CINCEUR for civilian occupation personnel of similar status. Payment must be made in US dollars. The term 'IRO personnel' as used in this agreement, is limited to US Allied and neutral employees of IRO and voluntary societies indicated in paragraphs 4 and 8. *d*, who hold valid IRO identity documents and who are paid wholly or in part in dollar backed currency;

(2) support IRO's requests of local Wohnungsamt for assignment of billets for displaced persons employed by IRO at installations remote from established assembly centers. Rent for these accommodations will be paid in Deutschmarks by the displaced persons concerned;

d. where possible, provide IRO personnel with access to occupation authority messes, subject to payment by individuals concerned, or provide bulk rations for sale to IRO units and IRO personnel subject to reimbursement in accordance with para-graph 11;

e. provide all IRO personnel with access to post exchanges, sales stores, laundry, dry cleaning and shoe repair installations, messes and recreational facilities on the same basis and subject to the same restrictions as those applicable to civilian employees, in like status, of the occupation authority;

f. provide to the extent practicable, necessary POL and spare parts for IRO vehicles, subject to advance payment of reimbursement by IRO in accordance with paragraph 11 for imported items and any items involving the expenditure of appropriated funds. To the extent practicable provision for spare parts and repair items will be from German sources;

g. provide garages and other maintenance facilities for IRO vehicles. Such main-tenance will, to the extent practicable, be provided from German sources. Where maintenance is provided to IRO from sources involving expenditures of appropriated funds such maintenance is chargeable against IRO reimbursement in accordance with paragraph 11;

h. without charge provide IRO with indigenous electrical (telephone, telegraph) and postal communications facilities for official use within the US area of control, together with appropriate priorities; such facilities will include telephone facilities at each assembly center and at all IRO offices and business installations. When communicating beyond the US area of control, IRO will comply with current regulations and tariffs as published concerning interzonal and international communications.

i. authorize the use of Army postal service facilities by IRO and IRO personnel subject to availability and to the rules and regulations prescribed by the occupation authority. Franking and free mail privileges will not be afforded IRO or IRO personnel through US Army signal and postal service facilities, nor to IRO personnel through the German telegraph, telephone or postal service facilities;

j. provide without charge to IRO rail transportation facilities within the US area of control for IRO personnel on official business. For leave purposes such facilities will be provided on the same basis as for civilian personnel of the occupation forces;

k. provide, against reimbursement on an agreed scale, medical, dental, hospital, and burial facilities for IRO personnel;

l. establish, in consultation with IRO, ceilings on numbers of IRO, voluntary Agency personnel and repatriation representatives permitted in the zone.

Section VII. FINANCE

11. *a.* No payment will be required for such German currency as might be expended by the occupation authority against an approved budget in accordance with para-graph 10. *a.*

b. Cash payments will be made in Germany by individuals or units for personal supplies or services. Payments for other supplies or services furnished to IRO in the theater may be made in Germany by agreement between CINCEUR and IRO or their designated representatives or by financial arrangements made between the US Government through the Department of State and IRO Headquarters, Geneva, or its designated representative.

c. (1) Both the occupation authority and IRO will maintain proper accounting records with respect to all supplies and services furnished to IRO in accordance with this agreement.

(2) Such records shall be in the form of invoices or receipts prepared at the time of the provision of the supplies or services. All such records shall specify both the quantity and the price of the supplies or service concerned, insofar as practical at time of delivery.

(3) The prices fixed in respect to such supplies shall include an agreed allowance to cover transport and accessorial charges.

(4) The exact form of accounting records and method of calculating price and additional charges shall be agreed between IRO and occupational authority, subject to approval by the Department of the Army.

(5) Voucher discrepancies will be adjusted by agreement between IRO and the occupation authority.

(6) IRO will relieve the occupation authority of any costs incurred in movements, referred to in paragraph 9. *b* of refugees and their effects outside the US area of control.

(7) IRO will purchase in advance or reimburse for bulk rations issued IRO units, under paragraph 10. *d.*

d. (1) Except as provided in paragraph 11. *b* above, advances or reimbursement will be made by IRO through the Department of State to the Department of the Army for administrative costs and all other expenses, involving appropriated funds, incurred by the Department of the Army in procurement and delivery of IRO supplies and/or services, facilities and equipment, to include:

(*a*) cost of merchandise, packing for shipment and handling in accordance with shipping instructions;

(*b*) inland freight (country of origin) storage, warehousing, handling, transfer, cartage, lighterage and loading, and other expenses necessary to deliver the goods at shipside at port of embarkation;

(*c*) overseas transportation to port of debarkation;

(*d*) applicable insurance costs, including Marine War Risk, etc.;

(*e*) such expenses involving appropriated military funds as may be incurred in the area of US control, including that cost involved in the delivery of supplies from the port of discharge to the point of final destination at assembly centers.

(2) (*a*) The form of accounting records to be maintained by the occupation authority for such procurement and the forms against which payment will be made shall be agreed at the time IRO requests the procurement of such supplies.

(*b*) The food supplies from German pooled resources (including both indigenous and imported) to IRO at approved assembly centers which is in excess of the indigenous availability level for non-self suppliers in the US/UK areas of control will be replaced by IRO in kind, landed in Germany as per 11. *d.* (1).

Section VIII. STATUS

12. *a.* IRO personnel are subject to Military Government Law and Courts for offences committed by them in the US area of control. IRO and IRO personnel shall have in

general the same privileges and immunities as civilian employees of the occupation forces who are in the same status.

b. The occupying authority assumes no financial responsibility for risk, injuries or death occurring to IRO employees, nor for any claim arising against IRO or its employees or agents except in cases in which the occupying authority would be liable under existing regulations.

c. Refugees eligible for IRO assistance in the US area will have the same legal status and will be subject to the same courts as UN nationals who have no official relation with the occupation authority.

d. IRO will be responsible, in agreement with the occupation authority, for the legal and political protection of eligible refugees. IRO will be recognized as the appropriate authority to safeguard the legitimate interests of such eligible refugees as may request its assistance.

Section IX. PERIOD

13. *a.* This Agreement shall become retroactive to 1 January 1948 and shall remain in force until superseded by an agreement between CINCEUR and IRO, or terminated after 60 days written notice from either party to the other.

b. Discussions for the purpose of reviewing the provisions of this Agreement shall be undertaken at any time at the request of either party.

ANNEX

HQ US FORCES EUROPEAN THEATER: STAFF MESSAGE CONTROL: OUTGOING CLASSIFIED MESSAGE, 21 APRIL 1947

PRIORITY

To FOR ACTION: OMGUS for Berlin Command; First Military District; Second Military District; Headquarters Command EUCOM; Continental Base Section [and all military posts].

To FOR INFO: Director UNRRA US Zone, Heidelberg; Civil Affairs Div Opns Section, Heidelberg; OMGUS; USFA.

FROM: HQ European Command Sgd Huebner.

Subject: Denial of UNITED NATIONS care and treatment to new applicants after 21 April 47.

1. The following are interim instructions.

2. Admission to UN Displaced Persons Assembly Centers, as well as any other form of gratuitous US Army assistance, will be denied, to all persons who enter the US Zone of GERMANY or the US sector of BERLIN on or after 21 April 47. There will be no exceptions to this policy unless specifically directed by this headquarters.

3. Effective 21 April 47, UN Displaced Persons or assimilees, who are already resident outside of assembly centers in the US Zone of GERMANY and US sector BERLIN, will not be admitted to UN Displaced Persons Assembly Centers, except as follows:

A. When there is evidence of extreme hardship due to disease, injury, or other similar factors;

B. When there is evidence of inability of family wage earners to secure adequate employment;

C. When they have been accepted by representatives of governments concerned for repatriation or resettlement, have received their exit permits when such permits are required, and have been otherwise cleared and are awaiting only transportation for out-shipment.

4. Persons falling into the categories of 3 A and 3 B above will be admitted to Displaced Persons Assembly Centers when they are otherwise eligible for UN Displaced Persons care and treatment and when local German welfare agencies are not able to provide care at a level at least equal to that given to Germans in similar circumstances.

5. UN Displaced Persons employed in Guard and Labor Service Units are considered to be in assembly centers. When released without prejudice, and otherwise eligible for UN Displaced Persons care and treatment, they will be transferred to UNRRA-operated centers.

6. Unaccompanied UN children discovered in the US Zone after effective date of this directive, for whom Displaced Persons care is desired, will be reported to this headquarters for decision as to disposition.

7. UN Displaced Persons already resident in approved assembly centers prior to 21 April 47, and who have been screened and found eligible, are not affected by this order. Pending further instructions, persons who leave assembly centers for the purpose of seeking employment in the German economy will not be considered to have lost their right to care in assembly centers. Persons quitting assembly centers for other reasons will be readmitted only upon the conditions cited in paragraphs 3 A and 3 B above, or as otherwise specifically directed by this headquarters.

8. Applications for admission will not be considered by individual assembly center directors. All such applications will be referred to existing control centers located at KASSEL, DARMSTADT, STUTTGART, REGENSBURG, MUNICH and will be passed upon in accordance with the foregoing provisions. (BERLIN Command will make necessary arrangements for receiving such applications.)

HQ EUROPEAN COMMAND: STAFF MESSAGE CONTROL: OUTGOING MESSAGE, 19 JUNE 1947

PRIORITY

To: OMGUS for Berlin Command [and all military posts].

FOR INFO: Director UNRRA US Zone, Heidelberg; OMGUS; USFA.

FROM: HQ European Command Sgd Heubner.

Reference ourad SX–4301 dated 21 April 47, subject: Denial of UN care and treatment to new applicants after 21 April 47.

1. Provisions of paragraph 5 of reference cable are extended to include bonafide dependants of guard and labor service company personnel when such dependants have been living outside assembly centers in order to be with their providers, and when they formerly lived and were registered in a UN DP Assembly Center in the US Area of Control.

2. Upon application, such persons will be processed for admission into UN DP Assembly Centers in accordance with paragraph 8 of reference cable.

HQ EUROPEAN COMMAND: STAFF MESSAGE CONTROL: OUTGOING MESSAGE, 26 JUNE 1947

PRIORITY

To: CG [and all military posts].

FOR INFO: OMGUS; USFA.

FROM: HQ European Command Sgd Huebner.

References: cable, this Headquarters, SX–4301, dated 21 April 47, subject: 'Denial of UN care and treatment to new applicants after 21 April 47', SX–5696, dated 19 June 47, same subject, and letter, this Headquarters, file AG 383.7 GSP–AGO, dated 19 June 47, subject: 'Discharge of Displaced Persons from organized Labor Service Units'.

1. Discharge orders issued to personnel discharged from Labor Service and Guard Units will henceforth carry 1 of 3 indorsements as follows:

A. Discharge *without* prejudice.

B. Discharged for the good of service.

C. Discharge with prejudice.

2. Reference paragraph 5 of reference cable SX–4301, personnel whose discharge orders are indorsed according to sub-paragraphs 1 A and B above will be considered without prejudice for purposes of admission to a UN DP Assembly Center.

3. Personnel discharged with the indorsement as per sub-paragraph 1 C above will not be considered as eligible for admission to a UN DP Assembly Center.

4. It is requested that all Admission Control Centers be promptly advised of the foregoing provisions.

AGREEMENT BETWEEN THE US HIGH COMMISSIONER FOR AUSTRIA AND THE PCIRO, 11 AUGUST 1948[1]

Section I

1. *Preamble.* In view of and subject to

(*a*) the mandate of the PCIRO with regard to displaced persons and refugees as provided in the IRO Constitution; and

(*b*) the authority of the US High Commissioner for Austria as the occupation authority and his responsibility for the maintenance of law and order in the US Zone, Austria, as hereinafter provided:

This agreement is made between the US High Commissioner for Austria (hereinafter referred to as 'the US High Commissioner') and the Preparatory Commission for the International Refugee Organization (hereinafter referred to as 'PCIRO') with respect to the activities of PCIRO in the US Zone, Austria and US Vienna Area (both hereinafter referred to as 'the US Zone').

2. *Purpose*

The object of this agreement is to define the respective functions of the US High Commissioner and PCIRO with respect to refugees in the US Zone of Austria.

---

[1] PC/LEG/31, 24 Aug. 1948. This Agreement supersedes the Agreement contained in document MPC/17.

3. *Persons to whom this Agreement relates*

(*a*) As used in this agreement, the term 'refugees' refers to displaced persons and refugees eligible for assistance by PCIRO under the provisions of Annex I to the IRO Constitution.

(*b*) PCIRO agrees to perform the functions hereinafter provided for assistance to refugees (whether inside or outside assembly centers) who have been admitted by PCIRO for its assistance. Such admission will be subject to the financial limitations of PCIRO; and PCIRO's financial undertakings with respect to refugees will have effect from the date of their admission by PCIRO.

(1) PCIRO will, at any time after the date this agreement becomes effective, cease to assist any person found by it to be ineligible under the provisions of Annex I to the IRO Constitution; and will notify the US High Commissioner of such findings.

(2) PCIRO may at any time admit for its assistance persons in the US Zone who are determined to be eligible. This provision does not, however, authorize PCIRO or any affiliated agency to transfer refugees into the US Zone without prior approval of the US High Commissioner.

4. *General Provisions*

(*a*) PCIRO will comply with applicable military regulations and Civil Affairs laws.

(*b*) PCIRO will establish a central office at Vienna, and appropriate subordinate offices in each Area Command in the US Zone of Austria.

(*c*) The central and subordinate offices will maintain close liaison with the US High Commissioner through Staff and Liaison Officers designated by the US High Commissioner, in matters affecting the administration of PCIRO personnel and the performance of programs of assistance to refugees.

(*d*) Reference in this agreement to PCIRO and PCIRO personnel will include voluntary societies and their personnel for whom PCIRO accepts administrative responsibility in accordance with paragraph 5 (*c*), unless the context clearly indicates otherwise. PCIRO will provide the US High Commissioner with current lists of such societies.

Section II. FUNCTIONS OF PCIRO

5. PCIRO will, within the limits of its constitutional power and available resources, perform functions authorized in the IRO Constitution relating to the care, maintenance, repatriation and resettlement of refugees in the US Zone, and the determination of their eligibility, subject to the authority of the US High Commissioner, as provided in paragraph 1 (*b*), including, but not limited to, the following specific functions:

(*a*) Administrative control of PCIRO personnel, who will be subject to security clearance by the US High Commissioner.

(*b*) The administration of assembly centers, camps, hospitals, and other aggregations of refugees (all hereinafter referred to as 'assembly centers') including but not limited to the following functions:

(1) The provision of administrative, supply, welfare and medical personnel.

(2) Determining eligibility and admissibility for PCIRO assistance, whether inside or outside assembly centers.

(3) Allocation and distribution of refugees within and between assembly centers, except that refugees will not be transferred by PCIRO individually or in groups into the US Zone without prior approval of the US High Commissioner and will

not be distributed or allocated within or between assembly centers in such a manner as to require additional facilities in such centers without prior approval of the US High Commissioner.

(4) Appointment and supervision of watchmen, fire fighting squads and internal police within assembly centers.

(c) The co-ordination, supervision and servicing of all voluntary societies or other national or international societies engaged in work among refugees, and of their personnel, and the distribution of the material resources of these societies, all in accordance with the provisions of agreements concluded between PCIRO and the societies concerned. PCIRO will request the US High Commissioner to permit entry of the personnel of these societies into the US Zone, subject to security restrictions prescribed in paragraph 6 (f) (3), and will make recommendations to the US High Commissioner concerning the numbers of their personnel required in US Zone.

(d) Take all possible measures to encourage and facilitate the repatriation of refugees, including arrangements for contacts with refugees by national liaison officers and repatriation missions.

(e) Assist to the greatest extent possible and as rapidly as possible with the resettlement and re-establishment of refugees; and facilitate the work of resettlement missions from countries of resettlement.

(f) Assist with the rehabilitation and vocational training of refugees with a view to facilitating their repatriation and resettlement, their re-establishment in Austria to the extent acceptable to the Austrian Government, and the interim employment in Austria of refugees who will ultimately leave Austria.

(g) Arrange for appropriate contacts with refugees by representatives of foreign governments authorized by the US High Commissioner to perform activities in respect to voluntary repatriation or resettlement of refugees, subject to security restrictions and authorizations prescribed in paragraph 6 (f) (4).

(h) Re-unite families, alleviate other cases of individual distress, and give priority assistance to unaccompanied children.

(i) Render legal and other appropriate protection to refugees as provided by the IRO Constitution, subject to the provisions of paragraph 9.

(j) The development and implementation of a program of maximum employment of refugees in suitable work under applicable labor laws and regulations, having due regard to protection of their interests under the IRO Constitution. This provision will not be construed to deny any refugee the opportunity for repatriation or resettlement when such opportunity exists. The procedure in effect in US Zone on 1 July 1947 (as contained in Letter, USFA Headquarters, AG 383.7 AGA/V, dated 31 August 1946, 'Charge for Food and Lodging Furnished Displaced Persons', as amended) covering payment by refugees employed in the Austrian economy direct to the Austrian Land Government for food and lodging furnished in assembly centers will be continued in effect.

(k) Obtain clearance for the transport of refugees, from the US High Commissioner, when such movements originate or terminate within or pass through the US Zone.

(l) Provide the US High Commissioner with statistical data on names, numbers and location of refugees as requested, but PCIRO is obligated to furnish such data only to the extent that it is compiled for or by IRO.

(m) Provide for the care, maintenance, repatriation and resettlement of unaccompanied children, in accordance with the IRO Constitution.

(n) Maintain ration levels for refugees in assembly centers at the level and of the composition established for Austrian consumers in similar categories, as mutually agreed by PCIRO and the Austrian Government, without prejudice, however, to the provision by PCIRO of supplementary rations in accordance with levels established by PCIRO for special categories of refugees such as tubercular patients and children.

Section III. RESPONSIBILITIES OF THE US HIGH COMMISSIONER

6. To the extent practicable, the US High Commissioner will:

(a) Designate a staff section in Headquarters, USFA and subordinate commands with which PCIRO will maintain contact.

(b) Take the following law and order measures:

(1) Restore law and order in assembly centers, using Austrian police or US troops, if disturbances occur which develop beyond the capabilities of PCIRO to control.

(2) Assist PCIRO if necessary in removing from assembly centers persons ineligible for PCIRO assistance.

(3) Take such action as the US High Commissioner deems necessary to enforce compliance with Civil Affairs law, having due regard to the safety and preservation of official PCIRO archives and documents.

(c) Take appropriate measures to facilitate the prompt compliance by PCIRO and the Austrian Government with the terms of the understanding arrived at in the exchange of letters as follows: Letter from PCIRO to the Federal Chancellor, dated 29 April 1948, file 99/2/AUS, signed by the Executive Secretary W. Hallam Tuck and the replies thereto of the Federal Chancellor, date 3 June 1948, file 113. 845–Pol/48 and 25 June 1948, file ZI. 114. 588–Pol/48 insofar as the provisions of these letters pertain to the US Zone.

(d) Authorize the issuance by PCIRO of identification papers to refugees based on their PCIRO classification, and the issuance by PCIRO of documents to organized groups of refugees being resettled, and permit the movement out of the US Zone of refugees being repatriated or resettled by PCIRO, after clearance as provided in paragraph 5 (k).

(e) Furnish such access as is practicable to files and records to USFA, to aid in determining eligibility of refugees for PCIRO assistance, provided military security is not involved.

(f) Accredit personnel to Headquarters, USFA as follows:

(1) Personnel of PCIRO stationed for work in the US Zone will be accredited to Headquarters, USFA within thirty days from the signing of this agreement, provided such members meet the requirements for accreditation of Headquarters, USFA. Replacement personnel for PCIRO will be accredited to Headquarters, USFA, subject to the above provisions, as soon as practicable after their arrival in the US Zone.

(2) PCIRO personnel who are not stationed in the US Zone but whose work requires visits to the Zone may be accredited to Headquarters, USFA, at any time for the period necessary to accomplish their mission.

(3) The US High Commissioner will permit the personnel of voluntary societies requested by PCIRO for work among refugees to enter the US Zone in reasonable numbers, and without expense to the United States subject to security restrictions prescribed by the US High Commissioner and, if eligible, will accredit them to Headquarters, USFA.

(4) Upon the request of foreign governments to USFA Headquarters, the US High Commissioner will, subject to security and availability of facilities, and as he deems it advisable and necessary, accredit and authorize the entry and presence in the US Zone of repatriation and resettlement missions.

7. PCIRO personnel, including personnel of voluntary societies operating under the

co-ordination of PCIRO as provided in paragraph 5 (*c*), will be subject to Civil Affairs laws and courts for offences committed by them in the US Zone. PCIRO and its internationally recruited personnel accredited to Headquarters, USFA, shall have the immunities and privileges in legal matters of civilian United Nations nationals employed by the US Government. This provision may be modified by mutual agreement in accordance with action taken under Article 13 of the IRO Constitution.

8. Refugees in the US Zone eligible for PCIRO assistance will have such legal status and will be subject to the jurisdiction of such courts as may be prescribed in directives issued by the US High Commissioner.

9. PCIRO is recognized as the appropriate agency to provide legal and political protection to refugees except that the US High Commissioner shall remain the sole authority to decide on matters involving the extradition or removal of refugees from the US Zone.

10. Personal services, supplies and facilities will be made available to PCIRO and PCIRO personnel in accordance with provisions of current directives of Headquarters, USFA.

Section IV. FINANCE

11. PCIRO agrees to guarantee that neither the US Government nor the US High Commissioner will be financially responsible for risk, injury or death occurring to PCIRO employees or for any claim arising against PCIRO, its staff, or agents, except to the extent Military authorities may be liable under existing regulations.

Section V

12. (*a*) This Agreement becomes effective as of 11 August 1948 and shall remain in force until 31 December 1948. This Agreement may be extended for six months periods by mutual consent of the parties concerned.

(*b*) When the IRO is established under the terms of the IRO Constitution it may, upon notice to the US High Commissioner, take the place of PCIRO as a Party to this Agreement.

APPENDIX II (*c*)

AGREEMENTS WITH RESETTLEMENT COUNTRIES

IRO/LEG/GOV/10 25 Mar. 1949	Agreements concerning the re-establishment of refugees concluded between the IGCR and Governments.	
IRO/LEG/GOV/10/Add. 1 25 Mar. 1949	Addendum to above.[1]	
	Subject	*Countries*
IRO/LEG/GOV/10/Add. 1	Resettlement in Belgium of displaced persons from the US zone of Germany.	Belgium/Occupation Authorities, US zone of Germany
IRO/LEG/GOV/10/Add. 1	Resettlement in Belgium of displaced persons and refugees from the British zone of Germany, 13 February 1947.	Belgium; Great Britain

[1] On 1 July 1947 the functions of the Intergovernmental Committee on Refugees were made the responsibility of the successor organization (PCIRO), and a number of agreements which had previously been concluded between the IGCR and the governments of various countries of resettlement continued to serve informally as a basis for the re-establishment of refugees in these countries. IRO, wherever possible, continued the resettlement of refugees into the countries concerned within the general framework of these agreements, subject to developments and changes in procedure which arose in practice.

	Subject	Countries
PC/LEG/19	Immigration of refugees.	Bolivia
PC/LEG/24	Immigration of refugees.	Brazil
IRO/LEG/GOV/10/Add. 1	Immigration of refugees, 7 February 1947.	Chile
PC/LEG/23	Immigration of refugees.	Columbia
PC/LEG/25	Immigration of refugees.	Ecuador
IRO/LEG/GOV/10/Add. 1	Resettlement in the Netherlands of displaced persons from the US zone of Germany.	Netherlands
PC/LEG/18	Immigration of refugees.	Peru
IRO/LEG/GOV/10/Add. 1	Immigration scheme to Tunisia, 9 December 1946.	Tunisia
PC/LEG/22	Immigration of refugees.	Venezuela

PC/LEG/14 16 Feb. 1948	Agreement between the Australian Government and the PCIRO regarding immigration into Australia of refugees and displaced persons, concluded 21 July 1947 (text).
PC/LEG/27 21 Jun. 1948	Agreement (administrative) between the PCIRO and the Government of Brazil, concluded 30 April 1948.
PC/LEG/28 25 Jun. 1948	Agreement between the Government of the Turkish Republic and the PCIRO relative to the immigration of displaced persons into Turkey, signed 24 June 1948.
IRO/LEG/47 1 May 1951	Administrative agreement between the Government of Brazil and IRO, signed 23 February 1951.
IRO/LEG/GOV/32 2 May 1950	Agreement (exchange of letters) between the Government of Ethiopia and the IRO concerning the resettlement in Ethiopia of refugees and displaced persons within the mandate of the IRO, March 1950.
IRO/LEG/GOV/8 14 Mar. 1949	Agreement (exchange of letters) between the Government of Guatemala and the PCIRO concerning the resettlement in Guatemala of refugees and displaced persons within the mandate of the IRO, concluded 6 September 1948.
IRO/LEG/GOV/22 1 Nov. 1949	Agreement between the Government of Israel and IRO concerning permanent provision in Israel for institutional care of refugees, signed 28 October 1949 (text).
IRO/LEG/GOV/16 30 Jun. 1949	Agreement between the 'Banco Del Paraguay' and the IRO, 12 May 1949.

AGREEMENT BETWEEN THE GOVERNMENT OF THE COMMONWEALTH OF AUSTRALIA AND THE PCIRO, CONCLUDED 21 JULY 1947[1]

The Government of the Commonwealth of Australia (hereinafter referred to as the Commonwealth) and the Preparatory Commission of the International Refugee Organization (hereinafter referred to as PCIRO) have agreed as follows regarding

[1] PC/LEG/14, 16 Feb. 1948.

immigration into Australia of Refugees and Displaced Persons within the Meaning of the Resolution adopted by the Economic and Social Council of the United Nations on 16 February 1946.

1. *Number and types of Immigrants*

(*a*) The Commonwealth will from time to time submit to PCIRO (at Geneva) particulars of the numbers and qualifications of desired immigrants. The first of these lists will be submitted within 30 days after the approval of the Agreement.

(*b*) The Commonwealth estimates that during the balance of 1947 the number of workers and dependants desired will approximate a total of 4000 persons.

2. *Selection of Immigrants*

(*a*) The Commonwealth shall have the full right of selection by officers of the Department for Immigration of the Commonwealth and the Commonwealth will advise PCIRO from time to time of the names and functions of officers nominated for this purpose.

(*b*) The Commonwealth agrees that selection of immigrants will be carried out without discrimination as to race or religion.

(*c*) PCIRO will be responsible for instituting such preliminary selection procedure as may be required by the Commonwealth.

(*d*) PCIRO reserves the right to allocate the recruitment of immigrants for final selection by officers of the Commonwealth to the various Occupied Zones of Germany and Austria, and to the Middle East, Italy or elsewhere.

3. *Relatives and Dependants*

(*a*) Heads of family units selected may be accompanied by all members of their immediate family and by such other relatives as are dependent on the head of the family and who live with him. Other cases deserving special consideration from humanitarian standpoints will be examined individually by the Commonwealth.

(*b*) Any selected immigrant who goes to Australia unaccompanied by relatives or dependants shall, after three months' residence in Australia, have the right to nominate such relatives and dependants for admission, and the Commonwealth agrees to grant such admission providing the worth of the immigrant has been satisfactorily demonstrated and provided the immigrant is in a position to receive and support the dependants after their arrival in Australia.

4. *Transportation*

(*a*) All expenses incurred in moving selected immigrants to Australia shall be met by PCIRO, and PCIRO will also be responsible for providing the means of transport.

(*b*) The Commonwealth agrees to make an ex gratia payment to PCIRO of an amount of £10 per adult towards the extra cost incurred by PCIRO in moving immigrants to Australian ports as compared with the cost of moving them to South American ports.

5. *Reception and Placement*

The Commonwealth will advise PCIRO regarding the port(s) of disembarkation and accepts full responsibility for receiving, forwarding, and the settling or placing of immigrants in employment in Australia.

6. *Legal status*

(*a*) Immigrants to Australia become subject to all laws of the Commonwealth and of the state of residence.

(b) The Commonwealth guarantees to immigrants all rights and liberties granted by law to foreigners resident in Australia.

(c) The Commonwealth agrees that immigrants may be granted Australian citizenship in accordance with the provisions of the laws of the Commonwealth.

7. Legal and Political Protection

The legal and political protection of immigrants after their arrival in Australia will be assumed by PCIRO acting under the provisions of the Constitution of the International Refugee Organization in such matters.

8. Conditions of Employment

(a) The Commonwealth will provide regular employment for all persons coming under this Agreement. It requires that workers agree to remain at least one year in the employment accepted.

(b) Immigrants will, after their arrival in Australia, enjoy exactly the same living conditions and wages as Australian workers performing similar work and will be treated in exactly the same manner and without discrimination in the case of unemployment. They will be allowed to join trade unions in the same manner as Australian citizens.

9. Conditions of Entry

(a) The Commonwealth agrees to issue visas and entry permits without cost to the immigrants or to PCIRO.

(b) The Commonwealth agrees to admit to Australia, duty free, all the personal belongings (including tools of trade) of selected immigrants and dependants.

10. Resident Representative

The Commonwealth agrees to the appointment by PCIRO of a resident representative in Australia.

AGREEMENT BETWEEN THE GOVERNMENT OF ISRAEL AND THE IRO CONCERNING PERMANENT PROVISION IN ISRAEL FOR INSTITUTIONAL CARE OF REFUGEES, SIGNED 28 OCTOBER 1949[1]

WHEREAS it is the policy of the IRO, in order to bring about a rapid and positive solution of the problem of those refugees and displaced persons who require permanent assistance such as institutional care, to put into execution plans for the future provision to be made for each category of such persons; and

Whereas the Government of Israel has consistently pursued a broad policy of accepting for immigration on its territory large numbers of refugees and displaced persons who are in need, without discrimination as to the economic or medical requirements of such cases, and has already placed under institutional care a high proportion of immigrant refugees and displaced persons who were under the mandate of the IRO; and

Whereas the Government of Israel has developed an extensive programme for the immediate expansion of its now over-taxed institutions and facilities for the permanent care of such handicapped cases in order to make possible the continued admission to its territory of those who are in need; and

Whereas the Director-General of the IRO was instructed by the General Council of the IRO in its Resolution No. 39 to formulate plans, in co-operation with the

[1] IRO/LEG/GOV/22, 1 Nov. 1949.

governments concerned, to further the permanent provision for institutional cases among handicapped refugees and displaced persons; and

Whereas the Government of Israel and the IRO have established principles, by an Exchange of Letters between the Foreign Minister dated 1 July 1949 and the Director-General dated 18 July 1949, concerning the equitable allocation of funds budgeted by the Organization for permanent provision for refugees and displaced persons requiring institutional care;

the GOVERNMENT OF ISRAEL and the IRO hereby agree as follows:

1. The Government of Israel agrees to carry out forthwith a programme for the construction and establishment of projects and facilities to provide for the permanent care of handicapped refugees and displaced persons under the mandate of the IRO, and agrees to establish initially the following institutions for the following numbers of such persons received in Israel during the period 1 July 1949 to 30 June 1950:

   (a) for the tubercular, with an approximate capacity of 800 persons;
   (b) for the chronically ill, with a capacity of 300 persons;
   (c) for the mentally ill, with a capacity of 100 persons;
   (d) for the aged, with a capacity of 200 persons;
   (e) for invalids, with a capacity of 200 persons.

2. In addition to the above numbers of institutional cases, the Government agrees to admit for permanent resettlement in Israel during the period 1 July 1949 to 30 June 1950 the families and dependants of all such persons admitted in accordance with paragraph 1.

3. In recognition of the substantial contribution thus made by the Government of Israel to the solution of the international problem of refugees and displaced persons under the mandate of the IRO, the Organization agrees to make an initial financial contribution towards a just proportion of the capital investment costs of this programme, in implementation of the principles established by the Exchange of Letters of 1 July and 18 July 1949 and within the funds available to the Organization under the allocations made by the General Council for such purposes. Payments will be effected in the following order:

   (a) the sum of $2,000,000 in US dollars at the rate of
      (i) $1,000,000 in the course of November 1949,
      (ii) $500,000 in the course of December 1949, and
      (iii) $500,000 in the course of January, 1950;
   (b) the sum of $500,000 in other currencies to be agreed between the parties, taking into account both the currencies available to the Organization and the funding needs of the Government.

4. The Government agrees to keep the Organization informed both of the nature and the extent of the facilities developed in accordance with paragraph 1 and of the numbers of persons within the mandate of the IRO admitted into Israel and into institutions under the terms of paragraphs 1 and 2.

5. The Organization agrees to consider with the Government, within the terms and spirit of the Exchange of Letters, further allocations of IRO funds against the capital expenditures under paragraph 1 to the extent that proves feasible within the remaining funds budgeted for the purpose. Any such discussions will take into consideration the scope and requirements of the similar obligations and expenditures of the Organization for institutional cases to be resettled or re-established in other countries.

6. The Organization likewise agrees to discuss with the Government, within the framework of this Agreement, any further projects for permanent provision for institutional cases which the Government may wish to submit in accordance with the possibilities of its immigration programme.

APPENDIX II (d)

AGREEMENTS WITH VOLUNTARY SOCIETIES

PC/CM/4 15 Apr. 1948 Corr. 1, 12 May 1948	Agreement between the PCIRO and the Ukrainian Canadian Relief Committee and United Ukrainian American Relief Committee, Inc. Exchange of letters, October 1947 (Germany and Austria).
PC/CM/7 15 Apr. 1948 Corr. 1, 12 May 1948	Agreement between War Relief Services–National Catholic Welfare Conference and the PCIRO. Exchange of letters, November 1947 (Germany, Austria, and Italy).
PC/CM/8 15 Apr. 1948	Agreement between the Boy Scouts International Bureau and the PCIRO. Exchange of letters, February 1948 (Germany and Austria).
PC/CM/9 15 Apr. 1948 Corr. 1, 12 May 1948	Agreement between the American Friends Service Committee and the PCIRO. Exchange of letters, February 1948 (Germany).
PC/CM/11 15 Apr. 1948 Corr. 1, 12 May 1948	Agreement between the Lutheran World Federation and the PCIRO. Exchange of letters, December 1947.
PC/CM/13 Corr. 1	Agreement between the American Polish War Relief of the US of America and the PCIRO. Exchange of letters, November 1947 (Germany, Austria and Italy).
PC/CM/14 15 Apr. 1948	Agreement between the Church World Service, Inc., and the PCIRO. Exchange of letters, December 1947 (Germany and Austria).
PC/CM/15 15 Apr. 1948	Agreement between the International Rescue and Relief Committee, Inc., and the PCIRO, December 1947.
PC/CM/17 2 Mar. 1948	Agreement between the American Joint Distribution Committee and the PCIRO, February 1948.
PC/CM/18	Agreement between the Unitarian Service Committee and the PCIRO, February 1948 (Germany).
PC/CM/19 3 Mar. 1948	Agreement between the World Council of Churches and the PCIRO, December 1947.
IRO/CM/19. 1 28 Aug. 1948	Extension of above agreement to Italy, August 1948.
PC/CM/20 Mar. 1948	Agreement between the American National Committee to Aid homeless Armenians (Germany and Austria), February 1948.
PC/CM/21 4 Mar. 1948	Agreement between the Jewish Agency for Palestine and the PCIRO, December 1947.
PC/CM/22 4 Mar. 1948	Agreement between the Hebrew Immigrant Society and the PCIRO, February 1948.
PC/CM/25 4 Mar. 1948	Agreement between the Italian Red Cross and the PCIRO, December 1947 (Germany).
PC/CM/26 8 Mar. 1948	Agreement between the US Committee for the Care of European Children and the PCIRO, January 1948 (US zone of Germany and Austria).

PC/CM/27	Agreement between the World ORT Union and the PCIRO,
9 Mar. 1948	December 1947 (vocational training).
PC/CM/29	Resettlement Agreement between the IRRC, Inc., and the
12 May 1948	PCIRO (financing of individual migration), April 1948.
PC/CM/30	Agreement between the World's Alliance of Young Men's
7 Apr. 1948	Christian Associations and the PCIRO, December 1947
Corr. 1, 12 May 1948	(Germany and Austria).
PC/CM/31	Agreement between the Jewish Committees for Relief
7 Apr. 1948	Abroad and the PCIRO, November 1947 (Germany,
Corr. 1, 12 May 1948	Austria and Italy).
PC/CM/32	Agreement between the International Social Service and
24 May 1948	the PCIRO, May 1948 (Germany and Austria).
PC/CM/35	Agreement between the World Student Relief and the
10 July 1948	PCIRO, June 1948.
PC/CM/36	Agreement between the Polish Red Cross and the PCIRO,
23 July 1948	May 1948 (Germany and Austria).
PC/CM/37	Agreement between the United Lithuanian Relief Fund,
24 July 1948	Inc., and the PCIRO, July 1948 (Germany and Austria).
PC/CM/38	Agreement between the Netherlands Red Cross and the
10 Aug. 1948	PCIRO, July 1948 (child tracing in Germany).

APPENDIX II (e)

AGREEMENTS MADE DURING LIQUIDATION PERIOD—2 MARCH 1952 TO 30 SEPTEMBER 1953

WITH VOLUNTARY SOCIETIES

24 Oct. 1952	Lutheran World Federation—Trust Fund on behalf of residual refugees living in Germany, Austria, Italy, and Trieste.
24 Oct. 1952	International Social Service—Trust Fund on behalf of unaccompanied children in Germany, Austria, Italy, and Trieste.
24 Oct. 1952	World's Young Men's Christian Association and Young Women's Christian Associations (YMCA/YWCA)—Trust Fund on behalf of residual refugees in Germany, Austria, and Trieste.
5 June 1953	World Council of Churches—Trust Fund to provide financial assistance to residual refugees registered with IRO prior to 15 February 1952, and living in Ethiopia and countries of the Middle East.
24 Oct. 1952	World Council of Churches—Trust Fund to provide supplementary material aid to residual refugees registered with the IRO prior to 15 February 1952 living in Germany, Austria, Italy, and Trieste.
15 Jan. 1953	World Council of Churches—Trust Fund to provide supplementary material aid to residual refugees registered with the IRO prior to 15 February 1952 and living in Hong Kong and Shanghai.
23 Jan. 1953	WCC—Supplement to above, providing grants for permanent care of aged and other hard core IRO refugees.

24 Oct. 1952	World Council of Churches in conjunction with Refugee Service Committees in Greece and Turkey to provide supplementary material aid to residual refugees registered with IRO prior to 15 February 1952. Trust Fund.
9 June 1953	War Relief Services—National Catholic Welfare Conference. Trust Fund—residual refugees registered with IRO prior to 15 February 1952 living in Hong Kong, Shanghai, Austria, Middle East—permanent care of aged and other hard core cases.
15 June 1952	War Relief Services—National Catholic Welfare Conference, Trust Fund—additional medical services, medicines, and accessory items for refugees in Italy registered with IRO prior to 15 February 1952.
31 Oct. 1952	War Relief Services—National Catholic Welfare Conference. Trust Fund—residual refugees registered with IRO prior to 15 February 1952 with supplementary material aid, and living in Germany, Austria, Italy, and Trieste.
29 Oct. 1952	American Joint Distribution Committee—Trust Fund for residual refugees registered with IRO prior to 15 February 1952, living in Germany, Austria, and Italy, with supplementary material aid.
17 Feb. 1953	British Council for Aid to Refugees—Trust Fund for former IRO refugees resident in UK, supplementary material aid in the form of repayable loans, thus providing a revolving fund.
12 Jan. 1953	BCAR—Grant of 5,500 US dollars for 11 aged refugees.
25 Sept. 1952 15 June 1953	Escrow agreement: the Chase National Bank of the City of New York—Trust Fund for three years, regarding reimbursement of United States Federal Income Tax as amended for year 1951 under provisions of Section 321 (a) (2) of the Internal Revenue Act 1951. See Form No. 843. US Treasury Dept. Internal Revenue Service (Revised June 1951).
June 1951	Expellee Bank Corporation, Bonn. Special loan fund for Displaced Persons.

WITH GOVERNMENTS

17 Jan. 1953	France—The Association for the Settlement of Foreign Refugees, 'l'Association pour l'Établissement des Réfugiés Étrangers'. The Fund is to provide assistance through reimbursable loans to 'intellectual' refugees, i.e. physicians, lawyers, &c., living in France unable to find occupation.
23 Sept. 1952	Provisional Intergovernmental Committee for the Movement of Migrants from Europe (Intergovernmental Committee for European Migration, ICEM)—Trust Fund, for the movement of refugees who were registered with IRO at 15 February 1952.
10 June 1952	Italy—The State Secretariat for Foreign Affairs. Settlement of all internal rail charges to the Italian State Railways. Settlement of all

expenses relating to IRO operation of Bagnoli Camp. Remaining balance to go to Trust Fund with the AAI for permanent institutional care in Italy of 100 TB cases from Trieste. Settlement of external rail charges. Additional grant by IRO to provide Trust Fund for assistance to residual group of refugees in Trieste.

19 Aug. 1952   Germany—Claims outstanding for charges for transportation and care and maintenance of DPs from outside Germany and *Volksdeutsche* from within and without Germany. Agreement reached whereby the above claims would be waived and cancelled in consideration of the final settlement of the IRO Food Replacement Account.

18 Aug. 1952   Allied Military Government British–US Zone Free Territory of Trieste. Trust Fund for the resettlement from the Free Territory of Trieste of aged refugees registered with the IRO prior to 15 February 1952 or prima facie within the mandate of the IRO.

CUSTODY OF DOCUMENTS

20 Aug. 1953   Peat, Marwick, Mitchell & Co., 11 Ironmonger Lane, London. Chartered Accountants to the IRO.
> Hold Final Liquidation Account—copy of which is in Liquidation drawer.
> Also documents as per Agreement held in their files.

12 June 1953   Archives Nationales—All archives pertaining to the IRO. Not to be made available to the public for a period of 10 (ten) years from 1 July 1953. Agreement signed by Oliver E. Cound and Charles Braibant.

APPENDIX III

SELECTED RESOLUTIONS OF THE PCIRO, THE GENERAL COUNCIL, AND THE EXECUTIVE COMMITTEE

RESOLUTIONS ADOPTED BY THE PCIRO

First Session		*Resolutions*	
First Part	11–21 Feb. 1947	1–5	PREP/27
Second Part	1–21 May 1947	1–24	PREP/90/Rev. 1/Add. 1.
Third Part	15–25 July 1947	25–42	PREP/126/Rev. 1.
Fourth Part	21 Oct–1 Nov. 1947	43–55	PREP/154/Rev. 1.
Fifth Part	20–31 Jan. 1948	56–73	PREP/195/Rev. 1.
Sixth Part	4–12 May 1948	74–84	PREP/222/Rev. 1.
Seventh Part	10–11 Sept. 1948	85–91	PREP/240

RESOLUTIONS ADOPTED BY THE GENERAL COUNCIL

Resolutions

First Session	13–25 Sept. 1948	1–30	GC/55
Second Session	29 Mar.–8 Apr. 1949	31–38	GC/77/Rev. 1.
Third Session	28 June–8 July 1949	39–44	GC/98/Rev. 1.
Fourth Session	11–20 Oct. 1949	45–55	GC/135/Rev. 1.
Fifth Session	14–22 Mar. 1950	56–67	GC/163
Sixth Session	9–13 Oct. 1950	68–79	GC/194/Rev. 1.
Seventh Session	9–13 Apr. 1951	80–90	GC/224
Eighth Session	22–27 Oct. 1951	91–99	GC/251/Rev. 1.
Ninth Session	11–16 Feb. 1952	100–110	GC/276/Rev. 1.

RESOLUTIONS ADOPTED BY THE EXECUTIVE COMMITTEE

First Session to Tenth Session	Resolutions 1–11	EC/64
Eleventh Session	(6 Draft Resolutions only)	

A. SELECTED RESOLUTIONS[1] OF THE PCIRO

1. Formal acceptance of the PCIRO.
2. Measures to secure the signatures and acceptances necessary for the institution of IRO.
3. Assistance to refugees and displaced persons in Italy.
4. To provide initially for the Working Fund of PCIRO.
1. Implementation of paragraphs 3 and 6 of the agreement on interim measures.
2. Budget for the period up to 30 June 1947.
3. Relations between the Executive Secretary and the Preparatory Commission.
4. Composition of the Advisory Committee.
5. The budget of the IRO.
6. Personnel policy.
7. Plan of remuneration for staff members of the IRO.
8. Appeal to governments in connection with the screening of individuals or groups of individuals whose activities hinder repatriation.
9. Appeal to governments in connection with the placing in employment of displaced persons.
11. Appeal to governments in connection with resettlement.
16. Austria.
18. Legal and political protection.
19. Standards of living and care.
20. Relations with voluntary societies.
21. Relations with governments and/or occupation authorities in occupied areas.

---

[1] The texts of resolutions of a purely formal nature such as those taking note of reports of the Executive Secretary and Director-General are not reproduced here.

FIRST SESSION, FIRST PART, 11–21 February 1947: Resolutions 1–5[1]

1. FORMAL ACCEPTANCE OF THE MANDATE OF THE COMMISSION

THE PCIRO HAVING TAKEN COGNISANCE of the text of the Constitution of this Organization, and

HAVING CONSIDERED the terms of the 'Agreement on Interim Measures to be taken in respect of refugees and displaced persons', which was adopted by the General Assembly of the United Nations on the fifteenth day of December nineteen hundred and forty six

RESOLVES to register formally its acceptance of the mandate as defined in this Agreement, and accordingly to take all steps necessary to put into effect the mandate of the Preparatory Commission for the International Refugee Organization.

2. MEASURES TO SECURE THE SIGNATURES AND ACCEPTANCES NECESSARY FOR THE INSTITUTION OF THE INTERNATIONAL REFUGEE ORGANIZATION

THE PCIRO HAVING CONSIDERED the question of the measures required to secure the signatures and ratifications necessary for the institution of the IRO

HAS UNANIMOUSLY RESOLVED

(1) TO DIRECT its Secretary to transmit by telegraph the following resolution to the Secretary-General of the United Nations:

'THE PCIRO IMPRESSED with the urgent importance, both from the humanitarian and the political point of view, of securing an early final solution of the refugee problem and,

'BEING AWARE of the serious difficulties which will arise, directly or indirectly, for all countries, if the IRO is not constituted in time to take over the handling of this problem before June 30 next

'REQUESTS the Secretary-General of the United Nations to make an earnest and urgent appeal to all those countries which voted for the constitution of the IRO at the General Assembly of the United Nations on December 15th last as well as to those countries which either abstained from voting or voted against the adoption of the constitution to sign and ratify the constitution at the earliest possible moment and thus to help to bring this important international organization into effective operation in time to enable it to carry out the purpose which it is intended to fulfil';

(2) TO SUGGEST that the Secretary-General of the United Nations in addressing this appeal to member nations should emphasize to those nations which voted for the constitution on December 15th last that the fact of their having done so makes it particularly appropriate that they should now take the lead in helping to bring the constitution into force by signing and ratifying it at the earliest possible date, while to those nations which abstained from voting or voted against it, he might express the hope that they will nevertheless in the general interest reconsider their earlier attitude;

(3) TO RECOMMEND to the Governments represented at its present session that they should instruct their diplomatic representatives in the various countries approached by the Secretary-General in accordance with paragraphs (1) and (2) above jointly or separately to support the Secretary-General's appeal and to urge the countries concerned to sign and ratify the constitution of the IRO at the earliest possible moment. It also recommends that those Governments should support the appeal by all other means in their power;

(4) TO DIRECT the Executive Secretary, as soon as he shall have assumed his functions, to neglect no opportunity to induce the countries which have not yet signed the constitution of the IRO and also those who have not yet ratified it to do so at the earliest possible moment, bearing in mind that unless the constitution of the IRO can

[1] PREP/27, p. 19.

be brought into force in sufficient time to enable the IRO to enter effectively into its functions by June 30th next the purpose for which the constitution was devised will be seriously jeopardised.

3. Assistance to be given to Refugees and Displaced Persons in Italy

(1) The PCIRO impressed by the disquietening reports it has received as to the position and conditions in which the numerous refugees and displaced persons in Italy who will be eligible for IRO assistance are likely to find themselves on the coming into force of the Peace Treaty with Italy and the departure of Allied troops from that country,

suggests that the Secretary-General of the United Nations should draw the particular attention of the Governments concerned to the gravity of this problem and should urge them to take, with the assistance of UNRRA and IGC, all appropriate and necessary measures to deal with it pending the coming into operation of the IRO.

(2) The preparatory commission further urges UNRRA and the IGC to ensure as far as possible the continuance of such care and maintenance as is at present being extended to a number of these persons until such time as the IRO is in a position to assume responsibility for them.

(3) The preparatory commission also directs its Executive Secretary to proceed in consultation with the Governments and the organizations concerned, to study this problem with a view to making recommendations designed to enable the IRO to assume responsibility for those refugees and displaced persons in Italy who fall within its mandate as soon as it comes into operation.

4. To Provide Initially for the Working Fund of the Preparatory Commission

The PCIRO recalling the interest which the United Nations has shown in the establishment of an International Refugee Organization, demonstrated by Resolution of the General Assembly on February 12, 1946, and December 15, 1946, and by Resolutions of the Economic and Social Council during its first three sessions,

recalling that the General Assembly authorized the Secretary-General of the United Nations 'to advance loans to certain specialized agencies repayable within two years, for the purpose of financing their initial operations, up to such amounts as may seem necessary and appropriate, having regard to the proposed financial resources of the agency concerned, provided that the concurrence of the Advisory Committee shall be required for loans aggregating more than $2,000,000 (United States), or in excess of $1,000,000 (United States) for any one agency,' and,

considering the serious social and political consequences which would follow any failure to complete without interruption or delay the work which the Preparatory Commission has initiated

resolves to transmit to the Secretary-General of the United Nations the following cable:

'The following message was unanimously approved by the Preparatory Commission at its session on February 19:

' "The Preparatory Commission for the International Refugee Organization has now begun its work and has taken steps to initiate the necessary measures to provide for its accomplishment.

' "The question whether this work is to be completed or is to be abandoned, now depends on whether the necessary funds can be secured to enable the Preparatory Commission to continue its operations and the Executive Secretary to be appointed and to undertake his task forthwith.

' "Although the expenditure involved will be very small in comparison with the expenditure hitherto incurred in preparing for a solution of the refugee problem and in comparison with the expenditure contemplated in the work of the International Refugee Organization itself, there are serious constitutional and practical difficulties in securing from the Governments concerned independent advances against their eventual contributions to the IRO.

' "In the opinion of the Preparatory Commission the only way in which the necessary funds can be secured is by means of an advance from the Working Capital Fund of the United Nations, as was done in the case of the Interim Commission of the World Health Organization and in accordance with the provisions of paragraph (c) of the Working Capital Fund Resolution adopted by the General Assembly on 14 December 1946.

' "The Preparatory Commission recognizes that no legal obligation falls on the Secretary-General to provide these funds and that the matter is entirely within his discretion.

' "It wishes, however, to point out that, if these funds are not available, the Preparatory Commission will be obliged to disperse, it will be impossible for it to appoint an Executive Secretary or for such an officer to undertake the functions incumbent on him, the prospects of the coming into operations of the IRO will be seriously jeopardised and may have to be altogether abandoned, the work on the refugee problem carried out during the past year will be wasted, and the grave social and political dangers which have long been foreseen if the refugee problem is not rapidly and satisfactorily solved will at once come about, with consequences the extent of which cannot be foreseen.

' "Moreover, the Preparatory Commission feels strongly that if the funds required to enable the Preparatory Commission to continue in existence and to accomplish its task are not made available, the United Nations will have failed in the first operational task which has been imposed on it or on any of its organs. The Preparatory Commission considers that such a failure would be gravely detrimental to the prestige and standing of the United Nations.

' "In these circumstances, the Preparatory Commission most earnestly appeals to the Secretary-General of the United Nations to hold at its disposal as an advance from the Working Capital Fund of the United Nations a sum not exceeding in all two hundred and fifty thousand United States dollars, in order to enable the Preparatory Commission to continue its work during the next four months and the Executive Secretary to undertake the task assigned to him with the least possible delay. The Preparatory Commission further urges the Secretary-General to make available to the Preparatory Commission and to the Executive Secretary accommodation in the United Nations building at Geneva sufficient to enable them to carry out their functions and to put at the disposal of the Executive Secretary such staff and such other technical assistance as may in the opinion of the Commission or of its Executive Secretary be essential for the accomplishment of this aim." ' '

(Signed) HENRI PONSOT
Chairman of the Preparatory Commission.

FIRST SESSION, SECOND PART,[1] 1–12 May 1947: Resolutions 1–24

1. THE IMPLEMENTATION OF PARAGRAPHS 3 AND 6 OF THE AGREEMENT ON INTERIM MEASURES

THE PREPARATORY COMMISSION HAVING CONSIDERED the status of signatories to the Constitution of the IRO and the Agreement on Interim Measures as adopted by

[1] PREP/90/Rev. 1/Add. 1.

Resolution of the General Assembly of the United Nations on 15 December 1946, and

BEING CONFIDENT that the necessary signatures and acceptances to enable the Constitution to come into force in accordance with the provisions of Article 18 will be forthcoming, but

BEARING IN MIND the possibility that the necessary acceptances may not be available in time to enable the IRO to come into existence by 1 July 1947 and the necessity of avoiding any breach in the continuity of operations, since it has been advised that UNRRA and the IGC will be obliged to terminate their activities on 30 June 1947, and

BEING SATISFIED that the taking over as from 1 July 1947 of certain functions, activities, assets and personnel of certain existing organizations dealing with refugees and displaced persons by the Preparatory Commission is essential in order to accomplish the orderly transfer to the IRO of such functions and activities,

RESOLVES:

1. to take over, as contemplated by paragraph 3 of the Agreement on Interim Measures as from 1 July 1947 such functions, activities, assets and personnel of certain existing organizations dealing with refugees and displaced persons as are considered to be essential in order to accomplish the orderly transfer to the IRO of such functions and activities, subject to the provisions laid down in the Resolutions of the Preparatory Commission;

2. to request that Governments, members of the Preparatory Commission should make contributions as contemplated by paragraph 6 of the Agreement on Interim Measures in order to finance the operations, as from 1 July 1947, of the Preparatory Commission until such time as the IRO is formerly constituted, which advances shall be deductible from their first contributions to the IRO;

3. to request that the appropriate constitutional organs of UNRRA and the IGC consider, as a matter of urgency, whether those organizations will have surplus funds available on 30 June 1947 which they would agree to transfer to the Preparatory Commission in order to help finance its operations and, if such funds are available, that they take the necessary steps to transfer them to the Preparatory Commission.

3. RELATIONS BETWEEN THE EXECUTIVE SECRETARY AND THE PREPARATORY COMMISSION

THE PREPARATORY COMMISSION RESOLVES

1. Subject to paragraph 2 below:

(a) to direct the Executive Secretary to conclude, in conformity with the Constitution and with the Resolutions adopted by the Preparatory Commission, agreements with certain existing organizations dealing with refugees and displaced persons in order to provide for the taking over of such of their functions, activities, assets and personnel as may seem desirable, as contemplated by paragraph 3 of the Agreement on Interim Measures;

(b) to authorise the Executive Secretary generally to exercise, in conformity with the Constitution and with the Resolutions adopted by the Preparatory Commission, the powers of the Director General and in particular to enter into agreements with governments and occupation authorities and to make such other agreements and commitments as may be necessary in order to accomplish a smooth transfer of functions and activities or to carry out the provisions of the Constitution and of the Resolutions adopted by the Preparatory Commission;

2. (a) to establish an elected advisory committee to meet at the call of the Chairman during the interval between meetings of the Preparatory Commission, and

(b) to direct the Executive Secretary to submit to such committee for its advice and subsequent report to the Preparatory Commission his plans for the organization of the IRO and his appointments of senior members of his staff.

4. The Composition of the Advisory Committee Established by the Preparatory Commission

THE PREPARATORY COMMISSION RESOLVES

1. that the Advisory Committee shall consist of representatives of Belgium, Canada, China, France, Netherlands, United Kingdom and United States of America;

2. that the Chairman of the Preparatory Commission, the representative of France, shall act as Chairman of the Advisory Committee;

3. that four members, including the Chairman, shall constitute a quorum of the Advisory Committee.

5. The Budget of the IRO

THE PREPARATORY COMMISSION HAVING REGARD to the grave effect of any failure to ensure the immediate assumption on 1 July 1947 by the Preparatory Commission of the responsibilities which it has taken upon itself under the Resolution on the implementation of paragraphs 3 and 6 of the Agreement on Interim Measures (document PREP/65) and

BEARING IN MIND

(a) the necessity to enable the Executive Secretary to implement the powers conferred on him under document PREP/74 which are necessary to secure the take-over without interruption of functions from the existing Organizations, and

(b) the need for the distribution of funds to banks before 1 July 1947 to meet operational requirements on or immediately after that date

RESOLVES

1. to authorise the Executive Secretary to make commitments against anticipated advance contributions in accordance with the 75% plan of expenditure set forth in document PREP/44 subject to necessary modifications as provided for in paragraph 2 of this Resolution;

2. to authorise the Executive Secretary to transfer by written order funds between sections within the administrative budget and to increase any section in the operational budget by not more than 25% by transfers from other sections, and to require him to report to the Preparatory Commission all such transfers together with a written explanation of each;

3. to direct the Executive Secretary to report to the next Session of the Preparatory Commission the details of advance contributions referred to in paragraph 1 above, and the expenditure and commitments made against them, together with a forecast of future expenditure within the budget as approved in the Constitution.

4. to direct the Executive Secretary, on behalf of the Preparatory Commission, in its operative capacity, to approach the Secretary General of the United Nations with a view to obtaining a further advance as required to cover the Executive Secretary's immediate needs.

6. Personnel Policy

THE PREPARATORY COMMISSION CONSIDERING that the IRO is a new organization and that its budget should be drawn up with paramount concern for economy;

that its main tasks should be repatriation and resettlement and that the greater part of its funds should be used for those purposes;

that the staff employed in the new organization should be thoroughly acquainted with the problem of refugees and displaced persons and should, above all, be efficient and devoted to their task;

RESOLVES

1. that the personnel of IRO should be recruited from the present staffs of UNRRA, IGC and the voluntary agencies, from candidates suggested by Governments, and from other sources;

2. that from 30 September 1947 the Executive Secretary should submit for its advice to the Advisory Committee referred to in the Resolution adopted by the Preparatory Commission on 14 May 1947 nominations for the Deputy Director-General and for the principal executive immediately subordinate to the Deputy Director-General or the heads of departments at headquarters and for heads of major operational organizations in the field. The Advisory Committee should provide its advice within one week. The extension of appointments beyond 30 September 1947 of persons appointed prior to this date shall be subject to this provision as from 30 September 1947;

3. that at the request of the Executive Secretary, Governments members of the Organization should, if possible, provide information regarding nominees for such posts which may serve as a guide for the Executive Secretary for making nominations:

RECOMMENDS TO THE GENERAL COUNCIL that the Personnel Regulations to be adopted by the General Council should embody the above principles.

7. PLAN OF REMUNERATION FOR STAFF MEMBERS OF THE INTERNATIONAL REFUGEE ORGANIZATION

THE PREPARATORY COMMISSION RECOMMENDS as a guide to the Executive Secretary in the development of a salary plan, the following principles:

1. that subject to the limited financial resources of the International Refugee Organization, the remuneration of the staff members should be such as to attract qualified candidates and ensure recruitment on an appropriate geographical basis. The compensation plans used by the United Kingdom Government for home and overseas duty should be given particular consideration. Supplementary payments may also be required for the recruitment of personnel from countries where prevailing salary scales substantially exceed the basic salary scale eventually adopted by the Organization. This basic salary scale should reflect the desirability of equal pay for equal work;

2. that a system of local allowances or other method of reflecting differences in costs of living in countries of employment and displacement expenses may be required;

3. that a substantial contribution by the Organization to a Provident Fund may be required in order to reflect the non-permanent character of the employment, and

4. that consideration should be given to the effect on the remuneration of staff members of the Organization of the applicable income tax regulations.

8. APPEAL TO GOVERNMENTS IN CONNECTION WITH THE SCREENING OF INDIVIDUALS OR GROUPS OF INDIVIDUALS WHOSE ACTIVITIES HINDER REPATRIATION[1]

THE PREPARATORY COMMISSION RESOLVES to direct the Executive Secretary to send the following message to the governments and authorities concerned:

'THE PCIRO IN PURSUANCE to the resolution adopted by the General Assembly of the United Nations on 15 December 1946 . . . RECOGNIZING the importance, in relation to repatriation, of the screening of all persons or groups who use duress or incite others to use duress with a view to preventing displaced persons from either expressing the desire to return to their homes or from getting into touch, orally or in writing, with the duly accredited representatives of the Government of the country of their nationality or former habitual residence:

[1] See Annex to Doc. PREP/83, paragraph 24.

'RECOGNIZING ALSO the importance of having such measures completed in the shortest possible time, so that the IRO may be in a position to ensure immediately and without hindrance the repatriation of displaced persons who wish to return to their countries of origin;

'EMPHASISING THAT THE COMPLETION OF SUCH MEASURES WOULD assist the IRO to avoid granting assistance to people who, according to its constitution, do not come within its competence;

'URGES the Government and authorities concerned to complete as soon as practicable the screening of the persons or groups of persons mentioned in the resolution adopted by the General Assembly of the United Nations on 15 December 1946 and referred to above.'

9. APPEAL TO GOVERNMENTS IN CONNECTION WITH THE PLACING IN EMPLOYMENT OF DISPLACED PERSONS

THE PREPARATORY COMMISSION RESOLVES to direct the Executive Secretary to send the following message to the governments and authorities concerned:

'THE PCIRO IN PURSUANCE of a decision taken at its Twenty-fifth Plenary Meeting held on 6 May 1947 at Ouchy, Lausanne, Switzerland,

'CONSIDERING that as regards displaced persons its main task is to encourage and assist in every way possible their early return to their countries of origin, or their resettlement in the countries likely to receive them;

'CONSIDERING ALSO that one of the most valuable means of promoting this repatriation or resettlement is to renew the capacity for work of the individuals and the skill which many of them may have lost;

'IMPRESSES on the governments and authorities concerned the need for the intensification of efforts for the placing in employment of displaced persons without delay.'

11. APPEAL TO GOVERNMENTS IN CONNECTION WITH RESETTLEMENT

THE PREPARATORY COMMISSION RECOGNIZING the urgent need for all governments, members of the United Nations, to adhere to the Constitution of the IRO in order that the international problem presented by the presence in Europe, the Middle East and the Far East of hundreds of thousands of refugees and displaced persons may be resolved in the shortest possible time

URGES those member governments of the United Nations which have not adhered to the Constitution to give immediate consideration to such adherence; and

INVITES such governments as may require further information concerning the obligations of membership in the IRO to request the Executive Secretary of the Preparatory Commission to supply such information, it being understood

1. that questions concerning the medium and manner in which contributions are to be paid are, under the terms of the Constitution of the IRO, to be resolved as a result of negotiations undertaken at the request of members between the Organization and such members; and

2. that the admission of refugees and displaced persons, as recommended by the General Assembly of the United Nations in its resolution of 15 December 1946, to territories of governments, whether members of the IRO or not, are matters of free negotiation between such governments and the Organization.

16. ON AUSTRIA

THE PCIRO HAVING EXAMINED AND DISCUSSED the report of the Executive Secretary on refugees and displaced persons in Austria (document PREP/47)

RESOLVES

1. to take note of the report, and

2. to instruct the Executive Secretary to make further studies on the question of the eligibility under the Constitution of the IRO of members of the various groups of so-called Volksdeutsche in Austria and to submit recommendations thereon to the Preparatory Commission at a later date.

18. LEGAL AND POLITICAL PROTECTION

THE PREPARATORY COMMISSION HAVING CONSIDERED the report of the Executive Secretary on Document PREP/41 relating to legal and political protection,

HAVING noted that Nansen refugees and refugees coming from Germany and Austria enjoy an international status laid down by various Intergovernmental arrangements and notably the Convention of 28 October 1933 and the Convention of 10 February 1938;

RESOLVES that the Executive Secretary be directed

1. to submit at the First Session of the General Council proposals concerning the modification of the terminology contained in Article 2 paragraph 1 of the IRO Constitution relating to protection with a view to facilitating an eventual amendment of the said Article of the Constitution according to the procedure laid down in Article 16;[1]

2. to take immediate measures as outlined in paragraphs 9, 10, 11 and 12 of document PREP/41 to ensure a smooth transfer without breach of continuity of the protective services at present entrusted to the IGO;

3. to secure, so far as possible, the extension of protective services to displaced persons and refugees in Germany and Austria under IRO mandate and to arrange, accordingly for the insertion of suitable clauses covering protective functions and the status of refugees, in any general agreements to be concluded between the Preparatory Commission/IRO and the Zone Commanders;

4. to secure, so far as possible, the extension of protective functions in Italy on assuming responsibilities now entrusted to IGC and UNRRA; and in particular the Executive Secretary is authorised to participate in the discussions on the agreement now being negotiated by IGC with the Italian Government with a view to IRO taking over such agreement; and to make suitable arrangements for the assumption by IRO of protective functions in respect of refugees and displaced persons under IRO mandate;

5. to pursue the consultations and surveys envisaged in paragraphs 15, 21, 22, 24, and 27 of document PREP/41, in order to facilitate the early assumption of protective functions by IRO in respect of other categories of refugees and displaced persons outside those mentioned in paragraphs 2, 3 and 4 of this Resolution.

19. STANDARDS OF LIVING AND CARE

THE PREPARATORY COMMISSION HAVING CONSIDERED Document PREP/34 and

BEARING IN MIND the necessity of establishing principles to guide the executive Secretary in preparing for the assumption of operational responsibility by the Preparatory Commission as from 1 July 1947

RESOLVES THAT

1. Document PREP/34 be accepted as information material.

2. The Executive Secretary should prepare, insofar as practicable and within the limits of the resources of the Preparatory Commission, for the assumption of operational responsibility as from 1 July 1947 for displaced persons and refugees falling within the mandate of the Constitution of the IRO and for whose maintenance the

[1] See Appendix I, p. 582.

Preparatory Commission will be responsible, in accordance with the following principles:

(*a*) The diet provided to displaced persons and refugees should not be lower than that of the local population. To the extent that the diet of the general population does not provide a minimum emergency standard of health, the Preparatory Commission should, taking into account climatic and other conditions, augment the diet of eligible displaced persons and refugees to the minimum emergency standards approved by medical and nutritional authorities. Particular consideration should be given to such special classes of displaced persons and refugees, as children, nursing mothers, sick persons and workers.

(*b*) Clothing should be provided as needed, to meet the conditions of the climate and should be of such a standard as to meet the needs of the individual in regard to occupation, physical condition, age and sex.

(*c*) Housing should be provided to meet minimum standards of health and decency; living quarters should, if possible, be reasonably heated, have sufficient lights and adequate sanitary facilities; and there should be adequate sleeping facilities for the persons to be accommodated with due respect to differences in age and sex.

(*d*) In co-operation with the governments or occupying authorities, the Preparatory Commission should maintain and safeguard health including health care during either repatriation or resettlement movements.

(*e*) In co-operation with governments or occupying authorities, and provided this does not tend to discourage repatriation and resettlement where such solutions are possible, an attempt should be made to ensure that as many displaced persons and refugees as possible have the opportunity to work at useful employment within their skills. Insofar as possible, vocational training and refresher courses should be provided to enable persons to learn new skills; to become adept again in previous skills, and such training should be related to the individuals prospective repatriation or resettlement.

(*f*) Attempts should be made to ensure that:
    (i) Schools are organized wherever appropriate;
    (ii) Children living in the community have the opportunity of obtaining a normal education;
    (iii) Higher education is encouraged;
    (iv) Arrangements are made for the vocational training of the youth whether living in groups or in the community.

(*g*) The development of community activities of the kind to which the particular groups are accustomed should be encouraged, and space and equipment for such activities should be provided.

(*h*) All groups should be provided facilities to conduct their own religious services and for persons not living in groups it should be the concern of IRO to ensure that they have access to religious services.

20. Relations with Voluntary Societies

Whereas national and international voluntary societies are providing substantial assistance both materially and in technical services and

whereas the voluntary societies' agreements with IGC and UNRRA terminate on 30 June 1947 and

whereas the Preparatory Commission recognises and appreciates the excellent services which are being given by more than sixty voluntary societies to the refugees and displaced persons in all countries where IGC and UNRRA are operating and

WHEREAS unless some immediate provision is made for their continuation with IRO, their services might not be available and

WHEREAS many of the voluntary societies have expressed their desire to continue their work with refugees and displaced persons in co-operation with IRO and

WHEREAS the Preparatory Commission is convinced of the desirability of continuing such services without interruption,

THE PREPARATORY COMMISSION RESOLVES THAT

1. The Executive Secretary shall have authority to negotiate new agreements with the voluntary societies or the extension of agreements existing between them and the IGC and UNRRA.

2. The Executive Secretary in negotiating new agreements or extending existing ones shall ensure that:

(a) the voluntary societies share the purpose of the Organization and observe the principles of the United Nations as contemplated by Article 2, paragraph 2 (f) of the Constitution:

(b) the established status and standards of performance are satisfactory for the purpose proposed, and that the various voluntary society programmes are co-ordinated with the activities of the Organization in order to provide an effective and integrated programme for refugees and displaced persons; and

DIRECTS The Executive Secretary to Study the possibilities of widening the activities of the voluntary societies and of strengthening their relations with IRO and to report with recommendations on these points at a later date.

21. RELATIONS WITH GOVERNMENTS AND/OR OCCUPATION AUTHORITIES IN OCCUPIED AREAS

THE PREPARATORY COMMISSION HAVING CONSIDERED AND AMENDED the statement of the Executive Secretary in document PREP/56 relating to agreements with governments and/or occupation authorities in control of occupied areas;

RESOLVES

1. to accept document PREP/56/Rev. 2 as setting forth the principles which should guide the Executive Secretary in making agreements with governments and/or authorities in control of occupied areas;

2. that the policies of the IRO should be implemented, in consultation with the governments and/or occupation authorities concerned, with a view to harmonising them with the necessary requirements of law, order and security and of the administration and economy of the Zones;

3. to authorise the Executive Secretary in cases where the government and/or occupation authority concerned decided that the general conditions in its zone are such that the harmonisation can be effectively carried out only by integrating the responsibility for the execution of the IRO policy in regard to refugees and displaced persons with the responsibility of the government and/or occupying authority for the administration of the zone, to negotiate an agreement in accordance with the provisions of Article 2, paragraph 2 (d) of the Constitution, by which the responsibility for material care and maintenance would be entrusted to the occupation authority under the supervision of the IRO;

4. to invite the occupation powers who are members of the IRO to urge their authorities in the zones to co-operate to the fullest extent of their powers in the execution of the policies decided by the Preparatory Commission and by the General Council of the IRO and to encourage the work of the IRO representatives in the zones especially in regard to the granting of facilities for close personal contact between such representatives and the refugees and displaced persons.

22. The Problem of Refugees and Displaced Persons in the Far East

THE PREPARATORY COMMISSION HAVING TAKEN NOTE of the report of the Executive Secretary on the problem of refugees and displaced persons in the Far East;

BEING CONVINCED that the principal obstacle to the completion of the repatriation of the European refugees and the overseas Chinese displaced persons in China is the problem of clearances by the countries of reception; and

FULLY REALISING the importance of the early solution of the problem;

RESOLVES

1. to appeal to the governments of the countries of reception to readmit as soon as possible those displaced persons in China who had their former habitual residences in their countries or territories and to maintain wherever possible their pre-war status under the existing immigration laws in order that their displacement because of the war may not operate to their disadvantage;

2. to direct the Executive Secretary to approach the governments of the countries which hold the possibilities of accepting the European refugees in China with a view to making the earliest possible arrangements for admitting them into their countries;

3. to authorise the Executive Secretary to take necessary steps for securing shipping facilities for those persons awaiting repatriation; and

4. that subject to the requirements of the semi-judicial machinery to be created in accordance with Annex I (paragraph 2 of the Constitution), determinations of eligibility shall be made by IRO with respect to displaced persons and refugees in China in accordance with such consultative procedures as may be agreed upon with the Chinese Government.

23. International Tracing Bureau

1. THE PREPARATORY COMMISSION TAKING NOTE of the recommendations made in the report of the Executive Secretary (Document PREP/37)

RESOLVES to send to the Governments concerned the following appeal:

'THE PREPARATORY COMMISSION FOR THE IRO, CONVINCED of the supreme importance of the tracing of missing persons, as emphasised by the Conferences of the National Tracing Bureaux in Brussels, September 1946, and Prague, March 1947;

'BEING ANXIOUS to ensure the continuation of such tracing,

'BELIEVING that the IRO, if it is to know at all exactly the scope of the task it will be given, should be in possession of lists of all persons for whom search is being made;

'INVITES the Governments concerned to have drawn up as soon as possible a list in alphabetical order of their nationals who have to be traced. For each person the following particulars (to which others may be added) should be supplied

'1. Name
2. Christian Names
3. Any other names by which known
4. Date and place of birth
5. Last official place of domicile (Country, Town, Street, Number)
6. Last place of residence before arrest or departure (Country, Town, Street, Number)
7. Date, place and grounds for arrest, or departure
8. Latest information available
9. Names and addresses of people able to give evidence
10. Address of the family or persons initiating the enquiry.'

2. THE PREPARATORY COMMISSION RESOLVES to ensure the continuation of tracing

activities by means of an International Tracing Bureau taking into consideration the suggestions made in document PREP/37 (paragraphs 14 to 19 inclusive);

DIRECTS the Executive Secretary to proceed to the organization of the said International Tracing Bureau;

DIRECTS the Executive Secretary to approach the Governments concerned in particular those of countries where tracing operations are to be carried out, so as to secure their most vigorous co-operation;

REMINDS the Executive Secretary of the necessity of maintaining the zonal tracing services in Germany and Austria.

FIRST SESSION, THIRD PART, 15-25 July: Resolutions 25-42[1]

30. REPORT OF THE ADVISORY COMMITTEE

THE PCIRO HAVING EXAMINED AND DISCUSSED the Report of the Advisory Committee (Document PREP/96) established by Resolution 3, paragraph 2 (a) and Resolution 4 of the Preparatory Commission

RESOLVES

1. to take note of the Report, and

2. to take note of the 'IRO Headquarters Organization Chart' submitted by the Committee, as amended by the Executive Secretary (Document PREP/96/Add. 1/Rev. 1); and

EXPRESSES ITS CONFIDENCE that the Executive Secretary, in making staff appointments, will be guided by the terms of Article 9 of the Constitution of the IRO

33. SEMI-JUDICIAL MACHINERY

THE PCIRO HAVING CONSIDERED the Report of the Executive Secretary on Semi-judicial Machinery (Document PREP/116)

RESOLVES to accept the principles set forth in the Report, as amended, and to instruct the Executive Secretary to prepare a draft constitution and draft rules of procedure and terms of reference for the establishment and operation of the semi-judicial machinery in accordance with the Principles of the Report as accepted.

34. IMPLEMENTATION BY THE GOVERNMENTS OF THE UNITED KINGDOM AND FRANCE OF THE NON-MONETARY GOLD PROVISIONS OF THE FIVE POWER AGREEMENT

THE PCIRO HAVING NOTED the Executive Secretary's oral report that no transfer has yet been effected by the Governments of the United Kingdom and France of non-monetary gold for rehabilitation and resettlement of non-repatriable victims of Nazi Action, pursuant to the undertaking given by them in Article 8 of the Final Act of the Paris Conference on Reparation of 21 December 1945, and in the Five Power Agreement of 14 June 1946, and

HAVING NOTED that funds are urgently needed for the purposes recognized by the Powers at the Paris Conference on Reparation on 21 December 1945 and at the Five Power Conference on 14 June 1946, and

HAVING BEEN ADVISED that acquisition and liquidation of non-monetary gold is a lengthy process from which funds cannot be realised in a short period of time.

DIRECTS the Executive Secretary to urge the Governments of the United Kingdom and France to implement the non-monetary gold provisions of Article 8 of the Final Act of the Paris Conference on Reparation and of the Five Power Agreement as quickly as possible.

[1] PREP/126/Rev. 1.

35. Transfer of Fifty Million Swedish Kroner to a Special Account of the Commission

THE PCIRO HAVING BEEN ADVISED that the Government of Sweden has, on the 12 July 1947, transferred the sum of 50 million Swedish kroner to a special account of the Commission pursuant to the Memorandum of Accord of 18 July 1946

RESOLVES to express its warm appreciation to the Government of Sweden for the payment of this sum, which will materially assist in the rehabilitation and resettlement of non-repatriable victims of Nazi aggression; and

EXPRESSES ITS HOPE that satisfactory arrangements may be made with the Swedish Government for the conversion of kroner to other currencies urgently needed for the assistance of non-repatriables, and

DIRECTS the Executive Secretary to forward to the Government of Sweden the terms of this Resolution.

36. The Implementation of Paragraph B of Article 8 of the Final Act of the Paris Conference and the Five Power Agreement of 14 June 1946

THE PCIRO RECOGNIZING that the Letter of Instruction from the Five Powers signatory to the Five Power Agreement of 14 June 1946 contemplated that 50 million Swiss francs would be made available by the Government of Switzerland to carry out the aims and purposes of the Five Power Agreement, upon liquidation of German assets in Switzerland; and

HAVING NOTED that this sum had not yet been made available; and

HAVING NOTED that funds are urgently needed as recognized by the Powers at the Paris Conference on Reparations of 21 December 1945, and at the Five Power Conference of 14 June 1946, for immediate assistance to non-repatriable victims of Nazi action to promote their rehabilitation and resettlement,

DIRECTS the Executive Secretary to urge the Government of Switzerland to transfer to the Commission as quickly as possible, for the purposes contemplated, the 50 million Swiss francs above mentioned.

37. The Implementation of 'Heirless Assets' Provision of Article 8 of the Final Act of the Paris Conference and the Five Power Agreement of 14 June 1946

THE PCIRO HAVING NOTED that pursuant to Article 8 of the Final Act of the Paris Conference on Reparation dated 21 December 1945, and to the Five Power Agreement of 14 June 1946, governments of neutral countries were to be requested by the Five Powers to make available for the assistance of non-repatriable victims of Nazi action assets in such countries of victims of Nazi action who have since died and left no heirs; and

HAVING NOTED that such assets have not yet been made available,

DIRECTS the Executive Secretary:

1. to urge the Five Powers, through their representative, the Government of France, to conclude negotiations with the neutral countries as early as possible; and

2. to bring to the attention of the governments of the neutral countries the urgent necessity that such funds be made available for the stated purposes.

39. Eligibility of 'Volksdeutsche'

THE PCIRO HAVING CONSIDERED the report of the Executive Secretary on the eligibility of 'Volksdeutsche' (Document PREP/97),

AND HAVING TAKEN NOTE of the discussions which followed consideration of this report,

TAKING INTO ACCOUNT on the one hand, the status of certain categories of persons known as 'Volksdeutsche' who are not excluded under the Constitution from eligibility for IRO assistance, and on the other hand, the inadequate resources which the Commission has at present at its disposal,

RESOLVES to instruct the Executive Secretary to consider as eligible for legal protection of the IRO and for the opportunities of resettlement offered by the Organization, the categories of persons known as 'Volksdeutsche' now resident in Austria who have not been and may not be transferred to Germany under the terms of international agreements and who are not otherwise excluded by the provisions of the Constitution, without prejudice as to further action which the Preparatory Commission might deem fit to take in this matter at a later stage.

40. RESETTLEMENT GRANTS

THE PCIRO HAVING CONSIDERED the Resolution adopted by the Intergovernmental Committee on Refugees in Plenary Session and submitted by the Director of the Committee to the Executive Secretary, and

CONSIDERING ALSO the Report and recommendations made by the Executive Secretary (Document PREP/94),

RESOLVES to authorize the Executive Secretary to make payments of resettlement grants, when and as the budgetary situation permits, in such manner as to encourage the permanent resettlement of refugees and displaced persons in family units.

FIRST SESSION, FOURTH PART, 31 October–1 November 1947: Resolutions 43–55[1]

43. EXPRESSION OF APPRECIATION FOR ACTION TAKEN BY THE UNITED STATES AUTHORITIES IN THE FIELD OF REPARATIONS

THE PCIRO RECOGNIZING the continued efforts by the Government of the United States to implement the non-monetary gold provisions of Article 8 of the final act of the Paris Conference on Reparation and of the Five-Power Agreement of 14 June 1946, and

HAVING BEEN ADVISED of the exceptional co-operation which had been and is being extended by the Government of the United States, and by the Commanding Generals of its Occupation Forces both in Germany and Austria, to representatives of the Commission engaged in preparing a joint inventory and accepting transfer of non-monetary gold from the United States Occupation zones

RESOLVES

1. to express its warm appreciation to the Government of the United States and to the Commanding Generals of its Occupation Forces both in Germany and Austria, and to their staff, for the speed with which non-monetary gold has been transferred to the Commission and for the full co-operation received and being received by the Commission's representatives;

2. to direct the Executive Secretary to forward to the Government of the United States and to the Commanding Generals of the Occupation Forces in Germany and Austria the terms of this Resolution.

[1] PREP/154/Rev. 1.

44. The Budget of the Organization

The pciro having considered the financial statement submitted by the Executive Secretary

RESOLVES

1. that, without affecting in any manner the contributions of Member Governments as set down in Annex II to the Constitution of the IRO and for the purposes of restricting expenditures within the limits of anticipated income, no expenditure shall be incurred in the period between the adjournment of the present Fourth Part and the convening of the Fifth Part of the First Session of the Preparatory Commission which would be estimated to involve a total annual expenditure in excess of that contemplated in the Administrative and Part I of the Operational Budget established by the Report of the Executive Secretary on Administrative Organization and Budget of the International Refugee Organization (Document PREP/44) as adopted in accordance with Paragraph 1 of Resolution No. 5 and as amended by the attached schedule hereby adopted, the total sum not to exceed $115,645,000;

2. that the Executive Secretary be directed to submit to the Commission at the Fifth Part of its First Session a further detailed financial statement relating to the year ending 30 June 1948, as well as a detailed statement of the expenditures incurred during the first quarter of that year, and such later period as may be practicable;

3. that the Executive Secretary be requested to examine the possibility of introducing further economies in expenditures on administration, to the fullest extent compatible with efficiency, and to report on the subject to the Commission;

4. that the Executive Secretary be requested to proceed at once with the preparation of a budget for the year ending 30 June 1949.

Schedule

Summary Headings for Plan of Expenditure

	$	$
Administration: Administrative Budget . . .	3,600,000	
Operational Budget, Part 1, Section 1 .	12,900,000	
		16,500,000
Care and Maintenance		80,480,000
Repatriation		4,500,000
Resettlement		14,020,000
Short Term Loans		145,000
Total		$115,645,000

46. Establishment of an International Tracing Service

The pciro recognizing the importance to the solution of the displaced persons and refugee problem of the fullest possible tracing of missing persons within the limits of the funds available to the Preparatory Commission and,

convinced of the necessity of co-ordinated and centralised international tracing procedures and,

having taken note of the commendable tracing work of the Central Tracing Bureau and the Zonal Tracing Bureaux as described in the Report of the Executive Secretary on the Establishment of an International Tracing Service (Document PREP/131),

RESOLVES to approve the principles of the proposals for the establishment of an International Tracing Service as set forth in the Report; and

DIRECTS THE EXECUTIVE SECRETARY

1. to take necessary measures in accordance with the principles of the Report for the conversion into an International Tracing Service of the present Central Tracing Bureau, its staff, facilities and functions, in order to eliminate to the maximum extent possible the present duplication of effort in the tracing field; and to extend the mandate of the International Tracing Service to include as far as possible the tracing of all non-German nationals, and of such German nationals as would be eligible under the Constitution of the International Refugee Organization, who have disappeared by reason of the War;

2. to invite all interested governments whether or not members of the Preparatory Commission, as well as voluntary societies engaged in tracing work, to relate their tracing activities with the work of the International Tracing Service; and to take steps in accordance with this invitation for obtaining the aid of, and establishing adequate liaison and co-ordination with both the National Tracing Bureaux and the voluntary societies; and for arranging suitable exchanges of basic tracing information and material between such governments and agencies and the International Tracing Service;

3. to notify all interested countries that, in view of the non-permanent character of the International Refugee Organisation, the International Tracing Service can continue to function for a maximum of two or three years, and will in the course of that period so organize its work as to make feasible the turning over to some more long-term body such tracing functions as remain incomplete at the conclusion of its own activities;

4. to negotiate with the occupation authorities for the amalgamation and full subordination of the Zonal Tracing Bureaux to the International Tracing Service, as well as for arrangements for the collection of necessary documents held by the military authorities or otherwise to be found in the occupation areas;

5. to negotiate with the control authorities of Germany for suitable arrangements whereby the Headquarters for co-ordinated tracing operations may remain in Germany;

6. to devote full consideration to every possibility for;

(a) the replacement of German employees of the International Tracing Service in the Zones of Occupation by displaced persons and refugees;

(b) the use of displaced persons and refugees as guards for the security of tracing materials and documents collected and retained by the International Tracing Service;

(c) the recruiting of International Tracing Service staff on an appropriate geographical basis within the conditions established by Article 9 of the Constitution;

(d) the establishment of a Zonal Tracing Bureau under the International Tracing Service in the British Zone of Germany, and early negotiation with the occupation authorities to that end;

(e) the establishment of adequate liaison with the governments of the non-member countries of Europe whence tracing data could be provided, together with suitable arrangements for the assignment of liaison officers from these countries to the International Tracing Service;

7. To express on behalf of the Commission its appreciation of the contributions made to the tracing function by the Vatican and to enquire whether the Vatican might envisage the possibility of placing at the disposal of the International Tracing Service its mass tracing facilities, including in particular its broadcasting services, for the tracing of missing persons.

47. Assistance to Spanish Refugees and Statutory Refugees

THE PCIRO, A. CONSIDERING

(1) that the Constitution makes the IRO responsible for:

'Spanish Republicans and other victims of the Falangist regime in Spain, whether enjoying international status as refugees or not',

'persons who were considered "refugees" before the outbreak of the second world war, for reasons of race, religion, nationality or political opinion', (Constitution, Annex 1, Part I, paragraph 1, sub-paragraphs *b* and *c*),

(2) that the position of these refugees calls for special measures of assistance and protection,

B. TAKING INTO ACCOUNT

(i) the very difficult conditions in which these refugees, particularly the Spanish Republicans and the Nansen refugees, are living;

(ii) the urgency of the need for help and the fact that until 1 July 1947 these refugees benefited by international measures of protection and assistance (IGC and the League of Nations High Commission on Refugees),

C. INSTRUCTS the Executive Secretary, to devote his full attention to organizing a programme of assistance to these refugees,

to put this programme into operation without delay,

to include in the budget, for that purpose, an adequate appropriation.

48. Limitations on Care and Maintenance

THE PCIRO HAVING CONSIDERED the Report of the Executive Secretary on the Status of the Organization and its Activities during the First Three Months (document PREP/130); and

BEARING IN MIND the intent of the Constitution to confer the maximum assistance possible upon all eligible refugees and displaced persons in need of care and maintenance;

CONSIDERS that the administrative restriction upon the admission of new cases to care and maintenance only upon proof of hardship is in principle undesirable; and

REQUESTS THE EXECUTIVE SECRETARY in the period prior to the Fifth Part of the First Session of the Preparatory Commission, or prior to any earlier date on which he is able in the exercise of his discretion to remove the restriction, to accord to the hardship exception the most liberal interpretation practicable; and

DIRECTS THE EXECUTIVE SECRETARY to make full report to the Preparatory Commission at the Fifth Part of its First Session upon the action taken in this regard.

49. Liaison with Voluntary Societies

THE PCIRO BEARING IN MIND the valuable work being done by Voluntary Societies for the welfare of displaced persons and refugees, and particularly the assistance being rendered to the work of the Preparatory Commission by these Voluntary Societies by means of personnel, supplies and special projects,

CONVINCED THAT THE INTEGRATION OF THE WORK OF THESE Voluntary Societies with that of the Preparatory Commission should be vigorously pursued,

REQUESTS THE EXECUTIVE SECRETARY to intensify the liaison between the Preparatory Commission and Voluntary Agencies and, if necessary, to call a Conference at Geneva of Voluntary Agencies in furtherance of this objective, and

INSTRUCTS THE EXECUTIVE SECRETARY to submit a report to the next session of the Preparatory Commission on this matter.

50. Issue of Travel Documents to Refugees and Displaced Persons
coming under the Mandate of the International Refugee
Organization

The PCIRO HAVING HEARD the most important statement made by the representative
of the Executive Secretary at the 44th meeting of the Preparatory Commission

NOTES

(1) that under the terms of article 20 of the Agreement of 15 October, 1946, all provisions of the said Agreement relating to the Intergovernmental Committee apply to
the Preparatory Commission for the International Refugee Organization, and shall
later apply to the International Refugee Organization itself;

(2) that in this matter there are at present in force

(a) the provisions under which, on the basis of the Arrangements of 1922, 1924,
1926 and 1928 and of the Convention of 1933, the signatory Governments undertake
to issue the so-called 'Nansen passport' to Nansen refugees;

(b) the Agreement of 15 October, 1946 initiated by the Intergovernmental Committee on Refugees, and providing for the issue of a travel document to certain refugees
coming under the mandate of the Intergovernmental Committee and who are now the
concern of the PCIRO. That Agreement was signed by the Argentine (ad referendum),
Belgium, Brazil (ad referendum), Chile, the Dominican Republic, Ecuador (ad referendum), France, Greece, India, Luxembourg, the Netherlands, Sweden, Switzerland,
the United Kingdom, and Venezuela, whilst the Governments of Australia, Canada
and Norway have indicated that although they are not prepared to sign the Agreement,
they will recognise the travel document issued in accordance therewith by any other
signatory.

(3) that the considerable task undertaken by the Intergovernmental Committee on
Refugees in order to remain closely informed as to the implementation and extension
of the Agreement of 15 October, 1946, is being taken over by the Preparatory Commission, particularly with regard to:

(a) all necessary notifications to the governments who have signed the Agreement;

(b) negotiations undertaken with a view to extending to the western zones of Germany and to Austria the implementation of the provisions of the said Agreement;

(c) approaches to be made to the three Governments who have signed ad referendum with a view to obtaining their final signature;

(d) further approaches to be made to some Governments in order that they should
sign the Agreement.

Furthermore, the Preparatory Commission,

CONSIDERING that the Intergovernmental Conference convened in London from
8 to 15 October, 1946, made the following recommendation:

'The Intergovernmental Conference considers it desirable that the Governments
concerned should envisage the possibility of applying the provisions of this Agreement to territories occupied as the result of the late war',

NOTING that the Governments concerned have not so far implemented the above
recommendation, with the exception of the United Kingdom Government, which has
given effect to the Agreement in the British Zone of Austria,

REMINDING the Governments concerned of the advantages offered by the travel
document established under the Agreement of 15 October, 1946 a document which is
internationally valid and has in fact already been recognised by a considerable number
of Governments,

DRAWING the particular attention of the said Governments to the substantial contribution that would be made to the solution of the refugee problem and to the resettle-

ment of refugees and displaced persons through the implementation of the Agreement in the western zones of Germany and in Austria.

ADOPTS AS ITS OWN the recommendation, quoted above, of the London Conference of 1946,

MAKES an urgent appeal to the Governments of France, the United Kingdom and the United States, for the simultaneous implementation, within the shortest possible time, of the provisions of the Agreement of 15 October, 1946 in the western zones of Germany and in Austria, and

INSTRUCTS the Executive Secretary to take, without delay, all appropriate steps to this effect.

In the event of its proving impossible to give prompt effect to the Agreement of 15 October, 1946, in some sectors,

THE PREPARATORY COMMISSION in view of the urgency of the situation

EXPRESSES the wish:

1. that the Executive Secretary should study, from a practical point of view, all appropriate measures to ensure the speedy departure of the categories of refugees and displaced persons in question, particularly from certain of the zones of occupation and from the Near and Middle East;

2. that the Executive Secretary should get into direct touch with the appropriate authorities to ensure that the refugees and displaced persons will be provided with the identity papers and travel documents without which resettlement and the delivery of visas by the potential countries of transit would be impossible.

54. IMPLEMENTATION OF THE LAST PARAGRAPH OF THE RESOLUTION ON THE CONSTITUTION AND INTERIM ARRANGEMENTS ADOPTED BY THE GENERAL ASSEMBLY OF THE UNITED NATIONS ON 15 DECEMBER 1946[1]

THE PCIRO BEARING IN MIND the Resolution of the General Assembly of the United Nations relevant to measures to be taken in respect of refugees and displaced persons, paragraph (e), adopted 15 December 1946, which urged each member of the United Nations to give the most favourable consideration to receiving into its territory at the earliest possible time, so far as may be practicable for permanent resettlement, its fair share of the non-repatriable persons who are the concern of the International Refugee Organization, and this in conformity with the principles of the Organization; and

CONVINCED that only through the effective implementation of the spirit of this Resolution will a rapid and realistic solution of the refugees and displaced persons problems be possible; and

CONSIDERING that the attention of the governments should be directed to the fact that thus far numerous resettlement programmes, while providing labour recruitment for the countries of reception, have not been sufficiently far-reaching to solve the larger social and economic need for group and family resettlement

INSTRUCTS THE EXECUTIVE SECRETARY

1. to consult with interested international organizations, in particular the International Labour Organization and the Economic Commission for Europe and with the Governments Members of the Preparatory Commission as well as with Governments of the other countries who voted for the Resolution of 15 December 1946, and any other Governments willing to assist, with a view to calling a Conference to determine the best methods of resettling refugees and displaced persons within a short period of time and relating their wishes and qualifications to the immigration requirements of the Governments of reception countries;

[1] See PREP/2, page 2, paragraph (e).

2. to present to the next meeting of the Preparatory Commission a detailed report on possible methods of implementing the Resolution adopted by the General Assembly of the United Nations.

FIRST SESSION, FIFTH PART, 20–31 January 1948:
Resolutions 56–73[1]

56. VOLUNTARY CONTRIBUTIONS TO THE LARGE-SCALE RESETTLEMENT EXPENDITURES OF THE ORGANIZATION

THE PCIRO HAVING REGARD to the intent of Article 10, paragraph 1 of the Constitution that the annual budget of the International Refugee Organization cover the necessary expenditures under three headings—to wit, administrative, operational and large-scale resettlement; and

NOTING the minimum sum of $5,000,000 fixed by Annex II to the Constitution for large-scale resettlement expenses, and the inclusion of a similar amount in the Budget for the period 1 July 1948 to 30 June 1949 for the same purposes; and

BEARING IN MIND the fact that Governments accepting the Constitution have contemplated contributing to the large-scale resettlement expenses, as provided in Article 10, paragraph 4 thereof, on a voluntary basis and subject to the requirements of their constitutional procedures and

BEING CONVINCED of the urgent need to make an early beginning in the field of large-scale resettlement in co-operation with countries receiving refugees for settlement on the land

RESOLVES to appeal to each Government Member of the Preparatory Commission to make every effort to provide a voluntary contribution to the large-scale resettlement expenses of the Organization for the fiscal years 1947/48 and 1948/49; and

DIRECTS the Executive Secretary

(*a*) to take the necessary measures for receiving and administering a voluntary large-scale resettlement fund in such amounts as may be contributed for the fiscal years 1947/48 and 1948/49;

(*b*) to communicate to the Governments Members of the Preparatory Commission the terms of this Resolution.

57. CONTRIBUTIONS TO A VOLUNTARY LARGE-SCALE RESETTLEMENT FUND

THE PCIRO BEING OF OPINION that Governments other than those which are Members of the Preparatory Commission may be willing to play their part in furthering the objects of the International Refugee Organization by contributing to the voluntary large-scale resettlement fund referred to in Resolution No. 56,

DIRECTS the Executive Secretary to communicate with Governments which, although not Members of the Preparatory Commission, are likely to be interested, informing them of the objects of the voluntary large-scale resettlement fund and inviting them to make a contribution to the fund.

58. BUDGET FOR THE PERIOD 1 JULY 1948 TO 30 JUNE 1949

THE PCIRO HAVING EXAMINED AND DISCUSSED the Budget Submission for the period 1 July 1948 to 30 June 1949 (document PREP/160 Annex)

RESOLVES

(1) that the Budget for the period 1 July 1948 to 30 June 1949 be the sum of

[1] PREP/195/Rev. 1.

4,797,800 United States dollars for administrative expenses and the sum of 150,229,258 United States dollars for operational expenses (except for large-scale resettlement expenses); and, in addition, a sum of 5,000,000 United States dollars for large-scale resettlement expenses; and that any unspent balance under these headings be carried over to the corresponding heading as a credit in the Budget for the succeeding fiscal year;

(2) that these sums (except for large-scale resettlement expenses) be contributed by Governments Members of the Preparatory Commission, subject to the requirements of their constitutional procedures, in the same proportions as established in Annex II, paragraphs 2A and 2B of the Constitution of the IRO;

(3) that contributions to large-scale resettlement expenses be on a voluntary basis and subject to the requirements of the constitutional procedures of Governments Members of the Preparatory Commission;

(4) that the Executive Secretary be directed to submit to the Governments Members of the Preparatory Commission the Budgetary Submission for the period 1 July 1948–30 June 1949, together with the terms of this Resolution.

59. Establishment of a Special Fund for Ocean Transport

THE PCIRO BEING CONVINCED of the necessity, in order to reach an early solution of the refugee and displaced persons problem, of increasing the rate of repatriation and resettlement, and of correspondingly reducing both the financial burden of the present heavy expenditure on care and maintenance, and the wastage of human resources from long continued residence in displaced persons camps, and

EMPHASIZING the crucial importance of placing adequate shipping at the disposal of the Organization if the numbers of refugees and displaced persons desiring repatriation or resettlement are in fact to be moved to the countries desiring to receive them, and

CONSIDERING that if advances could be made prior to the beginning of the next fiscal year by Governments Members of the Preparatory Commission out of their regular contributions to be paid to the Organization for the period 1 July 1948 to 30 June 1949, and again in the course of the latter fiscal year out of their contributions to be paid for the succeeding fiscal year, adequate funds could be made available to the Executive Secretary to permit the chartering of additional ships sufficient to increase the present rate of repatriation and resettlement overseas, to effect extensive economies on the care and maintenance expenditures of the Organization and appreciably to advance the date by which its essential tasks can have been carried out,

RESOLVES

(1) to direct the Executive Secretary to set aside in a special fund for ocean transport such sums as may be paid to the Organization prior to 1 July 1948 by Governments Members of the Preparatory Commission out of their regular contributions falling due for the period 1 July 1948 to 30 June 1949;

(2) to authorize the Executive Secretary to draw on such special fund for ocean transport, up to the maximum amount of 10,000,000 United States dollars, for the specific purpose of chartering in the name of the Organization ships over and above the amount of ocean transport provided for in the Budget for the current fiscal year;

(3) to request the Executive Secretary to report to the Preparatory Commission at the Sixth Part of its First Session (or to the General Council in the event of its having met prior to 1 July 1948) on the amount and disposition of the fund for such direction as the Commission or the Council may deem appropriate;

(4) to request the Executive Secretary to communicate to the Governments Members of the Preparatory Commission the terms of this Resolution.

60. Budget for the Fiscal Year 1947–48

The PCIRO having examined and discussed the Report of the Executive Secretary on the Status of the Organization and its Finances (document PREP/163) and the Budget Submission for the fiscal year 1 July 1947–30 June 1948 (document PREP/159); and

noting the earlier limits of expenditure which the Executive Secretary was authorized to make against the Budget for the fiscal year 1947/48 under Resolutions Nos. 5 and 44,

resolves

(1) to take note of the Report of the Executive Secretary and to approve the Budget Submission;

(2) without affecting in any manner the contributions of Member Governments as set down in Annex II to the Constitution of the IRO, to authorise the Executive Secretary to make expenditures in accordance with the Budget Submission up to a total annual amount not to exceed the sum of 119,088,320 United States dollars;

(3) to appeal to Governments Members of the Preparatory Commission to complete the necessary action for making available their annual contributions to the Administrative and Operational Budgets of the Organization in full.

61. Transfer of Funds in the 1947–48 Budget

The PCIRO having received the written report of the Executive Secretary (document PREP/163, paragraph 10, page 12) to the effect that a sum of $649,070 has been transferred from Section VIII (Repatriation) to Section IX (Resettlement) of the Operational Budget for the fiscal year 1947/48; and

noting that such transfer is within the authority granted the Executive Secretary under Resolution No. 5;

resolves to approve the transfer as reported.

62. Income Tax Exemption

The PCIRO having considered the Budget Submission for the fiscal year 1 July 1948–30 June 1949 (document PREP/160 Annex) and the allocation made therein for reimbursement of taxes paid on IRO salaries by employees who are nationals of those Governments Members of the Preparatory Commission not yet according exemption on such income; and

bearing in mind the importance to the Organization and to its staff of the preservation of a uniform and equitable scale of salaries, now calculated on a tax-exempt basis pursuant to Resolution No. 7; and

noting with interest the Resolution on Tax Equalization included in the Report of the Fifth Committee of the General Assembly of the United Nations and adopted by the General Assembly at its 121st meeting on 20 November 1947 whereby, *inter alia*[1]

(a) Governments Members of the United Nations not yet having done so are invited to take the necessary steps to exempt from income tax the salaries and allowances of their nationals who are employees of the United Nations Organization;

(b) it is proposed that the Secretary-General omit from future employment contracts any obligation to make reimbursement of income taxes of employees in the absence of special authorization from year to year; and

(c) the Secretary-General, in order to achieve equality among staff members, is authorized to reimburse them for taxes paid on salaries and allowances received from the United Nations Organization during the years 1946, 1947 and 1948;

[1] Note: See UN Doc. A/487 and *UN Journal* No. 59.

DIRECTS the Executive Secretary

(1) to make a further effort to reach satisfactory arrangements with those Member Governments not according income tax exemptions on IRO salaries paid to their nationals;

(2) to report to the Sixth Part of the First Session of the Preparatory Commission on the results obtained.

63. A Fair Share Plan

THE PCIRO HAVING TAKEN NOTE of the Report of the Executive Secretary on the Implementation of the last paragraph of the Resolution on the Constitution and Interim Measures adopted by the General Assembly of the United Nations on 15 December 1946 submitted by the Executive Secretary in accordance with Resolution No. 54 adopted during the Fourth Part of the First Session,

TAKING INTO ACCOUNT the necessity for adopting all possible measures to speed up the voluntary resettlement of refugees and displaced persons

INSTRUCTS the Executive Secretary

(1) to consult with the Governments Members of the Preparatory Commission and with those non-Member Governments likely to be interested, in order to determine what fair share of refugees, accompanied by their families, they are prepared to receive on their territory, in application of the last paragraph of the Resolution adopted by the General Assembly of the United Nations on 15 December 1946 concerning the Constitution of IRO and of the Interim Measure;

(2) to collect, in consultation with the experts of the Governments mentioned in paragraph 1, and with representatives of the international organizations interested (UN, ILO, ECE, etc), the data necessary for drawing up a 'fair share plan' for the voluntary resettlement of refugees and displaced persons;

(3) to take all possible steps, in collaboration with the Governments concerned, to speed up the voluntary resettlement of refugees and displaced persons, while at the same time taking into account the family and humanitarian considerations set forth in the Report of the Executive Secretary;

(4) to submit a report to the Preparatory Commission, at the Sixth part of its First Session (or to the General Council at its first Meeting) on the progress made in implementing this Resolution.

64. The Question of the 'Volksdeutsche' in Austria

THE PCIRO HAVING EXAMINED, in pursuance of Resolution No. 52, the Report of the Executive Secretary on the steps already taken or to be taken in implementation of Resolution No. 39 (document PREP/168); and

HAVING NOTED a special memorandum on 'Volksdeutsche in Austria' prepared by Professor M. W. Royse (document PREP/176); and

BEING OF THE OPINION that the issue is one of such scope and complexity that IRO policy will be of immediate concern to the General Council; and

CONSIDERING NEVERTHELESS that no decision should be taken to modify the principles laid down in Resolution No. 39

RESOLVES

(1) to submit the whole question of the so-called 'Volksdeutsche' in Austria mentioned in Resolution No. 39 for the consideration of the General Council of the IRO at its first session; and

(2) to direct the Executive Secretary to examine the eligibility of the persons in groups mentioned in Resolutions No. 39 and No. 52, as soon as the eligibility examination which is now being undertaken for the other categories is completed.

65. The International Tracing Service

THE PCIRO HAVING EXAMINED AND DISCUSSED the Report of the Executive Secretary on the Establishment of an International Tracing Service (document PREP/162)

RESOLVES

(1) to take note of the Report

(2) to direct the Executive Secretary to co-ordinate the work of the International Tracing Service with regard to tracing and search for children with the child welfare programmes of the Organization as a whole, with a view to ensuring the most efficient development of this important work.

67. Personnel and Establishments

THE PCIRO RECOGNIZING that the frequent changes in the establishments of the Organization, inevitable during its formative stage and made necessary by the imperative need for economy, have tended to militate against the creation of stable conditions of work for the staff;

RESOLVES

(1) to approve the intention of the Executive Secretary to give to the staff of each of the various establishments of PCIRO, as soon as he is satisfied that the necessary re-organization has been completed, an assurance of more stable conditions for the future; and, without neglecting the continuing need to combat any unnecessary expenditure;

(2) to request the Executive Secretary to express its gratitude to the staff for their loyal service during the formative period of PCIRO.

68. Implementation of Paragraph B of Article 8 of the Final Act of the Paris Conference and of the Five Power Agreement of 14 June 1946

THE PCIRO NOTING that one half of the 25 million dollar fund, intended by Article 8 of the Final Act of the Paris Conference on Reparation and the Five Power Agreement of 14 June 1946 for the assistance of non-repatriable victims of Nazi oppression, has not yet been made available; and

IMPRESSED that two years have elapsed since the eighteen Allied Governments recognized at the Paris Conference on Reparation that the non-repatriable victims of Nazi oppression '. . . stand in dire need of aid to promote their rehabilitation . . .';

DIRECTS the Executive Secretary to urge the Five Powers signatory to the Agreement of 14 June 1946, through their representative, the Government of France, to take appropriate steps for making available, at an early date, the remainder of the 25 million dollars for the reparations programme of PCIRO in favour of the victims of German action.

69. Concerning Limitations on the Assistance of the Organization[1]

THE PCIRO HAVING EXAMINED the Report of the Executive Secretary on Operations (document PREP/161) and the Report of the Executive Secretary on problems concerning the acquisition of refugee status and entitlement to care and maintenance (document PREP/169),

TAKING INTO CONSIDERATION that the protection and assistance of the Organization should normally be extended to all genuine refugees and displaced persons, according to the terms of the Constitution of the IRO;

TAKING INTO ACCOUNT on the other hand, the limited resources of the Organization

---

[1] This Resolution was not transmitted to the GC; cf. Res. 91 (PREP/240, p. 11).

DIRECTS the Executive Secretary

(1) to continue to implement the policy defined in Resolution No. 48;

(2) to ensure the legal and other protection of all eligible refugees and displaced persons by the Organization, according to the terms of the Constitution; and

RESOLVES to recommend to the General Council to consider at its First Meeting the desirability of restricting the benefits of the Organization, other than legal protection, to persons eligible under the Constitution who left their countries of origin or of previous habitual residence before 1 February 1948; and

DIRECTS the Executive Secretary to make as full a study as is practicable of:

(a) the number of persons now in receipt of care and maintenance who should not receive this assistance either on the ground that they are ineligible under the Constitution or that they are not genuinely in need of help;

(b) the number of eligible refugees considered to be in need of assistance not accepted for care and maintenance by the Organization on account of its limited financial resources; and to report the result of this study to the General Council at its First Meeting.

70. ELIGIBILITY AND SEMI-JUDICIAL MACHINERY

THE PCIRO HAVING CONSIDERED the Report of the Executive Secretary on Eligibility and Semi-Judicial Machinery (document PREP/165),

BEING OF OPINION that it is highly important to complete without delay the development of efficient administrative machinery (in the first instance) and semi-judicial machinery (on appeal) which will enable questions of eligibility to be determined rapidly;

HAVING NOTED WITH SATISFACTION the intention to preserve the full independence of the Eligibility Board in its dual role of hearing and determining individual appeals and advising upon questions submitted to it on the initiative of the Executive Secretary, and, in particular, the marking of this independence by the submission of a separate Budget for the main expenditures of the Board;

RESOLVES to request the Executive Secretary

(a) while bearing in mind at all times the need for economy, to ensure that the Board is properly staffed and its members provided with adequate assistance to enable the work of the Board to be performed efficiently and expeditiously;

(b) to present to the Preparatory Commission at the Sixth Part of its First Session (or to the General Council at its first Meeting) the report of the Chairman of the Eligibility Board on the activities and the working of the Board, together with his comments.

71. THE RESETTLEMENT OF DOCTORS, DENTISTS AND NURSES

THE PCIRO HAVING BEEN INFORMED that appreciable numbers of doctors, surgeons, dentists and nurses among refugees and displaced persons desire to emigrate to countries of resettlement where they will be permitted to continue their professional activities; and

NOTING the resolution passed at the Fourth Session of the Interim Commission for the World Health Organization on this subject,[1]

RESOLVES

(1) to express its appreciation for the action taken by the interim Commission for the World Health Organization concerning this problem; and

(2) to direct the Executive Secretary to address a letter to the Governments Members of the Preparatory Commission for the International Refugee Organization and

[1] See Doc. WHO/IC/124/Rev. 1.

to other governments interested in the reception of refugees and displaced persons, urging that favourable consideration be given to the admission of refugee doctors, surgeons, dentists, nurses and other qualified persons in the medical profession, and that they be authorized to continue to practise their professions provided they possess the required qualifications; and requesting such Governments to inform him of the conditions under which such refugees might be admitted to practise their profession.

FIRST SESSION, SIXTH PART, 4–12 May 1948: Resolutions 74–84[1]

75. ACTION WITH A VIEW TO THE CO-ORDINATION OF PROCEDURE FOR DECLARATION OF DEATH

THE PCIRO HAVING NOTED the Report of the Executive Secretary on Action to be taken with a view to co-ordination of procedure for Declaration of Death (document PREP/203); and

RECOGNIZING the urgency of solving the legal difficulties arising from the disappearance, due to war events or persecution, of large numbers of persons whose death cannot be conclusively established; and

RECOGNIZING FURTHER that such a solution would be in the interest of refugees and displaced persons who are the concern of the Organization and who are the persons most likely to be directly affected by the present difficulties; and

CONSIDERING that it is essential that this problem be solved by international action, the most appropriate form of which would be an international convention;

DIRECTS THE EXECUTIVE SECRETARY

(1) to prepare a survey of the problem;

(2) to transmit this survey to the Secretary-General of the United Nations and to request the latter to place this subject on the agenda of the next session of the Economic and Social Council of the United Nations; and

EXPRESSES THE HOPE that the Economic and Social Council will take all necessary measures with a view to the preparation of a draft international convention on the subject, or to some other form of international solution, in collaboration with the Executive Secretary of the Preparatory Commission for the International Refugee Organization (or the Director-General of the IRO).

76. PROPOSED DRAFT AGREEMENT TO ESTABLISH THE RELATIONSHIP OF THE ORGANIZATION WITH THE UNITED NATIONS

THE PCIRO HAVING REGARD to Section 2 (*a*) of the Agreement on Interim Measures, whereby the Commission shall 'take all necessary and practicable measures for the purpose of bringing the Organization into effective operation as soon as possible' and

HAVING EXAMINED AND DISCUSSED the Report of the Executive Secretary on an Agreement Between the United Nations and the International Refugee Organization (document PREP/205), together with the proposed Draft Agreement Between the United Nations and the International Refugee Organization (document PREP/206);

RESOLVES

(1) to approve the text of the proposed Draft Agreement as a basis for negotiation with the United Nations of a Draft Agreement defining the relationship between the Organization and the United Nations as provided under 3 of the Constitution of the IRO;

(2) to appoint a Negotiating Committee, to consist of one representative each from the Delegations of Brazil, Canada, China and Norway;

(3) to confer upon the Negotiating Committee authority to negotiate with the

[1] PREP/222/Rev. 1.

United Nations on behalf of the Preparatory Commission, subject to the instructions given to the Committee by the Preparatory Commission at the Sixth Part of its First Session, a Draft Agreement based upon the text of document PREP/206, as amended;

(4) to instruct the Negotiating Committee to submit the Draft Agreement as negotiated with the United Nations to the Preparatory Commission (or to the General Council upon the entry into force of the Constitution).

80. TRANSFERS OF FUNDS IN THE 1947/48 BUDGET

THE PCIRO HAVING EXAMINED AND DISCUSSED the Report of the Executive Secretary on the Financial Situation to the Close of the Fiscal Year 1947/48 as Forecast on 30 April 1948 (document PREP/202) with statement of Application of Estimated Resources and Approved Plan of Expenditure for the fiscal year, and Statement of Contributions as at 30 April 1948;

HAVING RECEIVED his report contained therein to the effect that transfers from the Health, Care and Maintenance Section of Part I of the Operational Budget have been made in the amount of $4,000,000 to the Resettlement Section, $1,572,548 to the Personnel and Establishment Costs Section, and $15,986 to the Review Board Section for the Fiscal Year 1947/48; and

NOTING that such transfers are within the authority granted the Executive Secretary under Resolution No. 5;

RESOLVES

(1) to take note of the Report and the Tables therein;

(2) to approve the transfers as reported.

81. AUTHORIZING INITIAL EXPENDITURE IN THE PERIOD BEGINNING 1 JULY 1948

THE PCIRO RECOGNIZING that Governments Members of the Preparatory Commission have not yet completed the necessary action for making advances on their contributions available for the period 1 July 1948 to 30 June 1949; and

NOTING that a detailed plan of expenditure based on actual anticipated income forthcoming for such period therefore cannot yet be prepared; and

BEARING IN MIND the possibility that the General Council may not convene prior to 30 June 1948, the last day of the present authority of the Executive Secretary under Resolution No. 60 to expend the funds of the Organization;

RESOLVES

(1) that in such case the Executive Secretary is authorized by the Preparatory Commission, pending the authorization of expenditure for the full fiscal year, to make administrative expenditures in the period from 1 July to 30 September 1948 in an amount not to exceed one-fourth of the approved Administrative Budget for the fiscal year 1947/48 and operational expenditures in an amount not to exceed one-fourth of the approved Operational Budget, together with amounts he deems prudent to expend from such funds as may prove available to be carried forward from the fiscal year 1947/48 in accordance with Paragraph 1 of Annex II to the Constitution;

(2) to direct the Executive Secretary to present to the next session of the Preparatory Commission (or the General Council) a plan of expenditure for the period 1 July 1948 to 30 June 1949 within the limits of anticipated income, indicating the allocations already made under the authority of this Resolution.

82. REPATRIATION AND RESETTLEMENT POLICY

THE PCIRO HAVING TAKEN NOTE of the Report of the Executive Secretary on the Policy of the Organization with regard to Repatriation and Resettlement (document PREP/211); and

BELIEVING that it is essential to bring to a speedy end a state of affairs in which large numbers of men, women and children are living as refugees and displaced persons in conditions of hardship; and

BEING CONVINCED that the needs of refugees and displaced persons who have valid objections to repatriation can in general be met only if the interested Governments are prepared to receive, in application of the last paragraph of the Resolution adopted by the General Assembly of the United Nations on 15 December 1946, a fair share of refugees and their families and, to this end, are willing to increase the pace and broaden the scope of present resettlement procedures;

DIRECTS THE EXECUTIVE SECRETARY

(1) to persevere in his efforts to arrange for the speedy repatriation of all eligible refugees and displaced persons willing to be repatriated;

(2) to continue, in accordance with Resolution No. 63, to seek the realization of a Fair Share Plan for the resettlement of eligible refugees and displaced persons who are unwilling to be repatriated and, as a first step, to negotiate with interested Governments new or amended agreements providing, *inter alia*, for

(a) the maximum feasible relaxation of technical immigration requirements and, in particular, of any medical standards which are unnecessarily exacting;

(b) the recognition of the family unit and the express restriction of the resettlement of individuals to refugees without dependents;

(c) all practicable measures to minimise the damage done to resettlement by the return of refugees from reception countries, including;

(i) the adoption of methods of selection which will avoid the inclusion in resettlement schemes of persons or categories who are unacceptable to the government of reception under their agreement with the Organization;

(ii) the institution of health and welfare schemes designed to assist the adaptability or resettled persons to their new environment, in co-ordination with other interested specialized agencies;

(iii) the responsibility for return costs to be borne by the Organization only if the circumstances so require;

(3) to give all possible encouragement to any governments who may be willing to receive, on humanitarian grounds, persons below the minimum standard for resettlement;

(4) to address to Governments Members of the Preparatory Commission a renewed appeal for contributions under Resolution No. 59 to the Special Fund for Ocean Transport, in hard currency or in such other form as would provide shipping;

(5) to address to Governments under Resolution No. 56 a renewed appeal for contributions to the Voluntary Large Scale Resettlement Fund.

83. PLAN FOR THE RESETTLEMENT OF REFUGEE STUDENTS AND PROFESSORS

THE PCIRO HAVING EXAMINED the Belgian plan for the resettlement of refugee students and professors (document PREP/212); and

CONSIDERING that the aims of this plan have great merit and are likely to stimulate public or private institutions in other countries to consider ways and means by which they could take part in carrying out this plan;

RESOLVES

1. to invite the Executive Secretary to make the scheme known to the governments and national and international institutions concerned, requesting them to examine it and then to inform him of the means by which they hope to be able to pursue the aims of the plan in their respective countries;

2. to ask him to report on the question at a later meeting, at the earliest possible date.

FIRST SESSION, SEVENTH PART, 10–11 September 1948:
Resolutions 85–91[1]

85. Convening of the First Session of the General Council

THE PCIRO NOTING WITH SATISFACTION the declaration on 28 August 1948 by the Secretary-General of the United Nations of the entry into force on 20 August 1948 of the Constitution of the IRO in accordance with Article 18 thereof, and

HAVING REGARD to the provisions of paragraph 2 (b) of the Agreement on Interim Measures

RESOLVES to convene the First Session of the General Council for Monday, 13 September 1948.

89. Concerning the Terminology of Article 2, Paragraph 1 of the Constitution

THE PCIRO HAVING REGARD TO Resolution No. 18 adopted by the Preparatory Commission during the Second Part of its First Session, on 21 May 1947 (document PREP/90/Rev. 1/Add. 1), in which consideration was given to the possibility of modifying the terminology of Article 2, paragraph 1 of the Constitution,

HAVING FURTHER DISCUSSED the desirability of such a procedure which might well be suggested with regard to other points,

CONSIDERS that in present circumstances it is not advisable to adopt such a procedure of revision of the Constitution, particularly for a mere question of terminology, since in such cases a sound interpretation of the Constitution is sufficient to ensure that its basic principles are respected, in accordance with the directives to be drawn up by the General Council,

RESOLVES not to transmit to the General Council for action the recommendation contained in the above-mentioned Resolution No. 18 and, in consequence not to include it in the Provisional Agenda for the First Session of the General Council.

B. SELECTED RESOLUTIONS OF THE GENERAL COUNCIL

1. Concerning membership in the Organization.
3. Agreement with the United Nations.
5. Constituting the Executive Committee.
8. Legal authority of the Director-General.
11. Determination of 'First Financial Year'.
14. Repatriation policy.
15. Limitations on care and maintenance.
16. Semi-judicial machinery.
17. The International Tracing Service.
19. Standards of care.
20. Resettlement policy.
22. The problem of the 'Volksdeutsche'.

[1] PREP/240.

23. Budget for the second financial year.
24. Budget for the third financial year.
25. Form of contributions.
27. Membership of states not members of the United Nations.
28. Contributions of new members for the second financial year.
29. Middle East refugees.
31. Privileges and immunities of the Organization.
36. Programme of the Organization.
37. Plan of expenditure for the third financial year.
38. Form of Contributions.
39. Completion of the programme of the Organization.
40. Future international action concerning refugees.
50. Plan of expenditure for the third financial year.
51. Budget for a supplementary period.
52. The International Tracing Service.
53. Exceptional measures which may be taken in respect to 'Hardship Cases'.
54. Completion of the programme of the Organization.
57. The International Tracing Service.
61. Plan of expenditure for the supplementary period.
62. Problem of international protection.
63. Status of refugees and displaced persons in Germany.
64. Care and maintenance for refugees in process of repatriation or resettlement.
66. Implementation of Resolution No. 53: refugees in Italy.
69. Assistance for the civilian population of Korea.
71. Amending paragraph 1 of Resolution No. 39.
74. Additional plan of expenditure for the supplementary period.
76. Completion of the programme of the Organization.
77. Electing the Executive Committee.
78. Continuation of the Organization's operations.
83. Extension of resettlement assistance.
84. Amending Resolution No. 78 on the continuation of the Organization's operations.
87. Proposed plan of expenditure for the supplementary and closure periods beginning 1 July 1950.
88. Amendment of the financial regulations.
89. The International Tracing Service.
97. Residual problems.
98. Remaining assets.
102. Financial statements for the fifteen months ended 30 September 1951 and future financial reports.
103. Final plan of expenditure for the supplementary and closure periods beginning 1 July 1950.
106. Disposal of assets.
108. Establishing a Board of Liquidation.
110. Defining the powers of the Liquidator.

FIRST SESSION, 13–25 September 1948: Resolutions 1–30. GC/55

1. MEMBERSHIP IN THE ORGANIZATION

THE GENERAL COUNCIL of the IRO

IMPRESSED by the importance of broadening the membership of the Organization to embrace the largest possible number of governments, in order that the Organization may have the most effective support in accomplishing its purpose of repatriating or resettling substantially all of the refugees and displaced persons who are its concern within the remaining two years of its lifetime: and

CONSIDERING that the continuity of the work of the Organization will best be served if those members of the Preparatory Commission which have not yet been able to ratify the Constitution nevertheless continue to take part in the deliberations of the Council;

RESOLVES

(1) to call upon all Members of the United Nations which have not yet adhered to the Constitution of the IRO, as well as all peace-loving States not Members of the United Nations, to take early steps to adhere to the Constitution;

(2) to urge those States signatories to the Constitution which have not yet ratified their signatures to be represented at the First Session of the Council by an Observer, and to invite all such Observers to be seated at the Council table and to take part, without vote, in the debates of the Council.

3. AGREEMENT WITH THE UNITED NATIONS

THE GENERAL COUNCIL of the IRO

HAVING CONSIDERED the draft agreement entered into between the Negotiating Committee of the Preparatory Commission and the Committee of the Economic and Social Council on Negotiations with Intergovernmental Agencies;

NOTING that the Economic and Social Council, by its Resolution of 24 August 1948, has recommended to the General Assembly of the United Nations that this agreement be approved without change; and,

TAKING NOTE of the Report of the Executive Secretary of the Preparatory Commission on the Draft Agreement with the United Nations (document GC/10);

RESOLVES to approve the agreement in accordance with Article XXII thereof.

5. CONSTITUTING THE EXECUTIVE COMMITTEE

THE GENERAL COUNCIL of the IRO

IN ACCORDANCE WITH paragraphs 2 and 3 of Article 7 of the Constitution

RESOLVES

(1) that the Executive Committee of the General Council shall consist of representatives of the following nine Members of the Organization, elected for a period of two years:

Australia, Belgium, Canada, China,[1] France, Norway, United Kingdom, United States, Venezuela;

(2) that the Chairman and Vice-Chairman of the Executive Committee shall hold office from the date of their election to the end of the regular session of the General Council next following, and shall be eligible for re-election, and,

(3) to transmit to the Executive Committee the draft Rules of Procedure of the Executive Committee (document GC/3), as amended.

8. LEGAL AUTHORITY OF THE DIRECTOR-GENERAL

THE GENERAL COUNCIL of the IRO

RESOLVES that, without derogating in any way from the authority conferred on him by the Constitution and by other decisions of the General Council or of the Executive

---

[1] At the Seventy-ninth Meeting, 12 Oct. 1950, the General Council nominated to the Executive Committee, Italy instead of China (Res. 77).

Committee, the Director-General, in carrying out the administrative and executive functions of the Organization, shall have authority in the name of the Organization:

(a) to acquire real property by lease or gift, to hold such property or to dispose of it by lease, sale or otherwise;

(b) to acquire, hold and convey other necessary property;

(c) to receive and disburse funds, and to call upon Members for the payment of financial contributions due, in accordance with the powers conferred on him by other decisions of the General Council and of the Executive Committee;

(d) to enter into contracts and undertake obligations;

(e) to conduct negotiations with governments, with intergovernmental bodies and with other public or private organizations, and to conclude agreements therewith, except such agreements as may require approval by the General Council under the Constitution;

(f) within the limits of the approved plans of expenditure and of the Financial Regulations, to undertake projects appropriate to the accomplishment of the Purposes of the Organization; and

(g) in general, to perform any other legal act appropriate to the purposes of the Organization.

11. DETERMINATION OF 'FIRST FINANCIAL YEAR'

THE GENERAL COUNCIL of the IRO

NOTING that the expenses of the PCIRO for the period 1 July 1947–30 June 1948 were met in part from advances on their first contributions made by Governments which had become parties to the Constitution during that period;

BEARING IN MIND that the terms of paragraph 6 of the Agreement in Interim Measures such advance contributions are deductible from the first contributions falling due to the Organization from such Members;

REFERRING to paragraph 1 of Annex II to the Constitution, wherein the provisional budget for the first financial year is determined to be 'the sum of 4,800,000 United States dollars for administrative expenses, and a sum of 151,060,500 United States dollars for operational expenses (except for large-scale resettlement expenses), and a sum of 5,000,000 United States dollars for large-scale resettlement expenses';

TAKING INTO ACCOUNT that those Member Governments which made advances under paragraph 6 of the Agreement on Interim Measures determined their contributions in the proportions set forth in Annex II to the Constitution as applied to the amounts of the provisional budget established therein for the first financial year; and

CONSIDERING that it was the clear intent of Article 10, paragraph 5 of the Constitution that only those Members of the Organization from which financial contributions would fall due for the first financial year should forfeit their vote in the General Council or the Executive Committee if such contributions were not paid within the expiration of a period of three months following the date of the coming into force of the Constitution, i.e. 20 August 1948.

RESOLVES

(1) that the term 'first financial year', as used in the Constitution of the IRO and in Annex II thereto, shall be interpreted as applying to the period 1 July 1947–30 June 1948;

(2) that, in accordance with paragraph 6 of the Agreement on Interim Measures, the advance contributions made by Governments during that period to meet the expenses of the Preparatory Commission shall be deducted from the contributions due to the Organization by operation of Annex II to the Constitution for the first financial year; and,

(3) that—in accordance with Article 10, paragraph 5 of the Constitution, and under the authority vested in the General Council by Article 10, paragraph 7 thereof—no Member of the Organization becoming a party to the Constitution in the second financial year shall be deemed to be liable to contribute to the expenses of the Organization for the first financial year, nor shall any such Member be deemed to lose its vote in the General Council or the Executive Committee by reason of non-payment within three months of the coming into force of the Constitution of any contribution for the first financial year.

14. REPATRIATION POLICY

THE GENERAL COUNCIL of the IRO

CONVINCED that repatriation operations must be carried on in the spirit of the Resolutions of the General Assembly of the United Nations and in particular of the Resolution of 12 February 1946 (Annex III to the Constitution) and of the Resolutions of the Economic and Social Council (especially of the Resolution adopted on 24 August 1948, document E/1027),

HAVING NOTED the Report of the Executive Secretary on the Policy of the Organization regarding Repatriation (document GC/14) and,

CONSIDERING that this Report follows the principles of the Resolution referred to above, and includes proposals to the effect that each refugee or displaced person should be given the opportunity to decide in complete freedom and after receiving full knowledge of the facts, including adequate information from the government of his country of origin, whether or not to be repatriated,

INSTRUCTS THE DIRECTOR-GENERAL to pursue his efforts with a view to ensuring the speedy repatriation of all refugees and displaced persons who wish to be repatriates; and

INVITES THE DIRECTOR-GENERAL to this effect, to give refugees and displaced persons wishing to be repatriated all assistance they may require, particularly by offering to each repatriate a food parcel corresponding to 20 days' supply of food, under the conditions of the above-mentioned Report.

15. LIMITATIONS ON CARE AND MAINTENANCE

THE GENERAL COUNCIL of the IRO

HAVING CONSIDERED the Report of the Executive Secretary of the PCIRO on the Limitations on the Assistance of the Organization (document GC/5/Rev. 1); and

BEARING IN MIND the intent of the Constitution that it should be the concern of the Organization that no *bona fide* and deserving refugee or displaced person be deprived of such assistance as it may be in a position to offer; and

TAKING INTO ACCOUNT that, within the funds available to the Organization, care and maintenance can be offered to all eligible applicants among refugees and displaced persons, over and above those now being assisted, only at the expense of a rapid and positive solution of the problem of *bona fide* refugees and displaced persons in terms of early repatriation or resettlement;

INSTRUCTS THE DIRECTOR-GENERAL to continue the policy of the Preparatory Commission in this matter, by:

(a) restricting the admission of applicants for care and maintenance to hardship cases, while according to the term 'hardship' the most liberal interpretation feasible; and,

(b) exercising his administrative discretion, at the earliest date at which it may prove possible, to remove the restriction.

16. Semi-Judicial Machinery

THE GENERAL COUNCIL of the IRO

HAVING CONSIDERED the Report of the Executive Secretary of the Preparatory Commission on the Eligibility Review Board (document GC/30); and

CONVINCED of the importance of a rapid handling of eligibility questions by means of efficient administrative machinery for determinations in the first instance and effective semi-judicial machinery on appeal;

RESOLVES

(a) to approve the proposals of the Director-General to continue the authority of the Eligibility Review Board in the dual role of hearing and determining individual eligibility appeals and advising on such eligibility questions as may be submitted to it on the initiative of the Director-General, while preserving in full the independence of the Board in its semi-judicial process of arriving at decisions required by justice under the Constitution, the decisions of the General Council, and the administrative interpretations and rulings of the Director-General; and

(b) to instruct the Director-General to maintain in force the established functions of the Eligibility Review Board in accordance with the principles set out in the Annex to the Report.

17. The International Tracing Service

THE GENERAL COUNCIL of the IRO

RECOGNIZING the importance of the fullest possible tracing of missing persons within the limits of the funds available to the Organization; and

CONVINCED of the necessity of co-ordinated and centralized international tracing procedures; and

HAVING TAKEN NOTE of the work of the International Tracing Service described in the Report of the Executive Secretary of the Preparatory Commission on the International Tracing Service (document GC/36);

INSTRUCTS THE DIRECTOR-GENERAL

(1) to continue the work of the International Tracing Service, seeking to eliminate to the maximum degree possible duplication of effort in the tracing field, and extending its mandate as far as possible to all non-German nationals and to such German nationals as would be eligible under the Constitution of the IRO, who have disappeared by reason of the Second World War;

(2) to maintain close relations with all interested governments whether or not Members of the Organizations, as well as with voluntary societies engaged in tracing work, in order to co-ordinate their tracing activities with the work of the International Tracing Service; to negotiate with those interested governments with which liaison has not already been established, with a view to their relating their tracing work to that of the International Tracing Service; and to arrange with all such governments and voluntary societies suitable exchanges of basic tracing information;

(3) to co-ordinate the work of the International Tracing Service with regard to tracing of and search for children with the child welfare programmes of the Organization as a whole;

(4) to take appropriate steps for the issuance of notifications of death of as formal or evidentiary a character as may prove useful, as well as of certificates of incarceration;

(5) to give particular attention to the difficulties experienced by the International Tracing Service in carrying out its work at its Headquarters in Germany, owing to the constant loss of its numerous refugee and displaced person staff through repatriation and resettlement; and,

(6) to consider in consultation with the United Nations, other international organiza-

tions, the occupying authorities, and all interested governments, the practicability of turning over to the United Nations or to some other long-term body as early as may be possible those important tracing functions which should continue after the cessation of the work of the IRO.

19. STANDARDS OF CARE

THE GENERAL COUNCIL of the IRO

HAVING REGARD to its function under the Constitution of providing care and assistance to genuine refugees and displaced persons until such time as their repatriation or resettlement is effectively completed;

BEING CONVINCED that early and effective repatriation or resettlement will prove possible only if minimum standards of health can be maintained among the refugee and displaced persons population; and

BEARING IN MIND that under the General Principles of the Constitution, on the other hand, it must be the concern of the Organization to ensure that its assistance is not exploited by undeserving persons or for purely economic reasons;

RESOLVES to instruct the Director-General to give effect to the following principles:

(a) All groups should be provided with facilities to conduct their own religious services; for persons not living in groups it should be the concern of the Organization to ensure that they have access to religious services.

(b) Housing should be provided to meet minimum standards of health, and decency; living quarters should be reasonably heated, have sufficient lights and adequate sanitary facilities; and there should be adequate sleeping facilities for the persons to be accommodated, with due respect to differences in age and sex.

(c) Every effort should be made to provide a diet for refugees and displaced persons necessary to maintain standards of health approved by medical and nutritional authorities. In view of the fact, however, that the Director-General reports that the caloric diet now prevailing in countries of Europe in which refugee camps are located has not been raised to such levels as no longer to require a differential ratio for displaced persons in those camps, the caloric diet for the occupants of such camps shall be no higher than that prevailing in the country in which such camps are located.

(d) Clothing should be provided as needed, to meet the conditions of the climate and should be of such a standard as to meet the needs of the individual in regard to occupation, physical condition, age and sex.

(e) In co-operation with the governments or occupying authorities, the Organization should maintain and safeguard health, including health care during either repatriation or resettlement movements.

(f) In co-operation with governments or occupying authorities arrangements should be made to ensure that as many refugees and displaced persons as possible may have the opportunity to work at useful employment within their skills. Persons gainfully employed should be required to make a reasonable contribution towards the costs of their maintenance. Insofar as possible, vocational training and refresher courses should be provided to enable persons to learn new skills or to become adept again in previous skills; such training should be related to the individual's prospective repatriation or resettlement.

(g) So far as practicable

(i) Schools should be organized wherever appropriate;
(ii) Children living in the community should have the opportunity of obtaining a normal education;
(iii) Higher education should be encouraged;

(iv) Arrangements should be made for the vocational training of the young, whether living in groups or in the community.

(*h*) The development of community activities of the kind to which the particular groups are accustomed should be encouraged, and space and equipment for such activities should be provided.

20. RESETTLEMENT POLICY

THE GENERAL COUNCIL of the IRO

REFERRING TO PCIRO Resolution No. 82 of 12 May 1948, to Resolution No. 157 (VII) of the ECOSOC of 24 August 1948, as well as to the stirring address by the Executive Secretary at the 6th Part of the First Session of Preparatory Commission;

NOTING that to accomplish its mandate it will be necessary to secure the acceptance by the countries of the world of not only those refugees and displaced persons who are themselves economic assets to the receiving countries but also their dependants, who by reason of age and physical or other handicaps make no present contribution or only a partial contribution to their own support and also of orphaned children and other persons without family ties;

NOTING FURTHER that heretofore immigration programmes have only partially secured this acceptance, and that, unless there is increased recognition and application of the principles of family resettlement with a view towards maximum assumption of responsibility for support by family members immigrating or already re-established, there will remain large numbers of refugees and displaced persons as a responsibility of the Organization at the time of the termination of its mandate on 30 June 1950; and

CONSIDERING that the moral reasons which originally inspired international action in this regard constitute a pressing obligation to complete the mandate of the Organization, and that, as indicated in the Report presented by the Secretary-General of the United Nations to the Economic and Social Council at its Seventh Session, a broadened and widespread effort would require but a minor sacrifice by each country towards the final solution of the refugee problem;

DECIDES to make a strong appeal to the conscience of individuals and nations, taking the lead in a worldwide effort with the co-operation of various organizations, national and international, public and private, and particularly religious organizations, with the object of obtaining the participation of individuals and countries in achieving a broad resettlement programme;

EXPRESSES THE HOPE that the United Nations will support this programme;

TRUSTS that all nations, whether or not they are Members of the IRO, will participate to the largest possible extent in this programme; and

REQUESTS THE DIRECTOR GENERAL

(1) to make a direct approach to Governments Members of the IRO and to all other governments of goodwill, in order to discuss with them the maximum share of refugees and displaced persons which they would be able and prepared to admit to their territories to effect the completion of the task of the IRO;

(2) to pursue the aims of the Preparatory Commission as defined in its Resolution No. 82, particularly in regard to the recognition of the principle of resettlement in family units;

(3) to continue the study of and put into operation schemes for large-scale resettlement, requesting in this matter the co-operation of all the countries concerned;

(4) to draw the attention of governments, when undertaking the discussions with them referred to in paragraph (1) above, to the special problem of intellectual refugees and displaced persons and to the importance of permitting them to continue to follow, in the countries of reception, their intellectual pursuits; and

(5) to formulate and submit to the General Council at its Second Session a plan for the disposition of such number of the refugees and displaced persons as it may then appear will require special measures of assistance for the completion of the mandate.

22. THE PROBLEM OF THE 'VOLKSDEUTSCHE'

THE GENERAL COUNCIL of the IRO

HAVING RECEIVED the Report of a special Working Committee appointed to study the problem of the 'Volksdeutsche' in Austria (document GC/40); and

HAVING DETERMINED that, under the terms of paragraph 4 of Part II of Annex I to the Constitution, only the 'Volksdeutsche' in Austria are under consideration; and,

BEING OF OPINION that the Organization is not at present in a position to take a decision concerning them;

INSTRUCTS THE DIRECTOR GENERAL while maintaining the status quo, to pursue the study of the problem, with a view to any further action by the General Council.

23. BUDGET FOR THE SECOND FINANCIAL YEAR

THE GENERAL COUNCIL of the IRO

HAVING RECEIVED the Budget for the Financial Year 1948–1949 transmitted by the Executive Committee with its comments, together with Schedules I, II and III thereof;

RESOLVES

(1) to adopt the Budget for the Financial Year 1 July 1948–30 June 1949, contained in Schedule I, as amended, to be the sum of 4,797,800 United States dollars for administrative expenses and the sum of 150,229,258 United States dollars for operational expenses (except for large-scale resettlement expenses);

(2) to allocate the total under each of these headings to the Members in the proportions set forth in Schedule III;

(3) to appeal to each Government Member of the Organization to make every effort to provide a voluntary contribution to the large-scale resettlement expenses of the Organization; and,

(4) to instruct the Director-General to submit the Budget for the Second Financial Year (document GC/56) to the Governments Members of the Organization, together with the terms of this Resolution.

24. BUDGET FOR THE THIRD FINANCIAL YEAR

THE GENERAL COUNCIL of the IRO

HAVING RECEIVED the Report of the Director-General on Budget Submission for the Financial Year 1 July 1949–30 June 1950, transmitted by the Executive Committee with its comments, together with Schedules I and II thereof;

RESOLVES

(1) to adopt the Budget for the Financial Year 1 July 1949–30 June 1950, contained in Schedule I, to be the sum of 4,500,000 United States dollars for administrative expenses and the sum of 150,060,500 United States dollars for operational expenses (except for large-scale resettlement expenses);

(2) to allocate the total under each of these headings to the Members in the proportions set forth in Schedule II;

(3) to appeal to each Government Member of the Organization to make every effort to provide a voluntary contribution to the large-scale resettlement expenses of the Organization; and

(4) to instruct the Director-General to submit the Budget for the Third Financial Year (document GC/57) to the Governments Members of the Organization, together with the terms of this Resolution.

25. Form of Contributions

THE GENERAL COUNCIL of the IRO

HAVING EXAMINED AND CONSIDERED the Submission of the Director-General concerning Form of Payment of Contributions to the Organization by Member Governments (document GC/35); and,

TAKING INTO ACCOUNT the importance of avoiding unnecessary delay in negotiations to be undertaken between the Organization and Members under Article 10, paragraph 2, of the Constitution, so that contributions may be payable in time to meet the anticipated expenditures of the Organization;

RESOLVES

(1) that the form in which advances have been made under paragraph 6 of the Agreement on Interim Measures by certain Members to the Preparatory Commission (as shown in Annex I to the Director-General's Submission) be approved, in conformity with Article 10, paragraph 2 of the Constitution, and that the amounts of the same be credited against the contributions of such Governments for the First Financial Year;

(2) that the form in which balances of contributions for the First Financial Year and contributions for the Second Financial Year have been proposed to be made (as shown on Annex II to the Director-General's Submission) be likewise approved;

(3) that the Director-General be authorized to undertake negotiations with remaining Members (including new members adhering to the Organization prior to the Second Session of the General Council) concerning the form in which their contributions shall be payable, having regard to currencies in which the anticipated expenditure of the Organization will be made from time to time; and

(4) that the Director-General be requested to submit to the General Council for its approval at its Second Session the results of the negotiations undertaken pursuant to paragraph 3 hereof, but that, pending such approval, he be authorized to accept payments against contributions of such Governments in the form agreed with each.

28. Contributions of New Members for the Second Financial Year

THE GENERAL COUNCIL of the IRO

HAVING ADOPTED by Resolution No. 23 of 24 September 1948 the Budget for the Second Financial Year, together with the proportions to be allocated to the Members; and,

BEARING IN MIND the importance to the full accomplishment of the purposes of the Organization of bringing in new members having the same proportionate financial responsibilities as the present membership;

RESOLVES

(1) that the contributions of any new members named in Annex II to the Constitution be allocated in the same ratio to the present Members of the Organization as is already established by Annex II; and

(2) that the proportions to be contributed by new members invited to adhere to the Organization by Resolution No. 27 of the General Council but not provided for in Annex II, shall be in the same ratio to the budgets as the following proportions bear to those set forth in Annex II:

	For administrative expenses	For operational expenses
Italy	2·40	2·27
Switzerland	1·30	1·10

29. MIDDLE EAST REFUGEES

THE GENERAL COUNCIL of the IRO

NOTES the receipt of a communication from the Security Council of the United Nations to the Executive Secretary of the Preparatory Commission for the International Refugee Organization with respect to Middle Eastern refugees and the transmittal of a similar communication to the Economic and Social Council, and

HAS EXAMINED with the deepest interest this communication and the record transmitted therewith.

The spirit which activates the IRO in the present task it is carrying on, committed to it by its Constitution, makes it deeply sensitive to the distress of any refugees such as is portrayed in this record.

THE GENERAL COUNCIL BETTER APPRECIATES the magnitude of the resources that must be obtained and the extensive organization which must be created to cope with the task of the relief of such distress, because of its own experience in attempting to carry through its task with the limited, and it is feared, inadequate resources, which are now and will be available to it.

THE GENERAL COUNCIL HEARTILY APPROVES of the action of the Director-General in having loaned the services of General Hardigg, one of the most experienced and able members of the IRO staff, to the Mediator and instructs the Director-General to lend such other assistance of this character that the Mediator may request and the urgent demands of its own tasks permit.

THE GENERAL COUNCIL ALSO REQUESTS the Director-General to inform the Executive Committee promptly of any action taken by the General Assembly of the United Nations pertaining to assistance to Middle Eastern refugees or of any request for any other form of assistance to the IRO by the Mediator, with a view to enabling the Executive Committee to consider whether any such further assistance may be practicable within the budgetary and Constitutional limitations of the IRO.

SECOND SESSION, 29 March–8 April 1949: Resolutions 31–38
GC/77/Rev. 1

31. PRIVILEGES AND IMMUNITIES OF THE ORGANIZATION

THE GENERAL COUNCIL of the IRO

HAVING CONSIDERED the Report of the Director-General on the Privileges and Immunities of the Organization (Document GC/66); and

BEARING IN MIND the requirement of Article 13 of the Constitution of the IRO that the privileges and immunities of the Organizations be defined in an agreement after consultation with the Secretary-General of the United Nations; and

TAKING INTO ACCOUNT the desire of the General Assembly of the United Nations that a unification of the privileges and immunities of the various specialized agencies should be achieved by means of the United Nations Convention on the Privileges and Immunities of the Specialized Agencies (Resolutions Nos. 22 (I) D of 13 February 1946 and 179 (II) of 21 November 1947); and

BEING CONVINCED that the privileges and immunities provided in that Convention are essential for an efficient exercise of the functions of the Organization; and

HAVING RECEIVED the Resolution of the Economic and Social Council of 9 March 1949 recommending to the Organization a draft Annex to the Convention;

RESOLVES

(1) to approve as the final text of the Annex the draft submitted by the Economic and Social Council, to read as follows:

'Annex X International Refugee Organization. The Standard Clauses shall apply without modification.'

(2) to accept the Convention in accordance with the Annex;

(3) to undertake to give effect to Sections 8, 18, 22, 23, 24, 31, 32, 42 and 45 of the Convention;

(4) to call upon the States Members of the United Nations and other States members of the specialized agencies which have not yet done so to accede to the Convention, indicating in their instruments of accession their undertaking to apply the provisions of the Convention to the International Refugee Organization;

(5) to call upon all such States which have heretofore acceded to the Convention to address to the Secretary-General of the United Nations a further written notification of their undertaking to apply the provisions of the Convention to the International Refugee Organization;

(6) to invite all such States, pending such action as they may take under paragraphs 4 and 5 hereof, immediately to accord to the IRO, as far as possible the benefit of the privileges and immunities provided in the Convention, as recommended by the General Assembly of the United Nations in its Resolution No. 179 (ii) C of 21 November 1947;

(7) to instruct the Director-General:

(a) to transmit to the Secretary-General of the United Nations the text of this Resolution and of the Annex as approved, in fulfilment of the conditions set out in Section 37 of the Convention; and

(b) to take such other steps as he may consider necessary or desirable in order to bring the provisions of the Convention into force for all countries where it will prove conducive to the more efficient exercise of the functions of the Organization.

36. PROGRAMME OF THE ORGANIZATION

THE GENERAL COUNCIL of the IRO

HAVING EXAMINED AND DISCUSSED the Preliminary Recommendations of the Director-General with a view to the Termination of the IRO Programme (document GC/W/3) and his proposals for Future International Action Concerning Refugees (document GC/W/4) and;

BEING IMPRESSED with the importance of early consideration of the rate of run-down of the present IRO programme and of such subsequent international action as may prove necessary;

RESOLVES

(1) to request the Director-General to circulate to the Governments Members of the Council further recommendations in the light of the discussions; and

(2) to convene a special session of the Council, at the call of the Chairman of the Executive Committee in consultation with the Director-General, to be held in Geneva on or about Wednesday, 22 June 1949.

37. PLAN OF EXPENDITURE FOR THE THIRD FINANCIAL YEAR

THE GENERAL COUNCIL of the IRO

HAVING EXAMINED AND DISCUSSED the Plan of Expenditure submitted by the Director-General, in accordance with Financial Regulation No. 8, for the Third Financial Year 1 July 1949–30 June 1950 (document EC/26, transmitted by the Executive Committee);

RESOLVES

(1) to adopt the Plan of Expenditure for the Third Financial Year as amended to provide for an allocation of $1,000,000 for residual cases; and

(2) to authorise the Director-General to incur obligations and to make expenditures against the Plan of Expenditure as approved, in a total amount not to exceed the sum of 4,500,000 United States dollars for administrative expenses, 140,732,581 United States dollars for operational expenses, and 199,537 United States dollars for large scale resettlement expenses.

38. FORM OF CONTRIBUTIONS

THE GENERAL COUNCIL of the IRO

HAVING EXAMINED the Submission by the Director-General on the Form of Payment by Member Governments of Contributions to the Organization (document GC/64); and

BEARING IN MIND the requirement of paragraph 2 of Article 10 of the Constitution that the General Council decide the form in which contributions shall be payable, having regard to currencies in which the expenditure of the Organization will be effected from time to time;

RESOLVES

(1) to take note that balances of contributions for the First Financial Year and the reported contributions for the Second Financial Year have been received in the form authorized by the Council in its Resolution No. 25;

(2) to approve the form in which it is proposed that the contributions of Members shall be payable for the Third Financial Year; and

(3) to authorize the Director-General to negotiate further agreements with Members under the terms of paragraph 2, Article 10 of the Constitution, and to accept payments against the contributions of such Members in the form agreed with each, subject to the approval of the General Council at its first subsequent session.

THIRD SESSION, 28 June–8 July 1949: Resolutions 39–44. GC/98/Rev. 1

39. COMPLETION OF THE PROGRAMME OF THE ORGANIZATION

THE GENERAL COUNCIL of the IRO

HAVING EXAMINED AND DISCUSSED the Further Recommendations of the Director-General with a view to the Termination of the IRO Programme (document GC/80); and

BEARING IN MIND that the IRO was established as a non-permanent organization for the accomplishment of its purposes in the shortest possible time, with the further understanding that its programme should be completed by 30 June 1950; and

IMPRESSED with the importance of taking all steps, within the time and resources remaining to the Organization, for the most suitable form of re-establishment open to those in clear need who remain the charge of the Organization; and

SATISFIED that the organization can effectively accomplish the immediate purpose for which it was created only if its remaining tasks can at once be defined with precision and finality;

INSTRUCTS the Director-General

(1) to discontinue on 31 August 1949 all registration whereby refugees and displaced persons may be determined to fall within the mandate of the Organization; provided, however, that

(a) unaccompanied children discovered after that date under the Child Search Programme may be declared to be within the mandate of the Organization;

(b) refugees leaving their countries of origin after 31 August 1949 and arriving in an area of IRO operations may be registered up to 15 October 1949 if, qualifying in all other respects, they are found to be within the mandate of the Organization;

(c) refugees and displaced persons in need of the legal and political protection of the Organization may continue to apply to be declared within the mandate for the sole purpose of receiving that form of assistance;

(2) to discontinue after 31 December 1949 admissions to the care and maintenance of the Organization in assembly centres and after 31 March 1950, admissions to care and maintenance of the Organization under cash assistance programmes; with the proviso however, that the Director-General may examine with Governments Members of the Organization means of establishing accountable increases which may result in their internal social assistance costs and making appropriate financial adjustments;

(3) to discontinue care and maintenance by 30 June 1950 for all persons other than

(a) refugees and displaced persons who are in process of repatriation, or resettlement (i.e. who are in a resettlement processing centre or for whom a resettlement nomination has been received by IRO);

(b) refugees or displaced persons who require permanent assistance such as institutional care and for whom other satisfactory arrangements will not yet have been completed;

it being understood that the decisions taken at the present session will not prejudice in any way the policy to be followed after 30 June 1950 if the activities of the Organization provided for in the Constitution are prolonged beyond that date;

(4) to institute immediately an intensive counselling programme, with the aim of interviewing by 1 November 1949 all refugees and displaced persons receiving care and maintenance whose future has not yet been provided for, in order to expedite their early decision for such suitable forms of re-establishment as are available in each individual case, and to withdraw assistance, as required by the Constitution, from those who unreasonably refuse to accept the proposals of the Organization; and at these interviews to make a general review of the individual relief cases,

(5) (a) to formulate in co-operation with the Governments and authorities concerned, and with all other interested organizations, and to put into the earliest possible execution, plans for the future provision to be made for those refugees and displaced persons who require permanent assistance such as institutional care, giving consideration to the most effective solution in relation to each area and each category of such persons;

(b) to allocate to Governments, authorities or institutions which undertake to make permanent provision for any seriously handicapped refugees as aforesaid, the equivalent of the care and maintenance costs, whether in currency or in kind, which would have been incurred by the IRO for such refugees up to 30 June 1950; and

(c) similarly, to transfer at his discretion IRO right, interest or title in such facilities, equipment or appropriately budgeted funds as the Director-General determines by written order will further the permanent provision for institutional cases among such handicapped persons including in particular an effort to establish by such means a 'TB Village Settlement',

(6) to draw up, and where practicable to put into execution, plans for the progressive closure of the Organization, bearing in mind such establishment as may be required after 30 June 1950 to complete the then remaining programmes;

(7) to report in detail to the General Council at its Fourth Session on the following:

(a) the numbers of refugees and displaced persons planned to be moved in the remaining repatriation and resettlement programmes of the Organization, and the date by which such programmes are to be completed;

(b) the arrangements made for completing the several programmes of the Organization in its different areas of operation; and the overall plan for its final closure;

(c) the action taken under the authority of paragraph 5 above including details of funds or property transferred and the progress made in the analysis of, and permanent provision for, the cases of refugees and displaced persons who require permanent assistance such as institutional care;

(d) the budgetary arrangements to be made in respect of those cases referred to in sub-paragraph (c) above which would not have been settled;

FURTHER RESOLVES

to direct an urgent and immediate appeal to all Governments Members of the IRO and to all governments of good will to do all in their power to extend their refugees immigration programmes and to liberalize in the broadest manner their selection and admission standards in order that the re-establishment programme of the Organization may be completed at the earliest possible date, and in particular in order that the smallest possible number of refugees and displaced persons may find themselves without firm provision for their future upon the closure of the IRO.

40. FUTURE INTERNATIONAL ACTION CONCERNING REFUGEES

THE GENERAL COUNCIL of the IRO

HAVING EXAMINED document GC/81 entitled 'Future International Action concerning Refugees',

DECIDES to transmit the attached memorandum to the Economic and Social Council of the United Nations.

Memorandum from the General Council of the IRO to ECOSOC

1. The General Council of the IRO has given consideration to the state of affairs likely to exist when the Organization terminates its services on 30 June 1950, the date usually regarded as that on which its mandate will come to an end.

2. The General Council was aware that the Economic and Social Council at its Ninth Session is due to consider a study made by the Secretary-General pursuant to its resolution 116 (VI) D dated 1 and 2 March 1948, concerning interim measures of protection of stateless persons. The General Council therefore felt it to be its duty to draw the attention of the Economic and Social Council to that state of affairs so that the responsibility temporarily assumed by the 18 Governments Members of the IRO for the fulfilment of a particular task, might in the event be transferred to some other international authority, without any break in continuity. The Economic and Social Council, having been duly informed of the various elements of the problem of refugees and displaced persons which is bound to present itself at that time, would thus be in a position to begin now to consider preparing and putting into effect the measures which might appear necessary.

3. While desiring to give the Economic and Social Council the benefit of all the experience they have acquired in the last two years, to help in solving this great human problem, these 18 Governments nevertheless wished to make it clear that whatever may be the position on 30 June 1950, or at any early date thereafter fixed for the termination of the activities of the IRO, they will consider themselves as being relieved at that time of the responsibility which will rest upon them until then as Members of the Organization. They will then consider themselves as having only the same responsibilities as any other state, arising out of their own national obligations and the general obligations which all countries of good will are called upon to meet at the international level, as well as those arising out of the specific obligations which derive from conventions or agreements to which they would have freely become parties.

4. The General Council unanimously recognized, that there will be a problem, of which the following will be the essential elements:

(1) when their mission comes to an end, there will still be in various parts of the

world, mainly in Europe, and more especially in Germany, large numbers of refugees at present under the IRO mandate, who for various reasons will not enjoy the protection of the government of their country of origin, and many of whom will not be capable of being completely and rapidly absorbed into the national community of the countries where they are living;

(2) there is every likelihood that in addition to these persons there will be new refugees for whom the very same problems will arise.

5. After examining document GC/81 which contains a study prepared by the Director-General on future international action concerning refugees the General Council reached the following conclusions:

(a) that international assistance in the protection of refugees should continue unbroken;

(b) that an organ within the framework of the United Nations should be entrusted with this responsibility;

(c) that it is not prepared to recommend a continuation of the life of the IRO in order to undertake this responsibility;

(d) that the question of the establishment of an international fund to be administered by the organ mentioned above for such purposes as may appear necessary and desirable for the material assistance of refugees after the termination of the IRO programme should be determined by the Economic and Social Council.

6. While document GC/81 was under discussion, various opinions were expressed by the Delegations of Member-States, making clear the attitude of their governments to the problem.

7. Although individual in character, these opinions derive special value from the fact that they were expressed by Delegations of States which have been working actively together for over two years, within the framework of the Organization, to find a solution to the refugee problem; the General Council therefore thought it advisable to attach to this document the summary records of the meetings at which this question was discussed.

8. The Economic and Social Council will see from these documents that:

(1) the need for international action, as mentioned above, was very generally acknowledged, and that such action has seemed essential in order to complement the protection given to refugees and stateless persons by the reception countries in the exercise of their sovereignty and out of their respect for the right of asylum;

(2) the General Council, having failed to reach a unanimous decision, did not find it possible to make a choice from among the four solutions put forward by the Secretary-General of the United Nations in document E/1112;

(3) several Delegations of countries of Europe whose opinion deserves special mention, in view of the very heavy burdens which they will have to bear on their own territories at that time, and the likelihood that these burdens will increase, and in view of the very liberal policy they have always followed in dealing with refugees declared themselves in favour of a United Nations High Commissioner. Such a High Commissioner who would enjoy a certain degree of independence and have a small headquarters staff, would be entrusted with the task of keeping in touch with the question of refugees and stateless persons throughout the world, or promoting international conventions defining the status of refugees, of enquiring into specific situations, of receiving and examining complaints and of making recommendations. A representative having international status, approved by the reception country, would be appointed to maintain the liaison between the High Commissioner and the national authority responsible for the legal protection of the refugees, to ensure that this protection was international in character;

(4) States Members of the IRO which are not Members of the United Nations expressed a wish, in view of the traditional interest they have always taken in refugee problems, to remain associated with any international work in this field and consider that the form of the future international organization should be sufficiently flexible to allow them to participate fully in its work;

(5) some Delegations, particularly European ones, indicated the very grave concern that they would feel if displaced persons were left in Germany after 30 June 1950 and desired to call this problem especially to the attention of the Economic and Social Council; they expressed the view that these refugees might have special need for assistance from the international fund mentioned in paragraph 5 (*d*) above if it were established. The purpose of this fund would be on the one hand, to make the international protection of these displaced persons more genuinely effective, and, on the other hand, by means of small contributions from all the countries willing to take part, to distribute as evenly as possible, the financial burden of relief for the large number of destitute refugees for whom countries represented by these Delegations will be responsible;

(6) the Delegations of certain European States, particularly those of Belgium and France, wished to make it clear that they considered the necessity for international actions to be as great in the field of assistance as in the field of protection, and that the establishment of the International Relief Fund seemed to them no less essential than that of the High Commission which they recommend should be created.

(9) In sending this document with its annexes to the Economic and Social Council, the General Council unanimously expresses the hope that the greatest possible number of nations will in future,

> on the one hand, help the IRO to bring its task to full completion by adopting the most liberal immigration policies possible,
> on the other hand, take into consideration the serious human problem which will inevitably present itself on 30 June 1950 or on the date soon thereafter at which the activities of the IRO will have been finally terminated, and which, by reason of its humanitarian character, concerns the nations as a whole.

FOURTH SESSION, 11–20 October 1949: Resolutions 45–55.
GC/135/Rev. 1

50. PLAN OF EXPENDITURE FOR THE THIRD FINANCIAL YEAR

THE GENERAL COUNCIL of the IRO

HAVING EXAMINED AND DISCUSSED the Report of the Director-General on the Plan of Expenditure for the Third Financial Year (documents GC/107, GC/107/Corr. 1),

RESOLVES

1. to take note of the Report; and
2. to instruct the Director-General to transfer from Section VII, Programme Reserves, to Section III, Care of Residual Cases, an amount of $9,000,000.

51. BUDGET FOR A SUPPLEMENTARY PERIOD

THE GENERAL COUNCIL of the IRO

HAVING RECEIVED the Budget Submission of the Director-General for a supplementary period subsequent to 30 June 1950 (document GC/121), together with Schedule I, II and III thereof, as transmitted by the Executive Committee with its comments,

RESOLVES

1. to adopt the Budget, contained in Schedule III, to be the sum of 2,506,893

United States dollars for administrative expenses, and the sum of 52,459,016 United States dollars for operational expenses (except for large-scale resettlement expenses);

2. to allocate the total under each of these headings to the Members in the proportions set forth in Schedule II; and

3. to instruct the Director-General to submit the Budget to the Governments' Members of the Organization, together with the terms of this Resolution.

52. THE INTERNATIONAL TRACING SERVICE

THE GENERAL COUNCIL of the IRO

HAVING CONSIDERED the Report of the Director-General on the International Tracing Service (document GC/111),

INSTRUCTS THE DIRECTOR-GENERAL

1. to re-examine in detail the programme and budget of the International Tracing Service, and to effect the maximum possible savings and simplification of operations in order that the main documentation functions of the Service may be completed by 30 June 1950, within the limits of the funds allocated;

2. to negotiate with interested governments and with occupation authorities for the transfer by 30 June 1950 of the then remaining tracing functions of the International Tracing Service to governments or to another international body.

53. EXCEPTIONAL MEASURES WHICH MAY BE TAKEN IN RESPECT OF 'HARDSHIP CASES'

THE GENERAL COUNCIL of the IRO

TAKING THE VIEW THAT, even if it is not possible to reconsider the date-lines laid down in Resolution No. 39, the Organization cannot remain indifferent to the fate of the new refugees who constitute hardship cases, before the transitional measures at present contemplated come into force,

INVITES THE DIRECTOR-GENERAL to examine with the Governments concerned means of alleviating the heavy burden imposed upon them as a consequence of their geographical position.

54. COMPLETION OF THE PROGRAMME OF THE ORGANIZATION

THE GENERAL COUNCIL of the IRO

HAVING EXAMINED AND DISCUSSED the Reports of the Director-General on Action Taken to Date with a View to the Completion of the Programme of the Organization (document GC/102), on the Resettlement of Refugee Specialists (document GC/108), on the Number of Refugees and Displaced Persons to be Moved in Repatriation and Resettlement Programmes (document GC/109), and on Action Taken by the Economic and Social Council of the United Nations on Matters of Concern to the IRO (document GC/104)

RESOLVES

1. to take note of the Reports;

2. to approve the steps taken and the measures proposed by the Director-General for the implementation of Resolution No. 39;

3. to address once again an urgent and immediate appeal to all governments of goodwill to do all in their power to liberalise in the broadest manner their selection and admission standards;

4. to authorise the Director-General to continue to seek solutions for the continuing care and permanent settlement of refugees proven to be institutional cases, by means of direct negotiations with governments and interested agencies;

5. to instruct the Director-General to pursue his efforts to reduce the number of

persons who have theoretically limited opportunities of resettlement by continuing to develop, with the help of interested governments, nominative resettlement schemes and by sending special representatives to countries of resettlement with a view to promoting individual sponsorship and employment offers;

6. to request all governments to facilitate the task of the special representatives of the Director-General, to give them full support in their task of promoting placement possibilities for refugees with specialist skills or with limited opportunities for resettlement, and to admit those refugees and displaced persons for whom resettlement opportunities will have been found;

7. to request the Director-General to transmit to the Secretary-General of the United Nations all the necessary resolutions, documents and records of the Fourth Session of the General Council, in order to assist the General Assembly of the United Nations in its urgent task of establishing a plan of organization to ensure the protection of refugees (and the administration of any possible assistance funds) after the IRO shall have terminated its activities; and

8. to transmit to the General Assembly of the United Nations the attached memorandum adopted by the General Council on 20 October 1949.

Memorandum to the General Assembly of the United Nations

1. At a time when the United Nations General Assembly has had the problem of refugees and displaced persons put before it, by the Resolution of the Economic and Social Council dated 9 August 1949, the IRO General Council at its Fourth Session desired to reaffirm the basic views set forth in its memorandum to the Economic and Social Council, dated 11 July, and to pass on to the Assembly the latest information in its possession.

2. This information mainly concerns the date on which the IRO proposes to bring its operations to an end, and the probable position at that time. It also relates to the special difficulties the IRO is encountering in completing its programme, and the assistance which the Organization expects from Governments.

I. DATE OF TERMINATION OF IRO OPERATIONS

3. The IRO General Council, anxious that the Organization should complete its programme as soon as possible after 30 June, 1950, the date on which in the ordinary way its mandate was expected to end, took important decisions during its Special Session in July 1949, with a view to setting limits to a problem which may never be completely resolved, and to preparing the final period of IRO operations.

4. The most important steps of this order taken at that time was the adoption of the date-line of 31 August 1949, from which date the Organization was to stop, and has indeed stopped, accepting any further registrations except for legal protection.

5. Taking into account the present rate of repatriation and resettlement operations and the new applications registered, it can now be estimated that by 30 June 1950 provision will have been made for the future of 970,000 refugees and displaced persons, and that there will still be about 292,000 for whom a solution remains to be found by IRO. In addition, there will be a very large number of refugees who will require legal protection.

6. In these circumstances, the General Council has agreed to propose to the Member Governments an additional period of nine months of IRO operations and has recommended their consideration of a budget to permit the continuation of the Organization's programme for the supplementary period.

7. Although the General Council agreed to recommend this extension to the Member Governments, it is not at present in a position to say definitely what action

Governments will take in the matter. While it was necessary for certain delegations to reserve their position on this question, the representatives of almost all Members of the Organization indicated that their governments would consider sympathetically this extension.

8. Being aware of the need to avoid any break in continuity in this field the Council recommends that the United Nations General Assembly should proceed immediately with the discussion of the problem which has been put before it. If there is an extension of IRO operations beyond 30 June 1950, it will still be necessary for the General Assembly to take decisions of principle forthwith and to make preparations for the establishment of the machinery which should come into force at a date no later than 1 January 1951.

9. It should be added, incidentally, that although this possible extension may bring about a change in some aspects of the problem, it cannot alter the principles in the light of which the problem must be considered.

10. On the one hand, the general principles of the question of international protection for refugees cannot be affected; on the other hand, although the problem with which the IRO has to deal will have been reduced in extent by the end of a supplementary period, it is none the less possible to state now that the work cannot be entirely completed and international responsibilities will definitely have to be met at the end of that period.

11. Lastly, the decisions which the Assembly may adopt might be of considerable assistance in the solution of a number of specially acute problems which the Organization has to face. At all events the consequence of such decisions would be a clarification of the position, since the Governments most directly concerned in the problem would be able to estimate now how much assistance they can reasonably expect to receive from the international community.

II. The Refugee Problem up to the end of IRO Operations

12. The work at present waiting to be done by the Organization, in terms of figures, apart from the legal protection of all refugees coming within its mandate, can be defined as follows: during the present financial year, the Organization hopes to repatriate or resettle 367,500 persons, so that by 30 June 1950, 970,000 refugees will have been provided for; at that date a solution will still have to be found for the cases of 292,000 refugees. Assuming that there is an extension there will remain at the end of that supplementary period substantial numbers of persons who will require continuing legal protection and others who may need other assistance.

13. These estimates however, are not enough to give an accurate picture of the position, for allowance must be made for the continuous flow of refugees to which the IRO will continue to grant its protection as long as it exists, but for whom it will be unable to provide care and maintenance or to organize resettlement.

14. Furthermore, it must be borne in mind that of the total number of refugees at present cared for by the Organization, about 150,000 are in circumstances which have so far made resettlement difficult, if not impossible, for them. They consist of people left alone in the world, unable to support themselves, requiring hospital accommodation or permanent care, or of individuals or whole families who, on grounds of age, health, occupation, etc., have not as yet been resettled in other countries.

15. The local re-establishment of these people has never seemed desirable unless it represents their own free choice. But the Assembly should be made aware of the fact that the Organization cannot achieve this aim alone, and that very far-reaching and energetic co-operation from the largest possible number of Governments is required.

16. The resettlement policy of the IRO has sometimes been misunderstood. The

General Council believes that it will only be facilitating the study of the problem put before the General Assembly if it takes this opportunity of informing the General Assembly, in an objective manner, of the true facts of the problem, as it appears to those who for the past two years have been bearing this heavy responsibility on behalf of the whole international community.

17. The General Council is aware of the difficulties Governments have had to face in regard to their resettlement policy. It must pay tribute to the constant efforts made by a large number of Governments, both to increase the quotas accepted and to liberalize certain of their regulations governing immigration. Appreciating as it does the magnitude of the results achieved, it expresses its gratitude and admiration to all the Governments which, looking beyond their own immediate interests, have in fact consented, in a true spirit of international solidarity, to receive on their territories refugees dependent on their material support. Without the help which came from these various sources, the IRO could have done nothing.

18. The Governments Members of the Organization have always been conscious of the humanitarian aspect of the problem, and they have always tried to find the fairest possible solution, both for those who are readily employable and for the others.

19. The General Council has, however, been forced to conclude, and to pass on that conclusion to the General Assembly, that in spite of all the improvements which have been brought about, a further effort will have to be made if the Organization is to complete its programme and set the seal upon its work by conferring upon the sum total of its achievements a character fully in harmony with the international ideal.

20. The General Council, anxious to do all it could in this matter, has just approved an initial allocation of 10,000,000 dollars for the solution of the 'hard core' problem, and an additional allocation, a larger one, is contemplated should the life of the IRO be prolonged for some months.

21. It is only if there is active support from the Governments, however, that these allocations can make it possible to achieve a just and complete solution, and the General Council must solemnly call the attention of the United Nations to the fact that if this support is not forthcoming, the General Assembly will be faced with vast problems when the IRO goes out of existence.

22. In this connection, the General Council again draws attention to the fact that in the above-mentioned message to the Economic and Social Council it expressed the unanimous hope that the largest possible number of countries would in future help the IRO to complete its programme by showing themselves as liberal as possible in their immigration policy. The Council wishes to express this hope again today, still more urgently, and with a fuller knowledge of the problem. It is convinced that a recommendation by the United Nations on the subject would meet with a response from a larger number of governments.

III. THE REFUGEE PROBLEM AFTER THE TERMINATION OF THE ORGANIZATION

23. The appraisal of the problem which will in fact exist after the closure of the IRO depends to a large extent on the collaboration which governments will give the Organization in the coming months.

24. But it can be stated already that in any event a problem of international responsibility will remain to be solved.

25. The General Council has already referred to the continuous influx of refugees to whom the Organization continues to extend its protection whilst unfortunately being unable to grant them more effective assistance.

26. It is to be feared on the other hand that in spite of the efforts of the Organization,

a relatively important number of refugees who are unable to support themselves may, upon the closure of the Organization, be left behind in conditions the adequacy of which is at the present stage open to doubt. It is clear that the existence of those refugees creates for the international community a problem which, as far as principles are concerned, does not depend on the number of persons involved, and that, on the other hand, the scope of the problem will vary according to the extent to which governments will until then contribute to its solution.

27. In this connection, it appears that if certain governments were sure that they would receive in the future some assistance, however small, for the care of the most deserving cases they would be more willing to receive or to keep on their territories refugees requiring permanent assistance; this would facilitate the solution of the acute problem of the 'hard core' which the IRO is endeavouring to achieve.

28. In appreciating the international responsibilities which are involved in this matter, it should be borne in mind that thirty countries had voted in favour of the constitution of the IRO and had thus recognized that the solution of the problem of the refugees was an international responsibility.

29. It is known that 20 months of efforts were needed to obtain the 15 acceptances required and that the establishment of the Organization was therefore delayed and its activity slowed up for a long period; and that in actual fact only 18 member governments bear the whole burden.

30. The IRO which is a non-permanent Organization, is facing a problem which in certain aspects appears unfortunately to be of a permanent character. Consequently the General Council requests the General Assembly of the United Nations to consider its responsibilities and if, in the absence of more precise data a final decision to be implemented forthwith in the matter of financial responsibility for assistance appears difficult at present, nevertheless to contemplate the possibility of such assistance, in case this assistance—as is unfortunately probable—might prove indispensable at a later stage.

FIFTH SESSION, 14–22 March 1950: Resolutions 56–67. GC/163

57. THE INTERNATIONAL TRACING SERVICE

THE GENERAL COUNCIL of the IRO

HAVING TAKEN NOTE OF the Report of the Director-General of the IRO on the International Tracing Service,

NOTES WITH SATISFACTION the efforts made and the results obtained in connection with the tracing of allied nationals dead or missing in Germany by reason of war,

CONSIDERING FURTHER that it is highly desirable that the work now proceding should be completed at a very early date,

INSTRUCTS THE DIRECTOR-GENERAL

(a) to take all necessary steps in order that the processing of the documents and other information material now held at ITS Headquarters at Arolsen, or which may be found in the future, should be continued and speeded up with a view to supplying the national tracing bureau concerned with information concerning their nationals;

(b) to undertake the necessary negotiations with the Allied High Commission in Germany, with a view to enabling the latter to take over, in such form as it may deem most appropriate, field tracing work, whether individual or not;

(c) to make provision in the Plan of Expenditure for the Supplementary Period of the IRO of the necessary funds for the maintenance at Arolsen after 1 July 1950 of a reduced IRO supervisory staff; in the understanding that such provision shall not exceed the amount of the savings which he can make in the sum allocated in the Plan of Expenditure for 1945/50 for the ITS, including Child Search;

(d) to enter into negotiations with the Allied High Commission in Germany with a view to arranging for the take over of the operations of the ITS and the Master Index and archives by the High Commission, at a date as early as possible before 31 March 1951 with the possible participation of certain governments, especially those interested in the tracing problem, in a Liaison capacity;

(e) to inform the Allied High Commission of the concern of the General Council that the security and preservation of the records and of the Master Index be assured and that the information contained therein be made fully available continuously in the future in the same manner as heretofore.

61. PLAN OF EXPENDITURE FOR THE SUPPLEMENTARY PERIOD

THE GENERAL COUNCIL of the IRO

HAVING EXAMINED AND DISCUSSED the Plan of Expenditure submitted by the Director-General, in accordance with Financial Regulation No. 8, for the Supplementary Period 1 July 1950–31 March 1951 (document EC/40/Rev. 1) as transmitted by the Executive Committee

RESOLVES

(1) to adopt the Plan of Expenditure, and

(2) to authorise the Director-General to incur obligations and to make expenditures against the Plan of Expenditure in a total amount not to exceed the sum of 2,506,893 United States dollars for administrative expenses, 52,459,016 United States dollars for operational expenses, and 199,537 United States dollars for large scale resettlement expenses.

62. COMMUNICATION TO THE UNITED NATIONS ON THE PROBLEM OF INTERNATIONAL PROTECTION

1. The General Council of IRO at its Fifth Session notes with satisfaction that with the undertaking on 1 January 1951 of the function of protection of refugees by the United Nations in which the 58 Government Members of the United Nations will hereafter participate—a function which has been heretofore the responsibility of the 18 Government Members of IRO—the affording of protection will pass into a new and different phase. In this connection, it desires to recommend to the United Nations that those refugees and displaced persons who have already been found eligible under the IRO Constitution by the IRO should clearly be regarded as under the competence of the High Commissioner for Refugees when he undertakes his duties.

2. The General Council of IRO also wishes to call the attention of the United Nations to the fact that IRO has been preoccupied with the enormous problem of refugees and displaced persons resulting from the war, with the movement of large numbers of persons in repatriation and resettlement and the overburdening problem of the care and maintenance of such persons; these services have been carried forward with resources inadequate to the task. These preoccupations of IRO have naturally influenced its decisions as to eligibility in a manner which should not be controlling in the broader perspective of the function of protection which the United Nations are now undertaking. Furthermore, it has appeared to the Council of IRO that certain sections of Parts I and II of Annex I—Definitions—to the IRO Constitution, which, it is recalled, was adopted in the light of the world situation of 1946, are no longer applicable with respect to the furnishing of protection in the light of the present day situation.

3. Pursuant to the foregoing, the General Council of the IRO has adopted the attached Resolution which it respectfully transmits to the Economic and Social Council.

Resolution on the Problem of International Protection

THE GENERAL COUNCIL of the International Refugee Organization

HAVING NOTED WITH SATISFACTION the Resolution of the General Assembly of the United Nations of 3 December 1949 with regard to the establishment of the Offices of the High Commissioner for Refugees as from 1 January 1951, and

HAVING GIVEN FURTHER CONSIDERATION to the problem of according protection to refugees under the auspices of the United Nations,

DESIRES TO ADVISE the Economic and Social Council of the conclusion, based on IRO experience, that certain sections of Parts I and II of Annex I—Definitions—of the IRO Constitution, such as, for example, Part I Section D sub-paragraphs (c), (d) and (e) and Part II, paragraph 6, no longer appear to be applicable to the furnishing of protection in the light of the present day situation; and that paragraph 2 (b) of Part II should be interpreted taking into account the real reasons which have inspired the persons concerned rather than indications of a purely formal nature,

RESPECTFULLY SUGGESTS to the Economic and Social Council that it give consideration to the adoption of a recommendation to the General Assembly of the United Nations that the General Assembly instruct the High Commissioner for Refugees

1. not to apply these aforesaid provisions of the definitions of refugees and displaced persons contained in Annex I of the IRO Constitution in the performance of his function of affording protection to refugees;

2. not to apply any decisions previously made by the General Council or the Administration of IRO restricting the services of IRO to refugees and displaced persons, such as the 'freeze order' and the date-lines which were adopted by IRO for purely financial or administrative reasons.

63. STATUS OF REFUGEES AND DISPLACED PERSONS IN GERMANY

THE GENERAL COUNCIL of the IRO

HAVING CONSIDERED at its Fifth Session the Memorandum of the Director-General on the problems relating to the protection of refugees and displaced persons in Germany,

NOTES WITH SATISFACTION the fact that the Allied High Commission in Germany have:

(a) adopted a law, determining the 'civil status' of refugees and displaced persons in Germany,

(b) requested the German Federal Government to prepare internal legislation defining the juridical, political, social and economic status to be accorded to refugees and displaced persons within the territory of the German Federal Government;

CONSIDERING FURTHER that, although the draft international convention relating to the status of refugees prepared by the ad hoc Committee cannot be submitted to the Economic and Social Council, and later to the General Assembly of the United Nations, until their next session, it does not appear desirable in the circumstances to invite Germany to accede to the 1933 Convention on Refugees, and

that it is none the less important that, at a time when the responsibilities of the IRO are reduced, the assurances which the refugees and displaced persons in Germany must enjoy should be fully safeguarded,

DESIROUS with this object in view, of advising the Allied High Commission in Germany, as the body responsible for the fate and the protection of the refugees and displaced persons in that country, as to certain aspects of the problem to which the Members of the General Council have given particular attention,

INSTRUCTS THE DIRECTOR-GENERAL to inform the Governments of the Occupying Powers of:

(a) the importance the General Council of the IRO attaches, in connection with the coming review of the Occupation Statute in Germany, to the retention by the occupying powers of reserve powers relating to refugees and displaced persons,

(b) the desire of the General Council that refugees and displaced persons in Germany be accorded juridical, political, social and economic status by the German Federal Government, substantially in accordance with the provisions already included in the draft international convention prepared by the ad hoc Committee of the Economic and Social Council,

(c) the desirability of inviting the German Federal Government to adhere to the future International Convention relating to the status of refugees, when the political and legal conditions necessary for the purpose permit,

(d) the desirability, in connection with the conclusion of the peace treaty with Germany, of including a clause in the treaty for safeguarding the rights of refugees and displaced persons.

64. CARE AND MAINTENANCE FOR REFUGEES IN PROCESS OF REPATRIATION OR RESETTLEMENT

THE GENERAL COUNCIL of the IRO

HAVING RECEIVED the Report of the Director-General (document GC/142) and of the Chairman of the Executive Committee (document GC/149/Add. 2) on the problem of the care and maintenance to be given after 30 June 1950 to refugees and displaced persons in the process of repatriation or resettlement, as well as on the means available for absorbing the costs involved in the continuation of such care and maintenance as may be necessary to promote repatriation and resettlement in order that the main objectives of the IRO may be accomplished before 31 March 1951,

RESOLVES

(1) to authorize the Director-General to give a liberal interpretation, within the practical limitations of the Plan of Expenditure for the Supplementary Period, to those provisions of Resolution No. 39 whereby he has been instructed to continue care and maintenance after 30 June 1950 for refugees and displaced persons who are in process of repatriation or resettlement, having regard for the total numbers which the Organization considers may be moved, on the basis of reasonably predictable resettlement opportunities, and

(2) to authorize the Director-General to negotiate with the Allied High Commission methods for meeting the costs of such care and maintenance in Germany out of the local currency funds made available for the support of refugees and displaced persons, taking into account the nature of the administrative arrangements made in each Zone for the progressive devolution upon the German authorities of responsibility for those refugees and displaced persons whom it will not have proved possible to repatriate or resettle.

66. IMPLEMENTATION OF RESOLUTION NO. 53: REFUGEES IN ITALY

THE GENERAL COUNCIL of the IRO

BEARING IN MIND the basic intent of its Resolution No. 53; and,

HAVING HEARD the Report of the Director-General on his examination with the Government of Italy of means of alleviating the heavy burden imposed on that country as a consequence of its geographical position; and

TAKING INTO ACCOUNT the very grave position, after the termination of the regular care and maintenance programme of the IRO, in which refugees will find themselves in Italy, a country already burdened by the presence of large numbers of Italian refugees from former territories and by the continued influx of new political refugees, as well as by overpopulation, unemployment and other economic difficulties; and,

NOTING WITH FAVOUR that the Italian Government, in accordance with its Constitution and traditions, has nevertheless continued since 15 October 1949 to receive upon its territory refugees from persecution;

RESOLVES

(1) to instruct the Director-General to negotiate with the Italian Government an arrangement whereby refugees who have entered Italy since 15 October 1949, who are within the mandate of the Organization for the purposes of legal protection, and who lack other adequate means of subsistence, may receive care and maintenance under Italian administration in the free enjoyment of an adequate legal status as envisaged in the international convention at present under discussion in the United Nations and at standards adequate to maintain health;

(2) to authorize the Director-General to credit against the contribution of the Italian Government for the Supplementary Period the difference between the present cost of care and maintenance and the cost (not to exceed the *per capita* rate heretofore incurred by IRO) of the arrangement to be negotiated in accordance with paragraph 1 above—subject to the approval of the General Council at its next subsequent session, and

(3) to invite the Director-General to take into account to the greatest extent possible the special situation of Italy when implementing his resettlement policies.

SIXTH SESSION, 9–13 October: Resolutions 68–79. GC/194/Rev. 1

69. ASSISTANCE FOR THE CIVILIAN POPULATION OF KOREA

THE GENERAL COUNCIL of the IRO

DEEPLY MOVED by the sufferings of the civilian population of Korea in their privation as the result of the conflict which has destroyed their homes and their material resources and has made a large number of them refugees, at least temporarily;

RECOGNIZING that, in the resolutions adopted by the Security Council and the Economic and Social Council of the United Nations on 31 July 1950 and 14 August 1950 respectively, the Specialized Agencies were requested to give whatever help the Unified Command of the United Nations in Korea might request, in order to assist and bring aid to the civilian population in that country; and

CONSIDERING the plight of the civilian population of Korea and the appeal to Specialized Agencies as a challenge to the effectiveness of international co-operation and humanitarian action;

ASSURES the Security Council and the Economic and Social Council of the United Nations of the readiness of the International Refugee Organization to consider with the greatest sympathy their appeals for assistance for the civilian population of Korea;

APPROVES of the action of the Director-General in offering to the Unified Command of the United Nations in Korea medical and other supplies and the loan of welfare officers and other trained personnel;

INSTRUCTS THE DIRECTOR-GENERAL to meet as fully as may be possible within the limits of resources available to the Organization any future request which may be received from the United Nations for assistance for the civilian population in Korea.

71. RESOLUTION AMENDING PARAGRAPH 1 OF RESOLUTION No. 39

THE GENERAL COUNCIL of the IRO

ANXIOUS to extend the services of the Organization to the greatest possible number of eligible refugees consistent with its resources and facilities;

AWARE that a substantial number of eligible refugees from political and religious persecution have arrived in areas of IRO operations since 15 October 1949, but have been deprived of the Organization's resettlement services because of the datelines established by the General Council at its Fourth Session;

CONVINCED that resources are sufficient to extend resettlement services to these highly deserving refugees during the Supplementary Period;

AUTHORIZES THE DIRECTOR-GENERAL at his discretion, to extend resettlement assistance to those refugees who arrived in areas of IRO operations in Europe and the Middle East before 1 October 1950, and who are not firmly established in those areas, on the understanding that their resettlement be carried out within the existing resources of the Organization and that it not prejudice the resettlement opportunities of refugees already registered, or the realization of the Hard Core Programme.

74. ADDITIONAL PLAN OF EXPENDITURE FOR THE SUPPLEMENTARY PERIOD

THE GENERAL COUNCIL of the IRO

HAVING EXAMINED AND DISCUSSED the Additional Plan of Expenditure for the Supplementary Period as contained in document EC/50 submitted by the Director-General in accordance with Financial Regulations No. 8 and transmitted by the Executive Committee,

RESOLVES

(1) to adopt the Additional Plan of Expenditure;

(2) to authorize the Director-General to incur obligations and to make expenditures against the Additional Plan of Expenditure in a total amount not to exceed the sum of 2,553,872 United States dollars for Administrative expenses, (of which 1,300,000 United States dollars are for closure purposes), and 29,188,715 United States dollars for Operational expenses.

76. COMPLETION OF THE PROGRAMME OF THE ORGANIZATION

THE GENERAL COUNCIL of the IRO

HAVING CAREFULLY REVIEWED the refugee problem with which the Organization is concerned, in the light of the information contained in the Annual Report of the Director-General (document GC/166) and his proposals for the conduct of operations during the Supplementary Period set forth in his Report (document GC/167) and presented verbally by him to the Council;

CONVINCED that with the invaluable assistance of governments and voluntary societies the IRO has accomplished a large measure of the task entrusted to it by the United Nations;

ANXIOUS that full use be made of existing resources and facilities in the short period of time ahead of it;

RECOGNIZING that the completion of the IRO programme will involve unusual difficulties and that the Organization is faced with especially complex problems;

A

AUTHORIZES THE DIRECTOR-GENERAL to take all administrative measures which he may consider necessary to bring to a successful conclusion the task of the IRO consistent with the objectives and general policies of the Organization as set forth in the Constitution, the resolutions of the General Council and the financial and other regulations;

B

EXPRESSES its appreciation of the unfailing support which the Governments of the Occupying Powers have afforded with the help of the Government of the Federal Republic of Germany and of Austria to the International Refugee Organization for the conduct of its operations in Germany and Austria, in terms of both programme and administrative facilities;

APPEALS to the Governments of the Occupying Powers for the continuation of such support until the end of the Organization's operations;

C

COMMENDS the humanitarian spirit which has animated governments and voluntary societies in assuming responsibility for the Institutional Hard Core cases, the most distressed group of the refugees under IRO care;

APPROVES the arrangements made by the Director-General for the long-term care of such cases, both in countries of their present residence and in countries whose Governments have agreed to accept a substantial number of such cases on to their territories;

INSTRUCTS THE DIRECTOR-GENERAL to seek further opportunities for the long-term care of Institutional Hard Core cases in countries of permanent asylum; or as an alternative, to make further arrangements *sur place*, similar to those which have already been made in Germany for the long-term care of such cases;

D

COMMENDS the attitude of the various governments and authorities which have agreed to assume as of 1 July 1950 care and maintenance responsibilities discharged up to that date by the IRO;

EXPRESSES its satisfaction with the arrangements made through the Allied High Commissioners with the German authorities whereby the latter have assumed full responsibility for the material welfare of refugees who are likely to remain in Germany;

WELCOMES the declaration made by the Government of the Federal Republic of Germany on the occasion of the submission to the German Parliament of the law governing the status of non-German refugees and the stated intention of that Government to adhere to the United Nations Convention relating to the Status of Refugees when it will have been adopted;

EXPRESSES its appreciation of the action of the international voluntary societies, which have undertaken by agreement with the IRO, to perform, in collaboration with affiliated German and Austrian societies, social casework among the refugees remaining in Germany and Austria;

INSTRUCTS THE DIRECTOR-GENERAL to afford to the authorities and organizations concerned the maximum assistance possible within the limited resources and facilities available to the IRO, in order to promote the well-being of refugees in Germany and Austria and to enable them to become assimilated into the local community, in the best possible conditions of housing and employment.

AFFIRMS that, in order to bring to a successful conclusion the task with which it has been entrusted, the Organization requires the continuing support not only of Member Governments but of all governments of goodwill.

RESOLVES therefore, to appeal again to all those governments to consider the possibility of admitting further groups of refugees on to their territories under the most liberal selection standards and of providing permanent asylum to the maximum number of Institutional Hard Core cases.

77. Electing the Executive Committee

The general council of the IRO

IN ACCORDANCE WITH paragraphs 2 and 3 of Article 7 of the Constitution

RESOLVES that, as from the end of the Sixth Session of the General Council, the following nine Members of the Organization shall constitute the Executive Committee of the General Council:

Australia, Belgium, Canada, France, Italy, Norway, United Kingdom, United States, Venezuela.

78. Continuation of the Organization's Operations

The general council of the IRO

DETERMINED to carry out the basic objectives of the Organization, to the fullest possible extent within the limit of resources now available, and in particular to achieve the firm re-establishment of the greatest possible number of refugees, to complete the solution of the Hard Core problem, and to aid to the fullest possible extent in the effective local establishment of those refugees who cannot be settled outside the areas of their present residence;

TAKING COGNIZANCE of unavoidable delays in the processing and reception of refugees by governments still willing to receive them, and of a considerable increase in resettlement opportunities resulting chiefly from new United States legislation; and

HAVING NOTED that, as a result of the slowdown in resettlement movements, sufficient resources still are available to the Organization for the resettlement of nearly all remaining refugees within the IRO mandate for whom opportunities are expected to be available, and to carry out the other objectives of the Organization, without the need for additional contributions by Member Governments;

RESOLVES TO AUTHORIZE THE DIRECTOR-GENERAL to carry on the approved operational programmes of the Organization, within the limits of existing resources, until 30 September 1951.

83. The Extension of Resettlement Assistance

The general council of the IRO

HAVING CONSIDERED the observations of the Director-General contained in his Outline of Plans for the Period of Operations after 1 April 1951 upon the implementation of Resolution No. 71 adopted at the Sixth Session of the Council in October 1950;

DESIRING to extend resettlement assistance during the short remaining period of IRO operations to as many eligible refugees as the resources and facilities of the Organization permit, irrespective of the date at which the refugees requiring such assistance arrived in the areas of IRO operations;

AUTHORISES the Director-General at his discretion to grant resettlement assistance, including hard core grants for resettlement, to any eligible refugees in areas of IRO operation in Europe and the Middle East who are not firmly established in those areas, on the understanding that their resettlement be carried out within the existing realisable resources of the Organization, that the resettlement of newly registered refugees shall not prejudice the resettlement opportunities of those previously registered and that the Director-General will so use the discretion granted to him as to minimise the risk of persons not now in refugee status being encouraged to enter that status.

84. Resolution Amending Resolution No. 78 on the Continuation of the Organization's Operations

The general council of the IRO

HAVING CONSIDERED the Outline of Plans for the Period of Operations after 1 April 1951 presented by the Director-General in document GC/213;

BEING OF THE OPINION THAT the Director-General should be authorised to complete, to the extent practicable within the limits of existing resources, the programmes proposed;

RESOLVES to authorise the Director-General to continue the approved operational programme of the Organization beyond the date limit set in Resolution No. 78 for so long as the existing realisable resources of the Organization permit and there are left any refugees within the mandate of the Organization who require resettlement assistance and for whom resettlement opportunities can be found.

87. PROPOSED PLAN OF EXPENDITURE FOR THE SUPPLEMENTARY AND CLOSURE PERIODS BEGINNING 1 JULY 1950

THE GENERAL COUNCIL of the IRO

HAVING EXAMINED AND DISCUSSED the Proposed Plan of Expenditure for the Supplementary and Closure Periods beginning 1 July 1950, as contained in document EC/56 submitted by the Director-General in accordance with Financial Regulation No. 8, and transmitted by the Executive Committee,

RESOLVES

(1) to adopt this Plan of Expenditure for the Supplementary and Closure Periods beginning 1 July 1950; and

(2) to authorise the Director-General to incur obligations and to make expenditures in accordance with the Plan of Expenditure in the manner prescribed by the Financial Regulations.

88. AMENDMENT OF THE FINANCIAL REGULATIONS

THE GENERAL COUNCIL of the IRO

RECOGNIZING the need for greater flexibility in the Organization's operations and consequently in the Plan of Expenditure during the remaining period of the Organization's activities,

RESOLVES that Financial Regulation No. 9 be amended to read as follows:

'The Director-General is authorized to transfer by written order funds between sections within the administrative part of the Plan of Expenditure adopted under Regulation 8, and to increase by not more than 25% any section in the operational part of such Plan of Expenditure by transfers from other sections thereof.

'The Director-General is also authorized to increase any section of the Plan of Expenditure by the addition, under written order, of Miscellaneous Income not previously included in the Plan of Expenditure.

'The Director-General shall report to the next subsequent meeting of the Executive Committee any such transfers or increases together with a written explanation of each.'

89. THE INTERNATIONAL TRACING SERVICE

THE GENERAL COUNCIL of the IRO

HAVING NOTED the Review of the History and Activities of the International Tracing Service submitted by the Director-General of the International Refugee Organization (document GC/198);

EXPRESSES its appreciation of this Review, which bears witness to the tremendous achievements of the Allied Authorities, National Tracing Bureaux, UNRRA and the ITS in the tracing of missing persons;

NOTES with extreme satisfaction that the ITS, under the IRO, and continuing the work of its predecessors has obtained outstanding results, in investigating one hundred tons of documents involving over 20 million names of Allied nationals, in achieving the classification of over 11,000,000 cards in the master card index of the ITS, the distribution to National Tracing Bureaux and other tracing agencies of documents concerning nearly 1,000,000 persons, the supplying of information concerning 155,093 persons after checking up on individual graves of Allied nationals, the publication of a two-volume catalogue of the concentration and labour camps organized by the Nazis in Germany, Austria and the occupied territories, the identification of 4,808 children;

PAYS TRIBUTE to the Director and Staff of the ITS for their unfailing devotion to these most important duties entrusted to them by the IRO;

NOTES WITH SATISFACTION that the negotiations entered into by the Director-General with the Allied High Commission in Germany, in accordance with Resolution No. 57 adopted by the Council at its Fifth Session, have been brought to a successful conclusion;

APPROVES the agreement concluded between the IRO and the Allied High Commission,

EXPRESSES ITS GRATITUDE to the Allied High Commission for agreeing to assume the responsibilities involved in taking over the functions and the safe custody of the records of the ITS as from 1 April 1951.

BEING ANXIOUS that the safety and preservation of the records and the master card index of the ITS should be assured in the future,

EXPRESSES THE HOPE that the Allied High Commission, guided by this concern, will take steps to ensure that the information contained therein be fully and continuously available in the future to the Governments having a special interest in the matter in the same manner as heretofore.

EIGHTH SESSION, 22–27 October 1951: Resolutions 91–99. GC/251/Rev. 1

97. RESIDUAL PROBLEMS

THE GENERAL COUNCIL of the IRO

BEARING IN MIND the invitation of the General Assembly of the United Nations, contained in Assembly Resolution No. 430 (V) of 14 December 1950, to transmit to it a communication on the problems of assistance to refugees; and

HAVING REVIEWED the residual problems which will remain at the termination of the activities of the IRO;

RESOLVES to request the Director-General to transmit the attached communication on its behalf to the General Assembly of the United Nations, for consideration at its Sixth Session.

Communication to the General Assembly of the United Nations

1. The General Council of the IRO in response to the invitation contained in paragraph 2 of Resolution No. 430 (V) adopted by the General Assembly of the United Nations on 14 December, 1950, transmits the following communication. This communication does not constitute a final report of the Organization, but aims solely to supply information to the General Assembly for the purpose of assisting the Assembly in its examination of the problem of assistance to refugees.

2. The General Council of the IRO at its Eighth Session (October 1951) determined that it had sufficient funds available to continue operations until 1 January, 1952, and that if additional assets arising out of operations are realized, it may prove possible to assist and to re-establish several additional thousand refugees in January and February, 1952. The Organization has already repatriated and resettled in excess of a million refugees, and will have made reasonably satisfactory provision for approximately 47,000 refugees and their dependants by the end of 1951, who, because of

age or infirmity, require permanent institutional or other forms of care. The problem of assistance to refugees in all territories where they have been established, both in Europe and overseas has been satisfactorily solved, thanks either to good conditions of employment in those countries or to the willingness of the receiving governments to help the refugees.

3. It can now be anticipated, however, that in spite of all efforts which the Organization has made or will make before termination, limited numbers of refugees will remain in certain areas whose problems, in the judgment of the General Council, will not have been satisfactorily resolved.

4. The Organization has devoted special attention to the resolution of the problems of refugees in the areas described in this communication, but because of limitations of time and resources and the presence of other factors in the situations set forth in this communication, must report that certain refugees will remain in their present areas of residence, facing doubtful prospects of achieving assimilation or self-maintenance in the immediate future. Generally speaking, the conditions under which they remain do not offer opportunities for the future; in some areas the level of economic activity is inadequate to meet the requirements of the indigenous population, and in consequence refugees presenting claims for assistance on purely humanitarian grounds cannot be integrated in the local economies; in other areas the refugees are unwelcome where they now are on political grounds but unable to depart, or local measures for their relief or institutions for their care are unavailable or inadequate.

EUROPE
Germany
5. In Germany the presence and continuing influx of large numbers of refugees of German ethnic origin, the shortage of housing necessitating the residence of substantial numbers in camps, unemployment and unbalance in the local economy make the assimilation of refugees formerly under IRO care difficult. Of 140,000 IRO refugees remaining in that country, 60,000 may be considered to be satisfactorily established, while the remaining 80,000 desiring emigration, have been unable for various reasons to qualify for resettlement and must, therefore, seek assimilation in Germany. The indigent among the latter group not only constitute a burden upon public relief rolls but present a problem which strains the capacity of voluntary agencies to meet. Although the situation of refugees in general tends to improve, with the rising level of the German economy, progress in this direction is slow and consequently the conditions under which the refugees live are not considered to be wholly satisfactory.

Austria
6. Approximately 24,000 refugees heretofore under the care of IRO will remain in Austria, some of whom will desire emigration. Austria has also received large numbers of refugees of German ethnic origin and suffers from overpopulation, a shortage of housing and unemployment. The refugees remaining in Austria will, therefore, face great difficulties in achieving assimilation and self dependence.

Italy
7. The presence in Italy of 24,000 refugees within the mandate of the IRO presents a very serious problem on account of the already existing considerable excess of manpower due to the natural increase in the population. The Italian Government, which has to face the unemployment of its own population, is consequently, not in a position to offer either assistance or employment to these refugees who, therefore, would prefer to emigrate if they were offered the possibility of doing so.

Trieste

8. The IRO has made intensive efforts to resettle refugees entering the Free Territory of Trieste, but some 7,000 will remain awaiting disposition after the Organization ceases operations. Of these, 900, including persons suffering from tuberculosis and other serious illnesses, present problems of continuing care. Some of these refugees are housed in Allied Military Government Camps and others are living in overcrowded private housing. These refugees are under the administration of the Allied Military Authorities, but the expense of their care is borne by the Italian Government. Moreover, the flow of refugees into Trieste continues at a rate slightly in excess of departures from the area.

Greece

9. In Greece, although the IRO has endeavoured during the year to resettle as many as possible of the refugees within its mandate, it has not been possible for these resettlement operations to keep pace with the rate of arrivals of new refugees. The Government of Greece is doing everything in its power to improve conditions for them, but it already has to provide for the refugees of Greek nationality or Greek ethnic origin whose presence in the country in large numbers is the result of the disturbed conditions prevailing on its northern frontiers. In view of the country's very limited resources and the difficult economic situation it has to face, Greece will be unable to absorb political refugees of foreign origin. It is therefore expected that some 4,500 refugees registered with the IRO will still not have been established by the time the Organization ceases to exist, and will consequently find themselves in a very difficult position.

Turkey

10. The situation of approximately 300 refugees in Turkey will continue to be one of insecurity. Internal resources for their care are unavailable, and Turkey is already beset by the influx of large numbers of refugees of Turkish origin from Bulgaria.

Spain and Portugal

11. The Organization has been unable to negotiate with the Spanish Government satisfactory living arrangements for approximately 500 refugees in Spain. Of these, fifty have been receiving assistance from the IRO which will be discontinued on its termination.

12. The Organization has also failed to make satisfactory arrangements with respect to 100 refugees remaining in Portugal. They will be unable to secure work and residence permits and will face an uncertain future.

New Refugees

13. It is estimated that from 1,000 to 1,500 refugees are entering Germany, Austria, Turkey, Greece, Trieste and Italy from Eastern European countries monthly. Their impact is felt also in nearly every country of Western Europe, where political asylum is an established tradition. In all of the areas of initial reception resources for their care are inadequate and many of these refugees must move on westward to find opportunities for a livelihood. This continuous influx underlines the permanent character of the refugee problem, particularly in Europe, which has been a matter of concern to international bodies ever since the end of the First World War.

MIDDLE EAST

14. In spite of the best efforts of the Organization with the assistance of selection missions sent to the area by three countries of reception, 250 refugees within the

mandate of the IRO remain in the Middle East, of whom 90 are receiving maintenance assistance from the IRO which will be discontinued by 1 January 1952. The countries of the Middle East already overburdened with problems of Palestinian refugees are unable to assist IRO refugees, and local facilities for their relief are unavailable.

FAR EAST

China

15. The situation of refugees in China causes the greatest concern. There remain there about 5,000 refugees of European origin, 2,000 of whom are at present receiving care and maintenance from the IRO. Four hundred of these will require continuing institutional care because of their age, illness or other disability. The number of refugees requiring assistance will inevitably increase as the present resources of the persons concerned are diminishing. In spite of the efforts of the Organization no authority or private agency or group has so far accepted responsibility for the assistance of these refugees when the IRO will have disappeared. If no assistance is given to them they will undoubtedly be in a most desperate situation.

Philippine Islands

16. In 1949 the Philippine Government, at the request of the IRO, offered temporary asylum to 5,500 refugees from Shanghai on the condition that the Organization would eventually remove them to other areas. The IRO has succeeded in resettling 5,350 refugees from this group. There will remain 150 refugees on the island of Samar, many of whom require institutional care. The Organization has found it impossible to place this residual group elsewhere. In view of its previous commitment, the Organization will endeavour in the time remaining to make the best arrangements possible, but the success of this effort remains in doubt at this time.

CONCLUSIONS

17. It must be borne in mind that in most of the countries mentioned above the situation of refugees coming within the mandate of the IRO is rendered precarious by the large numbers of refugees or other persons entering these areas, who, while outside the scope of the competence of the IRO, at the same time reduce considerably the opportunities of housing and employment available to refugees under the protection of the Organization.

18. In considering these residual problems for which it is not expected that satisfactory solutions will be found before the termination of IRO operations, the representatives of the Member Governments at the Eighth Session of the General Council were not prepared to present the position of their Governments as to measures which might be taken, in further efforts to resolve those problems by the General Assembly.

19. Nevertheless, they are agreed that, although the problem inherent in the situation as here set out are clearly not of sufficient magnitude to justify the maintenance of the IRO, they are so grave in terms of human suffering that they call for urgent consideration by the United Nations.

98. REMAINING ASSETS

THE GENERAL COUNCIL of the IRO

RECOGNIZING THE URGENCY OF THE EARLIEST POSSIBLE CONVERSION into utilisable form of all the assets of the Organization in order to enable it to resettle the maximum possible number of refugees from Germany, Austria, Italy and other areas, and otherwise to complete its programme and assigned tasks;

TAKING NOTE IN PARTICULAR that the Organization, under agreement with the occupation authorities, undertook at the commencement of its operations to replace to the German economy only the imported element of food consumed by IRO refugees;

TAKING NOTE of the Report of the Director-General that such replacement was necessarily carried out on the basis of long-range estimates, and that the final figures show that the Organization has supplied to the German economy a substantially larger amount of food-stuffs than was actually required to replace the imported element of commodities consumed by IRO refugees, that the value of such excess replacement is substantial, and has been made at the expense of Member Governments of the Organization;

TAKING NOTE that negotiations are in course with respect to other assets of the Organization which have not yet been placed at its disposal;

RECOGNIZING the interest of all Member Governments of the Organization in all such assets;

INVITES the attention of the Allied High Commission for Germany to the urgency of IRO's need to avail itself of all of its assets in a form which will permit their early use in completing the Organization's resettlement programme and its other assigned tasks;

REQUESTS the Allied High Commission for Germany to take all possible steps in conjunction with the Government of the Federal Republic to place at the earliest possible disposal of the Organization its assets arising out of the excess replacement to the German economy of food imports, which have directly benefited the German economy;

URGES other Governments and Authorities with whom negotiations are in process with respect to other assets of the Organization to take all possible measures to bring such negotiations to an early conclusion and to make available to the Organization agreed assets with the least possible delay and in a form permitting their utilization during the limited remainder of the Organization's lifetime; and

INSTRUCTS the Director-General to transmit this Resolution to the Allied High Commission for Germany and to other interested Authorities or Governments; and

REQUESTS the Director-General to take all measures appropriate to the earliest possible attainment of the objectives of this Resolution.

NINTH SESSION, 11–16 February 1952: Resolutions 100–110. GC/276/Rev. 1

102. FINANCIAL STATEMENTS FOR THE FIFTEEN MONTHS ENDED 30 SEPTEMBER 1951 AND FUTURE FINANCIAL REPORTS

THE GENERAL COUNCIL of the IRO

HAVING EXAMINED AND CONSIDERED the Financial Statements for the Fifteen months ended 30 September 1951 prepared and presented by the Director-General (document GC/253),

RESOLVES

(1) to accept the Financial Statements; and

(2) to approve the proposals of the Director-General as set forth in document GC/261 that the Balance Sheet and supporting statements as at 31 January 1952, and the Statement of Liquidation as at the final closure of the IRO, all duly audited, shall constitute the final financial reports of the Organization and shall be circulated to Member Governments as soon as possible after their respective effective dates.

103. FINAL PLAN OF EXPENDITURE FOR THE SUPPLEMENTARY AND CLOSURE PERIODS BEGINNING 1 JULY 1950

THE GENERAL COUNCIL of the IRO

HAVING EXAMINED AND DISCUSSED the Final Plan of Expenditure for the Supplementary and Closure Periods beginning 1 July 1950, as contained in document GC/265 submitted by the Director-General in accordance with Financial Regulation No. 8, and transmitted by the Executive Committee,

RESOLVES

(1) to adopt the Final Plan of Expenditure for the Supplementary and Closure Periods beginning 1 July 1950 in the amount of $102,827,440 representing the amounts of $102,530,237 shown in the Plan of Expenditure plus the additional payment of $297,205 made by the Government of Australia; and

(2) to authorize the Director-General and the Liquidator to incur obligations and to make expenditures in accordance with the Final Plan of Expenditure in the manner prescribed by the Financial Regulations.

106. DISPOSAL OF ASSETS

THE GENERAL COUNCIL of the IRO

HAVING CONSIDERED proposals for the disposal of any assets of the Organization over and above those included in the Final Plan of Expenditure

RESOLVES that such assets shall be disposed of in accordance with the following schedule of priorities:

(1) the first charge shall be to meet unforeseen claims against the Organization and to defray any additional costs of liquidation which might be incurred during the period of liquidation beyond those provided for in the Final Plan of Expenditure;

(2) the second charge shall be to reimburse the Provisional Intergovernmental Committee for the Movement of Migrants from Europe the costs of moving IRO eligible refugees who, by 1 February 1952 had been visaed, but not moved;

(3) the third charge shall be to provide, after consultation with the United Nations High Commissioner for Refugees, to the extent of assets realized from a satisfactory settlement of the Food Replacement Account in Germany and from any assets which may be realized in Deutsche Marks, grants for assistance to residual refugees, such as grants for refugees in Trieste, to the Displaced Persons Department of the Expellee Bank, to Voluntary Societies and to Refugee Service Committees;

(4) the fourth charge shall be to establish a revolving fund in the form of a trust, to be managed by the Provisional Intergovernmental Committee for the Movement of Migrants from Europe, for the movement of refugees who received visas after 1 February 1952. Priority will be given to refugees now registered with the IRO.

108. ESTABLISHING A BOARD OF LIQUIDATION

THE GENERAL COUNCIL of the IRO

HAVING CONSIDERED the plans for the liquidation of the Organization presented by the Director-General in document GC/262

RESOLVES

(1) that the IRO shall go into liquidation on 1 March 1952;

(2) that there be established as from 15 February 1952 a Board of Liquidation consisting of the Representatives of the following Member Governments of the Organization:

France, United Kingdom, Venezuela;

(3) that the Board of Liquidation, which shall be convened to its first session by the Director-General, shall elect a Chairman; and that thereafter the Chairman or

his Designate shall convene the Board upon the request of a Member of the Board or of the Liquidator;

(4) that subject to the ultimate authority of the General Council which remains unimpaired by this Resolution, the Board of Liquidation shall be vested with all the powers necessary to carry on and complete the work of the liquidation and dissolution of the Organization;

(5) that the Board of Liquidation shall conform to the policies established by the General Council and the Executive Committee;

(6) that the Board of Liquidation shall be authorized to dispose of any assets, property and records of the Organization in accordance with the directions of the General Council, and insofar as there are no such directions within its own discretion; and

(7) that the Board of Liquidation shall submit reports to all Member Governments of the Organization.

110. Defining the Powers of the Liquidator

The general council of the IRO

having created an Office of the Liquidator of the Organization as from 1 March 1952

resolves that

(1) on 1 March 1952 the Office of the Director-General shall be abolished and the Liquidator shall be the Chief Administrative Officer of the Organization;

(2) the Liquidator, who shall be responsible to the Board of Liquidation for the conduct of the Liquidation, shall administer all the activities of the Organization relating to the Liquidation of its affairs. His authority and responsibility shall include any action which the Director-General would have been authorized to take, or would have been responsible for taking, in relation to the disposition of claims and liabilities of the Organization, the receipt, management and disbursement of funds, the purchase and sale of securities, the opening, management and closing of bank accounts, the appointment, direction and termination of the Organization's personnel, the reporting of its current activities, and the preparation, presentation, confirmation, verification and completion of its accounts. The Liquidator shall have the authority to negotiate with Member and Non-Member Governments of the Organization, with appropriate Occupational Authorities, with the United Nations and its Specialized Agencies, with intergovernmental bodies, and with all other organizations, public and private, and individuals, and to conclude or determine agreements therewith;

(3) the Liquidator shall conform to the policy established and instructions issued, by the General Council, the Executive Committee and the Board of Liquidation with respect to the conduct of the Organization's affairs during the period of liquidation;

(4) the Liquidator shall, in addition, accept such other powers and responsibilities as the Board of Liquidation may confer upon him;

(5) any final assets property and records of the Organization, which may remain at the time of the completion of the liquidation, shall be disposed of by the Liquidator as determined by the General Council and the Board of Liquidation;

(6) the Liquidator shall have the same authority and powers as were previously entrusted to the Director-General, such authority and powers being limited to liquidation operations;

(7) to the extent that this Resolution varies in any way from the provisions of any previous Resolutions of the General Council, such Resolutions are to be deemed amended.

C. RESOLUTIONS OF THE EXECUTIVE COMMITTEE

1. Insurance programme of the Organization.
2. Assistance to Palestine refugees.
3. Immigration into the countries of the Middle East.
4. Appreciation of the action of the Government of the Philippine Republic.
5. Evacuation from China of European refugees within the mandate of the IRO.
6. Immigration into the countries of the Middle East.
7. Eligibility of refugees of Baltic origin.
8. Temporary asylum of refugees in the Philippines.
9. Assistance to the United Nations relief for Palestine refugees.
10. Resettlement assistance.
11. Disposal of records.

FIRST TO TENTH SESSIONS: Resolutions 1–11. EC/64

1. INSURANCE PROGRAMME OF THE ORGANIZATION

(Adopted at the 8th Meeting, 9 December 1948)

THE EXECUTIVE COMMITTEE of the IRO

HAVING EXAMINED the Report of the Director-General on the Insurance Programme of the Organization (document EC/4); and

HAVING NOTED the insurance arrangements entered into by the Director-General with commercial companies for coverage of certain specified risks on the one hand, and the reserves established by him on the other hand for self-insurance of risks which are commercially uninsurable or for which commercial insurance would be uneconomical

APPROVES the insurance arrangements made and

RECOMMENDS that if and in so far as it appears to the Director-General conducive to the efficient and economical discharge of the operations of the Organization, the Organization may carry its own risks, except as may otherwise be directed by the Committee.

2. ASSISTANCE TO PALESTINE REFUGEES

(Adopted at the 10th Meeting, 10 December 1948)

THE EXECUTIVE COMMITTEE of the IRO

HAVING RECEIVED the Resolution of the General Assembly of the United Nations of 19 November 1948 (UN document A/731) on the urgent problem of the relief of Palestine refugees; and

NOTING the appeal of the General Assembly to the International Refugee Organization and other appropriate organizations promptly to contribute supplies, specialised personnel and other services permitted by their constitutions and their financial resources, to relieve the desperate plight of Palestine refugees of all communities; and

HAVING TAKEN NOTE of the Report of the Director-General on Relations with the UN (document EC/10);

RESOLVED to approve, in accordance with Resolution No. 29 of the General Council of the IRO, the action taken by the Director-General, pending the establishment of the required UN administrative organization, in forthwith donating to the relief programme established by the General Assembly 100,000 blankets, in arranging a loan of 6,000 to 7,000 tons of flour for that programme, in turning over certain stores and vehicles of the Organization in the Middle East, and in proposing to examine with the UN the possible use in that programme of the procurement facilities and of members of the staff of the Organization.

3. IMMIGRATION INTO THE COUNTRIES OF THE MIDDLE EAST

(Adopted at the 11th Meeting, 11 December 1948)

THE EXECUTIVE COMMITTEE of the IRO
HAVING HEARD the declaration of the Director-General that he intends to countermand the instructions issued by the Executive Secretary of the Preparatory Commission on 18 May 1948 regarding the question of the participation of IRO in immigration into the countries of the Middle East; and
CONSIDERING the gravity and complexity of the question of principle involved,
REQUESTS the Director-General
1. to prepare and circulate to Governments Members of the Executive Committee a comprehensive memorandum setting forth the facts and considerations necessary for a just appreciation of the question; and
2. to suspend all other action in the matter pending a further meeting of the Executive Committee to be held on 25 January 1949 at a place to be fixed by the Chairman.

4. APPRECIATION OF THE ACTION OF THE GOVERNMENT OF THE PHILIPPINE REPUBLIC

(Adopted at the 14th Meeting, 26 January 1949)

THE EXECUTIVE COMMITTEE of the IRO
EMPHASISING the generosity with which the Chinese Government has for long provided a place of refuge to important numbers of European refugees; and
HAVING RECEIVED the report of the Director-General that the Government of the Philippine Republic has offered to the Organization a temporary asylum under appropriate conditions for refugees now leaving Chinese territory (document EC/17)
RESOLVES
1. to approve the action of the Director-General in accepting the terms proposed by the Government of the Philippine Republic;
2. to express to that Government in the name of the Organization its highest appreciation of the humanity and generosity of this grant of refuge;
3. to request the Director-General to transmit to the Government of the Philippine Republic the terms of this Resolution.

5. EVACUATION FROM CHINA OF EUROPEAN REFUGEES WITHIN THE MANDATE OF THE IRO

(Adopted at the 14th Meeting, 26 January 1949)

THE EXECUTIVE COMMITTEE of the IRO
HAVING TAKEN NOTE of the Report of the Director-General on the Evacuation from China of European Refugees within the mandate of IRO (Document EC/17)
APPROVES the measures taken to date; and
AUTHORISES the immediate evacuation of the eligible European refugees now in China whose lives or well-being may be in serious danger, subject to a careful control of their eligibility and assessment of the degree of their danger; and

RESOLVES that this evacuation be carried out in the following manner:

1. temporary reception under the conditions of asylum offered on the territory of the Republic of the Philippines, pending re-establishment elsewhere;

2. immediate steps toward establishment in countries of permanent or temporary reception; and

URGES Governments Members of the IRO and other Governments of good will to take their part in implementing the terms of this Resolution, in particular by providing opportunities of permanent, or (if this should prove necessary) temporary resettlement for the refugees evacuated from China.

6. IMMIGRATION INTO THE COUNTRIES OF THE MIDDLE EAST

(Adopted at the 19th Meeting, 28 January 1949)

THE EXECUTIVE COMMITTEE of the IRO

HAVING EXAMINED AND DISCUSSED the Report of the Director-General on Immigration into the countries of the Middle East (document EC/14); and

BEARING IN MIND the importance of assisting in every way possible the early resettlement of eligible refugees in all countries where they may be firmly established in accordance with their own best interests; and

TAKING INTO ACCOUNT the existence of a refugee problem in the Middle East, in aid of which the Organization has already made a substantial contribution;

RESOLVES to adopt the recommendations of the Director-General as set forth in his Report, with the following reservations:

(a) That before assisting the movement or making payment for the transportation costs of persons emigrating to Palestine and adjacent countries whose journeys originate after 31 January, 1949, the Director-General should consult the Conciliation Commission with respect to such transportation and that payment for same shall be conditional on verification of eligibility and on priority being given to refugees and displaced persons who are at present in IRO camps or who have been for some months in transit in various countries of provisional reception; and

(b) That in the event that by a date not later than two weeks preceding the Fourth Session of the Executive Committee, the results of his consultation with the Conciliation Commission have not been such as to enable the Director-General to make payment for the transportation costs of persons whose emigration to Palestine and adjacent countries originated after 31 January, 1949, he shall report to the Committee about such consultations as have taken place and shall make a recommendation for the consideration of the Committee at its Fourth Session with respect to the action to be taken by the IRO.

7. ELIGIBILITY OF REFUGEES OF BALTIC ORIGIN

(Adopted at the 25th Meeting, 30 March 1949)

THE EXECUTIVE COMMITTEE of the IRO

HAVING TAKEN COGNIZANCE of the report circulated to the members of the Committee regarding the eligibility of certain categories of refugees of Baltic origin;

HAVING HEARD the explanations given by the Director-General thereon;

CONSIDERED with the Director-General, that, in order that the interested persons be assured of a correct application of the provisions of the Constitution relating to eligibility, the policy advocated by the Director-General following the discussions which have taken place during the examination of this question should be approved.

8. Temporary Asylum of Refugees in the Philippines
(Adopted at the 45th Meeting, 12 October 1949)

The executive committee of the IRO

HAVING TAKEN NOTE of the Report of the Director-General on the Situation in the Far East (document EC/32), and

BEARING IN MIND the commitments of the Organization to the Republic of the Philippines and the conditions under which the Philippine Government generously offered a temporary asylum on its territory, pending their resettlement elsewhere, to European refugees from the Far East, and

BEING SATISFIED after a detailed examination of all the measures taken to date, that the Organization is doing all that lies within its power to expedite the removal of these refugees from their temporary haven to countries of firm re-establishment;

RESOLVES

1. to express its highest appreciation to the Philippine Government for the generous assistance already accorded to refugees in the gravest need, and to appeal to that Government, in the name of the Organization, to extend the period of the hospitality offered them; and

2. to instruct the Director-General to intensify his work with interested Governments in order to develop all possible programmes calculated to speed up the resettlement in countries of permanent reception of the European refugees now maintained on the territory of the Philippines, in full satisfaction of the assurances given by the Organization to the Philippine Government, and to report to the Executive Committee at its Seventh Session on the results achieved.

9. Assistance to the United Nations Relief for Palestine Refugees
(Adopted at the 48th Meeting, 20 October 1949)

The executive committee of the IRO

HAVING RECEIVED the enquiry of the Secretary-General of the UN as to whether the IRO could make available currencies or commodities to the United Nations Relief for Palestine Refugees (UNRPR), together with the report of the Director-General on the stocks available and the currencies not yet expended on the immediate programme of the Organization; and

BEARING IN MIND the generous assistance given by the UN to the PCIRO at the time of its formation, as well as the urgent needs of the UNRPR;

AUTHORIZES THE DIRECTOR-GENERAL

1. to donate to the UNRPR such of the quantities of the stocks listed by the IRO as the UNRPR may determine will materially assist in its programme, transfer to take place at the site of the several warehouses; and

2. to negotiate upon request an interest-free loan to the Secretary-General of the UN for the use of the UNRPR or of any successor agency established by the General Assembly of the UN, in amounts required to meet emergencies, but in a total amount not to exceed the equivalent of $2,800,000 and in such currencies as are immediately available to the Organization and as may readily be converted into the currencies of the countries of the Middle East; with the proviso that repayment of such loan shall be a first charge against any future contributions to the UNRPR or its successor.

10. Resettlement Assistance
(Adopted at the 66th Meeting, 13 October 1950)

The executive committee of the IRO

HAVING LEARNED of the particularly difficult circumstances of Russian Nansen or former Russian Nansen refugees in Austria, who have been eligible for international assistance for over 25 years,

HAVING REVIEWED the application to those refugees of the definitions under Annex I of the Constitution, in the light of the conclusion of the General Council, expressed in its Resolution No. 62 that paragraph 2 (b) of Part II of Annex I of the Constitution 'should be interpreted taking into account the real reasons which have inspired the persons concerned rather than indications of a purely formal nature';

HAS CONCLUDED that there is a prima facie presumption that the members of this group fall within the mandate of the Organization, subject to specific findings made in each individual case and URGES THE DIRECTOR-GENERAL to assist with the resettlement of refugees in this group, within the limits of available resources.

II. DISPOSAL OF RECORDS

(Adopted at the 79th Meeting, 25 October 1951)

THE EXECUTIVE COMMITTEE of the General Council

HAVING NOTED the Report of the Director-General to the Executive Committee of the Disposal of Records (document EC/60)

RESOLVES to approve the proposals of the Director-General on this subject and requests the Director-General to take action appropriate to the Disposal of Records in accordance with the Director-General's recommendations.

APPENDIX IV

OFFICERS OF MEETINGS OF THE PREPARATORY COMMISSION, THE EXECUTIVE COMMITTEE, AND THE GENERAL COUNCIL

Preparatory Commission—First Session, First to Seventh Parts

First Session	Date	Chairman	Rapporteur
First Part	*1947* 11–21 Feb.	H. E. M. Henri Ponsot (France)	Dr. E. M. J. A. Sassen (Netherlands)
Second Part	1–21 May	,,	,,
Third Part	15–25 July	,,	,,
Fourth Part	21 Oct. to 1 Nov.	,,	H.E. Mr. Helio Lobo (Brazil)
Fifth Part	*1948* 20–31 Jan.	,,	M. J. Schneider (Belgium)
Sixth Part	4–12 May	,,	,,
Seventh Part	10–11 Sept.	,,	,,

Sessions of the Executive Committee

Session	Date	Chairman	Vice-Chairman
First	Sept. 1948	H.E. Mr. J. Desy (Canada)	H.E. Mr. Rolf Andersen (Norway)
Second	Dec. 1948	,,	,,
Third	Jan. 1949	,,	,,
Fourth	Mar./Apr. 1949	,,	,,
Fifth	June/July 1949	H.E. M. Guerin de Beaumont (France)	Maj.-Gen. F. G. Galleghan (Australia) in the absence of H.E. Dr. Wu Nan-Ju (China)
Sixth	Oct. 1949	,,	,,
Seventh	Mar. 1950	H.E. Mr. Rolf Andersen (Norway)	Dr. V. Montoya (Venezuela)
Eighth	Oct. 1950	Mr. G. L. Warren (United States) acting during the illness of the elected Chairman, H.E. Mr. Rolf Andersen (Norway)	,,
Ninth	Apr. 1951	Dr. V. Montoya (Venezuela)	M. F. Leemans (Belgium)
Tenth	Oct. 1951	,,	,,
Eleventh	Feb. 1952	,,	,,

Sessions of the General Council

Session	Date	Chairman	Rapporteur
First	13–15 Sept. 1948	H.E. M. Henri Ponsot (France)	M. J. Schneider (Belgium)
Second	29 Mar. to 8 Apr. 1949	H.E. Mr. J. Desy (Canada)	H.E. Prince del Drago (Italy)
Third (Special)	28 June to 8 July 1949	H.E. M. Guerin de Beaumont (France)	,,
Fourth	11–20 Oct. 1949	Maj.-Gen. F. G. Galleghan (Australia)	Mr. B. Bøgh-Andersen (Denmark)
Fifth	14–22 Mar. 1950	Dr. P. J. Kanter (Netherlands)	,,
Sixth	9–13 Oct. 1950	H.E. M. P. Zutter (Switzerland)	,,
Seventh	9–13 Apr. 1951	M. R. Rochefort (France)	Mr. E. Dons (Norway)
Eighth	22–27 Oct. 1951	M. F. Leemans (Belgium)	Dr. P. J. de Kanter (Netherlands)
Ninth	11–16 Feb. 1952	Mr. George L. Warren (USA)	,,

CHIEF DELEGATES TO MEETINGS OF THE PREPARATORY COMMISSION AND GENERAL COUNCIL[1]

AUSTRALIA

MR. T. M. NULTY   PCIRO 1, 3, 4.
  Assistant Chief Migration Officer, Office of the
  High Commissioner.

MR. G. V. GREENHALGH   PCIRO 5, 6, 7.
  Senior Migration Officer, Military Mission,
  Berlin.

[1] The participation in the work of the PCIRO and the General Council is indicated by the numbers of the relevant parts and sessions of PCIRO and GC. For dates of the meetings see above.

BRIGADIER F. GALLEGHAN   GC 1, 2, 3, 4.
  Head of the Military Mission, BAOR, Germany.

MR. N. ST. C. DESCHAMPS   GC 5, 6, 7, 8.
  Acting Head, Military Mission, Germany.

MR. P. SHAW   GC 9.
  Permanent Delegate to the European Office of
  the UN.

BELGIUM

VICOMTE THÉOPHILE DE LANTSHEERE   PCIRO 2, 3.
  Minister in Switzerland.

M. J. M. SCHNEIDER   PCIRO 4, 5, 6, 7. GC 1, 2, 3, 4.
  Director-General in Ministry of Foreign Affairs
  and Commerce.

M. F. LEEMANS   GC 5, 6, 7, 8.
  Adviser, Ministry of Foreign Affairs.

M. J. L. DESY   GC 9.
  Fonctionnaire, Ministry of Foreign Affairs.

BRAZIL

M. HELIO LOBO   PCIRO 3, 4, 5, 6, 7.
  Ministre Plénipotentiaire.

CANADA

LT.-GENERAL M. POPE   PCIRO 1.
  Head of the Military Mission, Berlin.

MR. JEAN DESY   PCIRO 2, 3, 4, 7. GC 1, 2.
  Ambassador to Brazil, Ambassador to Italy.

COLONEL L. FORTIER   PCIRO 5.
  Associate Commissioner (Overseas Service)
  Immigration Branch.

L. D. WILGRESS   PCIRO 6.
  Minister in Switzerland.

MR. R. M. MACDONNEL   GC 3.
  Chargé d'Affaires in Czechoslovakia.

MR. C. RITCHIE   GC 4.
  Adviser, Embassy, Paris.

MR. G. K. MAGANN   GC 5, 6, 8.
  Ambassador to Greece.

MR. V. DORE   GC 7, 9.
  Minister in Switzerland.

CHINA

DR. WU NAN-JU   PCIRO 2, 3, 5, 6, 7. GC 1, 2, 3.
  Minister in Switzerland.

DR. HUA-CHENG WANG   PCIRO 4.
  Minister in Portugal.

DENMARK

MR. A. BøGH-ANDERSEN
Assistant Chief of Section, Ministry of Foreign
Affairs.

PCIRO 7. GC 1, 2, 3, 4, 5, 6.

MR. FINN T. B. FRIIS
Adviser, Ministry of Foreign Affairs.

GC 7, 9.

BARON J. H. G. ZYTPHEN-ADELER
Deputy Head of Section, Ministry of Foreign
Affairs.

GC 8.

DOMINICAN REPUBLIC

MR. CESAR PINA BARINAS
Minister to Italy.

PCIRO 1.

MR. CESAR RUBIROSA
Chargé d'Affaires, Switzerland.

PCIRO 2, 4, 5, 6.

DR. TULIO FRANCO Y FRANCO
Ambassador at the Holy See and Minister in
Switzerland.

PCIRO 3. GC 3.

COUNT M. HANOT D'HARTOY
Ministre Plénipotentiaire, Geneva.

PCIRO 7. GC 1, 4.

DR. B. GLASSON
Vice-Consul, Geneva.

GC 5.

MR. F. A. M. NOELTING
Vice-Consul, Geneva.

GC 8, 9.

FRANCE

M. HENRI PONSOT
Ambassador of France, Chairman, PCIRO.

All Sessions.

BARON LÉON DE ROSEN
Chef de division du groupe français, du Conseil
de Contrôle.

PCIRO 1, 4, 5.

M. GUERIN DE BEAUMONT
Ministre Plénipotentiaire.

PCIRO 2, 3, 4, 5, 6. GC 1, 2, 3.

M. PHILIPPE PERIER
Ministre Plénipotentiaire.

PCIRO 4, 7. GC 1.

M. ROBERT ROCHEFORT
Chef de Cabinet, Ministry of Foreign Affairs.

GC 1, 2, 3, 4, 5, 6, 7, 8, 9.

GUATEMALA

MR. A. DUPONT-WILLEMIN
Consul, Geneva.

PCIRO 1, 2, 3, 4, 5, 6, 7. GC 1,
2, 3, 4, 5, 7, 9.

ICELAND

MR. J. HAFSTEIN
Member of Parliament.

PCIRO 3.

MR. J. GUDMUNDSSON
Permanent Under-Secretary, Ministry of Social
Affairs.

GC 3.

ITALY

PRINCE M. DEL DRAGO   GC 2, 3, 4, 5, 6, 7.
  Ministre Plénipotentiaire.

M. C. SOARDI DI S. ANTONINO   GC 8.
  Ministre Plénipotentiaire.

MR. G. CAPECE GALEOTTA   GC 9.
  Adviser, Ministry for Foreign Affairs.

LUXEMBOURG

M. F. WEILER   PCIRO 7. GC 1.
  Adviser.

M. J. STURM   GC 2, 3, 4, 5, 6, 7, 8, 9.
  Chargé d'Affaires, Switzerland.

NETHERLANDS

DR. E. M. J. S. SASSEN   PCIRO 1, 2, 3.
  Member of the Second Chamber of the States
  General.

DR. H. VERWEY-JONKER   PCIRO 4.

DR. P. J. DE KANTER   PCIRO 5, 6, 7. GC 1, 2, 3, 4, 5,
  Deputy Director, Administrative and Legal   6, 7, 8, 9.
  Affairs, Ministry for Foreign Affairs.

NEW ZEALAND

MR. W. J. JORDEN   PCIRO 3.
  High Commissioner for New Zealand, London.

MR. T. P. DAVIN   PCIRO 4.
  Department of External Affairs.

MR. M. C. SMITH   PCIRO 5, 6.
  Immigration Officer, London.

MR. B. D. ZOHRAB   GC 7, 8.
  Assistant External Affairs Officer, Office of the
  High Commission, London.

MAJOR-GENERAL W. C. STEVENS   PCIRO 7. GC 1.
  Official Secretary, Government Offices, London.

MR. J. V. BRENNAN   GC 2, 3, 4, 5, 6.
  Chief Migration Officer, Government Offices,
  London.

MR. N. V. FARREL   GC 9.
  Assistant Migration Officer, London.

NORWAY

MR. R. B. SKYLSTAD   PCIRO 1, 2, 3, 4, 5.
  Minister to Switzerland.

MR. I. LUNDE   PCIRO 6.
  Division Chief, Ministry for Foreign Affairs.

MR. R. ANDERSEN   PCIRO 7. GC 1, 2, 4, 5, 6.
  Minister in Switzerland and Austria.

MR. E. DONS   GC 3, 7.
  Divisional Chief, Ministry for Foreign Affairs.

Mr. M. P. Anker   GC 8, 9.
   Minister in Switzerland.

Switzerland
Mr. Ph. P. Zutter   GC 2, 3, 4, 5, 6, 7, 8.
   Adviser, Legation.
Mr. P. Micheli   GC 9.
   Ministre Plénipotentiaire.

United Kingdom
Sir George Rendel   PCIRO 1, 2.
   Ambassador attached to the Foreign Office.
Sir Victor Mallet   PCIRO 3.
   Ambassador to Spain.
Mr. C. P. Mayhew   GC 1.
   Parliamentary Under-Secretary of State for
   Foreign Affairs.
Mr. C. J. Edmonds   PCIRO 4, 5, 6, 7. GC 2, 3, 4, 5,
   Foreign Office.   6, 7, 8, 9.

United States
Mr. A. Roseman   PCIRO 1.
   Bureau of the Budget, Washington, D.C.
Mr. George L. Warren   PCIRO 2, 3, 4, 5, 6, 7. GC 2, 3,
   Adviser on Refugees and Displaced Persons,   4, 5, 6, 7, 8, 9.
   Department of State.
Mr. G. H. Dorr   GC 1.
   Consultant to the Secretary of State.

Venezuela
Mr. V. Gerbasi   GC 1.
   Consul, Geneva.
Dr. Victor Montoya   GC 2, 3, 4, 5, 6, 7, 8.
   Permanent Delegate, Geneva.
Mr. O. Silva   GC 9.
   First Secretary of Permanent Delegation to the
   European Office of the UN.

SENIOR HEADQUARTERS OFFICIALS OF THE ADMINISTRATION

Executive Secretary:
   Altmeyer, Arthur J. (US)   Mar. 1947–Aug. 1947
   Tuck, William Hallam (US)   Aug. 1947–Sept. 1948

Director-General:
   Tuck, William Hallam (US)   Sept. 1948–July 1949
   Kingsley, J. Donald (US)   July 1949–Feb. 1952

Deputy Executive Secretary, then Deputy Director-General:
   Rucker, Sir Arthur N. (UK)   July 1947–Apr. 1951

Assistant Directors-General:

COHEN, Myer (US)   Oct. 1947–Jan. 1952
Department of Health, Care and Maintenance, then
Planning and External Services, then Budget and
Administration.

JACOBSEN, Pierre (France)   Sept. 1947–Feb. 1952
Department of Repatriation and Resettlement, later
Operations.

KOOLEN, Dr. Petrus N. M. (Netherlands)   Sept. 1947–Jan. 1952
Administration and Finance.

Office of Legal Adviser:

KULLMAN, Dr. Gustave G. (Switzerland)   July 1947–Mar. 1951
Department of Protection, Mandate and Reparations,
then Office of Protection.

General Counsel:

COX, William W. (US)   Oct. 1947–Apr. 1950
STEPHENS, Louis C. (US)   May 1950–Dec. 1951
KELLY, John D. R. (UK)   Mar. 1952–Aug. 1952

Special Advisers:

COX, William W. (US)   Oct. 1947–Dec. 1948
HOAGUE, George, Jr. (US)   Sept. 1948–Nov. 1950
Special Adviser on Shipping.

CHIAVARI, Marchese Gian G. (Italy)   Feb. 1949–Jan. 1952
Special Adviser on Italian Affairs.

LU, Dr. Kuang-Mien (China)   Sept. 1948–Aug. 1950
Special Adviser on Far Eastern Affairs.

LUSH, Brigadier Maurice S. (UK)   Mar. 1949–Oct. 1949
Special Adviser on Middle East.

POLLOCK, John R. (UK)   June 1951–June 1952
Special Adviser on Security.

PONSOT, Henri, Ambassador (France)   Oct. 1948–
Diplomatic Adviser. Counsellor, Liquidation Board.

SABALOT, Captain Abel C. J. (US)   Dec. 1949–June 1951
Special Adviser on Security.

Comptroller:

CAMPBELL, A. F. Desmond (Canada)   Sept. 1948–Mar. 1950
HYSSONG, Major-General Clyde L. (US)   June 1950–Apr. 1951

Chiefs of field missions:

Argentine

BURNAY, Jean (France)   Aug. 1948–Aug. 1949
WENDLING, Charles O. (France)   Aug. 1949–Dec. 1949

Austria
   MILLER, Charles S. (US)   July 1947–Jan. 1948
   WOOD, John S., Major-General (US)   Apr. 1948–Nov. 1951
   GIBSON, Peter L. (UK)   Nov. 1951–Jan. 1952

Australia
   LLOYD, C. E. M., Major-General (Australia)   Oct. 1948–Jan. 1952

Belgium
   HERMENT, Albert (Belgium)   Oct. 1947–Apr. 1950
   DE CROY-ROEULX, Etienne, Prince (Belgium)   July 1950–Jan. 1952

Brazil
   WOOD, Minter (US)   July 1947–July 1948
   STANSBY, Dumon, Brigadier (UK)   July 1948–Jan. 1952

Canada
   COLLEY, James (Canada)   Oct. 1947–June 1949
   ALLARD, Hector (Canada)   Aug. 1949–Feb. 1952

Czechoslovakia
   COLLINS, Ralph W. (US)   Oct. 1947–Aug. 1948
   VOLCKMAR, Alf. V. (Norway)   Sept. 1948–Feb. 1950

Denmark
   AARØE, Børge H. (Denmark)   Oct. 1948–July 1951
   VORSTRUP, Kristian T. J. (Denmark)   July 1951–Jan. 1952

East Africa
   CURTIS, Jubert A. (UK)   Jan. 1949–Oct. 1950

Far East
   COPE, Thomas (US)   July 1947–Dec. 1948
   WONG, Jennings (China)   Jan. 1949–July 1949
   ANDREW, George F. (UK)   July 1949–Oct. 1950
   THOMPSON, Frederick R. (Australia)   Nov. 1949–Jan. 1951
     (Philippines Office.)
   THOMPSON, Frederick R.   Jan. 1951–Mar. 1952
     (Philippines and Far East Office.)

France
   VALENTIN-SMITH, Victor (France)   July 1947–Jan. 1950
   GRIMAUD, Maurice A. (France)   Jan. 1950–Nov. 1951

Germany
  British zone
     FANSHAWE, Evelyn D., Major-General (UK)   July 1947–Jan. 1952

  French zone
     POIGNANT, Alfred (France)   Aug. 1947–Jan. 1952

United States zone

EDWARDS, Paul (US)	July 1947–Aug. 1948
RYAN, Philip E. (US)	Aug. 1948–Oct. 1951
JAMIESON, Thomas (UK)	Nov. 1951–Feb. 1952

Italy

KEENY, Spurgeon M. (US)	July 1947–Feb. 1948
MENTZ, George, Admiral (US)	Oct. 1948–June 1950
COUND, Oliver E., Colonel (US)	July 1950–Jan. 1952

Lebanon

STEPHEN, David C. (UK)	Feb. 1949–Nov. 1949

Luxembourg

MERSCH, Jean (Luxembourg)	July 1948–July 1951

Middle East

LUSH, Maurice S., Brigadier (UK)	Oct. 1947–Mar. 1949

Netherlands

SARK, Henry M. (Netherlands)	Oct. 1947–Aug. 1951

Poland

WIDDICOMBE, John S. (US)	Oct. 1947–Nov. 1949

United Kingdom

DOW, Leslie (UK)	Oct. 1947–Oct. 1948
GREENSLADE, Cyrus, Brigadier (UK)	Nov. 1948–July 1951

United States

WOOD, Walter A., General (US)	July 1947–Mar. 1952

Uruguay

WENDLING, Charles O. (France)	Jan. 1950–Jan. 1952

Venezuela

MEYER, Vincent, Brigadier-General (US)	July 1947–Feb. 1950
WILLIAMSON, Ten B. (US)	Feb. 1950–Dec. 1951

Liquidation Board:

COUND, Oliver E., Colonel (US)	Feb. 1952–Sept. 1953
DALLISON, Francis H., Brigadier (UK)	Mar. 1952–Dec. 1952
PONSOT, Henri, Ambassador (France)	Mar. 1952–

Delegates to Liquidation Board:

MONTOYA, Victor, Dr. (Venezuela)	Mar. 1952–
BEITH, J. G. S. (UK)	Mar. 1952–Jan. 1953
WARDROP, J. C. (UK)	Feb. 1953–
SERRES, Jean (France)	Mar. 1952–

IRO missions and offices

Country	Covered from headquarters at	Opened	Closed
Argentina	1. Buenos Aires	Aug. 1948	Dec. 1949
	2. Montevideo (Uruguay)	Jan. 1950	Jan. 1952
Austria (including Vienna)	1. Vienna 2. Salzburg	July 1947	Jan. 1952
Australia	1. Canberra 2. Sydney 3. Melbourne	July 1948	Jan. 1952
Belgium	Brussels	July 1947	Jan. 1952
Bolivia	1. Lima (Peru) 2. Montevideo (Uruguay)	June 1948	Mar. 1951
Brazil	Rio de Janeiro	July 1947	Jan. 1952
Canada	1. Ottawa 2. Hull, Quebec	July 1947	Mar. 1952
Chile	1. Lima (Peru)	June 1948	July 1948
	2. Montevideo (Uruguay)	Aug. 1949	Jan. 1952
Colombia	Bogota	May 1949	Nov. 1951
Ceylon	Colombo[1]	Feb. 1950	Mar. 1951
Czechoslovakia	Prague	July 1947	Feb. 1950
Denmark	Copenhagen	Sept. 1948	Jan. 1952
Dominican Republic	Ciudad Trujillo	July 1951	Sept. 1951
East Africa	Nairobi	July 1947	Oct. 1950
Eire	Dublin	June 1950	Feb. 1951
Egypt (see Middle East)			
Ecuador	Lima (Peru)	June 1948	Mar. 1951
Ethiopia	Addis Ababa	June 1950	Mar. 1951
Far East Office (China)	1. Shanghai 2. Hong Kong	July 1947	Feb. 1952
France	Paris	July 1947	Jan. 1952
Germany, US zone including Berlin	1. Heidelberg 2. Bad Kissingen 3. Munich	July 1947	Jan. 1952
Germany, British zone	1. Lemgo 2. Hamburg	July 1947	Jan. 1952
Germany, French zone	1. Haslach 2. Neuenbürg	July 1947	Jan. 1952
Germany, Liaison Office	Bonn	Feb. 1950	Feb. 1952
Germany, International Tracing Service	Arolsen	Jan. 1948	Operational responsibilities assumed by Allied High Commission 1 Apr. 1951
Greece	Athens	Nov. 1949 (previously dependent on Italian Mission)	Jan. 1952
Guatemala	Guatemala	Sept. 1948	July 1951
Iran	Teheran	July 1950	Mar. 1951
Italy	Rome	July 1947	Jan. 1952
India	1. Middle East	July 1947	Feb. 1948
	2. New Delhi[1]	Sept. 1950	Mar. 1951
Israel/Palestine	1. Jerusalem	July 1947	Feb. 1948
	2. Haifa	Apr. 1948	Dec. 1949
Lebanon and Syria	Beirut	July 1947	Apr. 1951

[1] Honorary representative.

APPENDIX IV

IRO missions and offices (cont.)

Country	Covered from headquarters at	Opened	Closed
Luxembourg	1. Brussels	Oct. 1947	..
	2. Luxembourg	July 1948	June 1951
Mexico	Mexico City	July 1949	Mar. 1951
Middle East HQ until December 1948 Egypt	Cairo	July 1947	..
Netherlands	The Hague	July 1947	Aug. 1951
New Zealand	1. Canberra (Australia)	July 1948	Aug. 1950
	2. Wellington	Aug. 1950	Jan. 1951
		Oct. 1951	Jan. 1952
Norway	Oslo	July 1950	Dec. 1951
Paraguay	Asuncion	Aug. 1949	May 1951
Pakistan	Karachi[1]	Mar. 1950	June 1951
Peru	Lima (Peru)	June 1948	Mar. 1951
Philippines	Manila and Samar	Apr. 1949	Jan. 1952
Poland	Warsaw	July 1947	Oct. 1949
Portugal[2]	Lisbon	July 1947	Oct. 1951
Spain[2]	Madrid and Barcelona	July 1947	Nov. 1951
Sweden	Copenhagen (Denmark)	Apr. 1951	Nov. 1951
Switzerland (Swiss Office)	Geneva	July 1947	Jan. 1952
Turkey	Istambul	July 1947	Mar. 1951
UK	London	July 1947	June 1951
US	Washington	July 1947	Mar. 1952
Uruguay	1. Buenos Aires (Argentina)	Aug. 1948	Dec. 1949
	2. Montevideo	Jan. 1950	Jan. 1952
Venezuela	Caracas	July 1947	Jan. 1952
Yugoslavia	Belgrade	July 1947	Aug. 1948

[1] Honorary representative.   [2] IRO represented by several voluntary societies.

APPENDIX V

CHRONOLOGY

1941

12 June. Declaration of Solidarity of the UN: Inter-Allied Meeting, stating among primary war aims the co-operation of free peoples in economic and social security, London, St. James Palace.

14 Aug. Declaration of Principles by Prime Minister Churchill and President Roosevelt ('Atlantic Charter'), incorporating in point 6 the principle of freedom from fear and want.

24 Sept. Inter-Allied Council Meeting in London, including a representative of the USSR, declared adherence to the principles of the Declaration and intention to co-operate in giving effect to them.

1942

1 Jan. Declaration by UN signed in Washington by twenty-seven states subscribing to the principles of the Atlantic Charter.

1943

19–29 Apr. Anglo-American Conference on refugees, Bermuda.

Aug. IGCR Executive Committee, extension of mandate and membership.

1 Nov. Moscow Declaration by President Roosevelt, Marshal Stalin, and Prime Minister Churchill concerning enemy atrocities in the course of the war.

9 Nov. Agreement to establish the UN Relief and Rehabilitation Administration, Washington, D.C.

10 Nov. Letter of President Roosevelt to the Secretary of War directing the army to prepare to assume 'the initial burden of shipping and distributing relief supplies'.

1944

12 Feb. Combined Chiefs of Staff defined the mission of the Supreme Commander Allied Expeditionary Forces (SCAEF) to re-establish civil governments in liberated countries and administer enemy territories.

10 May. General Conference of International Labour Office, Twenty-sixth Session, Philadelphia: declaration on social justice, included in the Aims and Purpose of the ILO. 'All human beings . . . have the right to pursue both their well-being and their spiritual development in conditions of freedom and dignity, of economic security and equal opportunity.'

1945

4–11 Feb. Agreements on occupation and control of Germany, reparations, and repatriation at Yalta Conference.

7 May. Creation of an International Refugee Organization first proposed at San Francisco Conference on International Organization.

24 May. Beginning of exchange of Russian citizens and Allied prisoners of war.

5 June. Division of Germany into four zones of occupation.

25 June. Establishment of four zones of occupation in Austria.

26 June. UN Charter signed at San Francisco, USA.

29 June. Bilateral agreement between the governments of France and the USSR for exchange of citizens on each other's territory.

13 July. SHAEF dissolved.

17 July. Potsdam Conference opened.

8 Aug. Charter of International Military Tribunal containing definition of war crimes and crimes against peace and against humanity signed in London.

17 Sept. Directorate of prisoners of war and displaced persons recommended to the Allied Control Council the establishment of a Central Tracing Service for UN nationals missing in occupied Germany.

20 Nov. Allied Control Council in Germany approved plan for transfer of over 6 million Germans and *Volksdeutsche* to Germany.

20–22 Nov. IGCR, Fifth Plenary Session, Paris.

21 Dec. Final Act of the Paris Conference on Reparations.

22 Dec. President Truman's Directive giving priority within the US Immigration Quotas to refugees and displaced persons.

1946

12 Feb. Resolution of the UN General Assembly laying down principles for the consideration of the problem of refugees. Resolution 8 (1).

13 Feb. UN General Assembly, Resolution on Extradition and Punishment of War Criminals.

18 Feb. First Session of the UN Economic and Social Council in London.

8 Apr.–1 June. Meeting of the UN Special Committee on Refugees and Displaced Persons in London.

25 May–21 June. Second Session of the UN Economic and Social Council, which submitted Draft Constitution of the IRO to governments.

14 June. Five-Power Agreement on allocation of a share of reparations for the benefit of non-repatriatable victims of German action.

6 July–20 July. Meeting of the UN Special Committee on the Finances of the IRO, London.

16 July. Extension of mandate of IGCR to include non-repatriable displaced persons in Germany, Austria, and Italy.

Aug. UNRRA Council authorized its Administration to adjust eligibility regulations to coincide with those of the draft IRO constitution.

30 Sept. The Economic and Social Council approved draft Constitution of the IRO and Agreement on Interim Measures.

3 Oct. Submission by ECOSOC to the UN General Assembly of the draft Constitution of IRO, the draft budget, and proposed scale of contributions.

15 Oct. Signature by fifteen governments of International Agreement on the issue of a travel document to refugees (the 'London Travel Document').

2 Dec. Economic fusion of the British and US zones of Germany ('Byrnes–Bevin Agreement').

9 Dec. Agreement between the French General Residency in Tunisia and the IGCR concerning the immigration scheme in Tunisia.

10 Dec. Sixth Session of the Council of UNRRA, Washington, D.C.

15 Dec. Approval of the UN General Assembly of the IRO Constitution and the Agreement on Interim Measures. Resolution 62 (1).

16 Dec. Sixth Session of IGCR, London.

31 Dec. Termination of the mandate of the League of Nations High Commissioner for Refugees.

      Agreement on Interim Measures came into force.

1947

1 Jan. Assumption of the League of Nations High Commissioner's responsibility by the IGCR.

6 Jan. President Truman's Message to US Congress urging legislation to permit admission of refugees to the USA.

23 Jan. Agreement between the occupation authorities, the Government of Belgium and the IGCR for recruitment of miners in the US zone of Germany.

5 Feb. The UK acceded to the Constitution of the IRO.

7 Feb. Agreement between the Government of Chile and the IGCR.

11–21 Feb. First Session of the Preparatory Commission for IRO convened in Geneva by the Secretary General of the UN.

13 Feb. Agreement between the CCG, the Government of Belgium, and the IGCR for recruitment of miners in the British zone of Germany.

3 Mar. Agreement between the Government of Peru and the IGCR.

10 Mar. Four-Power Conference in Moscow.

15 Mar. Agreement between the Government of Colombia and IGCR.

17 Mar. New Zealand acceded to the Constitution of the IRO.

1 Apr. Agreement between the Government of Brazil and the IGCR.

14 Apr. Transfer of Yugoslav refugees from Italy to the British zone of Germany.

21 Apr. Agreement between the Government of Ecuador and IGCR.

      Date after which the authorities in the US zone of Germany would not permit new applicants to receive UN care and assistance.

23 Apr. Four-Power Agreement, Moscow.

28 Apr. Special Session of UN General Assembly to discuss Palestine.

29 Apr. China acceded to the Constitution of the IRO.

1–21 May. Second Part of First Session of the PCIRO (Lausanne).

5 May. Agreement between the Government of the Netherlands and IGCR for resettlement of refugees from the US zone of Germany.

12 May. Iceland acceded to the Constitution of the IRO.

13 May. Australia acceded to the Constitution of the IRO.

15 May. Agreement between the Government of Italy and IGCR for the movement of refugees out of Italy.

10 June. Agreement between the governments of France and the UK for recruitment of refugees in their respective zones of occupation and their resettlement in the two countries.

27 June. Agreement between PCIRO and IGCR for transfer of responsibilities.

28 June. Agreement between PCIRO and the British occupation authorities in Germany.

29 June. Agreement between PCIRO and UNRRA for transfer of responsibilities.

30 June. Termination of IGCR, and of UNRRA's operations on behalf of displaced persons.

2 July. 'Freeze Order' on new admissions to IRO's care and maintenance.

3 July. The US ratified the Constitution of the IRO (Public Law 146, 90th Congress).

7 July. Further Message of President Truman to Congress urging admission of refugees to the US.

Decision of the Government of Turkey to admit Moslem refugees for settlement in Turkey.

9 July. Agreement between PCIRO and the US occupation authorities in Germany.

15–25 July. Third Part of First Session of the Preparatory Commission (Lausanne).

21 July. Agreement between the Government of Australia and PCIRO for settlement of refugees in Australia.

28 July. Guatemala ratified the Constitution of the IRO.

7 Aug. Canada ratified the Constitution of the IRO.

11 Aug. The Netherlands ratified the Constitution of the IRO.

18 Aug. Norway ratified the Constitution of the IRO.

6 Sept. Agreement between the Government of France and PCIRO on operations in the French zones of Austria and Germany.

8 Sept. Agreement between the governments of the UK and Yugoslavia on Yugoslav refugees (the 'Bled Agreement').

12 Sept. Temporary agreement between PCIRO and the US occupation authorities in Austria.

15 Sept. Italian Peace Treaty in force.

18 Sept. Instructions (General Bulletin No. 5) on formal relations between the PCIRO and voluntary societies.

26 Sept. Agreement between the Government of the UK and the PCIRO for settlement in the UK of refugees in the US zone of Germany.

Special meeting in Geneva on settlement of intellectuals and refugees with professional and specialist qualifications.

21 Oct.–1 Nov. Fourth Part of First Session of PCIRO (Geneva).

22 Oct. The Dominican Republic ratified the Constitution of the IRO.

Agreement between the governments of the UK and the Netherlands and PCIRO for settlement in the Netherlands of refugees in the British zone of Germany.

24 Oct. Agreement between the Government of Italy and the PCIRO.

3 Nov. First Session of the Advisory Committee on Specialists (Geneva).

26 Nov. Establishment of Review Board for Eligibility Appeals.

27 Nov. UN General Assembly approved plan for partition of Palestine.

1 Dec. Memorandum of IRO Executive Secretary to UN Commission on Human Rights concerning prevention of discrimination, statelessness, right of asylum, and the continuation of protection of stateless persons by an organization of the UN.

1948

1 Jan. Establishment of the International Tracing Service.

Establishment of the Division of Employment and Vocational Training at headquarters.

13 Jan. Agreements with the Government of France on the work and status of the IRO in France and on settlement of refugees in France and Algeria.

20–31 Jan. Fifth Part of First Session of the PCIRO, Geneva.

15 Feb. Evacuation of Christian Poles from Palestine.

26 Feb. Evacuation of Jewish Poles from Palestine and closure of office in Jerusalem.

28 Feb. Evacuation of Poles from India and closure of office.

1–2 Mar. Resolution of the UN ECOSOC on protection of stateless persons and right to a nationality.

3 Mar. France ratified the Constitution of the IRO.

15–17 Mar. Conference of senior medical officers, Geneva.

30 Mar. Belgium ratified the Constitution of the IRO.

17 Apr. Agreement with the Government of Venezuela on resettlement of refugees.

26–30 Apr. Conference on the Settlement of Specialists at Gwatt, Switzerland.

30 Apr. Agreement with the Government of Brazil on settlement of refugees.

4–11 May. Sixth Part of First Session of PCIRO, Geneva.

15 May. Termination of the British Mandate in Palestine. Establishment of Provisional Government of Israel, outbreak of war between Israel and the Arab States.

18 May. Suspension of the IRO's assistance in emigration of refugees to countries in the Near East engaged in hostilities.

1 June. Issue of 20-day food ration for repatriants instituted.

3 June. Submission to the UN of a memorandum on procedures for declaration of death of missing persons.

4 June. Venezuela ratified the Constitution of the IRO.

11 June. Agreement with the Government of Belgium for settlement of refugees from the British zone of Austria.

18 June. Currency reform in Western Germany. Formal beginning of counselling programme.

24 June. Agreement with the Government of Turkey for settlement of refugees in Turkey.

25 June. Enactment of the US Displaced Persons Act. Creation of the US Displaced Persons Commission.

8 July. Agreement with the French Resident Commissioner General in Morocco for settlement of refugees in Morocco.

28 July. Agreement with the US occupation authorities in Germany, superseding the Agreement of 9 July 1947.

2 Aug. Luxembourg ratified the Constitution of the IRO.

9 Aug. Agreement with the Government of France on settlement of farm families in France.

11 Aug. Agreement with the US High Commissioner in Austria for operations in the US zone.

20 Aug. The Government of Denmark ratified the Constitution of the IRO.
   Entry into force of the Constitution of the IRO.

21 Aug. Agreement with the Government of Switzerland on privileges and immunities.

6 Sept. Agreement with the Government of Guatemala on the settlement of refugees.

8 Sept. Loan of the IRO's Chief Officer for Supply and Transport to the UN Mediator in Palestine.

10–11 Sept. Seventh and last Session of PCIRO.

13–25 Sept. First Session of the General Council of the IRO, Geneva.

15 Sept. Agreement with the Government of Switzerland on the legal status of the IRO in Switzerland.

16–24 Sept. First Session of the Executive Committee of the IRO, Geneva.

30 Oct. First shipload of refugees admitted under the Displaced Persons Act of 25 June reached the US.

18 Nov. Agreement between the UN and the IRO became effective.
   Ration scales for IRO refugees became uniform in the British, French, and US zones of Germany.

19 Nov. Resolution of the UN General Assembly on relief of Arab refugees from Palestine.
   Agreement with the Government of Denmark.

17 Nov.–11 Dec. General Conference of UNESCO: resolution on the needs of refugee intellectuals.

7–11 Dec. Second Session of the Executive Committee, Rome.

10 Dec. Universal Declaration of Human Rights adopted by the UN General Assembly.

11 Dec. Agreement with the Government of New Zealand for settlement of refugees.

24 Dec. First large movement of Jewish refugees from Shanghai to Israel by the IRO.

1949

1 Jan. US occupation authorities in Germany closed Yugoslav Repatriation Mission.

13 Jan. Evacuation of White Russian refugees from Shanghai to the Philippines.

18–21 Jan. Conference of representatives of fifty-one voluntary societies working with the IRO, Geneva.

19 Jan. Grant of interest-free loan of £1 million (sterling) for assistance to Arab refugees.

25–28 Jan. Third Session of the Executive Committee, Geneva.

28 Jan. Resumption of assistance in movement of refugees to Near Eastern countries, and reimbursement of costs incurred by voluntary societies in moving Jews to Israel since 18 May 1948.

28 Jan. Agreement with the Government of Luxembourg on settlement of farm workers.

9 Feb. Deputy Foreign Ministers resumed discussions on Austrian State treaty.

25 Feb. Conference of IRO field officers on liquidation of the IRO's work.

26 Feb. Director-General met the UN Conciliation Commission for Palestine.

1 Mar. US occupation authorities in Germany closed Soviet Repatriation Mission.

3 Mar. The USSR repatriation mission left the US zone of Germany.

15–16 Mar. Discussions at Frankfurt between the Director-General and the Commanders-in-Chief of the three Western zones of Germany on the termination of the IRO's operations.

21 Mar. Initiation of rehabilitation and training of disabled persons in Austria, Germany, and Italy.

24 Mar. Italy ratified the Constitution of the IRO.

24 Mar.–7 Apr. Fourth Session of the Executive Committee, Geneva.

28 Mar. Switzerland ratified the Constitution of the IRO.

29 Mar.–8 Apr. Second Session of the General Council, Geneva.

7 Apr. General Council approved the allocation of $1 million for care of 'hard core' refugees in the Plan of Expenditure for 1949–50.

8 Apr. Signature of agreement between the governments of France, the UK, and the US on future treatment of Germany—formation of Federal Government, Occupation Statute, and formation of Allied High Commission.

21 Apr. Agreement with the Government of France on settlement of refugees in French Guiana.

27–29 Apr. Conference of chiefs of the IRO missions, Geneva.

12 May. Agreement for settlement in Paraguay of 500 refugees from Samar.

11 June. Resignation of Director-General, Mr. W. H. Tuck.

28 June–8 July. Third (Special) Session of the General Council, Geneva. Resolution on terminating IRO services, with certain exceptions, on 30 June 1950.

29 June–8 July. Fifth Session of the Executive Committee, Geneva.

5 July–15 Aug. Ninth Session of ECOSOC; statelessness, the future of international action concerning refugees, and procedures for declaration of death discussed in accordance with Resolution 116 (1) VI.

8 July. Appointment of Mr. J. D. Kingsley as Director-General.

13 July. The 50,000th refugee selected for settlement in the US under the Displaced Persons Act left Bremerhaven.

1 Aug. Protocol to amend the agreement of 19 November 1948 with the Government of Denmark.

Order establishing the intensive counselling programme.

5 Aug. The US High Commissioner approved the General Claims Law for Indemnification Procedure (for injuries due to Nazi action) in the US zone of Germany.

6 & 8 Aug. ECOSOC adopted Resolutions 248 A and B (II).

11 Aug. Adoption of the Geneva Convention relative to the protection of civilian persons in time of war.

12 Aug. The 50,000th refugee arrived in Australia.

10 Sept. Economic Union of three Western zones of Germany.

17 Sept. Memorandum of understanding with the Government of Norway on acceptance of hard core refugees.

18 Sept. Devaluation of sterling followed by devaluation of other currencies.

21 Sept. Allied military government in Western Germany was superseded by the Allied High Commission. Occupation Statute entered into force.

German Federal Republic established. Paragraph 2, clause d reserved to the Allied High Commission control over displaced persons and admission of refugees.

22 Sept. Visit to Geneva of the Sub-Committee on Immigration and Naturalization of the US House of Representatives, Committee on the Judiciary.

6–20 Oct. Sixth Session of the Executive Committee, Geneva.

11–20 Oct. Fourth Session of the General Council, Geneva.

18 Oct. Departure for the US of the 100,000th refugee to be admitted under the Displaced Persons Act of 1948.

General Council approved allocation of $9 million for the care of 'hard core' refugees.

28 Oct. Agreement with the Government of Israel concerning permanent provision in Israel for institutional care of refugees.

Appointment of Five Special Representatives of the Director-General to encourage placement of refugees with limited opportunities of establishment.

15 Nov. Agreement with the Government of Italy on identification and control of refugees.

16 Nov. Members of Czechoslovak repatriation mission granted political asylum in the British zone of Germany.

25 Nov. Promulgation of Allied Commission (Germany) Law No. 13 passing criminal jurisdiction over refugees to the German courts with effect from 1 January 1950.

26 Nov. Appeal of the International Tracing Service to thirty-seven governments to help find 20,000 children.

2 Dec. Agreement with the Government of Venezuela.

3 Dec. Resolution of the UN General Assembly concerning the establishment of a UN High Commission for Refugees from 1 January 1951.

15 Dec. Termination of Joint Committee of the Government of Brazil and the IRO.

20 Dec. Australian selection mission operating in Greece.

1950

14 Jan. Mission of Deputy Director-General to New York, San Francisco, Sydney, Auckland, Ottawa, New York, and London to further resettlement opportunities.

Agreement with the World Health Organization to make survey of the conditions under which children were transported by the IRO to Australia.

23 Jan. Mission of Director-General to European capitals for negotiations with the governments of Belgium, France, Denmark, Italy, Luxembourg, Netherlands, Norway, Sweden, and the UK as well as the Allied High Commission in Germany concerning the transfer of responsibility for care and maintenance and the acceptance of hard core refugees.

1 Feb. Increase of food rations for refugees in the IRO's care.

4 Feb. Swedish offer to provide permanent care for tubercular refugees and their dependants.

7 Feb. Agreement with the Government of the Netherlands for troops from Indonesia to be repatriated on IRO ships returning from Australia.

9 Feb. Meeting of the Director-General with the Allied High Commissioners in Germany.

10 Feb. Letter from the chairman of the Allied High Commission in Germany to the Chancellor of the German Federal Republic requesting legislation to safeguard the position of refugees who would remain in Germany after 30 June 1950.

27 Feb.–3 Mar. Meeting of experts of the UN and specialized agencies on the rehabilitation of the physically handicapped, Geneva.

28 Feb. Agreement with the Government of France about transfer of the IRO's responsibilities for care and maintenance.

8–21 Mar. Seventh Session of the Executive Committee, Geneva.

General Council voted $12 million for care of 'hard core' refugees.

13–24 Mar. UN conference on declaration of death of missing persons.

14–22 Mar. Fifth Session of the General Council, Geneva.

17 Mar. Promulgation by the Allied High Commission in Germany of Law No. 23 regularizing the personal status of foreign refugees in Germany.

23 Mar. Agreement with the Government of Ethiopia for resettlement of refugees in Ethiopia.

1 Apr. Registration of new cases by the International Tracing Service child search branch ceased.

Closure of staging and embarkation centre at Naples; transfer of functions to Bremerhaven.

6 Apr. Signature of International Convention on the Declaration of Death of Missing Persons.

24 Apr. Discussions with the Government of the UK about closure of missions in East Africa and Lebanon.

4 May. Announcement of the '2,000 scheme' for admission of refugees into the UK.

27 May. Agreement with the Government of Sweden for admission of tubercular refugees and their families.

1 June. Reorganization of Geneva Headquarters Administration.

13 June. Start of concert tour, sponsored by the IRO of refugee musicians.

16 June. Amendment to the US Displaced Persons Act signed by President Truman.

20 June. Agreement with the Government of the Netherlands for care of hard core refugees.

21 June. Inauguration of British Council for Aid to Refugees.

30 June. Transfer to local governments of responsibility for care and maintenance of refugees not in process of being resettled.

Protocol amending the Agreement of 19 November 1948 with the Government of Denmark.

1 July. Inauguration of Comité National Belge pour les Réfugiés.

1 July. Reorganization of Italy office and transfer of operational headquarters to Naples.

Transfer to Salzburg of operational headquarters of Austrian mission.

Establishment of Surplus Property Branch at Geneva headquarters.

4 July. Denunciation by the Government of France of Agreement of 13 January 1948 on legal and political protection of refugees in France.

10 July. Meeting of Deputies of Foreign Ministers on Austrian State Treaty adjourned.

24 July. Meeting in Paris of British, French, and US experts with delegates from various other governments to discuss means of relieving over-population in western Europe.

4 Aug. Loan of £1 million (sterling) by IRO to the UN Korean Reconstruction Agency (Resolution No. 69).

15 Aug. Submission to the West German Federal legislature of draft law on legal status of homeless foreigners.

16 Aug. Conference of field officers on problem of institutional hard core, Geneva.

8 Sept. Transfer from Bad Kissingen to Munich of headquarters for US zone of Germany.

1 Oct. Inauguration of Refugee Service Committees in the Netherlands and Turkey.

5 Oct. Enactment of Law No. 11, on unaccompanied children, by US High Commissioner in Germany.

5–13 Oct. Eighth Session of the Executive Committee, Geneva.

6 Oct. Agreement with the US Displaced Persons Commission for the IRO to transport (against repayment) ethnic Germans to the US.

8 Oct. Closure of Turkish–Bulgarian frontier as a result of Bulgarian expulsion of persons of Turkish ethnic origin.

9–13 Oct. Sixth Session of the General Council, Geneva.

18 Oct. Memorandum to the Government of Austria on residence permits for refugees in Austria.

19 Oct. Request by the Government of Greece for extension of resettlement assistance to refugees recently registered in Greece.

21 Oct. The Red Cross conventions adopted on 11 August 1949 came into force.

14 Nov. Supplementary agreement signed with the Government of Italy.

25 Nov. Transfer from Lemgo to Hamburg of headquarters for the British zone of Germany.

1 Dec. Decree of the Austrian Federal Minister of the Interior granting refugees the right to receive unlimited residence permits.

4–5 Dec. Conference on unaccompanied children, Geneva.

14 Dec. Appointment of Dr. G. J. van Heuven Goedhart as UN High Commissioner for Refugees for three years from 1 January 1951.

22 Dec. Agreement with the Government of New Zealand for immigration of 2,300 refugees.

1951

4 Jan. Technical Advisory Mission to Turkey in connexion with the reception of Turkish refugees from Bulgaria.

1 Feb. Discontinuation of Office of Protection at headquarters.

7 Feb. Designation of Mr. J. Donald Kingsley, Director-General of the IRO, as Agent-General for the UN Korean Reconstruction Agency.

15 Feb. Reorganization of Geneva Headquarters Administration.

23 Feb. Agreement with the Government of Brazil for a further selection of refugees as immigrants.

31 Mar. Termination of vocational training programme.

1 Apr. Transfer of International Tracing Service to the Allied High Commission in Germany.

4–12 Apr. Ninth Session of the Executive Committee, Geneva.

9–13 Apr. Seventh Session of the General Council, Geneva.
      General Council votes $20 million for care of 'hard core' refugees.

18 Apr. Sir Arthur Rucker, Deputy Director-General of the IRO, appointed as Deputy Agent-General for the UN Korean Reconstruction Agency.

25 Apr. Promulgation of German Federal Law on Homeless Foreigners.

9 June. Expulsion of members of the USSR repatriation mission from the US zone of Austria.

12 June. Agreement between the IRO and the German Federal Expellee Bank.

30 June. Agreement with the government of Canada for the IRO to transport (against repayment) non-refugee migrants to Canada.

2–25 July. Conference of plenipotentiaries on the Status of Refugees and Stateless Persons, Geneva.

28 July. Signature in Geneva of International Convention on the Status of Refugees.

24 Aug. The USSR repatriation mission left the British zone of Austria at the request of the British authorities.

21 Sept. Letter from Queen Juliana of the Netherlands to President Truman of the US appealing to him to initiate a new approach to the refugee problem.

2 Oct. International Migration Conference convened by the International Labour Office opened in Naples.

10 Oct. Publication of report *Migration from Europe*.

18–26 Oct. Tenth Session of the Executive Committee, Geneva.

22 Oct. Millionth refugee resettled by the IRO.

22–27 Oct. Eighth Session of the General Council, Geneva.

26 Nov. Opening of Conference on European Migration convened in Brussels by the Government of Belgium at the request of the Government of the US.

26 Nov. Provisional Intergovernmental Committee for the Movement of Migrants

from Europe established. Agrees to transport all IRO refugees in possession of visas, who have not been transported when the IRO ceases operations.

13 Dec. Agreement concluded between the IRO and the World Council of Churches whereby that organization assumed responsibilities for refugees remaining in the Philippines at the close of the IRO operations.

31 Dec. Last day for the issue of visas under the US Displaced Persons Act.

Additional protocol to the Supplementary Agreement, dated 14 November 1950, with the Government of Italy.

1952

31 Jan. Transfer to the UN High Commissioner for Refugees of all protection functions hitherto exercised by the IRO.

1 Feb. Operations of Provisional Intergovernmental Committee for the Movement of Migrants from Europe began.

7–13 Feb. Eleventh Session of the Executive Committee, Geneva.

11–16 Feb. Ninth Session of the General Council, Geneva.

15 Feb. Board of Liquidation established.

29 Feb. Director-General, Mr. J. D. Kingsley, resigned.

1 Mar. The IRO went into liquidation.

28 Mar. First Session of the Board of Liquidation.

16 June. Second Session of the Board of Liquidation.

30 June. US Displaced Persons Commission completed its regular programme of activities.

21 July. Last shipload of refugees to be admitted under the Displaced Persons Act reached the US.

7–8 Nov. Third Session of the Board of Liquidation.

1953

7 Jan. Fourth Session of the Board of Liquidation.

23–25 Feb. Fifth Session of the Board of Liquidation.

25 Mar. Sixth Session.

4 May. Seventh Session.

27 June. Eighth Session.

28 Aug. Ninth and Final Session.

30 Sept. Final Liquidation of the IRO.

BIBLIOGRAPHY

I. IRO DOCUMENTS AND PUBLICATIONS
II. UN DOCUMENTS AND PUBLICATIONS
III. UNITED STATES GOVERNMENT DOCUMENTS
IV. UNITED KINGDOM DOCUMENTS
V. BOOKS AND ARTICLES

I. IRO DOCUMENTS AND PUBLICATIONS[1]

IRO/COL/8   Subject analysis of the documents of PCIRO and the General Council of IRO (Feb. 1947–end of 1950).

LB/MISC/1–2 Subject analysis of documents of the General Council and of the Executive Committee of the IRO (Sept. 1952).

Reports by the Director General to the General Council:

PREP   1 July 1947–30 June 1948, Geneva, Sept. 1948.
GC/60   July 1948–Mar. 1949.
GC/100   1 July 1948–30 June 1949, Geneva, Aug. 1949.
GC/140   1 July 1949–31 Dec. 1949, semi-annual, 7 Feb. 1950.
GC/166   1 July 1949–30 June 1950, annual, 23 Aug. 1950.
GC/167   Report on the Plan of IRO Operation for the Suppl. Period.
GC/227/Rev. 1 1 July 1950–30 June. 1951, annual, 31 Oct. 1951.
GC/256   1 July 1951–31 Dec. 1951, semi-annual, 29 Jan. 1952.

IRO/LEG/LS/4 9 June 1949, German-British zone. Military Government Law No. 59, effective 12 May 1949 concerning Restitution of Identifiable Property to Victims of Nazi Oppression.

IRO/LEG/LS/5 3 Nov. 1949, Germany (US zone) General Claims Law: Law Concerning Redress of National Socialist Wrongs of 10 Aug. 1949.

Assembly Centre Nursing Manual, 64 pp., n.d. IRO/HCM/MED/47.
The Central Registry System, at Headquarters, Geneva, 1 Aug. 1950, IRO/ADM/12.
Classification Manual, Nov. 1950, 104 pp.
Constitution of the IRO, Agreement on Interim Measures, Geneva, 1947–8, 45 pp.
Detailed Survey of the Nursing Services in the British Zone of Germany, 42 pp., n.d.
The Forgotten Elite, the Story of Refugee Specialists, Geneva, Jan. 1950, 43 pp.
Italy, Camp Medical Services, *Handbook for Medical Services*, 54 pp.
Manual for the Eligibility Officers, 164 pp., n.d.
Migration from Europe. A report by the Director General to the GC of the IRO on experience gained in the field of migration through the processing and transportation for resettlement of more than one million refugees and other migrants, GC/199/Rev. 1, Geneva, Sept. 1951, 98 pp.
News Report, semi-monthly.
Office of Statistics and Operational Reports:
  Occupational Skills of Refugees, 31 Jan., 31 Mar., and 30 Sept., 1948, 39, 35, and 39 pp.; 31 Mar. and 30 Sept. 1949, 32 pp.; 31 Jan. 1950, 23 pp.
  Occupational Skills of Refugees in Italy, 1 Dec. 1950.
  Statistical Report with Three Years Summary, Geneva, June 1950, 48 pp.
  Statistical Report on Occupational Skills of Refugees, U.S. zone, Germany, IRO, US zone headquarters, Bad-Kissingen, 15 Apr. 1950, Employment Division, 55 pp.
  Statistical Report on Occupational Skills of Refugees, US zone, Germany, IRO, US zone headquarters, Bad-Kissingen, Resettlement Division, 15 Aug. 1950, 42 pp., and 1 Jan. 1951, 44 pp.
Operational Manual, revised, May 1951, 122 pp.

[1] For symbols and dates of these documents and other mimeographed documents see Appendix III, pp. 682–3.

Personnel Regulations and their Implementation, Geneva, 1 May 1951, 85 pp.

Professional Medical Register, compiled by Health Division, Headquarters, Geneva, 421 pp., n.d.

Rapport à Monsieur l'Ambassadeur de France, Haut Commissaire de la République en Allemagne, sur les activités de l'Organisation Internationale pour les Réfugiés en zone Française d'occupation en Allemagne, Jan. 1952, 69 pp.

Report to the High Commissioner for Germany on the IRO, US Zone Germany, 22 Oct. 1951, 22 pp. and appendixes.

Report of the Liquidation, Geneva, 31 July 1953, 27 pp., mimeographed.

Un aspect de son œuvre en France, 1952, 61 pp.

UN Conference on Declaration of Death of Missing Persons, *Final Act and Convention on Declaration of Death of Missing Persons*, IRO/LEG/36, Geneva, 16 May 1950, 12 pp.

Vocational Training Schools, detailed programmes, Nos. 1–28, IRO, US zone of Germany, Bad-Kissingen.

What is our Future? Published by the IRO, US zone, Germany, Jan. 1951, 54 pp.

II. UNITED NATIONS DOCUMENTS AND PUBLICATIONS

Yearbook of the United Nations, 1946–7. Lake Success, 1947, pp. 810–19 and following years.

UN, ECOSOC, *Annual Reports of the IRO*: 1st, E/1334, 17 May 1949; 2nd, E/1675, 2 May 1950; 3rd, E/2005, 6 June 1951; 4th, E/2211, 23 Apr. 1952.

—— *The Question of Refugees*, documents for the Special Committee on Refugees and Displaced Persons, E/REF 1, 1946, 75 pp.

—— *Report on the Progress and Prospect of Repatriation, Resettlement and Immigration of Refugees and Displaced Persons.* Submitted by the Secretary-General in collaboration with the Executive Secretary of the PCIRO. Lake Success, 1948, 67 pp. Doc. E/816, 10 June 1948 (Hambro Report).

Report of the Committee on Negotiations with Specialized Agencies. Proposal on Interim Arrangements on Refugees, 1946, Doc. E/228—Annexes 36–47.

UN, General Assembly, *Official Records* (First Part of First Session), 10 Jan.–14 Feb. 1946:
Plenary Meetings, Annex 17, pp. 601–3: Report of Third Committee (A/45).
Twenty-ninth Plenary Meeting, pp. 413–39: Discussion of Report, 12 Feb.
Third Committee, *Summary Records*, 11 Jan.–10 Feb. 1946, pp. 9–26: Fourth–Ninth Meetings, 28 Jan.–8 Feb.

—— —— (Second Part of First Session), 23 Oct.–16 Dec. 1946:
Sixty-sixth and Sixty-seventh Plenary Meetings, 15 Dec., pp. 1420–54: Discussion of Third and Fifth Committee Reports.
Annexes 96 and 97, Docs. A/265, p. 1595 and A/275, p. 1600.
Third Committee, *Summary Records*, 24 Oct.–13 Dec. 1946:
Fifth–Twenty-first Meeting, 4–12 Nov., pp. 81–120.
Twenty-fifth–Thirty-second Meeting, 16–25 Nov., pp. 137–88.
Thirty-fourth–Forty-first Meeting, 28 Nov.–4 Dec., pp. 193–254.
Forty-eighth Meeting, 12 Dec., pp. 312–20.
Annexes 9–10, pp. 321–64.
Fifth Committee, 1 Nov.–13 Dec., 1946:
Thirty-fourth–Thirty-ninth Meeting, 3–9 Dec., pp. 173–6.
Forty-third Meeting, 12 Dec., p. 276.
Forty-fifth Meeting, 13 Dec., pp. 281–4.
Annexes 12 and 12a, p. 384.

UN, ECOSOC, *Official Records, Summary Records*:
First Session, 23 Jan.–18 Feb. 1946.
Twelfth Meeting, 16 Feb., pp. 99–103.
Second Session, 14 Jan.; Spec. Suppl. No. 1, Report of Special Committee on Refugees and Displaced Persons, 7 June 1946, 176 pp. (E/REF/75); Spec. Suppl. No. 2, Records of the Committee of the Whole on Refugees, 15–20 June, 64 pp.

Third Session, 11 Sept.–10 Dec.:
  Thirteenth–Fourteenth Meetings, 30 Sept., pp. 83–90 and 92–97.
  Seventeenth Meeting, 2 Oct.
  Twentieth Meeting, 3 Oct.
  Spec. Suppl., 3, Annex 7, pp. 21–39.
  Spec. Suppl., 8, Annex 21: Rep. of *ad hoc* Committee on Finances (Doc. E/203/Res. 1);
    Annex 22, Final Report of the Committee on Finances of IRO (Doc. E/213).
Documents issued by Special Committee on Refugees and Displaced Persons:
  E/REF/1–89; E/REF/Fact Finding/1–39, Sub-Committee Fact-Finding, 1–16 May 1946;
    E/REF/Org.Fin./1–14, Sub-Committee on Organization and Finance, 3–23 May;
    E/REF/Fin./1–23, Committee on Finance, 6–22 July, 1946.
UN, Department of Public Information, 1948, Nos. 1–13, *What the United Nations is doing for Refugees and Displaced Persons.*
—— *Magna Carta for Refugees,* rev. edition, 1953, 54 pp.
—— *Protecting the Refugees, The Story of UN Effort on Their Behalf,* 1953, 24 pp.
UN, Department of Social Affairs, *A Study of Statelessness,* New York, Aug. 1949, UN Publications, 1949, xiv. 2.
Agreement Between the UN and the IRO, UN, New York, 1949, 22 pp.
Immigration in Brazil, Doc. E/CN12/169/Add. 1, New York, 1950.
Immigration in Chile, Doc. E/CN12/169/Add. 2, New York, 1950.
Immigration in Venezuela, Doc. E/CN/12/169/Add. 3, New York, 1950.
Definition of Refugee Status, 1950, Doc. E/1618.
Report of the *ad hoc* Committee on Refugees and Stateless Persons, 1950, Doc. General E/AC 32.
Yearbook on Human Rights, New York, 1951.
UN Conference of Plenipotentiaries on the Status of Refugees and Stateless Persons, held at Geneva, Switzerland, from 2 to 25 July, 1951. *Final Act and Convention Relating to the Status of Refugees,* Geneva, 1951, 59 pp.
Reports of the Social Committee, Special Committee on Statelessness, *Refugees and Stateless Persons*:
  First (E/1806, 1/8 1950).
  Second (E/1814, 10/8 1950).
  Third (E/1831, 15/8 1950): Resol. 319 (IV) of GA.

III. UNITED STATES GOVERNMENT DOCUMENTS

US War Refugee Board, *Final Summary Report of the Executive Director,* Washington, 15 Sept. 1945, 74 pp.
US President (Harry S. Truman), 'Immigration to the US of certain DP's and refugees in Europe, statement and directive', US Department of State, *Bulletin,* xiii, 23 Dec. 1945, pp. 981–4.
War Relief Control Board, *Voluntary War Relief During World War II.* Report to the President, Washington, March 1946, 73 pp.
US, 80th Congress, First Session, Senate Hearing, Committee on Foreign Relations, *International Refugee Organization,* Washington, 1947, 48 pp.
US, 80th Congress, First Session, Report of a Special Sub-committee on Foreign Affairs (Fulton Report), *Displaced Persons and the IRO,* Washington, 1947, 88 pp.
US, 80th Congress, First Session, House of Representatives, on House Report No. 2910: Hearings before Sub-committee on Immigration and Naturalization of the Committee on the Judiciary, *Permitting Admission of 400,000 Displaced Persons into the United States,* 4, 6, 13, 20, 25, 27 June and 2, 9, 16, 18 July 1947, Washington, 1947.
'The State of the Union; Message of the President to the Congress', US Department of State, *Bulletin,* xvi, 19 Jan. 1947, p. 124.
US 80th Congress, First Session, House of Representatives, 15 May 1947: Hearings before a Special Sub-committee of the Committee on Foreign Affairs on HJ Res. 207, *International Refugee Organization,* Washington, 1947, 71 pp.

US 80th Congress, First Session, Senate Report No. 51: *International Refugee Organization*, Washington, 1947, 4 pp.

US 80th Congress, First Session, House of Representatives Report No. 464: *International Refugee Organization*, Washington, 1947, 6 pp.

The Displaced Persons Problem, Washington, 1947, 25 pp. (Dept. of State Publication 2899. European Series 26.)

US 80th Congress, Second Session, Senate Report No. 950: Report of the Committee on the Judiciary pursuant to S. Res. 137 . . . , *Displaced Persons in Europe*, 2 Feb. 1948, Washington, 1948.

US 81st Congress, First Session, Senate Report No. 476: Report of the Committee on Expenditures in the Executive Departments pursuant to Public Law 601, 79th Congress, 8 June 1949: *United States Relations with International Organizations. III. The International Refugee Organization*, Washington, 1949, 54 pp.

US 81st Congress, First Session, on House Report No. 1344, 2, 4, 9 Mar. 1949. Serial No. 5 Committee on the Judiciary. 80th Congress, House of Representatives, Report No. 1854, *Emergency Displaced Persons Admission Act*, Amending the Displaced Persons Act of 1948, Hearings before the Sub-committee No. 1, Committee on the Judiciary, Washington, 1949.

US 81st Congress, First Session, 5, 6, 7 Apr. 1949, Chicago, Ill. House Report No. 581, Amending the Displaced Persons Act of 1948, *Proceedings of the National Resettlement Conference for Displaced Persons*, H. Doc. No. 220, Washington, 1949.

US Treaties and other International Acts, Series 1846, *International Refugee Organization: Constitution*, Washington, Department of State, Publication 3362, 1949, 119 pp.

US Public Law 774, 80th Congress, 25 June 1948, US Public Law 555, 81st Congress, 16 June 1950: *Displaced Persons Act with Amendments*, Washington, 1950, 18 pp

US 81st Congress, Second Session, House Report No. 1687: *The Displaced Persons Analytical Bibliography*, Washington, 1950, 82 pp.

US 81st Congress, Second Session, House Report No. 1507: Report of a Special Sub-committee of the Committee on the Judiciary House of Representatives pursuant to H. Res. 238 (Walter Report) *Displaced Persons in Europe and their Resettlement in the United States*, 20 Jan. 1950, Washington, 1950, 149 pp.

US 81st Congress, Second Session, House Report No. 1841: Special Sub-committee of the Committee on the Judiciary, *Expellees and Refugees of German Ethnic Origin* (Walter Report II), Washington, 1950, 87 pp.

US Displaced Persons Commission: *Memo to America: The DP Story, the Final Report of the US Displaced Persons Commission*, Washington, 1952, 376 pp.

US 83rd Congress, First Session, Senate Report No. 522: Report Committee on the Judiciary, *Escapees and Refugees in Western Europe*, Washington, 1953, 81 pp.

Whom We shall Welcome. Report of the President's Commission on Immigration and Naturalization, Washington, 1953, 319 pp.

IV. UNITED KINGDOM DOCUMENTS

The Parliamentary Debates (Hansard), *House of Commons*:
   1943, Vols. 387, 388, 389, 391, 393: for special reference see General Index in vol. 394.
   1945, Vol. 413, coll. 361–5: 20 Aug.
   1946, Vol. 423, col. 2113: 5 June.
      Vol. 426, coll. 961–4: 31 July; coll. 1260–79: 1 Aug.
      Vol. 427, col. 187: 9 Oct.
   1947, Vol. 433, coll. 2057–61: 26 Feb.
      Vol. 441, coll. 985–6: 4 Aug.
   1950, Vol. 441, coll. 325–6: 28 Mar.; col. 2034: 24 May.
      Vol. 480, coll. 205–8, 219, 247–9: 1 Nov.
   1952, Vol. 503, col. 30: 30 June; coll. 418–19: 2 July.
The Parliamentary Debates, House of Lords:
   1943, Vol. 128, coll. 836–72: 28 July.

1946, Vol. 144, coll. 1164–94: 19 Dec.
1948, Vol. 156, coll. 1154–82: 23 June
Ministry of Labour and National Service, *Report for the Year 1947*, Cmd. 7559, London, 1948.
—— *Report for the Year 1948*, Cmd. 7822, London, 1949.
—— *Report for the Year 1949*, Cmd. 8017, London, 1950.

V. BOOKS AND ARTICLES

AUERBACH, FRANK L., *The Admission and Resettlement of Displaced Persons in the United States*, Common Council for American Unity, New York, Revised 1950.
—— *The Immigration and Nationality Act. A Summary of its Principal Provisions*. Common Council for American Unity, New York, 1952, 103 pp.
—— 'The Refugee Relief Act of 1953', Department of State, *Bulletin*, xxix, 24 Aug. 1953, pp. 231–5.
AUSTRALIA, EXTERNAL AFFAIRS, *Current Notes on International Affairs*, xx, Feb. 1949, pp. 214–23.
—— 'The IRO and Australia's Contribution', *Current Notes on International Affairs*, xx, Nov. 1949, pp. 1163–70.
BENTWICH, NORMAN, 'IRO of the United Nations', *Jewish Yearbook of International Law*, 1948, pp. 152–63.
—— *The Rescue and Achievement of Refugee Scholars. The Story of Displaced Scholars and Scientists, 1933–1952*, The Hague, 1953, 107 pp.
BERGER, JOSEPH A., 'Displaced Persons: a Human Tragedy of World War II', *Social Research*, New York, xiv, Mar. 1947, pp. 45–48.
BIEHLE, MARTHA H., 'Sixth Plenary Session of Intergovernmental Committee on Refugees', US Department of State, *Bulletin*, xvi, 2 Feb. 1947, pp. 200–1.
BORRIE, W. D., *Immigration: Australia's Problems and Prospects*, Sydney–London, 1949, 105 pp.
BRACEY, BERTHA L., 'Practical Problems of Repatriation and Relocation', *International Affairs*, xxi, July 1945, pp. 295–305.
CANADA, EXTERNAL AFFAIRS, *Land for New Citizens*, Ottawa.
CAREY, JANE PERRY CLARK, *The Role of Uprooted People in European Recovery*, Washington, National Economic Society Planning Association, Planning Pamphlet No. 64, 1948, 85 pp.
CARTER, HENRY, *The Refugee Problem in Europe and in the Middle East*, London, 1949.
CITROËN, H. A., *European Emigration Overseas, Past and Future*, The Hague, 1951, 48 pp.
COIGNY, R. L., and STRAUS, P., 'Rôle de la gamma globuline dans la prévention de la rougeole —Résultats d'une étude épidémiologique', *La Presse medicale*, 59ème année, No. 31, 9 mai 1951, pp. 634–9.
COLDWELL, M. J., 'Refugees and the United Nations', *International Journal*, ii. 102–5.
COMMITTEE FOR CHRISTIAN GERMAN REFUGEES, *Ten Years of Stewardship*, New York, 1945.
Commonwealth Survey, 'Commonwealth Participation in IRO', 14 Sept. 1951, pp. 15–18.
Congressional Digest, 'The Controversy over Proposals to Bring 400,000 Displaced Persons to America', xxvii, Jan. 1948, pp. 11–32.
CONTROL COMMISSION FOR GERMANY (British Element), 'German Refugee Problem'. *Monthly Report*, 1949, No. 4, p. 20.
COPE, E. W., 'Displaced Europeans in Shanghai', *Far Eastern Survey*, xvii, 1948, p. 274.
COUNCIL OF FREE CZECHOSLOVAKIA, *In Search of a Haven. The Story of Czechoslovak Refugees*, Washington, 1950.
COUSINS, NORMAN, 'An Apology for Living', *Saturday Review of Literature*, xxxi, 9 Oct. 1948, pp. 9–12, 54–58.
DAVIE, MAURICE R., *Refugees in America*, Report of the Committee for the Study of Recent Immigration from Europe, New York, 1947, 453 pp.
DESAGE, RENÉ, *La Réglementation des étrangers en France*, Paris, 1950.
DRESDEN, MARIE LANE, 'Who Shares our Concern for these People? The Resettlement of

Unwanted Refugees by the IRO', *Social Service Quarterly Review*, xxvi. (No. 3). Sept. 1952, pp. 270–83.

DUGGAN, STEPHEN, *The Rescue of Science and Learning*, New York, 1948, 214 pp.

EISENHOWER, DWIGHT D., 'Displaced Persons in Germany, letter from General Eisenhower to the President', US Department of State, *Bulletin*, xiii. 21 Oct. 1945, pp. 607–9.

ELIAS, JULIUS A., 'Relations between Voluntary Agencies and International Organizations', *International Affairs Journal*, vii. 1, 1953, pp. 30–35, New York.

FERRIERE, SUZANNE, 'Role of Non-governmental Organizations in the Assistance of Migrants', *International Labour Review*, lxiv. Nos. 5 and 6, Nov.–Dec. 1951.

'Die Flüchtlinge in Oesterreich', *Berichte und Informationen*, iii, 1948, p. 1645.

FRIEDMANN, WOLFGANG, *German Immigration to Canada*, Canadian Institute of International Affairs, Ottawa, 1952, 63 pp.

—— 'Migration and World Politics', *International Journal*, vii. 3, Summer 1952, Toronto, pp. 196–203.

FRINGS, PAUL, *Das Internationale Flüchtlingsproblem, 1919–1950*, Frankfurt a. M., 1951, 295 pp.

GROSSMANN, KURT R., *The Jewish DP Problem. Its Origin, Scope, and Liquidation*, New York, Institute of Jewish Affairs, 1951, 43 pp.

—— 'The Perpetual Refugee Problem', *Congress Weekly*, xix, 1952, p. 9.

HARRISON, EARL G., 'Displaced Persons in Germany, Letter from President Truman to General Eisenhower; Report of Earl G. Harrison'. US Department of State, *Bulletin*, xiii, 30 Sept. 1945, pp. 455–63.

HOEHLER, FRED K., *Europe's Homeless Millions*, New York, Foreign Policy Association, 1945, 96 pp. (Headline series No. 54, Nov.–Dec. 1945.)

—— 'Displaced Persons', in Huszar, George B., *Persistent International Issues*, New York, Harpers, 1947, pp. 41–68.

HOLBORN, LOUISE W., 'The Legal Status of Political Refugees, 1920–1938', *The American Journal of International Law*, xxxii, 1938, pp. 680–703.

—— 'The League of Nations and the Refugee Problem', *The Annals*, May 1939, pp. 124–35.

—— 'The United Nations and the Refugee Problem', *Yearbook of World Affairs*, 1952, vi. 124–48.

HOLT, H. E., *et al.*, *Australia and the Migrant*, London and Sydney, Angus & Robertson, 1953, 186 pp.

HULME, KATHRYN, *The Wild Place*, Boston: Little, Brown & Co., 1954; London: Frederick Muller, 1954, 233 pp.

INSTITUT FÜR BESATZUNGSFRAGEN, *Das DP Problem, Eine Studie über die Ausländischen Flüchtlinge in Deutschland*, Tübingen, 1950, 201 pp.

INSTITUT ZUR FÖRDERUNG ÖFFENTLICHER ANGELEGENHEITEN, *Europe and the German Refugees*, Frankfurt a. M., 1952, 94 pp.

INTERGOVERNMENTAL COMMITTEE FOR REFUGEES, *Report of the Director, 1940–1947*, London, 1947.

INTERNATIONAL LABOUR ORGANIZATION, *Memorandum on Migration Policy*, Doc. Pinc/1/6, Rev. 1. Geneva 1952.

International Labour Review, 'Migration: Displaced Persons and Refugees', lv, May 1947, pp. 434–6.

—— 'Migration: Immigration into Canada', lvii, Mar. 1948, p. 242; Oct. 1948, pp. 530–1.

—— 'Migration: Displaced Persons in China', lvii. 4, Apr. 1948, pp. 378–81.

—— 'Migration: Immigration into Brazil', lviii, Oct. 1948, pp. 528–30.

—— 'The ILO and Migration Problems', lxv, 2 Feb. 1952.

—— 'The Resettlement of Refugees and Displaced Persons in the United States', lxvii, June 1953, pp. 559–76.

'The International Tracing Service in Arolsen', *Vierteljahrshefte für Zeitgeschichte*, Oct. 1953, p. 395.

Interpreter Releases, No. 24, pp. 228–32, 1 July 1947, 'Resettlement of Displaced Persons'.

'IRO to End Operations After 55 Months' Work', *World Affairs*, Wellington, New Zealand, viii, Mar. 1952, pp. 32–33.

JACOBSEN, PIERRE, 'L'Œuvre de l'Organisation Internationale pour les Réfugiés', *Population*, 1951, No. 1, pp. 27–40.

JOHNSON, A., 'Places of Displaced Persons', *Yale Review*, xxxvi, Spring 1947, pp. 394–404.

JOHNSON, R. H., 'International Politics and the Structure of International Organizations, the Case of UNRRA', *World Politics*, July 1951, pp. 520–38.

KEENLEYSIDE, HUGH L., 'Canadian Immigration Policy', *International Journal*, Summer 1948, pp. 222–38.

KENT, DONALD PETERSON, *The Refugee Intellectual. The Americanization of the Immigrants of 1933–1941*, New York, Columbia University Press, 1953, 317 pp.

KINGSLEY, J. D., 'IRO Transplants a Million Refugees', *United Nations World*, New York, 1950, iv. 42.

KOEHL, R. L., 'The Politics of Resettlement', *Western Political Quarterly*, vi, June 1953, pp. 231–42.

KOTSCHNIG, WALTER M., 'Problems of the Resettlement Program', Department of State, *Bulletin*, xx, 13 Mar. 1949, pp. 307–8.

KULISCHER, EUGENE M., *The Displacement of Population in Europe*, Montreal, 1943, 170 pp.

—— *Europe on the Move; War and Population Changes, 1917–1947*, New York, 1948, 377 pp.

LEHMAN, HERBERT, 'The "Joint" Takes a Human Inventory—The End of the DP Problem is In Sight', *Commentary*, vii, Jan. 1949, pp. 19–27.

LOCHORE, R. A., *From Europe to New Zealand, An Account of our Continental Settlers*, Wellington, 1951, 112 pp.

MACLEAN, MAJOR GENERAL, FITZROY, 'Responsibility for Refugees', *The Times*, 26–27 Nov. 1947.

MAKAROF, 'Das Internationale Flüchtlingsrecht', *Zeitschrift für Völkerrecht*, July 1952.

MALIN, PATRICK M., 'The Refugee: a Problem for International Organization', *International Organization* (Boston), i. 3, Sept. 1947, pp. 443–59.

MANCO, G., *Les Étrangers en France*, Paris, 1952.

MURPHY, H. B. M., 'The Assimilation of Refugee Immigrants in Australia', *Population Studies*, 1952, v. 200.

—— 'The Resettlement of Jewish Refugees in Israel, with special Reference to those known as Displaced Persons', ibid., 1951, v. 153.

NATHAN-CHAPOTET, ROGER, *Les Nations Unies et Les Réfugiés*, Paris, 1949.

OFFICE OF THE HIGH COMMISSIONER FOR AUSTRIA, *Report on Austria*, 1951, Vienna, 1952, 135 pp.

OFFICE OF THE HIGH COMMISSIONER FOR GERMANY, 'Political Aspects of the Refugee Problem', *Report on Germany*, 1950, Nos. 30–34.

—— ibid., 9th Quarterly, 1 Oct.–31 Dec. 1951.

—— ibid., 21 Sept. 1949–31 July 1952.

PARRY, CLIVE, 'Constitutions of International Organizations', *The British Year Book of International Law*, 1946, pp. 394–496 and 1947, p. 429.

PELCOVITS, N. A., 'European Refugees in Shanghai', *Far Eastern Survey*, 1946, xv, p. 321.

PHELAN, V. C., 'Organization of Migration into Canada', *International Labour Review*, lxv. 3, Mar. 1952, p. 27.

'Polish Refugee Camp in Mexico Closes', Department of State, *Bulletin*, xvi. 19 Jan. 1947, p. 138.

PROUDFOOT, MALCOLM, '"Displaced Persons" in Ten Eventful Years, a Record of Events of the Years Preceding, Including and Following World War II, 1937 through 1946', *Encyclopedia Britannica*, Chicago, 1947, ii. 141–4.

REES, ELFAN, 'The Refugee and the United Nations', *International Conciliation*, June 1953, No. 492, pp. 267–314.

Refugee Settlement in the Dominican Republic, the Brookings Institution, Washington, 1942.

'The Refugee in World Affairs', *Journal of International Affairs*, vii. 1, 1953, New York.

RINGLAND, ARTHUR C., 'The Organization of Voluntary Foreign Aid, 1939–1953', US Department of State, *Bulletin*, 16 Mar. 1954, pp. 382–92.

RISTELHUEBER, RENÉ, *Au Secours des Réfugiés*, L'Œuvre de l'Organisation Internationale pour les Réfugiés, Paris, 1951, 319 pp.

—— 'The International Refugee Organization', *International Conciliation*, Apr. 1951, No. 470, pp. 165–228

ROBERTSON, A. H., 'Some Legal Problems of the UNRRA', *The British Year Book of International Law*, 1946, pp. 142–67.

ROBINSON, NEHEMIAH, *Convention on Relating to the Status of Refugees. Its History, Contents and Interpretation, A Commentary*, New York, Institute of Jewish Affairs, 1953, 238 pp.

ROTHOLZ, 'Der Begriff der "Protection juridique et politique"', *Archiv des Völkerrechts*, ii, 1950, pp. 404 ff.

RUCKER, SIR ARTHUR, 'The Work of the International Refugee Organization', *International Affairs*, xxv. 1, Jan. 1949, pp. 66–73.

SCHECHTMAN, JOSEPH B., *European Population Transfers, 1939–1945*, New York, Oxford University Press, 1946, 532 pp.

SIMPSON, SIR JOHN HOPE, *Refugees: A Review of the Situation since September 1938*, London, 1939, 114 pp.

—— *The Refugee Problem—Report of a Survey*, London, 1939, 637 pp.

STADULIS, E., 'Resettlement of Displaced Persons in the United Kingdom', *Population Studies*, Cambridge, 1952, v. 207.

STUCHEN, PHILIP, 'Canada's Newcomers: the Displaced Persons', *Queen's Quarterly* (Kingston, Ont.), lv, Summer 1948, pp. 197–205.

SWETTENHAM, JOHN ALEXANDER, *The Tragedy of the Baltic States. A Report Compiled from Official Documents and Eyewitnesses' Stories*, London, Hollis & Carter, 1952, 216 pp.

TARTAKOWER, ARIEH, and GROSSMAN, KURT, *The Jewish Refugee*, New York, Institute of Jewish Affairs, 1944, 676 pp.

TOYNBEE, ARNOLD and VERONICA, ED., *Hitler's Europe, Survey of International Affairs, 1939–1946*, London, New York, Toronto, 1954, 730 pp.

TUCK, W. H., 'IRO Achievements and Tasks Ahead', *International Affairs Quarterly*, New York, 1949, xiii, 29.

UNRRA, European Regional Office, *Displaced Persons Operation in Europe and the Middle East*, London, Dec. 1946, 69 pp.

—— *Basic Field Manual*, Appendix A and B, Apr. 1946.

US DEPT. OF INTERIOR, *Token Shipment*, Washington, 1946.

US WAR REFUGEE BOARD, *Final Summary Report of the Executive Director*, Washington, 15 Sept. 1945, 74 pp., processed.

VERNANT, JACQUES, *The Refugee in the Post War Period*, London, 1953, 827 pp.

WAHRHAFTIG, ZORACH, *Uprooted, Jewish Refugees and Displaced Persons After Liberation*, New York, Nov. 1946, 219 pp.

WANDER, HILDE, *Die Bedeutung der Auswanderung für die Lösung Europäischer Flüchtlings- und Bevölkerungsprobleme*, Kiel, 1951, 81 pp. Kieler Studien No. 15.

WARREN, GEORGE, L., 'Aid to Escapees from Iron Curtain Countries', Department of State, *Bulletin*, xxvii, 18 Aug. 1952, pp. 261–2.

—— 'Interaction of Migration Policies and World Economy', ibid., xiv, 10 Feb. 1946, pp. 213–16.

—— 'Residual Problem of Refugees on Termination of IRO', ibid., Washington, 1952, xxvi, 24 Mar., p. 458.

WEIS, PAUL, 'The International Protection of Refugees', *The American Journal of International Law*, Apr. 1954, pp. 193–221.

WILSON, F., 'A New Pattern in Emigration: The Work of the IRO', *Listener*, xlvii, Jan. 1952, pp. 126–7.

WILSON, FRANCESCA M., *In the Margins of Chaos: Recollections of Relief Work in and between Three Wars*, London, 1944, 287 pp.

WOODBRIDGE, GEORGE, *The History of UNRRA*, New York, 1950, 3 vols.

The World Today, 'Refugees: An Unsolved Problem', Aug. 1952.

—— 'Progress in Refugee Settlement', Oct. 1953, pp. 449–59.

INDEX

Academic Assistance Council, 426.
accommodation, *see* billeting; housing.
Accommodation officer, 79, 101.
accountants, 101, 115, 519.
accounting, 89, 521, 523–4, 526, 549.
accounts of voluntary societies, 148.
Accueil Catholique Français, 162.
Acheson, Dean, 23, 24 nn. 1 & 2, 43 n. 1.
ACVFA, *see* Voluntary Foreign Aid, Advisory Committee.
administration, 68–84; finances of, 40–43, 51–52, 59–60, 103, 124, 125.
Administration and Supply Department, 70, 75, 76, 78, 79.
Administrative Committee on Co-ordination, 169.
Administrative Management Division, 93.
administrative officers, 79, 101.
administrative services, 550–7.
Administrative Services Division, 70, 74, 75, 77.
administrative services officer, 101.
adoption of children, 498, 507, 511, 512.
Aeriom Donaueschingen, 506.
Afghanistan, 45 n. 1.
age of refugees, 190, 197, 275.
aged refugees, 269, 481; care of, 226, 232, 261; homes for, 151, 218, 227, 244, 489, 492; resettlement of, 114, 153, 156, 393, 400, 424, 485, 486, 489, 490; travel arrangements, 240, 252, 256, 467; voluntary aid, 155, 156, 160.
Aglasterhausen, 505.
Agreement Between the UN and the IRO, 51 n., 167.
Agreement on Interim Measures, 54, 55, 61.
agreements, 56–57, 319, 322–4, 425, 445; between IGCR and PCIRO, 591–4; with governments and occupation authorities in Europe, 61, 117, 127–9, 133, 136–7, 141–3, 155, 185, 211, 221 n. 1, 318–20, 328, 517, 518, 594–674; with local settlement countries, 474, 478; with resettlement countries, 64, 366, 368, 370, 375–7, 383, 385–8, 391, 393, 400–8, 416, 674–8; on reparations, 118–19; regarding hard core, 485–7; with voluntary societies, 150, 151, 154, 155, 157–9, 300, 679–80; during liquidation, 680–2; *see* Byrnes–Bevin Agreement.
agricultural workers: housing, 195; resettlement, 64 n. 3, 383, 384, 386, 396, 397, 401, 403, 405–9, 411, 413, 414; statistics, 190, 274, 275, 305–8; training, 282.
AHEPA, order of, 165.

Aide aux israélites victimes de la guerre, 163.
air travel, 112, 394, 398, 424, 447, 453–7, 459, 462, 466–8.
Albania, 138–9, 175, 180, 388.
Albanians, 16, 100, 199.
Algeria, 14, 16, 141.
aliens' registration certificates, 317.
Allied Combined Travel Board, 324.
Allied Commission for Austria, 128, 129, 211.
Allied Commission for Italy, 137.
Allied Control Council for Germany (Control Commission), 77, 117, 128, 130, 186, 233, 286, 316, 329, 502.
Allied Council for Austria, 135.
Allied High Commission for Germany, 121, 135, 315, 317, 321, 332, 336, 475–6.
Allied Military Government for Occupied Territories, 17, 58.
Allied Post-war Requirements Bureau, 329.
allotments, 115.
allowances, 42, 60, 63, 81, 87, 89, 91, 92, 93, 231, 394, 419.
Altersheim Hospital, 260.
Altmeyer, Arthur J., 55, 59, 62, 99.
Amberg, repatriation centre, 343.
ambulance services, 242.
ambulance trains, 252.
amenity supplies, 21, 87, 126, 135, 220, 231, 477, 524, 532–3.
American Committee for the Resettlement of Polish Displaced Persons, 147, 162, 165.
American Committee for the Resettlement of Professionals, 160.
American Committee for the Welfare of Cripples, 160.
American Council of Voluntary Agencies for Foreign Service, 13, 152, 159, 302.
American Federation of International Institutes, 165.
American Foundation for the Blind, 160.
American Friends Service Committee, 146, 157, 162, 163, 165, 174, 302, 505.
American Fund for Czech Refugees, 147, 162.
American Joint Distribution Committee, 118, 146, 152, 157, 162–4, 189, 218, 236, 243; movements, 148, 151, 405, 415–17; relief programme, 14 n. 3, 149, 149 n. 1; in Far East, 422, 424; rehabilitation and training, 192, 221, 281, 282, 285, 296, 310, 334, 531; Report, 224; work for special groups, 483, 485, 491, 524.
American Journal of International Law, 311 n. 1.
American National Committee to Aid Homeless Armenians, 147 ,162, 165.

81; in Italy, 80, 137; necessary for legal protection, 313, 316, 324, 326, 327; of children, 503–5; of dependants, 395; of Saarlanders, 173; persons excluded from, 172, 175, 341, 351, 381, 393, 420; procedure, 266, 270; time limit for claim, 66; *see* Constitution; disqualification.

Eligibility Appeals, Review Board for, 65, 71, 74, 204, 208–10, 213–15, 381.

Eligibility, Office of, 73, 75, 205.

eligibility officers, 77, 79, 101, 268.

embarkation centres, 218, 238, 256, 257, 259, 302, 373, 374, 413, 417, 457, 460.

embezzlement, 548, 549.

Emergency Relief Appropriation Act (US), 14, 14 n. 1.

Emerson, Sir Herbert, 9, 11, 12 n. 3, 37, 39 n., 48, 58, 59.

emigration, 6, 8 n. 1, 9, 10, 43, 79, 81, 126, 142, 152, 326; *see* movements; repatriation; resettlement.

Employers Confederation (Norway), 156.

employment, 219, 272–82, 295; administration, 77, 124, 192, 223, 226; by IRO, 308; contributions paid by employed refugees, 126, 132; effect on venereal diseases, 250; for resettlers, 369, 370, 375, 376, 387, 388, 390, 391, 393, 396–8, 404, 406, 409, 412, 417, 421, 510; in Austria, 129, 132–3, 231, 478; in Belgium, 142; in Eastern Europe, 347; in France, 140; in Germany, 120, 129, 130, 132, 135, 195, 221, 476; in Italy, 194; information for, 60, 300; ILO help, 169; of rehabilitated refugees, 291, 294; statistics for, 309; *see* permits for work; Resettlement Placement Service; unemployment; workers.

employment officers, 79, 101, 273.

Employment and Vocational Training, Division of, 70, 273, 289, 290.

engineering, 225.

engineers, 388, 408, 429.

Entr'aide française, 163.

Entr'aide universitaire française, 163.

entry, control of, 133.

epidemics, 240, 242, 244, 254, 256, 257, 259.

Epirots, 138.

Equador, 23, 45 n. 1, 368, 401.

equipment, 532–3; *see* office accommodation.

Erivan Republic, 172–3.

escort officers, 101, 444.

Esslingen, 310, 331, 427, 502.

establishment, 42, 82, 124, 125.

Estonia, 177 n. 2; *see also* Baltic states.

Estonian Central Committee, 224.

Estonians, 189, 192, 199, 249, 339, 344, 357, 361–3, 390, 398; *see also* Balts.

Estorick, Eric, 'The Evian Conference and the Intergovernmental Committee', 11 n. 1.

Ethiopia, 45 n. 1, 113, 376, 429.

EUCOM, 117, 519, 522, 527.

European Payments Union, 115.

Evangelisches Hilfswerk, 477.

Evans, Myrddin, 29.

Eversburg, 310.

Evian-les-Bains conference, 11, 11 n. 1, 405.

exchange, 108–10, 113 n. 1, 114, 125; *see* British Exchange Control; currencies.

Executive Committee of IRO, 682–764.

Expellee Bank (Germany), 121, 477, 566, 568.

Export Control Law, 158 n. 2.

expulsion: of refugees from resettlement countries, 325; considered by Human Rights Commission, 326.

extradition, 32, 325.

factory workers, 383.

Facts about the Refugees, 542.

families: counselling of, 268, 270; in Belgium, 378, 381; in France, 383; living arrangements, 219; of Poles, 176, 392; of staff, 93; preservation of, 64, 207, 228, 232, 354; resettlement of, 168, 194, 255, 269, 370, 373, 376, 377, 385, 387–9, 391, 393, 395, 398–400, 402, 404, 408, 428–9, 481; travel arrangements for, 258; voluntary societies' help for, 152.

Family and Individual Services, Division of, 70.

Family Welfare Association, 164.

Far East: employment in, 278; IRO work in, 143–4, 208–9, 216, 217, 220, 237, 238, 287; movements from, 412, 421–6, 448; refugees in, 172, 202; voluntary societies' work in, 157; *see also under separate countries*.

Federal Law on Homeless Foreigners (Germany), 317.

Federal Security Agency (US), 359.

Fédération belge des femmes universitaires, 163.

Fédération des Œuvres Hospitalières de Caritas, 485.

Fédération des sociétés juives de France, 163.

Feld Afing, 505.

Ferrière, Suzanne, 'Role of Non-Governmental Organizations in the Assistance of Migrants', 157 n. 2.

field offices, 68, 69, 93; *see* missions.

Field Operations, Department of, 77.

Field Services Division, 73, 75.

films, 292, 299, 300, 349, 351, 542–4.

Final Act, 328 n. 1.

finance, 102–26; administration of, 82, 115–16; difficulties, 55, 56, 133, 227; in Austria, 135–6; in Germany, 134; in Italy, 137; in Middle East, 144; League of Nations, 5–8; of care and maintenance, 50; of movements, 416, 471; of tracing service,